PENGUIN BOOKS

THE HUGO YOUNG PAPERS

'A priceless record of recent history' John Rentoul, *Independent*

'He lays bare who really hated whom (mostly on the same side)
and aims a few choice slings at both parties along the way'
Anne McElvoy, *Evening Standard*, Books of the Year

'A treasure trove . . . unlike memoirs written with hindsight or
diaries edited for effect, these contemporaneous notes provide
an invaluable glimpse of how the principal players saw things at
the time' Philip Stephens, *Financial Times*

'A significant document by a single-minded man who loved good
political stories' Peter Stothard, *The Times Literary Supplement*

'An extraordinary contemporaneous record of the thoughts of
some of our most senior politicians' *Daily Mail*

ABOUT THE AUTHORS

Hugo Young was one of the most influential journalists of his generation. His columns, first in the *Sunday Times* and then for nearly two decades in the *Guardian* until his death in 2003, were essential reading for all who took politics seriously. Born in 1938 into a Catholic family in Sheffield, and educated at Ampleforth and Balliol College, Oxford, Young began his career on the *Yorkshire Post* before spending two years in America, first as a Harkness then as a Congressional Fellow. On returning to Britain he joined the *Sunday Times*, where he rose to become deputy editor, until moving to the *Guardian* in 1984. He wrote a number of books, including *The Blessed Plot: Britain in Europe from Churchill to Blair* and *One of Us*, the first authoritative biography of Margaret Thatcher. He was Chairman of the Scott Trust, owner of the *Guardian* and *Observer*, from 1989 to 2003. He married twice, first to Helen Mason, with whom he had four children, and after her death to the American artist Lucy Waring.

Ion Trewin is the editor of the Alan Clark Diaries. He is the author of *Alan Clark: the Biography* (2009). After a decade as literary editor of *The Times*, he became a publisher, retiring as editor-in-chief of a London publishing house. He has been literary director of the Man Booker Prizes since 2005.

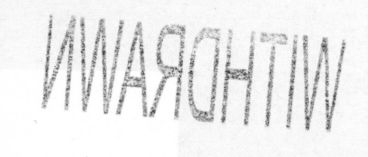

HUGO YOUNG

The Hugo Young Papers

A Journalist's Notes from the Heart of Politics

EDITED BY ION TREWIN
with Forewords by
Harold Evans and Alan Rusbridger

PENGUIN BOOKS

PENGUIN BOOKS

Published by the Penguin Group
Penguin Books Ltd, 80 Strand, London WC2R ORL, England
Penguin Group (USA), Inc., 375 Hudson Street, New York, New York 10014, USA
Penguin Group (Canada), 90 Eglinton Avenue East, Suite 700, Toronto, Ontario, Canada M4P 2Y3
(a division of Pearson Penguin Canada Inc.)
Penguin Ireland, 25 St Stephen's Green, Dublin 2, Ireland
(a division of Penguin Books Ltd)
Penguin Group (Australia), 250 Camberwell Road, Camberwell, Victoria 3124, Australia
(a division of Pearson Australia Group Pty Ltd)
Penguin Books India Pvt Ltd, 11 Community Centre, Panchsheel Park, New Delhi – 110 017, India
Penguin Group (NZ), 67 Apollo Drive, Rosedale, North Shore 0632, New Zealand
(a division of Pearson New Zealand Ltd)
Penguin Books (South Africa) (Pty) Ltd, 24 Sturdee Avenue, Rosebank, Johannesburg 2196, South Africa

Penguin Books Ltd, Registered Offices: 80 Strand, London WC2R ORL, England

www.penguin.com

First published by Allen Lane 2008
Published in Penguin Books 2009
1

Copyright © The Estate of Hugo Young, 2008
Editorial matter copyright © Ion Trewin, 2008
His foreword copyright © Harold Evans, 2008
His foreword copyright © Alan Rusbridger, 2008

The moral right of the author has been asserted

Printed in Great Britain by Clays Ltd, St Ives plc

A CIP catalogue record for this book is available from the British Library

978-0-141-03356-3

Photograph of Hugo Young on pii reproduced by kind permission of the *Guardian*

www.greenpenguin.co.uk

Contents

PART ONE

1969–1979

Early Years

PART TWO

1980–1990

The Thatcher
Governments

PART THREE

1991–1997

Major and the Coming
of Tony Blair

PART FOUR

1997–2003

New Labour in
Government

For Lucy,
and Hugo's children

Acknowledgements

For help most generously given:

Lucy Waring-Young, Hugo's widow, and her fellow Hugo Young trustees, who initiated this book and kept an eye on its progress: Harold Evans, Graham Greene, Anne Lapping and Alan Rusbridger.

Hugo's children: Dominic, Cecily, Victoria and Emily.

Tim Radford, *Guardian* journalist, who initially went through every file and wrote a valuable summary of what was discussed. His work on the time lines and the footnotes have added immeasurably to the authority of the final work.

Elisabeth Ribbans, associate editor of *The Guardian*, for her tenacity, untiring spirit and all-round support.

Stephanie Cross, who typed up much of the final book.

Also from *The Guardian*, Luke Dodd, Chris Elliott, Ed Pilkington, Richard Nelsson and the Research and Information Department, Mariam Yamin (archivist), Nicole Schultz, Holly Bentley, and those present and past *Guardian* journalists whose knowledge helped explain mysteries and fill in gaps.

Dame Elizabeth Forgan, successor to Hugo as chair of the Scott Trust.

Lord Hurd, who reminisced about his conversations with Hugo over a quarter of a century.

Stephen Fay, colleague and collaborator of Hugo's from the *Sunday Times*.

Those of Hugo's contacts still alive who gave their approval for his notes of their conversations to be included.

At Penguin, Stuart Proffitt, Richard Duguid, Phillip Birch and the tireless copy-editor, Bob Davenport.

Michael Sissons.

Alex Shapland-Howes.

Letters are reproduced with the kind permission of the authors or their families.

Abbreviations

BAOR British Army of the Rhine
BiE Britain in Europe
BSE Bovine Spongiform Encephalopathy
CAP Common Agricultural Policy
CBI Confederation of British Industry
CCO Conservative Central Office
CDU Christlich Demokratischen Union / Christian Democratic Union (Germany)
CJD Creutzfeld-Jakob disease
CND Campaign for Nuclear Disarmament
CPS Centre for Policy Studies
CRD Conservative Research Department
CSJ Commission on Social Justice
DES Department of Education and Science
DHSS Department of Health and Social Security
DoE Department of the Environment
DTI Department of Trade and Industry
EC European Community
ECB European Central Bank
ECHR European Court of Human Rights
EEC European Economic Community
EMS European Monetary System
EMU European Monetary Union
ERM (European) Exchange Rate Mechanism
ESDP European Security and Defence Policy
EU European Union
FCO Foreign and Commonwealth Office
FDP Freie Demokratische Partei/ Free Democratic Party (Germany)
FPTP first past the post
FT *Financial Times*
G8 Group of Eight (Canada, France, Germany, Italy, Japan, Russia, UK, US)
GATT General Agreement on Tariffs and Trade
GDP Gross domestic product
GLC Greater London Council
GMB The General, Municipal, Boilermakers and Allied Trades Union, now known simply as GMB
GNP Gross national product
HC House of Commons
HL House of Lords
HO Home Office
IGC Intergovernmental conference
IMF International Monetary Fund

ITN Independent Television
  News
LD Liberal Democrat
LEA Local education authority
MAFF Ministry of Agriculture,
  Fisheries and Food
MoD Ministry of Defence
MORI Market and Opinion
  Research Institute, now just
  MORI
MP Member of Parliament
NATO North Atlantic Treaty
  Organization
NEC National Executive
  Committee (of the Labour
  Party)
NHS National Health Service
NI Northern Ireland
NMD National Missile Defence
NSC National Security Council
NUM National Union of
  Mineworkers
NUR National Union of
  Railwaymen
NUT National Union of
  Teachers
OECD Organization for
  Economic Cooperation and
  Development
OMOV One Member One Vote
OPEC Organization of the
  Petroleum Exporting Countries
PCP Parliamentary Conservative
  Party

PLP Parliamentary Labour Party
PM Prime Minister
PMQs Prime minister's questions
PPS Parliamentary Private
  Secretary
PQs Parliamentary questions
PR Proportional representation
PSBR Public-sector borrowing
  requirement
QMV Qualified majority voting:
  a specified level of support –
  greater than a simple majority
  – required for EU proposals
RUC Royal Ulster Constabulary
SC Shadow Cabinet
SDLP Social Democratic and
  Labour Party (Northern
  Ireland)
SDP Social Democratic Party
SIS Secret Intelligence Service
SNP Scottish National Party
SPD Sozialdemokratische Partei
  Deutschlands/Social
  Democratic Party of Germany
ST Sunday Times
TGWU Transport and General
  Workers' Union
TU Trade union
TUC Trades Union Congress
UKIP UK Independence Party
WEU Western European Union
WMD Weapons of mass
  destruction
WTO World Trade Organization

Foreword
by Harold Evans

Hugo Young was deceptive. This is not to say he was deceitful: he was incapable of artifice. On first meeting him, many people – including me – got the wrong impression because his convictions and indeed his passions were subordinate to his modesty and forbearance. Reading this book with its historically important record of political leaders speaking with unbridled candour, I'm reminded of how I misread him in 1966.

I'd just joined the *Sunday Times*, supposedly being groomed to be managing editor, but in those early days very much the new boy from a provincial editorship, finding my way round the leading national newspaper of the day. On my first Thursday morning, I was invited to go along to the office of the deputy editor, William Rees-Mogg, for the leader writers' conference designed to decide the paper's attitude to some policy emerging from the rather frantic last days of Harold Wilson's Labour government, holding on with a majority of only 4.

The *Sunday Times*'s editor, Denis Hamilton, took no part in setting political policy: his trust in Rees-Mogg was total. I found the 'conference' consisted only of Rees-Mogg and Hugo, doubling as social-services correspondent and leader writer. He was a fresh-faced 28, another provincial newcomer, almost as new to the paper as I was. Rees-Mogg was a supremely confident columnist of fluency and wit, his reputation already made. Hugo, tall, bespectacled and reticent, looked like a head prefect, and in William's presence then had the deferential manner of one summoned to the beak's office. Both he and William were Roman Catholics, and I presumed that the absence of any cut and thrust that morning was in part because they shared a common faith; they were both of the liberal centre.

Hugo's manner gave no inkling of how he would translate such consensus as emerged into an editorial. The two qualities that took me by surprise when I read this leader and others from future meetings of the three of us was how faithfully he reflected the nuances of a discussion, but yet how forceful he was in expressing a conclusion. Rather rambling exchanges between us on the pros and cons of allowing television into Parliament or the minutiae of negotiations with the rebellious white government of Rhodesia or the falsification of a Hansard record or the hardy perennial of a prices-and-incomes policy were transmuted into crystal-sharp statements of policy in direct, vigorous English. How could a head prefect write with the authority of a High Court judge?

It was the same in all the fourteen years we worked together after I became editor of the paper in 1967. With Hugo as chief leader writer, I changed the way editorials were written. I had confidence in him, but wanted to draw more on the special knowledge of the experienced section editors, so I created and chaired an editorial conference of eight to supplant the troika, including a former editor, Harry Hodson, provost of Ditchley, Oxford; Frank Giles, deputy editor and foreign editor; and John Whale, religious-affairs editor and our expert on Northern Ireland. Hugo was surrounded – and not at all fazed. Peter Wilsher, the business editor, Ronald Butt, the political editor and columnist, and Eric Jacobs, the labour editor, were far more trenchant than Hugo in expressing their points of view, all speaking from their own positions of special knowledge.

These sessions were often disputatious on issues like trade-union law, immigration, the ill-treatment of prisoners in Northern Ireland, and especially the impropriety of the paper printing details of Cabinet meetings from the Crossman diaries. Hugo did not hold forth much and never flared up. He more often asked questions, mildly, propelled by a genuine curiosity rather than aggressive questions to expose the idiocy of the speaker. He wanted to know not so much what someone thought as why he thought it, even on the hot issue of the performance of the English cricket team. He didn't write all the editorials – John Whale, Frank Giles and I wrote a fair number – but I admired Hugo's distinctive style and integrity so much I invited him to write a weekly political column while continuing to share the editorial writing.

This made Hugo very nervous. He didn't want to upset Ronald Butt, whose regular column on the leader page I intended to retain. I assured him that Butt's column was safe and they approached politics from different perspectives. Then Hugo worried whether week after week he could maintain the relevance and readability of a personal column. Of course he soon proved he could. His style of informed reasoned vigour won him ever-increasing acclaim when he moved to *The Guardian* five years later, shortly after Rupert Murdoch took over Times Newspapers.

The reasons why his columns attracted a wide following were, I think, four: his fidelity to his values, his command of the language, his judgement of character, and his deep research. He had an absorptive memory. I never saw him take a single surreptitious note in group lunches at the *Sunday Times* with prime ministers, Chancellors, Foreign Secretaries and distinguished visitors; sight of a pencil and paper and they'd have clammed up right away.

We respected the confidences we'd promised – a point of honour to all of us – but Hugo made notes afterwards. Occasionally he'd share them with his colleagues, but rarely did anyone see the notes he made after his private meetings and which form the bulk of this volume. They are astounding. They put readers at the centre of things. We see the way politics – and the courts – really works, how individuals of varied temperament and status reconcile public duty and private ambition – or fail to. Unlike some diaries which are all gossip (Chips Channon) or intrigue (Woodrow Wyatt), Hugo's have an extraordinary combination of detached observation with acute perception of both the character of his interviewee and the intellectual context. The notes were the bedrock of the opinions in his columns, and the source of their major influence.

Hugo got so much out of these encounters because he put so much into them. He prepared as if for a finals examination. It was a relief to people in political life to talk to someone who thoroughly understood the complexities and the jousting personalities they wrestled with; who knew, also, that Hugo Young was a man without malice who would not betray them. In one of his diary entries (12 April 1981), Tony Benn, who was not, shall we say, an admirer of the *Sunday Times*, wrote, 'I must say Hugo Young had played it quite squarely. He had taken a lot of trouble, had let me check the quotes, and his own assessment wasn't really obtrusive and a lot of the argument got across.'

Hugo's name came to open many doors closed to other reporters; he had exceptional access to a number of senior civil servants and judges. He established the same rapport in the major interviews he did for the paper when I asked him to join one of our major group-reporting exercises, as he did with Insight in the Philby investigation and with other reporters writing on the moon landing and the Zinoviev Letter forgery.

When they surveyed the accumulated treasures of Hugo's notes and letters, his widow, Lucy, and the trustees of his literary estate were acutely aware of the ethical constraints in publishing discussions undertaken in the expectation of anonymity. As a trustee of the estate but not an employee of *The Guardian*, I can speak to the conscientious way its staff went about securing approval for the publication of selections from these once private notes. All involved, it seems to me, have cooperated to produce a book that is at once informative and entertaining, and a public service – very much in the tradition of Hugo's columns.

Foreword
by Alan Rusbridger

On 21 July 1997, Tony Blair, Hugo Young and I met for tea in the garden of Number 10. The Prime Minister was reasonably assiduous in talking things over with columnists and editors – I sense he preferred the former to the latter – and on this day we chatted over tea and biscuits in the summer sun for ninety minutes or so.

A couple of days later an immaculate record of the meeting arrived in the post from Hugo. He had taken no notes at all during the conversation – but here it was in perfect summary. It was the first time I appreciated this particular facet of Hugo's distinction as a political columnist. He was first and foremost a reporter: he believed in finding things out and cross-checking them before he wrote about them. He never lost his appetite for the basic job of asking questions and recording answers. I had often seen him asking penetrating questions – questions that hinted at the quality of his mind, his reading, accumulated knowledge and intellect. This was the first time I had seen how he systematically noted and ordered his reporting. (Had I been as assiduous a note-taker as Hugo, I would have recorded the day on which the controversial businessman Sir Gerald Ronson sat himself down in my office and delivered himself of the aphorism 'Opinions are like arse holes. Everyone has one.' As a proposition on journalism, this was hard to argue with.) If Hugo had simply been an opinionated stylist he would not have been revered as he was. Much rarer are the commentators who also report. Hugo was not afraid to express pungent opinions, but he believed in putting in the hours before he put pen to paper. As this book suggests, his columns were like icebergs. Readers saw a sunlit tip of crystal argument. They may have guessed, but they never truly knew or saw, what lay beneath.

Hugo died a working journalist. His last column was filed a few days before he died. A couple of weeks before the end he'd lain on his four-poster bed in Christchurch Hill, Hampstead, reading a handwritten letter from the Prime Minister passionately defending his position on Iraq. He was surprised – perhaps a little flattered – to think that the PM cared enough about his repeated attacks to engage in written correspondence. Not that it changed his mind.

He left that letter behind, together with all his papers – more than thirty years of meticulous notes of lunches, phone calls, meetings in which the great players of the age had discussed politics, the law, government, religion and culture with him. Any policeman or lawyer will tell you of the value of contemporaneous notes. Historians of modern British politics would have formed an orderly queue around the block from Christchurch Hill for access to those files.

After Hugo's death on 22 September 2003, his executors were faced with a dilemma. Most of the conversations with Hugo were off the record. One option would have been to destroy the papers. That is the preference of one veteran political journalist I know, who over the years has accumulated his own attic full of notes and diaries of meetings with the great and powerful. On his death, his wife has firm instructions to burn the lot. Hugo's stated preference was for his papers to be preserved and made available to scholars. But he gave no clear instructions about the circumstances, or timescale, under which they could be used.

In 2006 a small group of his family and friends met to resolve the issue. It would have been unthinkable either to have destroyed Hugo's papers or to have placed them immediately in the public domain. The papers themselves were taken to the *Guardian* archive – established with Hugo's enthusiastic support – where they were logged and indexed. A decision was taken to publish extracts from the papers so long as we traced every living participant in the off-the-record conversations and they gave permission.

Modern-day politics operates in an uncertain twilight domain of not quite public, not quite private. Since Richard Crossman and Tony Benn, there has been a torrent of diaries from people in British public life. Outgoing prime ministers rush into print with their memoirs. Diplomats spill beans; private secretaries tell out-of-school tales.

Time frames also have become compressed: where once it was considered officially decent to wait thirty years before opening the filing cabinets to public scrutiny, the main players themselves now rush to do deals with publishers before their market – or simple curiosity – value fades. The Blair government alone has already been chronicled by a swarm of the participants – political, diplomatic and mandarin. Robin Cook, Mo Mowlam, Clare Short, Alastair Campbell, David Blunkett, Jonathan Powell, Christopher Meyer, Cherie Booth, Giles Radice, John Prescott are among those who have published inside accounts of Blair's time in power – and Blair himself is working on his own version. Margaret Thatcher, John Major, Kenneth Clarke, Nigel Lawson, Paddy Ashdown, Menzies Campbell and a host of others have contributed to a small library of memoirs of life in government and opposition.

Freedom of Information legislation now allows journalists more or less immediately to prise open some doorways into public life that were previously sealed for decades. Today, even the thirty-year rule that once delayed the release of the vast bulk of public documents is being reviewed – having been made to look increasingly archaic by FoI and the lucrative trade in political memoirs.

But where does this new freedom for politicians and their associates to tell all leave journalists? Every day of the year – probably every hour of every day – politicians tell journalists things on a variety of terms: things that are 'unattributable', or on 'lobby terms' or 'for deep background', or 'off the record', or 'for guidance only', or on 'Chatham House rules'. Their motives may be mixed – from misleading and spinning via persuasion and advocacy to informing and enlightening.

Most journalism is about the here and now – telling readers as much as possible about the events of the day or week – and most journalists appreciate the trade-off whereby they can often get the reader closer to what is actually happening if they disguise or conceal their sources. Some of them (and not a few readers), however, nurse anxieties about the amount of information which is not above board and cleanly attributable. Some journalists are better than others at keeping records of, or even remembering, the daily interactions and conversations which inform their work. But a journalist who does keep a meticulous record of who un-attributably said what at a particular moment thereby creates an archive of information of potential journalistic and historical significance. Where that journalist is a figure of Hugo's distinction and access, the archive grows into something genuinely important.

It's fair to say that a small number of Hugo's former confidants and interlocutors thought that his papers should be kept under lock and key for a very long period indeed. Some considered their dealings with Hugo to have been so private that they should never be made public: that a fundamental accord between politicians and the Fourth Estate would be broken if the former believed that their off-the-record conversations would ever be published.

The overwhelming majority of those we contacted were, however, perfectly relaxed about the thought of publication, though they sometimes asked for minor passages to be excised. 'It was off the record at the time,' a distinguished former Cabinet minister rang me to say, 'but I'm happy for it to be published now. But can you take out one sentence about X? I stand by it, but he is currently very unwell and I have no wish to add to his family's unhappiness at the moment.'

Many were surprised that Hugo had taken such care over record-ing what were often long-forgotten exchanges, but several declared themselves 'fascinated' to be reminded of them, while others remarked on the 'excellent record' he'd produced. Some had quibbles about minor uses of language ('I think Hugo was paraphrasing what I said') or small details of fact. But most of those who lunched with, talked to or confided in Hugo were pleased that these exchanges should now be published, and some even offered their help in decoding cryptic abbreviations in his notes. One foreign diplomat went to far as to say he was 'honoured and touched' to see his conversation with Hugo included in the book, while another gave me his approval by declaring this 'a splendid undertaking', adding that 'Hugo was indeed one of the finest, most astute and most honourable journalists to grace the pages of a British newspaper.'

There are precedents. All of C. P. Scott's diaries, letters and notes have been in the public domain for decades now. Anyone can read his records of encounters and his correspondence with Lloyd George, Kerensky, Churchill, Woodrow Wilson, Lord Curzon, Lord Smuts, Ramsay Mac-Donald. The editor of his papers, Trevor Wilson, wrote of them, 'They are an account of what, during his periodic visits to the south, he learned about the affairs of state. Thus, their chief interest lies in what they reveal about the decisions that were being taken at the top and the men who were taking the decisions.' Similarly Alastair Hetherington, editor of *The Guardian* between 1956 and 1975, bequeathed all his papers to the London School of Economics. There you can read records of his many private conversations with statesmen including Hugh Gaitskell, Jim Calla-ghan, Jo Grimond, Edward Heath, Harold Macmillan, Presidents Kennedy, Johnson and Nixon, Henry Kissinger, Indira Gandhi, Robert McNamara, Le Ngoc Chan, Bill Bundy and Dean Rusk.

Hetherington's diaries reveal that he had 99 deeply off-the-record meetings with Harold Wilson, 54 of them during Wilson's premiership. Many of them took place with no one else in the room. Wilson talked about the major issues of the day, including Rhodesia, Vietnam, Profumo, the Middle East, nuclear defence, the press, the timing of general elections, economic and monetary policy, and future Cabinet appointments. An interesting doctoral thesis remains to be written comparing these exchanges between a prime minister and a leading editor both with the public pronouncements and policy of the former and with the coverage of that 'official' story by the latter.

Political memoirs are necessarily written with hindsight. Some politicians feel liberated to be a good deal franker in retrospect than they were able to be at the time. The value of Hugo's papers is that we do frequently glimpse what they thought at the time: what was happening behind the scenes, or what they thought was happening. That might be quite a different thing from the contemporary narrative of events that was publicly available, or from the narrative subsequently constructed by politicians with half an eye on history.

Besides this, the book contains a lesson for all aspiring, and actually practising, journalists in seeing how a great political writer and reporter such as Hugo worked. The painstaking making of notes and recording of meetings and conversations helped Hugo become the formidable commentator he was. How many of us wish that we could recall people or moments or utterances that may have seemed unimportant at the time but which later assume great significance? These notes were Hugo's hard disk.

At some point in the future it is *The Guardian*'s intention, and that of Hugo's family, to make all his papers available for scholars, just as Scott's and Hetherington's have been. Collectively they make the case for the eternal value of reporting. *The Guardian*'s centenary history claims that Peterloo, as recorded by the *Manchester Guardian*'s founder, John Edward Taylor, marks 'the debut of the reporter in English public life'. Hugo's work stands superbly in that tradition.

Introduction

Hugo Young is already considered one of the more remarkable political journalists of his time. His columns, first in the *Sunday Times* and then for nearly two decades in *The Guardian*, illuminated our understanding of the political scene. Just how he accumulated the knowledge on which his writing was scrupulously based is revealed in this book.

Before the age of electronic recording devices, reporters relied on their note-taking abilities and their memories. Most journalists who trained on provincial newspapers learned shorthand (usually Pitman's). But as, increasingly, it became possible to thrust a pocket-sized, handheld recording device in front of a speaker, Pitman's ceased to be a vital part of a journalist's armoury.

Hugo needed no such devices. In their place he relied solely on a phenomenal memory (not dissimilar to that of *The Observer*'s Kenneth Harris, who a few years before managed to reconstruct and publish interviews in a question-and-answer form). This had the benefit that his contacts never felt ill at ease at the sight of their host scribbling notes or checking that the tape was still running. Liz Forgan, whose connection with *The Guardian* began as women's editor, believes that 'Powerful people trusted him because he was of their clan, socially, intellectually and emotionally, but he was a better version of themselves. Less grubby, less ambitious, more dignified, less needy.'

His first interviewee, Douglas Hurd, remembers, 'His success was partly achieved by creating a conversation between two people roughly equal in status and knowledge, which is not compatible with note-taking. The records must have been made immediately afterwards. His own preconception sometimes appeared, as is natural in a conversation between equals, but never in a way which interrupted the even flow of discourse. He did not distort what he heard. The conversation was a pleasure in itself, which is why it was easy to accept the next invitation.' Hugo's fine memory also allowed him later to entertain his contacts at the Garrick Club (to which he had been elected in 1984), which forbids the use of notebooks or recording devices.

Douglas Hurd was right in his surmise. Once lunch was over, Hugo would sit down at a keyboard and type up what was said at the meeting. (Some of his subjects have been surprised to learn that he kept such detailed accounts.) Although these notes – never intended as verbatim minutes – were inevitably weighted towards those parts of the conversation that most interested Hugo, their accuracy was rarely questioned. In later years, when married to Lucy, his second wife, she recalled that on his return home after these lunches she 'would greet him often in the hall. He would smile and say, "Wait, darling, let me write down my notes," and from his office would stream the most rapid-fire typing sounds imaginable – ten minutes' worth? Then a smiling Hugo would appear to say hello. I am convinced after hearing the beautiful collection of sentences he spoke in the days before he died that he wrote by chasing his thoughts. It was almost trancelike his method.'

Emily, one of Hugo's three daughters, recalls: 'Our father's study was definitely his private domain, a careful system that might have looked like chaos to the outside eye.' Victoria, another daughter, says the study had originally been a bedroom (of the third daughter, Cecily) and 'sometime in the early eighties she and Dominic [the sole Young son] laboriously painted a massive rainbow on one wall. When it became his study, and was redecorated in nice neutral shades, he instructed the builders to paint around the rainbow – so it was still there all those years later.' Helen, his first wife, was a journalist by training. 'He always showed our mother everything he wrote before he sent it off, for her opinion on it,' Emily recalls. She remembers too, 'His intense concentration when working', and that 'somehow he managed to filter out the chaos of family life happening loudly outside his study door.' Mealtimes were the scene of 'regular heated family debates about lots of different subjects – politics, TV, why things were the way they were, how they should be.'

When these interviews began, in 1969, Hugo and Helen had been married three years and he was a leader writer at the *Sunday Times*. Thus meetings with the likes of Douglas Hurd – in 1969 private secretary to the Leader of the Opposition Edward Heath – helped ensure that his writing for the paper was well informed. In pronouncing on the issues of the day in the name of the *Sunday Times*, Hugo followed the dictum of C. P. Scott about comments being free and facts being sacred. Who would have guessed that his connection with the legacy of Scott, proprietor and editor of the *Manchester Guardian*, would have formal links two decades later?[1]

In his first decade in London he felt his way. Born on 13 October

---

1 In 1989 HY became chairman of the Scott Trust, owner of *The Guardian* and, more recently, *The Observer*. He held the post until his death in 2003.

1938 in Yorkshire with an inborn enthusiasm for Yorkshire cricket, he was educated at Ampleforth and read jurisprudence at Oxford. (The law remained a lifelong interest.) At twenty-three he had a spell learning the journalistic trade on the *Yorkshire Post* before spending two years in the United States first as a Harkness and later as a US Congressional fellow. He returned to Britain in 1965. When Harold Evans, a fellow northerner, who had made his reputation editing the *Northern Echo*, succeeded Denis Hamilton as editor of the *Sunday Times* in 1967 Hugo had been on the paper for almost two years. Evans used Hugo in a variety of roles, although officially he was chief leader writer, to which was added the role of political editor in 1973. The paper's decision in 1976 to reconstruct the events leading up to the 'Who Rules Britain?' general election in February 1974 gave Hugo and his colleague Stephen Fay the excuse and the opportunity to interview over a short period of time a range of politicians of all political persuasions. A few months later he and Stephen Fay collaborated again when sterling was once again in crisis. Fay remembers Hugo's typed-up notes, which were essential when colleagues were working together and needed to know what the other had discovered. Several of those whom Hugo met in these investigations became regular contacts in the future. Soon he began filing accounts of his interviews year by year. 'Will memoirs one day beckon?' he mused at one point.

As will be seen from this book, Hugo's note-taking gradually developed a style of its own. Some journalists and columnists make a brief record of an encounter – perhaps a few key words to remind them of what was said. Hugo's typed-up accounts became narratives, and as his confidence and knowledge of his subject grew so he added his own reactions, his opinions, and often his views on the individual he was interviewing. He was not always flattering – indeed, he could be withering in his comments: he described one official as 'a parody of a certain kind of civil servant: gawky, pompously orotund, trying to be agreeable but retreating into shell at the slightest excuse, repetitive; fingertips coming together, much throat-clearing, a tendency to add one more point – which turned out to be indistinguishable from points already made. I had the feeling that he hadn't talked to many journalists, that this was a bold new departure for him – but he was very determined to retain control.'

Hugo saw from the beginning that his job was not only to uncover what was really going on in government and in the opposition parties, but also to identify where political opinion and political PR (what would become known as 'spin') did not always agree with the facts of the matter. His was a role that was perfectly in tune with newspaper developments of the time.

As Hugo himself noted,[1] when he first read newspapers, in the 1950s, there were no political columnists. This might have had something to do with the continuing post-war paper shortage, which meant that the *Sunday Times* of the period was often restricted to fewer than twenty pages. But by the mid-1960s, with newsprint more widely available, the signed column was beginning to emerge, giving the columnist 'an oracular authority no journalist deserves'. William Rees-Mogg, later editor of *The Times*, made his reputation then as the *Sunday Times*'s only named political voice. Indeed, when Rees-Mogg wrote in 1966 that it was time for Sir Alec Douglas-Home to resign as leader of the Conservative Party, Home was, Young wrote, 'positively sheepish in his subservience to the prophetic word'. The political column quickly proliferated. In 2003 Hugo mentioned someone who was compiling a list of all the national newspaper columnists to whom Downing Street might want to get a political message across; with the job incomplete, he had already reached a figure of 221. As Hugo observed, however, the greater the number of columnists, the less the influence of any single one.

By the 1970s, several figures had become key, among them Peter Jenkins, political columnist and policy editor of *The Guardian*, and Hugo himself, who began a column in the *Sunday Times* called Inside Politics. With the liberal-minded *Sunday Times* under Harold Evans far outselling its broadsheet rivals, the influence of Inside Politics was quickly felt. However, when Rupert Murdoch acquired Times Newspapers in 1981 it did not take long for the *Sunday Times* to shift to the political right. Hugo felt increasingly uncomfortable. In 1982 Murdoch engineered his displacement as joint deputy editor. Meanwhile Peter Preston, editor of *The Guardian*, had been stalking Young as a columnist.[2] It took two years, but the moment arrived in spring 1984 when Hugo and the *Sunday Times* parted company. Hugo moved to *The Guardian*, and not long after Peter Jenkins, having spent twenty-seven years with *The Guardian*, went to the *Sunday Times* as its political columnist. For the next eighteen years Hugo would inform his readers on *The Guardian* twice weekly. It was never a burden. As he wrote in 2003, 'I enjoy every column day that comes around.'

To Hugo, most journalism had only a transitory value, much of a columnist's work being written for the next day's paper. He even questioned the prestige given to named columnists, noting that, while

---

1 Hugo Young, *Supping with the Devils: Political Writing from Thatcher to Blair* (London: Atlantic Books, 2003). Other quotations of Hugo's in this introduction are taken from his introduction to this volume.
2 I have included in the appropriate place chronologically Hugo's own view as well as an encomium from Harold Evans – who had by then moved to *The Times* as editor in succession to William Rees-Mogg – and a note from Peter Preston.

'reporting is the bedrock of journalism, columns seem more like the shifting sands of tide and fashion: undisciplined, unreliable and possibly, in the basic scheme of things, unnecessary'. As a columnist of many years standing, he decided that his role was one of 'explanation rather than persuasion'. He believed that the 'columnist should try for scoops of fact, but may more readily discover scoops of interpretation'. His own reporting, he felt, came through 'a distinctive prism'. Power and how it gets managed by the power brokers and the powerful had rarely been discussed openly. Hugo showed no such inhibition.

He quickly realized that he did not see sounding off as a primary purpose (although useful on occasion); rather he wished to 'convey some more or less important truths about present moods and future probabilities as seen by the actors in the political game'. He never bragged about the influence of his column, although, as he put it aptly, 'I'm happy to bask in the milieu that just occasionally says otherwise.' Those who bent his ear, and gave him insights and exclusive information in the hope that his column would reflect their policies and their thinking found that Hugo was not malleable. He was fastidious on that point: as he wrote, 'I don't see myself as a player, more as a watcher, a finder-out, a discloser, an alerter, a reporter.'

Hugo did, however, lend his weight to causes in which he believed, not least civil liberties, and felt that occasionally he had 'helped push the boulder back up the hill, shaming legislators into moving in directions the government did not want'. He did express views, too, on wider issues, supporting two wars, in the Gulf and the Balkans, although on Iraq he was 'an early dissenter'.

Liz Forgan recalls:

We needed an unassailable champion for Channel 4's plan in the 1980s to publish a long interview with a serving MI5 officer, Cathy Massiter. This brave woman, in breach of the Official Secrets Act, revealed systematic abuses by her colleagues including the bugging of trade unionists and leading civil-liberties campaigners, among them Harriet Harman and Patricia Hewitt, later to become Cabinet ministers. Hugo, who for all his magisterial qualities had a radical soul, was outraged and instantly agreed – at great risk to his reputation and to important relationships – to front the programmes.

For much of his professional life Hugo mused on the essential conundrum of his trade: how should he and politicians relate to each other? Politicians increasingly needed Hugo – as became clear following the death of the Labour leader John Smith and the emergence of Tony Blair and his New Labour cohorts. His contacts were now telephoning him. But gaining inside knowledge worried Hugo: even though, he wrote, the columnist 'owes it to readers to know as much as he can conceivably find out', his audience also needed 'to rely on us being outsiders, ultimately'.

Hugo's fascination with power was intense but quite narrow. Liz Forgan thinks that 'He never really got to grips with the women's movement or the emerging politics of race, but it would have been very easy to imagine him as an ambassador, a private secretary or a government minister (not true of many journalists). He loved those worlds – in those days still quite academic, quite upper class, very male – and he was completely at ease in them.'

As for Hugo's own political persuasion, that was a case of mind your own business. He never went further than admitting to being a liberal with a lower case 'l'. He was interested in the judiciary, and persuaded many a judge to talk to a journalist for the first time (he was the only journalist on the *Sunday Times* with a law degree). And he observed that 'Home Office issues – immigration, Freedom of Information, abuse of police power – are a category that puts all governments under the jaundiced eye of a liberal journalist.'

Most conversations were for background use, to ensure that his columns were well informed. Sometimes he was asked to withhold a specific piece of information or not to give any clue as to its source, but those he saw knew from the beginning that Hugo was a journalist: they knew why they were meeting, and that his intention was always to produce as knowlegeable a piece as possible. In a conversation with Alastair Campbell (in January 1998), he stressed that what he wrote would not in any way be seen as coming from Downing Street. 'It would just seep into my consciousness and seep out again as my wisdom.'

Throughout his career, most of Hugo's writing was about British politics, although this increasingly included Europe, but he was probably the only political commentator (rather than diplomatic specialist) to court ambassadors and embassy staff on a regular basis, in order to gain a less chauvinistic understanding of the issues. If some subjects appear to be ignored, or at best merely touched upon, remember that many matters that bulked large in Hugo's lifetime – Aids, Vietnam, sexual scandal in high places, politicians at the Old Bailey, foot-and-mouth disease, the conversion to decimal currency, and so on – might be political issues, but they seldom required much off-the-record briefing. Given his two years in the United States in the 1960s, it is surprising that he did not write more about American affairs before Clinton, but wars and the events that followed 9/11 changed that. And a development in his personal life was influential. Following the death of Helen in 1989, in 1990 he married an American artist, Lucy Waring. Although their base was London, they also spent holidays in the USA.

Lucy was an enormous support to him when cancer first struck. He continued working; indeed, even in the final year his interest in the world of politics never dimmed. He was writing until the end came, on 22 September 2003. The tributes to his qualities from all quarters, all political colours, were huge and heartfelt, and are referred to in the pieces by his editors included in this book.

Editing Hugo's notes into book form has been instructive. Although he and I first met more than forty years ago, it is only now, in reading the material he left behind, that I realize just how well informed he was and how widely read. I hadn't appreciated the extent to which cultural matters interested him – Lucy proved a considerable influence here – but from his writings it is clear that he long puzzled over the philistinism that ran throughout British political life. The Dome, to take but one example, was 'an abomination'. That he was a member of the Garrick provides a clue: of all London clubs, it has the most varied membership – not only from acting and the theatre, but from writing, publishing, the press, the law, and many other areas too. Many of his interests were represented there.

He and I were near contemporaries in the old Fleet Street. When he joined the *Sunday Times*, in 1965, I was already on the *Sunday Telegraph*. We first met because he and my *Telegraph* feature-writing colleague Helen Mason started going out together. They married in 1966, lived first in Islington, and more than once babysat for my wife and I after our son was born and I had moved to *The Times*. For a time they had a country retreat near Bury St Edmunds, and eventually they moved to a house in Christchurch Hill, Hampstead. Hugo and I renewed our acquaintance following *The Times*'s shift from Printing House Square, opposite Blackfriars station, to a brand-new building next to the *Sunday Times* in Gray's Inn Road, where Hugo was now the political editor. We shared many a taxi between our offices and the Garrick. He was discretion itself about his lunch guests and what they had told him. It was therefore instructive to open the *Sunday Times* the following weekend to see if one could marry what he was writing about with whom I had spied him entertaining.

In selecting what to publish in this volume I have been guided by two abiding principles: how interesting each account seems today and its historical value. Cuts have been made silently; misspellings have been corrected. In the early days a variety of old typewriters with ribbons of variable quality were available at the *Sunday Times*. Decades later, legibility of the surviving pages was therefore sometimes a problem. However Tim Radford – long-serving *Guardian* science correspondent, literary editor, and for this volume the researcher – as well as our keyboard operator, Stephanie Cross, and I were usually able to tussle out Hugo's intention, even when the occasional word was missing. Readers may sometimes pause when Hugo uses the first person in these narratives. 'I' is often the subject's voice, but sometimes Hugo's, although he gradually developed the style of inserting 'per HY' where he was expressing his own view. I believe that the sense soon becomes clear. If sentences fail the Fowler or Gowers test, one should remember that Hugo was preparing notes, not finished pieces. The ellipses that sprinkle the text are his, as are the occasional notes '(check)'.

In the first decade, the 1970s, there was less to choose from than later – not least because for eleven months from the end of 1978 the *Sunday Times* and *The Times* were not published thanks to a dispute between the management of Times Newspapers and the printing unions over the introduction of what was called, quaintly to twenty-first century ears, new technology. Not surprisingly, there was little incentive to interview politicians when there was no available vehicle to publish one's conclusions. This means that the build-up to the 1979 general election, which saw Margaret Thatcher elected to power, is unreported. Some years in the early 1980s are also thin in material, which may be explained by Hugo's move to *The Guardian*, with some files disappearing in the process.

From what must be at least one and a half million words, what has been left out? More often than not the minutiae of each stage of British negotiations with Europe – Maastricht, Lisbon, and much in between – which now seem only of interest to the anoraks of European Union history. There are other exclusions. Very occasionally Hugo was prevailed upon to conduct a formal interview with a tape recorder (Margaret Thatcher and John Major were two such subjects). Transcripts exist, but they lack that essential and unique Hugo Young ingredient: the narrative commentary on his subject and an account of the discussion that took place. There are also envelopes and menus with a few words scrawled upon them, but Hugo's handwriting at this distance is a tough call, as even his children admit.

To help the reader, a summary of events is provided for each year, and a list is given with career details of Hugo's interviewees; within the narratives themselves, footnotes explain the identities of those who do not figure in the cast of interviewees.

It is a testament to the quality of these edited narratives – and not just in the information and insights that they give – that they make such absorbing reading. Liz Forgan, who succeeded him as chair of the Scott Trust, says, 'The fact that he was a man of total integrity and a brilliant master of English prose was the bonus which made him one of the great chroniclers of twentieth-century British politics.' His memorial service was widely reported. One headline said it all: 'A beacon of enlightenment in what can seem a tarnished world'.

Ion Trewin
June 2008

Cast of Interviewees

AITKEN, JONATHAN Journalist, foreign correspondent, author, business-man; Conservative MP for Thanet East 1974–83, for Thanet South 1983–97; Minister for Defence Procurement 1992–4; Chief Secretary to the Treasury 1994–5.

ANCRAM, MICHAEL QC; Conservative MP for Berwickshire and East Lothian 1974, for Edinburgh South 1979–87, for Devizes since 1992; minister, Northern Ireland Office, 1993–7; chairman of the Con-servative Party 1998–2001; succeeded as 13th Marquess of Lothian 2004.

ARMSTRONG, SIR WILLIAM Cabinet Secretary and head of the Home Civil Service from 1968; influential during the dispute between the government of Edward Heath (q.v.) and the miners and during the three-day week – one Cabinet minister at the time described him as the 'deputy prime minister'; later Baron Armstrong of Sanderstead.

ASHDOWN, JEREMY JOHN 'PADDY' Commando, diplomat; Liberal MP for Yeovil 1983–2001; leader of the Liberal Democrats 1988–99; EU special representative in Bosnia and Herzegovina 2002–6; later Baron Ashdown of Norton-sub-Hamdon.

ATKINSON, NORMAN Engineer; Labour MP for Tottenham 1964–87; Labour Party treasurer 1976–81.

BAKER, KENNETH author, editor; Conservative MP for Acton 1968–70, for St Marylebone 1970–83, for Mole Valley 1983–97; PPS to the Leader of the Opposition 1974–5; Minister for Information Tech-nology, DTI 1981–4; Minister for Local Government, DoE 1984–5; Secretary of State for the Environment, 1985–6; for Education and Science 1986–9; Chancellor of the Duchy of Lancaster 1989–90; Home Secretary 1990–92; later Baron Baker of Dorking.

BALLS, EDWARD Journalist, economist; chief economic adviser to the Chancellor of the Exchequer 1997–9; chief economic adviser to the Treasury 1999–2004; Labour MP for Normanton since 2005; Secretary of State for Children, Schools and Families since 2007.

BEITH, ALAN Liberal then Liberal Democrat MP for Berwick-upon-Tweed from 1973; Liberal chief whip 1976–85; Liberal deputy leader and foreign-affairs spokesman 1985–7; Liberal Democrat Treasury spokesman 1988–94.

BENN, TONY Polemicist, memoirist, pamphleteer and diarist; renounced his hereditary title as Viscount Stansgate in 1963, Labour MP for Bristol South-East 1950–60, 1963–83, for Chesterfield 1984–2001; Minister of Technology 1966–70; Secretary of State for Industry 1974–5; president of the EEC council of energy ministers 1977.

BERNARD, DANIEL Diplomat; French ambassador to London 1998–2002; provoked a political storm after he was identified as the 'ambassador of a major European country' who at a party given by Lord Black of Crossharbour, proprietor of the *Daily Telegraph*, described Israel as 'a shitty little country' that had provoked an international security crisis; then became ambassador to Algeria.

BERTHOIN, GEORGES Civil servant; European Communities official and adviser; honorary international chairman of the European Movement since 1981.

BIFFEN, JOHN Conservative MP for Salop, Oswestry 1961–3, for Shropshire North 1983–97; Chief Secretary to the Treasury 1979–81; Secretary of State for Trade 1981–2; Lord President of the Council 1982–3; Leader of the House of Commons 1982–7; later Baron Biffen of Tanat.

BLACK, CONRAD Baron Black of Crossharbour; chairman and director of the Telegraph Group 1987–2005; chairman and chief executive of Hollinger International 1990–2003.

BLACKBURN, DAVID Solicitor, property consultant; also involved in the Kings Place development near King's Cross, new home of *The Guardian* from late 2008.

BLAIR, CHERIE QC (as Cherie Booth); married future Labour Party leader and prime minister Tony Blair in 1980; co-author of *The Goldfish Bowl: Married to the Prime Minister* (2004).

BLUMENTHAL, SIDNEY US journalist and author; assistant and special adviser to President Clinton 1997–2001.

BLUNKETT, DAVID Labour MP for Sheffield Brightside since 1987; Shadow Cabinet 1992–7; Secretary of State for Education and Employment 1997–2001; Home Secretary 2001–4; Work and Pensions Secretary 2005.

BOTTOMLEY, VIRGINIA Conservative MP for Surrey South-West 1984–2005; Secretary of State for Health 1992–5, for National Heritage 1995–7; later Baroness Bottomley of Nettlestone.

BOULTON, ADAM Political editor and presenter of Sky News since 1989; married in 2006 to Anji Hunter (q.v.).

BRITTAN, SIR LEON Barrister; Conservative MP for Cleveland and

Whitby 1974–83, for Richmond, Yorks., 1983–8; Chief Secretary to the Treasury 1981–3; Home Secretary 1983–5; Trade and Industry Secretary 1985–6; European commissioner 1989–99; later Baron Brittan of Spennithorne.

BROWN, GORDON University lecturer, television journalist; Labour MP for Dunfermline East 1983–2005, for Kirkcaldy and Cowdenbeath from 2005; Shadow Cabinet 1987–97; Chancellor of the Exchequer 1997–2007; prime minister from 2007.

BROWN, SIMON Baron Brown of Eaton-under-Heywood; High Court judge 1984–92; Lord Justice of Appeal 1992–2004.

BUDD, SIR ALAN Economist, university lecturer; chief economic adviser to the Treasury 1991–7; founder member of the Bank of England's Monetary Policy Committee, 1997–9; Provost of Queen's College, Oxford, 1999–2008.

CAMPBELL, ALASTAIR Journalist, sports columnist; political editor of the *Daily Mirror* 1989–93; press secretary to the Leader of the Opposition 1994–7; Prime Minister's official spokesman 1997–2001; director of communications and strategy, Prime Minister's Office, 2001–3.

CAMPBELL, GORDON, Baron Campbell of Croy Diplomat; Conservative MP for Moray and Nairn 1959–February 1974; Secretary of State for Scotland 1970–74.

CARLISLE, MARK Barrister, judge; Conservative MP for Runcorn 1964–83, for Warrington South 1983–7; Secretary of State for Education and Science 1979–81; later Baron Carlisle of Bucklow.

CARRINGTON, PETER, 6th Baron Carrington Leader of the Opposition in the House of Lords 1964–70; 1974–9; Secretary of State for Defence 1970–74; Foreign Secretary 1979–82; Secretary General of NATO 1984–8; became a life peer, Baron Carrington of Upton, after House of Lords reform in 1999.

CHAPPLE, FRANK General secretary of the Electrical, Electronic, Telecommunication and Plumbing Union (EETPU) 1966–84; Labour Party NEC member 1965–71; later Baron Chapple of Hoxton.

CHIRAC, JACQUES Prime minister of France 1974–6 and 1986–8; president of France 1995–2007.

CLARK, ALAN Historian, diarist; read law, but never practised; Conservative MP for Plymouth, Sutton 1974–92, for Kensington and Chelsea 1997–9; Minister of State at the MoD 1989–92.

CLARKE, CHARLES Labour MP for Norwich South since 1997; junior Home Office minister 1999–2001; Minister without Portfolio and chairman of the Labour Party 2001–2; Secretary of State for Education and Skills 2002–4; Home Secretary 2004–6.

COOK, ROBERT FINLAYSON 'ROBIN' Labour MP for Edinburgh Central

1974–83, for Livingstone 1983–2005; Opposition Treasury spokesman 1980–83; Opposition front-bench spokesman on European and
Community affairs 1983–4, on trade 1986–7, on health 1987–92, on
trade and industry 1992–4, on foreign and Commonwealth affairs
1994–7; chairman of the Labour Party 1996–7; Foreign Secretary
1997–2001; Leader of the Commons 2001–3; resigned from the
Cabinet over the Iraq war 2003.

COOPER, SIR FRANK Civil servant; Permanent Undersecretary at the
Northern Ireland Office 1973–6, at the MoD 1976–82; chairman of
the Institute of Contemporary British History 1986–92.

CORNFORD, JAMES Director of the Nuffield Foundation, 1980–88, of
the Institute for Public Policy Research 1989–94, of the Paul Ham-
lyn Foundation, 1994–7; chairman of the Dartington Hall Trust
2002–7.

CORNISH, ROBERT FRANCIS Soldier, diplomat; director of British Information Service, New York, 1996–90; head of FCO news department
1990–93; ambassador to Israel 1998–2001.

CUMMINGS, DOMINIC Head of research, and campaigns director,
Business for Sterling 1999–2001; director of strategy for Iain Duncan
Smith January–September 2002.

CURRY, DAVID Journalist; Conservative MEP for Essex North-East
1979–89; Conservative MP for Skipton and Ripon since 1987; junior
minister at MAFF 1992–3; at Energy 1993–7

DAVIES, JOHN Oil-industry businessman; director general of the CBI in
the 1960s; Conservative MP for Knutsford 1970–79. Edward Heath
(q.v.) appointed him Secretary of State for Trade and Industry 1970–
72. Enoch Powell, a Conservative critic of Mr Heath, likened this
to Caligula's appointment of his horse as a Roman consul. Became
Chancellor of the Duchy of Lancaster in 1972.

DE CHASTELAIN, GENERAL JOHN Canadian soldier; chairman of the
Independent International Commission on Decommissioning, Northern Ireland, since 1997.

DELL, EDMUND Labour MP for Birkenhead 1964–79; Paymaster General 1974–6; Secretary of State for Trade 1976–8; founder chairman
of Channel 4 TV 1980–87.

DENMAN, SIR ROY ambassador and head of the European Communities
delegation in Washington 1982–9.

DEWAR, DONALD Labour MP for Glasgow Garscadden 1987–97, for
Glasgow Anniesland 1997–2000; Shadow Cabinet member 1984–97;
Secretary of State for Scotland 1997–9; first minister of the Scottish
Parliament 1999–2000.

DIANA, PRINCESS OF WALES Born Diana Spencer; married Charles,

Prince of Wales, 29 July 1981; mother of princes William and Harry; divorced 28 August 1996; a campaigner for Aids awareness, she also supported the campaign to ban landmines.

DONALDSON, SIR JOHN QC; Baron Donaldson of Lymington; judge, president of the National Industrial Relations Court 1971–4; Master of the Rolls 1982–92.

DONOUGHUE, BERNARD Journalist, historian, academic, senior policy adviser to the Prime Minister 1974–9; as Baron Donoughue of Ashton, Opposition spokesman in the Lords on Treasury, Energy and National Heritage 1991–7.

DORRELL, STEPHEN Conservative MP for Loughborough 1979–97, for Charnwood since 1997; Secretary of State for National Heritage 1992–5, for Health 1995–7.

DUNCAN, ALAN Conservative MP for Rutland and Melton since 1992; PPS to the Leader of the Opposition 1997; vice-chairman of the Conservative Party 1997–8.

DUNCAN SMITH, IAIN Conservative MP for Chingford 1992–7, for Chingford and Woodford Green since 1997; leader of the Conservative Party and Leader of the Opposition 2001–3.

DYKES, HUGH Conservative MP for Harrow East 1970–97; MEP Strasbourg, 1974–7; chairman, of the European Movement 1990–97; joined the Liberal Democrats 1997; later Baron Dykes of Harrow Weald.

ELWYN-JONES, FREDERICK QC; Labour MP for Plaistow division of West Ham 1945–50, for West Ham South 1950–74; Attorney General 1964–70; as Baron Elwyn-Jones of Llanelli and Newham, Lord High Chancellor of Great Britain 1974–9; Lord of Appeal from 1979.

ERRERA, GERARD Diplomat; French ambassador to NATO, Brussels, 1995–8; ambassador to London from 2002.

FIELD, FRANK Campaigner, polemicist; Labour MP for Birkenhead since 1979; director of the Child Poverty Action Group 1969–79, of the Low Pay Unit 1974–80; Minister for Welfare Reform 1997–8.

FIGGURES, SIR FRANK Treasury civil servant 1946–74 and chairman of the Pay Board during the government of Edward Heath (q.v.).

FINKELSTEIN, DANIEL Director of the Social Market Foundation 1992–5, of the Conservative Research Department 1995–8; now comment editor of *The Times*.

FOWLER, WYCHE US Democratic politician; junior Senator for Georgia 1987–93; ambassador to Saudi Arabia 1996–2001.

FRASER, MICHAEL Deputy chairman of the Conservative Party 1964–75; later Baron Fraser of Kilmorack.

GAREL-JONES, TRISTAN Linguist, merchant banker; Conservative MP for Watford 1979–97; deputy chief whip 1989–90; Minister of State at the FCO 1990–93; later Baron Garel-Jones of Watford.

GEORGE, EDWARD 'EDDIE' Governor of the Bank of England 1993–2003; later Baron George of St Tudy.

GILMOUR, IAN Journalist, barrister, historian; Conservative MP for Norfolk Central 1962–74, for Chesham and Amersham 1974–92; Secretary of State for Defence 1972–4; Lord Privy Seal 1979–81; later Baron Gilmour of Craigmillar.

GODBER, JOSEPH Businessman; Conservative MP for Grantham, Lincs, 1951–79; Minister of Agriculture, Fisheries and Food 1972–4; later Baron Godber of Willington.

GOLDSMITH, SIR JAMES 'JIMMY' Businessman; French MEP 1994–7; founder of the Referendum Party, for which contested Putney in 1997.

GORMLEY, JOE Trade unionist; president of the NUM 1971–82; later Baron Gormley of Ashton-in-Makerfield.

GOULD, BRYAN Diplomat, university lecturer, television reporter; Labour MP for Southampton Test 1974–9, for Dagenham 1983–94; Shadow Cabinet 1986–92; vice-chancellor of Waikato University, NZ, 1994–2004.

GOULD, PHILIP Pollster, political strategist; later Baron Gould of Brookwood.

GREENSTOCK, SIR JEREMY Diplomat; political director at the FCO 1996–8; UK permanent representative to the UN 1998–2003; UK special representative for Iraq 2003–4; director of the Ditchley Foundation since 2004.

GRIMOND, JO Barrister; Liberal MP for Orkney and Shetland 1950–83; leader of the Liberal Party 1956–67 and briefly in 1976; trustee of *The Guardian* and *Manchester Evening News* 1967–83; later Baron Grimond of Firth.

GUMMER, JOHN SELWYN Publisher; Conservative MP for Eye, Suffolk, 1979–83, for Suffolk Coastal since 1983; Paymaster General 1984–5; chairman of the Conservative Party 1983–5; Minister of Agriculture, Fisheries and Food 1989–93; Environment Secretary 1993–7.

HAGUE, WILLIAM Conservative MP for Richmond, Yorks, since February 1989; Secretary of State for Wales 1995–7; leader of the Conservative Party and Leader of the Opposition 1997–2001; biographer of William Pitt the Younger.

HAILSHAM, LORD Formerly Quintin Hogg QC; Viscount Hailsham of St Marylebone; Conservative MP for Oxford City 1928–50; disclaimed a peerage as 2nd Viscount Hailsham in 1963 to contest the Conservative leadership and represent St Marylebone 1963–70;

Shadow Cabinet during the Wilson years; became a life peer and Lord Chancellor 1979–87 under Edward Heath (q.v.).

HAIN, PETER Anti-apartheid campaigner, activist; chairman of the Young Liberals 1971–3; Labour MP for Neath since 1991; junior Foreign Office minister 1999–2000 and 2001–2; DTI minister 2001; Secretary of State for Wales 2002–8, for Northern Ireland 2005–7, for Work and Pensions 2007–8.

HAINES, JOE Political journalist, author; chief press secretary to prime minister Harold Wilson (q.v.) 1969–70 and 1972–6, and to the Leader of the Opposition 1970–74; director of Mirror Group Newspapers 1986–92.

HARRIS, JOHN Journalist, polemicist; personal assistant to Labour leader Hugh Gaitskell 1959–62; director of publicity for the Labour Party 1962–4; special adviser to Roy Jenkins (q.v.) at the Home Office 1965–7, at the Treasury 1967–70; as Lord Harris of Greenwich, Minister of State at the Home Office 1974–9; joined the SDP, and became a Liberal Democrat home-affairs spokesman in the House of Lords 1988–94.

HAVERS, SIR MICHAEL QC; writer, judge; Conservative MP for Wimbledon 1970–87; Solicitor General 1972–4; Attorney General 1979–87; later Baron Havers of St Edmundsbury.

HEATH, SIR EDWARD 'TED' Conservative MP for Bexley 1950–74, for Bexley, Sidcup, 1974–83, for Old Bexley and Sidcup 1983–2001; leader of the Conservative party 1965–75; prime minister 1970–74; led Britain into the European Community in 1973. While Leader of the Opposition, he captained his yacht *Morning Cloud* to victory in the Sydney to Hobart race in 1969; in 1971, while Prime Minister, he skippered Britain to victory in the Admiral's Cup. He also conducted the London Symphony Orchestra and the Royal Liverpool Philharmonic at gala concerts.

HEALEY, DENIS Author, essayist, memoirist; Labour MP for South-East Leeds 1952–5, for Leeds East 1955–92; Secretary of State for Defence 1964–70; Chancellor of the Exchequer 1974–9; deputy leader of the Labour Party 1980–83; later Baron Healey of Riddlesden.

HESELTINE, MICHAEL Magazine publisher; Conservative MP for Tavistock 1966–74, for Henley 1974–2001; Secretary of State for the Environment 1979–83, for Defence 1983–6 (resigned over the Westland affair); contested the leadership of the Conservative Party 1990; Environment Secretary 1990–92; Trade and Industry Secretary 1992–5; deputy prime minister 1995–7; later Baron Heseltine of Thenford.

HEWITT, PATRICIA General secretary of the National Council for Civil

Liberties 1974–83; policy coordinator to the Leader of the Opposition 1988–9; Labour MP for Leicester West since 1997; Secretary of State for Trade and Industry 2002–5, for Health 2005–7.

HOGE, JAMES US journalist; editor of *Foreign Affairs*; chairman of the International Center for Journalists.

HOWE, GEOFFREY Conservative MP for Bebington 1964–6, for Reigate 1970–74, for Surrey East 1974–92; DTI minister 1972–4; Chancellor of the Exchequer 1979–83; Foreign Secretary 1983–9; Leader of the House of Commons and deputy prime minister 1989–90; later Baron Howe of Aberavon.

HOLME, RICHARD President of the Liberal Party 1980–81; chairman of the Constitutional Reform Centre 1985–94; as Baron Holme of Cheltenham, Liberal Democrat spokesman in the House of Lords 1992–9.

HOON, GEOFFREY Labour MEP for Derbyshire 1984–94; Labour MP for Ashfield since 1992; Secretary of State for Defence 1999–2005; Lord Privy Seal and Leader of the House of Commons 2005–6; chief whip since 2007.

HUNT, DAVID Solicitor; Conservative MP for Wirral 1976–83, for Wirral West 1983–97; Secretary of State for Wales 1990–93; Chancellor of the Duchy of Lancaster and Minister for Public Service and Science 1994–5; later Baron Hunt of Wirral.

HUNTER, ANGELA JANE 'ANJI' Special assistant to Tony Blair, both as Leader of the Opposition 1994–7 and as prime minister 1997–2001; married in 2006 to Adam Boulton (q.v.).

HUNTER, ROBERT US ambassador to NATO 1993–8; now senior adviser to the Rand Corporation and president of the Atlantic Treaty Association.

HURD, DOUGLAS Novelist, historian, memoirist; former diplomat; Conservative Research Department 1966–8; private secretary to then Leader of the Opposition Edward Heath (q.v.) 1968–70; political secretary to prime minister Edward Heath 1970–74; Conservative MP for Mid Oxon 1974–83, for Witney 1983–97; Foreign Office minister 1979–1983; Home Office minister 1983–4; Northern Ireland Secretary 1984–5; Home Secretary 1985–9; Foreign Secretary 1989–95; later Baron Hurd of Westwell.

JACKSON, ROBERT Journalist; fellow of All Souls 1968–86; Conservative MEP for Upper Thames 1979–84; Conservative MP for Wantage 1983–2005; Labour MP for Wantage since 2005; junior minister at Education and Science 1987–90, at Employment 1990–92, at Office of Public Service and Science 1992–93.

JENKINS, ROY Author, historian, biographer; Labour MP for Central

Southwark 1948–50, for Stechford, Birmingham, 1950–76; SDP MP for Glasgow Hillhead 1982–7; Minister of Aviation 1964–5; Home Secretary 1965–7 and 1974–6; Chancellor of the Exchequer 1967–70; president of the European Commission 1977–1981; co-founder of the SDP in 1981; chancellor of Oxford University 1987; later Baron Jenkins of Hillhead.

JENKINS, SIR SIMON Author, journalist; columnist for the *Evening Standard* 1968–74 and editor 1976–8; political editor of *The Economist* 1979–86; editor of *The Times* 1990–92; columnist for *The Times* 1992–2005; columnist for *The Guardian* from 2005.

JOWELL, TESSA Labour MP for Dulwich 1992–7, for Dulwich and West Norwood since 1997; Minister for Women 1998–2001; Secretary of State for Culture, Media and Sport 2001–7; Minister for the Olympics since 2005; Minister for London and Paymaster General since 2007.

KAUFMAN, SIR GERALD Author, journalist, political correspondent; Labour MP for Manchester Ardwick 1970–83, for Manchester Gorton since 1983; junior Department of Industry minister 1974–9; Shadow Cabinet and Opposition spokesman on environment, home and foreign affairs 1980–92.

KEDOURIE, ELIE Professor of politics in the University of London 1965–90; founder and editor of *Middle Eastern Studies*.

KEMP, SIR PETER Civil servant; Second Permanent Secretary in the Cabinet Office 1988–92.

KERR, SIR JOHN Diplomat; ambassador to the US 1995–7; Permanent Undersecretary FCO and head of the Diplomatic Service 1997–2002; later Baron Kerr of Kinlochard.

KINNOCK, NEIL Labour MP for Bedwellty 1970–83, for Islwyn 1983–95; leader of the Labour Party and Leader of the Opposition 1983–92; European commissioner 1995–2004; chairman of the British Council since 2004; later Baron Kinnock of Bedwellty.

KINSMAN, JEREMY Canadian high commissioner in the UK 2000–2002; ambassador to the European Union 2002–6.

KISSINGER, HENRY US Secretary of State 1973–7; Nobel peace laureate 1973; counsellor to the Centre for Strategic and International Studies since 1977.

KOGAN, MAURICE Civil servant; professor of government and social administration 1969–95 and from 1990 director of the Centre for the Evaluation of Public Policy, Brunel University.

LAMONT, NORMAN Merchant banker; Conservative MP for Kingston upon Thames 1972–97; Treasury minister 1986–90; Chancellor of the Exchequer 1990–93; later Baron Lamont of Lerwick.

LANDER, SIR STEPHEN Director general of the Security Service 1996–2002; director of Customs and Excise 2002–5; chairman of the Serious Organized Crime Agency since 2004.

LANE, GEOFFREY DAWSON Baron Lane of St Ippollitts; QC; Lord Chief Justice of England 1980–92.

LANG, IAN Conservative MP for Galloway 1979–83, for Galloway and Upper Nithsdale 1983–97; Secretary of State for Scotland 1990–95, for Trade and Industry 1995–7; later Baron Lang of Monckton.

LANSLEY, ANDREW Civil servant; Conservative MP for Cambridgeshire South since 1997; vice-chairman of the Conservative Party 1998–9; shadow Chancellor of the Duchy of Lancaster 1999–2001.

LAWSON, NIGEL Journalist; special assistant to prime minister Alec Douglas-Home 1963–4; editor of *The Spectator* 1966–70; Conservative MP for Blaby, Leicestershire, 1974–92; Financial Secretary to the Treasury 1979–81; Secretary of State for Energy 1981–3; Chancellor of the Exchequer 1983–9; later Baron Lawson of Blaby.

LESTER, ANTHONY QC; special adviser to Home Secretary Roy Jenkins (q.v.) 1974–6; chairman of the Runnymede Trust 1991–3; member of the Parliamentary Joint Human Rights Commission 2001–4; prominent Liberal Democrat; later Baron Lester of Herne Hill.

LIDDLE, ROGER Special adviser on European affairs to the Prime Minister 1997–2004; principal adviser to the President of the European Commission since 2006.

LILLEY, PETER Conservative MP for St Albans 1983–97, for Hitchin and Harpenden since 1997; Trade and Industry Secretary 1990–92; Social Security Secretary 1992–7; deputy leader of the Conservative Party 1998–9.

LIVINGSTONE, KEN Leader of the Greater London Council 1981–6; Labour MP for Brent East 1987–2001; member of the council of the Zoological Society of London 1994–2000; mayor of London 2000–2008.

MCALPINE, ALISTAIR Treasurer 1975–90 and deputy chairman 1979–83 of the Conservative Party; created Baron McAlpine of West Green 1984; defected to Sir James Goldsmith's Referendum Party in 1996.

MCCAFFREY, SIR TOM Press secretary 10 Downing Street 1971–2; director of information, Home Office, 1972–4; head of news at the FCO 1974–6; chief press secretary to prime minister James Callaghan 1976–9; chief assistant to Michael Foot 1980–83.

MCGAHEY, MICK Scottish miner's leader and a lifelong Communist; elected vice-president of the NUM in 1972.

MCINTOSH, SIR RONALD Civil servant; deputy Undersecretary of State at the Department of Employment 1970–72; deputy secretary at the Treasury 1972–3; director general of the National Economic Development Office 1973–7.

MACLENNAN, ROBERT 'BOB' Labour MP for Caithness and Sutherland 1966–81, then Social Democrat MP, Social and Liberal Democrat, and later Liberal Democrat MP till 1997; Liberal Democrat MP for Caithness, Sutherland and Easter Ross 1997–2001; president of the Liberal Democrats 1994–8; later Lord Maclennan of Rogart.

MACMILLAN, MAURICE Publisher, son of former Conservative prime minister Harold Macmillan, 1st Earl of Stockton; Conservative MP for Halifax 1955–64; Secretary of State for Employment 1972–3; Paymaster General 1973–4; later Viscount Macmillan of Ovenden.

MACSHANE, DENIS Journalist, trade unionist; Labour MP for Rother-ham since 1992; director of the European Policy Institute 1992–4; junior Foreign Office minister 2002–5.

MADEL, SIR DAVID Conservative MP for South Bedfordshire 1970–83, for Bedfordshire South-West 1983–2001; member of the House of Commons European-legislation committee 1983–97.

MAJOR, SIR JOHN Conservative MP for Huntingdonshire 1979–83, for Huntingdon 1983–2001; Foreign Secretary 1989; Chancellor of the Exchequer 1989–90; prime minister and leader of the Conservative Party 1990–97.

MARQUAND, DAVID Historian, professor, lecturer in politics, political commentator and biographer of Ramsay MacDonald; leader writer for *The Guardian* 1959–62; Labour MP for Ashfield 1966–77; British delegate to the Council of Europe 1970–73; chief adviser to the Secretariat General of the European Commission 1977–8;

MATES, MICHAEL Conservative MP for Petersfield 1974–83, for East Hampshire since 1983; Minister of State for Northern Ireland 1992–3 (resigned).

MATUSSEK, THOMAS German diplomat, ambassador to the UK 2002–6.

MAYHEW, PATRICK QC; Conservative MP for Tunbridge Wells 1974–97; Solicitor General 1983–7; Attorney General 1987–92; Secretary of State for Northern Ireland 1992–7; later Baron Mayhew of Twysden.

MEYER, SIR CHRISTOPHER Diplomat; press secretary to prime minister John Major (q.v.) 1994–6; ambassador to Germany 1997, to the US 1997–2003; chairman of the Press Complaints Commission from 2003.

MILIBAND, DAVID Head of policy, Leader of the Opposition's office 1994–7; head of the Prime Minister's policy unit 1998–2001; Labour MP for South Shields since 2001; junior minister at the Department for Education and Skills 2002–4; Secretary of State for Environment, Food and Rural Affairs 2006–7; Foreign Secretary since 2007.

MILLER, FRANKLIN 'FRANK' US Department of Defense official; senior director for defence policy and arms control 2001; National Security Council 2001–5.

MONKS, JOHN General secretary of the TUC 1993–2003; general secretary of the European Trades Union Confederation since 2003.

MOORE, JOHN Conservative MP for Croydon Central 1974–92; Secretary of State for Transport 1986–7, for Health and Social Services 1987–8, for Social Security 1988–9; later Baron Moore of Lower Marsh.

MORRIS, BILL Jamaican-born general secretary of the TGWU 1991–2003; president of the TUC 2000–2001; later Baron Morris of Handsworth.

MORTON, SIR ALASTAIR Former chief executive of Eurotunnel 1990–94; chairman of the UK Treasury's private-finance panel 1993–5; appointed by deputy prime minister John Prescott (q.v.) to head the Strategic Rail Authority 1991–2001.

MOWLAM, MARJORIE 'MO' University lecturer; Labour MP for Redcar 1987–2001; Northern Ireland Secretary 1997–9.

MURDOCH, RUPERT Australian-born publisher and chief of News Corporation (United States) and News International Plc, publishers of *The Times*, the *Sunday Times*, the *News of the World* and *The Sun*; chairman of Fox Entertainment Group and British Sky Broadcasting.

MURRAY, LIONEL 'LEN' General secretary of the TUC 1973–84; later Baron Murray of Epping Forest.

NANDY, DIPAK Lecturer, broadcaster, journalist; founder director of the Runnymede Trust 1968–73; deputy chief executive of the Equal Opportunities Commission 1976–86.

NEWHOUSE, JOHN Author; former Washington correspondent for the *New Yorker*; senior policy adviser on European affairs to US deputy Secretary of State Strobe Talbott 1998–2001; now senior fellow with the Center for Defense Information.

OWEN, DAVID Medical doctor, Labour MP for Plymouth Sutton 1966–74, for Plymouth Devonport 1974–81, then SDP MP for Plymouth Devonport 1981–92; Foreign Secretary 1977–9; co-founder of the SDP in 1981, and leader 1983–7 and 1988–90; appointed by prime minister John Major (q.v.) as EU co-chairman of the International Conference on Former Yugoslavia 1992–5; later Baron Owen of Plymouth.

PAKENHAM, SIR MICHAEL Diplomat; deputy secretary, overseas and defence, Cabinet Office 1997–9; chairman of the Joint Intelligence

Committee 1997–2000 and intelligence coordinator 1999–2000; ambassador to Poland 2001–3.

PALLISER, SIR MICHAEL Soldier, diplomat; ambassador to the European Communities 1973–5; head of the Diplomatic Service 1975–82; president of the China–Britain Trade Group 1992–6.

PATTEN, CHRIS Conservative MP for Bath 1979–92; Conservative Research Department 1966–70; Cabinet Office 1970–72; director of the Conservative Research Department 1974–9; minister in the Department of Education and Science 1985–6, in Overseas Development 1986–9; Secretary of State for the Environment 1989–90; chairman of the Conservative Party 1990–92; Governor General of Hong Kong 1992–7; European commissioner 1999–2004; later Baron Patten of Barnes.

PATTEN, JOHN Author; Conservative MP for Oxford West and Abingdon 1983–97; Minister of State for Housing, Urban Affairs and Construction 1985–7; Home Office minister 1987–92; Secretary of State for Education 1992–4; later Baron Patten of Wincanton.

PHILLIPS, SIR (GERALD) HAYDEN Civil servant; principal private secretary to the Home Secretary 1974–6; assistant secretary at the Home Office 1979–81; assistant Undersecretary of State at the Home Office 1981–6; deputy secretary at the Cabinet Office 1986–8.

PLOETZ, DR HANS-FRIEDRICH VON German diplomat; ambassador to the UK 1999–2002, to the Russian Federation 2002–5.

PORTILLO, MICHAEL Broadcaster and journalist; Conservative MP for Enfield, Southgate, 1984–97, for Kensington and Chelsea 1999–2005; Chief Secretary to the Treasury 1992–4; Employment Secretary 1994–5; Defence Secretary 1995–7; away from Westminster, has made several well-received television documentaries.

POWELL, JONATHAN Journalist, diplomat; chief of staff to the Leader of the Opposition 1995–7; chief of staff to the Prime Minister 1997–2007.

PRESCOTT, JOHN Trades unionist; a steward in the merchant navy and an official for the National Union of Seamen before becoming Labour MP for Kingston upon Hull East in 1970; deputy leader of the Labour Party 1994–2007; deputy prime minister 1997–2007.

PRESTON, PETER Novelist and journalist; editor of *The Guardian* 1975–95, co-director of the Guardian Foundation since 1997.

PRIOR, JAMES 'JIM' Conservative MP for Lowestoft, Suffolk, 1959–83, for Waveney 1983–7; Minister of Agriculture, Fisheries and Food 1970–72; Leader of the House of Commons 1972–4; Secretary of State for Employment 1979–81; Secretary of State for Northern Ireland 1981–4; later Baron Prior of Brampton.

PUTTNAM, DAVID Broadcaster, film producer; member of the Arts Council Lottery Panel 1995–8; chairman of the National Endowment for Science, Technology and the Arts since 1998; later Baron Puttnam of Queensgate.

PYM, FRANCIS Conservative MP for Cambridgeshire 1961–83, for Cambridgeshire South-East 1983–7; Secretary of State for Northern Ireland 1973–4, for Defence 1979–81; Leader of the House of Commons 1981–2; Foreign Secretary, 1982–3; later Baron Pym of Sandy.

RENWICK, ROBIN Diplomat; ambassador to South Africa 1987–91, to Washington 1991–5; later Baron Renwick of Clifton.

RHYS-WILLIAMS, SIR BRANDON Conservative MP for Kensington South 1968–74, for Kensington 1974–88; one of a group of occasional 'Tory rebels' during the Thatcher years. When he died, in 1988, Frank Field (q.v.), described him in *The Guardian* as 'Tory champion of the vulnerable'. Ben Bousquet, Caribbean-born Labour candidate for the same seat, served as an usher at Sir Brandon's funeral.

RICHARDS, SIR FRANCIS Director of the Government Communications Headquarters at Cheltenham 1998–2003; governor of Gibraltar 2003–6.

RICKETTS, SIR PETER Diplomat; director of international security at the FCO 1999–2000; chairman of the Joint Intelligence Committee, Cabinet Office, 2000–2001; political director at the FCO, 2001–3; Permanent Undersecretary at the FCO and head of the Diplomatic Service since 2006.

RIDLEY, SIR ADAM Foreign Office, Treasury; economic adviser to the Shadow Cabinet 1974–79; director of the Conservative Research Department 1979; special adviser to the Chancellor of the Exchequer 1979–84.

RIFKIND, SIR MALCOLM QC; Conservative MP for Edinburgh Pentlands 1974–97, for Kensington and Chelsea from 2005; junior Foreign Office minister 1982–6; Secretary of State for Scotland 1986–90, for Transport 1990–92, for Defence 1992–5; Foreign Secretary 1995–7.

ROBENS, ALFRED Baron Robens of Woldingham Labour MP for Wansbeck Division of Northumberland 1945–50, for Blyth 1950–60; junior minister at the Department of Transport 1945–7, for fuel and power 1947–51; chairman of the National Coal Board 1961–71; director of the Bank of England 1966–81.

RODGERS, WILLIAM Labour MP for Stockton on Tees 1962–74; Labour then SDP MP for Teesside, Stockton, 1974–82; Secretary of State for Transport 1976–9; co-founder of the SDP in 1981, and vice-president 1982–7; director general of the Royal Institute of British Architects 1987–94; chairman of the Advertising Standards Authority

1995–2001; as Baron Rodgers of Quarry Bank, leader of the Liberal Democrats in the House of Lords 1998–2001.

ROWE, ANDREW Journalist; Conservative MP for Mid-Kent 1983–97, for Faversham and Mid-Kent 1997–2001; consultant to Home Office 1974; director of community affairs, Conservative Central Office, 1975–9.

RUSHDIE, SALMAN Novelist, critic; the centre of a storm over his novel *The Satanic Verses*, his life was threatened after he became the subject of a fatwa by Iranian religious leaders.

RUSSELL, CONRAD 5th Earl Russell; historian; Liberal Democrat peer elected to the House of Lords 1999.

ST JOHN-STEVAS, NORMAN Conservative MP for Chelmsford 1964–87; arts minister 1979; Leader of the House of Commons and Chancellor of the Duchy of Lancaster 1979–81; later Baron St John of Fawsley.

SCHREIBER, MARK Conservative Research Department 1963–7; director of the Conservative Party Public Sector Research Unit 1967–70; special adviser to the government 1970–74, to the Leader of the Opposition 1974–5; lobby correspondent of *The Economist* 1976–91; director of Times Newspapers Holdings from 1991; as Baron Marlesford, member of the House of Lords select committee on the EU from 2003.

SEITZ, RAYMOND US diplomat; chief of mission at the US embassy in London 1984–9; ambassador to the UK 1991–4.

SHORE, PETER Labour MP for Stepney 1964–74, for Stepney and Poplar 1974–83, for Bethnal Green and Stepney 1983–97; Secretary of State for Economic Affairs 1967–9; Minister without Portfolio 1969–70; Trade Secretary 1974–6; Environment Secretary 1976–9; shadow Leader of the House of Commons 1984–7; later Baron Shore of Stepney.

SHORT, RENEE Journalist, Labour MP for Wolverhampton North-East 1964–87; chair of the Commons select committee on social services 1979–87.

SIRS, WILLIAM 'BILL' General secretary of the Iron and Steel Trades Confederation 1975–85.

SMITH, JOHN QC; Labour MP for North Lanarkshire 1970–83, for Monklands East 1983–94; Trade Secretary 1978–9; principal Opposition spokesman on trade, prices and consumer protection 1979–82, on energy 1982–3, on employment 1983–4, on trade and industry 1984–7, on Treasury and economic affairs 1987–92; Labour leader from 1992 until his sudden death in 1994.

SPARROW, NICK Managing director of ICM Research; pollster for the Conservative Party 1996–2003.

SPICER, SIR MICHAEL Journalist, novelist; Conservative MP for South Worcestershire 1974–97, for West Worcestershire 1997; deputy chairman of the Conservative Party 1983–4; junior minister in the Department of Transport 1984–7, in the Department of Energy 1987–90.

STEEL, DAVID Journalist, broadcaster, author; Liberal MP 1965–88, Liberal Democrat MP 1988–97, for Roxburgh, Selkirk and Peebles 1965–83, for Tweeddale, Ettrick and Lauderdale 1983–97; sponsor of a private member's bill to reform the law on abortion 1966–7; leader of the Liberal Party 1976–88, co-founder of the Social and Liberal Democrats 1988; presiding officer in the Scottish Parliament 1999–2003; later Baron Steel of Aikwood.

STEPHENS, PHILIP Journalist; *Financial Times* economics correspondent 1983–8, political editor 1988–94, political commentator 1994–9, editor of the UK edition 1999–2003, associate editor since 2003.

STEVENS, JOHN Conservative MEP for the Thames Valley 1989–99, co-founder of the Pro-Euro Conservative Party; later joined the Liberal Democrats.

TAVERNE, DICK QC; Labour MP for Lincoln 1962–72; Democratic Labour MP for Lincoln 1973–4; Financial Secretary to the Treasury 1969–70; chairman of the Public Policy Centre 1984–7; member of the national committee of the SDP 1981–7, of the federal policy committee of the Liberal Democrats 1989–90; later Baron Taverne of Pimlico.

TAYLOR, IAN Conservative MP for Esher 1987–97, for Esher and Walton since 1997; junior DTI minister 1994–7; science minister 1994–5; chairman of the European Movement 2000–2004; chairman of the Tory Europe Network from 2002.

THATCHER, MARGARET HILDA Research chemist, barrister; Conservative MP for Finchley 1959–92; Education Secretary 1970–74; Leader of the Opposition 1975–9, prime minister 1979–1990; later Baroness Thatcher of Kesteven.

THORPE, JEREMY Barrister, television journalist, Liberal MP for Devon North 1959–79; leader of the Liberal Party 1967–76. He was later accused and acquitted of conspiring to murder a man who claimed to be a former lover.

TOMKYS, SIR ROGER Diplomat; ambassador to Bahrain 1981–4, to Syria 1984–6; principal financial officer at the FCO 1986–9; deputy Under-secretary of State 1989–90; high commissioner to Kenya 1990–92.

VARLEY, ERIC Trade unionist; Labour MP for Chesterfield 1964–84; Secretary of State for Energy 1974–5; for Industry 1975–9; Labour Party treasurer 1981–3; later Baron Varley of Chesterfield.

VYVYAN, MAJOR-GENERAL CHARLES Soldier; former British defence attaché in Washington; now a businessman, strategic adviser to the Bank of America, and visiting fellow of the Eisenhower Institute.

WALDEGRAVE, WILLIAM Conservative MP for Bristol West 1979–97; central policy review staff, Cabinet Office 1971–3; political staff, 10 Downing Street, 1973–74; Minister for Environment and Countryside 1985–7, for Planning 1986–8, for Housing 1987–8, at the FCO 1988–90; Secretary of State for Health 1990–92; Chancellor of the Duchy of Lancaster 1992–4; Minister of Agriculture 1994–5; Chief Secretary to the Treasury 1995–7; later Baron Waldegrave of North Hill.

WALL, SIR (JOHN) STEPHEN Diplomat; press officer at 10 Downing Street 1976–7; private secretary to the Prime Minister 1991–3; ambassador to Portugal 1993–5, to Brussels 1995–2000; head of the European secretariat, Cabinet Office, 2000–2004.

WHITELAW, WILLIAM 'WILLIE' Conservative MP for Penrith and Border division of Cumberland 1955–83; Leader of the House of Commons 1970–72; Secretary of State for Northern Ireland 1972–3, for Employment 1973–4; chairman of the Conservative Party 1974–5; deputy Leader of the Opposition 1975–9; Home Secretary 1979–83; as Viscount Whitelaw of Penrith, Leader of the House of Lords 1983–8. Margaret Thatcher (q.v.) once famously said, 'Every prime minister needs a Willie.'

WILLEMS, LODE Belgian diplomat; ambassador to the UK 1997–2002, to Germany 2002–6.

WILLIAMS, GARETH WYN QC; member of the Bar Council 1986–92; junior minister at the Home Office 1997–9; Attorney General 1999–2001; as Baron Williams of Mostyn. Leader of the House of Lords 2001–3.

WILLIAMS, SHIRLEY Labour MP for Hitchin 1964–74, for Hertford and Stevenage 1974–9; SDP MP for Crosby 1981–3; minister during the Wilson government 1964–70; Shadow Cabinet 1970–74; Secretary of State for Prices and Consumer Protection 1974–6; for Education and Science and Paymaster General 1976–9; co-founder of the SDP in 1981, and president 1982–8; as Baroness Williams of Crosby, leader of the Liberal Democrats in the House of Lords 2001–4.

WILSON, DES Journalist, campaigner, publicist, novelist; *Guardian* columnist 1968–71; director of Shelter 1967–71; head of public affairs at the Royal Shakespeare Company 1974–6; chairman of the Campaign for Lead-Free Air (CLEAR) 1982–90, of Friends of the Earth 1983–6, of the Campaign for Freedom of Information 1984–90; president of the Liberal Party 1986–7; director of the general-election campaign for the Liberal Democrats 1990–92.

WILSON, HAROLD Labour MP for Ormskirk 1945–50, for Huyton 1950–83; leader of the Labour Party 1963–76; prime minister 1964–70 and from 1974 to his sudden resignation in 1976, after which the onset of Alzheimer's disease became apparent; later Baron Wilson of Rievaulx. A populist, Wilson smoked a pipe in public, holidayed every year in the Isles of Scilly, wore a Gannex raincoat, and gave the Beatles the MBE. He left office announcing a list of honours that caused uproar: one recipient was later imprisoned for fraud, and another committed suicide while under police investigation.

WILSON, SIR RICHARD Civil servant; Cabinet Secretary 1998–2002; later Baron Wilson of Dinton.

WINDLESHAM, LORD Minister at the Home Office 1970–72, at the Northern Ireland Office 1972–3; Lord Privy Seal 1973–4; director of *The Observer* 1981–9.

WOLFF, MICHAEL JP; journalist with the *Daily Express*, and the *Sunday Telegraph*; editor of the Conservative journal *Crossbow*; special adviser to the government 1970–74; director general of the Conservative Party Organization 1974–5; died suddenly.

WORCESTER, PROFESSOR SIR ROBERT 'BOB' Pollster, political commentator, author; chairman of Market and Opinion Research International (MORI) 1973–2005.

WRIGHT, DR ANTHONY WAYLAND 'TONY' University lecturer, political historian; Labour MP for Cannock and Burntwood 1992–7, for Cannock Chase since 1997.

PART ONE

1969–1979

Early Years

1969

1 January   Rupert Murdoch, second-generation Australian newspaper proprietor, takes control of the *News of the World*.

3 February   Yasser Arafat takes control of the Palestinian Liberation Organization.

2 March   Concorde's first test flight.

5 March   Kray twins jailed.

17 March   Golda Meir takes over in Israel.

19 March   UK invades Anguilla, a tiny Caribbean island, after an internal rebellion against its dependency partner St Kitts and Nevis.

28 April   French president Charles de Gaulle resigns after referendum.

20 June   Georges Pompidou is elected president of France.

20 July   *Apollo* astronauts land on the moon.

9 August   Manson 'family' murder Hollywood actress Sharon Tate and others.

14 August   British troops move into Northern Ireland in response to sectarian violence.

21 October   Willy Brandt becomes German chancellor.

Deaths   Ivy Compton-Burnett, Dwight Eisenhower, Judy Garland, Ho Chi Minh, Boris Karloff, Jack Kerouac

HY opened his notebook with Douglas Hurd, private secretary to the Leader of the Opposition Edward Heath (known to his intimates as Ted). The next general election was now considered imminent as Harold Wilson, twice elected prime minister since 1964, was thought certain to go to the electorate in 1970. The state of the nation's economy and the power of the trade unions were key issues. Within the Conservative Party, perhaps Heath's major problem was how to cope with Enoch Powell, whose views on immigration, and in particular his 'rivers of blood' speech in April

1968, had alienated him from the mainstream of the party and its leader. Heath sacked Powell from the Shadow Cabinet, and endeavoured to purge the party of its more extremist right-wing membership, particularly those who owed allegiance to the Monday Club, infiltrated constituencies and endeavoured to gain selection as parliamentary candidates.

For HY, aged thirty-one and the Sunday Times's *chief leader writer, Hurd provided an unrivalled insight into the way the party's leader was thinking. As Hurd rose through the political ranks, ultimately becoming a trusted Secretary of State in Thatcher and Major governments, he would prove an invaluable source for HY for a quarter of a century.*

DOUGLAS HURD[1]
Lunch, 5 November 1969

LEADERSHIP DH sees great significance in the fact that letters are now coming in regularly from around the country with expressions of support for Ted. Constituencies which pass motions backing him and wishing him well relay the information to him. This is good for his morale, as was his conference speech, which gained from the quasi-challenges presented to him. (Remember also the fact that as soon as Parliament reconvened the 1922 Committee passed a motion of confidence.) But of course this is all double-edged. It emphasizes that confidence in the leadership is not universal or automatic.

DH believes that what he calls the 'solid centre' of the party now believes in Ted. But DH has been brought up in this solid centre – i.e. the upper middle class, I think[2] – and is probably sensitive to what is going on in a certain kind of drawing room. Evidently, they are now accepting a man who is not one of them. The same goes for Barber,[3] who suffered from a similar disability.

ELECTION It would seem they are regarding a spring 1970 election, after the Budget and the GLC election, as a strong possibility. It would also seem they are worried especially about the kind of game Enoch[4]

1 Biographies of HY's interviewees are placed at the beginning of the book.
2 Hurd's father, Anthony Hurd, a Wiltshire farmer, was MP for Newbury 1945–64; later Baron Hurd of Newbury.
3 Anthony Barber: educated at King Edward VI's Grammar School, Retford, Notts.; Conservative MP for Doncaster 1951–64, for Altrincham and Sale February 1965–September 1974; Minister of Health 1963–4 in Sir Alec Douglas-Home's Cabinet; ran Edward Heath's campaign for leadership of the Conservative party in 1965; later Baron Barber of Wentbridge.
4 Enoch Powell, the most controversial Conservative of his generation. A scholar and lecturer, between 1937 and 1951 he also published four volumes of verse. At the time of the 1970 election he had been MP for Wolverhampton since 1950; a member of Macmillan's Cabinet (as Minister of Health) in 1962, he refused to serve under his successor, Sir Alec Douglas-Home. His views, not only on immigration but on monetary policy and national identity, made him a bogeyman within the party as a whole.

would play. They still seem to see him – I disagree – as determined to ferment popular feeling in his direction. They are just hoping that he will play it quiet when the time comes – which, if he wants the support of the parliamentary party, he clearly would be advised to do.

Compared with the 1966 election, Ted will do less. He will respond to fewer challenges, not be so constantly in the front line. This is on the sound principle that in 1966 he was new, unknown and needed to show himself. Now this is not true. They also recognize that it will become to some extent a personal contest, for which Ted has no taste and little aptitude. Therefore it seems a conscious decision has been taken to try to whittle down Wilson's image during these run-up months. Ted can be expected to attack Wilson personally, in the hope of reducing Wilson's advantage during the mano-a-mano of the campaign. But this will be done only when it is related to issues, which Ted constantly prefers. (They believe the 'personal thing' was started by Wilson at the Brighton conference.)

CABINET Ted plays the job permutations close to his chest. But Reggie[1] is perhaps a big problem: where to place him? Because the Shadow Cabinet have been so occupied by detailed studies, it will be harder to shift them to different responsibilities in government – though obviously not at all impossible. Ted is absolutely committed to reduction in size. There will be no Cabinet members without proper tasks (departmental responsibilities?). It will be fifteen–seventeen (as Ted said in the TV broadcast with Robin Day).[2] Junior ministries will be pruned. The other day in Brussels, Ted said to Hurd, 'Do you think it should be three or four?' He meant the FCO jobs. Hurd said four would be needed. Ted said, 'No, I think they could manage with three.' DH regards the Shadow Cabinet, rightly, as ideologically unified. Boyle and Rippon[3] are the only eccentrics, and one of these has gone. (I rather got the feeling that Ted was glad to be rid of Boyle. Not for ideological reasons, but because he was not a professional politician.)

---

1 Reginald Maudling: Conservative MP for Barnet 1950–79; Chancellor of the Exchequer July 1962–October 1964; Home Secretary 1970–72; his brilliance was marred by allegations of laziness.
2 Robin Day: television and radio journalist, at ITN from 1955, at the BBC from 1959. Television was now playing an increasing role in political reporting and debate.
3 Sir Edward Boyle: intelligence work at Bletchley Park towards the end of the Second World War; Conservative MP for Birmingham Handsworth 1950–70; twice a junior Treasury minister; Minister of Education 1962–4; later Baron Boyle of Handsworth and vice-chancellor of the University of Leeds. Geoffrey Rippon: Conservative MP for Norwich South 1955–64, for Hexham 1966–87; later Baron Rippon of Hexham. Although at one time a prominent member of the Monday Club, he was a pro-European and in the reshuffle following the sudden death of Chancellor of the Exchequer Iain Macleod he was appointed by Heath as Chancellor of the Duchy of Lancaster to negotiate Britain's entry into the Common Market.

CANDIDATES DH has an interesting private and unproven theory. He says that attempts to characterize candidates selected in opposition as right wing have been unsuccessful. But he proposes a new theory: that seats west of Salisbury and north of Lincoln (roughly speaking) have more right-wingers. And that this is because the further you get from London, the more the selection tends to be controlled by a small group of people. It is much easier there to effect some kind of putsch, if you have the alliance of the local chairman. Nearer London, the press pays more attention, and also the centre has more of a grip and can push Chataways and Raisons[1] rather more easily. A very interesting theory to test: look at safe Tory seats in West Country and Lancashire, Hurd says, and the theory gets some support.

OTHER GENERAL POINTS Strongly disputes any idea that the party has shifted to the right in any respect, including race. On race the policy at York and Walsall is fully consistent with the 1966 manifesto, just in more detail. Insists that Enoch's only effect has been to make Ted say more about the subject than he otherwise would have done.

---

1 Christopher Chataway: television journalist at ITN 1955–6; at the BBC 1956–9; Conservative MP for Lewisham North 1959–66, for Chichester May 1969–September 1974; a junior minister in Sir Alec Douglas-Home's 1963–4 government. Timothy Raison: journalist on *Picture Post* and *New Scientist*; editor of Bow Group journal *Crossbow* 1958–60; of *New Society* 1962–8; Conservative MP for Aylesbury 1970–92.

1970

12 **January**   Biafra surrenders; Nigerian civil war ends.
  1 **March**   Rhodesia severs the royal link with the UK and becomes a racially segregated republic.
 10 **April**   Paul McCartney announces the end of the Beatles.
 29 **April**   US troops invade Cambodia.
 18 **June**   Conservative leader Edward Heath wins the British general election.
  3 **July**   IRA snipers fight with British troops in Belfast.
  8 **October**   Alexander Solzhenitsyn wins the Nobel Prize for Literature.
  9 **October**   The Khmer Republic proclaimed in Cambodia.
 24 **October**   Salvador Allende elected president of Chile.

Deaths   John Dos Passos, E. M. Forster, Charles de Gaulle, Jimi Hendrix, Janis Joplin, Gamal Abdul Nasser of Egypt, Bertrand Russell

HY's first interview of 1970, with Conservative chief whip William Whitelaw, preceded the Conservatives' 'heavily publicized pre-election weekend' at Selsdon Park, which stressed 'the need for tax cuts, more selectivity in social services and above all a more vigorous approach to law and order'.[1] Harold Wilson, the prime minister, endeavoured to turn this to the Labour's government's advantage. He saw Selsdon Man, in HY's words, as 'a hairy, primeval beast threatening to gobble alive all the benefits which socialism had spread around post-war British society'. According to Wilson, Selsdon Man is 'not just a lurch to the right. It is an atavistic desire to reverse the course of twenty-five years of social revolution. What they are planning is a wanton, calculated and deliberate return to greater inequality.' The general election campaign was under way.

1 Hugo Young, *One of Us* (London: Macmillan, 1989).

WILLIAM WHITELAW
Lunch, 20 January 1970

ON POWELL W thinks he has now gone too far (with his proposal
to withdraw aid to urban areas), and will lose backing as a result. He
states categorically that Powell has long had the single ambition of leading
the Tory Party – this was absolutely clear in 1965. Moreover, he has the
dream of making it a working-class or 'ordinary man's' party. He has
two plans. Plan One: Tories lose by 20 or more seats (that is the necessary
margin to unseat Ted), and the fat is in the fire. Plan Two: Tories win by
20 seats, and Powell is 'the residuary legatee of everything that goes
wrong' and will make life very tough for the leadership.

Among the backing which Powell has lost over race are Michael Alison
and Nicholas Ridley,[1] who both favour many of his economic ideas.
Biffen ('one of the ablest young men on either side') remains loyal,
although privately uneasy. In general, support now is less than the 15
votes he got in 1965. For the future, no one could say how many votes
he could get at any one time. W believes that the new parliamentary
party, even if the Tories lose, will be very different from the present one.
On balance, candidates are always further right than members – but then
Parliament usually works its effect on them.

COMMON MARKET W believes this will be 'far harder than
anyone has yet understood' to get through Parliament. We will get the
terms and it will be up to us to reject them or accept them. One of the
dangers is that inexperienced candidates etc. will make commitments in
their campaigns relating to the detail of the deal. And then they will be
in trouble when the decisive vote comes.

THE PARTY How much it has changed. With the departure of the
squires there has been a departure of instinctive loyalty. Policy is no
longer made by the leader. The growth of the Bow Group, the Monday
Club and the rest of the PCP world testifies to the greater breadth of
policymaking or at least of those who feel that they merit a place in policy
discussion. (W did not deny that in the end policy was formed at the top.)
He said that the meritocrats on the back benches would be more difficult

---

1 Michael Alison: Old Etonian; after Oxford, spent several years in the City before joining the Conservative
Research Department in 1958; MP for Barkston Ash 1964–83, for Selby 1983–97. Nicholas Ridley: Old
Etonian; after Oxford, a decade as a civil engineering contractor; MP for Cirencester and Tewkesbury 1959–
92; Secretary of State for Transport 1983–6, for the Environment 1986–9, for Trade and Industry, 1989–90;
later Baron Ridley of Willimontswick.

to handle than the squires, just as the conference has become more difficult
to manage. There is, he suggests, a growth of scepticism and a decline of
deference to people just because they are ministers.

On the other hand, he defined the problem between the leadership
and the constituencies as in some ways less difficult than it might have
been. What worries the constituencies is how much they *want* Ted to
succeed. They worry about whether or not he is making an impression,
because they desperately want a leader to whom they can be totally loyal.
The Tories only know two positions: either this one or a ruthless decision
to do away with the leader. Curiously, although Ted has perhaps only
50–60 per cent support within his own party, he has more support among
Labour and Liberal voters than one might expect. He has made more
tours than any other Tory leader, his audiences are the biggest since
Winston; also, his manner of dealing with the constituencies has vastly
improved over the last years.

On some counts W here is open to question. First, the knights of the
shires could be a great deal more difficult than the self-made men today,
because they had roots, money, independence. They could write letters
and it meant something. Now the new Tories are more like the Labour
Party: held together, perhaps, essentially by the threat of an election. In
other words, the problem of management has not got more difficult, it
has simply changed. Likewise, the conference. W spoke of needing to
pay more attention to conference than the Tory leadership has been
accustomed to ('I have been urging this on the leadership for a long time').
But, with his sideswipes at the incompetent chairman at Brighton '69,
what he was really saying was that the rude voices from below need a
more sure and firm touch than ever before – i.e. that the *image* of unity
must still be preserved at all costs, and the party must not be seen to be
incompetent in its management. Yes, let the party rank and file have their
say, but no, don't let them be seen to vote the leaders down. Again – a
move in the Labour direction?

MEN AND POLICIES East of Suez is the leader's personal conviction, which he clings to with absolute assurance. (With all this talk of
Heath's conviction, stubbornness etc. are they frightened of another
Eden?) W will back Maudling utterly and totally if it comes to a show-
down over the leadership if they lose – but note that Maudling's loss to
Heath [in 1965] hit him more deeply than anyone knew. 'If you get
Maudling interested in something, then he is terrific. If he was leader, you
would see a new Maudling.' Another runner would be Barber, whom W
admires greatly. Rippon: 'a strange man about whom there are divided

opinions – he needs to prove himself in a big job'. Keith Joseph:[1] 'more an administrator than a politician'.

The Sunday Times *occasionally invited leading political figures to lunch in the board room at the newspaper's offices in Gray's Inn Road. Harold Evans, editor since 1967, would preside. The home team included political staff and leader writers. In the following instance Michael Fraser was a key figure in the Conservative Party – a former director of the Conservative Research Department and now deputy chairman of the party organization.*

MICHAEL FRASER
Lunch, Thomson House, 10 March 1970

ELECTION Canvasses September as possible date – partly on grounds that it will be Tories rather than socialists who are still on holiday. Believes 60 per cent chance of Tories winning by a 'modest' majority – i.e. 30–45 seats.

HEATH Believes that Ted may have the quality which Michael Fraser puts highest of all – constructive imagination: a vision of what sort of society he wants and a capacity to bring at least some of it about. When he became leader Ted was very green, having gone into the whips office very soon after getting into Parliament and remaining there until 1959. Adds to this the peculiar difficulties he has faced. One was that the fact that, alone with Disraeli, he is out of the Tory mould – that is, he is neither aristocrat nor industrialist/businessman, from which strains the party has broadly chosen its leaders since Peel. Likewise, he was taking over a losing concern – there never was more than the most minute chance that after 1961–3 the Tories would remain in power for long after an election, and they were certainly bound to lose the 1966 election, yet he kept going without any sign of breaking or quitting.

   Compassionate, involved, emotional – these are some of the adjectives Fraser uses about Heath. He listens to you, but it is hard to get him to change his mind – if you want to change his mind, go in with four good men and true. He can't stand cant, or people who do not speak their

1 Sir Keith Joseph: Conservative MP for Leeds North–East 1956–87; junior minister in Harold Macmillan's government; Social Services Secretary under Edward Heath 1970–74; one of the architects of what was to be known as 'Thatcherism', he served under Mrs Thatcher as Secretary of State for Industry 1979–81, for Education and Science 1981–6; later Baron Joseph of Portsoken. His political philosophy earned him the nickname of 'the mad monk'.

mind, or people who dabble in the fringes of an issue. What is Heath's vision of society? It is what you would expect from a man who has grown up from his origins and won the struggles he has won. He will not need to be spurred into action – that is one of the qualities he will have as PM.

JOHN BIFFEN
Lunch, 24 March 1970

THE PARTY There is a struggle beginning for the soul of the Tory Party. It *is* only just beginning. The principal focus, in JB's view, will be the Common Market, whose posing of the nationalist versus the internationalist conflict will continue for years after our actual signing of the Treaty of Rome. Will we fight every inch of the way, or will we lead the flight from sovereignty? JB believes there to be a strong 'almost primeval' force of nationalism in this country. He regrets that it was first tapped by the immigration issue, and would have preferred it to be on the Common Market first and the rest later. He thinks that this issue will dominate the next five years of British politics as the balance of payments has dominated the last five.

What he means, of course, is the challenge to Heath Toryism made by Powell Toryism. Internationalism is seen as perhaps the major identifying difference between the two – larger even than economic differences, and certainly larger also than immigration itself (one of the few points at which the Heath and Powell brands almost coincide! And have done since even before P's Birmingham speech).[1]

Biffen believes that the parliamentary party, assuming a Tory majority of 25–50, will be somewhat more favourable for Heath than it is now, with more people backing his version of Toryism. But he surmises that it would be more difficult now for a Heath Tory to be nominated than it was two or three years ago. A reason why the parliamentary party will be easier is that by and large the winnable seats chose their candidates some time ago, and hence fell into the Heath mould.

This, however, Biffen sees as steadily more unrepresentative of the country at large. He thinks he sees, without being dogmatic, a nationalism which is politically unrepresented, as well as support for the other limbs of Powellism: freedom and choice in the economic sphere and far greater community care of the old and incapable.

Significant changes have come about since 1964. One is the progressive decline of the Bow Group. ('There is a vital argument about the future of

---

1 On Saturday 20 April 1968 Powell made what became known as his 'rivers of blood' speech in Birmingham, where he talked of the consequences of unchecked immigration from the Commonwealth.

the Tory Party going on. Have you heard any contribution from the Bow Group?') The quality of work is not there, although he agrees that this is partly the fate of being party mainliners in opposition. This matched by a staggering rise in the Monday Club's membership and fortunes.

'Heath is basically a super management consultant, brought in to improve the performance of Great Britain Ltd by that marginal 1 per cent which makes the difference between profit and loss. Even the inter-nationalist in him conforms to this picture: he sees Great Britain Ltd as part of a limited trading company doing business with Germany Ltd, France Ltd etc.' He is the technocrat in politics, and this applies as much to his political techniques as to his policies and priorities. Among his more exact exemplars are Walker, Jenkin, Higgins and possibly most of all Heseltine, an absolute shit with great promise and rapidly rising.[1] These are men who are internationalists, believers in abrasive methods and supervised competition, and people who, crudely, are kind to the blacks (which JB puts in to exemplify a general posture, not because he disagrees on the blacks). He is an administrator. He is totally and irreconcilably different from Powell – 'The Poet'. They simply cannot understand each other, not only in their policies but in their methods and their priorities.

He is not all that popular in the country. Yes, he is with the activists, and so he should be. But what about the next layer out from there – the Tory voter, and the inarticulate floater (who is far more numerous than the articulate floater)? If he lost, he would not have the strength to rally the party. He has no resources of affection or respect to fall back on. As for his achievement in retrieving the party from the collapse of the Macmillan years, if he hadn't done that in all these years of opposition then the party did not deserve to be in business at all.

Clearly [Powell] will do nothing for the first year of a Tory govern-ment. But the issues are there to be exploited. For example, the party is clearly in a terrible mess with its entire social policy (education, health, even pensions, although EP has spoken on these), which EP has not yet chosen to concentrate on as he has on the economy. What should be his role? It is clear that EP has done a lot of thinking about this. He has told JB that he does not intend to follow Bevan.[2] He will not form a cave in the government benches, nor will he seek a gathering of Powellites. A

---

1 Peter Walker: Conservative MP for Worcester 1961–92, later Baron Walker of Abbots Morton. Patrick Jenkin: Conservative MP for Woodford 1964–74, for Wanstead and Woodford 1974–87; later Baron Jenkin of Roding. In 1974 he served briefly as energy minister in the Heath government, when he famously advised citizens to save power by brushing their teeth in the dark. Terence Higgins: former Olympic athlete; Conservative MP for Worthing 1964–97; Financial Secretary to the Treasury 1972–4; later Baron Higgins of Worthing.

2 Aneurin Bevan, architect of the National Health Service and one of the most important post-war Labour ministers, represented the party's left wing, and his supporters were called 'Bevanites'.

main reason for this is the fear of being surrounded by jackals. EP is very much a lone figure by choice. He does not see his influence being through numbers, nor even his return to a future decision-making role – not necessarily as prime minister but as maker of prime ministers – as depending on numerical support mainly.

(I deduce therefore that, after the first months of a Tory government, EP will open fire on the Common Market and social policy, although Heath will be pursuing Powellite economic policies – as Biffen foresees it – and these will be very unpopular.)

In the general election on 18 June 1970 the Conservatives polled nearly 1 million more votes than Labour and overturned a Labour majority of 98 in 1966, to gain a majority of 31. Seats: Conservative (including 11 Ulster Unionists) 330; Labour 287; Liberal 6; Others 7; (including one Scottish Nationalist). Edward Heath succeeded Harold Wilson as prime minister. Within a month of forming his government, Heath suffered a severe blow when Iain Macleod, Chancellor of the Exchequer, died suddenly aged 56, following a heart attack. In the reshuffle that followed, Anthony Barber became Chancellor of the Exchequer. The seriousness of the economic situation led to much discussion of the need for a national government.

JOHN BIFFEN
Lunch, 12 November 1970

INFLATION The situation is potentially disastrous. It holds the promise of the most awful social crisis, worse than any other peacetime phenomenon. The outlook is so bad that JB would contemplate a total authoritarian government for twelve months, with absolute clampdown on the money supply and even (although this would conflict with the ideal) a total freeze on wages, prices etc. If this meant Austin–Morris came out of business and similar events as well as high unemployment this would have to be accepted. Indeed, probably the most salutary thing which could happen now would be the collapse of Austin–Morris, an event which would drive the message home throughout the private sectors, and would have a special effect on engineering settlements. The government is probably right to be doing basically nothing, but it should have the courage to say that that is what it is doing. There is little doubt that this government is going to become exceptionally unpopular quite soon, and in this situation one of its most serious deficiencies will be its lack of parliamentary competence. To have lost Boyle, Macleod and Powell is to have lost three most competent parliamentary people as well as three who can sell unpopular policies outside the Tory Party.

ENOCH POWELL It is not out of the question to contemplate a reconciliation with the leadership, although this would never happen with Heath as prime minister. Enoch's temperament is to keep people at arm's length, therefore he will never attract a formal grouping like Bevan did. No doubt discontented and disappointed people will gather around him, but they would quickly become jackals who would make life very difficult for Enoch himself. He is a time bomb ticking away. No one, including him, knows whether and when circumstances will converge so as to make him a truly decisive menace to the leadership. He has followers who do not publicly admit to being such. It is a mistake to think of Enoch as being without any connection to the government, as if the government were sealed off from the contagion. In the Cabinet he keeps in touch with Keith Joseph and Margaret Thatcher, and may be expected to increase his contacts there. Among junior ministers there are many more contacts – Michael Alison, Nick Ridley, John Eden, John Peyton[1] etc. Note also that the One Nation Group includes a number of Powellites, and the group's meetings are one occasion when the faithful can get together, before or after dinner.

DOUGLAS-HOME[2] Most people, contrary to the conventional wisdom, retain the political beliefs they formed as young men. Home's earliest position of importance was anti-Communism. This has remained the thread throughout his connection with foreign affairs. It can be seen partly in his attitude to Munich, but became very explicit in his celebrated attack on the Yalta agreement, when he interrupted Churchill with great determination in the House of Commons. He does not see Russia as a Russian threat but as a Communist threat. It does not differentiate between Communist countries. It probably takes into account the possibility that Russia has changed from a hungry country to a satisfied country. It overlooks the immensely cautious and defensive and unconfident posture which is Russia's historical position (in contrast to the immensely self-confident impulse of Maoism and Chinese culture). Home's anti-Communism has led him into error, especially in his view

1 John Eden: Conservative MP for Bournemouth West 1954–83; Minister for Industry 1970–72; later Baron Eden of Winton. John Peyton: Conservative MP for Yeovil 1951–83; Minister of Transport Industries 1970–74; later Baron Peyton of Yeovil.
2 Sir Alec Douglas-Home, Foreign Secretary under Edward Heath, had renounced his peerage as 14th Earl of Home to become Harold Macmillan's successor as prime minister (1963–4). He served as Foreign Secretary throughout Heath's 1970–74 government.

of the Indian Ocean. Surely once we gave up India we gave up any strategic interest in the Indian Ocean or for India's alignment internationally. Moreover, on Home's analysis the British defence force should be clearly built up. It is a question of how seriously one feels threatened by Russian naval expansion. Personally I feel quite unthreatened by it. Among the many failures with which Home has been associated was the Central African Federation, which was the epitome of white paternalism – laudable but mistaken.

TONY BENN
At Thomson House, with Harold Evans,
30 November 1970

Long disquisition on his consistent theme about participation, control and the means of consent. Believes evidently that this is more than ever relevant. Among many thoughts, made the following propositions:

1. We now enter era of zero growth. Energy crisis puts everything on a new basis. No one realizes how serious the position is. Believes that a middle-term consequence of this will be a national government, led by Home, with Heath, Thorpe, Robens, Marsh, Brown, Gunter[1] et al. in it, but Labour not in it. Wilson would be invited but would not serve. Home the most likely man, being without ambition and old in years.

2. The government would usher in a totally managed economy, with controls and rationing on a wide scale. It would involve considerable sacrifices in democratic terms, but people would have to take it – it would be said – as the only means of survival. It would, however, cause serious social discontent. Like all governments, it would to some extend fail: and having failed, there would be no alternative government waiting to take over if Labour joined in it. (Obviously Benn, although totally opposed to participating in it himself, has doubts about Labour's and Wilson's reliability on this point.)

3. Among the many results of world recession will be collapse of the Common Market. 'We will all become autarkic.' Britain will simply see that it cannot be in her interests to let coal and oil go to the EEC, and this will mean the end of the EEC. However, by his present

---

1 Richard Marsh: Labour MP for Greenwich 1959–71; Minister of Transport 1968–9; chairman of British Railways 1971–6; later Baron Marsh of Mannington. George Brown: Labour MP for Belper in Derbyshire 1945–70; deputy leader of the Labour Party 1960–70; Foreign Secretary, 1966–8; later Baron George-Brown of Jevington. Ray Gunter: trade-unionist Labour MP for Southwark 1959–72; Minister of Labour 1964–8.

commitment to the EEC, Heath is debarred from 'playing the patriotic card' in his efforts to get the country mobilized on his side.

4. Here is an alternative to the rightist, control-bound national government. This is a radical new approach to politics and the business of consent. It is based on the observable fact that the workers' veto operates against any incomes policy: even a 'compulsory' one is seen to be voluntary. In all areas of society there is an absence of consent and of confidence. The only activity free from this is protest itself: see UCS [Upper Clyde Shipbuilders], see BAC [British Aircraft Corporation] workers in Bristol. Suddenly, having taken responsibility, workers find themselves looking at life in a totally new and invigorated way. One should give serious consideration to these models as pointing the way to the new politics. The essential price of consent, on this model, will be a really drastic approach to equality. Growth having stopped, we can no longer deceive ourselves that redistribution can be paid for by expansion. We must think at last about the roots of equality. This will mean, in Benn's terms, not so much an education of the unions to pay the low-paid at the expense of their high-paid members as an onslaught on the familiar targets of socialist attack: property, wealth, salaries etc. etc.

5. Benn believes that this kind of approach could create a different sort of Britain. I think he is sincere about this. He wants to end the 'trench-warfare' which is the root cause of us producing only two-thirds of our productive capacity. He sees industry in a condition where all the best people are fighting the system and opposing the management. He also believes that the workers could not make such a hash of things as management has. For instance, both miners and rail unions opposed the rundown of mines and rail against the concerted wisdom of the Civil Service, both parties, all Fleet Street (with an honourable exception) etc. They were right as it turns out.

6. The Labour Party. Only a few of the Shadow Cabinet agree with this analysis. He attacks their collective reticence about the real issues between them, broken now by Prentice[1] – Benn told Prentice that he was glad he had spoken as he did last week. He also rejects the attempt to consider all this in Marxist terms. 'The Labour Party has never been Marxist. Its origins are quite different, in Methodism and Nonconformity.' Finally he rejects the criticism of himself that he has only now seen the light. Claims to have been saying it in power – wanted

---

1 Reginald Prentice: Labour MP for East Ham North 1957–74, for Newham North-East 1974–7; crossed the floor to join the Conservatives, continuing to represent Newham NE as MP 1977–9; Conservative MP for Daventry 1979–87; Minister for Overseas Development 1969–70; Secretary of State for Education and Science 1974–5; a junior minister in the Thatcher government; later Lord Prentice of Daventry.

a Common Market referendum, but was shot down by the Cabinet; spoke about participation then; urged the 1968 mid-term manifesto, which was intended to admit where we had gone wrong.[1]

---

1 Tony Benn in his diary entry for the same day, writes, 'Went to *Sunday Times* (Harold Evans and HY) and they listen most attentively to my political analysis. I said "Look, both parties have failed. There is an energy crisis and there may be a slump . . ." ' Benn wanted more democracy, more equality – it was the time of national governments. 'HE asked "why are you so unpopular with the press?" "Because you write such unpleasant things about me." '

1971

The Sunday Times *had acquired the serial rights in the memoirs of Harold Wilson before they were written. When the newspaper received the completed typescript, HY was commissioned to read and report on the contents.*

PRIVATE NOTES ON WILSON MEMOIRS
31 March 1971

They begin by appearing to be magnanimous. He is kind to Home, for example, and admits one or two errors. But as they go on they become more and more acrimonious. The last two or three chapters are straight electioneering, with his parliamentary manner towards Heath reproduced on paper.

They read more like his personal *Keesing's Archive* than anything. He sounds like a man who has had before him his appointment diary, but not his personal diary. It sometimes seems as if every trip to Barnsley, every speech to a trade council, every proposal in every speech he ever made is there. Every detail from every Queen's Speech certainly is there, and most details from every Budget, every shift on pensions, and every famous crack he ever made against the Tories.

One is reminded how constantly he travelled. He seems always to be on the way to or from Moscow or Washington, not forgetting Ottawa, to meet people who he has known for years. Not an international dispute anywhere takes place without it creating an emergency for the British Cabinet, bringing Harold by emergency 'copter at first light from the Scillies: Middle East War, Rann of Kutch,[1] Czechoslovakia, Vietnam. The book conveys a very weird combination of compulsive self-dramatization and compulsive preoccupation with events of no importance. At times therefore it is comic. Wilson, of course, never sleeps (while at the same time he never loses a night's sleep): viz. 'I did not leave for Chequers until 3.15 a.m. During what was left of the night I thought the matter through, and awoke fresh and with a clear view.'

Events pass without discrimination as to their importance. The appointments diary is remorselessly recorded. There are few large ups and downs. It's all in a day's work. Two major omissions greatly lower its value. It contains virtually no characterizations of people; and I suddenly realized that this was not due just to discretion, but perhaps to the fact that HW is just not very interested in looking at people in any respect other than what they do to and for him. Secondly, it contains no assessment on anything, not for a single moment pausing to look at any event from any kind of historical perspective. Virtually no judgements are passed on policies which may not have survived the passage of time very well: no opinions are voiced in other than the narrowest party terms. The author sounds like a small, grey, strangely bureaucratic figure.

But also a venomous one. All the embarrassing interludes (and embarrassment is one clear response which one has to quite a few of the events recalled) are defended to the teeth. Winter emergency committees, southern Africa famine relief, Davies's mission to Hanoi[2] – it's all there. We are told that the Tory press dismissed them all as gimmicks. A great

---

1 Disputed territory – mainly salt marshes, but a source of natural gas – on the border between India and Pakistan, which partly led to the 1965 war between the two countries.
2 Harold Davies, Labour MP for Leek 1945–70, later Baron Davies of Leek, was dispatched by Harold Wilson in July 1965 as a special envoy on a peace mission to North Vietnam, with which he had connections.

deal of time is spent fighting old battles with the press. The increasingly frenetic note of defensiveness as the book advances is especially signified by increasing jeers at the press.

There are a lot of quotes from his speeches. It sometimes sounds like a cuttings book with so many favourable press references to him also recorded.

I go back to the lack of perspective. This is the decisive flaw, which makes this such an empty book. There is on the whole remarkably little revelation of detail, although there is some. I don't think this is as bad from a journalistic viewpoint than the feeling of it being his personal Reuters dispatch.

On the whole this seems to raise more acutely than ever the policy of buying memoirs sight unseen. These are shallow, tendentious and often of an almost unbelievable tedium. Would they have been if HW had had to earn his £100,000, instead of being able to extract a guarantee of it come what may? Why doesn't the NPA [Newspaper Proprietors' Association] do something useful and enter into a gentleman's agreement that no one will buy memoirs until they are written?

1972

30 January   Bloody Sunday in Derry, paratroopers kill 13.

30 January   Pakistan leaves the Commonwealth.

2 February   Irish rioters burn the British embassy in Dublin.

21 February   US president Richard Nixon begins a historic visit to China.

22 February   An IRA bomb hits Aldershot: seven killed.

24 March   Heath imposes direct rule in Ulster.

14 April   Nixon steps up bombing in North Vietnam.

30 May   Japanese terrorists kill 25 in Tel Aviv airport.

17 June   Five White House operatives are arrested for breaking into Democratic Party offices: the 'Watergate scandal' begins.

4 August   Idi Amin announces the expulsion of 50,000 Asians from Uganda.

5 September   Eleven athletes killed when terrorists storm the Israeli compound at the Munich Olympics.

7 November   Nixon wins a second term by a landslide.

Deaths   Maurice Chevalier, J. Edgar Hoover, Ezra Pound, J. Arthur Rank, Harry S. Truman, Duke of Windsor

Nothing of HY's has survived from 1972

1973

1 January The United Kingdom, Ireland and Denmark join the European Community.

23 January President Nixon announces the end of the Vietnam war with a peace accord.

20 March The UK government proposes to end trial by jury in Ulster.

4 April The World Trade Center officially opens in New York.

30 April Nixon aides H. R. Haldeman and John Ehrlichman resign over the Watergate burglary.

24 May Lord Jellicoe and Lord Lambton resign from the Heath government over sex scandals.

11 September Salvador Allende, president of Chile, dies in a military coup.

6 October The Egyptians reclaim the Suez Canal in the Yom Kippur offensive.

8 October The BBC loses its monopoly on radio broadcasting with the launch of LBC.

14 November Princess Anne marries Captain Mark Phillips.

22 November William Whitelaw agrees a power-sharing deal in Ulster.

12 December Edward Heath announces a three-day working week as disputes hit coal mines, railways and power stations.

23 December OPEC nations increase oil prices by 70 per cent.

Deaths W. H. Auden, Pablo Casals, Noël Coward, former US president Lyndon Baines Johnson, Pablo Picasso, J. R. R. Tolkien

As 1973 drew to a close, the Heath government was in crisis. To Conservatives everywhere it was Us and Them – or who ruled the country: the government or the unions? The best-laid plans of the Selsdon Park weekend in early 1970 had been overtaken by unforeseen events, which led to a statutory pay freeze and the creation, through the 1972 Industry

Act, of sweeping new powers for the Department of Trade and Industry
– the kind of intervention that the Conservatives had previously pledged
to obliterate. This 'U-turn' would haunt the Heath administration, as
would the phrase itself. HY later wrote that it was an experience that
'Heath was never allowed to forget'. Strikes in the mines – coal was still
the principal source of fuel for power stations – led to government
measures to reduce demand. Britain soon became used to power cuts
and a three-day working week.

BRW [1]
Simpson's Restaurant, the Strand,
6 December 1973

- We face ten years of fighting for our standard of living and for free speech: the two great battles.
- Oil embargoes are first threat by Soviet military might to our standard of living. This will go further unless we take care. Finlandization of Europe: Germany looks more and more east, with young especially disenchanted with the EEC; France now showing more interest in the EEC, but Socialist–Comm almost won last time; Italy – note the growing compact between the Vatican and the Communist Party, two authoritarians despairing of democracy (a CP deputy's speech at Strasbourg – against abortion); Sweden, Denmark, Belgium hopelessly riven by language. UK is the best hope.
- We must stand together on oil. Suggests oil-buying consortium, which would say to Arabs, We'll buy what you sell in 1974. If you sell us none, we will buy none. You will not pick us off seriatim. This is the only way to stand up to an overbearing supplier in any business. (HY: note that Israel is mostly a distraction from clear thinking about the Middle East and commercial politics thereof.)
- Next great Soviet threat is the death of Tito.
- The Tories should do two things: abolish the earnings rule for pensioners, thus releasing skilled and semi-skilled labour, at no real cost, and bring in higher family allowances, with abolition of income tax relief – as a precursor to tax credits. This gives money to wives, the vital political and social need – and one which, unlike anything else, pays attention to family size (cf. threshold clauses).
- Should be an election now, in February or so. Can't face eighteen months of election politics on small majority. Thereafter the Tory aim

must be to detach the Labour centre and right into the Liberal Party. Therefore we all hope for large Liberal poll – perhaps 20 per cent: enough to attract Jenkins and that real Tory Reg Prentice (patriot, order, discipline, common sense).

–   Can Ted be Moses? No he cannot. But nor can Wilson ever be a national leader again. Ted lacks breadth. The memory of the merciless Wilson of years ago is too deep – he feels obliged to pay in kind. He is never fatherly and broad at question time. The Tories have been a class party since 1931, although Macmillan got their highest vote ever in 1959. The tragedy was 1931 – allying with the Liberals and putting Labour in the cold. In truth the class war is dead: but being pressured by the tiny minority whose advantage it is to do this. The Liberal revival is a measure of people's feeling that class war is dead, but that other parties don't reflect this. (But – HY – surely it is the awakening of false expectations of equality which drive more people than BRW thinks into militant labourism.)

–   Enoch is dead. Will shortly join Mosleyites.[1] He has no answers. He is fighting to recover what the Tories have been fighting to abandon for a hundred years. He has no answer on race, his economics are mad – a certain recipe for political revolution and a general strike. He has his running dogs – Marten, the pathetic little Teddy Taylor, plus Biffen and Bruce-Gardyne, Fraser.[2] 'I interrupted him the other day, the ultimate insult. I was shouted down for minutes by the running dogs.'

–   John Davies has lost all confidence, that is his trouble. Doesn't know where he stands with Ted; has been told to make his speeches dull because the Cabinet is downplaying Europe until there are benefits to show for it. A tragedy if he goes, because he knows more about industry than anyone in the HC. But he didn't know how to resign over the Industry Bill, nor how to modify it to make it more acceptable. All the signs of an inexperienced politician.

1   Followers of Sir Oswald Mosley, pre-war leader of the British Union of Fascists, interned in 1940, returned to the UK to stand for Parliament after the Notting Hill race riots of 1958; he unsuccessfully contested Kensington North in 1959, and Shoreditch and Finsbury in 1966.
2   Neil Marten: Conservative MP for Banbury 1959–83. Sir Edward 'Teddy' Taylor: Conservative MP for Glasgow Cathcart 1964–79, for Southend East 1980–97, for Rochford and Southend East 1997–2005. John (Jock) Bruce-Gardyne: diplomat, journalist; Conservative MP for South Angus 1964–74, for Knutsford 1979–83. Sir Hugh Fraser: Conservative MP for Stone 1945–50, for Stafford and Stone 1950–83.

A GOOD GOVERNMENT SOURCE[1]
18 December 1973

By the weekend 8–9 December it was accepted by No. 10 that the
13 December measures would be necessary. (I am not clear precisely who
believed this, although Heath did; nor precisely what they thought would
be necessary.) On the advice of DTI officials, short-time working was
being prepared for. Those with responsibility for political information
were anxious to begin the process of alerting the public to the imminence
of crisis measures: finally, the upbeat nonchalance of official speeches was
about to be changed. Message was passed to the DTI: what was Walker
planning to do to this end? He said that he was only seeing the *Sunday
Times* (HY). Amazingly, however, at that briefing he made no attempt
to begin pushing the new line. Quite the contrary: short-time working
was mused about as a February–March possibility. When challenged as
a crazy optimist, he dimpled complacently and said that he realized that
if he was proved right no one would remember, but if wrong his name
would be mud – i.e. at the very least he still postulated his own optimistic
analysis as a real goer. The whole thrust of what he said concerned the
excellent situation which opened up once we had got over the little local
difficulty of the miners and the not so local one of the sheikhs. He reflected
upon the merits of an oil price rise (increased value of our exports as well
as imports!) and of investment prospects in Iran (cheap local labour,
available local raw materials, large British profits across the exchanges).

However, within this optimistic framework Walker let drop some oil
figures which confirm that he knew by 7 December that something drastic
was about to be done. He just refrained from underlining the significance
of the figures. They were as follows: without the coal crisis, power stations
were planning to use less oil anyway (has anyone really explained about
dual-fuel stations etc.?). When the oil crisis happened, Walker cut the oil
allocation to power stations by 50 per cent. Because of the coincidence
of coal and oil crises, the cut was reduced to 30 per cent. By 7 December
their oil cut was down to only 13.5 per cent. This was predicated on a
31 per cent coal production cut holding steady. But over Christmas the
coal cut would rise to 40 per cent. This might mean that the oil cut to
non-priority industries would have to be increased from 13.5 per cent to
30 per cent. (All this is a starting point for checking with the CEGB.)

It was apparent, between the lines, from my source that the government does not necessarily expect the three-day week to last a very short

[1] Unidentified. Memorandum to the *Sunday Times* editor, Harold Evans, aided by background from Michael
Wolff, with whom HY had lunch the same day.

time (although such cold-eyed intransigence is obviously a vital ploy for them to show). The equation was simply put: by cutting now, we ensure that there will be essential services through the winter ('There will be sewage'); by not cutting now, we come to a sudden grinding halt in mid-January. It was equally apparent that no detailed thinking had gone into the consequences of this: which suggests, in turn, that the real nature of the game *is* a gamble, pinned to the prospect of an early success.

When I asked where such prospects of success might lie, I was referred to Willie meeting the miners this week, and Ted meeting the TUC (Wednesday night). At both these settings, the unions would be 'put on the spot'. What did this mean? 'An offer would be made.' Otherwise, the two areas of Phase III[1] I was told to keep an eye on were its time span and its 'anomalies' provision. It may well be, I deduce, that a drastic curtailing of Phase III's duration (on the grounds that the energy crisis had changed all the assumptions), coupled with a favourable review under the anomalies procedure, might be a way out. The two would have to go together, because – on the Phase II model – any anomalies advantages offered the miners would have to be available only under Phase IV (v. this week's award to civil servants, under Phase II anomalies).

The Budget was very much a Heath exercise. For the fourth time (? previous occasions), Ted faced down the Treasury, with Barber in the background on his side. He refused to accept consumer deflation or any alteration of the precious Tory tax changes. Ted was adamant. And he went about the cuts in a very personal way. He saw the ministers mostly bilaterally and in total secrecy. (Since he was in Copenhagen 14–15–16 December – check exact dates – and up all night at Sunningdale[2] the previous weekend, the cuts must have been fixed around 10–11–12 December.) No opportunity was given for officials to mobilize inside departments for the defence of their own budgets – although that is now a battle being fought by individual ministers as the allotment of cutbacks is made.

The key ministry was Defence. Once Defence had agreed to one-sixth of the total package, the ground was cut from under the home spending departments. It seems there was little or no Cabinet or collective discussion of all this – so much for collective government applying to the dismantling as well as the establishment of priorities.

It is not true that Heath is badly tired, although Sunningdale was an

1 The Heath government's counter-inflationary policy involved two stages that imposed and continued a wage freeze, along with curbs on prices, a third that imposed a tight limit on individual wage rises, and a fourth that dealt with unfairnesses and anomalies.

2 The Sunningdale agreement was an attempt – at the Civil Service College in Sunningdale, Berkshire – to end violence and establish power-sharing between Unionists and Nationalists in a new Northern Ireland Assembly. The agreement collapsed in May 1974.

unaccustomed all-nighter for a man who needs and likes his regular sleep. What is true is that he is paying less and less attention to his public appearances. This disturbs the machine, who wish for more cosmetics to the words and context of speeches.

ELECTION The pressure from the machine is building up. It has only just begun – circumstantial evidence suggests that as recently as the 8–9 December weekend it was, if anything, being much discouraged officially. But Ted must be acutely aware of the unforgiving history of PMs who have chosen wrong. There is a strong feeling that they can win now. If they wait a year, the situation will almost certainly be less favourable to them, and great will be the curses heaped on him. The earliest possible moment – and on the most favourable interpretation – might be spring 1975. Against this I am told (ho hum?) of the real worries on the part of the post-war generation of Tories (i.e. Heath) of the consequences of a Tory landslide. What would this do to the Tory Party? Would it foreshadow a reneging on the Butlerism[1] which they went into politics for; and what would happen to the Labour moderates? There are lots of things to be said about this, but it is interesting that senior Tories are talking at all in these terms.

1 Richard Austen 'Rab' Butler: Conservative MP for Saffron Walden 1929–65; sponsor of the 1944 Education Act; later Home Secretary, Chancellor of the Exchequer and Foreign Secretary – but twice passed over for Conservative leader. He became master of Trinity College, Cambridge, and Baron Butler of Saffron Walden. Butler opposed hanging and flogging, he was an admired education minister, and his policies as Chancellor were so close to those of Hugh Gaitskell, who led the Labour Opposition from 1955 to 1963, that politicians and journalists alike spoke of 'Butskellism'.

1974

4 February Heiress Patty Hearst seized by a US revolutionary group; is later photographed carrying a gun in a bank robbery.

14 February The Soviet Union exiles writer Alexander Solzhenitsyn.

1 March A hung parliament after an inconclusive general election: Edward Heath attempts a deal with Liberal leader Jeremy Thorpe over power-sharing.

4 March Harold Wilson returns as premier after the Heath government resigns. The three-day week ends. The miners return to work with a 35 per cent wage increase.

1 April Cumberland, Rutland, Huntingdonshire and Westmorland all disappear in a reorganization of English counties.

19 May Valéry Giscard d'Estaing defeats François Mitterrand for the French presidency.

28 May The power-sharing experiment in Ulster fails.

17 June The IRA detonates a bomb in 877-year-old Westminster Hall.

8 August President Nixon resigns after the Watergate scandal; Gerald Ford is sworn in.

11 October In the year's second general election Harold Wilson gains Labour victory of just three seats.

24 December Labour MP and former minister John Stonehouse, presumed dead in a swimming accident in Miami, reappears in Australia.

Deaths Duke Ellington, Sam Goldwyn, Charles Lindbergh, Juan Perón of Argentina, Georges Pompidou of France, Oskar Schindler

The crisis between the government and the miners was the making of HY's political contacts book. He was now getting on well with Michael

Wolff, who included him in the distribution list for a letter from Heath to miners' leader Jo Gormley in which the Prime Minister set out the position as he saw it. The letter, dated 24 January, was published in full by the daily press. HY put his copy in his 1974 file immediately following an account of his interview with Len Murray, general secretary of the TUC. Heath was endeavouring to be conciliatory, as these two paragraphs from the end of his Gormley letter demonstrate:

We now have before us the possibility of a return to more normal working for industry. The extend to which we can realize this possibility, and with all the benefits to which it would lead, depends upon the decisions of your Executive and your Union. As Prime Minister, I urge most strongly that at your meeting your Executive should consider the position as it affects the rest of the country. I also urge that they should reflect, in the light of the serious economic situation which the country faces, upon the significance and advantages for your members of the offer which has been made and the other proposals which we have put to you. I very much hope that your Executive will conclude that, in the situation which I have described to you, acceptance of the offer and of the proposals which the Government has made would do justice not only to the aspirations of your members but also to the needs and circumstances of this country of which we are all citizens.

If the officers or the Executive of the Union would like to come and discuss the matter further with me and my colleagues at Downing Street, I shall be ready to arrange a meeting.

The Heath government's counter-inflationary policy involved several stages: a ninety-day freeze on most rises in pay, prices and dividends, followed by a second stage of £1 per week plus 4 per cent (subject to a ceiling of £250 per annum) and a third of £2.25 per week or 7 per cent. A fourth stage involved the establishment of a Pay Board and a Price Commission to deal with anomalies. Trade-union leaders were not happy.

LEN MURRAY
24 January 1974

TUC'S MEETING WITH TED, 21 JANUARY It was clear that the government's mind was made up before we went in. At least, I could see that, even if not everyone thought so. I knew I was right after a minute or two. Not so much from what they said but from other things – their general attitude. Carrington was present for the first time. His role was limited: to spell out the energy situation – i.e. to bring home the four-day week[1] and what it meant.

The main new factor was Heath's own attitude. At the previous meeting he had remained seemingly open-minded. At least he kept probing away at various things said by the other side. This time he was clearly not interested in this. 'He did not throw it over to us. There were three or four ways he might have asked us to take the initiative. But he didn't try any of them. Especially, he could have asked us what we thought the NUM would accept. But he didn't mention that. And I supposed by this stage he thinks that if he probed that sort of ground he would have the militants spotting the weakness and demanding the whole bag. Containment was the other big area. Asking us for more on that. But he didn't.'

At both meetings there were very long silences. Ted would sit for what seemed like minutes with his head sunk deep on his chest, pondering.

But at the second meeting, there was much greater identity between the ministers. At the first meeting it is true that Whitelaw and Barber had reacted differently. Barber's line of harsh insensitive questions much distressed Whitelaw. This time it was not so. In effect what had happened is that the meeting had come round to the Barber position, although in Heath's and Whitelaw's case with reluctance (this is my own interpretation – HY). According to LM, Barber's attitude throughout must be seen in the light of his first rejection of the TUC suggestion. Heath's repudiation of him nettled him badly. He felt let down.

(Further on that original TUC offer. It was made at the NEDC [National Economic Development Council] meeting in early January. High government source says it was done in an underhand way. In the good old days of Vic Feather,[2] top ministers feel, Ted or Barber would have been telephoned about it and there would have been a document sent round before the NEDC meeting. The devious Murray, showing what a deep-dyed politician he is, sprang it on Barber without warning. This is one reason why ministers are now saying the TUC offer was a political stunt.

(Stunt or no, Murray did immediately send it round to No. 10 after the Barber rejection. It seems to have arrived on Ted's desk even as he was being telephoned by Barber to tell him about the offer. And one story is that what Murray sent to Ted differed in important respects from what Barber rejected.

(What we do know is that it had a vital political effect. In retrospect it seems more and more clear that but for the TUC offer there would

1 The drastic solution of a three day week – intended to save commercial electricity use and reduce the risk of blackouts – did not include 'essential' enterprises such as newspapers, restaurants and so on. Once the restrictions had begun to bite, some members of the government argued that a four-day week would have been enough. It became a bargaining chip in Heath's negotiations with the unions.
2 Vic Feather: general secretary of the TUC 1969–73; later Baron Feather.

have been an election. It was this which put the government off its stride: led to the 14 January meeting, which in turn led to the 21 January meeting. Altogether a considerable political coup by Murray.)

LM contrasts Heath's general approach to these meetings with Wilson's. He has never started amendment in detail of documents put forward. Wilson in 1968 or was it '69, when he was abandoning his Industrial Relations Bill, spent sessions fiddling about with the wording of the TUC paper. Heath, by contrast, is very willing to go on verbally round the issue, but always in a negative rather than a positive way. I.e. instead of suggesting possible changes – or possible new offers – he would emphasize constantly the shortcomings of the TUC offer. LM was unwilling to say whether he thought Ted was merely embellishing his previous conviction that the TUC was useless, or whether he was genuinely seeking some glimmer of hope. Between the lines, LM clearly thought the former.

If there was one finally eloquent moment it was this, on 21 January. Some way into the meeting, one of the TUC side asked Barber, 'Are there any circumstances whatever in which you could conceive of moving outside Stage III?' The question was not dressed up or repeated. It hung in the air for a very long silence indeed. All the TUC eyes were on Barber. Eventually the silence was broken by Ted, who changed the subject. It was clear that in the end there was no such circumstance, although the government could not quite bring itself to say so in the starkest way.

Barber issued a statement at the end of the meeting. It appeared only 25 minutes afterwards (in written, mimeographed form??). It was not, says LM, the sort of statement which could have been put together in twenty-five minutes. He believes it was drafted before the meeting even began. Near the end of the five hours, the government side asked for a recess. They went upstairs for half an hour. LM believes this was to dot the eyes on the draft. When they came back, the meeting went on for only another twenty minutes.

THE TUC OFFER LM insists that it *is* a substantial shift, and also that it fulfils the negotiator's imperative of always finding another way out. 'Heath feels he must win. To him there must be a winner and a loser. We offered a way everybody could have won.'

He thinks Ted does not understand real life when he demands that the offer should be 100 per cent guaranteed. 'We could never offer anything 100 per cent. Perhaps we are too honest. We told him that we could not guarantee ABC Couplings in Walsall would not have an AEU [Amalgamated Engineering Union] shop demanding to go above Phase III. He seemed to think that made the whole offer worthless. He probably said to himself, The TUC can only offer me a 70 per cent guarantee so they are obviously useless. What he doesn't reckon on is the possibility that we would give him 95 per cent success in the event.'

What the government has rejected is not just a formula. 'It's an attitude of mind. There was a large shift, subtle but real, in the TUC's collective will to face the economic choices. This is finished from our point of view. We can't take it any further. Of course, if Ted wishes to take it up himself, or if he uses the relativities report,[1] that's a different matter.'

Did this mean that Heath and his government were finished altogether with the TUC? Of course not, says LM, the inveterate realist. The TUC goes on, but governments come and go. We have to keep at it. And get on with whoever we have to. We don't want to become just an electoral ally of the Labour Party.

CONFRONTATION   LM defines the famous 33¼ hours of consultation before the incomes policy was introduced. Ted makes much of these – especially the last quarter-hour. But the fact is that throughout, and right up to date, the government has not done more than the narrow consultation. It has said, Let's hear what you have to say, and then gone away and done what it wants. 'There has never been any negotiation, as I understand the term.' This government is not different from Wilson's and has not learned its lesson from those days: which is that governments are prone too easily to get into the position of saying, 'It is our job to govern.' 'That is not a negotiating position.'

EFFECT ON TUC   LM muses, Does Ted *want* to weaken the TUC? Certainly this is the one result of his repeated allegation that it is weak, and his final refusal of the offer. For it plays into the hands of IS [International Socialists] etc., who have been screaming that the whole deal is a fraud and the TUC had never been seen at No. 10. 'It will make it that much more difficult next time.' (See the *Worker's Press*, which LM obviously studies daily.)

The TUC has acted with great moderation and helpfulness throughout, he claims.

1. It has not followed Benn and Shore[2] into the wilder regions of the fraud rhetoric. It has not challenged the data more than by saying they may be 10 per cent wrong at the margin.

---

1 In January the government-appointed Pay Board produced its report on wage differences between groups within industry. The government and the Coal Board hoped that formal discussion of these differences might cool or settle the dispute with the miners.
2 Peter Shore: Labour MP for Stepney 1964–74, for Stepney and Poplar 1974–83; for Bethnal Green and Stepney 1983–97, Secretary of State for Economic Affairs 1967–9; Trade Secretary 1974–6; Environment Secretary 1976–9; later Baron Shore of Stepney.

2. It has not interfered with the three-day week. On the contrary the lads have obviously worked very hard for the three days.

3. The four million who the government says have settled within the terms of Phase III.

In the general election on 28 February 1974 the Conservatives polled nearly one and a quarter million votes fewer than in 1970, but this was still 230,000 more than Labour. In terms of seats, however, Labour moved ahead, but without an overall majority. Conservative 297; Labour 301; Liberal 14. Others included United Ulster Unionists 11; Scottish Nationalists 7; and Plaid Cymru 2.

Edward Heath endeavoured to form a government with the aid of the Liberal Party (led by Jeremy Thorpe),[1] which had nearly tripled its vote (from 2.1 million to 6 million), but only doubled the number of seats. Talks with the Liberals failed, and on 4 March Heath resigned. Harold Wilson returned as leader of a minority Labour government.

HY's confidence with his growing band of contacts now becomes evident in the accounts he writes up. The report of the Garrick lunch that follows is not merely information, but much more of a descriptive narrative, with the added value of his judgements, which until now he had added sparingly. These were to become a feature of his notes from now on. However, in this instance and at this distance it is not always clear which are Donoughue and Lester's views and which are HY's. The Labour Party's factions, even less than 100 days since the general election, are already visible, and with the benefit of hindsight, foreshadow the split that created the Social Democratic Party.

AL[2]
The Garrick, 24 May 1974

The Bernard Donoughue lunch, with Haines, plus sundry assistants, Garrick Club. BD intolerably grand. Nothing so appalling as the humble and low-born common man risen to the fruits of power. His postprandial cigar. The obvious purpose was to make sure Roy Jenkins[3] voted in Cabinet against any effort to raise the salaries of top people. As if AL would presume to 'influence' RJ on this: as if RJ would in any case be

---

1 The February negotiations were to prove the high point in Thorpe's career.
2 Coyly hiding behind the initials AL is Anthony Lester, now Lord Lester.
3 Roy Jenkins, having been Home Secretary, 1964–7, Chancellor of the Exchequer, 1967–70, and deputy leader of the Labour Party, 1970–72, had returned to the Home Office in the current Wilson government.

disposed to raise them. Not clear at all that this was Wilson's work. Just the little men around him pulling some levers. Atmosphere fraught with anti-civil servant paranoia, with Haines obsessed with his seat in Wilson's car ('I got in it at the palace, but they tried to squeeze me out since then').

Why don't the social democrats stand up? They do. But they lose. Why? Because the four lefties[1] are united and the right are less clear about their objectives, and less united on them, and fraught with personal rivalries (Healey, Jenkins, for example). Besides, what is the right thing to do? They cannot openly oppose the public. Wilson adopting a totally passive role in Cabinet, just lets things ride. The left is also dishonest and devious. For instance, it is the left quartet which back Concorde in Cabinet, Jenkins who opposes it. Benn bullshits away about the traumatic shock to the British people of giving it up etc. etc. Evidently the Left Four go along with him. But AL sure that the Government cannot go on with no other intellectual basis than the simple assertion that what they are doing must be better than what the Tories did. (Piece should explore not merely anti-Tory rationale but also anti-Civil Service one. Haines' palace experience caused him to think that this time the Civil Service was put in its place. It was all going to be different this time.)

JENKINS   One reason for the BD lunch was a belief that Jenkins was soft on civil servants, too easily their creature. Nothing could be less true. Gives them a hard time. They respect him even if they don't like him in all cases. He is enjoying his work, no longer sunk in the blues in post-election phase. He is bloody good at his job, and is backing up AL on sex discrimination but subtly so – a big meeting at which he showed no preference for AL but ended up not only by rejecting civil-servant arguments but in such a way as to lead to AL and civil servants getting together amicably on AL's terms. But how few ministers have any time to think. Take Lyon[2] – a dining room table with 150 infirm cases a week asking to come in. How long does he give each one – five minutes, he says. Constituency work. PQs. Departmental papers suggesting negative courses of action. I.e. ministers of State and below are case workers, utterly without time to think. Summerskill,[3] equally, has prison cases. Harris has police cases. Only if you have a view of what you want to do – as Lyon has, for immigration and race relations – have you any chance of playing a constructive role. Jenkins has such a view too. This is a big argument for departmental experts rather than the inspired generalist ministers. Generalists are meat and drink to civil servants.

1 These included Tony Benn, Barbara Castle and Michael Foot.
2 Alex Lyon: Labour MP for York 1966–83; minister at the Home Office 1974–6.
3 Shirley Summerskill: Labour MP for Halifax 1964–83; Home Office junior minister 1974–9.

PRICE SISTERS[1] When the father visited recently, with them by now emaciated, he simply gave them the clenched-fist salute. They are intellectual romantic Irish of extraordinary toughness. One – the younger? – is a good deal stronger than the other. When she resisted strongly last Saturday, vomit got into the trachea and she went black. Not quite clear whether doctors cannot or will not go on in such circumstances. In the end it doesn't matter. They cannot be expected to do it day after day. A terrible strain. The two are now down to a low level of subcutaneous fat. Could be serious by the end of next week. Comatose; then into hospital, intravenous feeding which brings them out of coma, and so on cyclically. They could last for several months like this, but in the end they'd die of kidney disease.

Labour party are crypto-withdrawers. For different reasons. They don't understand or openly back what Jenkins has done – which is to decide that the Prices won't be sent back now, but the case will be examined in a few months and they could be sent back then. In fact it is quite possible they will die. What will Brits think then? AL believes the main view is send them back, do anything to avoid bombs over here. On the other hand, hard to say that the government will be pilloried if they did die here. There *could* be bombs, however.

LORD WINDLESHAM
Lunch, 5 June 1974

HEATH The best metaphor is military: the colonel issuing orders down the line and incapable of understanding why they aren't always obeyed. During the three-day week W made a great effort to stop Ted talking about 'Phase III' – just to strike it out because it had become an irritant to the public. He simply could not understand the point. A story: Ted was going to visit the Vatican. In the FCO there is a man who is the world expert on the Vatican, and he prepared the speech that Ted was to make. It was carefully prepared in the language and style suitable for the Pope. Probably written in Italian first, to see how it sounded, and then translated back into English. This senior FCO man took the speech to Ted at No. 10. Ted read it with temper rising and said, 'Who wrote this bilge?' The author was in the room and humiliated. Ted insisted on putting this careful language into his own uniquely boring jargon. The FCO man went with him to see the Pope, was presumably the interpreter

---

1 Sisters Dolours and Marian Price, with others, were convicted of an Irish Republican car bombing and were imprisoned. They began a widely reported hunger strike – countered by force-feeding – to support their repatriation to prison in Northern Ireland.

between them. Ted delivered his speech, then went for a walk with the Pope. At the end of the day his only comment was 'I think this has been a good visit,' with not a single word of thanks or feeling for the wretched FCO man, who now rates Ted a major enemy.

Ted believes that policy is all that matters, despite having presided over so many policy reversals. He doesn't believe there is such a thing as political instinct. Will he go? W was amazed that he did not go immediately after the February election. Perhaps he will not quit willingly even if he loses again. W compares him with Maudling. Although very different figures, they have in common an absolute refusal to make political gestures to the party – viz. Maudling on capital punishment etc. (W is a strong Maudling man.)

WHITELAW The most probable successor now. A man of total political instinct – e.g. after the election, sitting in Cumberland, he at least saw that this was the end of the road. OK, he drinks too much and he has got various other shortcomings, especially on economics, but these are not very important. When he took over Ulster he chose W and Paul Channon[1] to go with him, not wanting more senior people like Julian Amery,[2] who would have argued too much. But he discovered that there was a breakdown between the Treasury and the Ulster Finance Ministry. He said to W, 'I know this is very important but I don't understand it myself.' Rightly suggesting that neither W or Channon understood economics either, he got David Howell on his team as well (Howell had been a Treasury civil servant as well as an economic journalist).[3]

KEITH JOSEPH Working full-time on his policy and ideology review. Totally committed, but without a party apparatus or committee. Therefore much better. But he won't write a book. Insists that speech is his medium. Would be receptive probably to the idea of a big *Sunday Times* piece some time – perhaps synthesizing his speeches which he is about to start making. A great appetite for politics, enormous energy, very highly strung and nervy, totally committed – despite being very rich, leads a humble life with no big car, no country house, but instead very, very close family ties. Note that he has been in the Cabinet longer than anyone except Heath, Home and Hailsham.

1 Paul Channon: Conservative MP for Southend West 1958–97; Minister of State at the Northern Ireland Office March–November 1972; later Baron Kelvedon of Ongar.
2 Julian Amery: war correspondent, soldier, diplomat; Conservative MP for Preston North 1950–66, for Brighton Pavilion 1969–92; was at the time Minister of State at the FCO; later Baron Amery of Lustleigh.
3 David Howell: resigned from the Treasury to become a *Daily Telegraph* journalist and then Conservative MP for Guildford 1966–97; Minister of State at the Northern Ireland Office from 1972 to 1974; later Baron Howell of Guildford.

Given his Oxford studies, it is hardly surprising that HY developed his interest in the way the legal system worked, as the latter part of this interview – and subsequent ones in future years – demonstrates.

LORD HAILSHAM
July 1974

Experience shows that at this rate of inflation, democracy cannot survive. There are also ominous signs everywhere: UWC [Ulster Warkers Council] strike, private beds action, Scanlon[1] and his Mr Fixit, NUM strike. The political strike is, as all these are in their way a political strike, the largest straw in the wind.

No, Parliament won't have the power removed from it, a more likely eventuality is a seizure of power by Parliament – i.e. a strong government forcing through Parliament a series of authoritarian measures and leaving individual MPs powerless. This is more likely than a seizure of power by a UWC-type seizure by the TUC. After all, the body which grew out of such a seizure would not be obeyed by the police or the army. But a mistake to see the UWC as totally *sui generis*: they did seize control; they did succeed in forcing the hand of the government; they set up a version of their own government. Admittedly, this did not succeed: they were abominated both by the government they replaced and by the government which replaced them. But they are an example. But he agrees that the mass support they attracted would probably not be repeated here: although the fact that they did it despite the total opposition of the existing and the British governments is significant.[2]

A middle-class backlash is inevitable. A populist movement. In the end people will not put up with the law being broken and factions of the workers getting away with it with impunity. People will take control into their own hands, or a strong government will use the public forces to seize control. People will get hurt. Quite likely there will be a lot of violence one way or another. But in the end there is a limit to what middle-class people will tolerate.

Does this make life difficult for the Tories? Certainly the Tories will not succumb to it. The Tory Party may break up, it will not be taken over. Just as Labour finds the Marxists difficult, the Tories will find the right-wing extremists difficult. It would create a resonance in the party,

1 Hugh Scanlon: president of the Amalgamated Union of Engineering Workers 1968–78; later Baron Scanlon of Davyhulme.
2 The Northern Ireland government had been suspended in 1972, but Lord Hailsham's 'existing' government is almost certainly a reference to the power-sharing executive that the UWC strike brought to an end.

but that resonance would not become dominant. The Tory Party is strong and totally resistant to that. The leadership is to the left of the party and has been for many years. It would be the same with the Labour Party: Marxists could break it up; they would not take it over.

A national government is very different from a coalition. It is formed before an election, goes to the country on a coupon, is returned, and becomes very strong having started as very weak. A coalition is always weak: a convenience to secure a parliamentary majority. History shows it would break up pretty fast. See Thorpe today. He says it would be for a limited time. 'Such governments break up under the weight of their own inanition.' (See Samuelites running so quickly on a tariff issue.)[1]

People feel (a) that the parties have failed, and therefore that there is room for dogmatism, (b) that the power base of the parties cannot cope with the present circumstances. So where does this leave the party politician? 'I don't know. Perhaps – I'm nearly 67 after all and an intelligent man – I might retire and pull the rug over my head.'

Ted is a very strong character, he has a vision still; he is alone among politicians – almost – in this. This makes him a hard man to beat. So if he loses next time, he won't have had it. The party may turn on him – but that is very different. The party can be a vicious beast when beaten. But Willie and Ted are a good combination, matching each other's weakness. So long as they are together, it will be hard to move Ted. No one else has the stature – the only man with vision is Joseph (although it is a little incoherent just now), but he lacks the strength and character to lead, let alone beat Ted. Willie does have the strength, although he lacks a clear idea of what he wants to do. I hadn't realized until recently how deep is the disloyalty to Ted: sometimes I have a go at them sometimes not. One can't be fighting all the time – not in the dining room anyway.

LIBERALS Respect for Byers, even Thorpe. But Pardoe and Smith[2] are just populist self-seekers. Poujadists.[3]

JUDGES I was determined to be a good Lord Chancellor. Therefore I made a deal with Ted. I was on the legislation committee, and any other committees where I had business to transact; but I did not occupy my

---

1 Ramsay Macdonald's national government of 1931 campaigned on the divisive issue of tariff reform. This certainly divided the government's free-trade supporters in the Liberal Party: it created a 'Simonite' wing, made up of followers of Sir John Simon, who favoured continued cooperation, and 'Samuelites' who followed Sir Herbert Samuel and eventually formed a minority opposition to protectionism.

2 Frank Byers: Liberal MP for North Dorset 1945–50; later Baron Byers; became Liberal leader in the House of Lords in 1967. John Pardoe: Liberal MP for Cornwall North 1966–79. Cyril Smith, Liberal then Liberal Democrat MP for Rochdale 1972–92.

3 Pierre Poujade: a populist politician in 1950s France, identified with the grievances of shopkeepers and other small businesses. The Poujadist movement became linked with nationalism and xenophobia.

time with Cabinet committees all the time. Gardiner, like Kilmuir,[1] was used as a housemaiden: there is dust in that corner, go clear it up, Dilhorne,[2] too, fancies that role. I wanted to be a big judge and a big politician. I dread the day when the LC is not a good enough lawyer to take his place as a judge.

Thinks it unlikely he would become a Lord of Appeal in Ordinary: although the salary is attractive – 'If you're offered a job at that salary you at least consult your wife' – and it is a haven from the storm. (He speaks with obvious regret about his political career being over; 'Whatever happens, I can't win.') Dilhorne did it 'by virtue of sitting whenever he was asked and saying nothing in the Lords'. I always wanted to be a judge, and you'll find I spoke very little in the Lords in the early days, with that in mind: and it cost me £50 a time.

HY was broadening his range, but Norman Atkinson, from the left of the Labour Party, did not become a regular.

NORMAN ATKINSON
10 July 1974

I now no longer believe I will live in a socialist society. I used to think I would live in an 80–20 situation – 80 per cent public ownership, 20 per cent private. I now doubt whether it will even reach 50–50. Even if we did everything ever listed at the most extreme of Bennery, we'd only have 10 per cent at the most.

Yes, the left is much too prone to sloganeering. But there is not enough time for serious analysis. I have too many other things to do, although I try hard enough. *Tribune* is run by three people who write it all, and it is certainly not good.

After the next election, Wilson will go. I have defended and backed him for twenty years. But now I'm finished with him. If we lose, that means we are in Europe for good. And in my judgement it means we'll have a European leadership. This means Roy Jenkins unquestionably. And I have a lot of time for him. That doesn't mean I'll support him, but I admire his stature and his ability. He is a more probable world statesman than Benn, although Tony has great mental capacities and a broad vision.

---

1 Gerald Gardiner KC, Baron Gardiner of Kittisford: Lord Chancellor 1944–45. Sir David Maxwell Fyfe QC, Earl of Kilmuir: Conservative MP for Liverpool West Derby 1935–54; Nuremberg prosecutor; Lord Chancellor 1954–62.
2 Sir Reginald Manningham-Buller KC, Viscount Dilhorne of Green's Norton; Lord Chancellor 1962–4.

Benn will be the left candidate; Michael Foot[1] will not run, Healey fancies himself as a leader of the Labour coalition, obviously, but he won't be the left candidate. But the broader question is election of the leader by the mass party. This is going to come. It has already gone through the procedure, brought up at the NEC twice etc. etc. It should be approved this year, but I doubt whether it will come into force for when Wilson goes.

I now think Wilson is bent. He is the greatest manipulator of the twentieth century, and not for good purposes. We learn more and more about the way he did things in the seven years – not just the policies – and personally I feel I must have failed badly in my duty.[2]

What I now fear is a fascistic economic set-up, with firms in private hands but directed and funded largely by the state and a total removal of freedoms of all kinds. This is the natural authoritarian response to an economic collapse. It differs totally from what I want, which is a system of freedom within state ownership, including competition between state-owned businesses, such as the Soviet Union is at least taking seriously. I am very aware indeed of the seriousness of the situation, but I reject the notion that it is due to unions or wage demands; after all in the last twelve months we have suffered a 4 per cent drop: 16 per cent price rise, 12.2 per cent wage rise. More deeply, the wage content of price rises is higher here, much higher than in many other countries, which is a fault of the economy and of investment and so on.

Talking to NA, like talking to Michael Foot, one is reminded once again of the quite different reality of left visionaries from the picture received from them. This is their own fault, by their class rhetoric, their slogans, their sense of social bitterness: but also the fault of the media and the Tory press and deeply received images. In fact the true leftist believes that his society will work better and create more wealth – and not merely redistribute it away from the indecently rich. Their analysis is serious. They propose themselves as a one-nation group, not ultimately as a tiny faction of destructive revolutionaries. And in Atkinson there is a lot of magnanimity, a lot of seriousness.

---

1 Michael Foot: journalist, critic, author, editor; Labour MP for Plymouth Devonport 1944–55, for Ebbw Vale 1960–83; for Blaenau Gwent 1983–92; Secretary of State for Employment 1974–6; Leader of the Commons, 1976–9; leader of the Labour Party 1980–83.

2 Norman Atkinson recalled when this book was in preparation, 'We labelled our criticisms of Wilson "Economic Appeasement".' He added, 'Some of us had worked for three years designing a possible National Enterprise Board encouraged by Wilson. It turned out to be vastly different when included in the Industrial Bill (1975), particularly the function of the Treasury. Tony Benn and myself have agreed in recent years that Denis Healey would probably have made the best leader.'

SHIRLEY WILLIAMS
12 July 1974

ECONOMY Works on the supposition that we can pull through between Scylla and Charybdis. Now gingerly leaping from the rock of underinvestment to that of inflation. Many things must go right: world commodity prices continue going down a bit more, TUC efforts paying off, most of all no crisis of confidence between now and the end of the year which could make people cancel investment plans.

Inflation, now running at 16 per cent, aims to peak out at 21–2 per cent, before receding to 16 per cent and even going lower later on most optimistic forecasts. Much therefore depends on what Denis [Healey] does.

CBI An engagingly patriot body. Mainly decent men who believe in the national interest. Adamson[1] a half-crown item on a tuppenny market stall, a man who thinks, not merely a moderate, although that helps.

EEC Jim[2] has never been pro-Europe. He is an English nationalist and a party man. He saw renegotiation as a way of keeping the Labour Party together. I think he is slowly beginning to see that a split is probably inevitable, because just as we pro-EEC people would stay in without renegotiation, the antis won't accept any renegotiation as enough. It is an ideological not a practical matter. But he has understood certain things. All the Commonwealth countries were asked what we should do, and all said, variously, we should stay in and fight for them, and that they didn't want to go back to imperial preference. This shocked Jim. American view, mildly, is that we should stay in, even though the US is much less pro-EEC than it was. This influenced Jim as well. He has become, despite himself, a strong advocate that the renegotiation must succeed. But can it? There will be a split whatever happens. If Tony Benn gets his special conference, it is likely to decide against staying in. If this comes after the government position is made known (in favour of new terms) then the position would be tenable. If it came before, then the Cabinet might go into a referendum in neutralist stance – a terrible thought. What we need is a major re-education campaign. That is what the Danes did. They sent 40,000 people to Brussels: planeloads every day,

---

1 Sir Campbell Adamson: director general of the CBI 1969–76.
2 James Callaghan: Labour MP for South Cardiff 1945–50; for South-East Cardiff 1950–83, for Cardiff South and Penarth 1983–7; Chancellor of the Exchequer 1964–7; Home Secretary 1967–70; Foreign Secretary 1974–6; prime minister 1976–9; leader of the Labour Party 1976–80; later Baron Callaghan of Cardiff.

to see the Danish commissioner, who was seeing three or four groups of several hundred every day for three months, just answering questions. But it was decisive in forcing the public to see and consider the facts. The government paid for the whole exercise. On balance, it is likely that Jim will favour the new terms he gets, but he could be railroaded by an early special conference, which would swing the referendum, probably. The only other person who could have proposed himself in the role is Denis, but he couldn't have done it so well. Jim played it absolutely straight, and I admire him for that.

BENN ETC   One must respect his open-government views, although I agree you can't do it selectively. He will be an electoral liability if the debate rather than its outcome becomes the issue. That depends on the press and the right to some extent. I believe Labour will end up looking very like Attleean Labour. But I very much fear that will be overlooked. It also depends a bit on whether Tony accepts the Cabinet compromise. He can fight like hell for his corner, but in the end he should accept the compromise or leave. Like I may have to do over the Market.

SCOTTISH NATIONALISTS   Very under-observed. Note: at every election since 1945 their poll has doubled – extraordinary thing. Plaid Cymru has gone up and down; the National Front has bobbled along. But the SNP has doubled every time. They could be the key to everything – but to what end? They are callow in Parliament. But like Berlin's hedgehog[1] they may get there in the end, unlike the fox. They do not really understand or acknowledge the argument about nation and all its implications. The Scottish Labour Party is in the last ditch and does not like being told to desert it by an English party which has ignored it all these years. An alliance with them is conceivable, although some of them are right wing.

Thinks a minority Labour government is most likely outcome. A Lib–Lab coalition is out: a battle not worth splitting the party over (unlike the EEC). The Libs are an unmanageable crowd even on their own: a real problem for the Tories if they coalesced.[2]

Maybe the disaster in Scotland won't be so great. But agrees the SNP is poised for a big leap.

1   Sir Isaiah Berlin in a famous essay divided writers and thinkers into hedgehogs and foxes. His inspiration was an ancient Greek fragment: 'The fox knows many things, but the hedgehog knows one big thing.'
2   Shirley Williams recalls that her reference to 'an unmanageable crowd' was in the context of Jeremy Thorpe's leadership of the party at a very turbulent time before his resignation.

In the second general election of 1974, on 10 October, the votes for the three main parties fell, but Labour lost fewer and emerged with 319 seats, giving them an overall majority over the Conservatives (276) and the Liberals (13). In Scotland and Wales both nationalist parties saw their votes and seats increase, the SNP returning 11 MPs and Plaid Cymru 3. Harold Wilson became the first Labour prime minister to gain a fourth term.

TONY BENN
Lunch, 5 December 1974

REFERENDUM

1. *Timetable*. At least five decisions of the greatest strategic importance have been taken. They are, in order: whether the terms are acceptable to Callaghan (although Benn seemed to take this for granted), whether the Cabinet takes the view before or after the special party conference, in what terms the conference reaches its own opinion, what influence the Cabinet allows the conference to have on this decision, and what will be the position of ministers who dissent from the Cabinet view.

2. *Argument*. Benn will accept the view of the people. But it is perfectly clear that he will be a loud anti-Market voice during the campaign. He will probably avoid overt anti-Market platforms, but his concern will be to drive home the loss of sovereignty. He is already impressed by the fact that over '50 per cent' of English law is outside Parliament's control. True or not, this will be a potent referendum point. It meshes beautifully into Benn's overall preoccupations, in three specific ways. First, the Cabinet's tactics will directly raise the balance-of-power question in the Labour Party. Second, he argues that 'consent' will be permanently at risk among workers who see the EEC commission running their lives, refusing to give Whitehall industrial grants, etc. Third, he speaks of the EEC 'breaking up the unity of the UK'. If we submit to Brussels, he believes there is no argument against Scotland becoming an independent kingdom (and, per HY, even if the UK votes 'yes' in a referendum, Scotland may very well vote 'no': which means that the nationalist question will be given another major boost).

3. *History*. Benn claims to have been an anti-Marketeer originally. He then changed around 1965/6 'out of despair' – i.e. he believed there was no alternative. He now rejects this argument absolutely. He did so with such exaggerated emphasis that I detected a basic uncertainty in his mind. However, as of now, the political fact is that he will devise

all the arguments he can to show that alternatives do exist – this is one more stand in his 'consent' obsession. To accept that there is no alternative is to accept that people do not control their destiny – which is anathema. Benn now takes great personal credit for his referendum idea. When he first uttered it, in 1968, he claims he was almost run out of the Cabinet. In December 1970, only Callaghan in the Shadow Cabinet admitted that 'Tony has launched a dinghy into which we may one day be very happy to climb, to escape from the storm.' He rejects all argument against the referendum, especially the idea that it infringes parliamentary sovereignty. A cunning distinction had entered the vocabulary: although 'omnipotence' is impossible, 'sovereignty' is imperative. Not long ago he had lunch with the Swiss Minister of Defence at Farnborough. The Swiss was urging him against having a referendum, saying that these things were possible in Switzerland, where the people were the most intelligent in the world, but not in Britain, where the people are not intelligent enough. Benn describes how at first he was riled, but soon was struck by the Swiss minister's immense confidence in the people. 'That is what we want here,' he says.

INDUSTRY   Benn said little in this field which we have not heard from him already, so it is not worth recording much. But he did say he was against (contrary to outward appearances) two-tier management structures with unions embroiled in the management process. He prefers to see their purpose as 'a widening of the bargaining process'.

It is perhaps more helpful to mention the inferences to be drawn from what he said. One is that, whatever anyone else may think, he has for the moment an immense and complete confidence in the truth of his belief in the idea of running industry by consent of the managed. He claims that some unions are gradually coming round to it, and that all are particularly excited by the opportunities of disclosure of company information which are now open for them to extract. He says that management too, whenever he talks to them face to face, see the force of his idea. He also insists – another neat dialectical success – that wage restraint and other industrial virtues are already most apparent in the workers' cooperatives which his department has financed.

It is also apparent that he is only concerned with the post-slump era. He talks of the defensive value of the Social Contract,[1] in warding off unemployment and preventing futile bankruptcies and the ultimate destruction of British capital. But to all questions about the next twelve

1 The Social Contract was a bargain between the unions and the Labour government: in return for a freeze on rent increases and a repeal of the Conservatives' 1972 Industrial Relations Act, the TUC would cooperate in voluntary wage restraint.

months he replied by referring to the next five years. He sees his vision as effecting a deep, permanent change in the structure and attitudes of industry. Whatever intervenes between now and then should only be used to assist the fulfilment of the vision.

Benn gave an impressive peroration, recalling how all his successes – abolishing the peerage and imposing the referendum were two he mentioned – were the result of patience. It takes ten years for an idea to come to fruit, although the referendum will have taken only seven. So it will be, he insists, with his industrial strategy. This was all very revealing, implicitly, about his political ambitions and how he expects to fulfil them.[1]

CHRIS PATTEN[2]
Lunch, 11 December 1974

REFERENDUM A very serious danger of a low poll. This especially bad for pro-Marketeers, since the antis are more committed. But the role the Tories ought to play is puzzling. Politically, can they seriously be expected to back Harold: not only that, but to back Harold is saying he got much better terms than the lousy Tories did (after all, it is the Tories who are meant to be good at dealing with foreigners)? Organizationally, what should the party do? Will it be good or bad for Tories to be stuffing letterboxes? Will this just off put the Labs and the Libs? And where will it leave the umbrella European groups? How much will these groups do, and will they be inclined to leave it to the Tories? Admittedly, there are only about two dozen constituency associations which are anti-Market. But this doesn't mean the rest are thirsting to win a referendum campaign for HW.

As James Margach[3] says, the Tories desperately want to get Wilson out, but generally want to keep in the Market, while Labour desperately want to keep Wilson in and don't want the Market. A confusing set-up.

CP has a yearning for Callaghan. Hopes especially he will be the big persuader on TV. 'We have no real communicators. They have them all.'

LEADERSHIP Seems very unsure how Heath will do. Although he has become a much nicer man, he has played it badly, especially re Shadow Cabinet appointments. Even Peter Thomas[4] and Heseltine (who

---

1 Tony Benn's diary for this date makes no mention of HY. He does, though, state that Harold Wilson was emerging 'more strongly as anti-union man'.

2 Alongside Douglas Hurd, Patten became HY's favourite Tory contact.

3 James Margach: long-serving political editor of the *Sunday Times*.

4 Peter Thomas QC: Conservative MP for Conway division of Caernarvonshire 1951–66, for Hendon South, 1970–87; Secretary of State for Wales 1970–74; later Baron Thomas of Gwydir.

expected to lose his) kept their places. There are a very large number of disappointed men and no-hopers about. After nine years it could hardly be otherwise, but Ted has made it worse than he needed to. Also, his painful lack of skill with the 1922 Committee. Should have responded to du Cann's welcome, urging warmly how much he looked forward to seeing du Cann on the front bench etc. etc.[1]

Thatcher will certainly run. Then du Cann comes in on the second ballot, after a mere stalking horse for him on the first ballot (M-Hyslop).[2] Much turns on what the Home committee[3] decides about(a) whether the winner must get a proportion of the college or of those voting. If the former, expect big abstentions on the first ballot. (b) Should new candidates be able to enter the field on the third ballot? If so, this would be a chance for the magic circle's compromise man (Pym? Prior?) to enter between the irreconcilable Heath, du Cann, Whitelaw forces. CP thinks it unlikely that the third-ballot entrant will be allowed. He regrets this.

Remarks how loyally WW and Peter Carrington have stood by Ted. But WW would be bound to step in on the second ballot, if du Cann did.

There is much talk of Ted putting up a stalking horse first time round. Also, if the committee decides on an annual ballot – and not just each Parliament – this improves Ted's chances this time. If they knew they could ditch him next time, MPs would be more inclined not to boot him out. And others would be less inclined to stand. This would also favour Soames.[4] On the other hand, if Ted *did* get enough votes this time, it could be interpreted as a vote of confidence, which would do him a dangerous amount of good.

1 Sir Edward du Cann: businessman, financier, influential backbencher; Conservative MP for Taunton Somerset 1956–87.
2 Sir Robert (Robin) Maxwell-Hyslop: Conservative MP for Tiverton, Devon, 1960–92.
3 A committee under the chairmanship of Sir Alec Douglas-Home – now back in the House of Lords as a life peer, with the title Lord Home of the Hirsel – was working on new rules for the election of Conservative Party leaders.
4 Sir Christopher Soames: son-in-law of Winston Churchill, Conservative MP for Bedford 1950–66; ambassador to France 1968–72; governor of Southern Rhodesia 1979–80; as Baron Soames of Fletching, Leader of the House of Lords 1979–81.

1975

DOUGLAS HURD
22 January 1975

REFERENDUM Certain gains have been made and the problem is to keep Wilson to them. What are they? That the question will be in the bill. That the committee stage of the bill will be taken on the floor. That the PM will recommend the terms if they are good enough. That there will be a Commons debate on the terms before the referendum debate, or at least as well as it (there is argument about whether this debate should be tight up against the referendum or immediately after the renegotiation). This debate is vital. It will be a major blanket against the Labour Party conference etc. etc.

Important things not yet gained. Particularly, will the Cabinet as such make a recommendation, whatever happens to the dissidents. This is very important: a government recommendation will establish a basic position, with dissenters clearly identified, which is much more influential on the people than would be a mere series of individual statements. It is, in any case, difficult for dissenters now. The split Cabinet is already showing at the dispatch box.

Money is another unanswered question. Will the government go for prohibiting spending, or for handing out taxpayers' money? Probably the latter, being easier.

PER HY   What happens after the verdict? If a No – is there any real reason for Wilson to resign? Why should he? Who would pressure him to? Not the Tories, who would be equally beaten. Not the Labour Party, which would presumably regroup around the new policy. But Benn etc. would not – so the ball would be with them. One might measure the devastation of the political scene which will result from a No vote in the face of government recommendation . . . and perhaps thank God Wilson has said he will not view it as a vote of no confidence in his government.

Again – technically, will the HC have to repeal the various laws which bind us to the EEC. Will this be a long process, and will it be open to the Marketeers to fight a rearguard action against withdrawal . . .

Will have little effect on the Tory leadership battle. All the candidates would keep the party in a reasonably offensive position, fighting for a Yes. This goes even for du Cann, H thinks. Du Cann is thought to have left anti-Marketry behind him. But clearly Ted has a unique impulse. There are anti-Market MPs who are pro-Ted and vice versa.

ON LEADERSHIP   Very opposed to du Cann. No convictions, very much a City man. Totally the wrong sort to win back the middle votes. OK in his present strange job.[1] But that is very different. In any case, the 1922 Committee is going to have to be much changed if it is to *decide* things. Never intended for that. But rules-change shows how it can be manipulated or at least get itself into a silly mess. Hugh Fraser got the

---

1   Even in opposition Edward du Cann retained a multitude of Commons positions in addition to the chairman-ship of the Conservative 1922 Committee: member, select committee on privilege; chairman, select committee on public accounts; chairman, select committee of select-committee chairmen.

idea going, on the grounds that the National Union should have a vote.[1] No one *wanted* to change the rules, but the 1922 sat around and let the Home committee be set up. When the Home report was debated, all but two of twenty-six speakers criticized the rules. Yet the press reports gave the totally false impression that the 1922 rubber-stamped the rules.

THATCHER Has gained stature since the October election and during it. Did not gain much stature in government, other than latterly and only among those who paid close attention to the DES. The objection to her is not simply that she is a woman, though this counts in Tory councils and also, more significantly, in the Commons. It is said she is often formidable, but only in the afternoon. The real case is her narrow horizons. No vision, no broad sweep. An inability – not unlike Ted's, but more acute – to put herself in others' shoes. Can you imagine her at a summit conference? it is asked. Very hard to see her performing well, because her forte is entirely the nitty-gritty. The comparison being made is with Bonar Law.[2]

Edward Heath resigned as leader of the Conservatives on 4 February. Following an election using the Home rules, he was succeeded by Margaret Thatcher a week later.

IAN GILMOUR
Lunch, 9 April 1975

THATCHER Not clear who she listens to except Keith Joseph. He is very close to her; it remains to be seen how close. Meeting of the Shadow Cabinet on Friday will launch a research programme which must get off in the right non-Joseph direction. SC is majority for Joseph, but with enough weight on the other side probably to stop it. Her own attachment to ideology is unclear. 'She has no ideas, not even views I think. She has some strong prejudices.' (This is supported by her distaste for speech-making.) Maudling is important as an anti-Josephite, but may be a burnt-out case. Physical deterioration is very startling. She wanted him inter alia as an Arab man (she was vice-president of Anglo-Jewish society or some such, and Finchley is Jewish). Unhappily the only evidence of her

---

1 The National Union of Conservative and Unionist Associations, a federation of the party's volunteers.
2 Andrew Bonar Law, prime minister 1922–3, became leader of the Conservative Party in 1911 as a compromise candidate.

flexibility is the housing-policy affair.[1] Should have been announced in July, but she resisted it. Yet she took all the credit in October. Otherwise the omens are poor. But she is an unknown quantity: that has been her strength. She only thought of the leadership when Keith withdrew, therefore has very little to show.

BALANCE Gilmour told her that he was a homosexual abortionist [i.e. pro gay rights, pro-abortion] and she should know what she was taking on. His only trouble is that Jenkins is so good at averting Home Office problem cases which suddenly erupt and would give him a chance for a row. On most issues Ian Gilmour is against the Tory tide. He expects to be purged in October, after he has been seen to be defective by one or two episodes between now and then. He remains utterly committed to a left Tory position. Believes no future in elections fought from the right. Heath's first two years were a disaster, he says, and claims to have said so at the time.

MORE ON THATCHER She has not made a mark in the country. She has the party solid behind her, unassailable position. But outside she remains curiously blurred. This is partly because she has said little, and partly because she has said support the strong. That is a bad message. It will get worse if Joseph triumphs over her.

HEATH If I were MT I'd be terrified of him. I think she is. Not that he could be leader if she fell under a bus today. But he is a force. He made some terrible mistakes. Mainly not going on 7 February.[2] We would have won then. But not having gone then, we should have stepped back and waited for the next fight, having conceded to the NUM on the TUC initiative. If it had been 7 February, we would have defeated the left, defeated the right, settled Europe, put the TUC in its place – altogether history would have been very different. It would also have vindicated an incomes policy. Alternatives: settle NUM by reference to oil prices, back in the autumn. Ian Gilmour didn't know how seriously this had been debated at the time ('I was toiling away at Defence'). To have taken up the TUC initiative would have caused trouble in the party, but it could probably have been pushed through. Ted also blundered in not going after February (although this is understandable), but even more so in not going on 11 October or at least announcing that he would go. This would

1 Late in 1974 the new Conservative leader, Mrs Thatcher, had first raised the prospect that tenants might buy their own council houses at below market value. This proved to be a popular proposal.

2 On 7 February 1974 Edward Heath had announced the general election that would be held – and won without a clear majority – on 28 February. Colleagues were later to argue that had he gone to the country in January, with a vote on 7 February, he might have won convincingly.

have sewn it up for WW. An unforgivable mistake. I think he has lost a touch of his arrogance, but only a little. (Per HY, *Sunday Times* obviously blundered in February in not backing the Tories. But, as IG agrees, it was understandable at the time . . .)

COALITIONS Agrees that Labour probably won't be killed by the EEC issue. But 3–1 against it being so by the economy. Of course, the most likely thing is that things blundered on as they are now. The agent, if it arrives, will be external: creditors, Germans, Arabs, IMF. Will be followed by a split which drives Labour left and right. What will Wilson do? If he goes right, allies with the Libs, then this poses problem for the Tories. If this was over an incomes policy, perhaps one-third of the Tories would go with Wilson. Quite unclear what Thatcher would do, although Joseph would obviously counsel against, and in favour of a hardline right party being preserved from contamination. There is then a centre party, and a real fragmentation. If Wilson goes left, into the siege economy (assuming we stay in Europe as well), not clear how it can be a siege if we stay in the EEC. But Labour probably stays more united. Heath would be more amenable than Thatcher to leading a Tory force into coalition. (Heath's other big blunder was in not making the supreme sacrifice, as he was supposed to do, on the Sunday before 10 October. Was meant to say clearly that he would go if he stood in the way. He was so unpopular this could have had a big impact. But he did not do it: recoiled at the last moment, gave a soft lobby meeting, followed on the Monday by a lot of woolly rubbish.)

DAVID MARQUAND
Lunch, 15 April 1975

ANTHONY CROSLAND[1] A broken figure in my eyes. I used to be a real fan. First awakening was during the effort to get him to sign the *Guardian* advert in 1971,[2] when he told us the Common Market was fifteenth on his list of importance. Crosland's real problem is a corrosive jealousy of Jenkins, starting from his failure to get the Treasury. This decision was probably merely bureaucratic. Jim wanted the Home Office and would take nothing else, so a straight switch was the simplest thing. Crosland has never recovered. His 'voters of Grimsby' stuff is repellent.

1 Anthony Crosland: Labour MP for South Gloucestershire 1950–55, for Grimsby 1959–77; Environment Secretary 1974–6; Foreign Secretary 1976 to his sudden death in 1977.
2 On 11 May 1971 *The Guardian* published a letter signed by Crosland, Healey and ninety-eight other Labour politicians supporting British membership of the EEC. At the time, Harold Wilson had not yet announced his opposition.

Not only ignorant but patronizing about the working classes, implying that they are incapable of taking a decent line about, say, race. Which is balls. He of all people has no place to talk like this anyway.

In the end his dishonesties must haunt him. Being a superb mind, he knows very well that his is being unstraight. This must worry him. Unlike Healey: a true Stalinist in his blithe willingness to use figures as it suits him, and to admit that it is pragmatic to change position. See especially his lurching around on the Market – and his justification of this to DM as a very persuasive argument: 'At least it's a better one than Harold has thought up . . . !'

JENKINS Probably cannot be leader. But such a decent man, and to have got so far. DM would vote for him . . .

TOM MCCAFFREY
Lunch, 21 May 1975

Jim Callaghan now has a closer relationship than ever with Harold, and a closer relationship than anyone else has. They see each other at least once a week for a private chat about the scene. At the Kingston briefing[1] when Jim not there, Harold would let Tom McCaffrey field the Rhodesian questions, saying this was really Jim's territory. Tom believes Jim's prestige will diminish slowly after the referendum. He will become less important once this fence is crossed, and his day leadership-wise may well be done.

Affirms that Benn will undoubtedly be offered something else. Also suggests that other troublemakers will be moved out. The bitterness towards Benn in the Wilson entourage is enormous, and should finally instil Harold with enough resolution. Several times between February and October, Benn went over the brink and just pulled back, leaving No. 10 without the opportunity they wanted to get rid of him.

Do not underestimate the vast importance now which Joe Haines occupies in Wilson's psyche. Many occasions when Wilson is about to start something and asks, 'Where's Joe?' He trusts his political advice; they have an intense personal loyalty to each other. Joe could have whatever he wanted. Wilson drives him hard, and wants to know where he is even if he takes a half-day off. But don't forget Joe has come a very long way from rowing the lightermen to work down the Thames as a boy

1 Commonwealth heads of government met at Kingston, Jamaica, from 29 April to 6 May 1975 to discuss, among other things, sanctions against Rhodesia.

(or some such trade), tea boy in the London office of a Scottish paper and so on up almost to the top in the *Herald*.

This contrasts with Jenkins's treatment of John Harris. Often drops Harris out of the car in mid-town, saying he is going on to a party, goodnight John, find your own bus fare.

Starting with the following account of a meeting with Dipak Nandy, HY occasionally introduced his solo encounters with a brief pen portrait of his interviewees. Not all would show him as so well disposed.

DIPAK NANDY
22 May 1975

Dipak Nandy is a highly intelligent academic/politician/administrator, former director of the Runnymede Trust, formerly in the Communist Party, well connected to the Labour Party, very knowledgeable about trade unionists, and very much a Jenkinsite in his location on the political spectrum.

He believes it is inconceivable for Jenkins to lead the Labour Party. He *is* an elitist, through and through. He will not descend into the marketplace to persuade and cajole people to his point of view, but prefers (a) lofty speeches, which are often very good but rarely if ever taking on hostile audiences, (b) the manoeuvrings of lieutenants like Harris and Rodgers (the latter much more substantial than the former) both among the press and in the PLP. He should be strongly contrasted with Gaitskell, much the bigger man, who fought for things he believed in in a wholly prominent, outspoken and exposed way – Jenkins prefers resignation, does he not? (As you will see, Dipak Nandy is rather bitter.)

He believes Jenkins is also the victim of the circle he has chosen to move in – 'all broken men, burnt-out cases, the Kensington intelligentsia who really live in a dream world'. The other inhabitants (and DN has witnessed this, an angle on Jenkins which Anthony L. [Lester], he says, would not have seen) include Noel Annan, Claus Moser and Isaiah Berlin.[1] Mark Bonham-Carter[2] acquires reflected glory by presiding over the *galère*. The natural conversational pabulum is nineteenth-century history, the worlds of Gladstone and Palmerston and endless speculations

---

1 Noel Annan, later Baron Annan, provost of University College London and then vice chancellor of the University of London. Claus Moser, later Baron Moser, statistician and chairman of the Royal Opera House. Sir Isaiah Berlin, historian, political philosopher and president of the British Academy.
2 Mark Bonham-Carter: Liberal MP for Torrington 1958–9; vice-chairman of the BBC; publisher.

about the three reasons why Palmerston was in the end a failure etc.
Annan, of course, has made this his literary territory (constant reviews in
the *New York Review of Books*). Jenkins is obsessed with it, but in a
socio-cultural way rather than as a hard-headed politico and of course
did that recent review of the Gladstone diary in the *Observer*.

But, says DN, one must remember that this is happening to a man
who has perhaps been one of the half-dozen best departmental ministers
since the war, I don't know how one tests this. But certainly at the Home
Office and the Treasury in the later sixties Jenkins acquired in Whitehall
terms a very high reputation. At the Home Office he also achieved quite
a lot of reform, as he is doing in a small way now. At the Treasury, of
course, his celebrity was acquired contemporaneously with a downswing
in his popularity in the Labour Party. At least in retrospect, that period
is one of the many counts against him.

Further, notes Dipak Nandy, it is characteristic that after 1970 Jenkins
should have written profiles of six political failures (or whatever the
number was – I've mislaid the book), whereas Crosland set down to write
essays and later a book about economic and social policy. Admittedly a
bad book, and not in the same league as *The Future of Socialism*. But
still it makes a pointed contrast with Roy.[1]

Harold Wilson appeared twice at the Sunday Times's *Gray's Inn Road
offices in little more than a month, first visiting the* Sunday Times *and
then at the invitation of the paper's Canadian-born proprietor, Lord
(Roy) Thomson, whose guests also included 'captains of industry', as
they were often called. HY clearly enjoyed recording each occasion.*

HAROLD WILSON (WITH JOE HAINES)
Lunch, the *Sunday Times*, 29 October 1975

Prentice is 'finished'.[2] He will lose his case even though Tom Bradley[3] is
chairman of the committee. He was a fool. Should have gone out with
twenty people each Sunday for a month and would have been in better
shape than he is now. Made a big mistake in converting himself into a

1 Roy Jenkins's *Nine Men of Power* began life as journalism, and was eventually published as a book in 1975.
Anthony Crosland, *The Future of Socialism*, 1956.

2 A high-profile victim of battles with left-wing constituency activists, in 1975 Prentice was 'deselected' for his
Newham seat. MPs and Cabinet colleagues backed him, but the Labour Party NEC endorsed the decision.
Prentice later appealed to the Labour Party conference, but failed to overturn the decision.

3 Tom Bradley: trade unionist; elected Labour MP for Leicester North-East in 1962, he eventually became a
member of the SDP, representing Leicester East 1981–3.

national campaign: representing the issue as between left and right in the party at large rather than in his constituency. If he had any sense he would have got Bradley to affiliate some branches, Tom Jackson[1] to do likewise, and so build up a counter force. If a man cannot rely on more than half his executive he has only himself to blame if he gets kicked out. But he will remain in Cabinet. Would have a good chance if he simply ran as the 'PLP' candidate at the next election. Frank Allaun[2] is in trouble from the other side in his constituency.

EUROPE It was going superbly well at Helsinki.[3] Me and Schmidt[4] and Giscard. Endless minutiae of Harold the statesman, Harold the behind-the-scenes fixer, Harold not being taken as anyone's fool. But it has got tangled over the oil business, where the real culprits are the French, who (a) refuse to join the IEA operation[5] and (b) tried to organize the whole conference down to the last detail. Only Jim and Harold got in the way of Giscard and Sauvagnargues[6] on this one. Noted that it was the Eight not the Nine in any case, because of France. 'But Jim has got to find some way to get himself off the hook' (this with the chuckle of an old operator watching a rival operator in trouble). The answer will be chairmanship of one of the most important commissions. Not necessarily finance.

DIRECT ELECTIONS Not ready with a policy yet.

In the Labour Party it is not an issue any more. Simply doesn't matter in party terms. Not even on the NEC ('What's that you said? NEC? NEC? What's that?') Multiple reminiscence about the brilliant triumph of the Islington conference . . . all a matter of timing . . . that is what politics is about . . . the telescope theory.[7]

DEVOLUTION 'A bore'. Of course I've always been a constitution-alist. But I wish more people would look at this politically, then it would all be easier. Trouble is too *many* people looking at it constitutionally.

But quite clear from Harold Wilson's words and manner that

1 Tom Jackson: general secretary of the Union of Post Office Workers during its national strike in 1971.

2 Frank Allaun: journalist, Labour MP for Salford East 1955–83; campaigner for nuclear disarmament.

3 World leaders met in Helsinki on 30 July–1 August 1975 for what would become known as the 'final act' of the Conference on Security and Cooperation in Europe.

4 Helmut Schmidt: German SPD politician and chancellor of West Germany 1974–82.

5 The International Energy Agency (IEA), made up of OECD countries, was established in 1974 in the wake of the OPEC oil-price crisis.

6 Jean Sauvagnargues, then Giscard's minister for foreign affairs.

7 Faced with a divided Cabinet and a promise of a national referendum on whether Britain should stay in the European Community, the pro-European Wilson allowed a special conference of the Labour Party membership at Islington's Sobell Sports Centre on 26 April 1975. Labour's anti-Europeans carried the day, but lost the referendum in June.

(a) There will be no PR [proportional representation] (it could be 'infectious').

(b) There will be no cut in Labour seats at Westminster. Arguments: seats are more scattered, bigger area to be covered; Westminster has 'override' power anyway, so Scottish must be fully represented there; also foreign affairs . . .

And this has weight: if Scottish rep at Westminster was cut, Scotland could claim more power for Edinburgh. If Scotland remains overmanned at Westminster, Westminster can claim override power more cogently.

Muttering about leaks at weekend. I know where they came from . . . Further obsession with leaks. But getting reckless. Lengthy chortling over his own successful leak to Harry Boyne[1] at the Commonwealth PMs' conference in Jamaica about I've forgotten what. 'No fingerprints,' he said joyously. And the correspondent already on holiday in the Caribbean when the story appeared . . .

I've got the best team since 1906.[2] Can't be matched for brainpower, I'm quite sure of that. (But doesn't reflect on how far removed from this will be the historical verdict on them and their ill-success.)

PRIVACY   Still wants his package: more privacy, less secrecy. Says the Home Office has got it all wrong. 'Roy wants something not a single one of his colleagues will support.' Wouldn't be drawn on Franks[3] – merely saying it didn't pay enough attention to privacy. Obviously deeply ruffled by land-deals stories,[4] and these appear heavily in evidence to Royal Commission on Press.

CROSSMAN[5]   Wants a ten-year rule. Before that, onus on the writer. After it, onus on the government. Obsessed with two examples, as at Blackpool. First, Amin. What would have happened to Hills if Amin had been in power in 1969, had been described as a nutcase by a Cabinet

1 Sir H. B. 'Harry' Boyne: political correspondent of the *Daily Telegraph*; director of communications for the Conservative Party 1980–82.

2 1906 was a significant year for the fledgling Labour Party, which achieved its electoral breakthrough with 29 seats at Westminster. The victors, however, were the Liberals under Sir Henry Campbell-Bannerman, whose 'ministry of all the talents' included David Lloyd George, Herbert Asquith, Sir Edward Grey, R. B. Haldane and Winston Churchill. Wilson (briefly a member of the Liberal Party at Oxford) may have had either success in mind.

3 Oliver Franks, Baron Franks of Headington, moral philosopher, civil servant, banker, in 1976 chaired a committee on ministerial memoirs.

4 Newspapers had reported in 1974 that Harold Wilson's secretary Marcia Williams and her brother Tony Field had profited from speculating in land. Wilson, who had denounced land speculation as 'the biggest single scandal, the ugliest of the faces of present-day capitalism', became the target of press attacks. The PM responded with libel writs against the *Daily Mail* and the *Daily Express*.

5 Richard Crossman, Labour MP for Coventry East 1945–74, had caused a political stir in 1975 by publishing his diaries of the 1964–70 Wilson administrations when he was in the Cabinet as, successively, Secretary of State for Housing and Local Government, Lord President of the Council, and Secretary of State for Social Services. The *Sunday Times* added fuel to the row by serializing the choicest entries.

minister reporting the Cabinet view in his memoirs, and then the same government had returned to power and Amin had taken in Hills.[1] Second, the royal family. They have no right to reply . . .

Claims that Trend's intervention was important in only two major parts of his own book.[2] First, Bhutto. HW had said he was the biggest crook unhung or some such.[3] Trend had asked whether he really wanted to say that, bearing in mind that he might return to power. Second, Harold Evans ignored advice to cut down a passage about the Soames affair, which reveals HW's rage at Foreign Office duplicity. (According to Haines, who intervened at this point, the Soames affair ranks second only to the *Yesterday's Men* affair in the annals of infamy.)[4]

LORD THOMSON LUNCH FOR HAROLD WILSON
Thomson House, 26 November 1975

A display of matchless vanity, but subtly different from his performance at the *Sunday Times*. Instead of parading his skill as a fixer of stories and coverage, HW parades his skill as a manipulator of economic forces. Thus does he think he appeals to his special audience. He talked for a very long time to each question, beginning with Rambouillet.[5] This, he said, was organizationally a shambles. Giscard insisted on having it there: 'Most of the others wanted it at Chequers.' Foreign Secretaries and finance ministers billeted in barracks. Ford ('Gerald') was furious. 'Gerald would have liked to have Simon[6] by his side, but I just about managed to get by without Denis [Healey].' Ford was furious, as we were, about the

1 Denis Hills, a British-born university lecturer, offended the dictator Idi Amin, who had seized power in Uganda in 1971, by comparing him to a 'village tyrant' in the typescript of his 1975 book *The White Pumpkin*. A Ugandan court sentenced Hills to death for treason, and his execution by firing squad was averted only after a visit by James Callaghan, then Foreign Secretary.

2 Under the convention of collective Cabinet responsibility, Sir Burke Trend, secretary to the Cabinet, had an interest in 'vetting' ministerial and prime ministerial memoirs published soon after the events they described.

3 Zulfikar Ali Bhutto was first president, then prime minister of Pakistan 1971–7. He was hanged in Rawalpindi on 4 April 1979 after a coup by the Pakistani military. His daughter Benazir, herself later to become prime minister of Pakistan, was assassinated after a party rally in Rawalpindi in 2007.

4 The Soames affair involved a conspicuous and damaging leak of secret negotiations – begun in 1969 and which came to nothing – between Sir Christopher Soames, Britain's ambassador to Paris, and Charles de Gaulle over the UK's relationship with France and other European states. Labour's election campaign in 1970 characterized the Tories as 'Yesterday's Men'. In 1971, after Heath's victory, the BBC precipitated a bitter row with Wilson's office when it used the same tagline as the title for a satirical programme about Labour, in which former ministers unwittingly took part.

5 Rambouillet: Heads of state of Italy, Germany, the UK, Japan and the US met as guests of President Giscard of France at the Château de Rambouillet, near Paris, between 15 and 17 November, 1975 to discuss the faltering global economy. It was the first of what would be known later as G8 summits.

6 William E. Simon, US Treasury Secretary, accompanied President Gerald Ford, and Chancellor Denis Healey accompanied Harold Wilson. But only the heads of state were accommodated in the château. Their ministers were billeted an 'inconvenient' distance away.

exclusion of Canada. In the end, however, it was a great success. People even talked about the spirit of Rambouillet. Was abusive, with elaborate faked apologies, about Giscard, also Ortoli.[1]

'Tell us about this economic policy of yours, which is doing so well,' says Roy Thomson. This launches Harold into a lengthy oration, maundering and partly inaudible, about the virtues of timing. Timing, he said yet again, was everything. His own had turned on the miners' conference. We couldn't do anything until after the referendum. 'I can't rock two boats – rather, I'm usually rocking half a dozen at a time, but I can't rock two liners at a time. We had to finish with the referendum, in which the timing in every respect ran for us.' Took a month and a week thereafter to get the pay policy right. I took great trouble with the miners. Of course I know them very well. I know the pits, I know the men. I know there were only three pits left in the West Midlands, Staffordshire and Shropshire, and those were undecided. I made them my first target. But every line of that speech (which?) had a hidden meaning, everything had its own inflexion. But you've got to know the miners like I do. I could see Ted was making a hash of it in February. I even wrote to him a personal note, 'marked confidential', telling him not to alienate the moderates (in February 1974).

What next, he was asked? Brunton[2] added that he thought the triumph was a big one, of getting the £6 policy[3] through and accepted. Wilson said it was all a matter of timing. The big thing was not just to have the £6 but to get acceptance for the idea that this kind of policy was the right thing to be doing. *That* was the big thing. It would be quite wrong for him to say what he thought about the economy, which is that the biggest problem is overmanning. You can't say that kind of thing in the middle of high unemployment. Also, he couldn't himself talk about the next phase, but it was a good thing Jack Jones[4] talked about it. (Weinstock[5] kept muttering that the £6 policy was nothing much. We had all succumbed to the illusion that it was an enormous sacrifice for the workers. For many, on the contrary, it gave them a lot more money. Like the equal-pay law. But, added AW, it was better than nothing. It has been made to stick. That was something.)

HW added that the need was for a few more big ones in the bag before he could claim success. The militant ones were the white-collar unions – power engineers.

1 Francois-Xavier Ortoli, a Frenchman and president of the European Commission 1973–7, did not attend the Rambouillet conference.

2 Gordon Brunton: chief executive of the Thomson Organization and director of Times Newspapers 1967–81.

3 Part of the Social Contract between government and unions in 1975 involved a £6 ceiling on wage rises.

4 Jack Jones: leader of the TGWU, and a force in the Labour movement. A 1977 Gallup poll found that 54 per cent thought him the most powerful figure in the UK.

5 Arnold Weinstock: head of GEC.

Why hadn't he said more about the need for diligence and hard work from the workers (this from Jules Thorn?[1]) Oh but he had, says HW. Often said it. Only the other day, a speech in his constituency club. Others did likewise. It was all a matter of timing.

I am accused of being a tactician, he said. Nothing could be further from the truth. Of course, I have to take precautions for the immediate situation. Anyone would. But the truth is I think very long term indeed. Nobody knows what my current long-term strategic thought is. (To make another speech about Dunkirk, says WR-M.[2])

Made various suggestions about investment. Mainly the State Unit Trust, which Harold Lever[3] is looking into. And personal investment in the NEB,[4] an idea pushed by Lady Falkender[5] on the analogy with the war, when people were asked to buy a Spitfire. They never did, of course. They just contributed to the general financial situation. But it was good for the country. Invest a pound for Britain.

There was a lot of discussion afterwards. Methven[6] opined that HW was the greatest parliamentary genius since Charles James Fox, 'And I speak as a constitutional historian.' Weinstock: 'He's the only man who can run this country at the moment. *That's* what's so bloody frightening.' Hussey[7] who had met him only once before, was appalled.

WR-M contested the view that he was the only man for the job. People think that, he said, but they only make it more certain. This is the great illusion Wilson has fathered on the nation, says HY. That the Labour Party can only be run thus. But Denis Healey would be different, says WR-M. He'd be the most likely successor, and at least he would have some intellectual idea about what he was doing.

He's like the Slater[8] of politics, says WR-M. So obsessed with the means that he totally gets the ends wrong. And in the end is tripped up by the means. But no, says HY. He is still there. He has made it work for him. Only by a fluke, says WR-M. Only by Ted Heath's classic blunder.

1 Sir Jules Thorn: head of the Thorn Group, later Thorn EMI.
2 William Rees-Mogg: editor of *The Times* 1967–81; later Baron Rees-Mogg of Hinton Blewitt.
3 Harold Lever: Labour MP for Manchester Exchange, then Manchester Cheetham, then Manchester Central 1945–79; Chancellor of the Duchy of Lancaster 1974–79; later Baron Lever of Manchester.
4 The National Enterprise Board was set up in 1975 to extend public ownership of industry. In 1981 it merged with the National Research Development Corporation to become the British Technology Group.
5 Lady Falkender, as Marcia Williams, was Harold Wilson's private secretary from 1956 to 1964 and head of his political office during his tenure as Labour leader and two terms as prime minister.
6 Sir John Methven: director general of Fair Trading 1973–6, then of the CBI 1976–80.
7 Marmaduke ('Duke') Hussey, who joined the Thomson Organization from Associated Newspapers as chief executive of Times Newspapers 1971–82. Later Baron Hussey of North Bradley, he was chairman of the BBC governors 1986–96.
8 Jim Slater founded the bank Slater Walker Securities with the Conservative MP Peter Walker, later Lord Walker. Walker quit the partnership in 1970, when he became a minister. The bank collapsed in 1975. In 1977 Jim Slater was acquitted of fraud. He is now chairman of Bioprojects International.

Wilson did not expect to fight an election and did not expect to win one. That was quite obvious. He had a whole new lease of life.

OWN IMPRESSIONS   He does bestride the scene. But what a scene to be so easily bestrode. He is a master of detail. Knows the pits, knows the men, knows his international finance, can bandy terms with anyone, a long accretion of knowledge and a long memory. He does *know* a great deal. He totally lacks self-doubt. And in a sense with reason. Politically, in *his* terms as a politician, he has won. All the derision and all the criticism does not reach him. He simply deflects it. This looks like a paradox with his obsession about the press. But it is explained by his constant fear that his own total self-belief may not be shared by the populace, which has been got at by distorted and biased media. Insouciance, conceit verging on total impudence (v. his lack of effort to make serious dialogue, refusal to answer questions, meandering verbiage etc. etc.). But flattering. David Brown[1] said he *was* flattered that HW remembered he had met in 1958, and in Huddersfield. But this is not the point, says Brown. Should *not* be Wilson's reflex.

1 David Brown: chairman of David Brown Holdings, and Vosper Ltd; his business career began in Huddersfield.

1976

29 January   Provisional IRA bombs explode in London's West End.
16 March   Harold Wilson announces his surprise resignation.
5 April   James Callaghan becomes prime Minister.
10 May   Jeremy Thorpe resigns the Liberal leadership after allegations of homosexuality.
4 July   Israeli raid frees hostages held in Entebbe, Uganda.
28 July   Tangshan earthquake in China kills more than 240,000.
24 August   After a heatwave dominates the British summer, Denis Howell is appointed 'Minister for Drought'.
26 October   National Theatre opens on London's South Bank.
2 November   Jimmy Carter elected US president.

Deaths   Busby Berkeley, Benjamin Britten, Agatha Christie, Howard Hughes, L. S. Lowry, André Malraux, Mao Zedong, Paul Robeson, Luchino Visconti, Zhou Enlai

Early in 1976 the Sunday Times *decided to reconstruct the events leading up to the February 1974 general election – when Edward Heath had been unable to form a government, even though the Conservatives won more seats than Labour.*

Not all the interviews are dated, hence the order in which they took place is unclear.

NIGEL LAWSON[1]
20 January 1976

Everything was geared up for 7 February ... [Then] 13 January, Chequers, Sunday ... for the first time Ted actually *expressed* scepticism about an election. It was impossible to tell whether this was him getting

---

1 Nigel Lawson had been hired by Conservative Central Office after the 1973 party conference. He was not yet an MP, but had advised Sir Alec Douglas-Home during his premiership. It was the second half of the parliament,

worried, or being a devil's advocate. (N thought the former.) . . . Here again Ted's style was revealed. He plays his cards so close to his chest. You'd sometimes think he was asleep. Meetings used to lack positive direction or chairmanship. His scepticism was expressed at Chequers in typically few words. You needed to be a Ted-watcher to notice it, but then it was obvious. But at this meeting, for the first time, it was clear that the price of oil was much on his mind. He wasn't sure what the implications were. But this now bulked larger in his mind than the miners . . . NL was instructed to do a redraft. He had already spent all Boxing Day writing a redraft. The contingency planning went on even after Ted's scepticism was pretty clear. NL did the final draft on 15 January. But then it all fizzled out. And we thought there'd be no election at all. It seemed that Ted had decided against. Nothing happened until 31 January. Then it started up again . . . Carrington took the lead. Lots of meetings. Other Cabinet ministers informed.

We would have won on 7 February. There wouldn't have been a miners' strike. The three-day week would have been a four-day week. The NUM would have had to decide to strike against an election. The Labour Party was pressing all the time, privately, to get the NUM not to strike.

Wrong to say Barber was totally hard-line. But he was convinced of the need for an early election, and was sceptical of the NUM, although he may have been lacking in astuteness to say so openly. He supported Carrington, though: chairman and former chairman together. He was the one most involved, plus the Treasury, with oil.

Ted's desire to achieve a kind of corporate state, giving the unions a big role in government, was absolutely genuine. There were problems of communication, which were very understandable. One problem was that the union leaders he spoke to spoke with different voices. Murray did not speak for the TUC, or Gormley for the NUM. This was bewildering. Unlike now, when if you speak to Jack Jones you speak to the union movement, by and large.

It was very difficult for the unions. Ted is such a silent person. He listens a lot, but he can't understand that the other side needs playback. The absence of playback totally disconcerted the unions. They are interested in negotiations, bargaining and compromise. This is what they understand. Ted sees politics as a search for rational solutions. Once found, all rational men will follow them. In that he was like William

---

and Lawson's appointment reflected the need to consider political strategy, although, as HY observed, he had no political brief. Late in November 1973 Lawson was instructed to draft the Conservative's general-election manifesto. This was tacked on at the front of an earlier Central Office work, as a 'crisis' package.

Armstrong, who also had no idea at all how the unions worked. He had no experience of them.

FUTURE   This was something new for the British people. They had never before had to resolve a constitutional issue. It was totally unfamiliar. They found the decision too big for them. Too hard to choose – which accounts for the Liberal vote. But it was a great educational process. Next time, the choice will be faced.

JAMES PRIOR
21 January 1976

17 January was the crucial date. This was when most people expected it to be announced. When it was not announced, there was an enormous sense of elation among Labour MPs down here at the House that evening. They felt they had been let off the hook. Yet the Tory Party in the country favoured an election by 90 per cent or more. The only Cabinet colleagues who were dubious were Whitelaw, Carr and Home. But the MPs were more so. Harmar Nicholls[1] an outstanding example of total opposition. He thought he was going to lose anyway, as did a lot of others who were either going voluntarily or saw retribution as a threat they'd rather not take on.

But by the date for deciding 28 February they were all resigned to it. The only qualms were felt by those who had wanted 7 February.

Ted never gave any indication what he thought. We were allowed to go ahead making preparations, but to my knowledge he did not once give a response when the arguments were put to him for 7 February. He later blamed Central Office for steaming up the machine for 7 February. My reply was that this could easily have been avoided if he ever told us before the last minute that February was off.

TED'S METHODS   (I put to JP that this lack of playback was also a key reason for his failure with the unions.)

That is the style of the man. He absorbs, he listens, but he plays his cards close to his chest. I didn't feel at the time that this was wrong, nor do I think so now. Went much further than many people in the party wanted him to go in making concessions. The party said enough was enough, and it was courageous of him to go as far as he did. He was more flexible than anyone else would have been. And others would have fallen

---

1 Sir Harmar Nicholls: barrister; Conservative MP for Peterborough 1950–74; chairman of Radio Luxembourg Ltd, and sometime president of the Wallpaper and Paint Retailers Association; later Baron Harmar-Nicholls.

into traps which he avoided, however much he may be criticized for the final failure.

REGRETS FROM IRELAND If only we had got little Willie back home earlier, and got him into the Department of Employment in time for the Stage II negotiations, I am sure we could have worked out much more. It could well have gone quite differently. Nothing could have avoided a strike, I now think. That is one thing on which the intelligence from the department was bad. If we had seen it like this from the start we could have adopted a different strategy.

Willie Whitelaw would have had much more finesse and much more power in dealing with the TUC than Maurice Macmillan could ever muster. Maurice never had the confidence of the Cabinet. It showed how, among other things, it is even more important for us than for Labour to have a very senior man at the Department of Employment. Maurice never carried the guns in public, in the Cabinet, or in consultations with Ted. Even though there was bound to be a strike, Willie could have man-oeuvred the TUC much more skilfully into a more solid offer, isolating the miners genuinely. The strike would not have been very long; we could have lived with it. Of course, I don't deny it would have been very difficult: Chapple has told me that his men would not accept a cut on the backs of the miners. I don't know how it would have been accomplished. But from a different start with a different minister I think it would have gone better.

However, there is no way I know of beating the miners. The only approach one can take is that they are slowly pricing coal out of the market. The industry has run down over the years, and the only logical way of curbing their demands is by showing how they are cutting the industry's throat and their own jobs as well.

Gormley is genuine enough. A genuine man. But he judged his colleagues wrong. When he gave advice, it was wrong. But I never got to the bottom of what passed between him and William Armstrong. (I put it to him that Ted had seen Gormley as well, and he said he did not know but would love to – HY.) He suspects, and the folklore says (as he put it) that Armstrong asked Gormley what was the minimum or maximum that the miners wanted, and Gormley told him the guts of Stage III, and they were both wrong.

LORD ROBENS
22 January 1976

Robens seems amazed that anyone should be bothering to rehash these events. It's all past, it's all over, what we should think about is the future . . . (I hope not the average reader response.)

Reluctantly, he delivered himself of this. (Harold Evans was wrong in thinking Robens played any part at all.) The problem lies back in the Robens period at the National Coal Board (1961–71). Covetous eyes were regularly cast on the manpower down the pits: coal was diminished in everyone's thinking: oil cost two bucks a barrel: manpower experts led by Frederick Bloody Catherwood (at Neddy?)[1] said there were too many men down the pits, but had no idea where the men should be.

In the Robens years the NUM had two choices: to go for big wage rises, and fast loss of jobs and closure of uneconomic pits (the American pattern), forcing up the relative price of coal even further. Or to go for moderate rises based on productivity, keeping price stable and jobs intact. The NUM went for the second option: jobs for many, not cash for a few. The NCB side of the bargain was increased mechanization to give the productivity. 'It was adhered to scrupulously throughout the 1960s.'

The effect of this was to shift the miners from top of the pay league to no. 11 in the early seventies. They had very modest pay rises. One year the East Midlands field accepted a shilling a shift as their total rise at the coalface. This was self-sacrifice, but pragmatism.

When the rise in the price of oil quadrupled, the *raison d'être* of low miners' wages instantly disappeared. Coal again became economic at a higher price. Having sacrificed money for jobs for many years, the miners, naturally, would do so no longer. The government, however, thought its incomes policy was more important than reality. Reality was the oil price plus the oil availability and the new need to make Britain more self-sufficient. Many people had foreseen that we could not go on living in the fool's paradise of cheap oil, (though not all admittedly: the 1967 Energy White Paper contained a classic phrase about energy policy needing to be based on the safe assumption of cheap Middle East oil for years and years to come). There was no real excuse for the government not perceiving the wholly new situation, even though they were already in the middle of their incomes policy and the miners' negotiations.

They should have treated the claim as an energy question not an

---

1 Sir Fred Catherwood: director general of the National Economic Development Corporation 1966–71; Conservative MEP for Cambridgeshire, 1979–84, for Cambridge and North Bedfordshire 1984–94; president of the Evangelical Alliance.

income question, because, taking the national interest as a whole, that would have been far better than the three-day week ('The beginning of the runaway inflation we are still living with'). R would have scrapped the annual negotiation and gone for a three-year contract: giving them the maximum in March but promising more in November, more in the following March, and more in the third year – all to put them back at the top of the league, which, he maintains, is their position in every other country in the world.

There are 200 million tons of coal here for the next 200 years. We know we can be self-sufficient, with this, with oil and with later nuclear additions. That is the reality we should try and capitalize on. But successive governments have a worse record on energy policy than on almost any other single area of policy.

Joe Gormley is a sane, sensible man who wants moderate solutions. There have always been Communists in the union, they have always occupied important positions (and I recall being lectured by Robens myself some years ago, and supplied with cuttings books and alleged inside information, when he was at the NCB, about the Commie wreckers – HY). But it is wrong to blame this on the Commies. The thing happened because the men knew they had made sacrifices which were now to be recouped. It was not a Communist plot at all, although of course they capitalized on the situation which presented itself.

MICK MCGAHEY
[no date]

Bathing time[1] was an idea of Joe's, based on an American system, and Joe was keen to get it solved because it was taking on a political connotation. The board tried to estimate bathing time in trials on a Saturday at three pits in Scotland. We thought it was an obscenity timing a miner bathing. We said we'd accept it as long as they based their experiments on Cyril Smith.[2]

WHITELAW He was too naive to be wholesome. He went right round the table shaking hands with every member of the executive. It was so obviously phoney. Story: Where do you live? Oh my father is

1 In a bid to settle the dispute without appearing to breach the government's pay policy, both sides discussed work-related problems, including the 'unsocial hours' involved in shift work, the 'winding time' spent getting down to and back from the coalface, and the time spent washing at the end of what was, notoriously, a dirty and dangerous job.

2 His huge size (he was by far the heaviest Member of Parliament) helped to ensure Smith's celebrity at Westminster.

buried there, I don't remember him. I was only 12. Friend of my mother
died when I was 8 but I remember her. Aye but you didn't go to boarding
school. (Whitelaw father surely killed in WWI?)

WILLIAM WHITELAW
22 January 1976

From August to early November there were the talks to set up the power-
sharing executive in Northern Ireland. I was desperate to see if it could
be achieved. It was very unfair on Maurice Macmillan that there was so
much pressure, including from trade-union leaders, for me to come back.
I said no. Ted was very impatient. He kept saying to me, Can't you speed
up the timetable? But I told him I couldn't. I had to take my time.
Sometimes I decided to make it an afternoon session, having told the
waiters to fill up the glasses at lunchtime. Sometimes it had to be the
morning, when everyone was clear-headed. They needed to be nudged
along in different ways.

I frankly never thought I would succeed. I rang Ted towards the end
of November, just before there was to be a statement in the House, and
told him we'd have to report failure. But there was one last effort. To my
amazement, they agreed, and this led to the Sunningdale conference.[1] But
who should run it? There were strong arguments for me to do it, but
other strong ones for Ted to do it and make it his triumph.

If I'd thought there was any chance of a February election, I would
have started opposing it much earlier. And if the move towards it had
gone on, I would have stayed in Ireland and not come back. To do what
I could to see that the power-sharing executive was as strong as possible
– although of course an election was certain to dish it.

There was a lot of indecision about the date of my return. What
decided it was a small thing. There was to be a Supply Day debate on the
Industrial Relations Act, initiated by the Opposition. It was going to be
very difficult indeed for MM, but as a new person with personal success
behind me I could answer the debate more easily. This was one thing
which determined the decision to move across.

Looking back, I didn't ever really appreciate the strength of my personal position at the moment. If I had, I might have said to Ted that I
would only come back if you give me permission to settle on the best
terms. I don't think he would have had me back on those terms. I would
have been regarded by my colleagues as impossible, and Barber and the

---

1 Sunningdale conference: see earlier footnote.

Treasury would have thought I was getting too big for my boots. But the fact is it never occurred to me to state any terms at all, big or small.

I was physically quite exhausted. I was mentally and emotionally affected by having seemed to have done something in Ireland. Not that I ever thought I had solved the Irish problem, but I might have got something going for a year or so. I was not mentally conditioned to home politics. *That's* what I'm trying to say. Look at the Pay Board. Before the report was published,[1] I never thought through the implications of it. Barbara Castle[2] said on the day the report came out that she couldn't understand why on earth I hadn't used it to settle the miners. She was quite right. I never really thought of it. I had taken on the conventional thinking of the government, and accepted the word of the report itself that it shouldn't be used for a single case. I'd have seen it if I'd been really attuned. It was very short-sighted of me to let it be published and then not use it.

When I got into the job, Ted was already in command. He knew the detail of the price code down to the last comma, and I could never understand it for a single moment. I agree, this gave me a weak position – the fact that Ted knew all about the policy and I did not, in that much detail. This meant I could not be a completely effective influence on him.

WILLIAM ARMSTRONG Armstrong got into quite a false position. He became more a minister than a civil servant. He was making political statements at our own meetings (i.e. meetings of the government team). This was very bad.

TED HEATH At all the inside meetings over the election, with Carrington, Barber, Prior and me, he never once showed his own hand. He bottled it all up. I'm sure he was troubled that I and Peter, his two closest colleagues, gave him different advice. But he has this extraordinary ambivalence. He was very nearly a very great man, but his trouble is that he cannot let his hair down in a crisis situation. He doesn't feel he should do, he doesn't know how to.

His great mistake was in letting Peter and Jim go on thinking he favoured 7 February, even though he never intended to have an election then.

---

1 Another reference to the January 1974 Pay Board report on relativities that some believed offered a potential mechanism for settling the miners' dispute.
2 Barbara Castle: Labour MP for Blackburn 1945–79 and a famous Labour firebrand. As Minister of Transport 1965–8 she introduced breathalyser tests. As Employment Secretary 1968–70 she introduced controversial legislation to limit union power and precipitated a Cabinet crisis. She was Social Services Secretary 1974–6, and became Baroness Castle of Blackburn.

LORD CARRINGTON
23 January 1976

I have no memory of anything. I kept no diaries, I can't remember details. But . . .

It is not true that Ted failed to keep his colleagues informed. They knew very well he didn't want an election on 7 February. (Here C's unreliable memory, plus loyalty to Ted, betrays him, I'm sure – HY.) But it's true that very often he thinks he's consulting when other people – like those he was consulting with – didn't think that was what he was doing at all. That's in the character of the man. It's quite clear, though, that he did get on with the union leaders. They greatly admired his resolution and intellect. Maybe they'd have liked him to behave as if he were one of them, on equal terms. But he was prime minister and had to make up his mind.

I still think it was right to do what we did. It is very fashionable to decry Ted and all he did. I don't agree with that at all. In fact it makes me bloody furious. You see, the prize of winning would have been absolutely enormous. And we jolly nearly did win. (I put to him the Wolff thesis that even winning would not have lasted long – HY.) I don't agree with that. Ted himself would have come through. The British don't particularly want to love their prime minister. He would have had their respect.

THE LESSONS The main one is never to tackle someone, or get yourself into a position where they can tackle you, if you can't win. There are very few sectional interests which can defeat a government. But the miners are one. In future it should be tackled differently. We should recognize that in a sophisticated society like ours some people *can* make government powerless. But you can so arrange things, or try to, to ensure that disagreeable things result from settling with them as you may have to do. It may not work at once, but you should be able to make it more difficult for them to do it to you again. With the miners, they should simply learn that they will price themselves out of the market and that's their funeral. In 1972, there was a strike of smaller port employees in East Anglia or somewhere. Flying pickets, the lot. There were so many pictures of strikers attacking policemen that they totally lost public sympathy. That strike was called off without getting what the workers wanted, because of public opinion. This is what you must do: get public opinion on your side. Government has been very bad at doing this. Of course, one problem is that you don't want to clobber the people you are trying to get an agreement out of. But one of the biggest features of the miners' strike was the way Len Murray had a field day. You should use TV, you should pick your ground very carefully, and you should not necessarily believe what the experts tell you. The Department of Employment told us what the miners would settle for. It was exactly the same in 1971–2. And they were wrong on both occasions. There were others who said they were wrong at the time. I wouldn't blame the civil servants. It was our fault for taking bad advice. But that is something we must come to a view about in future cases.

(PC doesn't believe that WW would have made any difference if he had come back from Ireland sooner.)

JOE HAINES
27 January 1976

Harold always knew that a Who Governs Britain election would be a hard one to fight. He therefore worked out the plans for such a possibility with some care a few weeks before it finally happened. He probably wanted May or June, but no Opposition leader can afford not to be ready for an election. Yes, the party machine was worried about having one at that time, but Harold was ready at any time. We were scared about fighting on the old register, however, and the machine was certainly not ready; it always takes longer to get going than the Tories. Ted Heath undoubtedly lost it by not going for 7 February. I think he would have won it if he had gone then.

I first heard of the possibility of an early election in mid- to late-November. I heard it much more firmly in mid-December. This was after Jim Prior had had a special lunch with a number of lobby correspondents to urge on them the virtue of an early election. (This must be the source of the December stories to that effect – HY.) When he said early, they said 'June?' He replied, 'April is the hump as far as the cost of living goes. Therefore there might be an election much earlier than June.'

This is why Haines insists that the miners' strike was 'the pretext not the reason' for the election – i.e. in the eyes of Prior and Carrington and the party machine, the indicators were that an election any later would run into terrible difficulties over inflation and prices. By October it would have turned much worse for them.

The heat was stepped up by Carrington, whose pro-election views were reflected in simultaneous pieces by Boyne and Shrimsley[1] floating an early-election line. (This presumably January – HY.) We hourly waited

1 Anthony Shrimsley: political editor of the *Daily Mail*. 1973–5; director of communications for the Conservative Party 1982–4.

for an announcement. Then it emerged that Ted Heath had gone into Cabinet and told them there would be no election.

But – would Heath ever have reached the position of having a Pay Board inquiry and an election simultaneously if the hawks had not driven him forward earlier on? To that extent, they were very influential. His closest colleagues, the ones he trusted most, were all telling him there must be an election. Without them there might never have been one, because Heath had not wanted one.

Further evidence that the miners were only an excuse, in Haines's eyes, was the discovery when the election had been won that the official projections showed inflation running at 17–20 per cent by the end of the year. Carrington and Prior knew this. They also knew that the threshold agreements, one of the hinges of the pay policy, triggered at 7 per cent: this figure was fixed at a time when they thought they would never be triggered. Then suddenly they faced the probability that they would be triggered ten times before the end of the year. It was the most inflationary deal any government has ever done.

MINERS JH confirms that Harold wrote *two* letters to Ted. One was public, backing the washing-and-winding-time idea. The other was confidential and personal, and not revealed until the *ST* lunch (see my note). This set out Wilson's long-standing acquaintance with the miners' leaders, especially the moderates, from way back (Len Clarke figured especially),[1] and wanted Ted not to confuse the moderates with militants, but saying to him that they were becoming militants under the influence of government policy.

HW was challenged many times to ask the miners not to strike. He always refused to do so, on two grounds. First, interference in what was not his affair. Second, and more important, the knowledge that they would take no notice of him, and thus he'd be exposed as having no influence.

ELECTION A few days before the announcement, Harold was talking to Haines. He compared the forthcoming campaign, as he so often does, to Marston Moor and Cromwell's triumph. Joe is a little unsure of the battlefield roles assigned to the various parties. But he recalls that HW said the centre must not give (i.e. we must hold the line against the Who Governs Britain charge), there would be trouble on the left wing (i.e. strikes, miners, incomes policy), and the right would come through for a smashing victory if the general could release it at the proper time

1 In 1974 Len Clarke was president of the 30,000-strong Nottinghamshire miners and linked with the moderates within the NUM.

(i.e. the big Labour issues: prices, especially food prices, Europe, housing). This was why all the Labour polls were issue polls: to show what issues were coming up and when to hit them hard. (This strikes me as heavy post-facto rationalization. The issues came up because, as everyone knows, and as both Heath and Whitlam[1] have been the latest to know, you can't fight a single-issue election.)

JH's view is that Ted thought you could fight such an election. 'One of the problems with a place like this is that you can kid yourself that what obsesses you also obsesses everyone outside.'

Wilson's campaign duly took off in Week 2, with his Manchester speech on prices.

FIGGURES[2] In Labour eyes the crucial turning point. This is what smashed Heath's centre. It was an instance, says HY, of the cock-up theory again, and bad communications at work. For Ted Heath did not find out about the Pay Board claim that miners were not at the top of the league until nearly 11 p.m. that night. There was a breakdown of communications between him, in Brum, and his staffman linking to No. 10. Wilson, on the other hand, found out at 6 p.m., via Roger Carroll [political editor] of the *Sun*. HW heard just as he was leaving for evening speeches in (?) Hampstead and Ilford. Put a passage in, which he prepared in car en route from Lord North Street [Wilson's home]. This dominated the nine o'clock news and next day's papers: Heath Got His Sums Wrong. On the news before the PM had even heard about it, and then he was slow to react, as was the lumbering Central Office (which Joe contrasts with the small mutually trustful team of Wilson–Haines–Marcia, always in total touch). By the time Ted commented, at next day's press conference, the story was irretrievable. It finally killed off the one-issue election.

BARBER BROADCAST Crude, untruthful – but very effective. The Tories cocked it up by apologizing for it. Yet it was a bloody good way of retaining the middle-class vote.

WILLIAM ARMSTRONG Has an unusual taste for publicity. He always likes being at the centre of things, being on the prime minister's team, even before 1970 (when he had just moved to the Civil Service).

1 Just as Edward Heath notoriously fought a 'Who Governs Britain?' campaign, the Labour 1972–5 Australian prime minister Gough Whitlam, who had problems with the Australian Senate, campaigned in 1974 on 'a mandate to finish the job' and with the slogan 'Give Gough a go!' He failed to win a majority in the Senate. On 11 November 1975 his government was dismissed by the Queen's representative, the Governor General Sir John Kerr.
2 Sir Frank Figgures: director general of the National Economic Development Office 1971–3; chairman of the Pay Board 1973–4. Described by HY, with no explanation, as 'the crafty old sod'.

When he was with Heath he liked to be associated with policy. It was especially improper for him to be a main architect and defender of the policy when, as head of the Civil Service, he actually had to send a letter on pay policy to 3¼ million civil servants. JH likened this to putting up Jack Jones to announce incomes policy to his members, instead of fighting for them.

WA caused much resentment among civil servants at the time. He should have been defending the service, but he was defending the policy instead. They also felt, or some of them did, that he was behaving improperly. To appear on platforms, become publicly identified. Not proper for the head of the Civil Service. Moreover, to be the prime minister's main policy adviser. This role should be done by the Secretary of the Cabinet. If Wilson has such an adviser now, it is John Hunt.[1]

JH further distrusted Armstrong because he had betrayed his background. I could never understand, says Joe, how a man born into a poor family and a Salvationist was never interested in the unemployment or Spain in the thirties.

WA has never been a central adviser to HW. Nor would Douglas Allen[2] ever dream of behaving like he did. It was a good job Armstrong arranged to get out before we came in. He could never have carried on as head of the Civil Service under Labour.

ENDPIECE At least by polling day, HW was sure they'd win (although JH loyally claims he thought so all along). Describes a visit with Harold to the Huyton polling stations in the middle of the day, where HW discovered the beneficial impact of the three-day week. There were 45 per cent returns already at a time when usually it was more like 25 per cent. Told JH to ring Birmingham and ask the same question. Discovered that at 6 p.m. some housing estates in Brum had polled 90 per cent. That wrapped it up as far as HW was concerned.

Felt sure the Liberal move would never come off. Ted's private secretary (Robert Armstrong)[3] phoned about 2 p.m. on the Friday, asking where Wilson would be. This seemed like a preliminary to getting out. By 7.30, no call. HW's people phoned No. 10, to be told there would be no call after all. This meant, says JH, that they would be trying to fix it up with the Liberals, but equally that the government was badly split.

---

1 Sir John Hunt: Cabinet Secretary 1973–9; later Baron Hunt of Tanworth.
2 Sir Douglas Allen: Permanent Secretary of the Treasury 1968–74; head of the Home Civil Service 1974–7; later Baron Croham.
3 Sir Robert Armstrong: principal private secretary to the PM 1970–75; Cabinet Secretary to Mrs Thatcher 1979–87. During the *Spycatcher* trial in Melbourne in 1986 he became famous for his phrase 'economical with the truth'; later Baron Armstrong of Ilminster.

HW knew that, just by keeping quiet, he would watch the Tories make a mess of it.

Ted was badly advised by the very people who had him call the election in the first place. The very people who had told him to go for a stronger majority were now telling him to hang on with no majority at all.

IAN GILMOUR
28 January 1976

Armstrong was taken by Ted as a special personal adviser, rather than Burke Trend or John Hunt. This was because he was tougher and more experienced than they were. What did this mean, I asked. He was 'like granite'. But how? In deciding to get his own way. IG tends to play down the view that WA was overly political. 'It doesn't mean very much to say he was political. Unless you want the man to be a mere stenographer, he cannot help being political.'

TED   Ian Gilmour disputes the suggestion that he was bad at negotiating. Cites the wide respect he gained among union leaders, who said they preferred doing business with him to doing it with HW.

EFFECT   Not the least result of the election was to destroy Ted's relations with the union leaders. We lost in October more than anything because people simply thought we could not handle union problems, we did not get on with union leaders etc. This was stolen by Wilson, but I have to admit it is an unsolved problem. We had thought an election was the answer to a political strike. We found out it was not.

Not surprisingly, the Sunday Times *wished Edward Heath to submit to questioning. HY wrote to him, and received the following answer, dated 28 January 1976:*

Dear Hugo Young,

Thank you for your letter of 18 January asking me if I would discuss the events of 1973–74 with you and your colleague.

I am afraid that I must decline the invitation to discuss those affairs at this stage. I am so sorry about this.

Yours sincerely,
Ted Heath

One of the key questions was the role played by William Armstrong. There had been criticism that he exceeded his Civil Service brief and became in effect 'part of the government'. HY asked his editor, Harold Evans, to approach Armstrong to see if he would agree to an interview. HE responded by office memorandum, copying in one of the Sunday Times's legal team, Antony Whitaker. Evans's memorandum also covered other matters of moment, not least the vexatious question of the publication of the diaries of Richard Crossman, a member of Harold Wilson's 1964–70 Cabinet.

H.E. to HUGO YOUNG, c.c. ANTONY
WHITAKER (in part)
29 January 1976

I talked with Lord Armstrong. He will talk freely to you I think.

On pits: They got the impression that Jack Jones and co. were throughout in league with the Labour Party (going from No. 10 to Wilson's room etc). Secondly, that Jack Jones felt he could be a statesman with Labour (emulating Ernie Bevin,[1] competing with the man who became Foreign Secretary – Bevin's bust in his room). But could not do deal with Heath.

He has great admiration for way Labour selling £6 now; feels that, after near threat of civil war, government has to treat with the barons (unions) until normality restored. Heath he referred to as 'divisive'. Don't say I said so . . . But see if he will relax.

Lady Armstrong told me that he [her husband] resents the criticisms that he became 'part of the government' – your point about Cabinet attendance. He did attend Cabinet meetings (and I recall he was in on the two big editors' meetings I went to at No. 10). Unfair to William to attack him for this, she says – and she says press did at the time – because he had to do what Heath insisted on. Got the strong impression that Heath ran Armstrong off his feet, and relied on him enormously.

CROSSMAN   Very interesting talk, of which key point is this:

The report very pointedly does *not* ask ministers to say they will observe the new rules. It merely asks them to sign to say they have read them. Very different thing: puts honour point more subtly. Radcliffe[2] insisted on this.

---

1 Ernest Bevin: general secretary of the TGWU 1922–45; Labour MP for Central Wandsworth 1940–50, for East Woolwich 1950–51; appointed by Churchill as Minister of Labour and National Service in the wartime coalition; Foreign Secretary in the Attlee government 1945–51.

2 Lord Radcliffe: Cyril John Radcliffe, barrister, privy counsellor, Lord of Appeal, had been director general of the Ministry of Information 1941–5. He headed a number of government inquiries, including a 1975 Privy Council committee on the memoirs of ex-ministers.

Radcliffe was chief censor in war and also utterly opposed to idea of Cabinet Secretary having any control over wording of memoirs. Hypocrisy to change sentences. Either let man say what he wants or prosecute him, says Radcliffe.

Again, says Armstrong, Radcliffe report is intended *not* to encourage Cabinet Secretary to bowdlerize but to make representation and leave it then to honour of the man and vestigial powers/check of Attorney General.

MARK SCHREIBER
29 January 1976

Hurd, Sewill, Wolff, Waldegrave, Jackson, Cope[1] and Schreiber began to meet regularly in Hurd's room at No. 10. Their purpose was to give Douglas advice on how he should advise Ted. This was prompted by their feeling – as special advisers – that the Civil Service was getting more of a hearing than political advice. Civil servants tended to treat the miners question and incomes policy and everything else as non-political.

WILLIAM ARMSTRONG 'You heard about his breakdown, I suppose.' He was in hospital. Then went to Victor Rothschild's villa in Barbados (?) to recuperate.[2] The culmination of his deteriorating behaviour came at a Permanent Secretaries' meeting, when he was said to have raved on about the Bible and sex among other germane topics. When he returned, which was not all that long after he left, he was a busted flush. In Whitehall it was being said, 'Poor William, we must make sure we don't put him under strain again.'

He had been acting in a very political role. (MS was at the time a special adviser in the Civil Service Department, therefore saw a good deal of things.) He was always seeing people privately. They would come in through the Golden Door (*sic*), which lets into the Civil Service Department from Horse Guards, accessible with a private key, so no one would know they had come. He saw several union leaders in this style. He was negotiating for Heath.

The moral, however, is not that he was acting improperly, but that (a) he should not have acted so *publicly*, (b) that Ted leaned on him so

1 Brendon Sewill: former director of the Conservative Research Department; Treasury special adviser. Robert Jackson: special adviser at the Department of Employment. John Cope: former special adviser at the DTI; Conservative MP for South Gloucestershire 1974–83, for Northavon 1983–97, and a minister in various departments; later Baron Cope of Berkeley.
2 Victor Rothschild, Lord Rothschild: intelligence chief, scientist, financier, oilman and director of the Central Policy Review Staff in the Cabinet Office 1971–4.

much. And listened to him too much. The only people Ted really listened to all the time he was in were Armstrong and Hurd.

Armstrong's advice was not always very good. But Ted wanted to be able at all times to convince himself that he had taken the best advice, that all he did was after the full deployment of rational examination – which he deemed to be reposed in the head of the Civil Service and not many others. Rothschild, for example, was not all that influential, because Ted regarded him as eccentric, which indeed he was. (This recalls the fact that Ted appointed him Think Tank without ever knowing him.) Ted was therefore a little fearful of Rothschild advice. Too much of a maverick.

Ted liked advice to come to *him* not to his colleagues, not a collective thing. This was partly the view of the field marshal saving the morale of his officers, as he saw it. Partly as a pressure of his intense personal style of governing, and his preference for the advice of the civil servants over that of politicians.

WILLIAM WHITELAW
29 January 1976 (second visit)

ARMSTRONG He had become the Prime Minister's right-hand man. He was in a false position. Why? I asked. Because he came out with political views at meetings with politicians. His mistake was not in having political views, nor in recognizing the political nature of what was going on. But he should not have come out as he did at meetings with us.

WW confirmed that WA had had a crack-up. It came 'towards the end' of the episode (I assume mid-January). Why did he have it? 'Because he had overreached himself. The strain had been too much in his false position. He had been the high priest of the incomes policy. He had taken a very firm stand about Stage III.'

JELLICOE[1] Was meant to be preparing contingency plans for keeping the country going in a major strike, especially the miners or the railways. But contingency plans are very difficult. Who is going to pull the switches in power stations? Certainly not soldiers. Who is going to dig the coal or transport it? This is an unsolved problem. Water, sewage and docks probably can be kept going.

ELECTION I was anxious to see the election run without bitterness. We had to avoid it at all costs. But, of course, to run a Who Runs Britain

1 George Patrick John Rushworth Jellicoe, 2nd Earl Jellicoe, Baron Jellicoe of Southampton: Lord Privy Seal, minister in charge of the Civil Service Department, and Leader of the House of Lords 1970–73.

election while restoring normality to everyday life was difficult to say the least. There was a real conflict here. I shrank from it, as did Ted. For the country it was a good thing we did. But it was not good for the party, probably. We were very high-minded.

The three-day week was adopted on the basis of 1972, when we got near to total breakdown. We said, This time we will not run out of endurance. We'll be able to run on to the summer. Once the weather was milder, our endurance was stronger. This could have let us run on. But why didn't it? That goes back to Ted. I know now that he didn't want to have an election; I didn't know that then. And Peter C and I got tired of arguing about it. We just gave up and left it to Ted. There was a general air that the election was going to happen. Why? We were pushed into it partly by our own propaganda. Having influenced the press ourselves, we then made the mistake of taking undue account of the press.

JIM PRIOR
4 February 1976 (second visit)

ARMSTRONG On the morning after we had taken the decision to go to the country William was missing. But hell, we were all under great pressure. Not just him. It is true that he had become far too political. Messianic was a good word. It had a terrible effect. He drove us along: some people thought here was this great public figure, this ice-cold civil servant, this dispassionate adviser – if *he* looks at it this way, we *must* be right . . .

MARK SCHREIBER
5 February 1976 (second visit)

Armstrong's crack-up was on 31 January, he insists. He kept notes, to which he has referred. I pressed him several times about the date. He had no doubt about it. Recalled talking to WA that morning (a morning on which he had breakfasted with Rothschild, which places it in his mind) and thinking that WA was finally off his head. Talking about the 'heff-alump traps' he was thinking up for the unions. That afternoon there was a regular meeting of Permanent Secretaries. The Permanent Secretaries vowed not to gossip about it, which they didn't. But MS heard.

SPECIAL ADVISERS MEETING Held at least weekly from end of November, in Hurd's office. They were acting as they were meant to.

By now they had found out a lot more about how Whitehall worked: that ministers saw only the papers sent to them, and it was the job of special advisers to find out what papers existed, and demand them. The general view of the special advisers was that the election should be on 7 February. But what distinguished some of them from the Ministers was that some of them argued that after 7 February the whole idea should be dropped.

At one point, John Hunt complained that Robert Armstrong, Heath's private secretary, was 'behaving too much like a Permanent Secretary' and getting above himself.

LANCASTER HOUSE CONFERENCE TO ANNOUNCE STAGE II   Yes, maybe WA only sat on the dais by a bit of an accident (see WA memo). But Ted said he could and should. It fitted Ted's idea that they were the philosopher kings: that having a Permanent Secretary on show proved that this was a policy backed by the best brains in the land etc. etc.

HY eventually spent several hours with William Armstrong discussing in detail (often tedious) developments in incomes policy. At the end of the interview Armstrong commented on other matters, but not his state of health.

WILLIAM ARMSTRONG
5 February 1976

No one saw soon enough the meaning of the oil price rise. Except one small voice at the back of the room, when the NUM executive first met Heath. In November. He said, 'If you can pay the bloody Arabs, why can't you pay us? We're British.' This man, says WA, who was not a Communist – don't know who he was – saw it all quicker than we did. We should have reacted much quicker at that time.

Asked whether he became ill, he said, 'Yes, I went off for a fortnight after it was over. There was nothing left for me to do.'

'I got a bit hot towards the end.'

ELECTION   'I put it to them. If you have an election, will you win? If you win, what will you do? I was always convinced the election would not be won. I thought they were running away from the thing by having an election.' But he adds that he was always exploring ways of settling.

LANCASTER HOUSE MEETING 'I came into the room and asked where I should go. They pointed to the dais. I asked the Prime Minister, and he said yes. So it was an accident, which I regret, that I was so publicly prominent.'

Was it unusual for a civil servant to be on Cabinet committees etc? 'Ted ran his committees in a different way. He ran this policy with a joint committee of officials and ministers. But it was unusual, yes.'

RONALD MCINTOSH
6 February 1976

Ted had the respect of trade-union people until just before the Chequers breakdown. Why? His infinite capacity for listening, and his manifest sincerity of purpose. Trade-union people know when they are dealing with an honest man and a straight man. They saw this in him. They thought the breakdown was due not to him but to the pressure from his Cabinet: that he was being imposed upon by the hard-faced men in the Cabinet. Therefore they came to think that no progress could be made.

Despite all that has happened, there are many who still much respect him, as someone larger than most politicians.

Heath made much use of a new technique of committeemanship. (This fits in well with my thesis – HY.) Unlike Wilson, he encouraged the growth of committees of ministers plus officials, instead of two separate layers. This is disapproved of by some civil servants – McI likes it. Also, ministers often dislike it. Heath applied it across the whole face of the government.

MENTAL FATIGUE

1. *Heath*. Sunningdale plus Copenhagen summit (early December) was too much for him. Copenhagen, HY recalls, was one of the most abject diplomatic fiascos of recent years. Heath exhausted, Pompidou dying.
2. *Barber*. Ronnie McIntosh heard lately from an excellent source that by Christmas Barber had found his stint at the Treasury too much for him. He was exhausted.
3. *Armstrong*. The exhaustion of the above two put William Armstrong in a stronger place. Ronnie McIntosh cautions us to recall that many prime ministers have had close advisers. If it hadn't been William Armstrong it would have been someone else. Agreed, however, that William Armstrong had got into this position by choice, not by chance.

The important thing is whether the judgement of the adviser complements the weak parts of the prime minister, rather than merely replicating them. The only trouble with William Armstrong was that he gave bad advice.

Some ministers made me sick. The talk of Munich was quite nauseating. (Carrington clearly in this class, in McIntosh's eyes.)

LEN MURRAY
6 February 1976

'Our view was that the three-day week was economically useless. That it was being used to split the trade union movement from the miners. There is no doubt about that. And as a tactic, it completely failed. We had no complaints from our members about our lines. The movement was not split.'

After the 16 January conference, the government must have known we were united in this, and that we would not be split. On the other hand, they could not believe we were united in our offer.

Heath was trying to believe us. We were trying to give him something – enough to let him tell Barber to sod off. We could see he was wanting desperately to believe we had something.

By 21 January the four-day week was proposed. Our judgement was that we had never needed the three-day week, and that this was another ploy. Having failed to split the trade union movement, they now wanted to split the unions from the consumers: brushing teeth in the dark etc. etc. Then reimpose the three-day week and say it was all the trade unions' fault. It's a well known negotiating technique: relieve the tension and then reimpose it. This was the meeting, however, at which, if Heath had only moved and decided, he could have had everything he wanted. This was the celebrated Scanlon intervention. Scanlon looked at Ted and said to him, 'Is there anything, anything whatever we can do which will satisfy you?' This had been a prepared move, said Len Murray. Behind it was the sincere willingness to do any little thing – some public statement, a bit of special publicity effort or whatever – which would satisfy Ted of their good intentions. Heath remained silent: his head sunk into his shoulders: wanting to say something but unable to do so. Then, after a few long seconds, Barber breaks in with cavils and complaints again.

This was Heath's big moment, and he muffed it.

'He had us where he wanted us. We knew the great risk we were running. We were putting ourselves in his hands. He could not lose. If he had taken the offer and it had failed, and other unions had broken through, he was home and dry with his Industrial Relations Act, with his incomes policy. If the offer had worked, it would have been a great political triumph for him. He could have said he got his settlement on his terms and the trade-union movement had come to heel.'

Return of WW from Ireland was seen by trade unions as a great gesture towards them: as indicating that a settlement was on the cards and desired.

One of the big results of it all was to give considerable fillip to the TUC–Labour Party liaison committee, which had begun in 1972 but now took on a new life.

WILLIAM WALDEGRAVE
10 February 1976

WILLIAM ARMSTRONG His crack-up was well before the election. He really did go mad. He used to talk about the phoenix rising from the ashes. This was a favourite line. He really believed in the ruination of Britain, to be followed by the resurrection. He talked about things like 'I'll move my red army this way and the blue army that way.' It was to be a total victory of good over evil. The final scene came after a three-hour afternoon with Rothschild, at which all of this and more disclosed itself and R diagnosed insanity. They knew that WA was already on some very serious drugs. He went first to the hospital, then to R's villa in Barbados.

How to explain his influence. He was a man who used his charm to the maximum. Great personal charm and charisma, and he knew it. A legendary reputation. What also distinguished him was a desire for publicity, a desire to be known, an appetite for the front line. He would hold audiences entranced with his fluency, his seeming candour. (Also a great man with eyes and gestures – per HY. Maximum use of eyebrows and left arm, painting in the truth.) He also drank a fair bit, which released in him a great talkativeness.

It was not entirely illogical for him to develop such a link with Heath. Heath needed someone for the job of overseeing the policy. Armstrong had always believed in a statutory incomes policy, as Ted probably knew. It was one policy objective he kept to, along with quite a few other people at the top in Whitehall. He got very close to Ted, but not so close as Robert Armstrong did – Robert became a close friend, utterly trusted.

William almost certainly did not address himself to the election as coolly as he now claims (I told WW about what WA had said). But WW not clear what view he did actually take about the election.

Another moment of his madness was lying full length on the floor in No. 10, waiting for an appointment to which Ted summoned him. Also present was someone like the president of the Institute of Accountants or someone like that, who witnessed an amazing declamation delivered from the recumbent position by the Permanent Secretary.

TREND His departure left Whitehall bereft, and for none more than William Armstrong. Together they had run the show. Trend was always the bigger figure, because he has policy objectives: maintaining the Anglo-American alliance, the intelligence agreement which went with it, the defence budget etc. Trend was a great constitutionalist, a very funny man, Irish in origin – and before him Ted was in almost total submission.

HUNT A less imposing man. Known as 'the smiler'. Yes, an Armstrong appointee, but also a Ted appointee.

HEATH One must never forget how exhausted he was. Trend's own mistake was to organize the 1973 Commonwealth conference on the wrong date. This was in the summer, coinciding with what should have been Ted's sailing holiday. He missed some big race. This meant he never had a proper holiday. This was a material fact later in the year after Sunningdale and Copenhagen. Ted was irritated with Trend over this error.

The proper analogy for his style is not with the Civil Service but the military, the only organization outside of politics of which Heath had any long experience. He saw the whole of life as a pyramid, of which the PM was the kingpin and all authority descended from him down the lines of command. The people were the privates, the Cabinet were his lieutenants. The union leaders, on this model, were slightly senior lieutenants – staff men above the rank of Cabinet people, but nonetheless subject to the commanding officer. Moreover, they commanded sub-pyramids of essential authority. It was on this basis that they were offered a part in what was undoubtedly going to be the corporate state, which they did not really understand they were being offered and did not have the wit to accept.

All Ted's real triumphs had been triumphs of authority: RPM[1] and Europe especially. He had done nothing, partywise, in the way of real *negotiation*. He was not a negotiator. Therefore WW agrees with my analysis of Ted as the non-negotiator, as the man who never understood why the unions did not see him as a negotiator.

1 Edward Heath had piloted the Retail Price Maintenance Bill through the Commons in the final months of Sir Alec Douglas-Home's 1963–4 Conservative government.

A vision of Ted at the top of the Downing Street stairs, surrounded by W. Armstrong, R. Armstrong, Trend and Hunt – this was the real Ted one felt. Surrounded by the Treasury.

At the end of the election, Ted said to an assembled gathering of friends, 'Well, I let you down.' No, no they all protested – Cabinet members and others among them – we all were in it together, we agreed on the election date, we all went along with not having 7 February. 'What I mean,' said Ted, a little resignedly, 'is having the election at all.'

He never wanted the election. He deeply disliked the confrontation. He saw the union people as people he ought to be doing government business with. Not as enemies.

ROTHSCHILD The CPRS [Central Policy Review Staff] had sent in a report in 1971 predicting a rise in the price of oil to $5 a barrel, were told by the DTI, – 'And where do you think the Arabs will put it, dear boys? In the sand?'

Then, in January 1974, R genuinely thought that he had got Ted off the hook. Sent a paper arguing that the fourfold rise in the oil price meant that the miners could be increased by at least three times on their present wage, with absolute economic justification. Thought this was a gift from heaven. But by then it was too late.

By early December – whenever WW went to No. 10 – the government was 'on a war footing'. That was the phrase, in a No. 10 paper. From that moment anyone who dissented in the smallest degree from the tough line was regarded as something of a traitor. Of course, it wasn't true. If we had been on a war footing, there would have been a manifesto, which there wasn't, and the party machine would have been prepared, which it wasn't.

EDWARD HEATH TO HAROLD EVANS
11 February 1976

From: The Rt. Hon. Edward Heath, MBE, MP
House of Commons

Dear Harold,

Thank you for your letter of 3 February.

I have considered carefully what you say. But after much thought my view remains the same as when I wrote to Hugo Young.

I am so sorry to send you what I know will be a disappointing reply.

Yours,
Ted

MICHAEL WOLFF
Phone, 12 February 1976

William Armstrong did have 'a minor breakdown'. But Michael Wolff claims rather lamely that he was all right before and after. He agreed, however, that WA had been deteriorating for some time. Insisted also that 'he wasn't alone', i.e. not exactly running the government. The other two Permanent Secretaries were still there, meeting, in the late stages, almost every day. 'It didn't all come out of his head.'

MAURICE MACMILLAN
[no date]

GORMLEY   It was impossible to have a confidential discussion with him. When we wanted to see him he would immediately go down the corridor and tell Daly[1] that he had been asked in. He was indiscreet and overconfident. I was dubious about his capacity to deliver, but the trouble was that elsewhere in Whitehall it was thought that the DEP [Department for Employment and Productivity] was overinfected by the cynicism of its professional civil servants.

Half the time dealing with the unions is like Napoleon dealing with his Italian generals. He gets them to go on a foray against the enemy when they are ordered; the trouble is to stop them going on a foray against the enemy when they are not ordered to. MM does not believe in taking the unions at face value; does not believe in regarding them necessarily as honourable men, and realizes that negotiation involves a great deal of wheeling and dealing. This, he says, comes from a long experience in the north in Halifax, and even memories of Stockton with his father.[2]

In normal circumstances we would have been able to sustain a longer strike. The problem was the miners' crunch. By the time they settled we would have had settlements with 70 per cent of organized labour. If we let them get away with too much that would have been a fine thing.

Ted took an immense amount of trouble to understand their problems, but he could not put himself in their shoes. He gave too much weight to what he heard, and he wasn't devious enough. He probably slightly over-intellectualized the problem. By establishing the relationship with

---

1 Lawrence Daly: leader of the Scottish mineworkers; member of the Communist Party until 1968; general secretary of the NUM 1968–84.
2 Harold Macmillan's first parliamentary seat was Stockton. When he was elevated to the peerage, he chose his title in memory of that time.

Gormley, he created a situation in which we went in with one barrel instead of two. He was too honourable and rational a man.

Ted overrated the effect of something being fair.

Bad intelligence from the department? Certainly not. We never said that we would automatically win a ballot. We said that if the executive recommended acceptance, that the miners would say yes; if they recommended rejection, the miners would say no; and that if they were neutral there was a chance that the miners would accept the terms, especially if there was some sort of sweetener.

Gormley still thought he could get a majority on the right, and some others thought so too, but that depended on him getting everyone there; on it being very well organized. In practice I think it was rather harder to get a majority than we thought.

It is quite obvious that if the right had had the will they could have done it. But they were intimidated by the effort of organizing support. If we'd had someone with Gormley's views and Daly's character none of this would ever have happened.

We were fighting a cold war all the time without wishing to destroy the enemy.

Inside the DEP they were not anti-union; they were pro-union and therefore a lot tougher than the other departments. They know that the unions are too powerful to be destroyed.

(MM says he had proposed an election immediately post-Yom Kippur War [October 1973] on the basis of settlement outside Phase III with the miners and the creation of a Department of Energy to get North Sea oil going. In the end he proposed going to the House with a Queen's Speech and then governing till defeated.)

Baldwin was right. There are three groups you should not pick a fight with: the Vatican, the Treasury and the NUM.

But I don't think we got it wrong, and we very nearly got it right.

KENNETH BAKER
[no date]

Armstrong had access to Ted. He had his ear, and he could always get in to see him when many of his ministers would be kept waiting for an interview. The work with Ted became so onerous that we had to get Bancroft[1] into the Civil Service Department to do his work for him there.

---

1 Ian Bancroft: second Permanent Secretary of the Civil Service Department 1973–5; head of the Home Civil Service 1978–81; later Lord Bancroft.

His memory for policy is phenomenal. When Geoffrey Johnson Smith[1] was brought in to head the government information service (January) Armstrong chaired a meeting for him and went back through the information policies of each government since the war. But he lacked the politician's ability to select, says Baker.

He shares with Ted an extraordinary ability to get through papers, masses of them, and shares with Ted and Wilson a great love for the technicalities and details of administration. The relationship between Ted and himself was extraordinarily close.

I first thought that he might be a little unbalanced when he read out Len Murray's letter about the possibility of TUC cooperation in Relativities Board work. He thought it was the greatest step forward in collective bargaining since the war. He broke down on a Friday, when he had to be taken out of a meeting.

Ted was able to establish such a close relationship with a civil servant partly because he was not a House of Commons man. He wanted to get things done, and the House did not appear to him the place to do them. I suspect this was because he was absorbed into the whips' office so early in his parliamentary life. They're technicians. He saw the House only as a place where you put bills through.

You must realize how much he believed in an incomes policy and how much he enjoyed working out Stages II and III. The mistake was not to go into the Relativities Board procedure as soon as the TUC suggested that they might be interested (what is timing here?).

Maurice Macmillan was an absolute disaster.

LORD CAMPBELL OF CROY
[no date]

I know all about Mick McGahey. In the previous miners' strike we had fought to keep the coal-fired station at Longannet[2] open, and we had succeeded. I thought it was quite a good thing that he did come through and say what he thought at Downing Street. He is a sincere man, and he does come through in such a way as to show people what they are up against. He is a Russian-type Communist – not like Jimmy Reid,[3] who is a likeable character with the gift of the gab. McGahey is a ruthless, determined man who says exactly what he means.

1 Sir Geoffrey Johnson Smith: journalist, BBC reporter, Conservative MP for Holborn and St Pancras South 1959–64, for East Grinstead 1965–83, for Wealden 1983–2001; parliamentary secretary for the CSD 1972–4.
2 Longannet: a Scottish power station fuelled by coal from its own mine.
3 Jimmy Reid: Communist shop steward who organized protests and helped stave off closure for the Clyde shipyards at Govan, Scotstoun and Linthouse in 1971; later joined the Scottish National Party.

I know Armstrong because he was private secretary to Rab [R. A. Butler] when I was private secretary to Lord Normanbrook,[1] and I knew that he could make a great contribution and it wasn't surprising for me to see him at meetings.

JOE GODBER
[no date]

Minister of Agriculture, and as such he had to argue things like exemption for breadwinners during the Cabinet discussion of the three-day week. It would have led to awful queues if only one bread shop had closed, and they did not then want panic of that kind to develop. At this time his official suggested that ration books should be printed, but he insisted that they should not be because the fact was bound to leak and lead to serious food hoarding.

A prime minister has to have friends, and Ted chooses his mainly from the Civil Service. He seems to like their minds, and he had a distinct preference for individuals. He has a certain feline quality which means that he makes very deep friendships, and is very loyal to them. It was natural that Armstrong should be one of them, because the Prime Minister is always overworked and he needs someone he can trust to share some of the burden. Though he didn't establish this sort of relationship with Rothschild.

Armstrong was not only involved with the wages side of the policy: he was also deep into the committee discussing boards. Godber did not much like it, but it is clear that there was not much he could do about it; also clear that Heath much preferred seeing him when he took his Permanent Secretary, Freddy Cairns, along with him.

The essential quality of Heath is indecision. He cannot make up his mind, therefore things can slip (and they obviously did during the negotiations with the miners).

FRANK FIGGURES
[no date]

A very politically aware civil servant, who says you can't understand it unless you remember what was in the back of the minds of the Tory ministers: specifically, stamp on local government two humiliating defeats

---

1 Lord Normanbrook, formerly Norman Brook: wartime and post-war civil servant and later chairman of the governors of the BBC 1964–7.

via Wilberforce.[1] The fact of their having happened made it more difficult for the Tories to deal with the issue.

He had been consulted during the planning of Stage III, and thought that relativities should come into it rather more since it is always difficult to make a special case for just one union, e.g. the miners.

It is clear that Figgures was willing to sanction large additional increases for washing and waiting time, but he felt he could not go to both sides and say, Now come on tell me that washing and waiting is custom and practice in the industry and I'll say it's OK to price it and pay out. The board was horribly unkeen about this idea. Figgures clearly thinks he could have settled the strike.

ARMSTRONG The thing that was wrong with the relationship was that it came out in public. Armstrong was shattered when he was called deputy prime minister. But all prime ministers have got their cronies. Bridges,[2] Brook and Trend were terrific cronies (Helsby[3] wasn't). When the Treasury and Civil Service jobs were divided[4] Armstrong had more time on his hands than the predecessors had, and so it was natural that he should spend more of it advising the Prime Minister on economic policy.

JOE GORMLEY
[no date]

He says he believes in negotiation, that's the job, and that he always wants a settlement without a strike, but when he has the tactical advantage he pushes it with an unscrupulousness which astonishes his colleagues. He says that he could have settled the '72 strike at 3 p.m., but he went to No. 10 and forced the Coal Board to disgorge even more.

HEATH–ARMSTRONG He says he was sent a note and asked if he would be willing to meet Heath. He replied that he would. He regards it as the job of a trade-union leader; he has to inform himself. They met in the garden of No. 10; Armstrong was there too. It was a summer afternoon; he is sure of that. He says that they discussed Stage III and

1 Lord Wilberforce: Appeal Court judge, who headed an inquiry into coal miners' pay during the 1972 strike.
2 Edward Bridges: Baron Bridges, son of Robert Bridges, Poet Laureate, and Cabinet Secretary 1938–46; his son Thomas, the second Baron Bridges, diplomat, became private secretary (foreign affairs) to the PM 1972–4.
3 Laurence Helsby: principal private secretary to the PM 1947–50; joint Permanent Secretary to the Treasury and head of the Home Civil Service 1963–8; later Baron Helsby.
4 Up to 1962, Sir Norman Brook (later Lord Normanbrook) had been Permanent Secretary to the Treasury and head of the home Civil Service, as well as Cabinet Secretary. He was the last to combine all three roles.

that he said that the way to settle with the miners was to allow a payment for unsocial hours in Stage III.

If that was done he thought the miners would not strike. He says that when the pay code for Stage III came out and unsocial hours was seen to apply to all industries, he no longer believed that the miners would settle. He had expected the government to keep this under the table, introducing it at the last minute to get everyone off the hook.

Could have settled the strike on three occasions; doesn't remember quite which they were, but bathing time was certainly one. He mentioned it to Whitelaw at the Brown's Hotel meeting, which was on a Sunday in a private room in December before Whitelaw saw the three leaders and then the whole executive. He saw H. Wilson negotiating this and claims that Harold blew it by making a statement on the subject in the House that afternoon. Gormley claims he gave Harold hell later on.

It is absolutely characteristic of Gormley that he said that the TUC had been helpful but why should the other unions not use the miners as an argument for their own claim? Perfectly clear that he would himself. That's what negotiation is all about.

Fascinating the way they all took credit for inventing the flying pickets. Gormley says that he started it by stopping trains coming out of an oil depot somewhere in Kent.

Claims he told Ezra[1] in '71 it would take £3.50 to settle that claim and Ezra was horrified. Of course it cost a good deal more.

A man of extraordinary low cunning.

Gormley defended McGahey stoutly, saying that he had been totally misinterpreted by the Prime Minister. And that he had not claimed that it was his intention to bring down the government, and that he would let No. 10 know this (how?).

A CIVIL SERVANT[2]

There is a certain *Schadenfreude* about Armstrong now. He is a victim of his myth. The view now is that he was not as clever as he seemed – that his reputation was so great that no one bothered to ask whether he was talking sense or nonsense; that he was not especially good at picking people; and that he had been subject to bouts of what later became described as madness throughout his career. He was known for his black humours.

In 1972 his problem was time: he had much too much of it at the Civil

---

1   Sir Derek Ezra: chairman of the National Coal Board 1971–82; later Baron Ezra of Horsham.
2   Unidentified.

Service Department, which is not the job for a grown man, particularly after the Fulton recommendations[1] had been implemented. He himself complained that there was not enough to do; he wanted to see how the post-Fulton organization ran for a few years, and then look at it again. He had been involved in incomes policy before, so it was natural that he should press himself on the Prime Minister.

Mixed committees were unusual but not new (what was different was the strength of Armstrong's emotional involvement). They had begun under Harold in 1964, when he came in believing that all the old ways were nonsense and that the split-level method of decision-making needed reform. But it was a bit embarrassing especially for someone like Armstrong who was included in and clearly knew a lot more about economic policy than Callaghan. He had lost all sense of embarrassment nine or so years later, however, when the mixed committees were used again for the prices-and-incomes policy by Heath. They had stopped under Wilson apparently, partly because he had his own cronies in the Cabinet Office and did not need them on Cabinet committees, though Kenneth Berrill,[2] the think tank man, comes close and is normally the Civil Service spokesman when one is needed on a Cabinet committee.

What had become different in '73 was the strength of Armstrong's emotional commitment. He himself had warned against it in a television interview ('one of his many television interviews'), saying that being a civil servant was a bit like being a small boy building sandcastles. You had to be ready for a bigger boy to come and knock it down, and be willing to start again. By '73 he could no longer bear to see the sandcastles knocked down.

JOHN DAVIES
[no date]

The parallel problem which nobody understood was the significance of the shift in oil prices. Yet there was the really big change in the circumstances of the country. Victor Rothschild knew it, and Ted knew it too, but very few others did. I did a paper for Ted in January. He had asked me to talk to friends in the oil industry, and it was clear from that that it

---

1 Harold Wilson appointment a commission, headed by Lord Fulton, chairman of the British Council 1968–71, to examine the workings of the home Civil Service, which was at the time, in Fulton's words 'fundamentally the product of 19th-century philosophy'.

2 Sir Kenneth Berrill: chief economic adviser to the Treasury 1973–4; head of the Central Policy Review Staff, Cabinet Office, 1974–80.

was prices and not the embargo[1] which were important, but it totally undermined everything we had been saying, which had been basically true, which was that we had every reason to be optimistic about the economy. Peter Walker is not a sound strategist on industry and he overstated it at times, but we had a virtual incomes policy, and investment was about to take off. What was not seen was how this was totally undermined by the oil situation. From October 1973 it was a different world. That was not clear even in the most sophisticated circles. I remember at Christmas in 1973 at home in Cheshire saying to my wife and children, 'Have a nice time,' because I believed deeply in my mind that it might be the last time.

HEATH In the end Heath took all the decisions himself. I think that from '70 to '72 I was a powerful influence on him. Barber never was. He acted dangerously only when Heath let him act alone. At the end of '72 I think the Prime Minister reckoned I was an election-loser because I was following a hard line and saying that's it's all going to be tough, which I think he'd felt too until the end of '72. In '73 his advisers were Willie W, Peter Walker, Carrington maybe. Carrington has great brevity and clarity, a distilling type of mind. But he's an imperialist, interested in our international political ability to dominate events. Walker is a propagandist, which is what a share salesman is bound to be. Willie is a chameleon. Victor Rothschild was Ted's strategist.

He's impenetrable, and one of the problems was that you didn't know what he was going to say in Cabinet until he said it. He has the appearance of great self-confidence. One of the biggest errors about Ted is that he was boosted as a man of principle. But he's not at all. He's a man of policies. A long-term view – I don't think he has one.

The Civil Service was frightened of him. Not Burke Trend, who was approaching retirement. But William Armstrong was dominated by Ted, which is a great pity. Allen was good. Rampton[2] was a technician. But when it came to major issues there was not a willingness in the Civil Service to talk back to Ted, except Victor R.

1 On 16 October 1973, OPEC nations decided to embargo crude-oil exports to those nations that had supported Israel during the Yom Kippur War.
2 Sir Jack Rampton: civil servant; Permanent Undersecretary, Department of Energy, 1974–80.

JEREMY THORPE
[no date]

The offer was never on. It was all mathematical. They had 296 and we had 14. It was not a majority, and even if a coalition had been formed it would not have lasted three weeks.

What is more, I had fought the election on the basis that it was totally unnecessary. And in no way had he changed his policy. I was not tempted in the slightest.

On the Saturday [2 March] the business side of our meeting was over in ten minutes. It was then Mrs Thatcher in reverse. He kept me talking for another thirty-five minutes to make it look good. We made two specific offers. We said that we were prepared to talk with any government, or that we would also always consider a government of national unity. That was my phrase: if I'd copyrighted it I would be a millionaire.

After I'd seen Ted I saw Frank Byers, Jo Grimond and David Steel in the evening. (I think Jo was tempted, but he knew it wasn't on.) And then a larger group in the morning, and at no stage was it suggested that I go in. I phoned Ted and said that there was no enthusiasm for him, that the government's industrial policy would have to change utterly and that we would have to have electoral reform. He said that he would have to put it to the senior colleagues. In the evening he phoned to say that there was no support for a change in the leadership and that he would offer only a Speaker's conference on electoral reform. Not enough.

The interviews over the 1974 election paid off. The Sunday Times *ran three extensive and much remarked pieces from February into March under a joint byline with Stephen Fay, with whom HY would collaborate on journalism and books in the future.*

HY had been embarrassed that he attributed some information he had been given by Nigel Lawson without first clearing it with him. Lawson, however, had no complaint. 'May I say that I thought your three pieces were the finest example of that particular genre of journalism that I have read anywhere for a very long time.'[1] Surprisingly, Lawson did not become a regular HY contact in the future.

1 Lawson, letter, 12 March 1976. HY archive.

CHRIS PATTEN
Lunch, 21 April 1976

THATCHER TEAM   Her trouble is she has never had a Rolls-Royce department.[1] This means she has no experience of a really hard private office. Therefore she does not know how good people ought to be and has too many second-raters working for her. Some of them she knows to be second rate or worse. The others she does not quite see as inadequate, e.g. Patrick Cosgrave,[2] whose speech-writing efforts so far have come to grief and been rewritten. In the immediate private office apart from those two were Richard Ryder and Gordon Reece.[3] She has very good PPSs: Adam Butler and John Stanley are vastly superior to Shelton and Montgomery,[4] who she had the sense to get rid of.

Patten himself and Adam Ridley are being drawn more and more into writing speeches, but she writes a lot herself, rewrites others, and altogether works fantastically hard all the time – but often at the wrong things. For instance, she will be found at two o'clock in the morning rewriting a badly drafted letter to some ordinary voter in Sunderland.

It is very hard to say which Shadow Cabinet people are close to her. She has so far got away without having an inner court, but this will surely have to come. Whitelaw sees her a great deal, but this is mainly because he was and always will be a chief whip (Humphrey Atkins[5] is thought to be useless). Airey Neave[6] is not close, although he has the pulling power of the man who put her in the big league. He is a ferocious and a dedicated schemer, much too prone to see mythical plots against her. To have him tunnelling around Westminster is probably counter-productive. Nor does it make much sense to reverse Heath's 'aloofness' by self-consciously but too mechanically asking MPs what they think about issues. Keith Joseph is kept at arm's length. Agrees that Geoffrey Howe also is not highly

---

1 From 1961 to 1964, Mrs Thatcher had held a junior post in the Ministry of Pensions and National Insurance. From 1970 to 1974, she was education minister.

2 Patrick Cosgrave: journalist, commentator, publisher; special adviser to Mrs Thatcher 1975–9.

3 Richard Ryder: journalist; political secretary to the Leader of the Opposition 1975–9; Conservative MP for mid-Norfolk 1983–97; later Baron Ryder of Wensum. Sir Gordon Reece: journalist, television producer; adviser to Mrs Thatcher 1975–9; director of publicity, Conservative Central Office, 1978–80.

4 Sir Adam Butler: Conservative MP for Bosworth 1970–87; PPS to the Leader of the Opposition 1975–9. Sir John Stanley: Conservative MP for Tonbridge and Malling since 1974; PPS to the Leader of the Opposition 1976–9. Sir William Shelton: Conservative MP for Clapham 1970–74, for Streatham 1974–92; PPS to the Leader of the Opposition 1975. Sir Fergus Montgomery: Conservative MP for Altrincham and Sale 1974–97; PPS to the Leader of the Opposition 1975–6.

5 Sir Humphrey Atkins: Conservative MP for Merton and Morden 1955–70, for Spelthorne 1970–87; was Opposition chief whip 1974–9; later Baron Colnbrook.

6 Airey Neave: soldier, prisoner of war, member of the British War Crimes Executive; Conservative MP for Abingdon 1953–97; head of Mrs Thatcher's private office 1975–9; he was killed by an IRA car bomb on 30 March 1979 as he left the Commons car park.

regarded by her. Reggie, however, has been waking up a bit and is thought to have made an excellent speech at the end of the defence debate.

One of the people she talks to a lot is Lady Young[1] – thought to be a highly sensible vice-chairman of the party.

THATCHER STRATEGY There is a lot of concern about the political problems of the next few months. Jim's honeymoon will last a while, and the forthcoming pay policy with Jack Jones will also be difficult to deal with. Thatcher's own honeymoon is virtually over, so something must be done on policy issues – this cannot be delayed any longer.

Expects the next manifesto to be a policy of 'common sense' and less of ideology than 1970 (despite this still expects Thatcher to be headlined as much further to the right than Ted Heath).

On incomes policy the party will probably have to support whatever the government agrees with Jones. There will be pressures to oppose it root and branch, as well as some people who want to support it outright (as opposed to writing an amendment, which would be the official tactic), or a few incomes-policy nuts who could oppose the policy because it wasn't strong enough, but on the whole there is very little fundamentalist criticism of the type which this government is running. Even John Biffen, who is intellectually opposed to it, always tries to find areas of agreement rather than disagreement (this style is unlike Joseph's). Joseph always homes in on the divisive point as well as being obsessionally ad hominem in style ('Ten years ago X was in favour of an incomes policy therefore he is a bad man').

In general, Patten does not get torn to shreds when he urges the Shadow Cabinet to take up 'common sense' rather than 'freedom'. Whitelaw pushed through support for the Race Relations Bill in the Shadow Cabinet without any discussion.

CHRISTOPHER SOAMES Coming back [from Brussels].[2] He will look for a seat. Epsom and Sevenoaks are the two which are being mentioned, with Epsom the front-runner. Peter Rawlinson[3] would go to the Lords and claims to be able to deliver Epsom for Soames. But, given Rawlinson's record of delivering anything to anyone, there are some people who doubt this. There is also the problem of Soames's own personality and numerous failures in the past, e.g. Chichester, where

---

1 Janet Young, Baroness Young of Farnsworth: created a life peer in 1971, vice-chairman of the Conservative party organization 1975–83; Chancellor of the Duchy of Lancaster 1981–2.

2 Sir Christopher Soames served on the European Commission from 1973 to 1977. He never contested another seat. He went on, instead, to negotiate the future of Southern Rhodesia, later Zimbabwe.

3 Sir Peter Rawlinson: Conservative MP for Epsom 1955–74, for Epsom and Ewell 1974–8; Attorney General 1970–74; later Baron Rawlinson of Ewell.

Home thought he could swing it for Soames because the Earl of Bessbor-ough was the local chairman. Also Honiton. Here Soames was not even shortlisted by the association but Tory Central Office persuaded the locals to interview him with difficulty. The Honiton chairman rang up the Soameses, where the telephone was answered by the butler, who enquired the name and occupation of the caller. This was relayed to Soames, and the reply came back that he was having lunch and would the man call back in a couple of hours. This did not show much sensitivity to the rights of the local chairman.

ADAM RIDLEY
Lunch, 9 September 1976

MRS THATCHER   Is she a radical? The answer is that she has strong instincts at a high and general level, but once she works down through the layers of argument to the detail she will not be intransigent. She needs to be persuaded at every stage of the argument. Thus she is not doctrinaire.

E.g. British Leyland: when Keith Joseph sounded off from the Centre for Policy Studies in hysterical fashion, she was rightly persuaded by the staff not to attack the bailing out. She saw the economic case as well as the human case.

E.g. public spending: although the party is against public spending growing, Margaret Thatcher is very scrupulous about details, constantly asking, 'Would we really cut this or that or the other?'

The trouble is that the issues are very big now. In the fifties and even the sixties they tended to be relatively simple: What do we think about SET,[1] or water metering etc. Now they are huge: the constitution, the unions, can the UK economy survive? etc. Does she have the aptitude for these at the right level? Probably not, but nobody else has either. Look at the government's record on devolution as a classic example.

But neither does she have the time. Nor does anyone. Some of her very consciously anti-Heath tactics mean that she has very little time for big thinking. For example, she makes a point of always being available to see people – both MPs and businessmen, but especially MPs. They can ring up to tell her what they have heard about something or to push a line of thought. She will always see them, unlike Heath. Secondly, she scrupulously involves MPs in policymaking, again to distinguish herself from Heath.

The policy groups have grown ridiculously. They are said to be

---

1 Selective employment tax, introduced by the Labour government in 1966.

seventy-five, but it becomes hard to distinguish a policy group from a couple of Tories who sit down and write a paper about water metering. Inevitably, the fruits of their work take her time. Thirdly, she is conscious of having to do a lot of self-education. Thus the foreign trips. The American trip was a very self-conscious exercise in advertisement. But the Australian trip is more a matter of genuine interest and fact-finding.

One important aspect to look at is her social life. This is extremely limited. In particular, there is almost no social contact whatever between her and her colleagues. This may be a more general phenomenon in circumstances where people are so busy. But it is a fact that the Shadow Cabinet meets only formally. Rather a long way from Macmillan's day, when he held two Cabinets, one with whisky and one without. The kind of casual and speculative conversations which could take place between colleagues at a country-house weekend. This probably reflects a common development in English life, but is acute in the Tory Party at the moment.

SHADOW CABINET Keith Joseph is much liked by Thatcher. She is grateful to him, and in some respects admires him. He still expects to get the Treasury, but this now seems outlandish. In his rather vague responsibility for shadow policy he does not actually control policy at all. His job is administrative, which is not his strong point, e.g. when an MP complains about not being on a policy group it is Keith's responsibility to find him a slot. Clearly this is not enough for him. He needs to be chairman of one or two key groups. But he is chairman of none. He is therefore wandering around in a vacuum and still devoting a lot of time to random pronouncements from the CPS. He has a butterfly mind.

Angus Maude[1] is also less influential than his position would suggest, not a very assiduous worker but a good unifier: can sit between Gilmour and Joseph and find some common ground. Also he has a lot of time available.

Hailsham is important and strong on all the big issues. Also, interestingly, Francis Pym, a constitutional radical.

But it is true to say that none of these people are seriously contemplating a stint of minority government or the need to make a coalition. They are just unwilling to think that far ahead, although some are more interested than others on the great constitutional questions.

CIVIL SERVICE Moving from the Civil Service to the Conservative Research Department revealed how pathetically inadequate the Research

1 Angus Maude: author, journalist, soldier; Conservative MP for Ealing South 1950–57, from 1957 to 1958 he sat as an Independent Conservative; Conservative MP for Stratford-upon-Avon 1963–83; Mrs Thatcher's Paymaster General 1979–81.

Department is. In this age of big issues, politicians need far more backup than they can get. It is becoming almost impossible to insert radical and speculative thinking into the agenda, even in opposition. The Civil Service is no better, as well having strong reasons for avoiding anything that might lead the way to change.

In the autumn of 1976 Britain faced an economic crisis. James Callaghan's Labour government had allowed the International Monetary Fund 'to impose rigorous disciplines on his Government's economic policies', as HY wrote in One of Us. *A full-page piece, edited by Hugo and headed 'A week in the life of the pound', appeared in the* Sunday Times *of 31 October 1976. The research continued, and another collaboration between HY and Stephen Fay took a while to ripen but finally bore fruit as a three-part series on the crisis of 1976 – entitled 'The day the £ nearly died', and with the opening sentence 'This is the story the Government does not want told' – in May 1978.*

POUND NOTES
1976

EDMUND DELL – 29 SEPTEMBER Will the party wear it? The party will have to wear it. There is no other policy but the one Callaghan described yesterday. This turns around one strategic objective to reduce the borrowing requirement. And one central need dominates everything, if we are to do this. The TUC support for the anti-inflation policy. It will help if the TUC come out with a statement in support of the policy behind the new loan.

I can see why the left think their hour has come. It does look bad. But they haven't really thought about what they mean by their economic programme. They talk about temporary specific import controls. We have those now. What they really mean is general and permanent import controls. But this would mean leaving the EEC. There is no possible way of remaining in the EEC and having the siege economy. Does the party really want to reopen that and leave Europe? I don't think so.

I think the main reason the pound has gone down so badly is not what has been said here, but what exchange dealers believe to be the likely effects of the seamen's settlement.[1]

---

1 In September 1976 the National Union of Seamen threatened to strike. The government, fearing a strike that could cripple trade and intensify the financial crisis, settled with a package of fringe benefits that almost matched the union's original demands.

SHIRLEY WILLIAMS – 28 SEPTEMBER (Caught momen-
tarily in the street, thoroughly distraught.)

It's all completely crazy. You can't stop bloody fools saying bloody
stupid things, and other people a long way away taking notice of them.
(This mainly a reference to Alan Fisher.)[1] If you're a democracy, this is
the price you have to pay. You can't possibly stop them saying things.
But of course, if it wasn't Britain, no one would give a damn.

DAVID OWEN – 29 SEPTEMBER (Now a Foreign Office minister, don't forget. Cool, intelligent, very right wing.)

Determination is everything. We have to stick to the policy, always
take a measured approach, not worrying about the next three days but
thinking in months not weeks. All that really matters is the support of
the German and US governments, and it doesn't help that they have
elections. But they are the only ones who really count, I think.

What the left don't recognize is that literally no policy can succeed
which does not have international support. This would be true of the
import-control way as well.

What we have to take comfort from is that governments are more
level-headed than financiers. After the German election it will be possible
to sit down and talk sensibly to the German government, although I have
no doubt that they will support the loan. After all, there is a European
dimension to all this. They can't afford the British economy to go deeply
adrift.

WILLIAM RODGERS – 29 SEPTEMBER   Any import scheme
of any kind would be a defeat for the policy. Even import deposits[2] would
be a bit of a defeat. We don't feel we've got to the bottom of the barrel
yet. But if we have to modify it, it will not be because of conferences or
the party. It will be because internationally there is literally no other way
of moving, even if the foreigners don't like it. (Implicit in this is the
government's belief that they *may* have to move in this way, but if they
do it will be with reluctant foreign acquiescence – HY.)

This conference[3] has been relatively docile. Compare it with the 1950s
and 1960s. People have said how much they regret what is happening,
and there've been motions passed against us. But the *mood* of conference

1 Alan Fisher, general secretary of the National Union of Public Employees 1968–82, had the previous day
condemned the Labour government's cuts in public spending as 'reactionary' and offered support for Labour
local councils that refused to implement them.
2 Companies were required to put down an advance payment on goods they were about to import. It was not
a surcharge – they eventually got the money back – but effectively this provided the government with a temporary
loan and eased a cash-flow crisis.
3 The Labour Party conference that week, in Blackpool.

has not been bitter and impossible. But of course I'm always an optimist, and I have never taken conference motions as seriously as many people.

One must never underestimate Jim's searing experience in 1966–7.[1] This went very deep. He is absolutely determined to avoid going down in history as the man who failed with the economy twice over. He sees economic problems in very simple terms. He talks about them to us in that sort of language. Not spending more than we earn; not living all the time on borrowed money – that kind of thing. It sounds very unsophisticated. But it is very deeply felt. He wants to erase the memory of ten years ago, very badly indeed.

From my conversations generally, I would divide the Cabinet into more than two groups. There are committed siege men: Yes-men. Then there are Yes, probably (i.e. those thinking it may be inevitable but not yet overt backers, being committed to the present line for the moment). Then – No, unless (those not ruling it totally out, but deeply reluctant. I include here those who will follow Jim wherever he goes). Then – No (the deep-rooted intellectual opponents).

These seem to divide roughly like this:

Yes: Benn

Yes probably: Foot, Shore, Silkin, Orme[2]

No unless: Crosland, Rees, Mason, Elwyn Jones, Varley, Mulley, Morris, Ennals, Peart, Millan?, Rodgers?, Hattersley[3]

No: Lever, Dell, Williams, Healey, Prentice

In discussing the shifts in the Cabinet we should not overlook how the left has in fact been weakened. Stan Orme is no substitute for B. Castle.

---

1 On 19 November 1967, after weeks of feverish speculation and a run on the country's reserves, Harold Wilson's government lowered the exchange rate by 14 per cent to make sterling worth $2.40. James Callaghan resigned as Chancellor and became Home Secretary 1967–70.

2 John Silkin: Labour MP for Deptford 1964–73, Lewisham Deptford 1973–87; government chief whip 1966–9; Minister of Agriculture, Fisheries and Food 1976–9. Stan Orme: Labour MP for Salford West 1964–83, for Salford East 1983–97; Minister of State for the DHSS 1976; Minister for Social Security 1976–9.

3 Merlyn Rees: Labour MP for South Leeds 1963–83, for Morley and Leeds South 1983–92; Home Secretary 1976–9. Roy Mason: Labour MP for Barnsley 1953–83; Secretary of State for Defence 1974–6, for Northern Ireland 1976–9. Fred Mulley: Labour MP for Sheffield Park 1950–83; Secretary of State for Education and Science 1975–6, for Defence 1976–79; later Baron Mulley of Manor Park. John Morris: Labour MP for Aberavon 1959–2001; Secretary of State for Wales 1974–9; later Baron Morris of Aberavon. David Ennals: Labour MP for Dover 1964–70, for Norwich North 1974–83; Secretary of State for Social Services 1976–9. Fred Peart: Labour MP for Workington 1945–76; later Baron Peart of Workington and Leader of the House of Lords 1976–9. Bruce Millan: Labour MP for Glasgow Craigton 1959–83, Glasgow Govan 1983–8; Secretary of State for Scotland 1976–9. Roy Hattersley: novelist, memoirist, columnist; Labour MP for Birmingham Sparkbrook 1964–97; Secretary of State for Prices and Consumer Protection 1976–9; deputy leader of the Labour Party 1983–92; later Baron Hattersley of Sparkbrook.

Equally, Millan instead of Ross[1] probably increases the Callaghan loyalists, as does the elevation of Ennals.

At second hand from junior Treasury men: the distinguishing feature of this crisis has been the loss of nerve of the Treasury mandarins. Previously they have been castigated by politicians for their orthodoxies. But at least they have been confident that these orthodoxies would work. Now, both at the Treasury and at the Bank, the remedies are put forward hesitantly by men who give the impression of being at the end of the line. Ministers find this very depressing.

1 William 'Willie' Ross: Labour MP for Kilmarnock, Ayr and Bute 1946–79; Secretary of State for Scotland 1964–70 and 1974–6; later Baron Ross of Marnock.

1977

3 **January**   Roy Jenkins, former Labour Cabinet minister and deputy leader, becomes the first British president of the EEC Commission in Brussels.

13 **May**   Prime Minister's son-in-law Peter Jay named as the British ambassador to Washington.

7 **June**   The Queen celebrates her silver jubilee.

15 **June**   Spaniards vote in their first democratic election for forty-one years.

5 **July**   Zulfikar Ali Bhutto, premier of Pakistan, is overthrown and arrested by the army chief of staff.

12 **September**   Black-consciousness advocate Steve Biko dies in police custody. South African police first blame a hunger strike, then say his head injuries were self-inflicted.

26 **October**   The last natural case of smallpox is recorded, in Somalia; afterwards the disease is declared eradicated.

21 **November**   President Anwar Sadat of Egypt addresses the Israeli Knesset.

24 **November**   Rhodesian leader Ian Smith accepts one-man, one-vote principle after ninety years of white rule.

Deaths   Wernher von Braun, Maria Callas, Charlie Chaplin, Bing Crosby, Labour minister Anthony Crosland, Anthony Eden, Groucho Marx, Vladimir Nabokov, Elvis Presley

TONY BENN
Lunch, the *Sunday Times*, 9 March 1977

The choice now is between the monetarist course and what he calls 'the manifesto choice' – i.e. the left perspective backed by the alternative strategy. The social-democratic course is finished – i.e. the public-expenditure way has had it. I saw Crosland facing this bitter fact about his own political philosophy. What is needed is a serious debate, freed from emotionalism and extremes, about this choice. Something which does not present the choice as between Stalin (me) and Chile (Mrs T).

The great issue of politics is who will reassert a full-employment policy and how this will be made credible. It can only be the Labour Party. Monetarists do not believe in full employment. What we are discovering is that we never really solved that 1931 crisis. The war deceived us into thinking we had. We should look at it over a forty-year period, not just the three years of Labour. [Political economist] Michael Shanks has forecast 2.5 million unemployed in 1982. Are we going to avoid that, or to face the political consequences of it for our society? No one has really thought about it.

Increasingly we have to realize that no negotiation is worth having unless it is with the person of ultimate power. On oil, no point in my trying to get out of Esso London what only Esso HQ can say or give. With unions, no point in getting Jack Jones to sign something which he cannot deliver. The key in my point of view is joint stewards committees, which general secretaries and employers join in disliking intensely. Yet this is the way to deal with disputes and with the forum of factories and plants where Labour power now lies. Similarly, no good my telling the NUM what I want to happen. Their view of what they can do with Stage III must be decided by them. I can propose nothing.

Britain's relevant social contracts are two: one with the unions, one with the IMF. The Callaghan solution has been a balancing act between the two of them, urging each not to wreck agreement with the other. Heath neglected one side of this balance, just as he thought that if he got agreement with union leaders he could force everyone else into line. We have seen that this simply will not work.

Open government is one key to widening the area of consensus you are seeking. This is the way Benn rebuts the notion that his own solutions are corporatist, a word he regards as the ultimate criticism. If the public knows more, it can contribute more. He has done this in energy – forcing choices into the public arena: e.g. his energy conference; e.g. his papers which he has published. He sees no reason why the Granada programme on Leyland could not have been screened a week before the decision was taken. (Also comments: there were a lot more heroes than I noticed round the table at the time.)

POLITICS OF ADVANCED TECHNOLOGY   Civil-liberties issues raised by (a) the news that all workers at the Shetlands terminal (?) which carries 40 per cent of all North Sea oil are under surveillance, (b) the news that at plutonium-using plants Benn has had to authorize guards with sub-machine guns, ID cards are in use etc. etc. Have we thought through these things?

LABOUR PARTY I'm not going to hound young people who join my party. I'm in favour of Rodgers having his say, of Prentice having his say etc. etc. (The right is divided into three: Prenticeites, who want to break up the party; Rodgersites, who want to clean up the party; and Croslandites, who have lost their way now that public spending has been shown to be definitely not the way out of the employment and economic problem.)[1]

FRANCIS PYM
Lunch, 15 March 1977

Scotland could yet tear the country apart. It is a real possibility. It was insane not to have inter-party talks before the bill fell, even before it was published.[2] For it is in no party's interest that things should turn out as they have done. Least of all, as it turned out, was it in Labour's. But they thought it would be in their interest to avoid inter-party talks at the beginning. If they had agreed on a sensible basis, they would have been in far less trouble than they are.

But they have approached it in a totally party-interest way, and have not secured their party interest, while at the same time they have grievously damaged the nation's interest. The statesmanlike thing to do was to see what could be done which was sensible and good for government. But this would have had to include reducing the Scottish seats at Westminster. This Labour was utterly unwilling to do.

The Tories, if they get back, will not be able to do nothing. But what to do is difficult. Pym is against joining in an 'auction' and against making competing claims which cannot, like this government's, be delivered. What is the point of mapping out great plans which then come to nothing? It only adds to the injury you do to the Scots.

But he implies that something more than the present Tory line may be necessary. It all depends, however, on the outcome of the talks. What

1 Tony Benn diary, 9 March 1977: 'Went to lunch with *Sunday Times* journalists Harold Evans, Hugo Young, Keith Richardson, Frank Giles, and Michael Jones; next to me Ronald Butt. I knew them all. I said Fleet Street didn't really operate under a market economy, nobody believed in it – the proprietors didn't, the editors didn't, the unions didn't. They said well we all live in an atmosphere of a market economy. I replied "We all live under the stars and the sun, but we don't worship them." '
2 In February 1977, Labour and Liberal backbenchers rebelled when presented with a Scotland and Wales devolution bill; it failed by 312 votes to 283. In March, the government began a series of all-party talks on devolution.

does the government want out of them? Does it even know what it wants? It seems very doubtful whether it does.

Long-term, Pym is a reformist constitutionally, although he recognizes that even in the next Parliament it is highly unlikely to come. He says this on the grounds that the system is simply not working, i.e. Parliament is not doing what the British people want. It cannot go on. However, the two-party system has broken down. We may regret it, but we must accept it. The main reason is not simply that electoral trends are breaking it up, but that as a *system* it has been ruined by the conduct of the Labour Party. In opposition, Labour backed every pay demand from any union or group. In 1970-74 they became totally irresponsible in this and other ways. In government they have become more and more the prisoner of the left. They are not letting the system work properly. It is only because of this that there is talk of Bills of Rights.[1] They wouldn't be necessary if Parliament was back in its proper place. I backed them for Scotland and Wales. But I won't necessarily support them for the UK parliament. How on earth would they work in practice?

We discussed elections. Agreed that a post-tax-cut-Budget election would not be off the cards. Jubilee interference would not matter. People wouldn't notice. An autumn election after Phase III agreement but before it was tested would also be sensible in some ways. Agreed that Jim's priority was to avoid an election after a parliamentary defeat. Would want to have one before the defeat, to maintain the illusion of control. It will be a very nasty election. Politics has got worse and worse, more and more extreme – the useless ding-dong and all that. Makes the country more and more ungovernable. I (HY) believe that there is a lot of rubbish talked about 'our great parliamentary tradition', and about our 'healthy' political system of vigorous debate between the extreme positions. Benn's case against PR, that he totally opposes it because it means that people don't know what they are getting as a government, is answered by the point that they do not know anyway: that they already vote for all kinds of odd reasons, not merely to give a mandate to the party.

THATCHER Doing very well indeed. Amazing reception wherever she goes. Weakness: talks too often to the party, not enough to the nation. Need more speeches like the one at Brighton – a national address. Biggest fear: that although she will be focused in Week 1, the long haul may weaken her commitments. But 'she is an exceptionally stubborn lady.' What she still needs is to depend on close political advice – she doesn't

1 In 1976 the Labour Party had produced a discussion document called *A Charter of Human Rights*. It supported the incorporation of the European Convention on Human Rights into domestic law. The Home Office also released a document on human-rights legislation that year.

take enough. Pym sounds sceptical about whether WW is really mattering much more than he did. Pym disclaims closeness himself.

TED PROBLEM Ted said eighteen months ago that he would not take office in opposition. So nonsense to continually speculate. What matters is what he does during and after an election. Especially during. Pym believes he will come on to the team in the end. But he is alone. He is also enjoying the fame and popularity of being a best-selling author,[1] going round the country, and still gets vast correspondence saying how much people regret his going – this is bound to do something to a chap.

DOUGLAS HURD
30 March 1977

DIRECT EUROPEAN ELECTIONS The die must be cast soon, certainly by the summit at the end of June. Tories are talking about finding ways of severing the issue of substance from the mechanics of election. The danger is of the issue collapsing merely because there is not agreement on an electoral system. But the PM's personal authority is at stake: he will not be chairman at the summit; it will look very bad if we haven't managed to get on the way to election by then.

In the Tory Party there are a number of MPs who are vaguely against direct elections who have come round to them, but will shy off if PR is also introduced in the equation. Equally there are others – like Paul Channon – who oppose PR very strongly but are so much pro-Europe that, if the government and the party backs it, they will vote despite their opposition to PR. One way would be to have a vote on the White Paper, after the government had stated a preference: but this unlikely owing to shortage of time for the government to make up its mind. More likely that the government will muddle along, delaying the moment of decision.

On balance thinks the Prime Minister is unlikely to come round. Says Dick Mabon,[2] the intermediary, claims that it is a tacit term of the Lib–Lab pact[3] that PR will be recommended by the government. But suggests the Liberals are being naive in thinking they will easily get it. Suggests

---

1 Ted Heath wrote three books in three years: *Sailing: A Course of My Life* (1975), *Music: A Joy for Life* (1976) and *Travels: People and Places in My Life* (1977).
2 Dickson Mabon: Labour and Co-op MP for Greenock and Port Glasgow, 1955–81; SDP MP 1981–3; Minister of State at the Department of Energy 1976–9.
3 Labour began power in March 1974 with a minority government, secured a majority of 3 in October 1974, but from March 1977 to August 1978 relied on a deal with the Liberals, who wanted electoral reform.

that Foot, and others who want to ditch Europe, will be only too keen to offer the Liberals a strong PR system, knowing that it will collapse in the House. This is the big danger.

Another big issue is whether the government will allow a free vote in Cabinet on the *principle* as distinct from the method. Last Friday (25 March) debate interesting: Brynmor John,[1] having first seemed to say that there would be a free vote on both, said at the end of the debate that the free vote applied only to the method. This was after a little man had arrived with a piece of paper, presumably from Downing Street. Therefore the government seems committed to solidarity in Cabinet. Therefore will this precipitate a resignation or two?

Thatcher is dead against PR in any arena. Mainly on wheeler-dealing grounds. DH has made speeches backing it, but has tailed these off after representations from Thatcher. However, DH deems half the Shadow Cabinet to be in favour now. He postulates losing the Sevenoaks by-election in 1982 as the moment Margaret will finally wake up.

Believes there will be no move to direct election if the UK refuses. France has problems, also Belgium. But thinks the Chirac commitment will hold good.[2] The UK problems are by far the worst.

When it comes, a lot will depend on who gets elected there. No early change in power is likely. But if some big men and some men with a future get there, this will raise its prestige automatically. The Tories have been besieged with candidates. And quite a few good ones: young men, a lot of journalists, who don't want to get into Westminster. Some of course are attracted by the money, others want something for their swan-song. But on the whole impressive.

EUROPEAN COMMISSION AND MINISTERS Jenkins has on the whole done well. Rather too much of a weakness for the glamorous intelligentsia over the less so. In particular, the Budget portfolio is becoming important, Tughendhat[3] had to fight for this against Jenkins, who had offered him something and wanted to ditch him with the Transport etc. But CT held out against Jenkins. Leaving the Irishman Burke[4] discontented with the ragbags. But CT had to operate cleverly for

1 Brynmor John: Labour MP for Pontypridd 1970–88; Minister of State at the Home Office 1976–9.

2 In 1977 Jacques Chirac, the prime minister of France 1974–6, had fallen out with President Giscard and been replaced by Raymond Barre. But Chirac had represented one of the nine governments that in December 1975 had agreed to direct elections to the European Parliament. By 1977 Chirac had founded a neo-Gaullist party called Rally for the Republic (RPR) and had become mayor of Paris, an office which had not existed since the Commune in 1871.

3 Christopher Tugendhat: politician, businessman, author; Conservative MP for Cities of London and Westminster 1970–74, for City of London and Westminster South 1974–6; European commissioner 1977–85; later Baron Tugendhat of Widdington.

4 Richard Burke: Fine Gael Minister of Education in Dublin 1973–6; European commissioner in Brussels 1977–81.

this. Went to see other commissioners and generally played his cards like a politician. ([John] Davies and Kirk[1] would not have been able to).

In the presidency, Britain has not excelled. The star has been Benn.[2] Rushed around Europe, displaying meticulous communicative spirit. All the capitals. Got things going. In particular, seems to have got the Torus[3] for Culham, with some concessions offsetting for the French in top scientific posts. Very skilful and energetic. Unlike Silkin, who has played it quite wrong, seeming to ask all the time for special concessions for the Brits. Instead of seeking a realignment of the CAP and using the Brit green pound as a bargaining counter, has simply put in for better subsidies and other Brit concessions, rather brutally and in the short term quite effectively.

UNIONS ETC Businessmen fear a Tory government more than the unions do. Jackson, Murray et al. are simply playing a predictable election game, saying that they could not work with the Tories. They back Labour and this is their way of doing it. But in fact they know very well that they'd have to work with Tories, and wouldn't actually dread it. In fact several things the Tories want reflect union wishes – especially a return to free collective bargaining. But businessmen think it would be a disaster simply because of their wrong interpretation of union actions.

Ted didn't see much of union leaders before 1970. Had been Minister of Labour, but much earlier. Later he became infatuated with them. Insisted on meeting after meeting. Was the only member of the Cabinet who actually enjoyed the meetings. Of course the union men loved them too: this was their way of life. Other Cabinet members used to moan to DH that yet another meeting had been fixed.

DH argues that Thatcher is realistic, and also that she does her best not to appear realistic. This is a pity. The way out must be to state objectives but admit – as is done in *The Right Approach*[4] – that they will take time and can only be done gradually. Prior knows this. He is rushing around the country seeing lots of factories and other people. Having some effect.

HEATH DH believes he will not serve in a Thatcher Cabinet, thinks the differences are too great. Not possible to envisage them getting on as a Foreign Secretary and a prime minister must. Also not possible to see

1 Possibly Sir Peter Kirk, Conservative MP for Gravesend 1959–64, for Saffron Walden 1965–77, who led the first Tory delegation to the European Parliament, in 1973. Kirk died suddenly in April 1977.
2 Not only was Benn Secretary of State for Energy, but also in Europe he was president of the energy ministers.
3 Joint European Torus, based at Culham, Oxfordshire: a massive fusion experiment to harness thermonuclear power.
4 A 1976 Conservative policy document.

him shutting up on other people's briefs. Will move in to slap down Sir KJ. Thatcher doesn't *want* to have him anyway. Only in certain circumstances would she have him. Perhaps if the result was close; and if a lot depended on Scotland – where Ted would have important standing.

Ted meetings are fantastically well attended. Went to speak to Young Conservatives at Winchester last week; Hurd also there. It was his twelfth speech of the week. Is doing this all the time. Gets full houses and much respect, without ever deviating from the party line except in his unwillingness to mention the leader by name. This is intoxicating, as are the letters. A big question is what he will do in a general election. DH thinks he will want to go up and down the country, and will certainly not do an Enoch. But, on the other hand, will not serve Thatcher: a nice point whether she will not invite him or he will not accept. But DH agrees that not to serve as asked would be bad for his reputation. For this reason his friends have put before him the Europe option: standing for the European Parliament, a big figure, alongside Brandt and Mitterrand, who will do so without leaving their home seats in their home parliament. Ted could do likewise, be his own man, be the biggest Brit there is. This has so far fallen on stony ground.

Ted prone to say to his former associates that they have moved far to the right. But this more in jest than anger. No loyalty tests. No Heathites either, and he has not wanted to organize such an equipe.

EDWARD HEATH
Lunch, 16 March 1977

The note of contempt for Thatcher and her team remains unabated. If they got in, Ted says, 'they wouldn't know what to do' about the unions and the economic policy. But they would be driven, he says, to a form of incomes policy. 'But they would have wasted all this time. We'd have begun all over again. Why won't people learn the lessons from the past?'

Claims there is a complete absence of sense to what he sees of the present Tory policy. This is against a background of many voices saying different things. 'It doesn't add up to anything.' There is no leadership, no coherent drive or policy. There are also contradictions – e.g. announce they are in favour of swingeing public expenditure cuts, yet table a motion (?) this week saying that there should be no cuts on the capital account. 'Anyone who knows a thing about public accounting knows that you cannot get instant cuts in current spending, and that all spending cuts are partly at least capital cuts.' Similarly, don't understand that monetarism will not work in an economy which is more than 50 per cent public. The cash limits idea is *not* a way of avoiding the reality of inflationary pressure. Believes it is a mirage to think it can be imposed as if it were somehow a magic escape from economic problems.

Also scathing about the implication that you can run a growing economy without running a budget deficit. Says the Japanese budget shows that at present 33 per cent of public spending is to finance a deficit! Far higher than the UK. Why? Essentially because people have confidence that the industrial future of Japan is secure. But, even in Britain, no business in the land runs on the basis that its business is financed out of current profits alone.

Unrepentant about any significant events of 1973–4, or even 1970–74. Those which he regrets are from the earlier period – 'when we were in the grip of the fashions of the 60s,' he moans, almost as if he had no responsibility for them. In particular, cites the abolition of the IRC[1] as a bad move, wasting a lot of time to a quite unnecessary end. The IRC's only real mistake was entering the market to take over Kent Instruments. Otherwise there was no serious reason to criticize it, still less dismantle it. The other thing he actually itemized was the mistake of making the NIRC[2] what Feather called 'a people's court' – i.e. the consciously proletarian decision to abandon wigs and flummery was a boomerang. Feather went on about the unions had never in their history failed to observe a High Court injunction – the last being the Torquay hotel case. Kept on to Ted about the NIRC not being 'a proper court'.

For the rest, he rambled through the events of that climactic time with scarcely a tremor of regret. Also reviled several loyal friends. Prior had been one of the big hawks, therefore not qualified to do business with the unions. WW, 'when he applies his reason to anything at all', is in his reason in favour of federalism. But since he hasn't thought about it, and is under pressure on all sides, he forgets that and now has come out against devolution of any kind (another for the politics of repentance), and also went though the insanity of putting on a three-line whip at the second reading of the Devolution Bill.

Noncommittal on whether he would take a place in government. (But Pym thinks he will, after sensibly preserving his position until he has to commit to it.)

Highly critical of [Foreign Secretary] Crosland over Rhodesia. Says the Kissinger/Vorster agreement was a miracle which should never have

---

1 Industrial Reorganization Council: a quasi-governmental state bank set up by Harold Wilson in 1966 to act – in the words of *Time* magazine in March 1968 – as 'Britain's official corporate marriage broker'.

2 National Industrial Relations Court, established by Edward Heath in December 1971 with the power to grant injunctions to prevent damaging strikes, settle labour disputes, and penalize unions. It was dismantled by the Wilson government in 1974.

been allowed to get away.[1] The Geneva conference was a nonsense, putting power in the hands of front-line presidents which was totally unnecessary. Britain should simply have said this is how we are going to proceed and kept Smith to his word.

Believes there will be a Phase III, and says it is essential. Otherwise sterling will run away again.

Goes on about typo errors in the 11 p.m. edition of the *Daily Telegraph*, which he gets nightly. Evidence of the country going to the dogs. But reluctant to admit that the *whole* place is like that – thinks the Japanese element not wholly out of the question (vivid account of the shipbuilder with 87,000 workers, 98 per cent on life contracts, all committed to finishing the ships on time etc.).

Obsession with the media. You can't do anything without getting the media behind you. Contrasts the old way with now, when politics is on every radio and TV show morning, noon and night in an election. In these circumstances no chance of running for a doctor's mandate.[2] You have to answer questions all the time. But further than that – stresses vital role of media in disputes. Scorns the *Sun*'s backing of the miners, which meant the *Mirror* had to do the same. This built up a climate. Similarly, the *Mail* backing the toolmen. Got to get the public on your side – although he agrees that the press does not equal the public . . .

Speaks of numerous dinners with businessmen, book signings, obviously feeds on the diet of letters. Whatever we may think, he has a public out there. That, if nothing else, buoys him up.

Claims to have made fifteen major speeches in the last twelve days.

The new boat: aluminium etc. etc.[3]

JO GRIMOND
28 April 1977

For my part it is not working well. We are getting drawn in. It is just what I warned them about. One problem is finding out far more than we really want to. We got a copy of some report the other day. If we were in

1 The winds of change blew fitfully in Africa. Long after other former British colonies had metamorphosed into independent African members of the Commonwealth, the whites clung to power in Southern Rhodesia. Ian Smith, leader of the Rhodesian Front party, made a unilateral declaration of independence in November 1965 and maintained control – in the face of guerrilla warfare from Robert Mugabe and other black leaders – until June 1979. In September 1976, US Secretary of State Henry Kissinger and South African premier John Vorster pushed Smith towards majority rule in what was then Southern Rhodesia, later Zimbabwe. The immediate outcome – a meeting between Smith's government and black African leaders in Geneva in October 1976 – ended in deadlock.

2 A reference to the national governments of Ramsay MacDonald, Stanley Baldwin and Neville Chamberlain from 1931 to 1940, which claimed a 'doctor's mandate' or free hand to put the economy right.

3 Mr Heath's ocean-going yacht *Morning Cloud III* sank during a Force 9 gale in the English Channel in 1974. Two of its crew – including Heath's godson – perished.

opposition, we could have used it. But being in cahoots with ministers tied our hands. This is happening a lot.

I have never been to see Benn. Of course not. I write letters to him, but I've always done that. I've never sat down at a table with any of the ministers. The last thing I want to do. I'm very worried about this oil slick from the blowout.[1] But what's the good of asking to be consulted? What could I do? The whole thing's absurd.

What is happening, in all this, to the Liberals as the party that wants to bust the system? How can we bust the system if we are part of it? From that point of view, the best thing would have been an election with a Tory landslide. Not because I want the Tories, but because it might have changed the whole pattern of British politics. As it is, what is changing about the Labour Party? Nothing. The deal would be all very well if we were having any effects on them. But we are not. The Labour Party is what it has always been, a socialist party. There is still a total difference between Helmut Schmidt and any Labour Cabinet member.

What I fear is that we will be landed with all the bad things Labour have done. We will be the people who let the shipyards be nationalized, let dock labour be protected etc. But what ice will we cut with our little concessions? Suppose we do even get PR for direct elections. That certainly won't help me much. Europe is totally unpopular. So is the Labour government. I am under threat from the Tories – not so much the SNP, whose candidate has changed. The anti-Grimond protest vote will go to the Tories now.

There are not many sceptics among my colleagues. Although there are quite a few who don't like all the work they have to do. My own work has not changed the slightest bit. But the trouble is, are we still an opposition party? It is hard to claim we are. I am used to being an MP for my constituents, and for the Liberal Party, but not being a member of government, still less quasi-government. I remember being on the race select committee, the only one I've been on. I resigned. I found that I was going round the country like a Royal Commission. That's all very well, but I haven't got the set-up to do that. I want £10,000 a year and a good staff if you want me to act like a minister.

What this whole arrangement overlooks is the value of ignorance. It's all too easy to begin to sympathize with ministers if you know all the arguments they know. Much easier not to know their problems. Now we all get the arguments, and when you've heard them you lose your clarity. How can you attack the government so strongly if you know why they are doing what they are doing?

1 The North Sea's biggest oil spill began on 22 April 1977 with a blowout at the Ekofisk Bravo platform on the Norwegian continental shelf. The well took seven days to cap.

JOE HAINES
1 June 1977

Robert Armstrong is of higher intellectual calibre than John Hunt. He will certainly be Secretary of the Cabinet.[1] There is no one else anywhere near it. And the Secretary of the Cabinet is the most important Civil Service job. Hunt has become more and more determined to try and influence policy. He is a devious and ruthless man. Very security-oriented. This is due to his background, which is strong on defence matters. I imagine that the first thing Hunt would do if anyone were presented for a job at No. 10 would be to send for his MI5 file. Hunt became very interested in Ireland, above all from a NATO point of view. What would happen to Ireland and to NATO if Ulster left the UK. This was his big interest . . .

R. Armstrong is less devious than Hunt, and also less capable of indiscretion. Tends to gain his way by sheer efficiency and intellectual power. Of course, all civil servants at the top are discreet and devious. But R. Armstrong would never let the mask slip as Hunt once did. He rushed into the room on the day Thatcher was elected leader, blurting out, 'I'll never vote for that woman.'

Joe says that honestly he hasn't a bad word for R. Armstrong. Nor, he claims, has Marcia [Falkender]. He is just so good. What do we mean by good? Extremely efficient administrator; able to read the Prime Minister's mind ahead of time; alert to all pitfalls; totally loyal to the prime minister of the day. He exhibited this to perfection in March 1974; after all, he had been extremely close to Ted. Not only the music etc., but also committed to the statutory incomes policy, which he was partly responsible for selling Heath on. In that fevered time, many people lost their heads and certainly a number of civil servants began to behave out of style. But somehow R. Armstrong was able overnight to assemble a loyalty to the opposing policy. He was retained by Wilson for quite a long time (see how long). Some of his assistants – especially Robin Butler[2] – found the intellectual problem of writing speeches for Heath and then for Wilson a terrible strain. But not R. Armstrong.

He got on with Marcia by being charming and considerate. But in practice he detested her and worked to minimize her influence. Allied with Haines and Donoughue to outwit her (be careful how this is put). In particular, backed their efforts (successful) to stop the attempt to kick

1 A correct forecast. Armstrong served as Cabinet Secretary 1979–89.
2 Sir Robin Butler, civil servant, later Baron Butler of Brockwell. He served as private secretary or Cabinet Secretary to five prime ministers between 1961 and 1998.

the Donoughue unit out of No. 10 into the Cabinet Office. Armstrong is remembered as the kind of man who would always be ready with the resignation letter *and* the reply, unbidden.

CROSSMAN R. Armstrong, Haines and BD were against legal action. But they arrived on Monday morning to find that Hunt had already consulted the Attorney General. They were aghast. Further, it is pure fiction to say that there was no consulting between Prime Minister and AG. Yes, it is true HW had not read the book – he hasn't read a book for years. But JH and BD had read it for him.

It was Hunt who most wanted to get Crossman. Not least because he foresaw the flood of future memoirs, including Joe's. Joe had quite a lot riding on Silkin's[1] failure. The Radcliffe committee was purely to appease Hunt. The thought of ministers actually pledging any signature to new rules was absurd: Castle, Jenkins, Benn, Healey all refused.

CHRIS PATTEN
15 September 1977

JOSEPH Is he really so disingenuous? One keeps saying this, but the evidence is not all one way. For example, last year he published his book of speeches the day before the launch of *The Right Approach*, over which we had spent a lot of time planning the right date, and he told nobody that his speeches were going to come out the day before.

Whatever else may be said about KJ, he has some nasty people around him. Alfred Sherman[2] is a pretty bad man: obsessed with race and immigration, very far to the right on economic issues, working at the CPS, and writer of at least some of Joseph's speeches (as he also is of some of Mrs Thatcher's). Possibly Bruce-Gardyne was also involved in writing.

THATCHER She retains a strong emotional affinity with the ideals of the right-wing party, especially as embodied in the NAFF [National Association for Freedom]. She has been heard to laud them as having done more for freedom in this country than anyone else in politics (this said at emotional moments). She was a friend of Ross McWhirter,[3] who

1 Sam Silkin: Labour MP for Camberwell Dulwich, 1963–74, for Southwark Dulwich 1974–83; Attorney General 1974–9; later Baron Silkin of Dulwich; brother of John Silkin.
2 Sir Alfred Sherman: journalist, political adviser; co-founder of the Centre for Policy Studies.
3 Ross McWhirter: journalist who, with his twin brother, Norris, launched and edited the *Guinness Book of Records*. The McWhirters held strong views on CND, the trade unions and the EEC, and launched the NAFF, later the Freedom Association. Ross McWhirter was shot and killed by two IRA volunteers in November 1975.

was murdered. She uses Robert Moss[1] to write speeches (check). Above all, perhaps, some of the people who make the NAFF tick and some of the MPs sympathetic to it believe they played a crucial part in putting her where she is, and believed at the time that what they were engineering was a right-wing putsch in the Tory Party. Thus, people like Tebbit[2] and George Gardiner[3] have been important in pushing forward the rhetoric of anti-union extremism, and they are people whose activities she looks well on. She thinks this kind of thing said from the back benches is important and useful. Especially does she like Tebbit, and listens to him. This is rather like Callaghan listening to Dennis Skinner:[4] Tebbit and Skinner are in the same class as gutter fighters. In practice, for the big speeches, Thatcher always falls back on the Patten–Ridley team, a Heath creation. But the Shermans and Gardiners loiter in the wings, and are sometimes favoured. Patrick Cosgrave, on the full-time staff, never writes speeches, or if he does they are not used. His function is to send her messages to local constituency dinners. But she keeps him on: again, an emotional bond, which she prefers not to sever. In her words, she is invariably cautious and moderate, at least on specifics. On the closed-shop issue,[5] she has kept strictly to the agreed line. But it remains open on the right to say, as they do, 'Ah, but she does not really believe it.' This is useful in party-management terms: it keeps the right happy. But, for precisely the same reason, it reveals her problem with the uncommitted voter she must be trying to attract.

ERIC VARLEY
House of Commons, 7 December 1977

STEEL   Six plants will have to go. He named East Moors, Bilston, Consett (?), Ebbw Vale and two others I did not recall. As well as that, there will have to be demanning at the efficient plants. All this will take time, but it has to come. He seems as though he is looking for much of it be done in 1978. Villiers[6] will continue until January–February trying to

---

1 Robert Moss: Australian-born journalist, author; member of the National Association for Freedom.
2 Norman Tebbit: civil-airline pilot, trade-union activist; Conservative MP for Epping 1970–74, for Chingford 1974–92; senior figure in Mrs Thatcher's subsequent Cabinet; later Baron Tebbit of Chingford. He was an outspoken figure: Michael Foot once called him 'a semi-housetrained polecat'. Tebbit was injured, and his wife, Margaret, disabled, by an IRA bomb at the 1984 Conservative Party conference in Brighton.
3 Sir George Gardiner: journalist; Conservative MP for Reigate 1974–97.
4 Dennis Skinner: miner, trade unionist; Labour MP for Bolsover since 1970; outspoken parliamentarian, affectionately labelled 'the beast of Bolsover' by parliamentary sketch-writers. His Who's Who entry describes him as born of 'good working-class mining stock'.
5 A. 'closed shop' was a business in which all employees were required to join a union.
6 Sir Charles Villiers: chairman of the British Steel Corporation since 1976; also a member of the National Economic Development Council.

do a deal with the steel-union federation. But after that he will have authority to go over their heads to deal on a plant-by-plant basis, which is what he wants to do and is the only way of getting anything done. Many union members are keen to go anyway – the older ones qualify for as much as £7,000 redundancy. I pressed him on total figures. He did not want to use a global figure, because it causes trouble. But eventually he said about 25,000 men.

Varley is a fervent proponent of decentralization. Wants to create a system which allows profitable steel plants in Rotherham and Sheffield to give higher rewards than the others. But admits the great difficulties. Thinks the shipbuilding set-up is right: with yards having a degree of management independence.

Thinks that coal will be the supreme example of the benefits of this philosophy. As he says, between 1926 and 1972 there was no strike in the coal industry (as distinct from pit strikes). Believes if they get back to pit by pit there will be no strike for another forty years. It was all Robens's fault – one of the classic wrong decisions of recent industrial history to have national bargaining. Also points out that the two major accidents, at Lofthouse and one other, were not due to pressures of productivity. One was a broken cable leading to a cage crash, the other to faulty maps of old workings. Mining is a safe industry, he declares.

He agrees, however, that not everyone supports him. Benn he named. 'Tony Benn sees all the workers as noble savages – to be treated as a group and class, and together.' (A classic middle-class piece of patronization, per HY.)

PAY   Interesting how all his fire, like that of other ministers, is directed at unions not managements. This I think is not because they love managements, but because they see unions (a) as their constituency and (b) as simply being inimical to sound pay policy. In particular, inveighs against the illusion of free collective bargaining. Points out that this envisages a free-market system of labour which simply does not exist.

CALLAGHAN   He really does mean what he says. He says that he need not stay in the job: he could easily take his prime minister's pension after being at it for two years and go off to his farm, and it wouldn't matter much to him if he did. This is sincere. Also, however, it is wrong to think of him in the short term. He thinks he can do something for this country; he believes in it in a very British way.

He is extremely tough when he wants to be. Over direct elections, he said to the Cabinet that the government would not have to oppose it, as had happened last time. When one member said this was outrageous, he said it was time to decide whether a man saw his duty as an MP as higher than his duty as a member of a government making collective decisions. Everyone else chimed in to say that this was the crucial point. And no one opposed a direct-elections bill.

He has not made many blunders. But one of them was Drax.[1] This commitment was made by accident. It was at question time, after he had been having a hell of a time over Peter Jay,[2] fighting like hell at QT, and suddenly this one comes at him out of left field and he gives it away. From then on the commitment was made. But Jim knows it is wrong.

CHRIS PATTEN
15 December 1977

CALLAGHAN Jim has a bad past and a doubtful future: but he is the man for now. Failure at the Treasury, not sparkling at the Home Office, not a brilliant Foreign Secretary . . . But a good prime minister . . . per HY.

How much will come out about Hodgery,[3] and about thuggery?

THE TORIES They have to get across the line that a Labour majority government is vastly different from a Labour minority government. The trouble with this, however, is that it may be an encouragement to vote Liberal . . .

Thatcher is better than she was on all this. True, Whitelaw had to move fast to counteract her sympathetic noises for the firemen.[4] He can move very fast indeed. He did well by going on television and saying something quite contradictory to what she had said. She is not in the habit of admitting that she boobed, but she takes the inference and acts on it.

There will be a higher profile in January, when she begins to take on board the increasing certainty of an October election.

What she now has to do is talk more about the things people care about and less about freedom. This means jobs and housing above all.

---

1 In July 1977 the government said that an order for Drax B power station, in addition to benefiting the power-plant industry, would be a mark of confidence in the UK's coal industry. Eric Varley, when Energy Secretary, had argued against such a decision.

2 Peter Jay, economist, journalist, broadcaster, was appointed as ambassador to the United States in May 1977. He was married to Margaret, daughter of prime minister James Callaghan, and the appointment inevitably provoked accusations of nepotism.

3 Sir Julian Hodge, accountant, banker and investor, whose name was often linked with powerful Labour interests. Jim Callaghan, Labour MP for South-East Cardiff, and later prime minister, had been a fellow founder-director of Hodge's Commercial Bank of Wales.

4 By 15 December the Fire Brigades' Union had been on strike for more than a month.

Simply don't believe that jobs are not an issue. They must be made one: we are the only reason why they have not been made an issue so far. If we were in power we would be crucified over them.

They are socially a major matter. The fact is that people who actually suffer unemployment are feeling it very hard. This is a cardinal reason for the rise of the National Front, backed by hordes of young people – although CP agrees with our line that they are not an electoral threat of any importance. Reaction in Bath after the Labour broadcast was that it was unfair to the National Party: that they are not quite so vicious as that.[1]

JAY   A difficult one to play. When CP made a speech attacking it, it was not well received. People thought it was personalities. Ditto attacks on Cinzano – the latest name for Owen, following a current jet-setting TV commercial.

Heath intervention in the PR debate was not helpful. Made it a leadership issue rather than an issue of substance . . .

People must stand for something.

Carrington and Prior lament the day Ted failed to put Thatcher and Joseph on the really important committees. Did not *meet* trade unionists. Would be very helpful now if they had. This was done entirely because Ted did not like them.

---

1   In December 1977 the Labour Party devoted a political broadcast to an attack on the National Front.

1978

18 January	The European Court of Human Rights finds the UK government guilty of mistreating prisoners in Northern Ireland.
24 March	The *Amoco Cadiz*, aground on the Brittany coast, spills 220,000 tons of crude oil into the Channel.
25 July	Louise Brown, the world's first 'test tube baby', is born at Oldham.
9 May	The body of former Italian prime minister Aldo Moro, kidnapped by the Red Brigade in March, is found in a parked car.
6 August	Pope Paul VI dies.
11 September	Bulgarian dissident Georgi Markov is killed in London by a poisoned umbrella.
28 September	Pope John Paul dies after thirty-three days in office.
16 October	Cardinals elect Karol Wojtyla of Poland as Pope John Paul II.
29 November	913 members of a religious cult commit mass suicide in Jonestown, Guyana.
1 December	The *Sunday Times* and its sister newspaper *The Times* stop publishing following a dispute with print unions over new technology.
11 December	Millions march in Iran against the Shah, calling for the return of Ayatollah Khomeini from exile in Paris.
13 December	Former Liberal leader Jeremy Thorpe committed for trial charged with conspiracy with three other men to kill Norman Scott, a former male model.
Deaths	Jacques Brel, Jomo Kenyatta, Golda Meir, Willy Messerschmitt, Norman Rockwell

GEOFFREY HOWE
Lunch, 20 June 1978

A sticky beginning, because he thought my piece of last Sunday was hostile,[1] and had been rung up by friends commiserating with him for such 'mean' journalism. But others had said it was kind. I explained to him that it was meant to be, and had therefore been a bad piece since it had been misunderstood.

Much obsessed with how newspapers decide what to publish of speeches etc. Sees our problems, but does not know how to lick them. Poses some of the problems of politicians: that they speak to different audiences in one and the same speech; that they say the same things in different form to many different audiences and have to, that the inadvertent remark can be seized on, that politicians can never determine what will catch attention.

A man deeply concerned about real problems. Above all, the fact that we in the Western world have learned to live for today not tomorrow. A journey north reminds him as he looks out the window of the massive extent to which the Victorian capital investment still shapes the economy. How much investment in the long term future are we now doing? We are heading for a really terrible time unless we can reverse this trend. He sees it as coming essentially through making risk capital more available and encouraging ventures in the private market. But he acknowledges that part of the Tory appeal is to give people more money, which they may decide to spend now rather than save. For him the prime effort is to get it into their hands, and not the government's. He says it will not necessarily follow that they will use it all up. Says that increase in indirect taxes, as long as it does not go overboard, will prevent consumer boom: says it is not proven that it will all lead to imports growth etc.

Evinces a sense of profound despair about Labour. Why?

- Their indifference to strikes and use of union muscle. See the hospital strike or threat. Inconceivable use of brute power. In the end Labour has to be passive about this: unwilling to stir it up.
- Healey's lack of a moral vision. It is remarkable how few things he has ever said about the kind of society he believes in. (Callaghan has said rather more.) A few ritual words about socialism. And about the

1 HY's Inside Politics column of 18 June 1978 was headlined 'What's wrong with the good Sir Geoffrey?' The occasion had been an economic debate in which the Chancellor, Denis Healey, likened an attack by Howe to being savaged 'by a dead sheep'.

arts. But as to the kind of political organization he believes in his career is a void.
- Their belief that more of the same is the only way to go. This will lead to a kind of Romanian or other East European economy (not re political rights, of course, but re economic control). This is the only way it can go.

But admits the Tory problem. He says that they must now 'unstitch the union argument without being too fearful', e.g. about closed shop and about hospital strikes. Must have faith that there is a majority in favour of the liberal position about all this. Hospital porters don't actually want to go on strike. But agrees that the countervailing force to that of the union leadership is needed to set up, around which they can rally.

THATCHER A mass of competing tensions, like all of us. Says she is a victim, like him, of media stereotyping. I agree, in part. But she is cool. Cites her dissent from the common Tory line at the time of the referendum on the EEC. She apparently demurred from the general line of attack on the very principle of the referendum, saying that it might not be such a bad principle. In this she was rather prescient. Claims that Gardiner is of little consequence; that Sherman is a good writer but an impulsive one and is in any case of diminishing importance.

TONY BENN
His office, 28 June 1978

THATCHER What she presages is a real polarization. Benn evidently relishes the thought. It fits in with his condemnation of the consensus politics of the last thirty years. He thinks she may sink like Goldwater,[1] or else change Britain's course pretty drastically. He acknowledges that the Tory programme is a long-term one, capable of being destroyed in the short term. He also relishes the disturbance Mrs Thatcher causes the establishment. Asked James Hamilton whether he is preparing Rhodes Boyson's education programme:[2] Hamilton grimaced. Similarly, at Energy, the officials would be utterly aghast at being asked to dismantle BNOC [British National Oil Corporation] if that is what is going to happen. Senses that Whitehall does not want her to win.

1 Barry Goldwater, Republican senator for Arizona, fought and lost a US presidential campaign in 1964.
2 Sir James Hamilton: Permanent Secretary at the Department of Education and Science 1976–83. Sir Rhodes Boyson: Conservative MP for Brent North 1974–97; junior Education and Science minister 1979–83.

MANIFESTO   Agrees with my column about Jim a few weeks ago. Describes Callaghanism as 'a militant vacuum'; i.e. confirms that the other side has an interest mainly in resisting the ideas of the left. Asserts that democratic socialism is dead. Hattersley still calls himself one; Rees and others are part of the Callaghan circle but they do not have any real ideas. On the other hand, says that it is not exactly an 'ideological' dispute. He believes that a good many of the NEC's ideas will get into the manifesto by the backdoor of the TUC. Instances particularly ideas on the economy and on Europe. Thinks planning agreements will be in: indeed, says that Jim appears to have accepted the need for them. He has seen Jim for a talk about it all. Says that he is receptive. Contrasts him with Wilson, very favourably. Says Jim is well aware of the danger of another 1970, when Wilson stole the walkabout idea from the Queen in Australia. Jim much shrewder. Gaitskell ran the Labour Party by trying to destroy the left. Wilson ran it by trying to destroy the unions. Callaghan is quite different. He believes in all his constituencies and wants to hold them together, especially the unions.

On the other hand, Benn concedes that 'even if Denis were to announce another four billion off the PSBR[1] the unions would still be fighting hard at the election.' Emphasizes the utter horror unions have of Thatcher Tories, and how they will strain every muscle to see that they don't get in. The same goes for the left.

CAMPAIGN   Sceptical about my suggestion that Labour will fight on the anti-Thatcher ticket mainly: thinks this would be dangerous. 'There must be some positive content.' People want something to fight for. He will make sure that he gets to Bristol as often as he can and go on the doorsteps.

He has been doing five or six meetings a week recently. Sees a welling-up of enthusiasm in the ranks, a keenness to come to meetings, a zeal to win.

LORD HARRIS
His office, 10 August 1978 (at his suggestion)

ELECTION   Will it be October? He thinks so. But it doesn't have to be. When I demurred and said it surely did, he replied quick as a flash that the government could survive by putting down an order for the

---

1 PSBR – public-sector borrowing requirement – is now called the public-sector net cash requirement. It could equally be called the Micawber measure, because it means the same thing: that government spending in the public sector exceeds income, and in an inflationary era it served as a crude index of economic stability.

Scottish referendum[1] on the Thursday after Parliament returns. This would mean a referendum perhaps in January. But it would keep things going, and there would be enough to put in a Queen's Speech. His assumption is that the Nationalists would not vote against the Queen's Speech if the referendum was fixed. Says he is quite sure Jim does not want to go in October. Also that a virtue of it is the scuppering of the Tory poster campaign.[2]

This, however, JH attaches little importance to. As the architect of Labour's most successful election advertising campaign, using professionals (in 1964), he doesn't think much of the Tory effort. Thinks they are quite wrong in going for unemployment.

(a) It is not a real issue, except for youth unemployment – i.e. the figures are a fraud, as people claim the dole and get two or three jobs on the side. This is why there are so many unfilled vacancies. He was talking to the chief constable of the West Midlands, who told him his main worry was non-recruitment to civilian posts in the police. This could not be so if the unemployment figures were real.

(b) The Tories will give rise to expectations they cannot meet. He asserts that within a year of the next government, whichever it is, there will be 2 million unemployed. This will really come home to roost against the Tories.

JH believes that inflation is the issue the Tories should be hammering without let-up. A much better one for them than jobs.

Thinks law and order not a serious issue – police pay matter[3] dead after one day. Immigration bad for Tories – Butt piece amazingly naive. He hears that Barney Hayhoe[4] thinks he may lose his seat because of the immigrant vote, among previous non-voters. (Might this be a good seat for Dilip Hiro[5] to cover.)

JH thinks the Tories will win. Says he cannot see Labour taking Home Counties seats like Watford. And thinks they have won all they can win in the north of England.

PRISONS Are in a desperate situation. Not entirely due to wages. Prison buildings are falling down. Went to Sheppey the other day and found that the floor of one of the Nissen huts had simply fallen through

---

1 In 1979 the people of Scotland were asked whether there was sufficient support for the Scotland Act 1978, which outlined a deliberative assembly for Scotland. Forty per cent said yes, but this was not enough and the Act was repealed.

2 A poster produced by Saatchi & Saatchi for the Conservative party simply displayed a long queue of people and the legend 'Labour isn't Working.'

3 In 1978 a pay review led by Lord Edmund-Davies recommended a 45 per cent pay rise for the police, given the special responsibilities of the force and an implicit obligation not to strike.

4 Barney Hayhoe: Conservative MP for Heston and Isleworth 1970–74, for Brentford and Isleworth 1974–92.

5 Dilip Hiro: Indian-born, London-based playwright, author and journalist.

with rot. This is repeated elsewhere. Meeting twenty prison governors tonight to beef up morale. Prison officers are in a pretty nasty mood. Dangerous industrial action being taken. We have almost reached the point on more than one occasion when it became impossible to receive more prisoners into prison, because of the officers' bloodymindedness. This is put down essentially to their sense of being an oppressed and undervalued class. He thinks that more money is needed for prisons but less for probation officers. Yet, because non-custodial care has become the vogue over the last five years, the growth of the Probation Service has become unstoppable. It is going to get annual tranches of extra public money. When it had to stand still, after the '76 cuts, it became efficient. The fact is that very few prisoners are suitable for non-custodial care. They are a rough lot. Yet I cannot alter the balance of priorities. Why? Because I have to work with them; they can appeal to the Home Secretary if I stand up against their growth; one junior minister can do little.

PUBLIC SPENDING   Only on the inside can you know the fantastic waste of public money. Even when the '76 regime was imminent, and the pound spiralling, civil servants put forward vast schemes of expansion. It is simply built into the system. Cuts in manpower are just not a high enough priority. Some top civil servants feel as strongly as I do about it. But without a severe, continuing and long-term priority established and driven home by the Prime Minister himself nothing serious can be done. The Civil Service unions are very militant, which is another major change. Spending ministers tend to think their job is to keep their clients sweet. The two biggest factors:

(a) The Treasury's loss of control over manpower, which has meant that the incentive which previously existed for a civil servant to be seen to cut back manpower – that it was good for his career – no longer obtains. The Civil Service Department has its own institutional thrust – it has no real incentive to cut back staff or restrain its growth.

(b) The Chief Secretary is vital. Joel Barnett[1] has been no good, Jack Diamond[2] was the best of all, simply saying that he was not there to argue the merits of a case, simply to say there was not enough money. He was very, very good. [Patrick] Jenkin also was useless.

To fashion major journalism out of this one would need: ex-civil servants, especially Sir D Allen; ex-ministers.

1 Joel Barnett: Labour MP for Heywood and Royton 1964–83; Chief Secretary to the Treasury 1974–9; later Baron Barnett of Heywood and Royton.
2 Jack Diamond: Labour MP for Blackley 1945–51, for Gloucester 1957–70; Chief Secretary to the Treasury 1964–70; later Baron Diamond of the City of Gloucester and leader of the SDP in the Lords 1982–8.

Despite mounting speculation, aided by the Prime Minister himself, Callaghan kept the date of the election so close to his chest that even his closest colleagues were surprised when on 7 September he came to Cabinet and announced his decision that it would be in spring 1979, letting the government run its maximum legal term. He thought Labour had at least as good a chance of winning next year as this. He had, however, bargained without there being what became known as 'the winter of discontent'.

SHUFFLE MUSINGS – HY HIMSELF
[no date]

The next Callaghan Cabinet will probably look a lot different from this one[1]. What intrigues, more than speculating about who goes where under the Labour majority, is what Jim would do if he had to look to the Liberals again. Would Steel be content to spend another four–five years on the fringe of power? I suspect not. I would expect him to be given a Cabinet job – Home Secretary perhaps. Look at his speech last weekend again. He was talking about 'a common programme', 'a joint programme'. Cledwyn Hughes[2] tells me that Callaghan and Steel are now mutually very admiring. They will each go into the election talking about their own way forward. But afterwards, says Cledwyn, Labour moderates hope very much to see the pact renewed as a way towards their big dream – a realignment of the parties and a dropping of the *Tribune* and ultra-left fringe. They see Steel as an indistinguishable social democrat – more now than ever before. Cledwyn accepts that much depends on the party arithmetic after an election, but says it would be the height of cynicism for a victorious Jim to throw Steel over simply because he didn't need him and 'after all he's done'. To which I said such things do happen.

Back to Labour – any shuffle must start with what happens to Healey. This sort of consequences game, by the way, is how Callaghan, ever the tactician, says he does it. Does Callaghan see Healey as the next PM? In say two–three years? What sort of PLP will there be? My hunch is that Denis will go to the FCO and ponce around as a world figure, whatever he says about fag ends. It's an unfulfilled ambition which must appeal. And he did start as international secretary to the party at Transport House, he is fond of reminding one. And he does keep up very

---

1 Commentators expected a shuffle, but in the event practically the only change that autumn was a simple one: Edmund Dell stepped down as Trade Secretary, and the young John Smith replaced him. However, the reshuffle speculation went on till March.

2 Cledwyn Hughes: Labour MP for Anglesey 1951–79; later Baron Cledwyn of Penrhos.

closely with the American domestic scene above and beyond the needs of a Chancellor – lunching US contacts at No. 11 as they pass through London.

Owen could go to Defence – his prime interest before office. Mulley, who he says has never done anything long enough to take either the blame or credit for anything that has started, could keep up his record by a stint somewhere else – it hardly matters where.

The big problem is who to put in the Treasury. Joel I think not. He wants a big spending department, he told me. He could go to Environment, or Education, or Health and Social Security. I would put a small bet on Hattersley. He is a right thinker to the Callaghan camp, not admired by Healey, the right age, and had been brought on by Jim as stand-in chairman of the Cabinet incomes-policy committee. Healey would push Shore for the job, but what about his siege-economy ideas? PM also admires Shore and wants to advance him at the expense of Benn. Merlyn [Rees] is due for a change. He could become Lord President easily – he likes charging about the Commons and being gregarious. What about Foot for the Treasury? Has tired of leading the Commons, but must have some ambition. And the Prime Minister owes him a lot. Depends on what he wants I suppose. I must lunch him. Maybe Owen will go to the Treasury – what a dreary prospect! If he does, it would clearly mean that Jim sees him as the next-but-one leader, which would mean that Owen would have to build a party base fast at Westminster and start saying hello to Labour hacks in corridors instead of looking through them. All the signs of Jenkins grandeur ruining him I fear.

Shirley, alas, doesn't have much credit to cash. The moderates despair of her. Say she's likely to throw it all in and become principal of some college, I forget which. Who succeeds Rab?[1] Benn must have a change. And he has behaved himself. Something where the fact that he is nuts won't matter too much – Environment maybe. Poor man. Jim's chances of success could ruin Benn for ever. No Labour wreck to take over for a long time. Employment would be a good job for Benn. Let him solve the lack of it and find a way of coping with the coming silicon chip revolution, about which Jim is already much perplexed and Benn very agitated.

Stray thoughts – Bruce Millan, colourless man but rated a top-flyer in the Whitehall game, 'absolutely brilliant with civil servants and mastering complex briefs' I'm told, could be advanced. That would let John Smith in as Scottish Secretary.

John Silkin must expect promotion. He's so full of beans about his Brussels games and is terribly ambitious.

---

1 Lord Butler of Saffron Walden (formerly R. A. Butler), now master of Trinity College, Cambridge.

Roy Mason could get a big job – Home Secretary is an obvious one. Has got a lot of mileage in him. Still shuns a political adviser. Reads all his Cabinet papers every Wednesday night and seems to do all right.

I think Jim would break up the DHSS by the way. Orme told me it's very much on the cards. Also talk of splitting Treasury functions, says Denzil[1] – giving the Chief Secretary his own department.

Where's the next Labour Lord Chancellor? John Morris maybe? He's rated highly in the same way as Millan and is also a creeper and a member of the government's Welsh mafia.

WILLIAM RODGERS
[no date]

CALLAGHAN The offices that Jim has held in the past have been very important. Having held the three great offices below prime minister, he has a degree of sheer knowledge which is not easy to match. Maybe we don't remember more than 10 per cent of what happened five years ago, but in his case it is a large 10 per cent. In particular, he knows the Treasury, and how to protect Chancellors – both against their colleagues and also against their officials.

Given his own failure at the Treasury, the legacy is important. First, he is quite determined to erase his memories of 1967. Secondly, and touchingly, he likes to parade his economic knowledge. For some reason he thinks I know something about economics. This is quite erroneous. But on one occasion he was chatting to me and taking enormous pleasure in regaling me with some recondite explanation of a corner of monetary economics, as if to prove that he really knew what the Treasury was all about.

A minor consequence of his never having held junior office (per HY) is that he does not know what it is to be a minor member of the Cabinet: the geography of the table is such that, if you are not one of the eight people right in front of him or one of the two at his side, it is very hard to say anything unless you have a paper to present. The casual nod or word is virtually impossible. Especially for me: sitting at the end of the table with Lever and Hunt between me and him. The one is always leaning back, the other leaning forward. On the other hand, Jim is exceptionally good about giving a hearing to even the meanest member of the team. Even the stupid and unimportant (e.g. Peart)[2] is given his say if he wants

1 Denzil Davies: Labour MP for Llanelli 1970–2005; Minister of State at the Treasury 1975–9.
2 Fred Peart: Labour MP for Workington 1954–76; later Baron Peart of Workington and Leader of the House of Lords 1976–9.

it. In this way Jim brings everyone along with him. I think it is not entirely for show, either. On big issues, he genuinely wants to hear what everyone thinks, he does not necessarily know exactly what he wants to do, he genuinely wants to take the voices. He is a very good listener. On small things he likes to get his way. But the big things get discussed.

Another feature of his style is that the Cabinet makes decisions. Very rarely does something come back for a second time. This contrasts with Wilson. A similar contrast relates to their treatment of people. Wilson was a corrupter. He corrupted decent men like Varley and Kaufman, who have actually made something of a comeback under Jim's more appreciative and straightforward manner.

Related to this is the absence of faction. Although there are people who I agree with and who talk sense more than others – like Edmund Dell – we simply do not meet beforehand. There is no preparation of positions, despite important matters on which there will be disagreements. This again is inspired by Jim's own style. Unlike Wilson, who was always plotting, and thus inducing everyone else to plot, Jim is not.

I think I understand how political a person he is. For example, I have helped him over Benn, by consciously setting up right-wing positions as a polar opposite from Benn, so that Jim can claim to be taking the middle course. When the direct-elections business was at its height, I wanted to make a strong speech, and had prepared it. But Benn was also anxious to make an outright attack on the discipline Jim was imposing on us. So I said I would renounce my speech on condition that Benn renounced his.

Jim is a populist. He is conscious of this, welcomes the description. This means that on many issues he is well to the right of me. But nevertheless he is a man for the moment. He has produced stability, a stable style and stable government. What he believes in is the regeneration of industry. He likes the company of businessmen, feels at home with them, shares most of the same attitudes. He likes them almost as much as he likes the Labour Party. What he cannot abide is the long-haired intellectual and all his works.

His relations with colleagues are interesting. It is a quite young Cabinet, and when it assembled last year was quite a boisterous one. He lets us have our heads, but somehow we all keep in line. The only egalitarian relationship in the Cabinet is with Denis. I don't know quite how much interchange they have, but at the Cabinet they have a relaxed and mutually understanding relationship. Denis is no threat to Jim. Jim allows Denis to take the lead. In a recent discussion about something impossibly complicated, like pensions in the nationalized industries, Denis effortlessly took over summing up – 'Perhaps I could sum up for you, Prime Minister' – and Jim felt no acrimony, nor was any intended. (Mostly the

Cabinet proceeds on Christian name terms, and Denis likes to use 'PM' when it suits the chemistry.)

With Foot, JC manipulates him. There is no equality there. With Shore he has used fairly assiduous cultivation: giving him jobs, letting him in on talks, asking for his view. Shore is not a strong person, not very assertive, but Jim values him. His motive here has been to isolate Benn. It began during the IMF business, and has gone on. Benn is now totally isolated, a lone voice. With Varley – JC probably recognizes that he is not the most dynamic of men, and rather soft although totally upright. Knowing this, he allows him to continue. With Owen – Owen is a protégé. Also, says Rodgers, totally unprincipled: now, for example, talks hotly about Europe, but was nowhere to be seen in the earlier days when the going got rough for the Jenkinsites.

Has he made any blunders? No doubt that the Jay affair was a monumental blunder. No justification for it at any level. Based on quite a false notion of the importance of ambassadors anyway. Got talked into it by Owen. A big mistake.

People often get impatient with Jim. Dell, for example. Expresses a real intellectual disagreement. But Jim does not slap him down, will listen to him. He doesn't actually mind strong views. Cf. Wilson – who kept Rodgers out in the cold for years because of supposed disloyalties.

1979

16 January	The Shah and his family flee Iran for exile; Ayatollah Khomeini returns.
2 March	In a referendum, the Scots vote for a Scottish Assembly in Edinburgh; the Welsh vote against a separate forum.
26 March	Egypt and Israel sign a peace treaty in Washington.
28 March	The Labour government loses a parliamentary 'no confidence' vote and is forced to call election.
30 March	A terrorist car bomb kills Airey Neave, Tory MP and senior aide to Margaret Thatcher.
2 April	The Vietnamese invade Cambodia and reveal mass graves from the Pol Pot regime.
4 April	Military rulers hang deposed Pakistani premier Zulfikar Ali Bhutto.
24 April	Abel Muzorewa becomes Rhodesia's first black prime minister.
4 May	Margaret Thatcher becomes the first woman prime minister of the UK.
8 June	The first direct elections for the European Parliament.
22 June	Former Liberal leader Jeremy Thorpe is cleared of conspiracy to murder.
27 August	Earl Mountbatten and three others are killed by a Provisional IRA bomb.
4 November	Iranians storm the US embassy in Tehran and take 100 people hostage.
13 November	*The Times* and (days later) the *Sunday Times* begin publishing again after eleven months.
24 December	The Soviet Union invades Afghanistan.
Deaths	Gracie Fields, Reginald Maudling, Mary Pickford, Jean Renoir, Barnes Wallis, John Wayne

With the Sunday Times *not published until November, HY was under little pressure to interview even his regulars.*

In the general election on 3 May, the Conservatives won 339 seats – a net gain of 62 seats – and Labour 269 seats – a net loss of 50. But in votes cast the Conservatives were way ahead, with 13,697,000 against Labour's 11,532,000. All parties except the Conservatives generally made a poor showing, the Liberals losing 3 seats and the Scottish National Party 9 seats.

ANDREW ROWE
Lunch, 13 September 1979

CENTRAL OFFICE McAlpine is a demon for the cost of office space. This is one reason why the CRD is planned to move in. But it may yet not happen. The present CRD director, Alan Howarth,[1] was Thorneycroft's[2] personal assistant: definitely committed to right-wing economics, though perhaps not so politically motivated as Chris Patten! A former teacher (?). Superior in rank to Tristan Garel-Jones, a young man with a lot of money and now MP for Watford. Says he wants to move on well before another election is in the offing.

His department was seen to have done 'best of all' in the election. Best proportion of young voters, best proportion of TU votes, much better proportion of blacks than anyone thought possible. Cites Huddersfield East as one instance showing this.

THATCHER STAFF ETC. Says Hoskyns[3] not so bad as I paint him. But Rowe didn't know that he was the author of *Stepping Stones* – a document whose title he certainly recognized. Claims that Hoskyns has been educated. Says he was the first drafter of Thatcher's successful speech to the Tory TU conference (which fell during the election, I think): it was subsequently gone over by Rowe's department, but Hoskyns had a big hand in it.

Sees Hoskyns as evidence that Thatcher is very keen on businessmen. No doubt she likes people who've done well in big efficient firms (Rayner);[4] but she also believes that successful small businessmen are

1 Alan Howarth: private secretary to the Conservative chairman 1975–9; director of the Conservative Research Department 1979–81; became MP for Stratford-upon-Avon in 1983, defecting to Labour in 1995.
2 Peter Thorneycroft, former minister in the Macmillan government, and later Baron Thorneycroft of Dunston, was party chairman from 1975 (when Thatcher became leader) to 1981.
3 Sir John Hoskyns: soldier, businessman; adviser to Mrs Thatcher and the Shadow Cabinet 1977–9; author of the *Stepping Stones* document summing up the strategy for winning the 1979 election.
4 Derek Rayner: joint managing director of Marks & Spencer 1973–91; adviser to the PM on efficiency, 1979–83; later Baron Rayner of Crowborough.

great men. Hoskyns not only was one, but became one as a consultant advising others on how to become successful small businessmen. Says Nigel Vinson[1] is another; he mainly financed the CPS. Was successful by exploiting some kind of invention (plastic boxes).

These people, he claims, are much nicer than the odious Alfred Sherman, whose racist passions are unabated. Sherman went to speak to the FCS [Federation of Conservative Students] this year. Got a big reception for his Adam Smith economics. Thinking he had the audience in his hand, he then moved on to the racial question – and got hissed and whistled.

SELECTION   An interesting perception. Says that the constituencies who are best at it are the ones where it matters least – those which are safe Labour seats, therefore constantly selecting. The ones which matter, the safe Tory seats, only do it once in a while – and simply do not know how to go about it . . . With some bad results in consequence.

MARK CARLISLE
26 September 1979

He was astonished to get into the Cabinet. Even after last November, when he was made shadow DES, he still thought that Maude or even perhaps Joseph would get the DES. Also, both Boyson and Janet Young had been canvassed, and he has these two junior ministers who might have expected to have his job. He was a well-known Heathite, never close to Thatcher. He had been thinking that if all he was offered was again number two at the Home Office he might not accept it. Expected her, with her attractive loyalty to people who have been with her, to keep Havers and Percival[2] as law officers, which is what I guess he would really have expected. However – here he is.

June was hell, so was May. He was at the office until 11.00 at night the first Saturday, with Hamilton. He was on the brink of a teachers' strike, had to get two sides of Burnham[3] together, had to make a first-day speech in the Queen's Speech debate, had his first bill on the timetable. He felt very overdone. Now he is enjoying it, at last feels as though he knows what he is doing.

---

1 Nigel Vinson: businessman, financier; founder-director of the Centre for Policy Studies; later Baron Vinson of Roddam Dene. His *Who's Who* entry says, 'Plastic Coatings Ltd, started in a Nissen hut, 1952.'
2 Sir Ian Percival, QC: Conservative MP for Southport 1959–87; Solicitor General 1979–83.
3 The Burnham committee on salaries in secondary schools.

THATCHER   Did interfere a lot at the DES at the start. She knows the department very well. Less so now, as international commitments consume more and more of her time. She works fantastically hard. Her staff adore her because she cares about them (cf. Heath). She will probably have to accumulate more political staffing. She seems to have no kitchen cabinet, no intimates – a loner.

HAYDEN PHILLIPS
30 October 1979

In charge of terrorism, N. Ireland, Euro aspects of, at the Home Office. Had two years with Jenkins at the EEC, leaving last February: that made five years with one minister – the outer limit of what is advisable in a Civil Service career. Robert Armstrong gave him this job, which is what he wanted and what in a sense his Euro experience trained him for.

WHITELAW   is a joy to work for because he is, surprisingly, very decisive. Very keen on making decisions. Unlike Merlyn Rees, who tended to call two-day conferences on things, and then be quite unable to make up his mind. With WW, you can go in with a list of things to be decided, the pros and cons written down, and get him to talk and decide without referring to anyone else. A bit of a change in the Home Office as a whole – which used to be committed to endless upward referring, endless meetings. Hayden thinks it's the best HO team for many years, with Leon Brittan and Timothy Raison. No longer a parking lot for even one old sweat.

One of Whitelaw's greatest qualities is that the more serious the crisis he has to deal with, the more frivolous and jokey he becomes. A great defuser, very helpful to everyone in this way.

THATCHER   No other PM of modern times has been more prepared to live with short-term political unpopularity. That is her distinguishing feature, as observed by one civil servant.

JENKINS   Does want, HP thinks, to come back to politics. If drafted, he might stay on for two more years as president, but doesn't want to. In many ways Europe has not suited his style. In the end the creature of other governments, a responder mainly to their initiatives. A corridor, elbow-squeezing role, rather than getting out front and addressing the people. His whole being really is as a political man, and that presumably is what he would still like to do. But he knows the pitfalls . . . and he must get into Parliament . . .

EEC The [John] Silkin line was really hopeless. Literally used to go in
and start shouting. That was all there was to his policy. Other ministers
adopted a modified form of this. But others again, pro-Marketeers, adopted
quite a different line. There was therefore no concerted policy, and this
seriously weakened the credibility of Britain's presence in Brussels etc.

The Tory line is probably more useful. But they must be prepared to
carry out their threats. Mrs T will get something but not everything
from Dublin.[1] She should then actually refuse to pay all the budget
contribution . . .

The EEC has never been in worse shape. First the policies that are
manifestly running out of steam: esp. CAP, the best illustration being
lamb. But also the general image. Brussels as pork barrel plus the home
of sumptuous living. The EEC as a gravy train does terrible harm to the
whole operation.

WILLIAM RODGERS
8 November 1979

Who will succeed? R is for Denis, as of this moment. Denis is very tough,
very clever, and there is no young pretender who stands out. Therefore
both I and Hattersley would swing in behind him. Denis said to me the
other day, What happens if I get first, Shore gets second, Benn gets third,
won't all Benn votes go to Shore? The answer Bill gave him was that Shore
would never get second. He has relatively few first-place nominations, but
a lot of seconds. It is therefore more likely to be Healey–Benn–Shore. Of
course there is also [John] Silkin. Totally bogus figure, a wet and feeble
chief whip, who was sacked because of it (sacked by Wilson?); a man
who did not even do his Market thing at all effectively in reality: yet who
got such a large number of votes at the PLP elections. People simply don't
know the truth about him. It is useful, though, to have another left-winger
to divert the Benn movement. Denis would have virtues Callaghan does
not possess: in particular, he never bears grudges. Unlike Wilson and
Callaghan, who made it a lifestyle. Extraordinary how Denis does not.

ROY JENKINS There was talk of him wanting to return, via Speaker
Thomas's seat.[2] But apparently he says he does not really want to return
to Labour politics. What about politics, though? Bill admits that Roy
seems not to have lost the urge. But he says that he does not think in the

---

1 The European Communities summit in Dublin on 29–30 November.
2 George Thomas: Labour MP for Cardiff Central 1945–50, for Cardiff West 1950–83; Speaker of the House
of Commons 1976–83; later Viscount Thomas of Tonypandy.

end Roy is a big enough risk-taker. That he will not embark on the massive job which would be entailed in trying to mobilize a centre consensus. In his Dimbleby lecture he will be advocating PR, but Bill can't remember what else – nor whether it could be called a speech which was that of a big man trying to push his way in. Anyway, Bill says he would have to conspicuously not support Roy, much as he admires him and believes in his enormous skills, especially in Parliament. He thinks Roy may have missed the boat even as far back as 1968, when Roy said to Bill that he could at the moment unhorse Wilson. But he didn't try. For it to work, it would need a substantial defection led by Rodgers – who else? If Rodgers won't do it, who will?

When Callaghan took over, he offered Rodgers the no. 2 job at the Home Office. Rodgers refused, saying that he would only make one more move and that was into the Cabinet: also thinking that he would in no circumstances be corralled with Jenkins. Callaghan said this was very inconvenient. Rodgers said he didn't mind going to the back benches. Callaghan said, The thing about you is that you're a fighter, unlike Roy Jenkins. Six months later Bill was in the Cabinet.

SHIRLEY WILLIAMS He and Shirley ran the Oxford Labour Club together. He knows her better than anyone else in the world does, she says. They have a love–hate relationship, but more love than hate. He has promised to be her Chancellor, and she his – except that whenever the latter comes up in their speculations she seems to be backing off. She is the most ambitious person he knows in politics. For that reason, he was astonished and admiring at her reception to defeat.[1] Took it far better than anyone else he could think of, and far better than such an ambitious person normally would. Beneath her public hesitations, he thinks she is quite determined to get back into the House. She is doing lots of political things, stayed on the NEC etc.

---

1   Shirley Williams lost her Hertford and Stevenage seat in the 1979 general election.

PART TWO

1980–1990

The Thatcher
Governments

1980

22 January	Soviet scientist and campaigner Andrei Sakharov arrested in Moscow.
21 March	The US announces a boycott of the Moscow Olympics. Despite a plea from Mrs Thatcher, British athletes refuse to boycott the games.
25 April	A US bid to rescue the Tehran hostages ends in disaster.
5 May	The SAS storms the Iranian embassy in Knightsbridge to free nineteen hostages being held in a siege by Iranian Arab separatists.
4 March	Robert Mugabe is elected premier of Zimbabwe.
18 May	Mount St Helens erupts in Washington State.
17 September	The Solidarity trade union defies the Communist regime in Poland.
22 September	Iraq border war with Iran flares into open hostility.
15 October	James Callaghan resigns as Labour leader.
21 October	William Golding trumps Anthony Burgess with *Rites of Passage* in a contest which makes the Booker Prize a fixture on the media calendar.
4 November	Ronald Reagan, the Republican candidate, wins the US presidency.
10 November	Michael Foot takes over the Labour Party, with Denis Healey as deputy.
8 December	John Lennon shot dead in New York.
Deaths	Cecil Beaton, Billy Butlin, Alfred Hitchcock, Steve McQueen, Oswald Mosley, Jean-Paul Sartre, Peter Sellers, Graham Sutherland, Josip Broz Tito of Yugoslavia, Kenneth Tynan, Mae West

Margaret Thatcher's Conservative administration was learning to face up to what government, as opposed to opposition, actually meant, even with a majority of over 43. Inflation and the economy dominated much

*of the early 1980s, as they had the previous decade. Thatcher herself
had to cope with the 'wets', whose form of liberal Toryism she abhorred.
The phrase 'U-turn', already in the political language, rapidly became
a political cliché. Meanwhile the Labour Party faced an upheaval with
the call by Roy Jenkins for realignment.*

CHRIS PATTEN
3 January 1980

STEEL PAY Has all the possibility of a first U-turn. Of course BSC
[British Steel Corporation] can't afford it, but then things are never black
and white. The art of politics, says HY, is the search for the right shade
of grey. Therefore there will probably have to be another per cent or
two. And of course, they are not copping out; they can't. Not without
significance that both Joseph[1] and Thatcher gave substantial TV interviews about it.

However, they do make rods for their own backs. At the 1922 [Com-
mittee] before her Washington visit, Mrs T made a great virtue of not
having had beer and sandwiches sessions at No. 10.[2] A great plus point
she thought, and there were some cheers. But surely they need to talk to
people? Not saying that industrial relations should be conducted by either
Wilberforce or by a combination of Churchill and Monckton.[3]

PUBLIC SPENDING Looks as though they are looking for another
billion in '80–81, and another 2 billion in 81–2. There are three things
you can do, given the commitment to increase defence (and the much less
justifiable commitment to spend more on anything to do with law and
order – defence has got more sellable and more justifiable after Afghanistan: where will the Russians go next – Yugoslavia?). Either you can do
the old Treasury thing of 5 per cent all round: CP would strongly oppose
this. Or you can uncouple benefits from the RPI [Retail Price Index]. Or
you can take it out of public-sector pay. CP prefers the latter of course –
mainly because in vast areas of public sector, especially the NHS, there
is job security which no one else really enjoys. Better to squeeze public
pay than hit benefits, at a time when inflation is still bad and when
unemployment is going up – unemployment, moreover, of people who

1 Sir Keith Joseph, Industry Secretary since the election.
2 In the Old Labour world of Harold Wilson and James Callaghan, beer and sandwiches appeared so often as
refreshment during talks with union leaders that the term 'beer and sandwiches' became a form of shorthand for
government-workforce dispute settlement.
3 Sir Walter Monckton: Conservative MP for Bristol West 1951–7; Minister of Labour and National Service
in Churchill's 1951–5 government; later Viscount Monckton of Brenchley.

want to work (perhaps unlike the position hitherto). But the savings from uncoupling from the RPI are admittedly attractive. What *should* happen (but won't) is to take it out of public-sector pay and increase child benefit. On child benefit, note that Lawson (despite his complicity on Rooker-Wise)[1] is always a strong opponent of the 'family policy' reasons for increasing child benefit. In public-sector pensions – probably not worth doing. The benefits would be long in coming, and in any case you are not just hitting the permanent sectors, but thousands of nurses and other lower-level workers.

MRS T   How very like Heath she is. See the business in the summer of denying that there were any real cuts taking place. This was very much *her* line, and very Heath-like. One of the results has been that the back benches are still thirsting for more cuts – but only, of course, in principle. The early day motions asking for the savings of various particular items go on a pace . . .

FRANCIS PYM
22 January 1980

Thatcher will burn herself out unless she is careful: but must admit that the opposite seems to be the case at present – the more she demands and does, the greater the reserves of energy to do them. One failing: she takes a hell of a long time to dispatch the business very often. Wants to go through all the arguments – not so much to let everyone have their say as to get her own mind straight. This takes much time. It was just the same in the Shadow Cabinet.

DAVID STEEL
26 February 1980

Hoggart story[2] is quite untrue – that the Liberals are preparing to be submerged into a vast centre party under Roy Jenkins . . .

But: DS is interested in an alliance, willing to consider electoral pacts. Recognizes that to have Roy on the team also would add enormously to Liberal credibility. But knows RJ is not simply going to join the Liberals.

---

1 The Rooker–Wise amendment to the 1977 Finance Act, introduced by Labour MPs Jeff Rooker and Audrey Wise, ensured an increase in personal allowances in line with inflation.

2 A *Guardian* op-ed page piece on 21 February 1980, by Simon Hoggart, examined the 'tactical preparations for a marriage of interests' between Roy Jenkins and the Liberals. It was headed 'Pre-marital relations'.

Waiting for him to announce himself more clearly, which he thinks will not be until the end of the year (he did not know about the Birmingham speech).[1] Says Dimbleby lecture[2] came too soon, before any follow-through could be done. But 'his people are working away' (whoever they are).

The big plus about Dimbleby was the commitment to PR. This makes it possible to talk turkey. But it has to be done in a way that the Liberals can get something out of – they got nothing out of Lincoln, as Taverne now admits to have been an error.[3] Setting up new parties is not at all easy, as Taverne showed.

Moreover, it would be foolish to think that more than one or two Labours MPs will come across to Roy. Maybe some significant figures in the Labour Party in the country. In local government more likely.

Liberals are divided on the Jenkins issue: the purists will have none of it . . . DS disagrees.

HY had taken little interest in political matters outside Britain, but certain issues could not be ignored. Africa in general and now Rhodesia in particular saw him making notes. In the United States, Jimmy Carter was in what would prove to be his final months as president. Riding into sharp focus was his Republican successor, the former Hollywood actor Ronald Reagan.

IAN GILMOUR
7 March 1980

RHODESIA We did want Nkomo very badly. Nkomo is a bigger, though less intelligent, man than Mugabe.[4] I.e. he is a conciliator, a compromiser, someone who can bring people together. What happens now to him is the most important thing by far. The split between him

---

1 What – if anything – Roy Jenkins said in Birmingham was barely reported. But commentators already knew of his intentions. A commentary by Peter Jenkins in the *Guardian* on 30 January 1980 predicted that Jenkins might well serve 'as the midwife of a new politics'.

2 Roy Jenkins's 1979 Dimbleby lecture – entitled 'Home Thoughts from Abroad', because Jenkins was at the time president of the European Commission in Brussels – appealed to the 'radical centre' to save the nation from the sterilities of left and right, and led to the foundation of the Social Democratic Party.

3 Dick Taverne resigned from the Labour Party in October 1972 after ten years as MP for Lincoln, following a dispute with his constituency party over Europe (he was a pro-European). He regained the seat (as Democratic Labour candidate) in a by-election in March 1973, won again in February 1974, but lost the seat in October 1974.

4 Joshua Nkomo, the first modern nationalist leader in Zimbabwe, had been an ally of Robert Mugabe, who became the independent Zimbabwe's first prime minister in 1980.

and Mugabe has grown deep. It became pretty bad at Lancaster House,[1] but by the end of the election campaign Nkomo was saying he could never again work with Mugabe. Joshua, however, is a good old-fashioned Tory politician. However, Mugabe's win presents an opportunity. We must pile in with what we can. The problem is that they need money and we don't have much of it, or so the Treasury tells us. We can give military advice etc., and should do.

At Lancaster House Mugabe's line was often irritating. He is a great proceduralist, rather like Michael English[2] in the House of Commons. Forever making points of order, as a device. Very boring.

Thinks Nkomo must be a deputy prime minister, with a decent portfolio. The presidency is not much: only command of troops in a state of emergency. There was an argument about this at LH, with an argument being put for a powerful president alongside a powerful prime minister. This was entirely devised as an idea to accommodate two powerful people – Josh and Robert – who might need to have suitable jobs. But in the end it was not put in, and the British did not really believe in it anyway.

Negotiating with the PF[3] was sometimes amusing. One could have good arguments, and they enjoyed them. Unlike Smith, who is just a copper-bottom bastard, and Muzorewa, who could never say anything in the PF's presence – which is why all the talks had to be bilaterals.

Biggest bastard of all has been Nyerere.[4] From the start. It seemed he did not really want LH to succeed, or the election. A real little hypocrite. He was denouncing us for breaking the LH terms around Christmas, simultaneously with flying thousands of ZANLA[5] troops down to Mozambique to penetrate Rhodesia.

Amery[6] is a very bad man. We have evidence of really perfidious intriguing for a long time, quite unjustifiable on any basis whatever. But he is pretty sound on domestic affairs ... On foreign affairs he will no doubt start being bad on the Middle East now.

One perception of Nyerere: likened him to Libya or Algeria in re Palestine – a leader without any contiguous border with the scene of the action, therefore able to meddle with impunity ...

1 The Lancaster House accord, signed on 21 December 1979, resulted in the white southern Rhodesians accepting majority rule. It was chaired by Lord Carrington, then Foreign Secretary.
2 Michael English: Labour MP for Nottingham West 1964–83.
3 The full title: Zimbabwe African National Union – Patriotic Front (ZANU–PF), led by Robert Mugabe.
4 Dr Julius Nyerere, president of Tanzania, and a key player in the settlement of the Rhodesian crisis. When he died, the BBC called him 'the voice of conscience in Africa'.
5 The Zimbabwe African National Liberation Army, led by Mugabe: the military arm of ZANU.
6 Presumably Julian Amery MP (see earlier), member of the right-wing Monday Club, and co-author of a political paper Rhodesia and the Threat to the West.

A point about the Treasury team: it is the weakest in living memory.[1] Geoffrey [Howe] is not good, just not in command and not a real believer either. John Biffen is a very nice and sensible man, but quiescent and so deeply pessimistic about the value of anything. Lawson is brash and unpopular.

A point about the Thatcher style: one problem of having a majority of the Cabinet against her is that things are done in small groups . . .

DAVID OWEN
20 March 1980

Very friendly, open, anecdotal, pensive, a nice mixture of seriousness and less solemnity than before.

Has a lot of time for Benn, as always. Says he is all-square with him on anti-establishment politics and on open government. But the trouble is that Benn corrupts essentially good positions. For example, latest attacks on lack of control on police put him on a good issue, but he is crazy to go around saying there is some massive police plot. If the leadership is thrown to conference, then Benn would be in with a chance.

LEADERS Thinks Callaghan will go this year. Says he should do, and do so in some favour. Would be good to go out having had a much better year than last, having won at conference: esteem would rightly attach to him – the manner of his departure is vital, and if it is on a low note it can make a man nothing: see Wilson. If, on the other hand, JC has a bad conference there would be a case for him staying on. Wants Denis to succeed. DO would not stand if Denis was for real. Thinks that others wouldn't either. But no one can be sure. If the right wipes its slate down to one man, there will be an incentive for the left to do so as well. This could be Foot. Shore must be saying to himself, My time is not yet come. Benn would have to stand against anyone but Foot: and if he stood would be humiliated, therefore must like the idea of Foot as a stopgap. Silkin[2] thinks Shore owes him a favour – for he stood down for Shore after they tied in Shadow Cabinet elections in 1971 or 1972. They are, in a way, friends, those two. Shore the more intelligent politician – but a man who always comes late into an issue. Very important political trait. In fact a real nationalist, with attitudes very similar indeed to Enoch Powell,

1 Sir Geoffrey Howe was Chancellor of the Exchequer from 1979 to 1983; John Biffen was Chief Secretary to the Treasury 1979–81; Nigel Lawson was Financial Secretary to the Treasury 1979–81.
2 John Silkin unsuccessfully campaigned for the Labour leadership when James Callaghan resigned in 1980. Michael Foot emerged the winner.

including on race (says very little about South Africa, you will notice). On foreign affairs, only interested in Europe, it seems. Silkin is a man who would be a reformer on things like open government, if enough people were too. The only man likely to be PM who could be put in that category.

DAVID MARQUAND
3 June 1980

If Jenkins is serious, he should not retreat. I have dropped him notes to this effect. Of course he is not necessarily the central figure in any new party. He is a catalyst, however. Clearly he cannot start a viable new movement in British politics all by himself. It still really all depends on the other people: Bill Rodgers most of all, and Shirley. Especially Bill. Shirley is unlikely to do anything if Bill doesn't fit; if Bill does, that puts Shirley on the spot. Bill is the stronger of the two, the more likely to be decisive.

If Callaghan went in the autumn and Healey succeeded, that would be the worst possible scenario for Jenkins. That would presume the conference also went Callaghan's way. Bill might then feel that the Labour Party was sorting itself out. Also, Bill is the only key person in the HC. He could bring a few, perhaps very few, other MPs with him.

The thing about Bill is that he has always understood that it is really all about power. It is not just a matter of the constitution and the changes there. Therefore he is, of all of us, the least fastidious about the unions. He is in that sense an old-fashioned 1950s Labour politician. Isn't upset by winning via the unions. This is what he did with CDS,[1] which was founded twenty years ago. He in a sense still sees another Gaitskell being propelled forward with compliant union leaders. Shirley is much more scathing about the unions than Bill is. On the other hand, it follows from this that Bill is more tough-minded about the triviality of being saved on the constitutional question. Says that even if we win on that, the problem is not over.

LIBERALS will not take kindly to Jenkins coming in and taking over a plum by-election. DM used to think that it was necessary to fight a by-election. Now not so sure, because it just may not be possible. The reason for fighting one was twofold: to show that people will *vote* for a Jenkins-type party, and do not just show themselves to favour one in

---

1 The Campaign for Democratic Socialism, formed by Rodgers and others in the 1950s, during a divisive period in the Labour Party under Hugh Gaitskell's leadership.

opinion polls, which do not matter a damn. Also, Jenkins needs to descend into the arena and get some votes.

However, a fourth party must stand for something. What, in DM's view, it would stand for among other things would be a challenge to the two-party establishment, a revival of democracy, favouring political and constitutional changes, libertarian, decentralized. But to stand on this ground and walk in as a fat carpetbagger might be to get off to quite the wrong start. It's contradictory.

It would follow from this that the only way (per HY) might be that Labour must split. But what do you mean by split? says DM.

What Labour has to face is the quite frightening possibility that the Liberals now have more active workers than Labour does. Healey puts the Labour activist figure at 250,000. It may be far less. Liberals may be at least as high as that. So it is not exactly a question of splitting the Labour Party but of moving into a vacuum which exists in Labour-type politics.

The Liberals could say, What have you got to offer? Probably a fourth party cannot establish itself unless the Liberals are ready to accept it. Yet they want to keep separate. So what's in it for the Libs? One answer: You, the Libs, have been plugging away for years and have now established solid bases around the country but predominately in Tory areas. You are now better placed than in the equivalent period of 1970–71, but the experience of 74–9 shows how incredibly difficult it is to achieve the objective, which is PR. For this you need fifty seats. What a fourth party has to offer is the potential grass-roots support of Labour areas, which Libs cannot now tap. Libs are strong in mainly Tory areas. A breakaway Labour Party could deliver the inner-city vote . . . the dissident working-class vote which now on the whole goes Tory not Liberal . . .

SHIRLEY WILLIAMS
6 June 1980

Today she, Rodgers and Owen have put together a joint statement in response to Silkin.[1] It is the first sign of the formation of a 'critical mass' on the Right which the party could not afford to lose. It says that, if the Silkin resolution is passed by the conference, they can no longer stay in the Labour Party (or something like that). This is a serious statement of position, which she hopes will make various other groups concentrate their minds. Especially the unions. They must see that, while they could

1 John Silkin, Shadow Industry Secretary, had demanded outright withdrawal from the European Common Market.

afford to lose one of the three, they could not afford to lose all three: and that if there was a choice between this three and the Bennites, most unions of importance would not choose Benn. She does not overestimate the importance of the statement, but she thinks it worth taking seriously – i.e. they are thinking about a split as the option which would become credible if Silkin was passed. They disagree about minor nuances of the stance towards Europe, and these have been deliberately fudged in the statement: but on the whole they are of one mind.

How has this come about? Owen is the crucial one here. She and Rodgers had been pretty well of one mind before, Owen has been much shaken by his reception at the Wembley conference,[1] the fact that booing started even before he got on to the disarmament bit, the aggression shown by Silkin in putting his name to the anti-Market resolution. There are other reasons to be worried. One is the increasingly anti-parliamentarian rhetoric in which Benn engages. When he speaks about the primacy of the activists, he virtually parrots Lenin. He speaks a language which despises the ordinary party worker, again Lenin-like. The supremacy of party and activist is a central Leninist tenet, and Shirley believes she has read more Lenin and Marx than Benn has. She thinks he does not really know what he is saying. Also, that he is to some extent being used by people much harder than he is: Maynard-type, Richardson-type, Militant sympathizers.[2]

What the conference decides, in her view, will not be necessarily permanent. Labour conferences very rarely are. If it decides against all the Benn reforms and the Silkin resolution, these will not go away. The fight will be continued. However, it is clearly important that the conference gets it right. What should then happen is as follows. Healey should be elected leader. Callaghan must stand down – he is doing his reputation absolutely no good by staying on and obliterating the memory of what was, after all, a not-half-bad prime-ministership. Healey, however, has very little time. He does not want to be Leader of the Opposition, only to be PM – he has told Shirley this. This means 1984, not 1989, when he will be too old. Therefore he has only one year – 1981 – in which to knock the party into shape and dig a deep enough trench out of which Mrs T cannot escape. That is a very short time. He has to be brutal. He must first destroy the left by confronting them. How? By making the PLP

---

1 A special Labour Party conference on 31 May, attacking the government's economic strategy. It rapidly became a battleground between the Bennite left and the right wing over issues such as the House of Lords, Europe, union legislation, the police, defence policy, and nationalized industries. The Labour NEC summed up the issues with a document entitled *Peace, Jobs, Freedom*.

2 Joan Maynard MP: trade unionist; left-wing Labour MP for Sheffield Brightside 1974–87; nicknamed 'Stalin's granny' by political opponents. Josephine or Jo Richardson: Labour MP for Barking 1974–94; member of Labour's NEC and coordinator of the Keep Left group. The Militant Tendency was for a decade a significant Marxist force within the Labour Party.

assert itself and show some guts, viz. after last weekend's conference the PLP should have sent a letter to the NEC saying that it found the manifesto unacceptable, instead of pussyfooting around, which JC was eventually persuaded to do by Foot and others. The PLP has to stand up and accept a tough leadership which forces the unions to choose. SW believes that, faced with a choice, the unions must choose the anti-Benn group. But then comes stage 2. Healey must divest himself of union influence. Must detach himself from the politically damaging stigma attached thereto. This would be easier after stage 1: because on the whole unions respect strength and success, and besides not all of them actually want to run the government. But it is a twofold operation, which he has very little time to do. She believes that keeping the unions at arm's length is vital, not just politically but constitutionally. When she was at Education, they wanted to interfere in certain Education programmes, and were much displeased when she wouldn't let them. However, they respect a show of strength. She says she wouldn't go along with any closer relationship than existed last time around.

The Owen–Rodgers–Williams group would like Hattersley to join them, but would exclude Healey. They see themselves as having sunk personal ambition: to be lining up behind a set of policies, rather than jockeying for the leadership, which in any case none of them could get this time. This has happened at just the time the left are beginning to be riven by just these kinds of personal ambition. Silkin vying with Benn. Heffer[1] getting into the picture. And so on. They see Healey as the clear right-wing candidate, without in an energetic way backing him (since they think he is unreliable on Europe). They think that if they stick together – and go – then Mason would certainly be with them, and possibly Varley.

Further on Benn etc.: the appalling insularity of his position. Their loathing for EEC makes them forget that there is another world. Total preoccupation with Britain's domestic problems, as if these could be disconnected. Nothing about Brandt[2] (pathetic brevity of Third World references in the manifesto).

HY's interest in Margaret Thatcher, now in her second year as prime minister, would expand, resulting eventually in a book, One of Us, *widely judged one of the best assessments of her life and political beliefs. Here he describes a* Sunday Times *lunch with her.*

1 Eric Heffer: Labour MP for Liverpool Walton 1964–91; member of Labour's NEC 1975–86.
2 An influential report entitled *North–South: A Programme for Survival* was published in 1980 by a commission led by the German chancellor Willy Brandt.

MARGARET THATCHER
Lunch, the *Sunday Times*, 9 July 1980

Far less shrill than ever in living memory: cool, quieter, rather more galleon-like in appearance; very confident; very ready with facts and figures – but not to make special pleadings. On the contrary, she talks more like a woman who observes the economy from afar: who is therefore not remotely embarrassed by the short-term failures of the things to come right: who speaks of economic forces as if the government really had little influence upon their movement, and to the extent that it *did* have influence could only set the context within which the economic operators could move. Time after time she came back to the two great problems of the British economy: the monopoly nationalized industries and the monopoly unions. Also, she revealed the very fundamental attitude about Soviet expansion which she refuses to see in sophisticated terms but sees in very clear simple terms. She seems like a lady who considers herself to be doing a service to her country by letting it begin to exist within 'sensible' and 'realistic' economic disciplines: who sees her job as to lead public opinion in that direction, to achieve consent, to prepare the ground – but who is not ultimately responsible for the failure of particular firms to survive, or even of particular nationalized industries to settle at reasonable pay rates. She has no difficulty in keeping on with the policy: it's in her bones, and in her mind is her conviction that to take any steps back would be absolutely fatal for the country. She really does see herself finally tackling the legacy of numerous self-deceptions perpetrated on the economy by Labour governments. I found her impressive: in her lack of anxiety, above all, but also in her confidence. It was more a case of her sharing certain facts with us than trying to indicate, Wilson-like, that we poor fellows knew nothing and then blinding us with her own cleverness.

FOREIGN   Giscard is Olympian not patrician. You just have to work out the way to deal with each one of them. The most important fact is that there is a Schmidt–Giscard axis. This cannot become a three-sided axis, as I asked her, because it is Schmidt–Giscard not French–German. This is very worrying when one of the two is dubious about the whole alliance.

In the EEC, fishing is the next big thing. Remember, it was what almost kept us out in the first place.[1] Very difficult negotiation. Fishermen are not going to like it.

---

1 The Common Fisheries Policy, established in 1970 to share and conserve fish stocks within Europe's 200-mile economic zone, created political problems for nations with big fishing fleets, such as Britain and Norway. In the end, Norway stayed out of the EEC.

Scornful of HE's references to recycling of oil money etc.[1] Also, by implication, of Brandt. Says recycling has become a cliché. What is required for the poorest countries is straight aid. They cannot conceivably afford to borrow any money, even at soft rates from international institutions. All they need is aid. We give more aid per GNP than most countries, including Germany. We give more and more of it in multilateral aid, however. The Third World which comes to us for more often does not realize this. At Ottawa[2] we have agreed to look at the whole *structure* of aid, with this in mind. Says she is seeing Anderson[3] because it's a free world, and after all she was seen by many people when she was running for PM. Thinks US president is *not* an impossible job: thinks a lot of his problem is his isolation. Not being knocked about twice a week; not going to constituency, living in an isolated city and in an isolated enclave within that city.

Oil is the key to everything. Puts the inflation down mainly to oil rises.[4] Says the OPEC bust-up could be helpful because it is less of a cartel. Says the real sources of recycling of aid should be the oil countries. Iran is key to much of this, in turn. Japan and Germany, taking Britain's lead, have not taken Iran oil after it went up to 35 dollars.

HOME The sectors which are doing well, especially on exports, are those where union power is smallest. And vice versa. She sees a union stranglehold in various ways – notably in restrictive practices in the Civil Service. For example, why shouldn't a minister be able to say that ten of his undersecretaries are better than the other twenty: Second, pay them accordingly? Why shouldn't the Civil Service be able to pay computer people, who it is short of, more than others without there being a ripple effect throughout the grade? These are difficult problems. Wants them talked about, as a start. But a long-term challenge.

As well as the constant emphasis on the role of union power on the restrictive-practice front as well as the law front, there was a strange caution about what should be done next. At one point, in respect to me saying that perhaps the government should have done more while it could, she replied, 'I think we could have done pretty well anything this year.' She was wistful about this. Said it was a conscious softly-softly-catchee-monkey policy, repeated her doubts about it, said they would do more, but also said that it would not be next year.

1 Harold Evans, the then editor of the *Sunday Times*, writes, 'It probably is me. I wrote about Third World debt and ways to deal with it.'

2 Mrs Thatcher is looking ahead to the G7 summit in Ottawa July 20–21, 1981.

3 This is John B. Anderson, a former United States Republican Congressman who stood as an Independent candidate in the 1980 presidential election.

4 In July 1980 the annual rate of inflation – based on changes in the retail price index – was running at 16.9 per cent.

Always looking for ways in which to make the market work. Thus against nationalized industries because they destroy the market principle, unless imports can make a market, but said that coal and steel show how hard this is. Envies France, Germany and Luxembourg because they can simply get lorries in at numerous points around their borders. Make it far harder for really tough unions to keep rival black materials out.

Thinks that rates must be abolished. But this is yet another thing which cannot be done in this parliament. Says that one-third of ratepayers do not vote: businesses. Rates are biggest single tax on businesses. They have no vote. Also, claims that 44 per cent of council tenants either have rent subsidies or rate subsidies or are on social security which includes both. Quite amazing figure.

On redundancy, speaks of it as inevitable. But conscious of effects on people. A great proponent, it seems, of the black economy: speaks repeatedly of the cushioning effect this was having on unemployment. The only trouble with it was, it seemed, that it deterred people from moving to new jobs in different parts of the country. When challenged with the discrepancy between the Inland Revenue's attitude to scroungers etc. and to the black economy she said she had 79,000 Inland Revenue staff already and didn't want any more.

(In discussing public spending, her style was always to say, 'I've got so much here . . . I've got so much there.' Just like a housekeeper. More than 50 per cent is absolutely spoken for: OAPs and indexing of them, defence, police – absolutely untouchable.)

On Healey: totally amoral. Look at the way he has changed his mind. Clearly she finds such a man incomprehensibly bad. But she says that he would be the best leader in the House – although query the country: wouldn't they see through his lack of convictions?[1]

She'd rather have Tony Benn. But not much. Very acid about the fact that his children would have far more money than her children, and therefore had no business, we inferred, to be preaching egalitarianism.

'Biffenry' is one of my problems. His speeches are marvellous. But these phrases keep coming out.[2]

1 Denis Healey joined the Communist Party in 1937, left in 1939, joined the Labour Party in 1945, and acquired a reputation as a left-wing ideologue. He is frequently misquoted as having said, as Shadow Chancellor, that he would 'squeeze the rich until the pips squeak'. He subsequently negotiated an IMF loan during the sterling crisis and endorsed wage-control legislation, which was seen by the left as a betrayal.

2 John Biffen, then Chief Secretary to the Treasury, had a gift for memorable language not always appreciated by his Cabinet colleagues: in 1980 he warned the country to prepare for 'three years of unparalleled austerity'.

JAMES PRIOR
15 July 1980 (with John Fryer)[1]

As a result of developments, the Cabinet is more united now than it was a year ago. In a curious kind of way. A lot of people are 'building themselves up' in the Cabinet. Is this storing up trouble? I asked. Prior laughed and said, That's the question. The odd thing is, he added, that 'She hasn't really got a friend left in the whole Cabinet' – and yet it is in this way united. One reason she has no friend is that she subjects everyone to the most emotionally exhausting arguments; the other is that she still interrupts everyone all the time. It makes us all absolutely furious, says Jim. And there is also conviction while surrendering some of her policies. This, says, Jim is good politics: it helps her in the party, it helps her with the right-wingers there, it may also help her to avoid the blame when things go wrong (in Rhodesia or in the unions, for example).

One has to remember that the squeeze is tougher than any country in the world is facing. The measure of this is 21 per cent inflation as against 11 per cent top-level money-supply increase (and it is probably smaller in fact).

He agrees with me that she does not worry very much: less anxiety than Ted or Harold or Jim. But he hadn't thought of it before.

My own strong impression is again of the sides coming together. The hawks, as Jim says, now believe in wages and their importance. But equally the doves believe in money supply: they see it as measure of squeeze; they say that there should be no relenting at the moment because of the impact on wages – especially there should *not* be a cut in National Insurance contribution.

BERNARD DONOUGHUE
3 September 1980

LABOUR   Still thinks that JC will go. But BD has urged upon him the case for not going: which is that he of all people is the best man to oppose Thatcher – the calm bedside manner beside the raucous authoritarian figure. Also the best man to handle unemployment and make it an issue which really wins for Labour. JC really cares about unemployment, not in a soft bleeding way (like Ennals, Lestor,[2] Orme), but is affronted by it. Unlike Healey, to whom it is just another number. The case against Jim

---

1 John Fryer: labour correspondent of the *Sunday Times* 1971–82.
2 Joan Lestor: Labour MP for Eton and Slough 1966–83, for Eccles 1987–97; later Baroness Lestor of Eccles.

staying is that he would be too weak with the party. Does not see the need for NEC reform, because basically he thinks the NEC is irrelevant, as do the TUC. The TUC don't really want the NEC reformed, because as things are they reckon the Labour government and the General Council jointly run the country. That suits them nicely. Callaghan at bottom thinks that, as long as he has the six top men in the TUC on his side, Benn and everyone else don't matter. This leads him to avoid the hard line urged by the Williams–Owen–Rodgers trio – who attack BD for putting the pro-Callaghan line (although BD personally thinks that JC *is* too weak with the party). A great error to predict one month ahead what JC will do. He never says. See the 1978 conference and the election, which BD got totally wrong. It may well be that he has not decided himself. One day he may think it would be good to go out on a high note, the next that it's rather nice staying in when things are going well. In health he is very good – no change discerned in his appearance by BD from 1976. Audrey [Callaghan's wife] will be pushing for him to quit. Either way it should be clear that he either quits now or says he will stay past the election – but, says BD, that's not Jim's way.

COMPARISONS Jim cares more about the party, or rather the movement, than Wilson. Wilson was an academic, Callaghan a trade unionist. Their origins are very important. Wilson ultimately got fed up with the party because it became too much of a problem to control it. Callaghan never really has. Wilson was not at heart a trade-union man, Callaghan is totally a trade-union man or he is nothing. Further, Healey. At bottom Jim does care about certain things. He has a sense of direction. Denis seems to care about nothing save success. He just wants to be on the winning side at any given time.

He got beaten in Cabinet from time to time, but happily went away to do what he was told. No fundamental convictions, says HY. He was a good deputy minister, the very reason which may make him a bad PM. Conversely, JC was a bad deputy minister and yet a good leader. It is a commentary on the Labour Party that Healey has to keep quiet now, in order to keep MPs sweet – in the belief (correctly, no doubt) that even though they have seen him and what he is like for years they will somehow forget and swallow their objections to him when the election comes.

GOVERNMENT Is in terrible mess following the disclosure that money supply had not been under control all this time. That in effect it was running at 20 per cent growth last January and February and continued far higher than they thought. This evidently came like a bolt from the blue, BD has it from a high Treasury friend he saw in France. There is a campaign among the politicians to blame the Treasury for this. But the Bank [of England], if anyone, is to blame. Either way the effect is appalling. It is as though the Tories' first year never happened. They had high interest rates in support of monetary control. They had a high exchange rate because their policies were perceived by foreigners to be too rigorous. These two rates produced the austerity and unemployment and general grimness – but, it turns out, to no end. The monetarist package was fully defensible, in BD's view, as the short sharp shock to the economy. But we've had the penalties of it without any of the underlying benefit implicit in monetary control. What will happen now? Maybe the figures in September and October will show that the August figure was an aberration. On the monetarist analysis this should not be so, for if there has been *no* monetary restraint (as we now learn) then there should be roaring inflation. Still, maybe the figures will be better for both money supply and inflation. In which case the government will be able to sell stock once again, which it has been quite unable to in the last six weeks. In fact MLR [minimum lending rate] should be much higher now – up three points, let's say. Is any of this being discussed as an option among ministers? What are the Biffens and Powells saying now? And what are the wets saying now . . .

Labour seems not to have latched on to this. They are so obsessed with unemployment. Yet, from the government's point of view, that's not a failure. They bargained for it. What they have failed quite simply to do is to carry out their policies. Yet because Labour doesn't like the policy it's perhaps inhibited from saying too much about this.

CENTRE Jenkins is a pretty well dead duck, he thinks. Just unwilling to do the necessary. Always has been. A fatal flaw of social aspiration, elitism, etc. Thought the brilliant Roy Jenkins could get anywhere on his own while still preferring Covent Garden to the National Union of Railwaymen. BD says, Where Sid Weighell[1] goes, there go I. If you can't get Sid on your side, you haven't begun. With Sid would come Grantham,[2] and then Duffy[3] would start talking, and there would be Chapple and Lyons[4] might even affiliate. As it is, there is no one in the Labour Party who wants to be caught having even a whispered good word to say for Jenkins. He is a 60-year-old failure who no one wants to get committed to. Whereas he could have been the best prime minister we ever had, if he had any real idea of political seriousness. The best thing – the only

1 Sidney Weighell: general secretary, the NUR 1975–83.
2 Roy Grantham: general secretary of APEX, the Association of Professional, Executive, Clerical and Computer Staffs.
3 Terence 'Terry' Duffy: president of the Amalgamated Union of Engineering Workers 1978–85.
4 John Lyons: general secretary of the Electrical Power Engineers Association 1973–91.

thing – for him is to become Liberal. He might win a by-election on his own. He might even get some people with him. He could do the Libs a good turn. But there is no serious chance for a man so cut off from all roots and organization. BD now thinks it virtually certain that Owen etc. would never go with Jenkins. And indeed that looks certain so long as the Labour Party issue remains even slightly fudged. The conference looks like doing better than that.

JAMES PRIOR
18 September 1980

A story only for the memoirs. I was dining with Moss Evans[1] the night before the first Budget. I had been to MT and to Geoffrey earlier saying that I was worried about VAT going up too high. Margaret said it wouldn't. Geoffrey said he would think seriously about what I said. Moss Evans said he was worried about 15 per cent VAT. I said, Don't worry, I have been assured by the PM, etc. etc. Next day we got it. You can imagine what that did to my standing with Moss Evans.

Lawson is said to be very important in the Treasury.

I'm not going to be too critical, I'm a member of government, and I want it to succeed. I got a fourpenny one[2] in July for saying that I didn't believe in a sound money policy (not for use).

IAN GILMOUR
5 November 1980

REAGAN[3] IG ceased to have a view long ago. Says that he knows reliable judges who say that Carter had become so bad that Reagan could not be worse and might well be better. This rests on a fallacy, says Ian: things always *can* be worse, however bad they are now. However, he did think that Carter had been pretty terrible.

POLICY He denies authorship of the phrase 'economics of the madhouse', but uses it as his latest shorthand. Says, amusingly, that the weekend before last he told his wife that he didn't want to speak to anyone who rang up – and then was rather miffed when no one did ring up. The same thing happened last weekend. So at least he feels safe from

---

1 Arthur Mostyn 'Moss' Evans: president of the TGWU 1978–85.
2 A fourpenny one: outdated slang for a punch, blow or clip round the ear.
3 Ronald Reagan, former actor, had defeated Jimmy Carter in the US presidential election the previous day.

culpability. Thinks that the phrase and other similar ones may have come from Rippon (Geoff the Ripper) and been transposed on to the Cabinet minister.

How will the madhouse economics change? We talk about the back benches. He says she has done more to cultivate them than any recent leader. Very sensible of her, he says. She must surely know that they are shifting. The enthusiasts are becoming agnostic, and the agnostics are becoming sceptics. This is very important. Probably the back benches will be the critical element in producing change. But how, and when? IG simply thinks that there must come a point when unemployment becomes insufferable politically, although he admits he has been wrong before. 'Perhaps another couple of speeches by Geoffrey' will be what does it.

With the economy in a poor way, the Chancellor, Geoffrey Howe, put the squeeze on social services and the military. Francis Pym, the Defence Secretary, would have none of it.

FRANCIS PYM
8 November 1980

DEFENCE I have no doubt what my position is. I made it quite clear that if we went beyond a certain point, it would have to be someone else who did it. I think I know what is tolerable. I am in no doubt what I shall do if things go very badly wrong this week. (He said that tomorrow, Wednesday, would be important, but not necessarily decisive. He also said that he thought it was a good thing for people to take the alternative which our system gives them. Not enough had done it in the past, he joked, as we collected our coats.) He said that the possibility of his resignation had had the most profound impact on No. 10. It was deemed, in his words, to be likely to have the most profound consequences. He therefore thinks he has probably won. He said, by the way, that he had seen Thatcher only this morning, and was seeing a lot of her.

Says that the whole public spending exercise leaves a lot to be desired. Not enough of an overview is seen by everybody. Thinks it might even be better to be done by a smaller group (as long as he was in it). The Treasury has no idea what the implications of cuts will be. Biffen simply named a figure which bore no relation to programmes or effects. Says that officials, on the other hand, have a close connection and know what is involved. Kept going back to the point that no one had a real view. Raised the question of Joseph as a particular example of a man who knew what he wanted and then did something quite opposite when in power. All very well, says Francis, for him to be wringing his hands, but he announced from the start one set of policies and has been doing something quite different.

Worries about Thatcher: she is mad to cut off so many possibilities. Why the hell does she keep on saying that she's not for turning, etc. etc.? Maybe she's not, but why say so? Makes it far more difficult for herself. Also thinks she does not *really* understand the problems of real people faced with the present economy: the unemployed, the factory owners etc. etc. The more we talked, the more deeply critical and anxious he sounded about her political instincts, her breadth of judgement etc. etc.

1981

4 January	Police arrest Peter Sutcliffe, later convicted as the 'Yorkshire Ripper', for the deaths of thirteen women.
25 January	'The Gang of Four' – Roy Jenkins, David Owen, Shirley Williams and William Rodgers – issue the 'Limehouse declaration', announcing their break from Labour and the formation of the Council for Social Democracy, later the SDP.
13 February	Rupert Murdoch buys *The Times* and the *Sunday Times*.
25 February	Tiny Rowland buys *The Observer*.
26 March	Launch of the Social Democratic Party.
30 March	Attempt on the life of President Reagan by John Hinckley Jr.
11 April	Black youths riot in Brixton.
13 May	Attempt on the life of Pope John Paul II by Mehmet Ali Agca.
21 May	François Mitterrand becomes president of France.
5 June	First reports from the US of a new kind of disease among homosexuals: later to be named as HIV/Aids.
3 July	Riots in Toxteth, followed by riots in London, Wolverhampton, Birmingham and Reading.
16 July	Labour holds Warrington in a by-election, but Roy Jenkins slashes the Labour majority.
29 July	Prince Charles marries Lady Diana Spencer.
6 October	President Anwar el-Sadat of Egypt is assassinated in Cairo; Hosni Mubarak takes over.
26 November	Shirley Williams wins the Crosby by-election.
15 December	General Jaruzelski imposes martial law in Poland.
Deaths	Hoagy Carmichael, Bill Haley, Joe Louis, Jessie Matthews, Albert Speer, Natalie Wood

HY began the year by talking to key trade-union leaders. Bill Sirs, general secretary of the Iron and Steel Trades Confederation, left him unimpressed: a 'somewhat naive fellow whose heart was in the right place, knew where he stood, flirted with possibilities of change, but in the end cares far more and knows more about steelworkers'.

BILL SIRS
8 January 1981

Very much against the January conference:[1] it's going to cost us tens of thousands of pounds. It's only happening because one union leader didn't do what he should have done at the TUC congress. The Boilermakers' leader was evidently absent for the vote on the Labour leadership, and the union vote (200,000) was switched by his deputy. This meant that the wider franchise carried the day. Sirs contends that if it had gone the other way, unions (all unions?) would have come to Blackpool committed in favour of the status quo.

As it is, there will be a vote. Sirs favours the status quo. That won't be carried. He thinks it would be the best way of getting peace, and especially coupled with the TU statement pro Foot would do a lot of good. But it is not realistic. Therefore we fall back on 50–25–25. This would have the merit of bringing peace. Which is what the unions more than anything seem to be wanting. Whether it will be carried we cannot say. Much depends on the GMWU [General and Municipal Workers Union], which wavers all over the place. There is total uncertainty there. 'There is a reason for that, but it's not my business to tell you what it is.' (I threw Basnett's[2] personality at him, but he ducked it.) If the 40–30–30 thing gets through, that's where the trouble will come. There will not be peace.

What about a split? The NEC is much further left than Sirs would like, and some policies are unacceptable – he instanced unilateral disarmament. He thinks that in the constituencies there could be trouble, leading to rival candidates being run against Labour, etc. He does not contemplate the possibility of Thatcher ever winning an election, but sees a multi-party situation possibly arising with a substantial non-Labour left. But would unions be part of this? We could do it by ballot, says Sirs. We are not

---

1 A special Labour Party conference at Wembley on 24 January 1981 altered the voting procedures and increased the influence of the trade unions in an electoral college. The following day Owen, Williams, Rodgers and Jenkins announced their Council for Social Democracy.

2 David Basnett: general secretary, General and Municipal Workers' Union (later General Municipal, Boilermakers and Allied Trades Union) 1973–86; later Baron Basnett of Leatherhead.

quitters; we stay inside and get from within against what we don't like –
usually. But things now are a bit different. In the foreseeable future he
does not see a trend of disaffiliation. But, when I pressed him later, he
said it was not inconceivable. Disaffiliation has been talked about 'in
union circles' on grounds of policy, but perhaps even more on grounds
of inefficiency.

I asked him whether the leaving of Shirley Williams would be a serious
matter. He thought so. He described her as a person of real high quality,
who listens to arguments, can put arguments, and altogether was a regular
guy. If she and people like her were to go it would be a cause of 'great
consternation'.

Would *any* unions go along with it? Sirs said it was not totally inconceivable that unions might shift from one Labour party to a different
Labour party. They might join up, in certain circumstances.

We then spent some time talking about steel and MacGregor,[1] during
which he gave me what I suppose is a standard spiel about the destruction
of this viable industry. Quite impressive marshalling of facts and figures.
Says that the union membership will accept the corporate plan – or at
least not oppose it. His own stance is to neither accept nor reject it: which
leaves him free to negotiate its details step by step.

At his meeting with Joseph, Thatcher and Prior early in 1980, he
recalls Thatcher being astonished to hear that Consett was to be shut
down. Is it really? she asked turning to Joseph. And then it was.

FRANK CHAPPLE
22 January 1981

On Owen etc. he despises them for all the years they spent in not making
a fight: in refusing to take up the things he fought for, in allowing the left
to get control both nationally and in local parties. The reason we have
Ted Knight[2] is essentially that Shirley Williams didn't give a lead to the
kind of people who needed persuading that it was (a) possible and
(b) desirable to keep Ted Knight out at all costs. The G3[3] recognize the
error of their ways, says Frank – but they are never too explicit about it.
He also thinks they are politically in error in making these constitutional

---

1 Sir Ian MacGregor: Scottish-American metallurgist, in 1980 appointed chairman of the nationalized British
Steel Corporation by Sir Keith Joseph, then Industry Secretary. Within three years, and after a series of plant
closures, MacGregor had reduced the industry's workforce from 166,000 to 71,000.
2 Ted Knight: controversial leader of Lambeth Borough Council, frequently labelled as a member of the 'loony
left'.
3 Shirley Williams, William Rodgers and David Owen were the original 'Gang of Three' within the Labour
Party. Roy Jenkins, later the fourth member, was not at the time in the House of Commons.

issues the breaking point, and in getting into a frame of mind to resign from the party before seeing what happens. FC says that he personally doesn't care too much about the electoral college, or about reselection. Clearly he would prefer there be no change, but what really bothers him is the entryism at local level,[1] and also some of the policy points about which Callaghan and others have for so many years refused to have a fight. (He cited Europe as one example, and recalled how, when he was on the NEC, Shirley herself suddenly switched her vote at a crucial meeting to vote in favour of a referendum.) He clearly, as an old Marxist, has no time for the fancy footwork and liberal party-healing instincts of people like Shirley. Recognizes a gloves-off fight when he sees one.

However – he has also said a lot in the opposite sense: that the party had already moved a long way from where he stood; that if it went on denying people the right to be heard etc. it would become intolerable; that in the ballot of his members he is quite certain that there would be a majority for disaffiliating. He does not regard disaffiliation as at all inconceivable. He finds a degree of disaffection now which he would never have credited. He said he himself only got out of his chair and voted Labour at the last election because he was shamed into doing so by his wife and son.

Totally scornful of Labour's financial mismanagement. Says that they must be *more* than £500,000 in debt, and the time will come when the banks will cease to ante up.

RUPERT MURDOCH LUNCH FOR GANG OF FOUR
20 March 1981

Present: RM, Long, Evans, D-Home, Giles,[2] self – plus Roy Jenkins, David Owen, Bill Rodgers and Shirley Williams.

I meet Shirley at the door, and warn her that Murdoch thinks their whole operation is 'a lot of crap'. The four dribble in, with Roy arriving last, rather grandly. He looks fat and sleek and just like they say in the nasty newspapers.

When we get round to the general discussion, Roy opens, after

1 A number of Labour MPs feared 'reselection' – effect, rejection by their own constituency parties – and some of them blamed 'entryism', an infiltration tactic reportedly used by Marxist and Trotskyist hardliners to take control of the party at grass-roots level.
2 Gerald Long: managing director, *The Times*. Charles Douglas-Home: deputy editor of *The Times* since William Rees-Mogg resigned on Murdoch's purchase of the paper. Frank Giles: editor of the *Sunday Times* since Harold Evans moved across to *The Times* in 1981.

Murdoch asks him how they disagree with the present government and how they see their party up to the election. Roy canters through an easy attack on the government, saying that their policies are bound to be self-defeating, and that it is demonstrative that you 'cannot eliminate the PSBR during a recession without breaking the economic system'.

All four of them are very buoyant, although Rodgers is less so than the others. They have the serenity of people who think they've done the right thing, and are well past the stage of having regrets about the Labour Party. Synthesizing the points which emerged:

Their main attention is on the Liberals, and they fulfil my column of a few weeks ago which said this is what mattered most to them. They keep saying *they* are the major partner: that no one is joining the Liberals now, all are joining them: that Liberals are joining the Social Democrats: that the SDP organization will be impressive – county-based, computer-run, although not eliminating the doorstep. They are pretty scornful of Liberals of all kinds, imagine that the Liberal vote is very soft, insist that they are more than a centre party.

Shirley and David, especially, insist they are not centre. They are democratic socialists. But there clearly is some tension here. These two favour a wealth tax, Jenkins says it would cost more to collect than it would bring in – although he concedes that Shirley's interest in the Liberals' 'acquisitions tax' is worth looking at. This surely one of the reasons why they won't want to get too deep into policy. They insist that all they need is general agreement on broad positions. There are, says Jenkins, only about seven general issues in politics, and if you agree on five of them you are a party. Owen dismisses my suggestion that a crucial determinant of the durability of their present poll support will be the support which exists for their policies.

Owen is proud of the fact that their most pronounced positions are unpopular. Europe and NATO. Not a single vote in being dreamily pro-EEC he says. Mrs Thatcher's best thing has been her success in taking on the EEC: a very good policy. Equally, taking the line Owen has about defence is hardly a populist thing to do at a time when the CND position is gathering ground.

Shirley talks about their support. She says that it comes from people under 40. Great dividing line by *age*. Older people in the Labour Party cannot make the shift. Younger people, in and out, see the need for change: are thirsting for an end to the two-party system: want to get committed. She says they have heard from hundreds of people who have never had anything to do with politics before but who are excited to commit themselves to the SDs. (This confirmed by A. Lester's experience with the lawyers.) Shirley dilates upon the creativity of young people –

mentions arts etc. – and says that in business and politics their talents are suppressed, and this is what the SDs want to tap.

Murdoch sits mostly silent. But he then says, You sound exactly like the Callaghan government in your general line. Owen says the Callaghan government was a lot better than it is often said to have been. Remember the time before the winter of discontent, he says. Callaghan lost his nerve and should have called a state of emergency when the ambulance drivers went out. They would take a tougher line with unions. They would also, says Jenkins, have a tougher line about the priorities of public spending: about keeping the ratio fixed: and about admitting that if you want industrial support you couldn't also have new hospitals.

They make a virtue of being Four not One: people like it, they say – no cult of personality. But I think I heard Shirley admitting this could not last. There is a heated discussion about populism – with Gerry Long intervening with typical abruptness to declaim that they had no guts and therefore could not be populist. Assaulted by Shirley, he quickly changes this to 'gut' – and they claim that they have plenty of gut issues which could make them a populist cause. Is Thatcher the main populist? She was, says Shirley

We discuss PR. I try to draw them out to admit that in a hung parliament they would get PR out of the Tories not Labour. They are discomforted by this, and Shirley suggests it is impossible to say. For example, she says, in a situation where Benn and Hattersley were vying for power, Hattersley would have an interest in committing himself to PR at the next election – as a way of bringing the Social Democrats on board in a way Benn would not. I.e. there is a Labour as well as a Tory interest in PR (essentially based on keeping the far left out).

BY-ELECTIONS They say they won't need to contest every by-election. They expect three to be announced on the day they set up the party: Mulley, Bottomley and Ifor Davies (Gower)[1] all in bad seats for them. They admit they have to face the prospect of losing. Rodgers even says it would be a pity to win the first, because it raises expectations. Jenkins says he could imagine winning *any* by-election. But quickly denies that he'd be ready to run in any old seat. Says it would be silly for him or Shirley to run in a seat which might not be holdable at the general election.

Murdoch says afterwards that his main impression was of four people who hated each other's guts. He has got it quite wrong. Obviously they disagree, but the main thing is their excitement at having got the show on the road so fast and well.

---

1 Fred Mulley: Labour MP for Sheffield Park 1950–83; later Baron Mulley of Manor Park. Arthur Bottomley: Labour MP for Middlesbrough, later Teesside, 1962–83, later Baron Bottomley. Ifor Davies: Labour MP for Gower 1959–82.

By the way: they claim that if the other parties *do* move to the centre, they will have served their purpose. Ho ho.

A by-election at Warrington on 18 July saw Labour scrape home with a majority of only 1,700 over Roy Jenkins for the Social Democrats. The Conservative vote plummeted to 2,000. It was clear that the SDP had arrived as a new force in British politics. HY quoted David Owen, in a scribbled note, headed 'SDP Westminster', 'Don't want to be a Mark 2 Labour Party. But don't want to be a Mark 2 Liberal Party either.'

In September 1981 the Prime Minister reshuffled her government for the second time in nine months. Among the 'wets' to go were Ian Gilmour, Christopher Soames and Mark Carlisle; Jim Prior survived, but was moved to Northern Ireland. Those entering the Cabinet were three of the architects of Thatcherism in the years to come: Norman Tebbit (Employment), Nigel Lawson (Energy) and Cecil Parkinson (Paymaster General).

JOHN BIFFEN
Letter to HY, from Department of Trade,
19 October 1981

That was a disgracefully generous article[1] – thank you so much – but the praise was really more than I deserved.

Wasn't Blackpool awful? I wish I had a better stomach for such occasions. It will be interesting to see what happens next. The PM now has the protective covering of a Right Wing Cabinet which should enable policies to move towards a greater emphasis on the protective role of the state. The problem, I think, is her disbelief that politically, in some circumstances, it is more popular to spend and *tax* accordingly. This disbelief – much in line with Chicago and Laffer[2] – is rooted in a stray prejudice in favour of self-help and personal success.

Within all this there is a nasty phrase lurking about Methodism and Groceries: we need a new Tawney.[3]

Again so many thanks for the unmerited plaudits,

John

1 HY's Inside Politics column on 18 October 1981 was headed 'A sober voice to still the dance of death' and described Mr Biffen at the Tories' Blackpool conference as 'one of the most original and Spartan monetarists'.
2 The 'Chicago school', led by the Nobel laureate Milton Friedman, preached free-market economics. Arthur Laffer, a supply-side economist, was an influential force in Ronald Reagan's administration.
3 R. H. Tawney: economist, Fabian, social critic and author of the 1926 classic *Religion and the Rise of Capitalism*. Mrs Thatcher was brought up in the Methodist Church. She was the daughter of a Grantham grocer.

SIR MICHAEL HAVERS
Lunch, 15 December 1981

THATCHER Greets you with a joke when you come into room. Her throat infection persists, and makes her vulnerable to huskiness at any time, but in spirits she is at the top. Really amazing. Also in her mastery of briefs. Havers may spend most of a night getting into some big brief, and finds at next day's Cabinet that she is completely on top of it. Also, she is very acquiescent in his judgement. When the Attorney says no, she agrees – although she may disagree with his opinion about risk: say, the risk of getting taken to the European Court or whatever.

She was very good when his house was blown up.[1] She rang Madrid, and said she knew he'd be all right but what about Carol [Havers's wife]? At Cabinet she laid down that no minister blown up in this way should suffer financially. He was in fact underinsured. She insisted that the Treasury should get on and pay him the figure, which was about £7,000. When the Treasury man demurred (on Havers's inquiry), she was furious and put Armstrong [the Cabinet Secretary] on to it.

He recalls among other things an instance of bureaucracy at work. After [the explosion] was over he was staying with his son in the country. On Sunday morning he is asked to telephone Scotland Yard. They say they want a name of someone who will take responsibility for the flat now that the forensic people have finished. He says, That is absurd, I'm out of London and the flat has gaping holes in the walls and a lot of valuables inside. He says, that they must stay. They say there's no reason to stay. He says, Get me the Commissioner. In fact the Commissioner is not available, but he speaks to a deputy commissioner, who says it's all a ghastly mistake – but only after Havers has said to him to listen to him without saying a word, and warning him that if he gives the wrong answer he will be ringing the PM instantly. But he reflects to the DAC[2] that if his name had been John Smith what would have happened; and the DA says he *hopes* the police would not have been so silly. Havers says that it's especially maddening since, as he told the cops, he'd been lying for them all weekend by saying he'd enjoyed excellent protection. In fact the protection had been lousy. The house had not been protected at the back at all.

---

1 Sir Michael's Wimbledon home – empty at the time – was damaged by a bomb blast on 13 November 1981. The IRA later claimed responsibility. Four police officers were slightly injured.
2 Deputy assistant commissioner (DAC) is a rank in the Metropolitan Police equivalent to deputy chief constable.

1982

12 January   Mark Thatcher, the PM's son, last seen on 10 January in the Paris–Dakar motor rally, is reported missing; he is found on the 15th.

26 January   Unemployment in Britain passes the 3 million mark.

2 April   Argentinians invade the Falkland Islands.

5 April   A British naval and military task force sets sail for the South Atlantic.

May   A British nuclear submarine sinks the Argentinian cruiser *General Belgrano*; Argentinian Exocet missiles destroy HMS *Sheffield* and container ship *Atlantic Conveyor*; Argentinian planes destroy HMS *Ardent*.

29 May   British troops storm Goose Green on the Falkland Islands.

29 May   The Pope makes the first papal visit to the UK in 450 years.

14 June   The Argentinians surrender; President General Galtieri is ousted.

29 June   Israel invades Lebanon.

7 July   Michael Fagan is found in the Queen's bedroom, drinking a bottle of wine and asking for a cigarette.

20 July   An IRA car bomb kills guardsmen, spectators and horses in Hyde Park.

18 September   Bloody massacres of Palestinians in the Sabra and Chatila refugee camps in west Beirut.

1 October   Helmut Kohl takes over as German chancellor.

12 December   Twenty thousand women form a human chain around Greenham Common to protest against US cruise missiles.

Deaths   Douglas Bader, Ingrid Bergman, Leonid Brezhnev, 'Rab' Butler, Henry Fonda, Princess Grace of Monaco, Thelonious Monk, Artur Rubinstein, Jacques Tati

RICHARD HOLME
19 January 1982

COMMISSIONS He'd just come from the constitutional conference, chaired by Henry Fisher.[1] Fisher good at keeping the heavies in
place, and treats Jenkins as leader of SDP with Owen as a walk-on part.
Very smooth – so much so that it came as a shock when he abruptly
put down Lester. The Commission is making House of Lords reform,
devolution and a Bill of Rights the core issues – with Freedom of Information, local government and Commons reform as outriding isssues. One
person has suggested that they should put it all into one gigantic bill,
hustle this through an abbreviated committee stage, then entrench it and
make it unamendable. A quite fantastic notion – Jenkins has said that
this would hardly do from a reformist, open-government party.

ELECTION RH now puts 50 as the minimum the Alliance will get.
And the maximum is government-forming. But suppose 90, I say. This
means 34–35 per cent of the vote, he says. It would leave the Tories far
ahead, so how to get out of the PR bind? I.e. how to prevent getting a
pledge to PR out of the Tory leader, and then this being ditched by Tory
MPs – meanwhile the Alliance being locked into government and looking
stupid? Answer: give support on the back benches for, say, eighteen
months: which would mean that the Alliance would bring down the
government, not itself be brought down by Tory backbenchers. This
would put the government's survival on their commitment to PR being
pushed through the HC – hence a much better tactic than joining the
government on a condition not fulfilled.

This path, even so, is fraught with danger. For example, if there is
much horse-trading after the election, will this not confirm the belief that
PR equals a big mess? Look what the minor parties are doing even
without PR, the Tories will say. And the danger of fragmentation is great.
Beginning with how the palace plays it. Who will the Queen call first?
Which Alliance leader will be the leader? What part will be played by
party caucuses, of which British politicians know little? How can leaders
be sure of delivering? Will the Tories split? – on that, yes very likely to if
there is a 200–200–200 situation, but much less likely if the Alliance
only has 90.

Further, should and will the only coalition be with Tories? They have
noted that both Callaghan and Healey said just before Christmas that

1 Sir Henry Fisher: president of Wolfson College, Oxford, 1975–85; barrister, judge; served on the joint
commission on the constitution set up by the Social Democratic and Liberal parties.

perhaps Labour would have to get ready to look at our electoral system. But RH and I agree that the Labour option looks very unlikely: there are just too many hard-core lefties to make this feasible.

He reckons the likeliest outcome as of now is Tories 35 per cent, Alliance 35 per cent, Labour 30 per cent. His judgement is that in parts Labour is down to 10 per cent. The by-elections show that the Tory hard core is steady at 25 per cent, whereas Labour does go down that far. He thinks the Labour vote is much softer at the moment, and likely to remain so. He finds this also in Cheltenham, where he is the candidate, and from anecdotal evidence. This shows that people either hate Thatcher or like her very much: she has a solid hard core he puts at 25 per cent. But Foot is widely regarded as a joke, especially by the young. Labour's only hard source of strength, however, is the C2s and DEs male under-25s: this is the one area where the Alliance finds itself miles behind.

Back to PR. The second option is to go the referendum route, i.e. get a pledge that between the second and third readings of a bill there shall be a referendum. This, however, has its risks. The pledge must be made beforehand: or rather the Alliance must state its tactics beforehand, but if it turns out to be in the majority it would not want to go the referendum route. In any case, not quite sure that the British people would take PR so seriously as they do. (Today a new Tory pamphlet, with good gimmicky idea – in favour of Direct Election.)[1]

THE ALLIANCE   He feels sure that in the end the deals will stick, with just a very few outbursts where they won't. But he is worried about the rows, and thinks they will set back the momentum. Momentum is all, at the moment. All the time, he thinks the political logic should be drawing them closer towards merger (which Jenkins alone of the G4 wants), and which Liberal bigwigs including Pincham[2] want, and which Steel wants but cannot say. He regards it as imperative to present a united front at the election. They will be terribly vulnerable to charges from the other side if they can't get their own act together.

This means choosing before the election not only a SDP leader but an Alliance leader. People will want to know who is going to be prime minister. But this presents a problem. It means making that choice and sticking with it before knowing who gets most seats. It wouldn't matter if the Alliance did not come out on top – the leader could then be changed. But the die would be cast as far as the PM was concerned.

1   The debate about electoral reform and proportional representation was immediately complicated by a second argument about which system was more appropriate. In direct election, voters ballot for the person they want to see in office. A US president – or a British prime minister – is chosen indirectly: by an electoral college in one case; by the party in the other.
2   Roger James Pincham: consultant, businessman; chairman of the Liberal Party 1979–82.

Steel is inclined, or was, to let Jenkins have it. Lately he's become depressed at SDP indecision. But he respects Jenkins's huge experience. He realizes he's got no ministerial experience at all, no managerial record even. RH thinks that even at that Steel underestimates the appalling difficulties of running governments these days. (I interpolate that the Kennedy days are absolutely gone, when inexperience, youth, novelty etc. etc. were what America needed. Everything is utterly different now: more slogging, slow and doomed to failure.) We also agree that Jenkins would be supremely good at putting the line that the other parties were finished, without asking any promises at all. A good line in ridicule, tempered by experience, an amazing ability to present himself as something new – and yet something not off-puttingly new, indeed, someone very experienced indeed.

There is no doubt that Jenkins will get the SDP leadership. Shirley probably won't even run. Owen thinks his time is not yet come. Otherwise the SDP is wracked by the great problem of deciding what it wants to be. Owen's view is as a one-off coalition: but this is very damaging, says RH. Must stop thinking coalition, and start thinking party. But he confirms that, if the seats deal can be worked out, there will be few problems about policy. Each party will produce a huge policy document, but then appoint wise men to work out a platform of agreed priorities – whose constitutional provenance will be muzzy, and therefore whose 'statutory' force will be obscure.

As to whether it will really work locally, this depends in the end on the candidates. If the Liberal or SDP candidate goes out of his way to butter up the other party, it will probably be OK. But if not, not. Already the experience has been appallingly bruising for local Liberals. He cited Oxon, Berks and Bucks, whose negotiations he witnessed last weekend. To see the Liberal from Henley finally understand that Henley might have to be given up in exchange for something else totally horrified the Liberal. How would he go back and tell them? he asked incredulously. It has made men age overnight, says RH.

Further on candidates: he admits that an Alliance government will be a strange thing. To fill a twenty-man Cabinet will be hard enough, let alone a 100-man government. And he agrees that experience is all, when trying to put forward radical proposals. (But will they be all that radical? Will the Civil Service be all that hostile?) They toy with political appointees, but reject them – at least as far as the Civil Service itself is concerned.

JAMES PRIOR
30 January 1982

He asked about Murdoch etc., sympathetically. 'Does he not want it to be a thinking man's paper any more?'

Between 1978 and 1984, HY presented a series of radio programmes on the judiciary, and later on the Civil Service. He was to pursue his interest in legal matters, and gained some interesting material on the current state of the judiciary, which the press as a whole tended to ignore.

SIR JOHN DONALDSON
9 February 1982

DIVISIONAL COURT When [Lord Chief Justice] Lane took over there was a backlog of about 600 cases. He put me in the Divisional Court to get rid of this backlog. I discovered that the rate of input – a figure no one appears to have found out before – was thirty to forty cases a month. Elementary arithmetic showed that the backlog meant that two years would elapse before these new cases came on. This was plainly quite out of the question. I did a number of things. First, a very simple point, but surprisingly effective, and I don't think even the bar quite knew what was going on. As judges, we would wander, as usual, to the door of the court, but then enter it with great and unaccustomed briskness and sit down instantly and say with great energy, 'Yes, Mr so-and-so.' Oddly, this accelerated things immensely. It changed the whole tempo. Secondly, we decided to pre-read cases, to isolate what was *the* point – because there only ever is one point. In the past, the court always had the papers and usually skimmed through them. But they had followed the time-honoured judicial method of letting counsel tell them what the case was about. We decided to tell counsel what the case was about – and we probably indicated what our view of it was as well. This led to an enormous increase in speed. We often didn't hear the applicant at all – or, alternatively, didn't hear the other side. We could usually tell very soon whether they had a point or not.

Thirdly, we struck out quite a number of criminal appeals. We discovered they had often been so long delayed as to make it scandalous to continue them: prosecutor's appeals, that is. I first understood what this entailed in a case involving two boys caught with petrol inside a house, whom the magistrates had unaccountably acquitted. The magistrates were quite clearly wrong. But two years had elapsed since the case. Instead of being 14 and 16, the boys were 16 and 18: they were different people by now. So we struck out the prosecutor's appeal. This had a spin-off effect. It meant that the parties in such cases, if they were prosecutors, got on with the job much more quickly.

The result of my ten months was that we got the backlog down to below 100, which is where it should be.

My underlying attitude was this. We did what I did at the National Industrial Relations Court – that unmentionable court – which was to depart from the age-old idea that the courts are a public facility, there to be used at the convenience of those who want to use them. But when proceedings have started, the *court* takes over control, and especially control of the speed. I got every case colour-coded according to type – pink for habeas corpus, for example – and also according to the stage it had reached in the process: different shoeboxes for different stages. Thus if I came into the office and saw two pink cases which had been in the same shoebox for weeks, I did something about it. Terribly primitive, of course, but it hadn't been done before. People had no serious idea what cases were in the pipeline: it was left to the pressure of the parties to determine what order things came up in.

I would like to apply this kind of thing across our whole system. At least throughout the High Court. You could put every writ on a computer, programmed so that, from the moment it was issued, if it was not moved to the next stage by a given date the computer would print out a summons to the litigant to show cause why the action should not be struck out. This would put a great onus on the parties to get a move on. But I haven't talked to the Chief about this. No one really cares very much.

LANE Doesn't actually like the Divisional Court, although that is classically the LCJ's work. He thinks the main job for the LCJ is crime. He therefore leaves the Divisional Court to others. It is now run by Mr Justice Woolf.[1] Lane concentrates on crime, and circuit administration.

Widgery[2] had let things run down completely. He was a sick man for years – I never knew exactly what was wrong with him. The system had run down so that it was completely immobile. He just wasn't with it at

1 Harry Woolf became a High Court judge in 1979, Baron Woolf of Barnes in 1992, and Lord Chief Justice of England and Wales 2000–2005.
2 John Widgery, Lord Chief Justice 1971–80, was said to be senile in his final years, yet still presided. He dismissed the appeal of the 'Birmingham Six' in 1976 over their conviction for the killing of twenty-one people in two hotel bombings. It took fifteen years and further appeals, including one before Lord Chief Justice Lane, before the convictions were overturned. Fresh examination of forensic evidence showed that the police had (among other things) fabricated evidence.

all – for several years. Everyone knew he was not up to it, and yet for the good of the law and the profession – I suppose it was right – no one did or said anything. (Per HY: a major scandal story here, obviously: conspiracy of silence, with thousands of litigants victimized to save the face of one man . . .) We now have – this was pre-Widgery – a statutory provision to get rid of a judge for infirmity: two doctors, plus the heads of all three divisions of the High Court. Would be almost impossible to operate, but the power is there.

Lane himself is an excellent leader. Very approachable. Very receptive of ideas, gets on extremely well with all kinds of people. Has hugely restored morale, which had been destroyed by Widgery, through the length and breadth of the system. He's clever at making people think he's not really any great brain. This is a sheer pose, although not really intentional. He got a double first, I think. He's got a mind like a razor – although you'll find it difficult to engage him in a serious intellectual discussion.

THE PROFESSION is enormously resistant to any outside sugges-tions for change. Very very conservative. On the other hand, one must admit that this is a strength in one sense. It fortifies the law's indepen-dence. Governments would otherwise begin to get the law under control. But of course the profession never wanted to have anything to do with the Royal Commission.[1] It did so only because it realized that otherwise government might do something nasty. Nor does it have any serious intention of putting the whole commission package into practice. You must remember that the Bar consists of self-employed people with families to keep, who don't want to change things which might put their life at risk. Also, there are the Inns of Court. They are an incredible problem with their jealousies. If you put forty lawyers and judges together it is quite literally impossible to get them to agree about anything, from redecorating the Inn to reorganizing legal education.

LORD CHIEF JUSTICE LANE
17 February 1982

SENTENCING Had crept up over the years in many kinds of case where there was no justification for it. Has been trying to reverse the trend, and with some success he thinks. For a large number of cases a

1 Richard Beeching, after a career with the chemical company ICI, was called in 1962 by Harold Macmillan to overhaul Britain's nationalized railways. In 1966, as Baron Beeching of East Grinstead, he was then invited by the Lord Chancellor to chair the Royal Commission on Assizes and Quarter Sessions, and overhaul the legal system.

very short time indeed is all that is needed in prison – even a week is enough in those places stinking of sweat and piss (Dammit: I omitted to ask him how he knows the sentences are coming down, if he refuses to cooperate with Oxford research.)

He said that the judges are not unresponsive to policy guidelines. What were the inhibitions? Entirely the public, according to Lane. If the public think judges are going soft, they let us have it. But, I asked, surely in most cases there was no wide interest or publicity, and the judges could act quietly to lower sentences. Yes, he said, that's exactly what is happening. It has to be done very quietly. Rape, by contrast, brought him massive mail, with many requests for castration. He especially treasures a letter demanding that judges make all rapists UNIKS. The problem for the judge, and for the LCJ, is to get the minor crimes down to lower sentences without letting up on the muggers and private housebreakers.

One of Lane's innovations has been to instigate irregular meetings of all the LJJ[1] in the criminal appeal division to discuss problems and arrive at policy positions. He says they all share his opinion about sentencing policy without any reservation. No one has breathed a word of dissent. This came to a particular head during the prisoner officers' action, when the judges realized that everyone had an interest in the prisons not exploding, and the judges knew they should swim along with the Home Office. When I asked him why prison figures had shot up again as soon as the strike was over, he denied this, saying that this was mainly the overflow back into prisons from the police stations. He maintains that the prison population is fairly static, while the crime figures are rocketing, and says this is some evidence that judges are doing what he wants them to do.

People are turning down the bench more now than they ever did. He has had three or four cases of people turning it down flat, saying they never want it. Other cases of people saying, God give me the bench, but not just yet while I've got children to educate. This delay does not amount to a black mark against them. Rather the reverse. There is no doubt, however, that when people turn it down this means the appointment of people who are less excellent. And this is bad.

WIDGERY ET AL. I had absolutely no idea what I was walking into when I came here, said Lane. There were three/four years of arrears in the Divisional Court, and it took eighteen months to eliminate these (cf. Donaldson's figures). Donaldson was put in there to do it. The system was also changed, giving single judges more responsibilities and doubling the availability, thereby, of judge power. But of course you have a blitz

---

1 A single Lord Justice of Appeal is abbreviated to LJ. By legal convention, the plural form is abbreviated to LJJ.

on the Divisional Court and your criminal appeals begin to lag behind. We're getting them down too, I hope. Lane said his own preference and priority was for criminal work.

He stressed that he had no Civil Service to rely on. He had to rely on judges. They had to work a lot harder as a result of the need to clear the lists. Of course, they made things work quickly, deciding some cases in a matter of minutes. But there was a lot of homework, and all the extra work always had to be done by judges.

IN GENERAL He said he did not think there were seriously valid camps of liberal and conservative judges. We agreed that all judges were more or less conservative. I said that, even within that rubric, one might look for one or two more Dennings.[1] He sighed with some despair. Denning was a real trial. His latest run-in with the HL, over the use of Hansard in court cases, will do us no good, Lane said. He will reply with another fusillade – and so it will go on. I said, Well, take Denning in his palmy days. Could we not do with one or two more pale reflections of that? Lane quickly demurred: One Denning is quite enough, and after him you really must have a break. Our job, after all, is to interpret the law, not to make it. (Lane was wholly opposed, though not ferociously, to using the European Convention etc. etc. Simply acknowledged this when I put it to him.)

He enjoys his job hugely. He looked extremely fit and totally unbowed down by what is clearly a heavy workload. Very earthy, wholly without side, very realistic. What he would be like, however, in a big people-versus-the-state situation I'm not at all sure.

He attacked the barristers' clerks scandal. Said some people who had left school at 15 were getting £100,000 a year – more than most people in their chambers. It was shocking, but no one could do anything about it, because no one dared to antagonize their own clerk or anyone else's.

Lane leaves Hitchin at 6.45 daily, in his old Cortina with chauffeur. Gets to work at eight o'clock. There is a very heavy social side as well. He and wife have decided to refuse everything unless it is absolutely unavoidable – unlike the Widgerys, who went out every night and this is what partly killed him.

He concluded with this fascinating point. His absolute priority is to stop the huge colossus created by Beeching – namely the Lord Chancellor's Department – from swamping the bench. It bids fair to do so, he said. He

---

1 Tom Denning, Lord Denning of Whitchurch, served as a judge for thirty-eight years, including twenty as Master of the Rolls. Famously forthright, frequently quoted, and occasionally controversial, he retired in 1982 at 83 after making remarks that could have been interpreted as racist. He died in 1999, aged 100.

urges and supports presiding circuit judges to resist the constant incursions of the circuit administrators. How was this conflict important? Because the LC's Department was clearly keen to reduce and centralize the regional court system. To the tidy bureaucratic mind, to have vast court complexes in Leeds and Birmingham and Manchester and close down Norwich and Ipswich assizes was desirable. Judges had to resist this. It would make judges more and more seem like the servants of the LC's administrators, and lose their dignity and independence: people simply available to put in the lists as it suited the administrator. It would reduce High Court judges, the red judge of old, to a mere circuit judge. This was a big battle he was fighting. One might thus portray him in a profile, among other things, as being at war simultaneously with the Home Office and the LC's Department to protect the estate and dignity of the High Court judge.

LORD ELWYN-JONES
25 February 1982

Lane was pretty much the obvious candidate. The main rival was Bridge.[1] Lane is a superb judge, a masterful judge, especially on the criminal side. He has a strong streak of vulgarity, and a liking for coarse jokes. This is evidence that he has no side or pomp of any kind – but he has to be careful in what company he shows this streak.

As LCJ he inherited a void. John Widgery was gravely ill for two years before he retired. Why wasn't he eased out sooner? Nobody told me as Lord Chancellor how bad things were. The Old Pals Act operates powerfully in the profession of the judiciary.

Of course, the LCJ's job has changed. Pre-Beeching he was in charge of the entire court system. Parker[2] used to get in here by 6.30, and with just his legal secretary took the whole burden. Post-Beeching the administration work belongs to the LC's Department. The LCJ continues to send who where, and decide who takes what case. He's also vital in assisting the LC on appointments. The LC depends on him very much for support, and I didn't get it from Widgery.

The LCJ should also have close relations with the Home Secretary. It should be as close a relationship as the constitutional proprieties permit. Between Lane and Whitelaw things are very bad. Their mutual feelings amount to something considerably more than distaste. Lane is a prickly character, like a hedgehog. But he's taken against the Home Office in a

1 Nigel Bridge, Lord Bridge of Harwich, presided over the 1975 trial and convictions of the Birmingham Six.
2 Hubert Parker, Baron Parker of Waddington: Lord Chief Justice 1958–71.

big way, and this could be damaging. It's certainly unusual. (I interrupted to say that I knew a bit about this and added that I thought both sides were a bit to blame. Elwyn replied that this may be so, but he indicated that Whitelaw feels deeply let down by Lane.)

He has ability – three firsts. Common sense – feet on the ground. Commitment – very serious about his job. Compassionate – 'I think,' says Elwyn. But he added that Lane's agitation re emptying the prisons was not only because of the administrative shambles of overcrowding, but because he feels a sense of compassion for people locked up in these appalling places – especially Brixton, the remand prison, where people wait for months for trial – and 15 per cent are acquitted, and 25 per cent are never sent to prison.

Rupert Murdoch had now been in control of the Sunday Times *and* The Times *for more than a year. The musical chairs among editors was not working. Neither Harold Evans at* The Times *nor Frank Giles, his successor at the* Sunday Times, *was happy. In January HY had been, as he put it, 'removed from being the first deputy editor'. Would* The Times *be a more appropriate home?*

MEMORANDUM FROM HAROLD EVANS
2 March 1982

The Times
200 Gray's Inn Road

Why *The Times* Needs Hugo Young
BECAUSE he is a brilliant political commentator
BECAUSE he is a man of the highest integrity
BECAUSE he cares about serious reporting of public life in all its aspects
BECAUSE in circumstances improbable but not inconceivable he would be well-placed as an insider to succeed to the chair
Why Hugo Young needs *The Times*
Because *The Times* remains a pinnacle in journalism and its fate attracts commensurate attention
Because it would stretch his talents, engage his sense of duty, and enrich his experience
And because his editor would be utterly committed to him

HE

HY TO HAROLD EVANS
From the *Sunday Times*, 6 March 1982

I think *The Times* is a great institution, which we must all want to flourish. But if I move from here I don't at present think it makes sense for me personally to move in that direction ... I could not possibly take the job with other than a 100 per cent involvement with the task of being your deputy. I doubt if this would leave time to write columns – certainly not to work for them as I try to do (and have time to do) here ... I feel I can pursue my journalistic interests, and help maintain our shared values, here for the moment: while at the same time being open to other possibilities which might come along and which, in an uncertain world, it might be sensible to take up.

A week later HY wrote an account of the previous few days. Murdoch was intending to sack Harold Evans and replace him as editor of The Times *with Charles Douglas-Home. HY thought a change was necessary, morale on the paper was terrible, the paper could simply begin to disintegrate. He had talked with his old boss, who said he was willing to go, and give his successor a good start, but the terms were derisory. In the end he left the paper at the end of March.*

LETTER FROM PETER PRESTON
[undated and in felt pen]

[Guardian letterhead]
From the Editor [Peter Preston]

Thursday

Dear Hugo,

A friend of mine and yours at Brighton said he thought you were feeling a bit beleaguered again. Just to say (again) that unbeleaguered eagerness still lives here if ever existence at Murdoch Towers grows too dire

Best wishes
Peter

HY stayed at the Sunday Times *for two further years.*

DAVID STEEL
25 March 1982

The day of Hillhead.[1] DS now claims virtual certainty that Roy will win. Says he went there four times, and certainty about ten days ago the SDP were terribly down. He walked into the Pond Hotel and thought he'd have to do a morale job. But now he feels it has come back. There have been enough switches. According to our canvass returns, he says, it should be all right, and we've got quite a lot of experience and should be able to get canvassing right.

Victory will be a very considerable achievement. DS advised against running: was especially cautious about the SNP vote, saying he thought they'd pick a good candidate and fight a vigorous campaign (which they did) and thus would pick up a serious number of votes. He found himself actually having to introduce the candidate to this alien people, the Scots, to whom he himself belonged: a very strange reversal of roles – but it worked all right. He said the SDP had far too many English people in sensitive posts like answering the telephone. The Tory candidate, Malone,[2] who had fought Steel last time was an ideal Glasgow candidate: no great stature, but a good Glasgow fighter – a civilized version of Teddy Taylor (a bit unkind that, I think).

It has been a listening campaign. DS has never known an election when so many of the voters have personally heard speeches by the candidates and, if RJ is the winner, by the winner. RJ says 7,000 people have heard his speeches. And extraordinary desire to hear what he has to say.

This is the first campaign, save Warrington, that Roy or any of them has really had to fight – i.e. the first time it has not simply been a question of getting the nomination and waiting for the votes to come in. I.e. he is in the situation the Liberals are always in – without a tribal vote. This is a wholly new experience, and deeply exhausting. Behind the scenes, Roy shows a terrible weariness, it is taking so much out of him. (When I said to DS that on Tuesday Roy had looked less than confident, Steel put it down to this fatigue. And he added that, when the Gallup poll came in on Tuesday evening after their marvellous rally, with 1,700 people there, they simply could not believe it. It did not accord with what Labour and Tory camps, according to our spies, were saying in private about what they were finding. Labour simply could not be several points ahead.)

1 The Glasgow Hillhead by-election was called for 25 March 1982 after the death of Conservative MP Tam Galbraith. Roy Jenkins won the seat and became leader of the SDP.
2 Peter Gerald 'Gerry' Malone: solicitor, journalist; Conservative MP for Aberdeen South 1983–7, for Winchester 1992–7; later Minister of State, Department of Health 1994–7.

Losing does not bear thinking about. The consequences would be terrible. Not so much because, as some journalists say, I'd not be prepared to serve with Owen or Shirley and the others – I've never said that. But it would certainly cause a lot of personal frictions and difficulties. Roy is uniquely equipped to lead the Alliance. His campaign has been Alliance-minded rather than strictly SDP. He said the other night that he and I had been associated for the last three years. When someone pointed out that this took him back into his EEC days, he said there was nothing wrong with a little pre-planning. In fact he has been close to Steel since the last election – unlike the others, who spent some time thinking that Labour could be rescued for their side. (DS had not seen Owen's amazing quote in our paper last Sunday, talking about the SDP's epitaph).[1] I asked what his disagreements were with Jenkins. He thought for quite some time and replied a certain difference over Polaris etc. – he's not been strong enough against Trident. Also, he has seemed to be wavering on law and order – flirting with the Whitelaw sus law[2] by another name: to have sus by a new statute (the stop and search law proposed by Whitelaw) would make everything worse. But otherwise DS thinks that there is agreement: on how to get into incomes policy, how to run a mixed economy, etc.

Very anxious if they win Hillhead to keep up the momentum. It sagged because (a) there were disagreeemnts between Liberals and SDP last autumn–winter, and later about seats carve-up (the Rodgers démarche), and (b) because SDP MPs split three ways over the Tebbit Bill.[3] This leads to something else they have to learn, which is how to exist when there are only two lobbies to go into. The Liberals learned in 1950–51, or rather *from* that period, when they constantly split down the middle about giving or withholding support from the Attlee government. This dogged them for years and years. In 1959, when DS came into politics, and even in 1964, it was the most telling jibe against them; that they were split all ways. Since then they have learned that, unpleasant though it sometimes is in choosing between the bad and the worse, the choice has to be made *together*. An absolute prerequisite. The SDP have yet to understand this. Indeed, it may take some time. Some SDP MPs are merely reselection refugees, and have no understanding or feeling for

1 In the *Sunday Times* of 21 March 1982, David Owen admitted the possibility that the Labour Party might pull itself together – and the rug from under the SDP's feet. 'It could be that our epitaph will be "We saved the Labour Party," ' he told David Lipsey.

2 Random stop and search – the 150-year-old 'sus' law – was seen as a provocation by the black communities in Bristol, Brixton and elsewhere, and the practice contributed to a series of inner-city riots. 'Sus' was abandoned after a judicial inquiry into the 1981 riots, but law and order remained a popular political theme.

3 Norman Tebbit, then Employment Secretary, introduced the 1982 Employment Act which challenged the 'closed shops' close to the hearts of trade-union leaders: places of employment where union membership was compulsory. Tebbit later called the Act 'his greatest achievement in government'.

what the party is really all about. Privately Rodgers and Owen will confess that they regret that so many have come across – especially the ones who are the wrong type.

As to the Alliance leadership, the mechanism is not yet thought out. What DS is beginning to favour is a steering committee jointly chaired by himself and Jenkins, which at some point makes clear that Jenkins will be prime minister if they win. It is quite delicate. Clearly Steel is an electoral asset, and it would be counterproductive to submerge him under Jenkins. He must remain the clear leader of the Liberals at the election, and indeed hopes to perhaps take the lead in television etc. They may also have to select a shadow team – itself a delicate task.

One of Jenkins's great assets is his ability to sweep grandly across hard issues in a way none of the other people including Steel can do. He can obliterate disagreements with the sweep of his hand. It's his manner, and his experience, and his past, and his weight. He'd be much better than me at running the show if we got in – but I have fought an election campaign as a party leader, which none of them has done. And it is a very difficult thing indeed to do.

NEIL KINNOCK[1]
Lunch, 22 April 1982

FALKLANDS It's been the only subject at Shadow Cabinet for days. Our line is the only one we could take: i.e. back the task force, attack the Argentinians, but never forget that there will be major questions to ask after it's all over about the cock-up that began it. Because Mrs T knows that, the only line *she* can take is to make it a great issue of principle. That's the only way to transcend the cock-up.

When and if the shooting starts, Labour will again be moving for ways to attack the government, I deduced. If we fire first, that will be appalling. *Must* make sure they fire first. But even if they do, and we then get into military difficulties, the line of attack against the government will be that, apart from the major starting cock-up, the soldiers were let down by incompetent political leadership at home. Labour very keen to ensure that their line is always to attack the politicians, never the soldiers (or the generals?). Kinnock describes the Shadow Cabinet as having all the time to remind themselves that they are not the government. Their discussions quickly sound as though they are, as they map out what should be done, how to treat the Americans etc. etc. Also, Healey going to Washington.

---

1 Neil Kinnock was then chief Opposition spokesman on education.

What is the total party picture? He thinks Benn and Hart[1] have very little support indeed. Great solidarity behind the Foot line. (This surprised me.) Benn is making mischief, and Hart is falling into traps. Better respect for the Dalyell[2] and Lyon line: who have said from the start that the force should not be sent.

He thinks a mistake was made in sticking to all this paramountcy stuff: that the islanders' wishes are paramount. But he conceded that it may not matter, after this display of what the realities are. However, Kinnock thinks that if, even after this, the islanders won't buy a deal, then in honour we must stick by them.

The bigger problem is sovereignty. A concept, says he, which Mrs T *alone* has always insisted on, while all other ministers have found other words in the lexicon in order to avoid mentioning it. He sees her, however, at some advantage from the possibility of an election even a year from now. It disciplines the backbench troops.

LABOUR PARTY   It is being somewhat rejuvenated, at least in the SC, by the Falklands crisis. The breath of life. But he did not at all sound like someone who seriously thought Labour would win an election. He cited Dennis Skinner as proof of a widespread anxiety. At a recent meeting of the organizing committee of the NEC, Skinner declared that Labour was doing just as badly in the 1973 local government by-elections and national by-elections as they are now, and yet won in 1974. Kinnock has called for the figures of Labour's percentage of the poll in 1973 compared with now, which he knows will show a sharp drop. But the point is that even Skinner can see there is reason for worry. This means that the whole party may become a touch more realistic.

His scheme is to expel those who are employed by Militant, but not those who merely belong. The latter course would begin a witch-hunt that might never end, and which would be impossible to conduct. But by expelling the employees he strikes a blow at Militant's whole organization in the constituencies. It would mean that Militant people could not lay open claim to power in Labour parties. It would go underground, where it would find things much harder to operate. (When challenged with the thought that Labour could never actually police this, and the constituents would simply ignore it – also with the thought that the conference will see a huge fight about it, with constituents and unions miles apart – Kinnock basically shrugged.)

He thinks Benn a fading force, and especially likely to be when the

---

1 Judith Hart: Labour MP for Lanark 1959–83, for Clydesdale 1983–7; later Baroness Hart of Lanark; along with Tony Benn, argued for the withdrawal of the task force sent to the Falklands.
2 Tam Dalyell; Labour MP for West Lothian 1962–83, for Linlithgow 1983–2005.

leadership contest is fought. In three years' time, perhaps. He thinks Hattersley the most likely to succeed: a far more radical figure than Shore. He said Hattersley at around the age of 45 or 46 had decided that upwards progression was made by ingratiation. But at some point later had decided to stop this and simply be his own man. The latter Hattersley had been a much more impressive figure. But he added that the electoral college made the whole thing unpredictable. It depends on the received perceptions people have of the politicians, rather than the much deeper knowledge of reality which exists in the parliamentary party. God knows what these perceptions are – about Shore, for example. As for himself, he ruled himself out of contention, while saying he would have a terrible job to vote for either Hatttersley or Shore.

ON EDUCATION Labour will bring in two bills. One a quickie, in the first week or two: to abolish assisted places, illegalize local authorities buying places other than for handicapped children, and one other thing. The other bill, to replace the 1944 Education Act, would be huge: redefining comprehensiveness, setting up a lot of costs for private schools (including VAT on fees, abolishing charitable status etc. etc.).

A SENIOR MINISTER (CABINET)
23 April 1982 (evening)

(He is not in the War Cabinet, but is senior and sensible.)[1]

The Conservative Party is much more divided than the Labour Party. Labour is amazingly full of warmongers. When I said that we ought to be very careful indeed not to allow any action until negotiations had really broken down, I was told the story of one Labour MP who had come up to a minister and said we should be getting in there quick and rooting out the Argies. This was Stan Newens – in other respects something close to a lefty pacifist.[2] This demonstrates how hooked Labour has got on the fascist junta and all that.

The Tories are deeply divided. There are people who say we should bomb now, including Buenos Aires (Winston Churchill),[3] ranging across to people who say we should use no military force at all in any circumstances (David Knox).[4] Between them there is a great shifting mass. We

1 HY has written alongside this entry the name Prior.
2 Stan Newens: coal miner, schoolteacher; Labour MP for Epping 1964–70; Labour and Co-op MP for Harlow 1974–83.
3 Winston Churchill MP: war correspondent, journalist, broadcaster, Conservative MP for Stretford 1970–83, for Davyhulme, Manchester 1983–97; grandson of the wartime prime minister Winston Churchill.
4 David Knox: Conservative MP for Leek, Staffordshire, 1970–83, for Staffordshire Moorlands 1983–97.

won't escape without losing some of the right wing, who won't accept anything short of some great naval action. How big this group is I cannot say, and nor can they. But there are not too many of them. The majority of the party is very anxious, but won't rock the boat.

The situation is fraught with political peril for us. The worst disaster I envisage is taking an action that is relatively unsuccessful – I rule out total fiasco, but the trouble is that when you start trying to retake the islands and do not completely succeed, that could in fact be a failure. So the most plausible disaster is a relatively unsuccessful action, after which we have to accept terms less attractive than those on offer now. Then, below that, there are lesser gradations of failure. I think that if we could squeeze a bit more out of the Argies, with American economic pressure and Reagan coming off the fence, we could probably get an acceptable deal.

But the problem is time. It may be right to say that a speedy military action is against our world interests, but once you get the troops down there you can't have them hanging about. All they do is get seasick and become unfit for action: literally unusable. That's the great problem. The trouble is we're getting there too fast, although not being on the inside I don't know how fast.

I have no reason to believe that Margaret has been other than perfectly reasonable and understanding about what has to be done. She is not to be counted among the Churchillites. She does get carried away by her own rhetoric, and is egged on by others on the back benches, but, when it come to the point, she is sensible. She has been standing the strain with incredible stamina. A quite remarkable lady.

What would she stick at? I can't say. What does victory actually consist of? Well, if you have to go in and retake the islands, you retake them and then get the United Nations in to look after it, because you can't go on holding it against a belligerent Argentina 8,000 miles away.

Are there negotiating positions? I don't believe we can go on talking about the wishes of the Falkland Islanders. Francis [Pym] has tried to fudge this, and will go on doing so. We should remember, by the way, the wishes of the British nationals in the Argentine. There are ten times more of those than of islanders. What do we think is going to happen to them?

I have been appalled by the popular press, and the attacks on Carrington and the Foreign Office. Especially the *Daily Mail*. They are bitterly and deeply unhelpful, and have no respect for the truth. Actually, I think it may be the case that in the end the Tory Party would wear a more compromising solution than either the popular press or the Labour Party.

KEN LIVINGSTONE
Train journey from Harrogate, 3 June 1982

LABOUR PARTY Is certain to move to the left, and become a left-wing party. No chance of winning the next election. Who can possibly imagine Foot winning an election? Or Healey? They just will not bring out the Labour Party vote. They were responsible for the failures of Labour government. People still care very much about this, and still remember it. They weren't even any good as social democrats. Even if you forget about the economic stuff, they deported Agee and Hosenball, passed racist legislation and so on.[1] Corporatist and centrist and totally uninterested in party democracy. Foot is simply pathetic. I thought at one time the office would make him grow. But it hasn't. He doesn't give a lead on anything. Look at the Falklands.

It is all the more necessary to have a leader who will bring out the maximum party vote when we have some of the centre vote being siphoned off by the SDP. This just increases the need for a properly left figure who can convince people he actually believes in something. That's what Labour has been lacking for so long. And that's why Thatcher is such a bloody formidable opponent.

We would not want Foot to go before the election. Better for us to have a leadership election after defeat has finally proved that the old gang and the old ways won't work. Also after a new parliament, which, whatever the size of the Labour Party, will have a *better* Labour Party. Benn is the only possible candidate. I wouldn't bust a gut for Tony Benn, but he's all there is. Is he too unpopular? You'll find that, once he becomes leader, things will very dramatically change. I've found that at the GLC. The leader is by far the most important person: everyone has to relate to him one way or the other. If Benn is leader, he will be seen and will probably behave quite differently from now, when he is the permanent outsider. This would be even more true if he became prime minister. I suppose, Kinnock could get the reluctant support of the hard left – you never know, things may turn back for him by some stroke of luck. One just does not really know how much he is motivated by convictions and how much by opportunism. Probably a mixture – most politicians have mixed motives.

1 Philip Agee – a former CIA man – and Mark Hosenball, two American journalists working in London, wrote an article in the listings journal *Time Out* about GCHQ, the Cold War signals headquarters in Cheltenham. They were deported in April 1977 by the then Labour Home Secretary Merlyn Rees. The jibe about racist legislation could refer to the then Home Secretary James Callaghan's Commonwealth Immigration Bill of 1968, drafted to prevent Kenya Asians who held British passports from entering Britain, while admitting white settlers fleeing Kenya.

The most amazing thing about the PLP is how little talent there is. On the left as well as the right. I remember in about 1975, when I first met people like Varley and Rees. I just couldn't believe it. That they were Cabinet ministers, running the country. This means that in a left government there would always be a place for Hattersley, for example. He's able and he's an opportunist. He's done rather well as Home Office spokesman. I haven't disagreed with a thing he's said about the police, for example. He's also been a good anti-racist. Even Healey could have his car and a job for a few years. There was a time when I thought Foot was going to retire gracefully, to let in Shore. There was also a time when Shore seemed acceptable to the left. But I've been very surprised by the venom of his language against the left.

IN GOVERNMENT we would need to fill up a lot of top Civil Service posts with party people. More than just political advisers. You'd also find a number of younger civil servants who would want to come on board as party people: who'd be proud to sacrifice the rest of their Civil Service careers because they'd really enjoy five years with us. Also, larger number of MPs in departments, watching them. There'd also be the judiciary. Have to get a lot of early retirements there. Are there any radical lawyers to put in their place? There are plenty of solicitors in that category, if no barristers.

But we wouldn't achieve everything. The priority would be direction of investment. Also stopping the flow of capital out of the country. It all depends on how it's presented. I find if I go to a meeting and say we must stop five billion of British money going out of the country, it gets wildly applauded. Nothing in the direction of investment would be really unpopular either. Only the media would make it into a great issue. But we could only make a start. We might then get defeated, and then have another crack at the election after next.

ELECTIONS are very important. They are the only way of cleaning out the party and bureaucracy. The only creative things in politics happen after an election defeat. The party renovates itself. That's why the Russian system is so bad. A dead bureaucracy never cleaned out. That's why I'm in favour of parliamentary democracy. But there's also the point that an armed insurrection could never work in this country, like some of the loonies think. You'd never stand a chance. The British army and police is probably bettered trained to put it down than any other in the world – especially after Ulster.

MILITANT is a bad joke, not a menace. It's had eighty organizers, a lot of money and a selling newspaper for ten years, and where has it got? Nowhere. If I'd had that, I could have been in total control of the Labour Party by now. Militant is pretty irrelevant. Also, it's hampered by being a slightly secret organization. It can't speak out. I and Ted Knight have no restraints. We have no other affiliations. Therefore we don't have to watch what we say. We therefore probably get more support. Also, Militant is very conservative. I've been defeated a number of times on our executive because Militant has voted with the right: Ulster troops out, gay rights etc. Although the left will all be trying to stop Militant from being expelled – we're all against all expulsions – secretly we'll be glad if they've gone. They just confuse the picture at the moment. They've got no constituency control. Four constituencies in Liverpool and one in Bradford. That's all they've got.

SOCIALIST ORGANIZER[1] are a bunch of hard thugs. They just want to destroy even us at the GLC, to wreck the whole system. They're a bit of a nuisance, but no more than that.

Some of the Benn people are very ham-handed. Fancy putting out minutes – the Labour '82 lot – about their plans for packing the NEC. At the GLC we have been open, but we don't take caucus minutes. You're just a laughing stock if you do it so crudely. This will affect the NEC elections this year. Getting Kinnock and Lestor off is too public. Bad tactics. May backfire. The one to watch is Maynard. Can the right get rid of her? If they can't she'll be party chairman next year. Which gives the power of making statements. I like Joan. She's not an operator. But she's got sound ideas.

GLC AND LONDON LABOUR We've learned a tremendous amount – don't forget it was a tremendous change for us. Take the press. Suddenly, from years of trying to get the press to take any interest at all, they never stopped. Everything I said was reported. You had to take time to learn how to deal with it. That's one experience which will be useful when we get more national power. We've also learned how to deal with bureaucracies, to some extent. When I came in, the chief executive thought that, as usual, he could manipulate the leader to persuade the rest of the party to forget about the manifesto. He couldn't understand it when I insisted on making so many decisions group decisions and not letting the manifesto be screwed.

1 Also known as the Socialist Organizer Alliance, one of a number of Marxist factions that competed for ideological influence at the time. It took its name from an intermittent journal published by the Socialist Campaign for a Labour Victory.

I find the group very helpful. It's quite wrong for the leader to make single-minded decisions, especially when there is a sudden crisis. Only in the most extreme situations should you not take time to think and consult. That's what I do all the time. I've quite often changed my mind as a result.

The quality of my front bench is now very high. Better, I think, than the front benches on either side in the Commons. We changed some of them after a year. A bad right-winger was replaced by a good one, a bad left-winger by a good one. There's quite a party balance. The hard left does not have a majority. I have to keep the centre with me, which I do – without serious attack from the left. Benn would have to do the same thing. The reason the quality is high is partly because I spent quite a lot of time persuading people to stand for GLC election. For the first time we actually had some seriously contested nominations. People gave up jobs. About three-quarters (check) of the committee chairs are full-timers, who get all in all about £6,000 per year. Too little? I don't have time to spend any money. Look at this suit. I haven't bought any piece of clothing for a year – just no time. Must do something about that. You see, I'm an ideologist, so I don't care all that much about money.

REDISTRIBUTION ETC My first interest in politics was in the statistics of elections. I became a real expert. Poring over them all the time. In London the redistribution is not half so bad as we once thought. *ST* survey following the local election results was probably about right. One thing it showed very clearly was that the Alliance vote did not vary more than 11 per cent – i.e. it was very flat all across London with one or two exceptions. Whereas Labour and Tory votes varied about 40 per cent. This is the key to the whole SDP problem. Tower Hamlets is about the last of the really rotten Labour areas. And Hackney. This is why the Liberals are doing well there. Being Liberal is the only way to be anti-Labour, which are rotten, corrupt and showing all the worst side of old-fashioned Labour bureaucracies.

PARLIAMENT I want to get in. Actually, local government has never recovered from Crosland. The key speech about the party being over.[1] From then on the power has gone more and more to the centre. But I'll wait and see. I do think that, the election after next, there may be about twelve GLC people in Parliament. There hasn't been one for the last fifteen years. They'll be a good influx, with real experience of running left-wing government.

---

1 In 1975 Anthony Crosland, then Environment Secretary – a brief that embraced local government – is supposed to have said in a speech in Manchester that the party was over. He warned that government could not underwrite all council spending.

SDP made a great mistake in letting the Labour refugees like Islington Council[1] in. They may not win a single seat in Parliament next time. All their existing MPs may get beaten. Look at the redistribution in their seats. It's very unfavourable to them. Wherever you look. Owen may be the only survivor. Jenkins has had a bad turn of the die. Shirley Williams is getting bad material in, having already squeezed the Labour vote dry.

Maybe the Alliance plus the Tories will shut us out for longer than I think. But sooner on later we'll win, because sooner or later people will get fed up of them – the more so if they are a kind of centrist alliance.

IMPRESSIONS Humorous, decent, open, extraordinarily detached, very committed of course. A good political analyst. Very adept and knowledgeable with electoral figures. Also young. One remembers he can afford to wait, unlike Benn. I think he will be leader of the Labour Party before the end of the century.

WILLIAM WHITELAW
[no date] on lobby terms, for what it's worth ... (HY)

PALACE BREAK-IN, JUNE 1982 The first stage of the disciplinary process must come from McNee.[2] He's in charge of his own discipline. Home Secretary is an appellate position in all such cases. Therefore Whitelaw must be careful next week to avoid prejudicing that role. He thinks that calling for McNee's resignation is pretty futile, since he's going so soon anyway.

The irony is that we have spent large sums of money on new surveillance equipment at Buckingham Palace in the last two years. What this episode shows is that there's nothing you can do about human error, however good your equipment is. The human factor was incredibly lax, with just about everyone saying it couldn't happen here.

There certainly will be a new security chief. This has already been set in train and discussed, before Dellow.[3] WW wouldn't say what was in Dellow, commenting that it had already been leaked in bits and pieces and he didn't want to say any more about what was in it.

He personally was much concerned with finding out more about supervision. Who did the supervision of the palace policy? Did the head of a

---

1 In 1981 and 1982 all three Labour MPs representing Islington constituencies defected to the SDP. Islington Council was fiercely – even notoriously – left wing at the time.
2 Sir David McNee: commissioner, Metropolitan Police 1977–82.
3 Assistant Commissioner John Dellow led the investigation into security shortcomings.

division of the Met make regular visits to the palace to see that the men were working properly?

Was he under personal pressure to resign? The chief whip tells him he is in no trouble. His enemies, on this occasion, are actually not making much noise. They usually only start up when they think they've got the Prime Minister on their side. On this occasion they quite emphatically have not.

MRS T AT No. 10
27 October 1982

A reception for people who went to the Far East[1]. I arrive late. She happened to be at the door of the room. Escorts me with amazing solicitousness to get the right drink, sends for soda when there's only water, explains that she likes to do this kind of thing especially for the pilots and so on. She then leads me into a further room and begins a guided tour. I feel the envious eyes of the other hacks burning at my back. But the conversation is inevitably innocuous: or rather one-sided. Her explaining; me grunting with suitable interest. It *is* interesting. There was nothing on the surfaces when she arrived: 'Furnished flat to let,' she described it. She got silver from Lord Brownlow.[2] Many pictures were changed. She has all English painters, with a special emphasis on portraits of people associated with No. 10 etc. The first she showed me was a George I, who gave No. 10 to Walpole and yet who wasn't represented on the wall until she came. She also went out of her way to get a good Nelson. There was a very good Younger Pitt, other admirals and soldiers. She knew them all: the provenance of the pictures and of every item of silver (one or two pieces were 'govt hospitality fund'). The room was full of round tables – 'better for lunch,' she said That was the furthest room. Then a smaller room with a long thin table for ten at the most – almost in a sort of hallway between two bigger rooms. This was where she had working lunches: 'with Helmut Schmidt, for example, now it's Helmut Kohl'. This led into the 'pillar' room, where the drinks were being served. Beyond that were the blue room and the white room. She had by now been joined by various other hacks, and was doing the full works. There were several Turners and several Wilsons: she wanted to get the glass off, but they wouldn't let her. Also several Romneys. The only non-English painting was a small landscape . . .

1 Mrs Thatcher and officials visited the People's Republic of China in 1982, to discuss the future of Hong Kong with Deng Xiaoping.
2 Possibly a reference to Peregrine Cust, the 6th Baron Brownlow, once mayor of Grantham – a post later held by Alderman Alfred Roberts, father of Mrs Thatcher – or to his son Edward Cust, the 7th Baron Brownlow.

Altogether she has a very good eye, and obviously a lot of natural interest in her surroundings. She had made the beginnings of a science corner in the pillar room. Newton bust. Picture of Boyle (she recited Boyle's law).

A fairly endless recitation. Answers questions, but not a listener – never a listener, on the big things as well.

Talk to Alan Donald, Far East man at FCO. He likens her to Queen Bess. Her womanhood is vital. The civil servants are like Essex and Raleigh: favourites come and go; the Queen goes on regally for ever. Not dependent on anyone, owing no favours. He claims she *does* like a good old hammer-and-tongs debate, and therefore does *not* conform to the exact picture of someone surrounded by toadies.

1983

18 January   The Franks inquiry finds the Thatcher Cabinet 'not to blame' for the Argentinian invasion of the Falklands.

8 March   President Reagan calls the Soviet Union the 'Evil Empire'.

23 March   President Reagan announces a space-based 'Star Wars' missile defence shield.

9 June   The Thatcher government wins a landslide election and a second term.

21 August   Philippines opposition leader Benigno Aquino murdered at Manila airport.

1 September   Soviet MIGs shoot down a Korean airliner.

2 October   Neil Kinnock picked as the new Labour leader in succession to Michael Foot, with Roy Hattersley as deputy.

14 October   Trade and Industry Secretary Cecil Parkinson resigns after his mistress Sara Keays speaks to *The Times*.

23 October   Suicide bombers kill 241 US marines and 58 French paratroopers in Beirut.

27 October   US marines storm the former British colony of Grenada after a coup by Marxists with links to Cuba.

30 October   Military rule in Argentina ends with democratic elections.

Deaths   Luis Buñuel, Kenneth Clark, Jack Dempsey, Arthur Koestler, David Niven, Ralph Richardson, South African leader Balthazar Johannes Vorster, William Walton, Rebecca West, Tennessee Williams

DENIS HEALEY
Phone, 25 March 1983

THE DAY AFTER DARLINGTON[1] It's been good for Labour, the turn of the tide perhaps. It showed how much depends on the

---

1 Labour MP for Darlington Edward Fletcher, who had held the seat since 1964, died in February 1983. At the by-election on 24 March, Labour's Oswald O'Brien held the seat against a Conservative challenge.

candidates. We had a very good candidate here, a terrible one in Bermond-sey.[1] But the swing of under 2 per cent is not enough to get us very far. It's not enough. We've got a bad candidate at Cardiff, I'm told. But it's a 6,000 Tory majority and we wouldn't really expect to win there anyway. It's very bad for the SDP.[2] Will lead to tensions between Jenkins and his party, and between the SDP and the Liberals. Of course, SDP candidate was terrible, and was exposed totally.

The Tories will be relieved. But their vote again dropped by more than ours did. And there are 79 seats where the Liberals came second to the Tories. I think most of their pros – people like Parkinson [the party chairman] – will be getting very wary indeed about a June election.

The coming document is infinitely better than the *Labour Programme '82*. It's halfway to a decent manifesto. The exercise has been useful. We've got agreement with the soft left on the NEC about what should be in the manifesto. That's a good change.

The Conservatives won a landslide victory in the general election on 9 June, with 397 seats, Labour 209, and the Alliance 23. Mrs Thatcher, now in a position of enormous strength, made several changes to her Cabinet: Nigel Lawson became Chancellor of the Exchequer in succession to Geoffrey Howe, who replaced Francis Pym as Foreign Secretary. On 12 June Michael Foot announced his intention to quit as Labour leader.

FRANCIS PYM
Phone, 6.50 p.m., 11 June 1983

He rang to say the BBC had implied that he had resigned. This was untrue: I have resigned at the Prime Minister's request, he said not for attribution. The BBC also implied I had been offered another job and had turned it down. This also untrue.

Further, it has been said that I would take the Speakership. As I have always said, I am not interested in the Speakership. That remains the position.

HY asked him whether he had been asked to accept it. He said that it had been implied that he might let himself be a candidate.

---

1 Sitting Bermondsey Labour MP Bob Mellish resigned in protest at what he saw as the party's leftward drift. The local Labour Party fielded its secretary, Peter Tatchell, whose name was then linked with the Gay Liberation Front. On 23 February 1983 the seat was won by the Liberal candidate, Simon Hughes, with a majority of more than 9,000.
2 The Social Democratic candidate polled over 12,000 votes (the Liberal in 1979 polled 5,000) and came third.

He said, when I commiserated, 'I suppose my face just doesn't fit.' He added, 'You will keep in touch, won't you?'

JOHN BIFFEN
21 July 1983

Bumped into him at his party. The day of the cabinet meeting to discuss a cuts package for the first time. JB said: Lawson was mad; he wanted public spending cuts for the next ninety-nine years and wanted every saving to be channelled into tax cuts. JB thought this was bad politics, if not bad economics. The Tory Party likes its cottage hospitals, he said. Went on about protective public spending, as usual. Said he thought he should make another 'three years of austerity' speech. Said he thought taxes should rise – but was alone in thinking so.

JOHN BIFFEN
Phone, 16 September 1983

Has already written his speech to conference, defending the anti-PR attitude of the government. Says that he will do this, has done it, without compromising his personal position, which is agnostic and prepared to favour PR in some circumstances. Recalls 1929, when the minority Labour government prepared a scheme for an alternative vote (straight first and second preference). 'I will satisfy the leaderene without mortgaging my conscience.'

Says it is entirely a politician's issue. Could become a factor if an election produced a hung parliament. The map is changing. The Labour Party may lose votes in two-thirds of the country, but still get a good presence in Parliament on a much lower percentage of the poll than the Alliance. 'I will not be speaking in the Angus Maude caste.[1] But I've convinced myself of a good practical case. Four-fifths of the people there won't know what we're talking about.'

Why don't more people mind about PR? There is a lot of cynicism about Westminster. The rhetoric of hustings implies a stronger division between people than there really is. No sense of outrage and frustration such as the Chartists really did evince. People here are very acquiescent.

In Parliament: the usual channels work well when it's only two across

---

1 Angus Maude, no longer in Mrs Thatcher's Cabinet, was sometimes called 'the Mekon', perhaps because of a faint resemblance to Dan Dare's extraterrestrial arch-enemy with the bulging forehead in the 1950s comic *The Eagle*.

the table. Much easier to arrange things. Once you bring in formally the Liberals, why not the SDP, and why not the Ulster Unionists: bigger than the SDP – and especially since all Ulster business is done by order not by bills?

Note how all parties behave with whatever power they have at their disposal. In recent contests re manning of the select committee on Welsh affairs (check), Liberals (who have two Welsh MPs) were ruthless in keeping Plaid Cymru (who also have two) off the committee, despite Plaid's complaint that Wales was all they had.

JB concluded by asking himself to a meal in Blackpool. When I said I imagined he was full up, he announced his strategy for invitation: I accept them all, he said, and am then quite ruthless in deciding which ones to cancel.

PATRICK MAYHEW
2 November 1983

I tried hard to avoid becoming Solicitor General. When Margaret sees me, she asks me whether I'm enduring it. Maybe I have too high a regard for my political weight, but I'd rather be in a department. Unlike Michael Havers, who's never really wanted to do anything else. One does almost nothing in Parliament. I like being in the House. Not many people can really make it sing, at the dispatch box (implication: PM, who is a good commons performer, thinks he does). I have a passionate ambition not to get promoted (to Attorney General).

But the job is not without interest. Hoping to do the Trade Unions and Labour Relations Bill. The Department of Employment people are not very high class. Also, I'm getting involved in the EEC, and getting to know that blasted law. I'll be doing the Kent Kirk[1] case, where for once we are on the side of the Commission.

I've been lucky in the two men I've worked for, Prior and Whitelaw. Prior, alas, is getting jaded. Losing heart. Getting interested in this farm he's gone into with Sainsbury.[2] But his approach to trade-union law was absolutely right, as everyone now admits. We had some terrible fights to preserve the moderate approach, and especially against banning the closed shop. We would all have resigned if it had been forced on us. That bloody little Sherman kept coming in. Also the stiff campaign was being run in

---

1 Captain Kent Kirk, a Danish fisherman and a member of the European Parliament. His trawler was stopped by the Royal Navy just inside the then 12-mile limit for territorial waters. He went to the European Court of Justice to argue that Britain's fishing regulations were illegal.

2 Sir Tim Sainsbury: businessman; Conservative MP for Hove 1973–97; PPS to the Environment Secretary 1979–83. James Prior had farmed in East Anglia. He became a director of J Sainsbury in 1984.

the Lords by Orr-Ewing,[1] who of course has a closed shop in his own business, as I reminded him. I doubt if Tebbit would have done anything very differently. But certainly he thinks our approach, coupled with his approach, has been the right one: and effective (which it has).

WHITELAW had a tremendous sense of fun. I remember within about five days there was Fagan's break-in to the palace, the park bombs killing guardsmen, and the Trestrail business.[2] It was an appalling time. I went into Willie and he looked at the end of his rope one morning. But within about three minutes he'd seen the funny side of things. Both Prior and he were loose about words: insensitive to nuance. But both were people you'd follow and support, even if you disagreed. That is the key to being a good top politician, or one of them.

HAILSHAM is another great old man: a hero of mine. Much chortling over Havers's chances of success, owing to the fact that Wimbledon looks highly loseable, on the basis of the Penrith figures,[3] and hence it must be doubted whether he would be offered the job should Hailsham go – which itself looks unlikely. He has been better this year than last: full of beans. Incidentally, a Hailsham *mot*: 'If adulterers had been run out of public life we would never have won either Trafalgar or Waterloo.'

Hailsham, however, favours a law of criminal trespass, so the government will smile on a private member's bill coming up. Mayhew is strongly against it, on the ground that it will cause endless bother for the police without a compensating advantage.

LAW SOCIETY a dreadful body. The man who recently took a solicitor to court to get him struck off (recent South Wales case, involving six-figure sums) was a hero. The solicitor eventually surrendered before it actually got to court. But the complainant was using a clause in the Solicitor's Act permitting this. The Law Society had brushed it all aside, even though the taxing master had reduced the solicitor's claim from £160,000 to £80,000. A question which was decided by Vinelott J. was whether the Law Society should pay the costs. He said he had no

---

1 Baron Orr-Ewing of Little Berkhamsted: deputy chairman of the Association of Conservative Peers 1980–86.

2 All events of July 1982: on 9 July an intruder, Michael Fagan, was found in the Queen's bedroom; on 19 July Whitelaw announced the resignation of the Queen's bodyguard, Commander Michael Trestrail, from the Metropolitan Police, over a relationship with a male prostitute; on 20 July two IRA bombs killed 8 soldiers, injured 47 people, and killed 7 horses in Hyde Park.

3 The Penrith and the Border by-election of 28 July was caused by the elevation of William Whitelaw to the peerage, so that he could become Leader of the House of Lords. The Alliance candidate turned Whitelaw's majority of 15,000 at the general election into one for the Conservative candidate of little more than 500. Wimbledon remained a Conservative seat until 1997.

jurisdiction. All the same, it's been an important bomb under the Law Society with its inadequate approach to self-regulation.

Incidentally, Mayhew drew the Lloyd's analogy. If we hadn't given in to the Lloyd's demand to self-regulate, things would never have got so bad, he said. He actually voted, as a minister, against the self-regulation bill – Meacher's[1] I think – the only minister to do so. He said he did so because he couldn't be saying one thing about the unions and something else about Lloyds.

Mayhew was especially vexed at ever being called a Thatcher spy – which Prior certainly thought he was when they came in in '79.

---

1 Michael Meacher: Labour MP for Oldham West 1970–97, for Oldham West and Royton since 1997; Environment Minister 1997–2003.

1984

5 March   Miners' strikes begin: soon only 21 of Britain's 174 pits are working. The active mines are in Nottinghamshire.

23 March   Sarah Tisdall jailed for six months for passing cruise-missile documents to *The Guardian*.

17 April   Policewoman Yvonne Fletcher is shot outside the Libyan embassy in London; diplomats are later expelled.

23 April   Americans claim discovery of the Aids virus; this is to be disputed by France.

8 May   The Soviet Union announces that it will boycott the Olympic Games in Los Angeles.

29 May   Riot police and miners battle at Orgreave colliery, near Sheffield.

6 June   Indian troops storm the Sikh Golden Temple at Amritsar.

18 August   Civil servant Clive Ponting is charged under the Official Secrets Act for passing information to a Labour MP about the controversial sinking of the Argentinian training ship *General Belgrano*.

21 August   Filipinos march in Manila against the Marcos government.

12 October   A bomb blast devastates a Brighton hotel where Tory conference delegates are staying. Mrs Thatcher narrowly escapes injury; three die.

31 October   Indira Gandhi, prime minister of India, is shot by her Sikh bodyguards; riots in India as Rajiv Gandhi takes power.

25 November   Bob Geldof of the Boomtown Rats forms Band Aid; four days later releases 'Do They Know It's Christmas?' in aid of starving Ethiopians.

3 December   A fatal gas leak kills thousands around the Union Carbide factory in Bhopal, India.

Deaths   Soviet premier Yuri Andropov, Count Basie, John Betjeman, Richard Burton, Sir Arthur 'Bomber' Harris, Eric Morecambe, J. B. Priestley, François Truffaut

GERALD KAUFMAN
Office, 25 January 1984

BENN   Gerald Kaufman will be on call for Chesterfield.[1] He thinks
that the Tories will want Benn to win – and suggests they may play down
the campaign, not try too hard etc. etc., but the question is whether they
can control the situation in that way. Also whether the Tory press will
play it that way. Also indicates that Kinnock would prefer Benn to lose –
although when directly challenged says that the best interest of the Labour
Party is for a win by an increased majority. Says that Labour should
increase its majority by 10 per cent according to national opinion polls.
In fact says that the Liberal is the only one with a chance of winning.
What it will take is for the Liberal to edge ahead of the Tory in a poll,
and the Liberals will pile in and say that the only way to keep Benn out
is by voting Liberal. This is the big fear. Liberals are very good at this.
Have already got *Focus* into lots of Chesterfield homes for a ward by-
election.

Varley says that Labour will win because people hate the government.
This goes to the heart of GK's political analysis. Maybe people do hate
Thatcher in large numbers. The question is, Will they vote Labour? This
leads to . . .

ALLIANCE   Labour's total job, as he sees it, is to down the Alliance.
In a sense, the Tories don't matter. It is to get a larger slice of that 58 (or
56) per cent of the voters who were anti-Thatcher in June. I.e. if the
Tories stay the same, and the Alliance goes down to 14 per cent, then
Labour can win the next general election. If the Alliance gets even over
14 per cent (but less than 25) and the Tories go down, Labour can
also win.

KINNOCK'S STRATEGY   should be to play to his strength. One
of his biggest mistakes has been to talk about defence. He should totally
ignore it, until he's worked out what he wants. A small mistake was the
Elgin Marbles – typical of an imperfect idea of what his job is all about.
Which is to get 13 million people to wake up one Thursday in 1987 or
'88 and say to themselves they are going to vote for a Labour government
that day.

The positive sides to the strategy should be the NHS and unemployment. On the NHS, Labour can't lose, says GK. Their private polls show

---

1 By-election caused by the resignation of Eric Varley, who had been appointed chairman of Coalite Ltd. Tony
Benn, who had lost his Bristol South-East seat in the 1983 election, was the Labour candidate.

Labour miles ahead on this one. According to his theory of political conduct, Mrs Thatcher makes a mistake in even talking about the NHS because, whatever the truth of the matter, people just don't believe the NHS is safe with the Tories (the mirror of Labour on defence – people don't believe defence is safe with Labour, a foul lie). On unemployment etc., Labour has made the cardinal mistake from '79 to 83 of coming out as the most reactionary party in Britain, of defending every job and attacking every ancient pit closure. This must all change. Labour must and can emerge as the party best equipped to make the shift into new technology and to protect the British way of life in the process. It should favour the capital-intensive manufacturing industries, which are the only ones with growth potential, and favour them making huge profits from which to finance a growth of public investment. At the election, Labour got stuck, thanks to P. Shore, as the party which favoured borrowing – another thing the British don't like. Did any union leaders understand this? He said that union leaders' cooperation was vital, and that it would be important to have thrashed out this kind of policy within a year – since by then we would be halfway to another election. Basnett and C. Jenkins[1] were the main ones who understood it – but neither was likely to do anything much about it. Basnett never has, and Jenkins has regularly shown a gulf between his knowledge and his action – which makes him all the more deplorable.

THE STAKES are the highest possible. GK put it like this. The Tories can win only one more election. There's no way Thatcher or any successor will win in 1992. What matters is whether it is Labour or the Alliance which replaces them. If Labour does very badly in the next election, Labour is finished. His own measure of survival, as a minimum, is that they should regain 50 seats, even though this won't put them into power. If they don't do that, millions of Labour voters will decide that Labour is done for and will change allegiance. This could happen sooner. He painted a worse-case scenario. This showed Labour as treading water in a year's time: as having only just scraped home as the second party in votes in the European elections: Benn back in Parliament and creating more trouble than unity: some people, perhaps including himself, having not been reselected: the Tories remaining impregnably ahead in the polls then. This could build into a national psyche which persuaded some Labour millions to jump ship, saying that they thought Labour could not win, and that they could not stand another Thatcher win.

---

1 Clive Jenkins: general secretary of the Association of Scientific, Technical and Managerial Staffs.

MORE ON KINNOCK Not for use or hint: GK says that, sitting
in the House on the front bench, Kinnock makes good private jokes. Can't
resist them. About once a fortnight, GK has to say to him, 'Remember that
you are leader of Her Majesty's Opposition.'

A Kaufman theme: as learned from Hugh Cudlipp:[1] the British voter
cannot be persuaded to do something he doesn't want to do. All you can
do is push him harder in the direction he already wants to go. Thus,
politicians must at all times work with the grain of public opinion, not
try and change it very much. Hence his views above about the way to
play defence, the NHS etc.

DAVID STEEL
Lunch, the *Sunday Times*, 8 February 1984

To be at 19 or 20 per cent at this stage is very good. This time after the '79
election we were barely at 10 per cent. For Liberals this is something new.

We've found that former Labour voters switch more easily to Liberals
than to the SDP sometimes. Won't vote for 'those traitors', but will vote
for 'you people who are different'.

There won't be a prime minister designate next time round. This was
a Marquand idea, which we fell for. No one can lay a glove on Mrs
Thatcher at question time. She is amazingly good, with an extraordinary
memory for figures. So unfair to judge Kinnock about that. On the other
hand, he's failing. This shows (per HY) how little Labour's problem is
one of personalities. It is much deeper than that. He does not resolve the
Labour dilemma about what sort of party it is. Picking Benn at Chesterfield, the more one thinks about it, was a catastrophe for the party. Opens
everything up again.

Just back from Moscow, Steel was obviously given a happy time by
the Russians, who made him think well of them and of himself. Not
exactly naive – but certainly wishful.

---

1 Hugh Cudlipp, then Baron Cudlipp of Aldingbourne: journalist, newspaper magnate, former chairman of
Mirror Group Newspapers; author of *Publish and Be Damned* and *The Prerogative of the Harlot*, two memoirs
of the media.

NEIL KINNOCK
Lunch, *The Times*, 29 February 1984

BENN/CHESTERFIELD Tony's obviously going to win, but we
don't know how much above a majority of three and a half thousand.
He's fought a very good campaign. He will not cause me any problems
when he gets back to Parliament. The truth is that Benn may no longer
be a Bennite! He does not seem to be part of the hard and loony left,
which are my only problem. They need a thick ear. But when he gets
back, I don't think he will be part of that sort of effort. We've been
through such a long time of turmoil in the Labour Party so that anybody
who is going to try and restart it is going to come off very badly indeed.
Almost no one wants to return to the bad old years of 1981/2.

RESELECTION Will be much less of a problem than you people
make out. You should talk to people like Shore and Kaufman rather than
suggesting they are going to get deselected. A lot depends on personalities
and how hard the member works. Kaufman will survive in triumph I
expect. I believe the situation is turning in Peter Shore's favour. John
Silkin may be a different matter, but of course we don't know whether
he's going to seek reselection.

THE OLD LABOUR PARTY Has come to a cul-de-sac. This
affects two particular groups. First the far left, which is now in eclipse.
Secondly, the 'bureaucratic' left is also out of the window. We have got
to revise our positions about the state. The role of the state is certainly
open to a lot of rethinking. We want to see the state portrayed as the
body which enables individual people to increase their liberty, no longer
to be the vehicle for a kind of obliterating uniformity. (Pat Hewitt made
the distinction between the state as doormat and the state as trampoline.
After some discussion of this image, she said that of course she intended
the trampoline to be the benign image which Labour should seek after.)
As part of the shift, he said he was very happy to engage in serious
argument about the virtues of collectivism, although he fully understood
that this had become the main ground of argument in British politics and
that collectivism was at the moment in retreat. It would certainly be
Labour's job to make that argument much more compelling, and he was
eager to undertake the task – i.e. to defend collectivism and then to
redefine what the virtues of the state are and are not. In connection with
this he pointed out that at the next election, in 1988, there would be
4 million new voters in the 18–24 age group. These were a crucial new

group of people, likely to be pro-Labour at least according to the party's opinion polls – although a problem with this age group is how many of them turn out.

PRESENTATION Was a theme which Kinnock was quite un-ashamed about as one of his priorities. He though it was a dreadful word, but he appears well attuned to the extreme importance of it in modern politics.

My general impression was of an extremely nice man not yet corrupted by office, quite hard-headed, very good at presenting himself. He will no doubt charm numerous lunch parties, dinner parties and other sorts of audiences. It is a completely open question whether he is able to forget that he has never held a proper job.

DAVID OWEN
29 February 1984

CHESTERFIELD might have been won if we'd fielded a superstar.[1] But Shirley was the only one. Steel would have pushed hard for her, but not for Rodgers. Nor would Rodgers have won it, probably. He would have stopped the slide away from our candidate. However, I'm not too bothered. In a way, we don't want too many by-elections too early.

But debilitation is going to be the big danger. Too much bickering, too much scrutinizing of the relationship, too little pride in the Alliance and the fact that it's two parties. Also too feeble a leadership of the Liberals. Not a criticism of David Steel in this. But the fact is that he has left a lot of areas too free for the troublemakers, of whom the unilateralists are the worst. Don't want to go through that again. I showed them how to do it in my speech at Harrogate. Why can't they follow the lead? Liberals can be led in the right direction if the leadership tries hard enough.

However, Steel would be a catastrophic loss. My worst fear is that Thatcher buys him off with some nice public-sector job. There's no doubt he's gone down, and it's not just due to my arrival on the scene. Something much much deeper. (DO didn't speculate what it was, but I suspect he half knows.) But he will, I hope, recover his steam and ground. He is irreplaceable. After him there's literally nothing.

---

1 Tony Benn polled 24,633 votes, with Max Payne, the Liberal, the runner-up with 18,369 votes.

POLITICALLY   it will be bad for us if Labour overtakes the Tories this year. I think they may not, since the economy is doing nicely. This is the best possible position for us: with the Labour Party just failing to make an impact. After a year of this and still no impact, people will begin to ask what Labour is all about, especially if Benn etc. start making more trouble. However, I do not think it is possible to say that Labour is in irreversible decline. I once said publicly that it may be the historic task of the Alliance, or at least its achievement, to revive the Labour Party. However, I don't think they've got very much chance. Kinnock has wasted his honeymoon period by refusing to grapple with substance. He's been good at the presentation. But he's basically just a Bennite. (I put it to DO that in fact, although Bennery was Kinnock's origin, he'd decided to abandon all policy talk for a period, in the hope that when it came up again people would accept that some of the old totems had been abandoned. DO then made his remark about Kinnock having wasted his honeymoon.)

I taxed him with where he was to the left of Thatcher. He bridled. The whole of social policy, he said. Especially redistribution of wealth – 'which I have done. I've shown I can carry it through. I did RAWP[1] and took on the London teaching hospitals etc. etc.' – and the whole field of rights. The SDP has a policy well to the left of Labour on all questions of human rights. Where Thatcher had been right, however, was in facing the British up to economic competition, the need for modernization, the need to crack the unions. He also thought he was to her right on some foreign-policy issues. Hugely contemptuous of the British pull-out from the Lebanon.[2] 'Absolutely pathetic, Healey and Howe. There are the Americans and the French, taken major casualties, and we run away at the first sound of gunfire' (he said this striding up and down the room in a fine old state).

He said that he gets very exhausted. Can he carry it all? Just too much to do, and too few people to do it. But he thinks the party has done incredibly well to keep its head above water. Thought they'd be wiped out with only six MPs. But much better than that. Thinks media have been very kind, except the BBC, which is a national scandal of establishment thinking. Talks about 'squeezing their balls' as the only way to get anything out of them. The approach of reasonable men will not work. Hints at future legal action against them for being unfair.

Wholly disagrees that the Liberals are better organizers or have more

1 RAWP: Resources Allocation Working Party, which provided a formula for distributing health-care funding.
2 In February 1984 Britain and Italy both announced that they would withdraw peacekeeping forces from Lebanon. The US Marines withdrew to ships offshore and kept up artillery bombardment and air strikes on Syrian positions.

members. Says their membership figures (claimed at 140,000) are a fiction, which never stands up when you get on the ground. Says they're good in parts of the country, but so are the SDP.

Claims that he seriously discussed with Debbie [his wife] on the Friday after the June election, as they drove back to London, whether the SDP was a party worth leading. Sometimes he still wonders. Can't stand the waste of time on bickering. Mentioned Taverne, Wrigglesworth,[1] Holme, and several other well-known names as people who spend too much time picking away at the edges. Says he has more time for Meadowcroft[2] than for many Liberals, because Meadowcroft has been a practical politician, and if you make a deal with him it sticks.

Also says that the Steel–Owen deal over Trident and cruise was a minor masterpiece, however scruffy it looked. It would have been fatal to be in different lobbies. But the Liberals would never have compromised if they'd doubted whether I'd lead the SDP into the other lobby.

HY's final column for the Sunday Times *('The press we don't deserve') appeared on 25 March 1984, ending with the rubric that he was leaving the paper to concentrate on freelance writing and broadcasting. His first column in* The Guardian *('The politicians who are living on illusions of future power') appeared on 14 May 1984. In it he was prescient about the Labour leader: 'I do not believe that Neil Kinnock will ever be leader of a majority Labour government.'*

MICHAEL SPICER
At Jeffrey Archer's,[3] 28 March 1984

Thatcher is very conscious of her style, her image. She knows very well that people may get bored with her. She needs surprises to keep people interested. In that sense, she is certainly a calculating political operator.

Knows a lot about Parkinson. Asked me whether Cecil was playing it right, and whether I thought he would get back. Clearly every move by CP is calculated. For example, Spicer said he made a mistake being

---

1 Ian Wrigglesworth: Labour and Co-op MP for Teesside Thornaby 1974–81, then SDP 1981–3, then for Stockton South 1983–7; SDP spokesman on industry and economic affairs 1983–7.

2 Michael Meadowcroft: Liberal MP for Leeds West 1983–7; chairman of the Electoral Reform Society 1989–93.

3 Jeffrey Archer: author; Conservative MP for Louth 1969–74; deputy chairman of the Conservative Party 1985–6; later Baron Archer of Weston-super-Mare; a controversial figure jailed in 2001 for perjury, became famous for shepherd's-pie-and-Krug parties at his London flat.

interviewed by David Frost[1] a week or two ago. He had cancelled all TV etc. except this one and a *Question Time*, which he did well on.

DICK TAVERNE
Dinner at Dutch ambassador's, 17 May 1984

Disaster for the Alliance would be thirty seats being fought against each other. Success would be only three seats like that, a joint campaign, a joint manifesto and, if possible, one leader.

There should have been a merger, or near-merger, after the election. Would have been quite right: we have done well, scored 26 per cent, now is the time to drive home our position. But Jenkins was ill, Owen took over, too many forces against it. If the spirit of the Leeds Liberals and the extreme Owenites is maintained, there will be no hope. Meadowcroft, like Owen, thinks that separation is all, and that PR will make it possible for power to be gained separately but equally, as it were.

Owen may have become slightly less extreme recently. Hard to say. But certainly he has a long way to go to move enough for a proper working relationship. Owen has all the political gifts save the strategic sense. Steel has much better strategic sense, while being less accomplished at other things perhaps.

Taverne is pessimistic about Labour splitting again. He thinks Hattersley and Kaufman got far too committed against ever leaving Labour for this to happen. Stupid as it seems, these personal things matter very much indeed: as they do about who will work with whom. He thinks a union split is more feasible. That Hammond at EETPU and Duffy/Laird at AUEW[2] will go for the no-strike agreements, mainly to preserve their memberships. That this will precipitate vast rows inside the TUC, leading to some kind of split.

Says that Jenkins is ill with Heath-type thyroid condition. Reflects on the Jenkins saga of missed opportunities. These began with his failure to quit over the European Communities Bill in 1971, then his failure to challenge and fight Wilson when he did leave, then his failure to back Taverne at the Lincoln by-election, then the Labour victory in 1974, which he did not expect, and which meant that his plans then (although too late) to set up an SDP were in ruins . . .

---

1 David Frost, television presenter, claims to be the only person to have interviewed all six British prime ministers between 1964 and 2007, and the seven US presidents since 1969.
2 Eric Hammond succeeded Frank Chapple as leader of EETPU, the electricians' and plumbers' trade union. In 1982 Gavin Laird became general secretary of the Amalgamated Union of Engineering Workers, later the Amalgamated Engineering and Electrical Union.

SHIRLEY WILLIAMS
Her flat in Rochester Row, 8 August 1984

SDP I asked about Owen. She says that he is certainly authoritarian, certainly very impatient, certainly an enormously powerful personality which puts almost everyone else in the shade. Why, however, is he so opposed to progress with the Liberals? She cites two reasons:

(a) *Defence*. He thinks that if the SDP and Liberals merge, the drift to unilateralist defence policies will become irresistible. He could not live with that. He sees the Liberals as unsound on defence, which makes them an electoral liability and also impossible for him, Owen. Joint selection is much affected by this. He thinks that if joint selection were fully authorized – save in exceptional circumstances – there would be a tendency for unilateralist candidates to get chosen simply because they tended to be the more popular at the moment, and to accord with the easy fashion of Liberal circles.

(b) *Liberal decentralization*. DO finds the Liberal structure impossible to work with, because it makes it almost impossible for the Liberal leader to be able to deliver on quick commitments which would be needed in a crisis. The labyrinthine dispersion of power gives opportunities to all sorts of mini-Liberals to put spanners in the works, sometimes merely out of pique because they haven't been consulted. If we had a merger, therefore, the SDP would become plagued by all these problems which make the Liberal Party itself almost impossible to run, let alone a joint party. David, 'being very much a top-down person', couldn't live with that.

I ask whether there is also a deeper reason: whether it has something to do with Owen's idea about which voters he's trying to win. She replies, For quite some time, David has had the idea that the voters to try and win are defecting Tories. But he has begun to realize that Tories have a habit of returning to the fold in the end. So I think in the last few weeks he's been showing that it's less obvious that we should be going for those people. I personally, says Shirley, have always held that we must try to replace the Labour Party. I think David is more inclined to this view now.

But this affects trade-union policy. She agreed with me that Owen had now got an anti-union profile. This was a bit unfair, she said. True, he was unyielding on ballots and on political funds. But he claims that in his speeches it is now only the 'tough' parts which get reported, and the tender parts get left out. The SDP was certainly different from Tories in that it has no desire to see unions disappear. The whole picture depended very heavily on the unions' vote on the political funds, and later on their belonging to the TUC. Hammond may well lead them out. Hammond and Gavin Laird have a view of the unions close to the SDP's.

She also sounds a very alarming note, which she knows is extreme: does the miners' strike not show the forces of the revolution and the counter-revolution preparing for battle, and more and more people learning how to do it?

1985

10 January   Clive Sinclair, producer of Britain's first popular computer, unveils the C5 electric car.

5 February   Terry Waite, the Archbishop of Canterbury's envoy, negotiates the release of British hostages in Libya.

22 February   The pound falls to almost the value of a dollar.

3 March   Mineworkers call off their year-long national strike.

11 March   Mikhail Gorbachev becomes general secretary of the Soviet Communist Party and premier of the Soviet Union.

8 April   Rupert Murdoch buys the Hollywood studio Twentieth Century–Fox.

11 May   Soccer fans die in a blaze at the Bradford City ground.

29 May   Liverpool fans battle at Heysel Stadium; 41 Belgian and Italian fans die.

7 July   Live Aid concerts raise £40 million for the starving in Ethiopia.

10 July   Greenpeace ship *Rainbow Warrior* is blown up in Auckland harbour; French agents are later implicated.

19 September   Mexico City is devastated by an earthquake; 9,000 die.

21 October   Mrs Thatcher boycotts call for economic sanctions against apartheid South Africa.

13 November   The Nevada del Ruiz volcano claims 23,000 lives in Colombia.

Deaths   Laura Ashley, former Labour deputy leader George Brown, Marc Chagall, Robert Graves, Enver Hoxha of Albania, Philip Larkin, Michael Redgrave, Orson Welles

ROBIN COOK
The Guardian, 4 June 1985[1]

He denied there was any general drift to the right among the electorate. He pointed to opinion-poll figures on nuclear defence (although admitted these were ambiguous, even though they do show good support for getting rid of cruise and Trident); also on welfare-state issues; also, he claims, on public-sector industry. But he conceded that, on the TU question, 'unions are unpopular'. Even here, however, he was disposed to say that people might want unions to be within the law, yet this didn't mean they were unpopular. He pointed to the great success of campaigns for the political funds: unionists, once asked whether they wanted their unions to go on having a political voice, overwhelmingly said yes on the grounds that they were in favour of democracy, according to Robin Cook.

He also denied that the Labour policies constituted any drift to the right. However, he insisted that, because they would be starting with a different status quo, they might have to accept things. He instanced wages councils: if they are abolished, the last thing he would want to do would be to re-create them just as they are . . . Altogether he was highly tricky on this question of Labour and its changes.

One interesting point which emerged was the high importance of opinion polling. This reminded me that [Bob] Worcester has said that MORI were called in six weeks after an election, instead of six weeks before it. Cook was very big on the idea of finding out your strengths, then playing to them. He spoke with pleasure about the way in which policy statements were being presented – 'in a consistent livery', was his Saatchi-like phrase!

When I said that Fowler[2] welfare plans were a gift to Labour, he said that the real reason this was so was that it put Labour's best issues at the top of the agenda. This, he thought, was more relevant than the actual policies (another indication of how poll-conscious and non-policy-conscious he is).

He rather favoured black selections where, as in London, they were what the people wanted. He ascribed the opposition to them as essentially

---

1 *The Guardian*'s editor, Peter Preston, had established the practice of regular lunches – open to many of the staff – with politicians and other newsmakers. Cook was at that time Labour's campaigns coordinator.

2 Norman Fowler: Conservative MP for Nottingham South 1970–74, for Sutton Coldfield 1974–2001; Secretary of State for Transport 1981, for Social Services 1981–7, for Employment 1987–90; later Baron Fowler of Sutton Coldfield. Party Chairman 1992–4.

a generation thing. Bob Hughes,[1] for example, brought up on passionate ideas about apartheid, cannot abide the sense that anything is decided on racial lines. Kinnock has the same instinct. But also, as Cook said, it is rather offensive to have to have a race-identity before being admitted to any group.

He is very full of 'perspective', a real bullshit buzzword. I thought, after being once impressed, that he was rather a shallow fellow, rather too ready to agree with people in the room, and distinguish himself from party policy where that was convenient. But certainly a complete gutter strategist. The Tebbit of the Labour Party?

He was especially scornful about Benn. Referred to him as now being with the Communist Party tankies (the hardliners). Said he had no following.

TONY BENN
House of Commons, 7 June 1985

Came in with great ebullience and friendliness: even more voluble than usual: spent much of the time chiding me for my centrist views, saying that my position was that of giving an episcopal benediction to all shifts to the centre. He was as ever humorous, pleasant, and rather more self-deprecating than usual. Distilling an incessant ramble.

He sees himself as representing an underclass: wherever there are people in struggle, he will be beside them, without questions asked. Solidarity was crucial. These people represent a growing segment of society which are marginalized by the media, never heard from, yet have been educated by life under this government and especially by the miners' strike: who are deeply engaged, often very articulate, filled with fighting horror at the government: they often voted Tory at the last election (mortgage-owning miners), but their eyes are open now. These are the forces the left speaks for: they are far more numerous than anyone realizes: they are also the real lifeblood of socialism and the Labour Party.

At the moment Benn, representing these people, is playing it quiet. They don't in fact want or need a leader: that's important. There are about thirty-five members of the Campaign Group of MPs who think like this. What Benn is doing is publishing his bills – two so far, on Land and Reform – which the press automatically castigates as loony. The press is assisted in this by Kinnock, who seems to see a large part of his life as being involved in discrediting Benn. Not that I'm trying to under-

---

1 Robert Hughes, Labour MP for Aberdeen North 1970–97, trade unionist, had been educated in the Transvaal and apprenticed in Natal before returning to the UK. He later became Baron Hughes of Woodside.

mine him, Benn insists. Benn believes the leader has been elected and must be supported.

Kinnock knows he owes his position to Benn, in the sense that it was Benn who invented the leadership election system. If the election had been by the PLP secret ballot, Owen would have stayed in the party and would have slaughtered Kinnock in any contest. The fact remains that Kinnock now sees it as essential to dismiss everything Benn stands for. Benn says this without bitterness, more with the elder stateman's amused certainty that he is right.

The problem is that there is a consensus stretching back from Pym to Hattersley. This rests on the belief that once you get rid of Thatcher, everything will be all right. This is also felt by people like Hobsbawm and the *Marxism Today*[1] crowd: that Mrs T is a mesmerizingly fearful person who is the key to everything. The truth is that it is capitalism which is the problem, not Thatcher. There is no substitute for class analysis. You have to decide which side you're on there. Benn says he thinks of politics now no longer as right and left but as top and bottom.

Owen is a Tory. He should have made the switch straight across. He's deeply right wing. The SDP are quite different from the Liberals, who do have roots, and many of whom belong in the Tribune Group. Kinnock, however, made a mistake attacking Owen in personal terms, says Benn. Attack the policies, not the person. This leads him into a long statement about how the people will respond to policies which mean something, and not to personalities or soft soap.

He contends that only on his part of the left is any serious thinking going on about how to behave when we've won. What would the leadership actually *do* on day one? They don't know, says Benn. What about exchange controls, what about the economy etc. etc.? He instances especially what about the minority-government scenario? He's utterly adamant that you can't go into a smoke-filled room and do a deal. He therefore suggests that when Labour has got most seats, which is probable, they should get the House. When Owen asks to go through the Queen's Speech they should say fine: and write a two-line speech about my husband and I enjoying our visit to Papua New Guinea and goodbye. There should then be a real programme, and the government should put it to the House. If the Alliance defeated it, Labour should get a dissolution, when it would destroy the Alliance at the polls. History shows, says Benn, that the electorate takes vengeance on parties which deny the result of an election. When I suggest to him that perhaps the electorate will be different after an election in which the Alliance may have only 70 seats with as many

---

1 Eric Hobsbawm: distinguished historian, Marxist and regular contributor to *Marxism Today*, an influential journal edited in the 1980s by Martin Jacques.

votes as the others, he says first the 70 is too high but mainly that the people won't be seduced in those circumstances by PR arguments. He thinks it will be a tricky time for the Queen.

Claims a parallel with the 1945 election. Then, with peace, the people turned to Labour: a switch from fear to hope. If unemployment goes down you'll see the same thing: a switch from fear to hope, redounding to Labour's advantage. When I put it to him that another parallel might be with the defeat of the unions (leading to Labour's improved fortunes), he said no, the unions were going to be seen as the one essential instrument etc. etc.

Meeting Kinnock that summer, HY noted that 'While insisting all the time that he's not paranoid about the press, he does seem very exercised about the limited ability to have Labour issues and policies ventilated. Could quote chapter and verse of Guardian *transgressions. Said that columnists like me and Ian Aitken [political editor of* The Guardian *1975–90] and the other heavies "set the agenda" which was followed above all by broadcasting.'*

NEIL KINNOCK
The Guardian 25 June 1985

A distillation of nearly three hours:

ECONOMIC POLICY He began by talking pretty vapidly about the rewards policy, otherwise known as the incomes policy, the essence of which seems to be the National Economic Assessment, and the convenience of which is, as he describes it, that it should not involve any hard deal with anyone, but simply the unions seeing what is in their best interests. Neil Kinnock emphatically holds to the Wilsonian truth that one's man pay rise is another man's job, and rests much of his thinking on the expectation that most people will be able to see this. He wants wage bargaining to be done in a different way, observing that there is no universal method by which pay deals are done, and wishing to swap 'productivity bargaining', a dirty word, for 'costs bargaining'. He generally hangs in with what Roy Hattersley has been saying about the economy, putting much emphasis on 'go for growth'.

Here he wants to distinguish himself from both the Callaghan government and the Mitterrand government. In particular Mitterrand, who, he says, came in with the French economy working at 80 per cent of capacity, and therefore was hit by inflationary pressures etc. Labour would be coming in to an economy working at 60 per cent (*sic*).

On specifics, he spoke of 'some' import controls, to protect highly vulnerable industries: the Hattersley version of exchange controls – i.e. a tax on exported money – saying that 'old-fashioned' import controls should not and perhaps could not be brought back.

DEFENCE POLICY The policy is to get rid of cruise and decommission Polaris within a few months – he said six or twelve – of taking over. 'The nuts would be undone . . .' Also, of course, scrapping Trident. He insisted that this could be done without any major disruption of Anglo-American relations. David Fairhall [*Guardian* defence correspondent] pressed him hard about this, saying that any disturbance of Britain's nuclear position would have a seismic effect on Washington, and also jeopardize Britain's lead role, which it enjoys for historic reasons, in NATO policy-making. Kinnock insisted that he had spoken to Reagan, Schultz, Weinberger,[1] and they knew where Labour stood and accepted it.[2] There would be no reprisals, he insisted; it was in the American interest not to fall out with Britain, and also because within the NATO strategy it made sense for British resources to be released to fulfil her naval role in the Atlantic – which would be possible when Trident was scrapped. (Although, interestingly, he said that no one should have any illusions that scrapping Trident would provide billions for pensioners: said that not even the extremists on the NEC any longer argued from that position.)

Pressed further, he blurred the issue about conventional defence spending, but said the commitment was to get total spending down to the average of NATO countries' spending, as a proportion of GNP (I think he said 5.2 per cent). But he was ill at ease when Fairhall said he should be far more fully prepared for what would in fact happen when Labour began to put all this into action. He was also especially keen to de-emphasize the radicalism of what was proposed: quite explicit about this frightening off the troops . . . Incidentally, also placed emphasis on the fact that the US no longer needs Holy Loch for its subs. And he said quite explicitly that the American bases, if non-nuclear, would stay.

THE PARTY His line seems to be this. There is now only a small segment of splinters who are out beyond the fringe. These are the people he was referring to in his T & G speech, when he cast an anathema over

---

1 George Schultz: US Secretary of State in the Reagan administration. Caspar Weinberger, US Secretary of Defense.
2 Kinnock adds, 'Obviously without enthusiasm.'

the wreckers and loonies. Militant is among them, but also he seems to include the Campaign Group of MPs, or some of them. He distinguished between the people who are really crazy (Benn, by implication) and those who haven't the guts or the sense to stand up to them: who get led along out of a bogus fear that their seats will be at risk. He describes Heffer as 'unable to maintain an erect position on anything . . . pathetic'. He says that Livingstone has never been a loony, but is deeply flawed because he regards politics as 'a numbers game', which, says Neil, I never have.

Kinnock's position is that the party's first duty is to get elected. He explicitly condemned the idea that it should be a federation of the dispossessed and underprivileged, and said it must appeal to the affluent or it is nothing: people who haven't got major problems, who are successful, who are not underprivileged etc. He cited Tawney with a line about idealism without lunacy and realism without torpor, or some such. This is the vision we have to convey.

COALITION AND ALL THAT Very emphatic that Labour would do no deals. He sees it this way. In a hung parliament, the first problem will confront Mrs T. She will presumably have to decide what she will do, as the incumbent. Only after that will it be his turn. His line will be: we must set about doing things, getting on with the job. It will be up to the others to bring us down. He still seems to think that in any subsequent dissolution-cum-election, a Labour government which has been denied the chance to 'get on with the job' will be returned by an outraged electorate.

(Further points on this per HY: one argument made against the Kinnock line is that it would let Mrs T in rather than do a deal with the Alliance. Yet it will be true, surely, that if Mrs T gets less than a majority she will go without delay – which alters all the equations, including the willingness of the Tory Party to do deals with the Alliance.)

IMPRESSIONS It is a Kinnock axiom not to worry about things he cannot change. Therefore, for example, he refuses to get too vexed about what Maxwell[1] is doing to the *Mirror*, much though he regrets it. This same kind of economical insouciance applies to the spectre of the money markets rushing out of Britain if Labour gets ahead in the election polls. As with the US and defence, he supposes that in the end people will see it is not in their interest to act against the Labour Party: Britain alive will be better for them than Britain dead.

---

1 Robert Maxwell: former Labour MP for Buckingham, publisher, newspaper magnate and controversial chairman of Mirror Group Newspapers.

DAVID OWEN
2 September 1985

As usual, to me, he was jocular, unimposing, undomineering, quite humorous and very laid-back. Also, as before, much preoccupied with his children, the youngest of whom is in hospital with a broken leg, having had it badly set by the Doctor himself and a local registrar!

OVERALL POSITION   He is quite content to stay at 31 per cent. It is pretty impressive. We've had various plateaux which people said we would stick at: 20, 25, 28. But we have gone on up. We are also doing well in local by-elections. He reeled off Vauxhall, Grimsby, Nottingham and some in the West Country . . .

He was worried about the Labour vote. Especially that the performance at Nottingham in county elections had been bad by the Alliance. But the by-elections showed them thundering back . . .

He sees no reason why the fickle middle classes should desert. But he says that the first priority must be to keep them. A lot of them voted Tory in 1979, and a lot of those who voted Alliance in 83 had voted Tory before that too. These must be hung on to. The Liberals' great problem in the past had been the lack of adherence and loyalty.

He candidly speaks in terms of saying that the most winnable seats are in the south of England and are Tory seats. He talks in terms of getting 50–80–100 seats, although does not discount being the largest single party. Says that Labour cannot be reduced below 200 – it gets something like 130 even with only 18 per cent of the poll (check)! Quite possible that Labour could get 250 this time.

KINNOCK   however, seems to have peaked. There was a time when I began to fear that he was doing very well. Much better than I expected. But this was before he was tested. Then he failed. When was this? Miners' strike . . . Also, he must be bitterly regretting his personal attack on me. I am making a point of never making personal attacks, and I don't reply. This is integral to the coalition strategy. The Alliance must speak and act at all times as though it is prepared to do business with anybody. It is therefore not in the business of digging trenches round itself. This applies to Thatcher as much as Kinnock – although it is quite inconceivable that Thatcher will be part of any coalition. To have lost a majority of 144 would be utter humiliation and she would go immediately.

We say that we are ready to talk to the party with the largest number of votes – that's a ploy which gives us a bit of leeway in the event. But the major point is that we should have a strategy which is both well thought out and transparent and agreed between us. We don't want a repeat of March '74, when every Liberal under the sun was volunteering an opinion about what should be done. We want to have thought it out beforehand. We also think it important that people should see what we are offering and doing. No hole-in-corner deals, but open offers. This, in turn, affects our insistence that we only deal with people who will talk to us. Writing a Queen's Speech is not enough. That's easy. But it must be seen as something done under our influence, recognizing our power.

DISSOLUTION I talked to Wilson recently about 1974. He's so gaga you can't be sure he's understood what you're saying. But I wanted to know whether he'd thought of asking for an immediate dissolution. He said, No, we had to get a few months under our belt to establish ourselves. This is exactly what Kinnock will want to do. But we want to establish that, in the present circumstances, the royal prerogative does not require to be exercised towards instant dissolution. We want the Douglas-Home precedent in 1963 to become more ventilated. That is, not kissing hands until he could assure the Queen that he could form a government. Although that was an intra-party situation, it could apply to the present: with nobody formally becoming prime minister, and therefore acquiring the right to a dissolution etc., until he has gone back to Westminster and put together a coalition he can rely on.

THE SDP has become better. A remarkable percentage (at least 85) of continued membership: over 50,000 members now. Is it more political? That is a problem. You must remember how many people who came into it had never been in a party before. That was part of its appeal. Also, quite a proportion of them do not have time to be politicians. They pay, they attend meetings, they work – but they don't run for office. They are export managers or medical registrars etc. etc., who have jobs they must keep at. Mind you, some people have become county councillors who never dreamed of doing it, and have now got their teeth into it.

HOW DO WE DIFFER FROM THE TORIES? Quite a pause. Then: the major difference is over unemployment and the risks we would take on inflation. I would take more risks, but judiciously: because we feel far more deeply about the moral repugnance and waste of unemployment, and are more convinced that the figures can come down. Behind our inflation tax we would reinflate the economy. This is a big and deep difference.

A generally greater role for state activity in the economy.

More public spending on some things. Health service. Tories were doing pretty well until a year ago, but now it's declining. But we all know that choice-making will be tough.

DO disposed to make much of the 'competence' argument. Says that Thatcher Mark 1 was at least competent, if unpleasant. Mark 2 is incompetent. This is what most bugs the kind of business people coming into the SDP. They can't stand the inefficiency of government . . .

All the constitutional stuff . . . Which is one reason also why the SDP wouldn't want to take another stride down the union reform path. There'll be quite enough constitutional reform without that.

He wouldn't touch the privatized industries. But, back to the unions etc., would go in for much more industrial democracy of a non-union-based kind.

LIBERALS There is a good deal more coming together. I had to concede limited joint selection back in July '83, when I had no position – only a handful of MPs. I still don't like it, but it has only happened in about 10 per cent of seats. Also, I have to admit that both sides have learned from the other, e.g. our approach to the miners' strike would have been less tough if the SDP hadn't been there. Equally, the Liberals influenced us on that one as well. It is the fusion of preferences and traditions, the fashioning of joint ideas through a genuine process of discussion and compromise, that is the whole point about Alliance politics.

But undoubtedly the big problem is defence. It is a question of whether the Liberal leadership can lay down the law to the minority of activists who are running the unilateralist side. My position is most dictated by what Liberal voters want. Plainly they don't want unilateralism. Much now turns on what happens in the arms control talks, which in turn will greatly influence the German elections in April '87, which are the really important ones. Unless Reagan and his people are prepared to give enough to prove that multilateralism has a future, my kind of position is going to get difficult. Just like Kohl's position in Germany, he implied.

Of course, we don't know yet how big an issue defence is going to be at the election . . . Maybe we shouldn't get in too much of a lather about it . . .

He's also very full of his theory that people shouldn't be called 'Tory voters' or 'Labour voters'. They are people who voted Tory last time, and perhaps before. But the notion of the electorate as being largely composed of fixed groups of unalterable party votes is a fundamental misconception, which should not be allowed to over-influence political strategy.

MALCOLM RIFKIND
Lunch, the Garrick, 28 October 1985

A proficient young man on the rise, with a particular penchant for courteous but firm argument: in the Thatcher mould in the sense of seeing
political life as a contest that must be won. But far more civilized than
she is.

EUROPE He sees the Fontainebleau agreement as having two main
effects. The first is to remove the British grievance about how the British
debt was calculated (I think): ... i.e. to change the status quo, which
means that Britain is no longer fighting against the status quo which all
organizations are very unkeen to change. The second is to put the UK
and France and Germany into the same camp, with France becoming a
debtor country next year or so. Together with the arrival of Spain,
Portugal and Greece, the North–South divide will become more important, with the North siding together.

There is no effective opposition to the EEC any longer in Parliament.
But the anti-EEC Tories, though few, are persistent, will always be present
and vocal on EEC debates, of which there are many. Always the same
people, making predictable points, but they have to be dealt with.

SOVIET RELATIONS He finds these an example of Mrs T's sheer
pragmatism, a feature he discovered much to his surprise on entering the
FCO at Falklands time. The brief history is this. Although it is true that
for several years her Iron Lady posture was dominant, this was, even at
its height, essentially a stance directed at the British interest rather than
at attacking the Soviet Union within. However, it did not always sound
like that. In any case, what with Afghanistan etc, relations were very bad
for a long time.

The first sign of this changing came in early 1983, when Rifkind went
to Moscow. This was the start of a thaw. As a result of this, the FCO
and especially Francis Pym worked their way towards a new position,
saying that relations had become intolerably bad and it was up to Britain
to try and change them. This reached a big moment with a long-planned
'seminar' after the 1983 election, to discuss with the Prime Minister
present how to improve relations. Two important things about this. First
Pym had been replaced by Howe; but Howe, to Rifkind's knowledge,
had always been sympathetic to the idea of improving relations, even as
Chancellor. Second, MT put her cards on the table early by saying
that she was interested only in practicalities. Therefore not interested in

changing the Russians, or recovering Eastern Europe for the Western way of life. She might detest their system, but she did not want even to talk about anything except the strictly practical . . .

Out of this grew a series of events. The Howe trip round Eastern Europe, which was designed partly in order to recognize the fact that each of those countries is developing a separate identity, and partly as part of the big picture of getting on with the Soviets within the limits of the British interest. There was MT's trip to Hungary, after which she could have run for president of Hungary and been swept to power, said Rifkind! Another important step was the Gorbachev visit, and the personal chemistry which was established between them.

UNITED STATES   He thinks personal relations are as good as the Kennedy–Macmillan link. A strong personal relationship which survives many disagreements. Emphasizes British role in the Star Wars terms of reference, and the importance of Britain having insisted on the ABM Treaty[1] not being breached.

On Star Wars, he insists on the superior morality of Star Wars over mutual deterrence, and tries to put every objection to it into the category of 'practicalities'. He also insists on the civilian spin-off from the research, on the decidedly feeble argument that as long as the scientists are working out there on the frontiers we can never know what they will come up with.

THATCHER AND THE FOREIGN OFFICE   The bad relationship was entirely associated with her bad personal relationship with Francis Pym. When Carrington was there it was 99 per cent good. It is now good. Pym disagreed with so much of her domestic as well as her foreign policy. She therefore mistrusted him. The link wasn't helped by the importation of a personal foreign-policy adviser, which she was perfectly entitled to do.

Parsons,[2] however, did more to improve the FCO position in No. 10 than to strengthen No. 10 in the FCO. 'We were terrified that it would be Alfred Sherman' or even Hugh Thomas.[3] Someone entirely ideological. Parsons's success is due to his personal relationship. She admired him because he stood up to her with courtesy and knowledge. 'She will respect an adversary as long as they know as least as much as she does and

1 In 1972, in an effort to limit the arms race, the US and the USSR signed the Anti-Ballistic-Missile Treaty. The US unilaterally withdrew from the treaty in 2002.

2 Sir Anthony Parsons: diplomat; UK permanent representative to the UN 1979–82; special adviser to the PM on foreign affairs 1982–3.

3 Hugh Thomas: historian, author of *The Spanish Civil War* (1961); director of the Centre for Policy Studies 1979–91; created Baron Thomas of Swynnerton 1981.

preferably more.' But of course it is true that any department will observe a strong PM and respond accordingly, 'at least to the extent of clearing its lines before it does something it suspects she won't agree with'.

SOUTH AFRICA He made the case against sanctions. He said that they would be disastrous psychologically. The Brits knew more about the Afrikaner psychology than anyone in the world, and they knew that sanctions would just drive them into themselves. Botha[1] and co., the reformers, have a better case to make to their right wing if they can keep saying 'Look what the markets are doing,' rather than 'Look what the Commonwealth is threatening to do unless we abandon our policy.'

He insists that in all the discussions he has been present at, including No. 10, the British jobs situation has had only the millimicro importance. Barely mentioned at all. It has been entirely a question of what will have what effect in SA.

He denies that we are swinging in the wind with Botha. Insists that it is in our interest only to see major reform, leading in the end to One Man One Vote. But there must be stages towards that. Botha has at least begun. Should we act so as to make his job more difficult? We must assist his process. Further, he sees some form of loose federation with a weak centre as the main stage towards what the African National Congress wants. He also sees Buthelezi,[2] personally, as the best choice to rally round: a man who wants moderate progress, is against violence. But he recognizes that the ANC must be involved, as he categorically indicated MT did too.

SCOTLAND Says the SNP is irrelevant, although it might win 'two or three' seats from Tories in the rural area.

DOUGLAS HURD
Lunch, the Home Office, 2 December 1985

One of a series of one-to-one lunches he has at his desk, except that Brian Mower[3] and his special assistant Edward Bickham plus a private secretary are there too, to enjoy Civil Service cold meat and British Rail cheese. DH is still laid-back, but a conspicuously thinking person. Mower says

1 Pieter Willem 'PW' or 'Pik' Botha: prime minister of South Africa 1978–84; state president 1984–9.
2 Mangosuthu 'Chief' Buthelezi: chief minister of the Bantustan of KwaZulu, and seen by some members of the African National Congress as a collaborator with apartheid.
3 Brian Mower: civil servant; deputy press secretary to the PM and then director of information at the Home Office in 1982; head of the news department at the FCO 1990–92.

that after N. Ireland he's a lot less laid-back than he was in his first run in the Home Office.[1]

He says that the reading of material and need to master a vast range of things is especially difficult for someone without legal training, although he concedes it's easier than the Treasury would be . . .

INNER CITIES Says that the C of E report[2] overlooks what the government is doing. We have machinery in place, we are on to this one, he says. What machinery? I ask. He itemizes a Cabinet committee meeting called by him three weeks ago when the spending ministries came: then another called by the PM: then another Whitelaw is chairing as a result of all this to make sure something gets done.

Insists that government is well aware of the problems, but doubts whether more of the same – by way of local-government spending – is the proven answer. What has not worked in the past does not seem a good way of proceeding now. Says the partnership programmes with local authorities have not worked in places like Lambeth – but admits that there is a tendency to dub the whole of local government with the sins of the worst councils. This raises an interesting question about whether you can find ways of treating councils differently: whether the Docklands Board is a model to be extended, despite its lack of democratic base, as a mode of direct action.

PRISONS Says that of course the numbers are too high, and says things are being looked at to reduce them: something about fine defaulters, about bail, about remand, about community service etc. But judges are deeply resistant to being told what to do. He challenges whether public opinion is something they are sensitive to. But insists that, while serious crimes should receive heavier sentences, the Home Office is doing all it can to favour shorter sentences for lesser crimes. We agree that it is a matter of deep and complex interest why some societies have so many fewer people in prison . . .

PHONE TAPPING When I asked whether the famous tribunal had been set up, he had to call in Stephen, his private secretary, who said it would be in place in the spring . . .

1 Hurd had been Northern Ireland Secretary for a year, September 1984–September 1985, before he became Home Secretary.
2 The controversial 1985 Church of England report *Faith in the City* highlighted urban problems – and was denounced by some Conservatives as 'pure Marxist ideology'.

1986

1 January   Spain and Portugal join the European Community.

9 January   Michael Heseltine resigns over the Westland helicopter affair, followed fifteen days later by Leon Brittan.

20 January   Britain and France agree on a Channel Tunnel at a cost of £5 billion.

24 January   Rupert Murdoch switches production of newspapers to Wapping; riot police clash with trade union pickets.

28 January   Space shuttle *Challenger* explodes on take-off; seven astronauts die.

7 February   Jean-Claude 'Baby Doc' Duvalier quits Haiti, ending the twenty-eight-year Duvalier dynasty.

19 February   The Soviet Union launches the *Mir* space station.

25 February   President Ferdinand Marcos of the Philippines goes into exile after riots in Manila.

28 February   Swedish premier Olof Palme is shot dead in the street.

15 April   US air strike against Libya – from British bases.

26 April   Fire in reactor no. 2 at Chernobyl – the world's worst civil nuclear disaster.

8 June   Kurt Waldheim elected president of Austria.

9 October   Rupert Murdoch's News Corporation launches the Fox Broadcasting Company.

19 December   The Gorbachev government frees dissenter Andrei Sakharov.

Deaths   Simone de Beauvoir, Jorge Luis Borges, James Cagney, Jean Genet, Benny Goodman, Cary Grant, Harold Macmillan, Henry Moore, Otto Preminger, Wallis Simpson

'The Westland affair', as it became known, brought about the departure of two Cabinet Ministers: Michael Heseltine at Defence and Leon Brittan, who had been at Trade and Industry only since September 1985.

The issue was over whether Westland should join up with its traditional helicopter-manufacturing partner, the American company Sikorsky, or, as Heseltine wished, form part of a European consortium. The affair also highlighted Mrs Thatcher's dealings with certain of her ministers – particularly in the matter of the leaking of a letter commissioned from Sir Patrick Mayhew, the Solicitor General, which to some questioned her integrity. She was put on the back foot. HY talked to a number of his contacts as the affair all too speedily unfolded. What follows are extracts.

JOHN BIFFEN
Phone, 12 January 1986

[Heseltine] is Heath with a pretty wife and several children. A total *dirigiste*. And a capacity to use words which seem to encompass deep feelings. He's for the yuppies. He is a yuppy type. Plus a restless disregard for all who are in receipt of current public expenditure . . .

Thatcher herself . . . is bound to be a bit vulnerable. She's dogmatic by rhetoric to her colleagues, but then backs off. It's happened time and time again. This issue could have been settled like so many others, with adjustments by all concerned. Nothing inherent in it which debarred that. Certainly she was not adamant for the Americans from the very start. But there was something in the chemistry of personality, a deep ambivalence each shared about the other . . .

I'd be surprised if this accelerated her departure plans. But one thing is certain: if she does go, she'll make absolutely sure that she does so in a way which minimizes MH's chances.

'In mid-Heseltine row', as HY recorded, Douglas Hurd, the Home Secretary, had lunch at The Guardian, where he managed to concentrate on Northern Ireland, which he had left only four months before. But it was impossible not to talk, briefly, about Westland.

DOUGLAS HURD
Lunch, *The Guardian*, 14 January 1986

Northern Ireland. Says that in settling the Anglo-Irish deal[1] they had three cardinal points in mind as priorities. First, the power stations. Second, the morale of the RUC. Third, the Protestant paramilitaries. These three seem to have been all right, as it has turned out. The aim was to do everything to canalize the Ulster Unionists into constitutional paths. This has happened. We decided not to announce it when Parliament was in recess, for this reason, but to give them the parliamentary chance. They are taking it with these rather meaningless elections.

He crystallizes his Irish experience thus. That here and there people who are perfectly ordinary in every particular, do business in the normal way, go about life quite acceptably, but who have this totally unreasoning deformation when it comes to politics and religion.

On MH's actual exit from the Cabinet, he denies that there was any uncertainty about what had happened. But there was a typically British behaviour pattern: carrying on as if nothing had really happened. Thus they went on to discuss Nigeria for a while, before the coffee break, and then had a perfectly sensible discussion about rates.

The major impression is of a Home Secretary who does not want to do things very urgently. Slowtiming Popplewell,[2] slowtiming Peacock[3] outcome, desirous of not reacting like a scalded cat. Douglas is the genuine article of a Tory, the Rab Butler of our day. A deep person, who thinks a lot, who is good with words, who is humorously ambiguous, who is relaxed with journalists, who has a subtle view of what is possible and sensible: in temperament about as far removed from the hasty Thatcherites and the uneasy Brittans as it would be possible to be and remain in the same Cabinet.

CHRIS PATTEN
Phone, 26 January 1986

THATCHER/WESTLAND Summarizing his position: he really seems to think we are at the end of an era. Into the tomb the great queen crashes. Too many details still waiting to hit her re Westland. But also it

1 The Anglo-Irish Agreement, signed on 15 November 1985, recognized a consultative role for the Republic of Ireland in Northern Ireland, in the face of bitter protest from Unionist Party members.
2 Sir Oliver Popplewell chaired an inquiry into crowd safety at sports grounds, in the wake of the disastrous Bradford Stadium fire and the subsequent tragedy at Heysel Stadium in Brussels.
3 Professor Sir Alan Peacock led an inquiry into the long-term funding of the BBC.

shows us how we've been governed all these years. For example, the use of Ingham[1] for whispering campaigns against ministers (Jenkins, Rees).

But also how can she construct a defence? Couldn't blame L. Brittan, because LB knew too much: tried to save him. Perhaps can't put blame on Ingham and Powell,[2] because they know too much also.

Quite a few people will say that we can regroup over next two years, but not with her. Has she got the ability to restore our fortunes? Think of all those she has shoved on to the back benches, who have not been promoted, who have cause to resent her ... A biggish army ... Add in the other looming things: Lawson's economic miracle, Fulham by-election, local elections which could be as disastrous as the 1968 elections were for Labour (when the Tories won Islington ...)

DOUGLAS HURD   A good bet. CP isolates his understanding of the brutalities of power ... He is easy with authority, instances his handling of the Loyalist marches in NI last summer: brilliantly played hand with low cards ... A stiff public manner, but very very good in the HC.

JOHN BIFFEN
Phone, 26 January 1986

Sunday evening, day before Mrs Thatcher faces her biggest post-Westland speech in the House of Commons.

1. *How did he judge the present situation?* [Biffen] is winding up tomorrow. Has written most of his speech. Says that he believes she will say things tomorrow which will cause irritation because they were not said on Thursday. He believes that the advice then – which he is at great pains to insist he had nothing whatever to do with – was to make a short statement because there was bound to be a debate. For this reason, which he thinks was a decent reason, things were not said which with hindsight [should] have been said. This, he understands, will now be made good.

2. *Is she at risk?* He gives a wonderfully British reply. It is difficult he says to disentangle his own feelings from what other people may think. What *he* thinks is that Labour cannot defeat the government. The only thing that can defeat the government is the Alliance, letting Labour in and getting seats itself. Therefore he favours a far greater

---

1 Bernard Ingham: Mrs Thatcher's press spokesman 1979–90.

2 Charles Powell: private secretary to Margaret Thatcher 1983–1990; brother of the diplomat Jonathan Powell, chief of staff to Tony Blair as leader of the opposition 1995–7 and as prime minister 1997–2007; later Baron Powell of Bayswater.

concentration on the Alliance. He doubts whether she is temperamentally capable of ever doing that. Tebbit hardly more so, although he has made a few overtures towards the middle ground. Therefore, a question will be how many people see the upside of this pretty disastrous affair as being a growth in the numbers of persons who think like they do.

3. One notes how JB seems to be very much thinking about his own role as a possible leader, distancing himself from the Thursday statement, though admitting a role in her earlier speech in debate; not offering a straight prediction that she will survive; identifying the task as one for which he happens to be cut out . . .

WILLIAM WHITELAW
28 January 1986

The day after Thatcher's speech in the House of Commons. WW feels that she is 'just' in the clear . . . But he is unwilling to give an emphatic reply to the question of whether she will survive for ever.

He thinks that Leon Brittan made a big mistake in not telling her much earlier what had happened. He is sorry for Leon (his protégé, after all).

But his most enthusiastic references are for Douglas Hurd. Douglas, he says, is now in a position of enormous importance and power. He regards him as quite wonderful, especially on television. But he is at pains to say that DH was not his recommendation for Home Secretary. He was delighted that she gave it to him, but Douglas was her own personal choice, not in any way Whitelaw's foisting.

He accepts that the Alliance are the big danger. But he is undecided how to deal with them. His only tactic for now is to say that they are not an alliance, but are two parties. As for the counter-attack, his best suggestion is to 'put Douglas Hurd on television every day you can.'

The Westland affair was by no means over. In a letter initiated by the Prime Minister, Patrick Mayhew, the Attorney General, queried a warning given by Heseltine that Westland risked losing orders from Europe if the American deal went ahead. But selective leaks from the letter rebounded against Mrs Thatcher. Eventually Sir Robert Armstrong, the Cabinet Secretary, was called upon to inquire and report. HY's background conversations may seem patchy, but so much was also leaking into the public domain.

IAN GILMOUR
Phone, 2 February 1986

The government is pretty vulnerable. Will Atkins[1] be fixed? Even with a 'good' Budget (which is unlikely), there will only be a temporary respite. Of course she is a very lucky politician, and she may get lucky again this time.

He rates her survival as 50–50.

Gilmour is quite emphatic that her story is totally unbelievable at crucial points. He has absolutely no doubt about it:

- Now we know she asked Mayhew to write his letter. *Why?* Either to confront MH, or to leak. Since they didn't use it to confront MH, must have been to leak it.
- The excuse that Cuckney's press conference[2] imposed a 4 p.m. deadline is totally bogus.
- Impossible that Powell would have been party to the leak without talking to her. IG knows him, says that sitting a few feet away from her he would have been absolutely certain to have involved her.
- Inconceivable that they did not tell her the next day.
- Inconceivable that Brittan would neither have been asked nor told her very soon after.

SUCCESSION He would back Walker if Walker has a chance. But he's not well placed now. MH no chance. What happened to MH? He went mad like the rest of them: caught up in a mad frenzy, which is what the government had become.

MICHAEL MATES[3]
2 February 1986

Amid much that is transitory, including his criticism of government for not having put up the civil servants immediately to the select committee, he offers one insight.

He says that when MT first saw the Armstrong report on the leak,

---

1 Sir Humphrey Atkins (Conservative MP for Merton and Morden 1955–70, for Spelthorne 1970–87; later Baron Colnbrook of Waltham St Lawrence) chaired the select committee on defence, which sought evidence from ministerial private staff about the Westland affair. Mrs Thatcher argued that such a demand had 'major implications for the conduct of the government' and tried to prevent it.

2 Sir John Cuckney, chairman of Westland, had called a press conference at 4 p.m. on 6 January to outline the Westland board's recommendations to its shareholders on the latest bid for the troubled helicopter company.

3 From 1987 to 1992, Michael Mates was chairman of the Commons select committee on defence.

there were four people in the room. He implies that he has spoken to one of them. He recounts the scene: MT is reading the report for the first time and her jaw drops. She says, 'You mean Leon knew?!'

Mates is emphatic that the PM did not know more than she says she knew. 'I know that she is innocent. And as you know I am not likely to be the first person to say that.'

SIMON JENKINS
At Lelyveld launch,[1] 6 February 1986

SJ, who is close to LB, now says he reckons he knows what happened re Westland. It was this. On the Saturday, Mrs Thatcher instructed (asked? suggested?) Mayhew to write his famous letter to Heseltine, raising material inaccuracies in the Heseltine letter to Lloyds Bank. She said (thought? whispered?) that this would be the way to 'get' Heseltine on Monday . . . I.e. she even then contemplated a leak? Well, it was she who used the phrase 'get the information into the public domain'. So we know she intended this to happen, it would seem. Further, when she said in the HC 'I gave my consent,' this was possibly not the slip of the tongue which Armstrong, before the select committee, called it. At the least, it was odd . . .

When LB was telephoned at his restaurant on the Monday, and told 'neutrally, as RA said', by his private office that the letter had arrived, and was asked what to do with it, he apparently said either 'Tell No. 10 to release it' or 'No. 10 want it released.' He then put the phone down, unaware that this was the moment at which he had 'authorized' what then happened. He had no idea that his department would then get stuck with leaking it. Which it did because Bernard Ingham told Bowe,[2] 'I don't want the Prime Minister's fingerprints anywhere near this.' She, much alarmed, tried to reach Brian Hayes[3] to say what Ingham wanted her to do, but Hayes was out of town. Further evidence of MT's involvement is contained in the fact that on the Tuesday she came into the private office and said to Bernard, 'Well done, that's done the trick,' or some such congratulatory phrase.

When I told Simon what Mates had told me – that MT, on seeing the leak report, said, 'You mean Leon knew?!', he thought this confirmed his picture, i.e. that phrase, far from revealing a woman totally ignorant of

1 Joseph Lelyveld: *New York Times* journalist and Pulitzer Prize-winning author of *Move Your Shadow: South Africa, Black and White.*

2 Colette Bowe: head of information at the DTI.

3 Sir Brian Hayes: Permanent Secretary at the DTI 1985–9.

what had happened, revealed one who thought that what had happened was unknown to Leon . . .

So on this account Ingham is the real culprit. Maybe MT left the details to him, but the decision to get the thing into the public domain was hers.

This would explain quite a lot of what happened. It just about sustains the 'misunderstanding' point at the heart of Armstrong's case: but it turns out to be a different sort of misunderstanding from the one he makes us think about. The main victim of the misunderstanding is not Bowe but Brittan, who had no idea that he was authorizing anything. It also explains why the private office did not tell her what had happened. She knew what, in a general way, had happened from the start. For she had initiated it, if this account is right. Merely the details were out of her hands. And since the whole inquiry has been about the details rather than the strategy, she has just about been able to keep in the clear.

WILLIAM WALDEGRAVE
His office, 24 February 1986

Thatcher has resumed control. For example, we are about to announce the four sites selected for disposal of nuclear waste, one of which will be the final choice. We've been trying to do this for some time, but each time the horse has stopped at the fence. Now we are doing it, only because the PM is back in the saddle. Also because Hailsham has risen up and said it is a moral issue . . . (one of the sites is in Grantham).

WW is not among those who have thought that MT should go. He agreed with my column on the subject. He adds that he has asked people, Do you seriously want a change of policy, or what? He thinks, as I do, that even if she fell under a bus there would be no escaping her inheritance . . . Therefore, the only *election* strategy is to go to the electorate and say, This is our record, this is what we have done, the Alliance has done nothing, if you vote Alliance you will let Labour get in. Letting Labour in is the biggest message by far.

The problem for the government is competence. Making the best of all issues that present themselves. Take British Leyland. Could have been presented differently: we are not going to sell BL Trucks to these Americans. We will wait for General Motors' Bedford Trucks plant to go bust (which it will do) and make the market so much better for BL . . . Ditto the rate settlement. Because of Treasury massive squeeze on the rate support grant, rates in shires will rise massively – just unnecessarily harsh, with disastrous political results. (He had lots of figures and percentages on this which I can't remember.)

Ken Baker he describes as the Willie of the future. A real fixer, who understands the policy as well: a genial, endlessly good-humoured oiler of the wheels. At their meeting this morning, all the DoE ministers went through all the policies and agreed that every single one of them was wrong and the meeting broke up in roars of laughter led by Ken.

HESELTINE'S problem was that he was a single-issue man. Can only concentrate on one thing at a time, with great intensity.

HURD Note his apparently effortless rise. You hardly notice it. Yet note too his . . . brilliantly timed 'executive intervention' in the Westland affair. Just sufficient of a lordly rebuke without being insufferable. Note how at the same time G. Howe said nothing.

CHRIS PATTEN
His office, 25 February 1986

POLITICS The right have picked on the DES as the target for their last dying thrust. Because they know Keith Joseph will be going, and they see CP as his replacement. CP has never thought this, if only because she has already promoted enough people from the left of the party and won't want to do any more.

However, CP is the target. The Garel-Jones stories are true. Tebbit did go to Wakeham[1] as the emissary from the 92 Group[2] and demand G-J be fired and ask that more rightists be promoted. They are seeing defeat staring them in the face and realizing that in eleven years they haven't got anywhere in the party. Also they are wedded to the notion that MT is imprisoned by wets, and but for them would be doing the proper rightist things.

Boyson is at the centre of this. He doesn't go much to NI these days. Holds court in the HC, receiving delegates. He is their candidate for DES, with Bob Dunn as Minister of State and Jim Pawsey as no. 3.[3] Dunn, it is an absolute fact, was going to be fired at the last reshuffle but, according to Wakeham himself, was saved only by the accident that he was in Finland at the time. Pawsey defeated Madel for the chair of the Tory education committee.

---

1 John Wakeham: Conservative MP for Maldon 1974–83, for Colchester South and Maldon 1983–92; chief whip 1983–7; Energy Secretary 1989–92; later Baron Wakeham of Maldon, and chairman of the Press Complaints Commission.
2 The 92 Group, a right-wing faction of the Tory Party, was so called because it met at the home of Sir Patrick Wall (Conservative MP for Haltemprice 1954–83, for Beverley 1983–7) at 92 Cheyne Walk, Chelsea.
3 Robert Dunn: Conservative MP for Dartford 1979–97. James Pawsey: Conservative MP for Rugby 1979–83, for Rugby and Kenilworth 1983–97.

I put it to CP that perhaps the right should have had more jobs. He asks, Where are they? Only with an enormous effort could they find a rightist to become Minister of Trade, and the only man they could find was a protectionist, anti-American, anti-European lover of Hitler and Stalin. A joke maverick charmer.[1] At a lower level the problem is to find people who are not bent as a corkscrew and who can do joined-up writing. Peter Lilley? Hardly ever speaks in HC; said to be clever, but rarely shows it. OK, maybe: but who else? They just don't exist. CP nearly had Eric Forth[2] pushed on him as a PPS, until he pointed out that Forth had spent half an hour at the party conference in 1984 talking to CP's agent under the impression that he was the YC chairman in Bath and saying that CP should be ditched. There are plenty more like that.

The extraordinary thing is that, post-Westland, it is the right who are showing maximum disloyalty. The left had a choice: either try and ditch her or rally round her. To much surprise, they have pretty well decided on the latter course. Much loyalty. Yet not from the right.

CP thinks the political situation for the Tories is very dire ... Approaching the black hole – around 32, 33 per cent – where you can disappear without trace and without predictability. Even people in Surrey tennis clubs are saying they won't vote Tory. He had a chap in who said he had been taught to mistrust anecdotal evidence, but he'd found every single anecdote pointing in one direction.

The letters he gets become increasingly rancid. When we have lost hundreds of seats in local government, plus Fulham disaster, who knows what the feeling will be? He seems to agree with me that they are stuck with MT. Certainly cannot be pushed out. He still holds out hope of a voluntary and credibly voluntary exit. Thinks they would do better then. But a more likely possibility would be the removal of Tebbit as the man to blame for the local-election disasters ... that what Tebbit said the other day about the other parties as 'dirty little parties' was pretty close to Bevan's (?) famous 'lower than vermin' line, which lost Labour so many votes as it was thought ...[3]

1 Alan Clark, Parliamentary Undersecretary at the Department of Employment since 1983.

2 Eric Forth: Conservative MP for Mid-Worcestershire 1983–97, for Bromley and Chislehurst from 1997.

3 Aneurin Bevan, Labour MP for Ebbw Vale 1929–60, the giant of the post-war left, in 1948 at a public meeting recalled his youthful attitude to the Conservatives and said, 'As far as I am concerned, they are lower than vermin.' The British press – which he had recently described as 'the most prostituted in the world' – jumped on the remark.

GEOFFREY HOWE
Foreign Office, 11 March 1986

He saw me late, after much postponement, and today after having to delay for receiving jabs for a trip to India. He made a striking impression. One saw even more clearly than before the role of Geoffrey as timeless and tireless occupier of high government positions from which it has become inconceivable that he should be dislodged. He has become positively arrogant in his sureness not only that Thatcherism is all coming together but that there is a seamless link which binds the entire Howe political career, a commitment to ideas which he has always believed and which constitute some kind of objective and indisputable reality that nobody can now gainsay. This is demonstrated, he thinks, by the evidence that all other parties are moving towards these realities, and also by the shifts in foreign governments' positions. There had been, he considers, an 'interruption' in 1974. But before and after that, and on now into the immeasurable future, the ideas of freedom and incremental improvement which he has always stood for will hold their central place. In this, of course, he overlooks the other small hiccup – when he was architect of the Heath government's prices and incomes policy and altogether an apostle for the time being of corporatist government. No doubt he would have a talkout for that as well. He really does see his career as a coherent whole. Thus, when I ribbed him for the reference in his latest big speech to a pamphlet he wrote on decontrolling rents in 1957, he said I was meant to take precisely the inference I had taken from it. He added another example: that he and Elspeth [Howe's wife] had written a pamphlet in 1969 concerning the role of parents and governors in schools, which led (I think) to the creation of whatever body it is that now looks after their interests. He sees this pamphlet as finally gaining some flesh through the government's growing commitment to parental roles etc. etc.

DAVID STEEL
Lunch, RSJ Restaurant, 19 March 1986

SDP PROBLEMS   These are infinitely fewer than they were. Hardly any at all. In terms of seats, we have decided almost all: only about eight are left, which will remain open until after the local elections reveal which party would be better at them. Very good relations between Dick Newby and Andy Ellis,[1] which lowers the number of things that have to be decided by leaders.

Owen is receptive to private criticism and ideas, and dismisses the argument that he is autocratic by pointing out that constitutionally he has less power as leader than Steel has. Steel finds him humourless and very egocentric and not ready to be ribbed in private about how often he makes a point of his having held high office in government. He thinks Owen is a terrible public speaker but a top-rate Commons performer. In the Commons he manages to cut through the awful difficulties, of which DS is only too well aware, confronting anyone who has only a trifling number of MPs. Owen's sheer arrogance is a great help here. On the other hand, these off-the-cuff speeches at conferences are often disastrous. Owen is a puritan. He despises rhetoric, and does not think his audiences should have a fun time.

ELECTION An unresolved problem is how much S and O should decide to appear together. Quite a lot of evidence suggests that it is better for them to do so, because this removes from the interviewer the possibility of concentrating on what the other has said elsewhere. It also evidently pleases the folks. Steel has been in favour of it, and by a conscious choice they did a series of double acts on the different major TV shows last year. Owen was more reluctant.

A big factor they are looking to is the other parties getting rattled as the campaign shows they are not going to win an overall majority. This will make for splits and confusions which the Alliance can exploit. This especially relates to all the theology surrounding coalition etc. etc. Here, he contends, the Alliance will be the only party which has its act together, having thought through a united front.

The election will not be preceded by a great financing from big business. Steel has frequent meetings with business people, who are showing more interest. But he agrees with me that the best they can hope for is the odd firm that decides to give both to the Tories and to the Alliance. Only after the election, when the Alliance is plainly stronger, might this change.

Believes that the evident determination of the Tories to stick with the Tebbit approach plays into the Alliance hands. He seems very sure that the people will reject the uncaring government, and that the tax strategy

---

1 Richard 'Dick' Newby: politician; held various positions in the SDP 1977–88; chief of staff to Lib Dem leader Charles Kennedy 1999–2006; as Baron Newby of Rothwell, Lib Dem Treasury spokesman in the Lords since 1998. Andrew Ellis: Secretary General of the Liberal Party 1985–8; chief executive of the Social and Liberal Democrats 1988–9.

won't work politically. But he agrees that this is the line he is stuck with, just as MT is stuck with the opposite.

POST-ELECTION He agrees that it all depends on the number. But a key lesson he took from the Lib–Lab pact was that a pact was much less good than a coalition. If the Alliance has only 30 MPs, they will have to settle for a pact, owing to sheer shortage of numbers. But if they have more – and he is very confident that they will – he would favour a coalition government. This could be of various types. There could be a limited agreement for, say, two years. He doesn't favour that: look at the mess Israel has got into with this boxing into two years. He would prefer five years, contingent, of course, on something on PR.

He agrees that PR cannot be got other than by a substantial Alliance presence. Again, all depends on numbers. His disagreement on the referendum, which Owen seems to favour, has been overplayed. Owen has not actually committed himself strongly on that. Steel, although not favouring it, recognizes that it will be a bargaining option, although dependent on the numbers. He thinks that a lot of the Tories favour PR anyway – which could be one of the many points on which they are split apart as they panic at losing the election. He thinks that Labour ought to favour PR when it becomes apparent to them that Labour will never again form a majority government. The only source of Labour hostility has been that PR would put an end to socialism in our times. Since this will be shown to have ended anyway, Labour can afford to look again.

He agrees that different cons flow from a Labour and a Tory 'victory' – i.e. becoming the largest single party. If the Tories do, which is perhaps the most likely outcome, they will still be essentially a defeated party. They will have been refused another mandate. They will have suffered crushingly. MT will therefore have to go, he hazards. The key man then will become Whitelaw – a prospect WW has, it appears, thought much about and very gladly accepted: the role of kingmaker and caretaker rolled into one. Much assisted by WW being in the Lords and therefore not a contender. At this point, the Alliance have a crucial say in who becomes the Tory leader. Plainly Tebbit is out, and so is Lawson. The wets come into play. Interestingly, the name Steel mentions most keenly is Geoffrey Howe. Howe is seen as the very model of a chap the Alliance could get on with. They remember his Bow Group origins (from the days when the Bow Group was liberal in their sense). They see him as temperamentally unabrasive. This makes him different from Walker and Heseltine, both of whom are seen as difficult comrades. Hurd also would be acceptable. I add that Howe would have the further advantage of being, out of all these characters, the one most likely to enjoy trust on the Tory right. Steel says that the right don't matter – nowhere else to go.

A Labour 'victory' would bring in other considerations. Again, much would clearly depend on the numbers. But Labour could justly demand a second dissolution: which is one reason why the Tories, having been routed by the Alliance, might sustain them in office. However, how could the Tories defend that? And how could they answer questions about that during the campaign?

Labour is caught by its intense hostility to Owen. However, according to DS, the ice is very slowly breaking. DS himself is very conscious of having been courted by Labour people: understandably, because they think (wrongly) that Owen and Steel could be separated off. But on asking Owen the other day whether he had noticed any change at all in relation to himself, Owen said oddly enough he thought he had – i.e. some Labour people know they may have to do business with him.

Kinnock's own stance against deals and pacts is firmer than almost anyone else's. This puzzles the Alliance. How much does he mean it? They watch closely his words. They think (but aren't sure) that there has been more caution of late. Others, however, are becoming growingly more open about the prospect of doing business, though obviously they will never go public about it.

This fastidiousness, however, has its costs. It means that Labour is not prepared for what may lie in store. It means also that the party is highly vulnerable during the election to speaking with different voices, as a coalition comes to look more and more the eventual outcome. It means that important socialists, like important Tories, are not laying plans for the nature of any future deal.

Labour has a further problem, which may indeed be a cause of Kinnock's insistence that a deal will not be done. Perhaps he realizes better than the Alliance the possibly insuperable problems of getting the PLP to line up behind a deal and go into the lobbies night after night to preserve it. Certainly there will be a hard core which will reject it. How big will this be, post-election? Steel asserts a doubt about my suggestion that the Campaign Group will significantly grow.

The sum effect of all this on the Alliance itself is to commit them, at the least, to securing a vote of the relevant parliamentary party of their putative partners before a deal is done. Don't want to have it welshed on after being signed.

It also makes them wonder, in respect of Kinnock, whether he could be persuaded towards the Schmidt line: which was always to say that without the need for a deal with the FDP, he would have been the prisoner of his far left. Can Kinnock work out such a pragmatic compromise himself? Does he want to? Has he thought it through with anyone?

NORMAN ST JOHN-STEVAS
Lunch, White's, 13 May 1986

HISTORY He never heard MT arguing about the merits of Hayek.[1]
There was never anything of that kind. What she was was a very determined departmental minister, keen on defending and enlarging her
budget.

She was very keen to get out of Education. She knew it wasn't really
a political department (and still isn't). For this reason she wanted to move
on, and for the same reason Ted was determined to keep her where she
was. NS gave a party for her third anniversary at the DES, and Ted came
to it. He recalls her indicating then that she would like a move. But it
suited Ted to keep her in this offshore department.

Her relations with Heath were not good personally. But NS could not
confirm that Ted was in general bad about women.

Her relations with [Enoch] Powell and his ideas were crucial: but NS
didn't know what their actual personal relations were.

CHARACTER ETC He makes much of her womanish determi-
nation to be surrounded by the people she likes to have. No man, he said,
would have got rid of so many people as she has, quite ruthlessly.

As regards religion, he regards her as having no interest in the great
metaphysical questions. But he was surprised by my story of her claiming
to have Stuart Blanch's books[2] at her bedside. Describes her as a church-
goer for purely social purposes.

But what she is most interested in is money. She is absolutely fascinated
by people who have made vast amounts of it. This distances her from
people like Norman, who cannot understand such an interest. But there
is no doubt, he says, that it is her dominating drive: the thing by which
she judges people.

He says that he sometimes wonders why he ever was a Conservative,
the party has now become so terrible. Makes the interesting point that
interest has entirely disappeared from the party. No landed interest, no
social interest, no organized commercial or business interest even. This is
to be seen in how very few people (in fact none) have personal followings.
When I said that Tebbit could disappear without trace, he said, Anyone
could.

1 Friedrich von Hayek: Nobel Prize-winning economist and defender of free-market capitalism, later honoured
by both Mrs Thatcher and President George H. W. Bush.
2 Stuart Blanch, archbishop of York 1975–83, wrote a number of books, with titles such as *The Christian
Militant* and *The Burning Bush* (both 1978).

He instanced Pym: a great man in the party by any standards, with all the jobs he had held, and he could be dismissed without a whimper simply to satisfy her whim. Nobody much minded. It would be the same with anyone you could name. Heseltine certainly. The fact is that these days it is every man for himself. There simply are no personal groupings of any kind – not even, one might add, a Thatcher grouping. There are, in this sense (I extrapolate), no 'leaders' of factions or groupings, because there is nobody looking to be led.

He insists that all politicians want office, and rightly so. Office is what they came into politics for: to do something. For this reason he does not discount the chance of Owen etc. going in with Labour, or of Labour having him. Remember Fox and North, he says.

He notes with amazement that today *The Times*, obviously quoting Ingham, can describe Biffen as 'semi-detached' and Tebbit as 'fully integrated' members of the Cabinet. A new constitutional category seems to have been invented.

IAN GILMOUR
Lunch, the Garrick, 25 June 1986

Carrington was never wholly engaged. And he did not understand economic policy. The chief culprit was Whitelaw. IG coldly describes WW as 'the weakest man I think I have ever known'. IG could not recall any single thing that WW stopped her doing, certainly nothing important. Whitelaw did not understand the economic question, but more importantly would absolutely never get in her way. Would never give any support to Prior, Walker and Gilmour.

We speculated about how it might have been. Of course, if WW had been a different character, he would have run against her in 1975 and won. Which just about ruins any hypothesis. But undoubtedly if he had stood with them, things would have been different. The commitments would not have been made in the first place.

He also remarked that Pym did not become a dissenter until rather later.

Howe. A man without convictions. So IG did not regard him as a deserter during the post-Heath years. He had nothing to desert from. He had been sound on social policy but not really on free-market stuff, even though he had been in charge of the prices policy. Essentially Howe is a man who does what he is told. He's now being rather a good Foreign Secretary because he does what the Foreign Office tells him. When he was no. 2 to Walker at the DTI, under Heath, he did what Walker told him.

KENNETH BAKER
Lunch, the Garrick, 14 July 1986

As breezy and genial as ever. He hit on a word that well describes his style of politics: 'I'm a dealer,' he said. That's why he thinks that the DoE Permanent Secretary, Terry Heisler, is the best Permanent Secretary in Whitehall. Heisler too is a dealer, interested in what can be done and how. My sort of guy, says Baker.

Remarks that he is the only member of the Cabinet, save D. Young,[1] who was not in the government at all in 1979; and that two years ago – just think of it – he was Minister of Information Technology. Confirms that he was left out of the 1979 government by an oversight: the jobs ran out before they realized they hadn't given him one (perhaps that was Minister of State-ships).

UNIVERSITIES Says he told Mrs T at the moment she offered him the job that he would not close any university (including poly?). He had some leverage and used it. Not in the business of shutting things down. Some universities, however, are very badly run: e.g. Keele. And they must be willing to rationalize – i.e. no good having economics departments with only five dons. Italian is the latest to be rationalized, cutting down the number of departments. But languages are the soft end of the business. Other departments will put up more struggle.

Says that tenure has been very bad for universities, and that the best universities don't resist the changes. There is a kind of blight, as he agrees with me, on intellectual stimulation in many universities. One proposal is that dud maths dons should be shopped out to schools, to help solve school shortages.

On loans, it is back on the agenda. Walden inquiry[2] will report next autumn, after much travel and work. Thinks that the time is ripe for people to be made to understand that universities' resources need increasing, and this is one way of doing it. Also thinks that firms should be made to pay for the talent they get. No reason why a firm which gets a well-trained electronics graduate shouldn't write off his debt as part of the initial contract of employment. Ah, but what about historians and philosophers? I asked. He agreed this was more of a problem, but assumed they would get jobs too, and firms should pay for them.

---

1 David Young, Baron Young of Graffham: Secretary of State for Employment 1985–7.
2 George Walden, diplomat, writer; Conservative MP for Buckingham 1983–97; as higher-education minister, in 1986 began a comprehensive review of the student grant system and the pressures on the polytechnics and colleges.

He's very keen on the polys, he says, like an Oxbridge man who has only recently discovered their existence. The North Staffs Poly has the third best electronics department in England, after Imperial College and Cambridge. 200 teachers in it – more than the whole of Keele University. Huge output of students.

LABOUR PARTY he thinks is doomed. We agree about the analysis, which also applies to the NUT and teaching and points to the major split in British society, between the inner cities and the rest. The Labour Party shows this clearly. Manchester is controlled by Militant, as well as Liverpool, where they won't loosen their grip. Even short of MT, the hard left is in control, and represents substantially different aspirations from what Kinnock is talking about. The people nominated for most inner-city Labour seats will not sit idly by as Kinnock fails to deliver a left programme. Given the huge difficultly *we've* had, Baker says, in controlling public spending, how can one imagine Labour resisting the vast demands of the lobbies and pressure groups – and then somehow fighting off the financial crisis which will follow? The truth is (says HY) there is no real consensus inside the Labour Party about what should be done, about the limits of action, about financial discipline.

Notes. KB is a flesh-presser. Often touches one's elbow and arm to emphasize a point. Also talks about 'our country' quite naturally, in a way more often found in an American politician.

PETER SHORE
Lunch, Café Pelican, 15 July 1986

Regards Livingstone as about the most evil man to come on the political scene for many years: clever at mobilizing the minorities, but a preacher and stirrer up of hatred against most established institutions. By this means he has created a radicalized class which rejects almost everything. The politics of hatred. (PS says he is quite certain he is the only multilateralist left in London politics.) Other cities have had similar experiences. This has changed the Labour Party, making old compromises unavailable.

He says the only hope is that a yet newer generation, post-Livingstone, is emerging which reacts against all that stuff. There is a more sensible politics among the youngest elements in the party. But they will take time to come through . . .

All in all, he says that any party that wins the next election will face a difficult time. North Sea oil has been wasted, and is now running out. Where is the result of it? PS had hoped that we might at least be ahead in information technology, with small business etc. etc., but we've failed at that too.

When Patricia Hewitt – at this time press and broadcasting secretary to the Leader of the Opposition, Neil Kinnock – invited HY to lunch she chose the Gay Hussar in Soho, a long-time haunt of Michael Foot and a gaggle of Tribunites. He found Hewitt 'eager to please, trying to be charming, but also suitably fierce and oath-ful. Speaks with some confidence as a woman who expects to be in government soon.' HY's impression of the Kinnock camp, as represented by Hewitt, was 'confident, even rather complacent – piously sure that the nice people are finally going to take over government; extremely touchy about the apparent unwillingness of people who ought to be nice to behave nicely (e.g. The Guardian); consumed with a pretty nauseating sense of clubbiness, with name-dropping of suitable socialists and others round the world: much taken with a sense of NK as the new generation, new frontier even.'

PATRICIA HEWITT
Her lunch, Gay Hussar, 23 July 1986

Some salient points:

Does not dispute that the financial world has changed since Labour was in office. Says that exchange controls are totally out. Is not an expert in this area, but does not demur from the idea that here is one area of control which has gone.

NATIONALIZATION Rejects my thesis that even as social ownership this is not popular. Says that the purpose of social ownership for British Telecom would be: to get more control over prices (with ministerial veto), to ensure a British purchasing policy, thus having a major effect both on British jobs and on British advance in this vital new tech electronic area. Says that nobody is in favour of old-style nationalization, but people are attracted by the idea of social ownership especially of the basic utilities, which are the priorities.

UNIONS Will repeal all Tory laws, but replace them with better ones, including the balloting provisions – although these will now be under the control of unions not bosses. Demurs at my suggestion that the Tories have done everyone a favour by putting ballots into consciousness. Says the Tories' biggest favour was the political fund ballots, which comprehensively backfired.

Unions' involvement in government will come via the National Economic Assessment: a round-table assessment including employers. This will divide the cake, and there will be a big input on wages. However, the biggest thing on this front is unions' new willingness to back a national minimum wage – figure to be decided when they get in. Unions have always opposed this because of differential problems. Claims it has been thought out quite a lot – Henry Neuberger[1] is the expert. This would be latched into the tax changes, and the benefits changes for the unemployed and long-term unemployed . . . A complex package.

The whole poverty–low-paid nexus is a central part of Labour's targeting. It is only below unemployment as the priority by which all the other policies must fall into place. There is no row between Meacher and Hattersley, as reported.

DEFENCE   There is unity, very much including Hattersley, behind a non-nuclear policy which asserts deep support for NATO. The official line now seems to be that the cruise bases are militarily unwanted even by the US, and that the sub bases are hardly used anyway. Kinnock spends quite some time talking to military people, and discovers how desperate the BAOR[2] and the navy are for more resources. Labour will heavily emphasize that Britain will be better defended under Labour, not worse. When I pressed PH on the resources question she repeated NK: we will spend 'what is needed', without commitment to a figure. (A bullshit answer.)

She made clear to me, interestingly, how the Labour line now is that deterrence in no way works. This is their escape clause from the charge that it is intellectually disreputable to be relying on the US umbrella. Labour asserts that we are not doing this: that deterrence has nothing to do with anything that matters etc. etc.

ELECTION   She sees the chemistry of 1987–8 as quite different from 1983, owing to NK. Instead of the youthful Thatcher against the aged Foot, there will be bright young Kinnock against toiling, shop-soiled Thatcher. This changes the entire chemistry.

Addendum on defence. Claims that NK does talk to the Americans. Says that much depends on the presidential election. They've talked to 'Hart's

---

1 Henry Neuberger: economist and adviser to Neil Kinnock.
2 British Army of the Rhine. In 1945 an army of occupation, it gradually became part of the NATO front-line defence against the Soviet Union and the Warsaw Pact countries. In 1994 it became British Forces Germany.

people',[1] for example, and satisfied themselves that the US doesn't make anything of cruise or Trident. And altogether is quite happy with what will happen. And won't mind about pulling out nuke bases. Claimed also that the embassy people said likewise . . .

BOB WORCESTER
Mori, 23 July 1986

A panelled office, with Bob in a fine-cut suit, surrounded by his gadgets, plus the speedy, thick-piled staff of a very prosperous business. He is clearly doing very well indeed. One of his biggest lines is the privatization programme, which he is deeply involved in (British Airways and many others). Making a bomb.

Also working hard for Labour. Many meetings. Has been almost from the start of this period, even pre-Kinnock. He gives an impression of a far more switched-on party. Also a happy party. Walworth Road [Labour Party headquarters] is a place where jokes can be made, where there is a swinging atmosphere, where professional people believe they can win, where new technology is used not despised. He makes several key points:

A very important fact is that Robin Cook, at Shadow Cabinet level, is devoting himself full-time to election strategy and tactics. A tower of strength. Organizing the visits and the education of all candidates in target seats. Much done to them re practical business of running campaigns. Worcester addresses them about what people really think, and advises them to read *Sun* and *Mirror*, not *Guardian*, and to remember that 23 per cent of the country read no newspaper regularly at all.

Party is much into mailshots. Canvassing has changed its nature. Never ought to have been used for persuasion, but now even less than before. Technology now permits individualized mailshots relating to people's concerns. Thus, a canvasser should find out why a voter is worried, and a letter should follow which says that the party is concerned about her concerns, and will do something about them.

The party's only serious weakness is Kinnock's inability to be perceived as prime minister. How can he do something about this? He doesn't have to, as MT makes error after error and shows herself not to be fit either . . . Worcester says that the Kinnock profile is much more important even than policy.

He drew me a diagram to illustrate his latest theory, which boils down

1 Gary Hart, Democratic senator for Colorado, campaigned for the party nomination in the US presidential election in 1984 and was considered a front-runner for 1988. He withdrew before nomination.

to showing that the election will be decided by 800,000 to 1 million people: 20 per cent of the voters in the 120 swing seats (it being assumed that Labour and Tories are solid at rock bottom 30, Alliance at 20).

He also thinks, because of the mailshot etc. technique mentioned above, that TV is less important than it was, comparatively.

I reminded him of his opinion two years ago that Labour could not win. He said that he had not reckoned on MT doing so many silly things, culminating with Libya, which has much strengthened Labour's position on defence. He now thinks that it is virtually certain (his exact sense) that Labour will be the next government, either as a minority or possibly a majority. He doesn't believe in the convention that a government only six points behind at this stage can easily make up ground. That's like some of the silly 'rules' so often said to be axiomatic about politics – which almost never are. E.g. that the Labour Party is terminally finished.

He rather agreed with P. Jenkins's piece saying that the Tories had 'the smell of death' about them.

My conclusions:

– Bob has gone over in a big way to his duties as a Labour pollster. Very committed.
– One should certainly start writing in a way which reflects the measure of optimism with which he is clearly filling the Labour Party whenever he sees them.

WILLIAM WALDEGRAVE
29 July 1986

Nicholas Ridley is becoming very powerful. He makes a trio with Lawson and Tebbit, arguing against the wets. Against Baker especially, over the teachers' pay resolution. Tebbit must be waning, but Ridley is a powerful addition to the Thatcher camp. John Moore also helps that, although he simply does what he is told, and has no independence. Ridley also notably got a very quick deal out of MacGregor at the Treasury.[1] This too is significant. There was a different chemistry from Baker. A sign of favour that Ridley should have achieved this.

WW therefore believes the wets are mistaken to claim that they are now on top. He discounts their claims to be organizing better than their ancestors.

As between Baker and Hurd, there will at some point have to be a

1 John MacGregor: Conservative MP for South Norfolk 1974–2001; Chief Secretary to the Treasury 1985–7; leader of the Commons 1990–92; later Baron MacGregor of Pulham Market.

reckoning among the left of the party. WW has no doubt whatever who he would bring back: Hurd, who is head and shoulders the superior person. Baker is a nice affable fellow, the Whitelaw of the party in the nineties, as WW said before. But not in the same league or calibre.

Nor is there any evidence of mutual support between them. Nothing but tooth-and-nail fighting for funds between the Home Office and the DES, as one would expect between any departmental ministers.

Thatcher is not losing her powers. Getting a bit dottier, like all prime ministers do. The same strengths, the same weaknesses. The only truly remarkable thing is that there is only one thing more remarkable than the eighth year and that is the ninth year.

Notes how Biffen has lost his clout. Just one silly TV interview[1] which overstepped the mark, and suddenly he could be discounted. Stepping over the invisible but decisive line between candid friend who is taken seriously and big-mouthed overstater of a point and overdoer of his position. Just that one remark about 'the balanced ticket': intolerable to MT, as he should have seen before he said it (this per HY).

BERNARD DONOUGHUE
Lunch, Café Pelican, 28 August 1986

ECONOMY He is advising clients and Grieveson's[2] that it no longer makes much difference which side wins the election. Admits that a Labour victory would have some bad effects, but contends that the inheritance of either side looks bad. This is partly circumstance, and partly what the Tories are doing now. Circumstance is producing a situation which shows inflation easing up, growth easing down, balance of payments looking worse, unemployment no better. This is quite unlike 1983, when inflation was heading sharp down and growth nicely up: and these projections have been fulfilled in a way unparalleled for twenty years, with high growth and low inflation. But the lines look different now. Add in other elements – the tailing-off of North Sea revenues, and the absence of asset-sale revenues – and suddenly you are looking at a much bigger deficit, whoever is in power, and a prospect for the economy which is critically dependent on a sizeable cut in sterling. This is the only explanation for the present huge discrepancy between inflation rate and interest

1 On 11 May 1986 Biffen told Brian Walden, on the programme *Weekend World*, that a 'balanced ticket' was needed to fight the next general election, and added, 'No one seriously supposes that the Prime Minister would be prime minister throughout the entire period of the next parliament.' It was after this interview that Bernard Ingham famously described Biffen as a 'semi-detached member of the Cabinet'.

2 Grieveson Grant, stockbrokers. Bernard Donoughue, once an adviser to Harold Wilson, became head of research and investment policy there.

rates – a 10 per cent real interest rate, bigger than in memory. The only explanation for that is the government's desperate need to keep sterling up, lest a fall in sterling imperils its one unarguable success – the inflation rate. But the government is making these prospects worse by its promises on tax, which it clearly cannot pay for other than by fudging the figures. A giveaway Budget is therefore a perilous enterprise. What is happening is rather like what happened in 1964: all long-term problems being shelved in favour of short-term advantage.

SOCIALISM We discuss what is left of socialism in modern times. BD asserts his commitment to 'a way of doing things', and to 'the idea of government action' and to 'a bias always towards the underprivileged'. We agree, however, that these great ideas need to be broken down. And there are certain problems. BD, for example, is utterly scornful of the Hattersley notion that anyone with £27,000 a year is 'rich' and must be taxed more heavily. Yet, if that is not a determinant of socialism, what is? Further, he concedes that there may be a lack of concordance between what he calls socialism and what the productive economy needs to keep itself growing. BD's own 'solution' to this would have been to examine priorities in a deep and big way, an exercise which he would see leading to a conclusion that Labour could massively cut spending on defence and on agriculture, and could also start to tax corporations: and thereby could raise, he guesstimates, £6 billion. This would mean you need not talk about increasing personal taxation. And you could cut the top rate of company tax, while insisting that all companies should pay it. In sum, he would like to see the Reagan tax package brought into Britain, and sees this right-wing Republican solution, with the abolition of perks and dodges while cutting the rates, as an ideal socialist expedient. Has urged Hattersley to look at it.

I asked him, a City gent, whether Labour could tame the City. He said, basically, that Labour needed to equip itself with far more knowledge. He disliked Hattersley's criticisms not because they were critical, but because they would be discounted as revealing great ignorance. This had both a small and a large dimension. The small one was political: Hattersley needs to get his personal act together and get better advisers to make up for his natural lack of feel for the economic field. The large point concerns policy: the City and the market has become far more complex and above all far more internationalized since Labour were in power. Presents a far more intractable power centre, and this will become more so when, as BD thinks likely within five years, 60 per cent of the City is foreign-owned. A vast area of economic activity, which currently has a balance of £6 billion in earnings, can be subjected to only marginal control by the controllers of the macroeconomy, especially socialist ones who believe in a partly directed economy.

KINNOCK BD thinks he got the job too soon. Never thought anything of him, and now feels he's doing a lot better than he would ever have expected. But it is tragic that he never had even a couple of years in a job. The better course would have been for Healey to succeed in 1980, and lead into two failed elections, Kinnock taking over thereafter after a proper grooming. Kinnock is too Welsh: plausible, pleasant, fluent, talkative, but ultimately lacking in bottom. BD's highest regard is for John Smith: and he says there is a minute of his to Callaghan ten years ago to this effect.

HIMSELF Thinks that as director of the policy unit he had more power than any junior minister, and than half the Cabinet. He has therefore had enough of public glamour, unless in particular jobs. He would not easily take a junior ministry just to make up the numbers, although he admits he could be pressed by Kinnock to do so. What he would accept: Minister of the Arts, junior FCO minister, junior Treasury minister (unlikely in the House of Lords). But he is clearly angling for the Bank of England, Leigh-Pemberton[1] clearly having been designated for the sack. Says Labour will need a friend there, as Labour knows, and is utterly confident that he could do the job. If he was ineligible, he would advise Hattersley to go to McMahon,[2] or to some senior existing BoE man.

However, BD doesn't think it will happen. He and Barnett, who talk much, think Labour won't win. At best it will be a messy result. It seems he doesn't really think NK can run a minority government either. Looks, rather, to the 1950 precedent: when Labour lost a 186 majority down to 5 (check figs) and then the Tories won on the momentum. Could be the same now – though he admits that the third-party factor makes the equation different.

THATCHER RESIDUE He homes in on the unions. Sums it up: whereas previously it was socially acceptable only to concede, now it is socially acceptable only to stand up to the unions. That was a big sea change, perhaps starting with British Leyland.

Columnar questions:

– The real economy which means that the election could be a bit irrelevant (see above).

---

1 Robert 'Robin' Leigh-Pemberton, remained governor of the Bank of England 1983–93; later Baron Kingsdown of Pemberton.
2 Sir Kit McMahon: deputy governor of the Bank of England 1980–85.

- The inadequacy of Hattersley: perhaps combined with the Thatcher wipe-out of top Tories, leading one to see a paucity of top-raters, not enough to fulfil Hoskyn's complaint that you can't find twenty people good enough to fill a Cabinet unless by enormous luck.
- Why was Barnett made vice-chairman of the BBC? To pave the way for another Tory to succeed cancer-ridden Young?[1] To get B out of line as economic spokesman in the House of Lords, where he constantly embarrasses the government? He is the only Labour man appointed to any quango, it would seem . . .

JOHN BIFFEN
Lunch, 20 November 1986

ELECTION He thinks it should be October. Strongly hopes she is not persuaded into June–July, because that would look wrong. Equally, thinks she should not risk the winter. Therefore he would favour going in October, even if the Tories were two points behind Labour in the polls. Meanwhile, he says that basically she wants to govern without Parliament, i.e. make sure nothing big or disturbing happens. She keeps worrying about 'another Westland'. But reassures herself with the thought that, even if there were another Westland, there couldn't be another Heseltine, as she says.

HUNG PARLIAMENT He thinks it quite possible. If the Tories were the largest party, he thinks she would attempt to govern for as long as was necessary to ensure to her satisfaction that the reason she was going was not perceived as being at someone else's bidding – especially another party's bidding. Finds it impossible to talk about scenarios, since every figure produces a different possibility. But he is clear that it could not be a coalition with the Irish, although Ivor Stanbrook[2] would like it. Whether it could be with Owen would entirely depend on numbers. Agrees that the Queen is not obliged to give a minority Tory government a dissolution, although (I thought) his mind wasn't on the job in question.

THATCHER Is very nervous about 'something going wrong', i.e. Westland. What JB fears is that if she wins it will not be a humbling experience but the opposite, for her.

1 Stuart Young, an accountant and brother of the Cabinet minister David Young, was chairman of the BBC governors until his death from cancer in 1986.
2 Ivor Stanbrook: former colonial officer; Conservative MP for Orpington 1970–92; avowed right-winger; member of the Conservative parliamentary committee on Northern Ireland 1989–92.

He would like a Cabinet of duly humbled men, but knows it unlikely.

Says that Wakeham is by far the most important person around her – although denies that Tebbit is out of favour.

ADDENDA Thinks the Alliance has blown it. Blames Owen (for identical reasons to mine). Reflects how much Smith, Hattersley etc. must have been enjoying the spectacle of Owen behaving exactly as he did under Labour: an overmighty colleague, unwilling to make the necessary compromises . . .

WILLIAM WALDEGRAVE
Lunch, 10 December 1986

VICTOR ROTHSCHILD[1] With whom WW is close friends. Says that R was satisfied with MT's statement (giving negative clearance). After all, says WW (and therefore?), MI5 has files on vast numbers of people and prima facie notes which could amount to the beginnings of suspicion. The fact that MI5 says it has no reason for thinking R a Soviet agent is spookspeak for saying there's no file on him. However, WW was less satisfied, and thought MT's subsequent statement on TV was needed to clear it properly up.

R has been trying to help Wright[2] and some others for years. Thinks they have been disgracefully treated as to their pensions. In Wright's case, he went away to work for Marconi in order to find out about computers, on the specific understanding that this would not count as break-in-service from a pension viewpoint. However, the Treasury ratted on this and he was left with £2,000 a year. R has been disgusted about this for a long time, himself having been much involved with these characters.

WW surmises that R fixed up Wright's visit here and his contact with Pincher[3] as part of a deniable operation arranged by MI5 or a faction therein, as a way of getting him some money without using the Treasury. Wright had written a memorandum, which inter alia exculpates R (which is why R asserted in his letter to the *Telegraph* that MI5 had unambiguous proof that he was innocent). There followed chapters towards a book,

1 Victor Rothschild was friends at Cambridge with Guy Burgess and Anthony Blunt, both later and separately exposed as Soviet agents. He worked for MI5 during the Second World War (winning the George Medal), and later became a security adviser to Mrs Thatcher.

2 Peter Wright, former assistant director of MI5, was the author of *Spycatcher: The Candid Autobiography of a Senior Intelligence Officer*. The first attempt at publication in Australia triggered a three-year legal battle over questions of confidentiality. It was eventually published there on 31 July 1987. In 1988 the government lost the battle to suppress publication in British newspapers, including *The Guardian* and *The Observer*.

3 (Harry) Chapman Pincher: chief defence correspondent of Beaverbrook newspapers 1972–9; author of *Their Trade is Treachery* (1981), *Traitors: The Labyrinths of Treason* (1987) etc.

and finally the Pincher deal. This based on the feeling that Pincher was a trusty. WW surmises that the anti-Hollis[1] aim was a subsidiary and not the main aim of the MI5 faction who arranged the deal.

He says, plainly direct from R, that Wright has done very great service to the country.

The lesson, he feels, is that the bloody law officers should be made far more accountable. The idea that their advice is specifically confidential is absurd. He also says that it seems quite credible that the reason no action was brought against Pincher was indeed that the manuscript had been got by a break-in or some such. Which was doubly absurd. Fancy planning an operation to stop the book coming out, but using a method which rendered it impossible to carry out your chosen plan of seeking an injunction!

Thinks Armstrong should never have been sent.[2] Should have been a politician, most likely Mayhew. Mayhew very good on his feet. The very specific training of a politician is to work out how to foresee and avoid traps of the kind that Turnbull[3] constantly placed in Armstrong's path. A civil servant is not trained in that way, certainly not publicly.

RIDLEY Is a formidable fellow. As influential as anyone right now. Not a nice man. But an effective politician. For example, his apparent reversal on the rate support grant, to the displeasure of some Tory counties, was quite clever. He knew he would have to harm about one-third of the counties. He at first penalized two-thirds of them, knowing he would give way to half of these and thus seem to be consultative and make them feel better. But NR is very unsympathetic to all the regulatory stuff, which WW is concerned with – although, pending the election, has laid off things like the green belt.

SUCCESSION He too would go for Hurd. But thinks he will be too old. Which indeed he will – he's now 56 after all. Therefore sees Baker as the most likely bet.

THATCHER Has she got better? She's got more cautious. And he's impressed by her quite amazing energy. But she is surrounded by poor officials. Instances also Charles Powell and his wife [Carla]. Powell is impressive because the new principal private secretary is so bad. Also, see the story of Powell's wife. Powell was duty officer one weekend. His wife

1 The book aired speculation that Roger Hollis, once director general of MI5, was a Soviet double agent.
2 Sir Robert Armstrong, the Cabinet Secretary, represented the government in the *Spycatcher* trial in Australia and famously told the Supreme Court of New South Wales that he had been 'economical with the truth'.
3 Malcolm Turnbull, Australian barrister, Liberal politician, was the advocate who represented Peter Wright and *Spycatcher* in the Australian courts.

was monopolizing the phone and he was getting agitated. Kept saying she must get off the line, because the Prime Minister might ring. 'But I am talking to the Prime Minister,' she scornfully returned.

1987

PATRICK MAYHEW
Lunch, Bussola, 21 January 1987

Genial, heavy and eats a big lunch.

THATCHER He regards Prior as the absolutely key person to the success of the Thatcher administration, for which he was very badly treated. Prior's first bill was the crucial breakthrough with the unions, who were themselves the crucial enemy of the government. Her conduct in undermining him, encouraging resistance, getting Ian Gow[1] to work, plus the odious Hoskyns with his demands that they should outlaw the closed shop, altogether made Prior's task very hard. She is a deeply disloyal person in that way.

Prior, on the other hand, was careless with his career. The run-up to his Irish posting was terrible, and meant he arrived there having pretty well said he didn't want the job. Mayhew is inclined to blame Jane Prior for being too ambitious and a bad guide.

HAVERS desperately wants to be Lord Chancellor, and the only error he has made is making this too clear. But PM thinks MT wants to make him LC, so it will probably happen – although he implies without confirming that there may be a query about his health.

Mayhew regards himself as consigned to be Attorney General, much as he would detest the prospect. Desperately wants a political job, and felt bad about leaving the Home Office. Says he went into politics to get away from the law, and look what has happened.

He claims that Nick Lyell[2] is the best lawyer in the House (this very odd – HY). But says that MT wants to make Waddington[3] Solicitor General, which PM discreetly indicates is not a very happy idea.

THATCHER is very good about taking the law officers' advice, but he adds that this may be partly because she does not always seek it – much chortling re Wright etc.

Mayhew would clearly actually like the NI job. His family goes way back as southern Protestants, who classically despised the northern Protestants. He goes there a lot still. He thinks the Anglo-Irish agreement, however, is deeply flawed. I sensed a strong Unionist, at least in the emphasis he placed on the intensity of mass feeling among the Protestant community. Thinks MT has been led by the NIO [Northern Ireland Office] and FCO into underestimating this, and that the only policy is to have no policy, no intent to do anything much. Thinks Dublin has been the sole beneficiary of the agreement, not even doing the minimum of putting a senior Garda man in charge of the border.

---

1 Ian Gow: Conservative MP for Eastbourne 1974–1990; PPS to Mrs Thatcher 1979–83; assassinated by the IRA on 30 July 1990.

2 Nicholas Lyell: barrister; Conservative MP for Hemel Hempstead 1979–83, for Mid-Bedfordshire 1983–97, for North-East Bedfordshire 1997–2001; Solicitor General 1987–92; Attorney General 1992–7; later Baron Lyell of Markyate.

3 David Waddington: Conservative MP for Nelson and Colne 1968–74, for Clitheroe 1979–83, for Ribble Valley 1983–90; government chief whip 1987–9; Home Secretary 1989–90; later Baron Waddington of Read.

On the succession: he is strong for Baker – a warmer man than Hurd, who would be his second choice. Tebbit has no chance.

JOHN MOORE
The Guardian, 10 February 1987

A nervous starter. Very quiet-voiced. Very ad-man soft, full of jargonish abstractions. Very full of Americanisms at all times – 'you guys', 'rail-roads', 'treasurers' of companies. But he did get a lot better. He is very much a finance man, though not a City man, having been mainly working for US companies in the brokerage and finance field. This makes him, among other things, deeply shocked and unimpressed by City attitudes to regulation. Thinks the SEC system,[1] which requires the very rigid declaration and recording of all deals, and far greater legal supervision, is the only one worth talking about. 'When money is involved, "My word is my bond" is a lot of nonsense.'

Among his points of interest:

Deplores the complete lack of informal discussion in Cabinet and Cabinet committee. There is more discussion in Cabinet committee, but none of it is informal. Cabinet committees have agenda, have papers, have decisions to approve. Everyone always calls each other by his office name, not actual name. A structured formality which militates against informal debate.

Not even Cabinet committees often make decisions. The decisions are made before them, by the lead minister, if necessary negotiating done with another relevant minister. Cabinet committee, and even more Cabinet itself, is there to bless the decision. He alluded to the eighteenth-century Church (got his century wrong, I think) needing to give its benediction. Cabinet was rather the same.

If you were to ask ten Cabinet ministers when each had last spoken informally to the other nine in the last six months, you'd be shattered by the answer.

Thirty to 40 per cent of my time is spent in what I called defensive briefing. For PQs, for television, for meetings, for speeches. A fantastic amount of time getting ready to avoid traps, rather than thinking about policy. For example, went down to the Greenwich by-election this morning. Many transport issues there as it happens: cross-river crossing, Dartford Tunnel, Rochester Way widening etc. etc. He got deeply briefed on every one of them. A file that thick. Then not a single question at the

1 The Securities and Exchange Commission, a US government agency, has since 1934 regulated the American market in stocks and securities.

press conference (owing to the incompetence of the journalists, and the egotistical sparring of V. Hanna).[1] He seemed to be saying there is too much of a premium on getting tiny details right, not enough on the big picture.

There is no mechanism in government like the departmental prayer meetings. Here you get real exchanges and real thinking. Nigel Lawson, for whom Moore worked both at Energy and at the Treasury, was superbly good at them.

He is against having political advisers. Would not know how to use them or their material. He is against having a civil-servant private secretary who turns out to be adamantly committed and political on your side. He doesn't give you detached advice.

Was unable to name one occasion when Cabinet as such took a decision. It blessed decisions. Of course, things like AWACS [Airborne Warning and Control System] have to go through Cabinet, and there was a proper discussion, but no decision was made there.

Moore is highly political. For this reason appalled by Tebbit's attack on the BBC.[2] Just bad politics, bad vibes, bad emanations if you attack an institution which is regarded quite like the white cliffs of Dover, and one which you think has been criticizing you. He is dry, as a consumerist not a producerist. Admits to being bone dry on economic things, but not therefore on the 'right'.

Although HY could say that some of his best friends were Conservatives, he would not have included John Patten, whom he found 'pretty unhelpful. Full of patter, very pleased with himself, very unrevealing of anything he really thought. A hard-nosed cocky bugger, with all the necessary outer smoothery.'

JOHN PATTEN
In his office at the DoE, 11 February 1987

ELECTION   Says he thinks there was a change some time in later summer. He judges by his mailbag. Through spring and summer, there was very bad mail, about Westland, about Libya, about British Leyland. Worse than at any time since 1979. A series of specific issues that people

---

1 Vincent Hanna: reporter for the BBC and later Channel 4.
2 In 1986, Lord Tebbit criticized the BBC reporting of the bombing raids on Libya. He later produced a detailed dossier on the corporation's coverage, which he said was 'riddled with inaccuracy, innuendo and imbalance'. The BBC responded with a point-by-point rebuttal and a letter from the new chairman, Marmaduke Hussey.

felt bad about. The people, and even the party, were deeply discontented.

The party, above all, has now come back. People send money. People write fan letters. He feels the party is absolutely solid. The conference was very successful. Tebbit had asked for a positive approach, around the theme The Next Move Forward. But there was no vetting of scripts, either by Conservative Central Office or by senior ministers. So this shows a collective consensus naturally emerging, which somehow came together.

As for Thatcher: he says she was weak up to Christmas, and her unpopularity was not offset by signs of great competence. But now we are back to the time when they think she's a tough old bitch who knows how to get things done. She is very capable, people think. So she too is solid.

He favours 1 October as the date. Cut out all the conferences. Unemployment down; two months of non-Parliament. All to the good.

HY judged his next contact, Bryan Gould, to be a mirror image of Thatcher's press secretary, Bernard Ingham. Gould saw Thatcher as the major hurdle, just as Ingham saw her as the major asset. He found Gould speaking identical language to Ingham about the public appetite for toughness and competence in leadership, and the near-irrelevance of likeability.

BRYAN GOULD
Tea, 16 February 1987

He insisted that Neil Kinnock was very tough, especially to those around him. But acknowledged without my asking him that Kinnock had a problem in public perception in this area.

We are now closing her options. Thinks she won't go on 7 May, although we still have to keep saying she might, to make sure all is prepared. But the point is that if she gets a mere 20 majority this will be a crushing defeat for her. She not only wants to win but to win big. Therefore she won't go early on a marginal chance. Plus the fact that the Alliance may do better in the campaign. Alliance improvement is the big need. We could win at our present figure if the Alliance takes Tory seats in the south. Otherwise we only need 2–3 per cent in any case. It is entirely possible.

His line appears to be that there are issues where Labour is plainly ahead: welfare, hospitals, education. What they should concentrate on is where they are weaker – especially the business about tough leadership.

He is a rare Labour in being prepared to talk privately about defeat, with plenty of correct caveats about this being only personal opinion. He gave two (a) You can never say never in politics, and after a second election one must be open to possible deals etc. with the Alliance. (b) A defeat in which Labour got 280 seats would be represented as a massive triumph, Labour on the way back, one more heave, no longer a forgotten party, no longer in eclipse to the Alliance: But 250 or under would be a fast increasing disaster, with the left profiting the lower the number of seats.

The Greenwich by-election, caused by the death of the Labour MP on 24 December, took place on 26 February. The Alliance fielded Rosie Barnes, whose husband was a well-known local councillor. She romped home with 18,000 votes (53 per cent of the poll), leaving the Labour candidate in second place (a fall of 4 per cent) and, disastrously for the government, the Conservative vote fell by 23 per cent to 3,800.

WILLIAM WHITELAW
Lunch, 16 March 1987

At Buck's Club: suggested to him in recompense for his having ditched me at the last minute following the Tebbit writ.[1] WW came on very apologetic about this, saying that 'Norman is unbelievably touchy,' and merely for Willy to have been seen with me (by all Tebbit's friends at Buck's Club??) would have caused a 'major ruction'.

ELECTION The most interesting thing WW said was that he was uneasy about the state of the country. Since WW is nothing if not a 'feel' politician, his present feel that the Alliance was going to do quite a lot better than in 1983, getting more seats, is of some consequence, especially since he is in the inner Thatcher councils still. He thinks that several groups – he instanced especially the farmers – were so fed up with the government that they would certainly not 'work for us', and might even slide over and vote for the Alliance. He thought academic opinion was also that way inclined, and could have a ripple effect. He did not talk like a man who thought the party was odds-on favourite to win.

He says his view of Conservative Central Office is low ('and I can tell

1 Norman Tebbit issued a writ for libel after HY claimed in a January 1987 column that the then Tory Party Chairman once said, 'Nobody with a conscience votes Conservative.' *The Guardian* apologized and agreed to pay damages and legal costs after accepting that Tebbit had never made this remark.

you that Margaret thinks exactly the same'). They seem to have made a mess of things. They explained the Greenwich campaign by saying that they were 'saving everything for Truro'.[1] Ho, ho, ho. He is also much disturbed by the low calibre of by-election candidates the Tories seem invariably to put in the field. He thought the Greenwich man was the pits, and had evidently been given no political education by CCO.

This led him to remark that candidates in general are getting worse, and are marked by a single trait: their desire to do whatever their leader wants them to do. Thinks this is seriously different from how it was in 1970.

POST-ELECTION If it turns out to be a hung parliament, he said with some deliberation, his advice to Margaret would be to go. She should call it a day. 'We should go together, we've had a good innings,' he added. He also said that if Wakeham, for whom he has ecstatic regard, and he together went to Margaret about anything – including her own behaviour in that eventuality – she would think long and hard before ignoring it. Wakeham is a big man at court, still.

A further consequence, he has no doubt, would be 'the moment made for Geoffrey'. Seemed quite sure that GH would be the inheritor, in that situation. 'Douglas wouldn't be able to manage it, and Kenneth is just not senior enough. Geoffrey has alienated surprisingly few people. This would be his finest hour.'

Maybe it was a wily politician's caution, but he conspicuously declined to think much about the effects of a big Tory victory. But he said that he had still not made up his own mind to go, although claims he would really like to if she permitted it. Would have no hesitation in doing so if George Younger's[2] father conveniently died, leaving George with his hereditary peerage and the ideal man as the Leader of the Lords.[3] The Lords now need big men as leaders. They want it. This was why Janet Young, splendid though she was, was not up to it. Not senior enough. And thus came about a terminal falling out with MT. If WW did retire, and Younger was not available, they might have to fall back on Belstead[4] – nice chap, but simply not up to it when the peers are being such a bloody nuisance. (In that connection, by the way, WW is hugely pleased with what one might call the Whitelaw Kindergarten: Caithness, Brabazon, Beaverbrook

1 Following the death of rising Liberal politician David Penhaligon, MP for Truro since 1974. The by-election took place on 12 March. The Liberal candidate, Matthew Taylor, increased his Party's majority; the Conservatives saw their vote decline by 6 per cent.

2 George Younger: Conservative MP for Ayr 1964–92; Secretary of State for Scotland 1979–86, for Defence 1986–9.

3 Whitelaw had been elevated to the House of Lords in 1983 with a barony – hereditary, but he had no heir. He was Leader of the Lords until 1988.

4 The 2nd Baron Belstead, deputy Leader at the time, became Leader of the House of Lords and Lord Privy Seal 1988–90.

and one or two others – young men who are learning how to be politicians at his feet.)[1]

He thought Hailsham, Channon, Jopling[2] would be for the chop: Walker 'only if we have a majority of over 40.'

CRIME FIGURES had just come out. Poor Douglas, WW iterated – and launched into an account of his life and times trying to throttle the Tory right, who would always give a Tory Home Secretary a bad time. Dreaded the capital-punishment debate coming yet again, but said that at least Douglas knew what he thought. WW added that when he quit Penrith, every supplicant for his seat was asked what he thought about capital punishment: and if he was against it, he was instantly chopped off the list.

Incidentally, WW recalled that he had never in twelve years had a discussion with MT about capital punishment. They each knew where the other stood, and when the debate was big and hot she never once discussed it with her Home Secretary.

RENEE SHORT
House of Commons, 23 March 1987

She is chair of the social services committee, now embarked on its major Aids inquiry.

People have not realized how serious the Aids crisis is. People in government included. Not many people have come into contact with Aids sufferers or seen them when they have been hospitalized. They may be aware of drug addicts, but not of Aids people. They do not personally understand, even yet, the horrific sight and effect of Aids: the appalling physical symptoms, the physical degradation.

Those we have met in hospital are surprisingly open about how they have contracted it. Say they know the dangers. Maybe their candour is because of the hospital environment, away from their pals, their dealers, the druggie environment. ('It's really organized crime.') All those we saw are unemployed, all young, all started drug abuse while still at school, and many having homosexual partners who have all these problems as well . . .

1 Malcolm Sinclair, 20th Earl of Caithness: Minister of State at the Home Office, then Environment, 1986–9. Ivon Anthony Moore-Brabazon, 3rd Baron Brabazon of Tara: a junior minister at the Department of Transport and the FCO 1986–92. Maxwell Aitken, 3rd Baron Beaverbrook: government whip in the House of Lords 1986–8; treasurer of the Conservative Party 1990–92.
2 Michael Jopling: Conservative MP for Westmorland 1964–83, for Westmorland and Lonsdale 1983–97; chief whip 1979–83; Minister of Agriculture, Fisheries and Food 1983–7; later Baron Jopling of Ainderby Quernhow.

If more people did know Aids' full impact, maybe more parents would be urging their sons and daughters against drug abuse, and talking to them about the cons of getting on to drugs.

At a drop-in centre on an estate in Edinburgh we found a lot of people trying to help. GPs, voluntary workers, social workers, some ex-druggies all doing their best. More resources, far more, are needed: human resources as well as money. Hard-drug addicts need vast support, to be motivated to try and give up (best done with help of peer group who have succeeded in kicking it themselves). These people need to be trained. And have backup from GPs, psychotherapists, social workers. Social workers especially important: because after the rent has been paid, people still need to be fed and looked after. Victims need to be able to turn to the social worker rather than the drug pusher.

Government is not fully seized of the scale of the problem that is certain to develop. It is certain because of the numbers who contracted the Aids virus before all the campaigning began, and even assuming that the campaign is quite successful. Many more people are at risk, apart from those who had the virus, from contact with people who don't know they've got the virus.

Voluntary groups know more than civil servants. They see it at street level. Ministers, of course, are very worried. They carry the can for the shortage of resources. They are fending off the deluge, and hoping against hope that it may not be as bad as some people expect. This is understandable, in a way. They have to find some refuge. But the fact is that it is a quite horrendous situation, imposing wholly new pressures on all sorts of people.

The whole NHS and social-service network will be put under heavier and heavier pressure. The NHS doesn't have the hospital beds. We don't have the community resources if people are sent, as they will be after a week or two getting some remission, back to the 'community', to their families or quasi-families.

One question for Fowler: when will the government set up Aids hospices? How much money for them? Cancer hospices say they cannot and will not take this new class of patient. How many hospice beds is Fowler willing to pay for?

DAVID OWEN
The Guardian, 24 March 1987

Much chaffing at my accounts of the split over defence, and scoffing indignation at my attempt to say the issue didn't matter as much as he thought it did. But this was good-humoured, he was feeling very good, because the SDP is now on a high again . . .

SDP, LIBS ETC. 'It's important to say some fairly jarring things to the gravel-drive vote, which they may not like. But then we would hope to get their vote for more our general stance.'

Ashdown would be disastrous, but he might get the nomination. Has no judgement. Has not matured. Has not been heard from on education, even though it's the big subject. Has not grown up. Wouldn't get a vote from a Liberal MP, but this might not mean he wouldn't get the job if Steel went.

Beith would be Owen's favourite candidate, and he hardly demurred when it was snidely suggested that this was because Owen could control him.

Alton has got a lot better, and looks like maturing.[1]

Wallace is very good and very nice. Better than Malcolm Bruce.[2]

LABOUR He thinks Labour will get 30–40 seats more than they now have (!).

He quite rejects the notion that the best result would be another Tory victory, leading to the realignment we have all been waiting for. A lot of rot, he thinks. In politics you have to take the tide when it comes, and you can't be thinking about that kind of calculation. Besides, that analysis presumes Labour will wither away, but it won't. (Per HY: one begins to see more that Owen believes a coalition role to be the Alliance's best bet, and has realistic ambitions for their total presence in Parliament.)

He talks about the Alliance getting 40 seats.

He also says that he has no objection to doing a deal with any Labour politician. Thinks it vital not to let personalities enter into it. All about policies and deals.

1 David Alton: Liberal/Lib Dem MP for Liverpool Edge Hill 1979–83, for Liverpool Mossley Hill 1983–97; later Baron Alton of Liverpool.
2 James Robert Wallace: Lib Dem MP for Orkney and Shetland 1983–2001. Malcolm Bruce: Liberal/Lib Dem MP for Gordon since 1983.

HUNG PARLIAMENT Specifically declines to talk about the nature of deals that might be done. Insists on keeping it secret. But he contemplates a very deeply shifting scene, in which the Tories, say, defiantly propose to meet the Commons without any deal with the Alliance, but as days draw on towards the moment, things begin to shift and they have to think more seriously . . .

THATCHER How amazingly unchanged she is by office. Both as PM and as an international figure. A nationalist.

JOHN BIFFEN
House of Commons, 13 May 1987

RESULT The hypothesis we work on is as follows, propounded by him. Tories 350, Alliance 50, others 25, Labour 225. Tory majority of 50. He thinks this pretty likely, although the majority could easily be half that and he wouldn't feel he'd made a spectacular misjudgement. He does not see what is likely to upset a Tory victory, although he admits anything is possible except an overall Labour majority.

CAMPAIGN We have already seen two examples of disastrous error. First Tebbit saying they would 'walk it'. Second MT talking about 'going on and on', and dreaming publicly about the end of the century. The British public hates being taken for granted like this, hates such arrogance. He prays that this kind of thing isn't repeated, but fully expects it will be.

A CONS VICTORY Even if it is 50, there will be some problem about getting the business through. It will mean a big shift in the balance on standing committees, which could make backbenchers more tricky. He is completely unPymite in his views about big majorities. The bigger the better.

In that event, however, he is fully expecting to be ditched. He 'just has a feeling' about it. Interestingly, he says that the main significance will be if 'Peter' goes as well. Since Biffen has never been a friend of Walker's, and indeed regards him as an unregenerate Heathite of the kind Biffen went into politics to get rid of, their 'twinning' is significant. Clearly Biffen knows he is regarded as among the wets, even though Walker and he diverge so much about interventionism in all its guises.

If the majority is small, however, he thinks he could well be kept. He does not sound like a man absolutely desperate to stay in, although his wife told me last night that the thing they would really miss was the car and the driver. She rather regretted the fact that, whatever happened, JB would stay in the Commons. He told me he might even stay for another term after the next one, depending on circumstances.

OPPOSITION He believes they are bound, by some method, to go for realignment. He is well aware of all the problems, but he thinks they will come to see that the only way of getting the Tories out is through a rearrangement which deposits on the far left the successor body to the Independent Labour Party. The only property the Labour Party has with a market value is the name Labour. He would expect the left probably to keep possession of this. He sees that sooner or later the Smiths etc. would think the only worthwhile objective would be to fashion a new alliance. However complicated the process. (I got a whiff here of the absolute realism of the practising politician, as he assumes people like Smith to be and as he is himself: it's about power or it is nothing.) Looking at the polls, there are 50 per cent of the electorate to play for. An attractive proposition . . .

HUNG PARLIAMENT Clearly the situation which he most relishes, as an observer and an operator. He asserts with some severity that he is sure MT would carry on, if she was the largest party. He cannot imagine her going to the Queen and saying that she was the largest party but didn't fancy forming a government. Just not in her character to be so defeatist.

He also says that it might be a situation which would advantage the Tories in that there would be absolutely no chance of realignment being fixed up. All the left parties would be cutting each others' throats in the jockeying for the next election.

DES WILSON
Lunch, 14 May 1987

Des his usual amazingly ebullient self. The only supreme egoist whom I really like.

He is keeping the night watch. Office hours 10 p.m. to 10 a.m. He examined the situation to discover what were the critical decision-making moments and soon realized they were between 7 and 8.30 a.m. Therefore the supremely important time to be in control was the hours leading up to that. He will spend the night surveying the press, preparing briefs, preparing speeches, jokes, lines for the press conference. Instead of the leaders arriving at 7.45 to find a room full of people with armfuls of newspapers, they will have Wilson-prepared briefs which give Des, or so he thinks, supreme control over the thrust of the day.

He says he now gets on well with Owen. Owen now trusts him, having been at first very suspicious; Owen sees that Des can deliver like a true professional. Des also stands up to Owen, unlike some others. Des finds that Owen is ready to change his mind, is likeable and flexible. He also thinks Debbie Owen is the biggest asset any political leader could have.

There are basically two views about the desirable outcome. Des believes that it will be best if the Tories get 15 majority and the Alliance beats Labour on the vote. This will prepare the way for a big shift, difficult though that will be to achieve. It will mean that the Tories won't win the following election, and that the Alliance will be best placed to win it. The inner implication of this, unmentionable of course, is that this election is all about what happens at the second election.

The other view, Owen's, is that a hung parliament would be best, with the Alliance in power after negotiation. This fits in with Owen's passionate desire for office. But it overlooks the horrendous problems for the Alliance in being part of a government, especially a Tory government. Steel is highly apprised of that, and when Des put his own favourite outcome to Steel, Steel, while not overtly agreeing, indicated as much.

Can a strategy be devised which covers both these analyses, or are they contradictory? Happily, they both imply the same thing: that the main focus of the attack must be Labour. Owen will want to do that, for his own reasons, as much as the Wilsonites. (Although of course, as I tried to get Des to agree, anyone who imagines that this kind of thing can be finely controlled is about as realistic as he who thinks he can control the weather.)

POST ELECTION In the event of a hung parliament, arrangements have been made for consultation. This will be controlled by the president of the Liberals [Des]. There won't be a meeting of the council (200 strong), but Des will have to give his agreement, having consulted with the regional chairs. Steel at first resisted this. Des laid down the law, saying that he hadn't been coming to the weekly meetings of the parliamentary party all this time, only to be shut out when it had to make a real decision. He pointed out that any deal would only hold up if the parties both experienced genuine feelings of agreement at grass roots. The compromise is that Des will be present, but will leave the room before the vote.

In the event of something like the Wilson scenario, what will happen? Des thinks the case for merger will become irresistible. The essential precursor to any deals with a re-split Labour Party. But will Steel be there to see it through? A delicate question. There would have to be a leadership contest, and maybe Steel would win it. Would he actually want to? He has worked out another sort of life, in which he remains a backbencher and elder statesman, writing and journalizing. The truth is that Steel would not mind Owen becoming the leader, as long as this didn't come about either through his being beaten on a vote or his manifestly shirking the struggle. Somewhere in there is a path towards Owen becoming leader of the merged party.

At the general election on 11 June the Conservatives (13,750,000 votes, 376 seats) were returned with a 102-seat majority, down 42 on 1983, with a swing of about 1 per cent towards Labour (10,000,000 votes and 229 seats). For the Alliance the result was disappointing: 7,341,000 votes, but only 22 seats.

WILLIAM WALDEGRAVE
His office, 27 June 1987

POLL TAX   Agrees rather shamefacedly that he was responsible with others for getting the idea going. Says that his brief was to find something that wasn't the rates and wasn't Local Income Tax. LIT is regarded as bad because it is buoyant: i.e. rises without decisions being made, and thereby gives local authorities reasons for being less disciplined and less accountable.

Basically, he says, all the inequities of poll tax can be dealt with, by shifting the rules and figures around. The real and unique problem is collection. We have been accustomed to one of the least oppressive governing modes – re individuals – of any country. No papers, no cards, no registration etc. etc. This may now change. Of course, there would be a similar problem with LIT.

The underlying problem relates, of course, to functions. The only reason the rates have become intolerable is that far too large a burden has grown upon them. Other countries have property tax but don't require such a revenue from it . . .

OPPOSITION   Labour's 'brilliant' campaign was really just a very good campaign by Kinnock to preserve his own position. Which it succeeded in doing despite the fact that Labour did worse than at any election except 1983.

We were astonishingly lucky that the Alliance made such a mess. Crazy of them not to go all out for Labour at the start. This would have done far more damage to the Tories than attacking the Tories did. It would have seduced away many of the Tory voters . . .

WW is less critical of Lord Young, saying however that he very quickly climbs down when one of his wheezes is sat on. This shows the lack of tenacity of the elected politician, he thinks, but he finds Young a decent enough chap.

DOUGLAS HURD
Lunch, the Garrick, 27 October 1987

Very relaxed, a man unoppressed by his job (despite prisons), detached and amused by much.

EXTRADITION will, he hopes, be restored after the Lords defeat. Unagitated by this, but simply says that international factors (Ireland, Italian fascists holed up here etc. etc.) meant the change was needed. But said that poor young C,[1] ranged against the sharpest lawyers in the land, had all the odds against him: and that this was one reason why it was desperately important to have a functioning Lord Chancellor. Hailsham had simply refused to play the normal LC's part of seeing bills through. Hears good things of Mackay,[2] but doesn't know him.

POLL TAX was all over the place. He rattled out the usual defence, re accountability etc., but then said he thought the whole thing was pretty unnecessary. Believes an early priority should be to get it out of the headlines. Says that Ridley is 'nowhere near to getting it right yet'. Hurd personally favours phasing.

BROADCASTING The BBC was 'basically OK', i.e. it now knew where it was. The licence fee was known, and within that they could do what they wanted. The Hussey–Barnett duo – 'and they're very much a team' – was on the whole working, as was Checkland[3] ('although I had nothing to do with that').

ITV was a much bigger problem. Far more on the agenda. The new franchises, and how these should be handed out: Channel 4, ITN, possibly

---

1 Malcolm Sinclair, the 20th Earl of Caithness, born in 1948, was Home Office minister in the Lords 1986–8. A former estate agent and property developer, he had the uncomfortable challenge of confronting the law lords in an attempt to push through government legislation that permitted a relaxation of Britain's extradition laws. This was contested by civil-rights lawyers and by peers from all three parties.
2 James Mackay, Baron Mackay of Clashfern, Lord High Chancellor of Great Britain 1987–97.
3 Sir Michael Checkland: director-general of the BBC 1989–92.

Channel 5; the major problem of domination by the Big Five, against which TVS[1] is especially fighting hard. DH said it was one of those areas where there was never a right moment to make decisions, because the moment you got near to it 'someone else came in and said you haven't thought about this.'

This leads to a major theme: MT's *obsession* with television, even though she doesn't watch it except on Sundays. Has become a major feature of the colloquies. Always ranting on about how shocking things are, and reminding DH that he has small children and how *could* he tolerate them seeing some of the dreadful stuff. 'She's itching to get out the censor's scissors.' However, he considers it an important coup to get into the manifesto – 'when she wasn't looking' – a clause saying that the broadcasting authorities would be responsible for standards. Clearly there was a big pitch to make the new body full of teeth, which he now says won't happen: this body will be useful, however, in being a receptacle for the objectors to let off steam in.

WHITELAW is still a force, but a waning one. He has less interest in issues than he used to, and therefore less influence. But he is still an invaluable chairman, on countless occasions. Can actually secure agreements nobody thought existed.

TEBBIT came, surprisingly, into the same category. 'I shall rather miss him,' Douglas sniggers incredulously. NT was an inventive committee man, partly because he had time to think. He would quite often come up with an ingenious solution, out of his very sharp intelligence. (Has he written himself out of the script? I ask. Oh yes, says Douglas. That's why he's looking so happy.)

THATCHER is still a huge interventionist, and therefore a very bad chairman. Hopeless at taking the voices. But insisting on chairing all the big legislation-oriented committees.

But this doesn't touch Douglas too much, except on TV matters, 'where I realize that she will insist on trying to take the big decisions'. Otherwise, not interested. For example, completely unengaged by the subject which dominates Hurd's life: prisons. 'I don't think she's ever been to a prison in her life,' he says.

Still has a highly selective approach to facts and evidence. For example, completely uninterested in addressing herself to academic research which might show her that the TV issue was quite complex. ('If she was aware

1 Television South, the ITV franchise-holder for the south of England 1982–92.

of the complexities in general, she wouldn't be where she is today.') Even worse, she is amazingly susceptible to the power of a single letter. Seizes on one letter from one citizen – say, describing how terrible policing is in Hackney – and uses it to illustrate what she supposes to be a general problem requiring instant solution. This is quite a random process. 'Her contact with the real world is highly anecdotal. Perhaps most prime ministers are like that. But she now never reads a newspaper, never watches TV, and *says* she never listens to the radio, although we know from other things she says that she obviously does.'

Douglas points to a slightly frightening isolation which she now seems positively proud of. She tells them she doesn't listen to the radio as if to prove that she's rather above such unreliable frivolities.

In parallel with this is the new attitude to Parliament, a definite change. 'She dislikes Parliament, and only goes there when she has to.' This contrasts (per HY) with her obsessive feeling that she should be there every evening, buttering up the troops and lecturing them, in her earlier days as PM. He regards this tendency as 'dangerous'. 'She is getting more and more removed from daily life.'

Remarks that she is still highly emotional. Reacts in a very emotional way, quite often to the point of tears, when something triggers her off. He saw this most when he was NI Secretary and a soldier was killed. It's the same kind of emotionalism which reacts to some of the letters she gets.

As an example of her not being in touch, at the poll-tax meeting today Ridley unfurled his idea for phasing being a local option. This story had already been leaked to *The Times*, which splashed it the day before. When Ridley remarked that it had already been in the press, she showed absolutely no sign of knowing this.

Will she quit? DH can only guess. But says this. Believes she is *now* minded to go for a fourth term. But if things begin to turn sour for her, especially 'in the area where she's always weakest, which is personal relations', she may decide to stop. She is already heard to say, at moments, 'I don't know why I bother to carry on' (which, I remark and DH doesn't disagree, would have been unheard-of from her a year or two ago). This could become a more firmly lodged negative in her mind. (And, per HY, the slump and all it means could be exactly the kind of setback which makes her begin to think she'd served her purpose and the mission was complete as far as it could be.)

But, adds Douglas, when she gets to this point and begins to see who might be her successor, this might (whoever the successor looked likely to be) be enough to persuade her of her duty to carry on . . .

Her style and method remain a chronic problem for the government.

'She has always been incapable of distinguishing between the important and the unimportant.'

On the other hand, she does have many personal skills. When Kenneth Newman[1] came to her, for example, to explain why he wanted to rearrange her personal protection arrangements, and save a lot of money, she objected strongly. Gave him a real going-over. When he came back at her rather better than in his first crack, but conceded that he understood her point, her mood completely changed. She was gushingly warm, almost skittishly flirtatious. Thus she made Newman feel good, while winning her point 100 per cent.

I remarked on her choice of Butler rather than Whitmore[2] as Cabinet Secretary, and recalled Whitmore's unique relationship with her as private secretary, which had been closer than Butler's. How has Butler, the Harrovian mandarin, won out over Whitmore, the grammar-school workhorse? DH replied that it had, he understood, been a close-run thing. But we shouldn't be too surprised. She always has had a weakness for the old-fashioned sort of manly figure, as long as they've shown utter loyalty to her.

CHRIS PATTEN
At the Overseas Development Agency,
16 November 1987

POLITICS Thinks Lawson has reached his peak. We should be quietly selling Lawsons in the market, although acknowledging how very, very well he has done as Chancellor. 'His critics must now surely be eating humble pie.' He has become a very traditional Chancellor: managing exchange rate, managing interest rates – a very far cry from 1979–82. Cannot believe, however, that Lawson will rise any higher.

THATCHER

– Has remained amazingly unwilling to lean on advice. A constant and foolish trait.
– *Charles Powell*, however, is very, very powerful (CP's considered superlative). Across the board. He and Ingham are the heart of the court, and the court may in the end be her downfall. Thinks Powell must be able, but is also a courtier. Suggests something of 'the son she

---

1 Sir Kenneth Newman: commissioner of the Metropolitan Police 1982–7.
2 Sir Clive (Anthony) Whitmore: War Office and Defence civil servant; principal private secretary to the PM 1979–82; Permanent Undersecretary at the Ministry of Defence 1983–8, at the Home Office 1988–94.

never had' about their relationship. Declines to specify, but suggests I inquire at the FCO for a Powell rating.

- Thinks Powell will be well advised to get out of No. 10 before the return of Butler. CP surprised that Whitmore didn't get it, having had, by all accounts, a superb Falklands.
- When she is briefed and set in motion, she can be absolutely unbeatable as a performer. Cites the Russian trip as something that on every level was brilliant: as showmanship, and at a more serious level. Proof of real quality . . .
- Reason tells him that she will fight for a fourth term, but instinct says otherwise. Can the battling granny seriously carry on that long? However, if Labour really does look unelectable then perhaps she will be very heavily keen to do it again.

SUCCESSION

- *Major* is the lead runner of his generation. Very good indeed. Comes without baggage, a great advantage. The Tebbit background without the Tebbit chips. Very well-balanced, decent man. Very hardworking, very able. Worked the whole of August and September, didn't go away, determined to get wholly on top of the boxes and the subject. Said by Peter Mountfield, the undersecretary dealing with ODA [The Overseas Development Administration], to be the cleverest Chief Secretary of the Thatcher years. This confirmed by other civil servants at ODA.
- Moore cannot be taken seriously. Better at close quarters, but really . . . Perhaps the prospect of Moore is the only plausible reason for thinking that Lawson could be a serious candidate.
- Howe, of course, is far too old. Geoffrey's problem is that he hates making decisions. Calls for more and more paper as a way of avoiding decisions. Hates conflict and difficulty. Now, of course, there's no bolthole for him on the Woolsack. She's going to have to make a very hard decision about one of the top people some time this parliament.
- Clarke,[1] being a barrister, has difficulty in seeing that sometimes it is not worth squashing a bad case into the ground.

1 Kenneth Clarke: QC; Conservative MP for Rushcliffe since 1970; Minister for Health at the DHSS 1982–5; Paymaster General and Minister for Employment 1985–7; Chancellor of the Duchy of Lancaster and Minister for Trade and Industry 1987–8; Secretary of State for Health 1988–90, for Education and Science 1990–92; Home Secretary 1992–3; Chancellor of the Exchequer 1993–7.

1988

3 January   Margaret Thatcher becomes the longest-serving British PM in the twentieth century.

29 February   A Nazi document implicates Austrian president Kurt Waldheim in Second World War deportations.

2 March   David Steel quits as Liberal Party leader; Paddy Ashdown later takes over as head of the new Social and Liberal Democratic Party.

7 March   Three IRA members are shot at point-blank range in Gibraltar.

15 May   The USSR admits defeat and begins withdrawal from Afghanistan.

16 June   Stephen Hawking publishes *A Brief History of Time*.

24 June   US scientists warn of the beginning of the greenhouse effect amid a catastrophic US drought.

6 July   An explosion on the Piper Alpha North Sea oil rig kills 167 workers.

27 July   Mrs Thatcher rejects the vision of a united Europe proposed by Commission President Jacques Delors, along with monetary union and a European Central Bank.

19 October   Home Secretary Douglas Hurd bans the BBC from broadcasting direct statements by IRA leaders. Instead the BBC uses actors to read the words.

8 November   George H. W. Bush is elected president of the United States.

16 November   Benazir Bhutto is elected prime minister of Pakistan – the first woman to head a Muslim state.

21 December   270 perish in an explosion aboard Pan American flight 103 over Lockerbie, Scotland.

Deaths   Raymond Carver; Richard Feynman, physicist; Trevor Howard; Robert Livingston (the Lone Ranger); Kim Philby, journalist and double agent, in Moscow; Kenneth Williams

JONATHAN AITKEN
1 February 1988

CONSERVATIVE PHILOSOPHY GROUP   This was an evolution out of the 'Hugh Fraser Group', which in turn was set up after Fraser's unavailing bid for the Tory leadership in 1974/5. It had actually pre-dated that, in the sense that Fraser, a man of ideas even though that wasn't his public image, became friendly with Roger Scruton and John Casey.[1] Together with JA, these four were the kernel of a quite irregular group who began to meet.

After the Thatcher leadership election, the group evolved into something more, and became the CPG, a source of ideas when ideas were thin on the ground. MT came to the second meeting, and almost certainly the first as well: and to many others in the years '75–8 – by which time the party machine had got its research-cum-ideas act together better.

MT was at first a good listener. The proceedings usually began with a paper. The earliest was given by Robert Blake,[2] and very soon after that came Michael Oakeshott[3] with something about the withering away of the state.

JA remembers one or two specifics about MT at these meetings. One is that she did say at an early one, 'We must have an ideology. The other side have got an ideology, by which they can test things. We should have one as well.' Another contribution it made to her was giving her phrases. She was very keen on borrowing/stealing/taking over phrases.

Airey Neave was the person who made the link, when he heard about the Fraser Group. Said to Aitken that 'the leader' would like to come. Aitken had said something which displeased her, he recalls. Neave said she was distressed. Aitken said he was very sorry, and would happily come and see her to sort it out. Neave said don't bother, see her in the division lobby: 'She'll be wearing a green dress.'

The first time the CPG made an appearance in print was in the *New Statesman*, when a piece under the byline of James Fenton posed as a parody of its proceedings. In fact this was a dead-accurate account written by Frank Johnson, who gave it to Fenton.[4] There was much huffing about Fenton not having been present . . .

---

1 Roger Scruton: writer, philosopher, editor of the *Salisbury Review* 1982–2000. John Casey: Cambridge lecturer, *Daily Telegraph* contributor.

2 Robert Blake wrote the standard history *The Conservative Party from Peel to Churchill* (1970), later updated and reissued with the change in title '. . . *from Peel to Major*'.

3 Michael Oakeshott: polemicist, political philosopher, Conservative intellectual.

4 James Fenton: poet, *New Statesman* political correspondent, later *The Guardian*'s German correspondent. Frank Johnson: parliamentary sketch writer, *Daily Telegraph* and later *The Times*; edited the *Spectator* 1995–9.

A frequent visitor was Enoch Powell. But very rarely when MT was there. This was by arrangement, apparently, because of personal frictions and incompatibilites.

Thatcher, of course, is not an intellectual. But she eagerly seizes other people's ideas.

It took place in Fraser's drawing room. But this got too small, so it transferred to Aitken's mother's drawing room. Now it is in Aitken's drawing room, which is the biggest of all. Thirty-plus people exchanging ideas and eating.[1]

They reckon there are now six peerages out of the CPG, starting with Hugh Thomas.[2]

ALISTAIR MCALPINE
33 Cork Street, 24 February 1988

DENIS THATCHER is very important. Absolutely staunch. The *Eye* image probably gives him pretty useful cover. He is very shrewd, very good with money and figures. To her he is an absolute prop, mainly because he actually shares her sense of mission. He really does see her role as being the recovery of Britain. He says that the only thing he disagrees with her about is hanging. Nothing else at all. He is actually a very considerable character in his own right (cf. Aitken on his enormous ego).

McA is quite certain MT will run again, unless Denis for some reason blocks it. He would do this only because he was badly ill, or she was worn out. Would never do it for his own convenience. On the other hand, if he *did* put his foot down, she would very likely do as he asked.

Parkinson was always someone who thought instinctively like her. The sort of man who, even if he was at the other end of the country, would probably have exactly the same response as she did to a political situation, without any consultation. Agrees with me that CP is a good politician. His trouble, says McA, is that he is too kind. Not a big enough shit. This makes him unable to take really hard decisions sometimes.

Confirms as a total fact that Cecil was intended to be Foreign Secretary in 1983.

---

1 Jonathan Aitken lived at Lord North Street, in two houses joined into one – hence the enormous drawing room.

2 Aitken wrote, 18 May 2008, 'The six CPG members who became Peers: [Anthony] Quinton, [Hugh] Thomas, [Robert] Blake, [Peter] Bauer, [Marcus] Sieff and [Arnold] Weinstock. Although the last two clearly qualify as being industrialist Peers, rather than purely political ones, nevertheless Mrs Thatcher did meet them for the first time at our early CPG meetings. The same is true of Robin Leigh Pemberton (although not yet a Peer). As for [Alun] Chalfont I do not have a record of him being a regular CPG member, but I think I recall him coming once or twice probably as someone's guest.'

The test she really applies to judgement of people is *cleverness*. This is often the key to people she's not really rated. For example, take Carrington. Carrington's problem was that he wasn't really very clever. Didn't know much. There was a memorable occasion when – McA recalls – there was an argument in Shadow Cabinet about the vices and virtues of the nineteenth century, in which C was saying that it was a terrible time. He was routed by Joseph and Maude, so much so that he made an excuse and left after fifteen minutes. Carrington is supremely the person of the network, of the people he knew, of contacts etc. etc. This is very antipathetic to MT, who wasn't in same network and in any case thought that foreign affairs should be about more than that.

A lack of cleverness was also close to the heart of her despising of Pym. She just thought he didn't think fast and didn't know enough. Of course, in his case, his dissenting and manoeuvring played a part as well.

If you look at the non-clever people in her Cabinet (Jenkin, for example), they've mostly been inherited. Not all, admittedly. Fowler, for example, isn't very clever, although he is at least keen. He and Channon surely have not long to last. There are four or five people she wants to promote. Chris Patten is among these, a super-clever person she really appreciates: and with whom the falling out, according to McA, began with CP's resentment that he wasn't secretary of the Shadow Cabinet in opposition, but was displaced by Wolfson.[1] (I don't believe this is the whole of it – HY).

Another exception to the cleverness principle is admittedly Moore. Moore is a fool. Look at his being ill – a mistake in the first place (just as transport ministers shouldn't have car crashes) – and then not going to an NHS hospital.

But if you look around elsewhere, most of her people are clever. MacGregor, for example. And Major. And Rifkind.

This looking for cleverness links to her favourite recreation, which is arguing. If she was truthful, this is what she would put in a biographical entry. She has a genuine and insatiable love of good argument. Of course, she is terrifically good at it. Her capacity to absorb detail makes her almost impossible to beat. She is so well informed. You need to be absolutely briefed if you want to keep up with her.

HONOURS   McA denies that she is all that interested in putting her own people in the Lords. Says you'll find she's made fewer peers than most in the past. She sees the HL as Parliament, not an honour. The last lot of 'working' peers had to write a letter saying that they fully intended

---

1 David Wolfson, director of Great Universal Stores 1973–8, became secretary to the Shadow Cabinet and then chief of staff in the 10 Downing Street political office 1978–85; later Baron Wolfson of Sunningdale.

to come regularly and take part. She can also be easily persuaded, especially by someone like Whitelaw. If WW asked her to make so-and-so a peer, she's very unlikely to fight it.

FUTURE LEADER Heseltine has not got a cat in hell's chance of leading the party. Nor has Tebbit. Nor has Howe, except as caretaker and no other way. But never underestimate people's utter conviction that the prize can be theirs. Personally McA would put a small amount of money on George Younger as a possibility – as long as his father stays alive for a few more years.[1]

THE RECORD A point that McA made concerns the TU laws. He recalls going in to see her one day in 1980, and on this rare occasion being ushered into the Cabinet room, where she had just finished a meeting. She was sitting alone, and was in a terrible state. This was, she said, because 'Jim Prior just defeated me in Cabinet, a terrible day.' When McA tried to console her, she said he didn't understand: that it was impossible to carry on unless we got the programme under way and did what we know is the right thing to do etc. etc.

When I (HY) said that Prior had been right, McA rejected this. He said that he now thinks (which he admits he did not at the time) that if the attack on the unions had been faster, and sharper, the British recovery would have been faster and earlier.

GEOFFREY HOWE
The Garrick, 26 February 1988

EUROPE He made a general, interesting point. The Brits, he contends, are now superbly professional in their Euro dimension. The French are likewise; so are the Dutch and also the Luxembourgeois (who had an excellent presidency). The Germans, perhaps because of their coalition government, are much less so. (Dealings in the EC do put one off coalitions for ever.)

But what he stressed above all, with a small demurrer for modesty, was 'Margaret and I are very experienced working through texts.' They had shown this ability on numerous occasions: building from one text to another, working through and amending, seeing the power of three words to change a meeting entirely.

1 McAlpine would have lost his bet. Younger, son of the 3rd Viscount Younger of Leckie, was made a life peer as Baron Younger of Prestwick in 1992. He succeeded his father to the viscountcy in 1997.

When the UK is attacked for not 'doing enough for Europe', GH takes pleasure (mild but stubborn, of course) in saying that the three big things that have happened to Europe's advantage – developments towards the internal market, settlement of the budget question, start of a reform of farm prices – happened because of Britain's strategic determination. Therefore Europe owes Britain and MT a great debt.

REAGAN Denies that she would ever say, 'He has nothing between the ears, dear.' In fact GH states that RR, although not a detail man, does quite often make telling contributions of a large-minded kind.

SOUTH AFRICA The recent clampdown on peaceful opposition is bad news. But SA 'won't change overnight', he intones. We just have to soldier on. When asked what outward signs one could point to for the effectiveness of this strategy, he had nothing to offer, although he said that Robin Renwick, the new ambassador, was being tremendously active in making contact with all the relevant parties.

The big point he wanted to make was that MT is the only person in the Western world who has a public in SA. He claimed this was true on all sides of the argument. She had a clear view, which she had stated. Everyone knew where she stood. This made her better placed than anyone else. Besides, he added, the logic of the anti-sanctions argument has now been accepted by most people, including those who said they were most in favour.

DOMESTICALLY Goes straight to the NHS as the great unsolved and perhaps unsolvable problem. Claims that education policy already shows a lot of acceptance. Disclaims any radical desire to challenge the root assumption in this country that health care should be free.

SUMMARY Geoffrey talks like a man for whom all is pretty much for the best in a slowly evolving world, at which he is close to the centre. Everything happens in glacial, undramatic ways. At the heart of it is the British revival, the British presence, to which he, as Chancellor, made the foundation contribution, bringing prosperity and the sound economy for which we are respected and in which we have been widely imitated – 'There are no socialists now. I would hate to be a socialist. What is there left to be a socialist about?' – and as a result of which Britain has a unique standing in world matters, in which role he again is a central, plodding, remorseless, optimistic, never-downcast figure. The proof of this is to be seen all around: the Gorbachev connection so neatly fostered before G became the boss: the Euro role, as above: the leader on S Africa: the special links in Washington. We have somehow revived into a world position.

All this represents a kind of synergy: one strength adding to another strength, all the time with Geoffrey himself, Mogadon man or not, quietly but unendingly patrolling the frontiers of an enhanced British presence. Thus he remembers his tour of Eastern Europe as an early crucial element in the East–West glasnost (sometime in 1983–4): quietly, doggedly, undramatically done, with maybe nothing to show for it immediately, but paying dividends in the end. Similarly the essential rightness of the British position in Europe and on SA, built on the essential rightness of British economic policy, have all earned us respect and a big role. In the Middle East it was the same. We began the process which led to the UN resolution about Iran–Iraq[1] (as he has often insisted publicly). This reflects our historic role in the region. But also, he stressed interestingly, the need to justify our existence as a permanent member of the Security Council.

ELIE KEDOURIE
20 April 1988

Met at the Israel Diaspora Trust dinner. On the tube back to Hampstead he remarks that MT is by far the most intelligent person in her Cabinet. By which he means the only person actually interested in exploring an issue down to its base, partly for the sake of the intellectual adventure. Only Lawson, he judges, might have some of the same. The rest are place-seekers and operators. Not a bad judgement, I thought.

But he conceded her interest in ideas was mainly to find support for her gut prejudices . . .

On the occasion of the next meeting HY thought Kinnock 'pretty lack-lustre. Like a burned-out volcano. With the unusual feature that he has never had the chance to come alight. He was above all boring. It was terribly hard to look at him and say to oneself, Here is a leader whose judgement/knowledge/wisdom one would be delighted to trust.' He quoted his Guardian *colleague Ian Aitken as recalling that Kinnock had always been a deeply pessimistic character from his youngest days,*

1 Altogether the UN passed ten resolutions addressing the Iran–Iraq war. The first, in 1980, had noted the start of the war, two more called for an end to it; others condemned the violations of international law, and deplored the use of chemical weapons. The most recent, when HY talked to Howe, had been in July 1987, demanding an immediate ceasefire, while urging the UN Secretary General to determine how the conflict had begun. Three more resolutions were agreed in 1988: one in May, and two more in August.

behind the Welsh bluster. 'This certainly shows now – and there is rather
less bluster.'

NEIL KINNOCK
The Guardian, 21 May 1988

BENN[1] Not worth having an argument, a debate. It might be if the
argument was at all new. But the issues are well known, and any open
confrontation would simply disserve the party by creating the impression
of massive division. Therefore NK will carry on with his speaking programme. He thinks Benn will be easily beaten, getting the votes of the
loonies and some of the hard left and some who by August don't want to
see him humiliated. Hattersley will also win, with Prescott second and
Heffer utterly humiliated: question – Why has Heffer been prepared to
do this for a man [Benn] he detests?

EQUALITY This is just about the only interesting part of the morning. He comes somewhat alive when asked whether Labour still believes
in equality. Explains roughly as follows. Equality is a jerk-word (my
word), an incantation (his word) which has always been intoned but
never been delivered. It is therefore worth looking at closely. Most people
are against inequality – but fear 'equality', which they construe as meaning a levelling down. A better response is available from the word 'fairness'. That is a tactical, pragmatic fact. It means the same, for practical
purposes, but involves fewer risks, fewer misunderstandings . . . NK then
goes on to assert, parenthetically, that he understands why people say that
inequality cannot be fought without the firm, hard weapon of equality as
a commitment. But he sees it as probably nothing more, in practice, than
a rhetorical term always used but never achieved. This causes much
disillusionment. It would be more honest with ourselves, he went on, and
also with the public, to talk about fairness not equality.

This is part of a larger linguistic problem. There are other incantations.
One is 'democracy', which has been perverted to mean that the only
possible solution to anything under the sun is via a democratic process,
even if this means that such things as welfare and housing problems are
left to incompetent and overworked officials whose only merit is that
they are elected.

Another such term is 'collectivism'. NK says that he chooses to talk
about 'individual emancipation' – admitting that it is ugly jargon – but

1 In October 1988 Tony Benn and Eric Heffer mounted an unsuccessful challenge for the Labour leadership
and deputy leadership.

finds that some people rail and shout about this being a concession to Thatcherite individualism. That is nonsense. It is one more example of Labour confusing means with ends. We need to reflect a greater liberty of the individual, he insists.

Examination of language in this way will actually refresh and refine (his words) democratic socialism. It will be a long, hard job, he says, to turn these concepts round and rake them out of the politics of the 1940s, and redefine them for the 1990s.

Therefore, he recognizes the problem of gross inequalities, but says that there is no way of instantly removing them. It is just not practical politics. It would affect too many people. He cannot make a cavalry charge and with some splendid dramatic move take back from people what has rendered inequality greater over the last eight years. Much as he might like to. He will not promise what he cannot deliver: i.e. won't promise a grand return to less inequality. Instead the aim is more modest: to try and get back to 1979 levels of provision for the less well off – in housing, in welfare, in schooling (smaller classes) – thus acting out the Tawney dictum which urged getting rid of inequalities that are not material so much as institutional. There is no way in which millions of people are going to be persuaded to surrender whole chunks of their improved standard of living.

DEFENCE He virtually said there would be no change in policy. Noted that the scene was changing fast, and was quite interested in the [Peter] Preston suggestion that he should say nothing until just before the election. But said, re the US 'umbrella', which has raised its head again recently, that since US Poseidon obsolescence would mean that Holy Loch would disappear, and INF meant that cruise would disappear, and F1–11 was being replaced by Minuteman and an end to air-launched missiles, the whole US question would be changing.[1] It would not require such a big decision by Britain about stationing stuff here.

Re the British deterrent, he specifically rejected my suggestion that Labour would simply put Trident into SALT [the Strategic Arms Limitation Talks] and see what the Russians would offer in exchange (unlike MT, who won't put them in at all). Said that the Whitelaw mission to Moscow (Healey in the party) had shown that Gorbachev would offer a deal that made sense. I.e. we would get rid of them in exchange for quantifiable Soviet reductions, and this would be argued for on the basis that it would make defence stronger.

1 The Intermediate-range Nuclear Forces (INF) Treaty was signed by President Reagan and General Secretary Gorbachev on 8 December 1987. Once it was in place, cruise missiles could be phased out. Poseidon, a US submarine-launched ballistic missile, was later replaced by Trident. The General Dynamics F1–11 was a tactical strike aircraft and fighter-bomber. Minuteman was a land-based intercontinental ballistic missile.

(There seemed to be no change here. And when I urged that it would surely need to be spelled out and defended over a long period to avoid a rerun of 1987, he didn't seem really to agree.)

THATCHER He muses about the difficulty of dealing with her. The fact that she's a woman remains, after all this time, a problem. Makes it harder to ridicule her – too many sexist pitfalls. Ridicule, further, is very hard to pull off if the subject is unaware she is being ridiculed. It requires the subject to be felled by a lethal scoff for humour actually to have its effect. Since this arrogant woman would actually not be aware her arrogance was being mocked, what is the value of mocking it?

ALAN BEITH
(At his request) House of Commons, 24 May 1988

Agrees that a wholly parliamentary strategy will not be of use to the Democrats.[1] But says that the coming of TV[2] will mean that a convincing parliamentary performance and presence will be much more necessary that it was.

Thinks it wholly absurd to believe that Labour can be eliminated. There will always be 120 Labour seats even if they fall apart. Also seems healthily responsive to my point that such 'strategy' is often baloney, and not connected to consequences. He actually asserts that the Tory vote, besides being the more plentiful, must also be the more vulnerable, in the old way of Liberal surges.

The Democrats must present themselves as being economically competent, but also more interested in fairness etc. etc.

Also much mileage to be made out of the 'authoritarian' stuff: which applies as much to Labour in the cities as to the Tories at Westminster. See Meadowcroft in Leeds[3] for numerous examples of how the non-Militant Labour is just as much of a menace as Militant was in Liverpool.

Worries that Ashdown will be another Kinnock: quite good in full flood, much manipulated by advisers, unsafe to be let out without them, generally unsolid.

1 'Democrats' must have been HY's shorthand. Two decades on, Beith says he would not have used this term to describe the Social and Liberal Democrats. He was a Liberal MP, and had campaigned actively for the party to be called the Liberal Democrats (as it would later be renamed).
2 Debates in the House of Lords were first televised in 1985; Commons proceedings were first televised in 1989.
3 Leeds West had been a Labour stronghold since 1945. Michael Meadowcroft, a Leeds councillor, unsuccessfully fought Leeds West for the Liberals/Lib Dems twice in 1974, but took the seat for the Liberals in 1983. He lost it at the 1987 election, and failed to regain it standing for his independent Liberal Party (not Lib Dem).

Thinks the new party structure and constitution will be a great improvement in the policymaking process.

FRANK COOPER
Institute of Contemporary British History launch, Chatham House, 22 June 1988

JOHN NOTT[1] During the Falklands, Cooper says he 'had to send Nott down to Cornwall every weekend', because he was so wrought up. Recalls how he used to return each Monday in a terrible state about his herd of prize cattle: with two graphs showing the dpmt [sic: probably a reference to daily milk production] of the cows and the size of his loan and the dire prospect that they were not going to coincide without a heavy loss to him.

He was rather an amazing chap, says C. Had decided to leave politics before the war, on the grounds that he would not be prime minister. That he could be Foreign Secretary or Chancellor, but what was the point? Reckoned he wasn't good enough at getting on with the people to make a satisfactory PM. Also was very keen to make a lot of money.

Took a very weird line over the defence review, from which, says C, 'we' had to rescue him. Stirred everything up, giving the impression that absolutely everything was under review, but had no idea how to get out of it. The department, as per tradition, helped him towards an anti-navy solution. Why is the department anti-navy? Basically because nobody has ever been able to agree with the role it sees for itself: stretching worldwide, ready to step in all over etc. etc.

C believes that the government, by refusing to make choices, will get into deeper and deeper trouble over defence. It is complacent, he says. Insufficiently worried and realistic.

HESELTINE he regards as having had the thickest skin of any minister he'd ever known (strong words!). An amazing willingness to take an interest only in the time span he saw for himself at the department (confirming my own witness to this).

---

1 Defence Secretary for two years from January 1981.

MICHAEL HESELTINE
Lunch, the Garrick, 6 July 1988

Vigorous, ungreying, arriving in his chauffeur-driven Jag exactly on time: unpompous, almost a little supplicant even – or at least trying rather consciously to persuade.

THE PAST

- *Miners etc.* Always remember that Lawson played a very important part in the destruction of Scargill.[1] It was his strategy as Energy Secretary which first led to the build-up of coal stocks, and as a result of his strategy that Scargill was forced into the position of knowing that if he didn't go in March[2] he would have lost a number of militant pits by the autumn, and therefore lost support for the strike. The militant pits would have shut. This forced him to go at the worst time, with summer starting, and therefore to be smashed.
- *Westland.* Would MH still have quit if – which he still insists was the issue – he had been able to take the thing to Cabinet and had been defeated? He thought it quite possible (but only quite possible – HY) that he would not. He remains utterly sure that he was right about the substance and right about the whole matter of style. On the substance, he looks at Westland now, in deep trouble, and recalls that it was always clear that Sikorsky would never be in the business of bailing it out. It wanted it for narrow reasons, and naturally has no interest in its long-term survival. The Euro consortium would have had that interest. It has all worked out, he says, according to the map laid out in his resignation statement and associated speeches.

    On his own conduct at the time, he insists that he never had an interest in 'destabilizing' the government or MT. He didn't think that was on, or desirable – even from his own point of view. But clearly he had some hesitation as he considered his options, which were to destabilize, to say nothing, or to be helpful – which is what he decided to do on 27 January [1986, the day Mrs Thatcher had to face Parliament after the Westland debacle]. Despite this insistence, I (HY) had the impression that MH was at least in part deeply interested in how Kinnock performed that day. And, like everyone else, he saw that he had missed his chance. He asked the wrong question (check that back).

1 Arthur Scargill: president of the NUM 1981–2002.
2 Scargill declared the national miners' strike on 12 March 1984, after pit closures involving the loss of 20,000 jobs had been announced.

At bottom MH says his concern about propriety was most to do with 'the concert party'. I.e. the buying up of shares to assist the American bid, in a quite outrageous fashion, along lines we may never now know all about.

HIMSELF He wryly notes that as it happens he, MH, has been a key figure at the two times when MT was in serious danger. He has helped her get out of the mess. First was the *Belgrano*. Here he came in as an outsider, not having been at the MoD. It fell to him to go over what had happened, because of all the rows about the *Belgrano*. This involved him in much confabulation with her, and he found her at every stage supportive when he said that such-and-such had or had not happened and should be admitted. They had a very close and warm link at that time. MH then destroyed Ponting in the HC, which finally restored the position. But then also at the Westland time, he sees his own intervention on 27 January as very important for saving MT as well.

THE PRESENT/FUTURE MH sees the political process as evolutionary not revolutionary. Thus he sees the TU reforms as arising from the Heath efforts, the privatizations as a logical outgrowth from council house sales etc. etc.

On privatization and union changes there isn't a millimetre of difference between him and the Thatcherites.

Europe probably epitomizes his biggest disagreements. He sees the whole of the economy as dependent on closer European links in a world battle with the US and Asia. No way we can survive except in a European context. This requires far more positive thinking than she will ever be capable of giving. For she is a gut non-European, and will always remain so. Although he declines to say that she would 'never' agree to entry to the EMS.[1] Thinks that there might come circumstances when she was obliged to make the best of it.

Linked to Europe is the regional/north–south thing, on which MH has made much headway. He sees this as a five–ten year strategic need, to shift towards the north. One triumph he already sees is having made the south-east householders see the connection between their anxieties and the northern inner cities. That both are victims of population misarrangements (my word). He has grand plans about the possibility of reviving Liverpool as a European base, container- and railwise. (See his speeches probably.)

---

1 The European Monetary System (EMS), involving European units of currency and an Exchange Rate Mechanism (ERM), was created in 1979 to hold the franc, lira, Deutschmark and other currencies together. It was the precursor of EMU, European Monetary Union, which in turn preceded the minting of the euro.

Among other issues he's hooked into, Labour's plight remains a constant theme, constantly returned to. What an amazing piece of luck for her. Kinnock is utterly useless. Why, for example, hasn't he battered her senseless over the law-and-order failure?

MH says, incidentally, that he always thought Owen made a profound error in leaving Labour. Should have stuck in there come what may, to win people over to the nuclear issue, remaining on the back benches. He described himself as having done exactly the opposite to Owen, in a rather similar position. I.e. remained with the party, come what may.

1989

24 February	Ayatollah Khomeini announces a $3 million bounty on the head of Salman Rushdie.
27 March	First free elections for a Soviet parliament.
5 April	Leon Brittan confirms that Mrs Thatcher's office authorized the leak of a confidential letter that prompted Michael Heseltine's resignation in the Westland affair.
15 April	Ninety-five die in a soccer disaster at Hillsborough, Sheffield.
2 May	Hungary opens its border with Austria.
8 May	Slobodan Milosevic elected president of Serbia.
4 June	Chinese soldiers suppress pro-democracy demonstrations in Tiananmen Square.
19 June	Burma renamed Myanmar by its military government.
26 October	Chancellor Nigel Lawson resigns from the Thatcher government; John Major takes over the Exchequer; Douglas Hurd becomes Foreign Secretary.
7 November	The Communist government of East Germany resigns; border points along the Berlin Wall are opened.
28 November	The entire Czechoslovak Politburo resigns. Václav Havel is later elected president.
3 December	President Bush and Mikhail Gorbachev meet in Malta and declare an end to the Cold War.
5 December	Mrs Thatcher is forced into her first leadership contest in fourteen years. She defeats Sir Anthony Meyer – but fails to secure the support of 60 Tory MPs.
14 December	The first free elections in Chile for sixteen years.
22 December	Romania's Nicolae Ceauşescu is overthrown, and later executed by firing squad.
Deaths	Samuel Beckett, Salvador Dalí, Daphne du Maurier, Emperor Hirohito, Herbert von Karajan, Ayatollah Khomeini, Konrad Lorenz, Laurence Olivier

CHRIS PATTEN
Phone, 29 October 1989

HOWE SPEECH (in CP's constituency, as it happens) is surely not very meaningful. Can hardly be seen as a rallying point for dissidents. All far more modest than that. Really just a reaffirmation of last summer, when GH and NL tried to get her to take a more positive position on the ERM. She was forced to concede a bit. But she says it can't go on, and moved to deal with it by shifting GH from the FCO. Scalp 1. Then Nigel gives her Scalp 2.

Actually the way she got these scalps has weakened her politically. Therefore GH could be said to be trying to exploit that and rerun last summer's battle.

Is *Major* on Howe's side? Poor old Major. His only interest must be to be left alone to get on with his job. To hold the markets in the next two days, and then to get through the autumn statement. M himself is very pragmatic. Surviving these moments will be his early priorities. He would probably prefer not to get caught up in the EMS saga, which runs and runs.

LAWSON it is true, is amazingly pig-headed. To that extent, his going must help a bit. Over the poll tax, Patten came up against his pig-headedness. Although CP got a lot, he got less than he wanted. Lawson's line was that this is an absurd tax anyway, why try and make it better?

Interesting to see *Baker* giving himself a front-row role. The *Mail on Sunday* claims that Baker stopped M making King[1] Foreign Secretary. Patten totally disbelieves this. But notes one underlying motif of the whole thing has been to place Baker as a Very Important Person . . .

DOUGLAS HURD will be very pleased to be at the FCO. His biggest problem is the boat people. It's easy enough to say that they must be sent home, but what will happen when a couple – or even just one – TV picture is seen of British soldiers forcing them on to Vietnam planes or boats? The policy has been kicking about for a year, but now is coming the moment of truth . . .

EUROPE Hurd may be more robust on this than Howe or Major. Patten, from his DoE experience, thinks the trick is twofold. To keep it as far as possible away from No. 10. And to set your own agenda. To

---

1 Tom King: Conservative MP for Bridgwater 1970–2001; Employment Secretary 1983–5; Northern Ireland Secretary 1985–9; Secretary of State for Defence 1989–92; later Baron King of Bridgwater.

merely react to whatever Brussels proposes always ends in tears. Thus: an example of how not to do it is Norman Fowler's pathetic attack on the social charter (my words).[1]

ELECTION PROSPECTS Ten per cent [rate of inflation] must be taken seriously. There was already going to be a rough winter ahead:

– getting inflation down
– dealing with public sector disputes
– mortgage rates sky high (which, by the way, put the poll tax in the shade)
– NHS troubles

Then on top of that there comes the 'has she lost her marbles?' question. We could do without that. However, if by 1991 inflation is down to 4 per cent and the rates are in single figures and unemployment is coming back down again (check), we could still be in a very strong position.

LABOUR remains an asset. Kinnock remains an asset. He just doesn't come over as a man who knows what it's about. Hear him on credit controls and you somehow know he doesn't know what he's talking about. Additionally, they've still not got any tune for the 1990s, except that 'she's gone too far'. (Per HY: maybe the Tory mess will be so great that people look at Kinnock and think he's not the man to get it right. I.e. the ghastly paradox that the worse it gets, the more ineligible Kinnock seems . . .)

JOHN SMITH
14 November 1989

Tremendously ebullient, and absolutely convincing as a fit person now.[2] Also a very funny man. Real wit. Says that he and Rifkind knew each other at the Bar. 'The thing about us Scottish lawyers is that we may not be right but we're quick.'

---

1 The European Social Charter – which guarantees economic and social rights – was the first international document to recognize the right to strike. It also endorsed safe and healthy working conditions and a minimum wage, and EU member states were required to incorporate the charter provisions in national legislation. The charter (sometimes called the social chapter) became a political issue. On 22 October 1989 Norman Fowler, the Employment Secretary, introduced a pamphlet critical of new requirements in the charter and said, 'You cannot force people by law to cooperate with one another . . . There is no master plan which meets every firm's needs. That is why the Government has consistently opposed pressure for legislation which would impose rigid requirements in place of flexibility and diversity.'

2 John Smith suffered a heart attack in October 1988, while Kinnock's shadow Chancellor. The illness kept him out of politics for three months.

SCOTLAND   He starts here. Says that Labour looks to win perhaps five more seats.

NORTH WEST   A key area of failure the last time. Should have won 22 seats, won only 1. Lost seats which should certainly be Labour. This is a key area for advance. But so are the Midlands and the south.

WHAT ABOUT THE SOUTH?   He maintains there are vast swathes of people who are fed up with MT and all she stands for . . .

PROSPECTS OVERALL   Thinks that T really is just about on the down, if not played out. There has been a big, deep shift away from Thatcher and her values. He finds this all over, including in the City, where there is great shame about her European attitudes.
      Labour has done three key things:

1. Got Europe right, just about.
2. Got defence right.
3. Got an economic policy together, which has been done more by thought and argument (led by JS) than by brute force.

ON KINNOCK   Says that the attacks are very unfair. But cites Truman and Attlee as the models. I counter by saying that, while people may be fed up with T, they believe that leaders should be seen to lead, and be seen to be competent. He rather agreed. And also with my suggestion that NK should set about making some major speeches. But on the whole was disposed to be less gloomy than Hattersley.

SIMON BROWN
Middle Temple dinner, 23 November 1989

Simon told me a funny story about the jury he had in Maxwell's libel action against *Private Eye*, in which Maxwell sued because the *Eye* had said that he was doing favours to Neil Kinnock in exchange for the promise of a peerage. After two days, he got a note from the jury asking, 'What is a peerage?'

1990

7 February	Central Committee of the Communist Party agrees to give up its monopoly of power in the Soviet Union.
11 February	Nelson Mandela walks free after twenty-seven years as a political prisoner in South Africa.
13 February	East and West Germany agree on unification.
15 February	The UK and Argentina resume diplomatic relations.
21 March	Namibia becomes independent after seventy-five years; joins the United Nations and the Commonwealth.
31 March	Poll-tax demonstrations in London turn into riots.
4 May	Latvia proclaims independence.
2 August	Iraq invades Kuwait, eventually to trigger the First Gulf War.
3 October	The two Germanies reunite.
23 October	Parliament votes to join the European Exchange Rate Mechanism.
1 November	Geoffrey Howe resigns in protest at Mrs Thatcher's attitude to Europe.
13 November	In a speech to the Commons, Geoffrey Howe attacks Mrs Thatcher's style of government.
14 November	Michael Heseltine announces a challenge for the Conservative leadership.
22 November	Mrs Thatcher announces that she will not contest a second ballot in the Conservative leadership election.
27 November	John Major is chosen as Conservative leader, after Michael Heseltine and Douglas Hurd concede defeat.
28 November	Mrs Thatcher resigns; John Major becomes prime minister.
Deaths	Leonard Bernstein, Aaron Copland, Greta Garbo, Ava Gardner, Barbara Stanwyck, A. J. P. Taylor, Sarah Vaughan, Patrick White

NEIL KINNOCK
18 January 1990

An off-the-record chat in his office, in company with [Labour's press secretary] Julie Hall (all eager and trying unsuccessfully to be tough) and a man who appeared to be some kind of bodyguard.

This occurred a week after I had written a tough profile of Kinnock, which did not go down well with his people, although he himself was apparently uncomplaining. He certainly made no complaining reference when we met, and was trying hard to be nice and funny.

ELECTIONS ETC His latest pitch is to talk about the decade of the 1990s. All policy should have short-term appeal but, more importantly, should stand up to a decade test. Should point the way towards 2000.

He insists that at the heart of everything is 'making Britain more competitive'. Everything has to be subordinated to that. That is the message he wants to get home. It so happens, he goes on, that all the natural Labour priorities assist in that process, especially all things to do with infrastructure.

He further insists that it is essential for Labour to have clarified its priorities before getting into power, 'otherwise there will be mayhem'. He feels that they are getting there. He talks, by the way, all the time as though his role is to educate the party in all these things. Posits himself as fully conversant with everything that needs to be done, and only bedevilled by a party that is slow to learn. I could see how he thought this. His leadership has been marked by just such education and forceful imposition. But whether the same process applies to policy as has applied to party reform is debatable.

He sees Labour as being part of a process, to be seen at different stages all across Europe, of achieving the right mix of market-oriented and socially aware policies. Sees it in East Europe, in Sweden (in many ways the model). When I asked whether Labour had achieved the mix, he said yes. First, got Europe right: i.e. off the hook of anti-Europeanism. Second, got the US right: i.e. off the hook of anti-Americanism. Third, got into the disarmament process: i.e. ceased to be CND.

On the question of priorities, we discussed what would be at the bottom of the list. I mentioned defence. He replied he was against crock-of-gold economics, and against therefore giving anyone the idea that defence cuts could solve all problems. Was very aware of how easily he could be misinterpreted if he started talking about defence cuts, by both Tories and Labour. Therefore chose to say as little as he did. However, he hypothesized that if he were to give a defence lecture for forty minutes which went through the whole problem, looking at the rest of Europe and what they were doing (compared with which Britain is doing nothing), and which also reflected on the vast industrial dislocation which will be caused by defence cuts etc. etc., he might be able to do something useful. I strongly urged him to do this. He said, Watch this space.

This led to a wider question, of getting the message across. He said two interesting things.

First, he volunteered that they were all very reluctant to say things twice. Because they were democratic socialists, he seemed to think they had some special need to say new interesting things all the time, and therefore shrank from repetition. Perhaps there was a need for repetition. I told him that whenever I reluctantly repeated myself in a column, it was often only after the third time that one suddenly got a big response.

Second, he mused that Maggie T had done a lot of repetition in the 1970s. Banging away with the same message. Perhaps, he tentatively reflected, there was a lesson here. Which took us more or less exactly back to the end of my piece about him last week . . .

IMPRESSIONS A decidedly nice man. Resilient to fraud. Surprisingly large physically, when seated. Philosophical about the political game, about the tricks the Tories get up to. I found him, however, curiously inarticulate. Talks a great deal: with apparent conversational knowledge of everything: with deeper knowledge on other things, based on experience: but not a clear conceptualizer and not a deep thinker. Is it my age, or something deeper, which makes me disbelieve in him?

MICHAEL HESELTINE
The Garrick, 13 March 1990

He began by being extremely wary about talking about herself and the leadership election potential. But he warmed up . . .

ECONOMY He basically believes the government is in serious trouble because there is no light at the end of the economic tunnel. The inflation which will come out of German reunification will lead to ruthless interest-rate hikes by Germany to defeat it. Japan is also going for an anti-inflation line. All this will lead to slowdown, which will deeply damage British industry, which has no hope whatever of seeing a domestic-led growth. He thinks the government may have some success in getting inflation to turn down eventually – but who knows when? However, the important fact is that there may be very little room for a pre-election binge of the usual kind. Inflation may be too high to risk it. This makes for gloomy economic prospects.

He noted with grim relish that this very day we had showed, for the first time ever, a deficit on invisibles. But the point was that all this led to a gloomy economic picture, which meant that the government's normal electoral advantage may well have eluded it on that front.

EUROPE His big pitch, as ever. He puts the problem this way. Not so much that there are major moments for decisive action – although these do exist – but that in the million daily decisions taken in Europe which affect Britain in one way or another, our fundamentally anti-Euro attitude is a major factor. He reminds me that the difference between failure and success for a nation lies between 0.5 and 1 per cent annual growth, sustained for forty years, and relative to our main competitors. I.e. it is the accumulation of lots of small decisions rather than a handful of big ones which makes the long-term economic difference. In this the government's role is to create an atmosphere, to announce an intention. MT is seen to be so rabidly anti-EEC that this is the bias proclaimed and understood by British business as much as European. This is why her attitude matters so much. It is out of tune with the whole of the financial and business world, and with the majority of the Tory Party. But it is the one that counts.

If we belonged to the ERM we would be subject to more discipline. This would have made the present crisis[1] much less. He believes that Germany and France will go ahead with some form of monetary union (or some such, I can't remember). He thinks we simply slide slowly out of the picture, and mainly owing to one woman's prejudice – it is nothing more. He laments how few people she speaks to, how entirely absent are her friends in the Cabinet, how dependent she is on civil servants for chat. She is simply not exposed enough to people with a proper Euro point of view.

He instances Germany as one issue she has got hopelessly wrong. He marvels at the fact that now we have managed to make Germany an enemy. After forty years of brilliant reconstruction, and the mediating influence of NATO and the EEC, suddenly Germany is now the enemy. Incredible. And all because of her latching on to atavistic prejudices of the British people. An appalling absence of leadership in the right direction, which will once again isolate us from the mainstream.

1 In addition to anxiety about business confidence, there was a rapidly gathering alarm about the community charge, also known as the poll tax, imposed the previous year. This culminated in riots during a demonstration by 300,000 in Trafalgar Square on 31 March.

I ask whether his colleagues – Hurd, for example – aren't an antidote to all this. He replies that Hurd and he are very alike in their thinking about Europe and the rest. Not a cigarette paper between them. But Hurd in the end is not important. Nobody is important. He remarks, though, on the importance of the DTI being peopled entirely with politicians who don't believe in either Europe or an industrial policy: Ridley/Redwood/Hogg.[1] He also notes the malign influence of Alan Clark at Defence: already talking very un-European language about the return of British troops (which happens to coincide with Clark's long-held idea that BAOR should return anyway). MH insists that all these placements are highly deliberate, to preserve the Thatcherite view where it matters most.

He adds, on my prompting, that these Euro attitudes don't help when it comes to the US. He opines that Bush 'won't like' MT. Quite alien to his preppy East Coast nature. Probably Bush wouldn't like Kohl either: but Kohl has made himself *numero uno* in Europe, and that's why he is ahead.

DEFENCE   MH does not believe in an early wind-down. He thinks the Soviet future is not settled, and suggests that Islam may yet replace Moscow as the enemy we need to watch out for, especially in connection with the oil, of course. He also sees the future of US cutbacks meaning that Europe has to do more for itself, which limits the scope for cuts. He maintains that this is his objective analysis, and does not spring from party politics.

WELFARE   I ask whether he has big disagreements on this as well. He says that he is even now preparing a big speech. But he faces a problem. What he wants to say is that a lot of the policy is right, but that there is this area which is wrong. But he dare not say it that way, because he knows it will be covered only for the 'wrong' point, and presented as an anti-Thatcher speech. This is a real and general problem he finds he faces, and I didn't find out properly how he deals with it.

I remark that his books[2] are a decent substitute. At least they lay out a full position. I ask whether he had much help with them. He implied that he had a lot (although from memory they contain not a single acknowledgement of help received).

1 John Redwood: Conservative MP for Wokingham since 1987; at the time Minister of State at the DTI; later Secretary of State for Wales 1993–1995. Douglas Hogg QC: barrister; Conservative MP for Grantham 1979–97, for Sleaford and North Hykeham since 1997; Minister of State at the FCO 1990–95; Minister of Agriculture 1995–7; son of Baron Hailsham of St Marylebone; later 3rd Viscount Hailsham.
2 Michael Heseltine wrote his first book, *Reviving the Inner Cities*, in 1983. He followed this with *Where There's a Will* (1987), *The Challenge of Europe* (1989) and his memoirs, *Life in the Jungle* (2000).

LEADERSHIP Finally he brought this up, having deflected it earlier. He does so by asking me for my assessment of the parliamentary party. I say that I am not in the closest touch, but offer the view that there are now more people who feel pretty bitter and alienated, and certainly more (but how many?) who fear for their seats. However, I then recite the bones of my column,[1] which he apologized for not having read, which said that the fear of a split would be so great that it would ultimately put people off the battle. 'You mean that the extreme right has been more successful in establishing their position than the left?' he put it. That's about right, I replied.

He then said that he recognized this opinion. But he thought it was completely wrong. He said that the right's veto did not actually exist in the way I described – it existed at the early stage. It might indeed be enough to forestall a challenge. But there came a point down the line when it would evaporate in the face of the gut reality that people wanted to keep their seats. How would this make itself felt? I asked. Not by people standing up and saying so, he said. But the whips would be asking them at some stage, and the reply would come: 'She has done heroic work. She must be heroically sent off. But it would be better to have someone else.' MH talks like a man who feels utterly certain that a lot of the right will at some stage take this course. And when will the whips ask the question? 'When the pressure from you people becomes strong enough.'

MH obviously spends a lot of his time thinking obsessively about all this. He foresees the economy failing to recover so spectacularly that real possibilities arise before the autumn. He remarks how much earlier than usual the talk has begun. Usually it starts in June, and whips talk about the need to get round one more corner before the recess. This time it started in February, and there is no sign of getting round any corner at all.

He was also in closest touch, it seems, with the *Sunday Times*, and perhaps other of the weekend pollsters. He knew their figures immediately. He mentioned to me that the *ST* people had told him of a high number of the right who said that they would choose him as their favoured successor. On the grounds that he might win. He sees his support coming from all regions and all sections and all classes.

At the bottom of it all he sees the poll tax. This was, first, what had now certainly scuppered Baker. He noted with satisfaction – although claiming he had nothing to do with it – how the papers were fingering Baker as the father of the poll tax. Which was true enough. He reeled off

1 HY's commentary of 13 March was headed 'To the last ditch and back again'. In it, he reflected on the role of journalists in the leadership crisis. He also concluded that, though there were huge concerns about Mrs Thatcher, there would not be a leadership contest before the next election.

his own credentials as its enemy. It was in the 1981 Green Paper, but rejected as an option. He kept it out of the '83 manifesto: as indeed he kept out the whole question of local-government finance. His speech on second reading predicts every one of the disasters that have now occurred. He feels entirely clean on the issue. When I asked what was his alternative, he began to bluster. But he said that he wasn't interested in finance, only in structure. There would have to be a complete change of structure. He rather plausibly denied that there was any real accountability now, saying that from his DoE experience he simply 'knew' that this was all a conspiracy of deception between local and central government.

The poll tax, however, was finally crucial as Thatcher's very own tax. She was to blame for it. She had pushed it through Cabinet without proper discussion. There had been a vast amount of advice against it. But she deserved to be stuck with it now. It was working out as a catastrophe, and she was to blame. Plainly MH sees this moment, and this issue, as the one which may now sweep him to his destiny. The glint in his eye was enough to get this across!

LABOUR Suffered from the fact that Kinnock was unalterably trivial. This was a word not applicable to Smith, Brown, Cunningham,[1] Dewar and others. But Kinnock could not escape it. What he seemed to mean by this was that with Kinnock you would never know what he really cared about, and what he would stand up for. Callaghan had not been like this, still less Attlee. Wilson had been like it. Kinnock was another Wilson: spineless, media-conscious, trivial.

His bet at the election remains a hung parliament. Thinks that Labour cannot get the biggest swing ever, although he admits that they will now be fighting the Labour of '79 not '87: i.e. without the Militant issue etc.

DOUGLAS HURD
Foreign Office (at his request), 29 March 1990

Urbane, relaxed, immensely chatty and laid-back. The effortless superiority of Etonian man, but with none of the side. We had an hour, without a telegram or an official intervening, at the end of which he wandered amiably off home.

---

1 John Cunningham: Labour MP for Whitehaven 1970–83, for Copeland 1983–2005; junior energy minister 1976–9; Opposition spokesman and Shadow Cabinet member 1983–97; agriculture minister 1997–8; Chancellor of the Duchy of Lancaster 1998–9; later Baron Cunningham of Felling.

KOHL[1] DH was to be at Cambridge tomorrow, after the initial speeches by Thatcher and Kohl today. They have a bristling relationship, in which Kohl bristles worse than MT. Hurd has had two sessions with Kohl, one of them entirely alone, and Kohl has spoken severely of how he can't get on with Margaret. But things are better now than they were in February. Kohl now has moved on the Polish border, which was just as well, and we seem to have got over our (her) anxieties about reunification, which infuriated the Germans. MT 'still has too much of an inclination to say what she thinks'. But at least, says Douglas, we are part of the agenda and the discussion now. There was a time when we had no idea how to insert ourselves into the process.

EEC Is dominated by the German problem, which is indistinguishable from the NATO problem. An enormous amount of work is to be done getting the new Germany properly into NATO, wherein DH places high priority on getting France fully back into it. Now is the opportunity.

We seem to be working very closely with the French on several Euro matters, re Germany. But Mitterrand's style is not easy to deal with. He is prone to make grand speeches and declarations, such as his latest one on the European Union, which lead nowhere but have inserted themselves into the political realm.

Although *political union* is being talked about, it is the wrong question to ask, because nobody has an agreed answer to it. The fact is that neither the French nor the Germans know what they mean about it. For example, the French talk about the European Parliament, but as soon as they are reminded that all Euro MPs want this in Brussels they shake their heads and say impossible, must be in Paris. There is a tremendous amount of vagueness as to what people really want by way of political union.

EMS (MOST INTERESTING) Douglas said that we would certainly be going in, and moreover that the person who would decide this was the Chancellor. He was quite emphatic about this, and repeated it several times. The Chancellor used not to be keen on EMS but has now become intellectually convinced. More important, he 'carries the major weight of responsibility for the future of our government'. He is therefore untouchable. He has enormous influence and importance. Now that he has said, often, 'when', this means that he will decide. He may be cautious in his timing. But his decisive influence is not disputable. When he has decided the moment is ripe, says Douglas, 'there may be two or three days of argument' but we will then go in.

---

1 Helmut Kohl, the German chancellor, was visiting Britain.

He could not have been more emphatic about Major's power in all this.[1] Said that his (DH's) role was secondary. He would make the diplomatic arguments for it. He had told Rocard[2] only the other day that the diplomatic arguments were entirely clear, but that they would not be the ones that counted. He also said that Lawson's departure had certainly made all this much easier.

LEADERSHIP   Said he thought it extremely unlikely that she would be there at the election. She was very tense just now, and also tired. But for the most part he saw no sign of any flagging of character or commitment. The same old Margaret. He thought there would be a challenge again this autumn. The publicity is irresistible, he says. It could be another Meyer-type[3] (mentioned Hugh Dykes), or it could be someone of more substance. He thought they would get not many more votes than Meyer. He thought it very hard to imagine the scenario of great men waiting upon her and telling her to go. The only way she *might* go, he said, was simply deciding to herself. A lone, undiscussed decision, saying that she thought she had served her time and done her task. But he found this pretty hard to imagine.

It would be the more hard given *Heseltine*'s position (we spoke before Tebbit's démarche).[4] But DH saw problems for Heseltine. His tactics had been impeccable so far. But they could not last much longer. There were enough people in the party who are bitterly hostile to MT who will be saying to Heseltine (rather like G. Howe), 'Put up or shut up.' I.e. when are you going to move?: we fear for our seats: we want a real challenge to the lady. All this will perhaps smoke MH out in ways he does not desire.

Of course, MT will be deterred from resigning, inter alia, because of the Heseltine threat. DH volunteered that he thought MH was by no means sure to win, even after she had gone. But he agreed that the fear of his winning posed a risk MT would be unlikely to take. But he stressed his belief that this would be by no means the only factor bearing on her decision.

Could her position improve? When I postulated a 25 per cent Labour

1 John Major was Chief Secretary to the Treasury 1987–9 and Chancellor of the Exchequer 1989–90.
2 Michel Rocard: prime minister of France 1988–91.
3 Sir Anthony Meyer, baronet, diplomat, Conservative MP for West Flintshire, and a pro-European, made a challenge for the party leadership in 1989 as a 'stalking horse' for a later challenger such as Michael Heseltine or Ian Gilmour. He was roundly defeated, but Mrs Thatcher lost enough votes, Meyer said, for people to 'think the unthinkable'.
4 Tebbit, a Thatcher supporter already thinking of quitting politics, publicly declared that he would fight Michael Heseltine for the leadership if Thatcher stood down. Party chairman Kenneth Baker called Tebbit's intervention 'a distraction'. In a column on 3 April, headed 'A man out of temper with his times', HY wrote that 'the first man to put his hat in the ring not yet set up, and the first declared candidate for a job not yet vacant, has blown it. Good.'

lead until the autumn, he said that this would of course be quite unsustainable. Thought it wouldn't happen. The summer recess, it seems, is being yearned for even earlier this year, as Douglas ruminated about it 'being all right if we get through to summer with the car still on the road'. Which he thought it just about would be.

USA   Relations are still pretty close. The US concerns are almost entirely Germany, NATO and the USSR. On these, especially the first two, we share very close interests. Germany is the object of policy rather than the collaborator. Washington and London see eye to eye, mostly. Although DH admitted that MT's early line on unification had not been helpful. Now it is better. 'She remains very useful,' he said with an unconscious patronizing tone. Only yesterday she had talked not only to Gorby but to Bush, and had a conversation about Lithuania which they can't yet have on their own. A conduit still. She admires and likes Bush. Their relationship is much less prickly than with Kohl, but rather less cordial than with Mitterrand.

DH regards it as a prime aim of policy to get some of our troops out of Germany by our own volition, rather than have them pushed out by the new Germany. He thinks Washington should have the same aim.

DEFENCE   He adds that he has no doubt that defence spending must come down, despite his speeches about the new theatres of trouble (Iraq, Libya etc. etc.). Cutting BAOR will involve us in a mini version of the Soviets' massive problem: what to do about unemployed soldiers. But it will have to be done. There is a great deal of work going on about all this – 'although the MoD doesn't exactly move fast'.

SOUTH AFRICA   Douglas strongly recommended a visit to see the editor of *The Sowetan*: as a wise man who has spent a lot of time trying to persuade the blacks to be sensible. Recently back from Windhoek (Namibia independence), he described the scenes between de Klerk and Nujoma[1] as being unimaginable even a year ago. A sort of statesmanship descended on them. He also said the chaos at times was like Hillsborough, except the victims would have been Yasser Arafat and Robert Mugabe.

LABOUR   Is questionably electable. It is therefore being taken more seriously by the BBC and foreign governments. Quite noticeable how much more coverage they are getting – rightly. He assumes that Hattersley would be Foreign Secretary, at which he would be rather good, whereas

1 F. W. de Klerk: premier of South Africa, still under white minority rule. Sam Nujoma: president of newly independent Namibia, formerly South-West Africa.

Kaufman is terrible. He regards the electoral map, and electoral precedent, based on the number of seats where the Alliance were second last time, as entirely unreliable. He hopes devoutly that the Tories won't choose to attack Labour for being reds etc., but will goad them persistently for their absence of policy.

GORDON BROWN
Lunch, the Garrick, 6 June 1990

Genial, slightly nervous. Remembered, as a first gambit, that Stephen Fay and I had written *The Zinoviev Letter*.[1] He had been doing research on the dirty tricks played by the Tory Party against Labour over the years.

He thinks the Tories will be trying the same thing this time. The US examples will be learned from. I say that the situation is different, especially in that there is nothing further to discover about Kinnock (unlike Dukakis, who was a complete unknown and therefore vulnerable to the dirty tricks that Atwater and others dreamed up).[2] Also, the British electorate is just far better informed, and hence less likely to fall for surprise shots. Also, the absence of paid-for TV means that the ability to exploit dirty tricks is less. However, we agree that one part of the US technique has common application. This is to define a narrow single issue as 'the' issue, having previously discovered some small part of that issue on which the rival candidate is weak.

The most he would say about Labour was that it has a chance of winning. This was different from the last three elections. He asked anxiously how Labour could have done better, what chances it had missed. I gave him my usual burst about Kinnock and the speeches. To which he said that NK would reply that last year he gave four big speeches (including one on education) to which nobody paid much attention. I said, Tough. You have to say it five times. In any case, you need a dossier of speeches which accumulate. Since Kinnock's weakness is perceived to be in the area of substance, this is surely a good way of meeting it. Brown seemed to agree, but didn't seem to think Neil would be receptive.

I gave it as my opinion, to provoke him, that, when we got down to it, there would be no really thematic difference between the party manifestos: that both were in the business of managing capitalism, and trying

---

1 The story of the document that purported to show that the Bolsheviks were providing financial support to the Labour Party at the 1924 general election. The book, by Lewis Chester, Stephen Fay and Hugo Young, was published in 1967.

2 Michael Dukakis: governor of Massachusetts and 1988 Democratic presidential nominee. Lee Atwater was the Republicans' presidential campaign manager for George H. W. Bush.

to persuade the electorate that they could do it best. He demurred, and kept returning to the one theme he wants to push, which actually has a lot of credibility. He said Labour was in favour of the public–private partnership. This was not the old nationalization, but also denied the Thatcherite contention that the public side had only a residual role. He saw partnership in industry, training as crucial – and distinctive. He said he was getting a lot of resonance out of this when he spoke to business people . . .

Altogether I found GB pleasant, serious and uninformative. No doubt he is as good a politician as people say he is.

CHRIS PATTEN
Department of the Environment, 25 June 1990

POLL TAX He agrees that the poll tax is a major problem, but he is persuaded that it is not as big as interest rates: he is therefore sensitive to the Major–Lamont argument that nothing must impede their economic policy, which is to get interest rates down. But the poll-tax problem is massive. He illustrated the point from an encounter in his constituency surgery last week. A couple who had bought their council house on a £32,000 mortgage came in and said that their PT (which was double what the rates had been – about £600) was simply unpayable. It had broken their backs. They could not afford another £30 a week. Yet on examining their accounts, he saw they were paying £360 for their mortgage. He asked them what it had been when they took it out. They said £190. But they still blamed the PT for their problems. It confirmed his metaphor, which I've heard before, that the PT was like a heat-seeking missile, homing in on low-rated housing which contained exactly the marginal votes the Tories needed to keep or get.

THATCHER: A MANY-SIDED PROBLEM Her style remains unbelievably wearing. It works like this. You have a debate in committee, and you win the argument. It takes a long time, but eventually the weight of those present simply shows her she has not won. But this is only the start. When this happens, she reopens the matter, picks apart what has been agreed, gathers informal groups to rediscuss it, finds numerous ways of twisting and turning to get her view back on top. One instance he mentioned (if I got it right) was the recent argument about disposing of untreated sewage at sea – where, as I recall, CP was left in lonely isolation at the EC meeting, saying we would not sign up to a convention limiting disposal to treated sewage. He won the argument, but then found it countermanded, after Ridley's intervention. He had to take all the flak, unable to say how he had really won.

- Ridley is a major menace. He engages in quite unscrupulous tactics to undermine colleagues, Major as much as Patten. He feeds the lady's instincts, especially on Europe. He has a lot of clout with her, but uses it quite ruthlessly. Chris said that he rarely thought people were really bad, but made an exception for Ridley.
- He said it was absolute rubbish to suggest that the Thatcher technique sharpened her ministers' minds. Does anyone seriously suggest that with Douglas in the chair important decisions would be subject to any less thought and care?
- The post-Moscow Cabinet was a classic show. The first half hour was taken up with an account of her great journey. All that was missing were the slides, said CP. It was Travels with My Aunt. A wholly ridiculous performance.
- To illustrate the nature of Cabinet debate, he reported the opinion of a newish member of the Cabinet secretariat, which had been given to Norman Lamont. This official was remarking to Lamont how exceptionally difficult he had found it to make any sense of his notes, after a typical Cabinet meeting presided over by MT. He couldn't understand why it was all such incoherent gibberish. But suddenly he found the key. If he recorded what the PM said and no one else, suddenly it fell into place. The thread was continuous if you left out all the contributions which she simply failed to take any notice of.
- She wasn't reachable by normal intercourse, he implied. She fired off these policy commitments without any consultation whatever. A minister might be engaged in delicate diplomacy to see some policy through, only to find that she had swept it all into a different plan on *Jimmy Young* or to the Tory women. ('Private roads and banning Rottweilers. Doesn't sound like much of a programme, does it?')
- As an extreme example of her uncontrollable interventionism, she has two- and three-hour sessions with John Major every day, says CP. Not quite so bad as it was in April and May, when she really did think she was in big trouble.

Is she in trouble now? Probably not, said CP. But, if the polls start going back to Labour, then there could be a challenge in the autumn. CP himself sounded like a man desperately keen to get to the end of July, and not much impressed by my prediction that all bad news had been so discounted that, for once, this would not be a tough July.

Major is very important. He is trusted because he gets his figures right. But he is very political. CP withdrew a first remark that he is too political.

But anyone who thinks that what Major says is said without Downing Street clearance doesn't know how things are working.

Hurd is very important. He knows how to handle her. He is a complete master of his subject, and he has a strategic objective.

Howe is now unimportant. Completely on the margin. One has to ring up to find out whether he is supposed to be getting the papers. How can anyone want to hang on in there? For the sake of his sanity one must expect him to get out before the end.

Wakeham has become important again. She sees him as having rescued electrical privatization. He has never argued with her in his life. He is not really in charge of publicity. That was just invented to give him a reason to attend all the meetings.

So it's Hurd, Major, Wakeham – with Ridley behind the arras. These are the men who matter. Although CP, averring modesty, claims (I'm sure rightly) that if he hadn't argued with her very hard, the whole environment programme would be an incredible mess. When I asked how he was viewed, he said, She's not sure about me. Because he does argue (which he always criticized the early wets for never doing), he is less than fully favoured.

Baker (I almost forgot) is proving a good party chairman because he has the quality successful party chairman always need: meretriciousness. But he is not highly esteemed by the colleagues.

Homelessness is cited as a problem which the DoE has got through after a massive programme of educating her. 'Her instinctive solution was the hosepipe.' But CP thinks his programme has a kind of rationale which, though again not appeasing the lobbies, will do some good.

ELECTION He is torn between the bottomless pessimism of the born pessimist and incredulity that the tide really should have turned for Labour. He agrees, he says, with the theory of history which says that Oppositions win elections when there has been some kind of sea change in public attitudes. 1945, 1979 and perhaps 1964 were such moments. But he does not think the theory is fully workable when the aspiring Opposition has nothing more to say than that it is opposed to the government. It needs more than that, and had it on previous occasions. He sees no sign that Labour will speak for a genuinely different politics. All it is saying is that it won't be so beastly as Thatcher, while doing nothing differently.

On the bottom line, he thinks that if things get better, the Tories could win by 15 or 20 seats in a tight contest. He notes that, assuming the Liberals don't recover, the government will need a higher percentage of the vote than in 1979, 1983 or 1987.

ADDENDA

- On Major. He resisted enormous pressure in autumn 1989 to raise interest rates, and in the Budget to have a tighter fiscal stance. This was brave – and right. The retail sales figures are showing the size of the downturn. If the rates had risen further, there would have been a slump perhaps. Did MT back him then, or pressure him? 'We will know that when the effects of the policy become apparent.'
- Alan Clark and C. Chope[1] are the known Rottweiler owners in the government. CP corrected my earlier note, to the effect that the point about single white males was that they *were* more likely to vote Tory (which makes better sense than Parkinson's version).

On 2 August 1990 Saddam Hussein, president of Iraq, launched the invasion of Kuwait, ostensibly to protect Iraq's oil supplies. Fighting in the First Gulf War – sometimes called Operation Desert Storm – began slowly, after diplomatic pressure, economic sanctions and a United Nations resolution of 29 November that authorized a coalition force of thirty-four nations – led by the US and backed by Britain but including military muscle from Saudi Arabia, Bahrain, the Arab emirates, Oman and Qatar – to engage Iraqi soldiers and push them out of Kuwait. In fact fighting did not begin until 17 January 1991. The campaign, an occasion for pyrotechnic displays of high-tech armaments, ended on 28 February with the collapse of the Iraqi army and the return of the Emir of Kuwait.

ROGER TOMKYS
Lunch, Oxford and Cambridge Club,
10 September 1990

Saddam has to be evicted. If he stays, that is the worst-case situation. It's as simple as that. We (who?) were quite surprised, especially in retrospect when there had been time to think, that there weren't Arab countries who wanted to temporize: to say, OK he's got Kuwait, we don't like Kuwait anyway, we will do a deal with him, even though it means letting him control our oil output levels and so on. Maybe there were such countries. But events moved so fast that they had no time to put such a position together.

Saddam may have thought this would happen. He certainly miscalcu-

1 Christopher Chope, Conservative MP for Southampton, Itchen 1983–92, for Christchurch since 1997.

lated. He can have had no idea that Saudi would act as it did, nor that the Russians would make common cause with the US. He thought he could get away with Kuwait. Therefore he made no preparations for what has happened. His policy has been a succession of improvisations, getting faster and faster. Some have been quite skilful, and he has some able people with him. But he will soon run out of improvising possibilities.

The blockade has been pretty successful. Very successful against outward goods, rather less so against inward. He has played the food card. This has been directed especially at countries with many nationals inside – e.g. Pakistan and India. Has tried to tempt them to give food, on the grounds that their nationals will die. But they are under other pressure too. Pakistan desperately needs world recognition, therefore will hesitate to be blacklisted, which would result from any breach of the blockade. India might be able to put together some kind of non-aligned grouping. But they would risk Western aid if they broke ranks. RT implied that a lot of pressure was being applied by the UK and US.

Another effect has been via immigration. A million Egyptians have tried to get out, and lots of others. There are few people left to run the Kuwait economy. All this means that Iraq is not producing much, with dire economic consequences.

We think the blockade is working well. But it needs time, obviously. And, equally, there is the chance always it will begin to fray. That is the scene in which the war option looms. What RT specifically mentioned was the situation in which sanctions are seen not to be working, and Saddam is therefore seen as in some danger of getting part of what he wanted. This would be unacceptable. But he admits that deciding when that moment has come will be difficult.

It is, however, the context in which the UN argument has to be seen. He did not exactly dissent from my line that British public opinion would be far happier with a UN-decided war. And he agreed that the UN was in far better public odour. But he implied that perhaps the UN would never get together to agree on a war option. This was why, even though Article 51[1] is disputed, it had to be invoked and, as it were, (my image) kept warm.

Here the Thatcher position comes into play. RT describes her as being swifter than he would be to leap a few steps. He, in common with *Guardian* readers, would like to see an escalation from sanctions to blockade, to UN vote, perhaps to provocation by Iraq and only then hostilities. She apparently sees the danger in this caution, in some circumstances. By the way, RT has seen more of her, he thinks, than any FCO

1 Article 51 of the UN Charter outlines the inherent right of a member state to defend itself against armed attack, until the Security Council has taken measures to restore peace and security.

official for months. In the last three weeks, has been inside Downing Street more than any FCO official for years.

Saddam, says this strong Middle East expert, has been the object of assassination for Assad of Syria for years. For at least twelve years, each man has been trying to kill the other. They have failed, despite access to some of the most expert hired killers in the world. But RT made little bones about this being a real object of Western policy. He just regretted how slight the chances were. How would it help? No one could be sure. There was certainly no bourgeois party in Iraq, or any other discernible group of opposition people. But he said that the very fact of a change of leader would perhaps make it easier for Iraq to leave Kuwait. There would be a shake-up, which is better than what we have.

WAR he agreed, would be of uncertain duration. No one could tell how long Iraq would last. We didn't talk about this enough.

COMMAND in a war would in effect be American. There would be joint command under an American of land and sea forces. Sea forces would be more independent, ship by ship.

HOSTAGES He said they were fairly sure that the numbers of British were now far fewer than they had originally thought. Nothing like 4,000 in Kuwait. In Iraq perhaps 500. He said that there was no way they could be allowed to determine what policy there could be. Cold-eyed, he said that if there was war there would be a lot of people killed anyway, and indicated that if these people were among them – tough. No special arrangements could be made for them, or special considerations allowed to apply to them.

AFTERMATH/STRATEGY/CHANCES/OUTCOMES He is deeply involved in thinking about these things. I could not remember all he said, but among memorable items were these:

Oil price is up and will stay up. Very unlikely to drop again. We should be thinking about $25 (I think he said), with all the consequences this will have. Not least for Africa: goodbye Third World chances of relieving its debt. Goodbye also Soviet hopes of cash aid for its economy. This will have massive economic repercussions. More than once he adverted to the chances of a world recession, and all the horrors this would mean. (Although it could also be argued, as I did not talk about with him, that if oil was that high Saddam could claim that he had secured his main aim which was to increase Iraqi oil revenue – which he will have done by 30 per cent or so.)

A permanent and completely unsure redrawing of the Middle East map. Even in the best case, what will happen to the Gulf? Will the emirates etc. get together in some way, for their own defence in future? They will certainly not get involved in moves toward democracy, as the Americans might like. What is more certain is that they will try and expel all the Palestinians now working in the Gulf, whom they will regard as potential unstable elements. This will have massive repercussions for the whole Israel–Palestinian issue, of course.

One element of the outcome ought to be some commitment by the rich states to send money to the poor states, as a way of proving their togetherness.

What will the US do in any circumstances? Two interesting hypotheses are clearly on top of the FCO minds. One: they believe that Bush cannot survive as president after 1992 if the US gets out without something pretty permanent having been put in place with a fair chance of stopping a return of Saddam or whoever. In this sense, it seems, even the peace option seems fraught with peril. Secondly – looking knowingly over his glasses – RT said, Had anyone thought what might happen if the Saudis said that the US could not go, insisting that they could not survive?

Re Saudi Arabia, he thought there would be consequences of so many people finding out just what a terrible place Saudi really is. Not just Americans, but Egyptians, for example, seeing Saudi Arabia at close quarters, and asking themselves what are they fighting for? The Saudi royal family? The family rulers all over the Gulf? All in all, Saudi Arabia may not survive the permanent presence of US troops, may not be able to survive without them however, and either way faces a new world which the ruling family itself may not see for long.

A number of points arose concerning Israel. It was, of course, deeply important that the linkage should not be made. This was why it was wrong for Americans (journalists, professors etc.) to be talking about a complete Middle East settlement at this stage. For any kind of linkage to be made would mean Saddam being given permanent status as an Arab hero: the man who alone was able to force the Americans and Israelis to treat etc. etc. This clearly couldn't be allowed.

Equally, even if Saddam climbed down and a way was opened, one problem is that there would no longer be any peace faction in Israel nor anyone for Israel to talk to even if a peace faction re-emerged. Couldn't talk to Jordan, given Jordan's present role[1] (not to mention King Hussein's weakness). Who else in the Arab world? Couldn't do any business with

---

1 Jordan had backed a peace proposal that linked the withdrawal of Iraqi troops from Kuwait with the withdrawal of Syrian troops from Lebanon and of Israeli forces from Gaza, the West Bank and the Golan Heights.

Arafat now, because of his renewed assertions of the need to settle everything by force.

He also said, again solemnly, that if the Iraqis used chemical weapons
he (i.e. FCO advice to Thatcher, perhaps coming from SIS) presumed
that Israel might well use nuclear weapons. I was so startled by this I
failed to follow it up. Chemical weapons against the West or against
Israel? The implication was simply against the West, which would
provoke a pre-emptive strike by Israel.

In general, he described the situation as the worst world crisis since
Cuba, with no chance of it ending so clearly as Cuba did.

Nonetheless, it was interesting, amid all this pessimism, to hear the
FCO man thinking forward to the possibility, at last, of a general conference on the Middle East – which the FCO and others have been hoping
for for decades. Being a good diplomat, he must think about the upside,
which he gives a 15 per cent chance of beginning to happen in the wake
of this massive shake-up to the kaleidoscope. He sees some possibility of
all sides getting round the table, and the West saying to Israel, Iran et al.
that they have spent vast fortunes on a status quo which is no longer
tolerable and are not prepared to go on doing so. With clever orchestra-
tion he sees some chance of this getting somewhere: perhaps the more so
as chaos has been made manifest.

I asked who would be the statesmen in the Middle East, and who
might lubricate all this. He could not name any Middle East leader who
was free from sectarian interest, although he said that Mubarak, while a
stupid man, had done well so far. He said he thought Thatcher and Hurd
would have as good credentials as anyone – and he is far from a Thatcher
admirer himself. But maybe this was just the FCO's top-flight Middle
East man Walter Mittying himself into a key role. Thatcher's intense
pro-Jewishness might marry with the FCO's historic pro-Arabishness . . .

*Little has survived of HY's notes surrounding the deposing of Margaret
Thatcher as leader of the Conservative Party, but events – as foreshadowed here – moved at enormous speed. Some of the detail emerges
in conversations in the early months of 1991, when John Major was
settling in as the new Tory leader and prime minister.*

MICHAEL MATES
4 November 1990

There will be a leadership challenge, as long as there is no war. No one could justify putting their name forward as the bodies were starting to come back. However, nominations would have to be in by 29 November; first round is on 4 December. Bush is going to the Gulf for Thanksgiving (22 November). MM implies that if war hasn't started in the next week, it won't start before end of November. Bush seems to be signalling this by letting it be known when he is going out there.

Who will be the candidate? Who better than Geoffrey? says MM. What else has he left the Cabinet for? Just to expire slowly? Or to do something? We will know by the time he speaks in the Queen's Speech debate on Thursday.

If GH runs, then MH will run and probably also Tebbit. It will open the gates. There will be a real contest.

MH has only got one shot at the leadership. He couldn't make a challenge himself. It might not lead to victory. And in the course of it, he could terribly damage her, but also terribly damage the party. Which he doesn't want to do.

If there was a stalking horse, he would do better than last time. At least thirty people told George Younger last time that this would be the last time they voted for MT. Also there would be Howe, Lawson and sundry other sackees of the last year. It begins to add up. MM guesses the thirty might have risen to sixty. Therefore we could get well over 100. Which would be the worst of all worlds, perhaps. With MT mortally wounded but still alive and kicking.

ALAN CLARK
Phone, 4 November 1990

He is on MT's side, but with reservations. Had talked to her today, he said. MH is synthetic, appalling, cowardly. A terrible man, whom everyone should see through.

MH should see, being a *paysan rude*, that if we lose the election and it can in the slightest degree be attributed to him he is finished. He will never get it in those circumstances. He therefore has to tread very carefully. It would not just be his enemies who would round on him. Therefore, unless he can guarantee to win, he cannot really run (which rather, per HY, gives the lie to the cowardice point). His letter to his constituency chairman:[1] what the hell kind of game is this supposed to be?

MT will fight hard. No question of standing down. She really is amazingly resilient. I occasionally see signs of her being a little *distrait*, spaced-out etc. But she has great disdain for her subordinates. She sees no one else who has her experience. And yet she is also a political realist. Her trouble is, however, that however many heads she chops off, Medusa-like, she continues to find herself in a perhaps impossible position.

The Euro-elections showed how crazy it would be to try and fight an election on the anti-EC card. Now there is rumbling talk of a referendum. (It was clear from the way Clark put this that it had been talked about today between him and MT, or at any rate someone close to her.) Clark describes referendum talk as the talk of desperation, coming from people who talk and talk and talk, and can't see their way out of a problem until someone suddenly says 'What about the referendum?' as a brilliant way out. A result of fatigue, he thinks. He is doing his best to kill it off. The theory is apparently that they have a referendum which they win, followed by an election which is seen to endorse it. But he says, What if they lose the first stage of the de Gaulle tactic (q.v. de G's exit)?[2] Then they would be in worse trouble: if, say, people said yes to losing the Queen's head on the currency.

None of this would matter if we had four more years to go. But only one more summer.

As to the numbers, he says he can't count the ultras. He thinks nobody listens to Dykes, Cash,[3] Taylor. But of the middle people, not over-bothered by the issue, he says 150–60, i.e. 3–1 in favour of EC, taking what he calls a 'vaguely CBI view'.

He personally seems to think that if she would go quietly, with all trumpets blazing, was succeeded by Hurd, that would be a good outcome. But he thinks that if she went bloodily, the media would be saying in ten days, Come back Maggie. He regards the poll figures[4] as quite unreal.

---

1 Following Geoffrey Howe's resignation as Chancellor on 1 November, MH wrote to the chairman of his constituency association saying, 'The crisis is one of confidence. It must be quickly restored. There is only one way to preside over and lead a democratic political party, and that is to pay proper regard to the myriad of opinions and, indeed, prejudices that go to make up its support . . . We cannot countenance the sacrifice of Tory seats, needlessly lost in spite of the effort to win and nurture them.'

2 On 24 May 1968, at the height of national protests, President de Gaulle challenged France's 8 million striking workers either to support his reforms or to accept his resignation. They did not support him, and he resigned the following year.

3 William Cash: Conservative MP for Stafford 1984–97, for Stone since 1997; author of publications such as *Against a Federal Europe – the Battle for Britain* (1991) and *Europe: The Crunch* (1992).

4 An NMR poll published in *The Independent on Sunday* on 4 November 1990 revealed that 39 per cent thought Mrs Thatcher should go immediately, 25 per cent wanted her out before the next election, and 17 per cent thought she should resign after the election. The same poll gave Labour a 17-point lead. The *Mail on Sunday*'s NPO poll on the same day gave Labour a 21-point lead.

They don't take account of how feeling would move if she was kicked out bloodily.

POWELL takes on an ever more important role. He does more of the 'day-to-day' stuff than used to be the case. Charles is very clever. I think, says Alan, that rather than it being a case of Charles second-guessing her, it's quite often Margaret second-guessing Charles. Also, at Cabinet committees he almost sits as a member of the committee. He interrupts if not in mid-sentence, then certainly in mid-paragraph. Four years ago he was quite different, sitting silent, as civil servants are meant to do. But because he is so good, this is all right . . .

Gulf war. AC, a defence master, says that the plan is that there should be war, but it is always possible that the Iraqis will prevent it happening by pulling halfway out of Kuwait. This is the nightmare scenario. The reason there needs to be war is (a) Saddam has nuclear potential, and this needs to be dismantled rather than let him have it in two years' time, which is roughly what we estimate it would take. (b) Israel. Israel is feeling marginalized. Since the end of the Evil Empire, it is less important: no longer the only stable element in the Middle East with an interest in Western democracy etc. Israel of course won't tolerate Saddam going nuclear. So if we don't do it, they will – which would be fatal.

War itself. Could be over more quickly than people are saying. What is quick? Five days. AC says he can't see the Iraqi SAMs[1] lasting more than forty-eight hours. Nor does he think they have the reload capacity which modern warfare is all about. Don't have the Russians and East Germans and French to keep the software going. On the other hand, if it does go on longer, it could be horrendous. They have desert fighting capacity and can take far more casualties than we can. If they don't collapse, it will be appalling. 'I wouldn't be surprised if we had to use tactical nukes in the end.'

---

1 SAMs: surface-to-air missiles, relatively short-range weapons believed to have been supplied to Iraq from the USSR.

1991–1997

John Major and
the Coming of
Tony Blair

PART THREE

1994–1997

John Major and
the Coming of
Tony Blair

1991

16 January   Operation Desert Storm begins war in the Gulf with air strikes.

26 February   Saddam Hussein withdraws troops from Kuwait.

11 March   John Major declares Britain 'at the very heart of Europe'.

31 March   The Republic of Georgia declares independence from the Russian Federation.

3 April   A UN resolution for ceasefire in the Gulf calls for dismantling of chemical and biological weapons and long-range missiles.

29 April   A tropical cyclone kills 138,000 in Bangladesh.

21 May   Former Indian prime minister Rajiv Gandhi is assassinated.

12 June   Boris Yeltsin is elected president of Russia.

28 June   Mrs Thatcher announces her retirement from the Commons.

1 July   The Warsaw Pact is officially dissolved at a Prague meeting.

26 July   Written evidence to the Commons discloses that the UK exported military and nuclear equipment to Iraq up until three days after the invasion of Kuwait.

19 August   An attempted coup against Soviet president Mikhail Gorbachev triggers the collapse of the Soviet Union. Estonia, Latvia, Ukraine, Belarus, Moldova, Kyrgyzstan, Uzbekistan and Azerbaijan all declare independence during August.

5 November   The body of newspaper magnate Robert Maxwell is found floating in the Atlantic; Serious Fraud Office begins investigation into pension fund losses from his companies.

18 November   British hostage Terry Waite is released in Beirut; Serbian troops murder 200 at Vukovar in Croatia.

Deaths   Claudio Arrau, Peggy Ashcroft, Frank Capra, Miles Davis, Margot Fonteyn, Graham Greene, Sean O'Faolain, Isaac Bashevis Singer, Angus Wilson

Military action in the Gulf had begun on 7 August 1989, when US troops were deployed in Saudi Arabia to protect the desert kingdom from Iraqi incursion, and other Gulf states also went on the alert. Within a month they were backed by 6,000 men and 120 Challenger tanks from Britain. Over the next few months there arrived naval forces from 12 nations, combat aircraft from 4 countries, and ground troops from 8. Altogether, 34 nations joined the coalition against Iraq. Diplomatic initiatives and UN sanctions all failed to secure Iraqi withdrawal. On 16 January what had begun as Operation Desert Shield became Operation Desert Storm.

ALAN CLARK ON THE GULF
Ministry of Defence, 14 January 1991

Said he could not go into detail because operational knowledge merged with conversational assessment. However . . .

Would it be long or short? We certainly want it short. But it may not be. We won't begin to know if it is to be short until three or four days have passed. It will be that long before the ground engagements begin in a major way.

Air power won't do it. It never does, asserts this military historian. Cites Normandy, Battle of Britain, Vietnam. You have only to fly over the ground to see why this is never enough. There is just too much ground, too many sites.

The land engagement is hard to predict. Iraqis have a lot of second-league Russian material. Durable, competent. And they have a lot of experience. These will be armies with roughly equal numbers, and roughly equal armaments maybe. AC recalls how he read Cabinet minutes when G. Howe was predicting the imminent end of the Iran–Iraq war with Iraq's defeat.

If it is to be long, it will be shitsville. Major shitsville. Schwarzkopf's[1] biggest fear is being stuck between the first and second lines of defence, and then having gas unleashed against him.

A very large effect of the war will be in the markets. They have discounted the war in advance. They have banked on a short war. If it turns out to be wrong, they will panic. It may be something like Suez, when Ike[2] forced Britain out by letting sterling fall. This time, bankers may go to Bush and say there must be another way of solving our problems.

Tactical nukes. When I say I have written a piece backing war, he asks

1 General H. Norman ('Stormin' Norman') Schwarzkopf commanded the coalition forces during the Gulf War.
2 Dwight 'Ike' Eisenhower: US president in 1957.

whether I back tactical nukes. He says this is the logic. I say that I see them as a separate category it would be fatal to use. He says that they are the only way to establish air superiority. Suggests that a tactical nuke should be dropped on day 1, and let Saddam 'suck on that one'. But of course it won't. He says this would be better than waiting to retaliate against the gas, with days of fever on the hot line as people took positions. What is so plain from this is tactical nukes are far from having been ruled out . . .

AC remarks that Saddam has the strongest diplomatic position of any weak aggressor in recent history. Has gained more, potentially, than anyone could have expected. If he moved even a little way out, there would be no war. Everyone would back away and he would, in effect, have won. Yet he has not taken any of the chances he has been offered. This argues such a degree of lunacy as to make his other actions very hard to read.

ALAN CLARK
14 January 1991

(He has written it all down, he says.)

Before the local elections, the writing was on the wall. MT was rattled. AC had fairly regular contact with her – he would call every six or seven weeks, although he might see her more often on organized business. After the result, things changed. Ealing[1] in particular was sweet: the Kinnock homeland. But Westminster and Wandsworth also vital. AC rang her to say, 'You're strong again. You won't be hearing from MH this autumn.'

The results were a special blow to MH. He wrote a piece in *The Times* three days after the results. A ghosted piece saying how he would change the poll tax. It exposed the thinness of his thinking. You could examine it at leisure in print, and see how slight it was. But there was a history behind it. Originally he had intended to make a grand speech, in the wake of electoral disaster. Major political capitalizing. But the 'little victories' denied him the chance. He had to backtrack. Therefore the speech was reduced to this rather feeble article. He could no longer throw down the gauntlet.

Nothing much happened until the autumn that he could remember. Then there was the terrible conference[2] in that ghastly compound, out of

1 The Conservatives regained Ealing in the May 1990 local elections, even though the nationwide voting patterns – if repeated at a general election – would have put Neil Kinnock in No. 10.
2 The Conservative Party conference the previous year had been in Bournemouth. Clark was not famous for enjoying such occasions.

touch with the real world. Perhaps that was where the trouble began. However, he also felt no frisson when Howe resigned [on 13 November]. Nor when MT made her grand stand at Rome and later in the HC. He took the view that this was just Maggie doing her thing, which would be balanced against DH and JM, and that in that balancing lay a reasonable hope of Britain maintaining a position in the EC. Rickety, but under control.

However, the press were beginning to talk up the crisis for her. It reminded AC of what happened to Douglas-Home in 1964. She was getting such bad treatment that it was affecting morale. Everyone was waiting for the next poll. The party was restive. Just as in April. But this time, seemingly, it had to be lanced by a contest.

The Howe speech. AC didn't think it was anything other than a personal explosion from a man who had had enough. Probably unplanned. But ask GH. Elspeth, however, a member of the *bien-pensant* left, would surely have been important.

He says the story about Saudi disintegration after US occupation is nonsense. On the contrary, Saudi has become a purposeful, decisive leadership, compared with the nervous vacillators he once knew. Saudi now has a cause, which its sparse people rally behind. The ruling family is strengthened.

Jordan is a different case. King Hussein was beguiled by Saddam, fascinated by him. He also had a people who wanted to back him, because of the Palestinian issue. He therefore was pushed to desert his financiers, the Saudi and the Gulf bosses. He is paying for this, and will pay more heavily. He is desperately short of money, and now faces being militarily squeezed. A gallant fellow, a wonderful place in several ways. But in serious trouble.

The trouble with bringing democracy to the Arabs is that you let the fundamentalists into Parliament. This is what happened in Jordan, where they are in government too.

Beware of all the stories about what Saddam was really intending to do. DH has heard stories twice from Hussein, twice from the Saudis, once from Mubarak, all explaining how they had phone conversations, meetings promises etc. etc. They have, he says affectionately, a wonderful capacity for fantasy but should not be believed. The truth is that Saddam simply deceived them. He told them he wanted only his claims in Kuwait, but then thought he could get away by taking the whole of Kuwait.

DOUGLAS HURD
House of Commons, 16 January 1991

As it turned out, seven hours before the war began.

DH was very relaxed. Feet up on the table, confiding, cool, amiable, rather jokey. As always, exuding as much detachment as engagement in equal measure.

He found himself more optimistic. As the generals got more cautious, he got more confident. He thought they would not get bogged down, and had no doubt at all about the victory. But he was aware of the slightly risky aspect of such confidence.

Believes Saddam is likely to attack Israel, when the combat has got going. Israel's response depends on how bad the damage is. Will the missiles land in the sea or will there be casualties? Israel, however, will be targeting western Iraq, and will not become part of the operation to recover Kuwait.

Welcomes French promise, today, to fight. Vitally important that this should be not just an Anglo-American war with Arab trimmings, but a European effort. All the turmoil they have caused in the last few days is to be understood as necessary to the French process. They have to see themselves as *not* responding to the US or doing anything under US leadership. Also, we have to remember that Mitterrand has problems at home, in his party and the country. But there remains the problem of how, exactly, France decides to use its force. We will see.

DH does not understand exactly what the French were up to this week. When Major saw Mitterrand it was obvious something was up, but he couldn't tell what. In Brussels, meanwhile, the French junior foreign minister (she) was putting her name without reserve to a EC statement saying that no negotiation was possible. If the French had let us know earlier, we could have done something with it. Also, we had difficulty getting the US even to make a statement, Washington was so furious. The French, however, were being very cynical. They knew perfectly well that they would get nowhere. Perez de Cuellar[1] had shown that. They just wanted to be seen to be doing something, for their own mysterious purposes.

It should also be remembered that Paris–Washington relations are thoroughly bad anyway. Great hard feeling over GATT especially.

There will be a lot of bombing. (DH does not dissent from my suggestion – ex Clark – that it will be four days or more before we can tell

---

1 Javier Perez de Cuellar: retired Peruvian diplomat; UN Secretary General 1982–91.

whether it will be a short or a long war. Depends on how we smash their communications, their supplies etc. And then how the Iraqis fight. Some Arabs think the Iraqi soldiers will cut and run. If they dig in and fight, minefields will be a problem, as in the Falklands . . .

The other perils of a long war will be: casualties, disintegration of Arab support for the coalition, the peace movement especially in the US Congress. (He mentioned them in that order.) He did not mention the markets until I did.

A very difficult problem is what you do if you get all of Kuwait but Iraq is still defiant. Do you chase them all the way into Iraq? Do we have to occupy Baghdad? He made an analogy with the North-West Frontier, when people there said there was just one more tribe around the corner who needed to be tamed.

There was no evidence of Saddam being vulnerable to internal coup. Mubarak said that even if he went, someone just as terrible would take over.

Kuwait might be 'flattened', as the sheikh said and Healey made much of. But Kuwait City wasn't like London, didn't have ancient buildings in it etc. It was a new city built for people to make money. The romance of Kuwait lay in the desert falcons etc. etc. Therefore DH could see what the sheikh meant when he said that, even if KC was flattened, he didn't mind as long as it was returned to its owners.

Gassing is the only aspect I really fear. Even though Saddam would be mad to use it, he might do. The nuclear response? DH noted that we were bound by undertakings under the Non-Proliferation Treaty not to use nukes against a non-nuke state (he has testified today before the foreign affairs committee). The rules of common sense also counselled against it. If it was discussed it was at tea-room level. But gas would release you from the restraints of targeting. The proportionality issue would change. He thought there would be no chemical strike-back by the US.

It is essential to have a post-war plan. But the locals are not helpful. He was in Bahrain, where the sultan (emir?) told him that his big idea was for the British to go on protecting Bahrain indefinitely. He was in Oman, where the head man said that his big idea was that people who opposed you were your enemies, and people who backed you were your friends.

CHRIS PATTEN
Conservative Central Office, 8 January 1991

In his large office, where he looks overweight but jovial, and is still suffering from the culture-shock of no longer having a department of efficient civil servants below him. At the DoE, when you decided something, there were people who would by and large act it out. Here there is no such system. Just one or two good people, especially John Cope as a kind of executive MD. He expects one or two exemplary sackings, but no more. More worrying is money. Costs £10 million a year to run. Massive debts. Money-raising separate from spending: chairman is only tangentially in charge. But he expects to be spending a fair amount of time on it.

HISTORY   His overall line is that he is not very interested in elaborately denying that there was a conspiracy. His position is simple. He wanted her to go, and when the moment arrived he helped to persuade her. But if it was a conspiracy, it was a rum version of one.

'What if . . .' discussions were taking place, bubbling along through the autumn. People were aware of the poll position, knew the party's weakness, knew she had been there a long time, knew there could be a leadership contest again. So everyone was what-ifing . . . with Douglas Hurd a notable exception. He was very reluctant to get involved.

On the Monday and Tuesday of the final week (i.e. 19 and 20 November), there was a swelling concern that if she only just won on Ballot 1, or if she didn't win enough at all, we should have a clear idea who would be the most likely person to beat MH. Also we had to decide whether one or two candidates would be better to run against him. There was a half-formed decision to have a meeting on Tuesday evening, after Ballot 1, to discuss whether Hurd or Major would be the best one to run against MH.

That meeting never got further than being an idea. Because during the Thursday evening, several people, CP included, realized that there couldn't possibly be only one candidate. That would have looked far too like the Cabinet candidate against the parliamentary party candidate (Heseltine). Simply not on.

One of Lawson's big pitches was the poll tax. Wittering on about it. Yet his own role in all that was bad. It is true that the Treasury alone seriously opposed the poll tax at the start. But it is also true that Lawson and the Treasury always fought attempts to mitigate its political disasters. The worst sort of Treasury argumentation, plus Lawson pulling rank and generally obstructing. For example, when CP came to the DoE, they devised what he calls a sensible scheme to cut the effect on the poor, by proposing that no one should be more than £2 a week worse off (in year 1?). This would have cost about £1.5 billion. In the end, got £300 million. An utter insensitivity to the politics of it all. CP had a meeting with MT about it – the only unminuted meeting with her he ever had. He made his pitch, but got nowhere.

Poll tax, of course, is a voracious monster . . .

AFTERMATH It is amazing to see how the party has taken it all in. The waters have been allowed to close peacefully over the grave. About 30 MPs were in some trouble. Only one or two – Townsend, Cormack[1] – are in trouble still. It is significant that the only problem we have here, on the constituency front, is Cheltenham and the racists.[2] Nothing to do with backing MH.

This is obviously easier because Major won. Would have been different under MH. There were many people who, having cut the throat of the ruler, happily saw the blood offering drip on her son and heir.

It is amazing how different government is when you are able to have rational discussions. A prime minster who rings up, asks sensible questions, and listens to your answers. A climate in which there are no givens, no off-limit areas, few sensibilities in Downing Street that have to be taken account of. The other day we had a good discussion around the fireside at No. 10 about the poll tax. MH led off. We all talked. JM summed up. All very different.

Major, CP thinks, is being too cautious in his attitude about how much to emphasize continuity and how much change. JM is desperately keen to see it as a seamless takeover. He has taken up some good issues, and his caution may be right. But the polls say that the change issues are much better for us than the stay-put issues.

He still expects a sticky period, perhaps encouraged by ongoing trouble from the Thatcherite *arditi*. The Johnsons (Paul and Frank), Worsthorne, Wyatt et al.[3] I discount these, but CP says they can stir up

---

1 Sir Cyril Townsend: former personal assistant to Edward Heath; Conservative MP for Bexleyheath 1974–97; director of the Council for the Advancement of British–Arab Understanding 1995–2002. Sir Patrick Cormack: Conservative MP for Cannock 1970–74, for Staffordshire South-West 1974–83, for Staffordshire South since 1983; has been described as a 'Heathite' and a Thatcher rebel.
2 John Taylor, barrister, broadcaster and at the time special adviser to the Home Secretary, later Baron Taylor of Warwick, was Conservative candidate for Cheltenham in the 1992 election. He was of West Indian descent, and the Conservative campaign was marred by racist comments from party members. The seat was won by Nigel Jones for the Liberal Democrats.
3 Paul Johnson: historian, columnist, former editor of the *New Statesman*, whose political views had swung to the right. Sir Peregrine Worsthorne: editor of the *Sunday Telegraph* 1986–9 and of its comment section 1989–91. Woodrow Wyatt: Labour MP for Aston Birmingham for 1945–55, for Bosworth 1959–70; columnist, author, diarist, chairman of the Horserace Totalizator Board 1976–97, and yet another left-wing journalist who became an outspoken admirer of Mrs Thatcher; later Baron Wyatt of Weeford.

trouble. There will certainly be a period when people start saying we should not have got rid of her, and that the poll tax is still here, and that nothing has changed. This will perhaps lead to another flowering of conspiracy theorists, and more trouble brewing.

He also notes, by the way, that McAlpine has transferred his allegiance entirely to the Thatcher Foundation.[1] And that there are people who do believe that she can come back, and are feeding her in this.

Heseltine is much enjoying his return to government. He talks too much, but he is on the team. It is amazing to watch one's successor running one's old department. MH, as before, takes no boxes home. It is incredible. Patten used to take three or four a night. It must mean that he delegates a lot. But it is still quite incomprehensible. Major has given him a free hand on the inner cities, and we can expect to see him making a lot of noise about that soon. Good. He wanted DTI, Major wanted him at the Home Office. DoE a good trade-off: CP said (to me) he could not go back to the HC yet again to say there would be another review. But he won't care about the global environment, 'which is what kept me sane'. He will care about the built environment, which he owns some of.

ELECTION It is a problem. Keeping ready for an early one but preparing for a late one. Also, the Gulf makes all domestic bets unreal. Can make a case for early. If MH had won, he would have had to go early in order to assert control over the party. This not JM's problem. The Gulf might make it attractive, and inflation will be coming down. But CP argues out for me the case for 1992. Says that JM could not be accused of hanging on to power. Says that JM will want to go after having achieved something. Says that the boxed-in argument is not very strong. After all, most countries have fixed terms. You just get ready for an election on an appointed day. Further, to go early might look opportunistic. Plainly CP will be a big influence on all this, and is already turning the conventional wisdom around.

SIR GEOFFREY HOWE
House of Commons, 7 February 1991

RESIGNATION SPEECH 'I didn't want it to be a damp squib' was his reply to my asking whether he foresaw where it would lead. He was riled by the fact that, when he resigned, many people but most of all MT said it was nothing, that it was all about tone and style, when it

---

1 Provides a website – 'the largest contemporary history site of its kind'.

absolutely wasn't. He wanted it to be seen for what it was. He hoped the speech would have an impact on how the government performed, but he wasn't optimistic. After all, very little else had: e.g. the Meyer challenge in 1989, the Lawson resignation ditto. Each should have warned MT; neither did so. So GH did not think it would have the explosive results it did have.

Looking back, he still finds her conduct entirely at fault and her demise likewise. He positively erupted with passion when he remarked that NL, GH and MT had been, with KJ, the real architects of the economic policy. They had done it together. From the start, these were the real allies. The trouble really was that, from the start, she was unwilling to discuss with us any aspect of exchange rate policy and its relationship with the EC, ERM etc. This was her big blind spot. GH said that he thinks that if she had not been in government in 1971–2, she would have been in the Turton and Walker-Smith camp opposing Heath's entry to the EC.[1]

DOUGLAS HURD
Foreign Office, 21 February 1991

The day Saddam makes a TV appearance after the Soviet plan. Sounds as though he was ranting hopelessly. DH says he rather thought, as soon as it was a matter not of Aziz[2] in Moscow but Saddam on TV, that it would go badly.

I suggest that this Iraqi rejection rather lets the coalition off an awkward hook. The Soviet Union plan could have been tricky. DH denies this. Says that if Saddam had begun to pull out, he would have had to talk 'to us' about the ancillary conditions. He would have been let go with his tanks, but he would have had to do something about the PoWs, who are a major concern. Iranians are still held in their thousands, says Francis Cornish [FCO news chief]. But he could once again have secured something by quitting. He would not have been attacked by us. But he has again made the wrong decision.

Iran is not being unhelpful. Iran and Moscow are both trying to maximize their situation in the post-war Gulf. But Iran's action over the air force shows that it still has credibility in Baghdad. Note that Iran has

1 Robert (Robin) Turton: Conservative MP for Thirsk and Malton 1929–74; Minister of Health 1955–7; later Baron Tranmire of Upsall in the North Riding of Yorkshire. Derek Walker-Smith QC: Conservative MP for Hertford 1945–55, for East Hertfordshire 1955–83; Minister of Health 1957–60.

2 Tariq Aziz: Iraqi politician, close to Saddam Hussein; foreign minister 1983–91; deputy prime minister 1979–2003; sent to Soviet Union by the Iraqi leadership in February 1991 to discuss a potential political settlement with Mikhail Gorbachev.

insisted time after time that the Kuwaitis must not give up an inch of territory. Absolutely clear that this would be bad regionally (i.e. for Iran).

If the land war starts, which it will do soon, it should be very fierce but short. Days rather than weeks. The only caveat was chemical and its effects. We know we have interdicted a lot of his supplies, but his people at the front may be ordered to loose off whatever they have got. Apart from that, should not be long – so I am told by the military. But Schwarz-kopf was being too optimistic when he said that the Iraq army was half destroyed, or some such.

About the aftermath, DH was remarkably agnostic. Emphasizes how messy it is sure to be, whether by war or diplomacy. Nothing clear or clean about it. But for a short time there will be something we can call victory. He says that the Americans are agnostic too. It depends entirely on what happens. Bush, he insists, has no desire for a Pax Americana. The last thing he wants to do is sit in Baghdad deciding what sort of government it should be, and being sniped at by the entire Arab world. But the rest of the neighbours are deeply anxious that Saddam should not retain his military strength. There might be a coup, DH muses. Equally, SH might quit Kuwait but still be an aggressor with his radio. He might still trumpet the S. Arab cause, bidding for heroism. We just cannot tell.

ARAB–ISRAEL   DH is not at all optimistic. He thinks that once you have got the process in place, any deal is possible to sketch. But getting the process started is what has defeated everyone for so long. Many ideas about how Italy favours a massive thirty-five-nation conference. France favours something much tighter. The Soviet Union favours the Security Council five. But whichever of these ideas you use, it will be useless if you don't get Israel: and useless if you don't get a Palestinian representation which can speak for itself and be listened to by Israel. The PLO is weakened by all this. The Gulf states want nothing to do with Arafat, who has let them down. Jordan? DH thinks making Jordan the Palestinian home would satisfy no one, least of all the Palestinians. It should be possible to reach a territorial agreement, in which the Palestinians agree not to be armed, to pursue their statehood by peaceful means. Jerusalem would have to be unique. Unique in the world. Protected from each side by some special mechanism. But none of this makes much sense until you have a process going.

ELECTION   DH says he is not an early-election man, in his bones. They had a very depressing economic report this morning in Cabinet. But he has not looked at the figures, and the whole thing is a long way from his preoccupations.

CHRIS PATTEN
Conservative Central Office, 18 April 1991

POLL TAX This was the day of the final Cabinet meeting to settle the alternative. He thinks they have come up with an excellent scheme which, with great simplicity, meets most of the points. It will be a property tax, with a rebate for single people. This meets the good point about the PT. There will be banding to deal with the discrepancy in property values between north and south. One virtue of this scheme is that it will mean one bill, not lots of supplements. It is not son of poll tax. It is grandson of rates. It is definitely the end of the poll tax.

He claimed there had not been a great deal of Cabinet trouble. Said he would keep the arguments of the PT ultras for his memoirs. But the Scots liked it because they hated the rates.

Waldegrave, the veteran of the poll tax, is amazed at the speed we have progressed at. The PT took far longer to think up.

On centralization, CP says that selling council houses was decent, so was making schools responsible for their budgets, so are the new planning laws making district councils decide instead of foisting all the unpopular decisions on the DoE. The opt-out schools in his constituency do not complain about the heavy hand of Whitehall. On the contrary they are amazed to get the cheque in the post for money the local authority spent on admin. One school got £250,000 under this heading, and said they would need to employ one more part-time secretary, the rest could be spent on books and labs.

He agrees the capping means central control. Capping has to stay because of the macro effects of local-government spending. But note how effective the regime is. Not a single Labour County Council is capped this year, because they have taken note of capping. Two Tory councils, both of which are backing off.

Note, however, how much of the source of all this lay with the Thatcher government. GH and NL reduced the rate support grant every year. This threw more burden on local authorities to collect money. It was done, in theory, to make local authorities more accountable, their spending money more visible: but in practice to assist in reducing income tax. Further, NL then scuppered the poll tax in year 1 by giving an impossibly mean grant.

All in all, CP thinks they have done well finally to find a way of getting rid of the consequences of all these great errors by the Thatcher government.

THE RIGHT   Euro is one obsession. The reason why they have been so sneering about the Kurds is because they see it as a danger signal that the EEC has come together here.

Another obsession is Patten himself, the guru to Major playing (CP ironically reflects) the role of Tebbit to Thatcher. They think he is filling Major's empty head with lots of stuff about the social market. To which he replies, 'We do not make enough of our social record. The last time social spending went down as a proportion of GNP was in 1976. It is the same now as in 1979, with GNP having massively grown. Why not develop our ideas about choice and better provision as a genuine social policy we are proud of?'

Tebbit is the only man whom Major is worried about. He is the only one who could marshal some troops. So Major has taken a lot of massaging care to keep Tebbit sweet. Which he has been.

THATCHER HERSELF   CP has seen her twice. Once, after returning from Reagan's eightieth, she was on a high. The second time she was in terrible shape. She has suffered multiple bereavement. It doesn't matter a damn whether she stands for Parliament or not. Not the slightest interest. Her clout comes from herself, not where she is sitting.

LABOUR/ELECTION   Labour cannot do better than buggeration, i.e. screw it up for anyone else. Cannot win an overall majority.

Two things noticeable from the polls. First, Labour's lead in education and health immediately dropped when Major took over. Second, Labour is still very, very vulnerable on the trade-union issue. The thought of the country being run by the unions still scares people. Also, Kinnock still reckoned not up to it in the polls.

The gloss is coming off John Smith in the City.

JOHN MAJOR   The Kurds plus the poll tax should get rid of the dithering image. This should be a better week coming up! But note what he has done. Has settled Europe policy into far better mode, has knocked points off the Labour lead, has done sensible thing on mortgages. This hardly the work of an indecisive man.

What he needs is a period when people stop digging up the rose bush to look at the roots. Needs to settle in and become part of the furniture. Needs to be seen around being treated as prime minister. This is one reason for having a later election, as is the need to expose Labour's policy for what it is.

He is terribly lacking in confidence in himself, especially all the social things. When CP went to lunch at Chequers, he was sitting opposite

Major, who upset a plate of biscuits. He looked up at Chris with the expression of a man mortified to have committed a solecism.

With the probing of his background he is again far too sensitive. He should be more able to present himself as someone who has achieved amazing things. Over the probing of his residences when he was a Lambeth councillor, CP suggested he should toss it off by saying at the age of 25 who was always able to remember where they slept every night? Major was horrified at this very good idea.

Perhaps one of his problems, CP says, is that he has no one nasty around him. Not a single one. Does he need a bovver boy?

Note his exceptional ease of working with women. Hogg, Chaplin.[1] Likes it not, it seems, in a sexy way. But like Keith Joseph, who also especially liked women.

He is amazingly, irreducibly untheatrical. He could never do what MT did in Russia in 1987. She was, at her best, a megastar. He would never begin to do that kind of thing. Likewise he has a tin ear. The third leader running. Oh dear. No sense of language.

CP was tremendously vigorous and confident. Plainly he fits into his job with elan and style. Shows himself to be quite brutal enough. A man firmly focused on his main chance, which, for him, is winning with Major. Quite assured enough of his own judgement. Probably losing that fastidiousness of the younger man which it is essential to do at the top. Without, however, descending anywhere near being a shit. Above all, unrepentant about the end of Maggie and the way this saved the party.

RAYMOND SEITZ
Lunch, the US embassy, 7 May 1991

This is Ray's first engagement on becoming US ambassador. He arrived here last Friday, in time for the Falklands service in Glasgow. He asks Peter Jenkins [*The Independent*] Charles Moore [*Daily Telegraph*] Robin Oakley [*The Times*] and self to lunch, together with the press attaché, Sam Sheppard. A thoroughly agreeable occasion. Some insights on . . .

THE THATCHER FINALE   P. Jenkins says that in Paris MT was meant to say that she was a candidate for the second ballot but would be returning to London to consult her colleagues. But she didn't fulfil

---

1 Sarah Hogg, Baroness Hogg of Kettlethorpe: journalist for *The Times*, *The Economist* and Channel 4 News; head of policy unit for prime minister John Major. She is also Viscountess Hailsham, married to Douglas Hogg. Judith Chaplin: private secretary and personal assistant to John Major as Chancellor and then as prime minister; Conservative MP for Newbury from 1992 until her death in 1993.

the deal that had been done. She said she was a candidate (see what she actually said), but omitted to say that she would consult. This put Hurd in a difficult position. He was forced to endorse her on screen, as it were. Could not do anything else given her failure to make good on the deal.

P. Jenkins also says that it is not completely known what the purpose of her seeing the Cabinet individually was. She thought it was so that she could beat them into submission one by one, extracting loyalty pledges. Others thought that it was a better way of getting her to submit. Wakeham, however, seems to have been the undisputed author of the scheme.

When she came back from Paris, the first to call on her (Jenkins again) were the team of MacGregor, Renton,[1] Baker, Onslow[2] (Plus?? Wakeham). They were meant to give her the bad news, more or less. But she sailed in and took over the meeting, which ended with Baker going out and saying his piece about her carrying on. (Baker did not distinguish himself at all.)

When I mentioned my story about her saying what she said at Versailles, Robin Oakley said it was quite possible. She would say, on this as on other things, one thing one minute and one thing another.

Moore maintains it was important that Major got a head start. Certainly his team was operating far quicker than others. It mattered because his presence and activity instantly gave the people who were guilty about getting rid of MT something to hold on to. It made him real. (Don't forget, per HY, that he was until a very late moment almost an unconsidered candidate, certainly one not mentioned much in the press.)

P. Jenkins says that Wakeham has told him a key event was the polls on the Friday showing Major ahead of MH. Wakeham indicated that these polls had been rigged. He said this joshingly, but the story is about. However, all those here present agreed that they could not have been rigged.

There is still much agnosticism about whether MT will run again. She is dithering frantically. Those who advise are evidently Peter Morrison and 'people like Gerald Howarth' (says Oakley).[3] It is mainly the anti-Euro brigade who want her to stand. They even say that if she goes to the House of Lords they will still find a way to get her back again, if

1 Timothy 'Tim' Renton: Conservative MP for Mid-Sussex 1974–97; chief whip 1989–90; arts minister 1990–92; later Baron Renton of Mount Harry.
2 Cranley Onslow: Conservative MP for Woking 1964–97, Minister of State at the Foreign Office 1982–3. As chair of the Tory backbenchers' 1922 Committee 1984–92, he had the unenviable task of telling Thatcher that many MPs wanted a wider choice of candidates, after she had failed to win conclusively in the first round, following Heseltine's leadership challenge. Later, Lord Onslow of Woking.
3 Peter Morrison, later Sir Peter Morrison: Conservative MP for Chester 1974–92; leader of Thatcher's campaign team in the 1990 Conservative leadership election. Gerald Howarth: Conservative MP for Cannock and Burntwood 1983–92, for Aldershot since 1997; Minister of State at the Department of the Environment 1990–91; PPS to Mrs Thatcher December 1991–April 1992; shadow defence minister since 1999.

necessary! Oakley thinks that if the general election is delayed until October, she 'may' stand down.

NORMAN LAMONT
The Guardian, 25 June 1991

Said he was at first 'very alarmed' by what MT said in the US.[1] But is now not so sure. Thinks that the sight of Heath and Thatcher brawling may help the Major approach as being reasonable etc. The party, he thinks, is starting to turn against her. His party workers are talking to him about how she should shut up.

Sees significance in a poll showing that 55 per cent prefer Major's approach to Thatcher's on Europe.

Claims that he saw Major as the next leader several months before MT quit: at which time he also decided that MT would not be fighting the next election as Tory leader.

Says that Major is deeply interested in how to run the health service, and schools. Very interested in management details and theories, 'which I must confess I find boring', i.e. Major really does care about the things that must now form our main agenda.

Has always been a late-election man, not just because of the economy, but because Major needs time to establish himself. Emphasizes what an extraordinary shift it has been for Major, and insists that any man would need time to establish himself. Thinks he will emerge as being just as decent as Kinnock, while a lot more intelligent.

He is plainly much preoccupied by the election, the campaign etc. In chat, I make a speech about it being impossible to call, and therefore heavily dependent on the campaign, which only small events could shift. And Major has no record as a campaigner – did not even appear at a press conference last time, as far as I can recall.

What will be the issues, he asks? Will Europe? We agree that the bipartisan line makes this unlikely. It will be about exhaustion, competence, time-for-a-change etc. Swing of the pendulum? They hope they have met that with Major. (Incidentally, per HY, although it may be true that the tide – cf. Patten – is changing Labourwards, towards their issues, this does not mean that the Tories have to fight on Tory ground. They

---

1 In a speech in the US, Mrs Thatcher implicitly embarrassed her successor when she criticized the decision to join the European Exchange Rate Mechanism and called for a transatlantic economic community. She was also the subject of a bitter attack from her predecessor Edward Heath. In a 20 June column headed 'Politics of the playground', HY remarked that it was hard to say which of the two former prime ministers 'displayed the more flouncing egotism'.

have no choice but to go the way they are going . . . Therefore Thatcher, Tebbit etc. are bad counsellors.)

On the economy, he expresses a desire to get away for two months. Looking at the tea-leaves gets maddening. Especially since he cannot do much, except on interest rates.

HIMSELF   Still a fat little man, but a hard fat man rather than a soft fat man. Careful, agreeable, disarming in a way. Easily thrown, however, by a question away from the script from Will Hutton [economics editor], to do with lowering the PSBR by manipulating Bank of England reserves. Norman floundered.

Europe – a divisive issue for decades – slowly became even more explosive as member states began to discuss their future together. The decisions slowly being taken, and culminating in the 1992 Maastricht Treaty, were to dominate political debate for years to come.

CHRIS PATTEN
House of Commons, 23 July 1991

MAJOR   Has become more confident over time. CP discounts the retirement of MT as much of a factor. But the EC summits and the G7 have shown him that he is as good as the next man, and actually reads his briefs rather better than the older sweats. He is more at home with the hard ecu[1] than either Kohl or Mitterrand.

The Cabinet is a quite different place from before. Take today. We had three or four really difficult issues with sharp divisions. (It was, I think, the day of the first public-spending talks.) They were dealt with over three hours. Everyone spoke who wanted to; there was in each case a deal done with reasonable tranquillity. In general, we are able to raise all the issues. We have the ability to disagree without the lid blowing off.

Major is good at getting other people to do some of the work. E.g. put Macgregor in charge of getting the Treasury and DoE agreed on the local-government settlement. Had a clear strategy for keeping the Treasury onside.

But politicians get on a roll. He has been on a roll for a few weeks. Helped by G7 etc., but also by the polls, which show us creeping back. To have made a poll recovery with recession at its bottom is pretty good.

1   The European currency unit, or ecu, was a convenient form of accounting used by both Brussels commissioners and European finance ministers long before European Monetary Union delivered the euro as a banknote.

ELECTION   Polls are to be believed. The feel-good factor was down to minus three (check) but is now going back up. Major is 25 points ahead of Kinnock (cf. Wilson 25 points ahead of Macmillan in 1963). Robert Waller [research director for Harris, the polling organization] suggests that the polls overestimate the Labour support by 5 per cent, on the grounds that there are seats where people will not vote Labour but Lib Dem. CP takes little account of this gloss.

So why not autumn, with everything going so well. Two reasons, he says, 'to be honest'. One: don't want Labour to be able to say we are running away when we don't have one. Two: unless the polls show a startling Tory lead in September, we believe we can do better in spring '92.

Believes Labour frailties are now once again being exposed. They had it rather good in the early summer. Now Kinnock can see it slipping away again.

Mandelson[1] theory of politics is all very well if the tide is running with you. Very skilful. They will fight a slick campaign. But when things get rough and the questions keep coming, what does Mandelson have to say?

CAMPAIGN   We will fight on two issues. First, leadership. Second, economic competence. The two are subsumed in the question, Would you trust NK with the economy more than you would trust JM with the NHS?

Plainly they feel Major is a big hit. His polling figures, especially among women, are amazing. He is seen as honest, above all. And he will have a lot of achievement under his belt. The poll tax, the Gulf war, the end of recession, defence cuts grappled with, the Citizen's Charter[2] (which, by the way, CP characterizes as having been beefed up from a feeble start rather than vice versa – thanks to JM).

EUROPE   He sees as an asset not a disadvantage. Better to go after Maastricht[3] than before. Put the Maastricht deal in the manifesto and chalk it up as a credit. The deal is available. Thinks EMU will be no real problem, whether it is called the Delors Compromise or the Major

---

1 Peter Mandelson: Labour MP for Hartlepool 1992–2004. One of the architects of New Labour and a close ally of Tony Blair, who made him Secretary of State for Trade and Industry in 1998. Forced to resign six months later after he was revealed to have taken a secret loan of £373,000 from his ministerial colleague Geoffrey Robinson. Returned as Secretary of State for Northern Ireland 1999–2001, but was forced to resign a second time, after allegations of misconduct over the passport application of controversial Indian businessman Srichand Hinduja. (An independent inquiry exonerated him.) European commissioner for trade 2004–8. Gordon Brown brought him back to the UK as Business Secretary in October 2008.

2 The Citizen's Charter, involving new ways to measure public services, was John Major's big idea, introduced in July 1991. It introduced league tables for schools and waiting-time limits for NHS patients, among other reforms.

3 Maastricht: The 1992 treaty signed in the Dutch town of Maastricht confirmed an 'ever closer' approach to political union, amended previous treaties, and changed the name of the Community to the European Union.

Conditions. It will leave the thing open for the future. The political side will be harder, because we have few cards to play. We do want much tougher compliance. But as for the rest, we are the negative ones. Don't want more majority voting [QMV], don't want co-decision-making for the Parliament. But Mitterrand doesn't either. So there is the making of an alliance with the French on politics and the Germans on EMU. They really fancy themselves as negotiators.

Many MPs don't know the different between EMU and ecu. The party as a whole will accept whatever Major comes up with. No doubt about that. Honest Major and that nice Mr Hurd.

The Thatcherites on this add up to perhaps twelve people or less. What will the lady do? Be interesting to see. She was much attacked inside the party for her outburst in June. The two old dinosaurs made it better for Major.

BATH   No problem, says CP defiantly. A local poll last week gave him 45 per cent. They are bitterly anti-Thatcher, so Major will win it for Chris. The SDP got £60,000 from Sainsbury to fight Bath last time, and still didn't win with a good candidate. This time, the then SDP agent, a hotshot, has come to CP looking for a job. Perhaps the eighties generation who flirted with the SDP and Owen are coming back to base . . .

1992

6 January	Bosnian Serbs declare their own republic.
15 January	Croatia and Slovenia quit the Socialist Federal Republic of Yugoslavia.
7 February	The Maastricht Treaty marks the founding of the European Union.
5 April	The Bosnian assembly declares independence from Yugoslavia; Serb troops begin the siege of Sarajevo.
9 April	The Conservatives win the general election with a reduced majority of 21 seats.
13 April	Labour leader Neil Kinnock announces that he will stand down.
22 June	Skeletons exhumed at Ekaterinburg are identified as Tsar Nicholas II and his wife, Alexandra.
18 July	John Smith is elected leader of the Labour Party.
26 August	Chancellor Norman Lamont spends £300 million in support of sterling, and vows to stay in the European Exchange Rate Mechanism.
16 September	The British pound is forced out of the European Exchange Rate Mechanism in the Black Wednesday monetary crisis (as is the Italian lira).
3 November	Bill Clinton of Arkansas defeats George H. W. Bush in the US presidential elections.
11 November	The Church of England votes to allow women priests.
20 November	Fire damages Windsor Castle: the Queen later declares 1992 an 'annus horribilis'.
9 December	The Prime Minister announces the separation of Prince Charles and Princess Diana.
Deaths	Isaac Asimov; Francis Bacon; Menachem Begin, former prime minister of Israel; Willy Brandt, former chancellor of Germany; John Cage; Marlene Dietrich; Benny Hill; Olivier Messaien; Satyajit Ray

JOHN GUMMER
Agriculture, Fisheries and Food, 9 January 1992

Met me late because he had 'just solved the Russian meat problem': getting the Russians to accept British beef they suspected of being contaminated.

We moved, hastily, on to the EC. Gummer has always been a passionate Euro, always seen himself 'as a European and not an American'. But he insists that the British people as a whole remain sceptical. He finds in his constituency or at places he goes that he is often alone in the room in favouring the single currency and all that. Sees the anti-Euro stance of Brits as still very deep, based on a different view of their nation.

He asserts that there are two things on which Britain differs from any other EC country. First, it is the only parliamentary democracy, 'in the true sense'. Second, it is alone in ministerial submission to the rule of law. He says that the French agriculture minister cannot be taken to court in the way the British minister can. These two principles are the ones Major has preserved at Maastricht.

He sees the single currency emerging into public acceptance by long use: the ERM etc. He insists that the CAP has been reformed thanks to British work and pressure.

Historically he regards Attlee and Eden as the two worst post-war prime ministers, because of their European attitude. Attlee was to blame for not entering the ECSC[1] (and also for creating the welfare state before he produced the wealth-producing society). Eden was to blame for the missed opportunity in the fifties.

ELECTION He thinks the Tories will win. Has put his prediction of the majority in a sealed envelope three months ago. All he would vouchsafe about this was that it would be somewhat smaller than the present majority. But it would still be quite enough. Why the optimism? Because Labour should be far further ahead in the polls than they are. He asserts that the poll tax will not matter much because the bills will be so far down: and that the health service 'has been peaked satisfactorily early'.

He rushed off, despite starting so late with me, to a meeting with Heseltine about farming and the environment. In lordly style he affected to say to his staff that he would not be able to go, but this was an act for my benefit, compensated for by giving me a lift in his car and instructing

---

1 Formally established in 1951, the European Coal and Steel Community was the first of the European communities and the foundation stone of the European Economic Community, later the European Union.

his driver to take me where I wanted to go. All the same, he is bright, winning and, as a source, neglected.

CHRIS PATTEN
Lunch, Brown's Hotel, 28 January 1992

We talk about what will happen when they have won. He says he will do so, but only by breaking a vow not to count chickens. Major keeps trying to get him to talk about jobs etc. afterwards, and he declines to do so. So this is a kind of dry run . . .

It will be, he says, a traditional government – if anything can be called traditional after so many years of Thatcher. It will be traditional in methods. Although it is possible to overdo JM's 'Cabinet' style and forget that in the end he is a prime minister who can very largely get his way – with the formidable Mrs Hogg to make sure he does so – the fact is that at the big moments he has been careful to bring everyone along, make them feel they've had their say etc. These two moments were (a) the poll tax deal and (b) Maastricht. On the poll tax it may therefore have taken longer than it should, and given us a couple of weeks' bother in the middle. But all in all this is his style, and it pays off. It will presumably carry on.

The preoccupations will also be traditional. Getting down inflation will be the big idea – is there a bigger one? The nineties will resound less to the snap of the credit card or the checkout till. There will be less spending. The government will pursue the age-old effort to square the circle of a little bit more on spending and a little bit less on tax. All governments will have to do this. Labour would be less good at it than we would be, because their spending commitments really are greater. We are already having a lot of problems because of the ERM. It simply reduces your flexibility. When did you last see a government not having a pre-election boom? All this will be as important for Labour – they are even more committed than we are to the single currency, which puts them in even more of a box. Apart from this, we shall have bits of social legislation to complete, the Citizen's Charter to keep going, the privatizations to complete. But overwhelmingly our business will be to keep inflation down. It will be a low-inflation decade.

EUROPE Britain has suffered no downside because of leaving the social chapter out at Maastricht. What will happen is simply that the social chapter will become a dead letter. German business has already said publicly that it will be asking its government to get more active in stopping this kind of thing happening. If the Brits can stop things, why can't the Germans?

Major now treads the international boards with great aplomb. He very much likes it. He has a lethal combination of great personal charm and being very well briefed. He will also, if he wins, have the great advantage of having won while so many others are being shown the door. Wider than Europe, we should expect him to play a big part in the world environment conference this year: he believes Britain should put a lot into it. He also takes the Commonwealth seriously, which meant that the last conference was far better than most others. In Europe, we will have an active presidency this year. Major is very well in with the Italians, having taken them seriously on the defence issue: gets on very well still with Kohl: gets on fairly well with Mitterrand, despite Maastricht – the bilateral went well.

CP has no doubt at all that the single currency will come. None whatever, he emphasized. The advantages and normality of the exchange-rate fix via the ERM will be seen to have only one logical outcome. But it will be a big project, very painful and difficult. How can Italy possibly measure up?

Broader than that, he believes that the great Europe debate will now revolve around enlargement. The Euro fans, people like Heath, will probably want to slow down the widening, arguing that the EC as it now is must consolidate. CP himself thinks there is no moral or political case for excluding the EFTAs [European Free Trade Association] and no ditto for denying to Hungary, Czecho etc. when they meet the economic terms, having the same entry privilege as Spain and Portugal. Therefore the debate will be all about this.

Pursuing the post-election scenario, we come to Scotland. He foresees some turmoil here. Says that it is impossible for them to change their position before the election: would look slippery, would split the Scottish Tory Party, would not add many votes. And for the moment they have to pretend that they are doing no thinking about it. Not many of them are, anyway. But Patten himself is. He thinks that Tory politics have changed since the 1970s. English Tories are no longer so wedded to the unchanging union. They hear from Scottish Tory MPs that the Scots will come to their senses once they experience a period of Labour government and they regard this as rather too high a price to pay for Scots to be taught a lesson. Therefore they look more benignly on the prospect of becoming a more English party: it would be a natural follow-on from MT's achievement in making the Conservative Party an English national party anyway. CP himself sees nothing wrong with a Scottish parliament. But it must be a real parliament, with legislative and tax-raising powers.

And the consequence of that must be that Scottish representation is lowered at Westminster – as was Ulster representation when Stormont existed. All this, as I point out to him, means that devolution etc. would swiftly change from being a Labour issue to a Tory issue – but at the price of the Tories becoming a still narrower-based party.

(Per HY: note how this, plus the boundary shifts depriving Labour of 20 seats next time, set the odds even further against there being a pure Labour government ever again if they don't win this time . . .)

ELECTION If Labour loses, he speculates on a revival of the left. They'll be able to say they've kept quiet for four years and look where it's got them. The Benn amendment to the economic resolution a couple of weeks ago: could have been the Bulgarian economic plan of three years ago. Thinks also they're certain to take on PR, and will probably do so during this campaign. Also says that Straw, Blair[1] etc. might well decide that politics was no longer a life for a sane man.

CAMPAIGN One thing you can be certain of is that we will not be talking about a fourth Conservative term, he said. Not once. It will be all about John Major's first election. To drive home the renewal they got in 1990, and escape the thirteen years of Tory rule stuff. The manifesto will contain some new things: not *very* new, but some little surprises which we have been talking about and getting the PM to agree.

JOBS Major absolutely hates sacking people – I'd forgotten he'd done it to anyone, but apparently there was a minor junior reshuffle. Patten's one contribution so far has been to say to JM that for the first five minutes after winning he is more powerful than he will ever be. He can do absolutely anything, and should remember it. In CP's opinion he needs to clear four or five people out in order to give himself the necessary space. This will hurt a lot of people, but he just has to face it. Hurd will stay, for a couple of years at least: as long as he wants to. There will certainly be a woman. Gillian Shephard[2] is the one Major knows best, and she had her chance as deputy chairman of the party: will she take it? CP seemed doubtful, and noted the improving form of V. Bottomley. When we got to Lamont, this seemed almost unbearably delicate ground

1 Jack Straw: president of the National Union of Students 1969–71; barrister; Labour MP for Blackburn since 1979; Labour NEC member 1970–82; Home Secretary 1997–2001; Foreign Secretary 2001–6; Leader of the House of Commons 2006–7; Lord Chancellor and Secretary of State for Justice since 2007. Anthony 'Tony' Blair: Barrister; Labour MP for Sedgefield 1983–2007; Shadow Cabinet 1988–97; leader of the Labour Party 1994–2007; prime minister 1997–2007; married to Cherie Booth QC.
2 Gillian Shephard: Conservative MP for South-West Norfolk 1987–2005; Secretary of State for Education and for Education and Employment 1994–7; later Baroness Shephard of Northwold.

but CP accepted my suggestion that Norman was not good enough. Baker will clearly be one of the four – but CP hinted that Hong Kong could be a *bonne bouche* (there could be others): wouldn't Ken look good in the plumes? From the feeling with which CP talked about the problems at the Home Office – police and prisons – I had the feeling that he might be heading that way, although Clarke seems a more obvious choice, with Patten at Treasury perhaps. (The key to Clarke is that he is anti-establishment – any establishment. And always gets his retaliation in first. This is why he did well under MT. KC is also the one man who CP felt, especially at the time of the Great Defenestration, he would go into the jungle with. A really straight guy.)

Of himself at CCO he said that it was just a job that had to be done. He didn't especially like it, but there it was. Likened himself to Mellor,[1] who had to spend his time concealing the fact that he could give you a fuller account of Beethoven's late quartets than anyone in government, and instead keep chopping public spending etc. Likewise, Patten might prefer giving the Disraeli lectures etc., but had to find other media through which to get the message across. But what he looked forward to was a big job in good company.

ROBIN COOK
Café Pelican, 12 February 1992

HUNG PARLIAMENT Now more likely. Remember, RC was predicting a hung parliament three years ago, which was partly why he took up PR. He was then thought to be wildly optimistic, however. He now thinks Labour will be the government, but probably without a majority – although from time to time he put in the caveat that majority was not impossible.

This hypothesis will involve the Liberals agreeing to support but not being in government. Even if they win some more seats, they will not have enough clout. Naturally Paddy Ashdown has to take the line he does about making PR an absolute condition: it helps him for the duration of the election. But at the end, will he let the Tories in? It is inconceivable. This will be happening after a night in which David Dimbleby[2] has been intoning about more and more Tory losses. Whatever the arithmetical outcome, the Tories will have been rejected. The Liberals would be torn

---

1 David Mellor: barrister, broadcaster; Conservative MP for Putney 1979–97; arts minister 1990; Chief Secretary to the Treasury 1990–92; National Heritage Secretary 1992.
2 David Dimbleby, presenter of the BBC topical television news programme *Question Time*, has served as 'anchor' for all BBC election-night coverage since 1979.

apart if PA let them stay in office. Labour would be rended apart by its supporters if it did anything whatever to let the government survive.

So if the Tories are merely the largest party, they will still have real problems: if they are not the largest party but can govern with the Irish they will have even more (per HY that is presumably a situation where PA would have to back Labour, come what may). If Labour and the LDs make a larger party than the Tories but still without a majority – that's where it gets very tricky indeed.

The Queen could be placed in a tricky situation even after the first election if defeat of a Tory minority government was delayed. It seems to be agreed that if Major couldn't get his Queen's Speech through, she would have to send for Kinnock. But suppose he got it through, but then couldn't get his first controversial legislation? Would she then be able to deny the PM his request for a dissolution? Actually, RC thinks the Queen's Speech itself could be delayed a month or more, whoever is head of the coalition.

There would certainly be no problem agreeing a programme with the LDs. The anti-Tory parties agree on a great deal already. The pensions, the CB,[1] something on education, the Scottish parliament etc. (he mentioned more). In this situation, moreover, don't assume that NK wants to do another 1974. He may or may not. But he worries – RC has had this at first hand – about the second result not going right. Therefore he will be more interested in a deal.

In such a situation, the left will be no problem. They will be desperate to keep the government going. They will be much more trouble if Labour has a majority of 30. The left are not what they were in 1975, when RC joined thirty-five of them to abstain on the government's spending programme. Not so numerous, not so rebellious, much less power locally.

PROPORTIONAL REPRESENTATION The Liberals will not get what they want. But they could well get an inquiry. Speaker's conference or something. However, PR will come by other means. It will begin with Scotland. To its great credit the Scottish Labour Party has voted for PR to the assembly, so that will be going through. We don't know when the HL reform will be happening, but that is PR as well. If the Europeans get their act together, we could have PR for Europe as well. Thus there will be much PR debate in the HC, and it will come to seem nonsensical that we have it for all these other places but not for the HC.

RC will depict it as a vote for stability. Hattersley always says it leads to instability: but that won't stand up if first past the post produces only

---

1 Child benefit. The 1992 Labour manifesto promised an increase; the Liberal Democrat manifesto promised childcare vouchers.

short-lived governments. There will be the added, powerful argument deriving from the Boundary Commission. This was designed by the Victorians to achieve an update on representative government by ensuring greater equality among constituencies. It is ironic that it should contribute to even greater unfairness when it allots twenty more seats to the Tories, which is what it will certainly do. This has some justification, in that it increases the seats in areas of growing population, of course. But its overall effect is terrible. And something Labour cannot ignore, because it reinforces the injustice of first past the post.

He sees PR, incidentally, also as a weapon against the tabloid press. A way of creating more plural politics . . .

SCOTLAND The policy on which Labour has spent as much time as any other. Much deep thought, culminating with the Scottish Convention.[1] However, there are massive unresolved problems, as far as I can see.

It does depend on an argument for the English regions. He despairs of how only Geordieland sees itself in regional terms. He therefore doesn't put much weight on this as a way of reaching a British solution.

He says that once the assembly is working, then it would be inappropriate for Scottish MPs to vote on English issues, such as health and education: and English MPs ditto. (He also said on TV last Friday that it would not be right for Scots to be ministers in these roles, which caused a hubbub.) He sees, therefore, a Westminster parliament which is sometimes a federal parliament – almost all finance would be federal, it emerges, with only a fraction of spending being raised by the assembly, and John Smith therefore being quite free to be Chancellor – and sometimes an English parliament.

If the Tories win and set up the assembly, RC would likely leave Westminster and go up there. He would like to be PM of the first Scotland. A great excitement to be in at the birth. But otherwise he would be torn. He would most like to be Home Secretary, because of all the constitutional stuff.

ELECTION He believes that the increase in the Liberal vote shown in the polls is coming from the Tories. This he sees as the crucial question. Last time it came from Labour; this time it will come from the Tories – and the Liberals will do much better on the day than in the polls, even if they don't crack 20 per cent.

He sees the Tory campaign as having failed. They threw everything in and it didn't shift the polls. They have played their main cards and it

---

1 The Scottish Constitutional Convention, an association of politicians, churches and social groups, was founded in 1988 and helped prepare the way for the establishment of a Scottish parliament in 1999.

hasn't worked. They do have the Budget coming up. But he finds even his cynicism outdistanced by the thought that they will take 1p off the standard rate. However, he sees that they might. This would be the only way to make a difference before 9 April. Raising the thresholds would only come through at the end of April. Therefore they may do it.

KINNOCK Will be a strong leader, a poor delegator. Will make full use of the massive centralization of the machine which MT effected, with No. 10 becoming so much more important. It is not in NK's nature to disperse such power. He has been good and unWilsonian about keeping people in their posts. Wilson always moved them if they looked like developing an independent power base. If NK *did* lose, which RC is seriously not contemplating, he would not survive a full parliament.

TORIES Note that Major, Patten, Waldegrave etc. etc have never served in an Opposition. This adds to their hubris. It also adds to the important case which says for the sake of democracy we need something other than a fourth-term government.

MURDOCH RC went to Wapping (secretly) yesterday. Saw Andrew Knight[1] (who got him there), Murdoch et al. He put to them a simple point. Why was it that with 60 per cent of the public anti-Tory there was only one Labour tabloid? *Today* was slightly different – it is targeting younger women, who have a great interest in the social agenda, therefore it is more Labour-leaning. Murdoch's reply was that it was a matter of principle!

DAVID OWEN
At the Rushdie meeting,[2] 14 February 1992

Who will win? Hard to say. But he thinks the British people, when they finally go into the voting booth, will ask themselves whether they really want to vote Major out and vote Kinnock in. On this basis, he implies, Kinnock will not win.

His own plans? Trying to decide whether he will 'wetly' sit it out, or

1 Andrew Knight: chairman of News International 1991–4 and has held a non-executive position since; editor of *The Economist* 1974–86 and masterminded Conrad Black's takeover of the Telegraph Group in 1986, becoming its CEO and editor-in-chief.
2 On the third anniversary of the Ayatollah Khomeini's fatwa against Salman Rushdie, 150 writers, artists and other public figures – including Martin Amis, Kazuo Ishiguro and Bob Geldof – met at the Stationer's Hall, London. The author of *The Satanic Verses* made an unannounced appearance. David Owen – married to the literary agent Deborah Owen – had just given up the leadership of the Social Democrats and would become EU co-chairman of the International Conference on former Yugoslavia 1992–5.

make a contribution. It seemed obvious to me that he will not want to be wet. But he claimed to find it a bit difficult. He said the thought of eighteen years of Tory rule really was a bit much: this said with a disarmingly honest grin. It is obvious he thinks extraordinarily well of Major. But then, he says, one or other of Major's people says something stupid and you remember what awful people he has around him.

On the other hand, he plainly has an irreversible contempt for Kinnock. Unfortunately, he said, there are some decisions when a prime minister does not have his civil servants around him, and his own judgement becomes paramount. Then Kinnock would be on his own, and his judgement is so bad (he implied and almost but not quite said) that the risk would be too great.

He also thinks that Labour 'has not changed far enough'. There's need for another push. He thinks their conversion to the market is not reliable. Defence he sees as less important, these days. For the next four or five years, he said, nothing serious is likely to happen. What really fires him is the spectre of the United States of Europe. This is what he would like to go on using his efforts to stop. He thinks Major has the right approach. When I suggest that Kinnock would do very little different, he claims to believe that this is the one area – 'oddly enough' – where he thinks Labour's conversion to the party of Europe is all too genuine. He thinks Labour's commendable internationalism now pushes it towards dreams of a great socialist Europe, with all the social democracies getting together. Therefore they are not to be trusted to preserve British independence.

All in all, he sounded very pleased with Major's government. He thought they had shaken off the 'thirteen years of Tory rule' albatross (which is where he came into politics in 1964) and that Major should be bolder in making this clear.

He said that what was really needed was a decent French party of the right. In a sense, he half-joked, he had great hopes in Le Pen[1] as a man who would keep the flag of French nationalism flying. But what France needed more was someone hot to replace Giscard and Chirac. France was the key to stopping a United States of Europe, driven forward by the Germans. He regarded the idea that Germany needed containing by a US of Europe as folly: they would not be contained, whatever the arrangements. They would simply dominate even more than their own territory.

---

1 Jean-Marie Le Pen: founded the extreme-right-wing Front National Party in France in 1972; campaigned for presidential office in 1974, 1988, 1999, 2002 and 2007.

DOUGLAS HURD
19 February 1992

He is swotting up for the election. Much time being spent at No. 10, into housing and the inner cities. It is a strange time, he thinks. Not a great deal happening, but everything about to happen. H volunteers that this really will be a horse race, so the media will get what they want – and what they invented the last two times. He knows this will be very close. Incredulous at Worcester's prediction of an 80-seat Tory majority.

RUSHDIE He thought he had played his hand badly. It was a big mistake to equate himself with Terry Waite, at any level. His freedom is not being curtailed in the same way, he is not so popular with the public, he is not in such bad shape. All this said, DH said he had to cast aside his prejudices and grapple with the fact that Rushdie was being threatened in a way and that this was not tolerable. However, to my direct question about giving Iran full recognition with the fatwa still in place, he replied with a firm statement that he would make no firm promise. It was not his position that the fatwa had to be lifted. The fatwa was one thing, but there were others. The Iranian government was not in a position to lift the fatwa in any circumstances. Rafsanjani[1] cannot do it. The government can withhold public money for the bounty (I didn't ask him whether the bounty was official money or not). As it is, said DH, they wanted more from us after Waite's release than we gave them. They thought that would be enough, but we are still pressing. Also, we are losing exports because our systems are not in place but also, he implied, because of the Rushdie aspects. At any rate, he insisted twice that there was nothing in the wind, and he dismissed Rushdie's loud prophecies to the contrary.

HUMAN RIGHTS I asked him, If I was a voter concerned about the government's promise to link aid etc. to human rights, how would you persuade me that this had indeed been the government's policy? He replied that he would cite Burma, Somalia, Sudan (?) as examples where aid had been cut or delayed. He would cite Zambia, Kenya and Zimbabwe as places where we had been moderately effective in getting results. Kaunda[2] had gone (and his successor is very good – but terribly assailed by the lack of rain). Moi[3] has given a bit. Mugabe has been pressured.

---

1 Akbar Hashemi Rafsanjani: president of Iran 1989–97.
2 Kenneth Kaunda: president of Zambia 1964–91.
3 Daniel arap Moi: president of Kenya 1978–2002.

He wouldn't say on what exactly, and he said some of this was private and confidential, only some of it public.

MAASTRICHT   We did not feel until the end part of the second day that there was any chance of a deal. At breakfast that morning, Hurd and Major said to each other that the weight of undecided matter was just too great to be completed. Major was especially strong about this.

The breakthrough did come with the social chapter. The proposal to leave the Brits out was made by the Dutch and agreed by Kohl – the crucial factor. But even then there was a lot left to decide. We the Brits were briefed much more closely than anyone else on the small details. Some we let go, but others which seemed small we insisted on going through. Lubbers[1] would go round the table on point after point, and very often it was we who put up our hands. They were getting pretty impatient with us by the end.

At that stage, you must remember, there are no officials present. We were on our own, the two of us. You could ask for an adjournment, which we did once or twice. But mostly you have to decide yourselves. It is quite hair-raising, not something I would like to be doing again for a while. It is all down to you. You need to know your stuff.

We had, of course, worked incessantly on it beforehand with all the partners. John and I saw the Dutch twice, or was it three times? There were numerous meetings. We had gone over and over and over the points. So there were no surprises. This was the big difference from Margaret, who would often prevent any discussion beforehand, any ground-preparation. She liked to come with surprises up her sleeve.

The Dutch were superb. Lubbers was intelligent, swift, cunning, everything he should be. He knew the issues intimately. He drove us through at the end very fast, or tried to. This again was good chairmanship.

General-election result, 9 April: Conservatives 336 seats (375 in 1987), Labour 270 (229 in 1987), Liberal Democrats 20 (17 in 1987), Social Democrats wiped out (5 seats in 1987); others 25 (24 in 1987); Tory majority of 21. Kinnock announces his resignation. John Smith took over the Labour leadership on 18 July.

---

1   Rudolphus 'Ruud' Lubbers: prime minister of the Netherlands 1982–94; UN high commissioner for refugees 2001–5.

CHRIS PATTEN
21 May 1992

ELECTION AND AFTER His worst worries were at Christmas and after. They had thought that the pre-Christmas period would be hard, because of Maastricht and the committee stage of the council-tax bill. But both went well. However, it was around then that they had awful economic news and it became apparent that growth was not a-coming. They did quite well with tax as a January issue, but then in February there was nothing left in the locker except yet more bad economic news. So we had a bad time. However, we saw it through, and at no time did Labour get a decent lead.

When the campaign started he felt better. Deserves credit, he thinks, for not losing his head. As does Major. He concedes that he did not always think they would win. But he says he was right to think that the intellectual tide had not shifted.

We will now have a period of steady government, not doing anything very exciting. Major is a shrewd politician, He will be trying to get the business cycle and the political cycle back in sync. He will do the harder things first, like getting public spending back under control, bearing down on inflation.

But the conventional wisdom should not be trusted. This says that everything in the garden is rosy. It seldom is. Things crop up that nobody expects.

We discussed the commentator's problem. He sympathized with my deployment of this. He said one effect of the polls, among their all-pervasive effects, was to convince people we were fighting a bad campaign. The moment we fell behind we were fighting a bad campaign. ITN has a lot to explain, leading the news so often with the erroneous Harris poll. Subplot: note how different the Harris results were for CCO, for which they were polling at weekends, compared with the ITN polls taken on Sunday–Monday–Tuesday. Consistently different.

He implies that he would have been Chancellor if he had won.[1] Says that Lamont would not have kept his job 'if there had been another outcome'. Lamont was a disaster during the election. The whole of the first week's failures was, it turned out, due to the over-frequent appearances of Lamont on TV. Also combined it with his peevishness about status etc. Compare Heseltine, who was brilliant. One night turned out at CCO at 12.15, after Major rang Chris at 11.30 to say (on Hogg's advice) that next day's issue didn't suit him and could he think of another? MH

---

1 Chris Patten, Conservative MP for Bath, and party chairman, lost his seat in the 1992 election.

answered the call instantly. But contrast MH's behaviour over the DTI. An amazing amount of condition-making, of which the demand to be called President of the Board of Trade was the easiest to meet.

CP also implies he would have been Hurd's choice as his successor, and that Hurd would have liked him not to go to Hong Kong, but sit around, look for a seat, and then become Foreign Secretary. A tempting idea. But Hurd was very good once CP had decided, and said it was a better job than almost any ministry.

Of the Cabinet, Waldegrave arguably should have stayed on, because he was over the worst: although perhaps the press conference[1] did for him, and CP feels guilty about not being there to shepherd him through it. Thinks that Gillian Shephard, who sounds more like a human being than a politician, will do better than VB. Says look out for Portillo: a Castilian, cold, hard, ambitious. Right-wing on almost everything, although he doesn't know about Home Office issues: a Euro-sceptic.

HONG KONG Amazing *Yes Minister* stuff about the uniform and the gong. Especially the gong. Especially from people down the line in HK, who worry about the effect on their own CMG[2] of the governor being plain 'Mister'. Fussing already about invitations and 'how shall we describe the governor's wife' – a last bid to get her to become a lady. The ultimate pitch was to say that 'Lady' was far easier to frame in Mandarin (or was it Cantonese?). But CP says that being a PC [Privy Counsellor] is enough, and if people want to give him a reward after he's finished, well and good. Says that it has nothing to do with getting back into Parliament, and believes the chances of that ever happening again are less than 50–50.

He has been reading the secret history of the 1982 deal.[3] Says that it was plainly pushed far too early by the Brits, under pressure from HK business who wanted 'clarity'. But what was the point? There was only one form of clarity Peking would want. This early effort forced Peking to take a hard line sooner than necessary. People blundered into it all. Geoffrey Howe was the only man who made some sense out of the mess.

1 A reference to a press conference at which William Waldegrave, then Health Secretary, admitted to torpedoing an emotional Labour Party broadcast about a little girl who had waited a year for treatment for 'glue ear'. The girl's mother and grandmother turned out to be Tory activists and – after denials of involvement from John Major and Chris Patten – Waldegrave confirmed that Tory officials had put the girl's consultant and the *Daily Express* in touch with each other before the broadcast. The child was publicly identified, and the resulting accusations and counter-accusations of cynicism and political opportunism became known as 'The war of Jennifer's ear'.

2 Companion of The Most Distinguished Order of Saint Michael and Saint George.

3 In 1982, Mrs Thatcher opened discussion over the future of Hong Kong and the New Territories by proposing that the British continue to administer the colony. Negotiations ended in 1984 with the 'one country, two systems' declaration by Deng Xiaoping, the Chinese leader, that established Hong Kong (and its neighbour Macau) as special administrative regions.

Yugoslavia, a country that had existed first as a kingdom after the First World War and then as a socialist federal republic after the Second, had always been an imposed federation of separate cultures and national groupings. As its guarantor the old Soviet Union collapsed, the constituent parts of Yugoslavia, too, became unstable. The first to declare independence were Croatia and Slovenia. Bosnia and Herzegovina prepared to separate, but the Serbs of Bosnia had other ideas. Catholic Croats and the Orthodox Serbs also fought. The only country to achieve independence without fighting was Macedonia.

TRISTAN GAREL-JONES
Foreign Office, 22 May 1992

YUGOSLAVIA TG-J has a chillingly indifferent exposition of the case for doing nothing. He said there was nobody in the EC who wanted to send troops. To which side? In whose interest? You could take your pick between the Serbs, on the grounds that they were strongest, and others on the grounds that they needed more help. 'Arguably, the future of old Yugoslavia will only be determined when a lot of people have been killed and they've been forced to look at themselves.'

SIR PETER KEMP
Paradiso Restaurant (at his suggestion), 2 June 1992

Labour, he thinks, must embark on the most detailed preparation for government. They should model themselves on Thatcher. She did come in with very highly worked-out plans. Adam Ridley and Peter Cropper[1] had done a lot of detailed work. They had worked out resources effect, distributional effect, spending effect etc. etc. when they arrived at the Treasury. Labour should also leap at the entire Kemp package[2] of governmental reforms, including the [Citizen's] charter.

He is a heretic on the fast stream. Thinks it is bad to tell people that they are an elite. This doesn't happen in private companies. People may get noticed and earmarked, but the last thing the chairman does is tell them.

European fast stream. Has been half a success. Recruiting people for

1 Peter Cropper: financial consultant; special adviser to the Chief Secretary to the Treasury 1979–82, to the Chancellor of the Exchequer 1984–9.
2 Having congratulated the Civil Service on 'giant strides' towards reform, in 1987 Mrs Thatcher started to think about the 'next steps' to improving Whitehall efficiency. From 1988 Sir Peter Kemp headed her new Office of the Minister of the Civil Service and became the Next Steps project manager

Brussels, keeping them on hold in Whitehall by giving them jobs here on a central budget, then launching them into vacancies that occur. The previous scheme was hopeless. Vacancies being sent round on buff paper, and the Permanent Secretaries making sure that their best people never applied for them.

One of the curses of government is that intervention is held to be bad. Yet they know they can do it all the time. They can't admit it; they can't therefore formulate a rational policy for it. Canary Wharf is an example of them getting it halfway between one policy and another: neither a red-blooded private development, nor one that the government feels happy helping. If this were Paris, Mitterrand would have paid for the tube line[1] and defined it as a grand project. Instead we are bickering about 'intervention'. He sees an eerie possibility: that Canary Wharf, crumbling and empty, will be joined by County Hall, a Japanese hotel,[2] as two prominent monuments to the Thatcher period. He thinks, however, that the County Hall decision can be reopened . . .

POLICY ADVICE This was something the Thatcher period just about dispensed with. One of the great tasks of earlier civil servants was to receive and listen to the disputatious lobby, the counter-interest groups. They ceased in all but formal name. They were received politely, but the exercise was empty. PK wants to see a revival of this process.

GARETH WILLIAMS, BAR CHAIRMAN
Sandwiches at 3 Bedford Row (his office), 2 July 1992

A FEW SALIENT POINTS The whole system is a mess, highlighted by the miscarriages (with more to come), and the collapse of the legal-aid system. Collapse? In that Legg[3] (LC's Permanent Secretary) had to admit to the Public Accounts Committee recently that of the £1 billion legal-aid outgoings, he could not account for £330 million. It had literally got lost in the system. One aspect of this is the vestigial checking which is done for criminal legal aid. Almost everyone can get it. But civil aid is a different matter.

We have to improve our act, make things much less expensive, and

---

1 Although the Docklands Light Railway reached the huge office development at Canary Wharf, in London's deserted docklands, in 1991, London Underground's Jubilee Line, inaugurated in 1979, reached Canary Wharf only in 1999.
2 County Hall, on the south bank of the Thames near Westminster, was home to the Greater London Council, led by Ken Livingstone, and abolished by Mrs Thatcher in 1985. Since then the building has become home to a Japanese-owned hotel, restaurants and an aquarium.
3 Sir Thomas Legg: Permanent Secretary to the Lord Chancellor's Department 1989–98.

much quicker. What people want, whether they're charged with burglary or suing for a broken leg, is certainty: mainly certainty about when the case will be decided. The whole system is far too uncertain and far too slow. It delivers a lousy service.

Increasing the number of judges is one need. A fraction of the cost of not having them. These costs are borne by witnesses, accused, jurors: with delays and hanging about. They're also borne by people waiting for their case to come on, while their life is wrecked or blighted until it does. Judges cost very little compared with the cost of delay. Wants more High Court judges, saying it is quite wrong, indeed illegal, for people to sit as deputies except in an emergency. Wants more LJJ, saying it is quite wrong for High Court judges to sit alongside, pronouncing on the work of brethren who may have been sharing their lodgings a few weeks back – and without any chance to build up a body of sentencing practice.

Wants posts to be advertised, retirement ages to be fixed. Mackay has made moves on the retirement front to rationalize the 75 for High Court, 72 county court anomaly: but says that pension will require twenty years' service. This induces people to stay on longer. Moreover, Williams wants to abolish the idea of old judges turning up to fill in. Buckley[1] was still doing it at 83!

Wants more transparency in selection. Would probably lead to the vast majority of those now chosen still being chosen. But sees no reason why a selection committee shouldn't operate. Mackay offers as his big answer the 'constitutional' point that LJJ are appointed not by him but by the PM! How pathetic. And why can't the Bar Council be consulted on appointments anyway. They are, after all, the people who see as much as anyone. Were not consulted over Taylor.[2]

TAYLOR   A strong man, psychologically and physically. Prides himself on this. Not a radical. Never notable for critical propensities when at the Bar. But ordinary people can do remarkable things if they are there at the right time. Taylor has a great opportunity. Post-Lane, with much wind and tide favouring change, and the Runciman commission.[3] Made a mistake at his press conference saying that the Court of Appeal should be able to send out 'a posse' to get new evidence. A silly expression. But in general has real possibilities. Appears to have adopted several of the proposals the Bar Council put to Runciman.

1 Sir Denys Buckley, born in 1906, was a Lord Justice of Appeal from 1970 to 1981. He died in 1998.

2 Sir Peter Taylor, Lord Taylor of Gosforth: Lord Chief Justice of England 1992–6.

3 The 1980s were marked by a series of prominent miscarriages of justice. The Runciman Commission 1991–3, led by Baron Runciman of Doxford, examined the effectiveness of the criminal-justice system in England and Wales.

What is needed? The ending of confessions as admissible evidence unless tape-recorded or witnessed by proper lawyers (not the solicitor's office cleaner). This in turn would make it easier to accept the end of the right to silence: not perhaps so far as directly inferring guilt but certainly being a point admissible in evidence. Make it much easier and more inviting for people to plead guilty. People don't do it now because they worry they'll lose bail. This leads to huge clogging of courts. They already plea-bargain privately, inside the locker room, sometimes with the judge letting it be known what sentence he will give. Williams favours more formal plea bargaining, out in the open, at the pre-trial stage. With due protection this would help defendants and help the system. As part of this would like to see judges under obligation to pass sentence in one month after a plea. Would like to see victims being given some consultative role in sentence. It goes on already, in the sense that decent police officers will privately find out how much of a row it will cause to reduce murder to manslaughter. Also wants to abolish committal proceedings: hugely expensive and totally useless. Wants a review committee set up within the Court of Appeal system headed by a judge, with police officers assigned to it (as part of career plan, as is going to Bramshill)[1] and lay representatives, to investigate miscarriages of justice.

Has his eyes on the Inns of Court: which do matter – controlling a lot of money, the libraries, entrance to the profession. Why shouldn't benchers be elected? He suggested this, and received responses of absolute horror, which he patently enjoys.

MACKAY[2] Has come down from Scotland, where lawyers are paid less than here. No excessive respect for the English system: good. And responsive to a certain amount of change, though he went about it the wrong way, e.g. all this consultation about barristers' exclusive rights of audience. Should have simply announced it and gone away. But where he is very bad is where it hits him closest: re judges – see above. Very conservative in all that.

Notes the courage of the government in trying to overturn in the House of Lords the judgement which says that the present practice re life sentencing should be changed. By this practice, the judge gives life but writes to say secretly what the recommended minimum should be: the LCJ also writes (or responds to request for opinion?): a junior civil servant has a view: the Home Secretary has a view. All this is secret. For many years nobody even knew it went on. The government is going to the highest court to preserve it.

---

1 The Police Staff College at Bramshill near Basingstoke in Surrey.
2 Lord Mackay, the Lord Chancellor, had proposed a series of reforms of the archaic rules of the Bar Council.

Incidentally, it only came to me at the end that this chap Williams has been made a peer (Labour working variety). Maybe this explains the faintly old-fashioned look he gave me when I disparaged the merit of making speeches in the House of Lords, which he cited as one source of Taylor's likely influence.

JOHN BIFFEN
Dinner, 22 October 1992

A political salon, laid on by the tireless Sarah [Biffen's wife], in which JB exercises his modest desire to be the guru if not the formal leader of a cave of sceptics. Those present: Alan Duncan, Iain Duncan-Smith, Barry Legg, Bernard Jenkin, plus Adam Raphael and Caroline,[1] plus Alison Smith (*Financial Times*) and us.

These were all men elected in 1992. Duncan had put his house and office at the disposal of the Major people in the leadership election. Yet all four were deeply anti-Major. Jenkin even said that if Major continued to lead the party, the party would be split for a generation. When pushed for an alternative, he said Lilley, Baker or Howard,[2] and of these Lilley, a deeply underrated man who made a marvellous conference speech, was the best.

What unites them is Euro-scepticism, but this spills over into other things. They are passionately anti-Maastricht, a fever which grips them ever more completely as they think up new and yet more points against it: its attack on sovereignty, its irrelevance to Europe, its inherent war-inducing dangers in Europe. They say there is a two-speed Europe already, with the British opt-outs. They want France and Germany and Benelux to try their little experiment in single currency and watch it collapse. They saw the collapse of the ERM as a predictable event, confirming them in their self-righteousness. They want Maastricht delayed (this per Jenkin) simply because every day it is delayed chips another bit off Major's power: it is simply a mini-defeat for the leadership. Of the four, I judged Legg the least impressive, Duncan-Smith the most garrulous and perhaps the least simple-minded, Duncan the most conspiratorial, Jenkin the most recklessly extreme.

Why have they got it in for Major? None of them was in the party when he was elected, but they all agreed they would have voted for him.

1 Barry Legg: businessman; Conservative MP for Milton Keynes South-West 1992–7; member of the Treasury and Civil Service select committee 1992–6. Bernard Jenkin: Conservative MP for Colchester North 1992–7, for Essex North since 1997. Adam Raphael: political journalist on *The Observer*; married to Caroline.
2 Michael Howard: lawyer; Conservative MP for Folkestone and Hythe since 1983; successively Employment Secretary, Environment Secretary and Home Secretary 1993–7; leader of the Conservative Party 2003–5.

Also, all agreed that there was no reason to think him a proper Thatcherite. Yet they direct at him the vengeance appropriate to a man who has read Machiavelli (which Duncan is full of, and Major has probably never heard of): i.e. Machiavelli notes that the Prince will invariably neglect the faction that put him where he is, taking them for granted, and curry favour with his former opponents. They see Major doing this, and are determined to punish him. However, they have to agree that he did not set out a prospectus that he has now repudiated. He is not another de Gaulle in Algeria. Nonetheless, they insist, he got there because of the support of the right, and in a sense he must now pay the price for *their* folly. They try to make this a little more respectable by suggesting, rightly, that when he came in he had few opinions, especially about EC. In particular, they think he has been converted in the seductive halls of government to ideological belief in Maastricht and the follow-on necessity of a single currency: i.e. that he is in a sense not a man of conviction, but one who acquired a conviction in the teeth of those who put him where he is. They are deeply unforgiving.

A related element is all this has to do with time lags. They see them-selves as hardened – 'combat-trained' Duncan says – in politics at univer-sity during the Thatcher years. They are Thatcher's children, the first significant cohort of such people to get into Parliament. Meanwhile, however, Thatcher has gone and the party has drifted in a different direction. Hence there is a kind of mismatch. These people are self-confident, quite tough, seemingly not ambitious for power in the present dispensation, ready to wait their time for something more akin to their beliefs.

This connects with the question of why there are still so few Thatcherites with leadership cred. at the top of the party. They agree it is one of her real weaknesses. They home in on Tebbit as the unfairly lost leader. He was the man. Thatcher became convinced that he was manoeuvring against her, while in truth he was giving her his all. It was perhaps true that he was using the CCO as a power base. But this didn't make him an enemy of hers. She was fed a lot of poison, especially by K. Baker, about Tebbit's never having recovered from the bomb. She was also persuaded to let Lord Young loose at Tebbit's side, which was a killer. Apart from Tebbit, they concede there was really no one. True enough, the bright, capable people like Clarke, Hurd etc. rose to the top on ability, but they are men from another generation. They are in a kind of time warp.

All in all, a reminder that some politicians really do believe things. These men are serious fanatics. They have a high idea of their own importance in some future time, and want to keep their hands clean for that. They have very strong feelings about political direction, not just about power, and they mark the cards of the leadership cadres with ideological severity. Portillo is their probable man of the future, but they seriously think Major can be unhorsed before that. I asked them whether they were (a) spectators at the fight, (b) committed to getting Major out, (c) MPs who thought the leader must be made stronger to win the next election. They were very dubious about doing anything to make him stronger. They really wanted him to fail. But when I said what about the alternative? their first response tended to be that's not my problem. I said if they thought that, they were being frivolous. That was when Jenkin offered Lilley's name in refutation.

Six months on from the general election HY had the opportunity to discuss with one of Major's key Cabinet members the state of the govern-ment, the conflict in Yugoslavia, and the fall-out from the Matrix Churchill affair, a phrase that would dominate political discussion for some time to come.

MALCOLM RIFKIND
26 November 1992

Cabinet is indeed totally different from MT. Had just come from one. But the agenda is very loose. The regular Thursday meeting has parliamentary business, foreign affairs, Community affairs and one other category. We often do not know what will be specifically coming up. If a minister wants to raise an issue, the PM likes his office to be told in advance. But the fact that we can only guess what might be appearing does not really matter. Even though we will not come briefed, 'we never have to decide anything.' These meetings are almost always for general review purposes. Also, they may last forty minutes or three hours – you never know which. It really is very collegial. I sometimes wish Major would come out with his own view, which he almost never does. Exactly the reverse of MT, whose Cabinets consisted of bilateral interrogations with nobody else allowed to intervene. It would sometimes be helpful to know the PM's view earlier in the meeting, because he's the one who usually has to carry the can so you like to know what he's thinking before you make your intervention.

On Maastricht, by contrast, there was a lot of general discussion at every stage, including how to deal with the parliamentary situation. Am I really in favour of Maastricht? He began by ducking. But he offered this history. Asked me to recall that Britain never wanted a treaty in the first place. We thought it was not necessary. This is sometimes forgotten by those who attack us for being negative. It was of the essence that we had to be negative: to resist the parts we knew we couldn't live with. But equally, since there was a general will in Europe to have a treaty, it was essential for us to go along with that and try to protect British interests at the same time. In fact there are some good things in Maastricht. What? He instanced subsidiarity – just about the only thing they would be sorry to lose, it seemed. When I remarked that it was going to be a singularly weird spectacle to see Parliament staying up night and day to get this unwanted thing through, he replied simply that in all the circumstances this was the least bad alternative.

He regards the EMU part of Maastricht as dead and almost buried. He is personally against the single currency at any envisageable time in his lifetime. Maybe his grandchildren. He regards himself as a sceptic in the Cabinet – as long as sceptics are allowed to be thoroughly in favour of Europe. He thinks he and Major, among others, are proof that the fault line on Europe is not left–right. He adds Lamont to this list, lamely citing Lamont's one-time connection with the Bow Group. But he rightly hives off the real zealots – Gummer and Hunt – with Heseltine a more tricky case and Clarke nearer to zealotry than Major. For his part, he favours a currency mechanism but not EMU. To make himself believe that all has been for the best, he persuades himself that our ERM member-ship was another phase like the gold standard and Bretton Woods: and to make this likeness stick he keeps pretending that we have been in the ERM for 'three or four years' instead of less than two. His rationale is that there are times for fixed rates and times for floating: it was right for Major to fix and right for Major to float, each in different circumstances. This is the Vicar of Bray indestructibly persuading himself that he lives by a single guiding star.

On the broad historic sweep, he said that the reason for the Great Failure – the pretence that entry was vital but at the same time would change nothing – was part tactics and part error. The tactics were to keep alarming truths out of the public eye. The error was not to see that the EEC would evolve. 'We joined a static Common Market. We did not see how it would change.' On the still larger point of the sceptics, he concedes, as someone who was wholly in favour of entry, that there may be some things which always distinguish Britain from the rest. In this the Biffens were right, and the rest of us perhaps were reluctant to see it. Geography really does matter – no one else ever talks about 'joining Europe', and this speaks for a profound cultural difference permeating many issues. Equally, nobody else associates parliament so closely with national sovereignty. He contended that this was a popular feeling, while I replied that it was surely a politician's bias much more – at which he half climbed down.

On the Ministry of Defence[1] he remarks that it is a unique department in one respect. In every other department he has run, the inmates or interests invariably sound off about how terrible everything is – the necessary prelude to getting down to business. With the forces it is exactly the opposite. Everywhere he went they told him how shipshape and super everything was – and only then could he get down to the business of finding out the truth. He also said that people like himself, conscious of not having been in the army, tend to overcompensate and are in danger of buying the military line, especially about regiments and cuts, whereas Archie Hamilton,[2] the only ex-serviceman among them, takes a tougher line, knowing where the wool is being pulled. But they are engaged in the biggest defence cuts since the war, and this is hard all around.

When I asked him about NATO, he said that it would still be necessary for all the usual reasons, mainly the fact that Russia could be taken over by the generals. But he cited Yugoslavia, where NATO has given itself to the UN, and NATO buildings and HQs have merely been 'debaptized', as the way things might be. I suggested that educating troops to fight for the world and not for country might be one of the big long-term tasks. He half agreed, but again cited Yugoslavia and its rules of engagement – i.e. only helping aid get through, not taking on the enemy – as perhaps the maximum of what our boys could be expected to do. I.e. the idea of risking death for the world is not on.

MATRIX CHURCHILL AND ALL THAT He raised this keenly. Said it had been the subject of some very slack reporting and other journalism. His main point concerned the PII certificate,[3] which he signed. He said it was utter nonsense to say that he should have resisted signing it in the circumstances. The basic rule, he contended, was that the two classes of document – internal policy advice, and intelligence documents – were not shown outside, to courts or anyone else. This was the basic rule which it was his 'duty', as his officials minuted when they sent him the papers, to uphold. He did not disagree. For he could not possibly have known that the papers would be important for the defence case. Until he knew what the defence case was, how could he look through the papers and decide whether his primary duty should be overridden?

1 Rifkind had become Defence Secretary after the general election.
2 Archie Hamilton: Conservative MP for Epsom and Ewell 1978–2001; Minister for Defence Procurement 1986–7; armed forces minister at the Ministry of Defence 1988–9; later Baron Hamilton of Epsom.
3 Public-interest immunity certificates could be used to prevent disclosure of sensitive documents.

As it was, he didn't have time to look through all the documents – even the MoD ones alone were extensive – and in the circumstance it didn't occur to him to do so. That was up to the judge, who would be able to relate them to the defence case. It wasn't enough for the defence merely to 'want' the papers. It was a long way from that to showing the defence needed the papers as a crucial part of the defence case. In any case, since the prosecution had been able to consider all these papers and many more, and had concluded that the prosecution should go ahead even in the light of them, it was hardly for a minister to second-guess that, given his own limited knowledge. What all this means, as MR kept insisting, was that it was [Alan] Clark's change of evidence which screwed the case, not the papers.[1] No paper he saw had said that Matrix Churchill had been given permission to do what they did etc. etc.

He made a rather arresting point. The press, he said, is always claiming the right not to reveal its sources. What is the difference between that and the minister claiming the right not to reveal *his* documents? Each is doing his professional duty as he sees it. Each says his work would not be possible if such a revelation was made. Yet the editor claims the right to defy the court, whereas the minister, while maybe resisting revelation, always does obey a court order. Does this not put him on a higher moral plane than the law-defying editor?

MR would, however, alter the PII in one respect. At present the minister signs not only to say that the documents fall in the given classes but adds that in his opinion to reveal them would be against the public interest. He favours leaving out that second half, and simply asserting, for the benefit of the judge who must decide, that the definition of the document is as described.

On colleagues: thinks Heseltine has lost it. We were all quite astonished that he showed zero political touch over the pits.[2] At the Cabinet meeting, when at the very end MH said to Major, 'Oh Prime Minister, do you think I should mention the announcement I'll be making?', it was the first Rifkind had heard of it. He said to himself, This sounds pretty dodgy but Michael usually knows what he's doing. That's obviously what Major said to himself too, said MR. The amazing thing was that the *only*

1 Alan Clark, in the trial of the directors of the Matrix Churchill company on charges that they had illegally supplied arms-making equipment to Iraq, admitted under cross-examination that he had been 'economical with the actualité'. The judge brought the trial to an end on the basis that the accused now had no case to answer. The government appointed Sir Richard Scott, Lord Justice of Appeal since 1991, to inquire into the issues raised. On 9 September 1999, four days after Clark's death, HY wrote that he was 'the only serving minister to express the truth about the arms industry. His conduct over selling the tools of war to Iraq in the late 1980s personified it. As the Scott Inquiry discovered, Clark's words and deeds were the acme of evasion, duplicity, cynicism and outraged innocence in the service of the national interest.'

2 Michael Heseltine announced the closure of 31 collieries in 1992, including many of those that had stayed open – and loyal to government policy – during the year-long miners' strike in 1984.

thing MH thought about was his brilliant success in negotiating the
compensation arrangements.

MAURICE KOGAN
Harkness Dinner, 7 December 1992

(With Tony Bencher, professor of education at Sussex.)

John Patten is the biggest shit in a long line of education secretaries.
Completely arrogant, won't listen to anyone, disdains to explain or argue.

Government has been absolutely destructive. Its schools programme
is totally corporatist and anti-democratic. Its target is to make all schools
direct-grant, and its original plan to give parents a majority of governors
has been scrapped to make government appointees – drawn from specific
categories like local business – the majority. They will be dependent on a
funding council which is totally centralized, even though it will no doubt
be located in Sheffield. It has no capacity to think about broad local needs
outside the particular school, about education development etc. etc. (a
long list – ask MK). The aim is simply to abolish the meaning of local
democracy.

There is a big contrast with health reforms, which have at least been
subject to a lot of consultation. With schools they decided long ago that
consultation would be supping with the devil (HY phrase).

But this is (per HY) a supreme example of the inability of oppositions
to mobilize when the common perception has been successfully put about
that they are responsible for the state of things. There is a national opinion
– or at least a Tory/press/business conventional wisdom, supported by
enough pieces of the academic world – that not only has our education
been a disaster (which many people would partly agree) but that the
diagnosis is as simple as Sheila Lawlor[1] et al. suggest . . .

MK says how amazing it is that the Labour Party makes no contact
with his education quality group, who could help them a lot. Jack Straw
was 'intelligent but wispy'.

---

1 Dr Sheila Lawlor: deputy director of the Centre for Policy Studies, and critic at the time of the 'discredited
educational orthodoxies of the recent past'.

1993

1 January	Czechoslovakia achieves 'Velvet Divorce' to become the Czech Republic and Slovakia.
1 January	The European Community creates single European market.
20 January	Bill Clinton becomes president of the United States.
26 February	A bomb blast at the World Trade Center, New York.
16 April	Srebrenica falls in the Bosnian war.
30 April	World Wide Web is launched at CERN, in Geneva.
6 May	The Newbury by-election proves a catastrophe for the Conservatives. The Lib Dems win with a majority of 22,000 on a swing of 27.8 per cent.
27 May	Norman Lamont forced to resign as Chancellor; Kenneth Clarke takes over; Michael Howard is Home Secretary. Norman Lamont later describes the Prime Minister as giving the impression of 'being in office but not in power'.
13 September	Yasser Arafat of the PLO and Yitzhak Rabin of Israel sign a peace accord and shake hands.
30 September	The Maharashtra earthquake kills 10,000 in India.
5 October	Russian military quash an uprising against Boris Yeltsin.
8 October	John Major announces a 'Back to Basics' campaign at the Conservative Party conference.
19 October	Benazir Bhutto elected prime minister of Pakistan for a second time.
1 November	The Maastricht Treaty formally establishes the single European Union.
13 December	Former trade minister Alan Clark tells the Scott Inquiry that Parliament should have been told that export controls to Iraq had been relaxed.
Deaths	Anthony Burgess, Federico Fellini, Dizzy Gillespie, William Golding, Audrey Hepburn, Rudolf Nureyev, Frank Zappa

RAYMOND SEITZ
Breakfast, Winfield House, 29 January 1993

US is very ambivalent about Britain's Euro connection. On the one hand, has always encouraged it: sees Britain as desirably at the heart of Europe, pushing its shared ideas, not strong if outside the centre. Yet also on the other hand, since there is no foreseeable chance of Europe getting together in the security field, US wants to feel that Britain remains its reliable partner in the global theatre.

This is based on the US feeling that it can only get involved in places if others will do so too – whether the UN, or allies or whoever. There are very few countries which qualify as likely partners.

Yugoslavia is an unfortunate place for this to be tested. Much easier if it were Somalia, which is uncomplicated and doable. The real problem with Yugoslavia has been the tentativeness of the response. France has been much the best: getting the UN force going soonest, getting involved ahead of others, keeping at it having lost eleven soldiers. Britain is involved with 2,500 troops, but at each stage has been half-hearted. RS not necessarily critical of this: after all, US has no troops there – Britain is into Bosnia, US is into the no-fly zone but more for deterrent/political reasons than for actual military ones, and in any case is not doing anything about it.

More generally, notes the way interest and commitment go hand in hand. If you have not got the commitment, the interest withers – at least as much as vice versa. The commitment in the end has a high military component: the capacity to do things equates to the ability to count – and to show that one means to count. There is no debate about this in Britain. Everything proceeds (this per HY) by ad-hoc indirection, without an open engagement with the big issue of where Britain intends to see and defend its interests. A blur of aspiration, unevenly applicable in the real world. This is doubly assisted by the lame silence of the Labour Party – which (per HY) is another reflection of Labour's uncertainty always resolving itself into agreement with the government.

The UN seat. Began with Warren Christopher[1] answering questions from State Department staff meeting. A thing he casually mentioned. And plainly a necessary thing. How to get Japan and Germany involved in world politics: how to reconsider in 1993 what was sensible in 1953: whether Europe should have so many at the table: how to recognize the fact that since '53 scores of countries have become independent. Maybe

---

1 Warren Christopher: US diplomat, lawyer; US Secretary of State 1993–7.

the problem is not resolvable. Maybe leave well enough alone. Maybe expanding the Security Council will make it unwieldy. Certainly asking countries to leave is not practical. But at least there is an issue. The Brits seem paranoid about it even being discussed – unlike, he thinks, France, which at least pretends that it may not mind the replacement of France and GB by the EC.

Disagrees with Hurd that the new world is less orderly than the old. Cold War: Cuba, Vietnam, Angola, Lebanon, Czechoslovakia, Hungary, Korea etc. etc. All mighty messy. And very dangerous. But there was a framework – politically, militarily etc. – in which it was carried on. People knew where they stood. Perhaps the point – a point – is that the difference is messier for the UK than for the US, in that it all comes nearer home with the events in central Europe, which *was* relatively quiet during the Cold War.

GORDON BROWN
House of Commons, 2 February 1993

I was struck by the unreflective frenzy of his discourse. Addressed me not so much like a public meeting but like a TV camera endlessly turning. A flow of three-point analyses and three-point plans to meet them. Everything in three points, and everything repeated three times in barely different words. If opposition is meant to be a time for thinking, it is evident that the longer these people stay in opposition the more they are driven to mimic the hyperactivity of the ministers they may never be.

I asked him his view on the TU connection. Before saying carefully that he wasn't making any public statements about this, he stated that he was in favour of one person one vote for election of leader and selection of MPs. He was more blurred about the conference, the policymaking etc. On the issue of letting TU members become Labour members, he said it was important that at the end of the day every member should be a fully paid-up member.

On the issue of disillusionment, he pointed to the £18 membership fee. This puts lots of people off. He did an experiment in two weeks in his constituency, and offered membership for £2, with the rest of it being made up somehow. On this basis they recruited 400 members. But the problem of making it up became too great. It showed, however, that there is a demand out there.

ROBERT JACKSON
Lunch, the National Gallery, 3 February 1993

Major is very much a ladies' man, in what is probably an innocent sense. Very keen on them. A lot of physical contact, of a faintly dubious kind. RJ has seen him hug both Gillian Shephard and Judith Chaplin with an exuberance just this side of fondling. But he is at the same time rather PC for a Tory: very keen to employ women in preference to men if possible. (I put to him Rachel Lomax's[1] point that he was keen to have women around him to get their reassurance – which made her think that he was very unlikely to be having a steamy affair in the closet: he was too naturally at ease with them.)

John Patten is a creep. Something between the Duke of Dorset and Noël Coward. Absurdly patronizing in his [Oxford West and Abingdon] constituency (neighbouring Jackson's). Absolutely no idea how to get on with teachers. What game is he playing, what act is he putting on?

We discuss vision. His theory is that it has been imported from the commercial world. Mission statements, and all that. With PR men mediating as a conveyor belt between the two worlds. Politicians have by no means always needed to have a vision. (I recall Macmillan's 1959 manifesto as an example of anti-vision par excellence.)

We discuss the royal family. Jackson is distressed by the willingness of respectable Tory MPs to say that the Prince of Wales being an adulterer doesn't matter. He says there is such a thing as public morality, which sets standards that keep society on the rails. He fears a coarsening of Britain, as we accept more and more immorality, and say nothing of that kind matters any more. He cites as the image of 1992 a picture in *The Sun* of a Windsor workman with his trousers down sitting on a vast Byzantine (or was it Etruscan or whatever?) urn, as if he was shitting into it. I cite the benign evolution of the race issue as one example of how a public morality really does exist and grow – which in a way confirms his point but doesn't tell us what the Prince of Wales should be doing. The point RJ makes is that we do need hypocrisy, the cement of society and the proof that standards exist. Without hypocrisy you know there are no standards, and vice versa. He yearns for a return to 'respectability' as the cardinal national virtue.

Sees a lot of the problem stemming from the sixties craze for 'authenticity', i.e. what mattered was you, how you expressed yourself, how you made yourself real: not external rules etc.

---

1 Rachel Lomax: economist, Treasury official, later head of the economic and domestic secretariat in the Cabinet Office; became deputy governor of the Bank of England in 2003.

FREEDOM OF INFORMATION Waldegrave has proposed an ombudsman for government information, who would be an independent figure deciding what should and should not be published. This is radical stuff. They see it as much cheaper than the Freedom of Information regime, which would cost £100–150 million: which on other countries' evidence would be little used for serious purposes: which would increase the power of lobbies and make government more difficult even than it is already. Government is already beset by the combined power of lobbies and the media to generate leaks that make things impossible. The hope had been to get the ombudsman approved before the Fisher Bill.[1] But there has been no agreement. Hurd is in favour, others against, the PM has not said. So the whips now say they can't kill the Fisher Bill, which must therefore go into committee stage, which Jackson must run – without being able to say what the government position is, and hence being forced to say that they will be listening to all sides.

He cites this as an example of how open government could be very unhelpful. If we could get through this quietly, we might do so. If a lot of noise alerts other ministers to what is going on, you could suddenly get an uprising that killed it off.

If I consult Maurice Frankel,[2] I may be able to get the story out that way. RJ's worry – another instance of how openness is unhelpful – is that several people in Whitehall knew he is having lunch with me . . .

HIMSELF He is thinking of quitting. Thinks he will get no higher.[3] His face doesn't fit. Major ignores him in the lobbies: 'His eyes pass right over me.' Wants to go before he is pushed. It is a terrible time in government. Everyone is very depressed. This is endurable for someone who is really ambitious, but I am not. More can be done on the back benches, like learning German (which RJ is already doing, and to which end he and his wife had a six-hour lesson every day for a fortnight in the summer). He is thinking of looking for one of the six new Euro seats where, he thinks, he might matter more than he does now.

Once the government had signed the Maastricht Treaty that created the European Union and opened the way to a common currency and political cooperation, ministers, parliamentarians, business people,

1 Early in 1993, Mark Fisher, Labour MP for Stoke-on-Trent Central since 1983, introduced a private member's bill seeking a Freedom of Information Act. It was called the Right to Know Bill. It ran out of parliamentary time.
2 Maurice Frankel: worked with the Campaign for Freedom of Information since its 1984 inception; its director since 1987.
3 Robert Jackson's instincts were right. He was Parliamentary Undersecretary, Office of Public Service and Science 1992–3. It was his last government job.

*trade unionists and journalists slowly woke up to the full implications
and the challenge of implementing, amending or opting out of some of
its obligations. The common foreign and security policy explicit in the
treaty also faced its first challenge: the confused and bloody conflict in
the former Yugoslavia.*

DOUGLAS HURD
Foreign Office, 18 February 1993

EUROPE Concedes that the first legal position outlined by TG-J
should not have been so.[1] By 25 January he had become uneasy about
the legal advice. It was plain that another opinion should be sought. He
says that he wishes this had been done sooner, and the result been
made clear earlier. To my suggestion that it was almost incredible that
something around so long should have waited so late to be considered,
he had no real answer. Obviously it is an example of the pressure of
government business, the day-to-day horizon ministers have to look at.

It was not, even then, certain which position was right. It could be
argued both ways. There were 'two piles of argument', and one pile
turned out to be a bit bigger than the other. I said that I thought the law
officers were less capable than FCO legal advisers in the field. He
demurred, and likened the Attorney's advice to that of leading counsel
after the junior had given a first opinion. Ho hum! He still didn't sound
tremendously sure that the technicalities were beyond question. But he
seems to feel that a political problem has probably been surmounted.

But not completely. Still sees amendments being passed whose non-
passage was 'desirable if not essential', i.e. probably nothing that could
block ratification, but some that would be inconvenient and messy (a
favourite word). Amendment 27 on the social chapter would still be one
such. He declined to name any others. I had the impression that ministers
were genuinely shocked to find so many Tories willing to vote in favour
of the social chapter. Therefore they hadn't thought that this would be
an area where trouble was inevitable.

One effect of last Monday – the day of his changed mind about the
law – he feels to have been a shift of momentum. Now detects more MPs

1 On 20 January, Tristan Garel-Jones had told the House that approval of Amendment 27,
deleting the UK's opt-out from the social chapter, would make ratification of the Maastricht Treaty impossible. John Smith on
8 February urged Tory rebels to vote with Labour for Amendment 27, because it would not wreck the treaty.
Lord Tebbit on 10 February urged Euro-sceptics to vote with Labour because it would wreck the treaty. On
15 February Douglas Hurd told the House that, on advice from the law officers, a vote for the amendment would
not stop the government from ratifying the treaty. Academics dubbed the confused episode 'the parliamentary
siege of Maastricht'. The government won the battle eventually. The UK adopted the social chapter under
Labour after 1997.

who want to get the thing over with. A small number of sceptics seem willing to change their position. Government feels that now would be the time to press on fast, to take advantage of this change of mood. But the Danish referendum[1] is too late for that, to their regret. Foresees problems reappearing as momentum is lost. But a related development is that the business community is stirring up. Not just in London, but in Leicester and the provinces. People waking up to the horrible messing about. Among these types are the Japanese: I had a crowd of them in here the other night; in their Japanese way they were showing uncomprehending impatience.

He attaches much importance to a speech this Saturday, addressing the party to the Maastricht question. Continues to see Maastricht as essential. Sees it as precluding the danger of a two-speed Europe rather than advancing it. If there was a crack-up, perhaps the French would lure the Germans and Benelux into a single currency. But if Maastricht is in place, that is much less likely to happen. The Germans wanted and got the convergence conditions, very tough. This was in a way the equivalent of their opt-out.

Are the rest of Europe as keen as he said they were (before Edinburgh) on the decentralized picture? That remains to be seen. It is what the argument will be about. But there is already a lot less EC legislation than there was. We have a chance to build things our way. We are already getting the enlargement negotiations started, which DH never thought would happen by now. This is because the Germans dropped their condition which said that enlargement could not start until Maastricht had been ratified. That process will help the process we want, away from a tight little Europe.

A key to the entire project is that we should be seen to be trying hard and likely to succeed. The Continentals can't understand why our procedures allow for so much time for bloody-mindedness. But they are learning to accept them. The crucial thing is that they don't perceive us as backing off. As long as we don't do that, we are a full part of the game. But that would change, admittedly, if they thought we wouldn't succeed. Our influence would plummet out of sight. That wouldn't be malice or calculation, just a fact of political life (HY phrase, thought inferred).

YUGOSLAVIA The difference Clinton's position makes is negative and positive. The negative side is that he has abandoned, for the moment, the rather extreme position he seemed to take, especially about rearming

---

1 On 2 June 1992 the Danish people voted in a referendum on the ratification of the Maastricht Treaty. They rejected it. France voted on the same issue on 20 September. It was approved by 51 per cent – a half-hearted endorsement that became known as the 'petit oui'.

and bombing. They have listened to the nature of the problem. The positive side is that American oomph is brought to bear. This is especially important to help our efforts to impose sanctions on the Danube, where we now have agreements with Romania, Hungary and others. US can use its cutters and its political muscle to help a lot. The war-crimes stuff is still around: which the UK thinks is not relevant and rather unhelpful, so long as you haven't got the criminals in jail and are anyway trying to negotiate with them.

Will we be there indefinitely? DH insists, but meditatively, not. Of course, everything depends on a ceasefire, on Vance–Owen[1] in some form working, which is asking a lot. But the hope is exciting. This would be a form of UN peacekeeping force, blue berets: but run by NATO command, and with Russian involvement. This would be a great development, which is as yet only at the drawing board. What part the UK would play in this remains to be seen. Of course, if there's no ceasefire, that's another story. We should, however, expect to continue our humanitarian convoys.

We should remember that the British and the French are the only people with substantial forces there now. We have the most in Bosnia, although France has the most in Yugoslavia as a whole. In this field, our relations with France have never been closer, even though we are fighting tooth and nail over trade. Note, also, that these two Security Council members, which Labour is ready to chide for hanging on to their seats, are the only ones actually getting stuck in.

MORE CLINTON Trade will be top of Major's agenda when he goes into Washington next week. We don't see the Democrats being systematically protectionist. But case by case they have been taking it from the machine, where the lobbies have been important. Perhaps the most important early thing will be if they try and unscramble the painfully done deal by Delors and Andriessen[2] over agriculture at Blair House, which the French hate and which, if it is reopened, will lead to a general unravelling. This was a Bush-time late success.

Douglas had to admit that Clinton sounded like a man who could use words better than Bush. Actually, the half-heartedness with which he said this reminded me mainly of how very committed the Tories were to Bush

---

1 UN special envoy Cyrus Vance and European Commission representative David Owen in January 1993 devised a peace plan for Bosnia. They proposed dividing the state into ten semi-autonomous regions. The Bosnian Serbs turned it down and the proposal – known in diplomatic shorthand as Vance–Owen, to distinguish it from other initiatives – perished.

2 Jacques Delors was the European Commission's president, Frans Andriessen its trade commissioner. They were at odds over the complex matter of European agricultural subsidies, and with the US over the even more fraught General Agreement on Tariffs and Trade that provided the framework for world trade. They patched up a deal at the US president's official state guest house in Washington, and it became known in EU history as the Blair House Agreement.

and how wary they remain of the new regime. How could a words man like Douglas ever think Bush was remotely as capable as Clinton in that department?

CHINA Not raised with DH. But Francis Cornish says that the stories of new talks are premature.[1] They came out of Peking. But it does seem as though the temperature is being slightly lowered, mainly through the British embassy in Peking. They expect China statements saying that Patten has withdrawn his plan, which will be balls. They expect similar statements saying that Hong Kong has been cut out of the deal, because any new talks will be between Britain and Peking (as usual) with HK people on the team. This will also be a load of balls.

TRISTAN GAREL-JONES
The Guardian, 23 March 1993

POLITICS His latest theory. The reason why the Tories have been in power for thirty of the last forty years is that they got three big issues right. (1) Defence. (2) Private property. (3) Europe. The man in the Watford North Conservative Club (a working men's club in his constituency) believed that Labour would leave Britain defenceless, steal his property and – while the man wasn't mad about Europe – get Britain disastrously out of Europe. All three of these issues are no longer available in the same way. Defence: the end of the Cold War means an awful lot of new thinking needs to be done, of which the Tories aren't necessarily the masters. Property: the end of Communism means no longer that socialists are like Commies. Europe: Labour has now come round. This defines the challenge to the 1990s Tory Party. New thinking is needed. Labour hasn't a chance, because Labour is buried in its Thatcherizing phase, just catching up with a dead agenda.

Other issues. For example, he thinks the plight of beaten-up wives, which he sees a lot in his constituency, is something the Tories need to have a serious policy for. Otherwise it will get into the hands of the mad feminists. Similarly, he wants to see the Tories have a proper policy for the fair and decent treatment of gays.

MAJOR He thinks Major will come out of the Maastricht phase and prove himself to be the man his friends know him to be and his critics

---

1 Britain's lease in Hong Kong would end in 1997. The new governor, Chris Patten, angered the Chinese by proposing a limited form of electoral democracy for Hong Kong in 1997. By the close of 1993, officials in Beijing were calling Patten a 'criminal' and a 'troublemaker'.

simply will not accept he is. TG-J insists that we have underrated his amazing achievement in getting rid of the poll tax and sorting out Europe. He expects him to win the next election and maybe see in the millennium but not hang on for ever to power. He will retire early. His successor will be one of three: Portillo, Dorrell or David Davis.[1] His bet in the end is Davis (whom I am ashamed to say I have never heard of), who is now a whip. Davis is, though, pretty right-wing, a Tate & Lyle man. TG-J advises us to take his bet seriously, since he claims he always thought Major would get it.

Defending his view that the Tories should always win, he came out with what will clearly become the talk-out in the future. 'It doesn't matter at all, as long as they *think* they could lose.' The only bad thing would be if one party knew it was there for ever.

Asked about the up-and-comers in the party, he conceded that there were few people at Minister of State level who should get into Cabinet. Agreed that Dorrell and Young[2] were two, but that there were few others. Said that there should be a big reshuffle at the below-Cabinet level. Denied that the onset of the Thatcherites was anything very much to worry about: noted that almost all of the new people except Sweeney[3] ('completely mad') and Legg ('thoroughly unpleasant') voted with the government in the end, even though some (Jenkin) had to be 'roughed up behind the bike shed'.

On Patten, said that when Chris came back the world would be at his feet and he would have money in the bank. Could do an international job – why not a commissioner? World Bank? – which would be perhaps better than Cabinet. He had argued very strongly that Major should order Patten to fight Nick Scott's seat,[4] but Major had replied that he could give orders to pawns but not to people like CP: and that given what Lavender [Mrs Patten] had gone through, with people in Bath spitting on them – for several weeks after the general election she couldn't talk about it without crying – the family could not be ordered to do that again. Says that CP had told Major a long time before the day that he was going to lose Bath, and suggests that the HK offer was made before the result was announced.

1 David Davis: Conservative MP for Boothferry 1987–97, for Haltemprice and Howden since 1997; Foreign Office minister 1994–7; chairman of the Conservative Party 2001–2.
2 Sir George Young: Conservative MP for Ealing Acton 1974–97, for North-West Hampshire since 1997; Minister of State at the DoE 1990–94.
3 Walter Sweeney: solicitor; Conservative MP for Vale of Glamorgan 1992–7.
4 Sir Nicholas Scott: Conservative MP for Paddington South 1966–74, for Chelsea 1974–97; Minister for the Disabled until 1994. Often described as 'colourful', in 1996 he was fined for drink-driving and failing to stop after an accident. At the Tory conference in Bournemouth that year he was found in the gutter and was escorted away by the police. He was deselected; his seat, now Kensington and Chelsea, went to Alan Clark.

FOREIGN OFFICE/POLICY Notes that the FCO budget is a tiny fraction of the MoD budget. Closing embassies is becoming absurd. For a fragment of a tank we could keep posts open. He recalls saying to Sir Patrick Wright[1] when he came into FCO that the FCO didn't seem to feature much in the PESC [Public Expenditure Survey Committee] rounds of which TG-J had been intimately aware as a whip. Wright had replied, Well, the FCO has always had the virtue of settling early in the round. To which TG-J scoffed at the FCO's innocence. It seems to explain quite a lot.

He says this budget question has to be decided outside the usual PESC round. It involves major issues of the British role. Pressed by me as to why DH was so unambitious in discussing foreign policy in a broad future context, TG-J said that this would be the last thing he would do until he was ready. But he would be doing so in his own good time.

It is all closely bound up with defence policy, a neglected area of discussion. Should we keep all our Tridents? Should the British army, the best trained in the world, be at large in Yugoslavia rather than ill-trained Spaniards who come cheaper? Should we have 2,000 men in the Falklands? What about Belize? What is NATO for? Etc. etc. These are very large, very difficult questions.

He insists on the case for Britain not settling to be another Holland. He sees the case: cut down our commitments, cut down our embassies, define our role as totally EC-oriented. But he thinks the counter case based on history is stronger. 'History has dealt us a more important role.' We punch heavier than our weight. A Spanish diplomat told him recently that 'David Hannay runs the UN.'[2] Our foreign service is the hottest in the world, bar none. We must play to all that strength.

MAASTRICHT Says that Major's performance has been tremendous. John Kerr, our EC ambassador, said that Major's last two hours at the Birmingham summit, pulling it all together with everyone wanting to complain about the draft, was the most brilliant piece of up-summing chairmanship he had ever witnessed. Major really is very hot at this, and everyone knows it.

The social chapter. The reason the deal was done at Maastricht was essentially because the southern Mediterranean countries were happy to see us opting out. It meant they had effectively opted out too. TG-J insists that the agreement of the eleven will never mean anything: that no

1 Patrick Wright: diplomat; Permanent Undersecretary and head of the Diplomatic Service 1986–91; later Baron Wright of Richmond.
2 David Hannay: British ambassador and permanent representative to the EEC 1985–90, to the UN 1990–95; the UK's special representative for Cyprus 1996–2003; made Baron Hannay of Chiswick in 2001.

countries will be wanting to insist on vast new benefits for their people when these become anti-competitive. If we *had* signed, it would have been different: with Germany et al. putting pressure on Spain et al., and on us, to secure the level playing field.

The cock-up over Amendment 27 and its legal effect. TG-J insists, under much pressing, that it really was what it seemed, a cock-up. The FCO had divided all amendments into treaty-wreckers and the rest, and put this down as a wrecker. Only after the initial debate did someone in the FCO legal department – quite junior – ask the question whether this 'double negative' would actually have the effect everyone had thought. It dawned on them that their first advice was wrong. They went to the Attorney General for a final opinion. It is now the Attorney's position that he would rather not have Amendment 27 because it would be legally untidy.

He is very scornful of the Labour tactics. He thinks Smith has decided he wants to weaken the government far more than he wants the Maastricht ratification. Says he told Mitterrand, who he saw at the weekend, that Labour wanted EU but the best way to get Maastricht ratified was to get the government out and Labour in – which would then lead to the social chapter as well. (Did Smith really say this to M?) He cites Thatcher's vote for the defence estimates as proof that Tories sometimes vote [for?] the national interest rather than the party battle. Also notes that the Smith thesis is in all ways preposterous: not least the claim that Labour, even with a majority of 50, could ever get the social chapter through. Only thirty Tories would vote for it.

Asked who on the Labour side is to be feared he says: Smith, Boateng,[1] Blair are all good. And Robertson.[2] Who can say Labour has reformed itself if the MPs can still keep George out of the Shadow Cabinet?

A by-election at Newbury (caused by the sudden death of Judith Chaplin – former political secretary and assistant to John Major – who had won the seat at the general election with a majority of over 12,000) would prove a severe test of the government's standing.

---

1 Paul Boateng, Labour MP for Brent South 1987–2005, was already Opposition front-bench spokesman on legal affairs.
2 George Robertson, Labour MP for Hamilton 1978–7, for Hamilton South 1997–9, was Opposition spokesman on European affairs; he joined the front-bench team later that year as shadow spokesman for Scotland; later Baron Robertson of Port Ellen.

PADDY ASHDOWN
House of Commons, 30 March 1993

Newbury will be a different sort of fight. It cannot be another East-bourne,[1] i.e. cannot be fought simply for the protest vote, attacking the government on all fronts. This is mainly because there is such a small Labour vote to squeeze. We are looking to persuade 6,000 Tories to come across. It follows from this, also, that there must be no mention of Lib–Labbery. We must not scare off the Tory voters. We must offer a positive programme, which appeals to people's sense that there is a better way of running the country.

This will be done, perhaps and not for using yet, by a Newbury Declaration, which Paddy is thinking of putting together. It will be motherhood and apple pie reduced to a five-point programme. What they are looking for – another pregnant phrase – is Protest-Plus. A way of putting the Liberals forward as an unabrasive, unalarming party with a positive plan (these my words not his).

He does not think Newbury will be easy to win. He says that the Tory candidate, who fought Yeovil in '92, is young but sharp.[2] Maples[3] would have been much better for the Tories, but this man is not to be under-estimated. When Paddy took him on to see what he was made of he was quick on his feet. But if the Liberals do win, he will immediately convert it into the language of Lib–Labbery. Will be looking for ways to demon-strate to the country that this was a vote for lots of things that all non-Tories believe in.

REALIGNMENT AND ALL THAT   Believes his party is slowly coming along. He is getting it used to his language, post-Chard[4] and post-conference. It is slowly not rejecting him. Cites Alex Carlile[5] as one who was utterly opposed a year ago, but is now saying just the same as he is. But he knows it will be very difficult. He believes that essentially the strategy must be reversed. Hitherto the aim has been to secure a hung parliament, and thereby hope to demonstrate that coalition politics

---

1 Following the murder by the IRA of former minister Ian Gow, who had a majority of 16,900 at the 1987 general election, the 21 per cent swing to the Liberal Democrats at the 1990 Eastbourne by-election gained them the seat with a 4,500 majority.

2 Julian Davidson was the Conservative candidate. The winner, however, by a margin of 17,055 votes was David Rendel, the Liberal Democrat.

3 John Maples: Conservative MP for West Lewisham 1982–93, for Stratford-upon-Avon since 1997.

4 On 9 May 1992, in a speech at Chard, Somerset, Paddy Ashdown summed up the realignment of his party and warned, 'Labour can no longer win on their own.'

5 Alex Carlile QC: Liberal Democrat MP for Montgomeryshire 1983–97; later Baron Carlile of Berriew; appointed independent reviewer of terrorism legislation 2001.

works. Now the idea is to get people to accept the idea of coalition politics and hope thereby to increase the chances of tactical voting and a hung parliament. Because it all does depend on people accepting the hypothesis that coalition politics is better than one-party politics.

He is not propounding an electoral pact in any formal sense. He seems to doubt whether it would work, from top down. But he sees things happening at local level and believes that there will be examples of it at the next council elections – Labour standing down for Lib Dems and vice versa. The Lib Dem constitution says it must be a local option, and he will put his hand on his heart and say he is defending the party constitution. In fact he will be covertly delighted the more it happens, of course. The importance to all this of PR cannot be exaggerated. Ashdown is the route through which a Labour commitment to PR gets the seal of approval – if they go that way. If Ashdown says they are OK, they are OK.

The virtue of Labour adopting PR will be that it announces Labour's acceptance of coalition politics. It will prove that Labour is on the side of political reform. There will have to be a deal however. The deal must be that Labour gets Downing Street but we get thirty extra MPs. 'Otherwise there's no point.' How will this be accomplished before a new electoral system? Here Paddy gets more murky. But plainly what he wants is some kind of informal electoral pact where a lot of Labour people happen to stand down by local option (and Lib Dems ditto). Behind all this he senses, after his journeying round the country, almost as much impatience with the Opposition as the government. People ask, When the hell are you people going to get your act together? This is more specific, and more virulent, than traditional anti-politician feeling.

He hopes that the agenda of each party will become more and more obviously the same. He sees all of Labour's moves as being towards the Lib Dems. It is the Lib Dem agenda – especially 'community' and the constitution – to which Labour reformers are cleaving. He thinks if Tony Blair and he got into a room they would agree about almost everything.

He thinks the Labour position depends on certain developments. Labour need to absorb the fact that they probably cannot win. The Boundary Commission changes need to be there for all to see. The Lib Dems need to have produced a record and a policy programme that makes sense to most Labour people, even if only secretly. This he believes has partly been helped by Maastricht, where he believes Lib Dem tactics have been exactly right. The party has stuck together, albeit with some arm-twisting sometimes. They made their shift at the right time, incidentally crossing with the SNP going the other way (and exactly the wrong way). But more than that, he thinks he's shown how coalition politics of a kind can work out.

His view is that the time for delays for delay's sake has gone. This is why they let the government win last week on its timetable motion. But they will still vote for the social chapter whenever it comes up. Thinks Smith, by contrast, is losing some of his Euro credentials.

On the social chapter, still thinks Major could come to grief. If Amendment 74 is accepted, and if it is passed, it will mean a new vote, after royal assent, on the social chapter specifically. This could come at the end of July – the Lib Dems don't want a longer delay, so Paddy piously insists, and thinks the Lords won't be able to delay it by more than a day or two. This could face Major with a terminal problem, assuming that the Tory sceptics stay together and vote with Labour. Major could face either having the social chapter or losing the treaty. Which would he do? Could he survive either choice? Is this the 'Semtex amendment' Paddy is looking for?[1] He envisages Major losing either way, quitting the prime-ministership – and then a referendum being the only way for a new Tory leader to get out of his jam.

FRANCIS CORNISH
The Garrick, 30 March 1993

MAJOR   Regarded by Hurd as needing to stand back. Far too keen to get involved in every detail. Hurd accommodates him on this, they have lots of bilaterals, Major ticks off long lists of detail, wants to know. For example, wants to know everything about the two men held in Iraq: unwilling to let the FCO handle it alone: worried about public questions being asked that he can't deal with. All in all, Major is too prone to fly off the handle. Gets excessively het up. Announces that he will never talk to so-and-so again. Cannot be laid-back enough. Is *far* too bothered by the press. And by PMQs, on which he spends half a day each Tuesday and Thursday getting ready.

Confirms that Major is certainly a brilliant negotiator. Far outstrips the grand old men, Mitterrand and Kohl, because he knows a lot more detail. Thanks to the FCO machine, he is in intimate touch with what others have been saying around the world. Has very good backup with Michael Jay[2] and John Kerr.

1 Semtex: a plastic explosive much used by the IRA and other terrorist groups. The grim joke refers to an amendment that would have explosive results for the Conservative government
2 Michael Jay: diplomat; at the time, assistant undersecretary for EC affairs at the FCO; head of the Diplomatic Service 2002–6; later Baron Jay of Ewelme.

HURD Shows no sign of wanting to go, although he has a decision to make about the next election. The big question, according to FC (and therefore being asked in the FCO?), is what he would do if Major had an accident. The answer, surely, would be that if the party called him he would not refuse – even though (this per HY) this would make him an up-market Douglas-Home, not very good at adding up.

Hurd has a lot of clout. He is now the senior man in the EC. He has clout in NATO. Not that people sit at his feet, but what he says can matter. He likes all that. He enjoys making big, thoughtful speeches. But FC did agree with me that, for example on defence matters, which are so interconnected with all this, Hurd has not said much.

There is plainly a big bother brewing about the FCO budget. Gilmore[1] et al. have been very clever in squeezing more, mainly by sharply cutting out people on the communications side whose work can be done by machines. It is entirely owing to that that we have been able to open some mini-embassies in parts of the old Soviet Union recently.

CHRIS PATTEN
Dinner, Gran Paradiso, Wilton Road, 5 April 1993

In company with Jim Naughtie [BBC], Don MacIntyre [*Independent on Sunday*], Peter Riddell [*The Times*] et al. with Edward Llewellyn (political adviser) and Mike Hanson (press officer, who reminded me I had met him when he was in charge of Vietnam boat people).

BRITAIN He puzzles how it can be that the government is evidently the most unpopular in living memory, yet the Opposition appears to be nowhere in public esteem either. He thinks this says more about Labour than about the Tories.

An agenda for Labour: Britain's role in the world, manufacturing industry, further disconnecting from the unions (isn't this a bit out of date?), moral passion. He scoffed at Tony Blair's alleged 'big speech' about social values and crime, because it was only two pages long.

An agenda for the Tories: let the economy keep getting better, keep on trucking. Why is it that since Mrs T, but not before, it has been thought that feverish activity and a big message are the only way to do politics? Maybe it need not be like that!

We should never forget that Hurd and Clarke are two people, perhaps the only two, in the Cabinet who have breadth and some scale. Hurd can

1 Brian Gilmore: diplomat; civil servant in the Cabinet Office 1988–92.

stand back and ask big questions; Clarke has an opinion on everything and doesn't mind who knows it. (Again, I think his antennae are off-key a bit, not having picked up Clarke's decline.)

He said, a little mysteriously, that it was important if you had a majority of 21 to behave as if you had one of 100: to behave, I guess, like confident winners.

HIMSELF   Lavender says that the job has been quite a lot harder than he ever expected, with far more nastiness than he bargained for.

He insists he will be staying until the due date. But when someone postulates that in a couple of years things may have levelled out with the Chinese and if a period of calm is established he might then consider leaving the last two ceremonial years to Prince Charles he does not demur. Llewellyn and I guess that he and Lavender talk a lot about this. So maybe his time is not necessarily as long as he makes out.

He seems to think it unlikely that he would go back into the Commons. He will be 52 in 1997. He has already worked out that the EC Commission changes faces in 1995, and speaks in general of the timing being wrong for various other possibilities. So he 'can't see a pattern'.

He's lost a lot of weight. His suit seemed to sag slightly – always to be avoided. He talked to L a lot about eternal verities he'd faced in hospital,[1] when he did rather nearly die. Says he read the New Testament. But he looked and sounded in full vigour, Lavender even more so. Keeping a nice balance between enjoying the unreal luxuries and knowing they won't last.

DOUGLAS HURD
21 April 1993

BOSNIA   With any form of pressure you can only guess whether it will change the Serbs or stiffen them. In any case, it is not as simple as pressure on the Serbs. What about the Croats, now fighting the Muslims? But accepting that pressure on the Serbs is the issue, there are four kinds:

Tougher sanctions. With very great difficulty the Russians have been persuaded to agree to them, and they will come into force on Monday. But there is a tremendous amount to be done. These are so far mainly paper sanctions. By sea, the Adriatic is just about OK. No oil tankers up there for a long time. By river, the riparian countries are starting to stop ships, but only starting. There is no systematic structure. They have to

---

1   After complaining of chest pains, Patten was treated with angioplasty early in 1993.

have documents, but who knows whether the documents tell the truth about end-user. So the new resolution provides for monitoring. The WEU is also working up a plan, hatched for a long time, still under discussion with the riparian states. By land, theoretically now land sanctions are legal. But only in theory. There will be CSCE [Conference of Security and Cooperation in Europe] customs officers in different places to try and impose them. But they need beefing up. By finance. Owen thinks these more important than land. There are banks helping the Russians to give financial aid. Again on Monday this will become illegal. We need to try and do more to stop it.

To get these in place we had to talk very strenuously to Kozyrev[1] in Tokyo. The Russians have deep links with the Serbs. (Kozyrev said among other things that what was going on in Nagorno Karabakh was far worse than Yugoslavia and why did we take an interest in that . . .). The Russian veto was touch and go. But they are very important on the ground as well, because their oil (and Ukraine) is what keeps Serbia going. In theory, again, an oil embargo starts on Monday. But Moscow is not in control. It will probably be down to the oil terminal manager, looking for more dollars.

Extreme force. This would be a sure-fire success once we'd got it into place. With enough troops – 100,000 at least – we could separate the combatants and impose a political solution: protectorates. Done by NATO, under UN authority. It would be for an indeterminate time. Clinton will never do it. In all his twisting and turning, that is very clear.

Therefore there are two options under active consideration in Washington and London, and elsewhere.

1. Arms embargo lifted. There may be support for this in Washington. But don't forget that arms for the Bosnians would go through Croatia, who are taking a 30 per cent cut on all illegal arms shipments now. Arming the Bosnians would also be arming the Croats. Russia would have to be squeezed very hard to agree, and would not do so for a policy that didn't end the embargo on the Serbs as well. This would be a very big change in policy. Let them all fight it out. Instead of trying to stop the fighting, encourage it to redouble. A change to the negative option. Although this has powerful backing in Washington, it is strongly opposed by Vance–Owen (and ? Stoltenberg, who replaces Vance any day).[2]

2. Air strikes. Probably preceded by an ultimatum. The soldiers

1 Andrey Kozyrev: Russian foreign minister 1990–96.
2 Thorvald Stoltenberg, former Norwegian ambassador to the UN and special envoy to Yugoslavia, cooperated with Lord Owen on a second peace plan for Bosnia, after the failure of the Vance–Owen plan.

everywhere are opposed to this. First because the nature of the terrain makes it certain that civilians would be killed. Second because they don't believe there would be a clear military advantage without follow-up by ground troops. This military opinion might be over-ridden, and the soldiers told to get on with it, but Clinton hasn't indicated that yet.

In the event of air strikes or ending the arms embargo we would not instantly withdraw our humanitarian troops. But we would have to look out for their safety. We are at one with the French in all this – they even have a battalion in Belgrade, very exposed.

Clinton came in saying we must do better. In February he concluded that what the Europeans have been doing was right: humanitarian aid, political pressure, sanctions and war-crimes commission. Obviously he is the key player on our side, but we are in very close contact.

The Croats are much more subtle than the Serbs, have been coming on in on the Serbs' skirts. Tudjman[1] is a subtle bully. Thatcher's praise for them, however, looks pretty dubious in the light of their new fighting against the Muslims. How do you deal with the Croat problem? Nobody has an answer.

The real question is, Are you going to want a Bosnia or not at the end of the day? Must Bosnia exist? We and the US have always said that after Yugoslavia the only realistic frontiers were those of the old, pre-Tito, republics. That is still the case. As in Africa, the old colonial frontiers, however illogical and messy, are the most practical. But this needs the agreement of the nations/republics inside to agree them.

If there is nothing more than sanctions, and the Serbs make military advances – is an end in sight, however disgraceful? Not really. They are still a long way from both their north–south line (taking them to the sea at Dubrovnik?) and their east–west line, the Krajina corridor. Besides (this per HY), what exactly is the end if there is still a civil war raging?

The question the Serbs should ask is what sort of future they want: stability and recognition or a burning battlefield? The trouble is that the generals are following the latter line. They don't want compromise. (Karadzic[2] is their puppet?) They don't understand the need for some compromise – and Vance – Owen gives them a lot. Milosevic,[3] by contrast, is a calculator. Shrewd, brutal, calculating. Very good English, a debater

1 Franjo Tudjman: president of Croatia.

2 Radovan Karadzic: psychiatrist, poet, politician; first president of the Bosnian Serbs; long a fugitive, indicted for war crimes by the International Criminals Tribunal for the Former Yugoslavia at The Hague, he was finally captured in 2008.

3 Slobodan Milosevic: president of Serbia 1989–97; president of the Federal Republic of Yugoslavia (later Serbia and Montenegro) 1997–2000; died of a heart attack in his cell in The Hague, 2006, while on trial for genocide and war crimes.

in conversation, who never lets you know what is underneath. His main opponents are the fanatics. He has to decide whether the economic devastation is worth it. Belgrade announced today that imports are 8 per cent of what they were a year ago. The FCO estimation is that if Milosevic really wanted the war to stop, he could stop it – with difficulty and over time. He is perhaps 70/80 per cent in control.

DH does not regard the policy as undebatable. He doesn't see this as an issue that divides people in necessarily political or dishonest ways. Struck round the HC by the strange alliances and attitudes: Budgen[1] the isolationist, Labour left the interventionists etc. etc. No merging into the Maastricht camps.

Our policy has not delivered the goods, he says openly. The horror goes on. We have to keep looking at other policies. He agrees with Max Hastings[2] that only overwhelming force can guarantee success: but not that some other option might not be useful. (An air of agnosticism not cowardice.)

The lessons elsewhere (DH's Chatham House speech, on the need for developing the idea of intervening in internal affairs). The areas where it matters are the old Soviet Union and Africa. Four Soviet Union republics (inc. Georgia and Tajikistan), although some say every small Soviet Union republic is at risk. Then Somalia, Liberia, Angola, Rwanda, Burundi, Zaire, Sudan: places which are disintegrating through civil war (separate from starvation). The way through it is not West or British armies but much earlier strategies both positive and negative on the economic front – without necessarily abiding by the 'internal affairs' embargo.

On the whole, people are prepared to do something in the face of particular situations: and then only slowly. But theoretical discussion is very difficult. They resist it. See specially India and Indonesia – both of which have few regional problems but have their own reasons to oppose internal interventions.

Remember that different countries have different problems. Japan is much more concerned about Cambodia. Nigeria is much more concerned about Burundi and other African places.

Feel sorry for Boutros-Ghali.[3] At the January 1992 UN summit under our presidency we paved the way for the B-G document on peacekeeping (or whatever it was). B-G works under terrible difficulties. Has four or five good men near him. But a shortage of resources and good staff. Has to rely on NATO for any military organization. UN is fuller now of

---

1 Nicholas 'Nick' Budgen: Conservative MP for Wolverhampton West 1974–97; an arch Euro-sceptic, best known as one of the 'Maastricht rebels'.

2 Sir Macdonald 'Max' Hastings: author, historian, television reporter; war correspondent and columnist; editor of the *Daily Telegraph* 1986–95, of the *Evening Standard* 1996–2002.

3 Boutros Boutros-Ghali: Egyptian diplomat; Secretary General of the UN 1992–6.

generals, since people are being called on for military support. Argentina is happy to do this, as are others: gives the troops exercise, earns money, and keeps the army from meddling in politics.

JOHN SMITH
House of Commons, 22 April 1993

A little fatter than when last seen. Offered me a whisky and drank one himself (6.30) despite alleged dietary restraint (although Lucy says whisky is good for the heart). Talking very fast, as if to an agenda calculated to make me feel sympathetic. I almost had the impression that the team – David Ward, Murray Elder, David Hill,[1] all coming out of his room when I arrived – had had a little confab about the best line to take. But at least we were alone.

Began with 'government': good governance, on which he presented me with copies of three speeches on the subject. Said that the one on citizens' democracy was the one he'd slaved over most himself. But also Tawney, which was his personal moral philosophy. Took a lot of time to tell me how much he believed in morality in government.

Said his agenda for this put openness high on the list. Said he was operating such a policy as leader of Labour, often rejecting colleagues' advice to keep things under cover. More widely, lambasted the secrecy of Whitehall and the inadequacy of the Commons. The Commons was too weak, Whitehall too secretive. He said the Budget should be preceded by discussions on a much wider basis. When I asked how he would change the culture, he said it began and ended with the man in No. 10. No. 10 was the one place the machine could not turn, if the PM was strong enough. He'd been quite close to Callaghan when in the Cabinet, and continued to see him now – found his advice helpful. I asked whether he would need to have a clear strategy spelled out for all this, rather than firm intentions, and he rather blurred whether this would be forthcoming.

Was also very keen on constitutional reform. Proud to have come out on bill of rights. A big change for Labour. Now that he's done so, can't really understand why he had such suspicion of it before. Guesses it was because of suspicion of the judges, an old Labour feeling. But now thinks there are quite a few good liberal judges down here, as well as plenty of Labour judges in Scotland. Plainly sees it as especially important that

1 David Ward: chief policy adviser to John Smith 1988–94; later Secretary General of the FIA international court of appeal, judging on disputes involving Formula One motor-racing clubs. Murray Elder: general secretary of the Scottish Labour Party; chief of staff to the leader 1992–4; later Baron Elder of Kirkcaldy. David Hill: former aide to Roy Hattersley; director of campaigns and communications for the Labour Party 1991–3.

Labour drives home its commitment to the individual (see below on unions).

Regional governments a big part of the programme, because part of the decentralizing mission. Claims always to have thought that Labour's post-war drive for centralizing was a mistake. Now sees Scottish devolution as the centre of his programme for decentralizing. Regards the day of the 1978–9 referendum as a big disaster, when he was close to Wales too. Here is another thing on which he distinguishes himself from Kinnock very sharply, describing Kinnock as a centralizer at heart. When I asked about England, he brushes aside the problem of regional identity. Says he would start, however, with merely administrative devolution ('like Scotland'), a Council of the North with powers over education, transport etc., which he seems to think could be done without legislation. Political devolution would come later, as with Scotland. Sees St Andrews House as a model of how government can be localized: see the Scottish handling of schools testing.

All this is part of a Euro vision. Sees four tiers of government. European, for Europe, Westminster for national; regional for regions; local for localities. This would put the UK on all fours with several European countries. A good fit. 'Interlocking' was a word he used. It would, per HY, redefine the meaning of 'federal' along German rather than British lines.

EUROPE   He passionately believes in, always has. Alas, we didn't have time to discuss this much further. But he talked as though EMU was rather being put off by circumstance rather than principle. On Maastricht he vowed to defeat the government over the social chapter and Clause 74, which would be voted on between royal assent and ratification. The Labour amendment would, if passed, declare that ratification would not take place if there was no social chapter. When I pressed him to consider the cons of wrecking Maastricht, he replied that Labour had always been in favour of Maastricht only with the social chapter. 'Europe is about people, not just about business and markets.' We agreed, at the coarse political level, that Labour would be unlikely to lose many votes if it was seen as the wrecker of Maastricht. 'We are the Opposition, after all.'

HIMSELF   I was struck by how often he said or implied that he had big advantages over Kinnock. He dismissed Kinnock with faint praise, routine allusions to him being 'unfairly criticized'. But plainly he sees this as the biggest single factor that will have changed for Labour by the next election. Referred to the advantage of being a politician who had never changed his mind. '"You've always thought the same about most things," my wife remarked to me the other day.' Emphasized his middle-class origins. 'They see me as this interesting chap from Morningside, and a QC.' Says that the English are far less mistrustful of Scots than of the Welsh, when I put the Scottish point. (But he seems rather blithely unconcerned at the suggestion that, as a Scot, he may have difficulty empathizing down here. He actually volunteered with pride that Scotland had always been consensual, that many judges voted Labour, that there was this sense of community unriven by so much class segregation, without seeming to see that this made his English task possibly harder.)

LIBERALS, PARTNERSHIP AND ALL THAT His basic line is that it is just not on. Says he doesn't spend time thinking about the philosophical questions, because he knows that it cannot happen, so why waste valuable effort? With the utmost politeness he says that people like me, who have never been politicians, never experienced the struggle, underrate the importance of party: of tribal loyalties: of the need to be fighting for a cause and a group. All this makes the idea of deals quite impossible. He would lose control, apart from anything else. Many people in the party would be outraged, and if there was actually a pact he would find Independent Labour (or Independent Liberal for that matter) candidates running in seats where the party had cut out. He claims that Ashdown – 'not that I spend much time with the man' – probably realizes the same.

He also denied that there was entire congruity between Labour and LD ideology. LDs would back a small businessman against his employees. They are less interested in collective solutions. Their line on the minimum wage is disgraceful. Also, to the charge that people will find it hard to understand why the parties are now so close together and yet fight each other, he says that for Labour to take on the LD agenda is a good way of getting LD voters to their side. Stresses that all his close people – Gordon, Tony, others – all agree with him about all this.

The only crevices in this line were his delight in having ensured that the CSJ[1] has no politicians on it, and has two Liberals. Says he thought there would be outcry in the party at this, but nobody made a fuss. Also says that he has seen David Owen lately, about Bosnia. Not only did Owen back Smith's decision to support interdicting bombing ('Your line and its timing are right,' said the sage of Herzegovina[2]), but there was rapport. Owen showed yet again that he hated the Liberals. Smith always

---

1 The Commission on Social Justice, an independent review set up by John Smith and intended to catalyse new Labour policy initiatives.
2 The 'sage of Herzegovina' could only be John Smith's sardonic description of Lord Owen, architect of the Vance–Owen and Stoltenberg–Owen peace plans.

thought Owen, unlike Jenkins, wanted a Labour Party Mark 2, and this now means Owen is much closer to Labour. They had an amiable meeting, burying much past trouble.

However, is adamant that the only way for someone like me to help get the Tories out is to back Labour. Direct, uncomplicated, the only course. Why don't people back Labour, he enquires? What sways them as they tread into the election booth? I said the sense of economic incompetence was one thing, trade unions another, Kinnock another (actually, it was he who mentioned Kinnock first in this context).

On the economy, he is adamant, and I believe him, that recession is not good for Labour. People need optimism to vote for change. (And you could say that the 1992 election was the ultimate proof of this: the biggest recession, yet a victory for the government.) So he actually claims to have no interest in depression and its manifestations.

UNIONS Says that he will be having a lot of trouble from them at the conference. On what? Candidate selection. When I said that a fight with the unions was good for his public image, he doubted it was worth it. But he is proud to have put his head far above the parapet on all this. More widely, does believe that the union albatross may no longer be as heavy. Thinks unions may make a comeback. Is looking for more individual rights, to be defended by unions. Wants to write in, as far as I gathered, some kind of charter for individuals, but stressing that unions were necessary to defend them.

ADDENDA Has still not quite got instinctive command of the 'When I'm prime minister' usage. Said it to me thus: 'If I do get to Downing Street – well, I'm going to be prime minister' – showing that in his bones he was a little doubtful.

Much praise for George Robertson. But when I said it was a slur on the PLP that George wasn't in the Shadow Cabinet, he said that George was undiplomatic, ungood at the process of jollying people along, always laying down the law. This would make him a wonderful minister – he would 'shoot straight up the list' – but less good at the oiling of politics.

Plunging into the Smith office, one was back in the heated (foetid?) atmosphere of everyday politics, where everyday ups and downs dominate life. This was the day Major had really announced the end of the recession, and was all smiles at QT. 'From annus horribilis to annus mirabilis in one jump,' David Hill sweatily opined.

WILLIAM WALDEGRAVE
4 May 1993

SCIENCE POLICY Just had a meeting with top scientists. Reflects on how strange it is to live in a time when the vast majority of people – including ministers and policymakers – do not understand the basic laws that are now known to govern our time. Thinks scientists need to try much harder to make people understand the truths they hold to be self-evident: quantum physics and the like.

Major is beginning to do better. Gathering hardness. It is sad to see how our profession spoils a nice man, but it has to be. He will have some big sackings to do, maybe only next year. He is like an American politician, shot from nowhere up the lists, without gathering the experience. But he is now harder. The reshuffle question turns on what to do with Lamont. WW thinks it would be a disaster for him to be Foreign Secretary. Thinks he should be himself. Can't think of anyone else. Regards Dorrell and Young as promotable; fears Redwood may be too.

Hurd remains far above the ruck. At a recent discussion about WW's baby – secrecy et al. – a voice from the plebs was banging on about this not being something he found people talking about in the pubs. Whereupon DH murmured, 'Wouldn't it be nice to do something just because we believe in it?' Hurd is so good as Britain's foreign voice. He is listened to out of personal respect. Right now it has been fascinating to see how he had been gently bringing the Cabinet, the party, the country round to the terrible prospect of falling out with the USA. Asking people to consider how unthinkable it would be, as it might threaten to be, over Bosnia.

ON BOSNIA WW line is that it may well fail. But it is better to fail doing something than doing nothing. It would be more honourable. But he agrees that the problem is deciding when failure has to be acknowledged. How you avoid getting sucked in. Agrees that the Heisenberg factor comes into play: which I understood to mean the way in which reality is affected by what you plan to do about it – Serbs changing reality by more massacring if you threaten to bomb.

On the EEC, he agreed entirely with my thesis – that the amendment would be accepted, and then maybe tested in court. Have the Cabinet already decided this? It almost sounded like it – although WW is rather on the outside of the centre at the moment.

RAYMOND SEITZ
Breakfast, 14 May 1993

Bosnia hit Washington in campaign mode. Clinton took a long time to realize that office was different from campaigning. He wasn't at ease with foreign affairs generally. But he also wasn't immediately able to shift to office mode where what he said today needed to be followed by some kind of action. He had said things about Bosnia in the campaign which amounted to unwise commitments. (Perhaps the main and only way in which Bush would have been different from Clinton is that he had now been 'in town long enough to know how to avoid getting committed'. Otherwise Bush would likely have been in just as big a stew as Clinton is.)

Clinton has domestic worries. Apart from the conflicting pressures, there's also the comparison with Bush. Here was Bush making Canadians fight alongside Syria in the Gulf. Yet here was Clinton unable to get oldest allies together in Bosnia. Major had his domestic worries: not wanting to add the breakdown of the alliance to his list of failures.

So now we await another refinement of proposals for action. Certain background facts are worth emphasizing.

First, we do have the capacity to enter Bosnia and sort of save it. With half a million men, we could occupy effectively. Not to do so is a conscious choice among the range of possibilities. We shouldn't pretend otherwise.

Second, this is the first European regional conflict. It is different from Somalia, the Gulf, let alone Grenada etc. etc. To an extent it is therefore Europe's problem. Or rather, for the US to intervene there is quite different from going to Somalia, which is doable quickly, by massive force, without too many complications, and with no alternative power. For the US to intervene in Yugoslavia would be a big decision: a kind of statement that the US does have a role in the post-Cold War world which many Americans actually do not want it to have. For US planes to be killing Greek Orthodox Serbs would be somehow different from anyone else doing it. Moreover, for the US to start getting involved would be the start of something that had no obvious end.

Third, to do this, US needs to see its strategic interest engaged. RS's personal view is that it cannot just be a part of a humanitarian mission, harsh though it may sound to say that. What might happen in Greece, Albania, Bulgaria, Turkey etc. – the classic Balkan wedge – should determine what we do. Our effort should be to prevent an extension of the turbulence in those directions. He sees this as more important than the argument about precedent, which doesn't necessarily follow, he says.

All in all, what we have is a situation governed by far more complex pressures than the simple one of guts, courage and commitment. There is a very serious question about how much can be done, how much ought to be attempted, what the repercussions might be, what the peoples of our countries can be persuaded to accept. And through it, despite the twists and turns and uncertainties, you can see a Clinton determined not to act in face of the disagreement of his allies; also allies determined, at least in Britain's case, not to split from the US.

DAVID STEEL
The Garrick, 8 June 1993

Smith is a deeply conservative man. I was at Glasgow University when he was at Edinburgh University. We competed for debating prizes. He was always a wonderfully swift debater, fast on his feet, good with repartee. But the Scottish Labour Party is deeply conservative, and he is one of them.

He confirmed this at a long lunch he had at my house last Christmas, with our wives. On the day of the election as leader, I had chanced to travel up to Edinburgh on the same shuttle and we sat together. I said to him that he had my commiserations. He couldn't understand what I meant. But by Christmas he was telling me he understood exactly what I meant.

He also made clear that he wasn't interested in any kind of deals with the Liberals. It just wasn't on his agenda. He seems unable to face the party problems that might ensue. DS seemed totally pessimistic about Labour being willing to deliver anything at all.

What Smith should do, if he had the nerve and the sense, is to say publicly that he wasn't entering any deals nationally, but that if local people didn't want to fight a seat too hard that was all right by him. No doubt Labour would feel the need to stand, but there is a big difference between trying and not trying. It can seriously affect the outcome. At the last general election, Steel had a good Labour candidate against him who was about the place etc., and the Labour vote stood solid. If Smith would do that much, saying that he was interested in getting this government out by any means, it would mean something.

Steel was more in favour of this than of policymaking organs. There are already too few places where we get together anyway – he cited Charter 88.[1]

Ashdown's problem is that, with Labour not moving an inch towards

---

1 A pressure group founded in 1988 targeting constitutional reform in the UK.

him, it is very hard for him to make clear what is in fact the truth: that the natural alliance is between the Liberal Democrats and Labour. In truth the Tory option is unreal, says HY (confirmed by DS rather iffily). Why doesn't Ashdown make that clearer? Because, says DS, he will be left high and dry if he concedes that clear identity and then finds that Labour won't give him anything. But he recalls a key moment when the German FDP, under Walter Scheel, having existed as a 'centre' party throughout an election, suddenly announced on election eve that it would back the SPD (Schmidt, I think). This was done by Scheel very late on, without consultation, and took everyone aback: but it did the trick, it worked, it put the SPD–FDP alliance in power. It was also, incidentally, the way Schmidt kept his far left under control (which was what Callaghan well understood during the Lib–Lab pact).

He puts some but not much weight on the fact of coalition politics working at local level in more and more places. It links to the option Smith should, but won't, take up.

Surprisingly unbitchy about Ashdown. Says PA is much better than he, DS, was at the party machine: getting involved, making it work.

Told me a good story about Linda Chalker.[1] Chalker, the Mother of Africa, has been leading the field to get African countries to be more democratic. Kenya a notable target. Knows all the people (as does Steel – who feels he has more influence in Malawi than he does in England). During the saga of the Kenyan election, much pressure on Moi to accept defeat etc. etc. if it came. In the event, when some of his ministers were beaten, he promptly put them back in his Cabinet (check) as personal nominees. When asked to justify this he said he was simply following the model of Linda Chalker – who, when defeated at the election, was instantly put into the Lords to retain her post as Minister of Overseas Development. This is the best anti-House of Lords story I have yet heard.

SALMAN RUSHDIE
27 June 1993

A meeting at dinner with Udi and Judy[2] across the wall. Also present Eugene and Avis Robinson – he the correspondent of the *Washington Post*, she an economist who really wants to be in Washington, but has been in Argentina for four years and now London. Also a poetess called Ruth (I think): all of us – even perhaps Salman? – living in Hampstead.

---

1 Linda Chalker: Conservative MP for Wallasey 1974–92, made Baroness Chalker of Wallasey after defeat in the 1992 election; Minister of State for Overseas Development 1986–97.
2 Udi Eichler, a television producer, and Judith Summers, novelist, near neighbours.

We have to be there before Salman arrives, Udi calls to tell us at 8.10 just as we are leaving. On our way round the corner, a man sitting on the bench makes almost no attempt to disguise the fact that he is watching us – an obvious Special Branch heavy. Salman eventually appears about fifteen minutes after us. He seems relaxed, amiable and quite soon jokey. What most surprises is how extremely white he is – much whiter than me. White face, white hairless hands and arms, which he exposes by rolling up the sleeves of his jacket, which billows like an Armani. Actually, he says he was asked to take part in Armani ads but declined (though he thought about it for a day); and he admits to liking Armani trousers. He is also fat, an obvious liver of the sedentary life. His eyes strike me as cold, yet his temperament isn't at all: perhaps this is just some tiny physical deformity, the heavy drooping, rather like the off-putting double-layered lip which is such a distraction on television.

However, the main thing is that he is very much nicer than he ever appears, because in this company he doesn't need to be belligerent or complaining. He has lately seen Major, whom he found much more businesslike than he would have expected: well-briefed, direct, pleasant. He had feared their meeting would be just blah-blah, but it wasn't. He also thinks very well of Douglas Hogg, who he regards as a human being, unlike Hurd, whose commitment is overlaid with such realpolitik calculation (my phrase not his).

His main concern is to see that the governments (all), having made a lot of verbal commitment, are now prepared to act. In a sense, having made the verbal noises they may have exonerated themselves. They have removed from SR the right to complain about them. But what he wants is action where it hurts, which is on the massive (£42 billion, he says) debt: *they* cannot trade unless banks are ready to roll over and reschedule debts, which governments could deter them from doing. This is by far Iran's biggest weakness. It could yet be a route through which the mullahs are toppled. He sees the ruling mullahs as deeply unpopular, and vulnerable: the alternatives he sees as another group of mullahs, or a royal return, or some form of democracy. None of these seems to me especially promising. But he must live in hope and optimism. I have the sense that, although he has to spend much time thinking about politics and talking political language, he doesn't really understand it.

He seems to maintain his sanity, despite being the object, as he says, of something never before seen in the history of literature. He has written two books in his captivity. He could write another about the tradecraft of the Special Branch, but he is very wary of saying anything about that, and he behaves like the most obedient of operators in the secret world. He says the worst single hardship is that he can't get on a plane and fly anywhere without huge problems. Many airlines, including all British ones, refuse to carry him, even though the government has urged them to do so. But he obviously gets out and about more than he apparently used to. He worries about his family, and feels the pain of having to forbid them to take up his cudgels in the way the families of the hostages used to. Too dangerous to themselves, and to his son, who is now 14.

He reads a lot and knows the whole literary gossipy scene in an up-to-date way, as far as I could hear. Very bitter about Le Carré having slagged him off – one of only three writers, he says, to have done this. He believes it was inspired by his unfavourable review of *The Russia House* [1989], even though this was qualified by statements of general praise for Le Carré's work.

Before we left he made a special point of saying how much he appreciated things I had written. This was generous, given the fact that at an earlier stage I was not an absolutely uncritical member of the support club and had written, as he must have thought, unhelpfully. He encouraged me to contact him by phone.

Our final departure, the first to go, took us past two more Special Branch heavies sitting in front of the TV watching a video. Also left us thinking that we are now glad to have Udi and Judy as neighbours, after our first (and second) sense of how deeply irritating Udi can be. But even though he's a swine, he knows a lot of people and wants us to know it.

L sat next to Salman and had an individual talk with him.

HY noted Neil Kinnock 'Looking better than before, and showing no dietary restraint. He says that before he consciously lost weight, and this had an exaggerated effect on his cheeks – which have now come back to normality. He was cheerful, funny, full of funny voices – a particularly good imitation of the Spitting Image *Major.'*

NEIL KINNOCK
Café Pelican, 6 July 1993

ONE MEMBER ONE VOTE / UNIONS He says that the leadership vote doesn't matter. It will sort itself out pretty fairly. Whoever is going to win is going to win. On the myth which says that certain seats 'belong' to certain unions, this may have had some truth twenty-five years ago but it has been steadily more false ever since. Cites Sedgefield and Mo Mowlam's seat [Redcar], both of them selecting at the last minute, where Blair and Mowlam sailed through the middle despite the GMB's alleged claim on the seats.

Thinks that the hard choice for Smith will be whether to accept, say, 95 per cent One Member One Vote: whereby an affiliated union branch can claim, say, 1 vote for every 100 members who pay the levy, which might give that union a handful of votes alongside the One Member One Vote votes. It wouldn't make any difference, it would certainly pollute the system, but it might be necessary to save everyone's face: and it would simply be a stepping stone to proper One Member One Vote in due course.

Meanwhile, because of the Boundary Commission, constituencies can't start choosing candidates until late '94. This gives the party a fortuitous extra year, so the possibility of delay for the decision to be made. Smith has to decide whether to go for it this year, lose, and come back heroically next year: or what?

Edmonds[1] is totally preoccupied with becoming boss of the new G and T union.[2] This is the dishonesty of his new position on OMOV. What Smith needs to do is rub Edmonds's and [Bill] Morris's noses in it: forcing them to look at headlines saying 'Smith humiliated', and asking them whether this is what will get the Labour Party elected. To Kinnock the whole issue is one where there should be no losers: a rare political question where the right answer stares you in the face without argument.

He thinks the unions would not in practice exert financial penalties if they didn't get their way. He can't write the speech in which they justify not paying out the political levy for whole chunks of work the party does. But he admits that not all countries are the same. He is just back from Sweden, where he finds great political vitality (not just among the social democrats) in parties which are modern and lively. The social democrats do not get financed by the unions except at elections. Yet they are well breeched.

LABOUR GENERALLY He sees the party as ready to become adventurous. It had a long time when it wasn't trusted: Militant, the unions, wild policies, a leader who had changed his mind. Now it had got rid of all this. It was respectable. This meant it should be able to take some risks. The model was Attlee, who, because he had been deputy prime minister in the war, was entrusted with his amazingly radical programme. Smith should be able to take a similar advantage. (Note per HY: Kinnock is less carping about Smith than Smith is about Kinnock.)

---

1 John Edmonds, general secretary of the GMB, Britain's third biggest union, 1986–2003; president of the TUC 1998. Edmonds and Bill Morris of the TGWU both challenged John Smith's proposals to reform the Labour Party constitution.
2 The GMB and the TGWU hoped in 1993 to merge 'at some future date', but this eventually did not happen.

MAJOR / TORIES We agree that the European elections will be Major's test. NK thinks the Tories could win only if they change their leader not more than eighteen and not less than twelve months before the election and if Labour makes a colossal balls of it. He thinks it quite possible they will change leaders again, working the same trick twice. He agrees with me that JM won't go in the same scenario as MT, but probably after the 1922 Committee have told him support has run out. Even then he might fight. He looks at himself every day and says, 'Well, nobody else is prime minister.' (NK is especially mordant about having to live with the fact that Major beat him. 'After all, he's not Churchill, or even Thatcher.') He thinks Major is a leader who will fight for himself, but has no chance of leading the party or his allies over the top. He wasn't elected to be that sort of leader, and he sure isn't being it.

A story about Richard Eyre: the Ralph Richardson Room at the National Theatre: an uneasy first visit by JM, to see *The Rise and Fall of Arturo Ui*: Eyre expatiating about the wonderful Richardson, whose portrait is on the wall: JM asking about the NT finances: Eyre saying they were like Mr Micawber: whereupon JM says I wonder how often that great man played the part of Micawber. Mind-blowing embarrassment all round. Why does Major have to pretend that he's a theatregoer?

LIBERALS Thinks Paddy is a liability. Was absolutely right about Bosnia, but is terribly pompous in public. Campbell, Hughes[1] are better. But admits that the Liberals are doing well and might do better. Says, rather mysteriously, that if Paddy 'really wants it' he could get 50 seats in the next Parliament, no bother. How? Well, 25 in the West Country for a start.

He is against any sniff of a deal with the Liberals. If Smith were to say that Labour wasn't going to fight very hard in certain seats, he would be open to all kinds of trouble, beginning with collapsed morale in the local parties. What NK advocates is a quiet getting together. Let the half-dozen Labour MPs who are close to Liberals – Calum Macdonald[2] ('the playboy of the Western Isles, but very intelligent'), Frank Field, one or two others – keep close intelligence on them, relating to which ones are likely to take positions in the event of a hung parliament etc. etc. – i.e. preparing for a tactical game.

This led him to say that a hung parliament was far easier to manage

1 Sir Menzies 'Ming' Campbell: QC; former Olympic sprinter; Liberal Democrat MP for North-East Fife since 1987; Lib Dem foreign affairs spokesman 1997–2006, deputy leader 2003–6 and Leader 2006–7. Simon Hughes: Liberal Democrat MP for North Southwark and Bermondsey since 1983; party spokesman on the environment 1983–8 and 1992–4, education 1988–92, health 1994–7, then home affairs until 2003; Lib Dem candidate for London mayoral elections 2004; party president 2004–8.
2 Calum Macdonald: Labour MP for Western Isles, 1987–2005.

than a Labour majority of 8. Recalls being a Labour rebel in the Lib–Lab-pact time and how he was terrified to miss a vote in case it was he who brought the government down. Thinks it would be the same now. Says that Labour could count on 4 SDLP, and the Welsh Nationals. But he agrees that if the Liberals do get even 30 seats, that will change the ball game. Says that Liberals at 22 per cent matter greatly, at 18 per cent hardly at all.

EUROPE Thinks that Labour must go into the Euro elections as the party of confederation: actually, I mentioned that word, and it struck the chord that has plainly been twanging with him for quite a while. Labour should be ready for the fact that Major will fight the campaign hostile to Europe, drumming up anti-European feelings in the Tory Party and trying to unite his party on that line.

Is very self-flagellatory about his own role. Says that after the 1975 referendum he should have come out loud and clear and said the issue was over. If Labour had done that, it would have changed a lot. Is altogether ready to unload on all this in a more formal interview . . .

Critical of Michael Foot for still being anti-European (despite being culturally a European . . .).

GORDON BROWN
Breakfast, 20 July 1993

Arranged because he wanted to push his line on economic policy and express, I think, a frustration about the way this was seen. A document is coming out soon.

His basic line is that Labour must cease to be seen as the tax-and-spend party. It must place skills and training at the very centre of its policy, not on the fringe. This must be based on the analysis which says that, even if there is recovery, imports will come flooding in and there will be insufficient British capacity. Labour must be seen to stand for the things people want, namely a buoyant economy in which they can better themselves. It must exploit people's understanding that the Tories will not give them this: that the Tories are quick-fix merchants: perhaps most important, that the Tories serve their vested interests, who pay for the party but also (and more important) have simply got a lock on the Tory political class.

Labour, in other words, must cease to be seen as the party of reflex actions: as the party of state solutions over individual self-improvement, the party that will take your money away, the party that sees production as an afterthought. Must also refine its appeal about 'manufacturing' and extend it to prove that it cares about financial services as well.

He is very impatient with those he calls the people who want to go back to 1983. Gould chief among them, but also Edmonds et al. I.e. people who profess to believe that lowering the exchange rate, releasing another £15 or £20 billion will provide what Labour is failing to provide, namely an aggressive, constructive economic policy that really cares about job creation. This he calls grossly irresponsible, and a delusion. He sees Edmonds as partly using it to bolster One Man One Vote, rather than the other way round now.

When I suggested that perhaps Labour would need to do more of a Clinton to try and shed its stereotypes, he said this was the main thrust of what Smith was trying to do vis-à-vis the unions.

On the unions and money, he said that we should note that Labour was now 'less dependent on union money' – about 60 per cent rather than 90 per cent, from memory. The constraining factor here was the unions' own funds, which in some cases were putting them in real difficulty. He also said that it was not hard to get party members if people really tried, and that in the seats where there was a proper drive this was achieved. But it can't be done through the post or via newspaper adverts. Personal contact is essential. And the most successful parties, on the whole, were those that had fewest meetings to discuss the finer points of Labour policy as it might have been but for the betrayals of the 1980s etc.

I asked him whether the unions provided much policy input or simply sat on the sidelines sniping. He said that there was an economic-policy committee, which would be the body from which his economic document emerged.

I have given a poor account of what he said about economic policy. He kept coming back to it, and I fear I kept switching off. But I did experience a sense that this was a man who thought seriously about the political economy, was deeply keen to get his ideas across, did believe that Labour must change its image and therefore its reality, had a genuine desire to connect with the productive parts of the economy, fully understood that the stereotypes were deeply damaging. He made me think that the job of columnist ought to be to dispel the cynicism about Labour, if possible to make the best of what they are trying to put together.

JOHN (LORD) HARRIS
The Reform Club, his lunch, 13 September 1993

In his role as chairman of the Police Foundation, which was set up with his influence (I think) when he left the Home Office. Funding unenquired about. But he is lacerating about police reforms.

The [Kenneth] Clarke White Paper was full of rubbish. Clarke [Home Secretary since 1992] is fanatically opposed to local government, and also uninterested in listening to other people's views. The police authorities reflect this: 43 heads, all of them Tory supporters, with 5 Home Office appointees and 8 local-authority people (plus others?). This is politicizing the police. The chairs are paid posts, most of them business people bringing a business ethic to police work. One may anticipate that if the authorities don't knuckle under to the Home Office will, the local-authority majority will be wiped out by fiat.

This is in effect a national police force in all but name. No local differences are allowed for. The authorities are the same for small and large, as are the targets required for league tables, irrespective of the type of locality, the number of crimes etc. etc. The arrest rate/clear-up rate will predominate, together with times taken to get to the scene of incidents. Much of this is crackpot. Opposed by senior policemen. Speed of getting to the scene, for example, is often not critical, since most calls to the police are made after the incident is over. But the arrest rate (if it is that) is a bad idea. Top cops say that, even though they oppose the tables, they will be determined not to be bottom. Therefore the likely consequence is a rise in the arrest rate of the wrong people. The whole principle of league tables is in any case vitiated by the fact that, unlike with schools, the customer has no choice to go elsewhere. Can't relocate to the highest clear-up rate in the country (somewhere in Wales).

Also in the White Paper (I think) is the idea for the fixed-term contracts for chief constables. This is also disastrous, and a route to politicizing. When a chief's term is coming up for renewal, he must ask himself how he can please his politically appointed chairman. This insinuates him into the political game. Is more reasonable for senior officers below chief rank to have these terms: but the key is that their renewal should be done by policemen, not by politicians.

Next comes Sheehy.[1] A bigger scandal. Here is a man on £900,000 a year talking about the irrelevance of higher pay to incentives to work well. The most unacceptable element of it is the fixed-term contracts for policemen of all ranks. This ruins the public-service ethic at its root: the idea that you are serving the public for life. It is passionately opposed by all policemen – see the 20,000 who went to Wembley Arena:[2] a massive proportion of all those not on duty or sleeping before their next shift. Equally wrong is the lowered starting rate for pay. A feature of Sheehy is who was on it. Again a handpicked group of Tory sympathizers, including

---

1 Sir Patrick Sheehy: chairman of BAT Industries and, since 1992, of the Inquiry into Police Responsibilities and Rewards.
2 Over 20,000 police officers went to Wembley to protest against the pay proposals of the Sheehy Report.

Eric Caines,[1] a notorious hammer of the public services from an academic base that gives him the impression of detachment.

MICHAEL PORTILLO
The Guardian, 14 September 1993

He quickly impresses as a formidable figure. A serious man, totally at home with the economic debate: deeply into the figures and arguments, plainly able to take on the Treasury people on their own terms with time to spare. Fluent, careful, a drawer of distinctions and maker of the interesting categories. The person he reminds me of most is Chris Patten: articulate, precise, fresh, hard-minded.

But there is an interesting contrast between Portillo downstairs and upstairs.[2] To the meeting he comes over as all of the above, and rather agnostic in his approach. To the lunch he shows his rightist colours much more coldly. He describes his longer-term aim as being to hang on to an ideology – built around a diminishing state, deregulation, competitiveness, education and Euro-scepticism – on to which he wants the party to be able to fasten when it has lost its way: which it inevitably is doing, he implies, in the rush of daily business.

A few points from many he made:

'I am an old-fashioned politician of the right, who favours trying to balance the books and a government that does not live beyond its means.' He says that this summer there has been too much of a tendency to label people as taxers or spenders, which is not a true reflection of the debate.

He notes the history of the Tory Party over the last fifteen years: the right wing has shifted from being the sound-money group (see the 1981 budget) to the faction that wants lower interest rates and a low exchange rate – i.e. the outward signs of a laxer policy. This has happened under the influence of Maastricht, which is a fixed-rate, managed-money (my words) project, but is anathema to the right wing because of the European aspect, not so much because of the restrictive implications for economic policy – which, after all, they used to favour (again, my gloss). This has also made them the anti-tax faction. So all in all there has been a big turnaround. In these departments, people have lost sight of public finance as the starting point of the position.

1 Eric Caines: NHS director of personnel, 1990–93; professor of health-service management at Nottingham University 1993–6. Other members of the Sheehy inquiry included Sir Colin Campbell, vice-chancellor of the University of Nottingham; John Bullock, of Coopers & Lybrand; and Sir Paul Fox, former managing director of BBC Television.
2 After an encounter with a larger number of journalists, the guest would often be whisked off to a brief formal meal in the *Guardian* boardroom, with a small group of senior figures.

I asked him how deeply new his review was, and how much of it would actually be a new-mandate programme rather than immediate. He said that he wouldn't oversell what he is doing. But they had to face the fact that there were programmes that were demand-led – social security above all – and which would not reduce. They were not cyclically based. Moreover, evidence showed that, after any recession, recovery leaves many people beached: for example, they have moved on to invalidity benefit, from which they don't move when recovery comes (and which is earnings-related, by the way). These benefits have to be paid for. We have to face that. Moreover, people have expectations about what National Insurance was paying for: e.g. NHS and their pensions, which could not be torn away. But in the strategic field what interested him was pensions. It made sense to get people to see that pensions could no longer be a complete state service: that it would help them minimize the bump downwards by making some private provision. But this was a thirty-year perspective – which nonetheless it was stimulating for a minister to have to think about. In terms of mandate stuff, this was the only thing he itemized.

North Sea taxes used to contribute 4 per cent of GDP at their peak. Now they have almost withered away.

On the cuts this year. There can be cuts even when the total rises: e.g. in the demand-led social-security budget. 'We may be able to give them enough blood for their opposition to melt away' – of the right-wing Gardiners and Townends[1] for demanding blood.

He implied that there would, at least, be no rise in the standard rate. Evidence showed, he said, that the two points of sensitivity were that plus certain rises in VAT. He also was careful to say that all such tax rises would be considered 'only if we need revenue increase'.

He believes that the VAT on heat and power may turn out to be easier to see through in reality than in prospect. Pensioners have been led to believe their costs will rise £10 a week. In April they will rise only £1 a week, and £2 a week the next April. May be a case of the damage being done before it all happens.

On the particular subject of schools, he simply denied that pupil–teacher ratio was the determinant of good output from schools. (This from a man with no children.) He was also floored by Vic Keegan's[2] question: if that was so, why do private schools boast about having lower ratios?

---

1 John Townend: Conservative MP for Bridlington 1979–97, for East Yorkshire 1997–2001.
2 Victor Keegan: assistant editor and chief leader writer of *The Guardian*.

UPSTAIRS A strong attack on the need for public subsidy for the Channel rail link. Taking a few minutes off the journey time was not a good object of subsidy. It had to compete with air services, and rightly so. Why give businessmen a subsidy like that: either on track or on fares?

A defence of rail privatization. Noting that all plans had been opposed: that many had broken new ground which everyone said was impossible. Notes the maddening propensity of the British to be fed up with the NHS, BR etc. etc., but opposed to doing anything about them. (Actually: people not fed up with the NHS, only with BR, but don't believe that what privatization means holds a serious promise of bringing any improvement.)

As a general rule, thinks government must get on and do what it has to do, and not be driven from pillar to post by pressures, winds etc. etc. This is what has happened in the last eighteen months and is what has done the damage. On this basis, favours the tough fiscal line that is coming, however unpopular.

Plainly interested in mapping out strategic ground. As above, on the ideology. In this he puts great emphasis on the unused possibilities of running with the grain: e.g. of the police, who will favour a lot of the Sheehy ideas to do with top-heavy bureaucracy and paper-pushing. (He expressed amazement – which doesn't seem at all amazing – at the fact that there are 300 policemen at any one time 'filling in reports'. I'm surprised it isn't more.) Also e.g. the teachers, who, as professionals, can surely be induced to welcome the proving of professional standards that is all part of the testing regime.

When I asked how his general ideology would fit with Ken Clarke's, he said, 'Let's not take Ken. Let's take Stephen Dorrell.' And Dorrell, he says, is totally opposed to his line on the state and government. Actually does not fear the role of the state. (Incidentally, Will Hutton says that Dorrell is overjoyed to have Clarke at the Treasury: everything has changed for the better. Also, both KC and D. Hunt are pushing in a different sort of direction.)

But the big one is Europe. Here Portillo is plainly in the very sceptic camp. He makes no bones about this. He tied the alleged 'failure of the institutions' to Europe, in part. Europe apparently was rather eating away at them. But more concretely he says that Europe was bound to come up again, and soon. Didn't know how or when. Could be on the ERM, could be on an aspect of Maastricht – any number of occasions on which the 11 would re-express the momentum they wanted to achieve. His own line was explicitly anti rejoining the ERM. He is against a fixed currency at any level, not just the 2.95. 'You know the official government line,' he said archly, but then said he hoped we would never go back in.

Factored somewhere into all this was the sense that British self-irony had grown from minor to major in the pageant of decline. It began as the jokey diminishment of a nation confident in itself, but has now become the self-abuse (all these are my phrases) of a country that makes cynicism and non-patriotism a way of life. Why do so many Brits take positive pride in not buying British? he asks. Germans and French aren't like that. When someone says there is nothing British to buy, he says, What about cars?

On the right wing in general, he acknowledged the presence of right-wingers in the Cabinet, but asked us to note how they don't act as a unit. Redwood, he instanced, had been saying things about tax that were not at all the same as he was saying. On the right-wing/left-wing divide, he said things had moved a long way from the wet/dry divide of years ago. There was, he implied, less disagreement about economic management.

But he thought the position was still favourable to the right wing. At the end of the day, it was the terms of debate laid down by the right wing – the Tories as a whole of the last decade and a half – that Labour was taking up. Labour was trying to disguise itself as the Tory Party.

Talking by chance to John Biffen afterwards, for whom Portillo worked when JB was shadow energy minister. Said MP was a sound fellow. Was playing it long. The Tories would lose the next election, and Portillo was well placed to pick up the pieces, the very messy pieces, that would be scattered about after that. I.e. it was not the right wing – and especially the Euro-sceptic right wing – that would be seen as responsible.

PADDY ASHDOWN
His office, pre-conference, 15 September 1993

His fear is of being too excited. He made an ideal plan of where the party should be at this stage, and it is well ahead – both in polling and in positioning. In fact is it peaking too early? He would rather be here next spring. He thinks the party needs to somewhat downplay its excitements.

He agrees that Labour's position is dire. He thinks Smith wasted a year – the leader's priceless honeymoon period. He needs Labour to do well, of course. He regards their failure to do well now as a serious thing. He even said he thought it might be irreparable: which, if true, is bad for the Lib Dems. The Lib Dems need to avoid a situation where 'letting Labour in' is the killer line.

What he attaches most importance to for his party is developing a message. A message rather than a programme. We have always had programmes, he said. The need is to refine the message and keep on and on repeating it so that it eventually penetrates. The worst thing for third parties is having no message: then they always get squeezed.

The components of the message have in some cases to be strengthened. The economic stuff is weak, he freely concedes. But the biggest source of appeal is the alienation from politics. How to tap into this – articulating it, sympathizing with it, promising something better – is the key.

He agrees with me that it may be that broad-brush rather than micro detail is best. He even said he thought the election manifesto should be like that. Though he said he doubted they would be able to get away with it.

He has set up an economic commission under Ralf Dahrendorf,[1] to produce a Yellow Book (after Lloyd George): an economic inquiry about making Britain more competitive internationally, starting with a study of what the economic and industrial future is, before going on to map out a Lib Dem policy.

He is enormously taken with Dahrendorf's insight that the profound event that is happening now is the break-up of the middle class: the alienation this class is experiencing through the recession: the massive lay-offs affecting white-collar workers, not blue-collars. White-collars, moreover, who may never get their jobs back. Cites United Technologies in the US, whose chairman told Dahrendorf they were sacking 150,000 people, all of them white-collar, who would not be re-employed – whereas blue-collars might be needed again as and when.

At the conference, watch out for the debate on prostitution: connects with inner-city things he has seen on his travels: has come up from the grass roots: question is, Can the party have a mature debate about policy on this? Other main problem may be the carbon tax. Also, notice pensions – perhaps the main strategic issue.

Believes the party is in good shape. No massive disagreements. In fact, hardly any. Is solvent, is better organized than it has ever been, has good local bases. A fear may be whether some new LD councillors, inexperienced, will shout their mouths off, but there's no problem yet.

Believes there is a period of great turbulence going on. Indecipherable consequences. Somewhere near the heart of this is perhaps the crack-up of the Tory Party, though that is at the outer extreme. Still sees Europe as the igniting factor not yet dampened. But a crossover into tax-and-spend. Even without it, the movement is great.

Election prospects. In the West Country a Euro election tomorrow would give us Cornwall and Devon. But it looks as though the Boundary

---

1 Ralf Dahrendorf: German-born sociologist; director of the London School of Economics, 1974–84: adopted British nationality 1988; later Lord Dahrendorf.

Commission may be fiddling the lines to make this impossible (by shifting Yeovil into Dorset).

MICHAEL PALLISER
11 November 1993

Went to the Hong Kong meeting[1] yesterday. Was shocked by Major's line, and especially his lack of factual information and his patronizing attitude. Major said that we welcomed our friends in Europe investing in Asia, implying that we were miles ahead of them. In fact Germany already invests hugely, and more than us (check). France and Italy are already in China more than us (check). Who on earth lets him say things like this?

On Europe. It is all very well lecturing Europe about social conditions etc., but he seems to forget that all over Asia the economy has been based on sweated labour. In some places this is getting less true. But HK businessmen went to south China for lower wages: and now are moving further up because south China wages are rising. (All this from Palliser, the chairman or something of the official Anglo-China society.)

In general, Major is quite mistaken in his view of Europe. The complacency is unbelievable. The fact is that Kohl may not be entirely representative of Germans, but isn't that a problem not a source of glee? Shouldn't we be worried about German nationalism – the logically approved consequence of all the Major stuff about the nation state? In any case, he is mistaken. True, people are leery of EMU – but it is plain that EMU hasn't gone away. True, the federation enthusiasts are having a poor time, but that doesn't mean the idealism of Europe has vanished. It is still a project seriously believed in.

The danger of the present stance is that once again we are seen to be only negative. We refuse to take a single initiative. We are seen as hostile, which has reverberations around the whole community. People just don't trust us. Therefore our line is mistrusted, because it is seen as proceeding from congenital lack of enthusiasm.

---

1 Chris Patten flew back from Hong Kong to brief the Cabinet on negotiations with Beijing over the handover; before the Cabinet meeting he addressed a public conference on Hong Kong.

MICHAEL ANCRAM
The Garrick, 15 November 1993

He used to work a lot at the Bar with John Smith. A close friend and convivial exchanger of hospitality. Says Smith is far, far more fun than he ever lets on: a mimic, a bon viveur, an irreverent, a man with a big house. But not an understander of the English. A man who has been part of the Labour ascendancy in Scotland which began in the mid sixties, and was due to the swing over of the Orange vote in Glasgow from Tory to Labour (on class grounds), and the withering away of the National Liberal vote which gave the Tories their rural strength rather artificially. Smith therefore thinks the Scots trick can be repeated, and doesn't understand that the English situation is different.

RAYMOND SEITZ
Breakfast, 16 November 1993

MAJOR JM had been to supper on Sunday. Ray says he first knew him in the eighties. Had not known him in the seventies, although he had known many of the other class of '79 at that early time. Major was then invisible. But when he got to know him, he thought of him as a goer. A combination of social humanity with right-wing economics, and a capacity not to offend.

Ray also saw him last night at the Guildhall. He notes a change in the last eight months or so. Earlier, when they had one-to-one talks, which they did from time to time when there was nothing big on the agenda, Major was reasonably relaxed. He had spare capacity (HY phrase) for talk, and he had what leaders are meant to have: a bigger perspective, a new way of arranging the facts – noticeable compared with the lower levels Ray might have been talking to about any given issue. He was also humorous, and keenly future-looking. Now, Ray finds, he is more enclosed. He has lost a sense of fun. He is hard and bitter, and he hasn't got the same perspective. A tiny incident, not for use: they went on the terrace with the dogs and Major took a couple of tennis balls to throw for them, but he didn't get any pleasure out of it. Seemed totally unable to relax. Very tense, the conversation jumped sharply about. Ray thinks he has been very badly bruised by Maastricht still. And sore about the pounding he has taken from the press and 'the establishment'.

He thought the Tory conference was terrible. Rather like the Republicans in Houston. Seitz's private test is to say that as long as Lilley is in the Cabinet, Major will not be able to take the risks he needs to take. He has to have the courage to be wrong: i.e. to take a position, to give a lead which may turn out to be unpopular or not to fly. As long as he has to appease Lilley, this cannot be taken seriously. In fact, what he should have done after the speech was to sack Lilley.[1] Especially because there was an extra tweak in Lilley's speech, goading Major about 'bastards', in effect saying come and get me. Sacking would have created a fine effect, at rather small risk. But of course, he wouldn't think of it . . .

Further on Europe: perhaps the problem was that it was hard to disengage the substance from the politics. The substance Major wanted had something to be said for it, but the politics drove him to present it in the wrong way.

IRELAND We agreed that Major was trying hard, and taking a risk. And that he was depending on this issue for political breakthrough. He thought Mayhew in some ways not the ideal person, but broadly was doing good things. He especially liked Mayhew's notion that all Ulster politicians were died-in-the-wool oppositionists, and this was the problem.

CLINTON Not true that there is anything in his not coming to Britain in January. If he came here he would absolutely have to go to Bonn, and then to Paris, and then to Rome. That is just the hard, inescapable politics of the thing, the advice Ray would be giving in Washington in his old job. Since he is going to Moscow, and to a NATO summit, and to an EC summit (sort of), that would mean him making an eight-day trip or whatever. But the UK press unfairly took it up. Partly a way of rounding again on Major, and jeering at him. But partly also reflects the keen anticipation with which the first and smallest sign of the ending of the special relationship is nigh.

Believes that Clinton is beginning to see that international affairs cannot be divorced from domestic. US does not have the Japan option: to be a massive economic power while taking almost no political responsibility. But Clinton has poor people around him. Drew on the Carter generation, the only ones available. Christopher, unlike other department heads, was given a lot of freedom about who he took. So the old gang came in, having not been very good under Carter either. Ray didn't say any of this quite so starkly, but the sense of it was clear.

---

1 Peter Lilley's address to the Tory conference in 1993 had promised an attack on 'benefit tourism', by removing entitlement to those who could not prove habitual residence. The address was described by some commentators as xenophobic. John Major, when a social security minister in 1986, had specifically ruled out a blanket test for residence, because it would be cumbersome and unfair.

MARGARET THATCHER
US Embassy Christmas Party, 16 December 1993

A serendipitous encounter in the queue towards the Seitz hosting line-up. Somehow MT materialized with Denis alongside just as I was contemplating how to avoid us spending ten minutes alongside Virginia and Peter Bottomley.[1] MT, having appeared, alluded to the presence of the queue, and with only the barest reluctance acknowledged that she would have to stand in it. Fortunately, I had my wits about me – unlike yesterday. (Digression: Coming out of the Major–Reynolds [Irish PM] press conference on the Irish declaration, I chanced to be last in the line of the journalists before the line was stopped to let the PMs go by. I brushed across Major's front as he walked along, and he followed me down the stairs alongside Reynolds. Having no question prepared, I remained pathetically dumb. *L'esprit de l'escalier* rectifiable but left unrectified even as I walked down the *escalier*.)

I asked her whether she was travelling a lot for the book.[2] She reeled off the places, saying one owed it to one's publisher, and it was much harder work than a general election. I asked her how she wrote, and how she liked it. She said it was very hard work. She wrote and wrote, and dictated as well, and then others laid hands on it. It was vitally important, she said, to have it shaped by an editor who had not seen it beforehand. John O'Sullivan[3] had performed this role wonderfully. She said it was important to write as she spoke, and she found it hard to get the right inflections into print. She had moved lots and lots of paragraphs about. It had made a difference. She found it very difficult to make the right sort of match between narrative time and analytical theme – don't we all? She expressed herself envious of people like me who knew how to write and had done it for a long time. She said she had cut and cut. Now she was working on the second (preceding) volume. It would be done by next year. I told her I had aided her by giving her researcher a rare document. It took her some time to stop burbling on about how wonderful her boy was, but then she did make a rather stiff expression of thanks for my help.

As we neared the reviewing stand, Denis insisted on removing her glass. He needed to explain to her that it would not be seemly to shake hands while holding a glass. He also remarked that only last night they

1 Virginia Bottomley's husband, Peter Bottomley, was Conservative MP for Greenwich, Woolwich West 1975–83, for Eltham 1983–97, for Worthing West since 1997.

2 Margaret Thatcher, *The Downing Street Years* (London: HarperCollins, 1993).

3 John O'Sullivan (editor, *The National Interest*) was brought into Margaret Thatcher's memoirs team midway through their composition to provide a fresh eye.

had been to dinner with John Birt and what a splendid chap he was.[1] Mrs T allowed herself to say what a very good thing the BBC licence fee was, and that even Denis – evidently an inveterate opponent of it – would now be paying it more happily having seen Birt, who she agreed was very good news.

She seemed stouter than before, a little puffy to my eye, and not nearly so glamorously made up as on TV. She said, when I asked her, that she had recorded nineteen hours of interview (not forty, as some have said) and was very firm that she owned copyright after four years. When I asked where the vaults would be that held this historian's treasure, while Denis said the BBC, she said hers. She claimed that she hated seeing herself on the programmes, but I failed to ask her what she thought of them.

Lucy remarked that it was an odd experience to see this person without the trappings. A reminder that at bottom everyone is ordinary. You would never think, coming across her, still less passing her in the street, that she was the Iron Lady and all that. But she was gracious to me. She has plainly got it stuck in her head that I am a fine writer. This cannot be because she read the book, still less any of my columns from the last months of her time as PM or after. What she says she likes is that not only can I write persuasively, but that I always 'have something to say', a serious argument to make. I know she thought this a long time ago – circa 1986 – the last time I interviewed her.[2] This interview had been preceded by an off-the-record chat, facilitated at his own request by Ingham, which came about because I had been one of the few columnists to give her an even break against Heseltine in the Westland affair. That was the high point of her regard for me. This in turn was followed by Matthew Parris leaving the House of Commons and, in c. April 1986, recording his last visit to MT in *The Spectator*. Her advice to him then – he was a former retainer of hers – was to keep in touch with things, not least by 'reading H. Young'. *The Guardian* managed to make something of this, and so, I believe, did Macmillans. A double-edged accolade, in a way. But echoing what she also said to me in Hong Kong in 1982 (see *One of Us*).

What all this proved to me is the truth of a phrase attributed to her by I forget who,[3] and recorded in *One of Us*: 'I make up my mind about a man in 15 seconds, and I rarely change it.' Perhaps I should have made more of this misplaced regard in the researching on my own book!

1 John Birt: director general of the BBC 1992–2000; later Baron Birt of Liverpool.
2 HY interviewed Mrs Thatcher on 8 July 1986, in advance of the Commonwealth conference. The theme – her attitude to South Africa and the question of economic sanctions – was so substantial and so detailed that the interview was published in two halves, on 9 and 10 July.
3 The more frequent version of this quotation is 'I usually make up my mind about a man in ten seconds, and I very rarely change it.'

1994

6 January	PM John Major says 'Back to Basics' was not a crusade about personal morality.
8 January	Alan Duncan MP, junior minister, resigns over allegations about the purchase of a cut-price council house.
17 January	Northridge earthquake devastates the Los Angeles area.
7 April	Genocidal killings begin in Rwanda.
6 May	The Queen and President Mitterrand of France open the Channel Tunnel.
10 May	Nelson Mandela is inaugurated as the first black president of South Africa.
12 May	Labour leader John Smith dies after a heart attack.
10 July	Two Conservative MPs, David Tredinnick and Graham Riddick, are suspended as parliamentary private secretaries over allegations that they each accepted £1,000 to table a parliamentary question.
21 July	Tony Blair is elected Labour Party leader, John Prescott his deputy.
4 October	Tony Blair calls for the party constitution – including Clause IV, relating to public ownership – to be rewritten.
19 October	Two Conservative junior ministers, Tim Smith and Neil Hamilton, are accused of accepting payments for asking parliamentary questions. Both resign.
27 October	Jonathan Aitken, Chief Secretary to the Treasury, denies *Guardian* allegations that he had misled the Cabinet Secretary about the payment of a bill at the Ritz Hotel in Paris.
19 November	Launch of the National Lottery.
11 December	President Yeltsin orders Russian troops into Chechnya.
Deaths	Elias Canetti, Kurt Cobain, Ralph Ellison, Kim Il-Sung of North Korea, Burt Lancaster, Jackie Kennedy Onassis, Karl Popper

MICHAEL HESELTINE
His office, 1 February 1994

Department of Trade and Industry: Ashdown House. His own office, unlike that of most ministers, not dominated by The Desk. Instead, his desk is in a corner, the chair back to the room, almost a student's workplace, although the rest of the room is quite large, with meeting table and armchairs. MH in a sweater. Jovial. Said he'd heard I'd remarried.

EUROPEAN ELECTIONS   There is no need for a disagreement in the party. We have a good right-wing agenda, distinguishing us from Labour. All about competition, deregulation, the need for Europe as a whole to position itself vis-à-vis Asia and the US. So there is a good Tory campaign in the making.

That said, however, there are obviously some problems. But they are not my problems. Everyone knows where I stand, and if I had been able to speak at the conference[1] I would have made a European speech, as I did with some effect in earlier years. This department has its own European agenda, as everyone knows. People ask why I have not spoken out, in retaliation against the anti-European speeches. The answer is that, although Europe is important, party unity is equally important. Therefore my position is that I won't stir it up, unless I am forced to. If the other side stick with our party line, OK. If they don't, then it will be necessary to speak. Equally, although I have been successful in fending off interviewers who try to push me in the past, if I am asked the questions in that situation I will have to reply.

Douglas is in charge of all this. Douglas is a good man. (When I said that DH wasn't so keen on Europe as MH, MH said he was a good man, sound etc.)

How would all this affect Major's position? He said that Major had only to survive until 31 July [the start of the parliamentary summer recess]. He would be ticking off the July days as they passed. 31 July was the moment of peace and survival. After that, he could surely rely on the economy having boomed away (my phrase) by October, in which case he would be safe. Of course, MH added, if for some reason that wasn't the case with the economy, then JM might be in some difficulties.

If he survived, wouldn't he be under constant pressure all the same? Well, MH breathed. He had almost got away by January. It all went calm

---

1 He was not at the time a Cabinet minister, and he had not been forgiven by Thatcher supporters: he was unlikely to have been offered a place in the political spotlight.

– and then there was Yeo[1] and all that. That surely can't keep on happening, he chortled – but then he checked himself, and said, Well I suppose it could!

He mused about how Major might be challenged. There was nobody big, was there? Lamont? Ho, ho. 'It took us twelve years to get Margaret out.' Meyer got 70 votes . . . he mused further, reminiscing. Would anyone back Lamont to get anything like 70 votes now? On the whole, he felt that Major would last – but he would say that, wouldn't he?

He looked forward to the election campaign in which he, MH, made speeches about 'this man of steel'. 'I've written the speech already – man of steel, seeing off his enemies, seeing it through, worst attacks any prime minister had suffered.' And we will win by 60 seats. He looked forward to his next meeting with the *Guardian* editorial team to tell them so – a reference to his prediction last time, which as I remember was correctish.

I said, But the economy wasn't the decisive factor in '92. He said, Ah yes, but disposable income was. Taxes were low, interest rates were coming down, inflation was lowering, people were actually better off. This may have had nothing to do with the state of the real economy, but it is, and always was, the reason people vote. 'I may be very cynical, but I do believe cynicism in this area is justifiable.' He sees all this being more so in 1996 or '7.

The big proof of this is Clinton. Who is the only leader in the world who is popular? Clinton. Very high ratings, despite his personal problems. He has two arrows pointing at his heart – yet the people give him sky-high ratings. OK, the philandering was discounted at the election, but what about sleaze? Nonetheless, people are not bothered. Clinton's sleaze is far worse than anything affecting us. And the reason, of course, why he is doing well is the US economy recovering.

To all this I reply that the Tories are surely more divided now than ever in fifteen years. Oh no, he says. It was worse in 1986. He was staggered, when he returned to the back benches – where he had seldom been throughout his political career – to discover the extent of people's disenchantment. (I think this is a self-serving point. To justify his departure to the back benches. And it was a different kind of trouble. People were alarmed, and beginning to get fed up with MT, but there wasn't the splitting there now is. There wasn't Europe . . .)

---

1 Tim Yeo, Conservative MP for South Suffolk since 1983, was Minister for the Environment and Countryside in 1993, the year that John Major launched his 'Back to Basics' campaign. Yeo resigned in January 1994 after the revelation that he had fathered a child in the course of an extramarital affair.

EUROPE AS A WHOLE As soon as the recovery sets in, the momentum will resume. We are in a centralized entity, MH insists. That is a fact of life. Subsidiarity is important as a political selling word, and does have some real value. But as a description of what Europe is going to be, it is a second-order truth. It has been popular because Europe has been unpopular: Europe has been a scapegoat for the recession and has taken its buffeting along with all political organizations. But MH has absolutely no doubt that the progress towards a single currency will resume. Germany, France, Benelux, probably Italy, Austria – all will have their reasons for wanting to coalesce. The costs of a multi-currency outweigh the benefits. We will all see there is either a DM-dominated regime or a single currency, and for the UK the single currency is much better. If you have a single market, you have to follow the logic.

JOHN BIFFEN
House of Commons, 8 February 1994

Believes the Tories will lose the next election, because of tactical voting. He thinks it could be an outright Labour victory. But he seems rather mixed up about the virtue and vice of Smith being such a non-policy man. Describes Smith as having 'the worst aspects of a Conservative'. Says it will be quite nice as a Tory to fight a Labour leader who has nothing to say. But all the same, the Tories will not win.

There is a cross-cutting factor for the Lib Dems here (this more per HY). On the one hand, they need Labour to become acceptable. They want to make themselves invulnerable to the charge of letting Labour in: i.e. this must come to seem to the voters a threat they can live with. On the other hand, they must fear that if this goes too far the tribal loyalties of Labour people in Lib Dem/Tory seats may prevent them from backing the Lib Dems.

After the Tory defeat there will be the mother of all battles over the future of the Tory Party. Between those who fight for the Thatcher inheritance in economic and European policy and those who fight for, as it were, the Major line, 'the present lot'. It will be deeply fascinating to see how people position themselves.

JAMES CORNFORD
Café Pelican, 2 March 1994

SMITH AND LABOUR JC doubts whether the party is really committed to the right level of detailed pre-work. He says, on the field he knows most about, that they are not – at least Smith is not – ready with the constitutional detail. Much of this is due to their terror of Lib–Labbery. He confirms the Lester rather than Barnett version of Charter 88 row. (But AL[1] a poor politician: not liked by Labour, and very unlikely therefore to be Lord Chancellor – which, by the way, JC has absolutely no doubt he would accept if offered. JC says that Menzies Campbell for Defence is a much more likely companion for Ashdown in the Smith cabinet.)

He wonders whether Blair is more than an adept politician. Has he got real substance, can he cut the mustard on the big issues? A good question. Blair's two achievements have been One Man One Vote, preceded by his manoeuvring to get the unions round to a new perspective: and getting the Labour Party aligned behind a tougher law-and-order policy. Both formidable, but not the same as working out a new social-security regime.

ON LIB–LABBERY Recalling his experiences with Steel and the Lib–Lab pact, and especially his dealing as a Lib adviser to Johnston[2] when they were brokering a devolution deal with John Smith and Foot, his painful memory is of people who didn't know what they wanted. There never was a bottom line, which is one reason Smith despises them rather now. Therefore he says it is cardinally important that Ashdown should have thought all this out. What is his bottom line re electoral reform? Up with what will he not put?

In conversation, I come to the conclusion that by offering his referendum, which will happen whether or not Labour has a majority, Smith has conceded Ashdown's maximum credible demand. Is Ashdown still hooked on a post-legislative referendum? This is surely crazy. The only way to give himself even half a chance of forcing Labour MPs to back reform is by getting a national referendum in place beforehand . . .

---

1 Anthony Lester, Lord Lester since 1993.
2 Russell Johnston: Liberal MP for Inverness 1964–83, for Inverness, Nairn and Lochaber 1983–8, and then as a Liberal Democrat 1988–97; later Baron Russell-Johnston of Ninginish, having changed his surname by deed poll to allow his forename to be included in his title.

HY viewed Bill Morris as 'a rather quiet man. Not always speaking grammatically. But doesn't seem so dim as he is caricatured. By union standards seems very like many others: under-educated, watchful, unflamboyant.'

BILL MORRIS
Transport House, 15 March 1994

Check-off[1] seems to be going OK. It is a massive undertaking, to contact 1 million people at the workplace and get them to sign up. T & G didn't make it any easier by deciding to have their political-levy ballot at the same time (deadline end of this week). This was to save costs, but has been a practical problem, trying to get people to understand two things at the same time. Both these exercises are costly and irritating. They have no upside, save perhaps for some politicizing at the workplace as people think about the need for a political fund to match the power of the bosses. Moreover, government has withdrawn funding from ballots. Last year down by 25 per cent, this year 50 per cent, next year 100 per cent: all to save public money. Mailing 1 million members even at second-class post is very expensive . . . He thinks Labour will change this. It is a matter of bureaucracy not policy.

He spends much less time on politics than did Jack Jones or Ernest Bevin.[2] This is because they have virtually no access to the government. And for himself, he is not on any of the Labour Party bodies, although he sees Smith and Whitty[3] from time to time. T & G have their man on the NEC, of course.

If Labour got back, he would certainly expect to spend more time on politics. He would expect to be consulted on things to do with union and employment affairs (pretty broadly defined, I inferred). He wasn't bashful about this.

Now, he expects the next big argument to be about the welfare state. This is what they are gearing up for. Seems to see the Borrie Commission[4] as a threat, although he didn't say so. Wants to insist that the welfare state is more than an affordability issue and more than a safety net but must encompass all the things people care about – above all, jobs. When

---

1 Under the check-off system, union contributions could be deducted automatically from pay packets, along with National Insurance and tax.

2 Jack Jones and Ernest Bevin were, like Bill Morris, in their time general secretaries of the TGWU.

3 John (Larry) Whitty: general secretary of the Labour Party 1985–94; later Baron Whitty of Camberwell.

4 Sir Gordon Borrie: barrister; chairman of the Equal Opportunities Commission 1975–6; chairman of the Commission on Social Justice 1992–4.

I asked whether he was basically in favour of no change, he said no – but then said that he wanted a policy with 'vision'. 'Beveridge had vision.'

HUGH DYKES
17 March 1994

Douglas Hurd is getting very strange. Had dinner with him last week. He said that he believed that integration should go no further. He seems to be switching off. He is tired.

The big unknown is how all this started. HD thinks Cash[1] and co. are being well financed by secret business fanatics, on the lines of the National Association for Freedom. How do they get such good intelligence? They are better informed than we are. Duncan-Smith very sharp on a recent point, ahead of the game.

Ministers have caved in to the sceptics' veto for far too long. After Maastricht they said they would become tougher, that that was the end of the game. But they have gone on caving in, letting William Cash run the European policy.

There is a larger mistake. People haven't seen that the country no longer sees things in a left–right way. There is a sea change. People want government intervention etc. Therefore to fight the European election on these lines is missing the point and will be counterproductive.

On 23 March 1994 HY interviewed John Major, fresh from some demanding negotiations in Europe. The Prime Minister told his interviewer, 'I am more a European in my head than in my heart, but I want to see Europe succeed.'

DOUGLAS HURD
Foreign Office, 30 March 1994

The day after the 27/23 climbdown.[2] He was pretty cheerful, though chagrined about the intense waste of time that all this had caused.

I remarked that my Major interview had been part of the negotiating

---

1 Bill Cash MP played a key role in organizing the Tory rebellion over Maastricht.

2 A complex argument about the number of minority votes required to block European legislation. The British sought 23 but were forced to concede 27 out of 90 votes in the Council of Ministers. Hurd's achievement was to defuse a potentially explosive political climbdown. A sceptic was reported in *The Guardian* at the time as saying, 'Douglas was brilliant. He poured treacle over the fudge.'

process.[1] He said yes. And not just because of the 'willing to delay enlargement'[2] line, but also because it was apparently (unnoticed by me) Major's first indication that he would be prepared to compromise. This was important. DH said he had been given a free hand to 'protect Britain's national interest' by the Cabinet. But he implied that this line from Major had been helpful.

For it would, he said, have been a terrible mistake to delay enlargement (not his actual words, but his sense). People hadn't paid nearly enough attention to this. There was a tide in the four countries, which JM had done much to assist. At two summits, DH had watched him working cleverly and quietly to that end, getting the awkward details sorted out, pushing people along. To lose the tide would be a major failure for British policy. Was enlargement 'British'? He said it was really invented by Margaret. She got it going. For dubious reasons. But Major had for a time been the biggest pusher. Now overtaken by the Germans – despite their own ambiguous feelings.

On 27/23 and all that. He had told the backbench committee, his last words before he left the meeting, that it would not be solved at either a clean 23 or a clean 27. Yet the party had persisted in thinking otherwise and raising the stakes. He agreed, however, that the thing had been mishandled, 'for which we are all partly to blame'. It has been an important but 'confined' issue. The problem was it had escaped from its proper box.

The Germans in the end had forced the deal through. They had done very well. Kinkel[3] was good. They had virtually taken over the presidency, much to the chagrin of the Greeks – but they had been right to do so.

It had all been hugely preoccupying. He confirmed that Michael Howard had made the main statement of dissatisfaction: 'long and able'. There had been a good discussion. DH had circulated a paper beforehand. Shephard had been passionate for 27. JM summed up in a sense nobody objected to, and that was it. He thought Major had done well in the House, been fully in command of the subject.

His main concern is that the big issues have been neglected. For him the biggest concern is security – briefly alluded to but not picked up in his Plymouth speech. Sees this as the area where it is most absurd of all to ask the question 'Are we in or out of Europe?' Also one the Tories just don't think about. When he referred to it on Monday, in answer to a soft

1 HY's interview with John Major appeared in *The Guardian* on 25 March. It was headed, 'His head leads his heart on Europe: Hugo Young hears first hand from John Major that brinkmanship and compromise are par for the course in dealing with the EU.'

2 In 1994 Austria, Finland, Sweden and Norway had all applied to join the EU. Norway eventually failed to join because in a referendum the Norwegians voted No.

3 Klaus Kinkel: German foreign minister 1992–8.

question from Dalyell, a backbencher came up to him afterwards and said, How interesting, could he see something on paper? Douglas referred him to six unread speeches. He told me that it was in order to make progress on this across four fronts – NATO, EU, trade and one other – that he really wanted to stay in his job.

At the end, he reverted to the *Guardian* interview. Said he thought it had gone very well. So did the PM. Major had said he was surprised by this. 'He has often cursed the name of Young in my hearing,' Douglas chortled. But he evidently thought he'd got across what he wanted to get across.

MICHAEL PORTILLO
Treasury, 26 April 1994

He greets me rather stiffly, but personally coming into the waiting room rather than sending a flunky. Not a white-collar flunky to be seen at any stage. 'Mine's a mineral water,' he says.

SELF-RELIANCE AND ALL THAT He'd made a speech last week setting out the case for the 'quiet majority' and their concerns. I asked him how this fitted into any account of what had happened in the Thatcher years.

He wasn't talking just about Britain, he said. There was a general erosion of social cohesion. The US was worse. Another prime case was Spain, which not long ago had no family breakdown whatever. The assertion of old values was necessary; most people really believed in them. In the UK things have been slipping, after a period in which they had been getting better [i.e. Thatcher, but then Major].

His main case story at the moment is education. He thinks our education policy has been a failure. There should have been far more independence for schools. He sees schools where the head is in charge of his budget and his methods. He, and the parents, can make their own choices. These places are vibrant and wonderful. They should be the norm not the exception. Every school in the land should, ideally, be run like this. I said that communities and cities could not be served in this way, they needed planning etc. etc. 'So you're in favour of central control,' he said politely. He just disagreed. But then said he wasn't setting up in business as an expert in education.

He said that it was true that many places had opted against Grant Maintained School status. That was just a sign of people's blindness. They just didn't see how things could be better. I said that plenty of places judged their schools to be perfectly OK as now, and fulfilling all the Portillo criteria of excellence, which was why parents voted against GMS. He said with a wry smile, 'I grant you there may be some schools like that.'

He also thought that the national curriculum was a real problem. Obviously it was terrible that children were leaving school illiterate and innumerate. That was the condemnation of the system. But the curriculum enhanced the power of the NUT (I didn't quite get this – except the hatred of the NUT), which also undermined things by encouraging its members to believe that testing and league tables were somehow unprofessional.

I suggested that all this was out of its time: that we were at a moment when society was moving back towards a social-democratic option. Maybe only from the pendulum swing, but palpably so anyway. He rejected this completely. He said that of course society was very conservative. The British were bad at change. They had resisted each and every privatization, and were now trying to defend British Rail – the worst railway anyone could imagine. But British Telecom, electric, gas, water etc. etc.: all had vastly improved under privatization. Nobody gave us any credit, as time went on. They forgot the horrors of what went before. But he had the feeling that all the same the memory and the effect seeped into the public mind: that this was a government that had done some important and good things. The railways would 'without question' be much better when reformed.

He especially mentioned the NHS as a place where change had been of huge value. The British had this extraordinary habit of clinging on to institutions that did not work. The NHS had been amazingly inefficient, yet popular. The new trusts were far better, and budget-holding GPs now up to 36 per cent. I murmured that the customers were not being well satisfied. This was not his experience, he said.

PUBLIC SPENDING I said that perhaps this had ceased to be a matter of philosophy and become a matter of marginal detail. I.e. the Clarke tax rises showed that all our societies were high-spending high-taxing places, and the utopian dream of vastly lower tax was unsustainable. He rejected this.

In 1979 public spending took 48 per cent of GNP; in 1988 it took 38 per cent. This wasn't a marginal change. It was colossal, and enabled us to pay off part of the national debt. But the figure had gone up a lot, I said. Yes, it was now 45 per cent. (He said that Gaidar, the Russian,[1]

1 Yegor Gaidar: Russian economist and politician; acting prime minister under Boris Yeltsin June–December 1992; first deputy prime minister 1991–2 and 1993–4.

had been in here the other day, and said the Russian figure was 53 per cent – 'so we're pretty close to the Russians,' Portillo said humorously.) It was absolutely vital to get it down, and there were ways to have a dramatic effect.

He is very interested in 'process' in the public sector. Thinks it is woefully untechnological and unmodern. The private sector, he says, has made vast incentive gains from computer-driven organizational change. Believes the Benefits Agency, now employing 80,000, could be halved, without any damage to fraud-chasing etc. etc. It is just very old hat in its management. The associated 'computer clutter' in an old-fashioned system was horrendous. It all needed severely attacking. And there were other parts of public-sector management that needed the same treatment.

He had high hopes for the private finance initiative greatly expanding if we can get it right.

EUROPE I said that of all the sceptics at the top, he was the most organized and committed, from what I'd read. He had a very serious view that the UK should distance itself. He did not disappoint me:

The nodal case is against the single currency. This is what Maastricht was most seriously about. The Prime Minister had handled Maastricht brilliantly. He had got the party lined up before, during and after. He had his parliamentary backing in his pocket before he went, got it confirmed when he came back. So it was in the manifesto, an agreed policy, everyone was pledged to it. I wasn't in the Cabinet at the time, but he had got all the Cabinet pledged to it beforehand. There was no escape.

MP is completely opposed to the single currency. He does not accept that there would be a heavy price to pay for keeping out of it. He has been round the City and found people who don't want it. He says the pro-Europe people have again been clever, putting the frighteners on anyone tempted to the sceptic side by saying that the City would be finished if we were outside the EMU. But this is not true. The City depends on its expertise, its speed, its honour, its huge innovative skills – 'there are some wonderful new products being put together all the time.' Its location didn't matter, vis-à-vis Europe. People had the assurance that they could sue in the English courts – a rather better bet than French or Italian courts (shades of the exam cheaters!). Moreover, there were now more and more people in business who were anti-EU. Strange, I said, since they had been the earliest driving force for entry. He agreed, but said it was proof that the Tories should not listen to business – which had got them into the ERM. He also noted the 'large number' of important journalists who now wrote very hostile pieces about the EU.

There had been a sea change re the last qualified-majority-voting crisis. Many new people came out of the woodwork, who had really been against Maastricht. (Peter Tapsell[1] told me the night before that there had never really been a Tory majority for Maastricht anyway.) When I said that many of these were more against Major than against the QMV deal, he said, 'I'll grant you that maybe 60–70 per cent were due to the Grand Old Duke of York factor, but that still leaves a lot of new anti-EU people.'

I said that this put Portillo far away from Major and the mainline leadership. He did not deny it. He was very open about it. But he knew he could not argue for it publicly. He was to some extent stymied in the debate that would be raging around until 1996. But he then said that whoever was leader would have to take account of the state of the party. The only question he ducked in an increasingly candid hour was whether this leader would be Major. But he talked like someone who thought Heseltine was a very plausible possibility.

I said that MH could be relied on to conduct a totally astute progress towards the leadership, and he agreed. When I reminded him that MH favoured a single currency, he smiled derisively and asked when he'd last said so. ('Whereas Ken Clarke has been very courageous saying that he does favour it. It does him absolutely no good.') Hezza 'wore a Union Jack about his person, and you never could know when he would unfurl it'. I put to him a theory I've been thinking about: that Hezza could be Referendum Man. It's certainly the mode that would suit MH, though of course he would have to decide exactly what the referendum was about. The problem, said MP, was that he could never be sure the whole Cabinet would be on the same side. This, he added, was a big reason why Major had been against a referendum at any time: that it would split not just the party but the Cabinet. If Hezza had a referendum designed to seal in a crypto-federal answer, there would be massive trouble. On the other hand, MP agreed the referendum was something MH might find would work for him.

He thought it more likely, though, that he would shift the sceptics' way. He wouldn't do this at once. It would not be the basis for his election. But he would do it after being installed as leader. As for his health? I asked.[2] Again smirking, MP said that he could see the party voting for Hezza precisely because he was old and maybe sick: i.e. a transitional short-term figure whose virtues might win them an election – and who in any case they might think 'deserved' something.

<hr />

1 Sir Peter Tapsell: Conservative MP for Nottingham West 1959–64, for Horncastle 1966–83, for East Lindsey 1983–97, for Louth and Horncastle since 1997.
2 In June 1993 Michael Heseltine had suffered a heart attack in Venice, but he returned to active politics.

Returning to Major, he said that the *Economist* piece of 25 September 1993 (this date has become a kind of mantra) was a position Portillo found quite acceptable.[1] 'What he wrote there – or was prepared to put his name to (another smirk) – was a position round which the party can unite.' But, he implied, this had been shifted from – although I said, and he did not refute, that the QMV fiasco was not of itself a shift.

I said it was curious how little popular resonance this issue had had during Maastricht or since. It was confined to the political class. He agreed. But he said it was the job of politicians to make people care about it. He also said that most people simply didn't understand how Brussels affected their lives. When I said that to many people Brussels was no larger an object of cynicism than Westminster, he said that was a big pity. But he said the reason the political class was obsessed was very simple: 'The political class are interested in power. If power is moved elsewhere, they naturally become obsessed.' He also remarked, re the debate that should be taking place, on the difficulty the sceptics had, if they held office. But why, I asked, were the pro-Europeans so silent, so unable to speak clearly? 'Because it would do no good to their careers.'

HIS OWN CAREER Yes, he said, it was a 'serious disadvantage' not to have run a department. I suggested he might like Education. Yes, he said, that would be good. 'And then that might be the end of everything,' he laughed – almost the first genuine non-smirk of the hour.

Portillo strikes me as totally ambitious, utterly calculating, and perhaps not even as chastened as he should be by his lack of experience. He really believes he speaks for the Tory soul. 'I hold my opinions (about Europe) much more strongly than the Prime Minister does or Heseltine does.' But at bottom his calculation will surely be enough to make him see that his real chance, assuming Major does not survive, is not next – but next but one. It's a long time since I've met a more coldly dedicated politician – though his opinionation may yet destroy him.

---

1 Major argued that monetary union was unrealistic, and urged other leaders to think about the things that concerned ordinary people: among them, security, jobs and the other nations that shared the continent. 'The present Community is but a fragment of Europe. If we fail to bring the democratic countries of Eastern and Central Europe into our Community, we risk recreating division in Europe – between the haves and the have-nots.'

JOHN BIFFEN
Phone, 3 May 1994

Major will survive as long as he wants to survive and as long as nobody in the Cabinet moves against him – a more difficult condition to be sure of. He will survive past the local-authority elections, and almost certainly Europe too. In the European elections, JB thinks the Tory representation will be halved: c.15 seats.

At the party conference he will get very large support. There will be great resentment of people who show any sign of trying to unseat him. He will also have six months of better economic news behind him.

The crucial moment is whether a candidate stands against him in the leadership contest in November. JB takes the Meyer event as a guide: c.60 people acted/voted against Thatcher. It would be about the same now, perhaps: but again it's hard to tell six months ahead. He thinks there would be little difficulty in getting 30 nominators.

JB personally wants Major to stay. He declined to say anything adamant against MH, but said he personally never voted according to a man's position on the ideological spectrum. He regarded the Tory Party as still a broad Church. He favoured a leader who promoted his views but also would protect them from becoming part of a sectarian battle.

It will be far better for the party if Major takes us through to the election. He may – to JB's surprise – win it. If he loses it, he will have done the party the service off getting it to where it is, ready for a new leader to emerge as the natural consequence of defeat.

Diagnostically, he says that MH would lift the party for a few months. He would also lift the middle class for longer. Which is why the Euro results in the Home Counties and the south-west are very important.

PORTILLO Used to work for JB, when at CCO: his assistant as shadow energy secretary. He has shown daring – which is a good start. His daring lies in saying things that will irritate the other wing of the party, including the leader. He does so in language that makes it hard to sack him. But he won't back off his beliefs. This puts him ahead of the other bastards. He is also sophisticated. JB had a long talk with him on the train to Birmingham, and found him with a decent sense of history and of reality. But it is all happening too soon for him. He also has to make absurdly convoluted speeches, saying in code what he would like to say in clear – and therefore not being able to set out his position with a view to maximizing it in the event of election defeat and a real contest in which he would be a serious runner.

Christopher Meyer arrived half an hour late at the Garrick in May 1994.
HY described what followed as 'not a very satisfactory lunch. Though
apologetic, more to the point he was poor company, venturing little and
having no interesting ideas – quite apart from a natural mumness which
I quite understand. Pleasant, slightly shambling, a faintly affected sense
of shamblingness.'

CHRISTOPHER MEYER
The Garrick, 9 May 1994

The first thing he told me was that although he enjoyed the job [press
secretary to the PM] enormously (he started in February I think), it has
always been his intention to return to the FCO. Since he is working for
a loser, this seems a reasonable precaution but perhaps explains his
general caution (cf. Ingham, who at least knew he was working for a
winner).

LEADERSHIP 'It really sticks in JM's craw that here we have an
economic situation with the real prospect of inflation-free growth for a
long time and the party seems willing to hand it over to John Smith for
fifteen years.'

CM thinks there are analogies with Bush, handing over economic
growth to Clinton. But the difference is that Major had time to play with
– three years.

He says that if there is a challenge, Major will see it through to the
end. He would do what Thatcher didn't do. Insist on another ballot until
the majority was declared against him.

Meyer ventured it as his opinion that, instead of trying all the time to
balance the forces in the party, there was a case for Major taking a strong
stand and pushing the waverers into line behind him. Is this a hint of
things to come?

John Smith, the Labour leader since 1992, died suddenly on 12 May
1994 following a heart attack.

GORDON BROWN
His office, 7 Millbank, 24 May 1994

No. 7 Millbank turns out to be another palatial extension of MPs' offices. There are alleged by the doorman to be 2,000 people working there. It is well carpeted and well provided, but journalists are no longer allowed free access to it with their cards. GB says he is trying to change this. He remarks, however, on its low technology. No Sky TV, and no proper computer terminals – cf. the House of Lords, where evidently there is soon going to be a big stocking up with computers for selected peers.

GB seemed oddly liberated. No signs of the uptight, neurotic fellow I've seen before. Perhaps not a man desperately worried about the leadership? As with Margaret Beckett[1] last night on Channel 4, death seems at least to have released confidence if not energies. These two both seem noticeably less confined in their demeanour. Not that they are any more reckless with their words: they just seem less defensive. This is perhaps a legacy of the extreme discipline the sainted Smith succeeded in imposing on the party.

Smith had had a philosophy of one more heave. Above everything else he wanted to make sure the party stayed united, or was seen to be. To this end, he really did prefer that challenging questions were not addressed in public, or even in private (I inferred). This had presented real problems for Brown in addressing the economic agenda. He saw it was vital to get away from the simplistic image of Labour as the party of high, incentive-killing, joy-destroying taxation. It produced very little money, it did nothing for incentives or opportunity, it positioned Labour in its old-fashioned mode. Last summer in particular – and I have it from Mandelson that Smith was part of this – Brown was under a lot of private, and some public, attack from within the party for not having a grand economic strategy for growth, tax etc. This was no doubt partly due to Smith's jealous reluctance (this per PM) to concede that his own tax plan was a political disaster when presented just before the '92 election.

Brown feels that his large strategy has been justified. First, he got into terrible trouble for not attacking the government over the ERM in 1992. But he took the line that Labour must not be tagged as the party of

---

1 Margaret Beckett: Labour MP for Lincoln 1974–9, for Derby South since 1983; first female deputy leader of the Labour Party 1992–4 and briefly leader following John Smith's death in May 1994; came third in the leadership election of July 1994 and second in the deputy-leadership contest; shadow Health Secretary 1994–5; President of the Board of Trade 1997–8; Leader of the House of Commons 1998–2001 and Secretary of State for Environment, Food and Rural Affairs; first woman to be appointed Foreign Secretary 2006–7; returned to office, as housing minister, in Gordon Brown's October 2008 reshuffle.

devaluation – which it had so often been. He thinks he has succeeded. It will not be so tagged.

Second, he wanted to redefine Labour as not the party of high income tax. Nothing would have been easier than to go to the conference and announce the new top rate of tax. It would have got a quick cheer. But it would have been a gross error. Having sat tight on that, Labour has again been vindicated by the government's own tax record and its forced confession of how much it has been put up, and how much it takes from GDP. This has removed the tax issue from the Tories.

Third, he wanted to begin to reposition Labour's policy for employment, growth etc. This is what his recent speeches and pamphlets have largely been about: developing the Labour alternative.

FULL EMPLOYMENT He agrees that this is a bit of a mantra (my word). He is pressed to promise certain levels of employment in x years, and will not do it. This would be quite crazy and unbelievable. Therefore, the Edmonds line about making full employment the centrepiece of policy is not very meaningful. But levels cannot be predicted or promised. On the other hand, employment can either be left as the residual of all other policies – the Tory line – or it can be a focused purpose of policy, which is what Labour makes it. You can either have a policy for reskilling the nation, or you don't.

SOCIAL CHAPTER He is making a speech about this very soon. He thinks Labour is caricatured as the party of job-killing regulation. Somehow they have to get the proposition away from this Tory formula. He concedes that not all the SC is appropriate for Britain. He cited works councils – though perhaps only as an academic example – as perhaps something good for Germany but not for Britain. I said he should make an effort to say that Labour is not simply committed, as the manifesto says, to a blank instatement of the SC into Maastricht, but has more refined thoughts on the subject. He seemed to agree. But he said that Labour's overall position must be for basic labour protection etc. (I cite from unclear memory through the blur of lengthy speeches he made to me).

Overall, his position kept coming back to community. He cited the Charter 88 lecture[1] as the point where he began all this. It wasn't simply a matter of community, but also the relocation of relationships with both the individual and the state. A key Labour task is reviving the idea of government as good and benign.

1 Gordon Brown had delivered the Charter 88 sovereignty lecture on 9 March 1992. In it, he had directly addressed the position of the individual and the state.

I asked him whether there was a lesson from the Thatcher period, whereby in the late seventies, before getting into government, Thatcher cornered the zeitgeist and made it her own. He replied that Thatcher's main achievement was to identify what was wrong with what had gone before. It was more negative than positive – justifiably critical, says GB: there was a lot wrong. I said perhaps one of Labour's problems in imitating the Thatcher capture of Big Ideas was that they were ambivalent about what had been happening. They wanted to retain some of it, build on it, not abolish it. He didn't like to accept this, but I think it is true.

He said that Labour had to remember its past. He recalled (cleverly) that I had been critical of this – which I myself had forgotten! But for a Labour person it was essential to restate the values and apply new policies to them. You couldn't get away from the values, however. And this meant using the past for a future purpose.

POLITICS The [leadership] election will be in July. There is no need for a conference. The results can be counted without a gathering. But it will not be at all easy. The balloting will be variable. Someone said to GB the other day that he will have eight votes: as MP, as union member, as Fabian, as other affiliated body, as constituency member etc.

There are real inhibitions on it being an opportunity for serious argument. It will be very short, not starting until after the European election. There will be post-European exhaustion. There is a desire not to have too fierce an argument anyway, which is bound to be exploited and misinterpreted.

As to his own candidature, he said twice that his desire was to avoid any confusion about the modernizing project. He wouldn't say what he felt about Blair etc. He said he would decide 'quite soon'. He claimed to be less concerned with what job he held in a few years' time than with the question of what Labour stood for and how it was seen by the country.

PETER LILLEY
The Guardian, 24 May 1994

He seems clever, small, evasive, mean, watchful. He has a serious long-term agenda, which is the capture of the Conservative Party for his kind of Tory. He talked a lot about the minutiae of social security (a handful of notes attached). But over lunch upstairs, the following emerged.

EUROPE He wants no more integration, but the reverse. To my question, he said quite openly that he would like to see measures to dis-integrate. He cites Switzerland: a small country which survives very well. Which country in the world has the largest foreign reserves? Taiwan, he claims. This shows that small countries can prosper without belonging to any clubs, and just by selling services and goods that people want to buy. That should be the model for Britain. It is totally preposterous to think that a country with 56 million people cannot exist as a viable economic entity on its own, outside clubs. It could get a trade agreement with the EU. Because the trade balance is so favourable to the EU, there should be no difficulty about them negotiating a free-trade agreement. Switzerland has one.

He completely dismissed any need for political union. This only got in the way of free economic choices, the ability to run an economy in the British interest. He thinks that the trend on the Continent is this way as well. When Kohl and Mitterrand have gone, the old men – the post-war men – will have vanished, and their imperatives will fade. He doesn't believe the younger generation support the kind of EU that has developed thus far. There will be a pulling away. (Cf. Portillo, who does not believe the Hurd thesis that EU is moving Britain's way.) He sees the EU as entirely the product of Bureaucratic Man, a European construct who is the enemy of the free markets that are the only road to prosperity.

Single market. He places all his emphasis on the iniquities of the European Court of Justice. 'It's the court that has caused all the trouble.' Quite shameless saying that when MT went into the single market, they thought it would be entirely about the market. Expresses a fixed certainty that the extensions that have been made from it are malign, unforeseen, and supervised by a court that has an inexorable tendency to interpret every legal uncertainty in an integrationist direction.

TORY POLITICS   He began to speak quite openly about there being only three Thatcherites in the Cabinet. Why was this? Mainly due to the long conspiracy at CCO to keep rightists off the candidates list. He himself when chairman of the Bow Group was excluded from it. As were many others. Angela Rumbold[1] is the first vice-chairman i/c candidates who has believed in letting rightists in: Marcus Fox[2] did it for a short bit, but otherwise nobody. The No Turning Back Group[3] had attacked Mrs T about this during the 1983 parliament, when she came to dinner. Eric Forth had risked all with a strong attack on her for not promoting drys,

---

1 Dame Angela Rumbold: Conservative MP for Mitcham and Morden 1982–97; deputy chairman of the Conservative Party 1992–5.
2 Marcus Fox: Conservative MP for Shipley 1970–97; chairman of the 1922 Committee 1992–7.
3 The No Turning Back Group was formed within the Conservative Party during Mrs Thatcher's second government. It took its name from Mrs Thatcher's 1980 conference speech, in which she addressed talk of political U-turns and said, 'You turn if you want to. This lady's not for turning.'

and for keeping all the wets there: it was the era of consolidators (like Biffen) who the NTB Group worried about.

He wants Major to stay. Is pretty sure he will do so. Made some sardonic remark about Major's limited ability to rouse people to believe in real Conservatism, but insists he must stay and is the best man to win the election.

One of Lilley's bugbears is the business world (again, cf. Portillo, who says the same). They are lousy advisers on politics. They pushed for the ERM, an unmitigated disaster – putting 15 per cent on British exports. When they can't do business, they always blame politicians. If they can't sell in Germany they say it's due to a fix of some kind; ditto all over the world. Anything but recognize that it may be due to lousy goods at the wrong price. But he had little answer when confronted with the Tory obsession with placing businessmen in every corner of the health/education etc. world.

He would like Education as his next job, a stepping stone to the Treasury. Sees it as the great failure, despite all that's been done. Who else in the Cabinet? No. 1 candidate: Michael Forsyth,[1] to bring a touch of Tebbit and the jugular. Then Aitken, David Maclean: and Neil Hamilton as chairman of the party.[2] Wow!

You get a taste of the calculating sureness of the right. They know they are right. He said Labour's best chance would be to emulate Australia and NZ Labour, and get round to the right of the Tories on some issues. Frank Field should be their guide – the only man on the Labour side with any interesting ideas. He insists that the intellectual tide is all to the right. When Malcolm Dean [assistant editor] challenges this, remarking for example that David Willetts[3] on family policy is now alongside the left, he just dismisses this. He doesn't seem to recognize that after the bludgeoning of the Tory years, with the middle third of the people now assuming many of the insecurities of the bottom third, there is a powerful swing back towards a desire for state and collective help.

Also, the right are prepared to wait. He spoke with real passion about the horror of Labour getting in – but you can see it would be an opportunity for his lot as well. Especially on Europe.

Characterizes himself as 'Burkean'. Says that Redwood is one of the

---

1 Michael Forsyth: Conservative MP for Stirling 1983–97; as Secretary of State for Scotland 1995–7 led the campaign against the Labour opposition's plans for devolution; later Baron Forsyth of Drumlean.

2 David Maclean: Conservative MP for Penrith and the Border since 1983; Minister of State at the Home Office 1993–7; Opposition chief whip 2001–5. Neil Hamilton: Conservative MP for Tatton 1983–97; resigned as Parliamentary Undersecretary of State at the DTI in 1994 after allegations that he had taken cash to ask questions in the Commons.

3 David Willetts: Conservative MP for Havant since 1992; Paymaster General 1996; shadow Secretary of State for Social Security 1998–2001, for Work and Pensions 2001–5; nicknamed 'Two Brains' for his highly intellectual approach and perhaps his high hairline.

most original people in the Cabinet, and always gets a big audience. 'He will get 200 people at a meeting. You couldn't say that for Dorrell.'

CONRAD BLACK
21 June 1994

At a lunch given by Weidenfeld[1] at the Garrick for Harold Evans's new edition (the third) of *Good Times, Bad Times*. Also present: [Melvyn] Bragg, [Phillip] Knightley, [Trevor] Grove, Tony Loynes, [Anthony] Holden, [George] Darby, [Bernard] Donoughue, [Stewart] Steven.[2] Not clear why Black was there, but he was voluble and reeked of power thinly concealed under a veneer of listening. He's a good talker, enjoys language, and came on amiable. Darby said afterwards, however, that at that very moment there were ructions unfolding at the *Telegraph*, with Black-imposed changes at the top to compensate for Max Hastings's allegedly idiotic shift of the magazine editor.

Was mainly interested in Black (I sat next to him at the start). True to image, he called Murdoch 'Napoleonic' (though derisively) within five minutes. Said Murdoch, whom he liked doing business with, was a debt junky, who loved taking risks. People who had been in big debt (like himself) to get their business started either retreated from it into prudence (as he had done, he said) or they can't resist ever higher gambles. Murdoch was of the latter kind.

This meant that we should all assume he would carry on losing money on *The Times* indefinitely.[3] It was losing £20 million at present. The way round this was going to lie in Murdoch coming to grief, I gathered. Black said he has massive problems: huge risks and problems in Asia, a fourth TV channel in the US [Fox] which was a vast gamble and which he was losing on hugely because of the price he paid for the football deal, and now taking losses on UK papers.

Further, the US networks had finally decided to fight back. They were determined to take Murdoch down and if possible out. He had talked to them recently, and they were going to turn up the heat and 'not let Rupert get away with it'.

The case against Murdoch was that he was not a successful indus-trialist. Black defended the Sky licence, and didn't gripe at the scale of

1 George Weidenfeld, Baron Weidenfeld of Chelsea: Austrian-born London publisher and philanthropist, also noted for founding a policy organization, the Club of Three.
2 Many of these were either contemporaries or contributors to the *Sunday Times* under Harold Evans.
3 Rupert Murdoch cut the price of *The Times* from 45p to 30p early in 1994, forcing the *Telegraph* months later to cut its own price to match *The Times*'s. The *Independent* followed suit. Murdoch then lowered the price of *The Times* to 20p.

newspaper ownership. Tried to make a case for saying that these weren't in detail Murdoch-controlled, and portrayed Rupert as some kind of philanthropist for keeping two large loss-makers, The Times and Today, alive. Said that Murdoch editors were fairly independent, which was the way they had to be. ('I tend to take on people I can live with, and let them get on with it – like Max.') But the real case against Murdoch was that he was utterly cynical about the public: thought the public were trash who would always buy trash and watch trash if it was available. His TV stations in the US live down to that insight, have done real damage to TV standards.

In the UK newspaper business, he forecast 'terrible turmoil in September'. He said that maybe the only groups strong enough to stand up to it were the Rothermere stable [Associated Newspapers, owners of the Daily Mail etc.] and his own.

He thought The Independent was in the direst straits, from which the Mirror couldn't rescue it.[1] Their only salvation lay in his kind of deal, which he'd spent a long time talking to them about: to run the paper at arm's length under a collaborative agreement, with separate editorial and no interference. The Mirror didn't know how to do this. He was totally scornful of the Indy, saying that its original appeal was always fraudulent ('It was no more independent than The Guardian or the Telegraph'), and its pitch was to pious yuppies, who were never going to make a big enough market or be the basis for a true identity.

He asked me how we were getting on with The Observer.[2] I gave him an upbeat assessment, in which he appeared to be little interested.

I'm afraid that he (naturally) gave no indication whatever what his tactics were going to be. But he spoke like someone who was not faced with any sort of crisis, claiming that his sales were a level million (and therefore equally admirable with those of The Guardian, both of us having stayed solid against The Times's advances!).

We then had much talk about the Catholic Church, in which he showed frightening knowledge of English cardinals. He also said he had been a bit worried about people thinking the Telegraph was a Catholic conspiracy, since as it happened (even after the departure of Knight![3]) several of the top people happen by pure chance to be Catholics – now joined by Charles Moore (whom he accused of self-indulgence in taking up acres of Sunday Telegraph space to explain why he had become a Catholic).

1 Both the Mirror Group and Sir Tony O'Reilly's media group took stakes in The Independent in 1994.
2 Guardian Media Group officially took over The Observer on 1 June 1993.
3 Andrew Knight, chief executive of the Telegraph Group, had joined Murdoch's News International.

EDDIE GEORGE
The Guardian, 5 July 1994

He made it clear that he would strongly advise the government against a single currency, on the 'French' grounds: that it would be impossible to get out of structural unemployment.

He also said that, whatever new government came in, he would be advising the lowest band of inflation targeting by then: 0–2 per cent. He kept insisting that the biggest task was getting inflation expectations down and steady: establishing a pattern people could rely on. So often this had been lost before. If any government said they would allow 5 per cent, that would just be the start. It would be up to 10 automatically.

Himself. Clever, confident, deeply steeped in all the stats, which he has at his fingertips: an intellectual of the banking process, the economic process, the financial variables. His big line is that he just tells people to think about the consequences, to see the questions etc. etc. But he is too modest . . .

A very heavy smoker. How long will he last?

JONATHAN AITKEN
Lunch, his house (alone), 8 Lord North Street,
12 July 1994

DEFENCE COST-CUTTING To be announced on Thursday. The new procedure for this, which locates it in the cabinet committee on public expenditure (EDX) and no longer bilaterally, was disastrous for the MoD. Rifkind [Defence Secretary] got hammered. They had been thinking in terms of possibly squeezing £500 million out of the budget over three years in cash terms. In fact ended with a £1.2 billion cut. Aitken wasn't there, but his impression was that this was Clarke on the back of an envelope rather than any platonic debate about the needs of defence in the modern age. It was a residual. 'Defence did not have enough friends.' Rifkind was devastated. And at the start did not know how he could get the money out without touching the front line. Nor did the chiefs. There was a lot of talk about exercising their right to see the PM (did they?).[1]

Meanwhile there had been a series of management exercises going on

---

1 There are no reports that defence chiefs did lobby John Major. But in August, according to press reports, the heads of all three branches of the armed forces had briefed Labour Shadow Cabinet figures, no doubt anticipating a Labour victory in the next election.

behind the scenes. Looking at waste and mismanagement in many areas. Duplication, overlapping, lack of modernity. These had engaged quite a lot of outside people, including finance directors from firms small and large (Marks & Spencer was one). These either had already or were now geared to producing some startling savings. He instanced some:

The Airman's Working Month, by ancient designation, consisted of 117 hours, substantially less than a 30-hour week. It included long lists of designated specifics, even down to 7.6 minutes (say) for hair-cutting, and x minutes for waiting to see a commanding officer etc. Totally archaic, and wasteful. Just by getting it up to 130 hours, he said, you can save jobs by the thousand. He mentioned 20,000 jobs going: check.

Another wasteful scam is called Margins: the need for oversupply in case of sudden use, and more particularly the employing of extra manpower in case people are on courses or whatever. Nobody can be out of action for four weeks (or more than that?) without being provided for in Margins. I.e. an assumption of almost no standing in for colleagues.

Stores. An amazing story. Will save £275 million (check) by rationalizing. It turns out that there are vastly more stores dumps than could ever be needed, and that 70 per cent of the spares kept are *never* used. Leander frigates (check frigates) have 10,000 spares kept, of which 8,200 are never used. So there are very big savings here, all conducted by a brilliant old civil servant called David Jones,[1] who has just been waiting for the go-ahead and knows where all the bodies have been buried.

Recruitment centres are another waste. They will all be closed. It costs £13,000 for the navy to get each recruit, to just get him through the door. The employment service say they can do it for £300. There is a huge network of employment centres round the country, now usually well run, that can do a far better job than the ancient hulks that can be found in city centres almost totally unattended.

All in all, they have got more than the £1.2 billion savings, keeping the surplus up their sleeves. Rifkind, from being sceptical, has become the most zealous enthusiast. The forces brass are mixed. The army will suffer least: they have already modernized and updated a lot. The navy will give two cheers, and will be especially sad about the recruitment centres (strange, for the service that used to work by the press gang!). The real hit is taken by the RAF, which turns out to have been very badly managed for many years. (He reeled off figures: 3,000, I think, for the army, 7,000 (?) for the navy, 20,000 (??) for the RAF. Said they weren't exact, but gave an order of magnitude.)

The great compensation, of course, is a release of the equipment

---

1 David Jones: long-serving Defence civil servant; currently Director General Supplies and Transport (Naval).

budgets. There has been a reversal of the 'hollowing out' process, whereby people did less training than they should have, and ships were sailed at slower speeds etc. etc. This has been vital in getting the support of the brass. They can see that their equipment budgets are improving: it really is Front Line First. This is especially vital in a time when high tech is taking over. He instanced the total lack of need for the kind of bombing that Reagan did of Libya, which would now be done from a thousand miles away by cruise missile sea-launched, or by stand-off missiles from aircraft again miles away. Much of the equipment and some of the thinking in the RAF still, until recently, presumed a main purpose of attacking Moscow by low-flying, radar-hopping planes going to a great height and simply unloading. All that is entirely old hat. High tech is what matters: unmanned missiles, laser-beamed bombs etc. (This was all rather an elementary lesson, I thought.)

Another especially bad feature of the RAF was the use to which trained pilots were put. It costs £700,000 to train a Tornado (?) pilot, but because of oversupply they were rotated between desk jobs and flying – an absurd waste. (Incidentally, the Israeli air force has 610 pilots out of the total 30,000 people: we have the same size air force and c.76,000 people.)

On the plus side, watch out for great increase in amphibiosity.

The underlying truth is that a defence review is going on all the time. It is not necessary. It is a phrase reborn from Denis Healey's time, when we decided to get out of East of Suez. But the fact is that we now have rather few commitments. Hong Kong will end soon. Falklands is there, and has to be thought about – it is on a gently downward-sliding scale. The major truth is that we do not have a commitment-based strategy but a capability-based strategy. We have what we have, for our own defence, and for reasonable flexibility in face of the new NATO role – in which out-of-area is now regarded as the way of the future, whereas it used to be the strictest rule that NATO never went out of area.

In this exercise, there have been some very good younger civil servants put to work. The cuts work began with a committee on which Aitken, Andrew Turnbull[1] (then from the Treasury) and the M&S finance director were the only ones who believed that cuts could be achieved in this way. One of the hottest was Alice Perkins,[2] Jack Straw's wife. This has therefore been a Treasury exercise, but in a new sense. (a) Yes, it was Treasury demand that induced the cuts: but it was also a collective decision by

1 Andrew Turnbull: at the time, Second Permanent Secretary, Public Expenditure, at the Treasury; Cabinet Secretary 2002–5; later Baron Turnbull of Enfield.
2 Alice Perkins – a civil servant who married Jack Straw in 1978 – was at the time undersecretary, defence policy and material, at HM Treasury. She went on to become director general, corporate development, in the Cabinet Office 2000–2005.

EDX. (b) The Treasury has been represented on every committee in the MoD that has been charged with the work. A discipline on the inside.

Major has been a key player. Never forget that his Chief Secretary role was almost as formative as his whip role. He knows a lot about it. He also thought that it could all be done without touching the front line. He had the faith. In this respect, the Major–Portillo axis has been very important in the defence-cuts operation.

MAJOR   He describes a story he says he knows is true. When Major was elected leader, Lamont came to see him about his job. There had been no campaign promises to anyone except Hurd. Even though Lamont had been his manager, most people thought Chancellor was one step too high for him. But Lamont lived in hope. Major asked him a question. Tell me, Norman, he said, in your heart are you at bottom a Euro-sceptic? Norman was much troubled about how to answer this. It was rather like a faceless gunman in Ulster asking one which side one was on (per HY). There was no obviously correct answer. But Norman said, 'Well, yes, actually.' To which Major said, 'Oh, I'm so glad. That's a great relief.' And made him Chancellor. (Aitken vouches for this story twice: I guess he got it from Lamont.)

He believes Major now speaks for most of the party on the question. He sees no split, because he contends that 90 per cent of the party are now, in the old language, Euro-sceptic. Only a very few are 'federalist'. He also agrees that if the Tories lose, they will become much more anti-European in that sense.

On 21 July John Major reshuffled his Cabinet, with Peter Brooke, John MacGregor, John Patten and Lord Wakeham leaving the government. Michael Portillo, Gillian Shephard and William Waldegrave moved up. On the same day Tony Blair was elected Labour leader, with John Prescott as his deputy.

DAVID HUNT
The Garrick, 16 July 1994

A day or two before the reshuffle, which he claimed to know nothing about. Probably rightly. He was quiet, mannerly, correct, watchful, but then opened out a bit. We had not met before, and he apologized for keeping me waiting since last September for a reply to my invitation. Could he even have been slightly nervous?

RESHUFFLE   Said he thought Major was less sensitive about this than Thatcher, who had been almost physically sick, notably when sacking Hugh Rossi,[1] who thought he was coming in to be named Secretary of State for Northern Ireland and was in fact sacked. The reason for this lies partly in Major's training in the whips' office, which is a very toughening experience.

EUROPE   He spoke as a serious European, he said. He had gone into politics on the Europe issue, after the de Gaulle veto.[2] He had been at a French university for a year in 1961, which helped this commitment. He thought Europe should be together – as simple as that. There had been quite a lot of Europe in his political rise. He was a Christian Democrat, he kept insisting. (See his speech to that effect last year.) He had belonged to the European Movement, and to its predecessor body. What did Christian Democrat mean? I asked. He could do no better than talk about its attachment to the European movement, that general idea.

However, he had been seriously alarmed, as a European, about the way in which Europe had got out of touch with people. He reeled off the usual stuff – Danish referendum, French referendum, opinion polls. He put all this down to Delors. He kept coming back to it. Delors has overreached himself, had a personal agenda, wanted to make the Commission a personal power centre, had become a separate government or seen himself as such. None of this was provided for or meant. He had alienated many people. Made public statements which turned people off, expressed ideas about the union which were far ahead of what people wanted, initiated things that did not have the approval of the Council. Delors could claim no true credit for anything useful on the British side – e.g. the British opt-outs at Maastricht, for which Lubbers was responsible.

Additionally, the socialist aspect of Delors, as well as the visionary, was deeply antipathetic. Hunt is a serious anti-socialist. He believes the social chapter is a disaster, because it would put off foreign investors who come here because we don't have it. He thinks its benefits are illusory. When I press him about the works-council clause, which is the only one now on the table, he fills this out. What he tells his Continental partners is that the British unions have the habit of internecine dispute and of confrontation – unlike their own. Jimmy Knapp[3] would not sit down round a table in order to further the cause of modernization. Therefore,

1 Hugh Rossi: Conservative MP for Hornsey (later Hornsey and Wood Green) 1966–92; his final ministerial appointment was Minister for Social Security and the Disabled, DHSS, 1981–3.
2 In 1963 General de Gaulle vetoed Britain's entry into the Common Market.
3 Jimmy Knapp: general secretary of the NUR (later the National Union of Rail, Maritime and Transport Workers) 1983–2001.

Hunt says, we are not ready for it. We might be later. In his speech to the TUC he emphasized this, encouraged them to the role of social partners. Equally, he instances the myth of working hours as something very unBritish: not just anti-boss but anti-British, who like to work as long as they want to, and who don't like 'social' restrictions.

What was Hunt's own vision [on Europe]? He was a bit coy. But he eventually conceded it could not stand still. Although it had to keep to a speed which people 'feel comfortable with' – a phrase of Hurd's which he thought excellent – there did have to be movement. What sort of movement? Well, he said it does envisage the EMU – but only if people are ready for it. Needs time, he kept saying.

Kohl he thought a wonderful man. He had talked to him from time to time. He had this big vision of Europe, as a way of binding Germany in. Hunt admired him without agreeing with him. Hunt thought it was all too fast . . .

BLAIR He comes with less baggage than Smith. But with Labour baggage all the same. Hunt sees little difference between them. He says that the Labour baggage is important. He cited the minimum wage, which he is convinced Blair doesn't really agree with, and the Merseyside Militant problem, which he thinks wider than I do. (It is his area.) He thinks Blair suffers from his lack of office. He doesn't look like a heavyweight. If you asked people about Robin Cook, they would probably think he held some office. They wouldn't think that of Blair.

ELECTION With each election he gets more worried about the 'sick and tired of them' argument. It gets harder to beat. But he thinks that with three years to go – he would advise playing it long – a great deal can change. Major can get better. People like him, they think he's a decent chap, and they won't want to take a risk. The risk element may still exceed the time-for-a-change element. Especially after years of low inflation and steady recovery.

Thinks the sleaze factor is a chattering-classes issue. 'Most people think all politicians are in it for themselves, irrespective of their party, I'm afraid.'

DOUGLAS HURD
Foreign Office, 25 July 1994

Remarks how much the US suffers from having an unelected Secretary
of State. When [Warren] Christopher goes to the Hill he is consorting
with the enemy. When Hurd goes, he is somehow received as an elected
politician and of the same tribe. When he told WC he had seen nineteen
senators and it had all gone very well, WC was full of amazement and
asked him how he did it.

CHRIS PATTEN
19 Cowley Street, 27 July 1994

BRITISH POLITICS   My advice to the Tories would be not to
attack Blair, but let him float down naturally from his present high. He
will never be as popular again as he is now. It is a mistake to attack him,
still more of a mistake to try and pretend he is a lefty. On the other hand,
in a year's time his problem managing the Labour Party will be more
apparent, and the dissent from his rightward shift more strident, viz.
Margaret Hodge[1] wriggling on the *Today* programme about his statement
on the desirability of two-parent families: not agreeing while trying not
to disagree.

The Tory Party should be patient. There never has been such a thing
as a voteless recovery. They now have the certainty of two years of steady
growth, and this will bring rewards. On the other hand, at the next
election they will have been in for seventeen/eighteen years – a very large
problem. And Blair is an intelligent man – although his voice is something
people may get very tired of (no more so than Major's, I said).

In these circumstances, this was a silly reshuffle. Where's the excitement? Everything was amazingly defensive. A typical whips' reshuffle:
e.g. fancy making one of the few men in the Tory Party who has ideas,
David Willetts, a whip as his first job! Ridiculous. David Hunt should
have been chairman. Why wasn't he? Because Major does not trust him.
He is thought to be unreliable. CP had no trouble with him when at
Environment. Hunt was absolutely OK, was brave, took the shitty jobs,
did the hard interviews, never undermined him. Hurd is very sore about
Hunt's Cabinet role over QMV. 'You don't have to scratch Douglas very
hard to get him steamed up about that.' Even so, Hunt should have

1 Margaret Hodge: leader of Islington Council 1982–92; Labour MP for Barking since 1994; a minister in the
Department of Culture, Media and Sport since 2007.

had the job. In any case, making him the Whitelaw *de nos jours*, the compensation prize, is hardly a way of sidelining him.

What the government needs, he says, is a bit of style. Unfortunately only Hurd and Heseltine are capable of it. Clarke has chutzpah but no style.

'I can't understand why Europe has become such a massive issue.'

Major is more self-confident and cheerful than at any time since shortly after the 1992 election. We agreed that this was a bit mystifying, given the situation. He said that Major was still capable of bitterness and smallmindness. Said (but wasn't sure) that Major had been urged to send a telegram to Peter Riddell's wedding, where journos were sure to be. But hadn't done so. Riddell had evidently written something he hadn't liked. (The moral of this story, incidentally, doesn't seem to me the one CP draws.)

PADDY ASHDOWN
His office, 13 September 1994

After a summer to reflect, he feels very buoyed up. He thinks at last there is a shift, a rumbling, a shake-up, a crack in the system. At last the Tories are not calling the shots. Why? One must go back to the death of Smith. It took everyone time to settle down after that, but he recalls the scene at the memorial service when he looked down the lines and lines of Labour politicians and realized that he was looking at people not just mourning Smith but mourning the old Labour Party. It would never be the same again.

He greatly admires Tony Blair. He reckons there is very very little between them in opinions, in fact, nothing that matters except PR. They have been saying the same kinds of things for a long time. He sees Blair as using his position well, to remove more of the obstacles between Labour and the Lib Dems – and between Labour and the real world. Most of all, his line on unions, once again reinforced at the TUC conference. (Where, by the way, Monks was telling Blair not to say anything about arbitration of the signal dispute and he just ignored it – this from Patrick Wintour [colleague on *The Guardian*'s political staff].)

He sees the issues of the era as threefold: first, economics (this is why his pamphlet is heavily economic): a mixture of market plus. Second, governance: the revival of government in many ways. Third, the nation state: on which he sees the Tories as especially flawed – hooked to the nation state and therefore resisting simultaneously all the 'community' devolution and the international (EU) side.

Somewhere in the synthesis of this triangle lies a word, an idea, something that will replace all the isms. (Much taken with David Marquand piece in *The Guardian* saying that social democracy was coming into its own in the UK at just the time when as an idea it was finished.)

Paddy's line now is very much to make the statesmanlike pitch: that these developments are very good for Britain; that his party is the party of ideas; that what matters is getting them into play, not whether the Lib Dems are the party to do it. (I suggested this made him sound (a) impossibly grandly statesmanlike, but (b) diminishing of his own party.)

He believes that the LDs can benefit from what has happened to Labour. That in their pockets the Libs should get stronger. They did this very well in the local elections and European elections. He sees it as quite likely that they will get fewer votes nationally but more seats – 'perhaps quite a lot more', he says hopefully.

So why not get off the fence and abandon equidistance? It's all a matter of timing, he says. He certainly doesn't want to risk the party conference being stalled by some activist talking about betrayal and making it to the headlines on TV. He thinks that when he goes for it, there will be three MPs who will oppose, and maybe 30 per cent of the party conference. He can live with that. He declined to say which MPs, but said they were the ones with Labour-type seats and 'dug into traditional areas', whatever that means. Must mean Lynne[1] plus two.

Meanwhile, he insists on not declaring any dramatic shift. It may even not come to that at any time. It may simply arise from the grass roots, from the 'objective reality' as a Marxist might say. He thinks Labour has to go still further to make itself acceptable. How? By becoming more committed to 'pluralism'. What does this mean? Essentially, a commitment to PR – which Blair has withheld. But without PR there is no pluralism. He also wants still more distancing from the unions etc.

For Blair, he thinks, it is harder than it is for him to leap over to recognizing the other's legitimacy. But for him, all the same, there is more to lose: what Ashdown could lose if he gets it wrong is his very existence as a party anyone listens to. As it is, the 17 per cent is very respectable as a base they have kept despite the Labour surge. Blair, moreover, is far too sensible to think that his 53 per cent can anything like last.

Jenkins/Williams/Rodgers. What they said has been OK, although Rodgers was sharper than the others. I don't mind that, but I think they don't understand about the timing. Naturally they can't leave and go to Labour – which, as Rodgers told me yesterday (HY), would just lose them all credibility.

---

1 Elizabeth 'Liz' Lynne: Liberal Democrat MP for Rochdale 1992–7.

He thinks the Tories are utterly bereft of any ideas about society/community. Willetts and his Civic Conservatism is the exception – but they don't want to know.

BILL RODGERS, meanwhile, had said to me yesterday:

He has spoken in *The Times* (3 August). Ashdown is wrong to think of us as an SDP phalanx inside the LDs. We don't plan or conspire – though Jenkins did spend several days at the Rodgers' rented house in Tuscany in August.

Our approach is that we want a left-of-centre government which will govern Britain better: we do now believe Labour is electable: we think that equidistance is nonsense, and that it is silly for LDs to pretend that Blair changes nothing. We (the three) are interested in Big Politics. Many Lib Dems are interested in Little Politics. Many of them are happy enough to be a ghetto of local-council power.

I went to see PA before Blair was elected and told him that this would be a big event. I had not been a Blair fan, but now I am. Told him that he had to start thinking hard because Blair did mean change. PA seemed very sensitive about equidistance, implying that I was trying to get him off it – which I wasn't especially.

Blair should accept that there are two opposition parties: should accept that the Lib Dems have legitimacy. Ashdown should accept Labour as the preferred next government of Britain. Therefore, although we are different parties, we shouldn't emphasize the differences.

For my taste Ashdown is too keen on individuals, not enough on 'community' and all that. Underlying it all is the simple fact that the LDs will not be the next government.

Rodgers's purpose, he says, was precisely to stop the seepage by making PA see that something had happened. Unless he accepts that, there's a danger of being marginalized. Obviously it is some offence to his vanity that people are saying such nice things about Blair.

At the last election, when I spent election night with Roy, we were both depressed by the results as they came in. We didn't want another Tory government. But we thought Kinnock no good as a potential PM. Major, on the other hand, has turned out to be a disaster we didn't expect.

Labour is still too corporatist, and too prone to union domination – in spite of Blair's 'remarkably courageous' performance during the TUC week.

Bill sees fully the danger of 'making a fight of it' at the conference. Also sees that if they left the LDs they would have totally shot their bolt. They therefore roam rather at the edge (my phrase).

JOHN PRESCOTT
20 September 1994

On 20 September 1994 HY had a meeting with Labour's newly elected deputy leader, John Prescott, 'in his office, above the shadow leader's. A large institutional room with Pugin panelling formerly occupied by John Smith.' In fact HY's preface to the encounter is twice as long as the record of the conversation itself, which remains private at Mr Prescott's request. Snippets of the preamble show HY rather dizzied by the 'Niagara' style of discourse for which the Labour strongman would become famous, but he may have underestimated the career prospects of his subject when he judged that the position of shadow deputy leader was 'the very apogee – and far beyond it – perhaps of his realistic political career'. HY continues: 'His talk is quite incessant. He never stops. It floats along well-worn paths of rhetoric – about the Labour Party, about public–private funding, about Europe, about modernizing, about the rail strike – not quite on the surface, but hardly any distance below it. He has half taught himself a great deal. Latched on to his chippy self-confidence, this comes out with some plausibility. There's an almost lordly quality: and in the Labour world he has entered the baronage. He reels off the terms, the equations, the amendments, the clauses, sometimes the real significances. But the more you listen, the more you can't avoid thinking that the plausibility of style is a style of mind that is basically disconnected from reality, or at least from coherence. He has wild energy, great commitment and now a pretence of grandeur – lying-back-in-the-armchair Labour grandeur – all of which give him the right to talk ceaselessly to any captive audience that presents itself, especially one like me, who he sees as a toffee-nosed intellectual he needs to impress. The difference now is that he is sure he can impress. As Niagara continues to disgorge, a kind of serenity becomes apparent.

'I try to imagine this man in a senior office of state: or equate him with some of the autodidacts of Labour's past. The trouble is that most of the working-class politicians who became ministers had actually gone to Oxford in between times: Wilson, Healey etc. But compare Prescott with, say, Bevin or Callaghan as repositories of good sense and uneducated authority and you see how hopeless he will be. His role will be to bustle into the Department of Transport (or whatever), send out lots of ideas, supply a grinning-cum-deeply-serious demeanour, and have them sent back by civil servants who can rather easily point out that they are half-baked. It's just about impossible to see him speaking to the nation

without provoking a puzzled giggle: not because he's stupid, which he isn't, but just because the words, taken as sentences and paragraphs and then possible chapters, fail to add up.'

WILLIAM WALDEGRAVE
Ministry of Agriculture, 6 October 1994

EUROPE The CAP will certainly be bust wide open by expansion. With twenty countries, it won't work. (HY: interesting how often he spoke about the twenty – showing how deep is the strategic desire.) It will be bad all round. It will bust GATT, by forcing us to jump the vast oversupply: it will deter Poles etc. from going into industry and make them stay on the land: it will bust the EU budget by miles. It therefore must be reformed.

The Germans, yes, are more difficult than the French about this. The French have bigger farms than we do, in the northern part. For the Germans, the problem of security remains uppermost. When I said to a German the other day that it would cost £10 billion (or ecus or whatever) to finance CAP expansion, he said, 'So? Ten million? So?' The Germans think any sum is worth paying for the binding in of eastern Europe.

The Germans of the next generation are a problem. In his cups, Volke Rühe[1] says, 'The Ukraine is part of the German sphere of influence.' WW chides him with starting a new world war with this kind of talk. The Rühe view is quite common. It is what Kohl stands so hard against. Kohl is the last German leader who fears the German people.

This is one big reason why foreign policy etc. has to be one area where Euro-closeness develops faster. It is quite obvious that security should be the first priority. So this will enrage the Tories? We have to take on the Cashite wing some time. On the other hand, harmonization etc. has gone far enough or too far. WW says he feels quite Gaullist – remembering that de Gaulle was a pro-European. He feels quite at ease with the emerging position.

The Tory Euro-sceptics are *mad*. He had Christopher Gill[2] in here recently. Barking. A former butcher – nothing wrong with butchers, but just crazy. When I said to Richard Ryder [chief whip], What about Gill? he said, 'There are a lot of them like that.' I think the problem of this government is not that ministers are exhausted but that the back benches

---

1 Volker Rühe: German CDU politician; defence minister 1992–8.
2 Christopher Gill: Conservative MP for Ludlow 1987–2001; one of the 'Maastricht rebels'; joined the UKIP 2006.

are full of people who are disappointed, angry, frustrated, and going mad as a result.

The party divide, he thinks, is no longer about the economy. There will always be the spending problem – but both parties have that. There is no real question about ownership any longer. The tax issue is also rather out of it. What matters now is governance, the constitution etc. The need to show that such a thing as Civic Conservatism exists and is vital. A real difference between the parties.

Blair's message on all this is very radical. It promises a big shake-up. The weakest point for the Tories is local democracy. They need to find a new way towards that, which has eluded them. We just don't know how to do it. Simon Jenkins, who WW says is the leading Tory philosopher, is very sharp about this, says it is the party's biggest weakness. WW agrees. The poll tax was a way of trying to do it, saying to locals, You raise the money and then take responsibility for the consequences.

But the Tories can be respectably against devolutions, against House of Lords reform, against the Bill of Rights. This is at the heart of conservatism. Also linked to Europe, of course, where Blair has declared for a full Delorsian programme, the social-democratic Europe which we oppose. All this gives us a real avenue towards a message, if we can find it.

MAJOR Tremendously chirpy. Came back from holidays in good form. Amazing. Why?

The first reason is the economy. Terry Burns[1] told them that they would get export-led growth and low inflation, and it is happening. It is a US-style recovery of the mid-eighties. It would not necessarily reflect in popularity by now, but that would come. There will be inflationary consequences towards the end of the government, but that will improve the feel-good factor. (Interesting that this Treasury forecast is trusted, despite the huge errors before the 1992 election when they got the deficit all wrong.)

JM believes all this and believes it will pay off. Still sees it as the big determinant. He has done all the right things, obeyed all the rules. He is backed by the sense that the mid-term blues are always deeper now. The troughs are always deeper, and the rises steeper.

On Europe, he thinks he has found the right posture, although he knows he hasn't yet got the right language. This is where he misses Chris [Patten] so much. Terribly. He could put the words on it. What he needs to be finding is something different from multi-speed and closer to multi-agenda. He thinks he can make headway on Europe as long as he

1 Sir Terence 'Terry' Burns: economist; chief economic adviser to the Treasury and head of the Government Economic Service 1980–91; Permanent Secretary to the Treasury 1991–8; later Baron Burns of Pitshanger.

gets past the own-resources issue. He believes that the longer the debate goes on, and the closer we get to expansion to the twenty, the more his line will prove right.

Survival itself brings its own reward. A year ago, WW wrote to JM saying this. He has done it. It shows his doggedness. Going on so long, doggedness acquires a kind of moral quality. He is applauded for this. There comes a time when it is elevated.

He is invulnerable to a challenge. But his ratings in the internal party polls are going up. I.e. he is going ahead of the party, rather than going ahead of rival ministers. People are having to accept that he is the party's best bet, its great strength.

Who does he depend on? Has a funny relationship with Clarke. Not all that smooth. But he sees Ian Lang, Tony Newton[1] and Richard Ryder. Also me a bit. I get calls to come round at awkward times, like when I have a hangover, to talk about particular political problems. (A proxy Patten? – HY). But yes, he is isolated, he has a few cronies, he spends a lot of time alone – all of which makes his survival more impressive. He is still sensitive but reads less, has an inner resolve. Ultimately he keeps it in his breast.

Remember he is not hated. Not like MT. Might be seen as pathetic. Anyway, on the doorstep people don't talk about politics like we do. Don't even say they've had enough of the present lot. Just don't bother about that much. Don't think about sixteen years of Tory rule.

TRISTAN GAREL-JONES
His office, 6 October 1994

EUROPE Not long ago had a discussion with Portillo. Came on avuncular. Said to P that he should either be saying get out of Europe or stop talking such rubbish about the conditions of staying in. TG-J thinks P is basically an exit man. Puts this down to his Spanishness. He was Spanish until a late age, says T, not just a kid. He is Castilian, arrogant, cold, pistols-at-dawnish (my phrase). T likens him to a Jew overcompensating for foreignness. Thinks this is perhaps even more important than his intellectual objections to the European system.

In their talk, P had said there was no real reason why Britain should not get out and then negotiate a trade deal. T exploded. Did P think there was the slightest chance of getting a decent deal out of that? And even if there was, did he realize that we sent 60 per cent of our exports to Europe,

---

1 Anthony Newton: Conservative MP for Braintree 1974–97; later Baron Newton of Braintree.

whereas no one country sent more than 4 per cent of theirs to us (check)? And moreover, how did he think agriculture would be dealt with – our farmers would certainly not accept less via deficiency payments than they do via the CAP? And did he think dear old Australia would bail us out? And how did he suppose we would gain advantage by continuing to have Europe as our main market while withdrawing from influence over the market conditions? And if he thought the French had been tricky on keeping out Japanese cars, what would they dream up as revenge against the UK?

MAJOR I tell him he is technically the most accomplished prime minister since the war, perhaps since Salisbury. (TG-J taking some wild swipes at history here. What did Salisbury have? Who has been telling Tristan?) He's got it all. But he doesn't really believe it. He doesn't really behave like a prime minister, won't tell people to sod off (except Paisley),[1] is altogether too self-effacing. Likewise, I tell his closest people to boost him, to push him from their point of view – but they are too reluctant.

Yes, he does feel pretty good. This is because he feels he has done everything he could have done in the right way. He has nothing to be ashamed of. Lower-class chaps like him tend not to be shits. They are desperate to do the right thing. He thinks he has done.

The first area is the economy Nobody has lost an election after two years of increase in net personal disposable income. This will certainly have happened by the time of the election, and with control over inflation. (And, per HY, if inflation edges up, that is good for incomes.)

Ireland. TG-J told him two years ago not to touch Ireland. Major said it was the duty of every leader to try. So he set to it. Again he feels he's done the right thing. He's doggedly pursued it. It wasn't at all easy. But it was a prime minister doing what he should do.

All this makes Major at ease with himself. He feels that it should come right, even if it doesn't. There's a kind of mirror image of Blair (per HY), in that he thinks that doing the right thing will see him through. That fairness will come shining through the British people (another symbiotic thing, fairness). Because history will give a good verdict, so will the people.

The reshuffle. Yes, a whip's reshuffle. And a good thing. Nobody who stepped even a millimetre out of line got any promotion. That was the important thing. Portillo? No – not a promotion. Redwood is from planet

---

1 Dr Ian Paisley: moderator of the Free Presbyterian Church of Ulster 1951–2008; Protestant Unionist MP for North Antrim 1970–74; Democratic Unionist MP for North Antrim from 1974; resigned his seat in 1985 in protest against the Anglo-Irish Agreement and was re-elected 1986; first minister of the Northern Ireland Assembly since 2007.

somewhere else, and Lilley is pathetic. Howard has spent two years sucking up to all the loathsome right-wing factions.

The people he most likes and feels good with are Ian Lang[1] and Gillian Shephard. Tony Newton a little bit less so, because Newton is a worrier: three packs of Rothmans to decide even a small question. Also Ryder. Douglas Hurd is different: a crucial, magisterial figure. Will he retire? TG-J thinks he will see it out until the election. Why not? He loves it and is excellent at it.

Hanley.[2] TG-J now claims he thinks Hunt would have been better. He evidently had not seen my piece naming him as a Hunt no-no man. Admits Hunt is tricky, and can't understand why, because he has so many gifts and abilities. But TG-J claims he has recently found Hunt a straight ally on some awkward questions.

On the doorstep Major is not hated. He may be regarded as pathetic, and we have to find a way of dealing with that. But nobody hates him. People quite admire him, even though they may not see him as a leader in the traditional sense (HY). Also, on sleaze, TG-J takes the view that this is a supreme issue for the chatterers. It doesn't bother people outside. Mellor,[3] Yeo et al. are all cases drummed up by the press far beyond what they merited. Nothing to do with government sleaze. Government here is cleaner than anywhere in Europe. Quangos? A jolly good thing that they are run by our people. 'I am a Tory. I want another eighteen years in power. As long as people are frightened of losing power, that is enough. It is the beauty of our system.'

CHRIS PATTEN
Phone from Hong Kong, 9 October 1994

Claims that he has not been told any of this by JM, but this is his own view. I think some of it has been said by JM to him.

JM has rightly concluded that he is safe until the election. By then he will have been prime minister for perhaps 6.5 years. A decent stretch. After which he can at least look back and say he has achieved a few things. The economy especially: rather well sorted out. And Ireland.

Ireland has made a big impact on him. CP has encouraged it. If there's any chance, ever, of making progress it is well worth almost any risk

---

1 Ian Lang: Conservative MP for Galloway 1979–83, for Galloway and Upper Nithsdale 1983–97; Secretary of State for Scotland 1990–95; Trade and Industry Secretary 1995–7; later Baron Lang of Monckton.

2 Jeremy Hanley: Conservative MP for Richmond and Barnes 1983–97; party chairman 1994–5.

3 David Mellor resigned from his Cabinet post as National Heritage Secretary in July 1992 after the tabloid exposure of an extramarital affair with an actress and revelations that he had accepted free holidays from a woman connected with the Palestine Liberation Organization and from the ruler of Abu Dhabi.

to do so. And also, this plays to JM's greatest strength, which is as a negotiator.

Where did he learn to be a good negotiator? He was superb as Chief Secretary. He was better briefed than the minister – I found this at ODA [the Overseas Development Administration]. He was ready to have bilaterals without officials in the room if that was what you wanted. He has the gift of ensuring that people leave the room, even if he has got all he wanted, thinking that they have had a fair deal and been well treated.

He was quite superb at Maastricht – brilliant handling. (CP was minding the home base at the time.)

What he should say to himself is, If I turn out to be the man left holding the ball when the people decided finally it was time for a change, I can't help that. Just bad luck. But meanwhile I'll get a few things sorted out. In this way he is far more likely to win the election than if he gets Portillo to write the manifesto.

That said, he does still get depressed. He doesn't enjoy the job enough. He gets ordered around by his private office far too much. When CP was back in the summer, his office let No. 10. know he was coming, and suggested dinner. CP said he would like to take JM out. Office was horrified. Said he was free only between 8.30 and 9.15. CP arrived at 8.20 and JM was in a meeting to which CP was ushered in. At 8.30 went up to the flat for a beer. Was still there at 11.45. All JM wanted was a chance for a long gossip. But how much better it would have been if they had gone out to the Ritz.

He doesn't always understand what a prime minister can make happen. Too humble.

Should see Blair as a blessing. A reason to become fully prime-ministerial – his best bet for getting on top of him. Also, should not talk about Blair or criticize him, least of all for his past – which nobody takes seriously anyway. The only thing he should do is say how delighted he is that Blair wants to fight the election on issues that are Tory issues: that public spending, tax etc. etc. would never have been Labour's agenda but for fifteen years of Tory government. This is a disputable strategy, of course, but the best available.

He should also recognize that he is not good at the Big Theme. He should therefore forget about that. He should concentrate on two things: the economy and Ireland. Should not touch crime or the health service etc. with a barge pole.

People are wrong to talk about the election as if it is sure to be in 1996. 1997 makes much more sense given the Budget cycle. The 1996 Budget to cut taxes.

Of course there are very big problems. Sleaze factor especially unfair

given JM's own scrupulous character. (Mark Thatcher story adds to it.)[1]
And the seventeen-years-in-power factor.

DOUGLAS HURD
Foreign Office, 10 November 1994

Vast haste. He had just heard the Pergau Dam judgment,[2] therefore gave
me less than fifteen minutes amid much apologies. Plainly shaken by the
judgment.

ROBIN COOK[3]
12 December 1994

POLITICS Does tend to think the ebbing of the tide will not be reversed. The economy will not work for the Tories, because, while unemployment is going down, the sense of job insecurity, as measured by
polls, is going the other way: something that pollsters have not seen much
before. This is explainable partly by the fact that the unemployment is
declining because of part-time jobs, which in fact increases rather than
diminishes people's fear of losing their full-time jobs.

By the way, he said he had advertised in *The Guardian* for a research
assistant and had had 600 replies. He interviewed twenty-six people. Almost
all were depressingly right wing. He hired two, one of them, Ambrose,
who was the most leftish – but for a reason Cook found depressing:
that he got his radicalism, as a pious Catholic, entirely from liberation
theology!

EUROPE He has been talking to the pollsters (Kellner, Cowling,
Jowell).[4] They find that there are 20 per cent invincibly anti-Europe,
25 per cent who are pretty pro-EU (mostly A and B classes) and *c.*60 per
cent who are open to persuasion, and swing wildly. Moreover, in this
state, they tend to answer simply on Euro questions not re EU but re

1 On the previous day the *Sunday Times* had published allegations that Mark Thatcher received £12-million
commission on a £20-billion arms deal with Saudi Arabia, negotiated while his mother was prime minister.
2 The campaigning group World Development Movement alleged that British aid money spent on the Pergau
Dam project in Malaysia was tied to a £1,000-million arms deal between the UK and Malaysian governments.
The High Court ruled that the Foreign Office was in breach of the 1966 Overseas Aid Act, despite Conservative
ministers consistently denying the link.
3 Cook was at this time shadow spokesman on foreign and Commonwealth affairs.
4 Peter Kellner: journalist and political analyst for BBC's *Newsnight*; later president of YouGov opinion polling.
David Cowling: author of the *ITN Guide to the Election 1992*; became political research editor of the BBC.
Roger Jowell: co-founded what was to become the National Social Research Centre; now a visiting professor
at LSE.

the issue in question: if on immigration, anti-EU; if on industry, pro-EU.

Reminds me that he was strongly anti-EU. Campaigned for No in 1975. Made his shift after the 1983 election, where he ran Kinnock's leadership campaign and was then asked to run the European Parliament election in 1984. By that time we had been in since 1972 and there was no point in saying we must get out. We must therefore make the best of it.

His present position sounds rather comfortably pro-EU. Not hung up about sovereignty, he says. The task must be to attract the 25 per cent and persuade the 60 per cent. By saying that EU is in the British interest and keeping the message hard on that point. On the single currency, he doesn't see it as a big problem. I taxed him with John Humphrys's[1] failure to ask him about constitutional aspects in On the Record, and he agreed. But he seems to say that, if the economic situation is right, this is not going to be a make-or-break sovereignty issue. However, he is deeply concerned about the actual convergence terms, and notes that it is only by breaking the Maastricht instructions that recession has been diminished in some places.

Says that there are three groups of antis in the party. First: P. Shore and a tiny handful – who are basically still fighter-pilot-obsessed, Little Gallant England etc. Second, the hard left: Benn, Skinner etc. A diminishing band. Third, more interesting, Hain, Berry[2] et al., who are not anti-EU but are Keynesian economists and ask important questions about the EU economic trajectory.

He notes how very much easier all this is for a Scot. Scots are not so worried about sovereignty, having lived under Westminster bossism for so long. Shore once chided Cook and Smith as 'Nordics', and therefore unable to understand the English.

CONSTITUTION Accepts, without being over-disloyal, that Jack Straw is not fully keen on constitutional reform. Notes that he is strongly anti-PR. But also says that JS is probably OK on the rest of the agenda, while not being dead keen. Cook speaks with feeling because this is the post he most wanted, if he couldn't have the Treasury. He wanted to be i/c constitution – while admitting that Blair may have been right not to give it to him: anyway, he could hardly pretend that the FCO job is downgrading! A strength is that he knows the regionalism thing through

1 John Humphrys: broadcaster and journalist; fronted the BBC Nine O'Clock News 1981–7 and since then BBC Radio 4's Today programme and BBC television politics programme On the Record; renowned as a tough, tenacious interviewer.
2 Roger Berry: Labour MP for Kingswood since 1992.

and through, having been a local government spokesman. This is important because of . . .

DEVOLUTION The situation is that there can be absolutely no question but that Labour must produce a Scottish parliament. The support is overwhelming. If we don't get it, the SNP will ride high. It is, without question, the one way to keep the kingdom together. Anything less will produce crack-up and the danger of Chechnya, as it were.

He says that there is no commitment to a referendum on devolution. This would be on the grounds that there is vast support for it, and the election result will prove that: a very clear test.

He sees the only serious problem as being the question of Scottish MPs voting on English education, health etc., and subsidiary politics of that – the lessening or loss of Labour majority. I.e. the West Lothian question. He sees only one way out of it: claiming that the mandate in 1996 is for a whole parliament, that all MPs were elected for that, that all should therefore vote on everything – and having a change only at the next election. He recognizes that this would have to incorporate English regionalism etc. etc.

1995

1 January   Austria, Finland and Sweden join the EU; the World Trade Organization replaces the General Agreement on Tariffs and Trade.

17 January   The great Hanshin earthquake devastates Kobe, Japan, killing more than 6,000.

26 February   Barings Bank collapses after trader Nick Leeson loses more than £500 million on the Tokyo stock exchange.

26 March   The Schengen Agreement eases cross-border travel between European countries (but not Britain).

22 June   John Major resigns as Conservative leader to force a leadership election, telling critics to 'put up or shut up'.

23 June   Douglas Hurd announces his resignation as Foreign Secretary.

4 July   John Major defeats former Welsh Secretary John Redwood in the Conservative leadership contest by 218 votes to 89.

5 July   Michael Heseltine becomes deputy prime minister; Malcolm Rifkind becomes Foreign Secretary.

8 September   David Trimble becomes leader of the Ulster Unionist Party.

4 November   Israeli prime minister Yitzhak Rabin is assassinated in Tel Aviv.

16 November   A UN tribunal charges Radovan Karadzic and Ratko Mladic with genocide during the Bosnian war.

29 November   President Clinton addresses both Houses of Parliament, then becomes the first US president to visit Northern Ireland.

7 December   Prime Minister John Major tells the Commons there is no scientific evidence for a link between 'mad cow disease' BSE and Creutzfeldt-Jakob disease in humans.

Deaths   Gerald Durrell, Patricia Highsmith, Lord Home of the Hirsel (Sir Alec Douglas-Home), Ronald Kray, Ginger Rogers, Harold Wilson

DOUGLAS HURD
Foreign Office, 18 January 1995

Very spry and funny; untroubled. Just back from Washington, where he saw 30 legislators (was it?) in 24 hours, and thinks Warren Christopher hasn't seen 30 legislators in 24 months. Much admires them. Trent Lott: 'The best sort of American politician – courteous, solid, knowledgeable, calm.' Gingrich:[1] 'A funny Keith Joseph – Keith was never funny. Full of ideas.'

BOSNIA   This was DH's main agenda. He thinks he made progress. The problem is there are two foreign policies in Washington, and too many people think that the President's is not the one that counts. Especially do they think this in Sarajevo, which is very dangerous. They are waiting for Gingrich, as it were. But DH evidently spent time explaining to many people, and they are starting to understand, he says, that once the US lifts the arms embargo, and the Serbs start attacking in consequence, the immediate demand from Sarajevo will be for more help: where are the bombers? etc. etc. The US will get sucked in, says Douglas with the cheerful glee of someone who thinks people are beginning to see sense.

But Dole[2] won't press for the arms embargo until April. There is time to play with . . .

YELTSIN   Faces disaster in Chechnya. The worst-case outcome is that he becomes under the thumb of some very nasty military people. This is all too possible. Yeltsin, however, is not drunk. But he is very explosive. He proceeds by explosion: seems reasonable, and then thumping the table. Literally. Thump thump thump, as he lays down the law: DH has been able to watch this several times. He likens Yeltsin to Chernomyrdin[3] to de Gaulle and Pompidou, and invites me to play with it: de G was explosive, and Pompidou the calmer technocrat.

Further to this worst case is a series of Russian defections. Why is this bad? Because the foreign offices of the world like order, don't like explosions etc. etc. Also, look at Afghanistan: money pours in; heroin and arms pour out. It is an absolute disaster area, basically without a government – though nobody bothers to report it these days. There would be more Afghanistans (e.g. Tajikistan) if Russia breaks up.

---

1   Newt Gingrich: member of the House of Representatives from Georgia, USA, 1979–99; Speaker of the House 1995–9.
2   Robert (Bob) Dole: Kansas senator 1969–96; Republican candidate for president in 1996.
3   Viktor Chernomyrdin: prime minister of Russia 1992–8.

MICHAEL PORTILLO
Department of Employment, 13 February 1995

Once again greets me with familiarity, coming into the waiting room
personally. Much chuntering about shaking hands, which he denied was
a purely Continental thing to do. I am not certain he doesn't read a word
I write, since he behaves like someone who hasn't got the smallest idea
how much I disagree with him – still less how acidly I have written about
him.

THE POLITICS I say, Don't you sometimes fear that, although the
Tory Party is deeply split and passionately engaged, the people might not
be? He replied, Well, that may be so now, but they will begin to be aware
of an ever more intense argument about the IGC,[1] in which sides will be
taken about the nation state and what it means. There will be a great
deal of passion on television, in newspapers and so on.

But then what about Major and his politics?

We agreed that his whole being was concerned with balancing acts.
That's what he is entirely about, I ventured, and MP did not disagree.
But then he said, We always say that, but what does it mean he will
actually do?

LABOUR He said that he had begun to 'have some hopes' of Labour
– i.e. that they would be more Euro-sceptic. Sees Cook as being more so.
(Hadn't thought of but agreed with my saying that Cook, like all Scots,
was less bothered about sovereignty.) He thinks Labour in office will find
two things. (1) That their Euro attitudes have been entirely a way of
getting at the government, of having influence, of getting their policies
into Britain by another route – which will now not be necessary since
they will be in power. (2) That, like all ministers, they will become very
irked on finding that there are numerous things they want to do which
they cannot do because they are decided elsewhere.

He did not know, nor did I, exactly how divided Labour might prove
to be.

He said he thought Cook was, fortuitously, a good placement. Would
have been wasted on Clarke, who was having lots of trouble anyway with
economic argument. But on the Euro issue Cook gives Labour a more
sceptic feel, which may pay off for them.

---

1 Proposed amendments to European treaties (Rome, Maastricht, Nice and so on) are discussed by an
intergovernmental conference (IGC), which then concludes with a meeting of the European Council.

But he said that if Labour won, and acted in a pro-EU way, it would meet a Tory Party which without doubt had become unanimously Euro-sceptic and make it hard to get things through the House of Commons (depending on the majority, of course).

IMMIGRATION   Towards the end he alluded to this as the second great issue that had been the subject of deception and delusion, where there had been a lot of misleading of public opinion. I said that Powell had been wrong on his prognostications in the sixties. He immediately pulled back and said that's as maybe, but all the same, wasn't it interesting that immigration was now linked up with the Europe question?

Throughout good-humoured and very open. He sat there for an hour and twenty minutes, after his secretary had said I might have half an hour. He had begun by saying that he didn't have much to do – that, as under Tebbit, for example, there was a big bill (job-seekers, in his case), which was handled by a junior minister at committee stage. Likewise, junior ministers had to have their share of the media work: Cabinet ministers did the *Today* programme and the main news; juniors did the five o'clock Radio 4 etc. But he, as the Cabinet minister, had time to spread round other issues – as had Tebbit. (This set us off on a line about whether junior ministers shouldn't be cut down: and him saying that the costs of junior ministers were great, that the backup was excess-ive, that the private sector wouldn't be so luxuriant, that it all needed to be looked at.)

He was fluent and well organized. His position is that the mess in the party is bigger than when we last spoke (April '94), and he seems confident it will move in his direction. Though he doesn't speak in personal terms, he just rejoices in the fact that it will be quite impossible, whatever Clarke wants, to get the party to support any more integrationist moves whatever. He is reflective, confident, likes pressing his ideas, which he does with unfailing courtesy, entirely unvindictive about an opposing view (which again confirms he may not have read my stuff), a believer in the exchange of ideas and the winning of arguments by reason. But there is also something watchful about him, of course. And perhaps something callow. He is very full of his sense of mattering, yet also aware of the uncertainties of the political life.

He said he had had the Belgian ambassador in, sitting in my seat. The Belgian had said that the point of the EU was to stop war. He went on about France and Germany etc. etc. MP said he didn't think that was a necessary reason for the EU any longer, but in particular denied that it meant the EU should continue to integrate. The Belgian was utterly against this. The only way to stop war was for complete integration, he said. This put MP in mind of the fact that Britain, and now Sweden, was the only EU country not to have been disrupted by insurrection or occupation or dictatorship in the last sixty years. He regards this as a quite vital fact, utterly differentiating us from the rest of Europe.

A REFLECTION This talk again reminds me of the lassitude of the pro-EU people, compared with the fighting edge of the antis. It is perhaps not so much that the British are inherently anti-European any longer, but certainly it is true that all present discontents can with some ease be laid at the EU door, and thereby become a rich source of nationalist politicking. I think the pro-Es have probably underrated the strength of the antis' line on the currency, and thought flabbily about its political consequences. Clarke's line that EMU is not a concomitant of more political union will not really wash, but shows that the pro-E's see their weakness – but are trying to get round it in a way that has become discredited: namely by pretending, as so often in the past, that nothing truly serious is taking place.

Remember that Max Hastings told me the other day that if Portillo became leader of the Conservative Party he would personally leave it . . .

MICHAEL PORTILLO
Lunch, Parkinson's, 4 June 1995

SOCIAL CHAPTER Believes that the value in not being in it does not arise from the freedom from the parental-leave directive etc. etc., but from the ability we have to be a new alternative pole round which others can gather. By our failure to join, the social chapter has effectively been put in abeyance. There have been few if any developments. We have managed to paralyse progress. If we join, under Labour, the whole dynamic will change. It will be a signal for more momentum, which others will progress.

SINGLE CURRENCY The right position for Britain to take now is to assert it will not join. The social chapter has shown us how this could work. If we said we would not join, other countries would change their attitude. Instead of being seen as holding out against what Germany wanted, they would be taking a more positive attitude: joining a group which said they were happy for Germany to go along with the currency but their interests were different. Britain could be a leader. Even France, he speculated, might in those circumstances review their position. We would certainly not be alone. This illuminated a larger point: which was that the only times we ever had influence was when we disagreed with Germany – whereas the FCO thought the opposite. This was the cardinal error of FCO thinking.

LABOUR Asked how Britain would be different if Labour won, he muses and says, Public spending mainly. Cites [Enoch] Powell for the aperçu that only a party for whom the cutting of spending is a prime objective has any chance of cutting it all. Labour will not have this objective, and therefore will get into trouble quite soon.

Adds, Perhaps Europe. But notes that Blunkett, Straw and Cook will be making much trouble, and Lilley, Redwood and me over the single currency.

TORIES ELECTION ETC. Much talk about Heseltine making a run, which obviously fascinates him deeply. He thinks Lamont is soiled goods, 'never quite rises to the occasion' and therefore is unlikely to be the stalking horse. Talk of Budgen. He offers that the strongest candidate might be Nick Bonsor[1] – but doubts he will do it. The problem, as he concedes, for many of them is why should they do it in order to help MH? We talk about the scenario of say 50 votes against Major and 50 abstentions. He doesn't disagree that JM will hang on if he possibly can. He believes, says MP, that he alone can unite the Tory Party: which is his abiding obsession, and rather more important to him than making the assessment that he is a wonderful PM. But MP says that if powerful people – KC say – went to him and said they would resign if he stayed, then he could not carry on. He said this is what dished MT (although my memory is that very few people said they would quit, though several said they thought she would lose if she fought – a rather different proposition). But it was not certain at all that people would behave like that anyway.

He went on to say that he now thought it would be better if the party formally split. He said it was now in a sense 100 per cent divided. Everybody was arguing with everyone else, and the leadership was trying to straddle what had become an impossible divide. He now wishes, he said, that the leader would take a clear EU position: this would at least mean clarity. He said 80 per cent of the party would doubtless go along with the leader. Admittedly, people like him would 'be off immediately'. When I pressed him on whether this would really be better for the party

1 Sir Nicholas Bonsor: barrister; Conservative MP for Nantwich 1979–83, for Upminster 1983–97; Minister for Foreign and Commonwealth Affairs 1995–7.

than the present situation, he said, amazingly, yes. The time had come. The divide would be formal, but in a way less damaging: a 20 per cent splinter, with everyone having to decide where they stood.

We agreed, as volunteered by me, that Europe was one of the few possible election aids to the Tories. He was glad to hear it, he said. But in that case, he wondered, how on earth could people think MH was a rescuer? I volunteered that perhaps, under a new leader, Europe would become less important: the leader would be the issue. He said that he did not agree with people who said that MH was so ambitious he would ditch his Euro commitment. Said that all the signs in private were of MH being just as pro-European as ever: he gave him that much credit for consistency, and said that Tories who thought they could have MH and an anti-EU stance were making a big mistake.

HY summed up his next interviewee as 'jovial, youthful, dull, low wattage. Decent chap, serious. Made me think how on top of it ministers always need to be, however. Not just on their subject (which I guess he is), but on the project, on the self-projection, on the commitment to dynamic futures, on the thrill of the game. I think Dorrell is a very committed politician, but somehow the lights don't shine.'

STEPHEN DORRELL
Department of National Heritage, 21 June 1995

The Tories can come back if they can get a hearing for the line they should be taking. This is to make a virtue of stable house prices, low inflation, and a platform for growth. This has been an extraordinary achievement, unmatched in my lifetime. It is very, very important. We have somehow to explain first that the recession was a price of the successes of the eighties, but then show we are on track for a much better form of growth. House prices, instead of being bemoaned for negative equity, should be presented as the basis for more home-owning.

The second strand of the message must be taking Labour apart. Showing how they would risk the above. Exposing Blair's two-faced attitude to the social chapter, which is to say to the unions he's in favour of it, while saying to business that he is in favour of an environment for business.

But all this is impossible to get across until the Tories have decided once again that they want to be a party of government: to unite, and to behave sensibly. And this, of course, is all about Europe. He notes that the Cabinet have 'shut up' for the last three months (1 March Major speech[1] being the benchmark). He especially notes that the key phrase in Portillo's Welsh-conference speech was about uniting around the EMU opt-out (strong words, SD thought, which he had verbatim). Portillo, whom he had known for a long time, was more interested in power than a cause. In the end, that's what had moved him. He probably didn't want to be leader of a small faction of the party. On the other hand, SD conceded that he had been behaving rather like that. He had been encouraging the factionistas (my word). SD agreed with me that if MP was sensible he would be urging them to cool it. The fact that he is not doing so is interesting, and not helpful to him.

This led on to the post-election scenario. If the Tories lose, what will happen? Depends on the scale of it. If a loss by 30 seats, then perhaps nothing very sensational. Major might even carry on for a while. But if by 100, then it would be less predictable. SD noted, though could not pretend to rely on, that there were analyses which said the larger the loss, the fewer the sceptics who remained.

SD regards the single-currency issue as a line in the sand for the sceptics, more than as a commitment they seriously expect Major to make now. They are the anti-integrationists, who think they have rather few places to stand on. He was utterly scornful of the (Portillo) analysis which pretended that Britain could be a magnetic pole against Germany on this question. Countries were not going to decide their attitudes by reference to what Britain did. It was a joke. But he also spoke as though it was totally understood by everyone that the UK would not go into a single currency at the start. Further, he argued, once it was shown that the single currency was good for exports, for inflation, for growth, it wouldn't take many months for the message to get home. He also said he had no problem with a referendum on the single currency: such a big change that neither party could get through it without that.

He thought on balance there would still not be a challenge. The old inexorable logic would present itself. Note how things change week by week. Two weeks ago, it seemed certain. Last week, after the rowdy meeting with the sceptics,[2] it swung the other way, as Major dug in his

---

1 On 1 March 1995 John Major addressed the Commons about Europe in a speech that *Guardian* reporters and commentators variously described as cryptic, ambiguous and 'the most detailed and significant he has yet offered'. Mr Major narrowly avoided defeat on his European policies with a majority of 5, even though former Chancellor Norman Lamont voted with Labour.

2 On Tuesday 14 June sixty of John Major's Conservative critics – members of the Fresh Start group of MPs, who met each week to discuss Europe – confronted him in his sitting room at Westminster to ask him to rule out a single European currency. In a column headed 'The Tory sleep of reason begets the incredible', on 20 June HY considered the strengths of Michael Heseltine as a potential challenger and summed up the sitting-room confrontation: 'It is unimaginable that such a leader would permit 50 of his party critics to harangue him, as Mr Major did last week, only to have these rude tormentors deride him for his lack of leadership in failing to throw them out.'

heels. This week, in the aftermath of that, the thing is subsiding. No doubt it will swing to and fro again.

Claimed to be quite unmoved by criticisms that he never went to the theatre. That's not what the job is about. The job is about getting better policies and resources for leisure (he didn't quite put it that way).

On the afternoon of 22 June John Major gave the officers of the Conservative 1922 Committee his letter of resignation as leader of the party. He would, he said, fight an immediate leadership election. Shortly afterwards, in the garden of No. 10, he told the press in a statement, 'I've now been prime minister for nearly five years. In that time we've achieved a great deal, but for the last three years I've been opposed by a small minority in our party.' Rather than put up with further threats of a leadership challenge, he was taking the initiative. 'The Conservative Party must make a choice. Every leader is leader only with the support of his party ... That is why I am no longer prepared to tolerate the present situation. In short, it is time to put up or shut up.'

DOUGLAS HURD
Foreign Office, 29 June 1995

Almost certainly our swansong, after so many conversations, usually (as with this one) prompted by him, arranged weeks ago but falling six days after he announced he would be quitting at the next reshuffle. As ever, he is spry, sardonic, pretty open, enjoying this kind of talk.

The party, he says, is demented, more than he has ever known it. He does not know what it will do. He thinks Major will win, but openly concedes it may not be by enough. He thinks all results are possible. Remarks that he got the Thatcher result in 1990 quite wrong, thinking she was going to win quite easily. So he does not make predictions.

People's intentions are not clear. You very soon run into the sand when you try to work it out. To my question, he states quite clearly that the party cannot be led from the far right. But he also does not rule out the possibility of that happening. They are so demented. What will Major do? It will be up to him to make the judgement about the vote he gets. DH agrees with the Matthew Parris piece [in *The Times*] last Monday (which, as I happen to know from Parris, came pretty much from Major, though MP in his piece said rather elaborately not): that Major's instinct will be to quit. So why might he not? 'Because he will be told it is his duty not to do so.' DH was splendidly emphatic about that, letting the phrase ring round a silence neither of us broke. He then said that Major would be told (by him, and by others, I inferred) that he owed it to the party not to precipitate the total divisive crisis that would eventuate from his retirement. The rot set in when the Fresh Start group came to see him. They were very rude, it was a big mistake. It meant that any lingering tendency he might have to move a bit towards them had vanished. He would not move an inch, would not listen to people who had previously (from positions of some influence close to him) been pushing him in that direction. Then, he brooded a lot at the G7 in Halifax, Nova Scotia [on 15-17 June]. He took DH into his confidence. The choices were three: resign, muddle on, or resign and fight. He did not seriously think he might resign. But he decided to fight. (This sequence of thinking, not previously known to me, may alter the way he may be persuadable to do his 'duty' next Tuesday evening [the day of the leadership election].)

A neglected cohort in all this are the junior ministers, who never appear on television and some of whom are able men and women. What do they think, I wonder?

When Redwood was launching, K. Clarke and I did a pre-emptive strike from Cannes, which turned out to be wrong.[1] We thought he would be putting out a right-wing platform, which he didn't. On the other hand, everyone knows his tax-cut ideas and public-spending stuff is nonsense.

Portillo is more obdurate (his word) about Europe than Heseltine is. DH had two conversations alone with him round the turn of the year. 'I didn't know the man.' But DH says he did not succeed in getting through. Portillo has very decided opinions, which he will not yield. (Earlier, by the way, Nigel Sheinwald[2] told me while we were waiting for DH that he had been at school with Portillo, had always kept up with him, but had never had a conversation in which MP revealed his true feelings about Europe, although they had very often talked. I warned NS that P had it in for the FCO. They know the wife better, by the way. She comes from a prosperous, cushioned, middle-class family with lots of children and a mother who never worked: Michael from a mother who worked hard as a teacher, and a father who was a rather elderly dreamer.)

If Major carries on (and even if he doesn't) and the party insists on not settling into a comfortable Euro position, then says DH we will lose the election, and be relegated into unimportance, and become I fear very much the anti-European party. I have told Delors about this, Douglas

1 John Redwood was the only other candidate. The European summit at Cannes on 26-7 June was attended by both Hurd and Clarke, who, in the words of *Guardian* reporter Stephen Bates, 'waited disconsolately' for Mr Major, who arrived late. At the end of the summit, Mr Major publicly asked his two ministers if they wanted to stand against him. *The Guardian* reported that Mr Hurd shook his head, and a blushing Mr Clarke mouthed, 'No.'
2 Sir Nigel Sheinwald: diplomat, head of FCO news department 1995-8; later foreign-policy adviser to Tony Blair; UK ambassador to Washington since 2007.

said: told him he must be aware that one of the British parties may become anti-European – a very serious matter. Delors went away thinking hard. DH says he fears that this would make British politics terrible. Blair's positions are a bit naive, but no doubt he will get past them. The problem is that Blair will have his day, Labour will get inflation-prone, the figures won't add up, they will get into a jam over Scotland, and one day they will be replaced. That is the moment to be horrified at, says DH. 'I am reasonably optimistic in a twenty-year perspective, and even ten, but what happens in between could be very bad.'

DH insisted that the phobes were misjudging public opinion. He finds, wherever he goes, that sensible, dull business people cannot understand a party that wants to create clear blue water between us and Europe. He is going to the north-east tomorrow, and knows he will find a real world entirely distant from the world of William Cash. Likewise in his Oxfordshire villages, while there are people who grumble about Europe, there are very few who see it as the defining issue. He says the polls steadily show 10 per cent who want out, 10 per cent who want a federal Europe, and 80 per cent who are in the middle: about half of whom would go a bit further in, and half of whom are happy about where we are now. The phobes, he is sure, are victims of their own propaganda. Why can't we get the party back to reflect that kind of reality on the ground?

But he reckoned the press were very important. The Murdoch press, and half the *Telegraph* and all of the *Mail* added up to a lot of votes. They do not reflect the public, however. OK, people can be stirred up to blame Europe for things that go wrong. But there must be a limit to how long this kind of mirage can be perpetuated (my words). And to how long newspapers can go on misrepresenting the views of their readers.

In the Conservative leadership election on Tuesday 4 July, Major polled 218 votes and John Redwood 89, with 20 abstentions. In the ministerial reshuffle that followed, Michael Heseltine became deputy prime minister and First Secretary of State; Douglas Hurd retired, and was replaced as Foreign Secretary by Malcolm Rifkind, who in turn was replaced at Defence by Michael Portillo.

Three weeks later a by-election at Littleborough and Saddleworth (caused by the death of the Conservative Geoffrey Dickens) saw a Liberal Democrat gain, with the Conservative vote falling by 20 per cent and the Labour vote increasing by 14 per cent. The Liberal majority was 1,193.

PADDY ASHDOWN
His office, 1 August 1995

Littleborough and Saddleworth was the worst by-election, the worst election, he has ever known. The Labour tactics were disgusting. Three weeks of sustained vilification of the Lib Dem candidate, without any mention of policies and very little of Tony Blair. Moreover, the main case against the candidate was that he had voted for a Royal Commission on drug use at the last LD conference. This was American-style politics: personal assassination. Is this what Blair wants? They have even said that this is the way they will carry on during the general election. (But where, I asked? He was vague.) My party is absolutely furious. It makes my task much more difficult, if we are going to have sensible cooperation.

We have taken a very big step by quitting equidistance. It took a long time, trudging round the party, explaining, cajoling. It has now been backed unanimously by the federal executive. By the parliamentary party too? I asked. He said there had been disagreers, but it was now accepted. It is a necessary but risky thing. It means our identity needs, more than ever, to be maintained. That means that 'I have to maintain a position of tension between the Labour Party and the Lib Dems. We have to show that we have not become a small sub-branch of Labour. Just as the other parties have to maintain the tension between them.'

What is our role? That is the question. We have to be ourselves, have our policies, and above all make them sharper than the other parties'. 'We have to be the party that makes clear what the others keep fuzzy.' Especially Blair. He is fuzzy.

The first area is Europe. PA dismissed my suggestion that Labour was different from the Tories because, although its line was similar, its good faith was so different that it would be much better at securing allies. The Lib Dems say very clearly that they want a single currency if the terms are right, that they believe in strengthening the Euro parliament, that they desire an extension of QMV. Including foreign policy? Yes, with the exception than no country should be forced to send its troops against its will. We had a long diversion on Bosnia. Paddy, who should be respected, is quite convinced that if there had been a better foreign-policy process, with a CP, the early decisions would have been far better – and in particular that we would not have fallen into the trap of not discriminating between aggressor and victim.

The second area is taxation. We are the only party making it clear that we favour an increase in tax for a specific visible popular purpose. PA ridicules the Labour statement, which was evidently made by someone at

Lit and Sad, that there would be no increase in income tax (or was it tax at large?).

The third area is constitutional reform. PA said that he doubted whether Blair really had it 'in his soul'. If he is in favour of pluralist politics, how can he possibly not remake the pledge to a referendum on PR? I reply – it is a secret subtext of our conversation, known only to me since I had seen Blair that very morning – that the 'soundings' I had indicated that the pledge was still being stood by. Also, that Blair did seem to me to be personally committed to pluralist politics and constitutional reform.

We talked about Blair. Ashdown said there was a danger that Blair thought that his simple arrival in Downing Street, all sweetness and light, would bring sweetness and light about. I said I thought he underrated Blair. To which he replied by withdrawing, and indeed admonishing me for even suggesting that Blair was less than wholly committed to doing something big. Rather confusing – but reflecting Ashdown's perplexity about what Tony will really do to him.

There was a contradictory role. First, to tame the left. Second, to put 'spine' into Labour and hold it to its commitments. PA agreed with me that the second role was far more important. I said the first was pretty out of date. Ashdown was very ready to doubt whether Blair would do all that much, and therefore it was all our duties to push him. But when I said that he should quit the 'taming the left' line as bad politics, he remonstrated with me, saying that I mustn't deprive him of his ability to win a Winchester. I.e. he confirms the LDs needed to keep that line going in order to win the Tory south. When I chided him with thus confirming the old charge that the LDs spoke out of different sides of their mouth to different audiences, he said with a straight face, 'We are all regional parties now.'

I said that the old LD role as a party of ideas seemed to be waning. He said he would be mortified to lose that role, but admitted it was true – and, moreover, for the moment, correctly so. 'If I had to choose between being a party of ideas and a party of commitments, I would unhesitatingly choose to be a party of commitments.' What does this mean? That people should know what we stand for (see above), which is based on ideas we have had for some years and are taking many years to get through to the people. Ideas that define us, that make people vote LD, that help LD politicians know who they are and what they are asking.

PADDY ASHDOWN
27 November 1995

(Deep deep background he dramatically insisted. Only you etc. etc. . . .)

I am desperately worried, he says, about what is going to happen in the next few months. I regard the next three months, about, as crucial. They will determine whether there can be a great reform movement in politics or not. The country desperately needs it. Is crying out for reform. But it may not happen.

What is needed is for Labour to show some willingness to work together in the project, the process. What this means, in turn, is that they move on PR. I cannot possibly do anything without something on PR. It would give away for nothing our biggest card; it would be suicide for my party.

I am not looking for a big U-turn by Blair. I just want an indication that the referendum will not be launched with a government pledge to advise a No vote. That would be utterly intolerable. But I don't need Blair to change his public mind yet. I do need a private word that at some future stage, after saving his face and securing his base, he will indicate that Labour would at least not oppose PR, and preferably of course support it. (Note: PA wasn't precise about what he wanted Blair to commit to, but said he would be willing to make his own judgement and take it upon himself to validate the undertakings Blair might secretly give to him.)

Blair wants a two-term government. He has often said so. We are his ticket to a two-term government. PR is his ticket to that: it would (or might well) keep the Tories out for twenty years or more. It might also lead to a Tory split. (What about a Labour split? PA said he thought Blair has thought about that and could live with it quite happily.) Blair can surely see this, says PA. Why can't he make a move, which would guarantee such a two-term future?

One reason, PA believes (has been told by a good source, he says), is that Blair worries about losing the Murdoch endorsement. He thinks that both Murdoch and Black are keen to see the Tories lose, in order to shift the Tory Party to the right – but then see the Tories back in again. If Labour introduced PR, this would not happen. Therefore, Blair dithers and worries.

It may also be the case that he thinks he can do everything with Labour alone. But Blair, says PA (and I agree), is obsessed with the narrowness and difficulty of winning at all. Does not believe in the landslide theory. Therefore, cannot really believe in the ease with which he can get things through without the Liberals.

What is needed is a great reform bill. It should encompass Scotland, incorporate a Bill of Rights, Freedom of Information and PR. Wales, says PA, is a second-order problem. But there is a vast amount of work to be done. Labour is showing every sign that it is looking up to but not beyond the election. It has not done the work. Least of all on the constitutional stuff, which will be very difficult to get through.

What I am saying, Paddy says even more conspiratorially, is that we should do in England what we did in Scotland: have a constitutional convention. I can't be caught dead saying it, but this is the right way forward. With political and extra-political components.

Paddy speaks mostly about the national interest: the thirst for reform: the cynicism of the voters: the need for a fresh start. He is also desperately worried about Gingrichism[1] coming here, after another Labour government has failed. We simply cannot afford, as a country, for Labour to fail.

But I also get a whiff of his fear for the Lib Dems. They historically do well under Tory governments, and badly under Labour governments. This is why, it seems, he wants to be incorporated into the next Labour government. I asked him how his party would wear it. He said, Divided. He would have to stake his leadership on it, if we got to a convention. The usual people would be against such a deal with Labour. But the overwhelming fact is that the Lib Dem strength, with just a very few exceptions, is not in Labour areas. That is what we have to keep remembering.

Incidentally, he insisted that the overwhelming majority of New Labour favoured PR. And most of the people around Blair, he said.

Blair desperately needs to switch from New Labour to New Britain. He has fantastic talent. Wonderful way with words, great charisma, and he's already done a lot that took courage. Where is it now being applied, however? The past is done with. He should look forward. But at present he's like a man carrying an incredibly expensive delicate vase – the prospect of election victory – and fearing to move at all in case he drops it.

GORDON BROWN
12 December 1995

His office, my request. He was more relaxed, less sound-bitey than I can previously recall. Perhaps because I said I wanted not to talk about immediately present things.

---

1 Newt Gingrich in 1994 backed a 'contract with America' promising welfare reform, tougher crime laws and a balanced budget. That year, the Republicans won control of Congress for the first time in forty years and Gingrich became Speaker of the House of Representatives 1995–9.

Brief headings of a forty-five-minute talk:

'Getting our betrayal in first'. I told him Blair had used this phrase to me. He said it would be better to say that the message had to be about the long term. We had to change the perceptions of Labour very deeply. We had to make people understand we weren't about tax and spend.

I asked him what the chances were of getting the city and industry to understand and behave like this. Short-termism etc. How on earth could this fundamental aspect of British capitalism be shifted by government, unless by tax arrangements etc.? He didn't sound too optimistic. But he had floated the idea of institutions promising to stay with companies they invested in for a certain length of time – perhaps backed by inducements.

Labour had to get rid of the sense that it existed entirely to compensate people for the failure of capitalism to give them what they wanted. This, he said, was almost entirely the way it was talked about and thought about in the post-war decades.

He was much taken with *Trust* by Francis Fukuyama.[1] He sounded as though he'd read it all. It showed that, whereas the eighties were dominated by individualism, the German, Japanese and even US models of the economy showed that trusting communal relations were more important in the long term.

Access to knowledge was the big challenge, not access to capital. Because capital was global, it was far less of a problem than it once had been. Not just a way of improving the supply side, but a way of improving the performance of national economies.

That said, investment was still appalling here. Only 1 per cent this year, three years out of the recession. The low level is unprecedented.

The basic reason for short-termism is uncertainty. One big contributor to that has been the decades-long argument about public/private issues. The demarcation of the line has been far far more important than the real performance on either side of it. Inflation has been another cause. Germany and Japan have suffered from neither of these destabilizing perceptions. Talk about the 'mixed economy' was really a way of saying that demarcation was what mattered.

In polls, and especially in focus groups, we find that the fact that Britain has slipped from thirteenth to eighteenth in the prosperity league has a great impact. Time and again, this is the button that really counts.

Are we getting ready for government? We have done a lot of detailed work in some areas. Youth unemployment is one. Monetary policy and the Bank of England is another. The University of Industry is another.

---

1 Francis Fukuyama, *Trust: The New Foundations of Global Prosperity* (New York: Free Press, 1995).

But he agreed that more needed to be done. He implied that much was already in train on tax, with academic and other help.

He insisted he did believe in a faster growth rate being possible. This would take care to some extent of the welfare problem: the problem of 'compensation' being seen as Labour's purpose. He also said, Because the world economy is indeed global, things can change much faster than they used to. (What can this mean? That the UK can change as fast as China?)

As we parted, he said he would like to have a whole extra session on tax. Remarked that decreasing the bottom level to 10 per cent was as progressive as raising the top level to 40. Yes, progressivity was important. But, again, he seemed to be groping to get away from that simple model. He even said something like that tax should be seen as a source of necessary public money – and not at all meritorious in any other light (which seemed to me to be almost denying the progressive purpose – or at least any kind of penalizing purpose).

1996

11 January   Baroness Thatcher describes the pro-European One Nation Conservatives as 'no-nation Conservatives'.

15 February   The Scott Inquiry finds 'a deliberate failure' to inform Parliament about the relaxation of guidelines on sales of equipment to Iraq.

13 March   An unemployed man kills sixteen primary-school children at Dunblane in Scotland, then shoots himself.

20 March   The British government admits a connection between BSE and a new form of CJD, triggering a crisis in UK beef industry; European nations begin to ban beef imports from Britain.

18 April   Fishermen burn the EU flag in a London protest against the Common Fisheries Policy.

30 May   The Duke and Duchess of York are divorced.

4 June   Mary Robinson becomes the first Irish president to make an official visit to Britain since the founding of the Irish Republic.

10 June   Northern Ireland peace talks begin without Sinn Fein.

15 June   An IRA bomb kills 200 and devastates a shopping centre in Manchester.

20 June   A Commons committee clears former Cabinet minister Jonathan Aitken of involvement in the illegal exporting of arms to Iraq.

5 July   Scientists announce Dolly the sheep, the first cloned mammal, at Roslin in Scotland.

11 July   President Nelson Mandela of South Africa addresses both Houses of Parliament.

28 August   The Prince and Princess of Wales are formally divorced.

15 November   The Stone of Scone, after 700 years at Westminster Abbey, is ceremonially returned to Scotland.

Deaths   Spiro Agnew, James Bond producer Albert Broccoli, Claudette Colbert, Ella Fitzgerald, Gene Kelly, François Mitterrand, Gerry Mulligan, Carl Sagan

STEPHEN DORRELL
11 January 1996

(Ran into him at *Newsnight*.)

ON SCREEN His amazing ability to pretend that Thatcher wasn't a problem. Drawing out what she said that he agreed with. Above all, the key thing: that there was not a shift to the right. In that, says SD, she's absolutely right. But of course he comes at it from precisely the opposite position. She is saying (along with Portillo, Redwood and the right) that this has not happened because she wants (a) to get it to move further, (b) to get ready for blame-apportionment after the election. This is a carbon copy of the Bennite period in Labour Party. Did Labour lose because it was too moderate or too leftist? In the same way, Thatcher says we have not cut taxes, cut spending etc. etc., therefore how can we possibly be called right wing? Dorrell, though, must insist there has been no shift for the opposite reason: that he desperately doesn't want one, and desperately needs to assure everyone that it hasn't happened.

(Interestingly, Lilley, on the *Today* programme [the following morning], was a carbon copy. Insisting that the entire Thatcher speech was an attack on Blair and accusing the BBC of virtually making up the story that the speech was all about Tory differences!)

OFF SCREEN In make-up, SD says that Portillo and Redwood have totally overreached themselves, the right will be suffering more and more for their behaviour, that Thatcher is out of touch with modern realities. Notes how little she has to say – nothing, except approval for Lilley's line on welfare – about present and future issues.

MICHAEL PORTILLO
Ministry of Defence, 25 January 1996

He is just back from the US. Says that the serious distancing that was apparent a little while ago, especially with the Senate, over Bosnia has altogether vanished. There is now total accord. Bosnia is being fantastically well run by NATO. It has been a huge operation. Admittedly, it has drawn on the big plans that had been laid for withdrawal, which would have involved 50,000 troops. But it is still very impressive. The kit available is tremendous. Just about anything that moves is watchable from the Pentagon. When the US pilot O'Grady was downed, the opening up of

Serb radar, which was the preliminary to him being shot down, came up on Pentagon screens and was back in Yugoslavia in seven minutes. But he was shot down in five. It should have been quicker. It can be a matter of seconds.

MP is obviously in love with the military potential. Remembers being there on handover day from the UN to NATO, and seeing the British general – Jackson[1] – on his theatre, who he describes as a Brit who is very dark – the prince of darkness, he lovingly says he is called – instead of the UN officers, who were often dark men who were whitely innocent, sending his helicopters with gun batteries slung underneath them down both sides of the line and getting emplaced, and the fact that the Serbs were as relieved as anyone to find that they were going to be protected.

EUROPE He said his activities as Defence Secretary haven't specially brought him into contact with the issue. But, in a general way, he believes EMU will happen. He doesn't see that the deadline is absolutely significant, and notes that it will be important for those who take part for the deadline to seem to be real almost until the last minute. There is good EMU and bad EMU. Good EMU means keeping strictly to the terms laid down, thus keeping inflation under rigid control. It is in everyone's interest that Germany should stick to this, otherwise there will be a crack-up at some stage.

I asked him whether he was in all circumstances and in perpetuity against sterling belonging. He said, It could depend on the circumstances. If we were in and it was a fait accompli, then we would live with it. He speculated, surprisingly, that it could turn out to be something that happened almost unnoticed. He remarked that there were cycles of fashion about fixed and floating currencies, which went in ten-year bits (roughly). When I said that by admitting that the EMU could glide unnoticed into our lives he was admitting that the political case against it – that it would remove sovereignty for ever – was less than he usually pretended, he immediately back-pedalled and said he was 'just trying to be fair'! He insisted that it would change things for ever. He thought the Central Bank would actually start to dictate tax as well as deficit; that there would be a quite perceptible change in what a country could do on its own.

I said, Are you against an independent Bank of England, in that case? No, he said. He hadn't thought about it for a while, and didn't know whether he actually favoured it. But he saw a fundamental difference between anything run from the Continent and run from here – irrespective

---

1 General Sir Mike Jackson, British army commander in Bosnia, retired in 2007 as Chief of the General Staff.

of whether it was the government or the Bank. Perhaps the governor of the Bank could be given a five-year contract by Parliament, which would include an inflation figure he had to meet, and he would be accountable then to Parliament. But in any case, as long as it was run from the UK, that was ultimately what mattered. He added, though, that he was a great admirer of the German economy, delivering growth and low inflation for so many years.

As to whether sterling keeping out would be disastrous, he was emphatic that it would not. He didn't believe the possibility of a decline in sterling should be decisive. He agreed that our economy might be less well run. But that was preferable to it not being free. He thought this would be favoured by foreign investors, who would continue to enjoy the advantages of being inside the EU – while knowing that if the government wasn't run very well, we would have to devalue, which would help their trade, which is what matters to them. If we were inside, and not being governed well, devaluation would not be an option – though he insisted, of course, that he was not a devaluer.

All this was said in mild and agreeable tones – almost academic. You can see how forced and out of character, in a way, his conference speech was: but he does like to be forced!

LABOUR Between us we worked out that Labour couldn't afford to go into EMU. When I said that Blair was all but committed to a referendum (on the latest Frost), he was taken aback. He said Labour would surely not want to have a referendum after three years in power, when they were bound to be unpopular. Yet equally they wouldn't want one early either, because that would be a hellish distraction from what they were wanting to do. Blair would surely know that he could get it through his party, and certainly get it through the House of Commons, if the timing was right. On the other hand, if he went for a referendum too soon, the Tories could unite around the proposition that the time was all wrong. He also made the point that Blair surely doesn't need to get involved in a referendum. No advantage to him, because he will say the same if he does. I point out to MP that Blair will never think the election is in the bag.

This (the week of Harman)[1] had been a godsend to the Tories. A real turnaround. What mattered wasn't Harriet's school, but the fact that the Tories had for the first time since 1992 looked like a party that might want to win the election. They spoke as one. Major was a hero. He had

---

[1] In January 1996 Harriet Harman, shadow Health Secretary, announced that her son would go to a 'selective' grant-maintained grammar school – an announcement that provoked charges of inconsistency. The previous October, shadow Education Secretary David Blunkett had told the Labour conference, 'Read my lips. No selection, either by examination or by interview, under a Labour government.'

done terribly well. The party felt good – the first time in ages. Elections are great concentrators of minds.

Could this be spoiled by Europe? He thought there was a possibility of minor inflammation, but perhaps nothing more. But there was absolutely no point in going for Major now. It would make things much worse. It was impossible to see a challenge. He is a proud man, so he won't go of his own accord. He thinks he won the last election, and he has great faith in the 'changeability of politics'.

Contrast this with earlier MP talks. Much calmer. And above all much more sanguine about Major. Though there was a hint of irony in his saying that 'Major is a hero.' He has the option of waiting happily for defeat . . .

He was infinitely courteous, almost familiar. Said how very grateful he was for my coming.

MORE PORTILLO   The point about Blair is that it has given us the issue of hypocrisy, which matches nicely with sleaze. It's the same kind of issue. It has a chance of cancelling out the other.

On Scott.[1] The things that have been said in the media about ministers have been quite disgraceful (he said this academically, not indignantly). To say that ministers have actually been ready to send people to jail by concealing evidence is grossly unfair. These are honourable men. And they are also careful men. At the very least, they would take care not to be caught doing something like that.

I remarked that ministers could in principle be honourable, but for *raisons d'état* do things that were not entirely honourable. He said he had not yet been in that position. I said he had not been long enough as Defence Secretary. It could yet happen – and he said he supposed it might.

He remarked that those who were supposedly in the dock did not give the impression of men hanging their heads in dread at the Scott verdict.

ROBIN COOK
1 Parliament Street, 5 February 1996

CAREER   There's no doubt that opposition is frustrating. I've spent sixteen years – the prime of my life – 'doing' nothing. Remaking the Labour Party, I suppose, is doing something. But I am 50 this month.

---

1 Lord Justice Scott's inquiry into the Matrix Churchill affair, in which four directors of a machine-tool company were prosecuted for having illegally sold equipment to Iraq. The case collapsed when it became clear that they had been advised by government officials on ways in which this could be done. Sir Richard Scott's lengthy report was not published until 15 February 1996, but the thrust of evidence, conjecture and several leaks had already made it clear that the report would not reflect well on the government.

Politics has got far more difficult in that time, because of the media. When I started, there were three terrestrial channels. Now there are four nationals, many locals, several satellites. This requires many responses, often very fast. One aspect of all this is that one has to learn to say less and less. Even the smallest subclause can be taken out of context and exposed as some 'policy' commitment or another by the other side. The result is that one says things very briefly, and always with a need to avoid saying anything that commits.

One reason it is good to go to Europe is that politics is a little more about discourse. When Tony went to the Austrian election he did a press conference with the local party leader, who began with a half-hour speech and there was then a discussion moderated by a professor.

EUROPE Speaking off the record, I think it is likely that there will be a single Euro currency within my lifetime – perhaps by 2010, or maybe later.

I am a sleeping member of the Keynesian wing of the party, and that has to be our priority – though as chair of the Policy Forum (check title) I have to be careful what I say in public.

The Keynesian wing is important. These are by no means anti-Europeans. Actually, almost all Labour politicians have a sympathy with Europe, because they see it as a place where community, collectivism etc. are recognized and upheld. Also, the trade unions have become almost to a man and woman pro-European because they have standing in Europe and many contacts and in some cases a lot of cross-border interests. This is one area where the TU influence is progressive. It is where quite a lot of union leaders do their work.

There is hardly a Labour politician who is anti-European in the old sense and under 50. The old right – Shore, Spearing[1] – are leaving. (Is Denzil Davies? Is Dunwoody?)[2] The hard left have few followers. Alan Simpson,[3] who is pretty hard left, is a younger man and much more intelligent than the old ones, and not anti-European in the Skinner sense.

All this means that, in power, we would have many fewer problems than the Tories. We would probably not go into a single currency first time round. We are also English/British politicians, which means that we will take the appropriate attitude towards immigration (he emphasized that quite strongly). But we are not hung up on sovereignty. We don't make a sovereignty argument against EMU (if we make it) but an econ-

---

1 Nigel Spearing: Labour MP for Newham South, May 1974–97.
2 Gwyneth Dunwoody: Labour MP for Exeter 1966–70, for Crewe February 1974–83, for Crewe and Nantwich 1983–2008.
3 Alan Simpson: Labour MP for Nottingham South from 1992.

omic one. As to a referendum, RC thinks in practice it would be almost impossible for either government to get EMU without a single currency – though Blair keeps the election option open. If the Tories commit to a referendum in the White Paper[1] (which he expects), we would slide in behind.

SCOTT INQUIRY The three years' duration have been a gift. I couldn't have asked for more – even though in another way (and publicly) we said it should be done in a year. The three years have exposed Whitehall operations with endless detail and embarrassment to ministers. It has shown how things get done, especially in the whole area of the arms industry.

I don't agree, he says, that this long period has taken the heat out of the final report. It may well be that, given the arrangements, which favour the government by giving them six days' notice, they will have a talk-out for the first two days. But that will not last. The systemic rot (HY phrase) will be impossible to cover up, as the report is trawled through. Of course, much will depend on how well we in the Labour Party handle it, how well we make the case, and how well government people do it. But I'm very confident it will do them enormous harm.

If the leaked version in the *Sunday Times* even half remains, WW[2] will have to go. It shows he wrote twenty-seven letters saying the guidelines had not changed when he knew they had changed. Scott isn't going to accept WW's line that they did not change.

But the main thing is the exposure of the system. Rehashing of all these civil servants talking about economies with the truth, the need not to keep people fully informed etc.

This links very much with our line on the new politics: openness, decentralization etc. etc. It is fortunate that Blair is making his speech on the new politics this week. (I asked whether Labour really would be different. He said, perhaps a little sardonically, that if the new politics means anything it must mean that things would be different.)

---

1 On 12 March 1996 Mr Major's government produced a White Paper in preparation for the forthcoming Turin intergovernmental conference on the Maastricht Treaty. Critics pointed out that it failed to address the three issues that divided Conservatives: monetary union, the social chapter, and measures against mass unemployment. That did not satisfy the Euro-sceptics. In a commentary on 21 March, in advance of a formal debate on the White Paper, HY wrote that attacks on the European Court of Justice by Conservative politicians suggested 'a profound and reckless ignorance. Perhaps these people are actually going crazy.'

2 William Waldegrave remained as Chief Secretary to the Treasury until the general election in 1997. In a Treasury statement issued on the day of the report, he said, 'Sir Richard Scott clears me of lying to Parliament or intending to mislead anyone in letters I signed.' Three days later Michael Heseltine told John Humphrys of the BBC, 'I know that William Waldegrave would never deceive anybody ... He is simply not that sort of person. But I can't expect anybody who doesn't know him to accept that judgement.'

POLITICS/ELECTION   We are bound to go down in the polls. But people out there do not really bother much about where Harriet Harman sends her son to school. It was certainly a bad week. But what matters is the quality of services, the security of jobs, the basic things that affect every-day life. Yes, it's made the Tories feel better, and that's not unimportant.

(Robin had a date the next day to attend the weights-fixing for the Grand National. This was a private engagement. 'We all have our vices,' he muttered, pleased with himself.)

DAVID BLUNKETT
House of Commons, 6 February 1996

Alone in his room in Speaker's Court. He is friendly, relaxed, notably fluent, desiring to be thoughtful, a solid citizen. He ends by saying to me that he committed himself body and soul to Tony Blair ('and what used to be called "the project"'). He says this without irony. He talked about what a job it had been, these last fifteen months, 'pulling chestnuts out of the fire'. He obviously thought he had done it rather well.

Much on education.[1] He says selection is the only question he is ever asked. He finds himself amazingly relaxed about it. If the policy of the Labour government, and for that matter the Labour opposition, is determined by what happens to 160 (grammar) schools, we will be dead ducks. He sees diversity as one of the values most to be cherished, and says that the great failure of comprehensives as conceived in the sixties was that people thought they were all meant to be the same. He seems especially keen on the idea of local schools sharing what they are good at (though his example, which concerned the teaching of Russian in Sheffield, hardly seems relevant to the core subjects).

He said that if he had three or four years in the job, he would hope to achieve something tangible. He would want to look back and say what he had done. But he didn't seem quite decided what the priority would be. Yet he is tremendously committed to doing well. To this end, he expects to come in with a detailed plan, not least about how he will use the delegated legislation which gives ministers much power. This will be the Tory inheritance he can exploit. He doesn't want to arrive at the department to be told that he can't do things, or that he must wait a year to get the Act passed. He also intends to come in armed with a lot of his own experts – unclear where they would fit in, though he mentioned that he didn't mean a clear-out of existing civil servants.

---

1 Blunkett was shadow spokesman on education and employment.

You get from Blunkett an important sense of someone who has run something, namely Sheffield City Council. He understands quite a lot about money, funding, capital receipts etc. etc. He is a governing man of the best kind. When asked in future who are the classy operators in the Shadow Cabinet, I will add his name to the shortlist.

PETER LILLEY
His office (with Steve Reardon, press officer),
27 February 1996

The reason to vote Tory comes down to constitutional matters. These are things that are irreversible. A financial crisis – on which Labour administrations have a 100 per cent record – can be reversed. Constitutional change cannot. This includes Europe, and all the rest, including hereditary peers.

Labour flatters us by making the only areas for reform the things we have not touched. Everything we have done they will leave in place. This is an enormous compliment.

If Major loses by only a little, he's not necessarily going to quit. If he does quit, after losing heavily, then the chance of a rump rebellion against whoever becomes leader will be very great.

Disputes that the Tory Party needs to rethink its positions. We agree that Europe is the one thing on which it is not agreed and pretty clear on the whole about where it wants to go.

His wife wants the Tories to lose, so that he can 'make some money'.

Conservative Central Office is in better shape than he can ever remember it. The money is starting to come in, at constituency level anyway. Finkelstein and Lewington[1] are very good.

Why will things get better? (1) The economy is getting better, and people at last feel it to be so. Whereas two years ago political rhetoric was ahead of public awareness about the economy, now it is behind. (2) The party is more united, and money is coming in, and CCO is good. (3) An election is getting nearer, voting is a less speculative matter.

Where will a Labour time be really different? (1) Public spending. At the edge, they won't be able to resist. They'll be softer. Smith[2] is softer than Dewar, who was careful never to commit and knew the subject very

1 Charles Lewington: *Daily* and *Sunday Express* journalist: director of communications for the Conservative Party 1995–7.
2 Chris Smith: Labour MP for Islington South and Finsbury 1983–2005; Opposition spokesman on national heritage 1994–5, on social security 1995–6; Secretary of State for Culture, Media and Sport 1997–2001; later Baron Smith of Finsbury; Britain's first openly gay MP.

well. Pensioners is the next big welfare target we have to look at, having done the first big three – invalidity benefit, housing benefit, lone parents, which are the three generating most growth until 2000, whereas pensions start growing after 2000. (2) Europe. The European project has taken the place of socialism which failed. It will therefore be a shock to Labour to find how little it offers. They have to face the fact that Britain feels different, and is different. He cites the Maastricht Cabinet debate, before Maastricht. Major went round the table, asking each man whether he was in favour of more integration. Every single one, from Patten to Lilley, said no.[1]

MICHAEL HESELTINE
2 April 1996

Many more complaints/philosophical resignations re the media. Remarks on how many of his speeches don't get reported. Instances serious personal efforts re urban policy, IT, and the Civil Service which haven't seen a line of print. Admits they should be issued earlier, complains about the need for them to be cleared, but says the press isn't interested in serious issues. We discuss the effect of competition in lowering standards – a feature he wholly rejects, but without any very convincing argument.

Re paternalistic Toryism etc. Wholly rejects my proposition that this is all over. Says he has always been of that wing, and it lives on very flourishingly. Cites two main efforts of his own which attest to this. (1) Urban policy: a Heseltine invention, going strong, a total public–private partnership, which has transformed our cities, and is doing so at a pace still. (2) Industrial policy. Again an MH obsession, now worked out in all sorts of ways, like Business Links and multiple other programmes, which involve thousands of people helping small businesses. Five thousand a month are coming. It's true he got rid of Neddy [the National Economic Development Corporation] – 100 people. It has been replaced by something far bigger and more productive, virtually the whole of the DTI.

He is amazingly vitriolic about Blair. The greatest con job of modern times. Blair is a total cynic. He has entirely rejected what he once believed in, and for that reason is never to be trusted. He belonged to CND, he campaigned to get out of Europe, he took the whole of the 1983 manifesto. He gave no reason for anyone to doubt that he agreed with them.

---

1   Peter Lilley has a different memory of this episode: 'What I recounted was how Major went round the Cabinet table asking each of us whether, from the point of view of our departments, what was on offer in the embryonic Maastricht Treaty was beneficial, harmless or acceptable. No one – even those who favoured European integration, like Patten – reported anything potentially beneficial.'

He has now rejected everything he stood for, purely for the sake of office. So how, he is asked, could Blair convince MH that he had really changed his mind? Only by joining the Tory Party, says MH. Was there anyone in the Shadow Cabinet, he was further asked, who he in any way approved of? After silent thought, he said that Gordon Brown had been the one he quite admired and thought was the best candidate for the leadership.

He goes on to say that Labour remains entirely the party of the producer lobbies. It is therefore against change. Change is the only route to survival and security for our people, and Labour is compelled to be against it, or at least certain to want to slow it down. You only have to look at Labour in the Commons to understand, if you know how politics works, that they have not changed. See last week's statement on rail privatization: a pathetic compromise, which we would have been torn apart for if we had presented any such thing, and which adds up to no policy at all. A very clear example of the compromises that destroy any consistency about Labour policy.

On Europe, he declines to be drawn into detail – saying very candidly that anything he said about the Tory Party or the Cabinet would not be treated as off the record. But he stated that he was confident that in ten years' time it would be clear that the political consensus had gathered round a pro-European position – and that the momentum of Europe would have been continued. He thought there was no alternative, and that everyone knew that. He would not specify on detailed policies, e.g. the single currency. He also declined to say anything about the referendum, still less about Clarke. But he observed that politics was always a matter of securing different constituencies, and there had always been a sceptic constituency in Britain – ever since Churchill. Incidentally, he made much of the fact that Churchill had talked only about 'a kind of' United States of Europe. This made it possible to say that Churchill has been right in his vision from the start.

MH's own position, he says, is reflected in his book title: *The Challenge of Europe – Can Britain Win?*[1] The last phrase was the important one – the one round which the Tory Party could unite. He has a lot of success making speeches of a uniting kind, on this theme. OK, for the moment the British think that the nation-state argument is the way to answer yes to the question, but he implied that this need not last.

1 Published by Weidenfeld & Nicolson, 1989.

JOHN BIFFEN
Phone, 10 April 1996

There's grudging recognition that the government is competent in the economic sphere. The strategists will be advising Major to go to the very end, to get this impression strengthened.

There's this sense that the government has been there too long, plus an absence of confidence in general if not in the particulars of economic management.

There are no serious divisions in the Tory Party, save on Europe. We are all Thatcherites now.

Blair is very good at showing he's the boss. He's like an intellectual Arthur Deakin,[1] slapping down harmless lefties. This is very effective, and politically valuable.

I see no reason why Major shouldn't go through to 1997. It will last to July, when it will doubtless face the ritual no-confidence vote. But it will survive, not least because Paisley doesn't want to be in the same lobby as Trimble. There will be no more defectors.

Labour are squeezing the Lib Dems even in the south-west. I really don't expect some radical growth of tactical voting. I predict, which P. Kellner agrees with, Labour 350, Conservative 250, others 50 – though others is more fluid. I expect the Labour vote to save some Tory seats from the Lib Dems. The Lib Dems are like the Parti Québécois: in the end, faced with Armageddon, people hold back at the very crest of the big moment.

Blair, I'm sure, would like a hung parliament: do a deal with the Lib Dems, let in PR, and guarantee a decade of right-wing social-democratic government, with the Tories perhaps split.

Between the Clarkeites and the Portillos? JB rather sardonically remembers that I think well of Portillo. I qualify this a little. JB says he can't see Portillo ever leading. I say I can't see Redwood doing so. We part – as he says he has to make lunch for his mother, which is worse than a three-line whip – with my reflection that All Souls, as is appropriate, is the graveyard of Tory aspirant leaders!

Princess Diana was an unlikely guest at The Guardian. *HY made a full note.*

---

1 Arthur Deakin: trade unionist and a fierce anti-Communist; general secretary of the TGWU 1940–55.

PRINCESS DIANA
The Guardian, 11 April 1996

[Michael] White, [Martin] Kettle, [Roger] Alton, [Sabine] Durrant, [Georgina] Henry, [Paul] Johnson, [Paul] Webster, [Edward] Pilkington, AR [Alan Rusbridger, editor], HY.

She arrived in the boardroom with practised poise. Good handshake, good eye contact, the veteran of a million such encounters, so one would expect at least this. Strikingly tall. Pink jacket, black skirt. What strikes you most of all are the eyes, which she uses a lot to good effect but which are in any case unusually impressive. But she's elegant in every way, good skin, delicate face, hands a mite chubby perhaps, complexion healthy, and gym-toned (she only goes three times a week, she lets us know later).

The point of this occasion is to talk about the media. This is her agenda: AR lets us know before we start, and additionally Ed Pilkington, who is *The Guardian*'s part-time royal watcher, knows Jane Atkinson [Princess Diana's press secretary] and also knows what they are wanting out of this. She has been to the *Telegraph* and the *Standard* ('Dear Max,' she purrs). When she was at the *Standard*, which shares offices with the *Daily Mail*, Nigel Dempster was literally sidling alongside every desk she stopped at. JA, by the way, seems the right person for her: middle-aged, level-headed, the right relationship with her, and sounds as though she has plenty of experience.

We start right in. The snappers (*sic*) are one obsession. Every time she leaves her house they are tailing her. All are freelance, therefore editors can't be approached to lay them off. Wherever she goes they follow, but now a few cars behind, 'because they know I get very cross with them'. There were a couple outside *The Guardian*. (Later, I heard that the *Big Issue* man who's always outside the office had been alerted to thrust a copy at her when she came out – but I never heard what happened.) The two papers she least likes and would never visit are *The Sun* and the *Mirror*. She and her adviser still can't decide how to get a better press going for her, and especially to get less probing. We discuss the idea of making bigger overtures to the heavy press (i.e. why not write a piece for *The Guardian*?). She says anything she says or writes will always be sliced up and exploited by the tabloids. We discuss forcing them to correct errors: she says that the danger is of thereby giving the story more life. The recent one was something about her having taken against Sophie Rhys-Jones,[1] who in fact she's only met twice. 'It's very hurtful, but what can you do? My brother-in-law,

---

1 Sophie Rhys-Jones married Prince Edward, Earl of Wessex, youngest child of the Queen and Prince Philip, in 1999.

Ed, was very cut up.' We discuss litigation, if there are big lies (much pressed by Rusbridger). She says she was all ready to go into the witness box in the *Mirror* case, whatever that was, before they settled it.[1]

The big story this week has been cellulite. She expresses incredulity that 'my legs' could matter to anyone, and affects amazement that so many papers could find so many ways of writing about the matter. JA's life is one long litany of phone calls from all sorts of people whenever a particular story like this surfaces. This morning she had had a German magazine on, earnestly telling her that they had a remedy for cellulite which they would be happy to give – in exchange for an interview. That kind of things goes on and on and on.

I sense that she is ambivalent. Although she laments the incessant publicity, I wonder how she would survive without it. I ask the question direct – again, she has heard it before. She says that if she knew that for a year nobody was going to pay any attention to her, she would feel massive relief. When I push her, she insists it is so – saying that the ever-present need to be on display is an enormous pressure. The three/ four months when she had announced her withdrawal from public life had been a great relief, though we never got to the bottom of why it was that the snappers respected it. Anyway, it ended, and now she has a permanent trail of people she mostly detests. She sees it as all about money. The 'ceasefire' (my word) broke down because somebody wanted to make some money. The cellulite picture that started it all was sold for £15,000 she said with absolute certainty, and when asked how she knew she said that she had good contacts in the trade. But, at another level, this is what has made her a world figure. We discuss whether the press might not ever get exhausted, whether the selling power of Di might ever see diminishing returns. Probably not, she sighs, as does JA: but in her sighing you can see at least a trace of *Schadenfreude*.

Other royals are discussed in the media framework. The Princess Royal is mentioned, as one who has had an excellent press, has somehow 'got the media on her side'. This wasn't always so, says Mike White [political editor]. A reason for it, adds HRH, is that she works enormously hard. She advises a scrutiny of any day of the week of the Court Circular, and expresses astonishment at the exhausting round that Princess Anne goes in for. I have the tastelessness – such is the laid-back mood of the lunch by now – to murmur that Princess Anne has the further feature of not being glamorous – which was quite obviously music to HRH's ears, as she openly smirked.

1 In November 1993 Princess Diana's lawyers obtained an injunction preventing the *Daily Mirror* and *Sunday Mirror* from publishing photographs of her at a gymnasium. Through her lawyers, she called the photographs a 'gross intrusion' on her privacy.

The conversation is pretty easy. She is quick and relatively open. Not very deep, and not interested much in conceptual questions, but fluent and intelligent, and enjoying jokes. Apart from the media – an all-engulfing obsession, the ocean on which she is destined to live for ever – three main subjects engage her.

One is the monarchy itself, coupled with the name of 'them' at Buckingham Palace. This mysterious 'they' features a great deal, without ever being reduced to names. In this respect, we have a repeat performance of the *Panorama* interview:[1] about which, incidentally, she has no regrets whatever – saying that it was a case of the right reporter turning up at the right time, when she had been advised by unknown advisers that an interview would do her some good, and Bashir, whom she had got to know over several months, proved to be 'very sensitive'. 'They' are totally out of touch, live in a sealed-off world, have no idea how real people live, are oblivious to their very bad press, seek comfort from the few triumphs like VE Day, and blame everything on 'the girls' – i.e. Diana and Sarah.[2] She obviously has a friendship with Sarah, though doesn't see her much. One reason why Sarah is less in the news is that she lives in Surrey, not London, and 'the snappers are pretty idle'. One reason why Di gets a marginally less prurient press than Sarah, however, is 'I haven't got an overdraft' – this said with an acid little jokey air.

She thinks the palace have no idea what a problem the monarch has. The death of the Queen Mother could be a platform for reform, but it will be wasted, she predicts. At the same time, she is hardly a revolutionary in her opinions. She says vaguely that the monarchy could be 'tighter' and 'fewer'. Asked what the model monarch is, she offers Norway – because it is small and well run, though she demurs about cycling and all that. She thinks in the UK there are too many semi-royals without a proper role, and sometimes there's a mad scramble to get in on things. She offered to go to Dunblane – this was said with lots of knowing glances at JA – but hinted that she had been stopped from going owing to rivalry. She clearly hadn't thought on the constitutional level about all this, but she just knew that the palace was a fusty old place where, from the beginning, she had been frozen out and looked at askance. There were 100 people there every day, most of whose lives were totally dedicated to keeping things as they are.

I asked her whether she thought Charles would change things. She said that when they had discussed all this, their views had been exactly the same.

---

1 In a November 1995 *Panorama* interview, Princess Diana told Martin Bashir that 'there were three of us in this marriage, so it was a bit crowded.'
2 Sarah Ferguson married Prince Andrew, Duke of York, third child of the Queen and Prince Philip, in 1986; they were divorced in 1996.

But that wasn't to say that he would be able to change things very much when he succeeded. Though, incidentally, when asked whether she had intended to imply on *Panorama* that he might not succeed, she repeated the gnomic opinion that he wanted to be happy – and the implication that the kingship would not make him happy. I should add, re *Panorama*, that she said instantly that it had been 'a tremendous relief' to get it all out, to have the sense that she was sharing the terrible things 'they' had done to her, to get more public awareness of the problems she had lived with.

A second thing she talked about was what her role would be. This was for the moment entirely on ice 'until we have decided about the divorce'. Nothing could happen until then. She felt that after that she would be less trapped (not her word) by the palace and would be freer to take things on, à la Princess Anne. One suggestion was that she could bypass the tabloids by becoming a more publicly serious person in this way: she clearly thinks divorce will make this easier. She wanted to clear up what she had meant about 'ambassador':[1] this wasn't a question of taking an embassy or anything like that, but of being available to do things that helped the country. I said that governments would surely want to treat her as a national asset, and she confirmed that politicians had not been unhelpful. But there was more to think about than that.

Amplifying this, she said that from the start she had wanted to get close to people in trouble. She thought she had a gift for talking to the dying and the helpless. When she had come into the royal family, at age 19, she had never done anything like that, but she quite soon saw it as a role for her. That is also what she can do abroad, and had done with some success in Argentina. She repeated this line a lot during the lunch – helping the people who needed her presence, being able to give them comfort. It sounded mawkish, but I think it is genuine: an escape she has found from the psychological and career problems that have emanated from her unfortunate marriage.

Incidentally, asked who she thought had leaked the fact that the divorce was coming (which was a *Sun* exclusive), she dimpled and said, 'A certain other lady.' Everyone took this to be Camilla Parker Bowles.

The third subject she went on about was her children. This was also very obviously genuine. She claimed that they were being brought up with far more awareness than either she or Charles had had as children. They went with her to hospices, for example. Yes, they had two lives – one ordinary, one extraordinary. Yes, William read the history of the kings and queens, though perhaps not the debates about the future of the monarchy. Asked what she thought about blood sports, she said she

1 Martin Bashir had asked her what role she saw for herself. She said, 'I'd like to be an ambassador for this country. I'd like to represent this country abroad.'

didn't like shooting and wished the boys weren't doing it – though she had been brought up with it herself, and was a very bad shot. Asked whether they had hesitated about Eton, she said not for a moment – and didn't seem to get the point when someone gently took her up on earlier remarks about being in touch with ordinary people. Asked whether she was a feminist, she said definitely not. But asked how she reacted to the sense, after *Panorama*, of being taken up as some kind of inspirational leader of women in similar positions, she said that she was glad to think that. She also said they'd had 10,000 letters in the first week after the interview.

ADDENDA   She calls the Queen 'Mama' (with emphasis on the first syllable).

She sees and talks to the Queen, about whom she has no criticism whatever, saying that the 'they' at the palace are the bureaucrats – though when I suggest she should become our Deep Throat in writing the definitive book about the palace, she clearly hasn't any idea what reference I am making.

She finds the gym a haven, a relaxer, an absolutely vital aid to sanity.

Mike White was the only person actually to call her 'Ma'am', which he did once: his defence afterwards was that he had always wanted to say the word to somebody (without any ironic overtone such as he applies to V. Bottomley when he wants to put her in her place).

She had been offered a de-luxe apartment by Donald Trump, which had been the start of one of the many rumours that she was going to live abroad, which she has absolutely no intention of doing. She said Trump's wife, Marla, was very nice. When someone confused Marla with Ivana, HRH remarked, 'They say second ones are better,' chuckle chuckle.

She thinks Tony Blair is a nice chap. Mentioned his Dunblane reactions as especially sensitive. As she said it, you could almost tell she sort of fancies him, unlike Major.

She realizes she will never be free of fame – thank God, I'm sure she feels. She will also never be free of the palace, 'because of my sons'.

She was, all in all, better value than I had expected. Within her limited field of interest, she has thought quite a bit. She was surrounded by politesse, but quickly established that it was possible to be reasonably daring in one's attitudes and questions. She liked the cut and thrust, turning on the charm and girlish giggling when appropriate. I don't really think she suffers all that much, though the snappers are a great nuisance. I think she actually likes most of the attention she gets. She clearly loves fencing with the palace officials and getting the better of them, and about this shot many a knowing grin at her PR adviser. I think she's taken on, in her own mind, the role of modernist, youthful crusader against the fuddy-duddies who think that the only problems the monarchy has faced have been Diana and Sarah. She gets a lot of mileage from this line, especially with this kind of audience.

It was interesting how many people in the *Guardian* building were straining to see her, waiting by the windows to see her leave. She took a tour with Alan, and many shook her hand. Georgina Henry [deputy editor] declared herself still a republican, but said HRH had certainly been very winning.

DAVID MADEL
2 May 1996

There's a general view here in Bedfordshire that we will do about 2 per cent better than last year. But we will see . . .

People are utterly furious about the beef ban. They say Major should have walked out at Turin, done a de Gaulle, produced an empty chair, saying he would not carry on until the Commission and Union had lifted the beef ban. At street level, people simply do not understand how it can be that Kohl eats beef at Downing Street and yet the ban remains. A classic example, it seems, of a stunt that had the opposite effect to what was expected.

People say on the doorstep, If you do win next year, what will you do? What will the next four years be filled with? The answers they give themselves are worrying. At present, there are two things we are on tenterhooks about. First, the nursery voucher scheme: will it work, will these pieces of paper link up with actual places? Second, the self-assessment of tax, which a lot of small shopkeepers and small business people and self-employed worry about. They say, Will these be schemes the government has made a cock-up of? They expect them to be. There's a deep fear that when this government does something important it won't come off, it won't work. There you go again, they say.

There is a large category of non-voting Tories. People who say they're Tory but tell you to your face they won't vote for you.

Disunity is like creeping treacle. This constant arguing and quarrelling. These repeated disputes about who is in charge.

(Per HY: this is all the stuff that happens when a government is falling apart. It reminds me how delicate is the business of power: how much of a confidence trick: how easily the illusions on which it is built can evaporate: how power depends on power – and loyalty and cohesion on the belief that power exists and will be used . . .)

JM is much more popular than the party. Compare 1974. I told my people never to mention Heath on the doorstep. As for Thatcher, never mention her at all. I wouldn't say that about Major. On the contrary.

I worry about whether he should do a TV debate. (HY says he should.)

I think I know that what he wants is a general election on 1 May 1997, the day of the council elections.

There can only be one confidence motion in a session. If Blair has one in June and loses it, he can't have another in July. We then adjourn on 11 July, the aim. Back in October. No overspill. A Queen's Speech early. A Budget early rather than late November.

But behind all this there is terrible anger. To what end? You might well ask. Anger is pointless, but it is real, especially about the beef. As well as anger, there is total uncertainty about what to do. In that situation, we should take it week by week, think about things, don't dig the hole any deeper.

TONY WRIGHT
Lunch, Café Pelican, 2 May 1996

Has been told by Blair that he would rather have him on *Newsnight* than serving in some lowly position on the front bench. When I liken this to Frank Field, TW says that Frank probably presents more problems for Blair than he does.

BLAIR Has done rather well. He is good at being a man of his time. That is to say, he well expresses the fact that there is no Big Idea. Maybe the Big Idea is that there is no Big Idea. (Wright reminds me that I am the father of the Big Idea thing, which he remembers much better than me, and urges me to remind people of this and make something of it. Plainly in his circle I have been tagged with this, and it is rather embarrassing not to recall it myself. But by the end of the meal I dimly remember a column written from the Lib Dem or Alliance or SDP conference in Harrogate sometime in the late 1980s.)

We are in a time, says Wright, when there are few certainties. And when people feel insecure. They know there are no systemic solutions, no large-scale plans that will work. Therefore what they ask of a leader is that they should trust him, find him reliable and decent, and a spokesman in part for their own uncertainty – i.e. tolerate, perhaps even desire, his absence of categoric certainty himself, as long as he seems an honest man who will do his best, perhaps on the small scale.

An example of Blair's incremental method is the fact that Lib–Lab manifestations have just quietly happened. Cook–Maclennan on the constitution, Cook–Maclennan on Scott, a joint line on transport policy. These have happened in public, and the world has not collapsed. This is much more effective than big declarations.

The Lib Dems want big declarations, and they are mistaken. They have got a great deal. If they had been told five years ago that Labour had adopted their constitutional agenda and pledged a PR referendum they would have been amazed. They have big problems, however. The old ones: their leadership is centre-left and their support centre-right. Most Lib voters put Tories as second choice. This is a fundamental fact they find it hard to accommodate, most of all in a Lib–Lab arrangement.

Blair, curiously, is not a good speechmaker. They are confections, addressed to TV, and have their value in that. But he seldom takes an issue and commits convincingly to it in a persuasive way. He did this with Clause IV. Reform of the party was something he passionately believed in, and he came over heart and soul as a risk-taker. There is nothing similar in his national agenda. What should attract such passion is the constitutional stuff. We need a John Bright,[1] and all we get are shopping lists. They need to take this as a really big commitment, which they send out with a trumpet call (HY phrase). Otherwise we will have missed a point, and anyway people need to be educated and infused on a subject they don't much care about.

Who can make really good speeches these days? Robin Cook sometimes. He does believe, and he has an edge, he takes risks, he doesn't need a script, he is not nervous about the slightest mistake.

ELECTION   We could be on the brink of a major change, even a near wipe-out. That is one of the possibilities. Let's face it. Goodness knows what would flow from that. A Labour Party with a huge majority could be very hard to handle. And the Tory Party that survived might be an appalling spectacle.

TRISTAN GAREL-JONES
2 May 1996

Saw Major two days ago. Though doesn't see him often. Also saw Clarke recently.

JM is mildly depressed. At times, I can't conceal it, he gets into black despair, very black moments. He is surrounded by lunatics, and it is hard

1 John Bright: Quaker, radical; Liberal statesman 1811–89; emerged as a famous orator during the campaign to repeal the corn laws.

to bear. Toby Jessel,[1] I ask you! A nice enough chap, but absolutely certifiable. Why does he matter? He's our majority, dear boy.

JM has managed to remain sane, despite it all. I can see what he will say at the next election. Here is my record, take it or leave it. Behind that is his belief that he has done nothing dishonourable that he can think of, and his conviction that on important matters he has done the right thing to good effect. If he is elected, he will be a hero. If he is defeated, he knows his stock will rise every month for the next fifteen years as they get into a bigger and bigger mess.

'You have to be David Mellor or Alan Clark, a cad or a bounder, to say you don't care what the media are saying about you.'

I told him that in Watford people are very critical of the government but not of him.

There's no question of him jacking it in. But MPs like Edward Leigh[2] and Bernard Jenkin and plenty of others go round talking like that, and the lobby – quite rightly – picks it up.

'If we're going to lose, it's important we should lose in a moderately decent way.'

Ken Clarke. He was extremely cheerful on every subject until I mentioned the Conservative Party. He thinks they've all gone barking mad.

The more I think about it, the more my mind goes back to 1986, when I was pairing whip. I could say to 100 people take the night off, unpaired. The crazies could be told to go away for a week – Winterton,[3] Jessel et al. With that majority it didn't matter. But this time I got it wrong. I thought that with a majority of 20 we would be OK. I never believed that the crazies would get into the larger double figures.

Redwood is utterly despicable. His programme in 1995 was sixth-form debating-society stuff; his people were loonies like David Evans and Tony Marlow[4]. Redwood said that was all a mistake. But it happened. And he is still backed by the crazies. His behaviour since 1995 has been no better.

Portillo, for all his weaknesses and his terrible mistakes, is much better. He has been a terrific minister. Very competent indeed. Europe is his Achilles heel. But he has a kind of Castilian integrity. There's something decent about him.

By May 1996 the Conservative government was fragile, and both commentators and parliamentarians were aware that it might be possible to

1 Toby Jessel: Conservative MP for Twickenham 1970–97.
2 Edward Leigh: Conservative MP for Gainsborough and Horncastle 1983–97, for Gainsborough since 1997.
3 Sir Nicholas Winterton: Conservative MP for Macclesfield since 1971.
4 David Evans: Conservative MP for Welwyn, Hatfield, 1987–97. Anthony Marlow: Conservative MP for Northampton North 1979–97.

*topple it on a vote of no confidence. The old Conservative allies, the
Ulster Unionists, were disaffected. John Major had enemies on the right
wing of the party, and there had always been a small core of rebels
prepared to challenge from the left. The arithmetic was tempting, but
the outcome uncertain.*

DONALD DEWAR
The Guardian, 7 May 1996

There will not be a confidence vote just for the hell of it. He was eloquent
on the difficulty of getting every one of the anti votes into the lobby. He
said that Trimble wanted to keep the government in for the foreseeable
future, until he could get some capital out of ditching it. Noted that
Labour had failed to defeat the government by two votes last week (on
leasehold reform, I think) with Trimble and co. in the opposition lobby.
Getting all these people together isn't easy. Add in Thurnham,[1] Paisley
etc. All in all, I had the impression that they are unlikely to go for a
confidence vote. He said they certainly wouldn't unless they were certain
they could 'get to single figures' – i.e. single-figure defeat. Not very
ambitious. They were unswayed by the fact that the Tories were being
regarded as a rabble on their last legs, not expected to survive etc. etc.
He remarked on the columns that would be written in derision of an
Opposition trying and failing.

People should not underestimate how fragile the Union now is in
Scotland. He was surprisingly emphatic about that, when I pushed him
to correct his sepulchral language. The SNP regularly got 25 per cent in
the polls. That was about their standard support across the country. But
it could grow. Moreover, the SNP is strong across the board, in all
regions and kinds of seat. The polls show that both independence and
devolution support are rather soft – i.e. 30 per cent of the SNP vote says
it wants devolution, and 30 per cent (check figures) of the Labour support
says it wants independence. He reckons the SNP are not expecting to
have a good election this time. A Labour surge will carry Labour through.
But the 2001 election could be a different matter if Labour messes it up.
He thinks Salmond[2] is waiting for that period, and could well be right to
expect an SNP surge. The Tories will always collect around 22 per cent,
but probably few seats.

---

1 Peter Thurnham: MP for Bolton North-East – Conservative 1983–96, independent 1996, Liberal Democrat
1996–7.
2 Alex Salmond, SNP MP for Banff and Buchan since 1987; SNP leader 1990–2000 and since 2004; Member
(Scottish Parliament) for Gordon since 2007; first minister of Scotland since 2007.

However, the four-way contests make it hard to predict. Rifkind will probably survive, Lang might well survive. Forsyth is less likely to – and Labour has an exceptionally good candidate – but being the Secretary of State he gets a lot of publicity that will help him.

Forsyth, incidentally, is a rabidly right-wing figure, whatever pleasant noises he now makes. His latest wheeze is for a league table of sheriffs giving their sentencing record, which not even Michael Howard has thought of. He is clever, committed and formidable. The non-flying of the EU flag[1] is small stuff, by his lights. But also remember that he has recently said that if a Scottish parliament is created there's no question of the Conservatives abolishing it. That was an important development.

DD said they were not totally committed against a referendum. But he feared it being decided on other matters, and generally confusing the issue. He understood the other argument: that as a way of nailing down the legitimacy it had its merits.

He declined to offer an answer to the West Lothian question, and insisted, like a good Scotsman, that there was no logical reason to cut back the number of Labour MPs.

Affable, humorous, discreet, human, articulate: a real passion for the processes of politics, the management of the House of Commons, the heart and soul of the Labour Party – but in a faintly irreverent way. Remarked on how often he had come second in nomination fights with people thirty years ago.

HY judged Daniel Finkelstein – his next interviewee – to be the ultimate policy geek: 'rimless specs, oval face, young mind, cocky and yet unsure, seeking the approval of older men. We had met years ago (c.1985) at the Tawney Society, when he was [David] Owen's young man. Still looks back admiringly on Owen, whom he now describes as a man who "wants right-wing policies and a left-wing party" – which neither DO nor DF seems to think expresses the fullness of his absurdity. DF's solution was to join the Tories, where he is now head of the research department. All in all, rather an unimpressive young man. Perfectly decent, and on the ball, and aware of what his job must be. But rather agitated – not a lot of bottom, I felt. Not a repository of wisdom. Very keen on working out his own positions, and telling you that he had done so – most of all how he had made the switch from left to right and how this was entirely justified by real-life events. But I don't think he will go all that far.'

1 As a gesture of protest against the European ban on British beef, Michael Forsyth, the Scottish Secretary, refused to fly the EU flag on 9 May 1996 to mark Europe Day.

DANIEL FINKELSTEIN
Café Pelican, 4 June 1996

He is very interested in the state, though denies that he is a minimal-state man. His guru is David Willetts, as he says quite openly, and Willetts's pamphlet *Civil Conservatism*, which he published when running the Social Market Foundation, is his bible. He says that he doesn't like paying 60 per cent tax on his upper income, which he tots up by including VAT on everything except housing and food. He is interested in finding private ways of doing state things. Thus sees the private hospitals doing NHS work as a good example, accepted by the public. Longish term he sees this as the way to go, including pensions.

He is open and easy about the main task of the CRD. It is to analyse and demolish Labour policies. This has been done badly hitherto, certainly up until the last party conference, where there were numerous failures in this field. He says there have been at least four confused attitudes towards Labour on the part of the Tories. (1) That Labour hasn't really changed. (2) That Labour has no policies. (3) In combination with either of these, that Blair may be OK but his party is not. (4) That Labour is now the Tory Party, therefore why not vote for the real thing? His own line, which he claims is now widely accepted, is to say that New Labour is New Labour, and its policies are bad policies. This was agreed at the political Cabinet a few weeks ago. He mentioned only Ken Clarke – who wants to say that Labour has no policies – as a significant dissenter from his line.

New Labour should be taken at face value, and Blair should be analysed as someone who wants Prescott, Dobson[1] and Meacher in his Shadow Cabinet – needs to keep them happy; wants to keep them happy. Therefore the line isn't so much that Blair is one thing, and they are another, but rather that the consensus that binds them all contains many bad things. He adds Gordon Brown to this list, saying that his latest statements about youth unemployment were totally non-credible. He also says that Straw on a children's curfew was a prize example of policy being made without thinking out any of its consequences. It will, he said, be attacked by the party.

He says, incidentally, that Labour is making a mistake in going for the Tories on tax. If they had any sense they would not pretend they are lower-taxing than the Tories, just as the Tories have learned there is nothing to be said for talking about health – that just plays to Labour's

---

1 Frank Dobson: Labour MP for Holborn and St Pancras since 1979; Secretary of State for Health 1997–9.

strength, however seriously we do believe our policies have been very good for health.

Tax-and-spend will still be the main issue. And the feel-good factor must surely come back into play. But he concedes that of course he is worried that it may not do so.

Another big thing is the constitution. He sees this as something all Tories agree about, and it has the special virtue of being something they can project as in the national rather than the party interest: a statement of principle which has a passion behind it. This reminds him to say that Major believes in it very strongly, and that one of the problems at the 1992 election, and later, was too many people imagining that Major would do what he was told. He won't. He is very stubborn – more so than MT (who was quite malleable when it came to presentation). There's been a tendency at CCO to work out what they think should be said, and then just assume Major will say it with conviction. But the words have to match his beliefs. Incidentally, the Major-in-the-round of the last election was a failure: played badly on the TV, which lost interest after the first bite at it.

More on the constitution. It should play bigger than last time. It is a reason to vote against Labour, because their changes will be permanent. It gives positive vibes to people who want a reason to vote Tory for the fifth time. Constitutional reform seems to be something Labour hasn't thought through. Also, because it is something Major himself believes in. That will come through as well.

He regards Europe as a dangerous issue for the Tories. People might agree with your basic attitudes, yet be worried by the extremity with which you express them and the disturbance your line seems to be promising. It is also, obviously, dangerous because it is divisive.

ROBIN COOK
House of Commons, 2 July 1996

The Road to the Manifesto. Published this Thursday. RC was candidly caustic, behind the usual professorial 'I'm bound to say's etc. He thought the policies as such were not vacuous (my word). There were a lot of decent things in them. The focus groups, he said with some exasperation, showed often that people wanted small, doable policies, not big promises they didn't believe the politicians would keep. The policies are in line with that. They had thought, at the NEC today, about publishing the 100 or so policies that have been listed, and decided not to do so on the grounds that the enemies would pick and choose the ones they wanted to attack; but these policies would be out in bits and pieces (largely repeating what is already known) before the conference.

His objection to the document is that it is defensive (he has used that word to Blair, so don't pin it on an SC member). It is still preoccupied with saying what Labour is not. Still beguiled by the fear factor (my word). In thrall to it. I said, Does it make you proud to be Labour? Good word, he said. The party will get restless, worried about all this. Still not enough which does make you proud, says where we stand in an unambiguous way.

Notes linguistic giveaways. Says the introduction announces that this document is 'uncompromising and un-something else', two negative prefixes – very revealing, he says. Shows the cast of mind. Like the Scott report? 'Yes, you'll find a lot of double negatives.'

He says that Blair spends too much time talking to business audiences, as someone has noted. Never talks to a TU audience. This seeps into his consciousness, of course. Pleasing business is more important than pleasing the party. Pleasing the *Daily Mail* is more important still. The document shows the signs of all that. Trying to suss out what the *Mail* will like (my word, not his). He likens this Blair trait – talking to business audiences – with Benn talking to audiences of 500 in 1981–3, when he never took questions and never talked to an audience of twelve. So he never got down to challenges. He believed what he was getting back, which was adulation. RC doesn't put Blair in quite that category, he says, but there is a danger.

Have you seen today's Tory effort? he asks. (*The Road to Ruin*.)[1] Yes, juvenile. It reminds him that we have been told nothing about what the Tories will do with a fifth term. Perhaps the time has come to fill in the blanks. We will start doing it.

Said he had never, oddly, known the party to be in a more perplexed state of mind. (He talks about 'the party' with real meaning and even reverence. This is one of the real divergences from Blair, and plainly a source of Robin's chronic disdain for him.) This was a paradox. It had also never in his lifetime been on the brink of perhaps a landslide victory. A really odd experience for all. Were these things connected?

Looking at the programmes as a whole, the most radical part will undoubtedly be the constitutional stuff. Not the economic or social. If we get that through, we will have done a lot. (Interesting to compare this with Clare Short,[2] seen just before. CS said that she was most reassured

1 The Conservatives' rejoinder to Labour's *The Road to the Manifesto*.
2 Clare Short: MP for Birmingham Ladywood – Labour 1983–2006, since then independent. Labour Party NEC member 1988–98; front-bench spokesperson 1985–97; Secretary of State for International Development 1997–2003.

by Brown's statement on youth unemployment and long-term unemployment, when he committed the windfall utility tax[1] to that end. For her,
this, combined with a commitment to greater fairness, would be enough
to feel Labour was doing something that mattered. Though she also said
that the constitution, in the form of PR, was radical stuff.)

Said that the response to the BSE problem has been too cautious. Or
rather – I think I heard him say (I've forgotten the timing) – if we had
said anything else, Peter Mandelson would have been on to Tony saying
we had sacrificed the patriotic vote.

For such a strong arguer as Cook, with such a high regard for himself,
he alluded with amazing relief to the fact that 'Mandelson hasn't got it
in for me at the moment.'

RICHARD HOLME
Lunch, the Garrick, 8 July 1996

Sees the Blair manifesto as thin. This helps the LDs. Makes it more
striking for them to be crisp and more specific. They can say more positive
and hard things about tax, with specific limits and specific purposes laid
down – this gives the LDs a profile.

Increasingly, the LDs will be seen not as the guard against the left but
as the spur to action. But they can play it several ways: the critical
opposition (as the Tories are spending two years cutting themselves to
pieces); the spur to action; the guard against the leftish extremes. Whatever suits.

But the important thing is to maintain an identity. This will be easier
if we avoid talking at all about post-election deals and structures. Happily,
if Labour is well ahead, this kind of question won't become top of the
agenda. We can therefore keep going on our own track, with our own
agenda.

Believes very clearly that there are excellent chances of winning between 30 and 40 seats. LDs have target-seats strategy more clearly than
before, and their organization in these 100 seats is excellent. (Almost all
are Tory seats.) The structures, the newspapers, the teams, the computers
etc. On the ground we are ready.

Has done a lot of focus-group work with groups who have no fixed
intention to vote for any particular party. Finding that for the first time
the Blair problem is just starting to define itself: that he is seen as a bit

---

1 Labour promised a 'windfall levy on the excess profits of the privatized utilities', arguing that they had been
sold too cheaply, that dividends were much higher than profits, and that water, gas and electricity companies,
along with BT, the British Airports Authority and so on, had been able to exploit monopoly power.

slippery, a bit surface. This is probably unfair. But it's the price he pays for being so good at it. It almost disguises the depth he has. But it is a factor. One of the lessons to emphasize Ashdown as the man of experience: the longest-lived leader, Bosnia man (even womanizing man, RH laughed).

Thinks the gap is bound to narrow. But by no means enough to save the Tories. What then for the Libs? You should ask Blair that question – he seems to say different things at different times.

Sees Labour as hopelessly unprepared for constitutional reform. Just declining to use the large number of people who have thought about it all. Neither Straw nor Richard[1] is up to it. Speaks with heavy omen about HL reform. Could be a morass. No certainty about what they will really do with hereditary peers. Cranborne[2] is no fool. See the Douglas-Home report in the early 1970s, which RH thinks was an excellent piece of work – Labour has nothing to match it today. The CU report[3] is not political, just technical. We agree that Robin Cook would be much better as the overlord.

In general, thinks the HL could cut up very rough.

WILLIAM WALDEGRAVE
House of Commons, 15 July 1996

If we lose, JM will go. Unfortunately, he has been telling people on aeroplanes that he wants Chris Patten to succeed him. This makes it impossible for Chris to do so: anyway a difficult task, by all objective tests. If we win, it will be very narrow and nobody will want to have a by-election. Anyway, Major will continue. If we lose, who will want to humour Major by letting him delay until Patten is available? And who will want to make it at all easy to let Patten in: who will want to have a by-election, which even in opposition may be problematic? All these things make it seem pretty certain that Chris is blocked. The idea of everything hanging fire while he is readmitted is an almost certain recipe for him being turned down. People think, in any case, that he should do some time back here, get back in touch with the party and the Commons.

In defeat, Redwood and Portillo will be candidates. JR is utterly unrealistic about public spending. Not only the farce of contingency

---

1 Ivor Richard; barrister; Labour MP for Baron's Court 1964–74; UK permanent representative to the UN 1974–9; as Baron Richard of Ammanford, Leader of the Opposition in the House of Lords 1992–7.

2 Viscount Cranborne, heir of the 6th Marquess of Salisbury: MP for Dorset South 1979–87; Leader of the House of Lords since 1994; managed the successful leadership election of John Major the year before.

3 The Constitution Unit of University College London delivered a report on House of Lords reform in April 1996.

reserve, but all kinds of money-business with other things. He is simply groping for populist issues (cottage hospitals) that don't add up. Lang was the first name WW mentioned as a centrist candidate, if he keeps his seat. Forsyth: a good knockabout operator, who has done well with Scotland, but even if he had the safest seat in the land he wouldn't be real as a leader. Shephard is now shown to have feet of clay.

He thought Clarke had played the Europe issue quite wrongly. Courageous and straight, but unwise and unnecessary to flaunt it quite so much. But WW agreed that KC felt worried about what JM would do, and used speeches to fence him in. Also that Hezza was not the force he used to be, mainly because he 'got bored quite soon'. Hezza was now bored with Europe, perhaps.

We got to a wider discussion about Europe. WW rethinking his positions, though very personally. As he sees it, the EMU will mean that a federal core does emerge, and faces us with a choice. The choice will face any government, and will be the defining issue of the next few years. France, Germany, Netherlands, Luxembourg, maybe Austria, maybe Belgium: these will go ahead. And once they have got the EMU they will want to do more: all in a federalistic direction. Foreign policy included. That is the only logic of what they want. For some countries – Spain, Poland – the position can be taken that we want to get in once we qualify. For other small economies, the loss of independence won't matter much anyway or (conversely) their economies don't matter to the project. For us, a large economy, it is quite different.

The choice will be hard to present. There is no language for it yet. But we could become a large offshore trading nation, making our own rules within the WTO and not burdened with the Brussels weights. This would, thinks WW, also involve us shedding our world-powerdom aspirations: all the baggage of boxing above our weight, all the grand notions that came from the nineteenth century. In Conservative historical terms, he sees the party going back to Burkean roots, where public spending was the one thing people cared should be kept to a minimum, and rather disapproved of imperial ambitions. Now that the imperial era has passed, there is a case for saying we should follow the whole logic of that and become the Japan of Europe. Or the Norway/Switzerland of the former EU. Settling for a smaller world role, cutting our defence commitments, cutting our FCO ambitions and size, altogether downsizing. A key to all this is an attack on protectionism. The EU is a protectionist cabal. We would speak and act for total free trade.

One of the most pernicious nonsenses of the EU is the belief that the single market means a level playing field for labour as well as trade. This is profound nonsense. It is the death of employment. And if you argue that, socially, the most corrosive evil is long-term unemployment, you should try to get labour costs down as the highest priority. As the way to keep people in work. He is struck by the sheer brutality with which the US does this, and doesn't propose we should do the same: leaving able-bodied men with literally nothing, no welfare at all. He also thinks the NHS is a vital service to be preserved, so as to protect people's deepest fears. But the social costs of jobs in Germany as against here are massive, and a huge deterrent – as the wisest German employers and economists well understand.

He sees welfare as necessarily being the object of any governmental concern, and the need for change. Thinks it inevitable that there must be a move towards the insurance principle, together with an element of compulsion – i.e. people being obliged to provide for themselves.

He was off to give a private dinner for 'Dukey' Hussey, his brother-in-law. Duke is now delighting in being thought a man who was the golden age of the BBC. Birt is dealing with the World Service without any consultation with the FCO – so WW says.

He notes how Major has remained a very decent man, despite it all. If he wins, nothing much will change. Perhaps we are discovering that politics these days is just that: an endless grind against the odds, with few friends.

JOHN GUMMER
Lunch, the Garrick, 24 July 1996

Frisky, energetic, creative, keen, quite garrulous about himself (as I encouraged). Only as we were leaving the Garrick did he say, with faint apology, that he had meant to ask me about what was happening at *The Observer*.[1] The great thing about JSG is that he has a sense of history, and a serious interest in his subject of the moment – Environment.

What was the hardest thing to drive through? He answered immediately. It was reversing the trend to out-of-town shopping centres. Which he claimed he had fully achieved by changing the planning arrangements, and getting the agreement of many of the bigger stores. The bigger ones have just about got all they need, and therefore have an interest in assisting in a change which will keep out the newcomers. The case for reviving inner cities is very strong. Gummer obviously has quite a knowledge of how to do this: making it attractive to superstores (who can backhaul with the same lorries that bring their stuff, and who gain from the 'just

---

1 In 1996, *The Guardian*'s economics editor, Will Hutton, took over as editor of *The Observer* from Andrew Jaspan.

in time' concept of delivering – i.e. not having as much space taken up with storage as with shopping, but keeping the lines going just in time).

All this had enraged lots of the lobbies and interests. But Gummer is proud of what he has got through. He sees it as good for the car-type environment problems as well.

His other big thing was getting Britain to exceed the targets she agreed to at the Rio summit. Other countries lagged behind, but we are ahead. He is very up on global warming: see his recent speeches and attendance at the summit. Altogether, he has taken this subject very keenly on board, unlike Howard, his predecessor, who was interested mainly in local government and its surrounding laws. A good example of how an individual minister's zeals and keenness can change a whole policy stance.

For JSG it is also attractive as an object lesson in European values. He is going to make a big conference speech linking the two: this is the one area where being 'European' cannot be gainsaid – as anyone knows who has thought about or looked at rivers, acid rain, air, birds etc. The RSPB [Royal Society for the Protection of Birds] has one million members: a voter group worth cultivating. He plans a humdinger at Bournemouth.

The other thing he is heavy on is London. Disagrees with Simon Jenkins. Says his London office has in fact been able to do more than a GLC would, because it crosses frontiers. It has just about got agreement for a plan for the Thames from Teddington to the sea. It is also getting closer to traffic and planning changes for the whole of central London: Trafalgar Square, Parliament Square, Horseguards, Strand. One of his biggest things is the new Thames bridge – 'live-on' bridge I think is the name: a bridge on a prime site which will thus pay for itself. The one to the South Bank will be announced soon. He hopes for another from the City to Bankside – although the City and the *FT* are now planning merely a walkway, to which JSG is very opposed.

Thinks on Europe that the Cabinet consensus will not crack. There are far more than three ministers in favour of it. The sceptics are up to their usual tactics, by pretending otherwise. The great bulk of the Cabinet is pro-European, and certainly in favour of the wait-and-see line on EMU. Gummer can simply see no case whatever for the other line – other than the view (itself mistaken) that such a line would help the Tory Party. Nothing whatever to do with the national interest.

He does not take a very romantic view of the British people having become more internationalist. Just a bit, he thinks. But he is strongly of the view that the Tory Party grass roots are not anti-Europe. Cites his own speech at the Welsh party conference, when he made an environmental speech that caught much fire, and – perorating with the line about being proud of being Welsh, proud of being British, proud of being

European – got an unstoppable standing ovation. Says that both he and Hezza have experimented recently at meetings with strong pro-European speeches and got the same response.

Is very confident of winning the election. Cites local by-elections with 15 per cent Tory swings as the secret evidence of change. People will come round as long as we can avoid seeming disunited. They will look at Labour and at Blair and wonder what the point is of changing. They will have the weaknesses of Labour's constitutional plans pointed out to them.

He is cogently scornful of Labour's environmental policy. *The Road to the Manifesto*, which I mentioned to him, has only two sentences, both cliché-ridden, but neither containing the two clichés you should mention – the biosphere and global warming. There seems no genuine interest there whatever. Blair's speech, much heralded, was empty. Dobson is Old Labour personified, and Old Labour is not interested in the environment, or at any rate in its modern problems. He even thinks Labour has been talking with the superstores with a view to changing his line on out-of-town stores – an amazing anti-historical line for Labour to be taking, if that is what it is doing.

Says that via Tom Burke, his recent adviser, he keeps contacting Labour, through the Green movement, to try and encourage them to assist in bipartisan lines. But there has been no response.

As an example of Old Labour's incorrigible presence, cites the impossibility of getting the local councils to make genuine partnership agreements. They will never surrender control. They will let NCP [National Car Parks] run their car parks, but not let NCP decide the tariffs or the opening hours or the wages of the man on the gate. Won't hand over property or the business. Insist on keeping control for the politicians and the bureaucrats. He sees local car parks as a kind of symbol of how retrograde Labour will be at all levels when they get into national power.

More broadly, expatiates on the classic historic errors for which the Tory Party has been responsible. We have got Ireland absolutely wrong at every stage from Gladstone's efforts onwards. And we have got our international role wrong very often too, most typically in Europe. Of the EMU, he says he is determined to try and avoid a repeat of the many previous instances of climbing aboard too late. He is vocal about the vital role we have played in the Uruguay Round – himself cooped up in a Chicago hotel on call for McSharry,[1] even though the UK was no longer the EU president. It was British pressure and influence that got the EU position clearest, and the EU which alone mattered in the WTO when dealing with the US. It is utterly crazy, he says, to imagine that outside

---

1 Ray McSharry: former Irish finance minister, and EU commissioner for agriculture.

the EU we would have mattered at all in that negotiation, or in any other trading matter.

SIR JAMES GOLDSMITH
Wilton's Restaurant, 18 September 1996

Ebullient, warmly greeting, already schmoozing with others in the restaurant. Accompanied by his flunky, Patrick Robertson. Wearing scrappy brown loafers with his dark suit. Bronzed, much grinning – until roused to almost foaming fury by the power of his own arguments and the way they are ignored by most influential people. Didn't ask me a single question – but then why should he? Made himself available for me to ask him any question I wanted, he said. Robertson silent and simpering beside me, laughing excessively loudly at Jimmy's rather old jokes. I got on early terms by talking about Wyche Fowler,[1] which came to me only as I sat down. JG said he was a very old friend, a great admirer. WF had often come to see him. They disagreed on much, but agreed about the environment and also about free trade etc.

FREE TRADE/PROTECTION   This is what really seems to turn him on. He has a well-organized, passionate line against 'universalism'. This seems to subsume a lot of things, but is mainly based on a belief that Third World countries must not be overrun by transnational companies and values. A strong belief that McDonald's should not rule the world. JG says he travels round the world for two months each year, goes into the heart of many countries, sees what is happening (he cited China), and is appalled.

He is equally appalled by the injustice of the American and transnational version of capitalism. Foams and rants about the profits being made on the back of cheap labour, the stock-market rise which is due to the same thing, the effects on domestic labour in the US, the real-term cuts of 20 per cent over a long period in salaries. He sounds, on this track, like a businessman version of Tony Benn.

This is part of a still wider view. He sees the future world struggle being between godless individualist materialism and 'rationalism', against spiritualism which is mainly but not solely represented by Islam. The wars of the world in our time hitherto have been between two godless powers, East and West, mercifully. Now Islam will have the power behind it. American religion is not spiritual, it is an offshoot of capitalism. He

1 Wyche Fowler: Democratic senator 1987–93 from Georgia, USA; US ambassador to Saudi Arabia 1996–2001.

has advised Wyche, incidentally, who is about to take up his Saudi appointment, that the first thing he should urge is a US withdrawal. The troops should be placed in Cyprus. The US must understand that Saudi has to reflect the general Islamic hatred of the US. In any case, he fulminates with a knowing grin, the West lost the Gulf War in all important respects.

His biggest case against Clinton is that he gave way to the cartels. He let big business tell him what to do about world trade. There are 100 companies that dominate the world, before which the politicians lie down.

When I ask, Aren't the Third World countries entitled to prosperity? he says, Yes, of course, but this doesn't have to be on the transnational capitalist model. Cites the US itself as a country that grew without world trade, and Singapore as one that grew behind protection walls. I didn't have the prepared equipment with which to take all this on, but busked my way through. He is a perfectly good conversationalist, even though he gets carried away by his own rants – well-tried orations he has given many times before.

EUROPE AND HIS PARTY   Sees himself as a pro-European who has been betrayed. He voted Yes in the referendum, was a keen supporter, but had not read the documents. When he read the documents, and when he watched EU develop, he became very shocked and determined that it must stop. He says that Europe will blow apart, and there could be war – unless we abandon the superstate. When I said there was a large element of uncertainty when Heath joined and a genuine sense of ignorance about the future, he said Monnet[1] knew what was happening. I said Monnet didn't matter then. He replied that there was a whole class of political people who had an idea about what they wanted to happen, but had never put it to the people.

He reeled off the list of what it is to be an independent nation, and shouted that we had lost them all. (He is very fluent, and well-practised with lists, quotes and speeches.) I said that NATO represented a sacrifice of sovereignty. He said that NATO was something we could always leave, which the EU was not. I said we could certainly leave the EU, but he said only by war. One of the fairly few moments when he seemed totally ridiculous and paranoid.

But he is very insistent that he is a European. This is why the UKIP detests him, and why the British National Party recently wrote a rather well-written editorial attacking him. He wants to stay in the EU; he wants

1 Jean Monnet: considered by many the founder of the European ideal; never elected to office, but president of the High Authority governing the European Coal and Steel Community 1952–5, forerunner of the Common Market; founded the Action Committee for the United States of Europe 1955.

a union of governments that are independent. He seems to want more foreign-policy collaboration in that context.

He has got an answer to Spicer's discovery that French and English versions of his book say different things.[1] They were never meant to be exactly the same. There have been editions in several languages, tailored to different cultures. But the kernel message is the same. He insists that the selected bits of contradiction result from mistranslation or selective editing. Can cite speeches etc. etc. when he has been going on about all this for years, and never changed his message about the superstate.

WHY DOES HE DO IT   Says that between 1989 and 1993 I will not find a single cutting about him. He was off the map. He wanted to do his own thing; he had left business. But then he got drawn into it, for the above reasons on the issue.

Notes that he is one of the few people who had the necessary advantages to do something: he had time; he had the money ('resources'); he could take the flak ('I don't like it, but I can take it, it doesn't mean anything to me'); and he doesn't mind if he fails. I remarked that the last was the thing that most distinguished him from politicians. I do it because I can do no other, he says. Somebody has to do it: to give the people a chance to say whether they want to be part of a superstate in which they have signed away their independence. Even if I knew I would get only 0.2 per cent of the vote, I would still do it. It has to be done.

Here, in other words, is a very dangerous creature. An other-worldly man, in many ways, who has more of the resources of the world than almost anyone else and wants to change the world with them. He is inoculated against criticism, incapable of succumbing to deals. He is in part an anarchist, he is counter-typical as a business tycoon, he is the loosest of all cannons at large in a system he detests.

He has a very low opinion of almost all politicians. Gave a party for Kissinger's seventieth birthday here, to which were asked the lions of the British scene. They made him think what total pygmies we have now. Spoke to Healey, and told him he had always disagreed with him but at least he was a man of stature. So was Callaghan. But now? 'I vomit on the government.' (There was quite a lot of vomiting – his favoured mode of contempt.)

If anyone epitomizes what he detests it is Hurd. Hurd was head boy when Goldsmith arrived at Eton, though he doesn't say Hurd beat him.

1   In his book *The Challenge from the East* (1996), Sir Michael Spicer, Conservative MP for South Worcestershire 1974–97, for West Worcestershire since 1997, and himself a Euro-sceptic, raised the question of the apparently linguistically differing views in Sir James's self-published book *The Response* (1995), about the chaotic consequences of the GATT.

But Hurd is a typical bureaucrat, willing to do anything, a civil servant, a man without convictions, a man who will be the tool of the trans-nationals very willingly.

Major he sees as a joke, and obviously has done for years. Thatcher was at one time a great person, but he doubts whether she has the vision to see the truth about the world as it is now. Blair he is waiting to see about: gives him the benefit of the doubt. Thinks he might come to something.

This contempt is especially vast for France. Sees the whole system as deeply corrupt, and likely to explode for that reason. Government, business, media are interlocked. Media are pathetic. He cites *Figaro* and *Le Monde* as in the pockets of government and business people who want things from each other. As a national press, they have a circulation of barely 1 million, so they have no power. He gave a big talk to the French Senate in which he ranted on about all this with chapter and verse, and he was heard in silence – they had never heard anyone saying anything like this before – before being given a standing ovation.

Listening to him, you get a weird sense of selflessness – combined, though, with utter self-belief in his rectitude: the belief that he alone tells the truth. I really don't see anything much in it for him. This is a rich man's folly, a bit of serious fun, a gesture that costs him small change while letting him ventilate his passions, a ploy that places him right outside conventional politics because he has no interest in winning and therefore in doing deals. He does want to win the argument, and he would like a referendum – but the main thing is to have taken part.

Does talk about Perot[1] in the same breath. Knows him. Says he is very intelligent 'but certifiably insane' – this said not as a glib line but meant with seriousness.

THE CAMPAIGN ITSELF The party is agnostic; he is not. The party contains federalists and separatists, and therefore has no line about what to campaign for in a referendum. But he himself has these strong feelings, which he makes very clear.

Denies that there are problems. Nationally they have 2,000 people seeking 650 candidacies. They announce a batch each Friday. They have some wonderful people. He meets them regularly. Among other things, this exercise is a way for him to meet the people.

Denies that the issue is a low priority for most people. Says there is passion all round, at every meeting. I say it is the obsession of a small class, who deceive themselves. He totally disagrees.

1 Ross Perot: American businessman; stood as an independent candidate for president in 1992, receiving 18.9 per cent of the popular vote; ran again in 2006, for the Reform Party.

Also reminds me that in the only poll – NOP a few months ago – they got 14 per cent support. So to that extent he is a normal politician, talking up the polls.

When accosted with the charge that he will be letting Labour in, he says that there is no big difference between the parties. He is essentially equally contemptuous of both, though he has always voted Tory. So whether Labour get in doesn't matter to him very much, at least on Europe. Notes that their positions have got closer together.

ROBIN RENWICK
17 October 1996

Believes that the UK will not go into EMU in the first round. It is too risky. He cites what is becoming perhaps the familiar proof: that there is this crucial difference with the USA. If there's a recession in Michigan, there may be jobs in Florida, and people can easily go there. Moreover, there's a balancing out of welfare, done by the federal government. These are the marks of one country, one money, one language, one sense of identity which can produce a kind of flexibility. None of this is true in Europe. If the British economy goes into slump, there's no chance of workers migrating to Germany even if they wanted to. And so on. This is bound to be a very big inhibitor – though he didn't explain why it wasn't the same inhibitor elsewhere in the EU: presumably he would say (with some justice) that there is greater willingness to cross frontiers between Germany and France and Benelux. Though what about Spain, Portugal etc.?

Says that Britain's position now is worse than under MT. At least with MT they had to pay attention. The BSE thing, in particular, was a complete mess. Blaming Europe for something that was almost entirely Britain's fault lost us all respect.

Thinks Labour will find out how incompetent a lot of its frontbenchers are. Blair will do well in government – but Blunkett? RR had heard his uttering what he regarded as wholesale rubbish about privatization on the radio. I rather agree, though not about Blunkett. The front bench is full of opportunists, trained in that mode only. It will await the emergence of a true governing cadre – who by definition will have had less time on the Opposition front bench. Equally, however, he said the Tories are totally exhausted. How can any government have Hogg, Gummer on the front bench?

HY thought that Virginia Bottomley's defence of the government in the following interview must reflect her colleagues' views, since she 'doesn't have an original thought in her head.'

VIRGINIA BOTTOMLEY
21 October 1996

We will hang on to the end, because the whole point is to let the economy improve, and to let people see that it is improving. The figures are so good, let people understand what they may be about to lose.

Blair is hopelessly thin on policy. His conference speech should have laid out a programme, and failed to do so. This is because the party is so badly split that he dare not do so. 'We all know what Labour's *really* like.' She explains that pretty well the whole of policy splits Labour from top to bottom, including Europe, which she regards as the biggest division of all. (Though when I gently chide her for this, she says maybe she is living in too small a circle – and maybe she is believing what the circle has convinced itself is true.)

She insisted what a straight arrow Major was, what a decent man, compared with glossy Blair. Again, the official line actually being seriously believed by the people at the top . . .

GORDON BROWN
5 November 1996

His new office, West Cloister, off Westminster Hall, a long corridor of Gothic arches, with his own circular office leading off it: must be the grandest set in Westminster.

ECONOMIC PROGRAMME He begins, without my asking a question, to regale me with the need for a programme which provides equal opportunity. He remembered that I had declared that relieving poverty was the main test, but said there was much more. Equal opportunity to work was a central part of it. This was more than training, University of Industry etc. It was the fundamental reform needed to employment and the welfare state.

The objective had to be to take note of how the employment pattern had hugely changed. There was no longer any question of becoming unemployed, then being floated back into the same or a similar job as demand increased. That is the old pattern, now outdated. More likely now was the need to accept a lower-paid job when returning, and then to try and surf upwards from there. Many people who returned to work do so for very low pay. Many went in and out of the employment market. (He has become a tremendous expert in the refinements of all this, understands employment patterns very well, has a very deep and impressive concern to deal with this prime and desperate economic need: truly an *homme sérieux*.)

Reforming the welfare state to this end was a huge but vital requirement. (I understood, incidentally, why he wanted a lackey, H. Harman, at Social Security rather than Chris Smith.) He kept coming back to this whole thrust of policy: training, restructuring the welfare system, providing if not jobs then the better means to qualify for jobs.

One of his key statistics is that 20 per cent of all households have no employed person in them, even though unemployment is running at about 7 per cent. This means that there are lots with several adults unemployed, and that single-parent families abound, and these are matched by the very large numbers where two or more adults are working. This had to be a very major issue that any government has to address: cannot just stand around and do nothing.

The minimum wage is vital in this context, as a floor. What matters is not the fact of it but the way it is done: i.e. the rate it is set at. He takes the US example, where as many as 80 million people are on wage supplements of some kind. But employers are nearer to having to pay a decent baseline wage. If there is to be a welfare system that does more to encourage work, then we have to make sure that cheap labour is not being bottomlessly subsidized by the state.

He reiterates his impatience at people who still equate tax-and-spend with socialism. He admits he once thought this himself – 'we all did' – to some extent. He sees there is still a great gap of understanding about the above, and a need to educate the public to see it. It needs to be 'the next stage' of our campaign of persuasion.

BUDGET AND TAX   He recalls what happened before 1992. First we made our spending commitments: child benefit and pensions. Then we said we would put up National Insurance for people at *c.*£20,000 – a 9 per cent rise. Then we said we would have a top rate of 50 per cent, without saying where it would cut in. This gave the Tory press two years to run all kinds of scare stories, bringing the cut-in figure lower and lower. All this was a disaster, a lesson. People said afterwards we lost because of Neil Kinnock. In fact, as John Smith readily admitted later, the shadow Budget and its forerunners were the heart of the problem.

There will be no shadow Budget this time. There will be an indication of tax position. We have begun this with the promise about VAT on fuel.[1] He talked, though, mainly about the low rate of 10 per cent, rather than anything at the top.

He agreed that it would not be satisfactory to talk about 'waiting until we see the books'. I added that, since they were committed to not increasingly public spending (except the youth unemployed, funded by the utility windfall tax – many billions more than the 1 per cent on income tax), the 'books' argument was a poor one for not indicating whether the 'fairness' symbols would come in.[2] He did not seem to disagree.

EMU AND ALL THAT   He said that hardly anyone in the Labour party objected in principle. He insisted that the Maastricht criteria were directions in which we would want to go for our own reasons: each was very sensible and necessary.

He maintained the referendum/election alternatives. He obviously remembers with meaning the 1978–9 Scottish events, where the devolution package was defeated on a low turnout. The thing he gets from that is the capacity of *fear* to be mobilized against change. The 1975 Euro referendum was a status-quo proposal. I added that it was backed by the press and the Opposition. All this would be different. He countered by saying that *The Sun* – he mentioned it about three times – was in favour of a referendum, and pretended to be neutral on the issue: therefore the press would not necessarily be launching itself for a No. He added that if EMU went ahead with the others and was a fair success – he thought, by the way, that it would happen, maybe a bit late, and would be held together – the pressure from business would become very strong indeed for the pound to get in.

All that said, when I asked if there could be a mandate at the 1997 election, he said no. There might be slight differences, but they would not be enough. When I said that a referendum on the Euro issue writ large might be a better way of handling it, he said that people might not accept that – to which I said that, with a large majority, that was a problem that could surely be finessed. He didn't either agree or disagree.

All in all, here is a serious man. With some patience. Realizes that the hard messages he wants to get across, about the long-term nature of what needs to be done, will themselves take a long time. He can say them endlessly. He also sees EMU as a complex subject, which again will be hard to get across.

1 In 1996, Gordon Brown and Labour colleagues outflanked the government to stop Chancellor Kenneth Clarke from imposing VAT of 17.5 per cent on fuel.
2 'Fairness' was a word much on Labour lips in 1996. Gordon Brown promised the trade unions 'fairness not favours'. Tony Blair defended the minimum-wage proposals on the grounds of 'fairness and efficiency', and offered 'decency, hard work and fairness' in a speech in Swansea.

When HY was asked by the New Yorker *to write a long profile of John Major, he undertook formal, taped interviews. There is no place for them here, not least as taped interviews often show up the verbosity of HY's subjects. But Norman Lamont, who had been Major's Chancellor of the Exchequer at the time of Black Wednesday, talked over a Garrick lunch, which allowed HY to write up the account in his own inimitable style. HY also wrote about Major in his constituency – a colour piece that shows that his reporting skills had not deserted him.*

NORMAN LAMONT
Lunch, the Garrick, 12 November 1996

MAASTRICHT   There was never any question of a veto. We decided to go the opt-out route, therefore we never discussed a veto. As for Lubbers's suggestion (which I told him about), it is flattering nonsense. I was never in a position where I could recommend that, nor did I seriously think it was an option.

A basic reason for this was that JM was convinced from way back that EMU would never happen. He told me that in explicit terms several times. So he misjudged it. He thought the opt-out was an opt-out from a non-event. But this makes it all the more puzzling that he should have worked so hard to keep Maastricht on board after the Danish referendum. Why did he bust a gut to save the Danes and to save Maastricht? The answer can only be vanity – and pride of authorship. I prefer to say vanity rather than stubbornness, says Norman. JM is not particularly stubborn.

Lamont recalls telephoning Major after the Danish referendum and making a remark about the Danes having pulled the building down and now there were the ruins left on the ground – and implying (saying?) that this was a good outcome. Major totally disagreed. But then Major, having wanted a Yes from the Danes, wanted a No from the French. In less than six months he had turned round. This was a reflection, no doubt, of the parliamentary pressure on him – or whatever. The simple fact is that he had changed his mind. This speaks oddly for the conviction that he had about Maastricht, even then.

THE ERM FIASCO   Norman himself says he has never been a fixed-currency man in the way that Nigel Lawson was. They agreed on opposing a single currency, but Lawson was stronger about the currency. Lamont was agnostic-to-sceptical. But he went along with it because it was what he inherited. It was government policy. He became Chancellor only weeks after we went into it, and he says that up until that time he

cannot remember having any attitude really about it, and certainly knowing nothing about it. He was totally immersed, as Chief Secretary, in
public spending. He wasn't asked for his opinion, and he didn't volunteer
it. He only remembers feeling it was rather odd, when he was told
about it. He recalls asking Terry Burns why we were doing this, and
Terry said, 'It's all political.'

Lamont says his July speech strongly backing ERM was his one big
mistake; he looks back on it with embarrassment. He reports that the
Treasury, long after, and after he had left office, had done an analysis
of it, and found it to be very prescient. But he still thinks it was a mistake, to be so strong. It was a very emphatic, unguarded speech. Major
had been imploring him to give it. So he did. But it did not look good,
later.

When we were forced out, Lamont says he did not feel it to be
traumatic. It was a conclusion which he actually desired. So he felt
comfortable at the turn of events. He had thought we would be forced to
devalue, not that we would be forced out. Major, by contrast, was deeply
troubled. The only light NL could shed on Major's condition at the time
– in face of the (unmentioned) rumours about JM having somehow had
a brief nervous collapse – was that when NL went to seek him just before
the exit, Major refused to talk about it. He says there is a minute on file
at the Treasury which records him as saying to his officials that he 'would
come back to that on another occasion' – i.e. he couldn't tell them
anything the PM had indicated.

Why was Major so committed? Pride of authorship again. And vanity.
Was this not a sign of him having a conviction? No, says NL. How can
you have a conviction about the value of the pound? It was a practical
matter. But he had become carried away by it (not his word). He had had
quite a long engagement with the issue, first as Chancellor. And somewhere in there was a sense that here was a thing he could invent and stick
to – something of a substitute for the economic wisdom and the deeper
knowledge/education that JM was very conscious of not having.

MAJOR HIMSELF He does not like argument. This too is part of
his insecurity. NL agreed that this sat rather oddly with him also having
few if any real opinions about anything, but he said it was the case. He
avoided real confrontations (e.g. the ERM story).

He does have opinions, says NL derisively, about blacks and whites,
about human rights, about UN-type things (i.e. the lefty ticket, it would
seem). But elsewhere it is hard to say what he stands for, what he really
believes in.

NL bets that, if the party does have a bust-up after the election, Major will side with the philes and not the sceps. He just expects this. (I agree with him.)

He says that the leadership election may well not be until November. Though it could be in June if people want it then. That would be the Redwood strategy. But Portillo will want it later, to enable him to make use of the opposition period. NL himself said he would favour Portillo over Redwood, and when I goaded him with Howard he said, to my surprise, that he would probably prefer Howard to either one of them. He thinks Howard is 'genuine'; that what he is doing at the Home Office about prisons is crazy and cannot go on, but is nonetheless done from some kind of conviction.

Major is certainly very intelligent. He has a high IQ. But he is also very insecure.

Why did I run his campaign? Because I thought him the most sceptic of the three, and because I was absolutely anti-Hezza. I had backed MT vocally to keep Hezza out, and told her I would have backed her again if she ran in the second round – while telling her in private that I would advise her to pull out. NL worried about this being thought 'dishonourable'. I told him I could not see it.

He maintains that nobody knows the inner Major – if there is one. There is no kitchen Cabinet. He is just a very mysterious person, a politician without a real core that one can see (my words).

THE FUTURE/EUROPE ETC. NL believes that Europe must either move forward or break up. In that he is like the federalists. He thinks the UK position is 'immoral', as well as impractical. We should not be saying we are part of it, while resisting everything they want to do.

His basic belief is that the thing is likely to grind to a halt sooner or later through sheer unworkability. He is less obsessed with 'sovereignty', a word he wants to curtail the meaning of (to 'power'), and which he admits is sliding away in many ways anyway. But he thinks that the right to pass our own laws is what counts. I say we still can, across a vast field. Which he doesn't deny. Suggests that each Whitehall department should do an audit of where they are free and where they are not free. Health and Education would be just about wholly free, DTI just about wholly unfree, Treasury 'a sword of Damocles' above it all.

He thinks Labour will move towards Europe – until they find out more about it.

Says that Europe is a much bigger issue than it appears. Concedes that in Harrogate, in his local poll, it came seventh in line. But those who feel about it feel passionately. Our talk makes me revise my own line a bit:

I think that maybe it's an issue that comes low on an unprompted hierarchy, but would be much higher once raised. This means that a referendum will be hard for the pro-Europe side to win, perhaps.

He asks me what I think Labour will do about a referendum. I say that my guess is that Labour wants to keep a 2001 election open as the test, pre a 2002 entry, and that Blair does not want a referendum. He thinks Labour will lose votes for this. I say, Yes maybe – but not many.

He says that the Tory Party will and should become the anti-federalist party, now that the left–right issue was dead with Marxism. We should be like the US in the nineteenth century, with a fed and anti-fed party as the big divide. He could see nothing wrong with this, though when I said he would be driving KC and his followers out of the party he did not have much of an answer. He also agreed that all the time there had been a natural pro-European majority in Parliament – though, as I said, EMU was at present the first exception to that.

JOHN MAJOR
Huntingdon and environs, 15 November 1996

THE ST NEOTS CONSERVATIVE CLUB, 9 A.M. A breakfast. 120 present. Solid local business people, not all Tories. A spacious club which can seat that many, and has plenty of other rooms. Tetley's pint for £1.20. Membership at £7 a year. The best place in a scruffy, crime-ridden town to drink.

They'd paid £19 a head for breakfast, on the day the Lib Dems were found to have charged £195 for councillors to meet possible council contractors at a buffet (check) meal at the LD conference.

How much would it cost to breakfast with Clinton?

Lots of suits. Middle England incarnate. An Asian in the food-manufacturing business who says that he's been banned from using a red dye by trading-standards officers interpreting EU regulations: the same dye the French use without trouble for glacé cherries.

Major comes in, greets me: Good morning, very nice to see you. Firm, fat handshake, as he rounds the corner of the table.

He is at ease here. Lots of people like him. If he had been sitting down at the table he would have been entirely at home, unlike Blair, Clinton, Thatcher. He banters easily with those around him. *Primus inter pares*, but the *pares* are very *par*.

St Neots is a new place in his shifting constituency. He cultivates it as if it is new and alien territory, worried about losing it. Peter Brown, his agent, tells me later that the re-districting will cut the majority from

36,000 to 22,000, but Major sees it as a marginal seat. He is just fantastically concerned about his base.

Plainly these people and this place are his lifeline, his base camp. He comes here a great deal. Later I found out from local reporters and Special Branch that he has a constituency day one Friday in four – i.e. a day when he does meetings, openings, talks. But he does surgeries (advice bureaux) more often that that. The policeman says that he takes three or four hours at it, and sees only about eight people: often sees a case for thirty minutes – five times longer than the average GP.

Sit near two Tories: they both volunteer that it will be good for the Tories to lose next time: (a) it won't make much difference, (b) the party needs a 'blood-letting' or perhaps a 'time to think', before the palace coup gets rid of Tony, and the Tories have to return in four or five years.

The sense among those I spoke to is (a) that Europe interferes too much and we the Brits obey the laws like nobody else, but also (b) we can't sanely afford to get away from it.

MAJOR HIMSELF A complete lack of aura. But also a sense of ease and relaxation here. Not in any way a fount of superior wisdom, not a philosopher. As far away as you could imagine from Mitterrand, Thatcher, Clinton. Perhaps also Blair, who it is hard to see as an ordinary bloke, who is unable to rise above the sense that everything is calculated – even if it is not. Major, by contrast, is unable to appear other than real. A very strange faculty. Blair is the more typical, it should be said.

The speech. No cameras. No journalists except me. Yet a text, sort of. Uncertain status: semi on the record, I suppose (though later he tells the man at Stibbington, whose conversation I had been eavesdropping on, that I was just following him around and treating it as all off the record).

The speech was the inaugural breakfast meeting of the Avery branch of the Huntingdon Tories.

The terms on which HY was accompanying the PM that day appear unclear, so the notes that follow here have been abridged to remove HY's record of conversations which John Major and others may reasonably have considered to be private.

EATON SOCON POST OFFICE The caravan moves a couple of miles down the road to Eaton Socon. The task is to visit a post office, which appears to be organized to mark the second anniversary of the Lottery. I arrive before him. There are two local-radio reporters and no writers on the scene, a couple of Special Branch police, no public. He arrives. Someone is coming out of the PO, who falls back with astonishment to see him coming though the door: a moment which he savours, while rushing to put them at ease with his ordinariness. He likes both aspects: the noticing and the reassurance.

He goes in, has a glance at the Lottery desk, talks to two women behind it, wanders round the little shop, is admitted behind the glass grille where the PO stamp-sellers do their work. Seen behind the glass, he can be seen making very little impression on the women. By now, ordinariness is ascendant. No shock effect at all. It is as though this man, who they had long ago decided by his television appearances was the acme of the ordinary, did not disappoint. Their judgement turned out to be absolutely correct. No star quality (cf. Thatcher in the estates: people backing off into corners of the stairwell as the star appeared).

They look like people who wonder why he is there. Which is fair enough, because he then returns to the door. Before he leaves, the radio reporters approach. He starts by putting a hairy hand over their two microphones, until he is ready. He then gives a little interview about how wonderful the Lottery has been, what a triumph, everyone knows it, money to the arts and charity and sport.

But he hasn't bought a ticket. I ask whether he's going to. Oh no, he says knowingly. Can you imagine what people would say if I won?

This seemed a bad piece of handling. He could have bought a ticket and given it to the nearest pensioner. He could have said that, in the unlikely event of winning, he would hive the result to the cats' home. Instead he rendered the whole occasion pointless by not buying a ticket: but since there was no journalist there except me, it became a non-event. It didn't happen.

It put me in mind of newspaper competitions which stipulate that members of staff and their families may not participate. Perhaps it was as though Major, as the founder-owner of the Lottery, felt that it was improper for him to take part. That it might be thought he knew the result. Or something. More likely it was an extreme manifestation of anxiety about sleaze roaring away at the time: to be whiter than white: not caught with hands in the Lottery till.

STIBBINGTON HALL This is the new headquarters of Ethical Holdings Plc, a pharmaceutical development company. In Major's constituency. It has grown from nothing in eleven years into an international business that specializes in technological innovation, with products now marketed in 43 countries. It's exactly the type of signature company for the Thatcher era: entrepreneurial, international, new tech. Employs about 180, a high proportion of them scientists. Quoted on NASDAQ [the

(US) National Association of Securities Dealers Automated Quotation System] since 1993.

Crunchy gravel, perfect lawns, again a low turnout of media (for the simple reason that it wasn't publicized, and the local radio/print people get notice only the night before, for security reasons). Major arrives, goes round the offices of the little stately home, engages with Dr Geoffrey Guy in well-informed conversation about drug royalties, company relation-ships, development as opposed to mere thinking-up, and liability for drugs they invent but do not market (Guy very admiring of this tricky question; Major well briefed, but also perhaps just quick-witted and thoughtful).

This is a better-suited crowd. There are Koreans, Japanese and Argen-tinians, all of them flown over by the company. This, says the man who sits next to me, is a great coup. The foreigners are fantastically impressed that the company, a small one in a remote part of Cambridgeshire, can get the PM himself to open their building. They don't mind not talking to him: they are just mighty pleased to have him in the tent, and mighty impressed that Ethical Holdings have got him there.

Actually, this has been Major's big line of activity. His constituency has been a big beneficiary of all kinds of development, being near Cam-bridge. And, driving round, I've never seen so much road development, producing interim chaos. If this were North Carolina, you'd know who'd got at the pork-barrel, though it doesn't work like that in the UK. My neighbour says that Major has brought more business to Huntingdon than anyone could have imagined. Another aspect of his being a good constituency MP. He is always available for companies like this.

The constituency, incidentally, used to be rolling green lands; now, over the last two decades, it's more of a sprawling overspill from London and an extension of Cambridge and Peterborough. All of the developing towns within easy reach of London. A few signs, like Stibbington Hall, of the graceful old England, on the edge of Fenland, with the dreaming spires of Cambridge over the flat horizon. But heavy roads, and many Happy Eaters and Little Chefs, which are Major's famously preferred eateries.

In his speech – off the cuff and pleasantly light – Major notes that Ethical has made £70 million in its eleven years, and says that he has been in the government for thirteen years and has not made £70 million. 'I sometimes wonder if this was a wise career choice.' Talks of Stibb as this 'wonderful hall I've known for so long'. Talks of the pharmaceutical industry as fascinating because it is all about R & D, has a long payback period, and is a huge UK success. (Plainly sees 'my constituency' as a kind of microcosm of the expanding life of Britain Plc.) Talks about 'an industrial revolution every bit as profound as in the eighteenth century' (the philosopher speaks). Notes that he couldn't have come to any company in his constituency in 1979, when he started, and found it had so many international connections.

He makes a verbal slip-up, and reiterates it to show it is not accidental – only a glimpse of his lack of education. 'We're not an empirical power any more. Alas, but we're not an empirical power.' Empire has gone. But our prospects, through Europe, are wonderful.

(All this can be placed in the context of the build-up to the British success story. This is going to be his big election theme. He's warming it up. Everything fits into that context . . .)

As he opens the velvet curtains covering the stone that marks the opening, he notes that there are two cords. He has a 50 per cent chance of getting the right one. 'A 50 per cent chance of getting *anything* right is a damn sight better chance than you have in politics.'

It has been a most amiable occasion, in which everyone was satisfied, as far as I could see. Without making any political points, he had impressed the audience with the larger political contention – that Britain is a success story to trumpet round the world.

We leave. As I depart, Peter Brown approaches and says that the PM suggests I should travel down in his car to Huntingdon. What were my arrangements? I said I had my car here, and would have to stay with that. He said, Come and talk to him anyway. I find him on the gravel. He is by now concerned for my enterprise. Had previously expressed concern that I hadn't walked round the upstairs offices with him – 'I should have arranged that,' he said. Now he asks, 'Have you got a driver?' Alas, I hadn't. And I didn't have the presence of mind to forget about that, jump in the Jag, and make my own way back up the appalling A1 to retrieve the car later. This was partly because I was already booked to interview him – something he didn't seem aware of. He obviously thought this was my chance. When I told him I was coming later, he said fine.

He went, at press request, to stand by a Rover car, part of his retinue. Rover had announced that morning a new infusion of investment for engine-building. Major complied. There were children hovering round the gate. He told staff to bring them in. He obviously likes children, again perhaps for the same reason as at the post office: both the impression he can make ('I met the Prime Minister,' I heard them chirruping as I drove out myself) and the awe which he can then excuse them. He asked them some multiplication sums (seven eights), bantered about another three hours in class. And then took off.

He was going to Huntingdon, for the advice bureau. There he spends three to four hours once a month, finding out about the problems at grass-roots level. It is his way of keeping close to reality – the reality he is most interested in, the one he's most at home with. This is the genuine concern of a modestly horizoned man, but also the level at which he can be quite certain he is not being patronized.

January–April 1997

15 January   The death of Conservative MP Iain Mills leaves John
Major's government a minority administration.

20 January   Labour MP Martin Redmond dies, and the government
is no longer a minority.

4 February   US sports star O. J. Simpson is found liable in a civil
court for the death of his ex-wife Nicole Simpson and
her friend Ron Goldman, and is ordered to pay $35
million damages.

23 February   Fire aboard the Russian space station *Mir*.

17 March   John Major announces a general election on 1 May.

22 March   The closest approach to Earth of the comet Hale-Bopp.

24 March   Former Scottish Office minister Allan Stewart withdraws
his election candidacy after allegations of an
extramarital affair.

26 March   Former Northern Ireland minister Tim Smith resigns as a
candidate over the 'cash for questions' furore.
Conservative MP Neil Hamilton refuses to stand down.

26 March   In San Diego, thirty-nine members of a cult called
Heaven's Gate are found dead after a mass suicide.

4 April   BBC broadcaster Martin Bell announces that he will
stand in Tatton, Cheshire, against Neil Hamilton as an
'anti-sleaze' candidate.

Deaths   Deng Xiaoping, Alan Ginsberg, Fred Zinnemann

ANTHONY LESTER
29 January 1997

All private.

Yesterday a meeting of the Lib–Lab constitutional commission. He
leaves it very depressed. Says it is clear that on electoral reform Labour
will give nothing.

A red-haired, close-cropped young man called Pat came from the Blair Office: one of the Blair police, asking about agendas and minutes etc. When anything came up that seemed to invite a concession, it was clear that Blair personally was resisting it. Cook very good on all the issues: very able: very sharp. The rest – Dewar, Robertson, Taylor,[1] Straw – are hackish. Dewar like an old woman pulling back her skirts at the slightest complication. They are clearly thinking we will not get many seats and they will get an easy majority. They don't therefore need us. So they will give no ground whatever that might detract from the leader's sole authority.

Actually not too bad on Scotland, or on the European Court of Human Rights. But on the House of Lords, for example, where Libs were trying to help towards some kind of possible PR formula for indirect election, Labour were obtuse and stubborn, spent half an hour arguing about 'to' or 'towards'.

A general disillusionment. Shirley almost wants to break off all talks. Jenkins, Rodgers, Cornford etc. etc. are all disillusioned. Cornford said to AL, Have you ever seen Blair without the smile? We saw him today (a reference to the red-haired young man).

What does Paddy think, AL wonders? To us, it all looks as though we are being hoodwinked on electoral reform at least: which for us is the big one. What should we do? Cut out completely? No, says AL. But say we have only got 25 per cent of what we can deal with, and await the other 75 per cent.

DAVID BLUNKETT
His office, 10 February 1997

He comes in late, seemingly cheerful, having just been with Chris Woodhead[2] (of whom he says, 'He's pretty good, but it's one thing working without direction, another when he's got a strong political lead – you can't have two Secretaries of State'), but complaining about the incessant pre-election pressure. 'Win or lose, let's get it over.'

EDUCATION   He thinks the fair time to judge the government will be after three years, though he would prefer two. He has his priorities: class sizes, early-years programme plus another. But almost the main thing he emphasized was making a difference to the under-25 group (the

1 Ann Taylor: Labour MP for Bolton West 1974–83, for Dewsbury 1987–2005; shadow Leader of the Commons 1994–7; later Baroness Taylor of Bolton.
2 Chris Woodhead: head of the Office for Standards in Education (Ofsted) 1994–2000.

beneficiaries of the utilities tax). That is where a real difference might be made.

Thinks the DfE[1] (or whatever it's called) is good. Much better than the old DES, which employers despised. Now they are quite supportive. Michael Bichard[2] is also very good indeed. He ran the Benefits Agency before, said Blunkett with a kind of conspiratorial smile, as if to say he shook it up well.

On the question of radicalism, he remarked that when he ran Sheffield his strategy was to ensure that the basic tasks were being as well done as possible, but then himself to take charge of the more risky things which were at the edge. He implies this as a way-of-being in central government.

As regards grammar schools, on which this week he seemed to renege on his 1995 conference pledge about lip-reading,[3] he said that in 1995 he had been under great pressure. It was a difficult conference. He had to satisfy Hattersley and others. He slightly got the words wrong, by not saying no to 'further' grammar schools. Also, when he said about the lips, he was parodying George Bush as a joke, he said. People have written this week as though he had never heard of George Bush!

ELECTION/TORIES   The Tories' best strategy will be to make the campaign last as long as they can. They are stretching us to the limit. There is always the chance that we will make a mistake. We keep needing to find new initiatives, he implied. A question of dominating the agenda, which is hard to do. Major has a great advantage in being able to control the time, even at this late stage.

We are already very stretched. There's only Tony, Gordon, Jack Straw (in his own odd way) and me, carrying the burden. Robin Cook? Oh yes, Robin is a brilliant politician, but the brief doesn't take him, week in and week out, to local-government conferences where he has to face a tricky audience, or do a lot of television.

Mandelson (I'd asked specifically) is very important, yes. But he's 'a bit jiggered' now. What? Tony is putting him under a lot of pressure to keep coming up with things. What are we going to do now? Tony asks him – more as time goes by. He's in a difficult situation. Will he be in the Cabinet? Nobody knows, says David. In fact there are Cabinet problems – he recites the familiar thing about the numbers, saying that you have

---

1 DfE: The Department for Education, successor to the Department of Education and Science (DES); it later merged to become the DfEE or Department for Education and Employment, which in time became the DfES or Department for Education and Skills.

2 Sir Michael Bichard: civil servant; Permanent Secretary to the Department for Education and Employment 1995–2001; chaired the inquiry into the Soham murders 2004.

3 In his 1995 party-conference speech, David Blunkett had told the party faithful, 'Watch my lips, no selection, either by examination or interview, under a Labour government.' George H. W. Bush had said at the 1988 Republican national convention, 'Read my lips: no new taxes.'

to add Irvine[1], Foster[2] ('and there had to be some kind of job for John Prescott'), and also Mandelson. 'A lot of people who think they're entitled to be in the Cabinet.' As to Mandy, though, he murmurs National Heritage, but then keeps saying that nothing, he thinks, has been decided.

We are all very tired. We have to avoid killing Tony. At the election, he should do two engagements a day: one very media oriented, one to meet the people. Thatcher was brilliant in her early decisions at doing heavily media-exposed things, but not too many of them.

RADICALISM AND GORDON BROWN We are certainly being very cautious. Personally, he says, I make a point of only saying what is practicable. That is why he has dealt with the grammar schools in the way he has. His object is to avoid controversy in the press. To avoid a distraction from the main task. He was very candid about that. And very cool.

On the wider front, there is of course a great restraint about money. But some people are not being careful about the pledges. Who? I asked. Gordon, he said. He instanced Brown's line about the review bodies' pay proposals,[3] which he says was not discussed in Shadow Cabinet, and DB himself was about the only colleague to be graced with forewarning. Others heard it on the *Today* programme.

It was not thought through. It was a sudden position by Gordon. And foolish. Also, Gordon's commitment to Clarke's Budget and spending for two years is unnecessary. One year OK, two years overdoing it. DB was quite alarmed about that.

Says that Blair's relations with Brown go back a long way, of course. And there is no argument about 'the project'. But the processes are a different matter. Gordon does seem to jump Tony into things that haven't been discussed. It is, he implies but did not say, to do with power and standing. A kind of rivalry, in which Gordon is determined not to be sidelined.

Said that Blair was very cautious, and likely to remain so. When I told DB that Blair had said, 'Watch me in government,' he replied that he thought Blair would be just as cautious when he got in, because he wanted a second term.

---

1 Derry Irvine: Baron Irvine of Lairg QC, Lord High Chancellor of England and Wales 1997-2003.
2 Derek Foster: Labour MP for Bishop Auckland 1979-2005; chief whip 1985-95. After Blair became leader, in 1994, Foster agreed to stand down, with the promise of a Cabinet post if Labour won in 1997. After Labour's victory he was given a non-Cabinet position, Minister of State at the Office of Public Service, which he resigned after just three days, claiming that Blair had broken his word. Created Baron Foster of Bishop Auckland 2005.
3 On 5 February the shadow Chancellor Gordon Brown warned that a future Labour government would 'freeze' top salaries – those agreed by the public-sector pay-review bodies for judges, senior civil servants and so on – in its first year in office.

EUROPE He alluded to EMU as the biggest decision of the next
parliament. 'I am a Euro-sceptic who is in favour of going in in the first
round.' His argument is that the stability pact and the interest-rate effect
will mean that we are deeply affected by EMU whether in or out. He
hopes deeply that Kohl's plight will mean it is put off for a bit.[1] But if it
happens, he thinks we should be at the table influencing how it is conducted. Look at it this way, he says. We should get the pain over early.
The pain will come from the massed opposition of the press, and from a
phobic Tory Party. But we will be able to defeat that more easily at the
beginning than the end.

In the first eighteen months, if we have a decent majority, the PLP will
not be difficult. They won't want to start making trouble for a government
after eighteen years. The line will be carried by the new entrants. Of course,
we would have to win a referendum, but I think at the early stage we could
do so. After three or four years it would be impossible. It would become a
referendum on us as a whole. We would have made mistakes, faced
troubles. To be in a situation where we said we wanted to get in at some
stage but not yet would be a source of derision and growing weakness as
the press took us apart. It would make no sense at all to wait that long.

Do others feel like this? He said they did. Cook? Yes, I think so, he
indicated. It is a growing feeling. But he did agree that the referendum
commitment put a serious obstacle in the way. It meant that the political
calculation was loaded against rather than in favour, at the margin (that
is my sentence, not his).

ROBERT MACLENNAN
Phone, 12 February 1997

INTERESTING BLAIRISH STUFF He doesn't think the Blair
commitment on a PR referendum in the first session is slipping away.
Blair is very concerned that the Murdoch press will rend him apart if he
speaks in favour of electoral reform. (I've heard this before, and Bob is
not clear whether it is a priori or he has heard it from a source – though
he may well have heard it from Blair himself, since he has been speaking
to him over the months.) They might tolerate him for one term, but not
if they knew he was interested in a project that was arranged to put the
progressive left in power for a long time, excluding the Tories by a new
voting system.

1 The Maastricht Treaty and the Stability and Growth Pact required the EU member states to contain spending
and prevent currency speculation. Kohl's plans to cut spending triggered a summer of strikes by German
public-transport workers, refuse collectors, postal workers and civil servants.

Blair's difficulty, though, is that the more he talks negative, the more he puts a gap between himself and the LDs. Driving a wedge between them and Labour. The logic of his position, however, is that he has the referendum and he advocates change himself. For him, as prime minister, to lead the government through the tedious and difficult parliamentary process of getting a referendum PR bill through the House of Commons and then to say he was not in favour of change himself would look very unconvincing from every point of view. For him to be on the fence would be an abdication of leadership, for which he would be pilloried.

Further, Maclennan thinks the trend in favour of PR is growing in the Labour Party. They will win a lot of seats which they would lose if they were refought on first past the post at the next election. So there will be self-interest.

He adds that AV,[1] though commonly said to be the only possible runner, is not by any means so. Cook thinks it is not the one that will favour Labour. AV would keep them out of a lot of seats in the south of England. So there is a lot to be argued about as to the system – though it is not fruitful or necessary to be doing that now. Incidentally, Maclennan was reading a lot into Blair's last interview with David Frost, in which he noted that AV was not proportional. Although some would read this (as I did) as a signal that he was against even the AV form of electoral reform, others (Maclennan) could read it as a subtle way of saying that something more than AV would be needed. (But cf. Cornford, the other day, who scornfully told me that the LDs were a hopeless divided bunch, who would cling to PR, split themselves over it, behave generally in an unrealistic way.)

Remember, Labour is committed to PR by the Scottish parliament.

As to the constitutional talks, Maclennan says they have been a two-way learning process. Some LDs have never seen Labour people at close quarters and have learned a lot. But, equally, the Labour people have learned from us. Perhaps the main way is through having to think seriously about the programme. (A. Lester said this morning, while being very cagey, that he was more optimistic than he had been: that the seriousness had grown over time: that Cook was excellent: that there was a certain bonding, and a real commitment to trying to find answers.)

Clearly, said Maclennan, this committee cannot write the Queen's Speech. We cannot expect to lay down the ranking of the order of bills. If Freedom of Information has to come behind Scotland and the House of Lords, so be it.

But Maclennan has abandoned his one-time line for a great reform

1 Alternative vote top-up, or alternative vote plus – another potential weapon in the arsenal of electoral reform, and recommended by some for election to an assembly or legislature.

bill. The point of that, he now says, was to emphasize that these things were all interconnected, not necessarily to say they should all be done together. He thinks that point has got across. The important part of the exercise has been to ensure that we are both fully attached to the constitutional project. In this, he thinks, it has been quite successful. He wants Labour to take courage, to see the scale of what they are doing, to be as brave as the 1945 government was in a different direction.

Will it all evaporate when they get into power? Not entirely, he says (with Scottish caution!). Scotland will come first, and will succeed in getting through. This will give them courage for the rest: will help them see themselves as a great reforming government. But much does depend on there being a big man in charge of it all, whose career is pinned to success. If it was Robin Cook, then it would sail through! But even under someone else, the crucial ingredient will be their commitment.

He thinks the LDs will matter whatever the size of their majority. If small, obviously. If large, Labour will factionalize 'if it's anything like its dear old self'.

I asked him if he thought that Blair has the big project inside him: did he, despite everything, have an idea about a great progressive government, a large project? Maclennan said he had asked him that very question face to face. 'I wish I could feel he really did believe it.' He might believe it, said Bob, but one could not be sure. There's a sense in which he feels the Labour/Lib Dem divide is regrettable. And certainly a sense in which he finds the Lib Dems irritating – as they often are, said Bob.

But the problem is that he may not be a pluralist. (And I agree with that.) I add that there are plenty of signs that he finds the Labour Party irritating. He does not revere the party as such. What he seems to believe in, I add, is a movement. This is inescapably a presidentialist attitude. He thinks that the whole country can be mobilized in progressive directions, but that parties are a problem not a solution. (This is all me, though Bob agrees.) And it bodes rather badly for the kind of party collaboration the Lib Dems envisage.

'I do have a kernel of optimism,' Bob concludes. What is governing all Blair's thinking is concern about muffing the election. It absolutely drives him. And it drives his entourage even more. He is surrounded by intensely short-termist people, whose interest is managing the next headline. It is very difficult for him to stand back, in that atmosphere.

Bob thinks the Blair model is of Republicans and Democrats, not of three or more parties. But the Rs and the Ds are federations, coalitions, only leadable by presidents. It is a defective model for the British system, and for the history of British parties.

ROY JENKINS
Speech at Andrew Duff book launch,[1]
17 February 1997

Remembers the many false dawns of the British resurgence of Euro-enthusiasm. Recalls that this was supposed to happen after the 1975 referendum, and never did. There were, *mirabile dictu*, people who said in 1979 that the Tory victory would return to power the party of Europe. When Major came in, he talked about the heart of Europe. Now Blair is being expected to move in that direction. It is imperative, says RJ, that he should do so – or the disenchantment with GB would be terminal. If that happens, they will set up another club which will keep us out.

He said that if EMU did not go ahead, he had the greatest fear that enlargement would not happen. If momentum stopped, France in particular would be prone to getting into the bunker. France has never been very keen on enlargement, and if the EU showed that it wasn't prepared to make the leap into EMU, France would take it as a signal to retreat (or might do so).

Recalling ERM, he listed it among the missed opportunities: the psychology of getting in late, after all the others. He said that before Britain entered, ERM had existed for 138 months (check), and Britain had chosen the eighth-worst month it possibly could have done to make an entry. If it had got in much earlier, a great deal of the history would have been different, he asserts.

WILLIAM WALDEGRAVE
Treasury, 17 February 1997

Rather muttering, hard to hear, heavier than he used to be.

Major only takes umbrage against people he thinks are supposed to be allies. Thus he won't mind about *The Guardian*, but he minded a lot about the *Telegraph*. Charles Moore regards himself as a kind of drill sergeant of the Conservative Party, perhaps justly. But Major can't stand the patronizing attitude. He thought the same about Max Hastings; Rees-Mogg is the same (though that was HY's name, not WW's). He thinks the *Telegraph* will support them. *The Sun* will, the *Mail* will, *The Times* will. All this will be editorially. There won't be the wham-bang front-page support.

---

1 Andrew Duff produced two books in 1997. One was *The Treaty of Amsterdam*; the other was *Reforming the European Union*. Both were published by the Federal Trust for Education and Research.

The Labour Party has become a serious disappointment. It is bad for politics to have a great congealing centre, where there is no longer the yin and yang, the two ends of the rope that are being pulled. He instances Gordon Brown and Jack Straw. It was pretty contemptible of Brown to say he would assail the very few public-sector employees on top salaries while being afraid to raise income tax. WW also cites the utilities tax, which has been put in instead of a corporation tax. A totally cynical manoeuvre, he says.

As for Straw, is there nothing Michael Howard can't do? If nobody is standing up for the other side, it is a grave situation. For those of us on my side of the Cabinet, the riposte to any objections we make is 'So you're to the left of Jack Straw, are you?'

There is such a deep dishonesty about the Labour Party. I was at a meeting in my constituency, a three-sider. Labour said they would improve education, but would pay no more money. The Lib Dems furiously attacked Labour for that, saying they (the LDs) would raise tax. I, the Tory, said we wouldn't pay any more money either, but were experienced in making ends meet and making improvements at modest cost. I got quite a decent round of applause.

Labour are going to get into deep trouble with public finances. They will also become very unpopular. We will get very tired after eighteen months of that *de haut en bas* voice of Blair. At that point Major will become an object of nostalgic popularity: a decent man who did his best etc. etc. Major will become a kind of hero.

Do I hate the idea of losing? Not really. But we should be winning. It is against all history that we are losing. But if we do, we should in theory be pleased because we have entirely won the argument. We have seen the Labour Party convert entirely our way. In that sense, Major is the most important prime minister of this century. If he had not won in 1992, Labour would not have changed sides in the ideological argument. The last few years have cemented in our view of society (my words).

Is there not a case, therefore, for change? Well, throughout our time the Opposition has been very effective. I have never felt any slackening of pressure. We always have to pay attention. The last four years have been very hard. The system, therefore, is working. And, since the other side don't want to do anything very different, why should one think that government will work better or that the system will somehow be better served by their winning?

If we lose, it depends on the margin. If it is a hung parliament, as some people are saying, then that will be terrible. John will have to stay on, I suppose. But otherwise he will surely go – but when? He will be in a strong position even if he loses by 50 seats – it will be so much better than it looked at one time. So people will have to pay attention to his opinions. I think he would never favour Redwood or Howard. He might favour Portillo – who has been a good minister, and who is now tacking sharply away from his extreme line on Europe: he now says that it is axiomatic that we must stay in. But more likely it will be someone from the middle – though certainly not Gillian Shephard. Rifkind, he ventures.

Chris Patten: it all depends whether he is passionately keen to get back. If he is, he will, somehow. But he will need to be utterly committed. He is, remember, a thug, as well as a nice guy. The most important thing about him is that he is very tough. The right cannot understand that, but it is true.

The prospect of a Labour government in permanent thrall to the *Daily Mail* is a pretty appalling thing to contemplate.

LIB DEM DINING CLUB
The White Tower, 17 February 1997

Richard Holme said he only wanted to use Jenkins sparingly, on grounds of image. But he would be doing the Harrogate rally on Lamont's doorstep with much relish. Shirley Williams will be used a lot.

Holme had a bet with William Hill that the Lib Dems would win more seats than they now have, and expected to get beyond 30. If Labour wins by 100 seats, the Lib Dems will get 60.

Dick Newby said he had been to see Roger Liddle on Sunday, and found David Miliband coming out. What were you doing? he asked. Oh, we were writing the Labour manifesto. Newby confirmed that they really *were* doing that. They said, moreover, that nobody would be checking it except Blair, Cook and Brown. Oh how far the party has come from the Callaghan days . . .

Some around the table were much more pessimistic about the election. Doubted whether Labour would get more than a tiny majority.

Taverne and Rodgers, and several others, said it was imperative to accept AV, or any form of PR, without being picky. And that the Lib Dems should be alive to any Blair offers. But there was also a general feeling that the Lib Dems had to say their own piece, stick to their own line, and go for it. Taking the high moral ground where necessary.

Alan Leaman[1] cringed at the suggestion that the Lib Dems were 'to the left' of Labour. Left is a word he never likes to use (even though it is true). The way they like to think of themselves (Holme says this too) is

1 Alan Leaman: high-ranking Liberal Democrat official, the party's candidate for Dorset Mid & Poole North 1997; director of strategy and planning 1995–7, and previously head of leader Paddy Ashdown's office.

as a party that has stuck to its guns, has clear policies that haven't changed.

'Lib Democrats make the difference' is going to be the slogan. A nice double meaning there.

On 17 March John Major announced the date of the general election – 1 May. HY's contacts concentrated on fighting the campaign.

PART FOUR

1997–2003

New Labour in
Government

May–December 1997

2 May   John Major resigns as leader of the Conservatives. Labour leader Tony Blair is invited to form a government.

10 June   Kenneth Clarke wins the first round of voting for the Conservative Party leadership.

17 June   Kenneth Clarke wins the second round of the Conservative leadership contest.

19 June   William Hague wins the final round, to become, at 36, the youngest leader of the Conservatives since 1783.

25 June   Supply ship *Progress* collides with the *Mir* space station.

30 June   Britain formally returns the colony of Hong Kong to China.

1 July   The royal yacht *Britannia* begins its last foreign mission, conveying the last governor of Hong Kong back to the UK.

3 July   The Parliamentary standards commissioner finds that five former Conservative MPs had accepted money from Harrods proprietor Mohamed Al Fayed and had failed to declare it.

31 August   Diana, Princess of Wales, dies in a car crash in Paris, along with Dodi Fayed and their driver.

6 September   Princess Diana is buried after a funeral at Westminster Abbey.

11 September   Scotland votes to create its own parliament.

4 November   The government declares Formula One motor racing exempt from a ban on tobacco sponsorship.

10 November   The Labour Party returns a donation of £1 million from Bernie Ecclestone of the Formula One Association.

28 November   Parliament passes by a majority of 260 a private member's bill to ban hunting with dogs.

Deaths   Sir Isaiah Berlin, Jacques-Yves Cousteau, Toshiro Mifune, Robert Mitchum, President Mobutu of Zaire, James Stewart, Mother Teresa, Gianni Versace

*Labour's landslide victory on 1 May 1997 ended eighteen years of
Conservative government. Labour 418 seats (a gain of 147), Conservatives 165 (a loss of 178), Liberals 46 (a gain of 20), others 30 (which
included a gain of 3 by the Scottish National Party). The Conservatives
were left with no representation in either Scotland or Wales. Among the
ministers who lost their seats were Malcolm Rifkind, Michael Portillo,
William Waldegrave, Ian Lang and Michael Forsyth.*

*With Labour in government for the first time in eighteen years, HY
quickly readjusted. Now that many of his long-standing contacts were
no longer at Westminster, he broadened his base, creating more European and American relationships.*

PADDY ASHDOWN
Phone, 9 June 1997

Re PR and all that. (I knew, though he concealed it, that he had seen
Blair at least once in the last week: Maclennan told me.)

On the gloomy scenario I gave him, he replied that he would have
agreed with it this time last week, but now there were some glimmerings
of hope – i.e. that the 1999 PR Euro election would take place. There
had been some signals. He thought the arguments were weighted.

The main objectors are the MEPs, but Blair owes them nothing and
sees them as the last outpost of Old Labour. (But actually, according to
Bob Maclennan, when the Cook–Maclennan committee was sitting,
Cook accepted that a PR election would be good for Labour, probably.)

On the other hand, with only 42.5 per cent of the vote, Labour can't
be sure of doing all that well by first past the post in a Euro election, and
also need something to conceal their falling off of performance, which
the PR confusion would certainly supply.

Remember: they know they will have to do something on the PR front.
Paddy regards the Cook–Maclennan report as something that Labour will
have good faith towards. Still believes it is an important document. And it
did say that the members of the PR commission should include only those
who favoured PR: not people who wanted AV and supplementary lists.

What is Blair's personal attitude? I ask. Ashdown says he heard that
Blair has said to people (Labour MPs?) that 'what God has given God
can take away', i.e. that the electorate – God – could easily reverse itself.
PA thinks Blair's attitude is 'purely pragmatic'. Which, he agrees with
me, is good and sensible – though with the caveat that Blair needs to
decide if he is a pluralist or not. That is a slightly larger question – a
ten-year pragmatism as it were.

ROBERT MACLENNAN
Same day (earlier)

Says that my pessimistic description is somewhat countered by secret talks Ashdown had with Blair last week. Blair told Paddy that the Euro elections would be 'all right'. Not to worry. But, says Bob, Jack Straw doesn't think that way.

Affirms that presence of anti-PR people on the commission will not be acceptable. They would be a 'Trojan Horse' – something Cook–Maclennan specifically ruled out. That is to say, deciding the second question, which is the commission's essential task, must exclude the possibility of AV.

As to whether Blair recognizes any leverage against him, on the part of the LDs, Bob says that there is, of course, no immediate leverage. But he needs to keep in with us. 'He needs to stop us becoming a straightforward opposition party' – which would happen if he reneged on the Cook–Maclennan document.

Remember the bad blood created by all this in the 1970s.

Cook did work out that PR at Euro elections would do Labour good rather than harm.

Bob contends that PR at Euro elections would have no vast domestic effect, except to show that PR elections were 'not catastrophic'. But he agrees when I add that it would legitimize one of the options in a referendum.

There are no technical legislative or administrative difficulties about setting up a PR election. That is a red herring – as long as the decision is made quite soon. But there is a problem for the parties: arranging the lists, selecting the candidates. That will take time and finesse.

IAN TAYLOR
Phone, 17 June 1997

Last night, Hague tried too hard to appear a real leader, trumpeting about what people in his Shadow Cabinet would have to do: posturing: absurd. He showed an alarming ability to modulate his position according to his audience (cf. the Positive Europe Group the other day). Yet this shifting position is supposed to be what everyone has to sign up to in the SC! He also showed amazing ignorance about the EU. He doesn't say we will leave, but he does talk about negotiation and all that, about veto rights etc. etc., oblivious of what this means, how catastrophic it would be other than as a prelude to exit.

If Hague wins, what will happen at the weekend? Either KC will have been offered an SC place, says thanks very much but only if he is free to take his line about Europe, and Hague climbs down, or KC fails to sign up. Either way, you get Hague starting off disastrously, with a split story or a climbdown story.

Why can't they take the point that (a) we will not be signing up to EMU but Labour may be, in which case we will be free to oppose if that seems right and it is an academic issue now, (b) the conditions at present are clearly not suitable. This would be a perfectly good basis on which to put the whole thing on the back burner. Instead of which it is being made into the great test which precedes and surpasses all other tests.

Ancram is the acceptable face of Hague, to offset the unacceptable Duncan. Duncan will get the Tory Party into big trouble one way or another.

ANJI HUNTER
Phone, 20 June 1997

Spoke to Anji Hunter: I got the message that they thought Hague was the more worrying choice for them. Not that she said as much, but she quietly rejected my analysis that the Tories had picked the wrong man, and moved to the right. What she wanted to say was how amazingly these people just do manage to come together when it counts.

CHRIS PATTEN
Ritz Hotel, 24 July 1997

I said I was letting him down lightly, back to real life. Hence the Ritz. The dining room noticed him: John Peyton was oozily sucking up; others said hello; a waiter grovelling, almost speechless, asked him (but not me) to sign some bigwig book, saying he had worked at the Conrad Hotel in HK for some years.

CP was in good shape, though physically heavier. Hands heavy. Jowl heavy. Girth heavyish. A few points:

Began by saying how wonderful *Britannia* had been. The first morning, they found the largest deployment of the Royal Navy for decades awaiting them. Elaborate filing and grouping, with *Britannia* steaming through the middle of the drawn-up convoy, and all ranks on deck and saluting, and planes flying over in salute – and Chinese watchers at the edge of the squadron, to make quite sure he left the premises. All this going on in

private, in secret, unrecorded, yet terribly elaborate. Interesting. He said
life on *Britannia* was like a very good country weekend, Chas very nice
indeed (he had three couples who were his friends), and along with the
Pattens were Edward Llewellyn and Martin Dinham.[1]

Is not contemplating an instant answer to Howe–Cradock.[2] But will
do one chapter of his book on it. He doesn't want to get typecast as
someone who can't leave the subject alone, yet he wants to have his say.

He has a complicated talk-out especially concerning what was and
was not done and promised in 1988 and 1989. The [manoeuvrings] of
Cradock et al. about what they were trying to achieve, their desire to
[show] they were not entering into secret agreements etc. etc. But his
bottom line appears to be, What damage has it done to HK? The question
I asked Jim Prior the other day. CP says he did a lot of careful work
about trade, which showed that Anglo-China trade rose during his time
and had fallen in earlier times. There seems to be a reverse correlation
between the rates of trade and levels of hostility.

He did not disagree with me when I said it was unfortunate that
Jonathan Dimbleby[3] had become his apparent Boswell. Said that JD had
plenty of other sources, including two very good FCO people and also
people in the HK government.

Regards Cradock as a man with a brutally good mind, but immensely
self-regarding. Incapable of thinking there is any other answer, once he
has worked out the answer that satisfies him. Reminds me that Cradock
was in East Germany, and was utterly opposed to Brandt's Ostpolitik –
a real submitter, it seems, to totalitarian governments. This is Cradock's
version of 'realism'.

Says he regards Howe's and Cradock's pieces as very thin. By the way,
the China policy was always Cradock's rather than Howe's. Howe got it
from Cradock, who exerted a great power over the FCO and the Whitehall machine.

His book will be about Asia and Europe. He also wants to do more
BBC films, of which he has three in mind. I told him he would need more
than a year to do all this. He said he would mostly write the book in
France, mainly on the grounds that he could perhaps get away from the
huge weight of correspondence. He also said that he didn't miss having

1 Martin Dinham, senior civil servant at the Department for International Development, had been seconded as
an adviser to the governor of Hong Kong 1992–7.

2 Sir Percy Cradock, diplomat, had been ambassador to the People's Republic of China 1978–83; Sir Geoffrey
Howe, as Foreign Secretary, had brokered the deal with Beijing over Hong Kong. Jonathan Dimbleby's book
The Last Governor (1997), about Patten's role in Hong Kong, talked of 'a motley array of superannuated
diplomats and politicians' and of 'appeasement'. Geoffrey Howe had called the book's allegations 'grotesque'
and 'unjust', and Cradock called them 'grubby' and 'groundless'.

3 Jonathan Dimbleby, *The Last Governor: Chris Patten and the Handover of Hong Kong* (London: Little,
Brown, 1997), and a five-part television series.

someone to clean his shoes, but did miss his PA, who would arrange every aspect of his practical life.

He seems to have had lots of possible offers. Named a university post among them. Lavender has told him that all this would mean would be raising money from all the people he was looking forward to getting away from. I told him it would be death. He said Peter Sutherland[1] had told him that the only really interesting jobs were big public-service jobs – but obviously there are not many of these, and they become available largely by chance.

He kept mum about his own future. Said he would decide nothing for a year. Had been approached to do Bosnia, but wanted time off to do his book. I asked him if the House of Commons was attractive. He said he was 53, and did not fancy a long stretch in opposition. When I outlined the Hague-collapse scenario, he said that in that event it would no doubt be Portillo who would get it. I cautioned about the huge effect of PR, and said 1999 was the year of truth for Hague.

He was going to see Hague, at Hague's request, this evening. He thought the Tories had a very hard row to hoe. The Ashdown–Blair thing makes it harder – both doing it at this moment of their greatest strength (my point not his). But he thought perhaps Blair was vulnerable: on the Budget, on the likely rows between Old and New Labour about public spending, and about Blair's own apparent piety. All of which we discussed. He finds Blair very sensitive and political: behaved very punctiliously and sensitively to Patten's position when in HK for the handover. Also very impressed by Cook playing it absolutely straight. And being very thorough and knowing about the issues.

On current politics, says he cannot understand the Tories' inability to be seizing the constitutional agenda for themselves. Should be pushing Labour to devolve *more*, because it is through other agencies than the House of Commons that Tories have a chance of running something and proving they can do it. On House of Lords reform: should be saying that all MEPs should belong to it – if they are serious about scrutiny and all that. Etc. etc. Hopeless to be saying entirely negative things.

Says he has difficulty knowing which Tories are still in the House – but Major had the same difficulty. When C and Lavender took John and Norma to dinner at Green's in May, Tapsell was sitting at the bar and Major couldn't remember whether he was still an MP or not.

1 Peter Sutherland: director-general of the GATT, later the WTO, 1993–5; chairman of Goldman Sachs International since 1995; chairman of British Petroleum, later BP, since 1998.

Labour ministers were quick to start calling HY. Here the new Foreign
Secretary wanted to give a briefing on his first visit to Bosnia.

ROBIN COOK
Foreign Office, 28 July 1997

He is going there [Bosnia] today, he said, to read the Riot Act.[1] We
are at the end of tolerating their failure to make any serious start at
implementing the Dayton Agreement[2] for an integrated state. It is three
ethnic groups in two entities, and they are not trying to change that.

The Bosnian leadership has failed to come to sensible agreement about
the use of airspace, into Sarajevo airport. There is no telecoms system
between Pale and Sarajevo. They haven't agreed to a joint-ambassador
system rather than three separate ambassadors. They maintain road-
blocks; they are recalcitrant against letting refugees return, and we have
evidence of them being beaten up by police.

They are also not yielding up war criminals. On this, to my question,
he said the UK had clean hands. Had promoted and helped finance a
second courtroom at The Hague, to speed the through-put. And had used
UK troops at Prijedor the other day, picking up a war criminal and killing
another.

There are, he freely admits, practical problems about seizing Karadzic.
But there is a commitment under Dayton to do so.

We are deeply concerned at the poor progress on Dayton. The US,
Germany and the UK have made it clear to the Bosnian leadership that
they cannot continue with international support for the Dayton Agreement when the main participants on the ground are not even trying to
implement it. Albright,[3] Kinkel and now Cook have been there and said
this.

He is highlighting three issues:

1. War criminals.
2. Media freedom, especially television. He actually thinks this is 'the
   key to the renewal of Bosnia'. Vital that the people should have
   some other diet than straightforward ethnic nationalism. The High
   Representative has tried to pressure them on this. 'Unless people can
   escape from nationalist politicians, there is no hope for the politics of

1 HY commentary of 29 July was headed, 'Robin Cook steps into a land of hatred.'
2 Under the Dayton Agreement of November 1995, Bosnia and Herzegovina, Croatia and the Federal Republic
of Yugoslavia all agreed to fully respect one another's sovereign equality, settle disputes peacefully, and assist in
the prosecution of war criminals.
3 Madeleine Albright: first female US Secretary of State, 1997–2001.

integration.' Among other things, RC will be challenging Pale TV to report his speech.
3. Attack on corruption. The level of accountability, whether about money or power.

Who will be listening? I ask. He replies: the international press. But then, I say, Who will deeply listen? He instanced Tuzla and Banja Luka as places he will be going to.[1] Tuzla has a tradition of more openness and less tribalism. Banja Luka also. But don't have any illusions, he says, about Mrs Plavsic,[2] Karadzic's rival.

There must, he keeps insisting, be an alternative to ethnic politics, ethnic apartheid. Can he mobilize mass support for this? Of course, he doesn't know, he says. But remember that at the donor conference in Portugal[3] the meetings produced a lot of linkages. For example: if the common ambassador wasn't produced, the world would cease to recognize the separate ones. For example vehicle licence plates, if not unified, would cease to be accepted internationally.

More fundamentally, unless there is a common economic and bank system, they would not go ahead with another donor conference. At the very last minute, and grudgingly, they agreed. And have developed such a system.

I propose a comparison with Hurd, saying DH fundamentally didn't want engagement, and all his aloofness stemmed from that. Well, says Robin, we are certainly engaged. We have been there four or five years. We have the largest European contingent (and, according to Ray Kyles, press officer, have spent $1 billion so far). It would, says RC, be a big failure if after all that time we didn't 'see the job through'. 'It must be made to succeed.'

In modern Europe, with the ease of travel and communications, everything has its effect elsewhere. If you accept the repugnant situation of a state divided on ethnic lines in Bosnia, there's a danger it will spread beyond Bosnia. It will do bad damage to the whole concept of a pluralist country. If you tolerate ethnic apartheid in Bosnia, that's a signal to other politicians elsewhere. It has no place in the Europe of the twenty-first century.

These people talked about building the Europe of the post-Communist world. Actually, they are building the Europe of the pre-Communist era, in which nationalism and divisions reigned.

---

1 Tuzla is the fourth largest city in Bosnia and Herzegovina; Banja Luka the second largest, after Sarajevo, and 90 per cent of its population is Serbian.
2 Biljana Plavsic: Bosnian Serb politician later indicted and sentenced for war crimes.
3 On 30 May 1997 foreign ministers met in Sintra, Portugal, as the 'steering board of the peace implementation council' to review the peace agreement for Bosnia and Herzegovina.

What we need to do is develop a momentum in favour of the right sort of politics. (This was in answer to my scepticism about how he could engineer change. He didn't sound very optimistic, but he didn't sound despairing either. Has the freshness and the indignation of a new political leader.)

The US has said it will get out in June 1998. We may be looking, by Christmas, at ways to get them to stay. Is it axiomatic that if they leave, we leave? 'It's an axiom, Hugo, in the sense that the moment we stop saying that, the US will feel free to leave.' Very important to keep the pressure on the US. And the fact is, it's easier to envisage them staying longer. If this was happening in 1992–3, there would be far more difficulty.

Germany is especially keen on all this. It took 200,000 refugees during the war. It wants to get them to return. But Bosnia is being very difficult, Izetbegovic[1] demanded £10,000 for every refugee he took back from Germany! Amazing! As if the roles were reversed, and he rather than Germany was the one dispensing the favours!

EUROPE ETC. As a social democrat rather than a Marxist, he thinks that things will evolve more by incremental stages than by some big-bang blueprint.

As regards France and Germany, he first says that he is signed up to the need for good relations with all the small countries, all of which save Ireland have socialist governments (and Belgium, though not socialist, has a socialist foreign minister): 'our sister parties'.

That said, though, there *are* openings for us if France and Germany are falling out. But I have to be careful in saying any of that. The fact is that when Mitterrand departed, the German link with France weakened. There were openings. He spoke in terms of a possible triangle as being very desirable and possible – though not expecting to crack the special France–Germany relationship.

We had done well at Amsterdam.[2] This alone meant that our role in all this was 'modified and modifiable further'. Indeed, Kohl and Kinkel got into trouble with the SPD on the grounds that Blair had outwitted them at Amsterdam. 'This was rather embarrassing.'

There is nothing for us in getting involved in the divide between France and Germany over EMU. We are very comfortable where we now are. There would be bad consequences for Britain moving heavily in.

---

1 Alija Izetbegovic: Bosnian lawyer, author, politician; member of the Bosnian-Herzegovinian presidency 1996–2000. At his funeral, in 2003, Paddy Ashdown described him as 'the person who did more than any other to ensure the survival of the modern state of Bosnia and Herzegovina'.
2 The European Council met in Amsterdam on 16–17 June 1997 and agreed what would become known as the Treaty of Amsterdam, dealing with questions of political union, citizens' rights and common foreign policy.

(1) Would lead to Britain being criticized, and perhaps the object being more likely to happen. (2) Would give France and Germany somebody to blame if EMU didn't happen. But were there people looking for that? I asked. He said yes, there were – though he conceded that they perhaps were not at the very top. He instanced Stoiber.[1]

He was extremely agnostic about whether EMU would happen on 1 January 1999, noting that those who wanted it to happen had an interest in putting it about that if it didn't happen then it might never happen. He was also not very interested in using the Euro elections as a dry run. Said, I think honestly, that they are not thinking about the tactics. It is all too far ahead.

ADDENDA Note that Kyles said Cook's interest in drawing in outside people – e.g. re defence sales, human rights, defence strategy – was important and big. A real sense of getting other people to 'own' decisions. Per HY: a fascinating further glimpse into the way this government is truly seeking to co-opt all opposition . . .

IMPRESSION Cook was immensely relaxed. Wholly on top of the job. Obviously rejoiced in by officials – as he is by Albright, and Blair! Still the same man: unpompous, witty, serious – swift. I have seldom seen a politician so obviously relishing what he had been waiting to do – even though in this case it is not the job he would have really wanted; he is not 'born' to be Foreign Secretary (cf. D. Hurd). Perhaps this shows that such born men are not the best . . .

ALAN BUDD
The Garrick, 17 September 1997

He is about to leave the Treasury to become an almost full-time member of the Bank of England monetary committee. He will have much time to reflect, and then decide. It seems like a total change from his Treasury life, where, as he puts it, he regards 6 p.m. as the time when he is able to start 'my own work' – by which I think he meant his economic advising. For the rest, it was all meetings and paper-writing for short-term reasons.

He is still quite amazed at Brown's reception at the Treasury, the day he walked in. The unorganized massing of officials up the stairs when it was known he was approaching, plus the move of the crowd from Downing Street to the Treasury. (Were there echoes of Diana here, one

1 Edmund Stoiber: German politician; chairman of the Christian Social Union 1988–2007; minister president of Bavaria 1993–2007.

asks oneself? If so, how can politicians remotely get a grip on it?) AB regarded this not as a display of Labour-supporting officialdom, but as a sense of relief at the end of total impasse. Officials like to do things, and they had had a government that could do very little (despite KC) for five years.

Brown could not have been more welcoming and supportive to Budd himself, despite Budd's origins as a Tory-appointed adviser (even though, as he is careful to point out, it was a Civil Service Commission appointment, not a political one).

EMU At my request, and in deep background mode, he gives me his account of the EMU argument. As an economist, he doubts whether the project will do what is needed, i.e. in a continent whose biggest problem by far is unemployment, it will be a distraction. People will be so preoccupied with making it work that they will not be able to give time to unemployment. EMU, moreover, will have no real effect on unemployment, except perhaps indirectly. He therefore feels, as an economist, that EMU would work better later: when some of the unemployment problems had been diminished by national means.

He thinks, however, that it will happen on 1 January 1999. This has become, rather suddenly, more apparent in recent weeks. It rather surprises him. He says it would be best if it were begun with the serious core currencies that qualified: to create a bedrock on which others could later rest. This would maximize the chances of surmounting the very considerable problems that will certainly attend it.

He notes, an under-noted point (he thinks), that the European Central Bank will be far more independent than any existing central bank. Far more so than the Bundesbank. It will have no proper political control over it. These people will have massive power.

On the British side, he says that Brown has been careful to avoid ruling it out, but he would be extremely surprised if we went in in the first round. On the whole, he downplays the bad effect this would have on our economic importance; he rather scoffs at the familiar notion that without Britain being at the centre of the design process, the thing will not work well. But he does say that, as well as the cyclical problems – the EU coming out of recession and having 3 per cent interest rates; the UK at the top of a boom and having 7 per cent interest rates – there are structural differences that will certainly cause problems: our much heavier investment in housing.

He thinks that the chance of the UK going in must be high, as long as it doesn't crack up. The reason for this, in the end, will be political. It will be like the ERM: the sense that one cannot pretend to be a player in Europe if one is excluded from the central project of the moment. That was an argument that persuaded even Margaret Thatcher. It is a geo-economic-political truth.

The particular British issue is when (more than whether, I gathered) we say that in principle we are in favour of entry. Will this be combined with the statement that we are not going in in the first round? – a position, he says, that will need to be established before the end of this year.

K. CLARKE He has said he had unbounded admiration for KC. I asked him exactly why. He said, KC has more strength of conviction, and a greater power of decision, than any politician he has ever met. He got this from within him. He was an amazing operator. I doubt, said AB, whether he has ever in his life at the Treasury asked for a paper. He will read a paper if it is sent, or at least scan it. But he would never ask for one. Cf. G. Howe, an obsessive asker for papers. He also made decisions, often on complicated things, very fast. And lived with them. It went back to all his previous jobs: Health, Education, Home. Never had any respect for the experts; never felt bound to follow them. Eddie George was the last expert to be dealt with, always very politely, in this way. Another KC trait: he never minded anyone arguing with him, very, very strongly.

CHRIS PATTEN
Phone, 24 September 1997

He calls from his London flat, prior to return to France and preparing for the move to Barnes [in south-west London]. Says that the move to Barnes is being interpreted as a retirement from politics – going to live in the country!

Has been writing ten lectures/speeches, using his old material, knowing that when he turns up there will either be 1,500 people when he expects 30, or vice versa. But he is getting down in earnest to writing a 100,000-word book, to be finished for HarperCollins by the end of March, which will start with a Hong Kong chapter (i.e., I gathered, taking on the critics), but will then be about lessons and problems: authoritarianism 'versus' economics, human rights in government, businessmen in politics etc. etc.[1] He says that the BBC have also just about decided to have him front three or four programmes, mainly Asia-based.

All this is convenient timing for him. It absolves him from politically

1 This was Patten's book *East and West*, which early in 1998 Rupert Murdoch instructed should be dropped by HarperCollins. It was published by Macmillan in September 1998, and became a best-seller in the UK and the Far East.

intervening. He will be too busy. At the present time, such interventions would be awkward.

What about Mr Hague? 'He's a good boy.' But ... I say that KC would surely have been much better, from which he does not demur. Says that Hague's test is whether he can lead the Tory Party away from its fixation that the way back is to become more right wing. They should forget about any idea that the reason they lost the election was that they were not right wing enough – or, indeed, that it had much to do with policy at all. It didn't. (N.B. It occurs to me that I am having this talk a day or two after CP was with J. Major and W. Waldegrave at T. Garel-Jones's house in Spain – so say the papers.)

They could have been much more effective as an Opposition. This is what their job should be. He would have made a big thing out of the robbing of pension funds[1] – a very big issue, that has not been attacked nearly enough.

He says that Hague must indeed try and reform the party, but again should not pretend that the answer is the wholesale Mandelsonization of it. Emulating Labour is not the way forward. Should concentrate on the rudimentary tasks (my words) of straightforward opposition. There is enough to go at.

He says that people say he should return to politics: that the Shadow Cabinet would be so much stronger with myself, Rifkind, Portillo and Forsyth aboard. I say he should not be seen in the same breath as Rifkind – and he agrees that MR has 'walked on too many pavements'. More than that, though, he says that the problem is, Do I want to belong to this club? Plainly the thought of Howard and Lilley as the bigshots is not comfortable for him. (I had said that Hague was surrounded by baddies. He muttered about A. Duncan – I said what I meant was Howard.)

DAVID MADEL
Phone, 5 October 1997

It's going to be a very difficult week. People don't like the two-in-one question. Happy to vote for Hague, but think they are being bounced on the reforms. But DM agrees that in fact this is not so: the arguments will be free to go on long after the ballot. However, these are the feelings.

Hague's biggest problem is the people around him, notably Alan

---

1 In his 1997 Budget, Chancellor Gordon Brown raised £5 billion when he imposed what the Conservatives were later to call 'a stealth tax' on pension funds.

Duncan, who sets the teeth on edge of at least half the PCP. A high-octane, excitable right-winger, unable to keep out of things.

The overwhelming feeling about Hague in the party is that nobody knows him. DM has been talking to many of his locals, because of by-elections etc. They are not hostile, but they are anxious and uncertain. They say, time and time again, that they know absolutely nothing about him.

This will be the first conference Hezza has missed since 1951.[1]

Howard is still aggrieved that Hague went back on his word about backing him, and ran himself. If he had been on the Howard ticket, Howard could even have won.

Thousands and thousands of activists (*sic*) think Clarke should have been the leader, but will not say so, out of a desire not to rock the boat.

The new constitution should be based round an electoral college, in which the MPs have a slice and the constituencies have a slice. Constituencies should have votes in accordance with their membership, i.e. like US states in the primaries. If Oldham West has the same vote as South Beds, it will be entirely wrong. Also, the centre should not supplant the associations. Members do not like to be written to by the centre, and prefer the locals to associate with.

Archie Norman[2] is on *Question Time* this Thursday. Is he fit and ready? He does treat us as though we were units in his Asda marketing path to the stars.

ANTHONY LESTER
Phone, 12 October 1997

He likens the British state of things to the Singapore government. A People's Progressive Party, which, having eliminated its enemies by Leninist means, is building an autocracy.

Robin Butler told him very recently how wonderful it all was. This is government by concentric circles, says RB. An inner – which consists of Irvine and Mandelson – and then outer ones with lesser ministers. Irvine and Mandelson are the only ones that count. Butler thinks both are wonderful. He is delighted by Mandelson, and hugely admiring of Irvine, who, he says, starts early, is very diligent, frames the right questions to clarify the issue, has a strong point of view, and gets things expedited.

1 Following his recovery from a heart attack in June 1993 Michael Heseltine had returned to active politics, but recurring heart trouble in 1997 kept him out of the Conservative leadership contest.
2 Archie Norman: businessman and politician, Conservative MP for Tunbridge Wells 1997–2005; chief executive of Asda 1991–6 and chairman 1996–9, credited for its transformation from near-bankruptcy to the second-largest supermarket chain in the UK.

Butler also says that the Cabinet Committee system is a dead duck. Forget all that, he tells Anthony. It is all run by the innermost circle. Ministers do not count for very much at all. Irvine, in particular, gets it all done, says Butler. All this, too, Butler much admires. He is not, one might infer, a very good guardian of the proprieties.

This links, I say, to the Gordon Brown triad – Balls and Whelan[1] – overriding the Treasury. A government of insiders, contemptuous of the existing machinery (which presumably spills over from their contempt for the Tories, with which they confuse the existing Civil Service).

Irvine himself is going even more power-hungry. He has let it be known that he will not appoint a lawyer to be the Permanent Secretary at the Lord Chancellor's Department – for the first time. This will clearly be a populist move, which will play to lawyers' unpopularity. But it is designed to give Irvine himself more power. Not to have a Perm. Sec. who can meet him on anything like equal legal terms.

This also connects with Irvine's plans for the appointment of judges, where he has dropped the Lab–Lib idea of a Judicial Appointments Commission. The left wanted such a commission to get more ordinary people on the bench; AL wanted it to insulate the judges from political interference. Irvine now says he hasn't got time to bother with a JAC. Combined with having a non-lawyer Permanent Secretary, how can this fail to deepen the complications of the LC's tripartite role as judge, minister and legislator?

NOTE TO SELF, 12 OCTOBER 1997 Further to Lester memo. This government is despising the Civil Service because they see it as part of the Tory disaster. This explains, perhaps, their willingness to override it (Treasury, especially). Yet the Civil Service were overjoyed when Labour won ... And Labour will need the Civil Service ... when things get tough. It is very ill-advised ...

GORDON BROWN
Treasury, 14 October 1997

All on Europe, just about.

He denied that little had been done by way of preliminary persuasion since the election. His strategy was as follows. First, get the Europe question away from ideological extremities. In particular, get EMU discussed in rational and cool terms. De-heat the thing. This has been done

---

1 Charlie Whelan: press secretary to Gordon Brown 1994–9.

via the Currie paper[1], via a consumers' advisory group (check) on the practicalities of EMU, via an understanding of the fact that the business cycles need to be in sync. He thinks quite a lot of groundwork has been laid.

But the key, no. 1, is to change the nature of British perception. To make the British think of Europe as an opportunity, as a way of finding a new role for Britain in the world. You might flirt with the old idea of Britain as a roving peacekeeper – some have done so – and as the junior partner to the US. But that is not very real; Europe must be seen, in a large sense, as the future. The place where Britain can score.

Another prior thing is for the Brits to think well of themselves: to feel Britain does count, is not a basket case, can lead. This, also, has begun to happen. The British are more self-confident. That is vital.

Along with this you do need to believe that the Brits are not irretrievably anti-Europe: that the Tory picture of Britain as a Europhobic country is false. I believe it is false, says GB. If you believed otherwise, you would regard a referendum as impossible to pass in any circumstances.

The heart of the British case for leading in Europe at present is on the jobs front. That is Brown's own personal crusade. He has had some success. He believes that almost all EU governments agree. Since twelve of these are now socialist or have social participation, that is impressive. The language of Europe is becoming more and more open to liberal ideas – Jospin[2] being the key exception. But he excuses France as being 'in transition'. In Germany he thinks the SPD is more open to this than the CDU.

On the EMU issue itself he declined to be drawn. He was being very, very careful – he said so in as many words – saying that he had to watch it because of the current stories about rifts between him and Blair (see today's *Independent* story by [Anthony] Bevins), which of course he denied. He gave me a very cool assessment.

He said that in the short term we could be a 'leader' in Europe without being in EMU. That is the right question, he said. But in the longer term it was another question. However, we could not make a decision at the moment which was based on that. There was a lot of preparation to do.

We jested about his caution. I said he sounded like a sceptic. He was saying that the convergence of business cycles could not be guaranteed – though he explained why the logic suggested it ought to happen. He also said that he could not say 'what words we will use at the end of the year'.

1 The economist David Currie, by then Baron Currie of Marylebone, later dean of the Sir John Cass Business School in the City of London, wrote a paper in 1997 called *The Pros and Cons of EMU*. It was published by the Treasury.
2 Lionel Jospin: prime minister of France 1997–2002.

What I got from this was a sense of genuine puzzlement in government circles about what is going to happen. He thinks there is almost no chance that EMU will fail, since the core countries are now locked together already and raise interest rates in unison. That is now accepted. So the political problems of all that – the northern-Spain, southern-Italy problems, if you like – are already to some extent accommodated. He clearly gives very little chance of it collapsing.

As to our membership, this would have to await developments. It was reasonable to see how it worked, and he would not say how long this investigation might take before a conclusion was reached. He said that the 'British terms' were very important, that the whole thing would turn on the British national economic interest. That was the way to look at it and present it.

On the political side, he said that the independence of the European Central Bank was already approached by his big decision about interest rates at the Bank of England. And this, he noted, had gone off without any fuss. It was better than politicians interfering, almost everybody could see.

When I raised the issue of political control and the visceral attitudes to that, he did not deny it. He emphasized, as Clarke used to do, the fact that neither fiscal details nor tax levels would be under ECB control. He had heard people talking about those things, but he seemed to reject the possibility. Indeed, he claimed that once the monetary framework was out of our control, then the other decisions would somehow make the Chancellor more rather than less important: or at least able to make decisions.

There was certainly a problem with the press. He notes that on all previous occasions, the press backed Labour against the party in the leadership's modernizing project. This time would be the first when the press was against it. It was clearly a factor. But he felt that as long as we said it was in the national interest, and could make a good case, then the people were not prejudiced against it. When I said that business would be important, he said yes – there seemed to be many businesses that were getting the message – but noted that they had yet to get into the serious persuasion business.

He spoke with somewhat bemused scepticism and doubt about the core issue of imbalances between the regions: the fact that the EU was not like the USA, could not easily transfer massive resources, was not flexible as to labour markets between countries – i.e. the whole sceptic ticket, so it seemed. I thought this was interesting. It was another sign of his puzzlement – rather than the adamant position he is represented as taking.

As to how the presidency could be used to further the British cause,[1] he said that we had to be careful. Using the presidency to further nation-state interests was not a good idea, as others (unspecified) had found. Hence, though he had the sense that this was the time to press for CAP reform, he knew it had to be done either before or after the presidency, not during. He sensed that the time was right, and the allies were there (among the interests as well as the powers). But he was in baulk as to the timetable. However, he didn't deny that in giving EU matters a high profile, the presidency had to be used.

In other fields, he went back to welfare-to-work as what he regards as the key to everything – or rather his conference pledge on full employment, which was much derided but which he seriously means. He says that it is what politics should be all about. He didn't make the pledge before the election, because he did not know if the means could be put in place – i.e. didn't know the size of the majority. Sensible minimum wage, welfare-to-work etc. But now they know they can get these things right, he sees full employment as a project worth working for.

The message to the Europeans is for a 'third way'. Not the US, not the old EU. But a European way . . .

ALL IN ALL GB was relaxed – we had an hour – and discursive. Very interested in my book[2]. But he took that as the basis on which to wander away from the questions, as he has always tended to do. Usually this is due to his desire to brain-bang one with his current obsessions. This time it was plainly for more defensive reasons.

---

1 The presidency of the Council of the EU rotates around member governments on a six-monthly basis.
2 *This Blessed Plot: Britain and Europe from Churchill to Blair* (London: Macmillan) was to be published in 1998.

1998

16 January   The government orders the aircraft carrier *Invincible* to the Gulf after Iraq restricts the movement of UN weapons inspectors.

17 February   Parliament votes by 493 votes to 25 for the use of force against Iraq if diplomatic efforts fail.

20 February   Iraqi president Saddam Hussein allows UN weapons inspectors to return to Baghdad.

28 February   Serbian police begin to eliminate 'terror gangs' in Kosovo.

1 March   More than 250,000 march in London in protest against a bill to ban fox hunting.

10 April   The Good Friday Agreement between the British and Irish governments on the political settlement of Northern Ireland.

5 August   Iraq suspends cooperation with UN inspectors.

7 August   Bombs at the US embassies in Tanzania and Kenya kill 224 and injure thousands. The blasts are linked to Saudi exile Osama bin Laden.

15 August   A terrorist car bomb at Omagh kills 29 and injures 200 people.

19 August   President Clinton finally admits an 'improper relationship' with White House intern Monica Lewinsky.

16 October   General Pinochet of Chile is placed under house arrest in Britain.

21 December   Trade and Industry Secretary Peter Mandelson admits borrowing £373,000 from Paymaster General Geoffrey Robinson, whose business affairs were the subject of a DTI investigation. Both resign.

Deaths   Gene Autry, Ted Hughes, Akira Kurosawa, Pol Pot, Frank Sinatra, Benjamin Spock, Michael Tippett, Tammy Wynette

ALASTAIR CAMPBELL
Phone, 19 January 1998

I rang and he called back. I stressed that this was the very conversation which would not be in any way used as coming from Downing Street. It would just seep into my consciousness and seep out again as my wisdom.

He said that the Blair–Brown row was overblown. Blair was not 'angry' about the Routledge book,[1] because he knew the reality of the relationship underneath. But if Gordon thought now was the time to encourage a book that said he should have been the leader, this was clearly a foolish thing to do. However, Charlie Whelan may have been more responsible than Gordon.

Once this kind of thing starts, it is inevitable that papers will write stuff that asks what it all means. Which is not helpful and is not necessarily right. My sense is, he says, that it will soon blow away: perhaps is already doing so.

There is the wider problem of unattributable briefings. He himself, he said, had gone over to attributable briefings in order to try and get things straighter. He claimed (!) to say virtually nothing off the record that he would not say on – 'except the swearing'.

But Charlie Whelan was different. There had been plenty of problems, especially with the *FT*. The Treasury give *FT* people a briefing, and then I rubbish it – and then quite reasonably the *FT* journalist says what the hell is he meant to make of that . . .

He believes that the basic necessity to have been learned from this is that people should not talk about each other. It was all very well in opposition, but Charlie still behaves as though we are in opposition. In government it is much more sensitive.

The fact is that GB's relations with colleagues are not good. Blunkett, Straw, Cook, Prescott: they don't trust him – and that is Whelan's fault (AC just about said).

---

1 Paul Routledge, *Gordon Brown: The Biography* (London: Simon & Schuster, 1998).

FRANK FIELD
His office, Department of Social Security,
20 January 1998

A large, pleasant office, in the old part of Richmond House,[1] redecorated by the Tories at untold expense: wood panelling, with British heroes – Shakespeare, Florence Nightingale et al. – chafed into the timber. Boring pictures by Henry Lamb. But Frank behind a fine desk in a well-proportioned room. Anxiously greets me; apologies for not coming down to meet me. Richard Thomas, a *Guardian* journalist on detachment, in his outer office: I failed to recognize him.

This is in the shadow of the Brown–Blair turbulence.

FF's basic desire is to work against means-testing. He sets out the short-term attractions of means tests, which he regards as a snare and delusion. They make good bullet points on a paper, but they are not going to solve the problem. They encourage fraud, they keep people out of work, they do not work. The man who recognized this most recently was Peter Lilley, who has said the Tories made a big mistake going down that route.

He insists he is not 'silly' about this. There have to be some means-tested benefits. Especially in the immediate term. (I have already forgotten which!) But he is especially keen on the development of stakeholder pensions.

He says he has no personal trouble with Brown, but it is obvious, talking to FF, that he is a rather second-league player. He is a knowledge-able boffin, who has deep commitment and a moderately clear picture of where we should be going. He is also patient, decent and wise. But he is not a heavy-hitter. He was, for example, dumbfounded that Brown should have swiped £5 billion by removing tax credits from dividend payments (Advance Corporation Tax), which at one fell swipe took away a lot of money from pension funds which will be needed if we are to improve the stakeholder pension regime.

In general, he says that there was no consultation about that. Nor was there about the ISAs, which he first read about in the papers, and which would have done such damage to the PEP idea, which many people chose to save by.

The question for now and the future is whether Brown can be reined in. The working of the welfare committee is the test. Is Blair a dignified or an efficient part of the constitution? The committee has its first meeting

---

1 Richmond House, Whitehall.

this Thursday (22 January). Blair is chair. Prescott, bizarrely (though FF
didn't know), is supposed to chair it if TB is away, but may not himself
be a regular attendee at the meetings!

I ask if there are fundamental differences between Blair and Brown on
all this. FF says he does not really think so. But he notes that TB is not
yet decided. TB seems to be feeling his way (he cited my *Guardian*
interview last Saturday as one example),[1] and to be vulnerable to the
means-test way of redistribution. As for Gordon, FF says that his main
interest seems to be in the accumulation of power and placemen rather
than in pushing a genuinely different set of ideas.

LODE WILLEMS
Lunch, his residence, 2 February 1998

He was especially interested in Blair's welfare reforms. Wants to meet
Frank Field, and is planning to take to see him some Belgian student at
Oxford who is doing a DPhil in an aspect of welfare reform. LW says he is
struggling to get to grips with the subject himself, but was much impressed
by the fact that when the Belgian deputy prime minister came here recently
he spent ninety minutes taking notes of what LW could tell him.

His own 'take' on Blair is that he and his government have calmed
down. They are making fewer grand effusions (my word): he notes this,
inter alia, about Europe. Claims that Blair has become less lectury –
though I rather dispute this – and that the presidency is now seen for
what it is: not an opportunity for grand achievements, but a six-month
period in which to help things forward. So all the early rhetoric is seen to
be bullshit: though I recall that Lode himself was once rather full of the
issues which he hoped Blair would move forward.

In fact I come up with my own view of the presidency, which LW
agreed with. Maybe its main effect will be to immerse the government in
the ways of Europe far more deeply than would otherwise have been the
case. For the presidency does involve great dealings with the Commission.
Brown, especially, is evidently rather frustrated to have forgotten that
only the Commission can actually take initiatives: hence much of what
he was saying about jobs etc. cannot be a British initiative. But the depth
of contact is very great. It means that a lot of ministers will know exactly
how Brussels really works.

For him, he says, Blair's 'conversion' will only be convincing when he

---

1 HY's interview of 17 January was headed, 'Vision for our future: Reinventing Labour was a huge challenge.
Now Tony Blair has taken on an even bigger task. He talks to Hugo Young about why we must transform our
idea of what the state can do for us.'

is heard to say something that no British leader has said: that such-and-such a policy or event or whatever is good or bad *because it is good (or bad) for Europe*. Every British leader has talked in terms of victory. So far, this seems to be the language that Blair still talks. We are watching closely, says Lode, for when he begins to change. (This is a good test.)

He says that when Santer[1] was here last week, he had found things very different from two years ago. Said that two years ago hardly anyone in the UK was serious about the euro, including the City. All said it was not going to happen. Now, Santer finds, the City is up and ready to go. As are other people.

Remarks that Geoff Martin[2] had warned him that a lunch with the editor of *The Times* was useless.[3] He was absolutely unpersuadable. Geoff had evidently had such an experience himself. In that connection, LW says that Peter Riddell, with whom he had lunched recently, had said that Murdoch was primarily motivated by his total dislike of what he called 'cross-border' forces and arrangements. (This seems a useful formula. It so exactly identifies what it is about the EU that he hates: an even bigger cross-border force than he is himself.)

On Iraq – which I happened to be writing about today[4] – he said he had just had a briefing from a US embassy person he used to know, who told him about the Albright/Cook talks this weekend. Albright is evidently hostile to the new attempt at a Security Council resolution, which Britain is keen on, which looks to have language asserting that Saddam Hussein is in 'material breach' or whatever of the earlier UN resolutions: Cook is seeking a freshened mandate. But the US is only keen on this if it is a 'very strong' resolution: which, almost by definition, means it will be rejected by China and Russia.

On Robin Cook himself, he says that on the Continent he is in no trouble for his private life.[5] Belgium's own foreign minister has been through an identical passage. But LW agrees with me that perhaps RC is somewhat damaged in his public persona. He notes that, in the HC, Cook is still Oppositionist: still turns majestically towards his own troops when he speaks. (Caution: did he get this point from Riddell?)

---

1 Jacques Santer: prime minister of Luxembourg 1984–95; president of the European Commission 1995–9.
2 Geoffrey Martin was head of representation of the European Commission in the UK.
3 Peter Stothard was editor of *The Times* 1992–2002.
4 HY's commentary of 3 February was headed, 'Bill and Tony's big adventure' and addressed the 'submissive respect' shown by British leaders to US presidents 'highlighted now by Britain's solitary, potentially catastrophic, part in a joint venture against Iraq'.
5 Robin Cook's marriage ended after he revealed that he had an affair with Gaynor Regan, a member of his staff. He married Gaynor in 1998.

SCENES FROM THE HELMUT KOHL
FREEDOM OF THE CITY
18 February 1998

Conrad Black said that it was vitally important that we should stand together against Murdoch on the pricing. The McNally amendment[1] was rubbish, but there needed to be new words in the Competition Bill to say that predatory pricing consisted of charging less than half the production cost for more than half the year. CB claimed that Murdoch had 'given me the run-around for a couple of years', but said that he was now thoroughly enjoying the price war. Gushed with stats about how much *The Times* was losing on Saturdays and Mondays, and noted that *Daily Telegraph* Saturday sales not hit at all by the *Times* Saturday price cut. He also said that he had 'taken over the writing of the leaders' on this subject. I remarked that he had been a restrained proprietor, normally confining himself to writing letters to his own paper. He said he had written a total of five leaders in the *DT* – over the years, I guess.

Lucy talked to Lenny Hoffman,[2] who was going to Hong Kong for ten days as an appellate judge: something the Thatcher deal provided for, that a UK or Australian or some other judge would sit for a few days, and have his judgment published – even though he would be only one among five. He wonders whether he will get some charter-party case, and the human-rights case will be left to the Chinese!

We talked to Cherie Blair, who had made a special note to the City of her desire to speak with me at the reception. This turned out to be simply that on a list of guests she had been asked to tick people she was keen to meet. We spoke briefly, as she was surrounded by sycophants. She wanted to say that she still read *The Guardian* and much admired, as she remembered she had told me before, my stuff. But her real message was a gripe: that people (Ros Coward[3] she mentioned) wrote nasty things about her professional life, including the puerile point that she took cases that were at odds with government policy. When I said that writers had a lot of freedom and the editor did not control everything, she clearly thought this was a sign that the editor wasn't doing his job properly – very revealing little New Labourish moment about the necessity for control!

---

1 The Liberal Democrat peer Lord McNally in 1998 proposed an amendment to the Competition Bill which was designed to outlaw Murdoch's predatory pricing of his newspapers, which in turn was intended to crush *The Independent* and the *Telegraph*. It received no support from the government.
2 Leonard 'Lenny' Hoffman: senior judge; became Baron Hoffman of Chedworth 1995.
3 Ros Coward: *Guardian* columnist and research fellow at City University.

Paul Lever, ambassador to Bonn, who I met long ago when he worked for Christopher Tugendhat, was nearby. He made some good remarks about leaders. Said that Thatcher, with whom he had much to do, made it an iron rule that the word 'compromise' must never appear in any briefing paper. It was simply forbidden. The FCO therefore had to find ways of couching their strategic suggestions round the unfailing notion of battle and victory. He said she never really knew when to stop. The art of negotiation, he said, was to know just the moment when you had got the best deal, or alternatively when the other side had had enough and the best thing to do was quietly retreat in order to come back the next day. All a matter of timing and feel. She seldom got it right. He recalled Carrington, in an early such negotiation, saying to her that she should stop for the night, everyone was tired, there was no deal to be had then: she replied by insisting on going on for two more hours. I asked him whether things were very different now. He said, I think so. But he added that Tony Blair had no experience of difficult meetings. He had run the Labour Party as a commander, he had a huge majority in the government, he did not have to do much brokering or fighting. So he had not been fully blooded, PL implied, in the reality of European deal-making.

He also noted animatedly that Kohl, Major and Blair had been talking at dinner in the crypt. This, he said, would be impossible in Germany. Kohl must have been astonished to see Major and Blair getting on so well. But, said I, the Germans and all Continentals are much better at coalition government, which surely points the other way. He agreed, but said there was this strict line between business and socializing. At the business level, yes – they have to make their deals. But that would not mean they would all have dinner together with a visiting statesman.

Talked at the end to John Major. Lucy found him amazingly sexy, getting close, very switched on, also very relaxed. He said his speech yesterday, on Saddam, was the first speech he had ever made from the Opposition back benches.[1] He now sees what a doddle Opposition is. So easy to make a speech when you are able to say what you actually think.

He said what a wonderful man Kohl was, as he had said to me before. Emotional, direct, big. He went on to talk about his Euro-trials, when I told him I was writing a book.[2] He immediately said he would read anything I wrote about him, and put it right.

---

1 Mr Major had been elected to parliament as Conservative MP for Huntingdonshire in 1979. He had never before been in an opposition party.
2 *This Blessed Plot*, published later in 1998.

What people did not understand, he said, was the problems he had, the constraints he was under. This, he said, was because 'I love the Conservative Party. All the time I wanted to do what was in the interest of the country and of the party.'

When I told him John Redwood had issued a statement attacking the whole Kohl freedom etc. he said, 'What do you expect?'

DAVID PUTTNAM
Causerie Restaurant, Claridges, 25 February 1998

A lunch arranged by him, following a rather acrimonious exchange of letters arising from a jibing piece I wrote before Christmas about the House of Lords. However, all is sweetness and extreme amiability . . . he was fresh from five days on Paul Getty's big yacht in the Grenadines, for which 'I paid not a penny.' Someone else, it seemed, had taken it for a celebratory holiday. Seventeen crew and six guests.

LOTTERY/DOME/MILLENNIUM EXPERIENCE DP is much involved, especially on the education side. He is a great apostle of learning, and sees his job as being to push this. It has been a hard task. His idea is that 'learning' etc. should infuse (he wanted Mandelson to say 'suffuse', but they agreed on 'infuse') every zone of the Dome. This reflects, in turn, is derived from and was connected with the 'Euan test': a reference made in August to Blair's son, and him being a benchmark for what should go on in the Dome, the conclusion being that it should be, above all, 'fun'.

This, says DP, was a big error. First, it was absurd to think that a child would be the guide. Children want to be stimulated, want to be excited, but depend on the adult world to find ways to do this. They cannot be guides. But, second, 'fun' was a slight and demeaning basis for the Dome. It was changed, therefore, to education in its broadest sense – but only after wasted time which DP reckons at six months. It took a lot of shaking down into a new mode.

An aspect of this was a battle for power. More than just a turf war. But once you mention education, David Blunkett and Michael Bichard want to get involved. They see it as a way of getting pet schemes launched – for example, the idea of 'family learning centres', based on the indisputable fact that homework etc. is better done when parents can help. Blunkett has wanted this, but there is no money. The millennium, however, provides money which is not Treasury-controlled. One (neglected) aspect of that is that there develops a kind of ministerial free-for-all for the pot.

LABOUR PARTY/BLAIR Brown seems to be the person Puttnam knows best. Regards him highly but, as we all say, he has a double personality. Can be very petty. This pettiness is what set him against Chris Smith, with whom, I gather, there is an enmity that goes back to some row they had when Smith was doing Health or Social Security in opposition.

Very interesting on Tony Blair. Claims not to know him 'as well as you do', but offered the following thesis. Blair, he says, is not physically very robust. Also, he is very interested in money. Therefore, perhaps he will quit after eight years. 'I can't see him ever doing more than eight,' says David (which, by the way, opens the door for Brown if he behaves properly and doesn't seem too worried about ensuring he gets it). DP says that Blair could then 'get any job he wanted'. He could get a lot of pay, 'with a private jet attached'. The two possibilities he proposed were boss of News International or boss of a merged Glaxo and Smith Kline (which had today announced they were not merging – but because of personalities, which Blair could finesse). A few years in that job could get in £20 million in the bank. DP kept repeating, to my question, that Blair was very aspirational.

After that, he could become president of Europe – when he was still barely 60. Could return to public life and fulfil his even grander ambitions – having got his money.

This was all very stimulating. I agreed that Blair was not in politics for ever – unlike Brown. Not the bone and blood of it. You could see Brown going on for ever, but not Blair. I wondered (to myself) how much Puttnam had discussed the thesis with others: say, Mandelson, who he obviously sees quite a bit of.

HOUSE OF LORDS He said he believed government was interested in a second phase.[1] But he said that Mandelson had recently expressed alarm at 'what we may have unleashed'. Fears a second chamber of second-raters, failures, rejects – councillors from South Notts. etc. But DP and I agree that the only way to avoid this will be by giving the HL more power. Otherwise, it is a real problem.

Notes that there are good people in the HL who want to do something.

1 A government White Paper of December 1998 promised to end by statute the automatic rights of hereditary peers to vote in the second chamber. 'This will be the first step in a process of reform to make the House of Lords more democratic and representative,' the document promised. But further proposals for reform would be left to a 'wide-ranging committee of both houses'.

Says that a handful of his group – Lords Paul, Stone, Sainsbury, Lady Kennedy,[1] others – are a kind of group who propose, unless things change, to go at some point to the government (perhaps Blair) and say that they had signed on for something that has not come about, a meaningful role in the HL. OK, he says, I have to spend Thursday night in the HL in order to vote. But where is there somewhere I can do my work? Is there no other business I can do?

Cites the Bishops Bar as the quintessence of what he detests. Doesn't drink much, can't stand the smoke, can't stand standing around reminiscing. The culture divide seems to be between professional retired politicians and people like him. On the whole, the old politicians are happy with things as they are. Others – Irvine, he says, is one – are genuine reformers, if they have a chance.

Said that on the Tory side he finds much to talk about with people such as Richard Ryder and Ian Lang (and suggests *The Guardian* invites a batch of them to lunch, to discuss HL reform).

PADDY ASHDOWN
His office, 10 March 1998

He is about to face the Lib Dem spring conference, which will be of some importance. There is an amendment down which has four points, two of which are important: that he should not be able to take further his Cabinet committee[2] without the approval of his federal executive, and that the party should not go into a coalition with Labour. He regards both as crucial not to lose. For even though coalition is not on the agenda, it would send the wrong signals – that his project was rejected by the party.

I asked him whether he would make it an issue of personal confidence. He replied that one did not do that sort of thing. On the other hand, he tried to make me not mention it (which I declined to do on the grounds that it is my idea) – which indicated to me that he is thinking of making it at least an informal subtextual reality which the party will become aware of.

He understands why people are worried. They think the LDs will be

---

1 Swraj Paul, Baron Paul of Marylebone: chairman of the Caparo Group since 1978. Andrew Zelig Stone, Baron Stone of Blackheath: director of Marks & Spencer 1990–99. David Sainsbury, Baron Sainsbury of Turville: parliamentary undersecretary at the DTI (and science minister) 1998–2006. Helena Kennedy, Baroness Kennedy of the Shaws: barrister; chairman of the British Council 1998–2004.

2 A joint Cabinet committee of Labour and Liberal Democrat politicians was established by Labour in 1997 to discuss electoral reform and other cooperation issues. It established a commission under Roy Jenkins, which in September 1998 proposed the alternative top-up, or AV-plus, system of voting.

absorbed, and sunk. He sees that if you have been fighting corrupt Labour machines in the inner city, it is incomprehensible to be working alongside them in government. He knows – but most particularly despises – the argument that Blair is really a Tory: which he most manifestly is not. He realizes that many people see Blair as not being a pluralist – which he freely admits has yet to be established, though he believes that when it comes to the point Blair will be forced in that benign direction.

The case made on the other side is, Do you want to look back on ten years and see us as simply on the margin? Look where we were ten years ago – nowhere. We have got back into a place of importance. We have a strong party. But what is this for? We have got Labour to make the most of our agenda – should we stand aside and let them get on with it while we snipe? There must be more to public life than that, he implies.

This sounds like something of a top/bottom argument. The top people do want office, do want to count, believe this is what they have been working for, imagine they can secure LD aims by getting closer to Labour. The bottom people in the end are not seduced by that, because it will never happen to them – apart from all their other tendencies to 'stay in the burrow where they have lived for a decade'.

Therefore the role for the LDs is to be probing, pushing, ginger-grouping (my word). For this is a shared project. (But it shows that the crucial thing they have not actually got over is the contradiction between having the same project and not being the same party.)

However, there is a new twist in PA's discourse, in that he now talks about 'anything can happen' in a few (number unspecified) years. He can't lay down the future. 'No politician can possibly pretend to know what will happen in ten years.'

There was one school of thought (Charles Kennedy)[1] which he found especially hard to follow in his own party: that the LDs should aim to take over from the Tories as the party of official opposition. This is so wildly improbable: how can anyone suppose that Toryism will become that much of a fringe party, that Hague won't be trying to get back to the centre ground, that lots of Tories who have 'lent' us their votes won't be taking them back again?

ALL IN ALL Repeats his old point that Blair is on a journey, the end of which he does not know. Says that Blair never gives an ideological answer to anything. His first reaction is *always*, Will it work?

He said he was getting much more out of the Cabinet committee

---

1 Charles Kennedy: SDP then Liberal Democrat MP for Ross, Cromarty and Skye 1983–97, for Ross, Skye and Inverness West 1997–2005, for Ross, Skye and Lochaber since 2005; leader of the Liberal Democrats 1999–2006.

than Blair was. How come? I asked. He said, We got PR for the Euro parliament. And we got the word 'proportional' put into the Jenkins commission's terms of reference. This was opposed root and branch by Jack Straw, and took Paddy two weeks to negotiate with Blair, but he won.

More broadly, Blair knows that if we walk out this will hurt him more than us (though it will harm the LDs too). Certainly Blair knew that earlier – to have walked out soon after the thing was set up would have been a blow. It still would be – if Blair is serious, as he is, about the whole progressive project.

LODE WILLEMS
Phone, 16 March 1998

Rang to alert me to the editorial in *The Sun* today, which he regards as proto-fascist. About immigration and asylum. (I had urged him to start reading *The Sun*, to get close to the mind that Blair cares so much about.) He is absolutely horrified. He says we should say to Blair, Is this the mind you are trying to appease, is this the place where you really need to insert your pieces?

Says he talked the other day to Roger Liddle. Both Blair and Mandelson believe that the main reason Labour lost the 1992 election was *The Sun*!

FRANK FIELD
Phone, 18 March 1998

BUDGET He describes the two competing images. (1) GB is determined to be a tight-belted Chancellor. Yet (2) there is clearly money available. We have already lifted the Tory spending limits for health and education – which was done without any accountancy subterfuge, just a straight lift, which the Tories perhaps felt they could not complain about.

I describe my thesis about Gordon Brown: the most remarkable Chancellor in our time in his power, his overbearing presence, the dislike he strikes in many hearts, the contempt he has for his colleagues.

He agrees with this – yet says that the Prime Minister remains wholly in charge. That is crucial. GB is a dark figure, a big presence. But the PM controls the minutes of the welfare committee meeting. It should be noted that there have been no leaks from the welfare committee – which suggests, does it not, that Gordon is not winning. Also notes that Tony is 'incredibly nice' to Gordon. Could not be nicer. Always looking for ways to make him feel better – rather than to keep him sweet. Almost like a therapist (my word).

But Tony is the boss, because Tony is the chairman, which Gordon much resents. Gordon himself is a very good chairman, brilliant: gets meetings over fast, demands hard thinking and decision. But Tony is in control here.

FF says that this split personality of Gordon's is very worrying. In the end, can he survive? Add in Robin Cook: he has 'down-graded' himself by what has happened. People just do not look at him in the same formidable light. This is why it is such a pity that Dewar is going to Scotland: the obvious man to step into RC's job, a safe pair of hands, good talker, etc. etc.

The bad thing is that this is all about personalities, and hardly at all about policies. It's not like having a ding-dong about the euro, and then going off to the pub for a cool-down chat. Personality disputes are more destructive because (per HY) there is no natural end to them.

JOHN KERR
Foreign Office, 17 April 1998

One of the richest conversations I ever had with someone I had never met before . . .

JOHN MAJOR JK feels that, as late as 1995, if Hurd had been prepared to really frog-march Major towards a more sensible Euro policy, he could have done so. Clarke certainly wanted to. This links with Helmut Kohl. Kohl started off by being very pro-Major. Partly because he wasn't Thatcher, partly because he seemed very can-do, very sound policywise, altogether a good thing. This lasted for some time. But then there was a great cooling of relations.

The high point of the Kohl–Major relationship was at Maastricht. Kohl was very helpful there. It was quite a spectacle. Major, to everyone's incredulity, took a very tough line. As Lubbers kept raising issues in the last six hours, Major would say, to item after item, I don't mind being in a minority of 11–1, we don't want this treaty anyway, it's you who want the treaty, so I'm sorry I'm not going to agree. Very often there would be guttural signs of admiration heard from Kohl as this performance was going on. Kohl was helpful therefore in prosecuting the British line.

ROBIN COOK Robin is the opposite of Hurd. He will not take 100 papers home at night; he will take only one. Some of the lower people at the FCO don't like this, want him to make decisions. But he is very happy to leave people like me, or a junior minister, to take a lot of the small decisions. He likes the big subjects, and he likes thinking about them, which he does to good effect. He has got, as far as JK sees it, deeply involved in big foreign affairs. He is intrigued by the problems, getting more and more engaged. They have an intellectual appeal for him.

Cook, having thought, is prepared to fight for his position. Cook is more like Healey used to be at the Treasury. Healey would have an almighty battle and row. Cook's stance is more like that – potentially. He will certainly not give up without a lot of discussion, and will insist on going back to have it again.

BLAIR, in turn, seems very wary of Cook. No. 10 talks as though Cook is the top man on the Old Labour side. Both JK and I express a certain incredulity at this. What, any longer, is Old Labour? Cook surely doesn't have a constituency that would worry anyone – as he himself would be the first to recognize. Nonetheless, JK insists, No. 10 thinks this way. I rehearse another aspect of this to him: Blair's obsession with *The Guardian*. (Interestingly, JK murmurs that he knows about that as well, and equally can't really understand it.)

One thing Cook enjoys, as an example, is engaging with Madeleine Albright and pointing out where she is wrong. They have a good relationship (I inferred). JK cited Iraq as an interesting area. Here, Cook was plainly very worried about the bombing policy actually having to happen. He would keep asking the same question: Have you thought what we do the next day? He asked Albright about this. She took it from him, and developed something of the same position about it.

This position was that it was right to threaten Iraq, but would have been disastrous actually to carry out the policy. In each case, the top people, Clinton and Blair, were more hawkish. JK observed No. 10 getting decidedly keen on the attack mode, as did Clinton. He worried about this. He also thinks of it as one area where Cook got close to a conflict with No. 10 – though it never in the end arose. Cook put this position in bilaterals, and also in the Cabinet, where he got support from people like Dobson and Short.

One of the misfortunes, on Iraq, was that when Blair went to Washington, for what was a very, very successful visit, Clinton was in the middle of the Lewinsky affair. This meant that at the press conference Clinton talked about Lewinsky and Blair about Iraq. This made Blair seem like the hawk on Iraq. He said a lot of strong things, the more so since Clinton was sort of on something else. It did not look good (I inferred) especially to the Europeans. It certainly means, since Blair did so well from the US point of view, that Clinton owes him a big one.

What is Cook's line on Europe? JK says more than once that he does not really know. He reckons that on EMU Cook has said enough to make it clear that he is not an enthusiast, but being a realist knows there may come a time when we have to join. (Kerr himself is not dissimilar, though he makes the crucial extra statement that he thinks that if it works it will actually be desirable – which Cook has not done.)

Cook is a very good chairman on the Council. He swots it all up carefully on the weekend, goes to Brussels, and has a dinner with some other foreign minister – makes the dinner part of the preparation for the meeting. He then knows who he is going to call on each subject, indicates how he is going to call them in a certain order, and then sums up again without notes. His summings-up are generally accepted as a decent first shot at least. All in all, he impresses people a lot by his performance.

IN THE FOREIGN OFFICE   JK disagreed entirely with my line about C. Meyer and the Bonn/Washington problem. Meyer should never have been sent to Bonn. He was a 'platform man' – i.e. he liked the big stage, the big show. Bonn was never the place for such a person. Meyer had actually wanted Rome – but that wouldn't have been big enough for him. (JK said Meyer was his oldest friend in the FCO.)

Meyer was therefore the ideal man for Washington. Lots of show. And Paul Lever was ideal for Bonn – a true Europeanist. But this was part of a bigger picture. JK said that his biggest hope in his five years in the job would be to finally rid the FCO of this 'Atlanticist vs European' stuff. He would do this, as far as I could see, by ensuring that Europeans got all the big jobs, which they mostly had now. He sounded very pleased at this. There was Lever in Bonn, Jay in Paris. But also David Wright in Tokyo – a complete Euro man. Then there was Jeremy Greenstock in New York – totally European. Another backroom boy rather than a platform man: the FCO candidate for Washington. JK said, by the way, that he thought Labour had wanted a politician, or possibly a business-man, in Washington, but never came up with a name: I said (without naming Mandelson) that I had been told that they did have one business-man in mind, whom they could not persuade to do it.

He said that the old signs of Atlanticism did still crop up. If there was a crisis in some Ruritania, the first instinct of some people was to think about Washington's view, and not about collecting a meeting of the EU political committee, hacking out a position, getting agreement etc. etc. He hoped gradually to change these instincts.

Among the ministers, JK volunteered Derek Fatchett[1] as first class, but no one else.

JK is entirely opposed to having a separate Secretary of State for Europe in the Cabinet. It would never work. The General Affairs Council is becoming more and more important – and reaches out beyond the EU affairs. It deals with Russia, with Bosnia, whatever. Any plan which said that the Europe Cabinet minister handled Community affairs, and the Foreign Secretary everything else, would therefore immediately cause confusion. It would relegate Europe to being supposedly less important than the big stuff – while actually violating the true hierarchy of work and interest any Foreign Secretary has. (That last part is all HY, but JK agreed.)

So, says JK, he would love to have Peter Mandelson as a minister for Europe, but he should not be in the Cabinet.

On EMU itself, he believes that Blair's fundamental position is pro but wary. That's fine. But he thinks the British position is not sustainable for long. Not beyond the end of the year. To be out and yet striving to be close is not sensible and will not work. But he has no clear idea about how that might be altered. He thinks the government has got itself into a bad box. This strikes me as the most important of issues: how we will be able to shift an untenable position, given the box our politicians have set themselves in.

He asks me what I think should happen. I say that at the very least they have to start making the famous 'preparations' which Brown spoke of last October.

On that decision, incidentally, JK took some trouble after returning here to find out who had been consulted, and in particular whether Cook had been. The record shows no contact or consultation with Cook of any kind.

He thinks we made a total mess of the Euro-X affair[2] – thanks entirely to Gordon Brown giving bad advice to Blair about how to play it. Brown became obsessed with demanding a British place at the table even though we weren't inside. This was never going to wash. Strauss-Kahn[3] proposed a perfectly sensible compromise, which we should have accepted. Instead of which Blair went pitching for the unattainable. This had a bad effect on several counts – not least that a summit which was supposed to be all

---

1 Derek Fatchett: Labour MP for Leeds Central 1983–99; a junior minister at the FCO 1997.

2 The Euro X committee was the body set up to coordinate economic policy in those countries that planned to join the single currency in 1999. Britain was not one of those countries, but wanted a seat on the committee anyway.

3 Dominique Strauss-Kahn: French economics minister 1997–9; director of the International Monetary Fund since 2007.

about enlargement (as we wanted) was half taken-up with the Euro-X question, which we were sure to lose anyway.

GORDON BROWN He thought the tension between No. 10 and Brown was far more important than anything about Old Labour. He, too, could not understand it. He said it was pretty well unique in his experience, since there was so little policy content in it.

It was quite foolish and wholly erroneous to have fallen out with Terry Burns. For some reason, Burns has been cast out. Burns is Sunderland/ Newcastle, he is QPR [Queen's Park Rangers] every Saturday; he is one of the lads. Equally, all the ideological stuff is years off the map, so it can't really be that. Whatever the reason, it has been bad for government. Both the Budgets, he said, contained things which, had they been handled through the normal channels, could have been done much more effectively. (He did not specify.)

Even more foolish, if anything, was the freeze-out of Nigel Wicks.[1] Wicks is a superb public servant. He has been re-elected not once but twice to the chairmanship of the monetary committee which has been setting up the EMU. Here is this Brit – coming from a country which could well have been suspected of seeking to wreck EMU – who gains the trust of all concerned. He is very clever; he is seen as very fair, and a complete master of the subject. He is accepted on all sides, perhaps as a kind of umpire through not being nationally committed – yet, more impressively, as someone who could have been unhelpful, yet has been wholly positive.

The monetary committee finishes at the end of this year – so Wicks will be the last chairman. A piece would be in order. But NW would be horrified. JK was once travelling with him in Europe, on a plane where journalists were present. Wicks put a newspaper over his head, for fear of being seen. He is that remote. JK, who has talked to him often and had him to stay in Brussels numerous times, has absolutely no idea what his opinions are on any private matters. He is a complete mystery, but one of the most important of all British public servants of recent years. He is the best Treasury man on overseas policy JK has ever known.

MALCOLM RIFKIND An ambitious Scot on the make – like me, says Kerr.

When JK heard that Rifkind was going to make his tour of Europe, he knew it would be a calamity. He messaged London accordingly. Said

1 Sir Nigel Wicks: civil servant; Second Permanent Secretary and director of International Finance at HM Treasury 1989–2000.

that it broke the rule which Major had been quite good at following – which was that you should refrain from telling the Europeans how to run Europe, because if you did there was a somewhat greater chance they would do what you advised them not to do. But, wider than that, the Rifkind project was doomed – especially and above all by going to Bonn and lecturing the Germans.

JK recalls meeting Rifkind in Washington during the BSE fiasco. He asked him what the British were going to define as victory in whatever interim dispute was then on the table. Rifkind replied that that would be decided by the Ministry of Agriculture: i.e. British foreign policy had been subcontracted to Douglas Hogg. Kerr couldn't believe what he was hearing, but MR proved unreceptive to criticism of a point he must have known was hopelessly indefensible.

BRITAIN'S ROLE IN EU/US While accepting my suggestion that in lots of micro-ways a government could register a shift towards Europe, he said he thought our 'broker' role was significant. We really could go to the EU and get it to change its position if we were clever about it by saying that we thought the US would be more amenable to such-and-such rather than so-and-so. And vice versa in Washington. We did have a role in the middle. I adhere to the Seitz thesis, he said more than once.

It is, by the way, from the Netherlands and not from Minnesota or Wisconsin that the Blair social policy has come.

BLAIR AND THE FUTURE It was a pity that the relations with Jospin were not much good. Probably could not be greatly improved. They just did not hit it off very well. Though JK says that Blair's speech at the Assemblée,[1] which at first he thought disastrous as he heard the cheers coming from the wrong people, was on reflection a great success and well worth doing.

By far Blair's most important and closest collaborator in the EU is Wim Kok.[2] Blair has a lot of time for him. He also thinks Prodi[3] is pretty good. And he went on holiday, as I remark, with Aznar.[4]

Schröder, if he gets elected, will be the key. Another reason why our EMU stance will get less sustainable by the end of the year. Schröder has

1 Tony Blair addressed the French National Assembly on 24 March 1998, and declared that ideology was dead: there was no longer a left-wing way or a right-wing way of running an economy; there was only a good and a bad way. The French left reacted coolly. *Le Monde* praised Blair's perfect French.

2 Willem (Wim) Kok: prime minister of the Netherlands 1994–2002.

3 Romano Prodi: Italian politician; prime minister of Italy 1996–8 and 2006–8; president of the European Commission 1999–2004.

4 José María Aznar: centre-right politician; prime minister of Spain 1996–2004.

taken a clever line about EMU, quite critical, but not hostile. When he gets elected, there's no way he will be anti-EMU. But he will be asking Blair, by then, what his policy is, what he wants etc. etc. There will be an SPD leader in government with whom we can and need to relate closely, for the first time. Schmidt was the last one – but had an ambiguous relationship, of course, with Thatcher.

JK said he was more worried about Conrad Black than Murdoch. One of his little stratagems was to get Richard Perle[1] to place a pro-EMU piece in the *Telegraph*. He thinks maybe Barbara Amiel [Mrs Black] is the way to the *DT*.

I try to persuade him that Murdoch matters much more, because *The Sun* matters more than the *Daily Telegraph*. JK seriously seemed to think that the *Daily Telegraph* readership was so massive as to be vital. I said Murdoch might be more easily seducible pro-Europe because all he cares about is money (we agree), and Black has Beaverbrookian aspirations and would be unregenerate in his attitude. JK said he now understood he had to read *The Sun*. (I told him I'd given the same advice to Lode Willems – whom he obviously thought rather well of.)

ROBIN COOK
Foreign Office, 6 May 1998

He wanted to say, in general, what a good year it had been for the UK in foreign affairs. Began to reel off his list.

CHINA I raised this first, because it was in his list. He said we now had developed a 'more realistic' relationship with China. They were now willing to engage on human-rights discussions. There have been twelve people named as human-rights prisoners; two have been let out. I'm not saying, he said, that this shows some huge transformation. But it is interesting that they are now ready to fight their corner in discussion.

This was different (I think he said) to Middle East discussions of the same kind, which were more formalistic. Middle East countries engaged with him on the disgraceful fact that London allowed terrorists to run their campaigns from here, and RC had to give them elementary lessons in freedom of speech etc. (Not quite clear about this.)

---

1 Richard Perle: neoconservative thinker, US lobbyist, political adviser; served in the administrations of President Ronald Reagan and, from 2001 to 2003, of President George W. Bush.

EUROPE   I asked him first about France. He said that it was noticeable how distant Jospin was keeping from Chirac. Jospin, he said, was a rather maligned man, seen as an Old Labourish sort. This was not true. He is an intelligent, subtle man, who is being rather effective.

He repeated what Mandelson had said earlier in the day about the centre-left grouping of leaders – the first time there would have been progressives in power in Paris, London, Bonn and Washington at the same time. (He wholly took my dry point about ideology seeming to matter at this level of discourse, whereas not at the domestic level!) He said that Blair was especially close to Kok. But also mentioned the Portuguese leader. If Schröder wins in Germany, there will be a big change (of a rather unspecified kind).

His main thrust here was to say that while we, the Brits, would never be so crude as to welcome a Franco-German divide, the fact that Chirac and Kohl had fallen out was a situation we could take account of . . .

It was in this context that the 'leadership' question should be thought about. 'A leading partner', he said (I think) drily, was 'the approved phrase'. The fact was that Blair had great acclaim in Europe. Because he was young, because he had this socking great majority, and because he had a lot of ideas, he had standing. On the other hand, nobody could deny that not being in EMU meant that you could not lead EMU. However, RC seemed disposed to play down the sense in which this seriously relegated us in 'Europe' as a whole.

He claimed that the effect had been very fast, once Labour had taken over. The switch from Rifkind to himself, for one (as Sheinwald, who served them both, confirmed when walking me through the yard), had been important. They had hated Rifkind's lectures, his sense that he was just trying to win a court case. Cook brought a new impression.

Interestingly Cook said, when I asked about the changing of popular attitudes to Europe, that these too had been shifted by Labour's mere presence. After all, the people had been used to British ministers returning from Europe and proclaiming their failure. They had rejoiced in failure, have been positively bashful about success. People do not like their leaders telling them about how much they had failed. That simple shift had already been important in changing the Labour image: that they weren't always talking about failure.

When I said I hadn't heard a British politician talking about something being good for Europe, he gently but correctly reminded me that he made a point of always saying, as did Blair, that something was 'good for Britain and good for Europe' – this was necessary to draw the sting from the tabloid sceptics et al. Anyway, it was the right way to see things, was it not?

His own practice as presidency chair has been to have dinner on the Sunday night before the General Affairs Council with one foreign minister. This has worked out well. His meeting with Hubert Védrine, the French foreign minister, was especially good. (Sheinwald said that Védrine, who is a civil servant, was at first chilly, unclubbable, but this has improved.)

Seeing him in the FCO is still rather odd. He does lack physical gravitas, an impression which is added to by his desire to be man-of-the-peopleish, eating in the FCO canteen – how often? – and the shirtsleeves greeting in the corridor. Hearing some music and singing coming from somewhere, he invites me to set off on a search, and we find this quartet practising in a room. He looks in for a couple of minutes and pronounces it rather good, though I doubt he can tell. What I mean is that, for all his intellectual ability, he seems almost in himself to be a little doubtful as to whether he is in the right place. He no longer bestrides, as he used to. This of course is in part due to his domestic chaos. But it is also because, as leader of the left, he has had every tooth drawn by the Blair triumph. Therefore he does not really have a constituency in the party. He therefore, perhaps seeing this, settles for this big job, and for being heavy in his praise for Blair – a different song from the one he used to sing. But, for example, there is still something unreal about hearing him say, when I ask for the latest state of play on the Middle East dealing, 'Have I heard from Tel Aviv this afternoon?'

USA/ALBRIGHT He comes right out and says what a good relationship he has with MA. I need to ask him more about the basis for this. He puts it down, I think from memory, to them having a common view of the world. I put to him the thesis that he and Albright had been dovish over Iraq – desperate to avoid conflict – whereas the leaders had got more bullish and gung-hoish. He did not entirely deny this. But he said that in Washington power was so diffused that you couldn't think about that without thinking of Congress and the Pentagon.

The big story is really about EU expansion. Within ten years there will be another ten or so members. This will mean the whole of the land mass, just about, is included. Most people have not begun to think about that, especially in the UK. It will be an immense development – which RC seems to regard more seriously than the NATO expansions, about which, all of a sudden – five years too late – this batch of grandees has suddenly spoken up in a negative sense.

ADDENDUM 'They're erecting statues to me in the Middle East' –
a reference to his clash with Israel.[1]

HY didn't mince words as far as his next contact was concerned. Alan
Duncan was one of a new breed of Conservative MPs. Before entering
the Commons, in 1992, Duncan had been an oil broker. He had moved
rapidly up the party organization, becoming a vice-chairman, and by
now was shadow spokesman on health.
  'Bitter and vicious, rather nervous with me, I thought, with his tight-
lipped little grimacing, but making up for it with an overemphasis of
numerous hatreds which I have seldom come across,' wrote HY.

ALAN DUNCAN
The Garrick, 18 June 1998

He began straight in on Europe, before saying, after a few minutes, 'We're
not going to spend all this lunch on Europe, are we?' He wanted to say
that to be against the EU was not to be anti-Europe: that he himself was
as global as any man: that the EU as an institution was intolerable, and
was what the argument was about. He simply did not come near to
accepting that, whatever the purist truth of that, in the real world one
did show oneself to be 'anti-Europe' by being anti-EU, since the EU was
the only game in town.

His line is that the EU is certain to break up. This will be forced by
EMU. EMU was a constitutional 'obscenity' (a word he is fond of), and
would lead to the crack-up of Europe. 'I fully expect to find myself in
uniform before my life is over,' he said proudly. (He looks to be about
40 now.) There would be bloodshed through this forcing of peoples to
pretend they were part of a single political entity, this denial of their
independence.

I pressed him to say how much the British economy would be 'independent' outside the EU, and he did not answer. The question didn't
seem to have occurred to him, so virulent is his dislike of Brussels and
all that.

The only 'positive' note he struck was about Germany, but this had
its own sting. He said (like the *Telegraph* recently) that his great wish

---

1 In March 1998 Robin Cook visited Israel, representing the EU as well as Britain, and arranged to meet a
Palestinian official at the disputed Har Homa settlement on occupied Arab territory in East Jerusalem. Israel's
premier Benjamin Netanyahu subsequently cancelled a dinner with Cook, and the Board of Jewish Deputies in
Britain withdrew an invitation to Robin Cook to speak at their annual dinner.

was for Germany to become a proud nation once again. He thought they were demeaned by sheltering behind this 'Europe', and this denial of their own nationhood. (This is somewhat different from the Cash line, for example.)

When I ventured that the European Parliament would become more important, he almost spat with disgust. 'The place will be blown up some time – I mean that literally,' he said. Elected by PR, it has no legitimacy. This opened up the electoral-reform subject. One of his pathological disgusts is at PR in any form: I would rather lose an election by FPTP than ever win one by PR. I asked him if that was Hague's line too – he coyly said he couldn't tell me. But when I said that psephologists agree (as per Lipsey[1] the other day) that the Tories need to be 6 per cent ahead in order to get the same number of seats as Labour, he said he had no idea of such a thing, and I think he genuinely did not know about it. He was therefore unable to receive with any intelligence at all the notion that the Tories should take an interest in PR.

He went on to talk about Blair. Here his hatred really boiled over. He regards Blair as a deeply evil man, a poseur, a power-mad centralizer, a serial liar at PMQs, someone who is perhaps the worst man ever to have risen high in British politics. All these expressions were used. He kept coming back to try and renew and enrich his language of detestation. Blair has no ideas, no centre, no purpose, no principles – nothing except a desire for power, which he had got by lying through his teeth at the 1997 election.

On top of this, he was now ruining the country very deeply with constitutional reform: this was another 'obscenity'. It was breaking up Britain, with no thought whatever for the consequences. They had thought nothing through, and meanwhile were inflicting on the country a great variety of bodies elected by a variety of systems so confusing as to drain people's lingering faith in democracy. The PR systems for Europe and for devolution and for London were guaranteed to have this effect. People would no longer know who their MEP was, would no longer have the faintest idea who was responsible for what, would no longer feel they, the people, played any relevant part in the democratic system.

I asked him if any Cabinet ministers were exempt. He said there were two ministers he admired. One was Chris Smith (the pink mafia?), who had been shamefully traduced. The other was Jack Straw, who was the steadiest, most statesmanlike man in the government. (It emerged later that he was in deep talks with Straw because one of the paedophiles was

---

1 David Lipsey: member of the Prime Minister's staff 1977–9; journalist; political editor of *The Economist* 1994–8; later Baron Lipsey of Tooting Bec.

being placed in a village in his constituency, and Duncan was trying to take a responsible line about it.)

On William Hague, he said that he had done far more than Thatcher in her first few months. He had wiped out the enemy, which Thatcher had never been able to do. He had decentralized the party, and reformed it far quicker than Blair had done with his. He was a man of very exceptional ability, as people would in due course discover. But he did not get anything like enough exposure. He had less exposure than any main party leader in memory. This he had to rectify. On the other hand, his main task was simply to wait. Labour would start dividing: there would be anti-Blair bitterness: the public would get disenchanted. William had to be ready, but had to wait.

He had inherited an appalling situation, which Major had brought about. But the rot went back to Thatcher. She should have sacked Lawson for shadowing the Deutschmark, should have refused to enter the ERM on any terms, and should never, of course, have been sacked. That was a catastrophic error, from which the party has still not recovered. What her departure did was deprive the party of a clear sense of identity. It still does not know what it is. Major had made this far worse, by listening to the terrible people around him, mainly Hurd, Heseltine and Clarke. Hurd was one of the most evil men in post-war politics: an appeaser, a despiser of the party, a man who ran away from all hard decisions, and who patronized Major, patting him on the head.

Then came Maastricht. Duncan says Major was correct to have got his opt-outs, which were a triumph. And we were right to say in the 1992 election that we would ratify Maastricht. But we should have reacted quite differently to the Danish referendum: seen it as the moment of rescue from this terrible, anti-democratic project. That was the great missed opportunity, from which much else flowed. Yes, to pull back from Maastricht would have been a big choice, an aggressive break with the past, and was therefore unimaginable to Major. But it should have been done. From the failure to do it sprang all the bitterness that marked the rest of his government.

Hague could not now expect to do everything at once. But he has to get rid of the faces who are associated with the failure of Major. When I mentioned Howard, Duncan implied it was only a matter of time before he went. There needed to be new people. When I asked how many of the PCP were Europhile, he said 10 per cent. How many of the new MPs? 10 per cent. It is an entirely marginal opinion: which indeed it has been for many years, screened by the hideous control which the three (Hurd, Heseltine and Clarke) exerted over Major.

He could not let the lunch finish without attacking *The Guardian* over

Aitken etc.[1] He thought the paper's entire conduct had been despicable. But he quite soon climbed down from this when I said that Aitken had been given the chance to walk away from the case and rejected it. Was this the Saatchi deal? he asked. I said it preceded the Saatchi deal. He said JA had told him the Saatchi deal wasn't really a deal. (I had forgotten that AD came out early as a friend of Aitken, spitting public blood about the campaign against him.) When he turned to Hamilton, I said we had the evidence etc. etc. He said, Fayed is polluted. I said, That is not the point. I asked him if we should simply not have exposed either Hamilton or Aitken. He turned the question by asking why we didn't do the same to Blair – 'the million quid from Ecclestone'. He also said the Tories were compiling a dossier of Blair's lies at PMQs which we should use.

Overall, the position degenerated simply into saying that because Aitken was his friend he felt he must defend him, and because Aitken was a major public servant, who had done much for his country, we should not have got him on such trivia. I told him that I knew Aitken of old, and knew in particular how he had lied on oath in the Biafra OSA case.[2]

He concluded by saying that I could probably see Hague by asking Sebastian Coe,[3] who should be reached at CCO. He would put in a word. He said, however, that there would be time problems. I said, But he is not running the country, and he needs to see people like me . . .

1 In April 1995 Jonathan Aitken promised to fight with the 'sword of truth' when he sued The Guardian and Granada TV for libel in a row over his extra-parliamentary activities, including the claim that an Arab associate had paid for his stay at the Paris Ritz in 1993 while he was Minister for Defence Procurement. In spring 1997 Maurice (Lord) Saatchi attempted to broker a peace deal – inviting Aitken and The Guardian's editor, Alan Rusbridger, to a private meeting in Wilton's restaurant in London. Aitken pushed ahead with the action, but the trial collapsed dramatically in June 1997 when evidence proved he had lied to the High Court in insisting that his wife had paid the hotel bill. In 1999 he was sent to prison for seven months for perjury. Neil Hamilton, Conservative MP for Tatton 1983–97, and corporate-affairs minister, was another prominent Tory involved in a libel action against The Guardian. In 1994 the paper claimed that he and another minister were paid cash 'in brown envelopes' to ask parliamentary questions on behalf of Harrods owner Mohamed Al Fayed. Hamilton sued The Guardian but dropped the case a day before the hearing in 1996. He lost his seat in 1997 to the BBC war correspondent Martin Bell. In November 1999 Hamilton lost a libel suit against Al Fayed, who had claimed in a Channel 4 documentary that Hamilton demanded cash payments, gift vouchers and hospitality at the Paris Ritz in return for parliamentary services.

2 As a young journalist, Jonathan Aitken was charged with – and cleared of – breaking the Official Secrets Act (OSA) when he published documents that showed that the then government was arming the Nigerian side during the Biafran civil war late in the 1960s.

3 Sebastian Coe: athlete, politician; Conservative MP for Falmouth and Camborne 1992–7; chief of staff to William Hague 1997–2001; chairman of the London Organizing Committee for the 2012 Olympic Games since 2005; made Baron Coe of Ranmore 2000.

GORDON BROWN
Treasury, 1 July 1998

This was a meeting asked for by him at short notice. I was irritated to find that there was a long unexplained delay when I'd arrived, which left me pacing the singularly tedious waiting room, before, after 30 minutes and no word from anyone, barging into the officials' room and saying, without preliminaries, 'How much longer must I wait?' The people in there – all women, I think – flapped and burbled about him just having left No. 10, and how they didn't know, and had no control etc. etc. I pressed on, restraining my temper but letting them know that other people had time problems as well as the Chancellor.

Perhaps this had a good effect. When he did arrive, he was tremendously apologetic, saying he didn't have a watch and had been straining to see the time on the clock in Blair's office. But it had been an important meeting, which he couldn't get away from.

He was, after all this, the soul of geniality. It was perhaps the best meeting I have had with him, even though it lasted only half an hour.

He began with welfare-to-work, rather inconsequentially. I suspect this was because, at some much earlier stage, he got it into his head (perhaps as a result of a single column I wrote when they were in opposition) that I am immensely interested in this. I'm afraid this is not so. However, he rattled off the figures to show how well it was already working, and how it was expanding from young people to the long-term unemployed etc. etc.

I asked him if it was true that they had been disappointed to find how little could be saved. He replied by saying that the differential performances between regions and places was huge, and there was therefore a good reason to make the worst as good as the best. He instanced hospitals especially – a 20 per cent differential. But the same principle could be applied to housing – a Housing Inspectorate has already been announced, which will tell us more about the very different performances of different authorities.

He volunteered also that there would be a lot more selling of assets, especially (I think) property holdings, which there was no reason to own. This was a way of releasing assets we don't need in order better to use assets we do need.

EUROPE He defended the government's position over EMU, very genially. He said he thought we were in exactly the right position: very fully engaged, without yet being on a dated course for membership.

If they had had a referendum earlier, it could only have been on the principle. This would have had several disadvantages. It might not have been accepted as definitive, because there would have been perhaps a three-year gap before entry, in which time a lot of trouble could have been made. By being *only* about the principle, it would have elevated the constitutional issue to unique status, without it being mitigated by the economic and financial case. By holding it later, there will be a better economic story to tell. The economic case, as seen on the Continent, will have got better. And there will have been a lot of preparation.

This preparation is going on. We have an educational/informational (not propaganda) programme in train this summer and autumn. There will then be a 'draft national changeover plan' early in 1999 (which is being worked on by the CBI, TUC etc. etc. as well as the Treasury).

I pressed him to agree that what he wants is to be in by 2002. He said he couldn't say that, it would contradict the stance he had taken about waiting to see the economic data. 'It's not a position I could take,' he said – though this sounded almost entirely tactical rather than substantive. I pressed him further: that he might want the election early in order to achieve 2002. He said, The election doesn't have to be after the full five years (or some such words) – almost (but not quite) hinting that an election timed to permit an EMU referendum that let us in by 2002 was one of the strategies being actively discussed.

When I said that there would have to be a decent time for preparation *after* the referendum he rather scoffed at that. Yes, the French had taken five years to prepare. But he would not need anything like so much time, given the arrangements we will be setting in place long before that – though he did seem to say that the notes and coins aspect was more time-sensitive.

When I said that the problem would come if Labour failed to win the election, or won only by a small majority and couldn't get their referendum bill through, he said immediately there was no chance of that. They would win, and we would see that the anti-Europe faction in the party was very small: as well as, by now, entirely based on the economic (Keynesian) argument, which would, we must hope, have been changed by events between now and then.

He believed that one of the tasks was to get people to understand that being pro-British and being part of a strong international economic community were not two contradictory tendencies. But it needed time to get this across.

ALL IN ALL I was impressed by GB's coolness, his unbothered air. Rather different from the impression one constantly gathers from others

(FF, PM) about his overbearing manner, his paranoid attitude to colleagues etc. Was he concealing something? Perhaps the truth is that he
plays his part – does not resist it – in the essential, inevitable process of
politics, which is so much about personal rivalry and creative tension.
When I said to him that it *was* all about personalities, he immediately
referred to Thatcher and her completely broken relationship with her
Chancellors. There was nothing like this on the present scene. I think
there was *something* a little beseeching, a little consciously agreeable, in
his attitude to me in this conversation: but also, behind that, no doubt a
full awareness of the power he has in the project which, undoubtedly,
they both share.

BLAIR–BROWN It was he rather than me who raised this: perhaps
it was supposed to be the key subtext of the meeting. He said the stories
about their relationship were based on a lot of myth and misunderstanding. He said this with total equanimity – in fact, I realized, this is one of
the keys to his approach to people like me. He is the soul of pleasantness,
and would never think to venture any kind of rebuke, merely a gentle
prod that might help us to get things right: a stoical, philosophical acceptance, far less agitated than Blair himself has sometimes been, about the
unavoidable ignorance in which the press operates.

He said he saw Blair constantly. They had just met for an hour and a
half, to talk about many serious matters. If he doesn't see him, he probably
talks on the phone every day. They are very close, as they have to be. If
No. 10 and the Treasury do not get on, what happens is immobilization,
a word he kept repeating. There had been no such immobilization, from
the start. Did anyone think that the independence of the Bank would
have been done by him alone? Or that the Budgets could have been done
that way?

People liked to take these dichotomies – fairness/efficiency, pro-EMU/
anti-EMU etc. – and pin each side of them on Blair and Brown respect-
ively. He thought they were artificial differences. There was no way Blair
and Brown differed on these lines. It was quite untrue to say that Blair
was less pro-Europe than Brown was. Again, I should stress, all this was
said with absolute calmness and ease, a sense of relaxation, of tolerance
for journalistic error – which didn't really matter, I suppose, because they
are in such a commanding situation.

PADDY ASHDOWN
21 July 1998

I put to him my thesis about the paradox Blair was in, and the hazard therefore faced by the great project. He said it kept him awake at night. But he countered with a rival thesis.

Blair, he said, was a man for the big project. He thought big and long term. He was also, at heart, a Liberal. He was a non-tribal politician. He had an interest in reversing what he regarded as the historic error as a result of which the twentieth century had belonged to the right and not the left. He saw that the way to do this was via what Paddy calls a '*rassemblement*' of the progressive left.

Further, he was quite sure that in his personal heart Blair was a pluralist and not a control freak. Paddy had seen his pleasure at the creation of the Scottish Assembly – a real sense of willingly devolving power. This could not have come to a power-mad centralizer. So what was needed was for Blair to be able to let this, his true nature, emerge in the context of Westminster and national politics as a whole.

Plainly the key event would be the Jenkins commission. Paddy sees this as the make-or-break moment for everything he and the Liberal Party have lived for ever since Jo Grimond. He claims not to know what Jenkins is proposing. He said he thinks Jenkins sees this as his great monument. I said, He wants the monument actually to be built, and this is the problem. I repeated my thesis as to why Blair might well not back PR in a referendum.

Paddy said that for Blair not to do this would be a reversal of his own character, and of much of what he has been seeming to indicate. It would reaffirm the old politics, in a way that betrayed his interest in new politics (my phrase). If the *rassemblement* was to happen, there had to be a new voting system, and a new recognition of the validity of rival parties as part of that. Blair could surely see that, if we were to reverse the false and unnecessary developments of the twentieth century, something like the *rassemblement* of the progressive left had to happen.

In essence this would, he said, be a continuation of what happened on 1 May. Blair would say to his people, You did this, on 1 May 1997, and now is the time to take that logic further and make more secure the progressive-left majority for which you voted. In other words, Blair would have to bring to the cause of PR the same reformist passion he was able to get support for in 1997. It would have to be portrayed, correctly, as the necessary next stage of political reform on which the country embarked in 1997.

I said, This means arguing for PR more on political than on fairness grounds. It means saying, rather openly, that the purpose is indeed (as the Tories complain) to entrench the 'true' will of the British people as an anti-Conservative country. That is quite an inflammatory proposition, and one which seems to be the reverse of high-minded. It would give the Tories a lot of ammunition, rather reversing the 'fairness' argument. Much, therefore, would depend on how the Tories were seen at the time: whether Hague had retrieved popularity enough to ignite a winning campaign against the 'gerrymandering' of the Lib–Lab plan. Quite possibly a PR campaign *could* be won (this is HY not PA talking) against a still hopelessly unpopular Tory Party. But the risk is pretty large that such a campaign would be the best way of reviving the Tory Party's fighting qualities.

He conceded – without actually going into it – that, for the LDs, PR was an essential prerequisite: i.e. that if Blair backed off, he could never hold the party to its present line of accommodation.

I said, It will be hard to fight a PR referendum at the same time as the LDs are fighting Labour as the main opposition in many big-city local elections next May. He quickly agreed that to coincide the two votes would be very difficult. But he then began to flirt with the idea of some grand 'day of democratic decision' (my phrase), on which not only PR but the euro would be folded into a grand campaign in parallel referenda – perhaps even as well as local or Scottish elections. I said I thought this was crazy, and therefore wouldn't happen. It was just a way of Paddy trying to make good his belief that the euro referendum not only should but will take place before the election.

He went on to refer me to his tenth-anniversary speech tomorrow. He is pushing the party to make a proper choice between (a) moving left and (b) getting out ahead, as he puts it. (A very ingenious way of dissolving the right–left paradigm!) Cutting across and around this will be a fight with the LD's strong local-government faction. Paddy wants to direct the party more towards a national agenda, and to get backing for various thrusts at the party conference in favour of initiatives that will in effect take away some power from local authorities. He instanced especially what Don Foster[1] is doing in schools policy.

The conference will be a huge policyfest. The party will be asked to make a series of choices, roughly between the above two tendencies. 'There will be reputations made and lost, according to how the votes go.' It will be almost all based on debate and votes on the big policy document that is coming out in August. He is quite aware that he may lose

---

1 Donald 'Don' Foster: Liberal Democrat MP for Bath since 1992; spokesman on education 1992–9.

some votes, but is determined to lead the party into a more national vein.

He spoke often and passionately about the huge excitement of all this. He was lucky, he said, to find himself leader when all this change was on the verge of happening. There was so much. This was a 'defining moment' – Jenkins really – for the kind of politics not only he but the majority of the British favoured.

I asked Paddy how often he saw Blair. He said, 'Quite often.' I said, 'When did you last see him?' He said, reddening, 'Do you mind if I don't answer that question?'

DAVID MILIBAND
10 Downing Street, 15 September 1998

THIRD WAY   Blair's pamphlet comes out on Monday. It's a serious effort, trying to say what we are, not just what we are not. Trying to redefine social democracy for a modern time. It has been a long time in the making. The aim is for a 'modernization' of social democracy, and to show it is 'not just splitting the difference between left and right'.

The pamphlet 'rehearses the value base' of the Third Way. Talks about the key dimensions of change. It is 'work in progress', rather than a finished project. He likens it, in that way, to Thatcherism, which didn't really kick in until the second term, he says.

One reason we have done it is because we need a 'core narrative' for ministers and departments to see and think through in their implementing of policy. A basis on which they know how and where to take their policies forward. Part of this is getting people 'to understand what we are, no longer just what we are not'. Another purpose: to 'draw in the strands of progressive thought'. We need to 'stimulate more understanding' of what we are trying to do. An aspect of this is getting properly connected to *the intelligentsia*: but that word doesn't mean, for this purpose, just academics and their type. It means heads of local education departments, senior civil servants, hospital-trust executives etc. etc.

His own tasks at the centre can be divided into three (of course): implementation, innovation, communication. (He really does rattle the mantra off.)

Implementation is what they're worried about right now. Can departments really drive things through, after the laws have been passed? How to get the main actors all moving in the same direction. The four main areas are education, health, crime and New Deal.[1] Driving the programme

---

1 The 'New Deal' programme to reduce unemployment by training, subsidized unemployment and voluntary work was introduced by the Labour government in 1998.

through the LEAs, the health trusts, school governors, teachers, parents etc. is a big task. 'Blunkett and Straw have been very good at giving coherence to their Balkanized departments.'

But then innovation is just as important. In the policy unit, likes to think of 75 per cent being implementation, 25 per cent looking forward to new areas. Very important not to get bogged down.

Communication. We must have a 'story'; equally 'a journey' to describe.

EUROPE   I repeat my chiding about them getting the EMU timing wrong. He shows he has not forgotten this, but sticks to the point that it would have been impossible last October.

Tony takes the view that you have to show people the practical benefits of Europe – e.g. doing something on BSE, on improving the environment – before you can hope to start changing national attitudes. DM said, by the way, that the social chapter has far more in it than people realize: four weeks' holiday, days off for sick children (check). So the HY version of the strategy – getting people gradually to understand that Europe is good and harmless – is correct, though DM doesn't accept that the low profile of it is likely to be costly.

Also, however, there has got to be reform of Europe . . .

A successful launch of the euro is very important . . . He thinks that asymmetric shocks are unavoidable – not countries, but regions – and doubts if people are ready for them. He also says that Japan – not Russia – is by far the greatest threat to stability for the euro's launch.

ELECTORAL REFORM   I tried to draw him with my thesis about the referendum being hard to win. He played a straight bat. Said that Tony would be saying to him now, Just hear what Hugo has to say and say how very interesting, and don't reply. Said that it was in the end very personal to Blair. Blair's interest was much more in the philosophy than in the mechanics. The fact that Ashdown and co. agreed with New Labour on many things was what interested him.

HOUSE OF LORDS   He made an especially passionate plea with me about the HL. 'I really hope I can persuade you that getting rid of the hereditaries is a massively important thing to do.' I had to understand how the Tory peers were going to fight tooth and nail. Cranborne will goad them on, whatever Hague says – why doesn't Hague sack him . . . ?

I argue that there should be some indication about stage 2, at least. He said that this was still being discussed 'in here'. But he insisted that if we argued for the two-stage plan to be fully connected, we would never get rid of the hereds. The hereds are getting ready to fight every inch of the way.

There was the usual stuff about *The Guardian*. But he gave a spectacular example – that we had apparently entirely failed to report the substance of the health White Paper. Can this be true? In general he had a wider point: that the news pages were too full of comment, and were unreliable as to factual detail.

MICHAEL PORTILLO
Lunch, the Garrick, 24 September 1998

He is still making his TV films, though the series has started. He says that Channel 4 agreed to do it on the unspoken basis that he was apologetic enough about how the Tories had allowed themselves to be seen. His speech at last year's party conference, which said some of this, was what caught their attention. Against that background of contrition, evidently, Channel 4 felt at ease letting him have what amounts (says HY) to a few hours of Portillo propaganda showcase for himself – 'Oh, you noticed, did you?' he said wryly.

He adds, by the way, that the same production company has been commissioned to make a series with John Major – presumably to coincide with the Major book.[1] Says he believes this will be heavily interview-based, whatever that means.

THE TORIES   To my suggestion that the Tories are making no mark because they have nothing to say about anything except Europe, he ruminates to the contrary. He agrees it is too early to make a mark, but says there are some areas where important ground exists.

One is the constitution, though 'we don't really know where that is going.'

The second is welfare reform, and the need to somehow find a way of decentralizing this, making individual assessment of needs more common, and getting away from the sense of entitlement, which is very ill-policed and is usually not cash-limited. He would like to find a way towards more locally based assessment, which involves having the discretion to deny claims. He says such a scheme has worked pretty well with the Social Fund (replacing the special-needs payments, or whatever they were called – money for cookers etc.). There has been some progress in this direction

1 John Major, *The Autobiography* (London: HarperCollins, 1999).

with the Jobseekers' Allowance, and also the New Deal – but he thinks far more will be needed and should be thought about.

He thinks there must be something also in the field of health: de-entitling; making real the public–private partnership idea, with more to the private. Ditto schools. Labour has not done much in this way at all.

HAGUE has done quite a few things that are subterranean but will be effective, especially re the party organization. The fact that people are ringing up now and saying they haven't had their ballot (for the party referendum) is a way of them finding out they have lapsed their subs, and so becomes a way of recruiting. The central database is helpful.

On Hague generally, MP is routinely loyal. Not by a word disparaging. But somehow unenthusiastic. His main criticism is for John Major. Says that it was disgraceful to resign when he did. Totally selfish. It meant that Hague had to try and make his name while the UK was basking in the Blair ascent. An impossible task. No good reason for Major to do this, except that he thinks only of himself. I reply that Major was so obviously preparing for exit that this was to be expected, psychologically as much as anything else. MP obviously does not agree with the conventional wisdom that Major, if nothing else, is a decent fellow. Remarks sardonic-ally on the wonderful press he has had for eighteen months – quite undeserved, he implies, and one of the many aspects of politics one has to be philosophical about.

Very critical of the Shadow Cabinet for poor support, and of Hague's office for not demanding it – e.g. not turning up when he makes a big speech, and thereby diminishing the occasion so much that no media people turn up either. This was the case with a very good speech Hague gave about welfare and social security.

BLAIR   I ask him whether he thinks Blair is an opportunist, or some-body better than that. He pauses for a long time, and then mutters that he is more of an opportunist. Why? He has no sense of history, nor any sense of the future. He is only for the present, the immediate effect. I reply that I agree about the history, but suggest the ten-year programme bulks very large for him, in a non-opportunistic way. Agreed, there is little intellectual structure, but there are pragmatic goals that are more than opportunist, and are all about incremental gains.

He was very interested in why I thought a PR referendum would not be won. He obviously was very worried about it. We discussed whether the Tories should openly campaign on the grounds of it being unfair to them – designed to exclude them for ever. I said yes; he seemed more doubtful.

EUROPE He thought the Hague referendum served the purpose of giving the leadership legitimacy for its position – 'like all referendums'. It would mean that the position was clear. However, it could have been clearer. He regretted that the line was not starker. You mean, I asked, that Hague should say 'Never' to the euro. No, said MP. Just 'No'. We should simply be saying that we are in principle against the euro, ultimately for political not economic reasons. I said, i.e. never. He again protested. Why should we say that, any more than the Labour Party was thought to be committed when it used to say it was against trade-union-reform laws? The point is, we will take the situation as we find it. If the euro has come about, that is a new situation. But, I asked, won't you at least admit that your line – 'Just say no' – means that if you were leader of the Tory Party and prime minister, you would in no circumstances take the UK into the single currency? He just about conceded that much.

Did he think a national referendum could be won by Blair? Yes, he said. He thought the anti case would be eroded by the least worthy of arguments – that EMU was inevitable, and that we couldn't afford not to be inside it. This would be a strong force. It would probably gain the day.

On the wider point, his line is that there could have been – could still be – two poles of EU: ours and theirs. It was open to us much earlier to make that clear. A competitive set-up almost. We would thereby have gained great influence, which we entirely lost by always sniping at what was proposed but then going along with it. We are therefore not taken seriously, after that history. Did this mean, I asked, that Maastricht should have been vetoed? He didn't think so. Major got his opt-outs, and the party accepted them. But his crucial error was not to seize the moment of the Danish No to say the whole thing should be renegotiated. Instead, he decided as a matter of honour that Maastricht must be saved.

This was utterly perverse. It was a golden opportunity to save himself a great deal of domestic trouble, which it was already clear was looming. The irony is that he then wanted the French referendum in September to be defeated. MP recalls watching the results coming in, at a Cabinet gathering at Admiralty House, where Major had temporarily decamped after the IRA bomb and the window-repairing of 10 Downing Street that was going on.[1] As the results began, Major came up to MP, of all people, with fingers tightly crossed, saying that perhaps it would be all right. By which he meant that the French would say no. What had happened in three months? He had become far more aware of the trouble in the party.

---

1 On 7 February 1991 the IRA fired a mortar shell from a white van parked in Whitehall. The projectile exploded in the garden of 10 Downing Street, and blew out the windows as John Major presided over a Cabinet meeting.

HIMSELF He wants to get back in the House of Commons. He thinks the leadership would have a problem if he got back before the next election, or tried to win a big by-election then. He sees himself as more likely to get a nomination than Patten, but less likely to win the result. (This was my point, which he agreed with – didn't volunteer it.)

He talks like a man who is seriously ambitious. Indeed, he is a serious man. He is interested in serious questions, wants to have serious talk – though not above gossip about Major, and about journalists and editors.

Incidentally, MP was totally opposed to the idea of Clinton being forced out of office. Disgusted by Starr,[1] appalled by the Republican witch-hunt. Not one of Clinton's natural supporters, but feels strongly that the office would be far more weakened by his going than by his remaining as a two-year lame duck. Noted that when talking recently at a school he had asked the class whether C should stay or go. 100 per cent said he should stay.

Extracts from HY's **This Blessed Plot: Britain and Europe from Churchill to Blair** *were published in* **The Guardian** *and* **The Observer** *between 24 and 27 October. On 7 November the book was reviewed in* **The Guardian** *by A. N. Wilson, who called it 'excellent and carefully researched', but who also observed that 'Young is so in love with the European ideal that he frequently made me feel petty and insular for not being carried away with it, as he is.'*

JONATHAN POWELL
Lunch, the Garrick, 18 December 1998

Brisk, a little rough, a little simplistic, a mite unsophisticated, a trifle hesitant despite the speed of his answers: he seemed perhaps unreflective, certainly unmandarin, but very on the ball, of course, and in the end pretty open.

IRELAND He has spent a great deal of time on this – most recently last night, when a biggish deal was made, the virtue of which was that the parties fixed it themselves, without prime ministers coming to push them on, though he, Powell, was a proxy PM in some ways, shouting at Trimble, as he put it, and shouting at the SDLP.

---

1 Kenneth Starr: American lawyer whose report, submitted to Congress, led to the impeachment of President Clinton in the wake of the Monica Lewinsky scandal.

The key to the latest shift is that the Ulster Unionists agreed to ten ministries, which means two for Sinn Fein. This was more than they wanted. But it helps everything along. It means that we only have to get IRA decommissioning and we will have made serious progress. Will this happen? He seemed just a little optimistic, talking about the feel and the signs and the sense he had that, despite the extremely hard-nosed politics dictating everyone's postures, there was some hope. He thought the LVF decommission[1] insignificant detail. He said that nobody thought, of course, that decommissioning meant disarming: it is *entirely* about face – not about capability. I asked whether McGuinness and Adams[2] sincerely wanted it. He said, They are politicians, and play it very tight. But he had had an interesting talk with Adams last night . . .

It takes up between one-third and one-half of his time, and also of Blair's.

EUROPE I asked if there was now a concerted plan to 'take on' the press. He said, No. If there was, it would be done in a rather different way from what has so far happened, which has been a somewhat dis-organized (my word) effort to correct certain inaccuracies and chide the papers that make them.

He mused about why it was that the papers were so hostile to Europe. Said that the one that worried him (them) was not *The Sun* but the *Mail*. *The Sun*, they feel, is taken for granted: is not much listened to: is not surprising. But the *Mail* has turned against the government on several fronts. Is this just Dacre[3] having oppositionist fun? Is he seriously anti? I said I thought he was. JP said that the previous proprietor of the *Mail* was pro-Europe,[4] which further deepened his puzzlement about who was calling the shots. But plainly the *Mail* and its twisting – its persistent anti-Europe position – is what worries No. 10.

On Murdoch, I said I thought that if he changed his business mind, *The Sun* would change but *The Times* would not. He agreed. But he also said it would have been pretty nice if Murdoch could have bought some of Berlusconi's[5] empire – that would have made him see the advantages of European integration. He seems to be of the school, though he didn't say so, that says Murdoch may change his mind for business reasons.

He was more bemused by the pro-Europe press, mentioning *The*

---

1 The Loyalist Volunteer Force was a breakaway faction of the Ulster Volunteer Force. In 1998 it handed over a small quantity of weapons to the Independent International Commission on Decommissioning.

2 Martin McGuinness: former Provisional IRA commander; Sinn Fein MP for mid-Ulster since 1997; Sinn Fein chief negotiator in the months leading up to the Good Friday Agreement of 1998; education minister in the Northern Ireland assembly 1998–2007. Gerry Adams, president of Sinn Fein in Northern Ireland since 1983.

3 Paul Dacre: editor of the *Daily Mail* from 1992.

4 The 3rd Viscount Rothermere died in 1998, to be succeeded by Jonathan, his son, as 4th Viscount.

5 Silvio Berlusconi: media mogul and three times prime minister of Italy – 1994–5, 2001–6 and since 2008.

Independent and the *FT* especially. I told him about *The Guardian*'s ambivalence, following our Monday meeting. Though I said that AR would certainly be pro-Europe when it came to any kind of point. He wondered why the pro-Europe press, including the *FT*, so easily gets swept into the sceptic agenda. Their feeling about tax harmonization epitomized this: the way a virtual non-issue came to dominate the British coverage of the Potsdam summit. He says that the papers of other countries are so amazed by the British papers' coverage that they want to come to the UK press briefings to hear where it all begins!

On the Budget: he was again exasperated by the reporting. Nobody, he says, thinks they can change the British rebate. The only person who mentioned it at Vienna was Kok, who said he would like one too. We have a veto, and they know we will exercise it. What is going on now is everyone taking their negotiating positions. What will come out, probably at the June not March summit, is something back for the Germans, and for the Dutch, which they both should get; something less for Spain et al. from the cohesion funds; something less for France because of CAP reform. But it will be a big, fairly orthodox negotiation about money, of a kind the EU is well able to have and make succeed. (The unspoken implication, though, is surely the probable slowing-down of enlargement. As Roy Denman said to me this morning, remember that the accession of Spain took seven years to complete.)

AMERICA/IRAQ/CLINTON He is very insistent that seeing the US/EU as an either/or is deeply wrong. Just factually false. The US see us as a part of Europe, their link to the EU, their guarantor of sensible things being done there. As for the Europeans, Schröder falls over himself to praise our US links (and hopes to emulate them), whereas Chirac is very Gaullist. Jospin is not like Chirac, however.

Our role in Iraq is eased, EU-wide, by the fact that we took the initiative to get moving on a defence agreement. If France had done this, not us, imagine how it would have looked to everyone. The fact that Blair started this helps us in both hemispheres right now – good credentials on both sides.

Once we had started going down this path, of making the inspection process the test, there came to be nothing else we could do than attack. Otherwise we would never have been believed. Clinton decided – I know at first hand – that, even though it would be thought a distraction from impeachment, he should go ahead. Why should we allow the impeachment process to stop us doing what the US interest requires? That was the argument.

The Republicans, by behaving as they have, have backed themselves into a corner. Like the right in Europe. Do they seriously want Gore as a president?

By the way, it is utterly and wholly inconceivable that Clinton will resign. It would defeat every single thing he has wanted and done. He is only just over 50, has a life to lead. JP recalls having watched C's departure being so often predicted, from Gennifer Flowers[1] onwards.

Blair does get on very well with C. Generational, a shared professional admiration, like-mindedness.

On Iraq: since there has come to be no alternative, we are intent on destroying military capacity. We have hit a lot of it: little is in Baghdad; much is in the desert or on the edge of Baghdad. JP was at a briefing this morning which surveyed the wreckage. The targets are delivery systems not tanks of chemical-war material – for obvious reasons. We think we will have cut out his ability to attack his neighbours for at least two years: maybe longer, depending on his rebuild capacity. That has to be our main ambition, it seems (I infer). If his command and control system is knocked out, he knows he would be flattened by any neighbour he attacked.

Also, this morning JP heard Blair talking to Hosni Mubarak. Mubarak said that he knew Saddam and that he was exceptionally crazy. A very wicked person. A man who did invite allies and friends into his palace for the pleasure of shooting them. A man who believed in terror, and always had done. Beyond the reach of reason, or normal diplomacy. Mubarak is not alone in saying this from first-hand knowledge. Abdullah of Saudi,[2] more Arab than his westernized confrères, is equally horrified by Saddam's pathological villainy. The regime, says JP (echoing Mubarak and others) consists of 100 people, the inner-inner people round Saddam who impose his terror. If you got rid of them, not saying we would have democracy – but perhaps a process that produced a more benign reality.

---

1 Gennifer Flowers: former television reporter, claimed to have had a twelve-year relationship with presidential candidate Bill Clinton in 1992; denied by Clinton at the time, but eight years later he admitted having had sex with Flowers.

2 Abdullah bin Abdul Aziz al-Saud, de-facto regent of Saudi Arabia from 1996, when his half-brother King Fahd suffered a stroke, assumed the Saudi throne in 2005.

1999

DANIEL BERNARD
Lunch, 11 Kensington Palace Gardens [no date]

Exquisite occasion, among the finery. A perfect lunch laid for two in the utmost privacy of a small room, every detail of table and food tastefully done, a tailcoated waiter for each of us . . .

He began by wanting to talk about *The Tablet*.[1] He thought I was head of it. I explained I was head of the Scott Trust, but he wanted to know about *The Tablet*. Where did it fit into the British landscape? He was very interested, he said, because he is a serious Catholic. At the end of lunch, on this tack, he said he would love to be the ambassador to the Vatican. He feels he must leave his present job before the end of the year, being the longest-serving one-place ambassador in the entire French foreign service! But he would not be like the Germans, who alternate Protestants and Catholics in Rome. If France sent a non-Catholic, it would cause a sensation.

On Blair. He has been seeing him for four and a half years, therefore since before he became Leader of the Opposition. Like me, he notes that B has seemed totally unchanged by being PM. Still very much the same person, saying the same things.

However . . . He makes an exception for Europe. He recalls B saying so often that he would start preparing Britain for a more European stance from the beginning of his time. This, says the ambassador, does not seem to have happened. He thinks B has been too cautious. It was not as if one expected any grand, declared policy as such. But, as he notes, Labour is very good at getting messages across, at finding ways. Why have they not done so with Europe?

He feels that such caution could be a strategic mistake. He thinks that if Europe is not decided before the election, it is fanciful to think it will not be a big election issue. He agrees with me that to get the Murdoch problem out of the way in a pre-election referendum would have been better from all points of view.

I asked him how sure he was that EMU would work. Very? Or quite? He had an amusing side-take on the difference between quite and very, which at first he thought meant the same thing – which they sometimes do. But his verdict is that it is a risk, but one about which there is no alternative but to be confident.

He recalls how very stubborn the Brits have been in convincing themselves that it would never happen. Recalls a very particular meeting

---

1 HY was a director of the Catholic newspaper *The Tablet* from 1985 until his death.

between Major and Chirac at Bordeaux, in which Major spoke in this spirit, including offering the view that the whole thing, as well as being wrong for Britain, was wrong for Europe. (He said, by the way, that Hague was very silly – my word – in continuing to say this, and to say that Blair should be pressing the Europeans to stop it. 'This is why nobody listens to him,' said the ambassador.)

He said that Blair's French speech had been delivered in excellent French: very good accent, unlike most Brits. He had wanted to practise for fifteen minutes before. It is pretty hard to give a forty-minute speech in a foreign language, and do it so well.

As to Jospin and Blair – they had hardly met before they became PMs. The links between Labour and the PS [France's Parti Socialiste] were pretty thin in reality. They just did not know each other. But now they get on fine – though there is undoubtedly a gap between French and British versions of what the politics of the left are. For the Socialists, there is an enduring view about the value and role of the state which Labour, under the influence of Thatcherism, has shaken off. France has not had its Thatcher – though, he implied, it would slowly move in a Thatcherite direction. For example the privatization of Air France, once unthinkable, will very slowly be happening.

RICHARD HOLME
Phone, 19 January 1999

HOUSE OF LORDS REFORM   He believes Labour do not know what they want to do. They have no history of an interest in constitutional reform. They do not know how the pieces should fit together – indeed, Irvine, who seems to be most in charge, specifically disclaims any 'grand plan', and criticizes those who urge one.

The Lib Dems have thought about how Scotland, Wales, the regions, even Europe might fit into a new HL. Labour hasn't.

It is slightly clearer what they don't want than what they do want. They do not want the elected element to be more than 50 per cent. But this leaves open the question of how democratic the rest should be: should elements from Wales and Scotland be indirectly elected or appointed by the government (from the local assemblies), for example? And what about England, where there are just these vestigial chambers lying somewhere behind the regional development authorities.

RH says it is not true that Blair wants only 10 per cent elected. He was present when Ashdown said to Blair, 'So about one-third, one-third, one-third?' And Blair replied, Yes, that sort of thing. (Be careful about situating that.)

The Royal Commission could have been quick if the government knew what it wanted. But the White Paper, RH knows, will be very bland as to the terms of reference of the RC. Will leave much open. The wider the terms, the longer it will take (which means there is something dishonest about urging the RC to report by the end of the year).

The White Paper will refer to other countries' experience with second chambers. At which Blair said, 'For God's sake don't let them go swanning round the world.'

Irvine is the nearest thing to a person in charge. Margaret Jay[1] seems to be confined to talking about whether things can be sold to the other parties.

Robin Butler is entirely the wrong chairman. He has no lateral habit of mind. Would be OK if ministers knew what they wanted. But he is certain to be a minimalist, and his whole training is to give ministers what they want – laced with a degree of conservatism where it counts, such as freedom of information, which he was frontally opposed to. (It is his main mark on the constitutional-reform package of the Labour government, per HY.)

The HL reform, per HY, is actually the keystone, the final jigsaw piece, for the constitutional-reform package. To pretend that it can be considered without reference to anything else is crazy.

LIB DEMS AND ALL THAT It is significant that Prescott has never attended the meetings of the LD/Lab constitutional committee. The government side is a floating crap game to some extent. Mandelson will be sorely missed, his role being cut up into little bits of Falconer,[2] Cunningham, Irvine.

When I asked Richard if any other member of the Cabinet really believed in this aspect of Blair's project, he replied, Mo Mowlam. Cook favoured PR and the constitutional package, but was dead against coalition politics. No, he reluctantly had to say, there were no others he could think of besides Mo.

1 Margaret Jay: daughter of former prime minister James Callaghan; first married Peter Jay, subsequently British ambassador to Washington (divorced 1986); created Baroness Jay of Paddington 1992; Leader of the House of Lords 1998–2001.
2 Charles Falconer: Baron Falconer of Thoroton; Minister of State, Cabinet Office, 1998–2001; Lord Chancellor 2003–7.

WILLIAM HAGUE
Centre for Policy Studies Dinner, 19 January 1999

This was held after his lecture on the British Way, a well-attended affair, with lots of the Tory class in evidence – a gathering of the dispossessed. Howard, Saatchi, Forte, Ancram, Davis, Cluff, Duke of Devonshire. The German ambassador, who told me he didn't think it made much sense. I took along Paolo Romani, from the Italian mass-circulation magazine *Famiglia Cristiana*, who had just interviewed me at the Goring Hotel.

Dinner after was attended by journos like Riddell, Jenkins, A. Roberts, A. McElvoy, M. Ivens, T. Hames, P. David[1] et al. I sat next to Sebastian Coe, who was earnest, civil, attentive and tremendously serious – mainly about William, but also about Europe and about the Olympic Committee on which he sits. (Said that the Salt Lake scandal[2] was going to be by far the worst in the IOC history.)

IMPRESSIONS OF HAGUE The lecture was rounded, polished and, I thought, pointless. All about a phantom enemy: the sense that the British have lost their identity and are deeply worried about that. A vehicle for attacking the devolution plans, and also for repeating the line on Europe – but steeped in an unavoidable nostalgia (the more so as WH kept on denying it), and in the desperate assertion that we did not 'need' to do anything we did not want to do: that nothing was inevitable. A favourite word was 'authentically': what is authentically British, and also authentically Conservative.

Perhaps the serious purpose was to try and find ground beyond the Labour Party. To that end, he explicitly gave up on the economic argument, under the guise of wanting to say that the Tories cannot any longer be just an 'economic party' – seen as cruel if efficient (though by the end cruel and inefficient). This implied a desire to open up on the welfare and other social issues. But the only one he was at home with was the national issue – in which, once or twice, he got perilously close to saying that English nationalism was a necessary, even a good, thing (while pretending, perhaps sincerely, to be deploring that particular consequence of Scottish and Welsh devolution). Quite a lot about the St George's flag displacing the Union Jack.

---

1 Peter Riddell; Simon Jenkins; Andrew Roberts, historian and newspaper columnist; Anne McElvoy, *Evening Standard*; Martin Ivens, *Sunday Times*; Tim Hames, *The Times*, Peter David, *The Economist*.

2 In December 1998 it emerged that in 1995 cash bribes had been distributed to some members of the International Olympic Committee, to influence their choice of Salt Lake City, Utah, as the site of the 2002 Winter Olympics. One Congolese member of the IOC, who admitted receiving $70,000, free medical care and a share in a lucrative real-estate deal, called such arrangements 'normal'.

But there was something terribly old about it. For example, exalting the Brits as 'enterprising', he went back to the Industrial Revolution and then to the thirteenth century.

Likewise, he got Blair quite wrong. The need to think that Labour was class-obsessed, was very Old Conservative – and anachronistic. He seemed to think Blair's speech last week to the IPPR [Institute for Public Policy Research] when he claimed the middle classes for Labour was a throwback to class-based politics, when it was entirely the opposite. But Hague kept going on and on about this.

Perhaps his strongest ground is in saying that the Brits are not a regional people, but a local people. Presages a revival of local government, despite the ravages inflicted on it by the Thatcher–Major regimes.

He insists that the Brits were 'really' as he described them, rather than as Labour would have them. This flies in the face of the election result and continuing opinion polls, a quest for 'the real roots of Britishness' beyond the focus groups.

His main attack on the EU seemed to be that it was out of date: offering solutions to the problems that were real enough fifty years ago, but are now not on the table – i.e. war.

An insistence that 'the world is at our feet' – as Brits.

THE DINNER My main impression was that he is simply out of his depth. He is intelligent and committed, and lives for politics. But he is irredeemably young, without any of the charisma or brilliance or boldness or capacity for instilling fear that might make up for that. Beneath the rather strident exterior – the barking Yorkshire voice, the emphatic manner – there seems to be, pretty near the surface, a man who probably knows he should not be in the job. A rather fearful man, nervous, easily knocked off conversational stride by someone older (me). He sits there, presiding, and the centre of attention of course, but there is something play-acting about the scene. He has some of the manner, and all of the applied seriousness, of a new-man party leader determined to make his mark, and spouting the language of a new start and fresh thinking – but it seems hollow. He has no presence. He is a boy. He does not seem at all at ease with himself. The tone of riposte he invites is, in the end, respectfully pitying rather than a fierce engagement. The little resigned grin that is becoming his trademark as he delivers speeches (which he does with word-perfect rhythm) is also a conversational device – and is the opposite of impressive. I kept thinking how very different all this occasion would have been if Kenneth Clarke or even (God help us) Michael Howard had been in the chair.

On a lot of subjects – Lords reform, the details of local government, others – he kept saying that these were subjects for another speech. I asked about Europe, and tried to get him to admit that his whole position – which was to emphasize the separateness of Britain in every time frame and every aspect – led to a position where we might go on pretending to be a full member of the EU (which he insisted we must be), but were actually conducting a concealed withdrawal which would end up in a wholly unsatisfactory position – a position he had referred to in a private conversation with me as schizophrenic ('sometimes more in, sometimes more out') without showing any regret for that state of affairs. (Although he did acknowledge that Mrs T was the prime exponent of taking us further in and talking us further out: yes, he said, and she regrets it. But which part did she regret? I asked. He said it was all a question of drawing a line beyond which we could not go, and it wasn't quite clear where this line was.) His answer was simply to say, with the grin playing, that Britain 'could have it both ways'. Pathetic. When I proposed to him that perhaps after eight years he would want to join the euro, and in that case would he favour more democratic accountability, his reply was instantly to deny that he had ever said we might go in after eight years: what he was saying was that we would not go in for another parliament. He did say that he favoured more political control, but showed absolutely no interest – indeed, he showed total hostility – in starting to devise an acceptable political framework for Europe.

Against all this, however, one must always remember that he has a lot of heavy-hitters behind him: the press. Perhaps the thing to hope for is that he is so inadequate as an Opposition leader – doing badly in this year's elections etc. – that even the anti-Europe press cannot bring itself to back him at the next election, which is certain to be all about the euro, given the fact that the referendum will not be until after the election.

DAVID MILIBAND
Lunch, the Garrick, 8 February 1999

MEDIA He made a big pitch to me about the inadequacies of the media, especially the broadsheet press, especially *The Guardian*. We did not do justice to the simple facts of what the government is doing. He instanced the reporting of last week's new pension vehicle, which A. Darling[1] had entirely failed, I said, to explain adequately on the *Today* programme. He had an exact memory of the space and column inches

1 Alistair Darling: Scottish lawyer; Labour MP for Edinburgh Central since 1987; Chief Secretary to the Treasury 1997–8; Secretary of State for Social Security (later renamed Work and Pensions) 1998–2002; Chancellor of the Exchequer since 2007.

given by the *FT* and *The Guardian*'s relegation of it to page 20, down-page. There were lots of other instances of *The Guardian* simply failing in its task of telling the news – never mind the complaints about straight reporting etc. etc.

Another complaint about us was the fact that there had never been an op-ed piece about education except by Roy Hattersley.

I said that the announcement that No. 10 was going to retaliate against all this by giving more on-the-record interviews and generally longer time on TV and regional press, after being followed by B's appearance on the *Richard & Judy* show, was a contradictory signal. He replied this wasn't so. They asked a lot of serious questions, not just Hoddle.[1] These were not reported. But it gave B a long time to spell out things of a serious kind to an interested audience. This was what the press and Paxman[2] never supplied. They envied Clinton the fact that his eighty-one-minute State of the Union address was watched from start to finish by more than 70 million Americans.

Interestingly, when I rejected some of this, he said instantly that the focus groups show that the appearance on *R & J* was seen as a very serious and worthwhile performance. They also show the same re Frost. All of which reminds one that the focus groups are an ongoing tool of government just about every day.

PUBLIC SERVICES   He is much concerned, linking to the above, about how little is known about the dramatic things that government is doing to health, education, crime. He himself is at the heart of all this. He wonders why people don't understand what is going on, how very much has changed or is being changed.

He also worried about when they should start shifting from the present to the future. They are full of patterns and milestones. They see next April as a big moment when 'delivery' takes over from, I think, evaluation and policy-formation. This is when the minimum wage comes in, when kids can go free to museums, and a whole lot else. However, the next phase is when to end 'delivery' and start thinking and acting towards 'renewal' – these are the vogue concepts. He asked me, historically, how this compared with other governments. I reminded him that Thatcher never thought like that, because she was firefighting and deeply unpopular, therefore didn't have many of the Blair shapes and patterns.

1 England's football coach Glenn Hoddle was sacked on 3 February 1999 after making public remarks about disabled people. Tony Blair, in an appearance on *Richard & Judy* on 1 February, had been asked if Hoddle should resign. Opposition leader William Hague at Prime Minister's questions then asked Blair who should be the next England manager, and Hoddle became, so to speak, a political football.
2 Jeremy Paxman: sometimes abrasive television interviewer of politicians; since 1989, presenter of BBC2's *Newsnight*.

No other government had been so systematic in its thinking of this kind.

GEORGES BERTHOIN
Lunch, the Garrick, 19 February 1999

EUROPE AS A WHOLE One must always remember that the base fact about the EU is that all its members are in there for reasons of national interest, and nothing else. One should also remember how much the world depends on it staying together. For example, if there was no more EU, Russia would be utterly horrified: it would uncage Germany. If Germany wasn't in there, Germany itself would be horrified: the present generation knows as well as Kohl how vital the EU is for the restraint of Germany and the German people. Belgium would explode without the EU. Even Sweden, when outside, knew that the EU was a major balancing factor, and a vital element of stability to the south of them. Spain and Portugal would be unimaginable, to themselves, without the EU. And so on.

They have come to perceive their national interest by discovering that there is no alternative. In 1965, when de Gaulle imposed the empty chair,[1] the Five were furious and talked a lot about finding something else that would dispose of the French. But they could find nothing. Nobody else has found anything since that fulfils the national interests as outlined above.

One should also reflect on how much Europe has become the most stable centre of economic growth and maturity in the world very likely. More and more attractive, GB expects, to investors from all over. He cites all those billionaires who have had to sharply revise their orthodoxies about the Asian miracle and all that. People who, having once opposed institutional strength on the global scene, now strongly argue for it. George Soros[2] is one of the biggest players who has changed his mind and stance. But look also at Bill Gates[3] – setting up a massive foundation, and wanting to get things out of the Commission.

---

1 In June 1965, in a bitter argument with other member states over the Common Agricultural Policy, President de Gaulle withdrew the French representative from Brussels. The episode became known as 'the empty chair crisis'. It was resolved in January 1966 in what became known as the Luxembourg compromise.

2 George Soros, Hungarian-born financier, speculator and philanthropist, credited with having broken the Bank of England on Black Wednesday 1992, used his billions through the Soros Foundations to fund political change in the former Soviet bloc.

3 Bill Gates, founder of Microsoft, and one of the world's richest men, began a philanthropic career in 1994. The Bill and Melinda Gates Foundation, established in 2000, is the largest charitable organization in the world.

BLAIR AND THE EU   Blair certainly has the opportunity to make a great mark. This will not be seriously impeded for the next three years – the span within which it is reasonable to expect him to indicate more clearly what he intends to do. He has a considerable magic in Europe. Most of the centre-left want to adopt more market-oriented economic policies, and he has shown the way. They find it hard to do this, but that is the way they know they have to go, now that the euro is in place.

There is an equivalence between Blair and Jospin, in that both of them are awaiting their next election victory. Jospin cannot truly 'Blairize' until he has won again. Blair cannot fully 'Europeanize' until he has won again. That is the way they see it.

Jospin, by the way, is a wonderful second-in-command – that is why Mitterrand made him Secretary General of the party – but he is rather narrow. He is not a man of grand vision. He is, however, very good at explaining, and at patiently moving forward.

Blair has much to contribute to US/EU rapprochement. He could be the key figure, in effect. Moreover, he has an important role in the defence momentum.

But . . . Kosovo shows how inadequate the arrangements are. The Franco-British effort is simply a coalition. That is, not *communautaire* in any way. It is the essence of inter-governmentalism. It is proof that the EU as a whole is not working together. It is nowhere near producing a common action plan.

Milosevic is able to exploit this. What do you suppose he thinks when he keeps getting the American, the Russian and the Franco-Brit people waiting on him? There is no one voice. Holbrooke[1] was effective because he just said, Stuff the others, this is what I am demanding, and Milosevic bent to him. The Euros cannot do that.

GB has been much involved with Yugoslavia from the beginning (through efforts by the Trilateral Commission[2] to get things going in some way). He is knowledgeable about it.

But what this shows is the dire need for the Commission to have foreign affairs under its wing. There has to be a 'European' voice. All right, not one that cannot be vetoed, and does not take account of national opinions. But at least a single voice speaking for all, unless the voice goes too far. This has to come through the Commission, Berthoin thinks. But,

---

1 Richard Holbrooke: US foreign service; US representative to UN 1999–2001; US Council on Foreign Relations since 2001.

2 The Trilateral Commission is a private organization, originally composed of influential individuals from the US, Europe and Japan, to promote political and economic cooperation. Its membership has included, at various times in their careers, Jimmy Carter, George H. W. Bush, Bill Clinton, Dick Cheney, Edward Heath and Georges Berthoin.

whichever way it comes, it must represent the idealism and the constructive role that the EU plays. Which it is nowhere near playing yet.

After all, even the Contact Group[1] cannot agree. Another plus for
Milosevic.

THE COMMISSION Is in very bad trouble. Of course, there
always has been corruption. Ever since the Hallstein[2] days, when an
Italian travel agency was found to have an exclusive contract for all EEC
travel: a vast account. Hallstein stamped on it very hard.

It is a great tragedy that the Parliament did not do the proper thing
when given the chance to vote down the Commission. At one blow, this
would have given political life to Europe. You wouldn't have needed
declarations and treaties – it would simply have happened. The Parliament
would have asserted accountable power, the Commission would have
been forced to examine itself.

But the Commission is only part of the problem. The non-transparency
of the Council is indefensible. Not even possible to know what the Council
is discussing. Absurd. And very damaging to the whole notion of a
political Europe.

Meanwhile, the Commission is traduced. Its shortage of staff is a big
reason for the corruption which certainly goes on. The problem is that
the EU takes on more and more tasks, but doesn't have the staff to do
them or the staff to invigilate the consultancies which step in in place of
the non-existent staff. The consultancies, indeed, report on themselves!

Of the Commission staff, about one-third are in the linguistics department. Not just interpreters, but translators: and often qualified lawyers
who have to supervise the translation. The actual bureaucracy is thus
very small . . .

THE BRITISH CONTRIBUTION Could be in the field of political reform above all. Not in EMU: EMU will have been done. But
there is much to do with political reform, which the British are good at.
The Brits would be good at working out how you can have a Europe that
does more and yet is more accountable.

Agreed: this can probably only happen after entry to the euro has
settled the British existential crisis once and for all.

The foreign-policy field – and especially the large view of relations
with the US – is another field where the UK could be vital.

1 The Contact Group, made up of Britain, the US, France, Germany, Italy and Russia, had overseen the last
phases of the Bosnian conflict. After the fighting in Kosovo, it imposed sanctions on former Yugoslavia and
banned imports of equipment that could be used for internal repression.
2 Walter Hallstein: German politician; first president of the Commission of the European Economic Community,
1958–67.

A pet scheme of Georges's is for improving QMV without abolishing the veto. He believes in the veto. It is necessary, to retain a national government's right to protect vital interests. But it should work like this. Yes, a veto in the Council. But this then has to be defended in the European Parliament, where the Commission will also give its view, as will the other governments. There will then be a vote. It would return to the Council, where a majority vote would be enough to overturn the veto if the Parliament has not supported it. This would politicize and open up the whole thing miraculously. It would make governments wary of using their veto, since they would not control the Parliament or even their own delegation in the Parliament. They would have to think long and hard before doing it. But it would still leave a veto that could be defended as a weapon in the hands of a government that really cared.

GORDON BROWN
11 Downing Street, 3 March 1999, a week before the Budget

(Relocated from Treasury. Walking up Downing Street, I saw first the Cardinal,[1] then Clare Short, then Brown – they were giving a TV statement about Third World debt.)

WELFARE-TO-WORK This was Brown's reason for asking me to see him. He still believes – an *idée fixe* from long ago – that I am deeply interested in w-to-w – presumably on the basis of my having written one piece about it! Such is the way one gets labelled: Thatcher was rather the same. Sometimes it works in one's favour, sometimes against.

The Budget will be about work, enterprise, family.

The work part is welfare-to-work and the need to extend it. It has been amazingly successful, he says (paper attached). Youth unemployment is down 50 per cent since Labour came in; long-term unemployed down 57 per cent. Yes, this is much helped by the economy. But there is value in the programme as well.

The next stage is the harder group: the hard-to-employ group. 'For these we need . . . not so much advice . . . as, well, coaching. Mentoring.'

What is true of the UK is very, very obvious: the link between education and work. Very roughly: with GCSEs you get £100 a week more, with A levels £200, with a degree £250.

---

1 Cardinal Basil Hume: abbot of Ampleforth 1963–76; archbishop of Westminster and cardinal from 1976 to his death in 1999; had taught at Ampleforth College, where HY had been a pupil.

The programme has been welcomed by companies. And they do not want it just for the subsidies. Many people are taken on without subsidy: just having been through the gateway, having been mentored, advised etc. What firms want are people with commitment. Seventy-four per cent of the w-to-w jobs are non-subsidized. In the US, Clinton's State of the Union message was proud to say that 10,000 US firms had taken on youth unemployed in a similar scheme. Here we have 40,000 who've signed up.

'I am personally surprised by the fall in youth unemployment.' We must now make it even more effective (the programme).

I said that the Budget is not what it was: no longer a very dramatic and unique event. He replied, It certainly is big for me (with a laugh). Yes, the Budget used to be about dividing up the national cake. That's what it was about for a hundred years. And yes, what people are still most interested in is fags, booze and car tax.

But now it is about how you position Britain in the global economy: what you can do for the country to make it function better in the global environment. It's therefore to do with competitiveness, skill-enhancement and so on. And supporting enterprise.

One does float things before, he said. I asked him what. He wasn't very precise, but went on about enterprise. 'The Budget as the dividing of the national cake is over, but there is much else.' It is all about what is going on in the world outside.

There are still plenty of secrets. Until I stand up on Tuesday, nobody will know whether my November forecast is still right, what money will be going to which departments etc.

The old Budget secrecy was far more about protecting the Treasury from proper scrutiny, under the pretence that this was all about national security, markets etc.

The enterprise agenda has to address low British productivity: 20 per cent lower than Germany, 30 per cent lower than the US. This is a real challenge. Therefore, how to equip for new tech, how to encourage science and development, what to do to help small business, to equip for better e-commerce. A mixture of public investment, exhortation, private tax breaks. (All this was imperfectly scrawled in my notes.)

EUROPE You were unkind, he told me, to say in October '97 that we had run away from a decision. On the contrary, he went on, I felt I had moved the government on from a position of agnosticism to one where we had decided we wanted to join – if the circumstances were right. This was my pressure, my idea.

Also, I wanted Tony to make his statement last week. (HY had written the contrary.) I persuaded him to make it. Although there is no change in the words of the policy, it is more than a changing of gear: it signalled our commitment.

The Tory line is more and more ridiculous. There will be rows at Treasury questions tomorrow. They have moved from being against entry for ten years, to being against a preparation plan, to refusing to discuss it at all (by withdrawing D. Davis from the HC committee – check committee). They are behaving like Labour did in the early 1980s, just wanting to deny the world as it is.

I said that the press had done Blair a favour by painting him as so decided. They were forcing more to be said by the government. He replied that television was better than the newspapers. He said, I was rather amazed to hear, that TV 'did give the impression of inevitability – of the process'. Unlike the press.

He regards the Owen position[1] as being in effect wholly anti. It is, he remarked, totally absurd to be preparing for something that is only meant to happen in ten years' time.

More worrying is the state of the European economy. Growth in Germany revised down to 1.5 per cent, Italy 1.4, France 2.0 (check).

The real trouble is the Bank. Duisenberg[2] feels obliged to react very conservatively against every public speech made by a politico calling for growth. The ECB could change its own remit. It could define price stability in a symmetrical way; it could ask finance ministers to decide a target; it could introduce proper transparency; it could promote adjustments in the stability pact. All this could be done without a treaty change, in dialogue with finance ministers.

There is Lafontaine[3] grandstanding. L is hooked on several misfortunes. Tax harmonization, which nobody wants or will give. Currency zones, which the US won't agree. Interest-rate cuts, which Duisenberg, for the above reason, is very opposed to. GB believes, by the way, that a deal was done before the ECB began by which there would be the cut in December – but none for several months after that. This is a very bad policy.

Are we able to influence this? The trouble is that the finance ministers, who should talk about all this, find it hard to do so in Ecofin[4] because thereafter the press hype up the pros-and-antis zero-sum game aspect of all these meetings (not a phrase GB used).

1 David Owen supported UK membership of the EU, but publicly opposed some aspects of integration, and led a 'no to the euro' campaign.
2 Wim Duisenberg: Dutch politician; president of the European Central Bank 1998–2003.
3 Oskar Lafontaine: German finance minister 1998–9; chairman of the SPD 1995–9.
4 The Economic and Financial Affairs Council of the Council of the European Union, made up of finance ministers from the member states.

This is going to be a hard year for the euro, because of the lack of growth.

He is also worried by the ECB saying that they can't cut (or raise) rates because of their different effect in Germany and Spain (which apparently Duisenberg is tending to argue). This plays into the hands of the Euro-sceptics all over, and is a big mistake. What is the answer to it? To have symmetrical inflation targets . . .

(He went off in a great rush to see Blair, urging me to keep in touch and expressing himself ready to be of help whenever I wanted it.)

ALASTAIR CAMPBELL
Phone, 8 March 1999

The problem with the British press is that it is stuck in the past. Fighting old battles. Thus, at Petersburg,[1] when for the first time (?first?) the real story was about the Franco-German disagreement, they couldn't cope with it. Running around like headless chickens asking where was the story: i.e. where was the Britain-versus-the-rest story.

The European media are ahead of the Brits in understanding what our position is, and how our position is influencing the broader picture.

AC says he finds it very, very frustrating dealing with the incessant unwillingness of the British press to tell the story as it is.

Did you notice the News International papers at the weekend? he asked. They said that Tony was telling the Europeans to be more like the Americans – yet they overlooked the fact that the US has minimum wage, TU-recognition laws etc. Paint the US–Euro divide as black and white, which of course it isn't. But everything has to be fed through their anti-Europe frame of mind.

Another example was Blair's Milan speech, which was reported by several papers as a 'Lafontaine snubs Blair' story – because of L's apparent partial reaction.[2] Yet that wasn't the story, and the speech was carefully nuanced.

In these circumstances it is impossible to get a proper debate going.

He repeated the long-ago fact that when he brought Blunkett in to meet the foreign press, they were vastly impressed – whereas the British

---

1 Not St Petersburg, Russia, but Petersburg near Bonn in Germany, the scene of an informal meeting between European leaders, who were preparing for another encounter in Milan which would in turn be a preparation for a formal EU summit in Berlin on 24–25 March 1999.

2 At a congress of European socialist parties in Milan on 1–2 March, Tony Blair urged his colleagues to reject regulation and high taxes, and embrace enterprise culture. The *Daily Mail* on 3 March reported that 'German finance minister Oskar Lafontaine swept unexpectedly on to the platform and demanded a huge cut in interest rates and higher public spending – the opposite of what Mr Blair had advocated.'

press would regard it as unthinkable: or even, I surmised, a kind of sick joke.

MICHAEL PAKENHAM
Dinner here, 20 March 1999

KOSOVO THOUGHTS . . .   The worst rationale for bombing is that NATO's credibility will be ruined if we don't. Were you saying that NATO would then be disbelieved as a defender of the West against a resurgent Russia? Nonsense.

The only rationale is humanitarian (I think he said). If you know that Serb forces are gathered waiting to enter across a bridge, if you knock out the bridge you can do some good, and hopefully with little loss of life.

He seemed to say that we might have made mistakes in getting to where we have got.

He agreed that if we do start bombing, it will be the independence not the autonomy of Kosovo that will become the object. Yes, he said, not many people seem to have realized that that is the logical consequence.

But there was more, which I have forgotten.

WAR THOUGHTS (MY OWN)   This is the nature of modern warfare: that there are wars that cannot be decisively won. But that does not justify saying we should not, necessarily, fight them. This is a deeply messy, terrible event. It is pretty amazing that Clinton got the Senate to agree what it did agree . . .

ROGER LIDDLE
The Garrick, 28 April 1999

THE WAR   RL seems pessimistic. He talks about a deal between the US and Russia to be able to keep US troops out of the action, and take the rug from under the Europeans. He seems to think this is the way it might end. He asked me how I thought it might end. I said, Partition – which he frowned deeply at.

DEFENCE FUTURE   For the Brits, the main problem is the army. Very overstretched. That is why Northern Ireland is so important. The commitment, especially with the cycling of tours of duty, is very extravagant. If we got peace, that would free up the army, which is already stuck with 4,000 in Bosnia, with maybe 8,000–10,000 envisaged for Kosovo.

CABINET He remarked on the weak state of the Cabinet. There were so few strong people; he said that even Tony and Peter were now worried that there was too much non-dissent. I described Byers and Milburn[1] as robotic, and he said this was the *mot juste*. Nobody would break any new ground at all. Nowhere near like Crosland et al. Everyone staying on the narrow track. Far too much conformity.

He put this down to the price of the SDP still making itself felt (which Roger was part of, of course). Not only did it remove a cadre of good people, but it planted the demand for total allegiance in New Labour. Nobody wanted to repeat what had happened in the eighties: the trauma was still at large.

He kept repeating this point. That Gordon was just about the only one. Cook was a pretty broken figure, in an odd way. The need, therefore, for Mandelson to come back.

JOHN KERR
The Garrick, 7 May 1999

KOSOVO The meeting yesterday (German G8) was on the whole useful. We got a statement that held all our positions, with admittedly the exception that it did not mention NATO, and did not put down a deadline for the Serbs to leave. But it retained what we need and want. It was achieved, moreover, with important British input. First Emyr Jones Parry, political director,[2] had a big hand in the language. Second, Robin Cook, where others were drifting a bit, was able to take a very clear and strong line. Albright was quiet, Fischer[3] has his political problems, many of the smalls were anxious for softness. Robin is at his best at these times: it brings out his combative streak, he never likes ceding a point, and his parliamentary skill is deployed well. Also, he has the advantage of knowing his position very clearly, and of having a PM and a party at his back who he does not have to trim towards.

The Russians are now on board. This is important. They are not there taking Milosevic's side, and coming to NATO having taken his position. They are offering themselves as brokers, going to M with our demands.

1 Stephen Byers: Labour MP for Wallsend 1992–7, for Tyneside North since 1997; Secretary of State for Trade and Industry 1998–2001, for Transport, Local Government and the Regions 2001–2. Alan Milburn: Labour MP for Darlington since 1992; arch-Blairite; Secretary of State for Health 1999–2003.

2 Sir Emyr Jones Parry: diplomat; political director at the FCO 1998–2001.

3 Joseph Martin 'Joschka' Fischer: German foreign minister 1998–2005.

If they were in the former position, they would be unacceptable and ineffective.

They do seem to have understood that it would be unwise to tie themselves to M. They look to the moment when the cameras as well as the troops go in, and we begin to see the devastation that has occurred by way of cleansing. They don't want to be tied to this too closely. They also do not want to be taken for granted by M.

However, difficult times loom. In one week, perhaps two, Primakov[1] and/or Chernomyrdin will come back with something from Milosevic, and it will probably be unsatisfactory. For my part, says JK, I would refuse on principle anything they come back with. It will certainly be soft, and it will certainly give M something of what he wants. This will be a kind of moment of truth for the alliance.

The only judge and jury of a deal must be the Kosovars. Whether they will return is the issue. Will they see they are going to be defended, and that they will have a life free from Serb oversight and tyranny? This is the vital war aim. Rather than the disposing of M. That may happen as a collateral event, and should be seen that way – not least because we need M to make the deal, to be humiliated into accepting it, whether or not he survives (that is HY not JK language, but the sense was JK's).

For JK, avowedly not a military man but one who has obviously talked to military men, the idea of a ground advance is perfectly practicable as long as it is prepared for. Kosovo is no bigger than Yorkshire. You don't go in with tanks, along terrible roads and defiles. You go in with a lot of troops and yomp from one end to the other, à la Falklands. The de-mining takes place backwards – i.e. de-miners go quite far ahead and work backwards. It is quite possible. The armoured personnel carriers can then move forward. He sees no reason – a thought he expresses in unblustering language – why we cannot do this, if we have enough troops.

This would not require vast armour coming in through Thessaloniki. The port of Montenegro could be the launch point. (It is surprising, by the way, that Milosevic has not seized Montenegro or set out to destabilize Macedonia.)

JK talked about an invasion starting in August. But he also kept saying that the preparations had not been made. There were plenty of plans, he said, for the army deployment in face of a voluntary Serb departure, but the more aggressive model, he implied, was still not planned for.

He was sanguine also on the ground that the Serbs had no national memory of military victory for a long time. The conscript army would be getting worried. They faced a war having had a lot of stuff knocked out, a loss of petrol etc. Thinking about what was facing them over the hill, they would weaken. They were not hard to beat, he said.

Washington, obviously, is the key. He has nothing but contempt for Clinton in this respect. When McCain[1] introduced his motion to give the President all necessary powers – available, but not obligatory to use – C was the first US president who sent his boys up to the Hill to lobby against it. He didn't want to be put on the spot, having to decide to use his powers. As a result, he is in Congress's hands.

This is the end, due to his lack of authority. The Lewinsky saga goes on. He just lacks cred. Moreover, the Republicans know they botched the impeachment, but are determined that he must not get away with it. They also think he is a total sleaze. This means he is likely to be deprived of what eventually emerged over Bosnia: the segment of the Senate which, while not voting for US engagement, did not vote against it – saying, in effect, that if this is what the President has decreed, we Americans will not block it, because that would seem to imperil our boys. All that is now very much at risk.

Will the US people want to let the bogus peace be made? A great deal depends on the CNN factor. Will the news from Kosovo be crowded out by tornados or murders elsewhere, taking the cameras' eye off the ball? It could be a vital factor. We need to keep these pix of refugees constantly in front of the American people's eyes.

At present, JK says he is not too worried about this. The statements made at the NATO fiftieth are there. Clinton made his statement this week when over in Germany trying to help Schröder.[2] But much depends on how he reacts to whatever the Russians produce.

It is true that the UK is at the vanguard edge of hawkishness (my phrase not his). He agrees that Blair has a certain moralizing innocence about it all. But Blair is at bottom right. He is using his freedom. Italy? D'Alema is better than Dini:[3] much tougher and more enduring. Germany: Fischer faces the real possibility of the Greens denouncing him, and therefore either him having to change parties or the Red–Green coalition collapsing or both. Schröder is more straightforward about it, though he will suffer from a coalition collapse of course. France? The cohabitation is always hard. Jospin is basically anti-war, Chirac basically very pro-war, more so than he says in public. The French position will be related to the

1 John McCain, Republican senator for Arizona since 1987; 2008 US presidential candidate.
2 NATO's fiftieth-anniversary celebrations, which began in Washington on 23 April 1999, were overshadowed by the bombing of Serbia and a boycott by Russia – not a member, but invited as a guest. 'We meet to honour NATO's past, to chart its future, to reaffirm our mission in Kosovo, where NATO is defending our values and our vision of a Europe free, undivided and at peace,' President Clinton had said.
3 Massimo d'Alema: prime minister of Italy 1998–2000. Lamberto Dini: prime minister of Italy 1995–6; foreign minister 1996–2001.

American. If the US chickens out, then France will denounce the US and become more pro-war. If the US stays in, France will perhaps snipe at the way Washington is doing it.

You can be sure of one thing: if the US decides not to go in properly, the White House will be furiously spinning to the effect that this is all due to the feeble Europeans.

Blair's position is being much strengthened with the Europeans. Unlike Iraq, where arguably (though falsely, says JK) he could be seen as Poodle Blair, this is not the case with Kosovo. If the US pulls back, then Blair will score with the Europeans for his manifest refusal to be Clinton's poodle.

If it does fail, then NATO will be damaged. (1) Its aspirant members will see it as a paper tiger, and will be less keen to join and offend Russia by doing so. Note how Latvia and Estonia, to name but two, have been privately urging us to make sure we get rid of M: very hawkish: they don't want Russia to get any consolation. But the whole enlargement move will weaken. (2) The NATO Europeans will be seen to, or will start to, perhaps fragment. The internal disagreements will come more out into the open. The coalition governments will find their anti-NATO left becoming more important. (3) Relations with the US will be hard, with each side blaming the other for failure.

Will Blair suffer internally, domestically? JK is not sure. He agrees that perhaps B has got very far out in front, with language that cannot be seen to have been sustained.

GORDON BROWN
Treasury, 15 June 1999

AFTER THE EURO ELECTIONS He began, quite heatedly, saying that we always seemed to meet on days when I had done a column which he disagreed with. (I think in fact he was referring to a meeting we had in November, when he took the chance to criticize the last chapter of my book, which he had just read.) He said my piece today was quite wrong. Obviously, he said, I was referring to him when I wrote that ministers other than Blair had been idle and uninterested in the Euro election, and did not talk about Europe enough.

He said the fundamental error was to think that he or anyone else could now start talking direct about the euro. If we did, he said, people would continue to see the euro as something that enemy Europe was forcing on Britain. This would be self-defeating. The task was to talk about Britain in Europe, Britain in the world – get people to understand that Britain and Europe were bound together for all kinds of good and beneficial reasons. Only after that did it make sense to get on with the euro.

We had taken a very big step forward in October 1997, and another stride when Blair introduced the changeover plan. These were substantial developments, along with the several millions we were committing to changeover. But we also had to recognize weaknesses, and we had to be frank about them.

He seemed to instance two in particular. (1) The ECB and its lack of an economic strategy. Does anyone know, he asked, what Europe's economic policy is, what its attitude to debt is, what its inflation target is, what its monetary policy is, what its interest-rate policy is? The culprits here are very much the finance ministers. They do not get together; they have not worked out a policy. But, I asked, did this mean a form of European economic government? He shrank from the idea. But he did not really say how the finance ministers should get their act together. (2) The next problem was the need for economic reform in Europe. We had to keep pressing that side of the case. We needed to have more employment flexibility – he spoke with admiration of the fact that US tradition enabled people to think it natural to change jobs often, and not to hang around in between. And other such inflexibilities in the usual European methods.

Overall, he kept insisting that it was important for the pro-Europe side in the UK to be critical of the euro and the way it was run. He resented the fact that if he ever uttered a reform proposal this was construed as an attack on the euro. It was not. But he and we had to make clear our position and our case for reform.

He claimed that, shortly after Blair made his February statement,[1] Hague managed to conflate two groups of people: those opposed tooth and nail to the euro, and those who wanted to reform it. This was a bad basis for the discussion. But GB spoke for the first time as if Hague was setting the agenda – and GB was at the same time whingeing about it, along with the heavy sceptic press that backed him up.

He kept insisting that he was sure the argument could be won. 'We will win,' he said. But it would take a long time. You cannot undo twenty years of Euro-scepticism in a short time.

I asked him whether he still thought there would be a referendum shortly after the next election, He corrected me: 'in the first part of the next parliament – assuming we get elected'. But he repeated that the case had to be made. 'We will have to make a judgement.'

---

1 On 23 February Tony Blair addressed the House of Commons on the euro and said, 'Our intention is clear. Britain should join a successful single currency, provided the economic conditions are met. It is conditional. It is not inevitable. Both intention and conditions are genuine.'

I asked him what the consequences would have been if after another ten years we were not in the euro. He seemed unable to contemplate this seriously. But he said that inward investment would have suffered, and outward investment by British firms into the euro area would have drifted away from us. When I said that perhaps investment was more driven by deregulated flexible labour than by euro membership, he said he didn't believe it. In the medium to long term, he insisted, thoughtful business people will not take that line.

I proposed that we could get into the bizarre situation where our economy was doing too well to shock the Brits into getting the euro. He replied, Sensible business people would not take so short-term a view. He added that we should always remember that Germany and France, for all their alleged sluggardliness, have higher productivity than we do. They are not basket cases, he said.

He also dismissed my suggestion that perhaps people would say that our good war in Kosovo had proved we could be a leader in Europe without belonging to the euro. It was economic stuff that mattered, he said, not defence arrangements.

He said he thought Clarke et al. would be blaming him and the government for not coming out harder. But they were wrong.

All in all, GB was rather less impressive than usual. Assertive, rather complaining about the press, distressed by Hague's setting of the agenda in a dishonest way.

CHRIS PATTEN
26 June 1999

Phone, to discuss dinner. Also talked about the Cardinal Hume funeral, which he found to be English Catholicism at its best. Did Blair take communion? And Hague and Ashdown and Donoughue? He thought probably not: the service sheet had invited people to go up for a blessing if not communion.

IRELAND[1] It has been a very draining time, he says. Forty public meetings, all of them difficult, ten thousand people, all of them engaged. A very intimate kind of feeling. For example, at the end of one meeting, which he had concluded with soft words about reconciliation, a little lady got up as he was about to leave and said, 'I agree with you about

---

1 From 1998 to 1999 Chris Patten chaired the Independent Commission on Policing in Northern Ireland, also known as the Patten commission.

reconciliation. But I'd just like you to know that the man who killed my son is sitting two rows away.'

He agrees that the letting out of jail could give Blair some real problems (my thesis). Trimble has gone as far as he can. That was obvious to CP in his journey round Ulster. He is walking on very thin ground. His side see themselves as having made all the sacrifices. They think the other side's concession on the constitutional point[1] does not count. They forget about it – what they care about are more day-to-day things like killing and weapons.

He thinks Blair may be going through the stage common to all British prime ministers: start with every intention to make progress on Ireland and Europe, but then get turned off them both and thoroughly pissed off. But he agrees that Blair has probably gone as far as anyone could go on Ireland.

EUROPE He is worried that the generalized anti-Europe line is not being answered. It is making ground. He thinks his job will be not so much to talk about the euro too early in his time, but to make a lot of noise (my phrase) about the virtues of Europe and the EU, albeit reformed. He does believe that we need to start putting some new words and meaning round such concepts as subsidiarity and democratic deficit.

Leon Brittan is right about Blair: having gathered all this popularity, why is he not using it?

Prodi: Blair told him that he thought Prodi would be either very good or very bad – he couldn't tell which for sure. CP thinks P is being much advised by Sutherland, Davignon[2] and Delors, and that he wants to reform the Commission, make it stronger etc.

It is true that Kinnock will be vice-president for administration. NK is not best pleased, and is trying to add on a few things to that.

He himself has no idea what he will get. He wants competition, and knows van Miert[3] wants him to have that. Also knows that Prodi regards him highly. But the trouble is that the French may well oppose it, and want a small-country person in this very sensitive job. He thought the idea of his being the social-affairs commissioner was crazy. 'I have form,' he said. He was on the Cabinet committee that did Maastricht, including the opt-out.

He especially thinks the government is negligent in completely failing to rebut the argument about the strong pound. Should be saying thanks

---

1 Under the Good Friday Agreement, Sinn Fein formally conceded the legitimacy of British rule in Northern Ireland, if that remained the majority choice.

2 Étienne, Viscount Davignon: Belgian politician, financier; vice-president of the European Commission 1981–5.

3 Karel van Miert: Belgian politician; European commissioner for competition 1993–9.

to the Opposition for pointing out how successful their economic policies have been.

On the Tories, he says that they will be moving into Europhobia. It looks inevitable. What Hague does not understand is that the more he gives, the more they will push for. The editorials in the *D. Telegraph* are written by an elected MEP, Daniel Hannan,[1] who runs the line that they must get out of the EPP. This kind of thing will go on further.

PHILIP GOULD
7 July 1999

He said, very effusively, how wonderful my book was. Everyone had read it. It had captured the thinking of all of us, he said. The argument was entirely persuasive. It was a wonderful, very important book. He didn't actually say Blair himself had read it, but his message was that all the Blair people saw the point of it.

However, he then said, What can we do about it? Tony is very well aware of all the arguments, all the factors. But what can we do about public opinion? Every time I do a focus group I get the *Daily Mail* coming back at me. It is terrible. People going on about the pound and the Europeans and how much they dislike the idea of closer union. You get it all the time.

How are we going to deal with this? he asked rhetorically. He didn't sound as though he had any ideas, or any great urgency about answering. He said it was all very well saying that Tony should take the lead, but if he got too far out in front he would lose the people and lose the issue. It would make things worse, not better, if it went wrong. 'I could tell Tony to do it, but then he would lose his government. He would finish up with a majority of 10.'

I said I had written in October 1997 that the EMU decision was a mistake. I also said there should have been a referendum at that time (a referendum in principle, to be acted on when the economic time was right). He said, 'You may well be right, you may well be right.'

When I said, Maybe the risk would get less in the second term, he did not respond at all positively. He seemed to have almost given up on the possibility. I urged him to remember that the time-vice moved on the other side as well: the longer we waited for the British people, the more

---

1 Daniel Hannan: *Daily Telegraph* leader-writer; special adviser to Michael Howard 1997–8; Conservative MEP for South-East England since 1999; expelled from the EPP (European People's Party) in 2008, after a campaign against the Lisbon Treaty.

distant we would grow from the Europeans – and the very act of delay became a self-fulfilling prophecy of impossibility.

He asked what I thought should be done. I said it would be a start if many more ministers than Blair would talk about Europe as a normal part of their daily lives, reflected in their speeches. He immediately said, You mean, they should start challenging public opinion, taking an aggressive line (or something like that). I said, They should start steadily normalizing Europe, just as a start and a way of draining some of the poison out of the British mind.

CONCLUSION TO BE DRAWN This was the most revealing conversation I'd had on the subject for a long time. PG is very influential with Blair. His focus groups plainly do have a vitally influential role. He, whom MacShane vouches for as a gut-instinctive European, is not willing to advise taking any kind of risk.

I also learn that focus-group politics remains in general the instinctive benchmark which they reach for before anything else.

Also, the second term dominates everything . . . As if we didn't know it already!

DAVID MILIBAND
Lunch, Wilton's, Jermyn Street (very luxurious), 16 July 1999

We agree that this is a de-luxe establishment, which stretches to the limit the New Labour addiction to classlessness. But David is quite unabashed. He does try to remove his jacket, but the waiter restrains him. He says that some of his colleagues would have come in svelte tieless and collarless shirts, and would presumably have been excluded. But he himself is delighted to be here, remarking only that last night, his birthday, he went to the River Café.

ASHCROFT AND THE TORIES He opens with this, reflecting no doubt the party machine's preoccupation. He thinks the Tories are in trouble over Ashcroft.[1] We agree that MA's role as ambassador to the UN and to (also from?) the EU makes him a strange person altogether. He says the Tories have some questions to answer, and especially Douglas Hurd has questions to answer ('Not for the first time,' he mutters).

---

1 Michael Ashcroft: businessman, politician; treasurer of the Conservative Party 1998–2001; deputy chairman since 2005; principal donor to the party; made Baron Ashcroft of Chichester 2000.

DEVOLUTION This had been Hague's speech subject yesterday. DM thinks it dubious whether he can make mileage out of it. Though he notes it as part of the obvious Tory plan to make nation and identity a big feature.

He says the case Hague makes can be answered. Hague said that English MPs alone should vote on English issues. But many 'English' issues are about spending. This gives them a Scottish dimension, because 90 per cent of Scotland's money goes from Westminster, and its proportions and size are relative to and dependent on the English share of the total handout. Therefore all Scottish MPs have a right to a say in English money spent on education, for example. We must get this message across more clearly, he said – noting, as I admitted, that I had not really thought of it that way, and found it fairly convincing.

All these issues with Scotland, he says, would be much harder if the economy was doing badly. As it is, what impresses him is that devolution has been relatively trouble-free. The opening was a UK occasion, he thought. But he knows that it is because we are in good economic circumstances that the problems are muted.

EUROPE We begin by noting that the strong economy has its relevance here also. Very much so. I remark that compared with the 1970s, when the sense of economic crisis was so important in the referendum to stay in, now the economic perception is the opposite. He amplified this by saying, Yes, the better the Blair government does with the economy, the less cause there may seem to be to change. He recognizes the political problem. He puts it another way as well: that the Blair government is the only one that has given Britain self-confidence, is the only strong government available, is the only credible government available, therefore the only government equipped to take Britain in – yet for all these reasons may find difficulty in doing so. A rather grim paradox.

On the euro, he says the position has not changed: the intention is serious, the conditions are serious. Blair still wants to go in, as long as the economic case is good. I remark that the economic case will never be decisive. And therefore there is a problem in pitching everything on it. He doesn't disagree, but twitches his nose dubiously. The economic case has absolutely got to be positive, he said: i.e. it cannot possibly be negative – which it could be if we tried to sell the case right now.

Have we learned from other Europen countries? I asked. This arose from a talk DM has had recently with the deputy foreign minister of the Netherlands, who he says is an exceptionally good man. They had agreed that the collaboration and political project-building was no longer about grand rhetoric or ideological argument, but by benchmarking. The

Dutchman was very keen on this: each country taking the best from the other. It was by no means all one way. He agreed with me that we made a mistake in talking both to our own people and to the Europeans as if we alone had things to teach, mostly coming from America.

On the other hand, the American economy was a phenomenon. Still growing at 4 per cent a year – having been declared a basket case ten years ago. Vast increase of jobs. A complete refutation of the thesis that an increase in the workforce (via immigration, for example) leads to higher unemployment. In the US model it simply leads to higher growth – the system somehow copes with 2 million more people a year (check). There was a vast amount to learn from the US too, and the anti-Americanism, especially in France, was mistaken.

In addition, we should take care not to exaggerate our own brilliance. Austria, Netherlands and Denmark all have lower unemployment than we have. We still have lower productivity than France and Germany etc. etc. We have a long way to go.

All this bore on Britain's Europe problem. For, yes, our apparent prosperity helped to make Europe seem less essential. However, we needed a broad case stated for Europe, as Blair indicated when deciding to take part in BiE.[1]

He seemed to feel that the 'top table' argument for euro entry was not terribly persuasive to people. It did need to be couched in terms of the benefit, mainly economic, in the long term. Another problem of success: the whole Kosovo story – which appeared to show us leading the top table (my words) in the vital field of public defence cooperation. This was another way in which we appeared to be losing out in the public appreciation of how much we might lose by being outside the euro.

The battle for the 'Europe' case must definitely begin. What were the headings? I asked. He said: economic, role-in-the-world, the things we do better together (crime, environment), the issue of what it would mean for Britain if the EU went on without us.

He therefore urged much closer attack on the great hole in the sceptic case: the refusal to publicly address the real consequence of much of their rhetoric – exit. Reminded me that the Howard Flight accidental remarks a few days ago were very telling:[2] he is a frontbencher; he said the hidden truth; he brought out what Hague really seems to believe

1 Britain in Europe, a pressure group backed by Tony Blair, Michael Heseltine, Kenneth Clarke and big business. William Hague promised to drive a specially adapted lorry to every part of the country in what he called 'the battle for the pound, the battle for Britain'.
2 Howard Flight: Conservative MP for Arundel and South Downs 1997–2005 with a gift for embarrassing the Conservative leadership. In July 1999, while freshly a shadow Treasury spokesman, he discussed quitting Europe. In 2005 he talked about undeclared Conservative spending cuts, and the then Opposition leader Michael Howard withdrew the party whip.

but will not say. They need to be hammered on this far more than they are.

I asked him at the end, Will there be a referendum in the next parliament? He said, Blair's position has not changed – the intention to enter, the insistence on terms. Yes, he said, there has been no change in Blair's basic position – i.e. there should be a referendum. But I told him about Philip Gould's dire assessment. It made him reassert the need for much more to be said about the pro-Europe case generally. A real campaign needs to start to get public opinion turned round.

BLAIR AND GENERAL GOVERNMENT   DM is very much in the engine room. His main things are education, health, crime, transport etc. The centre he thinks has got more grip than it used to have. For example, there is now a monthly (?) meeting between the departmental minister and his Perm. Sec. with Blair and his people. This has never been done before (the Perm. Sec. bit). It is a way of coordinating the work better, getting commitments, getting departmental accountability, making sure everyone is on track.

The Cabinet does not meet for long. But that is a modern change of style to fit the way people operate . . . It is not a 'big meeting' era, he suggests. People do things on the phone and on the hoof, always being flexible, rather declining to have the big, formal, decisive meeting as a kind of grand peroration. Things are more supple (I am free-associating here). One coexistent fact with this is that there are not really factions. (I gave him a little lesson in the Wilson period, and we contrasted the two cultures there.)

But one thing which worries him is that people tend to get on with their own jobs. They are not encouraged to talk broad. Ministers have said to him that once they became ministers the thing they missed most was talking to other politicians. They become administrators. There are one or two exceptions, orchestrated from No. 10. The Social Exclusion Unit and the Innovation Unit. These involve junior ministers once a fortnight getting involved in things outside their departments but back in the truly political world they may specially understand.

A problem with the Civil Service is not understanding the importance B attaches to follow-through. They think that once a policy has been set in place, their job is to think about new policies. They have to be reminded that what is wanted is application to managing the existing policies into on-the-ground reality. He repeated his Miliband model of government which, if I remember it correctly, is (1) invention of policy, (2) implementation of policy, (3) development of policy. Or some such scheme.

Ministers are about to make a series of speeches which set their policies in a wider context. Dobson today, others next week. Blunkett, Prescott, Darling, Byers. (These will be ill-reported, because they may not have a story. But they are an effort, as the prelude to the annual report, to bring together the big picture, get ministers reflecting on their larger tasks. Urges me to write a piece.)

MICHAEL ANCRAM
Conservative Central Office, 19 July 1999

THE TORY POSITION I have always said, he said, that there is a mountain to climb and you do not climb it by looking at it. One step and then another step. The Euro elections and the local elections were steps.[1] They boosted morale around the country. People were no longer saying why do we bother? It was a beginning.

We will win the Cheshire by-election (Goodlad).[2] Note that Blair has now let it be known he will not be going there, whereas at one time they said he was. It would have been a nice boost to be associated with victory, after the trouble of the last two months – two good months for us. Now that he is not going, you can see what Labour is expecting. It is, by the way, a rather odd rural seat. Lots of incomes from Liverpool, therefore no deep rural interests. It should be Tory, but it did swing greatly at the general election – unlike my own seat, truly rural, where the swing was only 2 per cent (disguising, admittedly, a sharp Lib-to-Lab swing).

How will we make more progress? Mainly because Labour is entering the non-delivery phase. It took some time – two years – for our past to be able to recede. Now it has done. OK, there will be a longer period in which Labour can go on saying that they inherited a terrible legacy. But as far as the Tories are concerned, we are now freer than we were to start afresh – which is what we decided to do, drawing a line, in February last.

Non-delivery will be the big thing next. Schools, hospitals, tax. People feel poorer. When they go away on holiday, they know they have less in their pockets. We can tell them this is because of various taxes. Stealth taxes, as Francis [Maude][3] calls them. They experience that. They blame the government. Our job is to capitalize on that.

Equally, they know what their own experience is in schools and

1 The Conservatives gained 48 councils and lost none in the local elections of May 1999. They won the greater share of the European vote in June – 34 per cent compared with Labour's 26 per cent – despite a very low turnout. William Hague claimed 'a major breakthrough' for his party.
2 When Alastair Goodlad resigned as a Conservative MP in 1999 to become high commissioner to Australia, his former seat – Eddisbury, with a majority of only 1,185 at the 1997 general election – was seen as winnable by Labour.
3 Francis Maude: barrister; Conservative MP for North Warwickshire 1983–92, for Horsham since 1997; shadow Chancellor 1998–2000; chairman of the Conservative Party 2005–7.

hospitals. Although there will be arguments about the figures, and we know that Labour will not fail to find a set of figures that sustain their election promises, people's actual experience is what matters. If their hospital is full of waiting lists, if their child's class is still too big etc. etc.

Another big issue for us will be transport. People know that Prescott made these promises which he has not delivered. He talked big, and nothing has happened – as they say to themselves while fuming in a traffic jam.

He also said that William's speech on English rights to vote on English issues had caused much resonance. More than MA had expected. A very good issue, it seems. He said, under pressure from me (ex Miliband) that the Tories would have to find a way of making explicit the carve-up of English money rather than the carve-up of UK money (on which it would be OK for the Scots to claim a voting right).

I asked him, in general, whether they had to find broad ideological differences with Labour, or whether it would be a contest between superior pragmatisms. He replied, Labour is top down, we are bottom up. They want to impose, as Labour always had. We want to recover our tradition – admittedly lost, unintentionally, during the Thatcher years – for local option and local choice and local government.

And then, he said, there is . . .

EUROPE   He now felt very comfortable with the party's Europe position. More so than two years ago. In Europe but not run by Europe is a very good line, the right line. I am a European, he said. But I am dead against the euro, and dead against Europe having power over fiscal, monetary, foreign or defence policy – also the *corpus juris*.[1] These are the areas we mean when we say 'not run by Europe' – i.e. it is not quite Hurd's line about the nooks and crannies.

What does 'not run by Europe' really mean, in the real world? Renegotiating treaties? Or what? He replied, I am a great believer in renegotiation. Nothing is for ever. We must see what it could do for Britain.

But what if Britain is the only country that wants to renegotiate Maastricht and Amsterdam?

MA: We will see how badly they want us in. We do, after all, pay £4 billion into Europe. If we left, the others would have to find the difference. They all want us to stay. That will be a negotiating strength for us.

But you still have to face the possibility that Britain will be quite alone in this. It would be certain to fail.

MA: But that's where you are wrong. Negotiation is the essence of

---

[1] The body of civil law.

real life. Look at Ireland (I interrupted, Ireland is a bad example: it has not produced a deal. To which he replied, It is a damn sight nearer to one than when I was a Northern Ireland minister). And look at Scotland – where England has engaged in a negotiation that many people did not want, which got Scotland (to my regret) a lot of what it wanted. Nothing is fixed in stone. But this is typically English and British. Seeking a way out, a way of diminishing the relationship. (I then delivered quite a long burst about the history, explaining why we seemed, under the Tory vision, quite happy about being thrust to the edge and then off the edge.)

MA: I think the argument is between that line, on the one hand, and the argument that EU is inevitable, on the other.

I asked whether he was in favour of any more QMV whatever. He said, No. Even on environment? I asked. No, he pretty much said. This extended to a similar, revealing, attitude. If we did get into the euro, he said, we would have to do our best to make things work, and to try and stop Europe falling apart. But he said this as a grudging idea – which I said reflected very exactly the whole British attitude over a long period. He took this as no sort of criticism, saying that everything can change.

I said to him that I thought Hague, unlike Ancram, was basically anti-European: basically would be happier if there was no such thing as the EU and we could get out. He denied this – though he admitted that there may be a generational difference in how they saw Europe.

Re the euro referendum, he said that there was now a clear 75–25 split, across both main parties, against the euro. Was it imaginable that Blair would risk his position to defy that? I agreed in one way, saying that the case for the euro, and even for Europe, had not been put for twenty years. I reeled off my usual line about Thatcher–Major, plus the media – adding up to a situation in which public opinion had been totally brainwashed in one direction. I suggested, boldly, that if the government began to try and turn this round, it would find that people did not rate Europe very highly among their concerns, and therefore would be ready to see reason if it came from Blair.

ASHCROFT Like all Tories he was more interested in the peripheral than the central issues. (a) Why was *The Times* doing it? (b) Why did the FCO let its papers get out? Especially the latter. MA said it would be a bad day if the previous government's papers could be raided by the incomers, who would then spend their first six months leaking the contents. Kerr has assured him that there will be answers to his questions about who saw what when, and how therefore it might have got out.

As to Ashcroft himself, Ancram says he agreed to come only if the party got its financial act together, and did not go on spending more than it got in. He also, ironically, has been doing more than anyone to organize a system to get people to give one-, two- and three-thousand-pound donations.

The day after the Eddisbury by-election. Despite their best hopes, Labour did no better than at the general election. The Conservatives won the seat with a majority marginally up, at 1,606.

DAY AT CHEVENING (FOREIGN SECRETARY'S OFFICIAL RESIDENCE)
23 July 1999

A Robin Cook event, to discuss post-Kosovo. Among those present: J. Kerr, J. Goulden, F. Heisbourg, J. Sawers (No. 10), R. Liddle, John Chipman (IISS), Sheinwald. Journos: Simon, Stephens, Macintyre, Wintour.[1]

A few collective thoughts that stick . . .

ROBIN COOK Began with a personal impression. There's nothing like a victory, or a perceived victory, to put a spring in the step. Attacks the baseless efforts of others to say differently. But reminds one that, whatever the aftermath problems, and whatever the post-facto judgements about the bombing etc., a war is fought till the other guy backs down. That is the big thing. Clearly Cook (and Blair) are full of the cleansing and empriding fact that they did 'win'.

As the day goes on, I admire Cook more. He is a very good chairman. Plans the discussion, edges it forward, intervenes himself but not too much, is plainly thoughtful, and to the point. He is funny to keep the tone lightish, and also personally knowledgeable. Can make fine distinctions between Bulgaria and Romania, and between Latvia and Estonia.

Notes how absurd it is to see the immense sums being spent by individual Balkan countries, especially Bosnia, on military – while we are channelling substantial sums for their fiscal renewal.

Likens the defeat of Milosevic to the fall of the Berlin Wall, in Balkan

---

1 Sir John Goulden: UK permanent representative to the North Atlantic Council and the permanent council of the Western European Union. François Heisbourg: head of the French interministerial group on international relations; later director of the Fondation pour la Recherche Stratégique, Paris, 2001–5. Sir John Sawers: foreign affairs private secretary to the PM. Dr John Chipman: director of the International Institute for Strategic Studies. Sir Nigel Sheinwald: now EU director at the FCO. Sion Simon: *Daily Telegraph* columnist and associate editor of *The Spectator*; Labour MP for Erdington Birmingham since 2001. Philip Stephens of the *Financial Times*; Donald Macintyre of *The Independent*; Patrick Wintour, then of *The Observer*.

terms. The first real setback he has ever had. Also makes it clear that getting rid of M is prime target of policy now, though he speaks with some uncertainty about the democratic forces that might be lying below him!

One difference between the Balkans and the rest of Europe is that since the war, in the rest of Europe, borders have been sacrosanct, and the issue/problem has been to make them porous enough – as porous as possible, of people and goods and money – so as to enhance prosperity. But the border issues have been settled. In the Balkans, this is not at all so: not the given of anyone's policy. Many contests over borders.

Calls his meeting with Primakov 'Old Russia meets Old Labour'. But says the new man is different, and quite possible to do business with.

Notes that the alliance is in better shape after the war than it was before the war. When things started, they found out how rusty and worrying a state it was in. But 'the habit of nightly consultation' has formed relationships and built a lot of confidence.

On Europe as such, he says that there must certainly be a strengthening of the European defence capability. Not merely more money, but better deployment. We spend 60 per cent of what the US spends on defence, and get far less than 60 per cent of US defence capacity. We have 2 million men under arms, yet had difficulty getting 2 per cent of that number into Kosovo.

JOHN MONKS
At the TUC, 2 September 1999

(Where, incidentally, I found the first person smoking in an office at her desk that I can recently recall: a woman in the outer office beyond Monks's own. Itself an odorous symbol of the Old Labour world, one might think.)

TUC AND THE GOVERNMENT   Blair himself. The mysterious world of the Third Way and what it means. And what Blair says it means. Blair will come to the TUC and probably say only a line or two about what the government has done for the unions and working people. McCartney[1] will be there to talk about the twenty-eight new personal rights that have come to workers – a good record, but Blair never likes to mention it, or at least spell it out. He is worried, they all are at Millbank

1 Ian McCartney: TGWU-sponsored Labour MP for Makerfield since 1987; Minister of State, Cabinet Office 1999–2001; sometime chairman of the TGWU parliamentary group.

and Downing Street, about seeming to be losing their rapport with the business world.

I draw JM on to Blair himself. He has dined there a couple of times (Chequers, perhaps). Says it is noticeable what a real family the Blairs are, and what a hard time the boys and Cherie give him at the table, telling him to have a go at Rupert Murdoch etc. etc. He does not live in an ivory tower. JM agrees with me, also, that Blair has changed rather little with power. Had not assumed the grandeurs. Still talks like a man slightly bashful about the appurtenances.

However, 'Blair is a marvellous actor,' said JM. And a brilliant politician. He is very astute. He is also very good at measuring the balance of forces in the parliamentary party. He does yield to a show of force – as over the lone parents,[1] when the finished deal, though complicated, actually cost more than the sum originally removed from them.

JM believes that quite a lot of the new MPs are still well imbued with the social dimension of Labour, and want the government to do more. They are also ambitious and loyal to Blair. So they are careful not to make too much fuss. But they should not be seen as Millbank clones, totally cynical and lacking in the slightest sense of Old Labour values. They will be delighted with every move the government chooses to make in a pro-union or pro-people direction. They are not, I infer, anything like so deeply pro-business as Blair himself is.

We agree that Blair's own personal instincts, separate from his political strategy, are probably not interested in the hard-luck cases. He is a prophet of aspirationalism. He wants people to pull their socks up, says JM.

And what of Gordon Brown, in this field? He says Gordon is more mysterious. A complete enigma. He will roll off a three-part sound bite in private, just as he does in public. You never really know what he is thinking, deeper down, says JM.

Did he see Blair? Yes, but the timings vary. Recently, with Kosovo and Ireland, he has not seen him for three months. But in a year he might well see him four times or so, depending on what was on the agenda. Blair will always see him if he asks (as he would see Morris, Edmonds et al. on what was regarded as Labour Party business). Were these meetings usually at Monks's or Blair's suggestion? Most often at mine, says JM – unless Blair has a problem with us, in which case he will ask to see me.

EUROPE This is JM's real concern, it is quite obvious.

The social-Europe question is awkward for all parties, not just the

---

1 Government plans to cut benefits to single parents by £10 a week had triggered a rebellion by 47 backbenchers in December 1997.

left. Blair is in favour of the euro (and of being European) except for the social-Europe part of it. He sees social reform in a liberal, flexibilizing direction as the necessary accompaniment to the euro. Others (Edmonds et al.) want a more social Europe, a European not American capitalist model – the Delors vision of a non-American capitalism, forged in our own way.

It is this which has led to Edmonds letting it be known he will launch a Unions in Europe group at the Labour Party conference – to supplement the Britain in Europe campaign. Monks clearly saw this as pretty unhelpful (and I subsequently got a flavour, from back-reading of papers, about how messy was the half-announcement, in *The Guardian*, of Edmonds's effort).

I asked him about Brown's position. He said he thought Brown was being moved by two thoughts. (1) The economy is going pretty well: I, Chancellor Brown, am responsible for this: this must be our election platform, which I will lead: there must be no distraction from this over-arching and unique (in Labour history) fact. (2) Europe offers the only conceivable route by which Hague could storm the country: we must not let him have the slightest opportunity to do that. Gould's focus groups show a steady 60–25 hostility.

In Monks's opinion (unprompted) this leads Brown, or could do, to a position like Hague's: put it off for the indefinite future. When I say, But that will have to become clear at the election, if it is so, he reacted as though he hadn't quite thought of that – but did not disagree. Visions (unspoken) floated into one's mind of the 1997 Tory formula about 'not in the lifetime of the next parliament'.

Cook, by contrast, has been letting it be known that we cannot go into the election with a wait-and-see policy. It will be torn apart – and the more so if Hague really does make the euro his biggest issue. But it is not quite clear (says HY) what Cook really does want. (Not far away from this, maybe, is Cook's natural antagonism to every position Brown takes.)

There is a school, more Euro-minded than Cook, which says that certainly the Brown line will not do.

Blair, JM construes, is somewhat less sceptical than Brown. And would be appalled if one put to him the possibility of a strategy that actually intended not to be in the euro for ten years. But for Blair the referendum, at any time, is a massive risk. It cannot be lost. Wales, and even Scotland, could have been lost without excessively dire conse-quences. This would not be true of the Euro referendum. It would be a test, as much as anything, of Blair's character. Will he risk it, even after a smashing victory at the election? JM ventured that perhaps he might do so as his final throw in politics, before retiring to do something else. On the other hand, his potential successors would have something to say about such a risk.

But Blair does think that BiE is important. He thinks that we must get Europe itself de-demonized before there is any chance of getting the euro accepted. I say, Will there be enough follow-up? Will he keep going? We agree, that is the question – but JM is not wholly pessimistic about that.

Moreover, this is helped by the way in which exit has now become a subject for conversation in polite society. Incredibly, it is now part of the talk. Thatcher, Tebbit and Cash: all this makes Hague's position much harder, and is meat and drink to Blair.

What would be the effect, I ask JM, of Britain being perceived as no longer a pre-In, but an indefinitely Out? He thought that, although the State Department has always been a pro-Euro pusher of GB, and now favoured entry into the euro (Seitz etc.), the Treasury was different, and feared a successful euro would imperil the dollar, and thereby make the US trade deficit harder to finance, with awesome consequences. Perhaps the Treasury saw the UK's non-entry into the euro as a way of weakening it, to US advantage. As for Japan, he thought they were too weak to matter at the moment. But he did say that he thought there was no doubt that investment patterns would be damaged.

One should always remember the background truth, however, that for the members of the euro it was a done deal. It was happening. It had ceased to be a debate. When the actual currency came into people's hands, that would be another development. But it has ceased to be controversial. People are just getting on and making it work.

Moreover, the economies of the EU are getting stronger. It is all very well to talk about their unemployment being high, which it is. But this is a lot to do with their fantastic productivity, especially in Germany and France. Go into a German factory and you see a place of pristine modernity, where there is no need for floor-sweepers. They are state-of-the-art places of high investment, with a trained workforce of elitists (my word).

At the end, JM asked me if I had seen the film *Elizabeth*.[1] He said he was struck by how it could have been that the English switched from Rome so suddenly. He saw in some of the lines a prefiguring of the timeless British attitude of sod the foreigners, and quoted an especially rich one from Walsingham. Might it be, he pondered, that the British were just, through and through, nationalistic, insular and nation-proud and xenophobic – perhaps the miracle was (per HY) that we had ever gone into the EU in the first place!

---

1 *Elizabeth* (1998), directed by Shekhar Kapur, starring Cate Blanchett.

NICK SPARROW
7 September 1999

FOCUS GROUPS AND EUROPE   Any focus group you talk to
will tell you (a) that 'they' don't want us and we don't want them, (b) that
we (the group) don't know anything about it and can't understand it,
(c) that the euro will happen anyway, because that is what the business
world wants. Labour made a mistake in overreading the pessimism of the
focus-group results, and choosing therefore to try and duck the issue
altogether. A classic example (per HY) of the malign and unhelpful
influence of focus groups on policymakers.

(Per HY) NS says that the main purpose of focus groups is not to
make policy, but to help decide how to present it, what to focus on etc.
etc. The trouble with the euro issue is that the focus groups have decided
the policy . . .

JOHN KERR/ROGER LIDDLE
Lode Willems's Dinner for Prince Philippe[1],
8 September 1999

SOME GLEANINGS   JK insists that we have been very influential,
in ways he could never have imagined. Chirac politely asked him at the
Berlin summit whether the British leader could possibly spare him five
minutes. That kind of thing. Numerous instances he could recite of the
wholly changed atmosphere. The best time of his entire career. Instead
of everything out of Europe being seen as a threat, it is now seen as an
opportunity.

RL says the German situation is extremely worrying. He spent this
day in Berlin, talking to the SPD apparatus people. Schröder faces some
very tough elections, climaxing in the North-Rhine Westphalia next May,
which, if he does badly, will lead to a reassessment of his role as party
leader. Scharping[2] could take over, very likely, and pursue a more traditional SPD policy. If the German economy continues to be so heavily
unemployed, that is serious for the prospect of British support for the
euro. If Germany does not reform, the Blair argument will be much less
strong. All this, Roger implies, is absolutely critical and should be closely
watched.

---

1 Prince Philippe, duke of Brabant: Prince of Belgium; heir to the Belgian throne.
2 Rudolf Scharping: former SPD chairman, became German defence minister 1998–2002.

RL says that Blair is wholly committed now to British entry to the euro. Sees it as a political necessity and an economic virtue, though I had the impression that the former outdistances the latter in his mind. (This, if true, is quite a change in the strength of Blair's view.)

They do remain committed, however, to the notion that this need not be an election issue. Blair is convinced he can argue his way out of the idea that he has to commit before the election, or that, in an election, he will have to commit to the referendum and then say which way he will be arguing. All this, he believes, is sustainable. Apparently he thinks that the Tories can be painted as the ideologues and the crazy exit merchants – and that will be enough. However, I think (and said) that he overlooks the political cons of seeming to be a ditherer. I also said that the idea that the Tories could possibly win the election was false.

Another interesting thing RL said was that Blair deeply wants to maintain the relations with the Liberals, wants a grand progressive coalition – but does not know how to achieve it, given the fact, according to RL, that he no longer wants much to do with PR. Various things have contributed to this turn-off. One was a crucially timed call from Prodi, when Prodi got evicted as prime minister, in which P said to Blair, 'Tony, whatever you do, don't adopt PR.' Another was the collateral damage of the Kosovo war and the evidence that coalitions were hard to run. Another, presumably, is the sheer difficulty of getting PR past the Labour Party. Despite all this, however, Blair is still searching for a way to sustain and grow a progressive movement encompassing the two parties.

FOCUS GROUP
21 September 1999

MY PRE-THOUGHTS In one way, these are the arbiters of political decisions, the desperately sought test bed for political ideas, or at least priorities. Certainly for presentation.

Are they the substitute for ideas, and still more for convictions? Or are they, perhaps, the substitute for politicians' contact with real people such as they used to get through their surgeries: a sort of scientific, organized, carefully chosen group of men and women in the street – who are more useful than random whingers coming into the surgery? Perhaps the real value is about what they say on how to handle things, how to present them, what hierarchy of things to talk about.

Remember David Miliband saying that Blair's performance on the sofa – check – had played well with the focus groups.

A group of unsophisticated people being manipulated by very sophisticated experts, for results they know nothing about: their innocence being used for far more valuable purposes than they could suspect. (They do not know, when they are answering the questions, who the client is, or even that it is a newspaper or a political party. Nor do they know – check – that they are being watched by me from behind a one-way glass.)

How important is one focus group? What do they tell that an opinion poll, or common sense, can't?

The application of quasi-science to the normal business of government ... A betrayal, but if so – of what?

The group is gathered in Edgware; they come from the surrounding area. The condition given to the recruitment agency was that they should all have voted Labour or Lib Dem in 1997, and say they might consider voting Tory next time. This is at one with a more general rule: that floaters are of more interest in all circumstances (to political parties, anyway) than fixed-purpose voters. They are got off the street, and paid £30 for the ninety-minute session.

They are always mixed gender, though usually divided into different age segments. People under 21 are never included, since they are not interested in politics. People over 65 are rarely included. The group I witness are between 40 and 60, by the look of them.

They are to be interrogated by John Turner, who says he has done hundreds of focus groups for ICM, but (according to A. Travis)[1] is a politics lecturer (at Oxford Brookes University) in the daytime. He is sharp, intelligent, observant, and talks to more ordinary voters than anyone in the country, I should think. Certainly in a structured fashion. He is an interesting man. Quite young, classless (Estuary voice), long-haired, crimplene-shirted, totally unintimidating – which must be important.

The point of focus groups, he says – and remember, he does it for the Tories, on ICM contract – is not that they make parties change policies, but that they give them a feel of what people are thinking about at any given moment. What matters to them, what doesn't matter to them. Also how to present things, and not least how to present themselves – the leaders.

It is interesting, for example, how very often the first and only impression of Hague that people express is the picture of him at the Tory Party conference in the 1970s, with Mrs T exulting him as a kid.[2] (This proved to be the case tonight as well.)

---

1 Alan Travis: home-affairs correspondent of *The Guardian*.

2 William Hague first emerged in the Tory limelight at age 16, when he addressed the 1977 Conservative conference, telling delegates, 'Most of you won't be here in thirty or forty years' time.' He received a standing ovation, and was photographed with Margaret Thatcher, then Opposition leader.

In the case of Blair, the commonest image has been of Phoney Tony. Asked what sort of place he would be found in, people say a plastic pub with plastic beakers, drinking a designer beer. This is what comes to the fore – though there is also the sense of him being a family man (the children and the pix of them matter a lot – as Blair must be well aware). And of him being accessible: a chap you could go and talk to in his plastic pub.

In previous focus groups, says John, the commonest line about voting Labour was that it's time for a change. But they now ask, Did he really mean it? What has changed? And thus, Is he a phoney?

Re Europe. People always say they don't have enough information (this too was replicated tonight). I say that this really means they can't be bothered to read the vast amount of stuff that is around – mainly because they think this is an issue the politicians should decide. The irony is that the politicians insist on the referendum, but the people do not really want it and are not ready to equip themselves to answer the question. John pretty much agrees. But he says the gap is filled by prejudice: they don't like the Germans; they may be xenophobic. They also have the sense, he says, that Europe is all about the elite and the elite politicians – that is their business, the political class; stuff of which they, the people, are outside. Thus 'I don't need to know.'

This is compared with health and education, where the people are quite different, often very engaged, closely knowledgeable and opinion-ated from personal experience.

What focus groups are good for, says John, is helping politicians to fill in a jigsaw puzzle of which they have only some of the pieces. They are part of the pool's learning process. 'Politicos begin to understand better how fragmented and specific is the knowledge and reaction of people to political issues.' 'It's a humbling process, for politicians.' 'It also teaches politicians how to get things across better.'

I say to John, Do you see Blair doing things and saying things, and know, from your professional experience, that he is responding to the very focus-group thinking you are in touch with every week? Yes, he said. Very much so. He gave as an example Blair's criticism of public-sector workers, in July, which seemed to put him at odds with Prescott. They were picking up a criticism of public-sector workers in the focus groups.

Hague's image at the start: no one knew who he was. They thought him (amazingly) a toff, because of the party he came from. They saw him drinking a G and T in a wine bar, whereas Tony would be having a pint in his plastic pub. But this – says the Tory pollster – is changing. (Though I emphasize that J is not a Tory, and is a lifetime *Guardian* reader, by the way.)

THE GROUP

A female college lecturer	A housewife
A training manager	A boutique manager
An electrician	A technical writer
An accounts clerk	

All had failed to vote Tory in '97, and half of them said they had never voted anything else before that.

My overwhelming impression of them was tolerance. They had not expected great things from Labour, but they were not very critical of them either. One said that they had made a mistake in voting Labour, but the rest were waiting and seeing. That was the chief sense – it's too early to tell. Give them a chance.

There were gripes and complaints. A general sense that the NHS was not getting enough money (no mention at all of the vast funds Brown reiterates, for education as well). A strong button about there being too many managers, and not enough nurses and doctors, who should be better paid. Some detailed issues about local schools, and the inability to get the one of choice for their grandchildren – and tending to blame the government for this. But not strongly. It was all immensely charitable, and disengaged. You had the sense that, if they had not been got off the street for this conversation, they would not normally talk about politics: perhaps the men would, but not the women. Thus, when asked what was really good or really bad about the government, few had any answer at all. When asked to imagine and describe the kind of house Labour and the Tories represented, they were nonplussed, though 'crumbling' was the Tory word (as in Leeds, apparently), and 'unfinished' the Labour word.

Thus, on Blair, they thought he was trying hard. They thought he might have better backup. 'Can't do it all himself can he?'

Asked for single words to sum up the government's performance, they came up with 'sound bite', 'unaltered', 'slow', 'they're on a learning curve', 'too early to say'.

On the Tories: 'They've fallen apart.' 'They're marooned in an open boat without a compass.' 'They've got nothing to say.'

On Hague: 'All I can think of is that baseball hat.'

When asked what the Tories could do to make their message clearer, to add to their attraction, not one person mentioned Europe. Europe, in fact, featured little. Though admittedly two of the panel said they would vote No, and one of them said that the Tories were 'going not to take us into the Common Market, which I agree with them about'. But it was not a big issue.

On Hague: he has no charisma. 'He's well spoken, but he seems like a puppet put there.' 'He's changed his voice as well.' 'He's probably very clever, but he's not leadership.' 'We remember when politicians did have charisma, but now nobody has.' (Much nostalgia, when prompted, for Thatcher.) 'If he can't manage the party, how can he manage the country?' 'In that TV thing at the party conference, a clever, pretentious, obnoxious, bolshy kid.'

What can Hague do? 'Come up with something positive.' 'Get some decent people in the Shadow Cabinet.' (The only member whom anyone could name was Widdecombe[1] – and she with derision, as someone who was going to have a go at Straw over the spies, yet Rifkind had been the one who blew the whole thing open.)[2]

Along with this was the clear sense that the Tories were totally divided. Hezza keeps featuring in people's minds and talk. (Deep shock at the story Hezza told jubilantly about how to keep his cash flow going by post-dating his cheques.)

What these people wanted was leadership, rather than policies. Someone who said what he meant and got on with it. Someone who did not back down. Someone who was strong and clear. An irony, therefore: here is a focus group, designed to help politicians show how to calibrate their messages, and with the likely purpose of blurring and softening them – yet the group actually wants something different: a leader, in a sense, who does not listen to focus groups.

Thus, they are looking forward to an Archer/Livingstone contest:[3] real people, strong characters.

Much more feeling about illegal immigrants – and 'Venezuelans' coming over and getting into our hospital beds – than about Europe.

I get a better understanding of how responses are focus-group driven. Even this single group is quite reliable. E.g. on Hague, on 'crumbling' – it says identical things to the Leeds group.

Is this the fulcrum of democracy, of accountability? In a way, yes.

Asked to choose between parties, on specific policies, they are incredibly dull and unwilling to commit. Just generally vague. Could this be stoicism, or despair, or just realism?

---

1 Ann Widdecombe: novelist, broadcaster; Tory MP for Maidstone 1987–97, for Maidstone and The Weald since 1997; Minister of State at the Department of Employment 1994–5, at the Home Office 1995–7.

2 Two Britons – one of them a Scotland Yard detective, another an 87-year-old woman – had been identified the previous week as KGB agents, and three days before the focus group a lecturer at Hull University had been named as a spy for the Stasi in former East Germany. Six trunk-loads of material had been handed to MI5 by a KGB defector in 1992. Malcolm Rifkind, then Foreign Secretary, had been told of the documents in 1996 and authorized their release to a Cambridge analyst, but, he told the Commons on 14 September, he had not been informed of British spies. 'Why the security services didn't do that in this case that is a matter which certainly puzzles me.'

3 In September 1999 the novelist and peer Jeffrey Archer was the most likely Conservative candidate for the London mayoralty. By November Lord Archer had withdrawn, his reputation damaged by revelations that he had asked someone to provide a false alibi in a libel trial.

A sense that what they care about and notice more than anything is the character and apparent style of the leader. Image is overwhelmingly what matters. Hardly about issues at all: just about faith, or the lack of it, in who might do a better job.

ALASTAIR CAMPBELL
14 October 1999

He calls me. It is the day of the BiE launch.

We agreed that the launch went well. His main reason for calling was to further spin against Hague et al., though he talked about them as the Tory leadership.

Labour polling says that Clarke and Hezza are far more popular than any of the Hague people. Also shows that Major, although not exactly popular, is seen to have been very badly treated by the conference when it airbrushed him out of history. Major has sympathy among the masses.

AC remarked that KC was 'the most forward' of the people on the platform today. But he said that what was noticeable was that all of them said so much the same thing: they all seem pretty agreed.

He said that the people in the hall – the business world – probably had lost a lot of respect for the *Telegraph* and *The Times* already. They may be Tories, but they don't like the slant these papers always put on Europe. AC was especially scathing about today's *Telegraph* lead, a purported leak from the Prodi committee,[1] which carries no weight from the British or any other government. (George Jones [the *Daily Telegraph*'s political editor] despaired of it, says Alastair.)

He says that the broadcasters 'seem to be realizing they have a special responsibility', given the bias in the press.

We discussed the euro as such. He said that Tony was absolutely certain the larger battle had to be won first. But he volunteered that some voices in BiE will be 'forward of our position – and we don't mind that'. They will be able to take part in the real debate, not the fantasy stuff the sceptics keep putting out.

He made an analogy with the Scottish parliamentary elections, 'when people were urging us to get out and slaughter the SNP'. But we rightly

---

1 Prodi had just become president of the European Commission. The *Telegraph*'s page 1 splash was headed, 'Prodi unveils EU superstate. Blair embarrassed by plans to scrap British veto on tax' and went on to say, in the words of the paper's reporter, 'A radical blueprint of a more powerful European Union, in which Britain would lose its veto over tax policy and be bound by a joint constitution, is to be published next week by Romano Prodi, the new President of the European Commission. The document, co-written by Lord Simon of Highbury, a Government adviser and former trade minister, will be seized on by critics as evidence of plans to create a European superstate.'

bided our time. They knew they should hold on for the right moment. It was important not to be 'losing arguments at the wrong time'. The Euro-sceptics may be starting to do that now.

'Tony is not interested in having arguments, only winning them'.

Tony thinks they have held absolutely to the October '97 position. Perhaps rather closer than one might have expected. But he also notes that popular opinion is not yet showing a shift towards Europe. There is a lot of work to do – taking on the arguments that have become embedded in the British mind (my phrase) over many years. The argument about the US relationship, about the jobs and economic reform etc. etc.

Most sane people, he says, are beginning to see Hague is talking rubbish, but it takes time to sink in (my phrasing).

LODE WILLEMS
Lunch, Halkin Steet Hotel – plus bits from an evening with the Andreanis,[1] 19 October 1999

There is a waning of support for British sensitivities. This cannot be expected to go on indefinitely. The new German ambassador [Hans-Friedrich von Ploetz], in his first week here, made an intervention at a seminar in which he said some very blunt things. (1) The euro is there, it is working, it will not go away. (2) Its structure and conditions are evolving, and will not change for the sake of the UK. (3) We took the risks, which you did not take. (4) Do not imagine this is the end of further integration: it is just the beginning.

This was tough stuff. But it was a signal, with which most ambassadors in London agree.

Blair still seems very timid, very cautious, very unwilling to take risks. At the BiE launch he was more keen to say he was pro-British than pro-European. He couldn't come out with a straight statement (but check text before using).

He is, LW is beginning to think, less honest than Hague. At least Hague is pretty clear. But Blair, by refusing to defend the euro, and by being so inexplicit about future EU development, is concealing what he knows and intends to be the case. (But after lunch I went to hear Hague/Blair joust after the Tampere summit,[2] the first Commons day back, and B's words were actually pretty open about QMV, about polling, sovereignty etc.)

---

1 Gilles Andreani: head of policy planning, Ministry of Foreign Affairs, Paris, 1995–9. Pascale Andreani: based at the French embassy in London 1998–2000.

2 A special European Council meeting on asylum, immigration, crime, access to justice and the Charter of Fundamental Human Rights, held at Tampere, Finland.

Blair has proceeded by set-piece occasions. LW lists them:

- The election in 1997, from which much hope sprang. He started badly at Malmö, lecturing the others.[1] But he learned from that, and has stopped it.
- The 1997 euro announcement, October.
- The presidency. He had trouble at the launch of the euro, but it wasn't all his fault. The Cardiff summit[2] produced useful ideas and initiatives on employment. Quite good.
- St Malo.[3] This was the big one. The French took it as vastly important. They call it 'a Copernican revolution'. (I met David Manning[4] in the evening, who is at the heart of all this. He confirmed the phrase. He also said how exciting it was to work in a project that had the whole government behind it. It really is moving, says DM. A very big effort, which Blair fully intends to see succeed. Travelling with Blair, and talking to him, Manning has the very clear impression, which he completely believes, that Blair is serious about a European defence development. But he agrees that the hardware problem is a big one: that recent news about Continentals getting together and Britain not being part of it is bad: that the GEC–Marconi–BAe event[5] was very unfortunate – officials had tried to get ministers to intervene, but they had not agreed to do so.) But St Malo, said Lode, was becoming a bit less British. Involving most of the others as well. Moreover, it is arousing problems with the Americans – see Strobe Talbott,[6] who says they aren't opposed, and hears British officials saying, 'Trust us,' but asks them for more assurances than that. Tampere was OK. The UK was good. (See Blair's statement, which does not conceal what the Brits initiated, like meetings of police chiefs etc.)

NEXT EVENT The Lisbon summit in March 2000, which Guterres[7] has promised his friend Blair will be a thematic summit, devoted to the Third Way. But this is dangerous. Jospin, although doing quite a lot of

1 At the Congress of European Socialists at Malmö on 6 June 1997 Blair had told his audience, 'Modernize or die.'

2 European leaders met at Cardiff on 15–16 June 1998.

3 A Franco-British summit at St Malo, France, on 3–4 December 1998 agreed on military cooperation between the two countries.

4 Sir David Manning: diplomat; UK ambassador to Israel 1995–8; deputy undersecretary at the FCO 1998–2000; UK permanent representative to NATO 2000–2001; foreign-policy adviser to the PM 2001–3.

5 Marconi, which had merged with General Electric, to become known as GEC–Marconi, then became part of British Aerospace and became known as BAe Systems from 30 November 1999. GEC then renamed itself Marconi. The drawn-out process of merger and restructuring became a political issue, because both companies were intimately involved in European defence.

6 Strobe Talbott: US journalist, foreign affairs columnist, author; US deputy Secretary of State from 1994.

7 António Guterres: prime minister of Portugal 1995–2002; president of the European Council January–July 2000.

Third Way things (as confirmed by Gilles Andreani) cannot afford to have his grand political process disrupted by this being spelled out in so many words. Schröder, for his part, never understood how important Blair regarded the joint Anglo-German (Mandelson–Hombach) document to be.[1] And a German remarked – von Moltke,[2] I think – to Lode that there did not appear to be any SPD big names present at the launch. Moreover, as John Monks recently said to LW, Blair is surely missing a big populist trick by not emphasizing the social dimension, which makes the EU popular with workers who want more rights etc. etc.

I asked him about the apparent conflict in the Dehaene document[3] between (a) the statement that members cannot 'pick and choose', and (b) the statement that flexibility was always part of the EU system. He replied, 'Flexibility' is to be taken together with the words about 'cooperation'. This is meant to mean that countries can 'cooperate' or not, according to the situation of the moment – but must be assumed to have the intention, when the time is right, to move ahead into full engagement. Whereas Hague talks like a man who does not want any momentum: that his 'flexibility' is the right to remain permanently outside the momentum.

[GILLES] ANDREANI   said (at dinner at his house): the time will come when the British need to be shown the necessity of joining. But there are two ways to do this, both at the same time. (1) To enlist them, encourage them, defer to their sensitivities. But (2) to show them that they can be excluded, which makes clear to them they can't afford to be . . .

ROGER LIDDLE
The Garrick, 8 December 1999

HELSINKI   Yes, the withholding tax will be an important issue.[4] The presidency and Commission have just sent us a draft compromise proposal. At No. 10, at first sight, we think it has the makings of a deal. The Treasury are now poring over it.

1 Bodo Hombach: German politician; Minister for Special Tasks 1998–9; then EU special coordinator of the Stability Pact for South-East Europe; co-author with Peter Mandelson of *The Way Ahead for Europe's Social Democrats* (June 1999), a document that became known informally as the Schröder–Blair paper.

2 Gebhard von Moltke: German ambassador to London 1997–9.

3 Jean-Luc Dehaene, prime minister of Belgium 1992–9, was one of three authors of an October 1999 paper entitled 'The institutional consequences of enlargement'. It became known as the Dehaene report.

4 The EU commissioners proposed a savings tax: it became known as a withholding tax, because it was meant to withhold at least some of the income earned by savers on investments outside their own countries. Germany wanted it because German citizens could so easily deposit cash in Swiss or Luxembourg banks. The UK objected because the City of London was a tax haven for foreign investors. At the Helsinki European Council in December 1999 Blair managed to achieve a six-month delay.

Tony has said to me that if there is a compromise which preserves the bond market, he will accept a compromise deal. He wants to do that. (He is not afraid, by implication, of the rows that might ensue.) The new offer is being looked at by the City as well (the Bank??), by implication.

The problem with the tax is that it is mainly a German problem. They are losing money, Schröder has been under pressure from the Treasury head. But a further problem is that in Germany and Austria there are strict rules about bank secrecy. A feature that comes from the aftermath of the Nazis. This means that an information/disclosure route is more difficult. In any case, it seems, a full-disclosure route is very hard for the City, because of the great weight of trading, the variety of products, the many meanings of 'interest' etc. etc. Very complex to make the right definitions.

Gordon Brown himself is in favour of wiping out tax unfairnesses and evasion-holes. Dawn Primarolo[1] led the EU team that has agreed a code whereby a total of fifty-five tax loopholes around the EU have been disclosed. As long as there is no harmonization in the sense of harmonized rates of tax etc. Gordon is in favour. He does not like tax evasion.

Another route is via OECD. In which the US, surprisingly, is in favour of more action. A problem, however, is Jersey and Isle of Man – which, amazingly, are said by constitutional lawyers to be beyond the reach of the British parliament as far as setting their tax regimes goes, even though we have to provide their military defence etc.

Blair has undertaken, inter alia, to put pressure on Man and Jersey re any tax-loophole-closing that is needed.

BLAIR AND EURO: A SITREP There was a Chequers away-day last Friday for the policy unit. Geoff Norris[2] asked Blair if he had changed his position on the euro. Blair said no. He still thought that if there was not a disaster for the euro – collapse of Schröder; riots in France; rate going through the floor – and if the conditions were met, he would still plan for a referendum early in the next parliament.

He said, and I agreed, that Blair is a lot more consistent about big things than he is often given credit for. He does not change his mind very much. But he agreed also that in this case, within the rubric of consistency, it would still be open to him to deem the economic conditions not to have been met if he felt that the political situation was not ripe for a referendum.

Blair has a touching innocence about his own powers of persuasion.

1 Dawn Primarolo: Labour MP for Bristol South since 1987; Financial Secretary to the Treasury 1997–9; Paymaster General 1999–2007.
2 Geoffrey Norris: member of the No. 10 policy directorate and special adviser on trade, industry, energy and employment since 1997.

He still genuinely thinks he can persuade Irwin Stelzer[1] and R. Murdoch of the virtues of the euro. But the wiser course, says RL, is to assume the press will remain on the line it now holds.

As for the referendum pledge, it remains open not to make it. Brown definitely does not want to. Brown forbids anyone to make speeches about the merits of the euro, because that starts an argument with the Tories, which distracts from the economy. He wants to keep the economy at the centre, because he wants to be in pole position if Blair quits the leadership in the next parliament (which RL mentioned quite coolly as if it were a real possibility). But on the referendum, he says that the case for silencing talk about it would be sustainable – as long as nobody imagined you could hold a referendum, after such displays of agnosticism, immediately after the election (which might be tempting, if the Tories were lost in a leadership wrangle). There would need to be nine months (HY figure, agreed by RL) at least.

But, equally, there needs to be far more preparation of the public mind. This will be hard before an election run on the above lines. Moreover, *The Sun* may say to Blair, We will back you in the election – but not if you commit to a referendum.

Don't forget how tall Blair walks in Europe. He is still the king of the group. So much stronger than any of them. They look up to him. The reason we got a budget deal so easily in Berlin was that Schröder did not want to offend Blair. He has huge amount of capital still. Which is why he wants to keep it, by agreeing a compromise on the tax if that is tenable.

LODE WILLEMS
Lunch, 14 December 1999

At the Halkin Hotel. (Lode's chef had flu, as I think had he – though he said he was over it. He wasn't quite as animated as usual.)

After the Anglo-French summit, Bernard[2] was saying farewell to Jospin at Northolt. It had been a difficult meeting, what with the beef etc. He said to Jospin, 'You have put me in the shit,' to which Jospin relied, 'That's what you're employed to do.'

---

1 Irwin Stelzer: London-based US economic guru and business columnist on the *Sunday Times*, revered by Rupert Murdoch.
2 Daniel Bernard: French ambassador to London.

ROBERT JACKSON
The Garrick, 15 December 1999

ALL ABOUT EUROPE He started by challenging my belief that by being outside the euro the UK would be marginalized. He said we were central now to all the big things: Kosovo, defence, institutional reform etc. etc. There was nothing we were outside being a central player. When I said that this depended on our being seen as potential euro members, he doubted this. I was unable to name a particular item where we would be marginalized for sure. I said it was more to do with political atmosphere and collaboration – to which he was pretty scornful, perhaps rightly.

He thought the economic case for entry was in the balance. It was hard to guess which way foreign investors (who, by the way, he said amounted to 5 per cent of the UK economy) would jump. Would they stay, attracted by the City's power and size and English-speaking world aspects and our labour costs, or would they leave because of exchange-rate unreliability, accentuated by our being a small country? Hard to say.

His own reason for wanting entry, and soon, was what it would say about British psychology becoming more European. He wants this to happen, while being very conscious of the history that makes us different from the mainland (he is writing a *Times* column on Fridays throughout 2000, showing what it was like in 1000, which will include some stuff showing how little we were like the Continent even then).

The Pro-Europe Tories had a meeting with Hague yesterday. The big shots (Clarke, Curry, Taylor, Howe – as well as people like RJ et al.). A very serious group. He was impressed by how Hague, a young man, dealt with them. Very mature and sensible. When asked, patronizingly, by Ray Whitney[1] whether he thought they were federalists – and also how many of the European centre-right leaders were feds – he took the question on its merits and began to go though the European leaders, from Chirac downwards. He gave a good account of them, and the conclusion was that about half were probably pretty federalist. But he insisted he got on well with them, which Jackson says is true.

Robert believes that the answer to the British problem will be enlargement. This will set a geographical limit to the EU, excluding Ukraine etc. There will be a kind of finality. There is still no political finality, and that is a big problem which the EU must address. But enlargement will bring about reform of the CAP, institutional reform, an establishment of differ-

---

1 Sir Raymond Whitney: diplomat; Conservative MP for Wycombe 1978–2001.

ent groups having different kinds of union, a line drawn under new competencies[1] – all things that the UK wants. In that context, the UK will probably be among those inside the euro. Will all this take a long time? Yes, but what is fifty years in the history of Europe?

One of the inner truths about 1999 is how much better Britain is in her self-regard. A lot has happened in ten years. We now no longer see ourselves as a basket case, which we did in the sixties and seventies. We don't sit apologizing at Königswinter,[2] which RJ has been going to for thirty years. The Germans are now the ones who have some explaining to do. Beyond economics, also, we think better of ourselves. All this is important, and good – not to mention the cosmopolitan city London has become. Do you know that a net 500,000 immigrants came here this year – mostly EU people to work in the City or in lower jobs? To learn English etc. etc.

However, RJ notes that there is rather a lot of equating of the UK with the US under the rubric of Anglo-Saxon. We do not deserve to pretend we are as good an economy as the US! And, he admits, French and German productivity is stronger than ours . . . etc.

He believes the legal order is what matters in the EU. This is much more important than any misbegotten attempt to create a European demos, which he thoroughly opposes and which (I add) is quite impractical and hypothetical. The legal order, based on national assent, is what needs to be bolstered by every means. It will come not just (or perhaps at all) by the formal voting for a European parliament (though the EP is very important as a scrutinizing and check-up body, a policing organization, which it should do more of). It is the de-facto acceptance of the legal order by governments.

HAGUE AND THE TORIES He says that Hague is very reasonable in private. He says that there will be no renegotiation of past treaties. Though he has to admit (I guess) that the flexibility of future deals may involve unscrambling past treaties. What RJ expects is a series of solemn speeches – Hague says that the Maples speech to the CPS is the latest exact and reliable text – punctuated by tub-thumping xenophobia etc. etc., the coarseness with which we have to put up in a populist age, Robert sighs.

So RJ thinks the Tories could revert to a better public position. The pro-Europeans, he insists, are serious people. If there were the slightest

---

1 Eurospeak for the new challenges that arise from the Maastricht Treaty (foreign and military policy; criminal matters) as opposed to the old community responsibilities, such as the economy.

2 The Königswinter Conference, an annual talkfest of heavyweights from British and German politics, journalism, science, diplomacy and business, at Königswinter, near Bonn.

hint that Hague was on course to pull out, they would be heard from. I say, These hints were strong at the party conference – Hague says now, though, that the signals from there were bad ones, which apparently he regrets a bit. I also say that Hague's public position goes so far to emphasize the extreme position that it is hard to see him as a moderate who might even want to go into the euro.

RJ thinks the Tories may not do so badly at the election. Probing, however, I find this to mean a Labour victory by no more than 120 seats – in which case, he thinks, Hague may be safe. People will think he did a good job.

He says that the deselection bogey is already past. If Tony Baldry [MP for Banbury since 1983] can get reselected without a vote, which happened a few days ago (and just after the *Sunday Telegraph* had run a sleaze story about him), then surely the problem is not widespread. But he did say that Currie, an abrasive character, might have trouble. Ken and Hezza not, nor (probably) Taylor.

GOOD NOTIONS We should persuade Bertelsmann [the German-based media empire] to buy the *Telegraph* from Conrad Black.

One should always take a very cynical view of Murdoch et al. They just want to hold governments in thrall, with a threat impending over them to keep them in line for what the tycoon wants. Very effective . . .

2000

9 February	Alun Michael, first secretary of the Welsh National Assembly, resigns, and is replaced by Rhodri Morgan.
4 May	Ken Livingstone becomes mayor of London.
20 May	PM's wife Cherie Blair gives birth to son Leo Blair.
7 June	Tony Blair is heckled and slow-handclapped by the Women's Institute.
20 June	Police stop Home Secretary Jack Straw's official car for speeding at 103 m.p.h on a motorway.
26 June	Scientists and politicians announce completion of the Human Genome Project to sequence 3 billion letters of human DNA.
3 July	Police chiefs tell Tony Blair his proposal for on-the-spot fines for antisocial behaviour is unworkable.
6 July	Tony Blair's son Euan, 16, is arrested for drunkenness in Leicester Square.
25 July	A Concorde supersonic airliner crashes in Paris; 113 die.
5 October	Slobodan Milosevic leaves office amid widespread demonstrations in Serbia.
11 October	Scotland's first minister, Donald Dewar, dies of a brain haemorrhage after a fall.
2 November	A Russo-American crew move into the international space station.
7 November	George W. Bush of Texas narrowly defeats Al Gore in the closest US presidential election ever (it takes a month to decide the tally).
Deaths	Sir John Gielgud, Sir Alec Guinness, Reginald Kray, Hedy Lamarr, Walter Matthau, Sir Stanley Matthews, Patrick O'Brian, Anthony Powell, Roger Vadim

The controversial Millennium Dome in east London was launched with a Millennium New Year's Eve party attended by the great and the good,

*who arrived via the Jubilee Line Underground. But there was much
criticism of the arrangements. The Queen was filmed singing 'Auld Lang
Syne' with the Blairs.*

ALASTAIR CAMPBELL AND
PETER MANDELSON
At David and Janice Blackburn's dinner party,
2 January 2000

ON THE DOME[1]   AC agreed that getting to the Dome was a fiasco
that should never have happened. One thing we (New Labour) are good
at, he said, is putting on events. We should have done this one properly.
He didn't seem quite clear who had messed up, but said that 'we' should
have ensured that the travel details had been thought out properly.

He said that there had been a lot of big threats. Including 'some big
and serious ones'. But this clearly wasn't responsible for the fact that
only a single electronic gate was at Stratford station for the entire multi-
thousand crowd to go through.[2]

One had to remember, he said, that the overwhelming need was to get
the job done. When PM, TB and AC went to the site four months after
the election, it was a complete desert. Nothing there except poisoned
land. To have completed the thing was a vast achievement, and absolutely
necessary. This is what people were concentrating on.

I asked him whether there had ever been a chance of not doing it. Did
it come close to being cancelled? Yes, he said. It was close. If you had
had a show of hands at Cabinet before a discussion took place, there
would have been a majority for quitting it. But Tony was in favour, so
was Prescott, so was Straw. That was a formidable trio, he said. After
discussion we didn't have unanimity, but the decision was made. It was
obviously influenced, he went on, by the semi-pledge we had given to
Heseltine in January 1997 – the continuity pledge he extracted before the
early stages could proceed.

The police were magnificent . . .

---

1 Alastair Campbell cross-checked these notes with his original diary and found the following entry recorded
for 2 January 2002: 'We went out for dinner at the Blackburns' fantastic new house in Notting Hill. Peter M
was there with Reinaldo. Hugo Young was his usual charming self, said he liked the Dome but then wrote a
totally negative piece about it. Janice Blackburn got terribly worked up when I went on about how chattering
classes would now be hell bent on destroying it.'

2 Peter Mandelson comments, 'Alastair is wrong about the entrance to the Dome on its opening night (by which
time I had long lost my responsibility for it). There was not one single electronic gate for entire multi-thousands of
visitors at Stratford. This was a VIP gate, but the police still took a long time (and there were various newspaper
editors in the queue . . .)'

He would personally have liked more traditional stuff at the Dome. Especially the lack of build-up was wrong. Should have been more people in the middle, not just at the back. Better acts to get it really moving.

PM was clearly intoxicated by the details – the PlayZone was especially wonderful, he thought. Quite carried away by the ingenuities to be seen all over. They were both, also, very aware of who had given the thing a bad show (*The Independent* and the *Sunday Times*) and who had been nice about it after the first night. Saw the *ST* and *Indy* as just determined not to see the good side . . .

ON CONTROL-FREAKERY AND LIVINGSTONE AC
said that Ken Livingstone was being favoured by the press just because it would be one in the eye for Blair. They all understood this. But you watch: when KL has got the job [as London mayor], they will start screaming that Blair should have stopped him.

TB is 'passionately committed' to elected mayors as the way to revive local democracy. But we know it will take time for people to emerge who want to do the job – the right sort of people.

The more I see of politicians, Alastair says, having known only of journalism before I got there, the more I admire the good ones. They have a hell of a job, to secure compromises, produce real leadership, take risks and get people to go along with them (all this is my paraphrase).

We discussed businessmen in politics. But Branson[1] is inarticulate (it was suspected?) and like all businessmen has no idea about how to make democracy work.

Clearly the candidate they wanted was Mo Mowlam. But she wanted, quite understandably, to stay in the Cabinet, he said. Otherwise, he asked, who would you have chosen? I said, Trevor Phillips,[2] maybe. But clearly not a big enough personality . . .

On control etc. TB has sometimes said to me, says Alastair, that we may have a huge majority, but that doesn't mean we have got popular consent. We cannot do things just because we have a huge majority.

By the way, he said that the first Tony had told him about the baby was thirty seconds before Mike White and Polly T were due to interview him at Chequers (which was in early August, and I was meant to be there too). AC was gobsmacked. He spent the whole interview not listening, but furiously trying to work out how to handle the story, when to disclose it etc. etc.

He also remarked how much he admired Hague's resilience. In every

1 Richard Branson: founder and chairman of the Virgin group; knighted 2000.
2 Trevor Phillips: broadcaster and journalist; Labour member of the London Assembly from 2000; became deputy chairman 2001.

other way, he was making bad decisions and was a bad leader. But his toughness is unbelievable, says AC. Though, seeing him at the Dome, AC thought he was looking much the worse for wear – at last.

PETER MANDELSON All on Europe. I had said to AC that Europe was one subject where Blair, far from being arrogant, listened to the people too much: or what he thought the people were saying. I ranted a little about Philip Gould etc.

PM agreed with me that, apart from TB himself, nobody was talking about Europe, and this was very bad. I said what about Robin Cook? He said, Yes, Robin has begun to talk about it, but he lacks real confidence. The truth is that he has never recovered from what happened with his wife. He really lacks an independent voice. He has not been, as a minister, a compelling force – unlike when he was in opposition. This was a double pity, because Robin has such excellent officials in charge of the European policy: Colin Budd and Nigel Sheinwald (not to mention John Kerr).

He said, unprompted, that if we did not have the referendum in the first half of the next parliament, we would cease to be taken seriously by the rest of the EU. We would be seen to have withdrawn from the real leadership position we sought (my phrase, but his sense). It may be tempting not to have the referendum, but that would be the consequence.

He said to the effect (can't recall *ipsissima verba*, but pretty close) that if the referendum was not held, that would be the end of Blair's major credibility as a European leader: for that reason, a prospect that cannot be contemplated – it must be held.

He said that Tony, of course, is aware of all this. But he is worried about losing it. He is also worried about splitting the party. What this last point means is more dramatic than that: he is worried about Gordon Brown deciding, for purely personal ambitious reasons, to oppose entry into the EMU. Gordon sits there as an obstacle. Gordon could be very powerful, in a very strong position, if he split from Tony over Europe. It is a worry – perhaps whatever the size of the majority of the election. (I had offered my thesis that a majority of 150 would be fine, but one of 100 would be seen as enough of a Tory recovery to frighten us off the referendum – PM did not comment on that.)

What does this mean? I ask myself. Surely not that they would openly split in a campaign. Only, therefore, that Gordon, by posing this un-spoken threat, has the capacity, unless persuaded otherwise, to prevent a referendum being held. This is a mighty strength. Maybe Blair will have to take it on, sometime.

What is Gordon's game? Peter instantly dismissed the notion that he was ceasing to be European. Absolutely not, he said. It was all about personal ambition. Moreover, he now had Ed Balls in the position of chief economic adviser, a far more powerful position than before. Balls is a poisonous influence ... (Taking over the role of Whelan, perhaps, in the Mandelson demonology.)

He referred me to *The Sun*. This had followed up a nasty piece in *The Observer*, which said that PM had cost £20,000 by travelling to make speeches and do euro-type business in various places. Trevor Kavanagh [political editor, *The Sun*] followed this up, but more important there was a leader which drove the point home, while also saying what a delightful contrast such an extravagance made with the frugality of Gordon Brown, who never travelled anywhere ... PM seemed to see the hand of Brown behind this. But also *The Sun* praising a refusal to go abroad ...

Tony is also worried about the cost of winning, let alone losing. It would be an almighty battle, very expensive in material as well as political resources.

His own maturing idea is for a slight change of rhetoric. He says there's no way the basic position of wait and see will change. But he has been toying with new words that go something like this. To say, We think the euro is a good thing, but we are not ready to enter it: it is wrong for us at the moment – but when the circumstances are right, we will enter. This would subtly shift from the negative line now put forward, which simply stresses the fact we are not ready without saying anything positive about the euro. Gordon Brown is totally opposed to any such shift. He wants to keep it right out of the debate. He, as much as Blair, is the author of the line which says we have to convince the British people of the broader case for Europe before we can convince them of the case for the euro. Where, however, is a single Brown speech to that effect (we both said to each other)? Blair has made speeches, but not Brown.

Peter thinks there are two reasons for the shift. First, to keep the boiler turning over: stoke the fire a bit: keep it moving. Second, so that when you say the time is right you are more credible for having said earlier that the time is wrong.

He had recently had a conversation with Roy Jenkins (at Robert Harris's house).[1] Roy had been very critical of Blair; Peter had rejected this. He said we should remember the bad luck the pro-Europe side has had in 1999: the resignation of the Commission, the beef-war troubles, the weakness of Schröder, the revelation of Jospin as so very un-Mitterrand-like in his European attitudes, the European elections. This

---

1 Robert Harris: former political journalist (*Panorama*, the *Sunday Times*), who turned successful novelist (*Fatherland*, 1992); he and Roy Jenkins were friends.

had been a bad succession of things. He also said that Schröder, notwithstanding the possible collapse of the CDU, is a 'weak vessel'.

We finish up (per HY, with PM agreeing) in the paradoxical position that the strongest leader in Europe is hog-tied by his domestic position from being a leader who can steer Europe out of its present problems. He is emasculated . . .

This means, among other things, that the UK is not in a position to take a lead in the political reform of Europe, start a serious debate about a constitution for Europe, or anything like that. Until we go into the euro, we will not be taken seriously.

HY was asked to lunch by Neil Kinnock, now again a European commissioner, to discuss his anxiety about EU coverage in The Guardian. *'I'm afraid that Neil has hardly changed. He talks a lot, is full of abstractions, is not terribly sharp or interesting. But heart in the right place. He did say some recordable things.'*

NEIL KINNOCK
Lunch, the Ivy, 27 January 2000

SOME HISTORY   He happened to spend a lot of time talking to Blair after B was elected Labour leader in July 1994. They were apparently on holiday in the same place. Kinnock recalls telling Blair, in particular, not to bother about becoming the leader of Europe. This was because *anno domini* would take care of it. Kohl would depart, win or lose, by December 1999. France was weakened, with Mitterrand gone. All in all, he could look forward to a time when he was de facto the leading person in Europe, to whom everyone would look. Blair, NK recalls, grinned sheepishly and wondered whether this could be true.

BRITAIN AND THE EURO   I asked him what would be lost if it became clear we were out for a 'prolonged period'. He said, We would just be taken less seriously, listened to with less concern, our interest and request paid less attention to. It's not so much that we would be simply discarded – just that our interests would be seen no longer to require propitiating. This would be terrible. After all, it is still actually the European Economic Union. Economics is by far the largest thing it does. Defence is much smaller – after all, apart from France and Britain, who cares about defence? The sad fact is that nobody really does. Even Germany, now that it has the buffer of Poland and Hungary.

Blair had the chance at the start to make more of his relationships than he did: he never did get into the habit of ringing up everyone on first-name terms and schmoozing. Likewise, at these bilateral weekends too much time is spent cooking up a Monday-morning headline, or else conducting external policy, which just causes a lot of confusion.

Blair did have great cred. And it is still the case that he could call it in. People do still want to know what he thinks, and look to him for a lead. Now that both Germany and France are weakened there is a gaping chance ... But Jospin may become the leader, if he does become the president. This chance still exists, for Blair. But not if our absence becomes seen as prolonged.

SUNDRY   He made a lot of the need for Blair to win by 101, not 99. This would make all the difference to Hague. He agreed that perhaps the figure would need to be higher for the euro referendum to come about.

ED BALLS
The Garrick, 4 February 2000

SECRECY/BANK MINUTES ETC.   The Tories began this, of course, but they did it in a half-cock way. The Ken and Eddie[1] show followed a strange path. The minutes would show that the Bank made its statement, there was a general but unnamed discussion, and then there was a Clarke verdict at the end. Eddie was obliged to spell out his position in the open, but the Treasury did not reveal its position in the discussions (i.e. the records did not name names) and the Treasury never knew what Ken was going to decide by the end. One result of this was that, in order to get its point of view fully on the table, the Treasury would liaise with the Bank, sometimes extensively, beforehand, and get the Bank to make the points which the official Treasury wanted to make but could not, at least openly and by name, make.

This was certainly an improvement on the secrecy of what went before. But it was not well thought out. From 1992, after the ERM fiasco, what the Treasury and the process needed above all was credibility. The way to get this was by transparency. This was not really full transparency.

We changed the system again, and at the start Eddie was very against revealing the MPC [Monetary Policy Committee] discussion for six weeks. However, this has come down to two weeks, because they found that members of the committee of the Bank might well be having to testify

---

1   Kenneth Clarke (Tory Chancellor) and Eddie George (governor of the Bank of England from 1993).

before the select committee and, if the minutes had not yet been published, got into all sorts of trouble as to what they could and could not tell the HC. So, de facto, the two-week period has developed.

He agrees with my point that this has done no harm at all. The holiest of the holy, formerly locked in essential secrecy, has positively benefited from being opened up. No more rumours, no more caprice (as with KC), an orderly discussion, conducted in the knowledge that it has to be revealed in public. By general agreement, it has made a huge difference to the conduct of economic policy.

To take one example, if the Treasury and not the Bank had decided to lower interest rates seven times in a year, the policy would have been seen not as sensible and responsible but as grossly dangerous and 'political'.

On the other hand, Gordon does feel it is necessary and right to give the MPC guidance and support. So far it has been support. He has made it clear that he agrees with its decisions, from time to time. This is to give them political support, and to make good the thing they are weakest at – which is communication. They are not good at explaining the context of what they do etc. etc. (Unlike Greenspan,[1] who is brilliant at it.) The more mistrusted you are, the more explanation is necessary. Thus the Bundesbank hardly gave any explanation, because it did not need to. It has such a reputation. But the ECB should be giving more and better explanation, because it is untried. Likewise, the British economic policymakers will take time to develop a reputation for soundness, and the transparency of the MPC is a way of doing this.

I asked about the euro-11.[2] He said, The trouble is that the euro-11 is not well led. Gordon is already the second-most-experienced finance minister in the EU, such has been the turnover. Eichel[3] is not a heavy-weight, and neither is the Frenchman[4] – Strauss-Kahn would have been a transformative figure. But Amato[5] is probably the next of the big three, and Italy is not very big. All this means that the euro-11 has no proper idea about what it should be doing. This, from our viewpoint, is a great pity. We need and want the euro-11 to do well.

GORDON BROWN IN ALL THIS Gordon is strongly Euro-pean. It is nonsense to say otherwise. You will never find a piece by him that hints at anything else. If you look back to the 1996–8 period, you'll

1 Alan Greenspan: chairman of the board of governors of the Federal Reserve System 1987–2006.

2 Euro 11: the eleven countries that had adopted the euro as currency.

3 Hans Eichel: German finance minister 1999–2005.

4 Probably a reference to Christian Sautter, who became France's finance minister in succession to Strauss-Kahn, who had just resigned following a scandal.

5 Giuliano Amato: prime minister of Italy 1992–3 and 2000–2001.

find that Gordon was being depicted as the great European and Blair as the semi-sceptic. Somehow this perception has reversed. It is not correct.

Ed himself also talked like someone wholly committed to the project, in time. He explicitly noted that he had been tarred as a sceptic. This was not on the basis of anything he had said either in public or in private.

He was, however, willing to agree with my mild criticism of Blair's decision to put all his eggs in the Lisbon basket.[1] He rather agreed that 'reform' was not a message to ring the rafters with the B and C2 voters.

Gordon was playing a long game, I inferred – and he almost said. By positioning himself as the austere guardian of the economic tests, he was building credibility for when he said they were passed. Which, by the way, was moving well in the right direction, said Ed.

He referred to the speeches Gordon has been making – and will go on making – about Britishness. The inwardness of this, said Ed, is something G would not admit to: that his purpose is to remove Britishness from the ownership of the right. That is what it is all about: to show Labour as the party of patriotism, and a more sophisticated patriotism than Hague's. He thinks Hague made a big mistake in the autumn by equating the Tory Party with English identity, and saying (which he seems now to have backed off) that he favoured an English parliament.

I said, Why doesn't Gordon put more in these Britishness speeches about Europe? He replied, He does put it in a bit, but, because his main strategy is to get Britishness accepted as a Labour property, to mention Europe was not the best thing to do. That, I was meant to divine, would come later.

I asked about the common idea that, because the economy is strong, therefore the popularity/need for the EMU was less. He said Gordon took exactly the opposite view. By proving that we were strong and capable, we could present EMU as something to enter from strength: if we were saying we can't manage our economy on our own, and therefore need EMU, that would go down very badly, especially since the country as a whole is much more self-confident than it was in the 1970s.

PORTILLO[2] Had just taken over as shadow Chancellor, and announced his two U-turns on day 1 – the MPC and the minimum wage. Balls thought Portillo had handled this badly. Should have tried to get something in return: e.g. saying yes to the MPC, but on condition there was reform.

1 EU leaders meeting in Lisbon in March 2000 set themselves the challenge of creating 20 million new jobs in the following decade.
2 Michael Portillo had returned to the Commons as Conservative MP for Kensington and Chelsea in a by-election on 25 November 1999 caused by the death of the former Tory minister and diarist Alan Clark in September. The Tory share of the vote was slightly up.

Gordon will be happier with Portillo than Maude, because he likes a good opponent. Maude meant that Treasury questions passed without interest and without an audience. I informed him that MP was very, very anti-Europe – which seemed slightly to surprise him.

JOHN KERR
The Garrick, 15 February 2000

BLAIR–BROWN–COOK ETC. ON THE EURO   JK believes that, after a long struggle, the four relevant ministers (the above three plus Byers) have agreed to a position which will commit to a referendum early in the next parliament. They will do this, he hopes and expects, in speeches in the next four weeks or so. This was an important, hard-fought battle.

He is still not sure that Brown signs up to it. That will be the crucial voice. But there was a meeting recently, the first they have had to talk about the euro line. It was a short meeting. It was not very easy. But it did (presumably according to Cook) result in the formula being accepted.

Brown, on the other hand, does seem to be more and more distanced from talking about it. He snaps at people who want to do so. Cook gets rebuked if he says too much. JK wonders if Brown doesn't actually enjoy Blair having to take the heat for difficult things he can wash his hands of. An example was the withholding tax. Brown's formula, dreamed up on the plane to Helsinki, was never a starter. Didn't have a chance. But he left it to Blair to face the consequences of its failure to get any agreement. I said, in reply, that Brown certainly does not mind embarrassing Blair: that this is a way of the older brother getting his revenge.

JK added, Perhaps the deal at the Granita restaurant[1] was not really about the succession but about giving Brown total sovereignty over economic policy. Certainly, he said, Blair shows very little interest in domestic economic policy. And Brown has now decided that the euro is a matter of domestic economic policy, not of foreign policy – it would seem.

He says that Brown seems to bestride all economic policy. Today's announcement (or pre-announcement) on the minimum wage is an example. JK says that to his certain knowledge (though he wanted to check up about last week) the Cabinet has not discussed the minimum wage. Brown alone imperiously decides that another 10p will do. This after pre-spin that there would be nothing.

1 The Granita restaurant story is firmly in political mythology. During a meal together at a restaurant in Islington, Blair and Brown are supposed to have agreed that Tony Blair would stand for the leadership and No. 10, with Gordon Brown as Chancellor, but stand down for Brown after an indeterminate period. In her 2008 autobiography, *Speaking for Myself* (London: Little, Brown), Cherie Blair claimed the deal was actually made at a friend's house a few days earlier.

MO MOWLAM
23 February 2000

At Doris Saatchi's[1] last dinner before leaving her 2 Hays Mews house . . .
Jon Snow[2] et al. also present, but this was a private conversation.

Livingstone is probably going to win. I cannot see why he would pull out.

It has been a terrible mess, very badly handled from the start. The trouble is that Ken is cleverer than the people ranged against him, and a much better strategic thinker. He reminds me of Sinn Fein. Sinn Fein were brilliant at working out the future moves. They would make maximum demands, and then complain even if they got them. They knew each nuance of spinning to different audiences: to the US, to the republican movement, to the NI audience, to the GB audience and so on. I did eventually learn how to handle them, but I can't say I ever got on top of them. Even if I did something and then rushed off immediately to Washington, they got there first.

Ken thinks like that. He knows how to play his audiences; he can think quite far ahead. We should have been doing the same; we should be doing the same now, working out how to block off the moves he is going to make – for example, how to deal with the immediate complaints he will make about not having enough money or power to do a proper job for London.

Unfortunately, in a word, he is better at spinning. Why isn't Millbank, the home of spinning, as good? Because all the best people left Millbank after the election. There aren't enough people of experience and quality there now. They don't know what to do. They are easily outwitted.

In the Civil Service, likewise, there isn't enough political sense (HY: this is an old story). They will write my speeches, which will be very good on facts and commas, and then they will try to write a humanized (political) intro and tailpiece which will be hopeless. These will be redone by my advisers, and then redone by me. But one of my troubles is that my advisers are worked off their feet. They work for McCartney, Stringer[3] and Charlie F as well as me.

She denied that *The Guardian* story saying that she would be drafted had any truth.[4] It would be mad, she said. She did say that she was always available to do anything she could to heal the wounds. The process had

---

1 Doris Saatchi: first wife of advertising executive and art collector Charles Saatchi.
2 Jon Snow: television journalist; presenter of *Channel 4 News* since 1989.
3 Graham Stringer: Labour MP for Manchester Blackley since 1987.
4 A *Guardian* page-1 story of 22 February had been headed, 'Secret plan to ditch Dobson: Mowlam lined up to take on Livingstone'. Frank Dobson had previously come forward as Labour's candidate for the London mayoralty.

to be 'inclusive' – this was the basis on which she had insisted on being free to talk to Ken as well as Dobbo. She had done so. But she did seem to think that the story was a puzzle. We speculated about whether it had been leaked out by No. 10 or by KL. She cleverly analysed the possible motives of each, and concluded that No. 10 would have been especially stupid to have done it.

All in all, she thought that KL should never have been demonized in the way he was. Blair should have stuck with the OMOV process and accepted the result. KL should have been given enough rope, and he would have hung himself (as he always has before, she said). It would have been far better to live with him.

Tony Blair doesn't really understand the depth of the problem. He doesn't have the political instincts that Ken does. He thinks and acts like a lawyer: give me a problem, we will look at it, I will solve it. All very rational. But if he is out of control, he doesn't know how to react.

All in all, things are starting to look bad. The Tories are beginning to look different. I see it in the Commons, which I barely went to when I was in Northern Ireland. I hate it, actually. But now you can see from their faces that they are looking up. A bit of the old arrogance is returning. Portillo is a strength, and if he and Hague can work as a team they will be quite formidable.

JOHN DE CHASTELAIN
2 March 2000

Sat next to him at the Canadian High Commission dinner party (at which, also present, were Princess Alexandra and Angus Ogilvy, Renato Ruggiero, and Clive something, head of the CBI).[1]

A few gleanings from de Chastelain:

He is torrentially interested in talking about Northern Ireland. Far from being silent, he cannot stop talking. It has been, after all, his entire life for five years; he is an intelligent, thinking man; he has deep intimacy with every aspect of the process and all the characters involved. He is bursting to talk about it, and of course to get somewhere.

He had had long sessions with the man he always referred to as the intermediary. When I asked, he said this man was extremely intelligent and very hard and altogether of high calibre. He said he was surprised that this had been the person the IRA nominated to do the job. These talks had proceeded by fits and starts, with a great deal of ebbing and

1 Renato Ruggiero: director general of the World Trade Organization 1995–9; Italian foreign minister 2001–2. Sir Clive Thompson: president of the CBI 1998–2000.

flowing about what de C could say the IRA had done, what he could use rather than what he could not use etc. etc. (This sounded as though there was a lot of 'without prejudice' kind of dialogue between them.)

In answer to a question from Michael Forsyth, who took a belligerently hostile attitude to everything de C said, he replied that on prisoner release the process would never have started without it. It was basic. On both sides, and both sides have had their releases. They were out under licence, they knew they could go back in – but it was something that had to be done unless one said that there should be no peace process at all.

He completely refuted the notion that he had ever proposed, or been involved in, equivalent symbolic climbdowns by the security forces and the IRA.

I asked him whether Clinton had really been a key player. Yes, he said, without a doubt. First, the visa granted to Adams – which was opposed by many of Clinton's staff as well as the UK government – was the essential starting point for Adams to be able to show his colleagues that the political process could get somewhere. That was in 1994. Clinton was vilified, but it proved to be a kick-start. Second, Clinton was the man who got Trimble over to Washington and in a position to start changing the perceptions of many important Congressional politicians, who simply did not know that the Ulster Unionists were human beings. Third, Clinton has been able to put pressure on Adams et al. at crucial moments because of the cred he has built up with them.

His great hope is that Trimble and Adams both survive. He thinks if that fails to happen, it will be a tragedy – as well as perhaps a disaster.

The 22 May deadline for a settlement remains: he is counting the days. What will the governments do to revive it? His own mandate expires then (though he showed no signs of thirsting to get out). He has said to Adams and others that, given the range of weaponry and its geographical spread, it is not realistic to start decommissioning a day before the deadline (I paraphrase).

He is still an optimist. If he didn't believe the IRA were capable of doing something, he wouldn't stay. He is clearly hobbled by the decommissioning terms, but that cannot be changed. He reels off the gains the IRA have made and the reasons which have persuaded a lot of them to go the Adams route: the consent principle,[1] the stake in the government, the Patten commission, the prisoner releases etc. On the basis of this he feels that the IRA are not necessarily committed to the military solution any more. But he admits he does not know. He said this over and over again. I may be a Pollyana, he said . . .

1 The principle of consent, signed by all parties to the 1998 Good Friday Agreement, was that there would be no constitutional change in Northern Ireland unless a majority voted for it.

HY: A BLAIR NOTE
3 March 2000

In the first week of March 2000 (beginning, to be precise, on 28 February), Blair took personal charge of a committee to reform adoption law, personally made the statement launching a 20 m.p.h. advisory speed limit in built-up areas, attacked the ITN desire to confirm the ditching of *News at Ten*, attacked the banks for the new charging system for ATMs, submitted to a forty-minute grilling on the NHS by a group of patients, nurses and doctors chaired by Paxman on *Newsnight*.

Check out the complete list of distractions in all except the NHS (example above) from high politics.

An election is coming . . .

DAVID MILIBAND
10 Downing Street, 7 March 2000

LIVINGSTONE It has been a terrible mess.[1] It is now all up to Frank Dobson. Can he get his message together and across?

DM rather doubts if a KL victory would be disastrous, though certainly not helpful. The issue would be whether KL took it as a base from which to attack the government and blame it for everything that went wrong. I was surprised that DM had the slightest doubt that this would be how KL played it.

Nonetheless, the mayoral thing is still on. They call it civic entrepreneurship. DM says that Blair is totally undiverted by the London fracas from his general view that mayors and business people and voluntary groups etc. etc. could be at the heart of a revival of city culture. Look at the wonderful things the Victorians did in those big cities.

THE DEUXIÈME ÉTAPE He used this phrase several times. He thought of it like this:

The first term has been a journey of discovery on the big issues.

– Macroeconomy. We decided to concentrate on that, we did so, we did the MPC, we got the framework right – but this has just scratched

---

1 In November 1999 Ken Livingstone, former leader of the Greater London Council, won his battle with the Labour hierarchy to be allowed to compete to be the party's choice. In January 2000 the Labour Party backed Frank Dobson. In March 2000 Livingstone decided to stand anyway, and was suspended from the party. Livingstone was duly expelled from the party, in April, but eventually won the contest.

the surface of the microecon problems. The microecon therefore needs our next attention.
- Social policy. The key we fixed on was work. This has made some progress. But it has exposed the terrible state of British education etc. Just scratched the surface, again, of the real problems. Education has made a start, but health less so. Transport hardly at all. Etc.
- Political change. Decentralization and all that. Again we started, made progress, but the civic entrepreneurship, the more I think about it, becomes a big necessity for the next term.
- Europe. We were determined to change the mad isolation from Europe. We have made progress. Blair said some brave things at Ghent. We have done more than we might have expected – on defence, on environment, on crime. But again the next stage, the euro, has to be tackled.
- Spending round. This is what we are concentrating on. The big one. Far more in our minds than the election. It is a three-year process, moreover. Until 2004. This is quite new. We have a government not thinking about one-year plans, with election in mind. This reminds one how little we are thinking about election, in a way. And how we are assuming that we will win, that this is a long-term project, making slow but steady progress forward. Forces us to be long-termist.

GOVERNMENT The most striking thing I've learned in government is how long it takes to get results on the ground. Take class sizes, the easiest of all things for central government to change. It has taken for ever, and we will just about make the 30-max class size pledged. But we never thought about the practical difficulties – moving classes out, the buildings etc. etc. Numerous obstacles and problems.

As part of this it has been shattering to see how appalling our primary system has been for much of the century. We have made big changes here. There really is a whole new ethos and practice in all primary schools, as many users notice. Has been the priority for Blair and Blunkett. But compared with foreign places, what is striking is how diverse our range is. The average performance may be similar, but the gulf between the excellent and the appalling is striking and large.

SPINNING/FOCUS GROUPS ETC. One of the misunderstandings is how much we control the news. Alastair says 'If only . . .' Extraordinary myth that has taken on a life of its own, but which is at odds with the facts . . .

In particular, to my specific challenge, he said that he was worried that 'we very much under-poll.' 'When Chirac and Barak[1] come here, for example, they immediately want to know what our polls are saying. They are amazed to hear that we don't do much of it.' Philip Gould has a business to run; he doesn't do very much. Compared with the US and Clinton, where they look at every single issue through polling, we do very little. (Very HY; this reminds me that the parallel myth is that the Anglo economy really resembles the American. We should be so lucky . . .)

ELECTION He would not be drawn on what would credibly be the worst imaginable result. Said 'if we lost', but then spoke as though it was out of the question that Hague would ever be prime minister.

He agreed with me that expectations were important, and should not be talked up. But he then said – while shushing me about using it – that 'these psephologists who know much more than I do' tell us that all the best things are coming together for us in that field . . .

By far his biggest concern is turnout. How can this be dealt with? We have to have an urgent and good story to tell. And we must tell it. We have to give people reasons to vote, to get out there. The danger is of people thinking they don't need to vote. On the other hand, he said that Labour MPs who won Tory seat seems rather confident. A lot of people who voted for Labour for the first time are pleased with what we have done. It makes up for the heartland . . .

PUTIN Blair is the first foreign leader to be asked to go and see him. It is important to do this. Putin is regarded as seriously wanting to liberalize the Russian economy, but in a far better way than the terrible traumas of ten years ago (now denounced by their chief begetter, Jeffrey Sachs,[2] for wanting to create a futures market before even small businesses started to exist). That was a terrible thing, says David. Putin wants to do better.

UNITED STATES He was totally opposed to Bush, which presumably reflects Blair's own line. Strongly pro-Gore. But the worry was that much of the international agenda was being driven by the hard-Republican Christian right.

---

1 Ehud Barak: prime minister of Israel 1999–2001 and twice leader of Israel's Labour Party.
2 Jeffrey Sachs: American economist; adviser to governments in Eastern Europe, Latin America, the former Yugoslavia, the former Soviet Union, Asia and Africa.

ROBIN COOK
29 March 2000

The first time I had had a solo head-to-head with him, which I used to do a lot in opposition. Previously he has been surrounded by flacks [PR minders], or by other journalists, and the purpose has often been to show off to a group of journos who might write well of him. This time he was relaxed, personable, confiding – at his best.

LISBON SUMMIT This was quite an event. A real success. The British reporting was dominated on the first day by the absurd story about our three jets. Did they think Gordon should have gone twenty-four hours early? Did they think that Tony should have missed making his NHS statement, just to share a plane? The French had four jets – and nobody there would even dream of commenting on it.

The conclusions were guided by us, but achieved by Guterres, who is among the most effective of all the EU leaders, an outstanding man. They mean something. They are tight deadlines and precise benchmarks for achieving things – and Guterres has, to the discomfort of some, committed them all to meet every spring to assess where we have got. There is nothing that better concentrates the mind of a British civil servant than the knowledge that there will inescapably be a meeting which needs papers eleven and a half months from now.

The French, frankly, got sidelined. There was an interesting passage re the paragraph on liberalization. This refers, among other things, to 'airspace'. Until then, Chirac had been quiet, because in the divide with Jospin he has to let J do the domestic economic stuff. But airspace gave him his chance: this was about international and security affairs. Actually, we will need liberalizing here to make any sense of travel in the future. But it was interesting to see how Chirac got beaten. Tony made a dignified but telling reply – and then recited how the electricity in Downing Street came from a French-owned company, the water in his Northumbria constituency, the trains that Connex run in SE England. This began a tittering around the room. Statesmen can stand many things but not tittering. The French simply could not sustain their general case. Nobody in the room supported them, except little Belgium – which always supports them.

Védrine offered me a flight back in his plane, I get on very well with him. He took me to the Quai, and then to the upstairs room where George VI and the Queen stayed – with the most massive bathrooms I have ever seen.

EURO Tony is a political strategist who I would think long and hard before second-guessing (HY words, but RC thought). He is a brilliant strategist. So when he is convinced that the 'Europe' battle has to be fought first, I take him seriously.

There is a 20–60–20 split in the polls. Sixty per cent can be swayed either way. They will be swayed mainly by practical things, most of all jobs. If we can show that British jobs will be under threat by staying out, then that will be a strong argument. There, recent events – BMW/Rover – help this. Actually Rover did not collapse because of the exchange rate, we think. They just lost half their market share, no doubt due to BMW incompetence but also to history. However, the hard pound undoubtedly will have bad effects.

There are some hard nuts to crack, however. For example, in my constituency there is a chicken farmer (or was it horticultural business-man?) who has just shed (or is just on the verge of shedding) 500 workers. It is entirely due to the pound, he says. He has lost £30 million. If we were in the euro, for all the usual reasons about national sovereignty etc. etc.

Gordon Brown is 'not a natural European', said Robin. But he was always regarded as such, I replied. This was a wrong picture, he replied. Gordon has never been at ease in Europe, still does not talk easily to European politicians. At Ecofin, he spends time talking and acting on the lines of the 'British interest'. Defending his corner. Rather than collaborat-ing. Of course, with a man so secretive with his own colleagues, it would be surprising if he was any different with Europeans. Yes, he does have a veto on the economic terms. No doubt about that. This is quite a big worry for Downing Street. (Otherwise, by the way, Robin was generous to Gordon, talking about the Budget etc.)

ELECTION He agrees with me that anything less than a three-figure majority will be unfortunate, and could have an impact on the euro issue. But he seems to be quite serene about the outcome.

He has always pointed out, he says, that we could win more votes and fewer seats under the vagaries of the British system. But he is quite confident about the heartlands, for example. Yes, there is an issue about whether they will turn out. But at present the choice they are making in their minds is between the real Labour government and some Labour government of their dreams. That is not the choice. And when the election comes the choice will be between this government and the Tories.

Further on the heartlands, he looks at the record. This government has done far far better than any previous Labour government. Those earlier governments had bad records on employment, especially. This has a very good one – 800,000 new jobs, the New Deal, long-term unemployment halved. Look also at the minimum wage, trade-union recognition.

I said, What about the first-time Labour voters? He replied, At the Scottish and other elections, we did rather better in the middle-class seats than the rest. Why was this? Well, perhaps it is because we are seen to be speaking to the kinds of people the heartlands do not like! This is a serious point – about the heartlands. We have done a lot that they want, but our image, our perceived identity, is drawn from the world in which we are seen to be mixing . . . But this does us a lot of good with the middle classes.

Tony would string me up alive if he heard me talking like this – he has an iron rejection of any complacency whatever.

TORIES Portillo is not fighting this election, he is positioning himself for the next. That is what he is all about, and he is very skilful at it. We have come to something, haven't we, when he is the compassionate face of Conservatism? But that is how he has shifted. He has ruthlessly changed his stance on several things. Did you see that piece he did about being a porter at St Thomas's Hospital. Brilliant, well written, feeling etc. etc.

Hague is as Labour was in 1979. Labour said then we are not going to be dictated to by the electorate – a strange thing for a party to say. Only in 1983 did we start the road to reversing all that, with Kinnock. Kinnock lost in '87 – but he was seen to have a project that made sense. Hague has no such project. He has not said to the party a single thing it does not want to hear. That is the charge against him – not that he is miles behind in the polls. He has no project that will sustain him in office, even if he has a better-than-expected election campaign: he will go, whatever the result.

Portillo, on the other hand, plainly does have a project. The 1983–7 project. To engage with the reality of the voters . . . Etc. etc.

ANDREW LANSLEY
The Garrick, 3 April 2000

A smart, reasonable, intelligent youngish Tory, who seems shrewd, unsectarian and well aware of the issues of political management.

TORIES I put it to him that Hague had not done what Kinnock did after 1983: that he was stuck as Foot in 1979. Lansley said no. And he has a point. Labour after Foot was having to tell its heartland vote to stop thinking what it was thinking: to abandon its age-old positions. Even as late as 1994, Labour people still wanted to be the party of high spend and even CND. None of this is true of the Tories. Hague does not have to get the party to abandon any of its heartfelt wishes. He does have an electoral problem, obviously. We are far behind in the polls and in the seats.

EUROPE He said, rather surprisingly, that the referendum was a nonsense. He thought here was an issue that could perfectly well be settled by an election – the two parties had clear and opposed positions. Each party, as I said, had only a fragment on its edge that disagreed with its position. Therefore an election would be entirely satisfactory as a way of dealing with it.

As a result, as I put to him and he agreed, we have a dangerous situation. The referendum, whatever the words, will be seen as for or against Europe as a whole. And, whatever the words, a No vote would take us towards the margins – he agreed. It might even set up a strong exit call. All this would be disastrous. An election would avoid all that. A victory for the Tories would not have the effect of setting up an exit move to anything like the extent that a No vote in the referendum would.

He said Blair was in the worst of all worlds. He was buying the *Sun* diagnosis: yes to Blair, not to the euro. Giving in to *The Sun*'s position, its blackmail (my word). A very strange thing to be doing, storing up a lot of trouble.

I said that Blair needed a big victory, which would finesse all of this; he did not seem to disagree. After a big victory, a big second-term triumph, he could do what he wanted: Hague would be gone, the Tories in disarray – and the ground free for a big Europe debate, in which the hard currency and job implications (my point not his) would doubtless be prominent.

Labour's line about the referendum could be dealt with in two ways.

- By reminding people that Labour had promised a referendum on the euro during this parliament, and Brown had evaded that in October 1997. (He claimed that the focus groups showed that people remembered this and attacked Labour for it. I replied that I doubted more than one in a hundred people would remember it.)
- Using the fact that Blair is seen as a fixer, and twister, a manipulator of all procedures (London being the prime example).

JOHN STEVENS
Phone, 6 June 2000

OFF THE RECORD.

He has heard from Margaret McDonagh (via Peter Temple-Morris)[1] a list of places where they would welcome an intervention by the pro-euro Tories. This says, inter alia, that Labour now seems less bothered about keeping sweet and not splitting the Tories, prepared to be more upfront about that. And Labour is right, I say. KC takes his position, whatever happens. The chances of him needing to be kept sweet have diminished.

They plan to run candidates against hard-line Euro-sceptics (a list appears conveniently in today's *Telegraph*). But they will avoid seats where the LDs were second last time and have a serious chance of winning. Thus they will fight Wokingham, since Redwood is hard-line and the LDs are far behind. But other such seats in the south they will avoid.

Kellner has told him that he thinks the LDs will end up with the same number of seats, but lose 10 in the south and gain 10 in the north.

He has talked to Charles Kennedy at some length, and agreed the above formula about not hitting the Lib Dems.

I said the LDs are now a transit camp for Labour voters as they were for Tory voters before. He could see that, but still thinks the Libs are vulnerable. Actually, all in all, he claimed not to know what the hell was really going on . . .

He railed against Clarke, whom I had just seen (but blurred when this was). Says he cannot see why KC can't see that Labour need all the help they can get if the referendum is to be held. I say, Ultimately Clarke is slothful and comfy, being a big Tory rebel, sincerely believing in his plans, but lacking the moral energy to do what Jenkins et al. did in 1981.

GEOFF HOON
Lunch, Luigi's, 7 June 2000

Derry Irvine was the first man GH worked for as a junior minister. Regards him as a friend, Irvine has been to stay, knows his children. A good sort, says Geoff, with whom, if he ceased to be a politician, he would hope to keep up.

---

1 Margaret McDonagh: Labour Party general secretary 1998–2001; later Baroness McDonagh of Mitcham and Morden. Peter Temple-Morris: barrister; MP for Leominster – Conservative 1974–97, independent 1997–8, Labour 1998–2001; later Baron Temple-Morris of Llandaff.

MINISTRY OF DEFENCE   A very can-do department, the effect
of policymakers working absolutely next to the people who have to see
that things happen. Other departments are different. There, unless the
minister or the private office chases something, it may witter away into
the sand. But soldiers are not like that. They are also respectful of lines
of authority. GH has been having a huge argument with the CGS, who
is about to leave. Some policy matter. The CGS resisted it all the way.
But now that he is going he has acceded gracefully . . .

NMD   He was pretty cagey. But he did say one thing: that a European
ambition might be to get to Europe covered by the NMD system. This
would be a way of turning the Europeans round. I put the usual objections
to the whole thing. He half agreed with me, but talked about risk assessment needing to be taken further. North Korea did have capacity. Iraq
was unpredictable. These were dangerous times.

I said, Why can't we believe they will be deterred in the usual way? He
didn't have an answer. We talked about rogue states and the facile nature
of that definition. Altogether he did not seem well briefed or to be paying
close attention. Not a likely powerful critic of the Americans – yet anyway.

POLITICS   He is very keen about this. A natural counter of votes. I
asked for the majority. He said, Roughly 70. We could lose 50 seats on
the same percentage as last time – LD votes refusing this time to back
Labour (though he conceded that Labour voters might go LD).

But he thinks 70 would be quite enough to hold a referendum. On
that, he thinks business must get more engaged. Or rather that it will be
very hard to run a referendum campaign if substantial parts of business
are against going into the euro. He agreed that there are significant
companies with a handful of sceps on the board who call the shots.

He feels quite sure that it is not William Hague's destiny to be prime
minister.

I found him cheerful, relaxed, confident, down to earth. A sensible
fellow, but without charisma or, I suspect, the appetite to try and acquire
charisma.

*HY originally suggested the Garrick as the venue for his first lengthy
talk with Philip Gould, but this was rejected by Gould's secretary,
which HY took as a 'heavy hint' that Gould had been refused membership of the club.[1] HY described him as 'nervy, spasmodically garrulous,*

1 Completely false, says Gould: 'I choose not to go to the Garrick as it will not accept women as members,
which is to me unacceptable in modern Britain.'

uneasy in one way (but with me, I think), slightly incoherent, but very, very interested in the tides of opinion'. The lunch took place, as it happened, the day after Blair's fiasco at the Women's Institute, when he misjudged the mood of his audience and was treated to a slow handclap.

PHILIP GOULD
Savoy Restaurant, 8 June 2000

He thinks opinion is hard to judge and hard to move. But he notices from his frequent and fascinated engagement with focus groups that people are (a) disbelieving in 'responsibility' and (b) the same about 'opportunity'. 'People' – by which he means lower-middle-class Middle England types – simply think that responsibility has gone for ever. They also show a desperate poverty of ambition. There is a widespread sense that university, let alone Oxbridge, is 'not for us'. This is the class system alive and kicking, in people's minds. This depresses him. As it should. He contrasts it with the US, and even with Germany and France. He did focus groups in Watts (he didn't say when), and found that, although people were living in the pits, they believed they would get out and were determined to do so. Germany and France, equally, show more sense of expectation and confidence than we do. Somehow, too many people here think (a) they themselves have nowhere up to go and (b) that the country has little hope, is going to the dogs, is not a great country any more.

This was added to by the state of the press. He spent a lot of lunch going on about the media, about which he frankly said he was obsessed. He saw them as knocking everything the government did, making it impossible to get policies and achievements across, engaging in character attacks and general undermining all the time. He said he knew the liberal press had to be detached, but he wished the *Telegraph* could be *The Guardian*'s model sometimes (not said seriously). The *Mail* is his special obsession, mitigated by the discovery that only 13 per cent of its readers are Labour voters – perhaps we should reduce that to zero, he speculated.

He was present this morning at a meeting with Blair, Brown, Mandelson and Campbell. This is a good team, he said. When they are pulling together, a lot of good things get said and decided. They are now pulling together. In particular, Gordon is back on side. He is talking to Gould, which apparently was not the case for the last three years, and GB has the merit of being interested in much that Gould is finding, especially about class. A big difference between Blair and Brown is that Blair is not terribly interested in what focus groups etc. say. He will bash on with genetically modified foods or Europe, regardless. Brown is far more interested in the detail, and responding to it.

But the big point was that this is a good team. And the Tory drive has been a wake-up call. This is healthy. Someone said this morning that perhaps we should start talking the Tories up – to which Brown said they were doing it perfectly well on their own. There is a sense that tightening of the figures will help make people get real, help bring the party alive, force voters to look more closely at Hague and ask themselves if they really want this man governing the country.

PG said that now he felt rather good. Mainly because the top leadership was getting it together. There would not be another period like this, he avowed, We are pulling it together. We will get into a run, into a groove (he kept repeating). And the Tories will, for sure, make mistakes. The press will get bored with slagging us off, and turn their eye on Tory errors.

The Tories, he felt, would continue with populist lines. He reeled them off. Asylum-seekers, crime, Europe. These had all worked well for them. They were quite unprincipled, 'unlike us'. Neither Kinnock nor Smith nor Blair would have sunk to the depths they have, especially about asylum-seekers. But there was nobody on the Tory team who rang many bells. Hague did not, though he was good in the House. People just do not relate to him, can't imagine him being the leader.

He is himself fascinated by class in all aspects. He worries about the low aspirations of the British, but also about their susceptibility to the media, which seem to be the only agency that can shift opinion (he implied).

The problem for politicians in New Labour was to get the right mix between conviction and consensus. This was the whole art. This is also what the media make very much harder. If you try and draw people along, pushing at the edge of their desire for a soft life, and at their prejudices, the media will try and block it. Europe being the classic example, but it goes wider than that. Blair is engaged on this dual task, very consciously. An enormous amount of time and collective effort is going into the issue of how best to restart the process, get control of the agenda, get a few months in the groove where you pursue both tracks.

He said that crime is unavoidably a big issue for everyone – more so than asylum, which after all affects only a smallish number. He watches disgusted the cynicism of the Tories saying asylum-seekers are causing your NHS waiting lists.

It is, by the way, quite wrong to talk about a liberal elite. There is no liberal elite, and it is certainly not running the country.

He is very interested in quizzing me about Thatcher. How did her first term go? Was she in terrible trouble? Did she have a challenging agenda? I rehearsed the history, pointing out to him that she was in a far worse state than Blair, and after three years, until the Falklands War, was widely expected to lose the election.

I also made a big case that her greatest strength was that she didn't mind not being liked. That is a big difference with Blair. Ultimately she did not care about popularity.

Ah, he seemed to say, but she had the press on her side anyway, and that is true. They were part of her project. They gave her an easy time right through the decimation of the heartlands. I add, There were perceived problems of a massive scale to be solved – which is not the case with Blair. There was not a sense of national crisis when he took over. Moreover, in the absence of opposition, the press have undoubtedly gone exactly the other way – they have felt a duty to attack him, whereas under Thatcher, with the ultra-left and Foot waiting in the wings, they felt a duty to support her.

ADAM BOULTON
At Belgian-embassy dinner, 6 July 2000

Blair would be helped not damaged by the Euan incident, which happened today.[1] It made him seem better connected to ordinary life. Rebuffed the latest Tory charge, which they've been working on hard, that Blair is out of touch.

AB has always thought that Blair would quit in the second term. He is not, fundamentally, wedded to politics. He could even be said not to be a politician: certainly not a conventional one. He does have other things to do, and does believe in the family stuff and all that. Also, he and Cherie like money: the private helicopters and all that. Moreover, she has her career. It has been on hold. She cannot progress until he quits as PM.

He thinks that Brown really is psychologically flawed. I asked him what he thought Brown really thought about the euro, and about his career generally. Adam was pretty nonplussed, though he must watch and see him often. Noted that he had not got married, he had the chance to get married, marriage was coming, yet he backed off. That tells you a lot, he said.

On the euro, he said that Blair, Mandelson et al. would find it impossible not to hold the referendum. They would look so stupid with anything

---

1 Blair's eldest son was arrested on 6 July 2000, aged 16, having been found 'drunk and incapable' after celebrating his GCSE results; reprimanded by police.

like a decent victory, and especially bearing in mind the Lib Dem alliance. They just have to hold it., They would look like total cowards if they didn't. Their role in history would have expired.

What, however, will be Brown's role? Adam advanced the complex thesis – which I contested – that Brown would remain a sceptic: that the referendum would happen without his full participation, and he would then be able to pick up the pieces when the referendum had failed. He would have clean hands. AB even suggested that this could be part of an agreement with Blair, sanctioned by him – in the interest of the party. I said I disagreed with all that. But it is interesting, and Adam is a serious, sharp observer.

JOHN MONKS
At the TUC, 14 July 2000

EURO He saw Brown and Balls ten days ago, Blair three weeks ago about.

Brown, when talking about the euro, says that he must at all costs protect the stability that has been created. There are two ways to do this. (1) via the MPC [Monetary Policy Committee], (2) by going into the euro. When he is pressed on the latter, however, he shears away and the talk becomes circular. He emphasizes all that is going well with the economy, and how much would be at risk if we made the wrong choices. He has no answer on the strong-pound issue, which is the main reason why the TUC goes to see him. He talks, honestly, about the productivity problem, but less honestly about the way in which industry has performed well enough despite the high pound, including getting its productivity somewhat better. He has figures to give him encouragement about the employment levels in manufacturing industry being better than those elsewhere. All in all, says John, this is not the language of a Chancellor who is expecting there to be certainly a referendum soon after the next election. He just does not sound like that, or someone getting ready for it.

The economic tests, says John, are pretty well met by now. There is convergence of everything except the exchange rate. This really exposes the truth that the issue is political – both the politics of the Labour government and the politics of the British people (this last HY's phrase). Moreover, he said, to my plaint that the framing of the tests as economic was always a mistake, that that was the way the Chancellor kept control. He sees the five tests as a Brown invention, for Brown's own purposes: a power play.

Blair he sees as being in quite a lot of trouble. The spinning has been terrible, culminating with the annual report yesterday, which Hague was able to ridicule very effectively. Monks admired H's timing with the jokes (in a HC speech), but the material was offered to him on a plate by the fatuities of the report, its plain errors, and the openness of the previous year's report to ridicule, which Hague duly exploited. John was chuckling at the memory of it.

He sees Blair as being in difficulties. It is for the first time possible to talk, however remotely, about Blair not winning the election. JM thinks he will win, but the talk had changed drastically from when Blair walked on water.

I put it to him that one was beginning to think that Blair might not be all that tough. Certainly this is what is now being put to the test. He hadn't needed to be terribly tough, he hadn't faced all that much adversity, before. Winning over the Labour Party was bold, but in the end they ate out of his hand because they wanted to win the '97 election. Now it is different: they are snapping and sniping, and this will go on. Monks said he disagreed that Blair was not tough. He thought he would and could be. But the ways he had to show it might be very demanding, including the sacking of Campbell and the moving of Brown from the Treasury. John seemed to think Blair had it in him to do this.

He notes how sanguine Blair was, when last seen (as he had been with me earlier), about winning over the people. Thinks that in a few weeks the task can be done. Big business will weigh in, the government will unite, and they will win, says Blair. To Blair, the quality of the argument is what will matter, and he is very confident of his ground. JM was worried on all these counts. Thought Blair was not being realistic.

I asked him, if Blair won a majority of 60, what were the chances of having a referendum? In Blair's mind, he said, 95 per cent. But Blair would not be in exclusive control.

Monks continues to flirt with the notion of Blair going much earlier to the country. He could do this only on the basis of the euro: saying that the conditions were now met: that he should not hang about: that, yes, there would be a referendum, but that he wanted to settle the ground for that without delay: that we needed to get in sooner rather than later. JM is rather hoping that he will do this, a grand and unpredicted gesture, which would seize command from Brown and the others, and be a make-or-break initiative.

He thinks Blair needs the therapy of something like this. He noted how poor he was on BBC *Question Time* two weeks ago, until riled by someone from UKIP who really got him fired up, got the audience fired up, and made Blair perform at his best, not only on that issue but for the rest of the programme. Taking the initiative on the very difficult issue of the euro, says JM, is the only way Blair can reassert command and do something to recapture the dominance he had for his first thirty months.

However, he knows this is unlikely. We turn to Brown. I put to him my emerging thesis that Gordon is actuated entirely by ambition, and that all these questions we keep asking ourselves about his adherence to the euro cause, his euro-scepticism etc. are the wrong questions. What matters to him is whether the referendum can be won. If he thinks it can't be won, he will want to position himself for the situation where it is lost. He will need to establish his doubts, as a reason why he was right and Blair was wrong – though if the referendum was in fact held, Gordon could hardly campaign for a No vote.

JM was told recently that Brown had always been against the refer-endum, when Blair declared for it. Brown took the John Smith line, that elections were what mattered. He never wanted to get hung up on a referendum, because he immediately realized (as did K. Clarke and M. Heseltine) that it could be hard to win. Therefore, it is said, Brown explicitly argued against the pledge (in November '96, from memory).

This is fascinating. But the source was Charlie Whelan, in a recent talk with JM. Charlie is a europhile, but also a Brownite. He would want Gordon to be seen in the best light, and the revelation might be the first move in an attempt to distance Brown from what he thinks is about to happen. Therefore, I say, it needs checking. But with whom? Mandelson and Cook are scarcely reliable. Elizabeth Smith, suggests JM. Also Murray Elder, also Roger Liddle.

We agreed that if the referendum was held and lost, it would have a catastrophic effect on the whole UK–EU relationship. The next step would be a push for exit. The certain immediate result would be a popular veto, as construed by the media, against any further collaboration with integration. He contrasted us with the Danes. A Danish No would have little effect. Denmark has been in the DM area for many years and will remain in the euro area come what may. That is why the economic aspects of the decision count for so little, but also why the political consequences of a No are so slight. It would be a big defeat for the political establish-ment, and reduce Danish influence, But Danish influence is small already, unlike what we like to think of as British influence.

ROGER LIDDLE
Phone, 16 July 2000

I spelled out the Brown political thesis. RL said that the basic truth is that nobody knows what Gordon is thinking. Peter and I, he went on, have talked about all this, and he decided it does not make sense. I had just spoken to PM, who said the same.

RL said he thought GB would in the end go along with Tony's judgement about the referendum. The issue would be whether he chose to let it be known that he was not keen on the referendum, rather as Callaghan did in 1975 (rather more than Wilson, RL said, though I think that is not the case). For Brown to try this, if the referendum took place, would be as disastrous for him as it would be for the party. If Labour lost the referendum, what a disastrous inheritance would await the new leader of the party. The Tories would almost certainly win the next election. So RL says he can't see this scenario for Gordon. But a more plausible one is that Gordon tries to dissuade Tony from holding the referendum. Tony gets dispirited and then packs it all in, seeing his historic mission undone.

On the referendum pledge, RL said with certainty that Gordon was opposed to making the pledge – but this was before the Tories made theirs. Labour were obviously aware of what might be coming, and had their own inner discussions of it. Gordon was clearly against.

I asked RL if he was also against when the pledge finally was made, months after Major had made his pledge. Roger said he could not remember.

Roger said that Tony's attitude would have been most influenced by Roy Jenkins, at each stage. Roy thought the referendum was a good idea, that the British people needed to have their say etc. etc. Tony was very much influenced by Roy in many things.

NOTE TO SELF ON TONY BLAIR
17 July 2000

Some reflections on the day that his April memo[1] is leaked:

This memo is very revealing. It does show a man obsessed with how the government is seen, not how it is performing, and still less how its

---

1 In April, while at Chequers, in a confidential memo to his closest advisers, Tony Blair elaborated what he perceived as the weakness of his government, including his perception that he and his administration were 'somehow out of touch with British gut instincts'. It was the third such damaging leak in a month. HY on 18 July

leadership and ideas are according with how it is seen. It is the quintessence of a worried man, whose worries are not about his beliefs/policies/convictions not getting through so much as about how he discovers policies and wheezes that accord with what the public want, or, more bitterly still, with what the public can be persuaded looks good.

It recalls the line, way back, that Blair said to me: We will win the election as long as I am the only voice that speaks for the party.

Some new images of Blair begin to rise in my mind: of a man who is lightweight as a butterfly, skimming along the surface. He is not at all without serious ideas about what he wants to do, but he has a distorted idea about his own unique role in doing this. He does lack gravitas. Terribly so. This could be seen on Saturday in the Alastair Campbell film,[1] when the blokeish man stood around while Campbell sat down – no respect, no authority. Just two lads together. Serious lads. But, as it seemed, equal lads.

Suddenly you begin to remember that Blair has not a great deal of weight. Weight is given by convictions and programmes, projects, and in the end an ideological conviction. Blair despises ideology, has made the banishment of ideology one of the cardinal parts of his project: something he is most proud of – the removal of the left–right difference etc.

Another strand of this is the quite extraordinary fact that a man could be in big trouble who has a 179 parliamentary majority. This, just as much as Blair's evident uninterest in parliamentary procedures etc., reminds one how unimportant Parliament has become. It's not just the bypassing in order to get things done, it's the complete failure to deploy this giant majority in ways that remind the country of the government's authority.

He has therefore quite neglected Parliament, because he did not think he needed it. This doesn't necessarily mean that Parliament is in permanent decline (though see Peter Preston's good column today). Any government that has to rely on a majority of 20 will soon find the Commons reinvigorated, though the Blair reforms of the Commons (Beckett)[2] seem calculated to knock the wind out of the opportunities of opposition.

He has in the course of this neglect deeply alienated people more traditional than he is. Has overlooked the degree to which he would one day need the party. Showed that he is far above the way of life of his MPs. Insisted on developing a cohort of trusties and loyalists, who will do anything he wants because they are starry-eyed camp followers on the

---

called the memo 'terribly depressing. It shows the lengths to which a desperate man has been driven, away from the steady path of purposeful reform into the dead end of instant wheezes and bogus responses.'

1 *News from No. 10*, shown on BBC2. *The Guardian*'s veteran political editor Ian Aitken said that it revealed Alastair Campbell as 'a nice, cuddly loyal servant of Tony Blair ... endlessly tormented by beastly lobby correspondents'.

2 Margaret Beckett, as Leader of the House 1998–2001, introduced a number of reforms.

way up – and are themselves very often as contemptuous of the old party as he is.

One effect of this is that he becomes easy meat when he starts to fall. He has enough enemies waiting for his decline. They see him as having neglected them when he has this vast majority, and, being human, they can be easily drawn into repaying him when the time comes – unless he shows a great deal of muscle.

We get a sense, all in all, of Blair's fragility. Perhaps his lack of bottom – something that derives from both the thinness of his project and the lightness of his personality. Also coming into this, perhaps, is his strange relationship to politics as a life. On the one hand, he has been totally dedicated to getting to the top and to getting New Labour into the position of the new twenty-first-century orthodoxy. On the other hand, he lacks some of the traditional aspects of a politician: total commitment; obsession; no family concerns; the sense that there is no other life; ideological traces; above all, party, collegiality, collectivism.

One should not overdo this. Plainly he does have the power to compromise, has got the negotiator's skills (Ireland, Europe, Brown . . .). In his own mind, too, he does have a very definite programme and project. But he may lack stamina. And he may lack resilience. He has led a charmed life. Floated like a butterfly. Within this a contempt for much that has passed for politics in the past in this country. A belief that somehow he is above politics, that he is certainly above party.

All in all, the genius who was looked up to by so many European leaders is turning out to be a bit thin. Maybe not to be able to cut it in bad times as well as good; maybe not a man for the long haul (though he is very insistent on his being a long-term project, and he means it when he says so).

This could all climax after the election, if he does not win quite big. The euro referendum will be the end of him if he does not hold it, or does not win it. He is totally aware of that, I'm sure.

HANS FRIEDRICH VON PLOETZ
The Garrick, 21 July 2000

He was at the opening of our Berlin embassy earlier this week.[1] An amazing event. The Queen et al., and lots of politicians, including Schröder, Fischer, Biedenkopf,[2] Irvine (I think), others. Would it have

---

1 The embassy in Wilhelmstrasse was selected by open competition, and was the first embassy to be built by private finance initiative. The Queen opened it on 18 July, and is reported to have said of its architecture, 'I understand that some people like it.' When asked to comment on the design, the Duke of Edinburgh said, 'No.'
2 Kurt Biedenkopf: minister president of Saxony 1990–2002.

been the same turnout for the German embassy opening here? The German media coverage was amazingly full, and altogether positive. The British media coverage was very slight, and concentrated on the one piece of criticism of the architect of the embassy, in one German paper.

At this meeting he witnessed a deep talk between Biedenkopf and Irvine, discussing constitutional issues. B favoured a system to be termed 'diverse federation', Irvine something called 'structural diversity'. B had been outlining the fact that in Saxony there needed to be further downward delegation even from the provincial government. In respect of the economy, said B, the state government could do nothing. Therefore, for those purposes at least, there had to be something else, some new variant of federation. Irvine was terribly interested, and asked for B to send him papers on it all.

It seems that Hans had a recent meeting with *The Sun*, just three of them at the table. It must have included David Yelland [editor] and Trevor Kavanagh [political editor], though he discreetly did not mention names. Hans put it to them thus: The euro will go ahead. It will not fail, and it will have political implications, it will be at the heart of something big that is happening. What do you want for Britain? Do you really want to be on the outside looking in? Is that your version of British history as it moves forward? And so on. He said they really did not have an answer.

July had been a bleak month for the government. April's embarrassing leak of a memo by Tony Blair was followed by an equally embarrassing leak of a memo from Labour's guru Philip Gould, who warned No. 10 that New Labour's 'brand' was becoming 'badly contaminated'.

DAVID MILIBAND
10 Downing Street, 25 July 2000

He began by asking me how I thought things were going. What of present discontents? I said that July was bad for many governments, and had been bad for this one. He seemed to question that. I got the message that this was meant to be a corrective, positive, if ever so polite, piece of favourable self-spinning. And why not?

I began with the leaks. He admitted they were terrible. Really bad. But he protested that they were only a tiny slice of TB's mind, a memo dashed off on a weekend, which any of us might have done. They did not reveal more than a fraction of his state of mind and preoccupations. Nor was it true that Gould was a decisive voice: Tony does not have gurus, said David, so much as a group of people – admittedly quite a small group – who bring to bear different attitudes and advice, all of which he listens to.

I said that nonetheless the leaks were revealing. Especially the stuff that wanted to associate himself with everything – which the Tories have already begun to use mercilessly. DM's answer to this was interesting. He said that nobody could get the oomph behind any policy to anything like the extent that Tony could. This meant he probably did too much. It certainly looks odd to see him today launching the football challenge,[1] yesterday being at the G8, and Thursday doing the health launch. We have to decide and choose, DM said. It is always a balance to be struck.

On the whole, he said, he was happy with the ideological positioning of the party. Happier than he was last year. Clarity had arrived where there previously had been, he had to say, some mush. He cited two things in particular. First, tax-and-spend. We are now very clear here; we have got the bedrock of our position. (This seemed to be saying that tax-and-spend, albeit in approved Blairite mode, had returned as a Labour ideal.) It is, most important of all, distinguishable from the Tories. It is very clear. Second, the same is true of Europe. Oddly, he said, I am now happier with the Europe position than I was a year ago (he even said eighteen months ago).

There could be no doubt, now, where we stand and where we are coming from. The message could be clear – though there was a problem about how to get it across. (Our talk was littered with a number of moments when he asked me how the record could be somehow got across.)

I challenged him on Home Office affairs, saying the government's line here was far from distinct from the Tories, but was chasing after them. DM and his unit have obviously been working a lot on this recently, and made the following points:

Criminal justice has not been reformed for decades. It is a total shambles. Nobody has got to grips with it. Nobody has even informed statistics and data about the scale of the problem. We have been doing this.

As an example, take police witnesses. He has met policemen who say they've attended at court for twelve days and only on the thirteenth been called to give evidence.

There has been a huge problem of rivalry between the Lord Chancellor's Department, the Home Office and the Crown Prosecution Service. Each has been a fiefdom. Now there is a joint committee working together

1 On 25 July 2000, Kevin Keegan joined Tony Blair in Downing Street to announce a new project to invest in football's 'grass roots' with a network of school AstroTurf pitches and soccer minicentres around the country.

– although they retain their separate budgets. He had been to Bristol recently and spent time with the CPS, who told a tale of total frustration with court time, witness time, delays, total inefficiency on every side.

Judges should be administrators of time as much as they are dispensers of justice. Auld[1] should do for criminal justice what Woolf very effectively and importantly did for civil justice.

On prisons, the UK has the lowest proportion of prisoners to crimes committed of all European countries. This is the Home Office answer to overcrowding. It shows that the UK has more crime than any other (check) European country. But it is a sort of retort to the more familiar fact that the UK has the highest proportion of prisoners per thousand population. Added to this, 54 per cent of people on non-custodial sentences reoffend, and 56 per cent of those who've been to prison (or perhaps vice versa). This shows that the criminal population is relatively small. (Implication: put more of them in jail for longer and you will reduce the crime rate.) Burglary has shown amazing drops (over 20 per cent). But crimes of violence are up. He admits this is partly due to the counting and reporting of crime being all over the place. But domestic crime and race crime are more reported, which is good.

When I said that I objected to the anti-justice, anti-court bias in some measures (e.g. deprivation of benefit) he didn't take the point. On the interesting issue of mandatory life sentences (Tony Martin)[2] I explained the position and drew his attention to the numerous reports advising against mandatory sentences. He replied, Only when the crime rate starts going down will you be able to persuade the public that we are on their side, and can then start talking about sentencing. He instanced the US example, where he noted that at last there was a bit of discussion about capital punishment, which had been off the agenda for decades, but only because the crime rates in cities especially have gone so dramatically down – due to better detection, more people in prisons, demographic effects of fewer younger males around etc.

The issue, though, was that people had to believe that we are on their side in this crucial area before any liberal reforms (I gathered) could be contemplated. Otherwise they would simply not be accepted.

This led to the issue 'Out of touch'. Interestingly, he says that all social-democratic governments he is in touch with – which means most – have found this to be the charge most often levelled against them by the right. It is a convenient portmanteau way of mobilizing people's

---

1 Sir Robin Auld, Lord Justice Auld QC, conducted the Criminal Courts Review 1999–2001.
2 Tony Martin was the Norfolk farmer who kept a loaded gun by him and shot and killed one burglar and injured another – and was then imprisoned for murder, wounding and possession of an illegal firearm. On appeal, the verdict was reduced to manslaughter.

general discontents. If the hospital has done badly, it's because Blair is out of touch. Literally anything will fit under the umbrella (this is HY's elaboration of DM's point). It is a very common charge, and it is hard to deal with. (But, HY remarks, this charge is, in his opinion, a fiction. Not true at all that Blair is out of touch.)

On the Tories. He said we should not underestimate the loathing they have for us, the social democrats. They believe we have no right to be in power. They feel usurped. (This is v. interesting. Shows more about Old Labour paranoia than being a real account of the truth, in my opinion. Shows their underdog feel. Actually, my impression of the Tories is that they have entirely lost their sense of being born or entitled to rule. It is a far more naked power struggle between equals than that . . .)

DM finds their whole strategy amazing. It was just about understandable to the masses that they could make a tax guarantee. After all, Labour shows a downward path on taxing with their forward plans. You needed an A-level economics degree to see through it. But the £16 billion cuts guarantee is a disaster for them. You don't need any O levels at all to see through that. Portillo, moreover, was quite appalling in the HC in answer to Brown the other day – DM said it was the worst parliamentary speech he had ever heard from the front bench. They have no way of defending the cuts charge. It simply will not be enough to say that they would spend money better, or that GB is being irresponsible in his forward planning. The Tories are also, it seems to him, putting themselves in a bunker. They are only appealing to the hard right. Why is this? What do they hope to gain? Well, we both agree, cynicism is their greatest friend. The belief that politicians can make no difference. The belief that Labour has been cooking the books etc. etc.

Further on the Tories, he remarked that this must be the first time in history that the party of the right, anywhere, had lost contact with its business constituency. What is the Tory Party for if not to be the party of business? It had sacrificed this through its attitude to the euro. See below.

So how could Labour get back to real supremacy? DM says we are the most successful social-democratic government. Or at any rate we are being successful. We are doing lots of social-democratic things. Arguably we are the best in UK history since 1945, which was v. good for a while but ran out of steam. Yet we are not seen as such. How can this change? he asks.

We discuss the problems of spin, the dangers in having overclaimed, the instances of double counting (which he claimed, at least, he could not recall a single example of). I remarked, It is the fate of politicians to be (a) endlessly repetitive, always saying the same thing again and again, while (b) needing to pretend to novelty, freshness, new wheezes, a new start etc. These niches were in conflict. But over and above that, Labour's emphasis on presentation had made things worse: made it hard to be taken seriously. Certainly one answer to his dilemma, however, was for the Tories to become more and more clearly alien from the mainstream.

Another was to make the evidence of success much more local. To meet people's distrust of big numbers nationally by putting on the net what has been done for every postcode. (He showed me this for NW3 1LG on his computer.)

All this took place in the context of my saying that turnout was going to be the single biggest problem. He did not disagree. The 1992 turnout had been very high, because people thought it might be close. That was one message: if people thought this was not going to be close, they might not vote. But he agreed there were wider things – the refusal of first-time Labour people (almost entirely negative voters) to do it again, and the disillusion of real Labour voters and their refusal to vote for 'Labour Lite'. The second class could perhaps be got at, the first perhaps not.

I also said that the Lib Dems could do well. He did not disagree. Said, as I wrote at the time, that Romsey was significant.[1] Very worrying for the Tories. As long as there were more Romseys (and not by implication more northern switches), he was all in favour of Lib Dems doing well!

On Europe, he said that he was happier with the positioning of the government (as above), but worried about the Eurobarometer poll, showing much disillusionment with Europe. We had to think about this. We agreed that it was necessary for ministers to get started on some much more general pro-EU speeches.

Re the euro, he said, the anti argument was, of course, changing. Having spent a year or two saying the eurozone countries were dead ducks, they have lost that argument: the eurozone economies are growing fast (besides having had for many years 20 per cent better productivity). So the sceptics abandon that argument, and now start talking about the Germans' monstrous pensions situation, or whatever. They will always find an argument . . . But the underlying fact is that the economic case against the euro as originally stated will not run. Therefore the battlefront has broadened . . . The very issue of membership is in the frame.

I asked, If we are not in the euro in five years, what will happen to us? He said, The world will not come to an end. But we will find the others doing more things together, which we are out of, and that cannot be good. On the other hand, there were ways in which we were genuinely different anyway . . .

---

1 The Romsey by-election was fought on 4 May. The swing to the Lib Dems of 21 per cent saw their candidate gain the seat from the Tories with a majority of 3,000. Labour came a very poor third.

DAVID CURRY
Phone, 3 September 2000

Labour will win by a landslide, he says. Can't see anything that is going to change that landscape. The important thing, therefore, is for us (the Tory left) to be there with the right lessons to draw from defeat.

To see how the party is positioning itself solely for the core vote is very sad. My children, says David, are all bright and living in Putney and in their mid or late twenties, and probably natural Tories. But none of them would ever vote Tory. They think the party is totally out of touch. All the stuff about gays is totally incredible to them. Like the British people, they may not think all that much of Labour, but there's no way they'll vote Tory. They think we're a lot of shits.

Hague and his fourteen pints: his problem is not just saying what he said, but the fact that nobody believes him!

The man who fought Hague at the last general election for the Referendum Party is now fighting a local election as the Conservative candidate in my constituency![1]

We have not selected either a woman or an ethnic-minority candidate for a single winnable seat. That is the sort of party we have become.

I take some pleasure in saying that I am closer to Hague on the euro than many of the right. Hague says he has constitutional objections for only five years. I say the euro is a good thing and we should be prepared to go in. The ultras on the other side say, Never – which is far further away from Hague than I am!

Going back to tactics, and the post-election scene, I said to DC, Does this mean that you and KC have an overwhelming priority not to split the party and be accused of losing the Tories the election? He said, That is pretty important. But some of us are going to have a big problem with the manifesto. Personally I have always taken the precaution of never reading the party manifesto. It is the coward's way out, perhaps, but it has served me well. I fight on local issues. But then I have to have some bullet points on Where I Stand, and of course it will become apparent then that I disagree with most of what the party is saying.

Our trouble is that we have nothing to say about the central services of health and education. On crime, Widdecombe is actually a bit more liberal than the party. But on the main issues we are silent. Portillo has made some effort very slightly to soften the euro position – but to little avail.

---

1 Alex Bentley (Referendum Party candidate) gained 2,367 votes in the 1997 general election.

MICHAEL PAKENHAM
The Garrick, 8 September 2000

MP is between jobs. He thinks he may get Poland. We have our usual
easy talk. Some stuff of importance.

GOVERNMENT STYLE   Cook is the most articulate minister bar
none (MP has attended a lot of Cabinet meetings as well as much else).
Blair is by contrast a stumbler. The Estuary hesitations contrast with the
smart Scots sound bites. Gordon, for his part, desires to talk to no one.

But Blair's hesitations seem partly contrived. They seem part of his
way of getting the boys on side, making them feel he is interested in what
they have to say, purporting to show the situation to be open. There is a
marked difference between the period in which a decision has not been
made and when it has been made. After it is made, Blair is very clear and
pretty good at articulating it.

One of his special gifts was from the start – in fact more at the start
(especially over Kosovo) than perhaps now – the ability to change the
context. He would take problem X and say it was really about Y. He
would just frame an issue from a different point of view to make it seem
less painful. That was especially true of Kosovo. You could call it the
antecedent of spinning: the talent and tactic which Alastair has made
grow in many and excessive directions – so much so that everyone is on
the lookout for it now, and therefore it has ceased to be useful. (Per HY:
as something American I read this summer said, the moment spin was
mentioned it ceased to be effective. That was Joe Klein,[1] I now recall.)

ANGLO-AMERICA AND DEFENCE   (Remember that MP
was close in to defence for several years.) He said that one had to recall
certain things about the US defence reality. First, Schwarzkopf and
Powell,[2] who are now backing Bush, were two of the worst generals in
the recent history of the US. Schwarzkopf was just dumb. He did so much
damage to allied relations, during the Gulf War, that he nearly lost it.
Enraged the French and many others too (including us, MP implied).
A real political dunderhead.

Powell is the chief architect of the new doctrine which says that the
US must have the mightiest war machine, but must never go to war if
there is a chance of a single US soldier being killed. This is a devastating

---

1 Joe Klein: US journalist, political commentator; author of the satiricial political novel *Primary Colors*.
2 Colin Powell: US general; chairman of the Joint Chiefs of Staff 1989–93 during the first Gulf War; US
Secretary of State 2001–5.

limitation. Remember Addis Ababa – 18 Yanks dead and we all get out.[1] Remember Bosnia – they wouldn't come in if a single US man was likely to die. Instead, we have this strategy of air attack by precision guided missiles. In Bosnia, don't forget, they wanted to use these while we sent the soldiers in. In all future combat, that is going to be the only way the US will operate.

They back this up with numbers. For each killer in the US army there's a tail of eight force-protectors (get someone in the MoD to tell you about the theory of force protection). That is not bottle-washers, but military people, in that ratio, in or near the field, to protect the sharp-end fighters. No other army comes anywhere near it.

This means that an enemy group has only to nail a dozen Americans – a terrorist attack, whatever – and the whole US army can be relied on to pull out. The philosophy of not-a-single-body-bag, which Powell invented, has reduced the US army to that.

Moreover, Bush is promising far more spending on the army. This army that will not fight! The spending it wants to increase will be for another generation of battlefield weapons – but for people who won't go on to the battlefield!

However, one does need to be fully aware that the US are light years ahead of us in several fields. Intelligence. The future possibilities of ground-screening with close-up imaging of tiny sections of the globe is now on its way at speed, with the US perhaps likely to be ahead for fifty years. France might get something better in a few years, but it will only do what the US can do now! This is massively ahead of every other possibility. Heavy lift. When you don't keep troops on the German plain, to fight a static war, but need them all the time for lifting – and usually outside Europe – then transport becomes indispensable. They have it, and we by and large don't.

On a larger theme, MP is much taken with a thesis that the US is so rich that they will take over the world. They will soon buy up Europe – they have to do something with their money. His son-in-law is a very rich man with his own planes. To us he seems incredibly rich, picking us up from the Vineyard and flying us to S. Carolina in ninety minutes. But he is small fry compared with many. This, like defence technology, is out of the European league.

ADDENDA MP was standing outside the Cabinet room after Brown had told colleagues about the line he was about to announce on the euro.

---

1 Perhaps a slip of the tongue by Michael Pakenham or a memory failure by HY. Eighteen US soldiers died in the 'battle of Mogadishu' in Somalia in October 1993 (an event turned into a Hollywood film called *Blackhawk Down*). The last US forces left Somalia in March 1994.

Robin Cook spoke to him, and said in the most emphatic way how good a line this was – and how it would be one in the eye to the excessive Europhiles.

Note also MP saying, *in re* European attitude to defence etc., that the Europeans would certainly never be going to help the Americans if they felt the need to intervene in Venezuela or Colombia. We should keep this in mind in thinking about the defence relationship.

HY prefaced his notes of this address by the then Cabinet Secretary and head of the home Civil Service by saying that the speaker was 'clearly of the managerial school rather more than the "policy grandee" school of top civil servant. Although the subject was, it has to be said, about the reform of the Civil Service.'

SIR RICHARD WILSON
Fabian lunch–seminar, 17 October 2000

Out of an unprepared and pretty sketchy talk and questions, the following points stuck with me:

He had had a meeting this morning to look at research they had had done about perceptions in the Civil Service. It showed that 65 per cent of the service believed they were living through a period of vast change in both the world and government.

It certainly is changing very fast. Perhaps prime among the changes is the factor of public expectations. People are no longer prepared to wait patiently while a benign state hands out what it chooses to. 'People may be less interested in politics. But they are very interested in the ways that government makes a difference in their lives.' The public knows all about its taxes, demands value for its money, and is very vigilant about the quality of public services.

Another big change has been constitutional. The British habit, says RW, has been to undergo big changes 'under anaesthetic' (good phrase); he thinks this was especially so re entry into Europe. Suggests it may also be so re devolution (though not, surely, in Scotland). What has been going on is a dispersal of power – a reshaping of the way people see Whitehall and Westminster.

The media also represent a major factor of change. A lot more aggressive, and more powerful. He cited, oddly, the Passport Agency as a victim of this. Said that the agency had been 'a basket case' in the 1980s. But it had been subject to heavy reform. It had had the bad luck to have a few glitches (massive computer failure, as I recall), and because the media got on to this they had a terrible time. But now the agency is doing well.

The fuel crisis of September[1] 'repays a lot of study' . . .

Another source of change is e-government. The acceleration of government services available online. Raises also issues about the borders between central and local government . . .

CIVIL SERVICE REFORM, in the light of all this. Policymaking has vastly broadened its sources. When I started in W, says W, all policy was made in W and W. (Translates as 'When I started in Whitehall, says Wilson, all policy was made in Whitehall and Westminster.') Often hustled together in a few pages of elegant prose, and whisked through the Cabinet and into a press release. That is no longer at all true. There is far broader sourcing of policy advice. The Centre for Policy Management[2] ranges far and wide, abroad especially, for the best practice ideas. 'We no longer believe in central government that we are the source of all advice and all knowledge.'

He praises Sure Start[3] as a wonderful case of effective policymaking and delivery. He cited export services as a classic case of something it has been very hard to get right, split between departments etc. etc.

PRIME MINISTER'S DEPARTMENT Cited as a big constitutional doctrine that the PM should not have much executive power. The No. 10 machine is there to support the PM, and be the watching post for the whole of government, but not to exercise great executive power. He said, amazingly, that any deployment of a PM's department would have a major constitutional effect (bad) on the independent power and accountability of Secretaries of State. (This was challenged by Vernon Bogdanor.)[4]

If there was a PM's department, he would become more of a president, or else he would merely duplicate what departments are doing. He argued that Blair is not becoming in any way a president. 'It would be a massive change in the constitutional role of Secretaries of State.' The better model is of checks and balances (perfect Whitehall waffle), which on the whole 'works rather well'.

---

1 Rising petrol and diesel prices triggered a series of public protests beginning on 8 September 2000, when lorry drivers, farmers and motorists blocked oil refineries and terminals. Petrol stations began to close after motorists started panic-buying. The Institute of Directors later claimed that the episode cost UK businesses £1 billion.
2 In fact, the Centre for Management and Policy Studies within the National School of Government, formerly the Civil Service College at Sunningdale.
3 A national network of Sure Start Children's Centres, aimed at helping families with children less than five years old, launched by the new Labour government. By March 2008 more than 2,900 centres had been opened.
4 Vernon Bogdanor: professor of government at Oxford University.

GENERAL   The government had had McKinsey's do a survey, inquiring what motivates civil servants. Fascinating stuff. It turns out they are not motivated by money but (a) want to make a contribution to society, (b) want an interesting job. The jobs are very, very interesting, even at a low level. Think of it, he says: an ordinary immigration officer who has the power of detention without trial.

The government also has MORI assemble and question a People's Panel: 1,800 people questioned regularly about what they think of what government is doing. It has been done for two or three years. 'We publish the results.'

I asked him about Freedom of Information, and accused him of resisting any change at all in the rules about policy advice. He replied rather uneasily. Said he put it down to the ferocity of the party battle, which he thinks is more so here than in any other country. If advice was public, or became public, the life of the Civil Service with another government would become impossible; the whole Civil Service role would become politicized. He implied that he would like more openness. He thought, though, that it depended on the 'maturity of our political culture'. This had to move forward on all fronts, not just *in re* Civil Service advice and secrecy.

After the seminar, he approached me, saying we had not met properly (actually not at all). Said he was a reader of my 'collected works'. Was very cordial. Implied, without saying so, that the blockage on FoI had been entirely political (which I think I actually knew – with Falconer playing Blair's hand very toughly). And repeated that it was all about the way anything will be exploited by the other side.

Praised himself, by the way, for encouraging the release of cabinet papers to the Phillips inquiry on BSE – as if he had any real alternative.

PHILIP GOULD
The Ivy, 7 November 2000

American election day . . .

Having predicted to me in June (as he claimed to remember) that Gore would win, he now feels wholly uncertain. He talked to his associate Stan Greenberg[1] last night, who said that, reading all the polls taken in the last twenty-four hours, the total picture was dead even, with Gore moving up – but that the undecided voters bent for Bush.

He had been there in mid-October, for the debates, but had gone less

---

1 Stan Greenberg: author; US political scientist; pollster for President Clinton in 1992.

than he planned because the situation was too tense. Impliedly, Greenberg et al. were too busy. He remarked on the amazing calm and drive of US campaigns, unlike British ones. If this was the UK, he said, and Blair was behind, the blame game would be all over the papers. There is none of that in the US – yet.

Bush feels easy in himself. This is what shows. He therefore feels easy with the people. That has been true of other successful presidents, notably Reagan and Clinton. And not true of many others – Nixon and Carter conspicuously. The warmth, the self-confidence, the lack of inner tension: this shows Gore, by contrast, is obviously not at ease with himself.

One has to allow, therefore, that Bush may turn out to have been the better candidate for the times. Americans need to feel easy with people. That is the style which Clinton especially helped to advance. Bush has fought a very good campaign – winning the debates, and removing the issue away from his own competence on to his own alleged geniality, his decency, his dignity and all that stuff. People know very well that Gore is clever, better qualified. But that doesn't count.

Especially it doesn't count in view of people's loathing of Clinton as a man. This is a tricky dichotomy. They think he has been a good president, and done well for them. But they don't like what he did. They are therefore more than usually full of real haters, who will never be reconciled to the Monica business. This will have an effect on turnout perhaps: they are more motivated than the Gore supporters.

Will it have a read-across effect here? PG doesn't think it will have a direct electoral effect. But the fact is that without the US Democrats the progressive project will look thinner based. To be reduced to a few Europeans and Blair – what is there to keep it going?

So the right will have something to crow about. Not just the Tories, but the European right. The profile of the progressive case, its credibility, will suffer. Not to mention, of course, Blair's relationship with Washington . . .

BLAIR AND LABOUR   Blair himself no longer counts as a man at ease with himself, says PG. He used to be more so, and it has got better than it was earlier this year. But he is still basically mystified as to why a government that is doing well economically should not be popular. Can't understand what has happened to him – other than through the demonic role of the press. He is taut and tense.

I suggest, says HY, that one reason why he has been so knocked back by the press is because he counted too much on them. He believed they were on his side. He had a good press before, during and after the election, and did a great deal to try and sustain that – but too much. Was too bothered by it. And therefore, when it turns against him, is even more grievously bothered than he should be. I acknowledged, though, that it is easier for me to say this than for Blair to admit it to himself.

He sees the fuel protests in September as a Rubicon. It changed things definitively, he thinks – even though the polls show Labour back at a 7 per cent lead. It changed the perception of us, says PG. It also made people more cynical. You have a situation now where people evidently do not really believe in government's ability to deliver the rewards of high public spending: don't believe in public investment – because look at the transport situation, for example!

So, September did damage our reputation, our image, the impression we made, and the ideology we want to promote – of public support for more public investment. People tend to say, especially now when the country appears to be out of control and in flood/rail chaos,[1] Give us the money, we will spend it ourselves.

He also said that even now the fuel protests worried him a lot. The worst thing of all is for a Labour government to have let the country grind to a halt. It would be our very worst nightmare. And nobody can be sure what the public will do. I was saying to Gordon only this morning, he said, that we just don't quite know how the voters will react on the ground (as distinct from the ballot box).

The tax issue is the new one. Came up in the summer. The old issues are Europe, crime and asylum-seekers. These are the Tories' strong points. Big issues, especially the first two. But now tax is there. Tax, however, is defeatable. The Tory sums do not add up. We have to make that clear, time and time again – and people will probably get the point: that the Tories do not really believe in making public services better, and are pretending by sleight of hand to be able to cut tax and increase spending on vital services. This gives us an enormous opportunity, which we will, I am sure, take.

He kept coming back to the wisdom of my pieces. This turns out mainly to relate to a piece I wrote about Dick Morris,[2] which he thought the acme of wisdom. I confessed to him that I had forgotten that he quoted Morris in one of the spring memos which caused me to write the very hostile piece about Gould[3] – which he seems magnanimously to have forgiven! He said I had got the new politics right – closer than anyone

1 The month had begun with severe flooding and line closures. Heavy rainfall triggered more than 40 severe flood warnings on 7 November alone, and floodwaters had invaded Ashford International Station.
2 Dick Morris: US columnist, author, political adviser to President Clinton, and campaign manager for the 1996 US election.
3 HY's commentary on 20 July was headed, 'The leaks show whose head must roll: that of Gould.' HY called him 'an agent of exaggerated terror'.

else. (This seemed, likewise, to be a commendation for seeing politics, as I sometimes have, in the same light as he has.)

He makes an interesting point about the differences between Blair and Brown. Blair, he says, is actually impatient of opinion polls. He trusts his own judgement more than anything else. This is what led him to want to give more priority to transport and crime, says PG, not the polls – which Blair is poor at reading and impatient at being confronted with. He is, therefore, more an instinctive politician. He just somehow thinks he is in touch with the British people.

On the other hand, he also disclaims the kind of prophetic Clinton-esque role which Gould tries to press upon him. He says, impatiently, that it is not his job to be the psychoanalyst of the British people, their father figure, their mentor. He is in Downing Street to do a job, he has a programme, he is doing his best to see it through. That is all that can be expected, he implies. In PG's view this is a mistake. It leaves out the 'feeling', 'empathizing' aspect of political leadership which, like it or not, is important in modern politics.

Gould is very insistent that politicians must 'honour' the public, not despise their concerns. He says this doesn't mean jumping about to meet those concerns by changing policy all the time. In that, Blair is on the same line as he is. Blair also wants to keep in touch with the public. But he thinks he knows the public without this great reliance on polls and focus groups. Thus he lacks both the poetry of leadership (Clintonism, empathy, emotionalism) and, one might say, the ultra-science that he is offered.

Brown is different. He absorbs polls with great voracity. He thinks it's the only way he can keep in touch with the British, especially the English, mind. Being Scottish, he thinks he knows Scotland pretty well. But for the rest, he demands, commissions and sucks in polling material all the time. He also, in PG's view, has more of a sense of linking people's feelings with their brains. Is a more natural political motivator, understander etc. One might say (HY) that in this, as in other ways, he is more completely and deeply a politician than Blair is: more addicted to polling; more committed day and night to every aspect of what it means to succeed as a leader.

Mandelson, by the way, is more like Blair than like Brown in all this. He too is pretty indifferent to polling. By the way, he is also distancing himself in Northern Ireland. He wants to do that. He wants to succeed at it, but he also needs an escape from the quite terrible relationship with GB, which pains him a lot.

There is no doubt that they were all in deep trouble earlier this year. Did not know what was happening to them (in the spring, it began). Had no focus. Had not yet homed in on spending and investment as the key. For example, when Laura Spence hit out at Brown[1] he was utterly mystified, went on and on to Gould about how this could have happened: why it was that a simple sentiment should cause such a blast from the press. He simply did not understand it. There were other examples.

PG kept coming back to the leaked memos and all that. He said he thinks he knows what happened. First batch result of the bin-man being commissioned by an intermediary with links to the *Sunday Times* Insight people, to hit the bins of Gould and Levy.[2] But then the *ST* people fell out with him, so he went to the Tory Party, and gave them stuff. They then took charge of the leaking, via *The Sun* and *The Times*. *ST* people have told Gould that this is roughly what happened.

He said, by the way, that one consequence of the spring leaks was that he could not hold focus groups for two months. I asked why. Because I was too well known, he said. He said he did subcontract them to others, and had continued to do so now – though he did watch them (through that one-sided mirror I expect).

He says, all in all, that he does not feel worried about the election: he is happier than he had been at any other time this year. Yet he also shudders with anxiety when I talk insouciantly about 'when you have won a decent majority'.

The reason for this anxiety is the fickleness of the voters. Their cynicism, their instant demands – and our (Labour) failure so far to make clear our project. He tended to agree with me that more openness, more fearlessness, more conviction would do the government more good than endless backing and filling. Yet at the same time he plainly feels that they have to be incredibly wary of the press.

He comes back time and again to the press. They are very important, he says. And they are terrible. He has done some focus-group analysis of *Mail* and *Telegraph* readers, and proved to his own satisfaction that these readers are wholly turned off the government. By contrast the 'Labour' press – in which he amazingly includes *The Sun* and *The Times*, thus casting some doubt on his analysis perhaps – shows much less hostility among its readers.

That degree of science aside, however, he has always thought Blair makes a mistake in trying ever to woo the *Mail*. He himself is wholly hostile to the *Mail* and everything it stands for. That is why he got involved with the *Express*, which will now cease to be part of the small

1 Laura Spence was a comprehensive-school student from Tyneside who was turned down by Oxford University. So she got a £65,000 scholarship at Harvard instead. The episode stirred up another classic British political row about privilege, class and opportunity, and Gordon Brown told a TUC audience that the episode had been an 'absolute scandal'. Brown was then denounced for his 'ill-informed, opportunistic and unhelpful intervention'.
2 Michael Levy: politician; chief Labour Party fund-raiser 1994–2007; created Baron Levy of Mill Hill 1997.

left-centred press. Under my questioning he denied that he ever advised going after *Mail* readers. He now thinks Blair may finally have learned that there is no point in cultivating these people, like Dacre.

He clearly talks quite a bit to editors. *The Sun* will back Blair at the election, but give him a kicking until then – with the aim of keeping his majority down. That is their interest: encourage the voters to withdraw support from Blair without kicking him out (a) in order to narrow the race, (b) in order to dissuade him from holding the euro referendum.

EUROPE AND THE SECOND TERM   Tony will be a different man, to some extent, in the second term. He will be relieved of that terrible burden of winning it, which totally dogs him at present. He will have done it. He won't need to stay on for the whole term.

I asked whether this would mean Labour being more radical in the second term. Philip seemed surprisingly doubtful. He said that for him the entire justification of the first term was a more radical second term: and expressed clear scepticism about whether this would really happen. But he did reaffirm that Blair would change, after the victory.

How would he advise them to handle Europe? He began by saying, under my encouragement, that if Blair did not hold the referendum he would be a historical failure. He would look very bad, in his own eyes not least. The Third Way plus Europe are his two big things – he can't duck away from the referendum.

How can he win it? Plainly we have to start talking more about the euro – though we can't do it much before the election. There has to be a strong economic case made: people must be persuaded that it will be bad for their jobs and prosperity to stay outside. A hard but not impossible job. There is no other basic way, says PG. I add, But you have to address the political issues too, and not let them fester under a stone. He did not disagree.

We agree with each other that Brown is Delphic on the subject. He always trots out the party line to me, says PG. But what does he really think? I remark that he has an even bigger interest than Blair in not losing a referendum, but that would be the end of his chances of being PM.

He also said that this was the kind of thing where polling could be very useful: where you knew your objective very clearly, and wanted to find out how best to pursue it, what nerves to touch, what anxieties to address, what to avoid and what to push.

British politics were briefly forgotten when America went to the polls to choose the successor to President Bill Clinton. The Republicans fielded George W. Bush, son of the 1989–93 president George H. W. Bush, the Democrats Al Gore, Bill Clinton's vice-president. So close was the outcome that controversy over who was the winner in Florida meant that the outcome of the ballot hung in the balance for a month. Only after rulings by the United States Supreme Court and recounts in Florida (introducing in the process the concept of chads, a hitherto generally unfamiliar word to the election lexicon) was the election finally decided in favour of Bush, with 271 electoral votes to Gore's 266.

DAVID MILIBAND
Phone, 8 November 2000

Saw him at the embassy last night, at the start of the roller coaster . . . Now, in the amazing uncertainty that still prevails next day . . .

Talk of the army vote, the expat vote, the difference between 'absentee ballots' and 'oversees voters' etc. etc. Plus the rumour that 3,000 Jewish voters accidentally voted for Buchanan,[1] owing to some error in the voting machines . . .

The embassy has been scrupulous in avoiding all signs of British bias, and in developing contacts with both campaigns. We [the UK] have stayed out of it completely – as both sides recognize and welcome.

What the Bush people say is, of course, no pull-out from Bosnia by 22 January etc. etc. Insisting that nothing dramatic will happen, that they have been misinterpreted.

But the trouble is that Bush, for example, takes a very strange attitude to the military and what it is for. Favours, he says, a big military budget increase (though, per HY, someone recently pointed out that Gore was actually promising more), but on condition that it is not used. A standing army that does nothing. A vision, therefore, of defence forces in a very old mode: defending the country against attack – which even in Europe is not how they are primarily seen. This is not what defence forces are for any longer. Instead, they are an arm of foreign policy. That is the way Tony sees them: a way of projecting foreign policy, not warding off non-existent threats to the home country.

This is part of the interdependent world, not the nation-state world. A world in which no country, including the US (says Tony), can make much headway without engagement and mutual dependence. The aspect of that which especially matters is the sense of multilateralism, expressed vitally through the reform of multilateral institutions – the UN, the WTO and the host of international bodies that do not connect. Facing a lot of

1 Pat Buchanan, adviser and speechwriter to former presidents Nixon and Reagan, was selected as the presidential candidate of Ross Perot's right-wing Reform Party.

international problems that should connect: debt, trade, environment etc.

The Congressional Republican majority, though narrowed, will be a vital factor. Per HY: what we see is the routine expressions of normality and reassurance, but with two possible different undertows. Either a learning process, whereby these inexperienced hands, seasoned by people like Zoellick,[1] become aware of the complexity of the world and the need for engagement. Or the opposite: the arrival at the top, both in the White House and Congress, of powerful politicians who actually resist that world view: who are unilateralist, even isolationist, who don't like multilateralism. After the initial period, one or the other will come to the fore. I think the latter is more likely.

DM also sees protectionism factoring into this: another aspect of the contest for the soul of America. Clinton has not been especially good on this, though he got better. Will Bush be any more of a free-trader, especially with so close a result? Protection seems to be a consensus position, to some degree. Overlapping all this is the US economy. In a time of growth it is much easier to resist protectionism than in a time of recession . . .

And then again there is NMD. DM said he thought Colin Powell had expressed reservations about it. Bush has been very emphatic.

IF GORE WINS . . . The Clintonists have been trying hard to feel their way towards some kind of interconnected world, as above. In finance, defence, debt relief. Being 'helping hand' internationalists, rather than world policemen.

But remember that the Senate voted 96–0 against Kyoto.[2]

He believes that Gore would be better than Clinton on the environment. A serious commitment and knowledge there. Something to counter the present US position – which Bush would surely make worse – that tells the developing world that global warming does not matter because the US says it does not matter.

PETER HAIN
Foreign Office, 9 November 2000

AFRICA When TB appointed me in July 1999, he said he wanted to set up our engagement with Africa. I had a long talk with him early in 2000 – unusual for a minister of my rank – in which he developed this theme.

---

1 Robert Zoellick: foreign-policy adviser to George W. Bush during the 2000 presidential election campaign; president of the World Bank since 2007.
2 The Kyoto Protocol: the international agreement, made in 1997 in Kyoto, to reduce the greenhouse-gas emissions that fuel climate change. The agreement was eventually ratified by more than 170 countries – but not the US.

In the FCO, Africa had been long regarded as a third-order area. It got elderly ambassadors on their last posting; it did not get the best people. The Africa department in the FCO was demoralized.

My coming here, says PH modestly, has created a buzz around the Africa department. Younger people now want to get to embassies in Africa. I gave a speech back in September 1999, and then two others later, which set out a kind of line about Africa. These were important. Have a look at them on the website.

Following Blair's interest, a committee was set up by Blair under C. Short to examine our having a greater presence in Africa, i.e. especially about peacekeeping, training police, training army. South Africa and Nigeria seen as the linchpins. These initiatives to run alongside the usual and older issue of debt relief. A paper is about to be produced of the conclusions.

Separately from that, an Africa Partnership proposal is being worked up. At a very early stage. Again it began with Blair. The idea is that Britain and other OECD countries should go into partnership with the better Africa countries, and have a quid pro quo of good governance and democracy. This is to build a strategy for success.

PH has been identifying unsung but improving African countries. Botswana, Senegal, Mali, Mozambique, he said. Build on their success, which is real if modest – but again South Africa and Nigeria are pivotal. To help them sustain success, and at the same time hope for a spillover into more intractable neighbour countries.

This has yet to mature into a plan. But early next year hopes to start engaging other OECD countries.

The origin of this, says PH, is undoubtedly Blair's sense of moral duty and obligation. It can be, and not falsely, dressed up as fitting into a strategy of British interest: the need for stability, the selling of British goods in markets, the need to stall Aids etc. But the real impulse has been Blair's moral imperative. Add into that, also, PH's own idea that if there comes to be a peaceful Middle East, terrorism will spill out into Africa.

How did Blair's interest begin? PH does not really know. But in his early talks Blair showed a special interest in the Congo. PH seems to be commissioned now to produce a paper on the Congo. B seems much taken with the fact that it is the size of Western Europe and has vast mineral deposits. He sees it, rightly, as a source of instability to bordering states (though actually, at present, it is calm).

Angola is another important place. PH says that he personally was able to get the policy changed to take a far more proactive stance against sanctions-busters. He saw SIS reports every day talking about planes coming in from Bulgaria, and wanted to know what we were doing about it. We are now evidently doing more. Here, also, we are close to the US. Did you know that the US is taking more oil from offshore Angola than it was from Kuwait when the Gulf War began?

C. Short is wholly on board. She is really the Cabinet minister for Africa. Two-thirds of her budget goes to Africa. She was the first to help Museveni[1] in Uganda in a big way – and Uganda is the only (check) African country to reverse the Aids onset. DFID [Department for International Development] funds have been very useful and big there.

Malawi, where PH was recently: one-quarter of the Cabinet died of Aids and one-sixth of the schoolteachers have died of Aids.

MoD: Hoon and Guthrie[2] have both told Hain that the boys like going to Sierra Leone,[3] because it is real action. One of the few places where they do it. Our Rapid-Reaction Force got its first outing there, and did it in forty-eight hours, which even the US said nobody else in the world could have done. We have 500 troops there now, and with an indefinite time laid out ahead. A Brit is now chief of staff of the UN force, which slightly hooks us into the UN more than we were before.

ALASTAIR MORTON
13 November 2000

At the Jenkins party.

He works a lot with Prescott. He likes and admires him, but thinks he has lost his fizz. It happens to all of us, but I think I detect that it is happening to John, says A. The other thing about Prescott, he says, is his incessant interest in what 'will play', 'will work': how things work out politically. Never ceases to talk about that – in response to whatever plans A and others are putting up.

He asks, Are the chattering classes deciding that Brown is a better man than Blair? How long will it take for this to become a serious matter? A himself says that Brown's most conspicuous feature is his short attention span. If something doesn't interest him, he just puts it away. It's hard to get him to stay with things. This is a difference from Blair, who does have a big picture. He doubts if Brown looks more than a few months, at most, down the road.

1 Yoweri Kaguta Museveni: president of Uganda since 1986.
2 Charles Guthrie: Chief of the Defence Staff 1997–2001; later Baron Guthrie of Craigiebank.
3 UN forces intervened in the bitter civil war in Sierra Leone in May 1999. In May 2000, British paratroopers secured the airport in Freetown for UN troops and to evacuate British citizens.

*HY went through a spell of conversations with dispirited pro-Europeans.
Roy Denman was particularly articulate.*

ROY DENMAN
Lunch, the Garrick, 15 November 2000

The euro referendum will not happen. Blair will run away from it. The
venom of anti-European feeling is very deep. RD hears regular anecdotes
about the extraordinary hostility of people out there, especially in the
south of England – the insular, middle-class Middle England types are
coming further and further out into the open.

The result of this will be that Britain will slowly – perhaps not so
slowly – leave the table of high influence. The Europeans will get fed
up with being stopped from doing things by the Brits, and will take
measures to sideline a country that is plainly not going into the euro.
The brute fact is – glossed over now, and politely guarded – that, until
we are in the euro, nothing we have to say about the future is taken very
seriously.

This is a huge comedown, historically. The Brits are a subject of
shoulder-shrugging and not a little contempt already.

We will have to adopt the Norway option.[1] And then after perhaps
another ten years we will look at it again. Meanwhile the thing will have
moved further forward within terms that we have had nothing to do with
setting.

One does have to have some sympathy with British politicians.
For French and Germans the role of the state has been much more vital.
When you have the enemy at the gates, the state is what protects you.
There is much less demonology about the value of the state than there
now is here. They just have a different attitude to what we think of as
sacred sovereignty. The war, as in so many ways, was and is the crucial
memory.

But also remember: the idea that Washington will be an alternative to
Europe is a total fallacy. We will soon find that the new US president,
perhaps the one after the new one, will go to Berlin and not to London
for his first trip. We will be isolated on the fringe, a vessel of agreeable
history but little else.

---

1 Norway remained outside the European Union.

DAVID MILIBAND
10 Downing Street, 28 November 2000

He said they had been to *The Observer* last week (was this TB? or just AC and DM?)[1] for breakfast or something. And had said to *The Observer* that they had only eighteen more issues before the election, and how were they going to use them? They professed amazement at this, and there were many furrowed brows.

In the same spirit he asked me what my plans were for the forty columns I had between now and the election. I.e. he seriously seems to think that journos have the same kind of agenda planning as political managers! Perhaps they should do . . .

JOHN KERR
Lunch, the Garrick, 28 November 2000

THE QUEEN In the course of telling me about his part-time role accompanying new ambassadors to present their credentials, he said that the Queen does take an informed interest in people and certain issues. He says that in their brief conversations the things that interested her most are (a) the military and (b) the countryside.

AMERICA He claims, in typically Johnish fashion, to have predicted that Bush would win as far back as 1997. Under questioning, he admits he didn't get it quite so clearly, but did say he had outlined in a paper to the FCO why Gore would not win, though Gore would be bound to be the candidate. He congratulated me on my immediate post-election piece, talking about a Bush presidency – apparently under the impression that this was a serious piece of prediction on my part, rather than the desperate space-filling of a columnist who had no idea what was going to happen next.

He's not disposed to criticize Bush or lament his coming. Does say that Cheney[2] will have the right instincts – though was quite the wrong choice for V-P, who should have been McCain. Also, interestingly, what a pity it is that there never was a real argument about the role of the US in the world – as there would have been if Buchanan were the candidate.

---

1 A veteran journalist on *The Observer* writes, 'I'm sure it must have been Blair, as I don't recall any Campbell visits by himself, while Blair came in a couple of times.'
2 Richard 'Dick' Cheney: vice-president of the United States 2001–9.

Says that Colin Powell, who I said would be terrible, was at least strongly pro-English. Powell and wife lunched very regularly with Kerr and his wife in Washington. He loves England, feels at home here. Oh God, says HY, another special-relationship phase . . . JK says that Condi Rice[1] is very smart. But the main point he makes about both of them is that it is very good for the US to have blacks in these two top roles – especially via a Republican presidency.

The larger fact is one that either president would have to deal with. Middle America will never support US action overseas on the grounds of the moral case, or just to help Europeans look after their own backyard. The only arguments that work are (a) plain US strategic interest or (b) what he calls 'exceptionalism': i.e. that only the US can do the work. It is because this latter argument had to be deployed so heavily by Clinton that so many Americans – including C. Rice – had the impression that the whole of the Bosnian force was made up of Americans.

GORDON BROWN I said that GB was going to be pivotal on the euro decision. He replied, Why wouldn't Blair, in autumn 2001, close the doors of the Cabinet and declare to his colleagues that there will now be a referendum in 2002 – and pre-empt all argument? I said, Completely unrealistic. GB will make sure that doesn't happen. JK said that perhaps Blair will have the cunning to allow GB to appropriate the decision – to let GB think it is his decision, and thereby get him fully committed with all his formidable power.

His model for this is the withholding tax issue. At Helsinki, Brown made a complete mess of this. Put up a fatuous proposal, drafted on the plane, which got nowhere. On the plane back, they had a Treasury post-mortem and realized they had to do much better. As a result Gordon started doing a bit of travelling. Not just to Cape Cod! Went round Europe and got support. Did a lot of drafting himself. This reached the Feira summit[2], at which he was very dominant, and from which, by the way, the Commission was virtually excluded. Brown's own drafting hand was hard at work. Everyone recognized his mastery. This could be a model for another campaign.

1 Condoleezza 'Condi' Rice: US National Security Adviser 2001–5, US Secretary of State since 2005.
2 European leaders met in June 2000 at Santa Maria da Feira in Portugal to discuss the unresolved questions of enhanced cooperation, a charter of rights, security, and many other issues.

MICHAEL PORTILLO
At Cecil Parkinson lunch, 10 December 2000

He was courteous, fairly relaxed, pleased to see us. Also quite interesting.
Lucy thought he looked a bit beaten about, a bit down. No doubt sees
the political situation badly. He said some interesting things, and evinced
a state of mind.

The state of mind was pessimistic. But, although he plainly knows the
Tories are going to lose, he did not seem like someone who has given up
on politics. There were stories to that effect this last week, based on a
Telegraph interview. But he seemed much too keenly interested in how
the party was shaping, and in the exact difference between the mods and
rockers, to be someone on the verge of withdrawal.

We agreed that the mods and rockers were bad language. Totally
inappropriate, especially to Widdecombe. But there really is a divide
between the social liberals and social authoritarians. And he is plainly
very keen indeed on the victory of the liberals. He is strongly of the view
that in this sense society is liberal. He notes the fact that even old people
are liberal, through being forced by circumstance to have to come to
terms with the children and grandchildren who are single parents, drug-
takers or whatever. They may themselves be conservative and conservative dressers etc., but they are not prescriptively reactionary. They have
come to terms with a social reality they do not passionately reject.

He claimed that Mrs T, in her days of power, was a social liberal.
Look at Parkinson, he whispered. And look at St John-Stevas. And look
at the gays in her kitchen cabinet. Not to mention the Jews and Asians
she was keen on. She was very inclusive in that way. She was also someone
who looked to the future, not the past – though he agreed with my
contention that, when she left power, that did begin to change. He says
that now she is more out of touch with the future, and more out of touch
with Britain – though less so internationally. He had seen her on 21 or
22 November, the tenth anniversary of her sacking, and found her trotting
out remarks like being lucky to have had the privilege to have served etc.
etc. Very roseate.

Mary Ann Sieghart,[1] who was there, asked MP whether Hague was a
mod or a rocker. After some thought, Portillo, having first said he didn't
really know, said he thought probably a rocker. MAS said she had
recently talked to a Shadow Cabinet bod who had asked Hague whether

---

1 Mary Ann Sieghart: journalist, columnist at *The Times*, assistant editor.

he was prepared to make enemies on the right, and Hague had replied, 'I never make enemies on the right.'

MP had some memories of government. He said they never expected to win the '92 election. And that from '92 to '97 had been a very long slog. This led him to think that maybe the cycles of government were longer than we had thought. (I don't want to be quoted on this, he said.) I.e. maybe they are in for a long haul now: that even though, like the penultimate Tory government, they were constantly on the back foot, the electorate may be forgiving to them as they were to Thatcher–Major. When I said, Wasn't this because Kinnock was unelectable? he said, 'I understand the drift of your question!'

His own recollection of that government is of being hammered and hammered by Labour for sleaze, for division, for everything. On and on. Very wearing. Equally, he said that 90 per cent of the time in government – 95 per cent actually, he added – is spent not having time to think. Whereas in opposition the only thing you do have time for is thinking. Therefore the parliamentary attack and the other yah-boo politics is just about all the Opposition has to engage in – which is why it happens.

Cecil himself, meanwhile, told Lucy that what the party had to home in on, and never stop driving home in all their ads, was that Blair was a liar. Simple, and blunt, as that. When L asked him what the biggest lie that Blair had told was, all he could refer to was some story about B having said he attended a football match long ago which he couldn't have attended because he was too young, and which had one or two other salient details wrong. Is this the best they can do? Even if it is, it shows how they obsessively think.

GORDON BROWN
Treasury, 12 December 2000

A meeting it has taken a long time to arrange. But he gives me an hour at 10 a.m., which was generous. We had an excellent, focused conversation, of which I recall the following.

TORY PARTY He began on this because I had written a piece for *The Spectator* about how Hague might start to recover. This had been a deeply unhelpful piece, saying that the Tories had to abandon much of what they now held dear. Since GB obviously thought I had been trying to help Hague, I asked him whether he had actually read the piece – which he claimed to have done. (He had also, by the way, read my column this morning, as well as remembering what I had said about his October 1997 statement on the euro. An assiduous fellow!)

Did I believe, he asked, in the cyclical shape of politics? That there were individualist phases followed by collectivist phases? This was the rhythm he himself plainly believed in. One such phase lasted from 1979 to 1997. When I said that Labour should have won in 1992, he replied that Labour wasn't ready, hadn't reformed itself, wasn't credible. This determinism, it's obvious to me, makes him confident of winning not only this election but the one after it – an important context in which to place his own career ambitions post-Blair.

The Tory problem, he said, was that they had no idea what they were trying to be. They were hopelessly caught between wanting to be Thatcherite and yet not wanting to be unpopular – therefore lacking the nerve to follow through, for example, on a tax policy, or say anything that might imperil people's belief that public services were safe in their hands.

Yet actually they were getting hooked on some incredible positions. Portillo's speech last night plainly hinted that they would make health insurance tax-exempt, and put heavier weight on private health. They were going to abolish the New Deal, the Working Families Tax Credits and much else that helped the poor to get a start. They were going to substitute the New Deal with some piddling idea from America which has got only 300 people signed up in New York (he told me the name, but I can't recall it). They hadn't decided whether they were going for a balanced Budget or not: whether they would adopt his golden rule, or not: whatever framework, therefore, would accommodate their tax cuts and spending cuts. He was plainly incredulous that they could have allowed themselves to get into such a mess, offering policies that were so plainly unpopular and flying in the face of the real good that had been done to help the working poor.

He kept coming back to this deep strategic failure. It was more important, he thought, than their confusions over Europe – which were simply a symptom of the larger failure. They simply saw little opportunities and leaped into them – without considering the long-term strategic picture.

He thought Portillo had made a big mistake in coming back to the Shadow Cabinet. He had accepted a poisoned chalice. Unless he had been able – which is now too late – to compel the party to get its policies into strategic shape, he was always going to be the fall-guy.

EUROPE AFTER NICE[1] He went pretty well straight into the problem of legitimacy. He now sees this as Europe's main challenge, and

1 A meeting of the European Council, under the presidency of France, had just ended in Nice. It was held to reform the institutional structures of the enlarged EU, and resulted in the Treaty of Nice.

is not optimistic about its being met adequately. He didn't seem to think Nice had meant very much, certainly did not rate it as any kind of triumph. When I said that Blair's performance vs Hague's yesterday had been something of a triumph, he replied, 'You need more than some good jokes to win this argument.' This wasn't said contemptuously of Blair, but established the depth of the issue as he sees it.

There are a lot of arguments we have to win, and they begin with the Commission. The Commission is unaccountable and dictatorial (his words). It was exactly what people disliked about Europe, especially English people. Something had to be done about that. The future of the EU did not belong to the Commission. The Commission certainly should have a role, but as a regulator, an invigilator of rules made by national governments, more than as a layer-down of laws which the Council of Ministers then rubber-stamp. Countries should be allowed to develop their own regulations on lots of areas of economic etc. activity, which then needed to be looked at and pass muster – but not with a uniform standard imposed from 'outside', i.e. the Commission.

The Commission had played a disastrous role in his own battle on the withholding tax. They had argued that such a tax was essential, that there was no alternative to it. Even when he had turned all other governments except Luxembourg round, the Commission was still trying to dictate rejection of the scheme. So the Commission is at the heart of this lack of accountability that is now the core problem. We have begun to do something about it. What happened under the Portuguese presidency was important. The future should see more of that: of national governments determining the agenda and its pace – because only these governments are accountable. But there is still a very long way to go.

I asked him whether other EU countries were as concerned with this broad problem as he was, as the Brits were. He didn't give a clear answer, but implied that they were not. He said in terms that the British have 'always had' a different demand for accountability than the Continental countries. They were more bothered about it. That had to be understood, did it not?

He was very keen to insist, therefore, that the future of the EU would have to be more governmental, and certainly not federalist. It was through the governments that accountability might be made more real. He gave an interesting example, saying that the ECB was a prime case of a body that needed more political input. His own favoured method would be by the finance ministers setting an inflation target. He said that governments needed to be able to have a story to tell when recession or slowdown occurred. Their people would demand to know why interest rates were not being set to suit their country but to suit the collective. Only a finance minister had a chance of convincing them that this had to be done.

He is very keen on not having any unified tax arrangements, as far as I could see, even on issues at the edge of the field. He took up my mention of eco-taxes this morning. He thought that it would be quite wrong to move to unify these. Tax variations were an important safety valve (I agree with that). There was much pressure the other way. Eichel complained to Fabius[1] about France giving in to the fuel protesters. Fabius complained to Eichel about Germany lowering certain business taxes. These were problems for them. But the answer was not unifying of the levels. The answer was a much deeper understanding, to be gained from the British, about the intellectual case against uniformity – a lesson already imported to amazing effect in the saga of the withholding tax, where GB 'had won the intellectual argument' and not just secured a quick fix against the background of a threatened veto. The EU had been persuaded by him to see that instead of a great edifice of regulation, applied to everyone, which would have been at the heart of the tax, the regime of open information was much more efficient, much cheaper, and more respectful of national differences. Plainly the Brown triumph on this had bitten deep into his attitudes.

He spoke rather off-handedly about the 2004 IGC and the constitution-building it might bring with it. But he welcomed the opportunity for further British lessons to the EU in how to make the nation states function within a better functioning EU. Again we would have to win big arguments. Most of all, we had to defeat Fischer's argument for federalism. It wasn't clear whether Fischer spoke for Germany as a whole – probably not. But it was a picture of Europe that we could not share, and would have to challenge hard.

Somewhere in the course of this bit he made a number of warm references to Tony's Warsaw speech, where he had set out the right kind of line.[2] (There was nothing even subtextually anti-Blair in any of our talk – though the ghost of Mandelson lurked unmentionably.) The IGC would offer us the opportunity to press the legitimacy argument strongly: the need to make the EU understood and acceptable to the voters, in good times and in bad.

EURO REFERENDUM   He said that, whenever this happened, it would not be primarily about the single currency. It would be about the

---

1 Laurent Fabius: prime minister of France 1984–6; Minister of the Economy, Finance and Industry 2000–2002.
2 In a speech on European enlargement to the Polish Stock Exchange, on 6 October 2000, Tony Blair called for 'a superpower, but not a superstate'.

EU and its legitimacy. Just as in 1975 it had been about whether we wanted to belong to a body that was designed to stop a European war. There needed to be a big reason, big questions – not just technical questions. On the whole, he also said, when Britain went in in the early 1970s it hadn't really known what it was getting into. The referendum could only be won if people were able to be persuaded that the EU was not a dictatorial unaccountable bureaucracy, but was about democratic politics.

He noted that not a single referendum on the currency had yet been held successfully. (Since Denmark is the only case, I think, that wasn't saying much. But he said Sweden would say no now, as well. And the post-Maastricht French referendum didn't really count.) To get any country to say yes to the euro was a big task.

The argument had to begin with the five conditions. These, contrary to general commentary, were very serious conditions. The October 1997 statement had been a strong one – contrary to what I had written at the time. It promised an assessment soon after the next election, which is what will happen – by far the best course available then. The conditions had to be really met. I said, They are subjective, a matter of your judgement. He said, It's true they require judgement, but the judgement has to be serious. People have to have it 'proved' to them that entering the euro will mean more jobs, more prosperity. When I said 'proof' would never be available, he said, 'Well, what about "demonstrated"?'

When the assessment was made, the Treasury paper would be very very detailed, he said. A closely reasoned piece of work. When I said that there would still be a lot of necessary room for his personal judgement, he didn't deny it, but kept on insisting that objective terms had to be met. This was not just exchange-rate parity – though he said, sharply, that there wasn't a single EU central banker or finance minister who would advise him to take sterling into the euro now.

I said, Do you accept that if we choose not to go in, and are not in in five years' time, our influence over the large political debates about legitimacy will be much reduced? He dodged it, saying that our influence had been great over economic reform without being in the euro. I said, But we are still seen as a pre-in – which won't go on for ever. He still declined to admit that we might lose influence, though he wasn't very convincing.

His main message was that if the economic conditions were not right there would be no point in making the political case for entry. 'I am not going to sacrifice the British economy.' The idea that one had to think about dates for referenda, and timing vis-à-vis elections was beside the point. These, he implied, were hopelessly trivial matters, set beside the need (a) to prove the economic case and (b) to make the EU answer the people's deep anxieties about its own lack of legitimacy. These were much bigger tasks. By implication, until a great deal of progress had been made, it would not be right to ask the people the question.

I asked him if he wanted Europe to feature large in the election. He immediately said he was wrongly charged with trying to exclude it. But then he said there was no point in getting the election confused with the referendum. It could not be a substitute. It would, I gathered, be in some sense morally wrong to confuse the two – so the euro should not be there. But Europe, if that meant contrasting our internationalism with the Tories' isolationism, yes – that could be helpfully discussed. It would not, however, be a very big issue for most voters.

MY COMMENT I've tried to write this note rather carefully, without embellishment. Wish I had had a tape. During the course of the talk, I didn't quite realize what I was hearing. GB is reasonable, strong-minded, interested in ideas, and comes across as a sincere European reformer who wants the EU to work – which I'm sure he does. He is wholly seized of the importance of Europe to Britain. He sees it as a massive enterprise of which he wants to be part – which in fact we have no choice about.

On the other hand, he reveals a Thatcher-like determination that only the Brits really know what is good for Europe. I asked him more than once what, in exchange, we might have learned from them. He never gave me a single instance. All the time it was a case of the EU countries/ economies needing to reform along lines we had already trodden.

Above all, he takes the anti-Commission line further than any Labour politician I've heard. Maybe Blair reflects this too: I'll ask him next time I have the chance. Certainly Blair et al. are exasperated by the system (like all British PMs). But GB adds an extra dimension of seeming to believe that the referendum can't be held until this issue is much better sorted out. He poses as a kind of reformist campaigner for a better political Europe, which means a more intergovernmental Europe, run along British lines – above all with a British respect for true accountability.

All in all, Gordon is not a Euro-sceptic in the sense we've come to take that to mean. He's pro-Europe. And he considers it all at a high level of seriousness. But he has a lordly attitude to the EU. Wrapped up together with a genuine reformist impulse are obviously a lot of private calculations related to his personal ambition.

He is not rushing to get into the euro, barely seems to recognize the damage done by remaining indefinitely out of it, is far more concerned by the downside than the upside. I used to think he might be holding his fire, the better to carry weight when the Treasury assessment came out favourably. I now think he doesn't see it that way at all. He's not certain to say No – but he is certainly not preparing the ground for a clever Yes. Salutary, to say the least. After all, the test of 'accepted legitimacy' is even harder to pass than the proof of economic benefit. It could be put off for ever . . .

LEON BRITTAN
Lunch, the Garrick, 14 December 2000

I have talked to Hague, quite a long time ago, about Europe, he said. I said that I knew I would not persuade him, and he certainly would not persuade me, but suggested that his tactics were at fault. It was a mistake to make Europe such a big issue, and to discuss it so aggressively. Putting it so big was a way of signalling to the world outside that the party was out of touch: and was run by extremists. For Europe has become associated with an extreme position. I also said he should allow more variation of opinion.

He would not yield on any of this. What is his real Euro position? Leon thinks that he is a visceral sceptic, but intelligent enough to know that getting out would be bad politics to say the least. But under his position is a willingness to take the consequences of getting out. He has people close to him who actually want to get out. And of course he also has plenty of MPs who have that line as well. But none of them has the courage to say it in public.

I have also made the point that letting a pro-Europe voice be heard is an important way of maximizing the Tory vote at the election. There are Tories who will not vote Tory because of the anti-Europe line of Hague and the leadership. If Clarke et al. are excluded, these people will go to the Lib Dems. We discuss what this might be. Say 10 per cent of the Tory vote (matching 10 per cent of Tory MPs who take a pro-Europe line). That would add up to a lot of votes . . .

Leon says that people in the City are often not keen on the euro. They can sound indifferent. But this is because they don't need to assent or dissent from something that may not be going to happen. They deal with reality as they see it. Why waste energy on an issue that may be academic? Therefore, though, if Blair did declare for entry, they would all come round very fast.

Leon's own view about the rate has always been that it would come down naturally the closer our entry seemed. This was partly why he has always favoured government making a series of statements ratcheting up the euro commitment. Commenting favourably on developments, each time increasing the signals in a positive way. He thought such ratchets would be reflected in the markets, which are always about what is going to happen in the future. But there has been no ratcheting, therefore no fall in sterling – though it's noticeable that the convergence is getting closer by degrees. He claims that a clear signal by the government after the election that they were going for it would lead to a fall in the sterling–euro rate.

I gave him the gist of my Brown talk, without telling him the source. He seemed surprised to hear it. He has rather loose ideas about how one might minimize the effect of a No vote – but I think he was persuaded by my rather cataclysmic view of a Big No.

Will Blair jump? He thinks, like me, that it depends on the election. He thinks a Labour majority of 100 would be massive. In normal times even 60 would be very secure. But, by the same token, it would have an effect on the Tory Party. Would a narrow result make the Tories more realistic (centrist) or more hard? He would like to think the former. I contend that as far as the euro goes it would just harden them.

Re Clarke, he says the vital thing is how often Ken makes speeches and interventions. He will not stop talking, but he may not have the energy etc. to talk enough. That would be fatal.

2001

23 January	Northern Ireland Secretary Peter Mandelson admits that he had personally intervened in a passport application for a wealthy Indian businessman, then the next day resigns for a second time.
26 January	Gujarat earthquake kills 12,000 in India.
21 February	The first UK case of foot-and-mouth disease in twenty years is found in an Essex abattoir. Livestock bans are subsequently imposed, herds culled, horse-racing suspended.
1 April	Slobodan Milosevic surrenders to special forces, to face a war-crimes trial.
13 May	Silvio Berlusconi wins the Italian election.
7 June	Tony Blair leads Labour to a general-election victory for a second time, despite the lowest turnout since 1918.
8 June	William Hague resigns as Conservative leader.
20 June	Pervez Musharraf becomes president of Pakistan.
20 August	Baroness Thatcher supports Iain Duncan Smith as the next Conservative leader.
11 September	Two hijacked aircraft crash into the twin towers of the World Trade Center, New York. A third plane hits the Pentagon. Almost 3,000 are killed.
20 September	Tony Blair announces plans to send troops to Afghanistan to support the US in the war against terrorism.
12 November	Taliban forces abandon Kabul.
2 December	The US energy giant Enron files for bankruptcy.
22 December	Hamid Karzai heads an interim government in Afghanistan.
Deaths	Douglas Adams, Sir Donald Bradman, Lord Hailsham of St Marylebone, George Harrison, Fred Hoyle, Jack Lemmon, Anthony Quinn, Harry Secombe

ROGER LIDDLE
Phone, 2 January 2001

EURO AND ALL THAT The effect of Nice, he says, has been to give Tony more confidence that he can win an argument about Europe. In other respects it perhaps hasn't changed much. But it did have that effect, which is important.

In the election, it still seems to be the strategy, shared by both Blair and Brown, that they should talk as little as possible about Europe. Tony will come back robustly if attacked, but he is unlikely to make it a big pitch.

I put to him my Brown thesis (without sourcing it); he said he had never heard this line of argument from the Treasury or the Brownies. If Brown had said it to Blair, Blair would have said it to Peter, and Peter would have talked to RL about it. This has not happened.

Blair's own view is that the issue of the euro and the issue of EU reform are mostly separate. RL is quite sure Blair now wants to get into the euro – but not sure whether he will be able to do so. He thinks the plan is to stick with the early-in-the-next-parliament formula and carry it out.

I asked about who would make the test, when it would be done. He said, I don't think anyone at No. 10 has been thinking deeply about post-election planning of any of this. In fact Tony probably would not want to be doing so, because it would run counter to his strategy of not getting Europe involved in the election. To be hatching 'secret plans' etc. would be contrary to that.

He presumes, though, that Blair would like to start a long debate after the election; presumably, he offers, it would be a long campaign. I said I wasn't so sure about that.

He repeated that he had not so far heard of the idea that the referendum should be put off until after the 2004 IGC (which is an implication from what GB said). This would push it too late in the parliament.

RL said he knew that GB had been doing 'a lot of thinking' about Europe, and especially about the Commission. He got very excited about Commission interference in things he wanted to do, notably about venture-capital schemes in the regions, and one or two other things which the Commission is quite entitled to have a look at but which GB resents.

There is a sense, he says, that the parliamentary party wants to 'get it sorted'. Don't want another parliament where the thing is undecided. Most MPs support Tony's position to downplay it now but decide it soon after the election.

There is, it is true, no critical mass for Europe in the Cabinet. There are few enthusiasts apart from Robin, Peter and Geoff Hoon in a slightly lesser category. Mo is leaving. Byers won't be in the same job. Milburn is said to be rather unhelpful. Straw and Blunkett could be a little cave of semi-sceptics, though when I remarked that Blunkett would never organize against Blair RL agreed. He also thought Straw was not exactly a scep. Just not very helpful.

On the reorganization of the government: he thought Cook would stay, for the moment – until the euro issue was sorted out. PM had said to RL that the only thing Tony could do was send Brown to the FCO – but that Tony would never have the bottle to do so.

[Handwritten note] Prescott will be the key figure: getting him on board will bring others along.

CHRIS PATTEN
Dinner at 112 Station Road, 3 January 2001

Immensely agreeable occasion, with Anthony (and Clare) Cary, CP's *chef de cabinet* in Brussels. C relaxed, humorous, reflective – and enormously kind about my book, which he has read twice (first time a 'skim', but then a proper read).

ON BLAIR   Why is he courting Russia so heavily? And why sucking up to China (the Jiang Zemin horror event . . .)[1] CP thinks this is naïve and stupid. What has Putin got to offer him? What big deals will China be giving him?

He totally neglects places where trade could be big, notably Latin America (especially Brazil). Also, I think C said, India. This is all inexplicable.

On Brown, I outlined the thesis I had written in my piece tomorrow. C said that Brown is crazy if he thinks the Commission is full of non-liberalizers. He regards Mario Monti and Fritz Bolkestein[2] as more intensively liberalizing by instinct than almost any British politician.

1   China's premier, Jiang Zemin, paid a state visit to Britain in October 1999, and was welcomed at Buckingham Palace, despite protests by Chinese and Tibetan demonstrators. On 18 April 2000, after a visit by Vladimir Putin, HY wrote that Tony Blair 'was going to be a different sort of leader, standing for something new in the grammar of foreign policy, an ethical dimension. He raised expectations. These have been betrayed many times over.' HY ended his commentary, 'The case for sticks not carrots, against the perpetrator of Chechnyan barbarities, goes unheard, just as it did with Jiang Zemin, and might, in the right circumstances, with Saddam Hussein. Instead we get a lot of stuff about men of the same generation who are able to understand each other. New men. New bonds. Special chemistry. This has its possibilities. But ethics? Schmethics. A hard man is sucking up to a harder one, as Bismarck might have said.'
2   Mario Monti: Italian economist, politician; European Commission member 1999–2004. Fritz Bolkestein: Dutch politician; European Commission member 1999–2004.

He vows to arrange a dinner or two for Brown, so that some broader knowledge of these people can be knocked into him.

ON TORIES He is wondering by how much the Tories have to lose for people like himself to be able to say to Hague et al., Well, you tried it, you are the first Tory leader to have gone into the election in forty years as the anti-Europe candidate – and you have been heavily defeated. You surely owe us an explanation of what happens next . . .

CARY ON EURO To the surprise, and reproach, of both Chris and me, A. Cary said he thought there should not be a referendum for years. He thought the chances of losing it were too great. He also thought the margin needed to be big – or else it would be challenged all the way down the line.

Chris and I both said that a victory by any margin was enough. After all that time and debate, if it was won it was won. We also said that Blair could not run away from it. (I think, for once, that Chris was deferring to my judgement.)

JOHN MONKS
Phone, 8 January 2001

ELECTION FUNDING The unions will continue to fund the party. There is an instinctive umbilical connection when elections are coming. All the intuition brings them together. This even goes for the unaffiliated unions. There is a bond between unions who want to keep the hard left from gaining ground, which also has been meaning that debates about affiliation have gone quiet.

But he wasn't sure whether the unions would actually be able to produce the £10 million the party is expecting. Their political funds were drained out in 1997, and he doesn't know how well they have been rebuilt.

Also, the manufacturing unions have been losing members, owing to economic decline in their sector.

NORMAN LAMONT
Lunch, the Garrick, 19 January 2001

EUROPE NL is much more amusing and speculative in private than
he ever sounds in public. He is prepared to concede ground and ideas,
and to take the other side seriously. But he now has a serious fear of the
end of independent government in Britain. If I had to point to a moment
that was decisive for him it would be the ERM exit, and the terrible
trauma around that. There was also, as he has said to me before, the
process of negotiating Maastricht, when he 'found out what they really
wanted'.

He sees 'ever closer union' as an interesting and multifaceted phrase,
but one that we the Brits have never really understood.

On the euro, he makes the interesting point (also made by others)
that, unless the government has a referendum early, there will be a danger
of not getting the notes and coins until after the following election, in
which case the Tories would try to stop it happening. Another reason to
go in early is that the longer we do survive quite happily while the
Continentals have the coinage, the less necessary it will seem that we
should belong.

He doesn't like the Delors phrase 'a federation of nation states'. Says
that this reduces nation states to historical and cultural artefacts, rather
than proper self-governing nations. He feels it is rather meaningless. (I
said, Like Hague's 'In Europe but not run by Europe'. He agreed. He
heard Frederick Forsyth[1] at a recent dinner growling as a coda to that
'in other words, the policy of France').

I said, It will never be like the USA, a federation of wholly subservient
states that never were nations. But that doesn't mean it cannot work as
a confederation.

He thinks the NAFTA [North American Free Trade Agreement]
option is mad. Of course it would be nice if we belonged to the NAFTA,
among other things. But we cannot apply as long as we belong to the EU.
And in any case, to see NAFTA trade replacing our EU trade is just utter
nonsense. He believes, or has persuaded himself, however, that by leaving
the EU we would not lose much trade.

Is he an exit man? He was, after all, the first politician to say some
years ago that exit was on the table. He says, I am in favour of a
multi-speed Europe, which will certainly come about with enlargement.
Enlargement, he is sure, will stop the federalizing of the EU.

---

1 Frederick Forsyth: novelist (*Day of the Jackal*); articulate, with right-wing views.

Will the Tories give up their fight against the euro? No, he said. Even after a Yes referendum? No. He personally would recommend going on fighting until the last day when coins and notes come in.

TORY PARTY First of all, he talks quite openly about the second Labour term. There is absolutely no pretence that the Tories are going to win. But he admires Hague, and thinks he may do a bit better than expected. The conventional wisdom is that if he halves Labour's majority he is safe. But does this mean the overall majority or the majority over the Conservatives? Has to mean the latter, in which case he needs to win about 100 seats! Merely cutting down the overall majority simply brings a Lib Dem and Labour coalition nearer, and doesn't really solve anything.

He thinks Portillo is a man in personal crisis. Or was when he last saw him, which was in July. He doesn't see anyone else as being a very likely candidate. But he says that Widdecombe will win if Hague is challenged. The system is mad. Should have been, as Hague wanted, a totally member-based vote at all stages. Splitting it between the parliamentary party and the membership is illogical.

He says that Portillo and Maude are very fed up, because of the briefing against them by the Hague acolytes. I asked, rather innocently, They all seem a bit unhappy? He replied with a sucking gasp of extreme 'you-could-say-so' agreement. We agreed that acolytes are the big problem very often – as they have been with Blair and Brown.

LABOUR He says that Brown would never have become anything like so popular a figure as Blair. He thinks Blair is a very good populist, whereas Brown seems sunk in gloom and distanced from the people.

Jeremy Heywood, who was his private secretary and is now Blair's, says that the talk about Blair–Brown no-talk (cf. Thatcher and her chancellors, cf. Norman and Major) is nonsense. They see each other constantly; they talk on the phone a lot – though Norman doubts this last point, on the grounds that ministers are often hard to track down and on the move.

PINOCHET He said he was embarrassed to receive the medal, on his recent visit to Chile.[1] He had not been warned, and when it loomed he wanted no press. But there were twenty TV cameras, and he knows he looked uneasy. He had gone there merely, he says, to talk to people with whom he got friendly during the Pinochet campaign here – and then this

---

1 In December 2000, during a visit to Chile, Lamont had been awarded a medal by the Pinochet Foundation for his 'extraordinary and valiant attitude' in defending Chile's former dictator Augusto Pinochet. Lord Lamont had joined Margaret Thatcher in criticizing General Pinochet's arrest and detention in Britain in 1998.

landed on him. He claims that P is a maligned man. Agrees that the army tortured and should not have, but believes that P often knew little about it. He also believes Frei,[1] who said that if there had been no revolution against Allende, Chile would have finished up as a Cuban satellite.

THATCHER He sees her often, he says. She is writing a new book, on foreign policy.[2]

ROGER LIDDLE
12 February 2001

He had spoken to Peter Mandelson today. PM said his lawyer had seen the Home Office evidence, and found it to be very weak. In a normal court of law the case would be dismissed for want of evidence.

Therefore there is reason to expect that Hammond[3] may be helpful to PM. RL has seen Peter's own statement to Hammond, and found himself pretty convinced by it. It seems on the evidence unlikely that Hammond can find that Peter tried to influence the passport granting, or did anything very wrong. Hammond may be bound to accept the lack of evidence that Peter ever did make the relevant call to the HO.

Pragmatically, what needs to happen is that Peter is given some vindication, while Tony is not found to have behaved very badly. This may be asking a lot. May be unavailable. But it would be the desirable outcome – so that PM can remain a relevant politician. I hope that Hammond says that P did nothing wrong, and accepts P's own recollection of the facts. If so, this would lead to people being able to say that he handled it badly at the time, and also saying that No. 10 handled it badly at the time, but that now it could be forgotten and we could move on.

Blair's attitude. Roger remarked that Tony had been 'particularly nice and warm to me in recent days'. Doesn't know whether this might have changed, given the events of the last three days, but doubts it. Tony going out of his way – since Roger is a Peter ally and intimate – to show by this means that he is still warm to Peter.

RL thinks that Tony is desperately keen to be fair to Peter, and also would like to make sure he is not ruined. RL thus rejects the common feed in this weekend's press that Tony is 'furious' about everything PM

---

1 Eduardo Frei Ruiz-Tagle: president of Chile 1994–2000.

2 Margaret Thatcher, *Statecraft: Strategies for a Changing World* (London: HarperCollins, 2002).

3 Sir Anthony Hammond, Treasury solicitor and Queen's Proctor 1997–2000, conducted the Hammond inquiry into what became known as the Hinduja passport affair. On 9 March Hammond found that Mandelson had not deliberately lied about a phone call to Home Office minister Mike O'Brien about a passport application for the Indian billionaire businessman Srichand Hinduja.

has recently been doing. 'In a way, Peter is Tony's closest friend.' Tony will be desperately keen to ensure that some way is found to preserve Peter.

So why did Peter behave so foolishly this week? By going to the *Mail* and *Telegraph*. Peter would say, says Roger, that he had to go further than *The Guardian*, the *Indy* and the *FT*, and had to go to editors not commentators. His purpose was to prepare the ground for the reception to the Hammond report, and ensure that his side of the story was fully understood. RL agrees with me that this may have been a mistake – but perhaps an understandable one.

RL said he felt 'desperately worried and unhappy' about the situation.

DAVID BLACKBURN
Dinner at Kaspia, 27 February 2001

Ken Livingstone has three reasons why he is pushing tower blocks (see S. Jenkins's excellent, if preservationist, piece in *The Times* on Friday 23 February).

A tower block involves no car-parking. Because they are so huge, the issue never arises – as it does in lesser developments. Ken is anti-car.

One of his few powers is to intervene in what are deemed 'strategic' planning matters. It is easier to define a tower block as strategic than it is a lesser development. He can nudge, and also can make life harder for the planning authorities (the boroughs). Ego satisfaction. A mark on London.

LODE WILLEMS
Phone, 1 March 2001

BLAIR–BUSH Ambassadors had a briefing from John Sawers about the Blair–Bush meeting. (Daniel Bernard grandly declined to go – a sign, says LW, of his deteriorating health and enthusiasm.)

Sawers's briefing on B–B in effect presented the man as a genius. Of quite unexpected calibre. This was the impression he wanted to convey to us, and wanted us to convey to our capitals.

JS used the following adjectives: tough, friendly, hospitable, with a grip on the issues, interested, hands-on, spoke without notes at all times, had lots of questions about Putin, showed detailed knowledge of the Balkans.

Colin Powell was there at the start. CP talked about Iraq, and Bush said that was Colin's take on the issue 'but some of us aren't there yet'. Cheney was also seen: JS said he too was hands-on and knowledgeable, but a very different character from Bush.

The British were very pleased with the communiqué about defence, which they described themselves as steering (making) the Americans to agree to. Their support was not unconditional, but the meeting was the first important step in the effort to convince the US that the European Security and Defence Policy was good and vital.

On NMD, Blair and Bush evidently had a long discussion, but more of a conceptual than a technical kind, Fylingdales and Thule[1] were allegedly not even mentioned – which LW found hard to believe (and which rather contradicts the impression of Bush as a hands-on detail merchant).

It was important that the communiqué spoke about 'substantial bilateral discussions' on NMD before any move is made, which in any case will be a long time from now, as Cheney admitted, because it is technically so far off.

Sawers said of Bush, 'He is an extraordinary president.'

This call, by the way, had been placed by Lode, in order to find out about the effect of foot-and-mouth on the election date. If it goes back to October, this entirely throws off the Belgian presidency plans . . .

ROBIN COOK
Lunch, *The Guardian*, 14 March 2001

Capable, knowledgeable, assured. He knew the shape of the world and its details. He is a lot more confident than he used to be, even a mite Metternichian. On foreign affairs, thus, a rather admirable performer. But also quite blatantly shifty when it came to (a) the Vaz affair,[2] (b) the election, (c) Mandelson/Hammond – a necessary reminder of just how devious and furtive and altogether openly dissembling top politicians need to be. His hands were often tightly clenched, with white knuckles showing – although his words and manner seemed very laid-back. He did not eat his crusts – meticulously stacking them at the side of his plate.

In his opening *tour d'horizon*, RC began by saying that Europe would implode on the Tories if they made it a big issue at the election. Their divisions and their extreme position would become very clear, and Labour would make sure of that. The thing he is proudest of is the removal of

1 Radar stations built during the Cold War at Fylingdales, North Yorkshire, and Thule, Greenland, to warn of incoming missile onslaught.
2 Keith Vaz, Labour MP for Leicester East since 1987, and Europe minister, had also become embroiled in the affair after it was revealed that he had written in 1997 to Tony Blair and to Peter Mandelson about passport applications by Srichand Hinduja and his brother Gopichand, also a billionaire businessman.

Milosevic, which would not have happened without the NATO action in Kosovo.

We now had the most open system of arms sales of any country in Europe, and, to his surprise, the EU countries had accepted the code of conduct which seems to have been largely drafted in London.

His two chief worries were (a) the grind-down of the Middle East peace process and (b) the utter failure to reform the United Nations.

QUESTION PERIOD Washington was the first subject. He claimed that Colin Powell was a very creative and progressive man, further to the left than many ministers in European governments. It was only the accident of the Gulf War, which happened to be fought under a Republican president, that put CP into the Republican not the Democratic camp.

To me RC said that he was still a good friend of Madeleine Albright, but she did not have the support. CP has the clout, because he is the most popular man in the government, which means that, although Rumsfeld[1] may seem to have won some early turf battles, in the end Powell will have reserves to call on.

Almost everything, he suggests, depends on Putin and Bush making a rapprochement. Putin has indicated that he is not going to oppose any form of NMD just like that. But Russia is above all interested in not being humiliated. So anything that the US does needs to avoid that, and also to engage Russia.

Remember also, he slightly enthuses, that proponents of NMD in Washington are also in favour of deep nuclear cuts. He said he wasn't entirely in favour of this – though I didn't understand why. Perhaps it has to do with the consequential effects on the British deterrent: a wonderfully odd position for the former CND man to be taking!

He said he was especially depressed that the British line, which is essentially to engage with the rogue states, had been especially unsuccessful with Iran.

ZIMBABWE He said that there was now a case for expelling Zimbabwe from the Commonwealth. Engagement was the better way. He also said that Mugabe has simply no understanding of the way 'we' see him. He seriously sees himself as an elder statesman of Africa, and expects to be treated that way.

He was amazingly defensive of Vaz, insisting that he had been acquitted and rebuking those of us who denied it. Said Vaz had been the best

---

1 Donald Rumsfeld: businessman, politician; US Secretary of Defense 1975–7 and 2001–6; highly controversial figure, particularly in his leadership of the invasions of Afghanistan and Iraq.

'visa' minister he had had, trying hard to improve our systems on the subcontinent.

ADDENDUM I asked him if Labour would treat Europe as a pro-active issue in the election campaign, or confine itself to rebutting Hague's wild extremes. He seemed to say that Labour would do more than react, and he himself said we had such a good story to tell over Europe that it would be a waste not to use it.

DAVID MILIBAND
10 Downing Street, 15 March 2001

BUSH Did he think the talks had gone well? He was a lot less effusive than John Sawers had been – see my note from LW a week or two ago. But he said they talked intensely and got on well. Bush was no bozo. 'It is a wonderful gift for a politician to start by being underestimated.' It opens up so many possibilities. But DM felt that there were danger signs ahead. He mentioned especially the environmental reverse, which is a subject close to his heart. Yesterday Bush indicated that he would back off the Kyoto targets (contrary to a campaign promise). All this is very worrying. It puts the US in a totally different camp from a pretty concerted European position on Kyoto and post-Kyoto.

I asked about Clinton. Did Blair miss him? He said, reflectively, not. The thing about politics, he has learned, is that there is no such thing as personal friendship that survives the departure from office. Clinton is yesterday's man. And must be feeling terrible about nobody wanting to know him any more. But that's the way it is. When I instanced Major and [George H. W.] Bush as a rare counter-case, he was interested. He agreed with me that Clinton's shadow was a long one. The president emeritus is in a sense the leader of the opposition until they select a new presidential candidate. This gives Bush a huge leg-up.

DOMESTIC He said the second term would proceed on its long-termist course. He reproached me for my contention more than once that the government was neurotic. Quite the contrary, he said. The Budget, for example, is long-termist (as I had written) – *The Times*, he made a point of telling me, had written the best leader on the Budget, talking about the new social democracy.

He would not be drawn on Whitehall reorganization, beyond saying that anything that had been written was wrong. He said that what the Civil Service needed to find a way of doing was recruit/train people with different skill sets from the ones hallowed by practice and tradition. They needed delivery merchants, people who could relate to the problems on the ground, people who did things rather than just writing about them.

When I said that Richard Wilson was not the man to do this, being such a traditional civil servant, DM replied by saying that no doubt RW would say that he, DM, wasn't well qualified for his job either: a little glimpse, perhaps, of the friction between Civil Service and policy unit. He did explicitly say that Wilson regarded the policy unit as unqualified to make comments on how Whitehall should be run.

He insisted on his long-termist point. Once again he denied my point that the government was too attentive to opinion polls, remembering that he had crossly emailed me on that point. Tony, he repeated, hasn't got the patience to go through the finer points of what A and B voters in Glasgow want to do about house burglars. He is much more fingertip sensitive, trusts his instincts not the figures. DM ridiculed the notion that any policy detail was settled in this way. On the other hand, he could scarcely deny that Brown is intensely interested in all that, or that P. Gould is a poll man par excellence.

He especially instanced the criminal-justice review – *The Way Ahead*, I think it is called – which emanated from Downing Street, but is published by the Home Office, a really serious and interesting piece of work. It should be linked to Blair's speech at Pentonville, when he talked about repeat offenders and the need for paying attention to the fact that all but the lifers will come out into society and it was just not good enough that so many crimes were committed by so few people (DM had the stats at his fingertips).

We concluded with rather sharp exchanges about my piece this morning, calling for the election to be postponed.[1] This was interesting. He said, first of all, that once you started postponing you didn't know when to stop. You might have to wait a whole year. There would always be a reason. He also said that foot-and-mouth affected only 0.3 per cent of the people.

However, he then strayed into some far-out territory, saying the whole issue was got up by the Tory press. First, Blair had never said 3 May, and yet was now being accused of sticking to a date that he had never named. When I said incredulously that 3 May was the word put about for months by people very close in, he said that all these things were a carousel feeding on itself. What balls! Second, he seriously suggested that because the *Mail* had got into the act with two successive front-page editorials, we all had a duty to back off. This was obvious Tory propaganda, he

---

1 HY on 15 March 2001 wrote of a 'foot-and-mouth election' – the first epidemic in decades had broken out – and warned that 'Labour won't lose, whatever the date. But Labour will seem ruthless, and an agent of the very cynicism Mr Blair once looked as though he seriously intended to dispel.'

said. Playing the Tory game, to get the date put off for blatantly slight reasons. Forcing Blair to seem to be making an unreasonable decision.

The interesting thing about this was the sight of Miliband, no doubt spouting the general Downing Street view (a) that the whole argument was to be seen as purely Tory vs Labour positioning and (b) that anyone who purported to be a progressive should be forced by the *Mail* to come to the support of the government!

Incidentally, I dropped into the conversation a light question about whether Blair was still seeing people like me. No, said DM, he wasn't doing much press at the moment. But you haven't been dropped from the list, he volunteered. He was, however, surprised that I hadn't been in for almost a year . . .

He also, patronizingly, said he thought *The Guardian* was doing better than at our last conversation about nine months ago. It was a bit more serious, a bit more straight in its reporting. He was especially interested in the public-services project, which he felt was very important as a kind of landmark to equal the Thatcher privatizations of the 1980s: a way of reaffirming the value of the public services.

All in all, a forty-five-minute conversation does expose one to the different perspectives of the insiders and us. David sees himself as engaged in a massive project for the reform of Britain. Long-termist, progressive, a rebirth of social democracy, which includes the routing of the right, and will involve the remaking of the state in various deep ways: the reaffirmation of the public sector, the reorienting of politics to the left. He sees all the stories about sleaze etc. as a distraction from this: usually untrue, always exaggerated, all building into a picture that makes no distinction between the Tories and Labour, even though the stories about Labour are so thin by comparison with Aitken etc. (even supposing they are true, which he thinks they are usually not). Over it all hangs his plaint that 'it is always possible, in the hard business of politics, that abrasive things happen when people are doing their best for the country.'

I have a lot of sympathy with this. The contrast should never be forgotten between the doers and the writers. Also, one probably has to plead guilty to being critical almost to a fault, because the government has so much power, and because *The Guardian* needs to be, as it were, a loyal critic from the left. But ultimately what's clear is that people like David see no value in the journalistic function. They believe in a free press, of course, and they say things like 'You must write what you must write' and all that. But they basically reject the role of the press as critic, as scourge (though admittedly it occurs to me that he commended today's leader on welfare-to-work as an ideal example of progressive journalism: welcoming welfare-to-work, explaining it, describing how it could go further).

ROGER LIDDLE
Drink, the Reform Club, 19 March 2001

He said, quite abruptly and sharply, that 'of course Tony wants to have the referendum.' We discussed the role of Brown. RL said that in the end what could Brown achieve by obstructing it? He is not prime minister, and wants to be prime minister. The real problem – the only problem – is for Tony to be sure in his own mind what he wants to do. Once that has happened, it is hard to see GB having the clout to stop it happening.

But there may be an institutional problem with the Treasury, almost separate from GB. As history showed, the Treasury is not exactly anti-Europe but is sceptical in a true and permanent sense. The assessment therefore may be sceptical. I replied, GB runs the Treasury and can surely doctor the assessment to meet the demands of the prior decision about holding the referendum. RL did not disagree.

The important thing to remember, he said, was that you could make an economic argument against going in at any time. There will always be some economic obstruction based on uncertainty. This uncertainty drives the Treasury, which is chronically short-termist – the short term being the only thing it thinks it can safely measure and predict.

He thought most of the Cabinet would follow Tony. They do not like Brown, who has been beastly to so many of them. He has no residue of support on a personal basis. The only problematic name RL mentioned was Blunkett. But I said that Blunkett in the end was a softie who would cave in to the will of a Blair-led majority.

On the Cabinet, further, he said that he thought Cook would almost certainly stay at the FCO, though Blair had never discussed it with him. He thought Straw might go to the Prescott type of job, mainly because Blunkett was getting himself rather blatantly primed for the Home Office. Who, said RL, would go to Education? This was a big job, on which there was a radical agenda, especially re secondary schools. But who in the Cabinet could do it? A. Darling was an underrated man, but could you have a Scot at Education? He asked me what I thought of Charles Clarke. I said that I was against all the HO ministers, but we agreed that he had a bit of something about him, was prepared to get a small way out on a limb, did not scare as easily as so many others did. 'He's the best man I know at taking a complicated subject and making a good speech about it to a Labour audience.' The other 'able' person he mentioned was Patricia Hewitt.

On Mandelson: he thought PM would not come back at the start of the next government. But he also thought that after eighteen months the government would be in trouble, and people would be pleading for Peter to be brought back to save their seats. RL recalls TB going to a meeting of the party somewhere in Sheffield, talking to party workers and MPs, and at the back of the room a voice shouting out that he must bring back Peter – this was after the first resignation – because otherwise they were going to lose their seats. 'I think that's what persuaded Tony to bring Peter back.'

MoD BRIEFING ON NMD
20 March 2001

This was arranged painfully slowly, after several calculations, with Brian Hawtin, director general, international security policy, MoD. With him he had Commodore Tim Hare, who is head of nuclear policy. Along also came Andy Helliwell, who works for Hare on National Missile Defence specifically. Of the three, Hare was by far the best and most promising for the future: confident, articulate, understanding what I was getting at.

Do they think NMD is sure to happen? Yes, they said. But it was subject to a lot of problems. The US could solve the technical ones – but then later they implied the technical problems were so varied and so great that one was left doubting whether this was so.

Bush has indicated he wants a missile defence system asap, but he realizes it may be a long way off. He has to. He has no options yet ready for inspection. The Clinton system – trajectory intercept – is the only show in town at the moment. It is still at the conceptual stage, and even that is far from fully shaped, let alone starting on the technology. And the Clinton system is itself very doubtful. Three tests so far out of an intended nineteen, and a high failure rate.

One has to take seriously the fact of the threat, said Hawtin, echoed by Hare. There's a very simple question: why are these three countries[1] trying to build long-range missiles, not just short-range ones? As a threat to the US. The UK has already analysed the threat, in its paper (which I took away) on chemical and biological warfare eighteen months ago. We tend to agree with the US analysis. Even France cannot really dissent from the threat analysis – and doesn't do so. France, however, is stressing the deterrence doctrine as the way to handle it, far more than the US is.

The Bush scheme is a way of downgrading MD [mutual destruction] as the only form of nuclear defence. To depend on defence rather than offence seems a good idea, even a 'moral' one – tied in to Bush's campaign pledges to cut the nuclear armoury a great deal. Bush and co. will argue

---

1 North Korea, Iraq and Iran were all named as threats in President Bush's 'axis of evil' speech on 29 January 2002.

that MD is unsuitable to a world of multipolar rather than unipolar threat. What Bush wants could be called mutual assured stability.

Hawtin kept saying that the Clinton–Bush plan was vastly scaled down from the Reagan Star Wars. Same principle, but much more modest and specific. Star Wars was designed to prevent a first strike from the massive Soviet arsenal, NMD is designed to prevent an isolated rogue-state action. These are very different.

On the other hand, the more they talked, the more complicated and fanciful much of this seemed. For example, when the US talks about protecting the allies: which allies? how? where? – these are all questions, as they said, that come to mind. To develop a system that protects the US mainland alone is complex enough. To develop one that protects countries at infinitely different ranges from Iraq is something else again. Layer upon layer, not just one system but many systems, are surely involved. They did not seem to disagree with this. Hare was especially eyebrow-raising. How to integrate between the systems? What about command and control? Who would control it in a theatre? Not to mention who would pay for it. E.g. would Greece pay for the protection it might uniquely need from a certain range of Iraqi weapon? And how much radar would they need, and where would it be? All this made Hare expose a lot of sceptical body language – even though he was adamant about the real nature of the threat.

They said that the Republican right wanted a system big enough to aim at China – which the Clinton system did not aim to do. If that happened, China, with its small nuclear missile defence force, would have genuine alarm. Cf. Russia, with a massive armoury, which NMD could not touch.

A basic US thought, common to Clinton and Bush, is the sense that START has taken far too long.[1] Since 1992, it has moved very slowly. People expected to be on START 4 by now. Meanwhile, both sides insist on hanging on to vastly more missiles than they need, to be used as bargaining chips if START gets moving again.

This is the context. So it has induced a kind of reversal of priorities, which Bush is now proceeding with. I.e. step 1: think about security issues and threats; step 2: think about arms control. The present method, of putting arms control first, has demonstrably not worked well.

What about the allies? I got the impression that the allies are essentially freeloading, at present, on US work. We are watching and waiting, Hawtin ponderously said. But it turned out that there were some differences:

The UK is, as ever, more equal than others. 'Because of our history,

1 The treaties arising from the Strategic Arms Reduction Talks, between the US and the USSR in 1991, and then between the US and Russia in 1993, placed limits on the number of nuclear warheads on each side.

especially in the nuclear field', we are having closer talks. They sounded very smug and accepting about this. Really did talk about the network of relationships. This compared with France and Germany – though one should note that Germany sounded less sceptical than before, and even France admitted the threats were there. They thought that there had been quite a change in the last year, in which a greater collectivity of European countries were now accepting that the US wanted to do this – and were prepared to take a serious part in the consultation which the Bush people keep reiterating they want to do.

The Russians were key, of course. But Hawtin's view was that Putin would have no choice but to go along with a change in the Anti-Ballistic-Missile Treaty. Arguably the Soviet Union fell because of Star Wars and its inability to replicate that system. It has no chance of replicating an NMD system to the US level. Putin knows this. Moreover, the strategic background has changed. Russia may be as threatened by rogue states as the US is – geographically, indeed, more so.

I said, This is all taking a very long time, and the strategic background may change. If Saddam is felled, if Iran goes moderate, if Kim Jong-Il[1] softens, doesn't this change the analysis? They were all emphatic that it would not do so – even in the unlikely event that the three ifs turned out to be right. There was so much oomph behind it, not least from the military-industrial complex.

On the other hand, they contradicted themselves a bit by saying that the Chiefs of Defence Staff were very doubtful about the funding implications for other projects ... Could Bush and Rumsfeld and Cheney surmount that?

Cheney and Rumsfeld are especially moved by the threats, however. Rumsfeld talks about it a lot. They really do fear rogue states, and sarin in the subway.

ED BALLS
Lunch (with Alan Rusbridger and Sidney Blumenthal), Soho House, 30 March 2001

THE EURO   Yesterday's Treasury PQs (and a statement?) had been much on the euro, and preparations for entry. They had thought that the amount of money which has so far been spent – £24 million in all – would cause a big row. EB professed himself disappointed that there had not been more of one, from either the Tories or the sceptic press. What the

1 Kim Jong-Il: head of state in North Korea since 1994.

Tories had gone on, instead, was the illegitimacy of the referendum. This seems to be their strategy – or was it? And whose is it? At any rate, that is what Portillo went on.

It raises a much larger issue, which EB wanted to put to me. This was that the question of consent could not be settled simply by the referendum. There had to be an ongoing assent, not a period in which people were challenging the referendum result and vowing not to let it stand. We were going to be in the strange situation of perhaps having the referendum, yet not being able to see the project through to completion – notes and coins – until after another election.

It was possible that the Tories would announce, even at that late stage, that they would not accept it. This would be extraordinarily difficult. If the currencies had locked but we did not have notes and coins it would be deeply turmoilsome to try and unpick it. But they may be tempted to pledge to do that. So from our point of view we must aim for a situation where consent remains good not only at the referendum, but then up to the locking, and then up to the next election, and then up to notes and coins.

We will be the first country to have an election between the decision to join and the presence of notes and coins. Quite a bit may depend, as far as public sentiment is concerned, on how the French et al. handled their transition to notes and coins. It has the potential to be highly positive – but also could be a cock-up (this per HY).

I said, If they (the Tories) get committed to the bunker, this will surely make it easier for you to win the next election. He did not disagree, but quite sensibly said that events could destabilize everything. But I think we agreed that, as long as the Tories remained committed to this extreme anti-Europe stance, they were less rather than more likely to be able to present themselves as once again a party of the centre.

However, the danger remained. If it was a 51–49 result, perhaps on quite a low poll, that might be the beginning and not the end of the euro endgame.

He thought that the business community, by then, would be pro-euro, however, which would be another factor weighing against the Tories. If their business constituency deserts them even further, what will they do? Business, he judged, was divided, and smaller business very ignorant. But big business would come round – depending perhaps a bit on the sector they were in.

On the Government and Brown's policy, he said that yesterday's statement, in which GB had said inter alia that he looked forward to debating the euro during the election, was carefully worked out. He volunteered that that sentence, about debating the euro, was referred to as 'the Hugo Young sentence' – a pleasing reference to my banging on about it for so long.

He denied that GB was inserting 'a sixth condition', as I had written in January, following my pre-Xmas talk with GB. That talk, it turns out, had also been carefully programmed. In retrospect, EB says that, because it took place just after Nice, it found GB emphasizing rather heavily the shortcomings of the EU system which had been thrown up at Nice – i.e. its lack of accountability etc.

This, however, was not a sixth condition. It was just a way of emphasizing the kind of changes Europe needs to make. It needed to be moving in the right direction, in order to persuade people.

BUSH AND THE US Ed played rather the UK official, in face of Sidney's blistering attacks on Bush. He made one or two good points. Notably that, while it was true that Rumsfeld et al. were seemingly unilateralist, the appointment of Zoellick at Trade was positive. SB agreed. Zoellick was a very bright man. Lamy[1] and Zoellick had a good chance of doing business.

Ed said that a senior minister 'who shall be nameless' remarked earlier that maybe a Bush presidency would be more helpful to the UK than a Gore presidency. (Can this have been Blair? Either him or Gordon, surely.) This was because of the trade/protection issues, but also because of the remarkable and telling observation that Gore was 'too left wing' – and therefore his victory would have given the wrong signal to the UK and the Third Wayers! He noted that there was nobody from Wall Street in the top echelons. Amazing, said SB.

He had rather a good image which he could not quite place. He said there had been 'one of those monitoring groups' – was this GCHQ[2] land or what? – which had been an Anglo-American creation long ago. When they wanted to untangle it, they found it literally impossible to separate the wires.

UK GOVERNMENT AND THE TREASURY I was re-minded, talking to Ed, how much of their lives are spent trying to get delivery of services better. Service delivery is the game that really matters, and proves most frustrating. It is the unseen part of the Whitehall iceberg (HY), the grind of effort and challenge we never see much of and people do not talk about in exciting ways. Yet it is real life.

The Treasury ponders this a lot. The Chancellor has become a very strategic post, now that the MPC has taken over monetary policy. He has

1 Pascal Lamy: a French member of European Commission since 1999.
2 Government Communications Headquarters: the UK signals-intelligence establishment, based in Cheltenham.

oversight: that is his central task. Departments, on the other hand, often do not have a strategic vision, or distance. Cites Health as the big example. There, because ministers are liable to be called to account for a single hospital failure, they need to get involved in far too much detail. And it is a prime example of the PAC [Public Accounts Committee] system which puts officials not ministers on the stand – and leads to a risk-averse environment. He seems to be thinking his way towards a situation where top civil servants become more public figures – rather as Eddie George is at the Bank. Taking public responsibility for their decisions.

SIDNEY BLUMENTHAL Bush is not an ideologue. He and his people can speak the language, say the words when necessary. But essentially they are about power and money and nothing else. Reagan was an ideologue; they are not.

A story on excellent authority. Alain Richard, the French defence minister, recently went to see Rumsfeld. They began to talk about the ESDP. Richard remarked that Powell and Bush had both expressed support and confidence. Rumsfeld said, 'That's them. This is me.' Before going on to launch an attack on ESDP. When Clinton (to whom SB speaks very often) heard this story, he was staggered that anyone could be so dismissive of the president. But it shows a lot.

The real victim in all this is Colin Powell. Powell is a Republican mainly because his first exposure to politics was as a White House fellow under Nixon. At that stage, as a young army officer, he was a tremendous trophy, and has remained that way. That is what gave him his Republican links.

He is now being humiliated. John Bolton, one of Cheney's many men, has been put in there as a senior official to watch him. He has no clout. They cannot, of course, get rid of him. As a black and all that he is such a valuable property. But he is a man of great pride and dignity. SB thinks he will not last the first term, and will sooner or later resign because he cannot tolerate the way he is publicly (and privately) treated.

Cheney is the prime minister to Bush's monarch. This is the first time we have had a prime minister, and Cheney is the first V-P who has run the government. He has his people all over the White House, and many other places.

If Cheney dies or quits, what will happen? One answer would be to put Powell there. But that would mean nobody running the White House. On the other hand, it would deploy the emblematic things CP is most valued for. Alternatively, what about Rumsfeld? But would Rumsfeld want it?

These people are hard-wired to the 1980s.

The lesson SB has learned from working for four years in government is that nobody knows a great deal. Nobody knows everything. Clinton, who signed every paper, read everything, marked everything up, was intensely interested in everything, even he did not know by any means what other people were doing. He could not.

JOHN STEVENS
Phone, 1 May 2001

He had read my upbeat piece about the referendum being held, and he felt very worried. The risk is monumental, because of all that's happened – not least today's paper from the Germans, and the sense that the Europe debate is hotting up so much.

How can they hope to win it without making any preparations? They perhaps think that because they beat Major and Hague they can win this easily. They are wrong about that.

He suggests that Blair should go on TV and say that he intends to have a referendum, he knows the euro is not popular now, but that he will hold the referendum when he feels he can win it. Perhaps, says JS, this would be a way of starting the long campaign. It would be fatal to commit to a referendum in the present state of public opinion. Heseltine thinks that Blair should set a date for the referendum now, which would focus people's minds, but JS seems to think this could be fatal.

Everyone underestimates the danger of holding a referendum when the Tory Party is united round its opposition to the euro. The Tory Party needs to be cracked apart. A PR commitment would be the way to do this – why can't Blair see the issues are closely linked? Without a PR commitment, it is hard for the Tory left to break away – yet if the party seems to be united it will be a heavy obstacle to beat in the referendum. If Blair calls a referendum soon, the antis will break open the champagne.

It is vital that Hague gets smashed, and knocked out. There then needs to be a contest between Portillo and Duncan Smith, which IDS wins. This would put up front the intolerable right-wing side of the party on all matters, and make it insupportable by its leftists. It would also make plainer the real exit agenda, which would frighten people off.

The Owen fallacy[1] will not survive the referendum campaign. People will see through it. But they need all the help they can get – like IDS being the Tory leader.

---

1 Possibly a reference to the common Euro-sceptic belief that Britain could negotiate a better deal for itself on international trade if it was outside the EU.

GORDON BROWN (AND ED BALLS)
Lunch, *The Guardian*, 31 May 2001

One week before the election. Asked for by him, in response to a *Guardian* editorial written by Martin Kettle which accused the Labour government of planning a non-radical second term.

Some remembered gleanings, all about public spending/public sector/ 'radicalism'.

Very insistent on the fundamental point that radicalism does not equate with higher income tax and higher spending. That is 'an old paradigm'. It goes back to the old days when the Tories were for lower tax and cutting services, and Labour for higher tax and, allegedly, higher spending and better services – a programme which invariably ran into the ground because of bad economic management.

Instead of this, Labour now has a more complex picture to try and fulfil. This does not depend on higher tax, at least direct tax, but on higher growth, from which public services attract the highest priority (rather than lower tax). The purpose of a programme which advances enterprise and thus growth is to secure better public services.

A crucial element is *how* public money is spent. The Tories reached 44 per cent of national income, but the vast mass of it was on unemployment pay and debt interest. If you have a smaller percentage but give much higher parts to education and health, that is a much better way of being 'radical' in the public interest.

Challenged on 'radical' for the next term he kept coming back to child-poverty measures, the WFTC [Working Families Tax Credits] (which could add £3,000 to a family earning £10,000). Within a lot of economic measures are all sorts of ways of helping the disadvantaged which are not sufficiently understood in that light.

Challenged on categories of spending, GB did insist that we would reach the EU average of health spending by 2006, which is the target (an incredibly long time away . . .)

Challenged on the overall level, he reeled off expected growth patterns in the economy, which I did not follow. The overarching point seemed to be that no one should expect a steadily mounting curve of spending as a percentage of output. It would rise, as a level, and then level off, said Ed Balls, tracing his finger in the air.

As regards tax etc., he emphasized more than once the seemingly magic figure that 10 per cent of the taxpayers paid more than 50 per cent of the tax. But that is only income tax. Asked whether his objection to a

50 per cent rate was that it would yield too little or that it sent the wrong signals to entrepreneurs etc., he said, 'Both.'

On higher education, he said, 'It is no longer a relationship between the government and the parent, but between the government, the parent and the student.' I.e. student contributions. (Breathtaking to see how this has become quite normal in Labour thinking, yet such a change from not very long ago. The new realism. Rather like 'Labour is the party of the homeowner,' a phrase often heard from Blair and Brown in this election.)

He was very heavy on 'the ethos of the public sector'. He kept returning to it, as something vital to preserve. He dismissed our general charge that they wanted to 'privatize' everything. This was completely false. What they wanted to do was to ensure as best as possible that the massive sums being put into public services were handled and run as efficiently as possible. Sometimes this would be by public-sector people, sometimes by private. Actually, he added, the private sector would be relatively small as a proportion of the managerial effort. But it was absurdly doctrinaire, and scaremongering, to rule it out, as we appeared to want to do. (This was a fascinating difference from Blair. Although Brown said all of this, he did not really answer the charge that a quite different message had come out of the campaign, to the effect that private-sector management was the thing of the future. Which certainly *is* the message that Blair has been putting forward, in quite radical-seeming terms. Brown here was at least pretending this wasn't so. He was several times confronted with the very different message he seemed to be giving to this cosy audience from the one that came out in the wider public campaign.)

He was especially emphatic that the Kiley plan for the London Underground was quite wrong.[1] Here was the government giving perhaps £15 billion of investment – did it not have a duty to ensure this was well spent? If Livingstone wanted to do it his way, let the London taxpayer carry the strain. (This overlooked the point that Livingstone cannot raise tax.) As it was, the general nationwide taxpayer was underwriting the Tube, and it was vital to have an efficient system of management and oversight.

He was very severe about Kiley's claims and plans as being, he almost implied, a con. He also rejected, as did Balls in even more vehement terms, the notion that the Tube could not be safely run by the split between the constructors and the operators. In this connection, as in others, he said that in any case there was no difference between the people who would actually do the job on the ground. Whoever owned or ran

1 Bob Kiley, US citizen, former CIA agent, former head of the New York Transportation Authority, became chairman of London Regional Transport in January 2001. Both he and London's mayor, Ken Livingstone, challenged the government's plans for a public–private partnership to run London Underground. Kiley was fired as chairman of LRT in July 2001, by the Transport Secretary Stephen Byers, but stayed on as Commissioner of Transport for London.

the operation, the actual constructors would be Balfour Beatty and other construction companies.

There were only two areas where he seemed pretty uneasy about all this:

RAILTRACK[1] He really could not defend what had happened. He was chided with what Blair said on *Question Time* last night, which was apparently, when asked why Railtrack could not be renationalized, that it would take two years to have the argument, and would just waste time. I.e. that money was not the problem. Brown rather feebly said that money was a problem, but he couldn't really square that line with the fact that government is putting £6 billion (or whatever) in anyway, not to mention watching dividends being paid out of this huge loss-making business.

PRISONS Malcolm Dean and Polly Toynbee [*Guardian* columnist] chided him with the failure of his 'social' power, operated with vigour elsewhere as Chancellor of the Exchequer, to ask very hard questions of the Home Office policy of filling more and more prisons. He knew the costs of each prisoner (now nearer 30K than 25), and the costs of building prisons per inmate (70K). But his answers wittered into the sand.

As regards the political tactics, he was interesting. He felt very triumphant about the fact that 'we have occupied the ground that has driven the Tories to the extremes'. This was so on public service, and also on tax. That is another way of expressing, I suppose, the Labour strategy of commanding the centre ground. They watch the Tories going extreme, and see that they are vindicated. It's almost as if part of their reason for taking their positions is to force the Tories in that direction.

However, it was interesting to see how much he dwelt on the theory that the Tories were really 'minimal-state' people. When I contested this, saying the whole point was how little the Tories had talked about that, and did not dare to do so – ever since they abandoned the tax guarantee – he said that it is 'obvious' that, apart from Hague, all the Tory frontbenchers were adopting secretly the Letwin[2] line, of wanting to drive down the public figure to 35 per cent of national income.

To me, this shows a false appreciation of a Tory debate that has yet to be had. When Malcolm Dean joined in on my side of this, Brown slightly withdrew. But it was revealing of his inner belief – that his own progressivism is underpinned (proved?) by the Tories' extreme rightism!

---

1 After six years as a public listed company, Railtrack was in trouble: it would be forced into administration in October 2001. Network Rail took over in 2002.

2 Oliver Letwin: Old Etonian; Conservative MP for West Dorset since 1997; shadow Home Secretary 2001–3; shadow Chancellor 2003–5; shadow Secretary of State for the Environment, Food and Rural Affairs 2005; chairman of the party's policy-review and research department since 2005.

PERSONAL IMPRESSIONS I have seldom seen a less healthy-looking man. But he also has the sharpest mind, deeply engaged by this entire spectrum of issues. There has never been a more serious social reformer by his own lights, or a more powerful one in Labour's modern politics. Notable also is more about his inner relationship with Blair. Clearly he values the public service ethos more deeply (viz. the replay on what is private and what is public). But, equally, it would seem that all the stories about their differences over income tax are wrong. Brown defended the absence of the 50 per cent rate vigorously.

He was also, Blairwise, acutely conscious of, for example, a Blair speech last Friday (about patriotism), which had got a lot of publicity, and which had therefore occluded what Brown had said about poverty . . .

HENRY KISSINGER[1]
4 June 2001

A Weidenfeld breakfast, mostly journos. But also John Chipman and the Israeli ambassador.[2]

HK a brilliant talker: spacious, faultless memory, amusing, drawing on experience, and revealing a Metternichian sweep. Also rather original. Very, very strategic; very interested in power – and power alone.

BRITAIN AND EUROPE He says, as he must have said often, that the authorship of the phrase 'What is Europe's phone number?' (or some such) is something he cannot recall. But he doesn't mind having credit for it. It is a good question.

He thinks there will be a big difference between Blair–Bush and Blair–Clinton. He told this to Blair 'before the election'. Blair–Clinton was based on Third Way discourses. That was the way Clinton ran his foreign policy in Europe. It made the Italian prime minister and Jospin more important than the Spanish prime minister and Chirac. They were all social-democratic types. This was the wrong way to run policy, a very strange priority for the strongest country in the world – not to be interested in power.

He added on Clinton by the way of a lot of scathing remarks about him being 'more interested in psychology and sociology than politics or power', re the Middle East. And in the same theatre, about him being a lawyer not a national leader *in re* the last effort with Barak to get a Middle East deal.

---

1 Dr Kissinger gave permission to publish here, though he did not recall his two conversations with HY.
2 Zvi Shtauber: Israeli ambassador to the UK 2000–2004.

NMD   He was asked how Blair could better persuade the Europeans to agree to NMD. He set off on a long discourse about how NMD was an essential tool. All US presidents except Carter (and Ford) had been interested in missile defence. 'If you are in charge of policy, when you realize that its whole premise involves the killing of millions of people it makes you think very hard. That policy is not an acceptable one. That is why defence, rather than deterrence, has always been desirable.'

The US nuclear deterrence was at the very centre of its policy, and hence vulnerable to the above. He alluded *en passant* to British and French nuclear policy: 'It is all very well for Britain and France to have a nuclear weapon they might use only after they had themselves been attacked, as a kind of last desperate resort' (or some such thesis). But the US was very different. (Deeply interesting view of the UK deterrent . . .)

He thought Russia might be easier to settle than the European allies. Russia had an interest in scaling down the nuclear weaponry. Russia could maybe see the generic missile threat more clearly than the European allies. He believed that the ABM treaty was preferably (by Washington) to be dealt with not by an abrogation and renegotiation, but by an informal political agreement. ABM was a deeply complex thing, had been done in a way that gave a lot of intelligence to the other side. By implication, I think he said, it would be hard to unscramble.

ESDP   The Pentagon was sceptical, and so was Colin Powell. But the State Department institutionally did not appear that way, because it wanted to negotiate. The State Department saw it as a negotiating chip re NMD, and therefore was holding back its critique.

HK's own concern was not that ESDP should be created. He regarded it as a good thing if it did not disconnect from NATO. And had the tacit understanding that it could be withdrawn in emergencies. I.e. it should be like the force of a nation state (the UK in the Falklands, the US in the Gulf, France in Algeria).

What was proposed was different: something explicitly and exclusively for acting where NATO would not act. Under a command structure with a Finnish general, which was really a thumb in our eye. And what was this purpose? Hard to find out. He heard people saying, 'The EU does not have a military purpose' – in which case what was the new force for?

He sees it as more like an instrument whereby the EU may want to irritate and differ from the US, while keeping NATO as a safety net if things go wrong.

His basic thinking is that the EU and the US must be seen to retain a common destiny. But the trouble was how to sustain that view without there being a common threat. The tragedy would be if the covert purpose of the EU was to undermine the US connection. 'I am old enough to believe in something called western civilization. Or rather I am not young enough not to believe in it. It is worth preserving.'

RUSSIA This concept should include Russia. For Russia and re Russia, NMD is a peripheral issue. An intellectual but not a real issue – not compared with the biggest issue, which is of the Ukraine returning to the Russian Federation. This would cause terrible instability among the neighbouring states. It would be bad objectively; it would also do a lot for Russian psychology. A country with the GDP of Portugal would get ideas about itself – which could get more threatening when it got a bigger GDP than Portugal. I am not thinking of a new Cold War, but of a serious problem.

CHINA HK often said he thought China was not a military threat. Not for twenty years would it be worth reckoning with. Its internal problems are too massive. It is paying a defence budget of perhaps $20 billion – in the same league as India. Japan has $45 billion. Ours is much, much greater. It is spending resources it cannot afford. It has 100 million people on the road, looking for work. It is quite possible that China will break up – possible if not probable. He talked about the danger of a territory stretching from the eastern Polish border to the border of North Vietnam which was Mafia-run, drugs-dominated, anarchy and chaos.

FRANCE AND GERMANY France's needling of the US is obnoxious but not serious. It has the saving grace of French cynicism. They know they cannot go it alone. In Cuba, in Berlin, in the Gulf and in the Balkans, France always delivered in the end. But France overestimates American rationality. They think we know what the limits are. But we don't know what the limits are. That may be a problem.

Germany is more difficult. Unlike France, it has no experience of having a national foreign policy. No sense of being a nation. Yet. Adenauer,[1] Schmidt and Kohl were great men, who tolerated the division of their country for wider international purposes. Performed a great service. But Germany cannot yet define what it is about. Lots of ideas floating around – for example, somehow including a relationship much deeper with Russia. All this could be dangerous. Could cast a bigger threat than France.

EUROPE Remember that the EU may not be there for eternity. Italy, Spain, others may eventually have new ideas about it. This could give

---

1 Konrad Adenauer: first chancellor of West Germany (1949–63).

Britain an opportunity. (This is rather like de Gaulle in 1969 – which Ed Balls was very interested in the other day . . .)

IRAQ It had been a fatal error not to go and finish off Saddam. But now it was impossible to know how to deal with him. The danger of the EU line was that it would reward him for doing nothing. Yet this was an honest disagreement. 'I just don't know what to do about Iraq.'

IRAN was different. There was a danger that by helping Iran as is you were helping the extremists rather than pushing the reformers' case. He thought some kind of unofficial sherpas could be operating to map out a route march towards better relations which the leaders of both the US and Iran could accept.

NORTH KOREA Very scornful of the EU initiative.[1] They had had a good reception – but what did they expect? NK got rewards, and gave nothing back. NK relations with SK now cooler. This sort of competitive diplomacy did not work for anyone's good, except that of Pyongyang.

NATO ENLARGEMENT It made no sense to enlarge just to Slovenia and Slovakia. Should include Romania and Bulgaria. But the real issue was the Baltics. Here we should seek a clever way of putting the European states up front and leaving the US as a military guarantor further back – to save Russian face.

'In every country where there is no visible threat, domestic politics invariably dominates foreign policy.' For the worse.

At the general election on 7 June 2001 Labour won 413 seats (a net loss of 6), the Conservatives 166 (a net gain of 1) and the Liberal Democrats 52 (a net gain of 6). The overall Labour majority was 167. The Conservatives began a tortuous search for a leader to replace William Hague.

JOHN STEVENS
15 June 2001

Portillo treated Clarke badly. Their meeting angered KC, I hear. MP said that he would not win the leadership if it was obvious he was succumbing to Clarke, or would invite him into his Shadow Cabinet. Clarke is

---

1 The European Commission decided on 14 May 2001 to establish diplomatic relations with North Korea, in a bid to step up aid to the North and reconcile the two Koreas.

apparently very angry about the way he has been treated. What will he do? Further blows were the defection of Dorrell and, more importantly, Damien Green, who is to be P's press secretary. The left should want IDS to win. Ideally they should be urged to support him if KC does not run.

But what the euro campaign may need is something drastic happening. If the euro campaign is to be a long haul, then the need for pro-euro Conservatives becomes very important. Business especially will see the need for this.

A central figure is Chris Gent,[1] former Tory operator, now a v. rich man, very, very worked up about the euro. Would he come in behind Clarke if Clarke left?

In the short term MP is a more dangerous opponent than IDS. He seems reasonable. He can work out an Owenite rhetoric which makes the Tories seem just anti-euro, not anti-EU. It could be seductive.

In the medium term a different story. Would be seen to be a phoney and also divisive. Would not lay a glove on Blair in the HC, and the inclusiveness would have got nowhere (what will he do about Section 28,[2] for example?). The right would start stirring.

BLAIR Perhaps a key issue is what Blair will have been told this weekend by the EU prime ministers after his smashing victory. Will they be urging him to get moving? What will be his take on what he hears? It could be a crucial few days . . .

CHRIS PATTEN
Phone, 22 June 2001

BLAIR AND EUROPE Brown's speech[3] is depressing. It sends very negative signs. These will be read carefully by my colleagues in the Commission. Blair is beginning to look like John Major with a big majority: a ditherer, an uncommitted leader. My colleague Mario Monti says, 'What is this majority for?' To which one might add, Having won the election by a landslide, Hague having put Europe up front, is there not a lesson to be drawn about the overestimation of British Euro-scepticism?

1 Sir Christopher Gent: businessman; CEO of Vodafone 1997–2003.
2 Section 28 was a controversial amendment to the Local Government Act 1986 which stated that a local authority 'shall not intentionally promote homosexuality or publish material with the intention of promoting homosexuality'. It was eventually repealed in 2003.
3 The Chancellor's Mansion House speech – always one of the highlights of the financial calendar – on 20 June had confirmed that the government's approach to the European single currency would be 'considered and cautious'.

It is a complete illusion to think that we can be as influential outside the euro zone as inside it. Why doesn't Brown attend Ecofin with any regularity? Because Ecofin is no longer the place where euro business is done. It is precooked in the euro-zone committee. So Brown only comes when he has an opportunity for a bit of Euro-bashing – with careful stage-managing by the Treasury beforehand.

One of the follies is that we are missing the chance to make a natural alliance with the Germans. Their agenda is right down our street: subsidiarity, defence of the nation state, better connection between domestic politics and European politics. All the things we care about – and Schröder is moving strongly that way. Yet we are not making the alliance as we should.

If this is not changed, we will be totally marginalized in the 2004 process. Ian Buruma's book *Voltaire's Coconuts* makes the very good point that our ability to be influential on the Continent and use the Anglophilia there is dependent on our moderating our Anglocentrism at home: our complacency, our superiority, and delusion that we can be self-sufficient and the Continent doesn't matter to us.

See my piece in *Prospect* for the argument that we can matter more in Europe, but only by losing 'sovereignty', not hanging on to it. Of course we can 'survive' outside the euro. But we will lose our place, lose influence, lose the sense of really mattering.

I come back in the plane with Blair often, from Council meetings. He is always full of big statements about leading in Europe and all that. But what does it really mean? How serious is he?

Jack Straw is a man I like, though I don't agree with his civil-liberties position. But don't imagine there is any doubt where he is coming from. He is a Euro-sceptic.

Robin Cook. Many people I admire in the FCO couldn't stand him. He did them down, notably over Sandline,[1] obliging John Kerr to humiliate himself to save part of Cook's skin. But in Europe, among European

1 Sandline International described itself as a private military company; led by former British army lieutenant colonel Tim Spicer, it was involved in conflicts in Papua New Guinea in 1997 and in Sierra Leone in 1998. The 'Sandline affair' created problems for the Foreign Office and the Foreign Secretary when it became clear that arms were being supplied to Sierra Leone in breach of a UN embargo, and that officials had waited for two months before telling Robin Cook about a Customs and Excise investigation into Sandline. On 30 July 1998 HY had written, 'Mr Cook talked his way out of that pretty effectively, not least because the scandal, if scandal it was, was small potatoes. His response was straight from Sir Humphrey's rule-book: new committees and oversights and career-adjustments to prevent a repeat calamity, along with the bigger FCO budget that might allow some of this to happen.' On 29 March 2001 HY commented that 'Some officials still reflect bitterly on the responsibility which, as they see it, he failed to take for the Sandline affair in Sierra Leone, instead dumping them in the dirt.' Cook, however, had become an excellent Foreign Secretary. 'Cook made one calamitous error at the start of his term, which was to promise an ethical dimension to his foreign policy in terms that have led to him being ethically faulted ever since. It was an honourable but half-baked claim, hoisting to prominence the false assumption that his predecessors had always been unethical and carrying the implication that he, a principled foreign secretary, would address the harshness of the world from a more elevated position.'

foreign ministers, he is, I think, the best. He speaks well at the table, without constantly referring to notes. Has a grip on the issues. And he has never, I think, taken a line I disagreed with.

I (HY) described the feud between Brown and Cook, going back to the 1970s. CP alluded to the P. G. Wodehouse quote about there being nothing so terrible as Scotsmen with a grievance . . .

TORY LEADERSHIP   Given the third-division people coming forward, KC may be tempted to move in. If he thought he had a chance of making the final battle KC vs MP, he might do it.

But the trouble is that the party is very far gone. When I made a few sharp remarks after the election, I had half a dozen letters all saying that I had spoken disgracefully – as if I had been knocking a great victory! The party will take some saving.

How would KC manage it? Especially if there is a referendum – how could he lead it against the grain of its own feelings re the euro? And if there's not a referendum, how could he attack Blair for not holding one?

It is probably leadable only by a right-winger, who understands that the right-wing stance is in fact a no-no. Like Kinnock – a lefty who led Labour to the right.

Portillo is by far the ablest. Why do people dislike him? Because he used right-wingery to grease his way up the pole, as they see it. I recruited him, to the CRD, from Cambridge. He was 22, an eye on the main chance, charming, very clever, and quite tough. He was a good Minister of Defence, as Guthrie et al. will say.

David Davis was a useless Minister for Europe. Iain Duncan Smith is an uglier Hague, without the charm or parliamentary talent. Ancram is someone we used to call Norman Crumb. Once a member of the Blue Chip[1] group who said almost nothing.

Will Ken ever bolt the party? No (v. firm and immediate). He's like me. With us it's tribal.

Candidates for the Conservative leadership emerged: among them Kenneth Clarke, Michael Portillo, Iain Duncan Smith, Michael Ancram and David Davis.

---

1 The Blue Chip dining club, founded by Tristan Garel-Jones, consisted of a dozen Conservative MPs, all elected for the first time in 1979. Peter Oborne pointed out in a *Spectator* article on 12 December 1998 that eight Blue Chip members had become Cabinet ministers. One of them – John Major – became prime minister.

LEON BRITTAN
27 June 2001

KENNETH CLARKE   Talked to KC a few times before he went to Vietnam.[1] His main worry was whether he would have enough support to get past the very first stage of the ballot. I said he would need to get his people running around to make sure of this. His second worry was whether, if elected, he would be able to impose his leadership, as it were, from the party in the country to the party in Parliament. To which LB advised him to reply that it was they – the PCP – that chose the system, and they would have to live with it.

KC's statement yesterday was very good. Took everything completely head-on.[2]

The referendum, in LB's view, would be the easy situation. KC could simply emulate Wilson in 1975. What was more difficult was the Tory attitude to Nice, the Rapid Reaction Force etc., on which KC had very openly said he would tear up the Tory line.

The only way he can win is by persuading people that he can win an election. That is what the party wants, or at least what he can make the best pitch for offering.

If it got to the national vote, KC would run Portillo very close. KC would certainly find it difficult to deal with Europe. But the issue will be, Do they think his strengths are such that they are more important than the Euro troubles. There will go on being arguments, whoever is leader . . .

There's a theory that if MP is far ahead at the penultimate stage, he will switch some of his people to vote for the candidate he most wants to fight in the country. This would be scurvy but possible. TG-J very stirred up by this.

The Ancram factor. Unhelpful. Don't know if MA thinks he really can win.

FRANCIS RICHARDS
4 July 2001

At Lode Willems's Rubens evening . . .

A tall, balding, somewhat humorous-looking fellow who, though

---

1 Kenneth Clarke went to Vietnam as a director of British American Tobacco, to discuss a proposed cigarette factory. His visit was condemned by the pressure group Action on Smoking and Health.
2 At a press conference on 26 June Clarke called on Conservative MPs to abandon Euro-scepticism and rally behind him. 'Without this, the party will not be capable of winning an election,' he said.

FCO by pedigree (son of Brooks Richards, another FCO mandarin), seems ideally cast as coming out of the secret world ... Eton and Cambridge.

I asked about the absence of the American ambassador, still not confirmed by the Senate. He replied, 'There are many American embassies in London. Each of us has our own embassy. The one from the secret world just carries on' (or words very like that).

He may actually have said that within the segments of the secret world there were separate embassies.

CLUB OF THREE[1]
Lunch, Walbrook Club, 6 July 2001

This was a twenty-five-person lunch presided over by Jonathan Powell, with George Weidenfeld. The subject was EU relations with the US under the new Bush administration.

Main speakers were Liz Symons[2] (boring and governmentalist), François Heisbourg (brilliant) and Karsten Voight (also brilliant – coordinator of German–American cooperation at the foreign ministry).

POWELL 'Heath chose Europe and turned his back on the US. Thatcher chose the US and turned her back on Europe. We are trying to avoid both those mistakes.'

The US seeks invulnerability, and therefore puts its emphasis on military factors. Europe is aware of its vulnerability, and therefore puts emphasis on legal and political methods. The US these days is seen like Bismarck, Europe like Woodrow Wilson. The one self-interested, the other moralistic.

VOIGHT 'A country that doesn't matter inside Europe will never be taken seriously by the US. That is why I have never understood the British attitude to Europe.' (Note to self: this could be the keystone motto of my book.[3] The point can be redoubled: that Britain has seen the relationship with the US as a compensation for not mattering in Europe. A fatal error, the source of so much misbegotten policy. Thus it is not simply that Britain has misunderstood the American desire for the UK to be involved

---

1 Club of Three: A French–British–German forum organized by the Weidenfeld Institute for Strategic Dialogue.
2 Elizabeth Symons, Baroness Symons of Vernham Dean: former civil servant, Minister of State for Defence Procurement 1999–2003.
3 Having completed *This Blessed Plot*, his book on Britain in Europe, HY had already begun to gather material for a history of the transatlantic relationship.

in Europe. She has actively invested in her US special relationship a positive reason not to be involved in Europe. A double self-mutilating whammy.)

'Germany is for the first time in a century an angst-free zone.'

The NMD is different from the INF [intermediate-range nuclear forces] and cruise time. In that time, Germany was always fearful that the US would not come to defend it (and therefore wanted to support whatever the US wanted), while other Germans were fearful that the US would come and defend it! But now – there are no enemies to defend it against . . .

Re US–EU – we should distinguish between trade issues, which can probably be managed by the political class, and other issues which engage the mass populations and are therefore harder to manage. These include genetically modified food, gene modification, abortion, the death penalty. These are multilateral and cross-border, and therefore not easy to control.

HEISBOURG Although there are often blips in the story, the US, as history shows, always does come in on the side of greater European integration. History shows they will not be spoilers.

This year the US will be alone with Iran and China in refusing to ratify the verification protocols to the convention (check detail) on the prohibition of biological weapons. This is one of several examples to show that the US is unilateralist.

From 1941 to 1991, Pearl Harbor to the Gulf War, the US saw itself as facing a single enemy. Its defence posture was shaped accordingly, and its emotional/political strategy was defined that way. But now, as before 1941, there is no single enemy.

Never forget that though the US has 40 per cent more defence resources than the whole of Europe, a huge amount – and growing – of this is directed towards east Asia. (Statistic: the US spends 35 per cent of all the world's military expenditure.)

By 2003, let's hope, the EU Rapid Reaction Force will have run out of Balkan wars to fight. Serious decisions await as to what it will be used for.

OK, there is not a European army. But we should understand that there will soon need to be much more coordination and more integration if the RRF is going to be meaningful.

PHILIP STEPHENS
Indigo, Aldwych, 9 July 2001

Much about his not becoming editor [of the *Financial Times*], and about our website strategies . . . But also:

EURO He knows not a single person in either the Treasury or the Bank who believes we will or should go into the euro in this parliament. These are not Europhobes. They just believe the problems are insurmountable.

They have a point. The currency gap is far too wide to even think of going in now. Goldman Sachs thinks it is 20 per cent overvalued. Getting it down is far from easy. In fact it may be impossible. Talking it down now would be risking a real sterling crisis, running out of control.

The counter-argument, though, is important. Sterling, first, must come down anyway. Things cannot go on like this. Manufacturing is suffering very badly indeed. It will have to come down irrespective of the euro. The argument for the euro is that it would at least provide a floor below which sterling could not drop.

The part of the strategy that ministers constantly underrate is the length of time it will take to get ready. Blair does this (as he has made clear to both HY and PS). He thinks he can ignite and win the argument in six months (PS's figure – I had heard three or four from Chris Haskins).[1] One insider told Phil that he had never known any other politician who was so convinced as Blair of his own power to win a political argument.

Brown's strategy, PS is convinced, is to organize things so that entry does become impossible this term. The way to do this is to delay, and not to prepare – so that in due course (spring 2003, as they were spinning at the time of the Mansion House speech) it becomes impossible to have a referendum for the simple reason of non-preparation. I.e. they are right to say the country is not ready – but only because they have failed to make it ready.

Of course, if we decide not to go in, we have to go on pretending that we have not decided. Blair must continue to act and talk as though it is our intention – mainly for the sake of our European partners and their belief in him. This is what makes Phil suspicious of all these promises about 'speeches in the autumn' etc. etc. They are consistent with just stringing us along – though even P does not yet feel sure that it will not happen.

---

1 Chris Haskins: chairman of Northern Foods and Express Dairies; Labour donor; later Baron Haskins of Skidby.

How might it happen? Mainly if Brown suddenly experiences a Damascene conversion. He could just say he has now decided to go for it. If he did, the Treasury minions would come round smartish.

Against all this, it should be said that when PS wrote a pessimistic piece about two weeks ago, Jonathan Powell told him he was simply wrong. Campbell, with whom he had lunch recently, didn't talk about it much but also indicated he was wrong. The inner circle seems very ready to believe what Tony is saying to them. (Though Campbell also quite shirty, especially with P. Toynbee, about the way hacks used to attack them for going for the headlines, and now reproached them for *not* getting headlines and doing things, when actually 'we are just getting on with the job'.)

OTHER THINGS *The Guardian* is known in No. 10 as *The Gordian* – for its slavish devotion to Gordon Brown.

Re London Underground, one of the merchant bankers getting millions from the *government* for his advice said, 'It's like the government breaking an egg, and then paying us a lot to piece it back together.' I.e. nobody believes the PPP [public–private partnership] will work.

What is hard to read is the politics. Kiley is ready to play hardball with the contractors – delving into the thousands of pages of legal detail. Maybe LU will just bugger about, with bad effect. The issue is, Who will get the blame?

PS forgot to write in his column his wheeze that LU should post a picture of Gordon Brown in every train, saying, This is the man responsible for your being where you are.

JOHN BIFFEN
House of Lords, 10 July 2001

Looking quite well – certainly better than when last seen at his party around Xmas. But on three-days-a-week kidney dialysis for the rest of his life, unless he has a transplant – which he says he might try for, and is regarded as being suitable for since he is in good optimistic spirits.

TORY LEADERSHIP Who would want the job? It is very bewildering what is likely to happen, because the party has no sense of knowing where it wants to go, and no chance of winning the next election.

Part of its problem is that Blair has taken so much of its ground. Thatcher liberalized many things, and Blair has carried on in a competent way doing the same thing. He seems more competent than Thatcher and

Major were in that respect. For example, education. Whatever you may say about the education policy, it is not class-based: it is excellence- and standards-based. This is in no way socialist.

The Tories are crazy to be so obsessed with Europe. I am the original Euro-sceptic, but what is the point of focusing so much on what is an academic question – the future of Europe. We (the UK) do not have any powers of initiative: we are purely reactive to what the Europeans propose. This means that it should not be a central subject, and certainly not one on which the Tory Party chooses obsessively to divide itself. The euro may be rather different – it is a concrete issue, which may or may not come up for decision, but it hasn't happened yet. So for the leader candidates, and the MPs, to make it such a dominant issue makes no sense at all.

On Europe, by far the biggest issue is enlargement. How will countries with vastly less economic wealth marry with countries that have so much? The issues are not primarily institutional, they are economic. Talking about the finer points of the institutions – the Commission, Parliament – is not the point. The point is how Europe will be able to enlarge. The issue behind that is essentially the subventions from the existing members to the new ones. It is not trade, because trade is already pretty free across borders – it is whether the west will pay for the east. Still an open question, JB thinks.

On the candidates, he declines to say who he will vote for. Clarke used to be his deputy as shadow Industry, Portillo his CCO legman/researcher when he was shadow Energy. Knew them as smart young men. Doesn't sound very keen on them now. Spoke more warmly of David Davis and IDS, Davis being someone he noted some years ago as a man of talent.

The real problem for the Tories is possible near-extinction across large parts of the country. In many cities not only is there no MP, there is no party of any recognizable kind. No Tory MP in a city outside London. The great beneficiaries from this will be the Lib Dems, who do exist in the cities, and will be the likely beneficiaries from a Labour failure on public-service delivery.

If the idea of Ken is that he can give Blair a good kicking – well, Hague was very good at that, and look where it got him. Nobody will be able to do that better than Hague. So the problem is much deeper.

JOHN STEVENS
18 July 2001

The hard-line anti-Europeans have got the control they want. I have a mole inside the Democracy Movement,[1] and keep in close touch with him. They were saying last night, We now have the real fight we want: we are fighting him with a weak rival[2] – and we are going to win. This, they think, will lead to their capture of the Conservative Party for the 'never' line on the euro, and a totally anti-Euro line on other European things.

The Democracy Movement claims to have 60,000 members. And 340 Tory constituency chairmen. These are very big numbers. They are names and addresses and a database. They give IDS a big start on the organization front. They could mean that actually the IDS campaign does not need to be terribly upfront – the work is going on underground by the DM.

They may have the support of the *Daily Mail*; they will certainly have Thatcher and the *Telegraph*. JS reckons there are '60 hard-line Euro-sceptic MPs'. JS asked me, as a parting shot, who will they vote for if they want the greater chance of party unity? I replied, If that is the only question, then IDS. John agreed.

On the other hand, there was a sense among some people last night that Ken was going to walk it. This was a big mistake. It is going to be very close, says JS.

If KC were to win, this would transform the euro debate, in John's opinion. It would suddenly make the referendum much easier to hold. (Though, per HY, it would bring closer the fatal sense that the campaign was the establishment versus the rest – something the British European argument, unlike any others', had a chance of avoiding.)

KC is not popular with a lot of people. They just don't all like him. They think he is a bully and arrogant. But then, has one got to like politicians? The obverse case is how many of them will primarily be asking, How can we win the next election? (The real thing this is asking is, How can we win 70 seats back, the realistic option?) JS talked to friends in his old European constituency [Thames Valley] last night. The Reading seats are a good barometer. They were both lost in 1997, having been strong Tory places. One was supposed to be recovered in 2001.

---

1 The Democracy Movement describes itself as a non-party pressure group to defend liberal democracy in Britain and across Europe, seeing this as being 'fundamentally undermined by the single currency, the proposed EU Constitution, and the drive to create a Brussels-based system of government'.

2 A possible reference to a belief among some Europhiles that a weak leader would be a disaster, and would discredit the Euro-sceptic wing. In the event, Iain Duncan Smith defeated two strong candidates but failed to gain electoral ground, and was then replaced by Michael Howard, another Euro-sceptic.

Neither was. Talking around last night, he found the Reading parties – themselves much diminished in size from *c*.2000 to *c*.500 – split down the middle. The interesting divide is this: the young people coming in wanted Portillo, and were passionately anti-European. The older people cannot stand the fact of not having a Tory MP. One of these said he wanted to get out of the EU, but still wanted Ken as leader because he had a better chance of winning.

If KC wins, it will be a hairy ride. Can he possibly lead a deeply Euro-sceptic party? How will he ride it? He could seriously split it. It will be quite a spectacle. Because, whatever happens re the euro, the other Euro issues will be there to cause difficulty. The Rapid Reaction Force, the Nice treaty etc. etc.

JS feels that Tory MPs are far more obsessed about Europe than the Tory Party at large – though the Clarke vote suggests that even this is moderating.[1] On the other hand, there are these sixty diehards (at least).

The irony is that the battle for the euro will be fought out in the Tory Party leadership campaign – in which both rivals will not be wanting to talk about it very openly. Or say they don't. Actually, though, while KC says he doesn't want to talk about Europe, the truth is that IDS's best card is to attack him on the Europe issue. What else does IDS have to offer? What else is the case against KC? IDS may try and drum up an argument that KC has not got any original ideas about public services, but it is the drumbeat of Europe that will rally his troops.

The question is, Where will the Portillo people go? Where will David Willetts? After musing about this, JS thinks that 90 per cent of them will go to KC in the end. They will presumably have to tell their constituency associations, write to them etc. etc.

TESSA JOWELL
At the Blackburns' summer party, 18 July 2001

Noted that the rebellion on Monday over the committee chairs[2] was a sign of things to come. This is a very different PLP from last time, she said. If you look at the list, it included fourteen ex-ministers. Also it included a lot of people who had got in in 1997. These had at first been

---

1 On 17 July 2001, after the resignation of William Hague, Kenneth Clarke won the Tory MPs' leadership ballot, with Iain Duncan Smith second. Michael Portillo was eliminated. But voting within the Conservative Party at large would not begin until 20 August.
2 On Monday 16 July 2001 Tony Blair suffered his first ever defeat in a Commons vote, when 120 Labour rebels voted with the Opposition. This was a protest against the sacking of two Labour select-committee chairs, Gwyneth Dunwoody, chair of the Commons transport committee, and Donald Anderson, Labour MP for Monmouth, 1966–70, for Swansea East, 1974–2005, chairman of the foreign affairs committee 1997–2005, later Baron Anderson of Swansea.

anxious to be onside. But now they were less so. They had not got jobs. But also they were just less subservient. They thought the public were displeased with seeing them as lobby fodder. Also, and most interestingly, she said that on average the votes of the 1997 intake who were not ministers had gone up, whereas ministers' on average had gone down (or something like that). They felt more confident for that reason too.

This, she was sure, would repeat itself. It was a matter of self-respect, and also of asserting the role of the MP. She was in favour of this. But it needed a different response from government and media. Government should find a way of being more relaxed, of saying there needed to be discussion, of saying there were different views. Media needed to stop seizing on all such events as evidence of 'splits' and the like.

I.e. a kinder, humbler Tessa – how many more are there in the Cabinet? None, I think.

Following the general election, Robin Cook, Foreign Secretary since Labour returned to power in 1997, had been moved from the Foreign Office to become Leader of the House (widely seen as a demotion). He was succeeded as Foreign Secretary by Jack Straw.

ROBIN COOK
Lunch, Royal Horseguards Hotel, 20 July 2001

APRÈS FOREIGN SECRETARY It came as a very big shock. I am sure Tony did not decide until the Thursday night or Friday morning in Sedgefield, as the press have reported. He had given me absolutely no indication, rather the opposite. What he said to me I have no reason to disbelieve. He said the government needed to have a fresh look, that we would be criticized and bad-mouthed if we didn't – and he couldn't move Gordon, so he had to move me. He was very straight and upfront about it. However, it did not work out that way. He and they were very shocked by the terrible press it got the next day. They were criticized and I was not. They misjudged it quite badly.

Actually, I would not have gone to any other job but this one. It is a dignified last job to have. It was the job Michael Foot had in the Callaghan government (check). I was always more interested in constitutional matters, and the House of Commons. We will have a lot more reform to do, especially re the House of Lords. There is important stuff to do. It is a reasonably dignified (*sic*) way of ending my political career. I am enjoying myself. I have to admit I did not agree immediately, and I did not feel comfortable for the weekend after I agreed. But by Monday I had come to see the point of the job, even though I was sorry to leave the FCO. I had planned to stay there until halfway through another parliament and we had seen the euro through, 'if we were going to do the euro at all'.

When I (HY) said that there was the euro subtext to Cook's removal – that Blair did not want a Chancellor and a Foreign Secretary at odds with each other at the time when he was getting ready for the euro – Cook demurred. He claimed not to have had serious disagreements with Brown for a long time. He also pointed out that Brown had quite palpably not been consulted – provable, he claimed, by the total absence of Brown spinning in the Saturday papers (cf. the Sunday papers, when he was getting to work saying the euro would be delayed).

HOUSES OF PARLIAMENT   The Commons. He could not, he said, as a Cabinet minister, welcome the rebellion that occured on Monday. That would be a bad thing to be caught saying. He also thought Polly T had been unhelpful in heralding his arrival in the job as a triumph for the rebellious tendency. He thought there was a danger of them getting the habit, always to be avoided. On the other hand, there were lessons. One was that the 1997 intake thought well of themselves and would not be treated as easy lobby fodder. The election showed that the incumbency factor was big. The seats won in 1997 showed a swing to Labour of 2 per cent on average, and in the country at large 2 per cent against Labour on average. This is quite a big differential. Further, RC agreed with my point that these people were no longer star-struck, they were less compliant than in 1997, they were asking what this was all about, they were hence developing a state of mind that was more belligerent. He said, at this, Yes, there is a lack of zip and excitement.

He put this down partly (mainly) to the nature of Blair and Blairism. Said that things like incapacity-benefit talk, immediately after the election, was a red rag (my image). Also that the way the private–public issue was handled was not very subtle. He claimed that he agreed entirely with the need for private input into the health service etc. It was only modest, and it was necessary. But, he rather gnomically implied, the affronts to what Labour MPs think they are about is one reason why they are not walking about with a spring in their step.

Blair's deeds were still seen as (and were actually) a sop to the *Daily Mail* and *The Sun*. The role of the *Mail* still matters: its place as the benchmark audience. MPs knew this, and for that reason alone were more hostile to measures that seemed (however falsely) to be nothing more than sops to the *Mail*. (Behind this was Cook's long-time feeling, I believe, that Blair has been too centrist and is too lacking in leftist zeal.

Though it should also be recorded that he said, 'No other Labour leader in history could conceivably have scored two big victories like these two. He has been a brilliant leader of the party.')

The Lords. Clearly he sees this as a major issue for him. Says that Wakeham will provoke a lot of fury among Labour MPs, if it remains the government's line.[1] I.e. we have the curious spectacle of the Commons actually not opposing HL reform as a challenge to the HC, but opposing a HL reform that does not do enough to give the place more legitimacy (and therefore be more of a challenge to the HC) – though there is a limit to this thought: a wholly elected Lords would probably not be acceptable to any HC.

Wakeham is quite inadequate, says RC. Such a small number of elected members is ridiculous. It would not get public support, nor Labour support. There must, however, be a stage 2. If there is not, we face the absurd possibility that as soon as the next hereditary peer dies (of the Cranborne 92)[2] they will have an election for the replacement. Thus driving home that only the hereds are engaged in something like democracy.

He asked me what I thought about reform. I said, 50 per cent elected, and then a similar number appointed for one term of ten years or so. He said, That's about right: the elected should outnumber the appointed, but no need for them to be far more than that.

When I said that all existing life peers should be purged, he rather agreed. He talked about a cleansing. The problem, however, would be with the existing peers, who would certainly oppose this. However, the Parliament Act could be invoked to get round that. (I'm not saying he was proposing all this very keenly, he just said it would be possible.) The essential point about the Parliament Act was to ensure that, if and when it was invoked, it was in a case which public opinion agreed with. He and I said to each other that the public opinion in favour of the present life peers would be very small.

AMERICA, GEORGE BUSH ET AL. Missile defence, he insisted, was a long way off. We do not know what the question will be. So we do need to have an answer. The trend seems to be for Bush to

1 The Royal Commission on the reform of the House of Lords, chaired by former Tory whip Lord Wakeham, recommended a second chamber with 550 members, of which 67, 87 or 195 should be elected, with an independent commission responsible for all appointments. It should contain a substantial number of people who were not politicians. On 7 November 2001, the government produced a White Paper that 'strongly endorsed' the Commission's views but proposed the sacking of the remaining 92 hereditary peers and the election of 120 members. Two years later the consensus was for an entirely appointed second chamber.

2 Viscount (Robert) Cranborne, Tory whip in the Lords, did a secret deal with Blair and secured places for more than 90 hereditary peers in the reform package. William Hague, who did not know of the deal, then fired him.

favour a sea-launched and boost-phase programme, but that is a very long way off – far further than Clinton's scheme. It would also have the great merit of not involving Fylingdales. I do not regard MD as an immediate problem, he said.

I replied, What about the US demand for our political consent? Are they going to put pressure on us for agreement? He said they might, but said also that he thought Blair had already been careful in what he has said. He could continue to be careful, while sounding and seeming friendly. That was OK even for Cook, an old CND hand.

He was far more concerned about Kyoto.[1] Here Blair had been very firm in private and public. Said we just disagreed, and were determined to push Kyoto through as far as we were concerned. It was very important he should stick to this. Cook thought he would do so.

Further to Kyoto, he said that Powell and the State Department had been sent Bush's statement about Kyoto and were horrified. Very rapidly, they offered a couple of paragraphs to 'internationalize' it and make it sound less of a case of the US doing what the hell it liked. The redraft was sent: only for the White House to ring up and say that the statement had already been made. I.e. an amazing example of a major international position being taken without any reference to the State Department.

I asked about Clinton and Bush. He said that there were great differences. Obviously one was their different levels of interest in things. Clinton was very interested in lots of policy, was a Third Wayer, and talked a lot to Blair about that. There is no similarity with Bush. The trouble with Bush was that he depended on advisers, and by putting Cheney and Rumsfeld at the heart of government he had chosen bad advisers. They were running the government. The big issue would be how Powell managed to assert himself. His great strength is that he could have been president, as he well knows. Politically he is by far the strongest person there with the public at large.

The problem with Bush is that he is wholly unilateralist, and domestic. All his positions are taken by reference to domestic politics, almost none to the world's interest. This is further worsened by his links to the oil industry, which determine a great deal, as do other lobbies.

A major example of this was the refusal to ratify (check language) the protocol of the CBW convention.[2] Iran the only other country to do so, as well as China. The industry went to Bush and said we can't have

---

1 President Bush renounced the Kyoto treaty – signed by President Clinton in 1997 – in March 2001. On 11 June 2001, in a White House statement, he described the Kyoto Protocol as 'fatally flawed in fundamental ways' and 'unrealistic'.
2 Chemical and biological warfare are prohibited under two international conventions: the Chemical Weapons Convention, effective from 1997, and the Biological Weapons Convention, effective from 1975.

European inspectors making unannounced visits to our factories making CB weapons or capable of doing so. Thus a very decent measure, designed to impose rules on a place like Iran, and never likely to lead to any intervention in the US, is scuppered by a US interest that is wholly industry-driven.

ANGLO-AMERICA He said that the key bad example is the Iraq bombing. He opposed this, tried to do something about it, and failed. He is in favour of the sanctions, to keep some sort of pressure on Saddam Hussein, but says that the bombing is worse than useless. It is dangerous for our pilots, it achieves nothing, and it gives us a bad name in the world. So why does it continue?

Because of the MoD's fanatical determination to keep close to the Pentagon. They will never do anything that puts that relationship out of line. The truth is that it is the pivot of all military careers and a great deal of decision-making. Any military officer who has ambitions has to keep close to the Pentagon, because he needs to serve in NATO. The US and UK have dominated serious appointments in NATO for years, for this reason. It is the driving priority of the MoD to keep it that way. They do not think in terms of national interest, but of both MoD interest and the American interest.

The FCO at least thinks about the national interest first. It is not without other tendencies in the Anglo-American direction, but it is willing to ask questions. As it did over the Iraqi bombing. I asked, Is it up to Blair, and only Blair, to disengage from the bombing? He said, Yes. But he is unlikely to do it because it would be a strain.

Cook was sometimes asked – indeed, I think, always had to be asked – for target approval for each new bombing raid. Sometimes he tried to say no. Each time the MoD pleaded the terrible consequences of displeasing the USA.

From the US's point of view, we gave them cover. They could always say we were doing it too. But the consequences for us internationally and domestically are very bad.

EURO He said it was an example of the incorrigibly short-term way in which politics was thought about, and the extreme unwillingness of anyone to take a decision until they absolutely had to. That was a Blair feature – also, as he agreed with me, a common feature of much modern politics. He said it was at work in his own sudden dismissal. But over the euro it was very dangerous.

There is no overwhelming thing that is giving the euro decision the right amount of urgency, he said. It can slip and slip. And given the unfavourable indicators at the moment – the exchange rate, the euro weakness, the slowdown in the world economy – this could last some time: the absence of incentive to decide.

That had been the motive behind the Mansion House speech by Brown: an elaborate case for delay. Brown had, said Cook, been abso- lutely furious when Blair spoke about deciding within two years (which he said in the HC, I think). Brown had intended at the end of two years, a different nuance. He was livid. So at the Mansion House he restored the two-year span. Which carries it forward, if taken literally, into 2003, by which time a whole stack of other arguments will have arisen, mainly to do with the election.

In Cook's view (as in mine) the turning round of opinion will take a long time and depend on a new sort of argument. His big worry is not winning the old argument, the economic argument. It would be quite possible to win the five tests etc. etc. He seemed to have little doubt about winning the argument. But the trouble would be turnout. Look at Denmark and Ireland. It was the failure to get the voters to bother to come out and vote. So this gave a big advantage to the sceptics, who are more highly motivated. They are fired up. They will vote. On a 30 per cent poll, we could not win, he said. On a 40 per cent poll, ditto. On a 50 per cent poll, maybe, but it would be close. We need at least 60 per cent turnout.

So how do you set about achieving that? You have to start making the case for the British national interest in a wider way. Where do we belong in the world? What is the big future for Britain? That kind of thing. Something to get inside the British head and make it more excited. To make Mr and Mrs Smith, come 6 p.m. on referendum day, decide to go to the poll rather than not go to it. Are they seriously going to get out of their chairs because they decide we have passed the five economic tests? You must be joking.

This positive change in the discourse should start now. But who will do it? I (HY) said that when he (RC) and Blair had make speeches of a pro-Europe kind it was interesting to see how the sceptic media soon buckled in outrage. He cited as an example the response to his attacks on media bias. The *Mail* had been angry, but had perceptibly changed its tone of coverage for a while, he said. They knew they were vulnerable, he said.

If Clarke becomes Tory leader that changes a lot. It would make the referendum easier to win – though he cautioned (as I have said) that the danger of the establishment being seen as pro-euro might mean, Ireland and Denmark style, that everyone would turn against it for that reason. KC would have its downside. On the other hand, it would be embarrassing for Blair to find a more enthusiastic European across the dispatch box. It would be the first time. So far he had been able to coast in the middle indecisive ground, because of Major and Hague being sceptical and hostile. Almost anything would make Tony seem better than that. If Ken gets it, the equation would change.

I asked about our influence, outside the euro. He said, In the real world in which relationships are made and decisions taken, if you are outside you are not listened to. He cited the ECB. It was all very well for Gordon to be telling them how the Bank should be organized. But why on earth will they pay attention when we are staying out of it? This is a very good point.

GORDON BROWN RC said it was not true that he and Gordon had a bad relationship going back to the deep student past. He wasn't aware of it. He did not have an especially bad relationship now.

Gordon has been a very good Chancellor. A massive social reformer, a micro-manager of welfare etc. He is not a macroeconomic man, not interested much in that. Besides, he has subcontracted it to the Bank.

Gordon will never be leader of the party. If Tony goes on into the next parliament, which he surely will, the first thing that will happen when he stops is a Stop Gordon movement. GB has many enemies in the party, and in the Cabinet. He has trodden on many people. He is not liked, even if he is admired.

Besides, it will be seen as time for another generation to come up. As with Blair after Smith, and Major after Thatcher. If Blair has failed, or weakened or lost a referendum, Gordon – and Blunkett too – will be part of the old guard. It is more likely to be someone we have never talked about, who is not in Cabinet now. (This is quite cogent, though remember that Cook has an interest in excluding anyone who is remotely of his own generation – out of *Schadenfreude* if nothing else.)

CHARLES CLARKE
House of Commons terrace, 23 July 2001

He denied any deep significance in his title of party chairman. Has a well-worked-out 'constitutional' riff that explains that there is no problem. But he does seem to have a problem with the Civil Service, which dictates where he works. If he works on Labour Party premises, he cannot take government papers there. If he works in a Whitehall office, he cannot have party officials on his staff. The only place, therefore, is the House of Commons.

He confirmed that an object of the second term was to try and find a way of reducing spin, control-freakery etc. He was a key to that. Was trying to create an atmosphere, following a Blair instruction, which somehow permits/encourages people (MPs) to come up with ideas and even differences – yet restrain themselves from slagging off ministers who disagree. Blair says differences are fine, as long as they are not personalized – therefore leading to bad press.

Plainly they are still fixated on the press, and CC wants to urge the media to be less adversarial, less prone to seize on 'splits'. He says he is very critical of the media on many things . . .

Public–private will be an issue at the conference. But only one among many – the PFI [private finance initiative] as one way of delivering better services. He discounted the unions as any more than headline-seeking, and distinguished between Dave Prentis (Unison), who is constructive, and John Edmonds, who cannot resist a quick headline.

Plainly favours Ken Clarke as Tory leader. Mainly because it would shift the euro ground. But his main thought was that either KC or IDS had the high capacity to be disastrous: KC too careless and lazy; IDS too right wing.

CC is intensely practical, vigorous, quite belligerent, very brisk, totally engaged: after all, at last he is in the Cabinet, after all those years of futile slaving for Kinnock.[1]

DAVID MILIBAND
26 July 2001

He never intended to become MP for South Shields. If the election had been in May not June, it wouldn't have happened. But he did want to move out of No. 10 after seven years working for the Labour Party and writing two manifestos. His wife said he needed a change too. He thought about running some big charity. Or something. Wasn't at all sure what or where.

But then South Shields fell vacant, and he was offered the chance to go for it. He was still unsure. Blair told him to go for it now rather than later if he wanted to become a politician at all – in ten years we may not be here, said Blair. He had doubts, and these were confirmed by an unnamed MP who told him it was a terrible grind, and what was the point of being a backbench MP? But the same day that MP called back

---

1 Clarke was the head of Neil Kinnock's office 1981–92.

and said he had rethought. 'Treat it as a great adventure.' This is what drove David to do it.

It is fascinating to watch the backstage work, seeing the practical meaning and problems of policy at grass-roots level. He is utterly absorbed by that now. He looks at South Shields and sees a town with a lot of different bits to it, including many good bits – but not connected and not a satisfactory whole. There is lots to be done. He has the chance to see on the ground what the schools reforms mean. He is less clear about the hospital, he says. But in a way the scientist has now come into the laboratory away from the blueprint.

He is sceptical about 'delivery, delivery, delivery'. It is not wrong, but it is not enough. For one thing, it will always fall short (as HY said). There will never be enough delivery. For DM, therefore, delivery needs to be fitted into a more dramatic narrative about the rebuilding of Britain. The issue is much bigger than mere delivery. It is about how the country looks at itself, what it sees happening over a long term: all about direction as much as delivery.

He finds the decline of the Commons much exaggerated. Seen from the inside it still matters greatly in the sense that one does need to establish a reputation for competence on one's feet, and handling the HC atmosphere and rules and getting to know its ways. All this matters to the way one is seen, and the way one is seen has an effect on one's chance of building a wider reputation.

JOHN STEVENS
4 September 2001

The anecdotal evidence is that Clarke will lose. One cannot trust opinion polls, but they show that direction too.

If IDS wins, he should not be regarded entirely as a joke. It could be serious. After all, things might go very wrong for the government. Economy collapses, Ireland blows up, asylum becomes unmanageable, public-service promises fail, any of a variety of possible personal disasters for ministers. Plus losing the referendum. A fatal combination is not unimaginable which would bring a Tory party to power, however inadequate its leader.

Moreover, he is not seen as a joke as Hague was. He may be limited, but the way they talk him up has some cred. He is a real guy, he has a family, he is not a nerd. This could be built into something that offers better than Hague, for all his political inadequacies.

However, remember he is a man in uniform. That's all he's really done, outside politics.[1] The fascistic tendency is there behind him. The right is always more dangerous than the far left. See the comparison with Labour and the CND. Nobody in top Labour really wanted CND to succeed. We might have a Tory Party that really did want us out of the EU. Moreover, the voices outside the party but inside the ideology are far more extreme than they have been for Labour at its worst.

The strongest figure behind IDS is Michael Howard, who will have a comeback, along with David Davis, a less strong figure.

All this poses a problem for Clarke, if he loses. What will he do? Will he split and go with the Lib Dems as a way to save the moderate opposition? (HY: I do not think so. Not a Jenkins – same age when he did that – but a very different character: a long-termist, a political thinker and deep strategist. KC is a man of instinct and idleness, who only got into this contest by accident. Does such a man really want to be prime minister badly enough to start the huge endeavour of a split?)

On the morning of 11 September, Islamist extremists from the al-Qaeda terrorist movement led by Osama bin Laden hijacked aircraft on commercial flights in the US and, in suicide missions, destroyed the twin towers of the World Trade Center in New York and a portion of the Pentagon building in Washington. The shockwaves of the subsequent war on terrorism irredeemably affected political life worldwide, but particularly the relationship between the US and the UK. But first there was the matter of the Conservative Party leadership.

DAVID CURRY
14 September 2001

The day after Clarke has lost by percentages 39/61.

There never was an equivalence in the campaign. At the London hustings, Clarke got booed for having sat with Blair at the BiE launch. Large posters were circulated of the picture, plastered with the legend 'Lest We Forget'. Yet when IDS remarked at the same meeting that, yes, he had voted against the Maastricht Treaty eleven times, he got a standing ovation from two-thirds of the hall.

The chances of IDS being the man who leads the party back to the centre are scarcely made believable by his Shadow Cabinet choices.

---

1 Iain Duncan Smith had trained at Sandhurst and spent six years in the Scots Guards (1975–81) before joining General Electric.

Howard as Chancellor, Davis as chairman, MacLean as chief whip, and the rest of the SC save one or two being very hard-line. Not an inch of room for flexibility on Europe.

People are already saying that in eighteen months IDS will be out.[1] David Davis is seen as the threat. As chairman, he gets round all the constituencies. A perfect base for building his popularity. Yet this is hardly credible. A chairman is totally tied in to a leader's record . . .

HANS-FRIEDRICH VON PLOETZ
15 September 2001

After 9/11.

At Hella Pick's. (Harold and Judith Paisner, Sue MacGregor,[2] Hans and Paivi von Ploetz – no sign of the threatened Weidenfeld.)

The first question is what the US will ask. It is unprecedented for NATO to invoke section 5, within an hour of meeting. But this says only that members pledge to use 'all appropriate means' to aid a member state attacked. Cf. the WEU, which says something much more complete: 'all available means'.

It may be that the US will ask only for political support. If a state is going to act, it is easier probably to act alone. (But, someone objected, does that mean us being totally submissive to what the US decides to do, and having to back it politically?)

Hans sees this as a great opportunity for a new world order (my phrase) in which the US is obliged to seek and stick by real alliance. Hitherto all US engagement overseas has been military. The assertion or threat of military power. It has not been political policy. To have a policy, you have to have allies, you have to work politically. This is what now faces the US. Not just with NATO and the EU but with Middle Eastern states as well. It cannot hope to work this alone.

Maybe they can go in and get bin Laden. But that would not be a military action. Military action would be involved in something larger. Especially dealing with states that harbour terrorists. It might be possible to say, with a certain proof, that a country is harbouring known terrorists, to then insist on them being handed over, with the implied threat of reprisals if they don't.

Some of this surely links with my theme of the US being in certain respects a strong target but a weak power. Also with my theme that the

---

1 This forecast was only seven months out.

2 Hella Pick: Austrian-born foreign affairs correspondent of *The Guardian*. Harold Paisner: solicitor. Sue MacGregor: presenter of the BBC Radio 4 *Today* programme 1984–2002.

US has not explained itself to the world well enough: has not established why it is a harmless power, an innocent power; has allowed its defence of liberty to be outshone and overshadowed by its reputation for power and nothing else.

Blair has a big chance to prove to the US (along with other European leaders) that the EU is worth more than the US thinks it is. To make the EU matter to the US as a real ally. Needs to show that the EU has a common terrorist policy (even though Spain, Italy, Ireland, the UK and others all have different definitions of terrorism).

Note also, as several said, that the Security Council – though this has hardly been reported – has also come out more strongly and decisively than anyone would have expected.

HANS-FRIEDRICH VON PLOETZ
From his car, 17 September 2001

For all of Europe the security partnership is absolutely vital. This was not a fair-weather thing, but at all times. And it is reciprocal.

But it has tended to be the limit of our main activities. Security – military security – has been mainly what it has been about. One could call this a redefining moment for the alliance, because it now requires us to think about the far more subtle issue of terrorism, in the changed circumstances of the end of the Cold War. We need to dig deeper to see how to deal with things that go beyond the familiar military role.

The alliance has always had a military and political purpose, but the political has not been prominent.

The remarkable thing about last week was the instant and unanimous response of the European powers, within the EU and NATO. No hesitation. There has never been such a rallying. At the Gulf War time it was more difficult, and much slower. Now there were no second thoughts.

It is far too early to talk about military options, or what individual countries may have to do. The 'who shoots first?' issue is premature. Blair said yesterday keep a cool nerve, and he was right. Fischer said yesterday that we don't exclude anything: we are going to be faced with very painful decisions; we know what may be required of us.

ROGER LIDDLE
21 September 2001

At an especially riotous and jolly dinner with Lode Willems: plus Daniel Bernard, Hans and Paivi von Ploetz, Jim Naughtie, Caroline Thomson (Roger L's wife).

BLAIR AS WAR LEADER   This is doing Tony a lot of good. He has done well, hasn't he? It should greatly increase his credibility all round.

His object (and this was also said by Martin Kettle, who had had an hour with Blair at the start of the week) is to stifle the isolationist instincts of the American right. He wants the US to recognize its international role again, and bind it in to that – against isolationism. Equally, this is a chance for the EU to show America that it is not the wimp that the US thinks it is. (This was said by both Daniel and Hans.) A great opportunity to raise Europe's image in American eyes, as well as enlist more support for ESDP.

BLAIR AND THE EURO   Before September 11 the mood about the euro was distinctly up. Why? RL said it may have had something to do with the (unverified) impression that Gordon might be changing his position. But, anyway, the mood was up.

Tony's view before September 11 was that he would have to spend the next nine months attending to public services. Trying to get that right. And after that would turn his attention to the euro. Is this still the track? Who knows?

JAMES HOGE
Foreign Affairs, 15 October 2001

People ask if this whole coalition to fight Osama bin Laden etc. is a change of policy by Bush. That depends entirely on how long it lasts. Is it just an ad-hoc coalition, to suit temporary US needs? I think it is too soon to say that Bush and his people have changed their view about coalitions, about the world as a whole, about an essentially unilateralist US foreign policy.

There is a battle between those who want it to last, and are internationalists (Powell), and others who I do not think have changed their world view.

At its best and most optimistic, this action may produce an 'elegant' solution to Osama bin Laden, and even do quite a bit to destroy terrorism. But it is not going to change the minds of people who did not want the landmines convention, the ICC et al.[1]

Nor will it change their minds about nation-building. 'I'm a bit cynical about this, but I know the players. I do not think Wolfowitz[2] or Cheney have been experiencing any epiphanies.'

The State Department is still out of some of the loop. For example, it was only thanks to the *New York Times* that we learned that James Woolsey[3] and a team had gone to London to try and establish that Iraq was linked to the WTC disaster. The State Department were never told they were going. That is pretty startling.

BUSH   The press conference was greeted as a triumph.[4] Just because he got through it, and appeared to be talking with his own voice. 'But the hosannas have gone to his head.' 'I do not think he understands the difficulties that face him. He makes it all sound simple. But it is not simple. War is infinitely more difficult than he seems to expect. After all, he came in without any experience in this field of any kind.' 'War is harder to get out of than get into.' Also, 'He doesn't understand the difficulties with the economy, nor with what people may come to think about what is happening to civil liberties.' 'He has no third eye to keep an eye on hubris.' 'We have no idea how he will perform when things go bad, which they will.'

However, he does have men of great experience round him. Cheney, Rumsfeld, Armitage.[5] They have all done a lot, for many years. It must have been them, plus Powell, who got Bush to talk about the Palestinian State, something totally against what we know of his instincts.

The worrying thing about the peace process is not the fact that no solution has been found, but the daily violence that accompanies it now.

The danger re Iraq is that even (perhaps especially) the hawks do not understand, do not accept, that whatever we might do in Iraq it will fail

1 The Convention on the Prohibition of the Use, Stockpiling, Production and Transfer of Anti-Personnel Mines and on their Destruction – sometimes called the Ottawa Treaty or the Mine-Ban Treaty – has been signed by 158 countries. One of its most high-profile champions was Princess Diana, who in Angola in 1997 posed in a minefield for photographers. The ICC – the International Criminal Court – was founded in 1998.

2 Paul Wolfowitz: close ally of George W. Bush; US deputy Secretary of Defense 2001–5; president of the World Bank 2005–7.

3 James Woolsey: director of the CIA 1993–5; on CNN on 12 September 2001, claimed that Iraq might have been behind the atrocities of the previous day.

4 On 11 October 2001, at a White House press conference, President Bush reported on his discussions with Tony Blair about Afghanistan, on the search for Osama bin Laden and the war on terror, on homeland security, and on his recognition that a Palestinian state could be part of a political solution to the Middle East crisis.

5 Richard Armitage: US deputy Secretary of State 2001–5.

to enlist any Middle East support if it leaves Israel/Palestine untouched. There really cannot be any doubt that it is central. It is what Middle East leaders, for various reasons, have to see as the major issue for very many of their people.

If we were to do something with Iraq it would obviously be done by insisting that the inspectors go back in, knowing that Saddam Hussein will reject this and then using that as our *casus belli*.

The argument is now being made by Wolfowitz and Perle that Arabs will say, You mean the US is launching their vast power against this puny enemy, the Taliban, in a wrecked country? Is that what the US means these days in the Middle East? I.e. goading Bush to do more, on the grounds that the Arabs themselves are expecting it, and will take note of our failure to act against a man who is undoubtedly going to claim a victory if we do not act, and who is doing a lot of damage in Kuwait at the moment.

NMD JH, who says he knows Rumsfeld very well indeed, cannot believe that Rummy really wanted NMD. He knew what it would do to his budget, the number of cutbacks it would make him make, including to national preparedness. He thinks Rumsfeld only favoured it because he knew Bush was obsessed with it: he saw this as his way into the Bush group.

The man who is really hot for it is Bush himself. Often asked every day about progress on it: as if there could be daily bulletins to prove it was moving forward. But he is reinforced by Cheney.

September 11, however, has changed quite a bit of this, for budgetary reasons. There is now no need to hold back for budget reasons.

Rumsfeld, by the way, is the only bureaucrat who Kissinger says he was frightened of. HK had vast respect for Rumsfeld's cunning. R would sit in meetings and say nothing and then go away and shaft HK in ways the Doctor could only admire.

THE LEFT Note the importance of campus protest. It is building. They can get 100,000 into the streets in Seattle, and there is a linkage developing between globalization protest and war protest. See US corporations plundering the world, and as agents of world inequality. This has a lot of mileage in it, says Jim.

HENRY KISSINGER
New York, 16 October 2001

He remains obsessed with Christopher Hitchens,[1] and the book attacking him.[2] He thinks *The Guardian* should never have printed excerpts. This made our opening difficult! But since it had been the origin of our meeting (at George Weidenfeld's last June), it did not bother me. However, it meant he would adamantly refuse to talk on tape about the terror crisis. 'I would not make *The Guardian* the place where I say what I have to say – I am giving a lecture in London where I will be saying it.'

Incidentally, it became clear that the CPS (or whatever think tank is sponsoring the lecture) pressed him to give a lecture attacking Blair's attitude to foreign policy. Even before September 11 he thought this would be in bad taste – to come to an ally and attack its leader. After September 11 it was out of the question. So he said he would be offering some banal thoughts about the crisis – partly extempore.[3]

Some gleanings, however . . .

There will be no broad-based government in Afghanistan. That's what they always say – a broad-based government. If it was possible, it would have happened a long time ago. The history should tell people it is not possible. Evidently HK has been reading *The Great Game*[4] and another book. All about England and Russia manoeuvring showing that tribal complexities were deep and pervasive and chronic.

If Osama bin Laden is running round the hills next spring, that will certainly be a problem. But the issue will be, How to define victory? What will the government look like if OBL has not been caught? However, if they have found some way of defining victory in a more limited way, perhaps that will help. (This from an expert in the defining of victory and defeat!)

Will the people stay firm? The American people have always been united. They are now rock solid. I was here at the time of Pearl Harbor, says HK. The feeling is even more intense now than then: more united: more determined. (After all, per HY, Pearl Harbor did not kill off the anti-war lobby in 1941.) Even during Vietnam, unity remained.

The issue is whether the government will stay firm. Or will it be

---

1 Christopher Hitchens: English-born, US-resident polemicist.

2 Christopher Hitchens, *The Trial of Henry Kissinger* (London: Verso, 2001).

3 Dr Kissinger spoke to the Centre for Policy Studies on 1 November 2001 and told his audience, 'I know of no other leaders that have so identified the experiences of New York and Washington with the attitudes of their own people as those of the British government.'

4 Peter Hopkirk, *The Great Game: On Secret Service in High Asia* (London: John Murray, 1990).

increasingly in receipt of helpful advice from politicians about the more 'practical' solutions . . .

As for extending the campaign, he talked as though Iraq was the ultimate case. There were countries, he implied, who harboured terrorists and did not carry the complications of Iraq (Syria?). He said on TV later that day that there would certainly be a second stage of the campaign, which would 'separate the sheep from the goats'. To me he said that we would 'lose a few Europeans', but not the big countries. And what about the Arabs? 'The Arabs just back the winners.'

Re Blair, he said that he had opposed the Kosovo bombing – but once it had started he was totally behind it. He thought there was more to be gained against the Serbs by Holbrooke's efforts involving the UN in a big way. He was anxious about Blair's stance, and the influence he had.

ROBERT HUNTER
Phone, 18 October 2001

The American people certainly need OBL, dead or alive, and the thugs around him.

We have let Pakistan decide who will be the government of Afghanistan. Weird. They gave us the Taliban, and they will give us the new government. All in all, we are going to let Pakistan, Russia and Uzbekistan take us to the cleaners.

Some important shifts of emphasis. Bush now has slightly softened the priority on OBL, not very sensibly. More important: see Powell – who originally said a war on terrorism with a global reach, and now says just 'terrorism'. This was because he needed to say that to keep India sweet re Kashmir. Problem is: everyone piles in. Brits have said from the start, What about the IRA? Russia says, Now we can go after the Chechens with US support etc. A dangerous broadening, forced upon us by Powell being in India.

The issue is: do you broaden the campaign (a) to get the networks or also (b) to get the countries that harbour terrorists? These are two different ideas, the second much more ambitious than the first. Iraq is the obvious case. Wolfowitz has argued for ages that we should go for Iraq. Note the present effort being made to link the anthrax[1] to Iraq and provide a reason to bomb the hell out of them.

Another issue: the big terrorist thing is the two threats: (a) nuclear –

---

1 In October 2001 US scientists confirmed that the anthrax bacillus was being deliberately distributed in powder form by mail. Most of twenty-two cases of anthrax infection were people who handled letters, or worked in offices to which the letters were addressed. Five died.

but how would they deliver nuclear? – and (b) biological. Not chemical. Biological is communicable and invisible: two things not true of chemical. Therefore far more serious.

The anthrax-spreaders knew what they were doing. Knew who they were targeting. But these were all prominent people, or connected to prominent people. This has an important minimizing effect on public response. Not yet 'ordinary' people. Just as there would have been far less national horror if the only hit had been on the Pentagon, not the WTC. Who works in the Pentagon . . . ?

What all this has proved, though, is that we are one country, pulling together. The 1990s were the biggest single legal-immigrant decade in our history – never mind the illegals. Yet they held together.

JOHN KERR
Lunch, the Garrick, 25 October 2001

AMERICA He thought there was one error in my piece this morning, which was to misunderstand Cheney when Cheney had talked about the Afghan war going on 'for our lifetime'. This was failing to see that Cheney's lifetime was pretty short. JK was making a joke here, but also saying that the Cheney health state is bad.

I told him, what he thought he had already worked out a priori, that Tom Ridge[1] was, according to Washington gossip, being lined up as the successor V-P. He thought Ridge a perfectly sensible choice, though he said he had already been chopped off at the knees – and if there was another domestic terrorist outrage would become unappointable as V-P.

It is true, I told him Holbrooke had told me, that 'previous US ambassadors' had wanted to write the special relationship out of the script. JK had indeed banned the use of the phrase when he was ambassador. He thought it useless. It seemed to rule out of account the fact that we had a special relationship with Israel or France, with everyone. He said, though, that he thought in his time we were no. 2 as successful lobbyist on the Hill – Israel was better – and also no. 2 as media-successful, where no. 1 was Ireland. But we were doing pretty well . . .

He noted Blair's remarkable standing in the US. Yes, it was amazing that they had set aside time for his speech to the Labour Party conference without being able to be sure it would be a good one – which it certainly was.

1 Tom Ridge: US politician, Congressman and, 1995–2001, governor of Pennsylvania; assistant to the President for homeland security 2001–3.

AFGHAN WAR ETC. ETC.   JK is at the War Cabinet.[1] It meets
very early. Today he didn't know if Straw was going to get back soon
enough from Washington, therefore didn't know if he would be having
to stand in for him or having to brief him on what to say. Straw turned
up five minutes early, as it turned out.

He thinks Blair does retain influence. He certainly had influence in the
early days. If it had not been for Blair, perhaps, there would have been
an opening to Iraq. He also speculated that Blair would retain this influence, not lose it, as time went on – contrary to what I had said in my
piece today. Bush could never afford to have a public row with Blair,
needed his support badly.

Blair, as everyone but especially the Americans know, is rock solid on
the campaign. Therefore he has credit. It may be that other Europeans
will flag, as time goes on. Also Arab countries. But Blair will not flag.
This gives him his clout.

JK asked me how Colin Powell was regarded, and was doing. I said,
He seems to be seen by most Americans as a reliable and trusted figure,
the most such. Rumsfeld, however, was getting a much bigger show. JK
said how badly he thought Rumsfeld conducted his press conferences.

I asked JK about Iraq. He said he had never believed it would happen.
Ask the Pentagon, he says, and they have no war plan. What would you
hit? they are asked. They talk about command centres etc. But they have
no real plans for this, still less for the consequences of doing so. They
cannot hope to Get Saddam by such a method. So how can they map out
a military campaign against Iraq that makes any sense?

It is true that if there could be incontrovertible proof that Iraq was
behind the WTC, or behind the anthrax, that would be different. Especially it would be different for Blair. He would see the evidence and, if he
agreed, agree with what then followed. But even in those circumstances
it could be very difficult to know exactly what to do.

To JK (and presumably Blair) the division is quite simple. A military
campaign in Afghanistan; an economic and political campaign elsewhere.
Not an extension of the military campaign to elsewhere. The economic
and political throttling of any country that harbours terrorists should be
severe. But the military campaign, even in Afghanistan, is very difficult.

The Afghanistan campaign is already at a stage where the US has
command of the skies. They are flying over Afghanistan without knowing what to hit. Why are they bothering? 'To establish that they have

---

1 Its members included John Prescott, Jack Straw, the Defence Secretary Geoff Hoon, David Blunkett, Robin
Cook and International Development Secretary Clare Short. Admiral Sir Michael Boyce, chief of the defence
staff, Alastair Campbell, Anji Hunter, Jonathan Powell, Sir John Kerr, the former MI6 officer John Scarlett and
Sir David Manning were also there.

command of the skies', he said ironically. To him, there is absolutely no chance of getting OBL by these methods. Though he doesn't oppose the methods as a starter.

The real method has to be via intelligence and bribery. To this end, a lot is going on by way of efforts to assemble new coalitions. These sound very complicated and problematic. Various people are in Peshawar at this moment, trying to watch it being sorted out as various Afghan warlords and chiefs circle round each other, vowing to do the business. These include R. Cooper[1] – now removed from No. 10 and already author of a Green Paper on mercenaries, now deputed by JK to Afghanistan (his Green Paper is being eaten away by various Whitehall departments – six, to be exact – who have standing on it). Others include a UN man, Bashini, or some such, whom JK talks about as 'Gucci', there are a lot of Gucci types, who are good but will not get down into the dirt, which is what is needed to get spies and other shenanigans working our way. He seemed to be hopeful that something will come out of this coalition-building, but the Russians are dead against the Taliban, the Pakis dead against the Northern Alliance, Iran also dead against the Taliban. Additionally, there seems, he says, to be quite an overlap between al Quaeda and the Taliban. So a war strategy cannot talk about getting rid of one without the other.

Our declared objective nonetheless tries to do this. A public document, drafted in the FCO, and now in Parliament, talks about four objectives. (1) Get rid of OBL. (2) Find a better government than the Taliban. (3) Get rid of al Quaeda network. (4) Maybe get rid of Taliban altogether (check these details).

The point is that our military objective is strictly confined to Afghanistan, and our political objectives only include actually replacing the Afghanistan government in the event of the other three objectives not coming to pass.

He referred to the redeployment, in today's papers, of Mr Bergen,[2] former British ambassador to Uzbekistan, now recalled to public service and operating over there. Bergen speaks Uzbek, Tajik, Pushtun and Russian. Was SIS not FCO. A very interesting character.

Other Brits who know, by the way, are David Hannay and N. Barrington,[3] both of whom served in Afghanistan, though Barrington ended up as ambassador to Pakistan and is therefore 'our great expert' on the situation in Afghanistan now. He is back in service.

He thinks it quite possible that the US, especially the military, will

1 Robert Cooper: diplomat; director, Asia, in the FCO 1998–9; head of defence and overseas secretariat, Cabinet Office 1999–2001; government special representative for Afghanistan 2001–2.

2 Paul Bergen: former intelligence officer, academic; ambassador to Uzbekistan and Tajikistan until 1995; in 2001 became the Prime Minister's personal representative for Afghan affairs.

3 Sir Nicholas Barrington: ambassador then high commissioner in Pakistan 1987–94.

want to have shots at, say, Indonesia or the Philippines and Muslims there if they can find reason. Pacific Command, which is the biggest US command, is feeling left out.

BLAIR (AND STRAW)   Is certainly in his element; he learned a lot from Kosovo. But JK told me a story about that. Clinton was utterly furious about Blair's Chicago speech, which he regarded as B coming into his (C's) backyard and telling him what to do. There was a one-hour telephone conversation so virulent that the minutes were not passed round Whitehall. JK had to go into Downing Street to read them. And no wonder, he said. But it had the desired effect. Clinton sounded off at length – but then in effect complied: let it be known that US ground troops could well be used, which was a turning point in the whole war.

Straw is a far easier colleague than Cook, for Blair as well as the government + FCO. Cook was very good indeed at the HC, at foreign meetings, at Cabinet. Very quick, very clever. Very admired. But if things did not fit into that – were not needed – he simply did not bother. He never read anything for more than three hours – hence the FCO's less than besotted admiration for his brilliance in reading the Scott report so fast. He did not take a long-term interest in anything at all.

Straw, by contrast, holds meetings. He reads papers. He is a very nice man – though JK said that with a determined wink. He is interested in the long term.

Also, JS says he finds the FCO quite different from the Home Office in this respect: at the HO, if you (the minister) disagreed with them, they would simply take a note and go away and do what you said. At the FCO, twelve people in a room are ready to argue their corner and explain why you cannot do what you thought.

However, he has deformities. JK noticed that I (HY) was not on a list of a recent get-together JS had organized. He asked why I wasn't there – presumably a small meeting for commentators? He was told, HY was so terrible to me as Home Secretary I will not have him. JK thought this absurd. I explained to JK that I was terrible to all Home Secretaries, but that this should not matter at the FCO. I also told him about our meeting with Straw and Alice at Tate Modern. However, JK said he would be 'working on' Straw. He said I should do nothing: sit tight: wait for the call. And when it came I should keep our talk strictly to Europe, the euro etc. (He remarked, by the way, that wives always take it worse. His own wife had got far more stirred by Sandline and Sierra Leone than he had: to him, he claims, it was all in the line of business.)

I asked what JS thought about Europe. JK had a long talk with him in June when JS began. JS said he wanted to make it quite clear from the start that 'I am Tony's man.' He said that, though he wasn't a wild enthusiast for the euro, he would do what Tony wanted. It was going to come, said Jack. He would be in the campaign. He would trust Tony's judgement. That was all there was to it.

Straw is on the phone a lot to Blair. Much more than Cook ever was. They talk a great deal. They seem to trust each other. Whenever Straw has a problem he will talk to Tony. Whenever Cook had a subordinate with a problem – on Colombia[1] and sending arms to the anti-drug squad there was one such – Cook did not want to know. Lloyd tried to see him for six weeks, and was refused. When Kerr remonstrated, Cook said that it was precisely because Lloyd did not know what to do that he would not see him – i.e. he did not want to take any responsibility himself for a tricky problem a subordinate could not solve.

CIVIL LIBERTIES   He said he was a Hampstead liberal – I corrected this by saying Maida Vale liberal – but he was worried about the difficulty of getting rid of Siri, the latest Egyptian terrorist wanted for trying to kill Mubarak[2] in 1993, who has managed to shelter behind our laws for many years. We agree that the incitement laws should have been used more, but there remains a problem about what to do with people who cannot be extradited to death-penalty countries yet cannot be detained here. I agreed. Said that as long as the judges were involved, it should be acceptable to detain him – and that the incitement laws were being too softly interpreted.

He said that Blunkett would be far worse than Straw. A complete authoritarian. Also someone who, like M. Howard, totally mistrusted public servants and would always be looking for private outsiders to do the job.

BBC AND INFORMATION   JK said that latest figures showed the World Service had an 86 per cent credibility rating with its audiences all over the place. It had increased its Pashtu and Uzbek (maybe other) services very sensibly. The Voice of America had a less than 50 per cent cred.

Denis MacShane had foolishly said not long ago that the BBC should become part of the battle machine, a propaganda outfit in effect. This

---

1 Anthony Lloyd: Labour MP for Stretford 1983–97, for Manchester Central since 1997; Minister of State at the FCO 1997–9. He flew to Colombia in October 1998 to discuss human rights and investment, and arrived during a bitter series of accusations against British Petroleum after claims that a company officer was involved in arms deals and a spying operation.

2 Perhaps a slip of the tongue. Hosni Mubarak, president of Egypt since 1981, has survived at least six assassination attempts. But Yasser al-Siri, then living in Maida Vale, was sentenced to death in his absence for his alleged role in an attempt in 1993 to assassinate Egypt's then prime minister Atef Sedki.

would be disastrous. The credibility is hugely increased by allowing some criticism of the government.

KERR HIMSELF Planning to leave a month before he is due to, to let Michael Jay take over. He will spend, on government time, some weeks driving an old Jaguar to Santiago di Compostela, then driving down western Spain, which he has never been to.

LODE WILLEMS
Walking from FCO to the Bush–Blair conference,
26 October 2001

He and Ploetz had had lunch with Cook a little while back. Cook was staggeringly candid, they thought. He mentioned three things RC had said. First, that autumn 2003 was the very outmost edge of when it would be credible to hold the referendum. Second, that since September 11 the Treasury was in retreat re the euro. Third, that 'the pound had done well in its time, but it was now time to give it a decent burial.'

Blair said inter alia that there were four courses of action that were possible in Afghanistan: (a) bombing, (b) hit-and-run missions inside, (c) bringing the Northern Alliance into play, (d) finance – by which he presumably means bribery. This was said in candour yesterday when they met at 10 Downing Street. Blair was being very open, and exceedingly impressive thought LW.

DINNER AT LODE WILLEMS'S
5 November 2001

Star guest: Peter Mandelson. Also present Daniel Bernard, P. Riddell, J. Naughtie, Geoff Martin, Mort Dworkin (pol. counsellor at US embassy – check name), pol. counsellor at Belgian embassy.

THE NIGHT OF 4 NOVEMBER Blair arranged a dinner with Chirac (and Jospin) and Schröder.[1] The reason was that Chirac is seeing Bush on Tuesday, Blair on Wednesday. They were the three countries that the US had asked for specific military assistance. That was another reason to meet.

---

1 An impromptu meeting of European leaders over dinner at No. 10, to discuss the air war in Afghanistan: the assembly fuelled speculation about a ground offensive.

The meeting was fixed by Blair without subtle or deep calculation. Just thought it would make sense that they got together. Unfortunately he was due to see Berlusconi last Thursday in Genoa, on his way back from the Middle East. At this meeting, inter alia, he needed to make up for the fact that the three had met in Ghent – the directoire.[1] This had enraged Berlusconi. So Blair was ultra smoothie and consoling. They got on well (despite Blair's statement to me earlier this year that B was one of the few leaders he did not really care for). Lots of smoothing over. However, Blair neglected to tell B that he had planned this dinner with Schröder and Chirac. Another insult. So when B heard about this he flew into a rage and demanded to be present, aided by the fact that Bush had accepted the modest offer Italy had made of three assistant ships (check what for). Which put him in the category of the engaged countries.

Once Italy was in, Spain could not allow that to happen without them. So Aznar insisted also. Berlusconi had the excuse, moreover, that he was always being goaded by Amato and other Italian politicians that he was excluded because he was unfit for leadership. This added to his pressure. Against the background of the perfectly reasonable need for the Big Three to meet. Only the circumstance that led to B's demand made it all fall apart.

After Aznar came Verhofstadt.[2] As president, he insisted he should come. Along with Solana,[3] representing the presidency. This did not please Wim Kok, who thereupon said he would come even if not invited. He had his domestic reasons.

The result was that far more of the meeting was taken up with discussions of humanitarian issues and threats than with the military campaign. Chirac said he was sure a mosque would be bombed, and then what would they do? The military stuff was neglected.

A solution to this may be the conference call, said Daniel B.

Ireland, Denmark, Sweden were all quite happy to not be there, apparently. Let others handle it, they seem to have said. But Portugal and Greece were furious.

---

1 Blair, Chirac and Schröder had met the previous month in Ghent: Romano Prodi, president of the Commission, took umbrage at a meeting of the 'Big Three'. As a consequence, on this occasion other prime ministers were invited.

2 Guy Verhofstadt: prime minister of Belgium since 1999.

3 Francisco Javier Solana de Madariaga: NATO Secretary General 1995–9; EU high representative for the Common Foreign and Security Policy and Secretary General of the Council of the EU since 1999.

JACQUES CHIRAC
29 November 2001

A meeting between his summit engagements with Blair. Held in the ambassadors' waiting room at the FCO, with an interpreter; also present were P. Stephens, B. Johnson[1] and P. Riddell (all arranged by Daniel Bernard).

The reason he had time was that, under cohabitation, Jospin had to have a separate hour with Blair, after Chirac's. Chirac arrived with many a reverberation before him, the whispering of the wing, the aura of presence – after all he is a head of state, not just a prime minister. He comes in: immensely polite, younger looking than his 70, carefully tanned, hair black not grey, more than once saying how grateful he was to us for being there, these 'high journalists'. He talked in English for the opening greetings, but said his English was not good.

He has tremendous presence. He is exciting to be around. He is humorous, self-deprecatory, sweeping in his vision, wonderfully '*grande France*' in his horizons – though not at all Gaullist in the way he talks about France as such.

He arrives uncharacteristically carrying a black briefcase. Which, to judge from the next day's papers, must have been the Blair family's present to him for his birthday – presented by baby Leo.[2] Chirac clung on to it. He is apparently very keen on baby Leo – perhaps it makes him seem younger to his own audience.

I think my single best impression of him was how much more mature he is about America than Blair is. He swept aside questions about why the US was going it alone in Afghanistan, and betrayed no impatience with the fact that France (according to the British-embassy man who came in) had fifty-eight soldiers marooned in Uzbekistan who have not yet been given a role. Suddenly after the months and years of British obsession about their closeness to Washington you see it as a neurosis. France is more mature, without being on any surface level resentful. Therefore, I would say, France is able to take a more lofty, more distant and more wise view, unencumbered by the British desperation not to get out of sync with Washington. (There was an interesting aspect of this in Martin W's column next day – 30/11/01 – when he said that the Brits

---

1 Boris Johnson, editor of *The Spectator* 1999–2005, had been European Community correspondent on the *Daily Telegraph* 1989–94.
2 Now thirty months old.

could have forced the US to accept a UN resolution if they had tried, but did not use their clout to do so, and held back . . .)[1]

Chirac, by the way, talks to Blair in French and Blair talks in English. But on the phone they always have interpreters. Thus they do not really chat as easily as any Anglo/American leaders can always do. Even though they seem to have a very good relationship.

JOHN KERR
Portuguese-embassy dinner, 4 December 2001

AFGHANISTAN AND AFTER He agreed that Blair had wanted to do more with our troops. But we did have more in there than people are supposed to know (SAS). The person who was embarrassed was Hoon, not Blair, because Hoon had talked about them being on standby and had pretty well indicated they would soon move in.

Blair was anxious that this was going to be a reverse of Kosovo: in K he had been the one for land troops, and Clinton had resisted it. In Afghanistan, the Afghans have taken the lead and Tommy Franks[2] has been humming and hawing about any British role. Blair did not like this.

Our role will very likely be to be the core presence in a UN force which stabilizes the scene and keeps the early peace. The rules for this should be both territory- and time-limited. It should have a clear marker about the ring around Kabul where it will operate. It should last for six to eight months and no more. The Brits very likely will be the core, but with Muslim forces alongside, including Turks. Also French and Spanish (though probably not German). There should be a few of this and that countries. The Brits are good at this kind of thing. It is a decent role to play, and we do it – have done in Kosovo, in Macedonia. Also now in Sierra Leone (though note that our troops there are down to c.300).

The army will in fact love to do this. The pattern seldom changes. They grumble and worry: add a 0 to every manpower figure queried (400 into 4,000), talk about the dangers of mission creep – then take the money and run. They always get more money out of it.

---

1 In his column on 30 November, Martin Woollacott – former foreign editor of *The Guardian* – quoted Mort Halperin (a former special adviser to President Clinton) as saying that Britain could have demanded a Security Council resolution on Afghanistan: 'Britain could have said that we want a resolution on Afghanistan. The council would have said yes. If the UK had insisted the administration would have agreed to it.'
2 General Tommy Ray Franks, US Central Command, led the US attack on the Taliban in Afghanistan, and in 2003 the invasion of Iraq.

GENERAL STUFF   Jack Straw has accepted the need to negotiate a Gibraltar deal that Cook would not look at. Cook was obsessed with what the *Daily Mail* allegedly would not wear.

Gordon Brown at the War Cabinet. He comes in with piles of paper. He sits there, slightly turned away from the straight-on vision of Blair, opposite whom he sits; he scribbles all the time on his papers. He plays no part in the debate. Even when things were sharp and important, he had nothing to say. His only intervention was to join in the laughter once when Jack Straw managed to get a crack in against Robin Cook. It is very strange.

Gordon is also more and more unpopular. He always has been, but people have been afraid to speak against him. At the start, in the Autumn Statement in '97 or '98, he made some big shift in social-security payouts, on a rather technical but vital matter, which he had not consulted the DSS [Department of Social Security] about. They were furious. It meant a lot to their operations. But they said nothing. The big difference this time is that Alan Milburn has gone public with his objections. Other ministers have collected critical mass, and also gone a bit public. It is all getting out more. Perhaps pushed along by Downing Street. So all in all Gordon has his back somewhat to the wall – a good thing, for those of us who want to defeat him on the euro.

GORDON BROWN
6 December 2001

(His breakfast invitation to *The Guardian*: AR, PT, LE, MK, VK, MW, PJ.)[1]

Mainly a virtuoso performance by GB to persuade us of the need to join in the great campaign to argue more for public investment. We, *The Guardian*, had written big pieces about this for some time, including our special section on public service, and now we needed to get behind the government (he implied) in proposing much more spending.

There needed to be a big argument, he said. We need to persuade the people that investment in services is vital. When asked why the argument was only now beginning he rounded on the questioner (me) to say that the government had had to spend a long time persuading people that it could be trusted to run the economy. He referred back to the 1992 election and why it was lost – the tax-and-spend-and-borrow policy which

---

1   Alan Rusbridger, Polly Toynbee, Larry Elliott (economics editor), Martin Kettle, Victor Keegan, Michael White, Paul Johnson.

the people rejected. Evidently it has taken five years in power for the government to be ready to take their case out into the public. Amazing.

GB, moreover, does not want an open argument. He was asked why he had made up his mind about the NHS, which he plainly has. He said that the very worst thing would have been to start the debate by saying we had an open mind. It would be no good showing that we didn't know what we were doing. So we had to declare where we stood – while still being ready, he rather sheepishly conceded, to hear good cases for other methods. However, he said they had been through all the alternative methods of financing health and found them all far more expensive and far less effective than funding out of direct taxation.

He was asked how much the health plan would cost. He said Wanless[1] would reveal all in a few months' time. He was pressed on this: no point in trying to persuade people with percentages – they needed to know that the government had a figure in mind they could somehow latch on to. They also needed to know more about what taxes would be raised. Above all, they needed to know not so much about 'value for money' as about reliability of being able to get as good a service here as they can in France and Germany. Gordon was reluctant to be specific. He pleaded Wanless. Asked, also, if the Adair Turner review[2] was parallel to Wanless or what, he produced some blether about Turner being about structures. Polly directly remarked that this was another piece of No. 10 vs No. 11, and GB batted this off. It all seemed to come into the sweep of his general impatience with people who talked about personalities and not policies.

GB is a formidable defender of all this. He is a deeply committed and serious engineer of the public welfare and the welfare state guided by the principles of work rather than welfare, and very ready with numerous stats to show (correctly) what has been done for the working poor and their children. He can reel off with total facility – that of a very committed public servant in the best and uncynical sense – the stats for all kinds of social inputs. He understands the problems. He faces, for example, the huge housing crisis in the south-east with open eyes, even though he seems to be able to do nothing about it except set up working parties (which he can also reel off by name). He stares at the complexities, the irresolvable massive financial shortcomings of the public good and does not despair, but tries to do small and eventually large (as he would say) things to address them.

People (VK) ask why he would ever want to be PM having been such

1 Sir Derek Wanless: businessman, government adviser; carried out the 2002 Health Trends Review at the behest of the Chancellor, reviewing the future of NHS funding; later updated his report on behalf of health think tank the King's Fund in 2007.

2 Adair Turner: director general of the CBI 1995–9, later Baron Turner of Ecchinswell, in 2002 chaired a review of British pensions.

a brilliant Chancellor. VK does not understand politicians. The very fact he has been so brilliant as Chancellor can only lead to the demand to be PM – which may yet be frustrated.

He makes efforts to be 'human'. There's a certain loud hail-fellow approach as he walks in, but then he forgets he has done it to one person and does it again to the same person. It is rather hollow, even though well meant. He just does not know how to distract himself from the problems of state and come down to the level of humanity. Even so, though, he has a sense of humour. He can see the point of jokes. He can laugh, though seldom at himself. I think he is a bully, against whom if one were giving a serious argument one would need to come as well prepared as one did against MT.

We had also a bit about transport, in which he once again said that, since the taxpayer was funding the giant share of London Transport, the taxpayer (via him) had to keep control. When asked if he would favour the GLA [Greater London Authority] having tax-raising power – since he had proclaimed himself a strong devolutionist – he hedged, though. We would have to look at it, he conceded. But only just.

At the very end I asked, 'If the five economic tests on the euro come out positive, would the opinion polls deter you from a referendum?' He replied, with instantaneous and amazing speed, 'No.' And left it at that. It was very ringing, and very clear. Getting up from the table, he said to me, The polls would not matter, we could win the referendum, but only as long as people believe the euro will do them economic good.

LODE WILLEMS
19 December 2001

THE AFGHAN DEFENCE FORCE It is immensely complex, and could very well go wrong. We have the absurd situation of a sixteen-nation effort being based at Northwood.[1] Instead, we could have used established machinery in Brussels – mainly NATO. LW admitted that the EU defence machinery was not yet oiled. But SHAPE[2] was there, and we could have used it. Instead, we have this untried thing at Northwood.

There are big problems between the US and the UK on the one hand, Germany and France on the other. The US/UK want it run from Tampa;[3] the others do not. LW had just watched German TV on which Greenstock

---

1 The navy's fleet headquarters at Northwood, Middlesex, served as a 'nerve centre' for missile and other information.
2 Supreme Headquarters Allied Powers Europe, one of NATO's two strategic military commands.
3 Fort MacDill, Tampa, Florida, became the communications centre for the US forces in Afghanistan.

(UK ambassador to UN) said it would be run from Tampa, and the German UN ambassador said if that happened the Germans would withdraw their contribution.

The US, it is true, did not want NATO involved in the military campaign. Did not want a repeat of Kosovo, when many countries could have their say on targeting. But NATO as a peacekeeping force is another matter. SHAPE could have been involved. The US, says LW, would not have been against that.

The main architect of what is going on is Blair. It is he who has insisted on doing it this way. That goes back to his public pledge not to turn away from Afghanistan after the war. But he has to be (is) extremely worried about how it is going to work out.

There are big problems with the Afghans, who do not want so many Brits in their country. That is because of historic memories of the nineteenth century. They would rather have the Germans!

IDS has been asking some relevant and well-judged questions, which Blair may find it hard to answer.

2002

1 January   Euro notes and coins go into circulation in twelve European countries, but not Britain.

1 February   Kidnapped *Wall Street Journal* reporter Daniel Pearl is murdered in Karachi.

9 February   Princess Margaret dies after a stroke.

26 February   London's mayor Ken Livingstone announces a £5 charge for driving in central London.

28 February   Goodbye to the franc, Deutschmark, drachma, lira, peseta and other European currencies.

18 March   The House of Commons votes for an outright ban on fox-hunting.

19 March   The House of Lords votes to continue fox-hunting under licence.

30 March   The Queen Mother dies at 101.

5 May   Jacques Chirac is re-elected president of France.

4 June   The Queen celebrates fifty years on the throne.

12 September   President Bush tells UN of the 'grave and gathering danger' of Iraq.

24 September   Parliament is recalled for a statement on the Iraq crisis, along with a fifty-page dossier on Saddam's programme for weapons of mass destruction.

2 October   The French government ends six-year ban on importing British beef.

25 November   President Bush establishes the Department of Homeland Security.

18 December   Foreign Secretary Jack Straw claims that Baghdad's 12,000-page declaration of its weapons programme is a blatant lie.

Deaths   Rosemary Clooney, Stephen Jay Gould, Richard Harris, Thor Heyerdahl, Myra Hindley, Chuck Jones, Peggy Lee, Leo McKern, Spike Milligan, Rod Steiger, John Thaw, Billy Wilder

ROY DENMAN
Dan's Restaurant, 119 Sidney Street, 8 January 2002

BLAIR He made a big mistake trying to settle Kashmir, and waltzing round India as an adviser on how to make peace. Indians are very, very sensitive to the former colonial power giving them advice, and the trip was therefore a mistake. Pakistan is rather different.

And the US. He does not really understand that he is behaving like a lapdog. The US always acts strictly out of self-interest. That has been true for ever. It was true of Roosevelt, and one should note the coolness of the Roosevelt–Churchill relationship in the end. Also note the speech with which the US Senate tried to undo the lease-lend agreement even before the Japanese war was over: needed Truman's casting vote to stop it happening. Note also the coolness between Eisenhower and Churchill.

RD links this into the Americans' uninterest in the past in anything like the way the Brits are. Even attributes Americans' reluctance to write thankyou letters after dinner to this impatience to move on!

PETER HAIN
Foreign Office, 8 January 2002

REFERENDUM He has been given a lot of publicity lately for allegedly breaking the government line of non-committal on the euro. Much of this, he says, has been a case of journos extracting from tiny material large balloons of so-called importance. He was manoeuvred into appearing to be saying that entry was inevitable, when in fact he had said no such thing: this was a case of the Press Association putting to him the meaning of something he had said on the *Today* programme, asking him whether he said it was inevitable, he replying by saying that he had not used that word – and yet the whole thing still appearing as him saying entry was inevitable.

There have been other stories of the same kind. He was also said to have been slapped down by Jack Straw, again by reading into some Straw remarks the slapdown that never occurred. They greeted each other next day in the FCO with shared incredulity, PH said. (This reminds me of a related item re bad reporting: the episode when Mandelson was foreshadowed as saying that Gerry Adams should be seen as a freedom fighter not a terrorist – check clips for the exact words: but on seeing the offending TV discussion, chaired by J. Snow, I found he had said nowhere near any such thing, but had merely engaged in a somewhat academic debate (on this point) about the issue of freedom fighters.)

However, this may arise from the fact that he gets round the country and goes on radio talk shows. He finds several things here. First, that much of the questioning starts from an incredibly basic level. Second, that, because he tends to answer questions fairly directly, he find himself moving out of the Brown box of total non-talk. He says this is an essential thing to do – but that he is the only minister doing it.

He rather despairs of the media's inability to treat the Europe issue with due seriousness. The way they pick up on these tiny invented insinuations of disagreement is the enemy of enlightenment. (He proposes a piece for *The Guardian*, a light piece, he said, which would recount his experiences with the media, as above.)

GARETH WILLIAMS
15 January 2002

Finally we meet, after numerous cancelled lunches. One of the most civilized conversations one could wish for, by an urbane, clever and pretty straight non-politician who takes a rather distant view of what he sees, while being a totally loyal Cabinet member.

MAINLY HL REFORM He says that process is more important than composition. He is concentrating on getting peers to agree to morning sittings, and to committee stages being taken up, for many bills, in the smaller room, since only thirty or so ever turn up for most of them anyway (and the committee stage does not have a vote). He is finding this quite hard. Especially the morning sittings. Most peers bleat that they are part-timers, not professionals, not paid accordingly. He replies, You have come here to do a job of work, and the work is better done in daylight hours than at two in the morning. The talking goes on. He has sent questionnaires for them to reply to. His motive, he says, is to get better revision, more sensible outcomes.

He thought the IDS plan was absurd.[1] It was FPTP, which would guarantee a same-sense result as the HC, which was not in the public interest. The idea of fifteen-year terms was very dubious (though actually he said his scheme could mean twelve-year terms – three HC terms, which of course are flexible). IDS also paid no attention to how you get life

1 On 13 January 2002, Iain Duncan Smith, the Tory leader, proposed a 300-seat, American-style upper chamber – geographically based, like the US Senate – with 240 of the members elected for just one term of fifteen years. Tony Blair called it 'a recipe for gridlock'.

peers to vote for their non-existence. They would not do so. They have no pensions. Many have been here very loyally for a long time, and would get nothing. Many gave up pensionable employment. Perhaps we could get over that, with Treasury support. But it would be hard to get. There were other reasons he thought it would not wash, and was bad for the country and democracy. He did not commit self to PR for the HL, and noted it was among the undecided elements of the White Paper, as was the whole issue of terms. But I had the impression that there would certainly not be a reform that forced any life peers out.

More generally I had the impression that reform for the second stage would not command absolute priority. He said that September 11 had caused a big backing up of bills, because there had been both anti-terrorism and extradition to take account of. This meant the hunting and HL reform would surely be put back.

He made another practical point. The remaining life peers, knowing they were going to be ousted, would fight a hunting bill tooth and nail as a last-ditch effort with nothing to lose. They could delay things much more. Likewise, any reform that did not command HL consensus or something like it would imperil much else in the programme. Thus to say that the HC could pass a new HL and then invoke the Parliament Act would imperil all the legislation in the intervening eighteen months. Life peers like Serota[1] and other 80-year-olds, who totter loyally in now, would say, What is the point of staying up to midnight as part of an HL reform we don't like anyway? Etc. etc.

I remarked how Wakeham had become a semi-hero when in fact his report was so heavily attacked. He said, Wakeham makes a big issue out of what we have dropped from his plan – yet these are not real issues. Especially his notion that party people should be chosen by a non-party body, the Stevenson commission.[2] Wholly absurd. Is Blair to say we need another university chap from Wales, and Stevenson says we don't like that one so we propose a dentist from Cumbria who is also a Labour person? It's ridiculous. Also, we oppose his idea that HL people should be barred from going to the HC. Why should that be so? If a sprightly HL member gets backing in his city for the HC, why should he be barred? If he has made a name in the HL, why should the HC be blocked for him?

Williams's view comes from a decent and liberal man. He is against law lords being there, and wrote as much in a law-reform book before the 1997 election. He thinks there should be a supreme court, judges appointed by a commission etc. Derry Irvine just disagrees with him.

1 Beatrice Serota, Baroness Serota of Hampstead: Labour life peer since 1967.
2 The House of Lords appointments commission, a non-partisan, non-statutory body, headed by Dennis Stevenson, Baron Stevenson of Coddenham, that vets all nominations for the House of Lords.

One of his frequent mentions, in attacking IDS, was the prospect of a chamber that could do nothing about the Guantanamo-type thing. He seemed to say that a Tory HL backing a Tory HC could see things like that through on the nod. (Also, presumably, Labour ditto.) He often mentioned the value of genuinely independent people being there, for that kind of thing.

Likewise, he said that his own proposal about process allowed for the fact that on any one issue there were big experts – Winston,[1] for example – who have much to say in their field but not time or interest for other things. That replicated itself on many subjects with non-party and party peers too. I.e. they only want to attend from time to time. They have great expertise. He cited Richard Harries, Bishop of Oxford, for a brilliant speech on the stem-cell-research debate which traced the history of the consideration of these issues in the Christian churches over the centuries. You really want to hear that.

He remains, though, against establishment, and would like other faiths present. He cites Rowan Williams of the Church of Wales, which (I had not known) was fully disestablished: had women priests far ahead of the C. of E., and will have a woman bishop: appoints all its own bishops – and Williams himself. Thus Williams, cited as a candidate for Canterbury, would come from a more liberal tradition. Gareth thinks he will not want the job.

SIR STEPHEN LANDER
Goldsmith's/Civil Service Seminar, 25 January 2002

He spoke all the time about 'my organization', his preferred designation to MI5. He is small, neat, sharp, constantly locating his spectacles at the precise point on his nose, with long white French cuffs obtruding far beyond the suit arms. He warmed up, as time went on. Although I was sitting as far as anyone from him, and therefore he was not always audible, he seemed to say some interesting things . . .

He classifies the tasks of my organization as being:

– Collecting information, by covert means against covert threats.
– Processing, indexing, judging, sorting information.
– Using the information in a way to warn, advise and protect. Mainly the government, but also no fewer than 700 other clients, he said. I.e. businesses and enterprises that did things that impinged on national

1 Professor Sir Robert Winston, Baron Winston of Hammersmith: surgeon, scientist, author and television presenter.

security. Did they pay for this? No. Oil companies, utilities companies, big business (I got the impression) of many kinds, military bodies etc. etc. But 700? I confirmed with him, one to one, that this was indeed the figure. Amazing.

The origins of vetting, he said, were during the rise of the Communist Party of Great Britain in the 1950s. There were 60,000 CPGB members at its height. This vetting led to a purge (*sic*) of the Civil Service. But he implied (though did not surely state) that there had been no vetting after 1992. Can this be true?

You catch spies, he said, either by getting information from the enemy or by identifying their agents in our country and then catching them. This can mean watching a house for months on end. He cited an IRA agent – the IRA were much in the conversation – who had been seen at a wedding in Ireland on the arm of an English resident. The house of the English person was watched every day for four months to try and catch him.

One of his emphases was on the way the law has changed the environment totally. When he started, law hardly came into it. Now the European Court of Human Rights is a big driver, a big limiter.

Moreover 'the more there is law in the process, the more interest ministers take in it, the higher up their concerns do our activities become.' Asked to parse this rather gnomic statement, he seemed to say he was pleased at the notion of ministerial attention – whereas many of those at the table imagined that the further ministers stayed out, the better he would like it.

On the international front, he said that 'relations tend to be fantastically easy bilaterally, and fantastically difficult multilaterally.'

He also said that there were swings and trends in history. And at present the Atlantic line was less important than the European, in his work. When I asked *à deux* afterwards, he confirmed that this is what he meant. 'The French are very very close,' he said, 'and very good. The Americans are always important, but our work takes us further into Europe now.'

How many espionage prosecutions have there been since 1945? This he regards as a question that catches everyone out. There have been 67, of which only 3 were unsuccessful.

'It is much easier to get a case up into an American court than into a British court. Some of the 9/11 cases in the US would never get to court here, because the evidence is far too slim.'

'Since the end of the Cold War, most intelligence services have grown. They employ more not fewer people. This has not happened here –

one of the few exceptions.' This is essentially a reflection of the money politicians decide to make available.

Who decides priorities? He seemed to say that MI5 priorities were agreed by the Home Secretary, but that there needed to be a consensus among other ministers too.

Asked about the penetration of CND, he flatly denied that CND had ever been targeted. Amazing. It turned out he seems to have meant that they were only targeted in connection with the CP.

There was an interesting discussion about the meaning of national security and, for example, whether it included economic well-being, which he seemed to say it should not. This was part and parcel of his minimalist claims for MI5, its distance from the Greens etc. troubles, its desire to stick to a narrow agenda – even including keeping it away from drugs. A point challenged by Lawrence Freedman,[1] who said he was shocked that, given the close links between terrorism and drugs, MI5 had kept out of drugs.

He ended on a rather elegiac note about the 'importance of myth'. The myth of MI5 was in a way unhelpful: it meant MI5 could be demonized by Gerry Adams as being responsible for every kind of thing that happened: it perpetuated a name that we have been trying to get rid of for decades. On the other hand, the myth was useful 'if the IRA thought we shot to kill' – this last said with only a light laugh.

MICHAEL PAKENHAM
10 February 2002

EUROPEAN DEFENCE He said it was a fundamental error to say simply that European countries must spend more. Far far more important was that they should spend better, more collaboratively, more sharing of skills etc. etc. I said, If there is no EU defence force dominating everything in twenty years, there will be no defence for any nation. He did not disagree. But he said that any suggestion that EU countries should pool their purchasing, refine their skills etc. etc. was eyewash (check details though).

We did get quite near to something important about eight months ago. But then it was buggered up by the Turks. And when we satisfied the Turks it was buggered up by the Greeks. Neither Turkey nor Greece has any vision of NATO other than as a servant of their very narrow and bitter national purposes.

---

1 Sir Lawrence Freedman: professor of war studies at Kings College London.

BUSH ETC. Bush gets worse and worse, he thinks. Wolfowitz and Rumsfeld were people he knew in Washington long ago. They were always bad news, especially Wolfowitz. If you let Wolfowitz make or speak for your foreign policy you are in deep trouble. Increasingly that seems to be what is happening. People used to say that at least Wolfowitz is not Perle. But that seems to be an increasingly empty distinction.

Is it worth Patten and Jospin saying what they said in Saturday's papers – that the axis of evil was an error, that Americans should take a more sophisticated line? Unhelpful probably for a Frenchman to say it. But it is essentially correct, surely, says MP. That cannot be the view of the world that has any hope of leading anywhere useful . . .

JOHN STEVENS
Phone, 12 February 2002

The day of the EU fudging its response to the German deficit increase . . .[1]

PUBLIC SERVICES AND THE EURO These are umbilically linked, in a way the government refuses to recognize. The clarity of this is made more emphatic by all this talk about the US going into Iraq, acting unilaterally etc. etc. The collection of present challenges sharpens even further the issue about where the British destiny lies.

The only way to secure the future of public services on a European scale is by belonging fully to Europe. We need to make clear which side of that line we stand on. We do seem – per Blair, per Brown – to be arguing for European levels of spending and standards. Yet we decline to take the step into the heart of Europe that makes this choice clear. We still dicker on the edge, pretending that we can have European standards of services and American standards of tax: we don't really do that, because taxes are on the agenda, but the rhetoric continues to say that we are not for higher tax, in the American way.

How does this factor into the reform debate? That debate does not presume essentially an argument about public/private split. It is about making the single market work. It is about freeing up the possibility of cross-national big deals. It is about getting things done better, but not about issues of ownership in public or private fields. Until the Germans take over a French bank or vice versa, the market will be showing it is not open. But that will come before too long. The vanguard companies are the airlines. We have seen the death of national carriers. There will

---

1 In 2002 Germany breached the agreed EU ceiling on budget deficits. The European Commission asked for a formal warning, but eurozone finance ministers would not endorse the request.

perhaps be only four airlines in Europe before long. Maybe one of them will be based round Buzz rather than British Airways? But the big event is that national frontiers have been broken by market need. The same will happen elsewhere. Part of this is free market in labour. It will be painful, but the market will say that cheaper labour in Poland needs to make its mark, and will affect jobs in western Europe. That, too, is on the reform agenda, and has to be.

So it is all quite different from the Brown agenda, which seems to say that we the Anglos are model reformers with our US models in mind, and everyone else is lagging. The truth is that Europe leads the way in building the model of public-service state. It is public money, even in the vaunted French healthcare system. (And it is public money – 95 per cent government guaranteed – in the new deal on London Underground!)

All this is coming to a head on the US wing of things. Iraq may not be first, as we agreed from our various conversations. But we edge ever further away from the Blair idea that Churchill's concentric circles can be maintained as the UK model.[1] We cannot become a fully European type of public-service state without entering wholly into the European destiny. That destiny issue is being highlighted by US unilateralism in the terrorist campaign, and will go on being highlighted by US technical superiority in all defence fields.

Labour has the chance to declare itself the European party, as the Lib Dems have perhaps already done. The Tories are more and more clearly the American party, despite these absurd trips to Europe by their spokesmen to look for better ways of doing health without spending more money on it.

All that said, though, JS reiterated the line that we may not be sensible to have an early referendum. If the polls show 50 per cent by autumn, he'd be happier to go for it in 2003. But the more sure way is by seeing the Tories wrecked in another election – i.e. a result which shows that they cannot win in 2009. The saving grace for Kinnock after 1987 was that he was thought a possible winner in 1992. He nearly did win. If the perception of the Tories after 2005 is that they cannot win the next time, that would be the kiss of death to any prospect they had, including a No vote in a referendum.

---

1 Perhaps an indirect reference to HY's book *This Blessed Plot*, in which, according to its reviewer David Fromkin, in *Foreign Affairs* September–October 1999, 'Churchill left Britons a dazzling vision – but one that became an excuse for strategic indecision. In Churchill's view, Britain was to be at the center of three concentric circles: a Europe that would unite, a commonwealth and empire that would cohere, and a United States that would serve as Britain's partner.'

JOHN NEWHOUSE
Call from Washington, Saturday 16 February 2002

Rang to express general alarm and depression about the way things were going . . .

Blair is the only person who can perhaps rescue the US from the course on which it seems to be setting itself. The key alliance should be between Blair and Putin. Together they should put the pressure on Bush to press for a different way forward – though I know, says JN, that this will not happen.

Putin has been saying some sensible things. See a *Wall Street Journal* piece a couple of days ago. Our line is that we keep expecting P to bend to our will. Which he has done. But he needs things in return, which he is not getting. He needs the framework disarmament agreement to be serious, and not suddenly to talk about warehousing the dismantled warheads: needs something on NATO expansion: debt forgiveness: help with WTO etc. etc.

Now P says, about Iraq, You must not do this. It is a warning. What is his leverage? We need him. And remember those new bases in central Asia we have put down with his permission – Uzbek, Tajik etc. All supposed to be temporary.

JN had lunch with Chris Meyer, a very old friend. Was disappointed. Meyer took an absolute party line. He started by saying, 'This may surprise you but I'm in favour of the axis of evil.' He was not remotely critical of Bush, though JN thought his body language said differently.

Suggested Russia is the key. What Putin did on 12 September changed the world – by backing the US. NATO is now irrelevant. It is just a coalition, not an alliance. And coalitions are not popular with the Bush people. They want coalitions of temporary usefulness as and when. Russia is the only serious player. NATO has no longer got the clout it used to have, simply because the US does not need it.

Iraq. Having said all this, JN said he did not think an invasion was going to happen, though the talk gets more intense. Bush has two options: to go in and beat Saddam and win in 2004; to go in and fail to beat Saddam and lose in 2004. He is more likely to go for the second.

(The eternal severities . . .)

JN pushed Meyer hard about Iraq: if asked to support an invasion of Iraq, would London do so? Meyer said, London would go along, if the plan made real military sense, and if the neighbouring states would not be unsettled. Asked if he has seen such a plan, he said no. Asked if London expected to see such a plan, he again said no.

He recalled that Bush senior, in '91, before the Gulf War, sent a letter to Saddam saying that if he used any of his WMD he should expect a horror to be visited on Iraq such as it had never seen before. Saddam saw the sense of this and did not use them. Therefore it makes sense to assume that GB II would send the same letter – or at least make sense for Saddam to assume the same message stands.

One should also remember the US military. They will have something to say if Perle-like plans become serious. They will want to know exactly what they're getting into. They will know Saddam does have WMD and might use them: in which case they may say it is crazy to move in.

What the US needs is help in getting out of the box it has created for itself. Blair and Putin are the only people who might be able to supply it.

LODE WILLEMS
A brief phone call, 17 February 2002

Re Afghanistan – Manning and Tebbit[1] are very worried about ISAF [the International Security Assistance Force]. Britain will be giving up command to Turkey quite soon. Can Turkey do it? We desperately need more soldiers, but nobody wants to give them. R. Cooper went to Washington to get Rumsfeld to supply more, and Rumsfeld said simply no.

Tebbit thinks that 'axis of evil' was written into the speech by Bush himself, supported by Rice.

ANJI HUNTER
L'Escargot, 19 February 2002

AH very full of her BP [British Petroleum] job, which she had looked out for months earlier. Got to know John Browne [BP chief executive], whom she describes as being the only man she knew who was as visionary and inspirational as TB. He was not just an energy man, but an environmentalist. He deeply believed in the benign role of BP. BP was an amazing corporation of idealisms and business dynamics. She has been to Mexico and New York, and will be going all over the place, from gas stations to drilling hubs, to see the entire business at work. She is in charge of communications, both internal and external. She is plainly very excited that she made the career move she had to make at 45 or never.

1   Sir Kevin Tebbit, former director of GCHQ, was permanent secretary, Ministry of Defence, 1998–2005.

BLAIR Was very against her going. Told her it would be bad for her, not to mention him. It took two months to settle him down, and make him see it was what she wanted to do. But they still speak a lot. He had spoken to her just before coming to lunch.

He needs people – so do all politicians – with whom they can comfortably talk. She was his person. Alastair is not such a person, far too critical and harsh. (It is evident therefore that she continues by remote control to do it.)

After all, she had been with him for a long time. She was there throughout the leadership battle and after. She took quite a part in the '92 campaign, and a bigger one in '97, a full part in the election strategy. She was also the 'business' link – which was partly how she met Browne, and (I surmise) soft-soaped any number of Tony's business friends and admirers.

Tony has a terribly high view of his own probity, which is genuine. He is very, very honest. It's the religious thing, in part. He is appalled that people should think he might be corrupt in any of the ways now being insinuated.[1] It leaves him very gloomy, and he doesn't know what to do about it.

As regards the PR of all this, she says Labour's private polls show a bit more damage than today's *Guardian* poll. They are always a bit ahead. But her own role is being in touch with the Tory shires, which she continues to fulfil by regular calls all over the country to friends who form informal focus-group evidence. What these reveal is that for the most part people are getting on with their lives, feel fairly prosperous, low inflation, low unemployment etc. (She says more of her friends are Tories than Labour.)

She also notes – in what must be a Blair point – that compared with Thatcher's fate after two big elections – 1983 and 1987 – the country is at peace. Thatcher had the miners' strike and then the poll tax and Whitehall riots as her reward for winning big. Blair's situation is very different.

BLAIR–BROWN It is a very, very deep and strange relationship. It is one of total mutual dependence, even now. They are bound together. When in opposition, these two, plus Mandy, were as blood brothers, helping each other, defining the project, writing each other's speeches, brainstorming everything they wanted to do. But then there was a great falling out.

She thinks that Brown is best seen as a typical son of the manse. She

1 In February 2002 a parliamentary row erupted about a letter Blair sent endorsing the sale of Romania's steel industry to the tycoon Lakshmi Mittal – a donor to the Labour Party. The Prime Minister dismissed objections as nonsense. Even if he had known Mr Mittal was a party donor, Blair told the House, it would have made no difference. 'It is not Watergate, it is Garbagegate.'

was herself raised in Scotland, and knows the type. He is very tight, very closed in, very serious. But also very suspicious.

Brown has been telling himself since the age of six that he wanted to be prime minister and would be. It is totally on his brain. Half of him can think of nothing else. This is a reason why AH thinks he would turn out to be a good prime minister, because he would finally have made it, and all the psychological barriers would have fallen away. He would finally be able to reveal himself as a rounded human being, as well as a serious, clever politician.

However, this plays very much into the euro. Here she has told Blair many times that he must go this term. He knows, she says, that if he doesn't he will lose enormous credibility, at home and in Europe. It would be disastrous once it became clear there was to be no referendum in this parliament. Also, since everybody knows he wants to do it, believes in it etc. etc., the shame would be the greater.

Gordon, though, does represent a big block. In this area they do not trust each other. Can Gordon be trusted to come out wholly and completely in private and in public? Or will he find ways of hanging back, with a view to being carried in triumph by the right-wing press in the event of a defeat – a national crisis – from which he could rescue the nation? Equally, Gordon may not trust Tony. AH has told Tony he should not run for a third term. She thinks two is enough anyway. But the referendum, as I suggested, provides a mark at which he could leave. She said, He should do a deal, saying to Gordon that he will quit once the referendum is held. This is what Gordon may not trust, as an exchange for his support for the euro.

CABINET 'We are surrounded by pygmies' is the cry from the hard men in No. 10. I said, Alastair? She did not deny it. This is why the other Cabinet ministers are so often being second-guessed. They are not given a chance, because of the fear that they will drop the ball. There is an example this week – Blair, instead of staying at Chequers and working on the Budget, is going to do an NHS thing, simply because it is a big BBC NHS week. He could have sent Milburn, but now, he rather bleated to Anji when she remonstrated, 'It's too late.'

It is true, however, that there are not many giants. Most big people did not go into politics in the 1980s, because Labour was such a mess. Only Tony and Gordon. Cook was already there. Blunkett not yet there – and not yet seen as big, which he has certainly now become. So this cohort is caught between the generation that spent its entire time in opposition (Hattersley et al.) and the generation yet to come which has been drawn in by Blair's success.

The later cohort is going to be very strong. She instanced Miliband, Purnell, Ruth Kelly, Yvette Cooper[1] and Ed Balls, who would certainly be going into Parliament. You can think of a Cabinet in a few years' time which will be really strong, with clever big people who are also good public politicians. These are not yet in good supply.

Look, for example, at Jack Straw. He has completely lost his confidence. You must remember that all politicians read their criticisms very carefully, and Jack has had a bad time. Jack says his trouble is Tony: that Tony takes all the big work – such is the prime-ministerial role these days anyway. He should adjust, says AH. But who could be Foreign Secretary? Hoon just possibly. But the one she thinks very, very highly of is Peter Hain, who never puts a foot wrong in her opinion.

MANDELSON Cannot come back, she thinks. It is all very unfair. His final sacking was deeply unfair. She came in too late that morning to try and stop it. The court of [Richard] Wilson, Irvine, Campbell and Blair, a man's blackballing procedure.

Peter is terribly able. We have had big fights. From time to time he has gripped me by my jersey back and told me I am giving him terrible advice when I say to him what he should be doing is getting round the constituencies, speaking at chicken dinners etc. You want to bury me, he complains. But the fact is that he has somehow not made the right moves. He is still toxic (HY). It is a shame.

AFTERLIFE Tony is a very grounded person. He will not become too high and mighty – he is not that sort of person. His four children help keep him grounded, forever pricking the balloon. Would he, I asked, want to make money when he quit? Absolutely not, she said – bang goes a story I have been dining out on for too many years. He would not go into business, no way. He would want to improve the world. He might do something religious, she said first. She then said Kofi Annan's job[2] perhaps – but I replied that a Security Council permanent member would never have that job.

---

1 James Purnell: special adviser to the PM on culture, media and sport 1997–2001; Labour MP for Stalybridge since 2001. Ruth Kelly: former *Guardian* journalist; Labour MP for Bolton West since 1997; Economic Secretary, Treasury, 2001–2. Yvette Cooper: columnist for *The Independent*; Labour MP for Pontefract and Castleford since 1997; junior public-health minister 1999–2002.
2 Kofi Annan: Ghanaian diplomat; UN Secretary General 1997–2007.

JOHN NEWHOUSE
Phone, 16 March 2002

I asked him about the *Foreign Affairs* piece by Kenneth Pollack, former Clinton NSC Middle East man and well regarded by JN. It was an entirely hawkish piece advocating invasion of Iraq.

JN totally disagrees. Proposes the better line should be to pressure Saddam to let in inspectors for seriously random searching. This demand would buy time. Meanwhile a political strategy has to develop. He thinks a lead item in that should be the cultivation of Iran, which has *sub rosa* relations with Israel. There are deep possibilities in Iran, which could lead to the isolation of Saddam. Only after that might a military option have to be considered, if Saddam had not faced reality.

JN disagrees with the view that Saddam would start attacking Israel when faced by the threat of war against him. He wants above all not to be bombed – with weapons that are far smarter than they were in the Gulf War. So he will not want to give any kind of *casus belli* to the US and the world, especially one that brings the world back into the US orbit of support.

The fashionable theory at present in Washington is all about massive air strikes, which would lead to a huge uprising. This is surely a fantasy . . .

Russia and Blair have leverage. They need to persuade Bush that the US will alone is not enough.

Bush II is fixated, so I am told, on finishing the business that Bush I did not complete, with all the political consequences (Clinton) that allegedly flowed from that.

MAJOR-GENERAL CHARLES VYVYAN
17 March 2002

Met at a Sunday lunch party given by the Beaumans (Chris and Nicola).[1] Sat next to his wife, Liz, and then him. He has retired from being defence attaché in Washington. And now left the army. Balliol five years after me, a contemporary of Chris Patten. Thoughtful, irreverent, unsoldierly, intellectual, self-effacing.

He said he was accepted at Balliol to read history because his great-uncle was R. H. Tawney, and Christopher Hill thought a debt should be

---

1 Chris Beauman: senior adviser to the European Bank for Reconstruction and Development. Nicola Beauman: biographer of Cynthia Asquith and E. M. Forster.

repaid! Claimed not to have been very bright – but obviously is. Now works for the Bank of America, and other US-based businesses, which he advises on grand strategy and the world scene.

IRAQ/US Thought Chris Patten's *FT* piece was a real mistake, very hostile to US unilateralism.[1] The wrong approach. Should have said, We the five most sophisticated countries in Europe have all had experience of terrorism: we have discovered there is no military solution: there has to be a political approach: we can help to explain to you etc. etc. This would be a far better approach.

It is roughly the approach that Blair should be taking now. CV is clearly very critical of Blair's closeness to Bush, his willingness to follow on in line. I said, But if he were to break ranks, that would be a bit of an earthquake. To which CV said, It would be the first time since Wilson tried to be the honest broker over Vietnam and got out of line with LBJ. So, yes, it would be a big change. But CV said he thought it needed to happen. We needed to say that, while understanding the predicament, we did not have faith in the solely military way out.

He agreed with me about all the practical problems, which I listed. He regarded these as very important.

His own belief has long been, he says, that sanctions should be dropped and Saddam deprived of this easy alibi for his treatment of his people. Whenever he put this to the FCO, they said, 'We cannot do that. We would lose too much face.'

The most interesting thing he said, which I got him to resay, since he left Washington before Bush came in, was that Bush has no time for Blair. He has had this from several senior people in Washington – presumably on the military side – whom he knew very well from his last job. Blair is seen as someone who brought nobody else with him after September 11. He is still seen by the Bush people as a Clinton clone, therefore they do not really trust him, still less have fellow feeling with him. He may say the right things, but he is not regarded as someone who has added to the party, and is therefore quietly low-regarded.

CV said he regretted this. He said he had a great admiration for Blair (based on what I did not press him to say).

---

1 On 15 February 2002, Chris Patten's article for the *Financial Times* was headed 'Jaw jaw, not war war'. Patten, now EU external-affairs commissioner, criticized the US instinct for unilateralism and said the US success in Afghanistan 'has perhaps reinforced some dangerous instincts: that the projection of military power is the only basis of security, that the US can rely on no one but itself and that allies may be useful as an optional extra'.

JEREMY KINSMAN
19 March 2002

ATLANTICISM Blair is overreaching himself and getting it wrong (this in response to my spiel about Blair being in danger of getting isolated).

All of Blair's peer group, i.e. the other EU leaders and perhaps beyond, ask themselves why he is sucking up to Bush so hard. This is very obvious to them. It's the way they see it, whether or not Blair intends that. They really can't believe that he should be doing this.

A consequence, as we agreed, was that Blair may be losing influence all round. He sets himself up as the EU's contact man for Washington. He tells EU partners after 9/11 that he can keep Washington on the path of sanity and include their opinions; and he tells Washington that he can bring EU countries along. But actually he may be in danger of doing neither of these things. He has certainly lost influence with the EU peer groups, says JK. And, as Charles Vyvyan told me on Sunday, he may be less in favour in Washington than he thinks – for the very reason that he cannot bring the Europeans with him. This is surely a definition of being isolated.

JK wanted to speculate as to why Blair was doing this. His own hunch is that he really likes the limelight: that he is like a moth to power. He wants to be centre stage, and knows that is where Bush will give him a place. I slightly qualified that by saying that Blair is also a serious believer that he can persuade anyone of anything, including the obvious fact as he sees it of there being no real divide between Europe and America as regards their interests. That, however, is surely a fantasy. JK discusses it thus. Originally, he suggests, London thought that the Pentagon ultras were being allowed to do their macho thing in talks about Iraq, make bloodcurdling promises – but Bush all the time was just letting them come out front while actually himself being pragmatic, and being above all under the influence of Powell. Now, he thinks, the picture is the opposite: that Powell is the front man to keep Blair et al. on side, while the real influence is exerted by the Pentagon civilians.

However, he did qualify this by saying that the military were always much more cautious than the civilians. Yet, even on that premise, all he deduced was that no invasion of Iraq would be thought possible before the end of the year.

EU ENLARGEMENT His wife is Czech, so he has a bit of an inside view on the Czech position, which he regards as being increasingly sceptical – above and beyond the Sudeten German issues. Czechs do not like the huge transitional period beyond which there will be free movement of labour. They will have to wait seven years before they get jobs in Munich. Meanwhile, they have to satisfy very rigorous standards before they get anything out of it except the advantages, which they recognize, of the single market and absence of customs barriers.

Much the same is true of Poland, with the CAP a huge extra thing.

Meanwhile, he thinks France will drive an impossibly hard bargain (or was this David Davis talking? – I just had lunch with him). At any rate, JK was less optimistic than I said I was about the 2004 deadline being kept.

PETER RICKETTS
26 March 2002

AFGHANISTAN I asked him if he feared endless bog-down. He did not deny it was possible. True, he said, that at first the US talked about an interminable commitment: then they seemed to find it was all over fast: now they are finding there is much cleaning up to do. I said, Cleaning up is a euphemism. These are very difficult enemies and very bad terrain, and there is no easy exit. He did not disagree.

I said, Other European countries wanted to send troops and were not allowed to by the US. He said, That is true. Germany wanted to, and several others. But the US only wanted us to be there. Why? 'Because', he said ruminatively, 'I suppose they feel comfortable with us.' I.e. we will take their commands and know how to work with them.

IRAQ What is the heart of Iraq's imminence? He said, There is no doubt that the WMD problem has become more acutely perceived. People are more aware of it. Saddam is a proliferee rather than a proliferant: he takes WMD materials from all over, and also nuclear material. There is no doubt he wants that. PR would not be drawn on how close he was to getting it, though he did not demur when I quoted a German from the *New Yorker* saying three years. I said, How can Saddam's WMD affect this country? He fell to talking about global and regional instability.

I said, How strange that Hoon should have talked so openly about using nuclear weapons. He said that this was established and well-known policy. But when I said it was seldom if ever spelled out like that, he could not quote a previous example, though he clearly thought there was one.

I asked him if he thought that terrorism would dominate the rest of his professional life. He said just about yes, if you included general lawlessness, plus drugs and crime problems globally. Terrorism etc. was going to be with us for the foreseeable future. There were terrorists being bred every day.

We agreed, though, that Bush's recent speech pre-Monterrey, plus the very big rise in US aid money, did suggest an understanding that the causes as well as the results needed to be attended to.

MIDDLE EAST PEACE POLICY   I asked what hand Blair could play. He said, surprisingly, that Blair easily talks to Sharon,[1] and does so. Can pick up the phone.

PHILIP GOULD
The Ivy (mine), 2 April 2002

QUEEN MOTHER   Disagrees that the BBC got it wrong.[2] Says the *Mail* and *The Times* are quite wrong to say that the British people are deeply stricken by the death, and are horrified by disrespectful coverage. Says that he thinks most people (though he hasn't done any work on this) have got it right: i.e. that this was a remarkable woman, who lived a very long time, who did some important things for the monarchy, was quite a character – but not that her death was something that requires drooling over.

Says that *The Times*, and perhaps the *Mail*, have it in for the BBC for commercial reasons. Especially News International, which wants to promote Sky. Today's headline about Sissons's tie fits precisely into that campaign to discredit, which Sky needs to raise its credibility. (Was it also *The Times*, I ask myself, that did the photos of the Sky presenter wearing black tie and two BBC presenters not?)

TORIES   David Davis is a smart man, who knows what we did to get in and understands they have to do something like it. They would have had to be certifiable if they didn't move to the centre and rediscover the old paternalistic, leftish Conservatism. But unfortunately IDS is a dud. His Harrogate speech was terrible[3] – contrary to what most people said.

1   Ariel Sharon: prime minister of Israel 2001–6.
2   The *Daily Mail* attacked the BBC for its 'disrespectful' coverage of the Queen Mother's death on 30 March 2002, reporting that Peter Sissons, the BBC newsreader, wore a burgundy tie rather than a black one for the occasion. The BBC responded with an NOP survey that on 19 April reported that 68 per cent of viewers disagreed with criticism of the BBC's coverage – and that that included 61 per cent of *Daily Mail* readers.
3   In his speech to the Tory spring conference in Harrogate on 24 March 2002, Iain Duncan Smith jokingly compared the Conservatives to the hero of the television series *One Foot In the Grave*. 'We all laugh at Victor Meldrew on television, but you wouldn't want to live with him and you certainly wouldn't vote for him. If we don't reflect the Britain we want to lead we will never be asked to lead it.' Peter Oborne, in *The Observer* the

It went over appallingly on television, he can't deliver a speech, has no power, no charisma. Perhaps it read better (it didn't). But he is a real downer for them.

The chances are, though, that the Tory press will keep him in place, even though he is not a real asset. They've begun to invest in him, and will not let go.

LIB DEMS They thought the Lib Dems were going to win 20 or even 30 seats. And think they should have done so. The fault was Kennedy's: he is not a man of presence, he is not a big strategist. Thus they realize the LDs will be important next time – but not as important as they ought to be.

VOTERS He does a lot of focus groups, and finds that the party's real problem is with its core support, the C2 and D voters: the working-class heartland voters, who use public services a lot and know that we have delivered and really care about that. This is the government's biggest problem.

It connects with the wider Labour problem, which is that after five years people have forgotten the past and forgotten how much Labour has done – and also have seen the flip side of certain things begin to work against us. The one he mentioned most often was spin. Labour needed spin at the start. It had always had a terrible press; it needed to make sure it got its message across. But this did mean, he frankly admits, double-counting, misleading stats. Straining to put facts in the right way – which were found out to be errors. This is big stuff. It means we have a credibility problem, which he thinks Labour can address and deal with but which is obviously serious.

The media are like a vast storm. They are coming at you all the time. The temptation is to succumb to their claims and agenda. Like a prisoner under police interrogation, he rather nicely likened it to. If the prisoner is slapped around enough he eventually says yes, you're right, I'm guilty. The recent performance of Blunkett, admitting that people felt more unsafe on the streets, was a case in point. That kind of thing has to be avoided.

BLAIR AND BROWN Brown: In general, said Philip, I am more on Gordon's net than Tony's. Gordon is deeply interested in the detail of

---

following Sunday, wrote, 'Harrogate was a staggeringly radical speech. Chattering-class commentators, such as Hugo Young in *The Guardian*, who set about trashing Duncan Smith afterwards, simply missed the point or perhaps didn't bother to read the speech. Young's article was a manifestation of what has become a tedious, authoritarian and discreditable syndrome of the high-minded left, the axiom that whatever emerges from the Tories should be barred from serious debate.'

my work. GB is a deeply serious politician. He has had a lot of very bad throws of the dice. A troubled and pained man. A victim, even. He sees himself that way. I feel he deserves to get the big job, because he does deserve something after all his disappointments. He is a wonderfully able politician, who, after Blair, would be a great prime minister. He does, however, need Blair. He would not have been a very good prime minister if he had won the leadership. He is a far better politician now than then. He would not have done the Clause IV thing (as wouldn't I, said PG), because he is a real party man. Clause IV was the bone of the party.

Gordon is also a very cautious politician. He worries away at things. He is often unable to decide until the very moment he has to. He can keep contradictory paradoxes in his mind at the same time. He spends endless hours with Ed Balls and Ed Miliband[1] going over every aspect of policy and strategy, talking, talking, talking.

On the euro, he is plainly pro-Europe. He is New Labour. New Labour includes the euro, in reality. It is about the future. But his caution will make him delay. His indecision is more important than the belief that he is a sceptic – which he is not. His own strategy is therefore exactly the opposite of mine (HY's). He wants to keep utterly silent about it, the better to appear as the impartial arbiter when the time comes. Only that way, he thinks, will the economic tests be credibly adjudged. He then thinks, it would seem, that the campaign can be won quite quickly, without the need for all the preparation which I (and Tony) think may be needed – though Tony, per HY, has often said he doesn't think the campaign would take very long.

Blair: Much more sure of himself than GB. Much more likely to come in and say we are going for it (whatever it may be). Much less given to agonizing. More direct. More open. More confident.

Plainly does see the euro as historic. The only thing around that offers historic status. Which is why it is not false to say, as Mandy does, that Gordon wants to be the one who takes us in, and that is why he is playing hard to get now.

Blair will not move, PG said, if Gordon is wholly against trying for the euro now: but he agreed that it was a kind of poker game – in which Blair could not act with Brown, but Brown could not afford to let anything get between the two of them when it came to a campaign.

PG's dream: that Blair goes on for another four or five years, probably takes us in, hands over to Gordon, who has a few years of effective prime-ministership. The crucial thing, he says, is to avoid bitterness. The

1 Edward 'Ed' Miliband: special adviser to the Chancellor of the Exchequer 1997–2002; Labour MP for Doncaster North since 2005; Chancellor of the Duchy of Lancaster and Minister for the Cabinet Office 2007–8; Secretary of State, Department of Energy and Climate Change, since October 2008.

models to avoid are Thatcher and Clinton. Thatcher, had she been allowed to go on, should have gone on, then left, leaving Heseltine to become leader, which would have given Labour a very hard time. Instead we had Major's seven years: a total waste of time for the Tories.

Clinton is even more graphic. Gore very bitter against Clinton, did not use him or allot him credit in the campaign. Clinton knew that a Gore victory would set the seal on what he had done. Instead he saw Bush ripping up his fiscal prudence and much else – all because Gore was too bitter to use him. Clinton, in turn, has become very bitter against Gore for not having protected his legacy.

ALASTAIR CAMPBELL
Phone, 14 April 2002

TRUST AND ALL THAT A big problem now is that anything whatever can be called sleazy. This call we are having, which has lasted a few minutes, could well be called sleazy in that climate. A culture has grown up in which merely listing things – Ecclestone, Hindujas, G. Robinson, Mittal etc. – is thought to be enough. Overlooking entirely the fact that all these have different details. The details are long forgotten, against a climate in which a general perception is nurtured.

This morning it was extraordinary, with all the big stories around re the Budget and the Middle East, that the plum 8.10 slot on *Today* should be given to unverified charges about the smallpox vaccine and Labour donations.

Polls tend to show that politicians and the government in general are unpopular. But when asked about Blair and Brown as individual ministers you get a different verdict. People are much happier.

One can say that a lot of this stuff will settle down. The big facts and stories – above all the Budget and its cons – will take over. Cannot be held back when they happen. This Budget is as important as any we have done. Ultimately that is what will matter.

It is true that we were guilty of overclaiming, which admittedly has been a trust-loser. But we have changed. Why did we do it? Because we were imbued with an Oppositionalist mentality in which all we had were words. We went on doing that too long. The prime example was the idiot Whelan saying that there would be £40 billion more on health and education. Yes, there was a time when we were double-counting and overclaiming. But now it is different.

Tendency – see TB on JY [*Jimmy Young Show*, Radio 2] the other day – to try and wipe out what has happened (say on education) and move on to the rest, without admitting that anything good has happened.

The Jo Moore saga[1] damaged our conscious efforts to remove spin. And get back to the straight and narrow. But we are doing that.

The Tories get space for saying that reform must come before money. Yet that is exactly the argument we have been making for years, on which the whole of our strategy has been based so far.

LODE WILLEMS
Lunch, his embassy, 23 April 2002

BROWN PLUS EURO   Lode is fascinated by the fact that he has only had a single one-to-one with GB, compared with six or seven with Blair. I.e. he has accompanied Didier Reynders, his finance minister, only once to the Treasury. A sign of how badly Brown deals with, or likes, these bilaterals.

Lode was very struck by the Budget speech and the way Brown, with Blair sitting alongside, used the first-person singular on virtually every occasion. Not a collective but a personal project, it seemed. I told Lode that this was perhaps an assertion of Brown's power vis-à-vis his colleagues rather than vis-à-vis Blair.

BLUNKETT AND IMMIGRATION   The EU ambassadors had a meeting (lunch) with Blunkett the other day. It seems as though this was the occasion out of which came the B quote about Brown being 'the money god'. He was furious about the way public spending was being arranged, about the deprivation of police and the Home Office, about the decision to concentrate it all on health.

The most interesting thing was Blunkett's interest in ID cards. He says that this will be the only way he can counter illegal immigration. Said he has not got collective agreement for it, which must mean Blair agreement, but has got agreement to the consultation process, starting in July. Very big change, if it happened.

Blunkett asked European countries for any advice and stuff they might have which would make the argument easier in the UK. LW's own view is that it would enhance rather than diminish rights – as I too am starting to think. I think the lives of legal residents would be made simpler if they just had to present a card to show they belonged here. LW said, What is

---

1 Jo Moore, a political appointment to the Transport Department, had suggested in an email that 11 September 2001 would be a good day to 'bury' bad news. She left the department on 15 February 2002, along with the communications chief Martin Sixsmith.

the difference between accepting the security hassle at airports and just very occasionally having to produce a card?

But they also said to Blunkett that an ID card on the Continent is often the only travel document people have. They can move around on the basis of that alone. This, too, he finds quite OK – but it would knock a hole in the British passion for her own border controls.

The Brits say, But we are an island, and we must keep our frontiers. To which a Belgian leader says, I have borders on every side, and the way I must deal with that is more complicated, has to be realistic and administrative, and therefore to permit free travel with ID checks available.

(In any case, one might add, the island argument is pretty bogus. It does not show that islands need to have passport controls: only that it is easier for them to impose them.)

DENIS MACSHANE
25 June 2002

Note, he said, how the Tories have all stopped wearing their £ lapel badges. He saw this as deeply significant evidence of their further withdrawal from the issue: a decision to stop even gesturing about it, so as to let Blair simply be taken on by the press. Let the press do the dirty work, and let the Tories almost seem to be above the battle.

He hears from a German source – someone close to Schäuble[1] – that IDS has evidently been telling the Germans that he will take Britain into the euro, after Blair has been defeated!

DOMINIC CUMMINGS
Lunch, Villa Bianca, 26 June 2002

He is now director of strategy for the Tory Party, having been for three years the director of Business for Sterling. Looks around 30. Talkative; a winning mixture of youth and maturity, without a sign of pomposity.

We started on the referendum. He said my pieces were watched with eager attention and deconstructed for hints as to where either my or the government mood was. Who did I seem to have talked to? I was seen as the most telling of pro-euro contributors in this respect – partly, I confessed, because I wrote about it too much, for which I was sometimes criticized.

He said he thought the referendum would not happen. The problems

---

1 Wolfgang Schäuble: German politician; interior minister 1989–91 and since 2005.

were too great. He agreed that Blair has a strong historico-psychological desire to go for it, but there are other things stacked up against it: non-convergence, economic uncertainty, the state of the polls, the general unpleasantness inside many European countries.

The polls were now back to 53–35, he said (citing a poll today – where from?). There has been a blip pro-Europe in Jan.–Feb., when the gap had narrowed to 10. But all the evidence from all over the world was that a referendum held to change the status quo was certain to be lost if the polling figures started against you. In fact the evidence was of coalitions beginning to fall apart after the referendum started, and of a weakening not strengthening of the case. The crucial factor here was the status quo. Those who wanted to change always had the harder task. The 1975 referendum on the EU is therefore a bad precedent for a Yes vote now.

He said he had talked to Ed Balls (whose name I brought up), and confirmed that Ed had said that the polls needed to be far ahead before anything could be risked: and also said that the worry had to be not about whether there was convergence on the day, but whether this would endure for years afterwards, especially the first few years.[1]

That problem played into the issue of the majority. If it was a narrow margin on a low turnout, the solidity of the mandate would crumble, especially if the economic stats turned against it – a repeat of the ERM, for example. I asked how the Tories would react to a defeat on a low poll and just marginal: he said that this might depend on how the economy did. If there was a UK majority but a negative in England, that would be disastrous and would be seen as such by the Treasury and Brown let alone IDS. It could surely not stand, he opined. It would be far too destructive.

He said that Blair's problem was that he had developed no vision about Europe. The economic case was at best 50–50, and the political case had not been made. They were nowhere near changing the psychology and preference of the British people, and had not allowed nearly enough time to do so. (This seemed to me a telling point.)

He remarked, as I did, that this was a real shit-or-bust operation. He thought that whichever party lost, it would crack apart. The Tories, especially, would fracture. There would remain an important gang of ultras – perhaps one-third of the MPs – who were determined to fight another day even if this was twenty years away. They would feel honour-bound to carry on the fight, however long it took. That would wreck the Tory Party. It was a nice point which would call itself the Tory Party, but both would be hopelessly enfeebled.

1 Dominic Cummings says he never had a private conversation with Ed Balls, but that 'Balls said this privately to many people,' who told him.

If there was a Yes, there would be an indefinite future of Labour/Lib Dem government. A terrible prospect.

We discussed less what happened if Labour lost. But it would be the making of the Tory Party, of that there was no doubt. He seemed unsure that Blair would quit.

Moving on to party politics, I asked whether Brown would be a more fearsome leader of Labour than Blair at the next election. He thought firmly not. Blair, whatever you say about him, is seen as a human being, is a normal person, can smile on television, has won two elections, has got people reluctantly but clearly behind him, has done or can claim to have done a pretty good job. Brown is Scottish, grim, unsmiling, and not fully human, people would think.

He is clear that the Tories will have a terrible task to win the next election. They need such a radical reform at all levels, and are so unwilling to face that. Everything needs to change. There needs to be far more devolution, so that locals can think it is worth being a Tory member. He comes from Durham, where there is absolutely no point in being a Tory. Locals should have far more autonomy to decide things, including the MP. (This seems against the Portillo view, as told to Frost, implying the candidates should be centrally chosen to get a better spread.)

The key was somehow to make the Tory Party seem representative of the country. Normal people of all ages. Not just old and stuck. A huge task to make Tory politics interesting.

He contrasts the Tory Party with Business for Sterling, which consisted of a dozen people, all young, all working very, very hard, and all believing utterly in what they were doing: believing in the cause, able to make it sing. Getting excited by it. Nothing of this is apparent in the Tory Party. It is quite quite different: a dead place.

I asked about IDS. DC had gone to work for him because he thought him straight and decent. IDS is clever enough, if not exactly brilliant (HY), but he is straight. Not a geeky weirdo like Hague. Not locked away with Amanda Platell[1] and Coe. Open doors.

DC confirmed that the removal of the euro signs from the lapels was a conscious policy. So was the downplaying of Europe as a whole. This he attributed to himself. After all, he was the one who first publicly said that IDS should not lead the euro campaign.[2] This is clearly understood by all concerned – though he was evasive about who might be the

---

1 Amanda Platell: journalist on *The Independent*, the *Sunday Mirror* and the *Sunday Express* (which she also briefly edited); press secretary to William Hague 1999–2001.

2 Cummings gave an interview to *The Independent* three weeks earlier in which he tried to torpedo the idea of the Conservative leader being the leader of, or running, the referendum No campaign. It was assumed that this was authorized by IDS, but, says Cummings, it was not. The 'downplaying of Europe as a whole' was agreed by IDS and was supported by Cummings, but not 'attributable' to him.

co-leader, what businessman would do it. David Owen would definitely not do it. They want a businessman with a long record of social reform – and also, I guess, quite young.

JOHN STEVENS
28 June 2002

We agreed that the whole Europe case needs to be relaunched as a visionary and idealistic case. Based on big arguments about the need to match economic forces with political forces (globalization); the need to protect European civilization; the need for a large, coherent region called Europe to come together to increase the security and prosperity of its citizens. This has never been attempted in this country. BiE and the European Movement and all the others have been hopeless at this. Partly because badly led, partly because the political will has never been there from the loudest voices. Admittedly it is a massive task. It has to meet the forces of history with an equal force for the future. Has to overcome cultural and psychological pulses that are very deep.

All this has been underestimated by Blair and indeed by just about every pro-Europe politician. Always talk about it in minimal, defensive terms, and about economic arguments that will never be wholly believed. Never rise to the proper heights of persuasion and belief. This, says JS, and I am starting to agree with him, cannot be done in the short time that must now elapse between now and a referendum in this parliament.

Here is why he believes that delay is becoming essential. He sees it as having several elements. The crucial one is the next election, and the need to destroy the Tory Party then. Only when that has happened can the idealistic argument, made by Labour and Lib Dems and rump pro-Europe Tories, have a chance. I say, The party does not matter, compared with the media. He replied, The media need a political party to clutch on to, and even the *Mail* could not succeed if the Tory Party did not exist.

Meanwhile, at the Treasury (where he has a good source), he says that the line is being prepared. It is getting ready to say, says the Treasury source, whoever he is, that we are getting there but are not yet there. That three of the tests have been met, but the other two have not been met. As to which tests fall into which category, they will pick them out of the hat.

His source also says we should not expect anything until next March or so. I.e. there will not be a definitive moment before that: and even then they may just talk about delay for the next bit – not even saying it will not happen in this parliament.

I say, If they do not make their intentions apparent by the end of this year (November) that will be signal enough. Perhaps I should therefore prepare my way towards being an early mind-changer on this: announcing that there will be no referendum and using that as a platform to say the whole pro-Europe cause needs to be rethought, reorganized etc.

For the truth is that there are very few real pro-Europe *impassionati* in the UK. Nothing like the head-and-heart passionates of the anti side. The pro-Europe people have entirely lost the plot for many years. Have never talked about it as they should. Have never flown the flag – in a real as well as a metaphorical sense.

He goes back to his analogy with the miners' strike. That was the determining moment for Thatcher, and it was well prepared. It accumulated heart and head together in the Tory Party and the country. It took a long time. It was decisive. Nothing like that has been attempted re Europe – and yet it is an issue on an even bigger scale, which desperately needs an equivalent critical mass of politics behind it.

Which brings us to the Tories. He has had good talks with people close to Howard. Howard thinks as follows. He was stitched up by Hague when he thought he was offering Hague the deputyship in his leadership campaign and found next day that Hague was the candidate. Very bitter, and wholly contemptuous. Likewise thinks IDS cannot cut it. Sees a big chance for himself.

The background fact which many understand is that if they finish the next election still being regarded as incapable of winning the 2009 election then they will be finished. They must at least be like Labour in 1987, perceptibly on the way back. The Labour recovery began after the miners' strike. What is the equivalent for the Tories?

Howard's line is that he could lead the Tories back to credibility without winning the 2005 election. That should be their target, he says.

DENIS MACSHANE
7 July 2002

BLAIR AND ANGLO-AMERICA At the famous 'Clinton' weekend, where the Blairites got together with Clinton in some hotel a few weeks ago, and talked about the Third Way (D MacS was there), Blair, musing by the fireplace, said, 'Britain has got to be a partner, not a poodle.'

Denis fell off his chair, and is amazed this hasn't got out.

What it shows is that Blair is aware of the poodle jibe and pained by it, and really does want to be sort of 'equal'. Take this alongside his interview with Jon Snow,[1] and you begin to get a picture of a man struggling against the accounts of geopolitics, and trying desperately to escape the embarrassment he knows very well his situation exposes him to.

HY thought Iain Duncan Smith, now approaching his first anniversary as leader of the Conservative Party, 'a mild and decent bloke, informal-ish in manner'. He recorded that Duncan Smith collected him himself in the Central Office hall, and led him up to his office via the back stairs. 'But we sit across his desk, rather than in sociable chairs. His desk is completely empty save for some glasses and crumbs, which he clears away. We have a short conversation, with his aide, Andrew, coming in sharpish twice to let him know he had another date.' HY's verdict following their meeting: 'He is quite amazingly without charisma. He is not even very confident in what he says; he has absolutely no style, no air of danger. But he is diligently learning his job, more than going through the motions.'

IAIN DUNCAN SMITH
Conservative Central Office, 19 July 2002

On the party, he says he is clear what needs to be done: to connect it to a wider world, and make it less hated (HY). He gave a speech last night trying to lead it in that direction.

One impressive thing was his backing for Letwin. He expressed himself very turned-off by Blunkett and his criminal-justice review, his attack on jury trials. But he notes Blunkett's style: to come out raging with all kinds of half-thought-through ideas from which he then backs off.

Explained his slight delay by saying he had been with the US ambassador. When I murmured that Farish[2] had made little mark on London, he said he was intimate with Bush, which was what counted. They were 'family friends'. He was therefore a useful ambassador. But he was 'no intellectual', which perhaps accounted for him not seeing journalists much.

1 Tony Blair talked to Jon Snow on *Channel 4 News* on 2 July 2002. HY, in his commentary of 11 July, wrote the following: ' "Could you foresee yourself committing British troops to a ground war in Iraq?" Snow asked. "I suggest we have that discussion when the decisions are actually about to be taken," Blair replied. In other words, when the discussion can influence nothing. Blair's suggested timing is precisely wrong. Any serious debate taking place after Washington has decided where it's about to go can only be destructive to the alliance. The time when a European argument might be useful is now.'
2 William S. Farish: Texas businessman and family friend of George W. Bush; US ambassador to Britain since 2001.

IRAQ He went straight into this. Confessed he had few disagreements with Blair's stance and apparent attitude. IDS talks to the Americans, and has just seen a lot of Middle East ambassadors. His opinion is that many Middle East countries want to see the back of Saddam. Saddam is a brutal and disruptive figure.

He thinks the West (US) must get far more engaged in the Middle East. He has conventional ideas about the need to pressure Israel; on the settlements. Etc. etc. But his most interesting line was the terrible state of Saudi and the Gulf states. These people had financed al-Qaeda to a quite colossal extent as a way of getting them off their own backs. They were corrupt and deeply dangerous. IDS had seen the King of Jordan recently, who complained that the West did not appreciate how the 'good' Middle East countries, like Jordan, were in grave danger and suffering a lot from the Saudi et al. financing of terror. This would not in any case work. Saudi street was searing with potential violence. IDS even offered the thought that perhaps Saudi would be better off without the princes – though immediately pulled back to lines about the devil you know.

He has nothing interesting to say about what happens if the Iraq war plays out badly. But he said that the Republican Guard might very well cave in. Why should they give their lives for the hated Saddam, in a lost cause? But he said this could not be the premise of a war. He agreed meekly that the war might well lead to a prolonged occupation – done by the Brits and Europeans, as usual.

He said Blair's latest statements (Wednesday's PMQs, I think) needed clarifying, and he wanted to go and see him about that.

EURO He said that if Blair did not have the referendum he could justly be called a coward. It would be for entirely political reasons. IDS is clearly gearing for this kind of attack on him.

Logically, Blair should not have a referendum. But he may find his heart ruling his head. The electric moment would then occur. A huge choice, which would galvanize the nation.

IDS feels comfortable with his party and his line. The party is united. Of its 330,000 members, 300,000 are against the euro. They often want him to say and do more about it, but he thinks it much better to have let it take a less important place in his profile.

Would he lead the No campaign? 'I will lead the Tory Party's No campaign.' It suited him at present that he should not be aspiring to lead the entire No campaign. Should 'stand aside' from that. But he seems to have no illusions that, when it comes to the point, the television will stake it as a battle between him and Blair.

In any case, he said, we are by far the biggest players in the No campaign. If we win it, it will change our situation. If we lose, he said with a light despairing snigger, I suppose we will have to go back to the drawing board.

GÉRARD ERRERA
Lunch, 29 October 2002

He said that the basic situation between France and Britain is that we agree about many things, but it is always a struggle against history and psychology to feel easy in our agreements. We are always in danger of falling out because of this past and this psychology. That is true, just as it is true that we agree about many big things. It complicates matters.

HY went to the United States for a week of interviews.

WYCHE FOWLER
12 November 2002

If Bush goes for it and fails to get Saddam, it will be fatal for Bush. Saddam was so demonized during the first Gulf War that we have to get him, if we try. But it will be hard. When we were going after Noriega, in a country the size of a postage stamp and with stealth bombers knocking out everything in sight, it took us 22 days to get him. What price a country with allegedly 1,500 miles of underground passages, and 10 body doubles for Saddam?

Fowler doesn't quite agree that the US people have become internationalist. Because of the demonizing, a question about bombing Iraq would get 70 per cent acceptance. But he agrees that the beginnings of sophistication are apparent; people seem to understand we need allies, feel uncomfortable without them.

He says that the Israel element is terribly strong. But they should not forget that a civilian government in Iraq is very unlikely to abandon its desire for nuclear weapons. If Israel has 300–400 of them, and Iran is getting them, how can anyone say that Iraq should not be allowed to have them? This is storing up a big problem. We need to recognize that a democratic Iraq, were such a thing credible, is not going to do everything we would like.

FRANK MILLER
National Security Council, 13 November 2002

Charming, frank, chubby-faced, easy-going, bespectacled, a bureaucrat rather than a political appointment I surmise. Genial but also knowing. In the course of the talk he said he had been the man responsible for establishing the link between North Korea and Pakistan on nuclear: reasoning that the only way Pakistan, a country dead broke, could pay for NK missiles was by giving them nuclear stuff.

THE WAR Saddam Hussein will play his usual game. It will be the movie as before. He will pretend to comply, will actually comply in bits and pieces at the start of the inspection campaign. Maybe someone will be publicly executed for defying the regime and refusing to give up data to the inspectors. But he will be trying to hang on to as much WMD as he can. This will be partly by destroying old stuff he doesn't need, and then stuff that can easily be rebuilt: i.e. he will do enough to make the French and the Russians say, Look, he's complying, we are getting somewhere.

Two difficulties will emerge. People will say, if and when he does give up WMD, that he is complying, is coming through. This will lead to a fight as to whether or not he is in material breach. Also, when he starts obfuscating, people will start asking the wrong questions – trying to persuade themselves that he is actually not doing enough that is wrong to justify going to war.

Wasn't this a story of US concession? I asked. A far cry from what they seemed to start out doing and thinking? He replied, The President decided that in all circumstances it was best for the US interest to go through the UN. We could, however, soon be in a '93–'94–'95 situation, where there is steadily more obstruction. How long must the process last? I asked. He said, surprisingly, Six months at minimum I would say. I.e. there was a check moment after two months, but, unless he has been quite flagrant, that need not be the cut-off. Six months it may well be, or more – to give the UN process a full chance to work.

The wild card in all this is the change of opinion inside Iraq. There is evidence of this. The referendum shows he is not very confident, needed to get a show of support; the release of prisoners did not come out of the kindness of his heart, was quite risky, has shown a lot of people that their loved ones are no longer alive. Also, the demonstrations that recently occurred. Something is stirring. This may get more pronounced when the inspections start and carry out the intention to press hard. Further, the item in Res. 1441[1] which says that the inspectors can take people out of Iraq to question them has many possibilities. They could come and be given green cards by the US or Brits and they would start unloading.

Is it the UN ambition to have a collective, not unilateral, effort? Yes, he stressed. Unless governments persist in turning a blind eye to accumulation of evidence that SH is stringing us along.

He is plainly worried about Blix.[2] They think Blix is looking for the Nobel Prize. But his job is not to decide about peace or war. His job is to carry out the resolution and search and find WMD. He has to be tough with the Iraqis, which he may not be. He has to be seen not to let them get away with things. Plainly the US will be watching him very closely for being oversympathetic to Iraq.

He said that the conventional wisdom about war being only fightable before March is not true. He is a former military man himself (US navy, and has been a Department of Defense official for a long time). If we fought in the heat it would be slower, but not impossible says the military. (Also there's the night-fighting aspect.)

Do we already know what and where he has WMD? We are very confident we know a great deal about what, but not where. We know he has 10–20 Scuds from the previous war; we know he has biological weapons on wheels. But we do not know where. As to the nuclear, we know that if he has fissile material he might have them in a year. By the way, he praised the UK dossier on all this as a wonderful piece of work.

POST WAR I cannot give you a completed plan, but there is a huge amount of work going on, he said.

The analogy is not perfect, but Iraq is quite like Nazi Germany. There are lots of excellent resources; it is a rich country, and could be a prosperous one. There are lots of good civil servants. One of our sources has said that only the top two people in a particular ministry are Baathists. The rest are just competent people, who are desperate to get rid of Saddam. We know this from intelligence, and also through Kurdistan, where bright people are closely in touch with people in Baghdad. Agriculture and Justice might have a lot more Baathists, but the rest could be easily taken over, he thinks.

There will be many tasks: ensuring the defeat of SH and his secret service; restoring law; destruction of WMD; rebuilding the infrastructure

1 UN Security Council Resolution 1441, passed unanimously on 8 November 2002, offered Iraq 'a final opportunity to comply with its disarmament obligations'. The text, drafted by the US and the UK, took eight weeks to negotiate.
2 Dr Hans Blix: Swedish politician, diplomat; Swedish foreign minister 1978–9; executive chairman of the United Nations Monitoring, Verification and Inspection Commission (UNMOVIC) 2000–2003, which started searching Iraq for 'weapons of mass destruction' in 2002, ultimately finding none.

etc. etc. We have been making a lot of plans under each heading. But there is obviously an issue about how it will be done. In Week 1 [*sic*] the 'coercive general' who defeated SH will clearly have to be in command. There will be a transitional period, leading towards an interim government. Who will lead the interim government, how to build the consultative mechanisms, how to make clear that we are liberators not conquerors – these are all important issues, not easy to resolve.

But Saddam's ouster will itself have a good effect. It will reduce opposition to the liberators. The pleasure at Saddam going will far exceed the displeasure at the Americans et al. coming. The Afghanistan example is a good one: not a bad job, on balance. In Iraq, only a coalition force can begin to restore order and lead to political, military and security order. Ideally – I don't want to sound like Polyanna – we develop a regional, federal solution. I know one cannot look at Iraq like Nebraska and Iowa and the United States, but why not try and use that kind of model.

One thing we are already making clear, however, is there can be no independent Kurdistan. Absolutely out. The idea that the Kurds can pluck the oil wealth is not on (and, of course, Turkey would violently oppose).

Yes, there are very big problems. But these problems are as nothing compared to the consequences of Saddam remaining in power: and will be seen as such by very many Iraqis.

JEREMY GREENSTOCK
United Nations, 15 November 2002

It is integral to the US system that they get to the realistic position late in the day. The views and conviction positions come out early: in this case, the Pentagon civilians' position plus Cheney. Only after that does the President have to take account of realities. The realities in this case were represented by Powell. The US system gives an advantage to the person who comes in late in the day, the bearer of realism. This is what happened here. The UK position was reached much sooner, as our system invariably allows. The realities included the state of US public opinion, and the sense Bush must have that people want an international, not unilateral, solution.

The resolution was full of subtleties. One of the crucial ones turned out to be the issue of whether or not a member of the Security Council could bring a complaint against Saddam direct or had to go through Blix. The answer was that in one case (paragraph 4, I think) it had to be joint, and in the other could be either/or. This is the kind of thing that happens.

It helps resolve problems. The Americans made no fuss about one of the alternatives going the French way rather than theirs.

For the French, the crucial thinking all along has been to safeguard the UN process: to prevent the US taking over and going it alone. They have not differed much on substance. And now they are distant from Saddam. He has broken contracts with them, they have nothing left to protect via Saddam, they want him out; they will therefore probably not stop any next stage. As long as the process is observed.

It is not conceivable that the US will welsh on its commitment to come back to the UN SC. It was agreed in any number of informal conversations. They agreed to it, as a price for not having two formal resolutions.

One of Powell's major tasks was to disconnect the French from the Russians, which he succeeded in doing by degrees. The Russians knew they would get no support from China. China feels itself remote from all this, and does not want to jeopardize its bilateral relations with the US. Nor does Russia. So, in the end, the P5[1] came along for their different reasons, France holding out the longest for the sake of the procedural point they took so seriously.

There could actually be a second resolution anyway. Promoted by the US. If they thought they could get 9 SC votes and the agreement of the P5, that is the way they would like to do it. (I.e. JG disagrees with Holbrooke's analysis that the Pentagon would win over Powell and drive Bush to simply ignore the UN.) At the back of this is the fact that the US now knows very well that for all kinds of reasons it will be better to have international agreement, not unilateralism. This will be especially important after a victory: if they go it alone, they will pick up the mess alone – including the surge of terrorist anti-Americanism, not to mention the reorganization of Iraq. They do not want to do this alone. So, for the fighting as well as the aftermath, they need wide support.

The decisive moment is unlikely to come before 8 December, but after that the triggers will be cocked: the diplomatic triggers, that is. There would be no question, however, of the UN resolution taking anything like the time the other one took. It would be precooked. The Brits already did a draft, in case that made it easier to negotiate the first resolution (a way of getting 1441 through), but it wasn't needed.

A point that is overlooked in the media is that the inspections will at least put all future development on ice. SH cannot make any more weapons, or any more stuff. He will certainly have hidden/be hiding

---

1 The five permanent members of the UN Security Council: China, France, the Russian Federation, the UK and the US.

things he can hide: this is not easy to do with missile factories, but is easy with smallpox.

We know he has this stuff. The French know it too, from their own services. That he has bio and chemical agents, nerve gas especially. That is another reason why the French will probably agree, as long as the breach is obvious enough. The Russians may be different. The point about not being able to develop more is very important. It puts it all on ice while the inspectors are there. Cannot be moved around; cannot be developed. This is a big inhibitor to him. Irrespective of what they actually find.

It will not be possible to find everything. There is every chance to disperse, disperse (he emphasized) and bury, and without the assistance of insiders it is not realistic to think that we can find everything. It also may not be all that crucial that we have this detail in the resolution about people leaving the country to talk to the Blix team. Some have criticized this because it will mean, they say, Saddam putting a freeze on anyone talking. But the resolution does make such opportunities obligatory. (He sounded less than convinced that removing sources was going to be a realistic big deal.)

He will be stupid if he thinks he is not being watched very closely. He is. The US has many means of doing this. So if he moves things it will be seen. They have made many preparations for invigilation from outside.

Further, if he is blatantly in breach, Blix will report it. If he refuses access, Blix will come right back here and report it. He will probably, when it comes to making the declaration, declare 500,000 documents for us to look through: something like that. A snow job of things that are not what we need and want to know, but a pseudo-compliance we have to work through. That kind of thing. He will not be so stupid as to pretend he has nothing of interest to us.

Asked direct about war, he thought the odds against it were lengthening, i.e. it was getting more and more likely. Unless Saddam complied very closely, it was likely to happen. It would, he thought, be agreed by the SC, as said above.

As to the conduct of war, he said they would avoid urban fighting if they could. It was very hard and dangerous. More likely to secure the airfields round Baghdad, impose a curfew, and send out drones and other planes to bomb anything that moved. The US, however, could not bomb civilian targets. And, unlike Kosovo, they could not sensibly bomb major infrastructure targets, since it is they (the US) who will be committed to running Iraq after the war. They know that everything they destroy they will need to rebuild. But JG reflects the view that nobody can be very sure about the military prognosis. He remarked that the weaponry was now unbelievably sophisticated, far more so than in the Gulf War.

BLAIR AT HOME He made the interesting point that Blair has no idea how to delegate. This is not just an abstraction: he does not know how to make people own his policies – how to get people in ministries to feel these domestic reforms are theirs not his. How to energize and incentivize them. Mrs T did do that – whatever else one felt about her. She wanted to reform the Civil Service, and put her people into that kind of work. Blair does not put his people into ministries with a reform agenda and let them get on with it. This means there is a reluctance, a grudgingness, even an incomprehension of what is expected of them. That is a big reason why so little has happened, he thinks.

He applies this to international stuff too. We Brits are brilliant at formulating positions in Whitehall – none better. But we do not get out there and sell them. I try and do this all the time: it is what my job is about. But in general it is a failing of the British system that it believes mapping out a brilliant analysis and policy is all they need to do.

Blair has done a lot of clear and good things. Kosovo, Sierra Leone etc. etc. There is this striking contrast between his clarity abroad and his lack of it at home. Abroad he has a moral view, says HY, which clarifies things: something he shares with Bush, says JG.

RICHARD HOLME
Phone, 26 November 2002

CHAS KENNEDY I said, Here the LDs have an opportunity, the government is in big trouble, the Tories are off the screen, yet the LDs have not moved out of their niche position. They remain on the sidelines. They are not a national voice. Their leader has said nothing memorable and is not a major figure. This is all a missed opportunity . . .

RH replied, I agree . . .

There is a huge opportunity. This may not be strictly electoral. Electorally, the LDs need Labour to go on doing well, because the next tranche of LD successes, like the last ones, need to come from Tory seats. The swing against the Tories is what helps the LDs. This means that (a) LDs may be conflicted about how Labour should be doing and (b) there are limits to what they can expect electorally.

But the political opportunity is immense. The party is missing it. Somehow cannot believe where it is at. Ask yourself how things would be if Paddy was still the leader. Four points better perhaps? The fact is that leadership is on the wane, TB and IDS are not popular, there is an opening for leadership of the Ashdown kind. The country may be less confident in its leaders than it used to be, but that doesn't mean it doesn't want leadership.

CK's style has been good (says HY, agreed by RH) for a low-level ambition. Nice guy, ordinary bloke, unthreatening. But he has not become the voice of the country, in any way. And to measure up to the opportunity he needs to get bigger. Maybe he does not have enough confidence in himself.

The situation is actually tragic. People go round saying CK should produce a book of great thoughts, find some Liberal gurus etc. But the real problem is not coming out with clear, well-expressed positions on the issues of the moment. There is not enough edge in what he says. Therefore not enough is memorable.

Iraq gives him a great opportunity. A tricky issue, and will become more so if the UN agrees to go to war. But a chance to speak for England, in a way that Blair does not. By the way, though, when he made a very effective intervention about three months ago, it was on the back of a brilliant series of questions J. Major had asked on the *Today* programme, which CK's team had the wit simply to lift.

The LDs do have attractive positions. Very clear on the euro, and Europe. Genuinely libertarian on terrorism, immigration etc.

The new word is not 'replacing' the Tories, which carries a lot of baggage and overambition: too ideological, too many questions. But better, and easier, 'overtaking' the Tories.

CONRAD RUSSELL
Phone, 26 November 2002

CHAS KENNEDY is a Liberal to his fingertips. A genuine Liberal. With all the right instincts. But his problem is that he cannot do things too fast. The public will never move as fast as you want them to move.

His successes have always been when he has appealed to the non-political vote. The moment he breaks out of that and becomes more belligerent he tends to be seen as just another politician. Slagging people off, all that stuff. The voters do not like that. He is best when he is not doing it. Before I retired from London University, my students always talked like that.

Ashdown was a grand strategist, but when his strategy failed he had nowhere to go. When PR slipped out of focus, he had no alternative. His great Blair linkages came to nothing.

CK has no grand strategy. He is fast on his feet. He has to be. Has to be ready to take allies where he can find them – for example libertarian peers in the House of Lords (Mayhew). Helena Kennedy – could easily be Lib Dem but for that Glasgow root.

His ambition is to rerun the 1997 election, with Lib Dems as the party of change and Blair as the party of no change. That is the large ambition, I think.

2003

30 January President Bush and Tony Blair draw up a final warning for Saddam Hussein.

1 February US space shuttle *Columbia* burns up on return from orbit, killing seven astronauts.

15 February One million people protest in central London against a potential attack on Iraq.

20 March British and US troops invade Iraq.

14 April Tony Blair declares victory in Iraq after US troops occupy Saddam's power base in Tikrit.

6 May George Galloway MP is suspended from the Labour Party amid complaints that his opposition to the Iraq war brought the party into disrepute.

12 May Clare Short, International Development Secretary, resigns from the Cabinet and accuses the Prime Minister of ruling by diktat.

29 May BBC defence correspondent Andrew Gilligan claims that the government had 'sexed up' information on weapons of mass destruction in the so-called 'dodgy dossier' on Iraq.

9 July Geoff Hoon, defence minister, names David Kelly, a Ministry of Defence biological-weapons expert, in a letter to the BBC about the 'dodgy dossier' on Iraq.

18 July David Kelly is found dead in woodland near his home.

27 December The Bam earthquake in southern Iran kills 40,000.

Deaths Idi Amin; Johnny Cash; Leopoldo Galtieri, former dictator of Argentina; Katharine Hepburn; Bob Hope; Gregory Peck; Leni Riefenstahl; Denis Thatcher; Hugo Young

HY was hospitalized over Christmas 2002. He was being treated for cancer when he contracted pneumonia. On his return, the first interview he undertook was with Chris Patten. Some friends wrote letters.

CHRIS PATTEN
23 March 2003

BLAIR AND IRAQ NOW At the Brussels EU summit, Blair and Chirac did have a tête-à-tête for fifteen minutes. Their officials stayed at opposite ends of the corridor. But they did talk.

There was a surreal beginning. Simitis and Papandreou,[1] both decent and genial men, tried to get things going. Simitis said that he thought it better not to talk about Iraq over dinner. So they should do it now. He laid the floor open. Not one voice spoke up. Nobody wanted to begin the discussion. Nobody prepared to open up the divide.

The focus now must be on the aftermath. Here Blair has some big problems.

First, to his credit, he has put his name behind the proposal for a UN Security Council resolution setting up the civil administration of Iraq after the war. As happened in East Timor, in Afghanistan, in Kosovo. There are some good ideas about how this might be done – the International Crisis Group has been thoughtful especially.

In the US, the State Department is interested. But the Pentagon and NSC seem against it. Don't want to hand over Iraq to the French and the Russians, which they think is what the UN would amount to.

However, the EU is important here. Has been much the biggest financier of both Afghanistan and Balkan recovery. But CP says he will find it impossible to get the EU treasure house opened without a UN resolution underpinning whatever is done. I.e. rebuilding of Iraq in the medium to long term may fail at that kind of impasse, unless the US yields.

Humanitarian aid is different. Have already committed €100 million. But on the rebuilding side, Blair's ambition of doing it through the UN faces the big problem of US obstruction. Can he deliver? Not a done deal.

Second, we must get the inspectors back. If the WMD are discovered by US forces, will any Arab believe them? Never a chance.

Third, the Middle East peace process. Will the US really engage? Blair has pushed it very hard, but what does the US mean by it? They have ostensibly signed up to the road map of the Quartet. There has been talking ever since Bush made his June 2002 speech.[2] And we seemed to

---

1 Costas Simitis: prime minister of Greece 1996–2004. George Papandreou: Greek minister of foreign affairs 1999–2004.

2 The 'Quartet' were representatives from the US, Europe, the UN and Russia, working on a 'road map' towards the resolution of the Israeli–Palestinian conflict first outlined by President Bush in a speech on 24 June 2002. 'It is untenable for Israeli citizens to live in terror. It is untenable for Palestinians to live in squalor and occupation,' Bush had said.

have made some progress. But CP thinks that what the US wants is only something the Israelis will volunteer for.

There was another meeting, in Washington, in December. Powell said wait a bit, for the Israeli election. This was a bogus excuse, Patten thought – after all, Sharon attacked the road map during the campaign.

When CP asked Condi Rice if Bush's speech at the AEI recently[1] – the one that Blair seized on as so important – really meant sticking with the Quartet road map as seemingly agreed last year, she hummed and hawed, saying that it would depend on the participants – i.e. Sharon has a veto.

Edward Mortimer[2] said to Chris he thought the last week of the UN process was the worst week of diplomacy by the Brits that he could remember. The blaming of the French; the farce of the UK resolution. The fact is we couldn't get Mexico and Chile et al. to agree with us, and the French had nothing to do with that.

CP also said that the French know very well what the Blair people were playing at. E.g. that Campbell had Rebekah Wade[3] in the day before *The Sun* produced its headline about Chirac being a worm.[4]

Europe. The truth is that the EU can never work as an entity if France and Britain are miles apart. This is supposed to be what St Malo was all about, and what the Blair strategy is supposed to be all about.

Why did Blair have nothing to say when Rumsfeld likened Germany to Libya and Cuba? Because time and again he thinks that to utter a single word of criticism of the US is tantamount to disloyalty to the Anglo-American special relationship. The delusion that you can only be regarded as a good ally if you do not utter a word of criticism.

He could have gained a lot in Europe if he had been able to take a more distanced stance.

FROM LODE WILLEMS
[no date]

Dear Hugo

You had your best day writing it and I had mine reading your excellent piece! I will have to reread it carefully, because it is very dense, indeed. Blair must have

1 George Bush addressed the American Enterprise Institute on 26 February 2003, and outlined plans for Iraq after the invasion.
2 Edward Mortimer: director of communications to the UN Secretary General; fellow of All Souls; former *Times* and *Financial Times* leader writer.
3 Rebekah Wade: editor of *The Sun* since January 2003; previously editor of the *News of the World*.
4 On 20 February 2003 *The Sun* delivered 2,000 copies of a special French edition on the streets of Paris. The front page showed the head of Chirac on the body of a worm, and the headline read, 'Chirac est un ver.' The

been on your mind for all these difficult weeks, difficult for both of you. It is a very personal piece (as you indicate in your introduction). Will he still see you after this? That cannot be a criterium, I agree.

Belgium is now very firmly in the F–G camp. History explains it all. A couple of weeks ago I had a long talk with PM Verhofstadt. I commented that relations with Paris were 'pretty good' (I have learned the art of the understatement) and he replied 'too good'. That also says it all. I don't want Belgium, whose only repute is based on the transformation (which owes quite a lot to Belgium's skills in the art of constructive compromise) from European battlefield to capital of Europe and of transatlantic cooperation, to now take the lead (or, more humbly, stipulate) in wrecking the EU, not old, not new, just the EU defined as 'where Europeans live'.

I wrote to Stephen Wall, a man I like and possibly the most pro-EU in Blair's entourage. I agree with his answer. And let's stop the blame game, the situation is too serious.

Hugo, it gives me the greatest pleasure to be back in touch with you, both privately and publicly. Please don't rush things, and listen to Lucy. I embrace both of you,

Lode

FROM STEPHEN WALL TO
LODE WILLEMS
[no date]

Dear Lode

How good to hear from you. I was thinking of you only the other day (with wholly benign thoughts I promise).

What has happened over the last few months bears out my deeply held view that the problem with Europe is not that it is in imminent danger of becoming a superstate but that the whole project remains extremely fragile. The problem with what you call some of the wilder ideas for the happy old few is that, as the last few weeks have shown, the old order has gone. Some European countries have taken the same position as France and Germany, some have not. Those that have not are not in a British camp, but they, equally, will not be cast as any less European than France/Germany, and will certainly not want to buy into a vision of Europe which defines itself in opposition to the United States. A Europe that regarded Russia as a more natural ally than the US would have made a very serious error of judgement, in my view.

'splash' went on, 'We think your president, Jacques Chirac, is a disgrace to Europe by constantly threatening to veto military action to enforce the will of the UN against Iraq.'

But it does not have to be that way. And I agree that we have to strive to come together again. Because the alternative is not Europe remade in the image of the original six, but Europe not made at all.

Your PM's idea of a defence summit led by Belgium, France and Germany is understandable for domestic reasons. But some of us thought these issues were to be determined in the Convention set up under the Belgium presidency. I hope you guys have not got bored with your own invention already.

All the best,
Stephen

FROM LODE WILLEMS TO STEPHEN WALL
(Sent 24 March 2003)

Dear Stephen

I was in the train to Leipzig yesterday and was reading *Der Spiegel* when I saw a picture of Schröder and Blair and of you in the background. I was suddenly overwhelmed by a feeling of gratefulness for your kind and always constructive welcome to Downing Street and for the many hours I had the privilege to spend with you. I am also very sad about the state of the EU and think that advisers such as us should be trying very hard to stabilize the situation and then move things forward again.

My 'shop' here in Berlin is almost going too well: 'the questions with the UK, the answers with Germany', I advised the PM and he obviously believed and followed me. You may add Iraq, Afghanistan (ISAF [International Security and Assistance Force]). We are seeing 'old Europe' at work, but I am trying to slam the brakes now on some wilder ideas for 'the happy old few'; this will not be possible before Belgian elections of 18/5 and the end of the war.

I still steadfastly believe that the UK should be fully engaged in everything European. That is in Belgium's interest and it is good for the EU.

It would give Lindsay and me great pleasure to welcome you in Berlin any time you and your wife would like to come and stay with us.

Warmest greeting,
Lode

GÉRARD ERRERA
11 April 2003

Lunch at his embassy: AR, MK, ST[1] – and a fantastic meal, putting our pathetic sandwiches, which we served when he came to *The Guardian*, to shame.

POST-IRAQ EUROPE, FRANCE, AMERICA The French line, he said, should not be judged mistaken just because the war seems to have been won. It was always going to be won quite soon and easily. But the argument was about principle, about whether war was the best way to reduce/remove such threat as Saddam posed. France had its view, which remains defensible and is defended.

What America – and the British hawks (he recently had lunch at the *Telegraph*) – cannot understand is the possibility that France may have taken this line out of conviction and principle rather than by calculation of what might be gained. If oil really had been the French motive, she would have had a different policy: after all, if everyone knew the coalition would win the war, how would France get oil benefits from keeping in with Saddam Hussein?

It is true that it has had a disastrous effect on France's relations with Washington. The last time Chirac spoke to Bush was on 7 February. It is not clear when or why they will next speak – no doubt when they have some desperate need to. But France is now second only to Saddam Hussein on the US hate list. Where next for bombing? Why – France of course!

The large and inescapable fact is that the problems of the world can only be addressed collectively. France is as necessary as anyone to be part of this.

I asked for his reaction to the common view that France (Chirac) is concerned to set up a rival pole to the US, that she defines Europe in opposition to the US, as a counterweight etc. etc. He vehemently denied this, and launched into a lengthy historical discourse that began to assert that even de Gaulle spoke openly about 'Europe for the Europeans', which was not to be seen as specifically anti-American.

He said that Europe did not need to mean something. It has to be allowed to have different opinions. It especially needed a defence arm, for countries and continents could not be taken seriously if they did not have a military aspect. He noted that Schröder had recently said Germany must increase its defence spending – though whether Schröder will do anything about it is another matter.

---

1 Alan Rusbridger, Martin Kettle, Simon Tisdall (*Guardian* chief foreign leader writer).

All the time he kept including Britain in as a natural member of this European arm. Not only was there defence, of course, but he noted that the way the Brits had fought in Iraq had been more European than American. The cultural differences – not just down to Northern Ireland – were obvious, and personally he felt proud of the Brits for that. But he went on to specify a series of concerns – Middle East peace process, Africa, world economic justice, WTO etc. etc. – where the UK was ranged on the European side not the US side.

On the Iraq specifics, the issue would be whether the UN would be given a proper role a priori. Or merely asked to endorse a posteriori what the US had decided to do. He feared the latter. Where would Britain stand? For example, the US is determined not to let UNMOVIC back in. It wants its own inspectors, perhaps covered by a hand-picked handful of people to make them seem impartial and respectable. This is not right from any point of view. Will Britain insist on a different way?

Just as important, will Britain try and keep Bush to his word about the Middle East peace process? France knows that Bush is faking it. He was stringing Blair along. Both when he said in Belfast that the UN would have a 'vital role' – what exactly is vital? – and more importantly in the Azores, when he supposedly signed up for the road map. This was insincere. France knows that he told Sharon immediately after that not to take it seriously: that he just gave it to Blair because Blair needed something.

I said, The problem is that Blair faces no party pressure any more. It was thought he would need to mend fences, i.e. by keeping the UN angle heavily to the fore. Now that has been forgotten, just about. Nobody is really pressing for it. Blair is rising so high he can already forget about the pressures he was under just a month ago from the party. Will these ever be reassembled?

On Germany, Errera discounted the sense that Germany was scrambling to find an Atlanticist way back. This had been said before, after Schröder's tactical concession to win the election. It was widely said he would return. In fact the German anti-war line got stronger. The sense in Germany, beyond A. Merkel,[1] is of strong anti-war sentiment still. Therefore it seems unlikely that Germany will retreat back towards the US.

The overall point he kept coming back to was the great uncertainty of things. Nobody could know what would happen in the Middle East, in Iraq, in Europe, with enlargement.

But he did say that he thought only when Bush and Sharon had gone was there any hope of a road map to the Middle East peace process.

---

1 Angela Merkel: former scientist; Christian Democrat politician; chancellor of Germany from 2005.

THOMAS MATUSSEK
Breakfast, 8 May 2003

SCHRÖDER–BUSH A major problem is that B cannot stand S. Ever since the Iraq decision,[1] he detests him. Bush is a very straightforward man. I saw him more than once when I served in Washington and he was governor of Texas. I thought at the time he was direct, focused, on the ball, rather narrow, but smart politically. He remains probably all of these things. But he is not a man for shades of grey. So anyone who opposed him on Iraq is likely to be tarred for political life.

SCHRÖDER HIMSELF Always remember he is quite different from Chirac. No grandeur. An ordinary bloke. An instinctive politician rather than a strategist. A man of instinct, and sometimes courage. When we were agonizing about troops to Afghanistan (TM was running the German team at the Petersburg meeting), the officials were very careful not to commit Germany to anything. Then Schröder swept in and said, Why not? Without any consultation he just said, Germany will send troops to Afghanistan. He risked his job, and could have been defeated. But he did it by instinct. Always remember that S's whole popularity rating was around 30 per cent before the war. On the war itself it was 84 per cent.

SCHRÖDER–BLAIR is affected by this. They got on cosily as old friends and similar kinds of Third Way operators. When S got elected, Labour were overjoyed. The two men have an ease together when they meet (TM has witnessed this quite often). But TM admits that this may now have changed a bit, because of Iraq. S disappointed Tony. Tony may not be like Bush – he still wants to talk – but there is a bit more wariness, wondering where S really wants to go. However, again we should note that it is nothing like Chirac's larger problem with Blair.

However, S's belated commitment to a kind of reform agenda is important. For S it is make or break. He had to threaten to resign to get it through the party executive. Will know whether this has worked on 2 June – a special SPD conference. It may not be very big or enough – but it is a vital sign of a new direction for the German model which is under such severe stress. TM still flabbergasted to think of the scale of unemployment, and the social damage as well as economic that this does.

---

1 Neither France nor Germany would join the 'coalition of the willing' to invade Iraq. US Defense Secretary Donald Rumsfeld described the two countries as 'problems', and said, 'But you look at vast numbers of other countries in Europe. They're not with France and Germany on this, they're with the United States.'

THE FRENCH VIEW   Errera, TM's counterpart here in London, often says to him, Don't go wobbly on me. Meaning, Do not desert the logic of the position we both took during the Iraq/UN war build-up. The fact is, says TM, that France has an organized position it is determined to defend. Many people, including himself, thought that the run-up to the UN vote was the usual French tactic which would end with a climb-down. But in retrospect we see that that was not going to happen. Chirac has a position which is serious. It says, This is and should be a multipolar world, and therefore that the French vision has to be persisted with. The key to this is NATO, and the French view that there must be a separate European defence effort outside NATO, which operates without NATO (American) permission.

TM disagrees with this. As, he suggests, does Germany (though he is not speaking for his government here). It is unrealistic. The Brussels meeting of the four[1] was very badly timed and had the wrong people there. Until they commit to more defence spending, the idea cannot take off. They will not so commit. Germany, he implied, would not do so. So the whole thing is a bit futile (HY). However, the idea of a multipolar world is very key for Chirac. It is wholly different from the Blair view. That lies at the heart of the divisions in Europe.

WASHINGTON   I say that the US is itself ready to distance from Europe. Has done its business there. TM very anxious to disagree. The Germans, he insists, are anxious to restore Atlantic relations. He clings to the idea that beyond the neocons there remains an Atlanticist group – Lugar, Biden[2] et al. – who are quite different in their view about the exhaustion and irrelevance of Europe. But what if Bush gets a second term? I ask. He sighs with a recognition that this would indeed present some problems . . .

MY CONCLUSIONS   Germany and France are different, and Germany does not wish to get sucked into the Chiracian view of the world, which it thinks is in any case unrealistic. On the other hand, it does seem to want multipolarity, albeit without offending the US. The difference between France and Germany is that France wants to stick out its chest and make its mark; 'Germany has absolutely no desire to make its mark.'

---

1 Germany, France, Belgium and Luxembourg, all of whose governments had opposed the Iraq war, met in Brussels at the end of April 2003.
2 Richard Lugar: Republican senator for Indiana. Joseph Biden: then Democratic senator for Delaware, US vice-president from 2009.

GORDON BROWN
19 May 2003

Breakfast at No. 11: AR, LE, MW, GH, PJ, RR, MK[1]. Ed Balls.

Mainly an attempt to change the subject from the euro as such. Whenever the five tests were raised – mainly by me – he said we should not presume about what he was going to say on 9 June. But the whole tenor of his talk was the case for delay.

On the tests. He said, when I asked, that it was not a helpful hypothesis – see above – to ask whether within twelve–eighteen months it was realistic to say that the tests would be any less ambiguous. I had asked which ones would be. He muttered about all the tests being needed to be passed.

He launched his usual passionate case for the tests being essential. This was nothing to do with personalities, nor with 'soft' tests, all that drivel. These were hard tests, for the national economic interest. He did agree that they might not be 'perfectly' passed. But he did not agree that there could always be 'ambiguity' in the eye of the beholder. When I suggested there would always be ambiguity, he said, 'I don't accept that.'

He (backed by Ed Balls) said that the vital thing for the UK economy was jobs, stability and growth. We had to be sure we could make the case for that, that it would really happen inside the euro.

Ed Balls made the case he has made before – not heard so much recently. Because the political consensus did not really exist for Europe, that made the economic case even more vital to be solid. If there had been a pro-Europe consensus it might be different. But France, for example, said that because the Maastricht referendum was won by 0.1 per cent, that was the end of the story. Perhaps it was, in France. It would never be like that in Britain. (This harked back to the Balls thesis that we needed to win by 70 per cent . . .)

As to who was responsible for the failure of a consensus to have emerged, they were inclined to blame everyone but themselves. It was the media, it was business. They did not really deal with the point that their strategy – which said we would go in 'if' not 'when' the tests were passed – foreclosed them from making a heavy case for all aspects of Europe.

GB's big case, though, was that this was essentially a pro-Europe moment. Britain was leading the way towards a reformed European

1 Alan Rusbridger, Larry Elliott, Michael White, Georgina Henry, Paul Johnson, Randeep Ramesh, Martin Kettle.

economy. More countries were seeing the point of this. French protectionism and German labour laws were throttling their economies and
simply had to be liberalized. Everybody knew that, including them. He
waxed on about all that, saying that Britain – a reformist economy
without the US attitude to social protection – showed our pivotal role.
This was now a globalized world, not the inward-looking protectionist
world of the Six and the Nine. Europe had to be clear about that. Had
to become outward-looking, ready to do the deal with the world as a
whole. This was the fourth phase of the UK's European odyssey. First,
keeping out. Second, edging in. Third, failing to cement our bonds. And
now, fourth, the globalized context which we are best placed to oversee/
supervise.

Plainly this is another test that has to be passed. GB emphatically
denied that. But he kept coming back to it. He said that the spreading of
the word about this was the way to build a British consensus for Europe.
The key. To show the Brits that Europe was doing all the British things.
He claimed that at bottom this argument would defeat all the stuff about
sovereignty etc. etc. How fanciful can you get!

He rejected the notion that the UK message would be less easy to get
across from outside. Said we had already been successful – the savings
directive, as usual, being his display piece (the way he had persuaded the
Europeans that the savings directive was a rejection of the real world:
that if it had been passed, all money would simply have passed outside
the EU altogether to Switzerland etc. etc.). But he did not cite many other
examples.

Today, he and Blair start their meetings with individual Cabinet
ministers, to go through the eighteen papers they are supposed to have
read over the weekend. (Tessa Jowell told Polly that they were 'marvellous, absolutely marvellous' when they met at the River Café party last
night.) Larry talked about these being 'one on ones'. I corrected him:
'Two on ones.' GB: Why is that important? No chance of divide and
rule, I replied.

Charlie Falconer took over from Derry Irvine as Lord Chancellor on 11 June.

ANTHONY LESTER
11 July 2003

Nobody has noticed that the Lord Chancellor's Department has been taken over by the Home Office. Falconer, but also Filkin:[1] see also the HC ministers. Likewise, in reverse, Scotland,[2] a liberal and decent person, has gone to the HO to do the terrible Criminal Justice Bill.[3]

Falconer will always take the Blair–Blunkett line. Note that there is a B–B line. Blair thinks no differently from Blunkett, and always has done. Blair has never been a liberal except in more than selective words (as HY has often written). Blair made his reputation, don't forget, defeating the master HC debater M. Howard when he was Home Secretary. The period when he became tough on crime etc. etc.

Blair hates the Human Rights Act, take it from me (as does Blunkett). The HRA had its origin in the Lester campaign. Lester converted Irvine, who was in league with [John] Smith. Blair inherited it. Straw, to do him credit, did get together with Irvine, and together they pushed it through.

Note, as a recent example, Blair's cavalier promise to derogate from the ECHR if it got in the way of his asylum controls. Said so to Frost. Has also implied it again in answer to Richard Shepherd:[4] refusing to promise to stick with the ECHR.

Add to this a current and long-delayed issue about expanding international human-rights obligations, which is in the air. E.g. re racial discrimination. This is something 10 Downing Street has repeatedly indicated inside Whitehall it does not want. Obstructionist. Something may now be moving – but can one imagine that a combination of Blair, Blunkett and Straw would enthuse to push it through?

Irvine was a beacon of liberalism, albeit a limited one. He did want FoI to be done properly, when Blair sabotaged it. Did resist the Murdoch effort to exempt the press from the HRA. Would often be on the right side re criminal justice, notably in the independence of criminal courts.

---

1 David Filkin: Parliamentary Under Secretary, Home Office, since 2002. Labour peer since 1999.
2 Patricia Scotland: barrister; Labour peer since becoming Baroness Scotland of Asthal 1997; Minister of State for the Criminal Justice System and Law Reform 2004–6; Attorney General for England and Wales since 2007.
3 The 2003 Criminal Justice Act provoked controversy by altering the law relating to police powers, bail, disclosure, character evidence, jury trials etc.
4 Richard Shepherd: Conservative MP for Aldridge–Brownhills from 1979; select-committee member; Freedom of Information campaigner.

Was surely v. good in private in rebuking Blunkett for his repeated attacks on judges in general and Collins J in particular (asylum).[1]

There is a strong rumour that the government is trying to remove judicial review from all asylum cases. There are other ruses, notably in some new and obscure civil-contingencies legislation, which the consultation paper says will be secondary legislation but should be treated as primary legislation – a device to put it beyond judicial review.[2] Something similar could happen in asylum cases.

In the Cabinet, who might stand up for these basic things? Gareth Williams, but he has no depth. Hewitt in the old days. Attorney General not in the Cabinet.

The judges despise and detest Falconer and his pretensions. Look at him. Suddenly suggesting that judges be appointed at 30 – a good way of undermining judicial independence. They have stopped him calling himself the head of the judiciary. Who holds that job? You might well ask. Nobody knows. But for eighteen months Falconer will appoint. Also, he is reported to be wanting a commission that is lay-dominated.[3]

Woolf probably makes a mistake attacking Blunkett every week. And Blunkett fights back. He has the people's ear and knows how to catch it. Woolf should keep his powder for very special and rare blasts.

Derry is a wounded elephant. Nothing to do. Enraged by what happened.

Even the Callaghan government was not as illiberal as this. Partly because it was a minority government. But also because Jenkinsism has its place in Old Labour. Jenkins has no place in Blairism. Both Jenkins and Irvine ruthlessly ditched as valued advisers.

How can Cherie put up with all this?

On 8 July 2003, HY's commentary was headed, 'Blair has run out of steam. It is time for him to quit.' HY listed the legion of troubles besetting Blair and his Cabinet, and concluded, 'Three-term leaders outlive their usefulness, and Tony Blair is no different. People might have different reasons to be pleased to see him go, notably his terrifying faith in personal moral crusades as George Bush's henchman. But that would not be the big reason. The big one is the need to re-enliven sterile,

1 Mr Justice Collins had ruled in test cases in the High Court in February that the Home Secretary was in breach of human rights when he denied benefits to asylum-seekers. The *Daily Mail* and *Daily Express* described Andrew Collins as a judge who did not put the British first. In March, the Court of Appeal upheld the decision.
2 On 11 December 2003 *The Guardian* reported that lawyers were 'outraged by plans to axe the high court's powers to scrutinise immigration and asylum decisions by judicial review, and to bar claims under the human rights act in such cases'.
3 Lord Falconer, the Lord Chancellor, surrendered his role as the nation's chief judge in 2006. In that same year he established a judicial-appointments commission to recruit and select judges in England and Wales.

thankless government. All Blair passion spent, someone else deserves a turn.' It was not his last column, nor his harshest judgement on Tony Blair – but it led directly to the last encounter of which he left a record: and it was with Cherie Blair.

CHERIE BLAIR
31 July 2003

In HY's account of this conversation – at 'a tea proposed by her, in the wake of my Blair Must Go column in July' – he recorded that she 'received me in their dreary toy-scattered quarters in Downing Street. She wearing tracksuit trousers and T-shirt. But made up quite a lot. Very red lips. She certainly looks better in the flesh than she ever has done in a photo. She's also animated, intelligent, and without side. Just pretty normal.'

He noted that she 'wanted to talk for too long about cancer. I had to bring her back to the reason for the visit.' Cherie Blair asked for the record of her conversation that day to remain private, but HY's notes of his own remarks show him offering reassurance that his call for her husband to quit had not been personal: 'I said I didn't really support anyone in that sense, though it was true that I had been pro Blair when he started, and generally supportive over the years. But I reminded her that my thesis had been that two terms were enough for anyone.'

Index

Figures in **bold** indicate interviewees